THE HERITAGE SHAKESPEARE

EDITED, WITH AN INTRODUCTION TO EACH PLAY
AND A GLOSSARY, BY

PETER ALEXANDER

*Regius Professor of English Language and Literature
in the University of Glasgow*

COMEDIES

William Shakespeare

THE
COMEDIES

with an introduction by TYRONE GUTHRIE

and illustrations by EDWARD ARDIZZONE

NEW YORK ꞏ THE HERITAGE PRESS

Contents

EDITOR'S NOTE

To spare the reader a succession of footnotes, I mention here some of the studies I should otherwise have to refer him to in passing. J. S. Smart's *Shakespeare: Truth and Tradition,* 'a new landmark in Shakespeare scholarship' is the best introduction to a study of *A Life of Shakespeare* by J. Quincy Adams; the student will then be in a position to profit by *Shakespeare: A Study of Facts and Problems* by Sir Edmund Chambers. The best idea of the structure of Shakespeare's theatre is given by *The Globe Playhouse* by John C. Adams, of Shakespeare's audience by Alfred Harbage's *Shakespeare's Audience.* On dramatic questions Granville-Barker's *Prefaces* are most helpful. Bradley's *Shakespearean Tragedy* is still an important guide in interpretation, and those who fancy that recent 'historical or objective' criticism has outmoded his method should read Alfred Harbage's *As They Liked It.* Dr. Tillyard's *Shakespeare's History Plays* is a valuable study of Shakespeare's attitude to his material and of the implications it suggests; and in Dr. Ivor Brown's *Shakespeare* can be seen the reactions to academic opinion of one familiar with the modern theatre. All Dr. Hotson's works have added valuable touches to the social background of Shakespeare's life and his *Shakespeare's Sonnets Dated* makes further apology for the dates here suggested for Shakespeare's 'First Period' unnecessary. Pollard's *Shakespeare's Fight with the Pirates* is the ideal preparation for Sir Walter Greg's *The Editorial Problem in Shakespeare,* an authoritative review that will enable the reader to study with advantage Professor Dover Wilson's *Introductions* to the Cambridge 'New Shakespeare.' The views summarized in the introduction which is now before the reader will be found argued in some detail in the writer's *Shakespeare's Life and Art.*

General Introduction

BY PETER ALEXANDER

IT IS STILL TRUE in the study of Shakespeare that 'the dispersion of error is the first step in the discovery of truth.' The scholarly criticism of his plays, which found but casual expression in his lifetime and took systematic shape only in the eighteenth century when men of letters and scholars found the editing of his works a source of profit or reputation, began by remarking that he ignored the Rules. These rules or laws of the drama were generalizations from the practice of the Greek dramatists; and Renaissance critics and their eighteenth-century disciples regarded plays that failed to conform to these Laws as deficient in Art. Shakespeare ignored the Rules so constantly that his critics, however much they admired his natural powers, could not accept him as a great Artist. This opinion is still maintained to-day by men of distinction in letters; but it is an opinion born of a fashion in European thought that has passed away, and it survives only as a prejudice that will no longer bear critical examination.

It is now realised that this demand for the scholarly imitation of the external or accidental features of classical masterpieces is an appeal to the letter not to the spirit of Art. No one to-day will argue that Westminster Abbey is inferior as a work of art to St. Paul's because the Gothic builders were not so familiar as Wren with 'the four regular orders of Greece.' Indeed, the complete revolution wrought by the progress of European criticism is best seen in the attitude of the French, who were the most jealous guardians of what they considered 'classical' form. The French were in this phase of their culture as severe in their denunciations of their own early architecture as they were of the lawless Shakespeare. Now France is proud to reckon the buildings they once despised as Gothic as their greatest and most original contribution to the art of the world. And for the very same reasons the English may now claim that Shakespeare is the greatest artist to whom their race has so far given birth—a dramatist unsurpassed, as all acknowledge, in the gifts that nature alone can bestow, but as unsurpassed for the judgment that gives to work almost as various as nature itself the unity and commanding power found only in the world's supreme masterpieces.

When Rowe in 1709 and Pope in 1725 ventured on the systematic criticism of Shakespeare, so important did the Rules seem to them and their contemporaries that they deduced from Shakespeare's practice three important conclusions that were long accepted as almost self-evident. First: Shakespeare could not have received any instruction worthy of the name of education, and consequently Stratford where he was born and brought up must have been peopled merely by ignorant and unbookish rustics. Second: the form in which Shakespeare cast his dramas, not being prescribed by the Rules of Art, was dictated by the dramatist's desire to gratify, in his pursuit of gain, an ignorant and untaught audience. Third: so little interest, except financial, did Shakespeare and his even more ignorant fellow-actors take in his works that his plays were transmitted to posterity in so sadly mangled a condition, so full of interpolations from hands other than his own, that it was hardly possible to judge in many instances which were and which were not his writings, or to believe that we had them in a form even approximating to that in which he left them.

On the first and third of these issues modern criticism has shown that in general the truth is the very opposite to what was once so confidently maintained; on the second the wiser judgments of the great critics of the past are being gradually confirmed and developed.

STRATFORD

In Elizabethan England every self-respecting community made careful provision for the education of its children. Measured by this standard the inhabitants of Stratford could claim an honourable place amongst their countrymen. Education had in its beginnings in England been the business of the Church, but, like many other functions of the Church, education had in the course of the Middle Ages been transferred to lay administration; and the school at Stratford had passed from the Church into the keeping of the Guild of the Holy Cross, the organisation in which the social instincts of the locality, according to the fashion of the time, found expression. There has been a long-standing belief that the schools of England were largely the creation of the Reformation, but this serious historical error was exposed by A. F. Leach; and in his *Social History of England* Sir George Trevelyan has summarised the true course of events when he says that it was not the Reformation that made the Schools of England but the schools that made the Reformation. In 1553 the school at Stratford was renamed The King's New School of Stratford-upon-Avon; but the school owed nothing to Edward VI or his Council, and was not new by some centuries.

This renaming of the school merely marks the change from the old Guild system to a more modern form of administration in which Stratford became by Royal Charter a corporate borough under a Bailiff, Alderman, and Burgesses. The new Common Council, whose original members had all served on the Guild, now paid the Vicar and the Schoolmaster and administered the property and revenues of the Guild. It was during this period of transition that the poet's father, John Shakespeare, came to Stratford.

John Shakespeare must have left his father's home in Snitterfield, some four miles to the north of Stratford—where his father Richard Shakespeare worked as a yeoman farmer—at least seven years before 1552. In that year is found the first mention of him in Stratford records, and he is already in business as a glover in Henley Street; and to become a member of the Craft of Glovers, Whitetawers and Collarmakers, he must have served a seven year apprenticeship. By 1557 John Shakespeare had so prospered in business that he was able to return to the district of his birth to marry the youngest daughter of Robert Arden, the gentleman from whom his father, Richard Shakespeare, rented his land.

Further than Richard Shakespeare no one has yet traced with any certainty the poet's paternal connections. But on his mother's side he was related to one of the great families of the West Country, for Robert Arden came of a younger branch of the Ardens of Park Hall, a family settled in the Arden district of Warwickshire, from which they took their name, from before the Norman Conquest.

Of the marriage of John Shakespeare and Mary Arden there were eight children—four sons and four daughters. William, the third child and first son, was christened on 26th April 1564. The only member of this group to survive the poet was his younger sister Joan, who is mentioned in his will. The other three girls died in infancy, and though his brothers reached manhood they too predeceased him.

In the year of his marriage John Shakespeare was elected to the Common Council and soon took a leading part in its affairs. He acted as Chamberlain for four years—a term of office without precedent in Stratford—presumably because he was specially qualified for keeping the borough accounts. In 1568 he became Bailiff, and by virtue of his office a gentleman entitled to his coat of arms. In 1577, however, after twenty years of continuous service, he suddenly ceased to attend the Council meetings.

It has been conjectured that in his zeal for public affairs he had neglected his own business; and he certainly, at this time, was or wished to be taken for a poor man, mortgaging as he did a valuable property inherited by his wife. The authorities however took a different view of his circumstances: in 1580 he was summoned before the Queen's Bench in Westminster and fined £20 for failing to provide security that he would keep the Queen's peace; and on the same day he was fined another £20, as he had stood surety for another man in the same position as himself. That this was the outcome of the measures of John Whitgift, the new Bishop of Worcester, who had come to Worcester as he was later to go to Canterbury to restore church discipline, there can be little doubt. John Shakespeare's troubles therefore were probably political not financial, and that he was a 'recusant' there is no doubt, though the grounds of his discontent are unknown.

In 1582 his son William married Ann Hathaway the daughter of an old family friend. The licence was issued in November 1582; the first child of the marriage, Susanna, was born in May 1583. All attempts to show from an examination of the Bishop's *Register* and the circumstances of the marriage that it reflects discredit on either party rest on the unhistorical conjecture that the church ceremony was then, as it would be now, the marriage ceremony. The church ceremony, for which the licence was obtained, was in respectable Elizabethan society frequently no more than an after-ceremony to the marriage proper; the licence is in no respect out of the ordinary. Ann Hathaway may have been eight years older than her husband, but this is not absolutely certain, and even if it were this would be no proof of irregularity. Those who still insist that there was some impropriety in the matter may be asked to produce their evidence. In February 1585, the twins, Hamnet and Judith, were christened at Stratford.

How Shakespeare intended to support a wife and family is a natural question, and fortunately the only tradition about Shakespeare's youth that has any trustworthy pedigree behind it supplies the answer. The group of traditions that gathers round Rowe's account of Shakespeare's deer-stealing and of his prosecution by Sir Thomas Lucy has not only no pedigree but is contradicted by the fact that there was no deer-park at Charlecote at that time, the Lucy family establishing one there only in the next generation. The passage from the first scene of *The Merry Wives of Windsor* that is regularly cited as Shakespeare's reminiscence of this adventure is more probably the origin of the story itself; and, as Professor Hotson has shown, any personal reference in the lines may be directed towards a man very different in character from Sir Thomas Lucy. This and the other popular stories about Shakespeare's youth are the kind of conjecture commonly drawn in to fill the vacuum that biographers naturally abhor. The story however that the youthful Shakespeare was a country school-master rests on a quite different foundation. The antiquary John Aubrey, who made a valuable series of notes on the men of Shakespeare's generation, was advised to visit William Beeston, then an old man, but well informed about the history of the stage, for he, like his father, Christopher Beeston, had been an actor and actor-manager. His father, Christopher, had actually been in the same company as Shakespeare for a number of years. That

INTRODUCTION

Aubrey discussed with Beeston the observation by Jonson on Shakespeare's 'small Latin and less Greek' is revealed in Aubrey's note:

'Though as Ben Jonson says of him that he had but little Latin and less Greek, he understood Latin pretty well, for he had been in his younger years a schoolmaster in the country.'

In the margin Aubrey recorded that his authority was Mr. Beeston.

Shakespeare's next step—his departure to London—is a venture that needs no fanciful embroidery to make it intelligible. Conscious, like a later country schoolmaster, of the genius within him, he naturally sought the field where alone his talents could find their full employment.

LONDON

Those who think of Shakespeare as an ignorant youth driven by a wrathful landlord from his careless rustic existence have now to explain how he started on his new and very different career in London. It is not surprising that some look elsewhere, to Bacon or to Lord Oxford, for the author of *Hamlet* or the *Sonnets;* for the explanation usually offered is as improbable as the transformation it attempts to account for. Shakespeare began, we are told, by rewriting the plays of others, among them those of Robert Greene. Why the works of a writer who boasted of a degree from both Universities should have been turned over to an illiterate new-comer is hardly to be understood; and the evidence that was for long advanced by scholars in support of this story is now seen to indicate a different and more natural course of events.

Those, however, who accept Beeston's statement that Shakespeare had been a schoolmaster find no difficulty in understanding his beginnings and progress as a dramatist. No miracle except that of genius, no hidden hand, whether that of Bacon or Lord Oxford, need be invoked. Shakespeare began as any educated young man might have begun by adapting for his purposes the models prescribed by the fashion of his time, the Latin authors familiar to him from his schooling.

Before grouping his plays in the approximate order of their composition one important observation that emerges from such a chronological arrangement as almost self-evident must be considered. Viewed as a whole and as the successive episodes in the life of one creative mind his plays reveal in their creator powers of development and self-criticism found, whether the medium be music, or painting, or literature, only in the greatest masters— those who gave to their art the devotion of a life-time. To suppose that this development could come by chance or from the

xi

mere desire to gain the applause or money of the ignorant is to deny the evidence of experience. Shakespeare had of course to make the major contribution to the fortunes of a large and important Company of actors, and at times this part of his task affected his work, but such plays as *Hamlet* and *Othello* are clearly the creations of a man who had thought long and deeply about his art. A later and in its own opinion better instructed generation did not hesitate to deny to Shakespeare even the rudiments of stage craft. The more carefully, however, this side of Shakespeare's work is examined the more clearly it is seen to be skilfully contrived for his own stage; and, what is more important, the more clearly it is seen that his craft is not an end in itself but the technical mastery inseparable from any powerful manifestation of art.

Beginning then with plays fashioned on the models then approved—plays so little like his masterpieces that they are frequently attributed to other hands—Shakespeare soon developed an original style of his own that commanded the applause of a wide public. In spite, however, of his popularity and success he was not content to repeat himself but from about his thirty-fifth year started on the series of tragic masterpieces, matched, if at all, only by the drama of ancient Athens. Nor do the works of his later years echo in feebler tones these triumphs but bring with their colouring and glow the splendid evening to the noon-day intensity of his genius—a conclusion visionary and apocalyptic.

FIRST PERIOD

FROM SHAKESPEARE'S ARRIVAL IN LONDON (1584) TO HIS JOINING
THE LORD CHAMBERLAIN'S MEN (1594)

No definite date can be given for Shakespeare's arrival in London; but by 1594 he had a body of work to his credit that must have occupied a considerable number of years. Naturally no details survive of his London connections when he was still unknown to the world, but what evidence there is indicates that he was for a time at least a member of Lord Pembroke's Company, and that for them he wrote some of his early plays.

Before the end of this period Shakespeare had established himself as a popular dramatist and as a poet of whom much was expected. The first reference to him in print, from the pen of the poet and dramatist Robert Greene, provides, indirectly, evidence of his success. Greene had failed to find in London the reward he expected for his work, and his irregular life was closing in misery and want. He felt with much bitterness that a writer received but a small return for his plays compared with the drawings taken by the performers; and on his death-bed he wrote for publication a letter to some playwrights with whom he claimed

APPROXIMATE ORDER OF COMPOSITION OF SHAKESPEARE'S WORKS

PERIOD	COMEDIES	HISTORIES	TRAGEDIES
1584 I 1592	Comedy of Errors Taming of the Shrew Two Gentlemen of Verona	1, 2, 3 Henry VI Richard III King John	Titus Andronicus
1594	Love's Labour's Lost	Venus and Adonis } Rape of Lucrece } poems	
II	Midsummer Night's Dream Merchant of Venice Merry Wives of Windsor Much Ado About Nothing As You Like It	Richard II 1 Henry IV 2 Henry IV	Romeo and Juliet
1599		Henry V	
III	Twelfth Night Troilus and Cressida Measure for Measure All's Well		Julius Cæsar Hamlet Othello Timon of Athens Lear Macbeth Antony and Cleopatra Coriolanus
1608 IV 1613	Pericles Cymbeline Winter's Tale Tempest	Henry VIII	

acquaintance, warning them by his own fate against depending on such ungrateful employers as the actors.

'Base minded men all three of you, if by my misery you be not warn'd; for unto none of you (like me) sought those burrs to cleave—those Puppets (I mean) that spake from our mouths, those Anticks garnisht in our colours.'

Greene then, as the allusions indicate, goes on to attack Shakespeare not merely as an actor but also as an actor-dramatist whose success, though undeserved, was making it more difficult for Greene and his friends to gain a living.

'Yes trust them not; for there is an upstart Crow, beautified with our feathers, that with his *Tiger's heart wrapt in a Player's hide* supposes he is as well able to bombast out a blank verse as the best of you; and being an absolute *Johannes fac totum* is in his own conceit the only Shake-scene in a country.'

Soon after Greene's death his friend Chettle printed this letter in a pamphlet entitled *Greene's Groatsworth of Wit bought with a Million of Repentance.*

Marlowe, with whom Greene claimed acquaintance, was naturally displeased with the letter, for Greene like many self-confessed sinners found satisfaction in proclaiming the faults of his friends. Shakespeare also was annoyed. Chettle, three months later, in a preface to his own *Kind-Heart's Dream* refused to admit he had wronged Marlowe but made full apology for what he confessed was an unwarranted attack on Shakespeare.

'I am as sorry as if the original fault had been my fault, because myself have seen his demeanour no less civil than he excellent in the quality he professes. Besides, divers of worship have reported his uprightness of dealing, which argues his honesty, and his facetious grace in writing, that approves his Art.'

As Chettle's words indicate, Shakespeare was already highly thought of in courtly circles; and this is confirmed by the publication of his *Venus and Adonis* in 1593 and the *Rape of Lucrece* in 1594, with dedications to Lord Southampton, whose gracious entertainment of the poet is publicly and warmly acknowledged in the dedicatory epistle to *Lucrece*. Further evidence of Shakespeare's familiarity with courtly and learned circles is found in his *Love's Labour's Lost* with its copious allusion to personalities, events, and fashions, then current topics in such society. Shakespeare's poems were no doubt written during the years 1591-93 when the plague and other troubles had closed the London theatres and the Companies had to tour the provinces for a living. Shakespeare can hardly have been on tour during this period of composition, and it was not till the return to London of the leading companies, and after the extensive regrouping that it made necessary, that he joined the Lord Chamberlain's men.

Venus and Adonis, although Shakespeare's first published work,

INTRODUCTION

was that of a writer of recognised reputation. His success had been made on the stage; but actors were very unwilling to publish their pieces, partly owing to lack of copyright protection, partly owing to their belief that publication would lessen their takings at the theatre. In this policy Shakespeare acquiesced throughout his life-time, never hastening into print with new pieces. The straitened circumstances of the actors however during their enforced absence from London gave the publishers a chance to pick up some of these much desired productions, and versions, good and bad, of certain of Shakespeare's plays now appeared in print.

From this and related evidence one can with some confidence assign to the period before the poems: his first tragedy, *Titus Andronicus;* his comedies, *The Comedy of Errors, The Taming of the Shrew, The Two Gentlemen of Verona;* his history plays, *Henry VI* (in three parts) and possibly *Richard III.* The assumption that Shakespeare did not begin his work as a dramatist till 1591 rests on the misinterpretation by Malone of Greene's attack on Shakespeare. Malone interpreted it as a charge of plagiarism. Now that this interpretation is rejected the conclusions drawn from it are unsupported, and indeed contradicted not only by the evidence of Greene and Chettle but by the circumstances in which his poems and early plays were printed. Shakespeare must have been working as a dramatist for some years before 1590. This period of successful work explains how by 1594 he could take a leading place in the first company of the age.

SECOND PERIOD

FROM SHAKESPEARE'S JOINING THE LORD CHAMBERLAIN'S MEN IN 1594 TO THE OPENING OF THE GLOBE THEATRE IN 1599

The Company which Shakespeare now joined included Richard Burbage, who was to prove himself in the rôles Shakespeare provided for him the greatest tragic actor of his age, Will Kemp the popular comedian, and John Heminge and Henry Condell, who became the Company's managers and later Shakespeare's first editors. Their headquarters were at The Theatre, the first play-house to be built in England for theatrical performances.

During this period Shakespeare was living, as the subsidy rolls indicate, in easy circumstances in London; and there still survives a letter to him from a friend of his father, Richard Quiney, who was twice Bailiff of Stratford, that confirms the evidence of the subsidies. In 1596 John Shakespeare obtained from the College of Heralds a grant of arms. He was entitled to this as a former Bailiff of Stratford, but although nearly thirty years before the actual grant he had taken the preliminary steps towards this dignity, he had allowed the matter to lapse. It was no doubt considered

INTRODUCTION

proper in view of the poet's position in London to complete the necessary formalities, and the family shield now showed 'in a field of gold upon a bend sable, a spear of the first, the point upward, headed argent,' and above as crest 'a falcon, with his wings displayed, standing on a wreath of his colours, supporting a spear, armed, headed, and steeled silver.' The motto was 'NON SANS DROICT.' In 1597 Shakespeare bought New Place at Stratford.

Whatever his interests at this time in his personal and private affairs, Shakespeare's mind must have been unsparingly given to his work in the theatre. In 1598 Francis Meres in his *Palladis Tamia* describes him as 'the most excellent in both kinds [comedy and tragedy] for the stage,' and adds 'for comedy, witnes his *Gentlemen of Verona*, his *Errors*, his *Love labours lost*, his *Love labours wonne*, his *Midsummer night's dreame*, and his *Merchant of Venice*: for tragedy his *Richard II*, *Richard III*, *Henry IV*, *King John*, *Titus Andronicus*, and his *Romeo and Juliet*.' He also mentions his poems and 'his sugred Sonnets among his private friends.'

The period opens with a group of 'poetical plays,' *Midsummer Night's Dream*, *Richard II*, and *Romeo and Juliet*. The comedy is perfect in its kind and unsurpassed for the marvellous harmony it establishes among so many apparently discordant elements. The tragedy is another of the early masterpieces and anticipates in its spacious design and intensity of handling the works of Shakespeare's full maturity. But for some years to come comedy and prose were the main interest, and this, in the figure of Falstaff, overwhelms even the historical interest in the two parts of *Henry IV*. With Falstaff gone, there is little left for *Henry V* but pageantry; yet this opportunity for costume effects and patriotic verse may have been not unwelcome to Shakespeare as a suitable opening for the new Globe Theatre in 1599.

THIRD PERIOD

FROM THE OPENING OF THE GLOBE (1599) TO THE TAKING OVER OF THE BLACKFRIARS THEATRE (1608)

The Globe Theatre was opened about May 1599. With the lease of the ground on which the Theatre stood nearing an end, the Burbages bought the old dining-hall of the Blackfriars and furnished it as a theatre, but an influential circle who lived in the vicinity had this project defeated. The Burbages then acquired ground just over London Bridge on the Bankside. To this side, south of the river, they transferred some of the main timbers from the Theatre; force was necessary for the landlord hoped to retain their building for his own profit. To meet this additional expense they took into partnership as 'householders' five of the leading 'sharers' of the company, of whom Shakespeare was one.

The Blackfriars they leased to the Children of the Queen's Revels. The actors were choir boys and their theatre was described as 'private' to distinguish it from ordinary theatres where the charges were not beyond the vulgar purse.

Near the beginning of this period Shakespeare's father died, in 1601; at the end, his mother, in 1608. His daughter Susanna married the well-known physician John Hall in 1607.

The great public event of the time was the death of Queen Elizabeth and the arrival of James in London in May 1603. The King at once took over the Lord Chamberlain's Company and they were now known as the King's Men. The senior members became Grooms of the Royal Chamber and in that capacity formed part of the entourage of the Spanish Ambassador who came in August 1604, to negotiate a peace between England and Spain.

During part of this period, as Professor Wallace has shown, Shakespeare lodged with a Huguenot family in Silver Street. He was now in a position to make considerable purchases of land at Stratford and investments in the tithes of the parish.

As before, however, Shakespeare must have given unremitting attention to his art, for he was now from his thirty-fifth year to engage in the most sustained and intense effort of his career.

The plays that were to make the name of the Globe for ever famous were very different from *Henry V*. During the next ten years Shakespeare produced there his seven great tragedies: *Julius Cæsar, Hamlet, Othello, Lear, Macbeth, Antony and Cleopatra,* and *Coriolanus*.

Many explanations have been offered for this apparently sudden shift in Shakespeare's interest. Some have blamed the dark lady of the Sonnets and the conduct of the friend for inducing a mood of gloom and misanthropy; others have dwelt on Shakespeare's connections with Essex and Southampton, and the former's death on the block, as the cause of his disillusionment and pessimism; others again see in this tragic mood Shakespeare's infection with the spirit of a new age. The accidents of life undoubtedly provide the material on which the imagination operates; but the relationship between this accidental and the universal element in art is not so simple as cause and effect. The process of transformation is even more complicated and vital than that of digestion. But it is unnecessary to attempt an analysis of this psychological problem here, for the tragedies rightly interpreted do not reveal a spirit of gloom and disillusionment.

Many critics have dwelt on the bitterness and disgust in the works of this period. And it is true that nowhere can one find a fiercer invective and more withering scorn than that poured by these plays on the baser side of our nature. The picture of man dressed in a little brief authority playing his fantastic tricks be-

INTRODUCTION

fore high heaven with an effrontery that makes the angels weep
has never been drawn with more penetrating irony. And as a
background we have the cowardly or malignant complacency in
our natures that tolerates such shameless wickedness. Passage
after passage emphasizes the degradation to which men can sink.
It is summed up in one terrible line from *King Lear*—

A dog's obey'd in office.

King Lear has been described as a tragedy of ingratitude—an
ingratitude that divides parent from child and splits the very core
of human existence. And the elements seem to take part in the
confusion as the old and cast-off father rages on the heath with a
fury that out-tongues the elements. But those who find in this
fury the climax of the drama have missed half the vision and the
half that is greater than the whole. The design on which the
drama is constructed is one familiar to great spirits in all ages,
and is perhaps exhibited in its simplest elements in the old story
of Elijah fleeing from Jezebel's vengeance and how as he stood at
the mouth of a cave

a great and strong wind rent the mountains and brake in pieces
the rocks before the Lord; but the Lord was not in the wind;
and after the wind an earthquake, but the Lord was not in the
earthquake; and after the earthquake a fire, but the Lord was
not in the fire; and after the fire a still small voice.

The heart of Shakespeare's drama is not reached till the storm
and tempest are over and we come on the stillness of Lear's reconciliation with Cordelia. Here at last he recognises goodness for
what it is in its own right. And the play's real theme is the gratitude of the converted heart at such a revelation. To see the virtues struggling in a world where their very virtue is the cause of
their undoing is to be aware of tragedy; but—and this is the
touch of nature that makes the reader kin with the poet—this
makes us love the virtues not less but more. Had Shakespeare not
seen so clearly the hollowness of the world he could not have
created with such passionate brooding those spirits whom his art
has made the dwellers for all time in the imaginations of men.
He is not confounded by his terrible visions, for he sees in the
midst of them what walks unscathed; and we read his plays because, however unconsciously, we share in that triumph, and have
at least a sense, however our intelligence or conduct may later
deny it, of what the soul hungers to attain to.

This revelation which is the consummation of his art did not
come to Shakespeare suddenly or because a woman was false or
a friend disloyal. It is born of the modest and ceaseless years of
thought and labour which are not without their intimations of the
final triumph of this period. Viewed in retrospect the humour

xviii

and comedy, which his earlier critics found more natural to his genius, are only another aspect, a partial realisation, of his tragic vision. Philosophers have indeed maintained that tragedy and comedy have another and finer connection than that of contrast; but, though there have been great tragic artists and great comic artists before and since Shakespeare's time, nowhere are they found united as in his work, and in such a manner that each but adds a new force to its apparent opposite.

Viewed after the event, the tragic period is seen as the natural development of the previous periods and to be explained only in so far as we can explain to ourselves the growth and nature of Shakespeare's art.

FOURTH PERIOD

FROM THE TAKING OVER OF THE BLACKFRIARS (1608) TO THE BURNING OF THE GLOBE THEATRE (1613)

The manager of the Children at the Blackfriars Theatre was foolish enough to allow indiscreet stage allusions to royalty that led to the suppression of his company. The Burbages and a group of actors as 'householders' that included Shakespeare took over from him his lease, and the King's men now acted at the Blackfriars during the winter months instead of in the open Globe Theatre, to the very substantial increase in their takings. The King's men were now too well established in official favour for the old objections to their presence there to be raised again.

The plays of this period have happy endings; but to distinguish their peculiar colouring from that of his earlier comedies they have been called Romances.

Once again critics have dwelt on the contrasts between this and the previous period and denied any spiritual continuity between them, or have paradoxically asserted that the Romances are the flight into a world of make-believe that alone could save the poet from the madness in which his tragic thoughts would inevitably have engulfed him. Or again the fashion of the time is thought by some to have directed Shakespeare's interest to this type of play.

But the tragedies are the foundation on which the Romances rest. If Shakespeare had found the heart of man wanting in the fiery trial of the tragedies, what would be the hopes and aspirations in which human nature reclothes itself with every new generation as regularly as the flowers return with the spring—what would these hopes and aspirations be but will-o'-the-wisps to lure mankind to its destruction, or to leave it, should it survive, bogged in disillusion and a dreary materialism?

If fashion had anything to do with Shakespeare's return to comedy, it was because it gave him an opportunity for the expression of something he had now very much at heart, something that came naturally after the struggle of the tragedies, as naturally as Prospero's sympathies with Miranda's hopes and fears. There can be little doubt that the *Tempest*, considered in conjunction with what we know of Shakespeare's arrangements at this date for taking over his house in Stratford from his cousin Thomas Greene, the town-clerk, indicates that he intended it to be his farewell to the stage. Persuaded no doubt by the importunity of his old colleagues he returned to take a final bow in *Henry VIII*. During the first performance of the piece, on 29th June 1613, the Globe was burnt to the ground; and this accident, for lack of more precise knowledge, may be taken as marking the conclusion of Shakespeare's work as an actor and dramatist.

STRATFORD

Shakespeare seems to have passed his last days quietly at Stratford, though there is a record of at least one visit to London.

He made his will in January 1615 or 1616, and revised it on 25th March 1616, after the marriage of his second daughter Judith to Thomas Quiney in February 1616. He remembers amongst other friends his old colleagues, Burbage, Heminge and Condell, the last survivors of the group with which he had acted for some twenty years. He makes provision for Judith and for his sister Joan Hart, but the bulk of his estate is settled on his daughter Susanna and her heirs. His wife was obviously going to live with her daughter, who was, if what she put on her mother's grave gives any echo of truth, devoted to her.

Shakespeare died on St. George's day, 23rd April 1616, and was buried, having this right as a tithe-holder, in the Chancel of the Church at Stratford. The monument on the north wall was erected sometime before 1623. In 1623 his wife was buried beside him, and his daughter Susanna not far away in 1649. She left a daughter Elizabeth Hall who had married Thomas Nash and, on his death, Sir John Bernard, but was to die without issue. Judith Shakespeare had three sons who all died childless before her. From his sister only, and that through her second son Thomas, can those living to-day who are related to Shakespeare claim their descent.

THE FIRST FOLIO

In 1623, seven years after Shakespeare's death, his old friends and fellow-actors, John Heminge and Henry Condell, gave the world the first collected edition of Shakespeare's plays. This is now known as the First Folio, because of its format and to distinguish it from the Second, Third, and Fourth Folios, issued in 1632, 1663, and 1685 respectively. Each of these later Folios is in turn based on its predecessor. Heminge and Condell attributed thirty-six plays to Shakespeare, all that are included in this Heritage edition of his works except *Pericles*, for *Pericles*, although its omission by Shakespeare's colleagues is good evidence that it is not wholly his, undoubtedly contains scenes from his pen.

Their long friendship with Shakespeare, their admiration for his genius, their position of authority in the company, for they had acted as its managers for many years, made Heminge and Condell in some respects well qualified for their task. They, if anyone did, must have known what was by Shakespeare and what was not; their office in the company had made them familiar with his manuscripts. Yet their edition has presented students with problems for which reasonable solutions have been found only in recent years; problems that may be summarized here in the questions: Why did Shakespeare himself not supervise the printing of his plays; and why, since Heminge and Condell claimed to be Shakespeare's literary executors and to have used his papers, is the First Folio not accepted as the last and final authority for the text of all the plays? Why have there been so many subsequent editors, a line that begins with Rowe in 1709, and includes Pope (1725), Theobald (1733), Johnson (1765), Capell (1768) and Malone (1790), and threatens, like the phantom procession that appalled Macbeth, to stretch out to the crack of doom.

Shakespeare did not print his plays when he produced them because the actors did not favour such a procedure. They feared that publication might affect adversely their takings at the theatre, and the financial return from such publications, at least to the author or actors, was insufficient to overcome this fear. It was not because there was no reading public; publishers were only too ready to print his plays; but there was nothing in the nature of modern copyright to protect the author's interest; and to dispose for a pittance of plays that were drawing good houses did not seem sound policy. Yet in spite of these considerations nineteen of Shakespeare's plays were printed in some form or other during his lifetime, and a twentieth just before 1623.

THE QUARTOS

The Quartos, so called from their format, contained single plays and sold at sixpence apiece, compared with the pound charged for the First Folio. For their printing the initiative lay with the publishers rather than with the actors. Enterprising if unscrupulous printers were ready to issue even imperfect versions of the plays, whether put together by needy actors who had had parts in them, or vamped up by someone who had carried away from performances the drift of the plot. Seven plays were published in this manner: *The Contention, The True Tragedy* (these were pirated versions of 2 and 3 *Henry VI*), *A Shrew, Romeo and Juliet, Merry Wives of Windsor, Henry V*, and *Hamlet*—and *The Troublesome Reign of King John* may be an eighth. These are now known as the Bad Quartos.

This attack on their property inevitably provoked a reaction in Shakespeare and his company. They published in reply the genuine text of *Romeo and Juliet* and *Hamlet*, and they were not unwilling to print plays that had become well known through frequent performance. In contrast, then, to the seven or eight mutilated or distorted versions stand fourteen authorised or authoritative texts: *Titus Andronicus, Love's Labour's Lost, Romeo and Juliet, Richard II, Richard III*, 1 and 2 *Henry IV, Merchant of Venice, Midsummer Night's Dream, Much Ado, Hamlet, Troilus and Cressida, King Lear, Othello*. These are the Good Quartos. Even they, however, were treated as in some measure provisional publications. Shakespeare never revised the proofs for any of them, and the printer, although he was in quite a number working from a manuscript in Shakespeare's own hand, found difficulties he failed to master. The Good Quartos are therefore in places faulty or corrupt, and Shakespeare died before he cared to mend matters.

The actors, when at last they came to their task, had to provide the publisher with copy that extends in print to nearly 900 pages in double column. Their knowledge that many of the Good Quartos were set up from the author's manuscript or an authorised transcript prompted their use of some printed versions as copy for their own text; they took the precaution, however, of having the printed versions compared with manuscripts in their possession, but too casually to exclude all error. The manuscript copy they had to provide for the other plays was also defective for much the same reasons that the Quarto prints were not faultless: the scribe prepared his draft from material not originally designed for the printer's use, and only careful supervision could have prevented his not infrequent stumblings.

To the printed record of this large body of theatrical copy, often entangled as it were in Quarto and Folio, a modern editor has to address himself in an attempt to remove its corruptions. Heminge and Condell discharged their task honestly and with all the skill that could be expected of them; posterity can never be too grateful for their care and pains; but only those who read their Shakespeare regularly in the early versions can know how much the general reader owes to the subsequent editorial labours of those whom Johnson defined as harmless drudges.

ACKNOWLEDGMENTS

'All trustworthy restoration of corrupted texts is founded on a study of their history.' This principle, long established in the recension of classical and biblical texts, is implicit in the work of Shakespeare's earlier editors, but its full implications were first made completely explicit in the criticism of A. W. Pollard, R. B. McKerrow and Sir Walter Greg. Their study of Elizabethan books and theatrical documents in the light of collateral evidence hitherto neglected or misinterpreted enabled them to redraw on more probable and intelligible lines the history of the versions in which Shakespeare's work has been transmitted to us. The gap the earlier editors left between Shakespeare and his text, they closed: minutiae—such as the original punctuation—once considered negligible, they have made relevant for the interpretation of the text.

This development in critical method has prompted the present revision of the text of Shakespeare that Messrs. Collins first published nearly ninety years ago. That edition was based on the work of the earlier editors, and their contribution to the elucidation of the text is naturally still invaluable. For their great Cambridge edition, published in 1863-66, Clark, Glover and Wright made an authoritative survey of all previous editions. Digested in a compendious textual apparatus, this greatly facilitated subsequent work on the text.

The range of detail that now confronts a general editor is so extensive that he is necessarily indebted not merely to previous editors but more and more to scholars who have made an intensive study of some aspect or portion of the text. Of the many special contributions that I have found most helpful I must name Dr. Greg's *The Variants in the First Quarto of 'King Lear,'* and its sequel, Professor G. I. Duthie's 'old-spelling' edition of the play; Professor David Patrick's *The Textual History of 'Richard III,'* a study of a text that shares a peculiar history with *Lear;* Professor J. Dover Wilson's *The Manuscript of 'Hamlet,'* and its sequel, the critical study of the play by Professor Thomas Parrott and Professor Hardin Craig, an edition admirably adapted *editorum in usum.* In the interpretation of the punctuation of the early texts—for to reproduce this punctuation would merely confuse and mislead the general reader—I am indebted to Dr. Percy Simpson's *Shakespearian Punctuation* and to the studies of the late Alfred Thiselton. To the glossaries of Dr. C. J. Onions and R. J. Cunliffe I am conscious of owing much; and I have found helpful matter in the work of Professor M. A. Shaaber and Dr. Richard Flatter.

The complete editions I have consulted with advantage include those by Mr. M. R. Ridley and G. L. Kittredge and that by W. A. Neilson and Professor C. J. Hill. Lastly I must mention the edition still in progress edited by Professor J. Dover Wilson, although my debt to him is not the least I have to acknowledge; for whenever I have ventured to disagree with him on general principles or their particular application, I have not spared myself the expense of second thoughts.

My personal thanks are due to Mr. George F. Maine, 'the onlie begetter' of this revision, for his constant encouragement and assistance.

P. A.

xxiii

The Preliminary Matter to the
First Folio
(1623)

Heminge and Condell, who edited the first collected edition
of Shakespeare's plays, arranged their contents in three sections: Comedies, Histories, and Tragedies. That arrangement as well as the order in which they placed the pieces in
each section is preserved in this edition.

To their text the editors prefixed the preliminary matter
here reproduced. Opposite the engraved portrait of Shakespeare which stood as frontispiece—now known as the
Droeshout engraving after the name of the engraver—they
placed Ben Jonson's lines *To the Reader*. Then follow their
dedicatory epistle and the address to 'the great variety of
readers.' They also included Ben Jonson's famous lines to
Shakespeare's memory and short tributes from Leonard
Digges and John Mabbe, both of Oxford University, and
verses from the sister University of Cambridge by Hugh
Holland.

Their 'Catalogue' does not mention *Troilus and Cressida*,
for they were able to include this play, in a kind of no man's
land, between the Histories and the Tragedies, only at the
last moment and after the settlement of a dispute with the
publishers who had issued the Quarto version in 1609. Heminge and Condell originally intended to place *Troilus and
Cressida* among the Tragedies immediately after *Romeo
and Juliet*.

To the Reader

This Figure, that thou here seest put,
  It was for gentle Shakespeare cut;
Wherein the Grauer had a strife
  with Nature, to out-doo the life:
O, could he but haue drawne his wit
  As well in brasse, as he hath hit
His face, the Print would then surpasse
  All, that vvas euer vvrit in brasse.
But, since he cannot, Reader, looke
  Not on his Picture, but his Booke.

B. I.

TO THE MOST NOBLE

AND

INCOMPARABLE PAIRE

OF BRETHREN

WILLIAM

Earle of Pembroke, &c., Lord Chamberlaine to the

Kings Most Excellent Maiesty

AND

PHILIP

Earle of Montgomery, &c., Gentleman of his Maiesties

Bed-Chamber; both Knights of the most Noble Order
of the Garter, and our singular good Lords.

Right Honourable,

WHILST *we studie to be thankful in our particular, for the many fauors we haue receiued from your L.L. we are falne vpon the ill fortune, to mingle two the most diuerse things that can bee, feare, and rashnesse; rashnesse in the enterprize, and feare of the successe. For, when we valew the places your H.H. sustaine, we cannot but know their dignity greater, then to descend to the reading of these trifles: and, while we name them trifles, we haue depriu'd our selues of the defence of our Dedication. But since your L.L. haue beene pleas'd to thinke these trifles something, heeretofore; and haue prosequuted both them, and their Author liuing, with so much fauour: we hope, that (they out-liuing him, and he not hauing the fate, common with some, to be exequutor to his owne writings) you will vse the like indulgence toward them, you haue done vnto their parent. There is a great difference, whether any Booke choose his Patrones, or finde them: This hath done both. For, so much were your L.L. likings of the seuerall parts, when they were acted, as before they were published, the Volume ask'd to be yours. We haue but collected them, and done an office to the dead, to procure his Orphanes, Guardians; without ambition either of selfe-profit, or fame: onely to keepe the memory of so worthy a Friend, & Fellow aliue, as was our Shakespeare, by humble offer of his playes, to your most noble patronage. Wherein, as we haue iustly obserued, no man to come neere your L.L. but with a kind of religious addresse; it hath bin the height of our care, who are the Presenters, to make the present worthy of your H.H. by the perfection. But, there we must also craue our abilities to be considerd, my Lords. We cannot go beyond our owne powers. Country hands reach foorth milke, creame, fruites, or what they haue: and many Nations (we haue heard) that had not gummes & incense, obtained their requests with a leauened Cake. It was no fault to approach their Gods, by what meanes they could: And the most, though meanest, of things are made more precious, when they are dedicated to Temples. In that name therefore, we most humbly consecrate to your H.H. these remaines of your seruant Shakespeare; that what delight is in them, may be euer your L.L. the reputation his, & the faults ours, if any be committed, by a payre so carefull to shew their gratitude both to the liuing, and the dead, as is*

Your Lordshippes most bounden,

IOHN HEMINGE.
HENRY CONDELL.

To the great Variety of Readers.

FROM the most able, to him that can but spell: There you are number'd.
We had rather you were weighd. Especially, when the fate of all Bookes
depends vpon your capacities: and not of your heads alone, but of your
purses. Well! it is now publique, & you wil stand for your priuiledges wee
know: to read, and censure. Do so, but buy it first. That doth best commend a Booke, the Stationer saies. Then, how odde soeuer your braines be,
or your wisedomes, make your licence the same, and spare not. Iudge your
sixe-pen'orth, your shillings worth, your fiue shillings worth at a time, or
higher, so you rise to the iust rates, and welcome. But, what euer you do,
Buy. Censure will not driue a Trade, or make the Iacke go. And though you
be a Magistrate of wit, and sit on the Stage at *Black-Friers*, or the *Cock-pit*,
to arraigne Playes dailie, know, these Playes haue had their triall alreadie,
and stood out all Appeales; and do now come forth quitted rather by a
Decree of Court, then any purchas'd Letters of commendation.

It had bene a thing, we confesse, worthie to haue bene wished, that the
Author himselfe had liu'd to haue set forth, and ouerseen his owne writings;
But since it hath bin ordain'd otherwise, and he by death departed from
that right, we pray you do not envie his Friends, the office of their care,
and paine, to haue collected & publish'd them; and so to haue publish'd
them, as where (before) you were abus'd with diuerse stolne, and surreptitious copies, maimed, and deformed by the frauds and stealthes of iniurious
impostors, that expos'd them; euen those, are now offer'd to your view cur'd,
and perfect of their limbes; and all the rest, absolute in their numbers, as
he conceiued them. Who, as he was a happie imitator of Nature, was a most
gentle expresser of it. His mind and hand went together: And what he
thought, he vttered with that easinesse, that wee haue scarce receiued from
him a blot in his papers. But it is not our prouince, who onely gather his
works, and giue them you, to praise him. It is yours that reade him. And
there we hope, to your diuers capacities, you will finde enough, both to
draw, and hold you: for his wit can no more lie hid, then it could be lost.
Reade him, therefore; and againe, and againe: And if then you doe not like
him, surely you are in some manifest danger, not to vnderstand him. And so
we leaue you to other of his Friends, whom if you need, can bee your
guides: if you neede them not, you can leade your selues, and others. And
such Readers we wish him.

Iohn Heminge.
Henrie Condell.

xxvii

To the memory of my beloued,
the AVTHOR
Mr. William Shakespeare:
And
what he hath left vs.

To draw no enuy (Shakespeare) *on thy name,*
  Am I thus ample to thy Booke, and Fame:
While I confesse thy writings to be such,
  As neither Man, *nor Muse, can praise too much.*
'Tis true, and all mens suffrage. But these wayes
  Were not the paths I meant vnto thy praise:
For seeliest Ignorance on these may light,
  Which, when it sounds at best, but eccho's right;
Or blinde Affection, which doth ne're aduance
  The truth, but gropes, and vrgeth all by chance;
Or crafty Malice, might pretend this praise,
  And thinke to ruine, where it seem'd to raise.
These are, as some infamous Baud, or Whore,
  Should praise a Matron. What could hurt her more?
But thou art proofe against them, and indeed
  Aboue th' ill fortune of them, or the need.
I, therefore will begin. Soule of the Age!
  The applause! delight! the wonder of our Stage!
My Shakespeare, *rise; I will not lodge thee by*
  Chaucer, *or* Spenser, *or bid* Beaumont *lye*
A little further, to make thee a roome:
  Thou art a Moniment, without a tombe,
And art aliue still, while thy Booke doth liue,
  And we haue wits to read, and praise to giue.
That I not mixe thee so, my braine excuses;
  I meane with great, but disproportion'd Muses:
For, if I thought my judgement were of yeeres,
  I should commit thee surely with thy peeres,
And tell, how farre thou didst our Lily *out-shine,*
  Or sporting Kid, *or* Marlowes *mighty line.*
And though thou hadst small Latine, *and lesse* Greeke,
  From thence to honour thee, I would not seeke
For names; but call forth thund'ring Æschilus,
  Euripedes, *and* Sophocles *to vs,*
Paccuuius, Accius, *him of* Cordoua *dead,*
  To life againe, to heare thy Buskin tread,
And shake a Stage: Or, when thy Sockes were on,
  Leaue thee alone, for the comparison
Of all, that insolent Greece, *or haughtie* Rome
  sent forth, or since did from their ashes come.
Triumph, my Britaine, *thou hast one to showe,*
  To whom all Scenes of Europe *homage owe.*
He was not of an age, but for all time!
  And all the Muses still were in their prime,
When like Apollo *he came forth to warme*
  Our eares, or like a Mercury *to charme!*
Nature her selfe was proud of his designes,
  And ioy'd to weare the dressing of his lines!

Which were so richly spun, and wouen so fit,
  As, since, she will vouchsafe no other Wit.
The merry Greeke, *tart* Aristophanes,
  Neat Terence, *witty* Plautus, *now not please;*
But antiquated, and deserted lye
  As they were not of Natures family.
Yet must I not giue Nature all: Thy Art,
  My gentle Shakespeare, *must enioy a part.*
For though the Poets *matter, Nature be,*
  His Art doth giue the fashion. And, that he,
Who casts to write a liuing line, must sweat,
  (such as thine are) and strike the second heat
Vpon the Muses *anuile: turne the same,*
  (And himselfe with it) that he thinkes to frame;
Or for the lawrell, he may gaine a scorne,
  For a good Poet's *made, as well as borne.*
And such wert thou. Looke how the fathers face
  Liues in his issue, euen so, the race
Of Shakespeares *minde, and manners brightly shines*
  In his well torned, and true-filed lines:
In each of which, he seemes to shake a Lance,
  As brandish't at the eyes of Ignorance.
Sweet Swan of Auon! *what a sight it were*
  To see thee in our waters yet appeare,
And make those flights vpon the bankes of Thames,
  That so did take Eliza, *and our* Iames!
But stay, I see thee in the Hemisphere
  Aduanc'd, and made a Constellation there!
Shine forth, thou Starre of Poets, *and with rage,*
  Or influence, chide, or cheere the drooping Stage;
Which, since thy flight from hence, hath mourn'd like night,
  And despaires day, but for thy Volumes light.

BEN: IONSON.

Vpon the Lines and Life of the Famous Scenicke Poet,

Master WILLIAM SHAKESPEARE

Those hands, which you so clapt, go now, and wring
You *Britaines* braue; for done are *Shakespeares* dayes:
His dayes are done, that made the dainty Playes,
Which made the Globe of heau'n and earth to ring.
Dry'de is that veine, dry'd is the *Thespian* Spring,
Turn'd all to teares, and *Phœbus* clouds his rayes:
That corp's, that coffin now besticke those bayes,
Which crown'd him *Poet* first, then *Poets* King.
If *Tragedies* might any *Prologue* haue,
All those he made, would scarse make one to this:
Where *Fame*, now that he gone is to the graue
(Deaths publique tyring-house) the *Nuncius* is.
  For though his line of life went soone about,
  The life yet of his lines shall neuer out.

HVGH HOLLAND.

xxix

A CATALOGVE

of the seuerall Comedies, Histories, and Tragedies
contained in this Volume.

COMEDIES.

HISTORIES.

TRAGEDIES.

TO THE MEMORIE
of the deceased Authour Maister
W. SHAKESPEARE.

Shake-speare, *at length thy pious fellowes giue*
The world thy Workes: thy Workes, by which, out-liue
Thy Tombe, thy name must: when that stone is rent,
And Time dissolues thy Stratford *Moniment,*
Here we aliue shall view thee still. This Booke,
When Brasse and Marble fade, shall make thee looke
Fresh to all Ages: when Posteritie
Shall loath what's new, thinke all is prodegie
That is not Shake-speares; *eu'ry Line, each Verse*
Here shall reuiue, redeeme thee from thy Herse.
Nor Fire, nor cankring Age, as Naso *said,*
Of his, thy wit-fraught Booke shall once inuade.
Nor shall I e're beleeue, or thinke thee dead
(Though mist) vntill our bankrout Stage be sped
(Impossible) with some new straine t' out-do
Passions of Iuliet, *and her* Romeo;
Or till I heare a Scene more nobly take,
Then when thy half-Sword parlying Romans *spake.*
Till these, till any of thy Volumes rest
Shall with more fire, more feeling be exprest,
Be sure, our Shake-speare, *thou canst neuer dye,*
But crown'd with Lawrell, liue eternally.

L. Digges.

To the memorie of M. *W. Shake-speare*

Wee wondred (Shake-speare) *that thou went'st so soone*
From the Worlds-Stage, to the Graues-Tyring-roome.
Wee thought thee dead, but this thy printed worth,
Tels thy Spectators, that thou went'st but forth
To enter with applause. An Actors Art,
Can dye, and liue, to acte a second part.
That's but an Exit *of Mortalitie;*
This, a Re-entrance to a Plaudite.

I. M.

THE WORKES

OF

WILLIAM SHAKESPEARE

containing all his

Comedies, Histories, and Tragedies:

Truely set forth, according to their first

ORIGINALL.

The Names of the Principall Actors

in all these Playes.

William Shakespeare.	*Samuel Gilburne.*
Richard Burbadge.	*Robert Armin.*
John Hemmings.	*William Ostler.*
Augustine Phillips.	*Nathan Field.*
William Kempt.	*John Underwood.*
Thomas Poope.	*Nicholas Tooley.*
George Bryan.	*William Ecclestone.*
Henry Condell.	*Joseph Taylor.*
William Slye.	*Robert Benfield.*
Richard Cowly.	*Robert Goughe.*
John Lowine.	*Richard Robinson.*
Samuell Crosse.	*Iohn Shancke.*
Alexander Cooke.	*Iohn Rice.*

THE COMEDIES

Preface

BY TYRONE GUTHRIE

So much has been written about Shakespeare, his life and his work have been treated from so many different viewpoints, that I hesitate to add another word.

One thought emboldens me: the vast bulk of Shakespearean criticism is the work of scholars and teachers, or else of those historical sleuths who track down and bring to book evasive Facts. Comparatively little has been written about Shakespeare by members of his own craft; yet he was, after all, a man of the theatre.

It is known that he wrote his plays to be acted by a particular company, of which he was both a working member and a part-proprietor, that he cared so little about literary publication that only pirated versions of his plays appeared in print, until, seven years after his death, his two friends, Heminge and Condell, collected the prompt copies and issued the First Folio. All these facts were glossed over in the long years between Cromwell and the end of the First World War. The theatre was considered to be frivolous, at best; at worst, the Whore of Babylon. So, in place of the man of the theatre, the expert craftsman, in place of the man of affairs engaged in the highly speculative business of theatrical management and making out of it a substantial fortune, in place of the popular colleague in a closely integrated group of theatrical personalities, there was substituted the shadowy but impressive image of A Genius, A Superior Being, a breather of rarefied air, a creature far, far removed from the indisputable and rather bourgeois facts of William Shakespeare's life.

However, for some years now, the theatre, or at all events the sort of theatre which might conceivably tackle the work of Shakespeare, has been considered respectable, not only morally and socially, but even intellectually. Many universities in America, and even a very few in Europe, admit Drama as a subject of serious study; professional practitioners are invited to lecture to Students; Drama is now ceasing to be regarded as a sluggish backwater in the river of Literary Tradition, and is achieving recognition as a river in its own right, a tributary of Literature, but still a river with a character and tradition of its own, as the Ohio River is to the Mississippi.

Shakespearean scholars no longer regard with contempt the efforts of those who perform the plays. On the contrary, they are now inclined to overestimate the value of performance and the experience of performers; and we, the professional theatre people, are apt to underestimate the debt we owe to the scholars. In preparing a Shakespearean play for production, we plough through volume after volume of commentary and criticism, and, because much of it is pedantic and silly, we lose patience and confuse the wheat with the chaff.

We forget that in our own Mystery, or Craft, or even Art, we labour under one immense advantage: we are writing in water. Our silliness and pedantry are forgotten almost as soon as they occur. They do not find their way into print. Of our performances there remains only the Legend, preserved in the gilded terms with which eld recites its own youthful experience to the next generation: "Ah, my dear boy, you may think you have great acting nowadays, but I remember . . ." And then follows a description of Irving or Salvini or Modjeska or Barrymore or Laurette Taylor, but never the homely chronicle of someone going through his nightly routine. It is always thrilling, mysterious; great shadows are cast, great echoes resound. It is such stuff as dreams are made on—not journalism, not even history, but myth.

I shudder to think that the day is beginning to dawn when all important performances will be mechanically reproduced in some durable form. So that posterity, finding in Helen Hayes only a dated hair-do, in Laurence Olivier only the accent of the long-defunct British Upper Classes, will laugh at the feebleness of our attempts. Our theatre will lie like a corpse, exposed on a slab to the irreverent, analytical, and, worst of all, dispassionate scrutiny of students.

So it is with the scholars. Their work is embalmed, not in myth, but in print. It is there in black and white and all its naked, dated silliness.

PREFACE

And yet . . . and yet. As Feste says, Time brings in his revenges. The nineteenth-century scholars, who seem so dated now, will swing back into favour. Their moralistic currency will again appreciate. Freud will go out and good old Dr. Bowdler will come roaring in.

I feel that I owe it as a positive duty, not only to express gratitude for delicious, nourishing crumbs from the scholars' tables, but to prove that, in print, we practical craftsmen can be the scholars' equals, not only in love and reverence for The Bard, but in the gallantry with which we too commit our pigmy thoughts to paper, with which we too lay our corpses upon the cold, stone slab of Time.

If Shakespeare were a new dramatist, any critic worth his salt would recognise some genius, but would feel it his duty to scold the young man for prolixity, turgidity, untidiness. He would suggest that this promising lad go to the Greeks to study economy and simplicity, to Marlowe to give his verse sonority, to Tennessee Williams to learn about character development, to Molière, Wilde, or Coward to polish his wit. The critique would not be unreasonable, unfair, or deliberately unkind. It would merely annihilate any possibility of success by the implication of seven out of ten for genius, nought for neatness.

There is nothing neat about Shakespeare. But, paradoxically, it is when it is most sprawling that the author's genius is most apparent. It is fair to say that Shakespeare wrote no good plays, only great ones. There is not one of them without the evidence of either carelessness or inconsistency, or else of such corruption in the text as would utterly sink lesser work. In *Twelfth Night*, for example, the neatest of the Comedies, the Fool is "planted" as one of a team of confederates who resent Malvolio's arrogance and long for revenge. Yet, when it comes to the sequence of the forged letter and the yellow stockings, the Fool drops out altogether and is replaced by an entirely new and unexplained character called Fabian. I suspect that this is not due to careless composition; Feste was a character in whom his creator was obviously interested and whom he intended to be the *raisonneur* of the piece, rather in the way that Jaques is used in *As You Like It*. More probably the substitution was forced by the exigencies of production. Perhaps an elderly actor playing Feste was unequal to the running about and hiding involved in the letter scene, and had to be replaced by someone younger and more agile, for whom the sketchy role of Fabian was improvised, taking over the Fool's share in the plot but omitting whatever comment or philosophy Shakespeare meant the Fool to express.

In the study there is time to notice inconsistencies, to ponder over such problems as whether Shakespeare wrote "Oh that this too, too solid flesh" or "sullied flesh." In the hurly-burly of stage performance most of these problems vanish into air, into thick air. No one can distinguish the pronunciation of "solid" from "sullied" so clearly as to affect the meaning of the speech. Theobald's famous amendment to Mrs. Quickly's description of the death of Falstaff—"a table of green fields" amended to "a babbled of green fields"—was certainly a piece of crossword-puzzle genius, and makes intelligible what was, in the original, gibberish. But a good actress in full cry could say "a table of green fields" and so colour up the phrase that the emotional effect would be unaltered; she could say "a cauldron of pink snakes" and not one person in a thousand would be aware of any inconsistency. Audiences do not apprehend dramatic poetry word by word, or even phrase by phrase, but in great douches of emotion. Sometimes a single phrase—"Wash me in steep-down gulfs of liquid fire"—"A wilderness of monkeys"—itself produces this poetic emotion. But in spoken poetry, as opposed to read, the rhythm, pace, pitch, and especially vocal colour of the speaker have immensely more effect upon the auditor than the literary quality of the verse.

Moreover, the best actors are not so powerfully governed by the precise meaning of what they are called upon to speak, as by its "feeling" in terms of their characters, the situation, and the pure music of the speech. This is not to say that they do not know the meaning of what they are talking about; they know very well, often better than the grammarians, because *over and above* the literal meaning of the phrases is their musical and emotional meaning, *between the lines* of the author's conscious thought is the subconscious impulse which made him phrase it so.

Nevertheless, I absolutely am not seeking to decry the immense value of the scholars' work, but only trying to show that many points which seem important and significant in the study are of little importance on the stage; conversely, much of what is vital on the stage is often of insufficient concern to scholars.

When a production is being rehearsed, its interpreters must ask themselves what sort of comment they plan to make. No production can help making a comment, however little those concerned may be aware of it. Every reader makes his own comment, be it only by the emphasis with which this or that idea occurs to him. Every beholder of a picture is an art critic, although most of us are too ignorant and inarticulate to make our comment valuable. So, granted that every production must imply a comment, indeed a complex of comment, theoretic decisions must be taken as to what this comment shall be, and practical decisions as to how it shall be made.

It is possible to attempt decisions of many kinds. Here are five of the most important:

1. TO TELL THE STORY OF THE PLAY AS CLEARLY AND INTERESTINGLY AS POSSIBLE.

2. TO ILLUMINATE THE THEME OF THE PLAY.

Any play which has aspirations beyond mere theatrical journalism, has a theme, which its plot exemplifies. Precisely to define the theme, especially in Shakespeare, is extremely hard and controversial. But, if the play is to be seriously interpreted, the actors must have some clear and concerted idea, over and above the mere plot, about what the play is trying to say. For example, you might try to interpret *The Merchant of Venice* as an anti-Semitic pamphlet; many people believe it to be so. More reasonably, I think, you might try to interpret it as a love story, almost a fairy story, with strong folk-elements—the three Caskets. This is how the play is usually done, and this interpretation treats Shylock as the Wicked Ogre. More reasonably still, I think, it can be interpreted as a Fantasia on the Theme of Justice versus Mercy. Similarly, it can be suggested that *Twelfth Night* is a Fantasia on the Theme of Sad and Merry Madness; *Timon* on

PREFACE

Gratitude and Ingratitude; *Measure for Measure* on Sexual Virtue and Vice; Fantasias, in short, on Polarity, all of them powerfully indicting excess, powerfully pleading for moderation and tolerance. Also, throughout the whole body of Shakespeare's works may be found an insistence upon the importance and significance of Forgiveness.

3. TO ILLUMINATE THE CHARACTERS.

This, in Shakespeare, is grateful work, since each play is a portrait gallery of unique power, variety, and originality.

4. TO MAKE A PICTORIAL STATEMENT.

Again this is grateful work, since all the plays give a great deal of stimulus and latitude to the pictorial imagination.

In the nineteenth century, particularly during Irving's twenty-one-year reign at the Lyceum Theatre in London, the plays were presented with sumptuous pageantry. Often to compensate for the time taken to prepare the great scenic effects, and to enable successive scenes to occur in one set, the text had to be severely chopped and rearranged. Nowadays we regard the text as far more important than the scenery, and there is a growing tendency to present the plays, as nearly as we can, in the visual style which prevailed when they were written—an open stage with no illusionary scenery.

The absence of scenery need not, and should not, preclude a handsome spectacle. The Elizabethan Theatre spent lavishly on its wardrobe.

Under the heading of pictorial presentation must also be included Choreography, that is, the arrangement and timing of movement. In this age we are probably more aware than ever before of the composition of a picture and the arrangement of figures in relation to one another and to a given space. This is partly the result of the present vogue for ballet, partly because of movies and television, with their stress on camera-angles and the composition of a "frame."

5. TO MAKE A MUSICAL STATEMENT.

In the theatre of the early nineteenth century this had become the dominant aim in Shakespearean production. Leading actors directed their own companies, everything was subordi-

xl

nated to a "Star" performance, and the performance itself was a piece of virtuoso declamation. The great speeches were Arias. They bore little relation to the context of the play; the actor declaimed them straight to the house, waited for applause, bowed, and then went on with the play. It was just like early Verdi; in fact, Verdi accepted the theatrical convention of his own day, and by his genius crystallised it, so that in his works the convention remains, glitteringly preserved, like a Fruit Glacé.

Nowadays, still in reaction against our forebears' obsession with rhetoric, still influenced by our parents' obsession with naturalism, still obsessed ourselves with psychology, and disastrously influenced by the microphone, the camera, and robot engineers, declamation is in sad decline. But I must not anticipate. The question of verse-speaking comes later.

Between the five aims listed above there need be no conflict. A great production will be in the bull's-eye on all five counts; story, theme, character, picture, and music will all be harmoniously blended into one expressive whole. Nevertheless, The Theme is far the most important as well as the most difficult. Once a decision, wrongly or rightly, has been taken as to what is The Theme, then a host of subsidiary decisions will follow. For instance, if you interpret *The Merchant of Venice* as a Fantasia on Justice versus Mercy, then the Casket Motif becomes relatively unimportant, a mere decoration, which concerns the plot but not the theme, a rose in icing sugar on a substantial cake. Antonio, on the other hand, as the proponent of mercy, becomes a central figure. Everything must be done to build him up and make him important, including the unmistakable indication of a homosexual interest in Bassanio. Also the ironic point must be heavily stressed that the Christians who plead for mercy from the Jew when he is in the ascendant, show him none whatever in his downfall. This places Bassanio, Gratiano, Antonio, and, especially, Portia, in a very unpleasant light. If that is not to be so, then this interpretation falls down and another must be sought. It is my view, however, that Shakespeare certainly intended this irony; that Portia, like his other "heroines," is meant to be a human being, not a painted image of unalloyed purity and sweetness; that, if the Trial Scene has this brutal and unpleasant climax, then the key is set for the final scene, which otherwise becomes too sweet.

The more one searches for the themes in Shakespearean comedy, the more evident it becomes that very few of these so-called Comedies are anything but highly serious, though high seriousness does not exclude humour. Few of them come under any reasonable definition of Comedy, and I think that, except that they have now been known as Comedies for so long, most of them would be far better described as Romances. (The immature *Comedy of Errors, The Taming of the Shrew,* and *The Merry Wives of Windsor* do not deserve a more dignified title than Farce, for they make no more lofty attempt than to be funny, often by very stale, dull means.) In general, the plans of the Romances are similar. Two or three groups of characters manipulate two or three separate but interrelated stories, which are eventually brought together in a Finale. Many of the story-devices are the stock-in-trade of romance—shipwreck, used as a symbol of wrecked hopes and to account for lost identity (compare the use of shipwreck in *Twelfth Night, Pericles, Winter's Tale, Merchant of Venice,* and *The Tempest*); the twin motif; the masquerading of girls as boys. It is Shakespeare's magic, the combination of towering genius with extreme practicality, to create characters of such freshness, variety, and originality, and then to place them in exceedingly conventional and traditional environments. "Once upon a time there was an old King who had three daughters . . ." We are at the deep roots of storytelling. When the King speaks with the accents of Lear, when the Wicked Sisters are dames of the calibre of Regan and Goneril, we are well away. The familiarity of the armature enables Shakespeare to cover it with clay as strange, mysterious, and explosive as *King Lear.* Were the plot as strange and original as its treatment, we should be lost indeed. The startling revelation of human nature in an Angelo or a Leontes, the subtlety of Feste and Jaques, the touching absurdity and humanity of Armado, Malvolio, Parolles; the nobility and intelligence of Helena (*All's Well*), the wit of Beatrice and Rosalind—all these are so unconventional, so

xlii

essentially *not* "off-the-peg," that they are rightly placed in the Ready Made Department of conventional romance.

The plan of Shakespearean comedy requires an elaborate Finale in which all the chief characters appear and all the plots are tied together in a bow. These Finales must proceed like greased lightning and must swing, without any screeching of gears, from melodrama to farce, from farce to poignant emotion. The demands upon the small-part players are almost more exacting than upon the leading actors. In *Twelfth Night*, for instance, Fabian has to read aloud a long, explanatory letter just before the end of the play, just when the least drop in tension will have people reaching for their hats. In *Measure for Measure* Friar Peter, a part almost non-existent otherwise, sets the key and tempo for the whole great Finale Movement.

Every now and again the headlong speed is interrupted for a great moment of revelation or emotion—the recognition between the Twins in *Twelfth Night*, the meeting of Perdita with her mother in *Winter's Tale*, the forgiveness of Angelo in *Measure*, or of Bertram in *All's Well*.

I have never seen one of these great Finales played with anything approaching adequate brilliance. The technical demands are too great. But I have seen blinding flashes. I recall particularly, in a production of *Measure for Measure* by Peter Brook, the impact of Isabella's forgiveness of Angelo. Nothing is said. The text gives no indication of the moment. The effect is made by a sudden pause after whirlwind speed, by a profound silence after tumult, by stillness after movement—in short, by technical means inaccessible to a Reader, but which are the very fabric of good Theatre.

All of us, through previous encounters in the theatre, through reading, through pictorial representations of Shakespearean scenes and characters, most important of all, through oral tradition—all of us bring to our approach to Shakespeare a mass of preconception. For instance, upon the part of Lady Macbeth the imprint of Sarah Siddons has been set for nearly two hundred years. No student of the theatre, no serious actress approaching the part, can entirely rid themselves of the idea that Lady Macbeth should look like Romney's portrait of Mrs. Siddons as The Tragic Muse, should sound as we understand that Mrs. Siddons sounded. It is said that she asked a waiter to bring some mustard and the poor man fainted away, so thrilling was her tone.

Such legacies from tradition must not be accepted without thought. Does the text demand this formidable, massive, contralto version of Lady Macbeth? The answer is no. The fact that Shakespeare must have known that the part was to be played by a boy undermines the Siddons idea.

The so-called "comic" parts tend to be far too coarsely and obviously done. This is part of a British, post-Restoration tradition that representations on the stage of members of the Lower Classes or Foreigners—much the same thing—must be in broadly comic terms. So it is customary for Dogberry and Verges or the Clowns in *Midsummer Night's Dream* and *Love's Labour's Lost* to be performed in terms of vaudeville knockabout.

Then there is the tradition that the parents, uncles, and aunts of Principal Personages should all be from seventy-five to a hundred years old. I think this has come about because the "star" parts are generally played by mature heavyweights. There are two excellent reasons for this: first, the youngsters rarely have the experience and skill to support an evening; second, the public likes to see a celebrated "Name" in the lead. Therefore Romeo and Juliet, or Beatrice and Benedick, are customarily played by forty-year-olds in gold wigs and tons of rouge. So it is logical that the lesser roles of their seniors be played, either by very old character actors, also wildly rouged to suggest a sprightly sixty-eight, or by very young aspirants who, to disguise the fact that they are the right age to be Juliet's children, appear as living corpses, inexpertly wrinkled, crouched over canes, simulating, with all the enthusiasm of youth, deafness, palsy, and the falling sickness.

All this, however, represents only the unintelligent use of tradition. In fact, in the theatre, tradition is as indispensable as in any other human activity. The French Theatre is above all others fortunate in that the Comédie Française possesses an unbroken tradition from Molière to the present day. Intelligent innovation is ceaselessly made, but the tradition is there.

In Britain there was the fatal break after the suppression of the Elizabethan-Jacobean Theatre until the Restoration of the Monarchy nearly fifty years later. The Restoration Theatre had little in common with the old tradition. The physical, social, and commercial relation of the actors to their audience was now quite different; so were the aim and style of playwriting and, consequently, of acting. Not only had the old tradition gone, the new theatre was far less securely rooted as an amenity of civilised life than was the Comédie in Paris. Throughout the eighteenth and early nineteenth centuries the British theatre existed only on sufferance. It enjoyed no state subsidy, no official prestige, and continued to be the target of puritanical moral stricture.

Nevertheless Shakespeare continued to be played. Dryden first, then Cibber, then Garrick mutilated, rewrote, rearranged the works, but kept them alive. Kean was followed at the turn of the century by Kemble, Macready, Phelps, and, finally, Irving. With his extraordinary personal prestige, immeasurably assisted by the magnetism of his leading lady Ellen Terry, Irving restored the serious theatre to the status of a National Institution, an indispensable necessity for a civilised metropolis, not just a slightly naughty and entirely commercial form of amusement.

Meantime, during the two-hundred-year interlude, the serious study of Shakespeare had passed from the Theatre into the realm of Scholarship. Alas, almost all of this work has been done in complete isolation from the professional stage.

Since Irving, the Shakespeare Memorial Theatre at Stratford upon Avon and the Old Vic in London have been established as permanent homes of Shakespearean Repertory Companies. Through these, for a generation, has passed the cream of British theatrical talent. Hardly an actor or actress, director or designer of importance but owes them a debt for having been brought into working contact with the plays, and into a stream which, still too recent to be dignified by the name of tradition, is nonetheless powerful and continuous. This new theatrical Movement is not out of touch with contemporary

xlv

scholarship, and much is being done from both sides to bridge the gulf, which for so long had sundered study from stage.

In America Shakespearean scholarship has, during the last thirty or forty years, flourished exceedingly. Much is already owed by Europe to American research. The theatrical side, however, is another question. At present America hardly sees any of Shakespeare's plays, or for that matter any classical plays, except in productions imported from Europe or else performed, necessarily amateurishly, in colleges and Little Theatres.

Therefore, in the present state of the professional theatre in America, it would, in my opinion, be hard to cast a Shakespeare play adequately. There are plenty of brilliantly talented actors but hardly any of them know even the elements of how to handle dialogue in verse. They can argue the hind leg off a brilliantly intelligent donkey about Motivation or Subconscious Desire or How Many Angels Can Sit on a Libido; but they can't get up and fire off an Aria.

Weakness in declamation is not confined to America. It is, to a rather lesser degree, a weakness all over the English-speaking world, and probably for the same reason—the inimical reception of declamation by the microphone and the fact that current playwriting favours not the Aria, but the shrug and the grunt. I think too that we are shy of declamation because many of us remember the dregs of the old nineteenth-century tradition, the throaty, barnstorming Yawp, with elongated vowels, over-explosive consonants, and interminable, would-be expressive pauses: Elocution. But it is unfair and absurd to condemn the idea of Rhetoric because it is sometimes vilely executed. Its absence from our theatre is the sadder and the odder because there is so great a public appetite for Music. The wild success of a good Musical, and the considerable success of even indifferent Musicals, is proof of that.

Shakespeare's plays, too, are Musicals. We neglect this fact not just at our artistic peril, we are throwing away a box office pearl. These Comedies are full of music, not just the songs, with which Shakespeare has lovingly sprinkled them, but the spoken music of the verse. This music will continue to be unheard until we can learn again to make the lines "sing"; until, in fact, we more generally realise that singing is only speech raised to a higher power. Molière's *bourgeois gentil-homme* was delighted and astonished to find that, without knowing it, he had all his life been speaking Prose. Similarly, most of us go through life unaware that the gift of song is ours for the having. All we need is a little more awareness of what we are doing and a good deal more care about how we do it.

This loss of music is part of the high price which we of the English-speaking world must pay for having so long regarded our single greatest source of Melody as being suitable only for the study—literature, not music.

If this essay is anything, it is, quite inappropriately to a Connoisseurs' *literary* and *illustrated* edition, a plea for getting Shakespeare *off* the shelf, *out* of the study, and back *onto* the stage, where he belongs.

But the preliminary to this is a fuller realisation that Shakespeare's works are not the first-prize bores which they seemed to all of us at school. A fine short-cut to that end is their presentation, not in the drably utilitarian dress of a school-book, not in the "compendious," india-paper, double-column department—a secular Bible—but in a really handsome edition, a pleasure to handle and to read.

A Note on the Illustrations

BY EDWARD ARDIZZONE

I HAVE HAD, for many years now, a theory of what the illustrator's task should be, and it goes something like this: The illustrator's job is to create a visual background which the reader can people with the author's characters; or, to put it another way, to stimulate the reader's imagination rather than to do all his imagining for him.

It follows, then, that any too detailed rendering of a specific character should be avoided, lest it go between the reader and the author, creating a sort of third-party intrusion. Some delineation of character, of course, is essential; a Falstaff or a Malvolio has to be drawn. On the whole, however, I try not to impose my personality too much between an author and his readers.

In illustrating the comedies of Shakespeare, I found myself faced with two main problems.

The first arose from the very fact that the plays are designed to be acted on a stage. In visualising a scene, I put myself in the position of a member of the audience. But, alas! the tall, upright shape of a full-page illustration is a difficult medium in which to describe a stage scene. So I compromised. Of the two illustrations I made for each play, one is upright; the second extends from one side of the stage to the other. To see these latter illustrations you will have to turn the book ninety degrees. Actually the practice of drawing illustrations lengthwise, or at right angles to the type, has many honourable precedents; it flourished hardily, for instance, in the Georgian and Victorian eras.

The second problem was that of costume. The more one knows of Shakespeare the more one realises—such is the universal quality of his work—that one can dress his plays in any period one wishes. There have, of course, been many experiments in this matter of costume, such as dressing plays in modern clothes or Victorian clothes. But all the same, there has grown over the past century a traditional way which we have come to accept, and this, after some thought, I have tried to follow.

In general I have endeavoured to create a visual analogy of the chosen scene. How far I have succeeded in doing this I cannot tell. But if enjoyment is any guide to success, then perhaps something of the master's quality has come through.

xlviii

The Tempest

THE TEMPEST

THE TEMPEST can be dated within narrow limits, and can be shown to be, if not the very last, at least the last but one of all Shakespeare's works.

King James had the piece performed at court on 1st November 1611. So much the record for that period kept by the Master of the Revels makes certain.

Shakespeare must have written the play some time after September 1610, for not till then could the poet have been in possession of information he turns to account in the drama; for *The Tempest*, although one of the most personal of Shakespeare's works, was suggested in outline at least to the dramatist by an event that startled London and was for a season the talk of the town.

In June 1609 a fleet of nine vessels had set out from Plymouth for Virginia to reinforce the colony recently planted there. Towards the end of that month a storm scattered the fleet and the Sea-Venture carrying Sir George Somers the Admiral, and Sir Thomas Gates the newly appointed Governor of Virginia, had to be run ashore on the Bermudas to escape foundering. The other vessels made for Virginia, and reports were sent to England of the loss of the Admiral and Governor.

The missing ship's company however had a miraculous escape. They got ashore safely, were able to live on the island, and there built pinnaces that enabled them to reach Jamestown on 23rd May 1610, nearly a year after their departure from Plymouth. The news of their adventures and safe arrival reached England in September 1610.

The speculation aroused by this remarkable series of happenings Shakespeare took advantage of in the play he must have set about composing soon after the story became public.

It is not, however, merely externals, such as the shipwreck that opens the play or the very title of the piece, that the story of the Sea-Venture and affairs in Virginia suggested to Shakespeare. With the news of the fortunate escape of the Governor and his companions came reports of unhappy con-

ditions in Virginia, and of difficulties not due to the climate
or the soil but caused by the conduct of the colonists themselves. The scheme was more than a merely commercial venture, although those who financed it were not indifferent to
this aspect of the company's affairs: the leading members of
the Virginia Council however also regarded it as a political
experiment and they exerted themselves to obtain from the
King a charter that would give the colony powers of self-
government wider than those usually acceptable to the purely
official mind. What was now reported from Virginia disap-
pointed the hopes of the Patriots, as these members of the
Council were called, who hoped to erect in Virginia 'a free,
popular state, in which the inhabitants should have no government put upon them but by their own consent.'

The Council had not neglected public opinion. Early in
1610 when news of the disappearance of the Sea-Venture
first reached England and the fate of its company was unknown the Council had printed *A True and Sincere Declaration of the Purpose and Ends of the Plantation begun in Virginia*. By this and other means they hoped to quieten alarmist
rumours. Late in 1610 Silvester Jourdan, who had been in the
Bermuda wreck and had just returned to England, published
*A Discovery of the Barmudas, Otherwise called the Ile of
Divels;* this the Council followed up with *A true Declaration
of the estate of the Colony of Virginia, with a confutacon of
such scandalous reportes as have tended to the disgrace of so
worthy an enterprise*. They did not however make public a
letter from William Strachey, who went out with Gates and
acted as his secretary, for in this the condition of the colony
is examined without reserve. Only when the Virginia Company had been dissolved was this document put in print in
Purchas his Pilgrimes with the title *A true Repertory of the
wracke, and redemption of Sir Thomas Gates, Knight; upon,
and from the ilands of the Bermudas*. Of these four documents the public could read three; Shakespeare however had
read the fourth and confidential paper, and from it he drew
not merely details that might give vividness to his shipwreck
and to the picture of his island but incidents, or at least suggestions for them, involving idleness, treasons and want of
government.

Shakespeare then combined in his play the miraculous with the realistic; but he was not asking of his audience any special effort of the imagination in setting his scene on an enchanted island. The Bermudas had seemed to the stranded mariners a haunted spot; the climate was mild, the soil fertile, and good food abundant, but the place was still the isle of devils, a region given over to wicked spirits. Shakespeare's audience would have no difficulty in accepting Caliban as a native of Prospero's island, with Sycorax as his mother and Setebos her god. Setebos is the name given to a Patagonian 'devil' by one of the companions of Magellan; his account of the circumnavigation of the world Shakespeare would find in English in Richard Eden's *The Historie of Travayle* (1577). This and reminiscences from his other reading Shakespeare blended with the Bermudas story to make for his audience a wonderful but not incredible plot. Even the enchanter himself was a type not unfamiliar to their imagination, and remarkable parallels to incidents in Shakespeare's plot have been found in *Die Schöne Sidea*, a play by Jacob Ayrer of Nuremberg who died in 1605. Here also is the princely magician who has lost his heritage, his daughter who marries the son of his enemy, the ministering spirit, the log-carrying, the sword held by a charm in the scabbard. As English actors were frequently on the continent, some report of this play may have come to Shakespeare; but the resemblances are more simply explained by supposing that the English and German dramatists were drawing independently on a common stock of traditional story.

Shakespeare himself was at the end of his career, and it is hardly possible not to see, as the poet Campbell suggested, in Prospero's resignation of his magic a reflection of Shakespeare's own farewell to his art.

MIRANDA. *If by your art, my dearest father, you have*
Put the wild waters in this roar, allay them

(ACT I. SCENE II)

ALONSO, *King of Naples*
SEBASTIAN, *his brother*
PROSPERO, *the right Duke of Milan*
ANTONIO, *his brother, the usurping Duke of Milan*
FERDINAND, *son to the King of Naples*
GONZALO, *an honest old counsellor*
ADRIAN ⎱ *lords*
FRANCISCO ⎰
CALIBAN, *a savage and deformed slave*
TRINCULO, *a jester*
STEPHANO, *a drunken butler*
MASTER OF A SHIP
BOATSWAIN
MARINERS

MIRANDA, *daughter to Prospero*

ARIEL, *an airy spirit*
IRIS
CERES
JUNO ⎱ *spirits*
NYMPHS
REAPERS
Other Spirits *attending on Prospero*

SCENE:

A ship at sea; afterwards an uninhabited island

The Tempest

ACT I. SCENE 1

*On a ship at sea; a tempestuous noise of thunder
and lightning heard*

Enter a SHIPMASTER *and a* BOATSWAIN

MASTER. Boatswain!

BOATSWAIN. Here, master; what cheer?

MASTER. Good! Speak to th' mariners; fall to't yarely, or we
run ourselves aground; bestir, bestir.   *Exit*

Enter MARINERS

BOATSWAIN. Heigh, my hearts! cheerly, cheerly, my hearts!
yare, yare! Take in the topsail. Tend to th' master's whistle. Blow till thou burst thy wind, if room enough.

Enter ALONSO, SEBASTIAN, ANTONIO, FERDINAND,
GONZALO, *and* OTHERS

ALONSO. Good boatswain, have care. Where's the master?
Play the men.

BOATSWAIN. I pray now, keep below.

ANTONIO. Where is the master, boson?

BOATSWAIN. Do you not hear him? You mar our labour;
keep your cabins; you do assist the storm.

GONZALO. Nay, good, be patient.

BOATSWAIN. When the sea is. Hence! What cares these
roarers for the name of king? To cabin! silence! Trouble
us not.

GONZALO. Good, yet remember whom thou hast aboard.

BOATSWAIN. None that I more love than myself. You are a
counsellor; if you can command these elements to silence,
and work the peace of the present, we will not hand a
rope more. Use your authority; if you cannot, give thanks
you have liv'd so long, and make yourself ready in your
cabin for the mischance of the hour, if it so hap.—Cheerly,

good hearts!—Out of our way, I say.   *Exit*

GONZALO. I have great comfort from this fellow. Methinks
he hath no drowning mark upon him; his complexion is
perfect gallows. Stand fast, good Fate, to his hanging;
make the rope of his destiny our cable, for our own doth
little advantage. If he be not born to be hang'd, our case
is miserable.   *Exeunt*

Re-enter BOATSWAIN

BOATSWAIN. Down with the topmast. Yare, lower, lower!
Bring her to try wi' th' maincourse. [*A cry within*] A
plague upon this howling! They are louder than the
weather or our office.

Re-enter SEBASTIAN, ANTONIO, *and* GONZALO

Yet again! What do you here? Shall we give o'er, and
drown? Have you a mind to sink?

SEBASTIAN. A pox o' your throat, you bawling, blasphemous,
incharitable dog!

BOATSWAIN. Work you, then.

ANTONIO. Hang, cur; hang, you whoreson, insolent noise-
maker; we are less afraid to be drown'd than thou art.

GONZALO. I'll warrant him for drowning, though the ship
were no stronger than a nutshell, and as leaky as an un-
stanched wench.

BOATSWAIN. Lay her a-hold, a-hold; set her two courses; off
to sea again; lay her off.

Enter MARINERS, *wet*

MARINERS. All lost! to prayers, to prayers! all lost!   *Exeunt*

BOATSWAIN. What, must our mouths be cold?

GONZALO. The King and Prince at prayers!
Let's assist them,
For our case is as theirs.

SEBASTIAN. I am out of patience.

ANTONIO. We are merely cheated of our lives by drunkards.
This wide-chopp'd rascal—would thou mightst lie drowning
The washing of ten tides!

GONZALO. He'll be hang'd yet,

8

Though every drop of water swear against it,
And gape at wid'st to glut him.
[*A confused noise within:* Mercy on us!
We split, we split! Farewell, my wife and children!
Farewell, brother! We split, we split, we split!]
ANTONIO. Let's all sink wi' th' King.
SEBASTIAN. Let's take leave of him.
Exeunt ANTONIO *and* SEBASTIAN
GONZALO. Now would I give a thousand furlongs of sea for
an acre of barren ground—long heath, brown furze, any
thing. The wills above be done, but I would fain die a
dry death. *Exeunt*

SCENE 2

The island. Before PROSPERO'S *cell*

Enter PROSPERO *and* MIRANDA

MIRANDA. If by your art, my dearest father, you have
Put the wild waters in this roar, allay them.
The sky, it seems, would pour down stinking pitch,
But that the sea, mounting to th' welkin's cheek,
Dashes the fire out. O, I have suffered
With those that I saw suffer! A brave vessel,
Who had no doubt some noble creature in her,
Dash'd all to pieces! O, the cry did knock
Against my very heart! Poor souls, they perish'd.
Had I been any god of power, I would
Have sunk the sea within the earth or ere
It should the good ship so have swallow'd and
The fraughting souls within her.
PROSPERO. Be collected;
No more amazement; tell your piteous heart
There's no harm done.
MIRANDA. O, woe the day!
PROSPERO. No harm.
I have done nothing but in care of thee,
Of thee, my dear one, thee, my daughter, who
Art ignorant of what thou art, nought knowing

9

Of whence I am, nor that I am more better
Than Prospero, master of a full poor cell,
And thy no greater father.

MIRANDA. More to know
Did never meddle with my thoughts.

PROSPERO. 'Tis time
I should inform thee farther. Lend thy hand,
And pluck my magic garment from me. So,

[*Lays down his mantle*]

Lie there my art. Wipe thou thine eyes; have comfort.
The direful spectacle of the wreck, which touch'd
The very virtue of compassion in thee,
I have with such provision in mine art
So safely ordered that there is no soul—
No, not so much perdition as an hair
Betid to any creature in the vessel
Which thou heard'st cry, which thou saw'st sink. Sit down,
For thou must now know farther.

MIRANDA. You have often
Begun to tell me what I am; but stopp'd,
And left me to a bootless inquisition,
Concluding 'Stay; not yet.'

PROSPERO. The hour's now come;
The very minute bids thee ope thine ear.
Obey, and be attentive. Canst thou remember
A time before we came unto this cell?
I do not think thou canst; for then thou wast not
Out three years old.

MIRANDA. Certainly, sir, I can.

PROSPERO. By what? By any other house, or person?
Of any thing the image, tell me, that
Hath kept with thy remembrance?

MIRANDA. 'Tis far off,
And rather like a dream than an assurance
That my remembrance warrants. Had I not
Four, or five, women once, that tended me?

PROSPERO. Thou hadst, and more, Miranda. But how is it
That this lives in thy mind? What seest thou else
In the dark backward and abysm of time?
If thou rememb'rest aught, ere thou cam'st here,

How thou cam'st here thou mayst.

MIRANDA. But that I do not.

PROSPERO. Twelve year since, Miranda, twelve year since,
Thy father was the Duke of Milan, and
A prince of power.

MIRANDA. Sir, are not you my father?

PROSPERO. Thy mother was a piece of virtue, and
She said thou wast my daughter; and thy father
Was Duke of Milan, and his only heir
And princess no worse issued.

MIRANDA. O, the heavens!
What foul play had we that we came from thence?
Or blessed was't we did?

PROSPERO. Both, both, my girl.
By foul play, as thou say'st, were we heav'd thence;
But blessedly holp hither.

MIRANDA. O, my heart bleeds
To think o' th' teen that I have turn'd you to,
Which is from my remembrance. Please you, farther.

PROSPERO. My brother and thy uncle, call'd Antonio—
I pray thee, mark me that a brother should
Be so perfidious. He, whom next thyself
Of all the world I lov'd, and to him put
The manage of my state; as at that time
Through all the signories it was the first,
And Prospero the prime duke, being so reputed
In dignity, and for the liberal arts
Without a parallel, those being all my study—
The government I cast upon my brother
And to my state grew stranger, being transported
And rapt in secret studies. Thy false uncle—
Dost thou attend me?

MIRANDA. Sir, most heedfully.

PROSPERO. Being once perfected how to grant suits,
How to deny them, who t' advance, and who
To trash for over-topping, new created
The creatures that were mine, I say, or chang'd 'em,
Or else new form'd 'em; having both the key
Of officer and office, set all hearts i' th' state
To what tune pleas'd his ear; that now he was

The ivy which had hid my princely trunk
And suck'd my verdure out on't. Thou attend'st not.
MIRANDA. O, good sir, I do!
PROSPERO. I pray thee, mark me.
  I thus neglecting worldly ends, all dedicated
  To closeness and the bettering of my mind
  With that which, but by being so retir'd,
  O'er-priz'd all popular rate, in my false brother
  Awak'd an evil nature; and my trust,
  Like a good parent, did beget of him
  A falsehood, in its contrary as great
  As my trust was; which had indeed no limit,
  A confidence sans bound. He being thus lorded,
  Not only with what my revenue yielded,
  But what my power might else exact, like one
  Who having into truth, by telling of it,
  Made such a sinner of his memory,
  To credit his own lie—he did believe
  He was indeed the Duke; out o' th' substitution,
  And executing th' outward face of royalty
  With all prerogative. Hence his ambition growing—
  Dost thou hear?
MIRANDA. Your tale, sir, would cure deafness.
PROSPERO. To have no screen between this part he play'd
  And him he play'd it for, he needs will be
  Absolute Milan. Me, poor man—my library
  Was dukedom large enough—of temporal royalties
  He thinks me now incapable; confederates,
  So dry he was for sway, wi' th' King of Naples,
  To give him annual tribute, do him homage,
  Subject his coronet to his crown, and bend
  The dukedom, yet unbow'd—alas, poor Milan!—
  To most ignoble stooping.
MIRANDA. O the heavens!
PROSPERO. Mark his condition, and th' event, then tell me
  If this might be a brother.
MIRANDA. I should sin
  To think but nobly of my grandmother:
  Good wombs have borne bad sons.
PROSPERO. Now the condition:

This King of Naples, being an enemy
To me inveterate, hearkens my brother's suit;
Which was, that he, in lieu o' th' premises,
Of homage, and I know not how much tribute,
Should presently extirpate me and mine
Out of the dukedom, and confer fair Milan
With all the honours on my brother. Whereon,
A treacherous army levied, one midnight
Fated to th' purpose, did Antonio open
The gates of Milan; and, i' th' dead of darkness,
The ministers for th' purpose hurried thence
Me and thy crying self.
MIRANDA. Alack, for pity!
    I, not rememb'ring how I cried out then,
    Will cry it o'er again; it is a hint
    That wrings mine eyes to't.
PROSPERO. Hear a little further,
    And then I'll bring thee to the present business
    Which now's upon 's; without the which this story
    Were most impertinent.
MIRANDA. Wherefore did they not
    That hour destroy us?
PROSPERO. Well demanded, wench!
    My tale provokes that question. Dear, they durst not,
    So dear the love my people bore me; nor set
    A mark so bloody on the business; but
    With colours fairer painted their foul ends.
    In few, they hurried us aboard a bark;
    Bore us some leagues to sea, where they prepared
    A rotten carcass of a butt, not rigg'd,
    Nor tackle, sail, nor mast; the very rats
    Instinctively have quit it. There they hoist us,
    To cry to th' sea, that roar'd to us; to sigh
    To th' winds, whose pity, sighing back again,
    Did us but loving wrong.
MIRANDA. Alack, what trouble
    Was I then to you!
PROSPERO. O, a cherubin
    Thou wast that did preserve me! Thou didst smile,
    Infused with a fortitude from heaven,

13

When I have deck'd the sea with drops full salt,
Under my burden groan'd; which rais'd in me
An undergoing stomach, to bear up
Against what should ensue.
MIRANDA. How came we ashore?
PROSPERO. By Providence divine.
Some food we had and some fresh water that
A noble Neapolitan, Gonzalo,
Out of his charity, who being then appointed
Master of this design, did give us, with
Rich garments, linens, stuffs, and necessaries,
Which since have steaded much; so, of his gentleness,
Knowing I lov'd my books, he furnish'd me
From mine own library with volumes that
I prize above my dukedom.
MIRANDA. Would I might
But ever see that man!
PROSPERO. Now I arise.   *[Puts on his mantle]*
Sit still, and hear the last of our sea-sorrow.
Here in this island we arriv'd; and here
Have I, thy schoolmaster, made thee more profit
Than other princess' can, that have more time
For vainer hours, and tutors not so careful.
MIRANDA. Heavens thank you for't! And now, I pray you,
 sir,
For still 'tis beating in my mind, your reason
For raising this sea-storm?
PROSPERO. Know thus far forth:
By accident most strange, bountiful Fortune,
Now my dear lady, hath mine enemies
Brought to this shore; and by my prescience
I find my zenith doth depend upon
A most auspicious star, whose influence
If now I court not, but omit, my fortunes
Will ever after droop. Here cease more questions;
Thou art inclin'd to sleep; 'tis a good dullness,
And give it way. I know thou canst not choose.
           *[*MIRANDA *sleeps]*
Come away, servant; come; I am ready now.
Approach, my Ariel. Come.

Enter ARIEL

ARIEL. All hail, great master! grave sir, hail! I come
  To answer thy best pleasure; be't to fly,
  To swim, to dive into the fire, to ride
  On the curl'd clouds. To thy strong bidding task
  Ariel and all his quality.
PROSPERO. Hast thou, spirit,
  Perform'd to point the tempest that I bade thee?
ARIEL. To every article.
  I boarded the King's ship; now on the beak,
  Now in the waist, the deck, in every cabin,
  I flam'd amazement. Sometime I'd divide,
  And burn in many places; on the topmast,
  The yards, and bowsprit, would I flame distinctly,
  Then meet and join. Jove's lightning, the precursors
  O' th' dreadful thunder-claps, more momentary
  And sight-outrunning were not; the fire and cracks
  Of sulphurous roaring the most mighty Neptune
  Seem to besiege, and make his bold waves tremble,
  Yea, his dread trident shake.
PROSPERO. My brave spirit!
  Who was so firm, so constant, that this coil
  Would not infect his reason?
ARIEL. Not a soul
  But felt a fever of the mad, and play'd
  Some tricks of desperation. All but mariners
  Plung'd in the foaming brine, and quit the vessel,
  Then all afire with me; the King's son, Ferdinand,
  With hair up-staring—then like reeds, not hair—
  Was the first man that leapt; cried 'Hell is empty,
  And all the devils are here.'
PROSPERO. Why, that's my spirit!
  But was not this nigh shore?
ARIEL. Close by, my master.
PROSPERO. But are they, Ariel, safe?
ARIEL. Not a hair perish'd;
  On their sustaining garments not a blemish,
  But fresher than before; and, as thou bad'st me,
  In troops I have dispers'd them 'bout the isle.

The King's son have I landed by himself,
Whom I left cooling of the air with sighs
In an odd angle of the isle, and sitting,
His arms in this sad knot.
PROSPERO. Of the King's ship,
The mariners, say how thou hast dispos'd,
And all the rest o' th' fleet?
ARIEL. Safely in harbour
Is the King's ship; in the deep nook, where once
Thou call'dst me up at midnight to fetch dew
From the still-vex'd Bermoothes, there she's hid;
The mariners all under hatches stowed,
Who, with a charm join'd to their suff'red labour,
I have left asleep; and for the rest o' th' fleet,
Which I dispers'd, they all have met again,
And are upon the Mediterranean flote
Bound sadly home for Naples,
Supposing that they saw the King's ship wreck'd,
And his great person perish.
PROSPERO. Ariel, thy charge
Exactly is perform'd; but there's more work.
What is the time o' th' day?
ARIEL. Past the mid season.
PROSPERO. At least two glasses. The time 'twixt six and now
Must by us both be spent most preciously.
ARIEL. Is there more toil? Since thou dost give me pains,
Let me remember thee what thou hast promis'd,
Which is not yet perform'd me.
PROSPERO. How now, moody?
What is 't thou canst demand?
ARIEL. My liberty.
PROSPERO. Before the time be out? No more!
ARIEL. I prithee,
Remember I have done thee worthy service,
Told thee no lies, made thee no mistakings, serv'd
Without or grudge or grumblings. Thou didst promise
To bate me a full year.
PROSPERO. Dost thou forget
From what a torment I did free thee?
ARIEL. No.

PROSPERO. Thou dost; and think'st it much to tread the ooze
  Of the salt deep,
  To run upon the sharp wind of the north,
  To do me business in the veins o' th' earth
  When it is bak'd with frost.
ARIEL. I do not, sir.
PROSPERO. Thou liest, malignant thing. Hast thou forgot
  The foul witch Sycorax, who with age and envy
  Was grown into a hoop? Hast thou forgot her?
ARIEL. No, sir.
PROSPERO. Thou hast. Where was she born?
  Speak; tell me.
ARIEL. Sir, in Argier.
PROSPERO. O, was she so? I must
  Once in a month recount what thou hast been,
  Which thou forget'st. This damn'd witch Sycorax,
  For mischiefs manifold, and sorceries terrible
  To enter human hearing, from Argier
  Thou know'st was banish'd; for one thing she did
  They would not take her life. Is not this true?
ARIEL. Ay, sir.
PROSPERO. This blue-ey'd hag was hither brought with child,
  And here was left by th' sailors. Thou, my slave,
  As thou report'st thyself, wast then her servant;
  And, for thou wast a spirit too delicate
  To act her earthy and abhorr'd commands,
  Refusing her grand hests, she did confine thee,
  By help of her more potent ministers,
  And in her most unmitigable rage,
  Into a cloven pine; within which rift
  Imprison'd thou didst painfully remain
  A dozen years; within which space she died,
  And left thee there, where thou didst vent thy groans
  As fast as mill-wheels strike. Then was this island—
  Save for the son that she did litter here,
  A freckl'd whelp, hag-born—not honour'd with
  A human shape.
ARIEL. Yes, Caliban her son.
PROSPERO. Dull thing, I say so; he, that Caliban
  Whom now I keep in service. Thou best know'st

What torment I did find thee in; thy groans
Did make wolves howl, and penetrate the breasts
Of ever-angry bears; it was a torment
To lay upon the damn'd, which Sycorax
Could not again undo. It was mine art,
When I arriv'd and heard thee, that made gape
The pine, and let thee out.
ARIEL. I thank thee, master.
PROSPERO. If thou more murmur'st, I will rend an oak
And peg thee in his knotty entrails, till
Thou hast howl'd away twelve winters.
ARIEL. Pardon, master;
I will be correspondent to command,
And do my spriting gently.
PROSPERO. Do so; and after two days
I will discharge thee.
ARIEL. That's my noble master!
What shall I do? Say what. What shall I do?
PROSPERO. Go make thyself like a nymph o' th' sea; be subject
To no sight but thine and mine, invisible
To every eyeball else. Go take this shape,
And hither come in 't. Go, hence with diligence!

Exit ARIEL

Awake, dear heart, awake; thou hast slept well;
Awake.
MIRANDA. The strangeness of your story put
Heaviness in me.
PROSPERO. Shake it off. Come on,
We'll visit Caliban, my slave, who never
Yields us kind answer.
MIRANDA. 'Tis a villain, sir,
I do not love to look on.
PROSPERO. But as 'tis,
We cannot miss him: he does make our fire,
Fetch in our wood, and serves in offices
That profit us. What ho! slave! Caliban!
Thou earth, thou! Speak.
CALIBAN. [*Within*] There's wood enough within.
PROSPERO. Come forth, I say; there's other business for thee.
Come, thou tortoise! when?

Re-enter ARIEL *like a water-nymph*

Fine apparition! My quaint Ariel,
Hark in thine ear.
ARIEL. My lord, it shall be done.   *Exit*
PROSPERO. Thou poisonous slave, got by the devil himself
Upon thy wicked dam, come forth!

Enter CALIBAN

CALIBAN. As wicked dew as e'er my mother brush'd
With raven's feather from unwholesome fen
Drop on you both! A south-west blow on ye
And blister you all o'er!
PROSPERO. For this, be sure, to-night thou shalt have cramps,
Side-stitches that shall pen thy breath up; urchins
Shall, for that vast of night that they may work,
All exercise on thee; thou shalt be pinch'd
As thick as honeycomb, each pinch more stinging
Than bees that made 'em.
CALIBAN. I must eat my dinner.
This island's mine, by Sycorax my mother,
Which thou tak'st from me. When thou cam'st first,
Thou strok'st me and made much of me, wouldst give me
Water with berries in't, and teach me how
To name the bigger light, and how the less,
That burn by day and night; and then I lov'd thee,
And show'd thee all the qualities o' th' isle,
The fresh springs, brine-pits, barren place and fertile.
Curs'd be I that did so! All the charms
Of Sycorax, toads, beetles, bats, light on you!
For I am all the subjects that you have,
Which first was mine own king; and here you sty me
In this hard rock, whiles you do keep from me
The rest o' th' island.
PROSPERO. Thou most lying slave,
Whom stripes may move, not kindness! I have us'd thee,
Filth as thou art, with human care, and lodg'd thee
In mine own cell, till thou didst seek to violate
The honour of my child.
CALIBAN. O ho, O ho! Would't had been done.

Thou didst prevent me; I had peopl'd else
This isle with Calibans.

MIRANDA. Abhorred slave,
Which any print of goodness wilt not take,
Being capable of all ill! I pitied thee,
Took pains to make thee speak, taught thee each hour
One thing or other. When thou didst not, savage,
Know thine own meaning, but wouldst gabble like
A thing most brutish, I endow'd thy purposes
With words that made them known. But thy vile race,
Though thou didst learn, had that in't which good natures
Could not abide to be with; therefore wast thou
Deservedly confin'd into this rock, who hadst
Deserv'd more than a prison.

CALIBAN. You taught me language, and my profit on't
Is, I know how to curse. The red plague rid you
For learning me your language!

PROSPERO. Hag-seed, hence!
Fetch us in fuel. And be quick, thou 'rt best,
To answer other business. Shrug'st thou, malice?
If thou neglect'st, or dost unwillingly
What I command, I'll rack thee with old cramps,
Fill all thy bones with aches, make thee roar,
That beasts shall tremble at thy din.

CALIBAN. No, pray thee.
[*Aside*] I must obey. His art is of such pow'r,
It would control my dam's god, Setebos,
And make a vassal of him.

PROSPERO. So, slave; hence!   *Exit* CALIBAN

Re-enter ARIEL *invisible, playing and singing;*
FERDINAND *following*

ARIEL'S SONG

Come unto these yellow sands,
    And then take hands;
Curtsied when you have and kiss'd,
    The wild waves whist,
Foot it featly here and there,
And, sweet sprites, the burden bear.

Hark, hark!
[*Burden dispersedly:* Bow-wow.]
The watch dogs bark.
[*Burden dispersedly:* Bow-wow.]
Hark, hark! I hear
The strain of strutting chanticleer
Cry, Cock-a-diddle-dow.

FERDINAND. Where should this music be? I' th' air or th'
earth?
It sounds no more; and sure it waits upon
Some god o' th' island. Sitting on a bank,
Weeping again the King my father's wreck,
This music crept by me upon the waters,
Allaying both their fury and my passion
With its sweet air; thence I have follow'd it,
Or it hath drawn me rather. But 'tis gone.
No, it begins again.

ARIEL'S SONG

Full fathom five thy father lies;
    Of his bones are coral made;
Those are pearls that were his eyes;
    Nothing of him that doth fade
But doth suffer a sea-change
Into something rich and strange.
Sea-nymphs hourly ring his knell:
    [*Burden:* Ding-dong.]
Hark! now I hear them—Ding-dong bell.

FERDINAND. The ditty does remember my drown'd father.
This is no mortal business, nor no sound
That the earth owes. I hear it now above me.
PROSPERO. The fringed curtains of thine eye advance,
And say what thou seest yond.
MIRANDA. What is't? a spirit?
Lord, how it looks about! Believe me, sir,
It carries a brave form. But 'tis a spirit.
PROSPERO. No, wench; it eats and sleeps and hath such senses
As we have, such. This gallant which thou seest
Was in the wreck; and but he's something stain'd

With grief, that's beauty's canker, thou mightst call him
A goodly person. He hath lost his fellows,
And strays about to find 'em.
MIRANDA. I might call him
A thing divine; for nothing natural
I ever saw so noble.
PROSPERO. [*Aside*] It goes on, I see,
As my soul prompts it. Spirit, fine spirit! I'll free thee
Within two days for this.
FERDINAND. Most sure, the goddess
On whom these airs attend! Vouchsafe my pray'r
May know if you remain upon this island;
And that you will some good instruction give
How I may bear me here. My prime request,
Which I do last pronounce, is, O you wonder!
If you be maid or no?
MIRANDA. No wonder, sir;
But certainly a maid.
FERDINAND. My language? Heavens!
I am the best of them that speak this speech,
Were I but where 'tis spoken.
PROSPERO. How? the best?
What wert thou, if the King of Naples heard thee?
FERDINAND. A single thing, as I am now, that wonders
To hear thee speak of Naples. He does hear me;
And that he does I weep. Myself am Naples,
Who with mine eyes, never since at ebb, beheld
The King my father wreck'd.
MIRANDA. Alack, for mercy!
FERDINAND. Yes, faith, and all his lords, the Duke of Milan
And his brave son being twain.
PROSPERO. [*Aside*] The Duke of Milan
And his more braver daughter could control thee,
If now 'twere fit to do't. At the first sight
They have chang'd eyes. Delicate Ariel,
I'll set thee free for this. [*To* FERDINAND] A word, good
sir;
I fear you have done yourself some wrong; a word.
MIRANDA. Why speaks my father so ungently? This
Is the third man that e'er I saw; the first

That e'er I sigh'd for. Pity move my father
To be inclin'd my way!
FERDINAND. O, if a virgin,
And your affection not gone forth, I'll make you
The Queen of Naples.
PROSPERO. Soft, sir! one word more.
[*Aside*] They are both in either's pow'rs; but this swift business
I must uneasy make, lest too light winning
Make the prize light. [*To* FERDINAND] One word more; I charge thee
That thou attend me; thou dost here usurp
The name thou ow'st not; and hast put thyself
Upon this island as a spy, to win it
From me, the lord on't.
FERDINAND. No, as I am a man.
MIRANDA. There's nothing ill can dwell in such a temple.
If the ill spirit have so fair a house,
Good things will strive to dwell with't.
PROSPERO. Follow me.
Speak not you for him; he's a traitor. Come;
I'll manacle thy neck and feet together.
Sea-water shalt thou drink; thy food shall be
The fresh-brook mussels, wither'd roots, and husks
Wherein the acorn cradled. Follow.
FERDINAND. No;
I will resist such entertainment till
Mine enemy has more power.
                    [*He draws, and is charmed from moving*]
MIRANDA. O dear father,
Make not too rash a trial of him, for
He's gentle, and not fearful.
PROSPERO. What, I say,
My foot my tutor? Put thy sword up, traitor;
Who mak'st a show but dar'st not strike, thy conscience
Is so possess'd with guilt. Come from thy ward;
For I can here disarm thee with this stick
And make thy weapon drop.
MIRANDA. Beseech you, father!
PROSPERO. Hence! Hang not on my garments.

MIRANDA. Sir, have pity;
I'll be his surety.

PROSPERO. Silence! One word more
Shall make me chide thee, if not hate thee. What!
An advocate for an impostor! hush!
Thou think'st there is no more such shapes as he,
Having seen but him and Caliban. Foolish wench!
To th' most of men this is a Caliban,
And they to him are angels.

MIRANDA. My affections
Are then most humble; I have no ambition
To see a goodlier man.

PROSPERO. Come on; obey.
Thy nerves are in their infancy again,
And have no vigour in them.

FERDINAND. So they are;
My spirits, as in a dream, are all bound up.
My father's loss, the weakness which I feel,
The wreck of all my friends, nor this man's threats
To whom I am subdu'd, are but light to me,
Might I but through my prison once a day
Behold this maid. All corners else o' th' earth
Let liberty make use of; space enough
Have I in such a prison.

PROSPERO. [*Aside*] It works. [*To* FERDINAND] Come on.—
Thou hast done well, fine Ariel! [*To* FERDINAND] Follow
me.
[*To* ARIEL] Hark what thou else shalt do me.

MIRANDA. Be of comfort;
My father's of a better nature, sir,
Than he appears by speech; this is unwonted
Which now came from him.

PROSPERO. [*To* ARIEL] Thou shalt be as free
As mountain winds; but then exactly do
All points of my command.

ARIEL. To th' syllable.

PROSPERO. [*To* FERDINAND] Come, follow. [*To* MIRANDA]
Speak not for him.   *Exeunt*

24

ACT II. SCENE 1

Another part of the island

Enter Alonso, Sebastian, Antonio, Gonzalo, Adrian,
Francisco, *and* Others

Gonzalo. Beseech you, sir, be merry; you have cause,
So have we all, of joy; for our escape
Is much beyond our loss. Our hint of woe
Is common; every day, some sailor's wife,
The masters of some merchant, and the merchant,
Have just our theme of woe; but for the miracle,
I mean our preservation, few in millions
Can speak like us. Then wisely, good sir, weigh
Our sorrow with our comfort.
Alonso. Prithee, peace.
Sebastian. He receives comfort like cold porridge.
Antonio. The visitor will not give him o'er so.
Sebastian. Look, he's winding up the watch of his wit; by
and by it will strike.
Gonzalo. Sir—
Sebastian. One—Tell.
Gonzalo. When every grief is entertain'd that's offer'd,
Comes to th' entertainer—
Sebastian. A dollar.
Gonzalo. Dolour comes to him, indeed; you have spoken
truer than you purpos'd.
Sebastian. You have taken it wiselier than I meant you
should.
Gonzalo. Therefore, my lord—
Antonio. Fie, what a spendthrift is he of his tongue!
Alonso. I prithee, spare.
Gonzalo. Well, I have done; but yet—
Sebastian. He will be talking.
Antonio. Which, of he or Adrian, for a good wager, first
begins to crow?
Sebastian. The old cock.

ANTONIO. The cock'rel.

SEBASTIAN. Done. The wager?

ANTONIO. A laughter.

SEBASTIAN. A match!

ADRIAN. Though this island seem to be desert—

ANTONIO. Ha, ha, ha!

SEBASTIAN. So, you're paid.

ADRIAN. Uninhabitable, and almost inaccessible—

SEBASTIAN. Yet—

ADRIAN. Yet—

ANTONIO. He could not miss't.

ADRIAN. It must needs be of subtle, tender, and delicate temperance.

ANTONIO. Temperance was a delicate wench.

SEBASTIAN. Ay, and a subtle; as he most learnedly deliver'd.

ADRIAN. The air breathes upon us here most sweetly.

SEBASTIAN. As if it had lungs, and rotten ones.

ANTONIO. Or, as 'twere perfum'd by a fen.

GONZALO. Here is everything advantageous to life.

ANTONIO. True; save means to live.

SEBASTIAN. Of that there's none, or little.

GONZALO. How lush and lusty the grass looks! how green!

ANTONIO. The ground indeed is tawny.

SEBASTIAN. With an eye of green in't.

ANTONIO. He misses not much.

SEBASTIAN. No; he doth but mistake the truth totally.

GONZALO. But the rarity of it is, which is indeed almost beyond credit—

SEBASTIAN. As many vouch'd rarities are.

GONZALO. That our garments, being, as they were, drench'd in the sea, hold, notwithstanding, their freshness and glosses, being rather new-dy'd, than stain'd with salt water.

ANTONIO. If but one of his pockets could speak, would it not say he lies?

SEBASTIAN. Ay, or very falsely pocket up his report.

GONZALO. Methinks our garments are now as fresh as when we put them on first in Afric, at the marriage of the King's fair daughter Claribel to the King of Tunis.

SEBASTIAN. 'Twas a sweet marriage, and we prosper well in our return.

ADRIAN. Tunis was never grac'd before with such a paragon to their queen.

GONZALO. Not since widow Dido's time.

ANTONIO. Widow! a pox o' that! How came that 'widow' in? Widow Dido!

SEBASTIAN. What if he had said 'widower Æneas' too? Good Lord, how you take it!

ADRIAN. 'Widow Dido' said you? You make me study of that. She was of Carthage, not of Tunis.

GONZALO. This Tunis, sir, was Carthage.

ADRIAN. Carthage?

GONZALO. I assure you, Carthage.

ANTONIO. His word is more than the miraculous harp.

SEBASTIAN. He hath rais'd the wall, and houses too.

ANTONIO. What impossible matter will he make easy next?

SEBASTIAN. I think he will carry this island home in his pocket, and give it his son for an apple.

ANTONIO. And, sowing the kernels of it in the sea, bring forth more islands.

GONZALO. Ay.

ANTONIO. Why, in good time.

GONZALO. Sir, we were talking that our garments seem now as fresh as when we were at Tunis at the marriage of your daughter, who is now Queen.

ANTONIO. And the rarest that e'er came there.

SEBASTIAN. Bate, I beseech you, widow Dido.

ANTONIO. O, widow Dido! Ay, widow Dido.

GONZALO. Is not, sir, my doublet as fresh as the first day I wore it? I mean, in a sort.

ANTONIO. That 'sort' was well fish'd for.

GONZALO. When I wore it at your daughter's marriage?

ALONSO. You cram these words into mine ears against
  The stomach of my sense. Would I had never
  Married my daughter there; for, coming thence,
  My son is lost; and, in my rate, she too,
  Who is so far from Italy removed
  I ne'er again shall see her. O thou mine heir
  Of Naples and of Milan, what strange fish
  Hath made his meal on thee?

FRANCISCO. Sir, he may live;

I saw him beat the surges under him,
And ride upon their backs; he trod the water,
Whose enmity he flung aside, and breasted
The surge most swoln that met him; his bold head
'Bove the contentious waves he kept, and oared
Himself with his good arms in lusty stroke
To th' shore, that o'er his wave-worn basis bowed,
As stooping to relieve him. I not doubt
He came alive to land.

ALONSO. No, no, he's gone.

SEBASTIAN. Sir, you may thank yourself for this great loss,
That would not bless our Europe with your daughter,
But rather lose her to an African;
Where she, at least, is banish'd from your eye,
Who hath cause to wet the grief on't.

ALONSO. Prithee, peace.

SEBASTIAN. You were kneel'd to, and importun'd otherwise
By all of us; and the fair soul herself
Weigh'd between loathness and obedience at
Which end o' th' beam should bow. We have lost your
son,
I fear, for ever. Milan and Naples have
Moe widows in them of this business' making,
Than we bring men to comfort them;
The fault's your own.

ALONSO. So is the dear'st o' th' loss.

GONZALO. My lord Sebastian,
The truth you speak doth lack some gentleness,
And time to speak it in; you rub the sore,
When you should bring the plaster.

SEBASTIAN. Very well.

ANTONIO. And most chirurgeonly.

GONZALO. It is foul weather in us all, good sir,
When you are cloudy.

SEBASTIAN. Foul weather?

ANTONIO. Very foul.

GONZALO. Had I plantation of this isle, my lord—

ANTONIO. He'd sow 't with nettle-seed.

SEBASTIAN. Or docks, or mallows.

GONZALO. And were the king on't, what would I do?

SEBASTIAN. Scape being drunk for want of wine.

GONZALO. I' th' commonwealth I would by contraries
Execute all things; for no kind of traffic
Would I admit; no name of magistrate;
Letters should not be known; riches, poverty,
And use of service, none; contract, succession,
Bourn, bound of land, tilth, vineyard, none;
No use of metal, corn, or wine, or oil;
No occupation; all men idle, all;
And women too, but innocent and pure;
No sovereignty—

SEBASTIAN. Yet he would be king on't.

ANTONIO. The latter end of his commonwealth forgets the
beginning.

GONZALO. All things in common nature should produce
Without sweat or endeavour. Treason, felony,
Sword, pike, knife, gun, or need of any engine,
Would I not have; but nature should bring forth,
Of it own kind, all foison, all abundance,
To feed my innocent people.

SEBASTIAN. No marrying 'mong his subjects?

ANTONIO. None, man; all idle; whores and knaves.

GONZALO. I would with such perfection govern, sir,
T' excel the golden age.

SEBASTIAN. Save his Majesty!

ANTONIO. Long live Gonzalo!

GONZALO. And—do you mark me, sir?

ALONSO. Prithee, no more; thou dost talk nothing to me.

GONZALO. I do well believe your Highness; and did it to
minister occasion to these gentlemen, who are of such sensible and nimble lungs that they always use to laugh at
nothing.

ANTONIO. 'Twas you we laugh'd at.

GONZALO. Who in this kind of merry fooling am nothing to
you; so you may continue, and laugh at nothing still.

ANTONIO. What a blow was there given!

SEBASTIAN. An it had not fall'n flat-long.

GONZALO. You are gentlemen of brave mettle; you would
lift the moon out of her sphere, if she would continue in
it five weeks without changing.

Enter ARIEL, *invisible, playing solemn music*

SEBASTIAN. We would so, and then go a-bat-fowling.

ANTONIO. Nay, good my lord, be not angry.

GONZALO. No, I warrant you; I will not adventure my discretion so weakly. Will you laugh me asleep, for I am very
heavy?

ANTONIO. Go sleep, and hear us.

[*All sleep but* ALONSO, SEBASTIAN *and* ANTONIO]

ALONSO. What, all so soon asleep! I wish mine eyes
Would, with themselves, shut up my thoughts; I find
They are inclin'd to do so.

SEBASTIAN. Please you, sir,
Do not omit the heavy offer of it:
It seldom visits sorrow; when it doth,
It is a comforter.

ANTONIO. We two, my lord,
Will guard your person while you take your rest,
And watch your safety.

ALONSO. Thank you—wondrous heavy!

[ALONSO *sleeps. Exit* ARIEL]

SEBASTIAN. What a strange drowsiness possesses them!

ANTONIO. It is the quality o' th' climate.

SEBASTIAN. Why
Doth it not then our eyelids sink? I find not
Myself dispos'd to sleep.

ANTONIO. Nor I; my spirits are nimble.
They fell together all, as by consent;
They dropp'd, as by a thunder-stroke. What might,
Worthy Sebastian? O, what might! No more!
And yet methinks I see it in thy face,
What thou shouldst be; th' occasion speaks thee; and
My strong imagination sees a crown
Dropping upon thy head.

SEBASTIAN. What, art thou waking?

ANTONIO. Do you not hear me speak?

SEBASTIAN. I do; and surely
It is a sleepy language, and thou speak'st
Out of thy sleep. What is it thou didst say?
This is a strange repose, to be asleep

30

With eyes wide open; standing, speaking, moving,
And yet so fast asleep.
ANTONIO. Noble Sebastian,
Thou let'st thy fortune sleep—die rather; wink'st
Whiles thou art waking.
SEBASTIAN. Thou dost snore distinctly;
There's meaning in thy snores.
ANTONIO. I am more serious than my custom; you
Must be so too, if heed me; which to do
Trebles thee o'er.
SEBASTIAN. Well, I am standing water.
ANTONIO. I'll teach you how to flow.
SEBASTIAN. Do so: to ebb,
Hereditary sloth instructs me.
ANTONIO. O,
If you but knew how you the purpose cherish,
Whiles thus you mock it! how, in stripping it,
You more invest it! Ebbing men indeed,
Most often, do so near the bottom run
By their own fear or sloth.
SEBASTIAN. Prithee say on.
The setting of thine eye and cheek proclaim
A matter from thee; and a birth, indeed,
Which throes thee much to yield.
ANTONIO. Thus, sir:
Although this lord of weak remembrance, this
Who shall be of as little memory
When he is earth'd, hath here almost persuaded—
For he's a spirit of persuasion, only
Professes to persuade—the King his son's alive,
'Tis as impossible that he's undrown'd
As he that sleeps here swims.
SEBASTIAN. I have no hope
That he's undrown'd.
ANTONIO. O, out of that 'no hope'
What great hope have you! No hope that way is
Another way so high a hope, that even
Ambition cannot pierce a wink beyond,
But doubt discovery there. Will you grant with me
That Ferdinand is drown'd?

SEBASTIAN. He's gone.
ANTONIO. Then tell me,
  Who's the next heir of Naples?
SEBASTIAN. Claribel.
ANTONIO. She that is Queen of Tunis; she that dwells
  Ten leagues beyond man's life; she that from Naples
  Can have no note, unless the sun were post,
  The Man i' th' Moon's too slow, till newborn chins
  Be rough and razorable; she that from whom
  We all were sea-swallow'd, though some cast again,
  And by that destiny, to perform an act
  Whereof what's past is prologue, what to come
  In yours and my discharge.
SEBASTIAN. What stuff is this! How say you?
  'Tis true, my brother's daughter's Queen of Tunis;
  So is she heir of Naples; 'twixt which regions
  There is some space.
ANTONIO. A space whose ev'ry cubit
  Seems to cry out 'How shall that Claribel
  Measure us back to Naples? Keep in Tunis,
  And let Sebastian wake.' Say this were death
  That now hath seiz'd them; why, they were no worse
  Than now they are. There be that can rule Naples
  As well as he that sleeps; lords that can prate
  As amply and unnecessarily
  As this Gonzalo; I myself could make
  A chough of as deep chat. O, that you bore
  The mind that I do! What a sleep were this
  For your advancement! Do you understand me?
SEBASTIAN. Methinks I do.
ANTONIO. And how does your content
  Tender your own good fortune?
SEBASTIAN. I remember
  You did supplant your brother Prospero.
ANTONIO. True.
  And look how well my garments sit upon me,
  Much feater than before. My brother's servants
  Were then my fellows; now they are my men.
SEBASTIAN. But, for your conscience—
ANTONIO. Ay, sir; where lies that? If 'twere a kibe,

'Twould put me to my slipper; but I feel not
This deity in my bosom; twenty consciences
That stand 'twixt me and Milan, candied be they
And melt, ere they molest! Here lies your brother,
No better than the earth he lies upon,
If he were that which now he's like—that's dead;
Whom I with this obedient steel, three inches of it,
Can lay to bed for ever; whiles you, doing thus,
To the perpetual wink for aye might put
This ancient morsel, this Sir Prudence, who
Should not upbraid our course. For all the rest,
They'll take suggestion as a cat laps milk;
They'll tell the clock to any business that
We say befits the hour.
SEBASTIAN. Thy case, dear friend,
  Shall be my precedent; as thou got'st Milan,
  I'll come by Naples. Draw thy sword. One stroke
  Shall free thee from the tribute which thou payest;
  And I the King shall love thee.
ANTONIO. Draw together;
  And when I rear my hand, do you the like,
  To fall it on Gonzalo.
SEBASTIAN. O, but one word.   [*They talk apart*]

Re-enter ARIEL, *invisible, with music and song*

ARIEL. My master through his art foresees the danger
  That you, his friend, are in; and sends me forth—
  For else his project dies—to keep them living.
                          [*Sings in* GONZALO'S *ear*]

      While you here do snoring lie,
      Open-ey'd conspiracy
          His time doth take.
      If of life you keep a care,
      Shake off slumber, and beware.
          Awake, awake!

ANTONIO. Then let us both be sudden.
GONZALO. Now, good angels
  Preserve the King!   [*They wake*]

33

ALONSO. Why, how now?—Ho, awake!—Why are you
  drawn?
  Wherefore this ghastly looking?
GONZALO. What's the matter?
SEBASTIAN. Whiles we stood here securing your repose,
  Even now, we heard a hollow burst of bellowing
  Like bulls, or rather lions; did't not wake you?
  It struck mine ear most terribly.
ALONSO. I heard nothing.
ANTONIO. O, 'twas a din to fright a monster's ear,
  To make an earthquake! Sure it was the roar
  Of a whole herd of lions.
ALONSO. Heard you this, Gonzalo?
GONZALO. Upon mine honour, sir, I heard a humming,
  And that a strange one too, which did awake me;
  I shak'd you, sir, and cried; as mine eyes open'd,
  I saw their weapons drawn—there was a noise,
  That's verily. 'Tis best we stand upon our guard,
  Or that we quit this place. Let's draw our weapons.
ALONSO. Lead off this ground; and let's make further search
  For my poor son.
GONZALO. Heavens keep him from these beasts!
  For he is, sure, i' th' island.
ALONSO. Lead away.
ARIEL. Prospero my lord shall know what I have done;
  So, King, go safely on to seek thy son.   *Exeunt*

SCENE 2

Another part of the island

Enter CALIBAN, *with a burden of wood. A noise of
thunder heard*

CALIBAN. All the infections that the sun sucks up
  From bogs, fens, flats, on Prosper fall, and make him
  By inch-meal a disease! His spirits hear me,
  And yet I needs must curse. But they'll nor pinch,
  Fright me with urchin-shows, pitch me i' th' mire,
  Nor lead me, like a firebrand, in the dark

Out of my way, unless he bid 'em; but
For every trifle are they set upon me;
Sometime like apes that mow and chatter at me,
And after bite me; then like hedgehogs which
Lie tumbling in my barefoot way, and mount
Their pricks at my footfall; sometime am I
All wound with adders, who with cloven tongues
Do hiss me into madness.

Enter TRINCULO

Lo, now, lo!
Here comes a spirit of his, and to torment me
For bringing wood in slowly. I'll fall flat;
Perchance he will not mind me.

TRINCULO. Here's neither bush nor shrub to bear off any
weather at all, and another storm brewing; I hear it sing i'
th' wind. Yond same black cloud, yond huge one, looks
like a foul bombard that would shed his liquor. If it should
thunder as it did before, I know not where to hide my
head. Yond same cloud cannot choose but fall by pailfuls.
What have we here? a man or a fish? dead or alive? A fish:
he smells like a fish; a very ancient and fish-like smell; a
kind of not-of-the-newest Poor-John. A strange fish! Were
I in England now, as once I was, and had but this fish
painted, not a holiday fool there but would give a piece of
silver. There would this monster make a man; any strange
beast there makes a man; when they will not give a doit to
relieve a lame beggar, they will lay out ten to see a dead
Indian. Legg'd like a man, and his fins like arms! Warm, o'
my troth! I do now let loose my opinion; hold it no longer:
this is no fish, but an islander, that hath lately suffered by a
thunderbolt. [*Thunder*] Alas, the storm is come again! My
best way is to creep under his gaberdine; there is no other
shelter hereabout. Misery acquaints a man with strange bed-
fellows. I will here shroud till the dregs of the storm be past.

Enter STEPHANO *singing; a bottle in his hand*

STEPHANO. I shall no more to sea, to sea,
Here shall I die ashore—

This is a very scurvy tune to sing at a man's funeral; well, here's my comfort. [*Drinks*]

The master, the swabber, the boatswain, and I,
The gunner, and his mate,
Lov'd Mall, Meg, and Marian, and Margery,
But none of us car'd for Kate;
For she had a tongue with a tang,
Would cry to a sailor 'Go hang!'
She lov'd not the savour of tar nor of pitch,
Yet a tailor might scratch her where'er she did itch.
Then to sea, boys, and let her go hang!

This is a scurvy tune too; but here's my comfort. [*Drinks*]
CALIBAN. Do not torment me. O!
STEPHANO. What's the matter? Have we devils here? Do you put tricks upon 's with savages and men of Ind? Ha! I have not scap'd drowning to be afeard now of your four legs; for it hath been said: As proper a man as ever went on four legs cannot make him give ground; and it shall be said so again, while Stephano breathes at nostrils.
CALIBAN. The spirit torments me. O!
STEPHANO. This is some monster of the isle with four legs, who hath got, as I take it, an ague. Where the devil should he learn our language? I will give him some relief, if it be but for that. If I can recover him, and keep him tame, and get to Naples with him, he's a present for any emperor that ever trod on neat's leather.
CALIBAN. Do not torment me, prithee; I'll bring my wood home faster.
STEPHANO. He's in his fit now, and does not talk after the wisest. He shall taste of my bottle; if he have never drunk wine afore, it will go near to remove his fit. If I can recover him, and keep him tame, I will not take too much for him; he shall pay for him that hath him, and that soundly.
CALIBAN. Thou dost me yet but little hurt; thou wilt anon, I know it by thy trembling; now Prosper works upon thee.
STEPHANO. Come on your ways; open your mouth; here is that which will give language to you, cat. Open your

mouth; this will shake your shaking, I can tell you, and that soundly; you cannot tell who's your friend. Open your chaps again.

TRINCULO. I should know that voice; it should be—but he is drown'd; and these are devils. O, defend me!

STEPHANO. Four legs and two voices; a most delicate monster! His forward voice, now, is to speak well of his friend; his backward voice is to utter foul speeches and to detract. If all the wine in my bottle will recover him, I will help his ague. Come—Amen! I will pour some in thy other mouth.

TRINCULO. Stephano!

STEPHANO. Doth thy other mouth call me? Mercy, mercy! This is a devil, and no monster; I will leave him; I have no long spoon.

TRINCULO. Stephano! If thou beest Stephano, touch me, and speak to me; for I am Trinculo—be not afeard—thy good friend Trinculo.

STEPHANO. If thou beest Trinculo, come forth; I'll pull thee by the lesser legs; if any be Trinculo's legs, these are they. Thou art very Trinculo indeed! How cam'st thou to be the siege of this moon-calf? Can he vent Trinculos?

TRINCULO. I took him to be kill'd with a thunderstroke. But art thou not drown'd, Stephano? I hope now thou are not drown'd. Is the storm overblown? I hid me under the dead moon-calf's gaberdine for fear of the storm. And art thou living, Stephano? O Stephano, two Neapolitans scap'd!

STEPHANO. Prithee, do not turn me about; my stomach is not constant.

CALIBAN. [*Aside*] These be fine things, an if they be not sprites.
That's a brave god, and bears celestial liquor.
I will kneel to him.

STEPHANO. How didst thou scape? How cam'st thou hither? Swear by this bottle how thou cam'st hither—I escap'd upon a butt of sack, which the sailors heaved o'erboard—by this bottle, which I made of the bark of a tree, with mine own hands, since I was cast ashore.

CALIBAN. I'll swear upon that bottle to be thy true subject, for the liquor is not earthly.

STEPHANO. Here; swear then how thou escap'dst.

TRINCULO. Swum ashore, man, like a duck; I can swim like a duck, I'll be sworn.

STEPHANO. [*Passing the bottle*] Here, kiss the book. Though thou canst swim like a duck, thou art made like a goose.

TRINCULO. O Stephano, hast any more of this?

STEPHANO. The whole butt, man; my cellar is in a rock by th' seaside, where my wine is hid. How now, moon-calf! How does thine ague?

CALIBAN. Hast thou not dropp'd from heaven?

STEPHANO. Out o' th' moon, I do assure thee; I was the Man i' th' Moon, when time was.

CALIBAN. I have seen thee in her, and I do adore thee. My mistress show'd me thee, and thy dog and thy bush.

STEPHANO. Come, swear to that; kiss the book. I will furnish it anon with new contents. Swear. [CALIBAN *drinks*]

TRINCULO. By this good light, this is a very shallow monster! I afeard of him! A very weak monster! The Man i' th' Moon! A most poor credulous monster! Well drawn, monster, in good sooth!

CALIBAN. I'll show thee every fertile inch o' th' island; and I will kiss thy foot. I prithee be my god.

TRINCULO. By this light, a most perfidious and drunken monster! When 's god's asleep he'll rob his bottle.

CALIBAN. I'll kiss thy foot; I'll swear myself thy subject.

STEPHANO. Come on, then; down, and swear.

TRINCULO. I shall laugh myself to death at this puppy-headed monster. A most scurvy monster! I could find in my heart to beat him—

STEPHANO. Come, kiss.

TRINCULO. But that the poor monster's in drink. An abominable monster!

CALIBAN. I'll show thee the best springs; I'll pluck thee berries;

I'll fish for thee, and get thee wood enough.

A plague upon the tyrant that I serve!

I'll bear him no more sticks, but follow thee,

Thou wondrous man.

TRINCULO. A most ridiculous monster, to make a wonder of a poor drunkard!

CALIBAN. I prithee let me bring thee where crabs grow;
And I with my long nails will dig thee pig-nuts;
Show thee a jay's nest, and instruct thee how
To snare the nimble marmoset; I'll bring thee
To clust'ring filberts, and sometimes I'll get thee
Young scamels from the rock. Wilt thou go with me?
STEPHANO. I prithee now, lead the way without any more
talking. Trinculo, the King and all our company else be-
ing drown'd, we will inherit here. Here, bear my bottle.
Fellow Trinculo, we'll fill him by and by again.
CALIBAN. [*Sings drunkenly*] Farewell, master; farewell, fare-
well!
TRINCULO. A howling monster; a drunken monster!
CALIBAN.　No more dams I'll make for fish;
　　　　　Nor fetch in firing
　　　　　At requiring,
　　　　　Nor scrape trenchering, nor wash dish.
　　　　　'Ban 'Ban, Ca—Caliban,
　　　　　Has a new master—Get a new man.
Freedom, high-day! high-day, freedom! freedom, high-
day, freedom!
STEPHANO. O brave monster! Lead the way.　　　*Exeunt*

ACT III. SCENE 1

Before PROSPERO's *cell*

Enter FERDINAND, *bearing a log*

FERDINAND. There be some sports are painful, and their
labour
Delight in them sets off; some kinds of baseness
Are nobly undergone, and most poor matters
Point to rich ends. This my mean task
Would be as heavy to me as odious, but
The mistress which I serve quickens what's dead,
And makes my labours pleasures. O, she is
Ten times more gentle than her father's crabbed;

And he's compos'd of harshness. I must remove
Some thousands of these logs, and pile them up,
Upon a sore injunction; my sweet mistress
Weeps when she sees me work, and says such baseness
Had never like executor. I forget;
But these sweet thoughts do even refresh my labours,
Most busy, least when I do it.

Enter Miranda; *and* Prospero *at a distance, unseen*

Miranda. Alas, now; pray you,
Work not so hard; I would the lightning had
Burnt up those logs that you are enjoin'd to pile.
Pray, set it down and rest you; when this burns,
'Twill weep for having wearied you. My father
Is hard at study; pray, now, rest yourself;
He's safe for these three hours.
Ferdinand. O most dear mistress,
The sun will set before I shall discharge
What I must strive to do.
Miranda. If you'll sit down,
I'll bear your logs the while; pray give me that;
I'll carry it to the pile.
Ferdinand. No, precious creature;
I had rather crack my sinews, break my back,
Than you should such dishonour undergo,
While I sit lazy by.
Miranda. It would become me
As well as it does you; and I should do it
With much more ease; for my good will is to it,
And yours it is against.
Prospero. [*Aside*] Poor worm, thou art infected!
This visitation shows it.
Miranda. You look wearily.
Ferdinand. No, noble mistress; 'tis fresh morning with me
When you are by at night. I do beseech you,
Chiefly that I might set it in my prayers,
What is your name?
Miranda. Miranda—O my father,
I have broke your hest to say so!
Ferdinand. Admir'd Miranda!

Indeed the top of admiration; worth
What's dearest to the world! Full many a lady
I have ey'd with best regard; and many a time
Th' harmony of their tongues hath into bondage
Brought my too diligent ear; for several virtues
Have I lik'd several women, never any
With so full soul, but some defect in her
Did quarrel with the noblest grace she ow'd,
And put it to the foil; but you, O you,
So perfect and so peerless, are created
Of every creature's best!

MIRANDA. I do not know
One of my sex; no woman's face remember,
Save, from my glass, mine own; nor have I seen
More that I may call men than you, good friend,
And my dear father. How features are abroad,
I am skilless of; but, by my modesty,
The jewel in my dower, I would not wish
Any companion in the world but you;
Nor can imagination form a shape,
Besides yourself, to like of. But I prattle
Something too wildly, and my father's precepts
I therein do forget.

FERDINAND. I am, in my condition,
A prince, Miranda; I do think, a king—
I would not so!—and would no more endure
This wooden slavery than to suffer
The flesh-fly blow my mouth. Hear my soul speak:
The very instant that I saw you, did
My heart fly to your service; there resides
To make me slave to it; and for your sake
Am I this patient log-man.

MIRANDA. Do you love me?

FERDINAND. O heaven, O earth, bear witness to this sound,
And crown what I profess with kind event,
If I speak true! If hollowly, invert
What best is boded me to mischief! I,
Beyond all limit of what else i' th' world,
Do love, prize, honour you.

MIRANDA. I am a fool

To weep at what I am glad of.
PROSPERO. [*Aside*] Fair encounter
Of two most rare affections! Heavens rain grace
On that which breeds between 'em!
FERDINAND. Wherefore weep you?
MIRANDA. At mine unworthiness, that dare not offer
What I desire to give, and much less take
What I shall die to want. But this is trifling;
And all the more it seeks to hide itself,
The bigger bulk it shows. Hence, bashful cunning!
And prompt me, plain and holy innocence!
I am your wife, if you will marry me;
If not, I'll die your maid. To be your fellow
You may deny me; but I'll be your servant,
Whether you will or no.
FERDINAND. My mistress, dearest;
And I thus humble ever.
MIRANDA. My husband, then?
FERDINAND. Ay, with a heart as willing
As bondage e'er of freedom. Here's my hand.
MIRANDA. And mine, with my heart in't. And now farewell
Till half an hour hence.
FERDINAND. A thousand thousand!
        Exeunt FERDINAND *and* MIRANDA *severally*
PROSPERO. So glad of this as they I cannot be,
Who are surpris'd withal; but my rejoicing
At nothing can be more. I'll to my book;
For yet ere supper time must I perform
Much business appertaining.   *Exit*

SCENE 2

Another part of the island

Enter CALIBAN, STEPHANO, *and* TRINCULO

STEPHANO. Tell not me—when the butt is out we will drink
water, not a drop before; therefore bear up, and board
'em. Servant-monster, drink to me.
TRINCULO. Servant-monster! The folly of this island! They

say there's but five upon this isle: we are three of them; if th' other two be brain'd like us, the state totters.

STEPHANO. Drink, servant-monster, when I bid thee; thy eyes are almost set in thy head.

TRINCULO. Where should they be set else? He were a brave monster indeed, if they were set in his tail.

STEPHANO. My man-monster hath drown'd his tongue in sack. For my part, the sea cannot drown me; I swam, ere I could recover the shore, five and thirty leagues, off and on. By this light, thou shalt be my lieutenant, monster, or my standard.

TRINCULO. Your lieutenant, if you list; he's no standard.

STEPHANO. We'll not run, Monsieur Monster.

TRINCULO. Nor go neither; but you'll lie like dogs, and yet say nothing neither.

STEPHANO. Moon-calf, speak once in thy life, if thou beest a good moon-calf.

CALIBAN. How does thy honour? Let me lick thy shoe. I'll not serve him; he is not valiant.

TRINCULO. Thou liest, most ignorant monster: I am in case to justle a constable. Why, thou debosh'd fish, thou, was there ever man a coward that hath drunk so much sack as I to-day? Wilt thou tell a monstrous lie, being but half a fish and half a monster?

CALIBAN. Lo, how he mocks me! Wilt thou let him, my lord?

TRINCULO. 'Lord' quoth he! That a monster should be such a natural!

CALIBAN. Lo, lo again! Bite him to death, I prithee.

STEPHANO. Trinculo, keep a good tongue in your head; if you prove a mutineer—the next tree! The poor monster's my subject, and he shall not suffer indignity.

CALIBAN. I thank my noble lord. Wilt thou be pleas'd to hearken once again to the suit I made to thee?

STEPHANO. Marry will I; kneel and repeat it; I will stand, and so shall Trinculo.

Enter ARIEL, *invisible*

CALIBAN. As I told thee before, I am subject to a tyrant, a sorcerer, that by his cunning hath cheated me of the island.

ARIEL. Thou liest.

CALIBAN. Thou liest, thou jesting monkey, thou;
I would my valiant master would destroy thee.
I do not lie.

STEPHANO. Trinculo, if you trouble him any more in's tale,
by this hand, I will supplant some of your teeth.

TRINCULO. Why, I said nothing.

STEPHANO. Mum, then, and no more. Proceed.

CALIBAN. I say, by sorcery he got this isle;
From me he got it. If thy greatness will
Revenge it on him—for I know thou dar'st,
But this thing dare not—

STEPHANO. That's most certain.

CALIBAN. Thou shalt be lord of it, and I'll serve thee.

STEPHANO. How now shall this be compass'd? Canst thou
bring me to the party?

CALIBAN. Yea, yea, my lord; I'll yield him thee asleep,
Where thou mayst knock a nail into his head.

ARIEL. Thou liest; thou canst not.

CALIBAN. What a pied ninny's this! Thou scurvy patch!
I do beseech thy greatness, give him blows,
And take his bottle from him. When that's gone
He shall drink nought but brine; for I'll not show him
Where the quick freshes are.

STEPHANO. Trinculo, run into no further danger; interrupt
the monster one word further and, by this hand, I'll turn
my mercy out o' doors, and make a stock-fish of thee.

TRINCULO. Why, what did I? I did nothing. I'll go farther
off.

STEPHANO. Didst thou not say he lied?

ARIEL. Thou liest.

STEPHANO. Do I so? Take thou that. [*Beats him*] As you like
this, give me the lie another time.

TRINCULO. I did not give the lie. Out o' your wits and hearing too? A pox o' your bottle! This can sack and drinking
do. A murrain on your monster, and the devil take your
fingers!

CALIBAN. Ha, ha, ha!

STEPHANO. Now, forward with your tale.—Prithee stand
further off.

CALIBAN. Beat him enough; after a little time, I'll beat him too.

STEPHANO. Stand farther. Come, proceed.

CALIBAN. Why, as I told thee, 'tis a custom with him
I' th' afternoon to sleep; there thou mayst brain him,
Having first seiz'd his books; or with a log
Batter his skull, or paunch him with a stake,
Or cut his wezand with thy knife. Remember
First to possess his books; for without them
He's but a sot, as I am, nor hath not
One spirit to command; they all do hate him
As rootedly as I. Burn but his books.
He has brave utensils—for so he calls them—
Which, when he has a house, he'll deck withal.
And that most deeply to consider is
The beauty of his daughter; he himself
Calls her a nonpareil. I never saw a woman
But only Sycorax my dam and she;
But she as far surpasseth Sycorax
As great'st does least.

STEPHANO. Is it so brave a lass?

CALIBAN. Ay, lord; she will become thy bed, I warrant,
And bring thee forth brave brood.

STEPHANO. Monster, I will kill this man; his daughter and I
will be King and Queen—save our Graces!—and Trinculo
and thyself shall be viceroys. Dost thou like the plot, Trinculo?

TRINCULO. Excellent.

STEPHANO. Give me thy hand; I am sorry I beat thee; but
while thou liv'st, keep a good tongue in thy head.

CALIBAN. Within this half hour will he be asleep.
Wilt thou destroy him then?

STEPHANO. Ay, on mine honour.

ARIEL. This will I tell my master.

CALIBAN. Thou mak'st me merry; I am full of pleasure.
Let us be jocund; will you troll the catch
You taught me but while-ere?

STEPHANO. At thy request, monster, I will do reason, any
reason. Come on, Trinculo, let us sing. [*Sings*]

Flout 'em and scout 'em,
And scout 'em and flout 'em;
Thought is free.

CALIBAN. That's not the tune.

[ARIEL *plays the tune on a tabor and pipe*]

STEPHANO. What is this same?

TRINCULO. This is the tune of our catch, play'd by the picture of Nobody.

STEPHANO. If thou beest a man, show thyself in thy likeness; if thou beest a devil, take't as thou list.

TRINCULO. O, forgive me my sins!

STEPHANO. He that dies pays all debts. I defy thee. Mercy upon us!

CALIBAN. Art thou afeard?

STEPHANO. No, monster, not I.

CALIBAN. Be not afeard. The isle is full of noises,
Sounds, and sweet airs, that give delight, and hurt not.
Sometimes a thousand twangling instruments
Will hum about mine ears; and sometimes voices,
That, if I then had wak'd after long sleep,
Will make me sleep again; and then, in dreaming,
The clouds methought would open and show riches
Ready to drop upon me, that, when I wak'd,
I cried to dream again.

STEPHANO. This will prove a brave kingdom to me, where I shall have my music for nothing.

CALIBAN. When Prospero is destroy'd.

STEPHANO. That shall be by and by; I remember the story.

TRINCULO. The sound is going away; let's follow it, and after do our work.

STEPHANO. Lead, monster; we'll follow. I would I could see this taborer; he lays it on.

TRINCULO. Wilt come? I'll follow, Stephano.   *Exeunt*

46

SCENE 3

Another part of the island

Enter ALONSO, SEBASTIAN, ANTONIO, GONZALO, ADRIAN,
FRANCISCO, *and* OTHERS

GONZALO. By'r lakin, I can go no further, sir;
My old bones ache. Here's a maze trod, indeed,
Through forth-rights and meanders! By your patience,
I needs must rest me.
ALONSO. Old lord, I cannot blame thee,
Who am myself attach'd with weariness
To th' dulling of my spirits; sit down and rest.
Even here I will put off my hope, and keep it
No longer for my flatterer; he is drown'd
Whom thus we stray to find, and the sea mocks
Our frustrate search on land. Well, let him go.
ANTONIO. [*Aside to* SEBASTIAN] I am right glad that he's
so out of hope.
Do not, for one repulse, forgo the purpose
That you resolv'd t' effect.
SEBASTIAN. [*Aside to* ANTONIO] The next advantage
Will we take throughly.
ANTONIO. [*Aside to* SEBASTIAN] Let it be to-night;
For, now they are oppress'd with travel, they
Will not, nor cannot, use such vigilance
As when they are fresh.
SEBASTIAN. [*Aside to* ANTONIO] I say, to-night; no more.

> *Solemn and strange music; and* PROSPERO *on the
> top, invisible. Enter several strange* SHAPES, *bring-
> ing in a banquet; and dance about it with gentle
> actions of salutations; and inviting the* KING, &c., to
> eat, they depart*

ALONSO. What harmony is this? My good friends, hark!
GONZALO. Marvellous sweet music!
ALONSO. Give us kind keepers, heavens! What were these?
SEBASTIAN. A living drollery. Now I will believe
That there are unicorns; that in Arabia

47

There is one tree, the phœnix' throne, one phœnix
At this hour reigning there.
ANTONIO. I'll believe both;
And what does else want credit, come to me,
And I'll be sworn 'tis true; travellers ne'er did lie,
Though fools at home condemn 'em.
GONZALO. If in Naples
I should report this now, would they believe me?
If I should say, I saw such islanders,
For certes these are people of the island,
Who though they are of monstrous shape yet, note,
Their manners are more gentle-kind than of
Our human generation you shall find
Many, nay, almost any.
PROSPERO. [*Aside*] Honest lord,
Thou hast said well; for some of you there present
Are worse than devils.
ALONSO. I cannot too much muse
Such shapes, such gesture, and such sound, expressing,
Although they want the use of tongue, a kind
Of excellent dumb discourse.
PROSPERO. [*Aside*] Praise in departing.
FRANCISCO. They vanish'd strangely.
SEBASTIAN. No matter, since
They have left their viands behind; for we have stomachs.
Will't please you taste of what is here?
ALONSO. Not I.
GONZALO. Faith, sir, you need not fear. When we were boys,
Who would believe that there were mountaineers,
Dewlapp'd like bulls, whose throats had hanging at 'em
Wallets of flesh? or that there were such men
Whose heads stood in their breasts? which now we find
Each putter-out of five for one will bring us
Good warrant of.
ALONSO. I will stand to, and feed,
Although my last; no matter, since I feel
The best is past. Brother, my lord the Duke,
Stand to, and do as we.

Thunder and lightning. Enter ARIEL, *like a harpy;*

claps his wings upon the table; and, with a quaint
device, the banquet vanishes

ARIEL. You are three men of sin, whom Destiny,
That hath to instrument this lower world
And what is in't, the never-surfeited sea
Hath caus'd to belch up you; and on this island
Where man doth not inhabit—you 'mongst men
Being most unfit to live. I have made you mad;
And even with such-like valour men hang and drown
Their proper selves.
            [ALONSO, SEBASTIAN *&c.*, *draw their swords*]
You fools! I and my fellows
Are ministers of Fate; the elements
Of whom your swords are temper'd may as well
Wound the loud winds, or with bemock'd-at stabs
Kill the still-closing waters, as diminish
One dowle that's in my plume; my fellow-ministers
Are like invulnerable. If you could hurt,
Your swords are now too massy for your strengths
And will not be uplifted. But remember—
For that's my business to you—that you three
From Milan did supplant good Prospero;
Expos'd unto the sea, which hath requit it,
Him, and his innocent child; for which foul deed
The pow'rs, delaying, not forgetting, have
Incens'd the seas and shores, yea, all the creatures,
Against your peace. Thee of thy son, Alonso,
They have bereft; and do pronounce by me
Ling'ring perdition, worse than any death
Can be at once, shall step by step attend
You and your ways; whose wraths to guard you from—
Which here, in this most desolate isle, else falls
Upon your heads—is nothing but heart's sorrow,
And a clear life ensuing.

He vanishes in thunder; then, to soft music, enter
the SHAPES *again, and dance, with mocks and mows,*
and carrying out the table

PROSPERO. Bravely the figure of this harpy hast thou

Perform'd, my Ariel; a grace it had, devouring.
Of my instruction hast thou nothing bated
In what thou hadst to say; so, with good life
And observation strange, my meaner ministers
Their several kinds have done. My high charms work,
And these mine enemies are all knit up
In their distractions. They now are in my pow'r;
And in these fits I leave them, while I visit
Young Ferdinand, whom they suppose is drown'd,
And his and mine lov'd darling. *Exit above*
GONZALO. I' th' name of something holy, sir, why stand you
In this strange stare?
ALONSO. O, it is monstrous, monstrous!
Methought the billows spoke, and told me of it;
The winds did sing it to me; and the thunder,
That deep and dreadful organ-pipe, pronounc'd
The name of Prosper; it did bass my trespass.
Therefore my son i' th' ooze is bedded; and
I'll seek him deeper than e'er plummet sounded,
And with him there lie mudded. *Exit*
SEBASTIAN. But one fiend at a time,
I'll fight their legions o'er.
ANTONIO. I'll be thy second. *Exeunt* SEBASTIAN *and* ANTONIO
GONZALO. All three of them are desperate; their great guilt,
Like poison given to work a great time after,
Now gins to bite the spirits. I do beseech you,
That are of suppler joints, follow them swiftly,
And hinder them from what this ecstasy
May now provoke them to.
ADRIAN. Follow, I pray you. *Exeunt*

ACT IV. SCENE 1

Before PROSPERO's *cell*

Enter PROSPERO, FERDINAND, *and* MIRANDA

PROSPERO. If I have too austerely punish'd you,

Your compensation makes amends; for I
Have given you here a third of mine own life,
Or that for which I live; who once again
I tender to thy hand. All thy vexations
Were but my trials of thy love, and thou
Hast strangely stood the test; here, afore heaven,
I ratify this my rich gift. O Ferdinand!
Do not smile at me that I boast her off,
For thou shalt find she will outstrip all praise,
And make it halt behind her.

FERDINAND. I do believe it
Against an oracle.

PROSPERO. Then, as my gift, and thine own acquisition
Worthily purchas'd, take my daughter. But
If thou dost break her virgin-knot before
All sanctimonious ceremonies may
With full and holy rite be minist'red,
No sweet aspersion shall the heavens let fall
To make this contract grow; but barren hate,
Sour-ey'd disdain, and discord, shall bestrew
The union of your bed with weeds so loathly
That you shall hate it both. Therefore take heed,
As Hymen's lamps shall light you.

FERDINAND. As I hope
For quiet days, fair issue, and long life,
With such love as 'tis now, the murkiest den,
The most opportune place, the strong'st suggestion
Our worser genius can, shall never melt
Mine honour into lust, to take away
The edge of that day's celebration,
When I shall think or Phœbus' steeds are founder'd
Or Night kept chain'd below.

PROSPERO. Fairly spoke.
Sit, then, and talk with her; she is thine own.
What, Ariel! my industrious servant, Ariel!

Enter ARIEL

ARIEL. What would my potent master? Here I am.

PROSPERO. Thou and thy meaner fellows your last service
Did worthily perform; and I must use you

In such another trick. Go bring the rabble,
O'er whom I give thee pow'r, here to this place.
Incite them to quick motion; for I must
Bestow upon the eyes of this young couple
Some vanity of mine art; it is my promise,
And they expect it from me.
ARIEL. Presently?
PROSPERO. Ay, with a twink.
ARIEL.   Before you can say 'come' and 'go,'
    And breathe twice, and cry 'so, so,'
    Each one, tripping on his toe,
    Will be here with mop and mow.
    Do you love me, master? No?
PROSPERO. Dearly, my delicate Ariel. Do not approach
  Till thou dost hear me call.
ARIEL. Well! I conceive.   *Exit*
PROSPERO. Look thou be true; do not give dalliance
  Too much the rein; the strongest oaths are straw
  To th' fire i' th' blood. Be more abstemious,
  Or else good night your vow!
FERDINAND. I warrant you, sir,
  The white cold virgin snow upon my heart
  Abates the ardour of my liver.
PROSPERO. Well!
  Now come, my Ariel, bring a corollary,
  Rather than want a spirit; appear, and pertly.
  No tongue! All eyes! Be silent.   *[Soft music]*

Enter IRIS

IRIS. Ceres, most bounteous lady, thy rich leas
  Of wheat, rye, barley, vetches, oats, and pease;
  Thy turfy mountains, where live nibbling sheep,
  And flat meads thatch'd with stover, them to keep;
  Thy banks with pioned and twilled brims,
  Which spongy April at thy hest betrims,
  To make cold nymphs chaste crowns; and thy broom
    groves,
  Whose shadow the dismissed bachelor loves,
  Being lass-lorn; thy pole-clipt vineyard;
  And thy sea-marge, sterile and rocky hard,

Where thou thyself dost air—the Queen o' th' sky,
Whose wat'ry arch and messenger am I,
Bids thee leave these; and with her sovereign grace,
Here on this grass-plot, in this very place,
To come and sport. Her peacocks fly amain.
                              [JUNO *descends in her car*]
Approach, rich Ceres, her to entertain.

Enter CERES

CERES. Hail, many-coloured messenger, that ne'er
    Dost disobey the wife of Jupiter;
    Who, with thy saffron wings, upon my flow'rs
    Diffusest honey drops, refreshing show'rs;
    And with each end of thy blue bow dost crown
    My bosky acres and my unshrubb'd down,
    Rich scarf to my proud earth—why hath thy Queen
    Summon'd me hither to this short-grass'd green?
IRIS. A contract of true love to celebrate,
    And some donation freely to estate
    On the blest lovers.
CERES. Tell me, heavenly bow,
    If Venus or her son, as thou dost know,
    Do now attend the Queen? Since they did plot
    The means that dusky Dis my daughter got,
    Her and her blind boy's scandal'd company
    I have forsworn.
IRIS. Of her society
    Be not afraid. I met her Deity
    Cutting the clouds towards Paphos, and her son
    Dove-drawn with her. Here thought they to have done
    Some wanton charm upon this man and maid,
    Whose vows are that no bed-rite shall be paid
    Till Hymen's torch be lighted; but in vain.
    Mars's hot minion is return'd again;
    Her waspish-headed son has broke his arrows,
    Swears he will shoot no more, but play with sparrows,
    And be a boy right out.   [JUNO *alights*]
CERES. Highest Queen of State,
    Great Juno, comes; I know her by her gait.
JUNO. How does my bounteous sister? Go with me

To bless this twain, that they may prosperous be,
And honour'd in their issue. *[They sing]*

JUNO.   Honour, riches, marriage-blessing,
Long continuance, and increasing,
Hourly joys be still upon you!
Juno sings her blessings on you.

CERES.   Earth's increase, foison plenty,
Barns and garners never empty;
Vines with clust'ring bunches growing,
Plants with goodly burden bowing;
Spring come to you at the farthest,
In the very end of harvest!
Scarcity and want shall shun you,
Ceres' blessing so is on you.

FERDINAND. This is a most majestic vision, and
Harmonious charmingly. May I be bold
To think these spirits?

PROSPERO. Spirits, which by mine art
I have from their confines call'd to enact
My present fancies.

FERDINAND. Let me live here ever;
So rare a wond'red father and a wise
Makes this place Paradise.

    [JUNO *and* CERES *whisper, and send* IRIS *on employment*]

PROSPERO. Sweet now, silence;
Juno and Ceres whisper seriously.
There's something else to do; hush, and be mute,
Or else our spell is marr'd.

IRIS. You nymphs, call'd Naiads, of the wind'ring brooks,
With your sedg'd crowns and ever harmless looks,
Leave your crisp channels, and on this green land
Answer your summons; Juno does command.
Come, temperate nymphs, and help to celebrate
A contract of true love; be not too late.

Enter certain NYMPHS

You sun-burnt sicklemen, of August weary,
Come hither from the furrow, and be merry;
Make holiday; your rye-straw hats put on,

And these fresh nymphs encounter every one
In country footing.

> *Enter certain* REAPERS, *properly habited; they join
> with the* NYMPHS *in a graceful dance; towards the
> end whereof* PROSPERO *starts suddenly, and speaks;
> after which, to a strange, hollow, and confused
> noise, they heavily vanish*

PROSPERO. [*Aside*] I had forgot that foul conspiracy
Of the beast Caliban and his confederates
Against my life; the minute of their plot
Is almost come. [*To the* SPIRITS] Well done; avoid; no
   more!
FERDINAND. This is strange; your father's in some passion
That works him strongly.
MIRANDA. Never till this day
Saw I him touch'd with anger so distemper'd.
PROSPERO. You do look, my son, in a mov'd sort,
As if you were dismay'd; be cheerful, sir.
Our revels now are ended. These our actors,
As I foretold you, were all spirits, and
Are melted into air, into thin air;
And, like the baseless fabric of this vision,
The cloud-capp'd towers, the gorgeous palaces,
The solemn temples, the great globe itself,
Yea, all which it inherit, shall dissolve,
And, like this insubstantial pageant faded,
Leave not a rack behind. We are such stuff
As dreams are made on; and our little life
Is rounded with a sleep. Sir, I am vex'd;
Bear with my weakness; my old brain is troubled;
Be not disturb'd with my infirmity.
If you be pleas'd, retire into my cell
And there repose; a turn or two I'll walk
To still my beating mind.
FERDINAND, MIRANDA. We wish your peace.   *Exeunt*
PROSPERO. Come, with a thought. I thank thee, Ariel; come.

> *Enter* ARIEL

ARIEL. Thy thoughts I cleave to. What's thy pleasure?

PROSPERO. Spirit,
We must prepare to meet with Caliban.
ARIEL. Ay, my commander. When I presented 'Ceres,'
I thought to have told thee of it; but I fear'd
Lest I might anger thee.
PROSPERO. Say again, where didst thou leave these varlets?
ARIEL. I told you, sir, they were red-hot with drinking;
So full of valour that they smote the air
For breathing in their faces; beat the ground
For kissing of their feet; yet always bending
Towards their project. Then I beat my tabor,
At which like unback'd colts they prick'd their ears,
Advanc'd their eyelids, lifted up their noses
As they smelt music; so I charm'd their ears,
That calf-like they my lowing follow'd through
Tooth'd briers, sharp furzes, pricking goss, and thorns,
Which ent'red their frail shins. At last I left them
I' th' filthy mantled pool beyond your cell,
There dancing up to th' chins, that the foul lake
O'erstunk their feet.
PROSPERO. This was well done, my bird.
Thy shape invisible retain thou still.
The trumpery in my house, go bring it hither
For stale to catch these thieves.
ARIEL. I go, I go. _Exit_
PROSPERO. A devil, a born devil, on whose nature
Nurture can never stick; on whom my pains,
Humanely taken, all, all lost, quite lost;
And as with age his body uglier grows,
So his mind cankers. I will plague them all,
Even to roaring.

Re-enter ARIEL, _loaden with glistering apparel, &c._

Come, hang them on this line.
[PROSPERO _and_ ARIEL _remain, invisible_]

Enter CALIBAN, STEPHANO, _and_ TRINCULO, _all wet_

CALIBAN. Pray you, tread softly, that the blind mole may not
Hear a foot fall; we now are near his cell.
STEPHANO. Monster, your fairy, which you say is a harmless

fairy, has done little better than play'd the Jack with us.

TRINCULO. Monster, I do smell all horse-piss at which my nose is in great indignation.

STEPHANO. So is mine. Do you hear, monster? If I should take a displeasure against you, look you—

TRINCULO. Thou wert but a lost monster.

CALIBAN. Good my lord, give me thy favour still.
Be patient, for the prize I'll bring thee to
Shall hoodwink this mischance; therefore speak softly.
All's hush'd as midnight yet.

TRINCULO. Ay, but to lose our bottles in the pool!

STEPHANO. There is not only disgrace and dishonour in that, monster, but an infinite loss.

TRINCULO. That's more to me than my wetting; yet this is your harmless fairy, monster.

STEPHANO. I will fetch off my bottle, though I be o'er ears for my labour.

CALIBAN. Prithee, my king, be quiet. Seest thou here,
This is the mouth o' th' cell; no noise, and enter.
Do that good mischief which may make this island
Thine own for ever, and I, thy Caliban,
For aye thy foot-licker.

STEPHANO. Give me thy hand. I do begin to have bloody thoughts.

TRINCULO. O King Stephano! O peer! O worthy Stephano!
Look what a wardrobe here is for thee!

CALIBAN. Let it alone, thou fool; it is but trash.

TRINCULO. O, ho, monster; we know what belongs to a frippery. O King Stephano!

STEPHANO. Put off that gown, Trinculo; by this hand, I'll have that gown.

TRINCULO. Thy Grace shall have it.

CALIBAN. The dropsy drown this fool! What do you mean
To dote thus on such luggage? Let't alone,
And do the murder first. If he awake,
From toe to crown he'll fill our skins with pinches;
Make us strange stuff.

STEPHANO. Be you quiet, monster. Mistress line, is not this my jerkin? Now is the jerkin under the line; now, jerkin, you are like to lose your hair, and prove a bald jerkin.

STEPHANO. *Put off that gown, Trinculo* (ACT IV. SCENE I)

TRINCULO. Do, do. We steal by line and level, an't like your Grace.

STEPHANO. I thank thee for that jest; here's a garment for't. Wit shall not go unrewarded while I am king of this country. 'Steal by line and level' is an excellent pass of pate; there's another garment for't.

TRINCULO. Monster, come, put some lime upon your fingers, and away with the rest.

CALIBAN. I will have none on't. We shall lose our time, And all be turn'd to barnacles, or to apes With foreheads villainous low.

STEPHANO. Monster, lay-to your fingers; help to bear this away where my hogshead of wine is, or I'll turn you out of my kingdom. Go to, carry this.

TRINCULO. And this.

STEPHANO. Ay, and this.

A noise of hunters heard. Enter divers SPIRITS, *in shape of dogs and hounds, hunting them about;* PROSPERO *and* ARIEL *setting them on*

PROSPERO. Hey, Mountain, hey!

ARIEL. Silver! there it goes, Silver!

PROSPERO. Fury, Fury! There, Tyrant, there! Hark, hark!
[CALIBAN, STEPHANO, *and* TRINCULO *are driven out*]
Go charge my goblins that they grind their joints
With dry convulsions, shorten up their sinews
With aged cramps, and more pinch-spotted make them
Than pard or cat o' mountain.

ARIEL. Hark, they roar.

PROSPERO. Let them be hunted soundly. At this hour
Lies at my mercy all mine enemies.
Shortly shall all my labours end, and thou
Shalt have the air at freedom; for a little
Follow, and do me service. *Exeunt*

THE TEMPEST

ACT V. SCENE 1

Before PROSPERO's *cell*

Enter PROSPERO *in his magic robes, and* ARIEL

PROSPERO. Now does my project gather to a head;
My charms crack not, my spirits obey; and time
Goes upright with his carriage. How's the day?
ARIEL. On the sixth hour; at which time, my lord,
You said our work should cease.
PROSPERO. I did say so,
When first I rais'd the tempest. Say, my spirit,
How fares the King and 's followers?
ARIEL. Confin'd together
In the same fashion as you gave in charge;
Just as you left them; all prisoners, sir,
In the line-grove which weather-fends your cell;
They cannot budge till your release. The King,
His brother, and yours, abide all three distracted,
And the remainder mourning over them,
Brim full of sorrow and dismay; but chiefly
Him you term'd, sir, 'the good old lord, Gonzalo';
His tears run down his beard, like winter's drops
From eaves of reeds. Your charm so strongly works 'em
That if you now beheld them your affections
Would become tender.
PROSPERO. Dost thou think so, spirit?
ARIEL. Mine would, sir, were I human.
PROSPERO. And mine shall.
Hast thou, which art but air, a touch, a feeling
Of their afflictions, and shall not myself,
One of their kind, that relish all as sharply,
Passion as they, be kindlier mov'd than thou art?
Though with their high wrongs I am struck to th' quick,
Yet with my nobler reason 'gainst my fury
Do I take part; the rarer action is
In virtue than in vengeance; they being penitent,
The sole drift of my purpose doth extend
Not a frown further. Go release them, Ariel;

My charms I'll break, their senses I'll restore,
And they shall be themselves.
ARIEL. I'll fetch them, sir. *Exit*
PROSPERO. Ye elves of hills, brooks, standing lakes, and
    groves;
And ye that on the sands with printless foot
Do chase the ebbing Neptune, and do fly him
When he comes back; you demi-puppets that
By moonshine do the green sour ringlets make,
Whereof the ewe not bites; and you whose pastime
Is to make midnight mushrooms, that rejoice
To hear the solemn curfew; by whose aid—
Weak masters though ye be—I have be-dimm'd
The noontide sun, call'd forth the mutinous winds,
And 'twixt the green sea and the azur'd vault
Set roaring war. To the dread rattling thunder
Have I given fire, and rifted Jove's stout oak
With his own bolt; the strong-bas'd promontory
Have I made shake, and by the spurs pluck'd up
The pine and cedar. Graves at my command
Have wak'd their sleepers, op'd, and let 'em forth,
By my so potent art. But this rough magic
I here abjure; and, when I have requir'd
Some heavenly music—which even now I do—
To work mine end upon their senses that
This airy charm is for, I'll break my staff,
Bury it certain fathoms in the earth,
And deeper than did ever plummet sound
I'll drown my book. *[Solemn music]*

Here enters ARIEL *before; then* ALONSO, *with a
frantic gesture, attended by* GONZALO; SEBASTIAN
and ANTONIO *in like manner, attended by* ADRIAN
and FRANCISCO. *They all enter the circle which*
PROSPERO *had made, and there stand charm'd; which*
PROSPERO *observing, speaks*

A solemn air, and the best comforter
To an unsettled fancy, cure thy brains,
Now useless, boil'd within thy skull! There stand,
For you are spell-stopp'd.

61

Holy Gonzalo, honourable man,
Mine eyes, ev'n sociable to the show of thine,
Fall fellowly drops. The charm dissolves apace,
And as the morning steals upon the night,
Melting the darkness, so their rising senses
Begin to chase the ignorant fumes that mantle
Their clearer reason. O good Gonzalo,
My true preserver, and a loyal sir
To him thou follow'st! I will pay thy graces
Home both in word and deed. Most cruelly
Didst thou, Alonso, use me and my daughter;
Thy brother was a furtherer in the act.
Thou art pinch'd for't now, Sebastian. Flesh and blood,
You, brother mine, that entertain'd ambition,
Expell'd remorse and nature, who, with Sebastian—
Whose inward pinches therefore are most strong—
Would here have kill'd your king, I do forgive thee,
Unnatural though thou art. Their understanding
Begins to swell, and the approaching tide
Will shortly fill the reasonable shore
That now lies foul and muddy. Not one of them
That yet looks on me, or would know me. Ariel,
Fetch me the hat and rapier in my cell;   *Exit* ARIEL
I will discase me, and myself present
As I was sometime Milan. Quickly, spirit
Thou shalt ere long be free.

ARIEL, *on returning, sings and helps to attire him*

Where the bee sucks, there suck I;
In a cowslip's bell I lie;
There I couch when owls do cry.
On the bat's back I do fly
After summer merrily.
Merrily, merrily shall I live now
Under the blossom that hangs on the bough.

PROSPERO. Why, that's my dainty Ariel! I shall miss thee;
But yet thou shalt have freedom. So, so, so.
To the King's ship, invisible as thou art;
There shalt thou find the mariners asleep

Under the hatches; the master and the boatswain
Being awake, enforce them to this place;
And presently, I prithee.
ARIEL. I drink the air before me, and return
Or ere your pulse twice beat.   *Exit*
GONZALO. All torment, trouble, wonder and amazement,
Inhabits here. Some heavenly power guide us
Out of this fearful country!
PROSPERO. Behold, Sir King,
The wronged Duke of Milan, Prospero.
For more assurance that a living prince
Does now speak to thee, I embrace thy body;
And to thee and thy company I bid
A hearty welcome.
ALONSO. Whe'er thou be'st he or no,
Or some enchanted trifle to abuse me,
As late I have been, I not know. Thy pulse
Beats, as of flesh and blood; and, since I saw thee,
Th' affliction of my mind amends, with which,
I fear, a madness held me. This must crave—
An if this be at all—a most strange story.
Thy dukedom I resign, and do entreat
Thou pardon me my wrongs. But how should Prospero
Be living and be here?
PROSPERO. First, noble friend,
Let me embrace thine age, whose honour cannot
Be measur'd or confin'd.
GONZALO. Whether this be
Or be not, I'll not swear.
PROSPERO. You do yet taste
Some subtleties o' th' isle, that will not let you
Believe things certain. Welcome, my friends all!
[*Aside to* SEBASTIAN *and* ANTONIO] But you, my brace of
    lords, were I so minded,
I here could pluck his Highness' frown upon you,
And justify you traitors; at this time
I will tell no tales.
SEBASTIAN. [*Aside*] The devil speaks in him.
PROSPERO. No.
For you, most wicked sir, whom to call brother

63

Would even infect my mouth, I do forgive
Thy rankest fault—all of them; and require
My dukedom of thee, which perforce I know
Thou must restore.

ALONSO. If thou beest Prospero,
Give us particulars of thy preservation;
How thou hast met us here, whom three hours since
Were wreck'd upon this shore; where I have lost—
How sharp the point of this remembrance is!—
My dear son Ferdinand.

PROSPERO. I am woe for't, sir.

ALONSO. Irreparable is the loss; and patience
Says it is past her cure.

PROSPERO. I rather think
You have not sought her help, of whose soft grace
For the like loss I have her sovereign aid,
And rest myself content.

ALONSO. You the like loss!

PROSPERO. As great to me as late; and, supportable
To make the dear loss, have I means much weaker
Than you may call to comfort you, for I
Have lost my daughter.

ALONSO. A daughter!
O heavens, that they were living both in Naples,
The King and Queen there! That they were, I wish
Myself were mudded in that oozy bed
Where my son lies. When did you lose your daughter?

PROSPERO. In this last tempest. I perceive these lords
At this encounter do so much admire
That they devour their reason, and scarce think
Their eyes do offices of truth, their words
Are natural breath; but, howsoe'er you have
Been justled from your senses, know for certain
That I am Prospero, and that very duke
Which was thrust forth of Milan; who most strangely
Upon this shore, where you were wrecked, was landed
To be the lord on't. No more yet of this;
For 'tis a chronicle of day by day,
Not a relation for a breakfast, nor
Befitting this first meeting. Welcome, sir;

This cell's my court; here have I few attendants,
And subjects none abroad; pray you, look in.
My dukedom since you have given me again,
I will requite you with as good a thing;
At least bring forth a wonder, to content ye
As much as me my dukedom.

Here PROSPERO *discovers* FERDINAND *and* MIRANDA,
playing at chess

MIRANDA. Sweet lord, you play me false.
FERDINAND. No, my dearest love,
I would not for the world.
MIRANDA. Yes, for a score of kingdoms you should wrangle
And I would call it fair play.
ALONSO. If this prove
A vision of the island, one dear son
Shall I twice lose.
SEBASTIAN. A most high miracle!
FERDINAND. Though the seas threaten, they are merciful;
I have curs'd them without cause. [*Kneels*]
ALONSO. Now all the blessings
Of a glad father compass thee about!
Arise, and say how thou cam'st here.
MIRANDA. O, wonder!
How many goodly creatures are there here!
How beauteous mankind is! O brave new world
That has such people in't!
PROSPERO. 'Tis new to thee.
ALONSO. What is this maid with whom thou wast at play?
Your eld'st acquaintance cannot be three hours;
Is she the goddess that hath sever'd us,
And brought us thus together?
FERDINAND. Sir, she is mortal;
But by immortal Providence she's mine.
I chose her when I could not ask my father
For his advice, nor thought I had one. She
Is daughter to this famous Duke of Milan,
Of whom so often I have heard renown
But never saw before; of whom I have
Receiv'd a second life; and second father

This lady makes him to me.

ALONSO. I am hers.
But, O, how oddly will it sound that I
Must ask my child forgiveness!

PROSPERO. There, sir, stop;
Let us not burden our remembrances with
A heaviness that's gone.

GONZALO. I have inly wept,
Or should have spoke ere this. Look down, you gods,
And on this couple drop a blessed crown;
For it is you that have chalk'd forth the way
Which brought us hither.

ALONSO. I say, Amen, Gonzalo!

GONZALO. Was Milan thrust from Milan, that his issue
Should become Kings of Naples? O, rejoice
Beyond a common joy, and set it down
With gold on lasting pillars: in one voyage
Did Claribel her husband find at Tunis;
And Ferdinand, her brother, found a wife
Where he himself was lost; Prospero his dukedom
In a poor isle; and all of us ourselves
When no man was his own.

ALONSO. [*To* FERDINAND *and* MIRANDA] Give me your
hands.
Let grief and sorrow still embrace his heart
That doth not wish you joy.

GONZALO. Be it so. Amen!

Re-enter ARIEL, *with the* MASTER *and* BOATSWAIN
amazedly following

O look, sir; look, sir! Here is more of us!
I prophesied, if a gallows were on land,
This fellow could not drown. Now, blasphemy,
That swear'st grace o'erboard, not an oath on shore?
Hast thou no mouth by land? What is the news?

BOATSWAIN. The best news is that we have safely found
Our King and company; the next, our ship—
Which but three glasses since we gave out split—
Is tight and yare, and bravely rigg'd, as when
We first put out to sea.

ARIEL. [*Aside to* PROSPERO] Sir, all this service
   Have I done since I went.
PROSPERO. [*Aside to* ARIEL] My tricksy spirit!
ALONSO. These are not natural events; they strengthen
   From strange to stranger. Say, how came you hither?
BOATSWAIN. If I did think, sir, I were well awake,
   I'd strive to tell you. We were dead of sleep,
   And—how, we know not—all clapp'd under hatches;
   Where, but even now, with strange and several noises
   Of roaring, shrieking, howling, jingling chains,
   And moe diversity of sounds, all horrible,
   We were awak'd; straightway at liberty;
   Where we, in all her trim, freshly beheld
   Our royal, good, and gallant ship; our master
   Cap'ring to eye her. On a trice, so please you,
   Even in a dream, were we divided from them,
   And were brought moping hither.
ARIEL. [*Aside to* PROSPERO] Was't well done?
PROSPERO. [*Aside to* ARIEL] Bravely, my diligence. Thou
   shalt be free.
ALONSO. This is as strange a maze as e'er men trod;
   And there is in this business more than nature
   Was ever conduct of. Some oracle
   Must rectify our knowledge.
PROSPERO. Sir, my liege,
   Do not infest your mind with beating on
   The strangeness of this business; at pick'd leisure,
   Which shall be shortly, single I'll resolve you,
   Which to you shall seem probable, of every
   These happen'd accidents; till when, be cheerful
   And think of each thing well. [*Aside to* ARIEL] Come
   hither, spirit;
   Set Caliban and his companions free;
   Untie the spell. [*Exit* ARIEL] How fares my gracious sir?
   There are yet missing of your company
   Some few odd lads that you remember not.

   Re-enter ARIEL, *driving in* CALIBAN, STEPHANO, *and*
      TRINCULO, *in their stolen apparel*

STEPHANO. Every man shift for all the rest, and let no man

take care for himself; for all is but fortune. Coragio, bully-
monster, coragio!

TRINCULO. If these be true spies which I wear in my head,
here's a goodly sight.

CALIBAN. O Setebos, these be brave spirits indeed!
How fine my master is! I am afraid
He will chastise me.

SEBASTIAN. Ha, ha!
What things are these, my lord Antonio?
Will money buy 'em?

ANTONIO. Very like; one of them
Is a plain fish, and no doubt marketable.

PROSPERO. Mark but the badges of these men, my lords,
Then say if they be true. This mis-shapen knave—
His mother was a witch, and one so strong
That could control the moon, make flows and ebbs,
And deal in her command without her power.
These three have robb'd me; and this demi-devil—
For he's a bastard one—had plotted with them
To take my life. Two of these fellows you
Must know and own; this thing of darkness I
Acknowledge mine.

CALIBAN. I shall be pinch'd to death.

ALONSO. Is not this Stephano, my drunken butler?

SEBASTIAN. He is drunk now; where had he wine?

ALONSO. And Trinculo is reeling ripe; where should they
Find this grand liquor that hath gilded 'em?
How cam'st thou in this pickle?

TRINCULO. I have been in such a pickle since I saw you last
that, I fear me, will never out of my bones. I shall not fear
fly-blowing.

SEBASTIAN. Why, how now, Stephano!

STEPHANO. O, touch me not; I am not Stephano, but a
cramp.

PROSPERO. You'd be king o' the isle, sirrah?

STEPHANO. I should have been a sore one, then.

ALONSO. [Pointing to CALIBAN] This is as strange a thing as
e'er I look'd on.

PROSPERO. He is as disproportioned in his manners
As in his shape. Go, sirrah, to my cell;

Take with you your companions; as you look
To have my pardon, trim it handsomely.
CALIBAN. Ay, that I will; and I'll be wise hereafter,
And seek for grace. What a thrice-double ass
Was I to take this drunkard for a god,
And worship this dull fool!
PROSPERO. Go to; away!
ALONSO. Hence, and bestow your luggage where you found it.
SEBASTIAN. Or stole it, rather.
Exeunt CALIBAN, STEPHANO, and TRINCULO
PROSPERO. Sir, I invite your Highness and your train
To my poor cell, where you shall take your rest
For this one night; which, part of it, I'll waste
With such discourse as, I not doubt, shall make it
Go quick away—the story of my life,
And the particular accidents gone by
Since I came to this isle. And in the morn
I'll bring you to your ship, and so to Naples,
Where I have hope to see the nuptial
Of these our dear-belov'd solemnized,
And thence retire me to my Milan, where
Every third thought shall be my grave.
ALONSO. I long
To hear the story of your life, which must
Take the ear strangely.
PROSPERO. I'll deliver all;
And promise you calm seas, auspicious gales,
And sail so expeditious that shall catch
Your royal fleet far off. [*Aside to* ARIEL] My Ariel, chick,
That is thy charge. Then to the elements
Be free, and fare thou well!—Please you, draw near.
Exeunt

EPILOGUE

Spoken by PROSPERO

Now my charms are all o'erthrown,
And what strength I have's mine own,
Which is most faint. Now 'tis true,

I must be here confin'd by you,
Or sent to Naples. Let me not,
Since I have my dukedom got,
And pardon'd the deceiver, dwell
In this bare island by your spell;
But release me from my bands
With the help of your good hands.
Gentle breath of yours my sails
Must fill, or else my project fails,
Which was to please. Now I want
Spirits to enforce, art to enchant;
And my ending is despair
Unless I be reliev'd by prayer,
Which pierces so that it assaults
Mercy itself, and frees all faults.
As you from crimes would pardon'd be,
Let your indulgence set me free.

The Two Gentlemen of Verona

THE TWO GENTLEMEN OF VERONA

THE TWO GENTLEMEN OF VERONA was first printed in the Folio of 1623, although it must have been written before 1598 as Meres included it in the list of works he ascribes in his *Palladis Tamia* to Shakespeare. The evidences of style and versification seem to indicate that this was the earliest of Shakespeare's romantic comedies, and it is unfortunate that no clue has so far been discovered that would allow a more precise date to be fixed for its composition and enable the historian to pronounce with more confidence than he dares at present on Shakespeare's part in the development of this type of play.

In 1559 the Portuguese poet Jorge de Montemayor published his *Diana Enamorada*, a romance in Spanish, that was to enjoy a popularity not confined to the Peninsula. Nicholas Colin made a French translation in 1578 and in 1598 was issued the English version of Bartholomew Younge. Borrowings however from the *Diana* had appeared in various forms, and it has been thought that a play performed before the Queen in 1585 entitled *The History of Felix and Philomena* may owe its plot to Montemayor, for in the second book of his *Diana* he relates the story of Felix and Felismena. Whether the English play was indeed a version of this part of the Spanish romance must remain doubtful unless further evidence is discovered, for no copy of the play has survived; what is certain however is that Shakespeare directly, or indirectly through some version such as that here mentioned, drew on the story of Felix and Felismena for incidents in his *Two Gentlemen*. The romance of Proteus and Julia recalls the following episodes from the earlier story: Felix sends a letter to Felismena who, like Shakespeare's Julia, pretends to reject it and to be displeased with her maid for acting as a go-between; Felix just when he is enjoying the affections of Felismena is dispatched to Court by his father; Felismena follows him in male disguise, lodges at an inn, hears her false lover serenade Celia (Shakespeare's Silvia), who however is merely playing with him; Felismena then enters the service of Felix and in her disguise as a page acts as his messenger to

Celia. Here Shakespeare's plot and the Spanish story diverge. Shakespeare's Silvia has her own admirer in Valentine and has no need like Montemayor's Celia to fall in love with the disguised messenger, and eventually to die of a despairing passion. There are however in the exchanges between Julia and Silvia points that recall the conversation of Felismena and Celia. Finally Felismena and Felix are reunited after a combat in a wood, though the circumstances are quite different from those in Shakespeare's plot: Felismena is here the rescuer of her distressed and repentant lover.

Shakespeare also had in mind an Italian play or at least its plot; and it is probable that Montemayor had the same comedy in his memory when he wrote the Felix and Felismena episode. The girl disguised as a page in the service of the man she loves and carrying his messages to the lady he is for the time enamoured of was made an international figure by an Italian play that was performed at the Carnival of 1531 in Sienna. This was the famous *Gl'Ingannati* (*see* p. 931) written for and staged by members of the Academy of the Intronati. Many versions and imitations of this device were acted or printed, the most famous of all being Shakespeare's *Twelfth Night*; Shakespeare's first sketch however for this masterpiece is found in *The Two Gentlemen*. Shakespeare's interest in the various versions of the theme will be discussed when the Viola-Olivia episode in *Twelfth Night* is reached; meantime it will be sufficient to note that in 1595 a Latin version of *Gl'Ingannati* called *Laelia* (the name of the heroine of the Italian comedy) was performed at Cambridge before the Earl of Essex. As Shakespeare's dedications to his poems *Venus and Adonis* and *Lucrece* were addressed to the Earl of Southampton, and Southampton was a devoted member of the Essex circle, the question of a possible connection between Shakespeare's *Two Gentlemen* and *Laelia* has been raised, and it has even been suggested that *The Two Gentlemen* although it may have been written before 1595 was perhaps revised with the Latin version in mind. There is however no evidence that enables the priority to be determined, and all that can safely be affirmed is that Shakespeare was already meditating a theme he was to develop in its perfection only in later years.

73

Already in *The Two Gentlemen* Shakespeare's treatment of his sources shows the direction his mind was taking. Laelia, the heroine of the Italian intrigue, is a determined and astute plotter set on having her own will and quite without the delicate and indeed quixotic scruples of the Spanish Felismena. Shakespeare's Julia is much more like Montemayor's heroine than the unscrupulous Italian. Her lover on the contrary is drawn perhaps more after the Italian than the Spanish model; less brutal than Flamminio of *Gl'Ingannati*, he yet lacks the courtesy that mitigates the infidelity of Felix.

If Montemayor had the Italian plot in mind he gave it a tragic turn by depriving his Celia of the comfort her counterpart Isabella in *Gl'Ingannati* finds in Laelia's long-lost brother, who turns up, like Sebastian in *Twelfth Night*, to take his sister's place in the affections of the deluded girl. In *Two Gentlemen* Shakespeare has provided from the beginning for his second heroine: Proteus has a friend Valentine and this allows Shakespeare to add to the complications the theme of broken friendship. The manner in which the friends are reconciled in the final scene has seemed to some critics so outrageous that they suppose someone has rewritten Shakespeare's version. Valentine accepts the repentance of the false Proteus, although he has just caught him in the very act of disloyalty, and as a pledge of their renewed faith offers to surrender his own Silvia to him. Shakespeare is of course taking advantage of the David and Jonathan convention fashionable at the Renaissance to resolve the tangle of his plot. Such friendships as that of Valentine and Proteus were supposed to be superior to the loves of men for women, and Shakespeare finds in this commonplace a resource in his difficulty.

The play is doubtless on conventional lines, but there are many charming passages and the scene in which Julia listens to Proteus serenading Silvia reveals that combination of poetic and dramatic power that was to give Shakespeare's later work its characteristic excellence.

VALENTINE. *Cease to persuade, my loving Proteus*

(ACT I. SCENE I)

DUKE OF MILAN, *father to Silvia*
VALENTINE ⎱ *the two gentlemen*
PROTEUS ⎰
ANTONIO, *father to Proteus*
THURIO, *a foolish rival to Valentine*
EGLAMOUR, *agent for Silvia in her escape*
SPEED, *a clownish servant to Valentine*
LAUNCE, *the like to Proteus*
PANTHINO, *servant to Antonio*
HOST, *where Julia lodges in Milan*
OUTLAWS, *with Valentine*

JULIA, *a lady of Verona, beloved of Proteus*
SILVIA, *the Duke's daughter, beloved of Valentine*
LUCETTA, *waiting-woman to Julia*

Servants
Musicians

SCENE:

Verona; Milan; the frontiers of Mantua

The Two Gentlemen of Verona

ACT I. SCENE 1

Verona. An open place

Enter VALENTINE *and* PROTEUS

VALENTINE. Cease to persuade, my loving Proteus:
Home-keeping youth have ever homely wits.
Were't not affection chains thy tender days
To the sweet glances of thy honour'd love,
I rather would entreat thy company
To see the wonders of the world abroad,
Than, living dully sluggardiz'd at home,
Wear out thy youth with shapeless idleness.
But since thou lov'st, love still, and thrive therein,
Even as I would, when I to love begin.
PROTEUS. Wilt thou be gone? Sweet Valentine, adieu!
Think on thy Proteus, when thou haply seest
Some rare noteworthy object in thy travel.
Wish me partaker in thy happiness
When thou dost meet good hap; and in thy danger,
If ever danger do environ thee,
Commend thy grievance to my holy prayers,
For I will be thy beadsman, Valentine.
VALENTINE. And on a love-book pray for my success?
PROTEUS. Upon some book I love I'll pray for thee.
VALENTINE. That's on some shallow story of deep love:
How young Leander cross'd the Hellespont.
PROTEUS. That's a deep story of a deeper love;
For he was more than over shoes in love.
VALENTINE. 'Tis true; for you are over boots in love,
And yet you never swum the Hellespont.
PROTEUS. Over the boots! Nay, give me not the boots.
VALENTINE. No, I will not, for it boots thee not.
PROTEUS. What?

VALENTINE. To be in love—where scorn is bought with
  groans,
  Coy looks with heart-sore sighs, one fading moment's
  mirth
  With twenty watchful, weary, tedious nights;
  If haply won, perhaps a hapless gain;
  If lost, why then a grievous labour won;
  However, but a folly bought with wit,
  Or else a wit by folly vanquished.
PROTEUS. So, by your circumstance, you call me fool.
VALENTINE. So, by your circumstance, I fear you'll prove.
PROTEUS. 'Tis love you cavil at; I am not Love.
VALENTINE. Love is your master, for he masters you;
  And he that is so yoked by a fool,
  Methinks, should not be chronicled for wise.
PROTEUS. Yet writers say, as in the sweetest bud
  The eating canker dwells, so eating love
  Inhabits in the finest wits of all.
VALENTINE. And writers say, as the most forward bud
  Is eaten by the canker ere it blow,
  Even so by love the young and tender wit
  Is turn'd to folly, blasting in the bud,
  Losing his verdure even in the prime,
  And all the fair effects of future hopes.
  But wherefore waste I time to counsel thee
  That art a votary to fond desire?
  Once more adieu. My father at the road
  Expects my coming, there to see me shipp'd.
PROTEUS. And thither will I bring thee, Valentine.
VALENTINE. Sweet Proteus, no; now let us take our leave.
  To Milan let me hear from thee by letters
  Of thy success in love, and what news else
  Betideth here in absence of thy friend;
  And I likewise will visit thee with mine.
PROTEUS. All happiness bechance to thee in Milan!
VALENTINE. As much to you at home; and so farewell!
                                    Exit VALENTINE
PROTEUS. He after honour hunts, I after love;
  He leaves his friends to dignify them more:
  I leave myself, my friends, and all for love.

Thou, Julia, thou hast metamorphis'd me,
Made me neglect my studies, lose my time,
War with good counsel, set the world at nought;
Made wit with musing weak, heart sick with thought.

Enter Speed

Speed. Sir Proteus, save you! Saw you my master?
Proteus. But now he parted hence to embark for Milan.
Speed. Twenty to one then he is shipp'd already,
And I have play'd the sheep in losing him.
Proteus. Indeed a sheep doth very often stray,
An if the shepherd be awhile away.
Speed. You conclude that my master is a shepherd then, and
I a sheep?
Proteus. I do.
Speed. Why then, my horns are his horns, whether I wake
or sleep.
Proteus. A silly answer, and fitting well a sheep.
Speed. This proves me still a sheep.
Proteus. True; and thy master a shepherd.
Speed. Nay, that I can deny by a circumstance.
Proteus. It shall go hard but I'll prove it by another.
Speed. The shepherd seeks the sheep, and not the sheep the
shepherd; but I seek my master, and my master seeks not
me; therefore, I am no sheep.
Proteus. The sheep for fodder follow the shepherd; the
shepherd for food follows not the sheep: thou for wages
followest thy master; thy master for wages follows not
thee. Therefore, thou art a sheep.
Speed. Such another proof will make me cry 'baa.'
Proteus. But dost thou hear? Gav'st thou my letter to Julia?
Speed. Ay, sir; I, a lost mutton, gave your letter to her, a
lac'd mutton; and she, a lac'd mutton, gave me, a lost
mutton, nothing for my labour.
Proteus. Here's too small a pasture for such store of muttons.
Speed. If the ground be overcharg'd, you were best stick
her.
Proteus. Nay, in that you are astray: 'twere best pound
you.

79

SPEED. Nay, sir, less than a pound shall serve me for carrying your letter.

PROTEUS. You mistake; I mean the pound—a pinfold.

SPEED. From a pound to a pin? Fold it over and over,
'Tis threefold too little for carrying a letter to your lover.

PROTEUS. But what said she?

SPEED. [*Nodding*] Ay.

PROTEUS. Nod-ay. Why, that's 'noddy.'

SPEED. You mistook, sir; I say she did nod; and you ask me if she did nod; and I say 'Ay.'

PROTEUS. And that set together is 'noddy.'

SPEED. Now you have taken the pains to set it together, take it for your pains.

PROTEUS. No, no; you shall have it for bearing the letter.

SPEED. Well, I perceive I must be fain to bear with you.

PROTEUS. Why, sir, how do you bear with me?

SPEED. Marry, sir, the letter, very orderly; having nothing but the word 'noddy' for my pains.

PROTEUS. Beshrew me, but you have a quick wit.

SPEED. And yet it cannot overtake your slow purse.

PROTEUS. Come, come, open the matter; in brief, what said she?

SPEED. Open your purse, that the money and the matter may be both at once delivered.

PROTEUS. Well, sir, here is for your pains. What said she?

SPEED. Truly, sir, I think you'll hardly win her.

PROTEUS. Why, couldst thou perceive so much from her?

SPEED. Sir, I could perceive nothing at all from her; no, not so much as a ducat for delivering your letter; and being so hard to me that brought your mind, I fear she'll prove as hard to you in telling your mind. Give her no token but stones, for she's as hard as steel.

PROTEUS. What said she? Nothing?

SPEED. No, not so much as 'Take this for thy pains.' To testify your bounty, I thank you, you have testern'd me; in requital whereof, henceforth carry your letters yourself; and so, sir, I'll commend you to my master.

PROTEUS. Go, go, be gone, to save your ship from wreck,
Which cannot perish, having thee aboard,
Being destin'd to a drier death on shore.   *Exit* SPEED

I must go send some better messenger.
I fear my Julia would not deign my lines,
Receiving them from such a worthless post.   *Exit*

SCENE 2

Verona. The garden of JULIA's *house*

Enter JULIA *and* LUCETTA

JULIA. But say, Lucetta, now we are alone,
  Wouldst thou then counsel me to fall in love?
LUCETTA. Ay, madam; so you stumble not unheedfully.
JULIA. Of all the fair resort of gentlemen
  That every day with parle encounter me,
  In thy opinion which is worthiest love?
LUCETTA. Please you, repeat their names; I'll show my mind
  According to my shallow simple skill.
JULIA. What think'st thou of the fair Sir Eglamour?
LUCETTA. As of a knight well-spoken, neat, and fine;
  But, were I you, he never should be mine.
JULIA. What think'st thou of the rich Mercatio?
LUCETTA. Well of his wealth; but of himself, so so.
JULIA. What think'st thou of the gentle Proteus?
LUCETTA. Lord, Lord! to see what folly reigns in us!
JULIA. How now! what means this passion at his name?
LUCETTA. Pardon, dear madam; 'tis a passing shame
  That I, unworthy body as I am,
  Should censure thus on lovely gentlemen.
JULIA. Why not on Proteus, as of all the rest?
LUCETTA. Then thus: of many good I think him best.
JULIA. Your reason?
LUCETTA. I have no other but a woman's reason:
  I think him so, because I think him so.
JULIA. And wouldst thou have me cast my love on him?
LUCETTA. Ay, if you thought your love not cast away.
JULIA. Why, he, of all the rest, hath never mov'd me.
LUCETTA. Yet he, of all the rest, I think, best loves ye.
JULIA. His little speaking shows his love but small.

81

LUCETTA. Fire that's closest kept burns most of all.
JULIA. They do not love that do not show their love.
LUCETTA. O, they love least that let men know their love.
JULIA. I would I knew his mind.
LUCETTA. Peruse this paper, madam.
JULIA. 'To Julia'—Say, from whom?
LUCETTA. That the contents will show.
JULIA. Say, say, who gave it thee?
LUCETTA. Sir Valentine's page; and sent, I think, from Pro-
teus.
    He would have given it you; but I, being in the way,
    Did in your name receive it; pardon the fault, I pray.
JULIA. Now, by my modesty, a goodly broker!
    Dare you presume to harbour wanton lines?
    To whisper and conspire against my youth?
    Now, trust me, 'tis an office of great worth,
    And you an officer fit for the place.
    There, take the paper; see it be return'd;
    Or else return no more into my sight.
LUCETTA. To plead for love deserves more fee than hate.
JULIA. Will ye be gone?
LUCETTA. That you may ruminate.   *Exit*
JULIA. And yet, I would I had o'erlook'd the letter.
    It were a shame to call her back again,
    And pray her to a fault for which I chid her.
    What fool is she, that knows I am a maid
    And would not force the letter to my view!
    Since maids, in modesty, say 'No' to that
    Which they would have the profferer construe 'Ay.'
    Fie, fie, how wayward is this foolish love,
    That like a testy babe will scratch the nurse,
    And presently, all humbled, kiss the rod!
    How churlishly I chid Lucetta hence,
    When willingly I would have had her here!
    How angerly I taught my brow to frown,
    When inward joy enforc'd my heart to smile!
    My penance is to call Lucetta back
    And ask remission for my folly past.
    What ho! Lucetta!

Re-enter LUCETTA

LUCETTA. What would your ladyship?

JULIA. Is't near dinner time?

LUCETTA. I would it were,
That you might kill your stomach on your meat
And not upon your maid.

JULIA. What is't that you took up so gingerly?

LUCETTA. Nothing.

JULIA. Why didst thou stoop then?

LUCETTA. To take a paper up that I let fall.

JULIA. And is that paper nothing?

LUCETTA. Nothing concerning me.

JULIA. Then let it lie for those that it concerns.

LUCETTA. Madam, it will not lie where it concerns,
Unless it have a false interpreter.

JULIA. Some love of yours hath writ to you in rhyme.

LUCETTA. That I might sing it, madam, to a tune.
Give me a note; your ladyship can set.

JULIA. As little by such toys as may be possible.
Best sing it to the tune of 'Light o' Love.'

LUCETTA. It is too heavy for so light a tune.

JULIA. Heavy! belike it hath some burden then.

LUCETTA. Ay; and melodious were it, would you sing it.

JULIA. And why not you?

LUCETTA. I cannot reach so high.

JULIA. Let's see your song. [LUCETTA *withholds the letter*]
How now, minion!

LUCETTA. Keep tune there still, so you will sing it out.
And yet methinks I do not like this tune.

JULIA. You do not!

LUCETTA. No, madam; 'tis too sharp.

JULIA. You, minion, are too saucy.

LUCETTA. Nay, now you are too flat
And mar the concord with too harsh a descant;
There wanteth but a mean to fill your song.

JULIA. The mean is drown'd with your unruly bass.

LUCETTA. Indeed, I bid the base for Proteus.

JULIA. This babble shall not henceforth trouble me.
Here is a coil with protestation! [*Tears the letter*]

Go, get you gone; and let the papers lie.
You would be fing'ring them, to anger me.
LUCETTA. She makes it strange; but she would be best pleas'd
To be so ang'red with another letter.   *Exit*
JULIA. Nay, would I were so ang'red with the same!
O hateful hands, to tear such loving words!
Injurious wasps, to feed on such sweet honey
And kill the bees that yield it with your stings!
I'll kiss each several paper for amends.
Look, here is writ 'kind Julia.' Unkind Julia,
As in revenge of thy ingratitude,
I throw thy name against the bruising stones,
Trampling contemptuously on thy disdain.
And here is writ 'love-wounded Proteus.'
Poor wounded name! my bosom, as a bed,
Shall lodge thee till thy wound be throughly heal'd;
And thus I search it with a sovereign kiss.
But twice or thrice was 'Proteus' written down.
Be calm, good wind, blow not a word away
Till I have found each letter in the letter—
Except mine own name; that some whirlwind bear
Unto a ragged, fearful, hanging rock,
And throw it thence into the raging sea.
Lo, here in one line is his name twice writ:
'Poor forlorn Proteus, passionate Proteus,
To the sweet Julia.' That I'll tear away;
And yet I will not, sith so prettily
He couples it to his complaining names.
Thus will I fold them one upon another;
Now kiss, embrace, contend, do what you will.

Re-enter LUCETTA

LUCETTA. Madam,
Dinner is ready, and your father stays.
JULIA. Well, let us go.
LUCETTA. What, shall these papers lie like tell-tales here?
JULIA. If you respect them, best to take them up.
LUCETTA. Nay, I was taken up for laying them down;
Yet here they shall not lie for catching cold.
JULIA. I see you have a month's mind to them.

LUCETTA. Ay, madam, you may say what sights you see;
   I see things too, although you judge I wink.
JULIA. Come, come; will't please you go?   *Exeunt*

SCENE 3

Verona. ANTONIO's *house*

Enter ANTONIO *and* PANTHINO

ANTONIO. Tell me, Panthino, what sad talk was that
   Wherewith my brother held you in the cloister?
PANTHINO. 'Twas of his nephew Proteus, your son.
ANTONIO. Why, what of him?
PANTHINO. He wond'red that your lordship
   Would suffer him to spend his youth at home,
   While other men, of slender reputation,
   Put forth their sons to seek preferment out:
   Some to the wars, to try their fortune there;
   Some to discover islands far away;
   Some to the studious universities.
   For any, or for all these exercises,
   He said that Proteus, your son, was meet;
   And did request me to importune you
   To let him spend his time no more at home,
   Which would be great impeachment to his age,
   In having known no travel in his youth.
ANTONIO. Nor need'st thou much importune me to that
   Whereon this month I have been hammering.
   I have consider'd well his loss of time,
   And how he cannot be a perfect man,
   Not being tried and tutor'd in the world:
   Experience is by industry achiev'd,
   And perfected by the swift course of time.
   Then tell me whither were I best to send him.
PANTHINO. I think your lordship is not ignorant
   How his companion, youthful Valentine,
   Attends the Emperor in his royal court.
ANTONIO. I know it well.

PANTHINO. 'Twere good, I think, your lordship sent him
    thither:
There shall he practise tilts and tournaments,
Hear sweet discourse, converse with noblemen,
And be in eye of every exercise
Worthy his youth and nobleness of birth.
ANTONIO. I like thy counsel; well hast thou advis'd;
And that thou mayst perceive how well I like it,
The execution of it shall make known:
Even with the speediest expedition
I will dispatch him to the Emperor's court.
PANTHINO. To-morrow, may it please you, Don Alphonso
With other gentlemen of good esteem
Are journeying to salute the Emperor,
And to commend their service to his will.
ANTONIO. Good company; with them shall Proteus go.

Enter PROTEUS

And—in good time!—now will we break with him.
PROTEUS. Sweet love! sweet lines! sweet life!
Here is her hand, the agent of her heart;
Here is her oath for love, her honour's pawn.
O that our fathers would applaud our loves,
To seal our happiness with their consents!
O heavenly Julia!
ANTONIO. How now! What letter are you reading there?
PROTEUS. May't please your lordship, 'tis a word or two
Of commendations sent from Valentine,
Deliver'd by a friend that came from him.
ANTONIO. Lend me the letter; let me see what news.
PROTEUS. There is no news, my lord; but that he writes
How happily he lives, how well-belov'd
And daily graced by the Emperor;
Wishing me with him, partner of his fortune.
ANTONIO. And how stand you affected to his wish?
PROTEUS. As one relying on your lordship's will,
And not depending on his friendly wish.
ANTONIO. My will is something sorted with his wish.
Muse not that I thus suddenly proceed;
For what I will, I will, and there an end.

I am resolv'd that thou shalt spend some time
With Valentinus in the Emperor's court;
What maintenance he from his friends receives,
Like exhibition thou shalt have from me.
To-morrow be in readiness to go—
Excuse it not, for I am peremptory.
PROTEUS. My lord, I cannot be so soon provided;
Please you, deliberate a day or two.
ANTONIO. Look what thou want'st shall be sent after thee.
No more of stay; to-morrow thou must go.
Come on, Panthino; you shall be employ'd
To hasten on his expedition.
                    Exeunt ANTONIO *and* PANTHINO
PROTEUS. Thus have I shunn'd the fire for fear of burning,
And drench'd me in the sea, where I am drown'd.
I fear'd to show my father Julia's letter,
Lest he should take exceptions to my love;
And with the vantage of mine own excuse
Hath he excepted most against my love.
O, how this spring of love resembleth
The uncertain glory of an April day,
Which now shows all the beauty of the sun,
And by and by a cloud takes all away!

Re-enter PANTHINO

PANTHINO. Sir Proteus, your father calls for you;
He is in haste; therefore, I pray you, go.
PROTEUS. Why, this it is: my heart accords thereto;
And yet a thousand times it answers 'No.'   *Exeunt*

ACT II. SCENE 1

Milan. The DUKE'S *palace*

Enter VALENTINE *and* SPEED

SPEED. Sir, your glove.
VALENTINE. Not mine: my gloves are on.

SPEED. Why, then, this may be yours; for this is but one.

VALENTINE. Ha! let me see; ay, give it me, it's mine;
Sweet ornament that decks a thing divine!
Ah, Silvia! Silvia!

SPEED. [*Calling*] Madam Silvia! Madam Silvia!

VALENTINE. How now, sirrah?

SPEED. She is not within hearing, sir.

VALENTINE. Why, sir, who bade you call her?

SPEED. Your worship, sir; or else I mistook.

VALENTINE. Well, you'll still be too forward.

SPEED. And yet I was last chidden for being too slow.

VALENTINE. Go to, sir; tell me, do you know Madam Silvia?

SPEED. She that your worship loves?

VALENTINE. Why, how know you that I am in love?

SPEED. Marry, by these special marks: first, you have learn'd, like Sir Proteus, to wreath your arms like a malcontent; to relish a love-song, like a robin redbreast; to walk alone, like one that had the pestilence; to sigh, like a school-boy that had lost his A B C ; to weep, like a young wench that had buried her grandam; to fast, like one that takes diet; to watch, like one that fears robbing; to speak puling, like a beggar at Hallowmas. You were wont, when you laughed, to crow like a cock; when you walk'd, to walk like one of the lions; when you fasted, it was presently after dinner; when you look'd sadly, it was for want of money. And now you are metamorphis'd with a mistress, that, when I look on you, I can hardly think you my master.

VALENTINE. Are all these things perceiv'd in me?

SPEED. They are all perceiv'd without ye.

VALENTINE. Without me? They cannot.

SPEED. Without you! Nay, that's certain; for, without you were so simple, none else would; but you are so without these follies that these follies are within you, and shine through you like the water in an urinal, that not an eye that sees you but is a physician to comment on your malady.

VALENTINE. But tell me, dost thou know my lady Silvia?

SPEED. She that you gaze on so, as she sits at supper?

VALENTINE. Hast thou observ'd that? Even she, I mean.

SPEED. Why, sir, I know her not.

VALENTINE. Dost thou know her by my gazing on her, and yet know'st her not?

SPEED. Is she not hard-favour'd, sir?

VALENTINE. Not so fair, boy, as well-favour'd.

SPEED. Sir, I know that well enough.

VALENTINE. What dost thou know?

SPEED. That she is not so fair as, of you, well-favour'd.

VALENTINE. I mean that her beauty is exquisite, but her favour infinite.

SPEED. That's because the one is painted, and the other out of all count.

VALENTINE. How painted? and how out of count?

SPEED. Marry, sir, so painted, to make her fair, that no man counts of her beauty.

VALENTINE. How esteem'st thou me? I account of her beauty.

SPEED. You never saw her since she was deform'd.

VALENTINE. How long hath she been deform'd?

SPEED. Ever since you lov'd her.

VALENTINE. I have lov'd her ever since I saw her, and still I see her beautiful.

SPEED. If you love her, you cannot see her.

VALENTINE. Why?

SPEED. Because Love is blind. O that you had mine eyes; or your own eyes had the lights they were wont to have when you chid at Sir Proteus for going ungarter'd!

VALENTINE. What should I see then?

SPEED. Your own present folly and her passing deformity; for he, being in love, could not see to garter his hose; and you, being in love, cannot see to put on your hose.

VALENTINE. Belike, boy, then you are in love; for last morning you could not see to wipe my shoes.

SPEED. True, sir; I was in love with my bed. I thank you, you swing'd me for my love, which makes me the bolder to chide you for yours.

VALENTINE. In conclusion, I stand affected to her.

SPEED. I would you were set, so your affection would cease.

VALENTINE. Last night she enjoin'd me to write some lines to one she loves.

SPEED. And have you?

VALENTINE. I have.

SPEED. Are they not lamely writ?

VALENTINE. No, boy, but as well as I can do them.

Enter SILVIA

Peace! here she comes.

SPEED. [*Aside*] O excellent motion! O exceeding puppet!
Now will he interpret to her.

VALENTINE. Madam and mistress, a thousand good morrows.

SPEED. [*Aside*] O, give ye good ev'n!
Here's a million of manners.

SILVIA. Sir Valentine and servant, to you two thousand.

SPEED. [*Aside*] He should give her interest, and she gives it
him.

VALENTINE. As you enjoin'd me, I have writ your letter
Unto the secret nameless friend of yours;
Which I was much unwilling to proceed in,
But for my duty to your ladyship.

SILVIA. I thank you, gentle servant. 'Tis very clerkly done.

VALENTINE. Now trust me, madam, it came hardly off;
For, being ignorant to whom it goes,
I writ at random, very doubtfully.

SILVIA. Perchance you think too much of so much pains?

VALENTINE. No, madam; so it stead you, I will write,
Please you command, a thousand times as much;
And yet—

SILVIA. A pretty period! Well, I guess the sequel;
And yet I will not name it—and yet I care not.
And yet take this again—and yet I thank you—
Meaning henceforth to trouble you no more.

SPEED. [*Aside*] And yet you will; and yet another 'yet.'

VALENTINE. What means your ladyship? Do you not like it?

SILVIA. Yes, yes; the lines are very quaintly writ;
But, since unwillingly, take them again.
Nay, take them.   [*Gives back the letter*]

VALENTINE. Madam, they are for you.

SILVIA. Ay, ay, you writ them, sir, at my request;
But I will none of them; they are for you:
I would have had them writ more movingly.

VALENTINE. Please you, I'll write your ladyship another.

SILVIA. And when it's writ, for my sake read it over;
  And if it please you, so; if not, why, so.
VALENTINE. If it please me, madam, what then?
SILVIA. Why, if it please you, take it for your labour.
  And so good morrow, servant.   *Exit* SILVIA
SPEED. O jest unseen, inscrutable, invisible,
  As a nose on a man's face, or a weathercock on a steeple!
  My master sues to her; and she hath taught her suitor,
  He being her pupil, to become her tutor.
  O excellent device! Was there ever heard a better,
  That my master, being scribe, to himself should write the
    letter?
VALENTINE. How now, sir! What are you reasoning with
  yourself?
SPEED. Nay, I was rhyming: 'tis you that have the reason.
VALENTINE. To do what?
SPEED. To be a spokesman from Madam Silvia?
VALENTINE. To whom?
SPEED. To yourself; why, she woos you by a figure.
VALENTINE. What figure?
SPEED. By a letter, I should say.
VALENTINE. Why, she hath not writ to me.
SPEED. What need she, when she hath made you write to
  yourself?
  Why, do you not perceive the jest?
VALENTINE. No, believe me.
SPEED. No believing you indeed, sir. But did you perceive
  her earnest?
VALENTINE. She gave me none except an angry word.
SPEED. Why, she hath given you a letter.
VALENTINE. That's the letter I writ to her friend.
SPEED. And that letter hath she deliver'd, and there an end.
VALENTINE. I would it were no worse.
SPEED. I'll warrant you 'tis as well.
  'For often have you writ to her; and she, in modesty,
  Or else for want of idle time, could not again reply;
  Or fearing else some messenger that might her mind dis-
    cover,
  Herself hath taught her love himself to write unto her
    lover.'

All this I speak in print, for in print I found it. Why muse
you, sir? 'Tis dinner time.

VALENTINE. I have din'd.

SPEED. Ay, but hearken, sir; though the chameleon Love can
feed on the air, I am one that am nourish'd by my vict-
uals, and would fain have meat. O, be not like your mistress! Be moved, be moved. *Exeunt*

SCENE 2

Verona. JULIA's *house*

Enter PROTEUS *and* JULIA

PROTEUS. Have patience, gentle Julia.

JULIA. I must, where is no remedy.

PROTEUS. When possibly I can, I will return.

JULIA. If you turn not, you will return the sooner.
  Keep this remembrance for thy Julia's sake.
                                          [*Giving a ring*]

PROTEUS. Why, then, we'll make exchange. Here, take you
  this.

JULIA. And seal the bargain with a holy kiss.

PROTEUS. Here is my hand for my true constancy;
  And when that hour o'erslips me in the day
  Wherein I sigh not, Julia, for thy sake,
  The next ensuing hour some foul mischance
  Torment me for my love's forgetfulness!
  My father stays my coming; answer not;
  The tide is now—nay, not thy tide of tears:
  That tide will stay me longer than I should.
  Julia, farewell!   *Exit* JULIA
  What, gone without a word?
  Ay, so true love should do: it cannot speak;
  For truth hath better deeds than words to grace it.

Enter PANTHINO

PANTHINO. Sir Proteus, you are stay'd for.

PROTEUS. Go; I come, I come.
  Alas! this parting strikes poor lovers dumb. *Exeunt*

SCENE 3

Verona. A street

Enter LAUNCE, *leading a dog*

LAUNCE. Nay, 'twill be this hour ere I have done weeping; all the kind of the Launces have this very fault. I have receiv'd my proportion, like the Prodigious Son, and am going with Sir Proteus to the Imperial's court. I think Crab my dog be the sourest-natured dog that lives: my mother weeping, my father wailing, my sister crying, our maid howling, our cat wringing her hands, and all our house in a great perplexity; yet did not this cruel-hearted cur shed one tear. He is a stone, a very pebble stone, and has no more pity in him than a dog. A Jew would have wept to have seen our parting; why, my grandam having no eyes, look you, wept herself blind at my parting. Nay, I'll show you the manner of it. This shoe is my father; no, this left shoe is my father; no, no, this left shoe is my mother; nay, that cannot be so neither; yes, it is so, it is so, it hath the worser sole. This shoe with the hole in it is my mother, and this my father. A vengeance on 't! There 'tis. Now, sir, this staff is my sister, for, look you, she is as white as a lily and as small as a wand; this hat is Nan our maid; I am the dog; no, the dog is himself, and I am the dog—O, the dog is me, and I am myself; ay, so, so. Now come I to my father: 'Father, your blessing.' Now should not the shoe speak a word for weeping; now should I kiss my father; well, he weeps on. Now come I to my mother. O that she could speak now like a wood woman! Well, I kiss her—why there 'tis; here's my mother's breath up and down. Now come I to my sister; mark the moan she makes. Now the dog all this while sheds not a tear, nor speaks a word; but see how I lay the dust with my tears.

Enter PANTHINO

PANTHINO. Launce, away, away, aboard! Thy master is shipp'd, and thou art to post after with oars. What's the matter? Why weep'st thou, man? Away, ass! You'll lose the tide if you tarry any longer.

LAUNCE. It is no matter if the tied were lost; for it is the unkindest tied that ever any man tied.

PANTHINO. What's the unkindest tide?

LAUNCE. Why, he that's tied here, Crab, my dog.

PANTHINO. Tut, man, I mean thou'lt lose the flood, and, in losing the flood, lose thy voyage, and, in losing thy voyage, lose thy master, and, in losing thy master, lose thy service, and, in losing thy service—Why dost thou stop my mouth?

LAUNCE. For fear thou shouldst lose thy tongue.

PANTHINO. Where should I lose my tongue?

LAUNCE. In thy tale.

PANTHINO. In thy tail!

LAUNCE. Lose the tide, and the voyage, and the master, and the service, and the tied! Why, man, if the river were dry, I am able to fill it with my tears; if the wind were down, I could drive the boat with my sighs.

PANTHINO. Come, come away, man; I was sent to call thee.

LAUNCE. Sir, call me what thou dar'st.

PANTHINO. Will thou go?

LAUNCE. Well, I will go.   *Exeunt*

SCENE 4

Milan. The DUKE's *palace*

Enter SILVIA, VALENTINE, THURIO, *and* SPEED

SILVIA. Servant!

VALENTINE. Mistress?

SPEED. Master, Sir Thurio frowns on you.

VALENTINE. Ay, boy, it's for love.

SPEED. Not of you.

VALENTINE. Of my mistress, then.

SPEED. 'Twere good you knock'd him.   *Exit*

SILVIA. Servant, you are sad.

VALENTINE. Indeed, madam, I seem so.

THURIO. Seem you that you are not?

VALENTINE. Haply I do.

THURIO. So do counterfeits.

VALENTINE. So do you.

THURIO. What seem I that I am not?

VALENTINE. Wise.

THURIO. What instance of the contrary?

VALENTINE. Your folly.

THURIO. And how quote you my folly?

VALENTINE. I quote it in your jerkin.

THURIO. My jerkin is a doublet.

VALENTINE. Well, then, I'll double your folly.

THURIO. How?

SILVIA. What, angry, Sir Thurio! Do you change colour?

VALENTINE. Give him leave, madam; he is a kind of chameleon.

THURIO. That hath more mind to feed on your blood than live in your air.

VALENTINE. You have said, sir.

THURIO. Ay, sir, and done too, for this time.

VALENTINE. I know it well, sir; you always end ere you begin.

SILVIA. A fine volley of words, gentlemen, and quickly shot off.

VALENTINE. 'Tis indeed, madam; we thank the giver.

SILVIA. Who is that, servant?

VALENTINE. Yourself, sweet lady; for you gave the fire. Sir Thurio borrows his wit from your ladyship's looks, and spends what he borrows kindly in your company.

THURIO. Sir, if you spend word for word with me, I shall make your wit bankrupt.

VALENTINE. I know it well, sir; you have an exchequer of words, and, I think, no other treasure to give your followers; for it appears by their bare liveries that they live by your bare words.

Enter DUKE

SILVIA. No more, gentlemen, no more. Here comes my father.

DUKE. Now, daughter Silvia, you are hard beset.
Sir Valentine, your father is in good health.
What say you to a letter from your friends
Of much good news?

VALENTINE. My lord, I will be thankful
  To any happy messenger from thence.
DUKE. Know ye Don Antonio, your countryman?
VALENTINE. Ay, my good lord, I know the gentleman
  To be of worth and worthy estimation,
  And not without desert so well reputed.
DUKE. Hath he not a son?
VALENTINE. Ay, my good lord; a son that well deserves
  The honour and regard of such a father.
DUKE. You know him well?
VALENTINE. I knew him as myself; for from our infancy
  We have convers'd and spent our hours together;
  And though myself have been an idle truant,
  Omitting the sweet benefit of time
  To clothe mine age with angel-like perfection,
  Yet hath Sir Proteus, for that's his name,
  Made use and fair advantage of his days:
  His years but young, but his experience old;
  His head unmellowed, but his judgment ripe;
  And, in a word, for far behind his worth
  Comes all the praises that I now bestow,
  He is complete in feature and in mind,
  With all good grace to grace a gentleman.
DUKE. Beshrew me, sir, but if he make this good,
  He is as worthy for an empress' love
  As meet to be an emperor's counsellor.
  Well, sir, this gentleman is come to me
  With commendation from great potentates,
  And here he means to spend his time awhile.
  I think 'tis no unwelcome news to you.
VALENTINE. Should I have wish'd a thing, it had been he.
DUKE. Welcome him, then, according to his worth—
  Silvia, I speak to you, and you, Sir Thurio;
  For Valentine, I need not cite him to it.
  I will send him hither to you presently.   *Exit* DUKE
VALENTINE. This is the gentleman I told your ladyship
  Had come along with me but that his mistress
  Did hold his eyes lock'd in her crystal looks.
SILVIA. Belike that now she hath enfranchis'd them
  Upon some other pawn for fealty.

VALENTINE. Nay, sure, I think she holds them prisoners still.
SILVIA. Nay, then, he should be blind; and, being blind,
How could he see his way to seek out you?
VALENTINE. Why, lady, Love hath twenty pair of eyes.
THURIO. They say that Love hath not an eye at all.
VALENTINE. To see such lovers, Thurio, as yourself;
Upon a homely object Love can wink.   *Exit* THURIO

Enter PROTEUS

SILVIA. Have done, have done; here comes the gentleman.
VALENTINE. Welcome, dear Proteus! Mistress, I beseech you
Confirm his welcome with some special favour.
SILVIA. His worth is warrant for his welcome hither,
If this be he you oft have wish'd to hear from.
VALENTINE. Mistress, it is; sweet lady, entertain him
To be my fellow-servant to your ladyship.
SILVIA. Too low a mistress for so high a servant.
PROTEUS. Not so, sweet lady; but too mean a servant
To have a look of such a worthy mistress.
VALENTINE. Leave off discourse of disability;
Sweet lady, entertain him for your servant.
PROTEUS. My duty will I boast of, nothing else.
SILVIA. And duty never yet did want his meed.
Servant, you are welcome to a worthless mistress.
PROTEUS. I'll die on him that says so but yourself.
SILVIA. That you are welcome?
PROTEUS. That you are worthless.

Re-enter THURIO

THURIO. Madam, my lord your father would speak with you.
SILVIA. I wait upon his pleasure. Come, Sir Thurio,
Go with me. Once more, new servant, welcome.
I'll leave you to confer of home affairs;
When you have done we look to hear from you.
PROTEUS. We'll both attend upon your ladyship.
                              Exeunt SILVIA *and* THURIO
VALENTINE. Now, tell me, how do all from whence you
came?
PROTEUS. Your friends are well, and have them much com-
mended.

VALENTINE. And how do yours?

PROTEUS. I left them all in health.

VALENTINE. How does your lady, and how thrives your
love?

PROTEUS. My tales of love were wont to weary you;
I know you joy not in a love-discourse.

VALENTINE. Ay, Proteus, but that life is alter'd now;
I have done penance for contemning Love,
Whose high imperious thoughts have punish'd me
With bitter fasts, with penitential groans,
With nightly tears, and daily heart-sore sighs;
For, in revenge of my contempt of love,
Love hath chas'd sleep from my enthralled eyes
And made them watchers of mine own heart's sorrow.
O gentle Proteus, Love's a mighty lord,
And hath so humbled me as I confess
There is no woe to his correction,
Nor to his service no such joy on earth.
Now no discourse, except it be of love;
Now can I break my fast, dine, sup, and sleep,
Upon the very naked name of love.

PROTEUS. Enough; I read your fortune in your eye.
Was this the idol that you worship so?

VALENTINE. Even she; and is she not a heavenly saint?

PROTEUS. No; but she is an earthly paragon.

VALENTINE. Call her divine.

PROTEUS. I will not flatter her.

VALENTINE. O, flatter me; for love delights in praises!

PROTEUS. When I was sick you gave me bitter pills,
And I must minister the like to you.

VALENTINE. Then speak the truth by her; if not divine,
Yet let her be a principality,
Sovereign to all the creatures on the earth.

PROTEUS. Except my mistress.

VALENTINE. Sweet, except not any;
Except thou wilt except against my love.

PROTEUS. Have I not reason to prefer mine own?

VALENTINE. And I will help thee to prefer her too:
She shall be dignified with this high honour—
To bear my lady's train, lest the base earth

Should from her vesture chance to steal a kiss
And, of so great a favour growing proud,
Disdain to root the summer-swelling flow'r
And make rough winter everlastingly.

PROTEUS. Why, Valentine, what braggardism is this?

VALENTINE. Pardon me, Proteus; all I can is nothing
To her, whose worth makes other worthies nothing;
She is alone.

PROTEUS. Then let her alone.

VALENTINE. Not for the world! Why, man, she is mine own;
And I as rich in having such a jewel
As twenty seas, if all their sand were pearl,
The water nectar, and the rocks pure gold.
Forgive me that I do not dream on thee,
Because thou seest me dote upon my love.
My foolish rival, that her father likes
Only for his possessions are so huge,
Is gone with her along; and I must after,
For love, thou know'st, is full of jealousy.

PROTEUS. But she loves you?

VALENTINE. Ay, and we are betroth'd; nay more, our marriage-hour,
With all the cunning manner of our flight,
Determin'd of—how I must climb her window,
The ladder made of cords, and all the means
Plotted and 'greed on for my happiness.
Good Proteus, go with me to my chamber,
In these affairs to aid me with thy counsel.

PROTEUS. Go on before; I shall enquire you forth;
I must unto the road to disembark
Some necessaries that I needs must use;
And then I'll presently attend you.

VALENTINE. Will you make haste?

PROTEUS. I will.   *Exit* VALENTINE
Even as one heat another heat expels
Or as one nail by strength drives out another,
So the remembrance of my former love
Is by a newer object quite forgotten.
Is it my mind, or Valentinus' praise,

Her true perfection, or my false transgression,
That makes me reasonless to reason thus?
She is fair; and so is Julia that I love—
That I did love, for now my love is thaw'd;
Which like a waxen image 'gainst a fire
Bears no impression of the thing it was.
Methinks my zeal to Valentine is cold,
And that I love him not as I was wont.
O! but I love his lady too too much,
And that's the reason I love him so little.
How shall I dote on her with more advice
That thus without advice begin to love her!
'Tis but her picture I have yet beheld,
And that hath dazzled my reason's light;
But when I look on her perfections,
There is no reason but I shall be blind.
If I can check my erring love, I will;
If not, to compass her I'll use my skill.   *Exit*

SCENE 5

Milan. A street

Enter Speed *and* Launce *severally*

Speed. Launce! by mine honesty, welcome to Padua.

Launce. Forswear not thyself, sweet youth, for I am not
welcome. I reckon this always, that a man is never undone
till he be hang'd, nor never welcome to a place till some
certain shot be paid, and the hostess say 'Welcome!'

Speed. Come on, you madcap; I'll to the alehouse with you
presently; where, for one shot of five pence, thou shalt
have five thousand welcomes. But, sirrah, how did thy
master part with Madam Julia?

Launce. Marry, after they clos'd in earnest, they parted
very fairly in jest.

Speed. But shall she marry him?

Launce. No.

Speed. How then? Shall he marry her?

Launce. No, neither.

SPEED. What, are they broken?

LAUNCE. No, they are both as whole as a fish.

SPEED. Why then, how stands the matter with them?

LAUNCE. Marry, thus: when it stands well with him, it stands well with her.

SPEED. What an ass art thou! I understand thee not.

LAUNCE. What a block art thou that thou canst not! My staff understands me.

SPEED. What thou say'st?

LAUNCE. Ay, and what I do too; look thee, I'll but lean, and my staff understands me.

SPEED. It stands under thee, indeed.

LAUNCE. Why, stand-under and under-stand is all one.

SPEED. But tell me true, will't be a match?

LAUNCE. Ask my dog. If he say ay, it will; if he say no, it will; if he shake his tail and say nothing, it will.

SPEED. The conclusion is, then, that it will.

LAUNCE. Thou shalt never get such a secret from me but by a parable.

SPEED. 'Tis well that I get it so. But, Launce, how say'st thou that my master is become a notable lover?

LAUNCE. I never knew him otherwise.

SPEED. Than how?

LAUNCE. A notable lubber, as thou reportest him to be.

SPEED. Why, thou whoreson ass, thou mistak'st me.

LAUNCE. Why, fool, I meant not thee, I meant thy master.

SPEED. I tell thee my master is become a hot lover.

LAUNCE. Why, I tell thee I care not though he burn himself in love. If thou wilt, go with me to the alehouse; if not, thou art an Hebrew, a Jew, and not worth the name of a Christian.

SPEED. Why?

LAUNCE. Because thou hast not so much charity in thee as to go to the ale with a Christian. Wilt thou go?

SPEED. At thy service.   *Exeunt*

SCENE 6

Milan. The DUKE's *palace*

Enter PROTEUS

PROTEUS. To leave my Julia, shall I be forsworn;
To love fair Silvia, shall I be forsworn;
To wrong my friend, I shall be much forsworn;
And ev'n that pow'r which gave me first my oath
Provokes me to this threefold perjury:
Love bade me swear, and Love bids me forswear.
O sweet-suggesting Love, if thou hast sinn'd,
Teach me, thy tempted subject, to excuse it!
At first I did adore a twinkling star,
But now I worship a celestial sun.
Unheedful vows may heedfully be broken;
And he wants wit that wants resolved will
To learn his wit t' exchange the bad for better.
Fie, fie, unreverend tongue, to call her bad
Whose sovereignty so oft thou hast preferr'd
With twenty thousand soul-confirming oaths!
I cannot leave to love, and yet I do;
But there I leave to love where I should love.
Julia I lose, and Valentine I lose;
If I keep them, I needs must lose myself;
If I lose them, thus find I by their loss:
For Valentine, myself; for Julia, Silvia.
I to myself am dearer than a friend;
For love is still most precious in itself;
And Silvia—witness heaven, that made her fair!—
Shows Julia but a swarthy Ethiope.
I will forget that Julia is alive,
Rememb'ring that my love to her is dead;
And Valentine I'll hold an enemy,
Aiming at Silvia as a sweeter friend.
I cannot now prove constant to myself
Without some treachery us'd to Valentine.
This night he meaneth with a corded ladder
To climb celestial Silvia's chamber window,

Myself in counsel, his competitor.
Now presently I'll give her father notice
Of their disguising and pretended flight,
Who, all enrag'd, will banish Valentine,
For Thurio, he intends, shall wed his daughter;
But, Valentine being gone, I'll quickly cross
By some sly trick blunt Thurio's dull proceeding.
Love, lend me wings to make my purpose swift,
As thou hast lent me wit to plot this drift.   *Exit*

SCENE 7

Verona. JULIA's *house*

Enter JULIA *and* LUCETTA

JULIA. Counsel, Lucetta; gentle girl, assist me;
    And, ev'n in kind love, I do conjure thee,
    Who art the table wherein all my thoughts
    Are visibly character'd and engrav'd,
    To lesson me and tell me some good mean
    How, with my honour, I may undertake
    A journey to my loving Proteus.
LUCETTA. Alas, the way is wearisome and long!
JULIA. A true-devoted pilgrim is not weary
    To measure kingdoms with his feeble steps;
    Much less shall she that hath Love's wings to fly,
    And when the flight is made to one so dear,
    Of such divine perfection, as Sir Proteus.
LUCETTA. Better forbear till Proteus make return.
JULIA. O, know'st thou not his looks are my soul's food?
    Pity the dearth that I have pined in
    By longing for that food so long a time.
    Didst thou but know the inly touch of love.
    Thou wouldst as soon go kindle fire with snow
    As seek to quench the fire of love with words.
LUCETTA. I do not seek to quench your love's hot fire,
    But qualify the fire's extreme rage,
    Lest it should burn above the bounds of reason.
JULIA. The more thou dam'st it up, the more it burns.

The current that with gentle murmur glides,
Thou know'st, being stopp'd, impatiently doth rage;
But when his fair course is not hindered,
He makes sweet music with th' enamell'd stones,
Giving a gentle kiss to every sedge
He overtaketh in his pilgrimage;
And so by many winding nooks he strays,
With willing sport, to the wild ocean.
Then let me go, and hinder not my course.
I'll be as patient as a gentle stream,
And make a pastime of each weary step,
Till the last step have brought me to my love;
And there I'll rest as, after much turmoil,
A blessed soul doth in Elysium.

LUCETTA. But in what habit will you go along?

JULIA. Not like a woman, for I would prevent
The loose encounters of lascivious men;
Gentle Lucetta, fit me with such weeds
As may beseem some well-reputed page.

LUCETTA. Why then, your ladyship must cut your hair.

JULIA. No, girl; I'll knit it up in silken strings
With twenty odd-conceited true-love knots—
To be fantastic may become a youth
Of greater time than I shall show to be.

LUCETTA. What fashion, madam, shall I make your breeches?

JULIA. That fits as well as 'Tell me, good my lord,
What compass will you wear your farthingale.'
Why ev'n what fashion thou best likes, Lucetta.

LUCETTA. You must needs have them with a codpiece,
madam.

JULIA. Out, out, Lucetta, that will be ill-favour'd.

LUCETTA. A round hose, madam, now's not worth a pin,
Unless you have a codpiece to stick pins on.

JULIA. Lucetta, as thou lov'st me, let me have
What thou think'st meet, and is most mannerly.
But tell me, wench, how will the world repute me
For undertaking so unstaid a journey?
I fear me it will make me scandaliz'd.

LUCETTA. If you think so, then stay at home and go not.

JULIA. Nay, that I will not.

Lucetta. Then never dream on infamy, but go.
  If Proteus like your journey when you come,
  No matter who's displeas'd when you are gone.
  I fear me he will scarce be pleas'd withal.
Julia. That is the least, Lucetta, of my fear:
  A thousand oaths, an ocean of his tears,
  And instances of infinite of love,
  Warrant me welcome to my Proteus.
Lucetta. All these are servants to deceitful men.
Julia. Base men that use them to so base effect!
  But truer stars did govern Proteus' birth;
  His words are bonds, his oaths are oracles,
  His love sincere, his thoughts immaculate,
  His tears pure messengers sent from his heart,
  His heart as far from fraud as heaven from earth.
Lucetta. Pray heav'n he prove so when you come to him.
Julia. Now, as thou lov'st me, do him not that wrong
  To bear a hard opinion of his truth;
  Only deserve my love by loving him.
  And presently go with me to my chamber,
  To take a note of what I stand in need of
  To furnish me upon my longing journey.
  All that is mine I leave at thy dispose,
  My goods, my lands, my reputation;
  Only, in lieu thereof, dispatch me hence.
  Come, answer not, but to it presently;
  I am impatient of my tarriance.   *Exeunt*

ACT III. SCENE 1

Milan. The Duke's *palace*

Enter Duke, Thurio, *and* Proteus

Duke. Sir Thurio, give us leave, I pray, awhile;
  We have some secrets to confer about.   *Exit* Thurio
  Now tell me, Proteus, what's your will with me?
Proteus. My gracious lord, that which I would discover

The law of friendship bids me to conceal;
But, when I call to mind your gracious favours
Done to me, undeserving as I am,
My duty pricks me on to utter that
Which else no worldly good should draw from me.
Know, worthy prince, Sir Valentine, my friend,
This night intends to steal away your daughter;
Myself am one made privy to the plot.
I know you have determin'd to bestow her
On Thurio, whom your gentle daughter hates;
And should she thus be stol'n away from you,
It would be much vexation to your age.
Thus, for my duty's sake, I rather chose
To cross my friend in his intended drift
Than, by concealing it, heap on your head
A pack of sorrows which would press you down,
Being unprevented, to your timeless grave.
DUKE. Proteus, I thank thee for thine honest care,
Which to requite, command me while I live.
This love of theirs myself have often seen,
Haply when they have judg'd me fast asleep,
And oftentimes have purpos'd to forbid
Sir Valentine her company and my court;
But, fearing lest my jealous aim might err
And so, unworthily, disgrace the man,
A rashness that I ever yet have shunn'd,
I gave him gentle looks, thereby to find
That which thyself hast now disclos'd to me.
And, that thou mayst perceive my fear of this,
Knowing that tender youth is soon suggested,
I nightly lodge her in an upper tow'r,
The key whereof myself have ever kept;
And thence she cannot be convey'd away.
PROTEUS. Know, noble lord, they have devis'd a mean
How he her chamber window will ascend
And with a corded ladder fetch her down;
For which the youthful lover now is gone,
And this way comes he with it presently;
Where, if it please you, you may intercept him.
But, good my lord, do it so cunningly

That my discovery be not aimed at;
For love of you, not hate unto my friend,
Hath made me publisher of this pretence.
DUKE. Upon mine honour, he shall never know
That I had any light from thee of this.
PROTEUS. Adieu, my lord; Sir Valentine is coming.   *Exit*

Enter VALENTINE

DUKE. Sir Valentine, whither away so fast?
VALENTINE. Please it your Grace, there is a messenger
That stays to bear my letters to my friends,
And I am going to deliver them.
DUKE. Be they of much import?
VALENTINE. The tenour of them doth but signify
My health and happy being at your court.
DUKE. Nay then, no matter; stay with me awhile;
I am to break with thee of some affairs
That touch me near, wherein thou must be secret.
'Tis not unknown to thee that I have sought
To match my friend Sir Thurio to my daughter.
VALENTINE. I know it well, my lord; and, sure, the match
Were rich and honourable; besides, the gentleman
Is full of virtue, bounty, worth, and qualities
Beseeming such a wife as your fair daughter.
Cannot your grace win her to fancy him?
DUKE. No, trust me; she is peevish, sullen, froward,
Proud, disobedient, stubborn, lacking duty;
Neither regarding that she is my child
Nor fearing me as if I were her father;
And, may I say to thee, this pride of hers,
Upon advice, hath drawn my love from her;
And, where I thought the remnant of mine age
Should have been cherish'd by her childlike duty,
I now am full resolv'd to take a wife
And turn her out to who will take her in.
Then let her beauty be her wedding-dow'r;
For me and my possessions she esteems not.
VALENTINE. What would your Grace have me to do in this?
DUKE. There is a lady, in Verona here,
Whom I affect; but she is nice, and coy,

107

And nought esteems my aged eloquence.
Now, therefore, would I have thee to my tutor—
For long agone I have forgot to court;
Besides, the fashion of the time is chang'd—
How and which way I may bestow myself
To be regarded in her sun-bright eye.

VALENTINE. Win her with gifts, if she respect not words:
Dumb jewels often in their silent kind
More than quick words do move a woman's mind.

DUKE. But she did scorn a present that I sent her.

VALENTINE. A woman sometime scorns what best contents
her.
Send her another; never give her o'er,
For scorn at first makes after-love the more.
If she do frown, 'tis not in hate of you,
But rather to beget more love in you;
If she do chide, 'tis not to have you gone,
For why, the fools are mad if left alone.
Take no repulse, whatever she doth say;
For 'Get you gone' she doth not mean 'Away!'
Flatter and praise, commend, extol their graces;
Though ne'er so black, say they have angels' faces.
That man that hath a tongue, I say, is no man,
If with his tongue he cannot win a woman.

DUKE. But she I mean is promis'd by her friends
Unto a youthful gentleman of worth;
And kept severely from resort of men,
That no man hath access by day to her.

VALENTINE. Why then I would resort to her by night.

DUKE. Ay, but the doors be lock'd and keys kept safe,
That no man hath recourse to her by night.

VALENTINE. What lets but one may enter at her window?

DUKE. Her chamber is aloft, far from the ground,
And built so shelving that one cannot climb it
Without apparent hazard of his life.

VALENTINE. Why then a ladder, quaintly made of cords,
To cast up with a pair of anchoring hooks,
Would serve to scale another Hero's tow'r,
So bold Leander would adventure it.

DUKE. Now, as thou art a gentleman of blood,

Advise me where I may have such a ladder.

VALENTINE. When would you use it? Pray, sir, tell me that.

DUKE. This very night; for Love is like a child,
That longs for everything that he can come by.

VALENTINE. By seven o'clock I'll get you such a ladder.

DUKE. But, hark thee; I will go to her alone;
How shall I best convey the ladder thither?

VALENTINE. It will be light, my lord, that you may bear it
Under a cloak that is of any length.

DUKE. A cloak as long as thine will serve the turn?

VALENTINE. Ay, my good lord.

DUKE. Then let me see thy cloak.
I'll get me one of such another length.

VALENTINE. Why, any cloak will serve the turn, my lord.

DUKE. How shall I fashion me to wear a cloak?
I pray thee, let me feel thy cloak upon me.
What letter is this same? What's here? 'To Silvia'!
And here an engine fit for my proceeding!
I'll be so bold to break the seal for once.   [Reads]
    'My thoughts do harbour with my Silvia nightly,
        And slaves they are to me, that send them flying.
    O, could their master come and go as lightly,
        Himself would lodge where, senseless, they are lying!
    My herald thoughts in thy pure bosom rest them,
        While I, their king, that thither them importune,
    Do curse the grace that with such grace hath blest them,
        Because myself do want my servants' fortune.
    I curse myself, for they are sent by me,
        That they should harbour where their lord should be.'
What's here?
'Silvia, this night I will enfranchise thee.'
'Tis so; and here's the ladder for the purpose.
Why, Phaethon—for thou art Merops' son—
Wilt thou aspire to guide the heavenly car,
And with thy daring folly burn the world?
Wilt thou reach stars because they shine on thee?
Go, base intruder, over-weening slave,
Bestow thy fawning smiles on equal mates;
And think my patience, more than thy desert,
Is privilege for thy departure hence.

Thank me for this more than for all the favours
Which, all too much, I have bestow'd on thee.
But if thou linger in my territories
Longer than swiftest expedition
Will give thee time to leave our royal court,
By heaven! my wrath shall far exceed the love
I ever bore my daughter or thyself.
Be gone; I will not hear thy vain excuse,
But, as thou lov'st thy life, make speed from hence. *Exit*
VALENTINE. And why not death rather than living torment?
To die is to be banish'd from myself,
And Silvia is myself; banish'd from her
Is self from self, a deadly banishment.
What light is light, if Silvia be not seen?
What joy is joy, if Silvia be not by?
Unless it be to think that she is by,
And feed upon the shadow of perfection.
Except I be by Silvia in the night,
There is no music in the nightingale;
Unless I look on Silvia in the day,
There is no day for me to look upon.
She is my essence, and I leave to be
If I be not by her fair influence
Foster'd, illumin'd, cherish'd, kept alive.
I fly not death, to fly his deadly doom:
Tarry I here, I but attend on death;
But fly I hence, I fly away from life.

Enter PROTEUS *and* LAUNCE

PROTEUS. Run, boy, run, run, and seek him out.
LAUNCE. So-ho, so-ho!
PROTEUS. What seest thou?
LAUNCE. Him we go to find: there's not a hair on 's head
but 'tis a Valentine.
PROTEUS. Valentine?
VALENTINE. No.
PROTEUS. Who then? his spirit?
VALENTINE. Neither.
PROTEUS. What then?
VALENTINE. Nothing.

LAUNCE. Can nothing speak? Master, shall I strike?
PROTEUS. Who wouldst thou strike?
LAUNCE. Nothing.
PROTEUS. Villain, forbear.
LAUNCE. Why, sir, I'll strike nothing. I pray you—
PROTEUS. Sirrah, I say, forbear. Friend Valentine, a word.
VALENTINE. My ears are stopp'd and cannot hear good news,
So much of bad already hath possess'd them.
PROTEUS. Then in dumb silence will I bury mine,
For they are harsh, untuneable, and bad.
VALENTINE. Is Silvia dead?
PROTEUS. No, Valentine.
VALENTINE. No Valentine, indeed, for sacred Silvia.
Hath she forsworn me?
PROTEUS. No, Valentine.
VALENTINE. No Valentine, if Silvia have forsworn me.
What is your news?
LAUNCE. Sir, there is a proclamation that you are vanished.
PROTEUS. That thou art banished—O, that's the news!—
From hence, from Silvia, and from me thy friend.
VALENTINE. O, I have fed upon this woe already,
And now excess of it will make me surfeit.
Doth Silvia know that I am banished?
PROTEUS. Ay, ay; and she hath offered to the doom—
Which, unrevers'd, stands in effectual force—
A sea of melting pearl, which some call tears;
Those at her father's churlish feet she tender'd;
With them, upon her knees, her humble self,
Wringing her hands, whose whiteness so became them
As if but now they waxed pale for woe.
But neither bended knees, pure hands held up,
Sad sighs, deep groans, nor silver-shedding tears,
Could penetrate her uncompassionate sire—
But Valentine, if he be ta'en, must die.
Besides, her intercession chaf'd him so,
When she for thy repeal was suppliant,
That to close prison he commanded her,
With many bitter threats of biding there.
VALENTINE. No more; unless the next word that thou
speak'st

Have some malignant power upon my life:
If so, I pray thee breathe it in mine ear,
As ending anthem of my endless dolour.

PROTEUS. Cease to lament for that thou canst not help,
And study help for that which thou lament'st.
Time is the nurse and breeder of all good.
Here if thou stay thou canst not see thy love;
Besides, thy staying will abridge thy life.
Hope is a lover's staff; walk hence with that,
And manage it against despairing thoughts.
Thy letters may be here, though thou art hence,
Which, being writ to me, shall be deliver'd
Even in the milk-white bosom of thy love.
The time now serves not to expostulate.
Come, I'll convey thee through the city gate;
And, ere I part with thee, confer at large
Of all that may concern thy love affairs.
As thou lov'st Silvia, though not for thyself,
Regard thy danger, and along with me.

VALENTINE. I pray thee, Launce, an if thou seest my boy,
Bid him make haste and meet me at the Northgate.

PROTEUS. Go, sirrah, find him out. Come, Valentine.

VALENTINE. O my dear Silvia! Hapless Valentine!

Exeunt VALENTINE *and* PROTEUS

LAUNCE. I am but a fool, look you, and yet I have the wit to think my master is a kind of a knave; but that's all one if he be but one knave. He lives not now that knows me to be in love; yet I am in love; but a team of horse shall not pluck that from me; nor who 'tis I love; and yet 'tis a woman; but what woman I will not tell myself; and yet 'tis a milkmaid; yet 'tis not a maid, for she hath had gossips; yet 'tis a maid, for she is her master's maid and serves for wages. She hath more qualities than a water-spaniel—which is much in a bare Christian. Here is the cate-log [*Pulling out a paper*] of her condition. 'Inprimis: She can fetch and carry.' Why, a horse can do no more; nay, a horse cannot fetch, but only carry; therefore is she better than a jade. 'Item: She can milk.' Look you, a sweet virtue in a maid with clean hands.

Enter Speed

Speed. How now, Signior Launce! What news with your mastership?

Launce. With my master's ship? Why, it is at sea.

Speed. Well, your old vice still: mistake the word. What news, then, in your paper?

Launce. The black'st news that ever thou heard'st.

Speed. Why, man? how black?

Launce. Why, as black as ink.

Speed. Let me read them.

Launce. Fie on thee, jolt-head; thou canst not read.

Speed. Thou liest; I can.

Launce. I will try thee. Tell me this: Who begot thee?

Speed. Marry, the son of my grandfather.

Launce. O illiterate loiterer. It was the son of thy grandmother. This proves that thou canst not read.

Speed. Come, fool, come; try me in thy paper.

Launce. [*Handing over the paper*] There; and Saint Nicholas be thy speed.

Speed. [*Reads*] 'Inprimis: She can milk.'

Launce. Ay, that she can.

Speed. 'Item: She brews good ale.'

Launce. And thereof comes the proverb: Blessing of your heart, you brew good ale.

Speed. 'Item: She can sew.'

Launce. That's as much as to say 'Can she so?'

Speed. 'Item: She can knit.'

Launce. What need a man care for a stock with a wench, when she can knit him a stock.

Speed. 'Item: She can wash and scour.'

Launce. A special virtue; for then she need not be wash'd and scour'd.

Speed. 'Item: She can spin.'

Launce. Then may I set the world on wheels, when she can spin for her living.

Speed. 'Item: She hath many nameless virtues.'

Launce. That's as much as to say 'bastard virtues'; that indeed know not their fathers, and therefore have no names.

Speed. 'Here follow her vices.'

LAUNCE. Close at the heels of her virtues.

SPEED. 'Item: She is not to be kiss'd fasting, in respect of her breath.'

LAUNCE. Well, that fault may be mended with a breakfast. Read on.

SPEED. 'Item: She hath a sweet mouth.'

LAUNCE. That makes amends for her sour breath.

SPEED. 'Item: She doth talk in her sleep.'

LAUNCE. It's no matter for that, so she sleep not in her talk.

SPEED. 'Item: She is slow in words.'

LAUNCE. O villain, that set this down among her vices! To be slow in words is a woman's only virtue. I pray thee, out with't; and place it for her chief virtue.

SPEED. 'Item: She is proud.'

LAUNCE. Out with that too; it was Eve's legacy, and cannot be ta'en from her.

SPEED. 'Item: She hath no teeth.'

LAUNCE. I care not for that neither, because I love crusts.

SPEED. 'Item: She is curst.'

LAUNCE. Well, the best is, she hath no teeth to bite.

SPEED. 'Item: She will often praise her liquor.'

LAUNCE. If her liquor be good, she shall; if she will not, I will; for good things should be praised.

SPEED. 'Item: She is too liberal.'

LAUNCE. Of her tongue she cannot, for that's writ down she is slow of; of her purse she shall not, for that I'll keep shut. Now of another thing she may, and that cannot I help. Well, proceed.

SPEED. 'Item: She hath more hair than wit, and more faults than hairs, and more wealth than faults.'

LAUNCE. Stop there; I'll have her; she was mine, and not mine, twice or thrice in that last article. Rehearse that once more.

SPEED. 'Item: She hath more hair than wit'—

LAUNCE. More hair than wit. It may be; I'll prove it: the cover of the salt hides the salt, and therefore it is more than the salt; the hair that covers the wit is more than the wit, for the greater hides the less. What's next?

SPEED. 'And more faults than hairs'—

LAUNCE. That's monstrous. O that that were out!

SPEED. 'And more wealth than faults.'

LAUNCE. Why, that word makes the faults gracious. Well, I'll have her; an if it be a match, as nothing is impossible—

SPEED. What then?

LAUNCE. Why, then will I tell thee—that thy master stays for thee at the Northgate.

SPEED. For me?

LAUNCE. For thee! ay, who art thou? He hath stay'd for a better man than thee.

SPEED. And must I go to him?

LAUNCE. Thou must run to him, for thou hast stay'd so long that going will scarce serve the turn.

SPEED. Why didst not tell me sooner? Pox of your love letters! *Exit*

LAUNCE. Now will he be swing'd for reading my letter. An unmannerly slave that will thrust himself into secrets! I'll after, to rejoice in the boy's correction. *Exit*

SCENE 2

Milan. The DUKE'S *palace*

Enter DUKE *and* THURIO

DUKE. Sir Thurio, fear not but that she will love you
Now Valentine is banish'd from her sight.

THURIO. Since his exile she hath despis'd me most,
Forsworn my company and rail'd at me,
That I am desperate of obtaining her.

DUKE. This weak impress of love is as a figure
Trenched in ice, which with an hour's heat
Dissolves to water and doth lose his form.
A little time will melt her frozen thoughts,
And worthless Valentine shall be forgot.

Enter PROTEUS.

How now, Sir Proteus! Is your countryman,
According to our proclamation, gone?

PROTEUS. Gone, my good lord.

DUKE. My daughter takes his going grievously.

PROTEUS. A little time, my lord, will kill that grief.
DUKE. So I believe; but Thurio thinks not so.
Proteus, the good conceit I hold of thee—
For thou hast shown some sign of good desert—
Makes me the better to confer with thee.
PROTEUS. Longer than I prove loyal to your Grace
Let me not live to look upon your Grace.
DUKE. Thou know'st how willingly I would effect
The match between Sir Thurio and my daughter.
PROTEUS. I do, my lord.
DUKE. And also, I think, thou art not ignorant
How she opposes her against my will.
PROTEUS. She did, my lord, when Valentine was here.
DUKE. Ay, and perversely she persevers so.
What might we do to make the girl forget
The love of Valentine, and love Sir Thurio?
PROTEUS. The best way is to slander Valentine
With falsehood, cowardice, and poor descent—
Three things that women highly hold in hate.
DUKE. Ay, but she'll think that it is spoke in hate.
PROTEUS. Ay, if his enemy deliver it;
Therefore it must with circumstance be spoken
By one whom she esteemeth as his friend.
DUKE. Then you must undertake to slander him.
PROTEUS. And that, my lord, I shall be loath to do:
'Tis an ill office for a gentleman,
Especially against his very friend.
DUKE. Where your good word cannot advantage him,
Your slander never can endamage him;
Therefore the office is indifferent,
Being entreated to it by your friend.
PROTEUS. You have prevail'd, my lord; if I can do it
By aught that I can speak in his dispraise,
She shall not long continue love to him.
But say this weed her love from Valentine,
It follows not that she will love Sir Thurio.
THURIO. Therefore, as you unwind her love from him,
Lest it should ravel and be good to none,
You must provide to bottom it on me;
Which must be done by praising me as much

As you in worth dispraise Sir Valentine.
DUKE. And, Proteus, we dare trust you in this kind,
 Because we know, on Valentine's report,
 You are already Love's firm votary
 And cannot soon revolt and change your mind.
 Upon this warrant shall you have access
 Where you with Silvia may confer at large—
 For she is lumpish, heavy, melancholy,
 And, for your friend's sake, will be glad of you—
 Where you may temper her by your persuasion
 To hate young Valentine and love my friend.
PROTEUS. As much as I can do I will effect.
 But you, Sir Thurio, are not sharp enough;
 You must lay lime to tangle her desires
 By wailful sonnets, whose composed rhymes
 Should be full-fraught with serviceable vows.
DUKE. Ay,
 Much is the force of heaven-bred poesy.
PROTEUS. Say that upon the altar of her beauty
 You sacrifice your tears, your sighs, your heart;
 Write till your ink be dry, and with your tears
 Moist it again, and frame some feeling line
 That may discover such integrity;
 For Orpheus' lute was strung with poets' sinews,
 Whose golden touch could soften steel and stones,
 Make tigers tame, and huge leviathans
 Forsake unsounded deeps to dance on sands.
 After your dire-lamenting elegies,
 Visit by night your lady's chamber window
 With some sweet consort; to their instruments
 Tune a deploring dump—the night's dead silence
 Will well become such sweet-complaining grievance.
 This, or else nothing, will inherit her.
DUKE. This discipline shows thou hast been in love.
THURIO. And thy advice this night I'll put in practice;
 Therefore, sweet Proteus, my direction-giver,
 Let us into the city presently
 To sort some gentlemen well skill'd in music.
 I have a sonnet that will serve the turn
 To give the onset to thy good advice.

DUKE. About it, gentlemen!
PROTEUS. We'll wait upon your Grace till after supper,
And afterward determine our proceedings.
DUKE. Even now about it! I will pardon you.   *Exeunt*

ACT IV. SCENE 1

The frontiers of Mantua. A forest

Enter certain OUTLAWS

FIRST OUTLAW. Fellows, stand fast; I see a passenger.
SECOND OUTLAW. If there be ten, shrink not, but down with
'em.

Enter VALENTINE *and* SPEED

THIRD OUTLAW. Stand, sir, and throw us that you have
about ye;
If not, we'll make you sit, and rifle you.
SPEED. Sir, we are undone; these are the villains
That all the travellers do fear so much.
VALENTINE. My friends—
FIRST OUTLAW. That's not so, sir; we are your enemies.
SECOND OUTLAW. Peace! we'll hear him.
THIRD OUTLAW. Ay, by my beard, will we; for he is a
proper man.
VALENTINE. Then know that I have little wealth to lose;
A man I am cross'd with adversity;
My riches are these poor habiliments,
Of which if you should here disfurnish me,
You take the sum and substance that I have.
SECOND OUTLAW. Whither travel you?
VALENTINE. To Verona.
FIRST OUTLAW. Whence came you?
VALENTINE. From Milan.
THIRD OUTLAW. Have you long sojourn'd there?
VALENTINE. Some sixteen months, and longer might have
stay'd,

If crooked fortune had not thwarted me.
FIRST OUTLAW. What, were you banish'd thence?
VALENTINE. I was.
SECOND OUTLAW. For what offence?
VALENTINE. For that which now torments me to rehearse:
  I kill'd a man, whose death I much repent;
  But yet I slew him manfully in fight,
  Without false vantage or base treachery.
FIRST OUTLAW. Why, ne'er repent it, if it were done so.
  But were you banish'd for so small a fault?
VALENTINE. I was, and held me glad of such a doom.
SECOND OUTLAW. Have you the tongues?
VALENTINE. My youthful travel therein made me happy,
  Or else I often had been miserable.
THIRD OUTLAW. By the bare scalp of Robin Hood's fat friar,
  This fellow were a king for our wild faction!
FIRST OUTLAW. We'll have him. Sirs, a word.
SPEED. Master, be one of them; it's an honourable kind of
  thievery.
VALENTINE. Peace, villain!
SECOND OUTLAW. Tell us this: have you anything to take to?
VALENTINE. Nothing but my fortune.
THIRD OUTLAW. Know, then, that some of us are gentlemen,
  Such as the fury of ungovern'd youth
  Thrust from the company of awful men;
  Myself was from Verona banished
  For practising to steal away a lady,
  An heir, and near allied unto the Duke.
SECOND OUTLAW. And I from Mantua, for a gentleman
  Who, in my mood, I stabb'd unto the heart.
FIRST OUTLAW. And I for such-like petty crimes as these.
  But to the purpose—for we cite our faults
  That they may hold excus'd our lawless lives;
  And, partly, seeing you are beautified
  With goodly shape, and by your own report
  A linguist, and a man of such perfection
  As we do in our quality much want—
SECOND OUTLAW. Indeed, because you are a banish'd man,
  Therefore, above the rest, we parley to you.
  Are you content to be our general—

To make a virtue of necessity,
And live as we do in this wilderness?
THIRD OUTLAW. What say'st thou? Wilt thou be of our
consort?
Say 'ay' and be the captain of us all.
We'll do thee homage, and be rul'd by thee,
Love thee as our commander and our king.
FIRST OUTLAW. But if thou scorn our courtesy thou diest.
SECOND OUTLAW. Thou shalt not live to brag what we have
offer'd.
VALENTINE. I take your offer, and will live with you,
Provided that you do no outrages
On silly women or poor passengers.
THIRD OUTLAW. No, we detest such vile base practices.
Come, go with us; we'll bring thee to our crews,
And show thee all the treasure we have got;
Which, with ourselves, all rest at thy dispose.   *Exeunt*

SCENE 2

Milan. Outside the DUKE's *palace, under* SILVIA's *window*

Enter PROTEUS

PROTEUS. Already have I been false to Valentine,
And now I must be as unjust to Thurio.
Under the colour of commending him
I have access my own love to prefer;
But Silvia is too fair, too true, too holy,
To be corrupted with my worthless gifts.
When I protest true loyalty to her,
She twits me with my falsehood to my friend;
When to her beauty I commend my vows,
She bids me think how I have been forsworn
In breaking faith with Julia whom I lov'd;
And notwithstanding all her sudden quips,
The least whereof would quell a lover's hope,
Yet, spaniel-like, the more she spurns my love
The more it grows and fawneth on her still.

ACT IV. SCENE 2

Enter THURIO *and* MUSICIANS

But here comes Thurio. Now must we to her window,
And give some evening music to her ear.
THURIO. How now, Sir Proteus, are you crept before us?
PROTEUS. Ay, gentle Thurio; for you know that love
Will creep in service where it cannot go.
THURIO. Ay, but I hope, sir, that you love not here.
PROTEUS. Sir, but I do; or else I would be hence.
THURIO. Who? Silvia?
PROTEUS. Ay, Silvia—for your sake.
THURIO. I thank you for your own. Now, gentlemen,
Let's tune, and to it lustily awhile.

Enter at a distance, HOST, *and* JULIA *in boy's clothes*

HOST. Now, my young guest, methinks you're allycholly; I
pray you, why is it?
JULIA. Marry, mine host, because I cannot be merry.
HOST. Come, we'll have you merry; I'll bring you where
you shall hear music, and see the gentleman that you ask'd
for.
JULIA. But shall I hear him speak?
HOST. Ay, that you shall.   [*Music plays*]
JULIA. That will be music.
HOST. Hark, hark!
JULIA. Is he among these?
HOST. Ay; but peace! let's hear 'em.

SONG

Who is Silvia? What is she,
    That all our swains commend her?
Holy, fair, and wise is she;
    The heaven such grace did lend her,
That she might admired be.

Is she kind as she is fair?
    For beauty lives with kindness.
Love doth to her eyes repair,
    To help him of his blindness;
And, being help'd, inhabits there.

121

Then to Silvia let us sing
That Silvia is excelling;
She excels each mortal thing
Upon the dull earth dwelling.
To her let us garlands bring.

HOST. How now, are you sadder than you were before?
How do you, man? The music likes you not.
JULIA. You mistake; the musician likes me not.
HOST. Why, my pretty youth?
JULIA. He plays false, father.
HOST. How, out of tune on the strings?
JULIA. Not so; but yet so false that he grieves my very heart-strings.
HOST. You have a quick ear.
JULIA. Ay, I would I were deaf; it makes me have a slow heart.
HOST. I perceive you delight not in music.
JULIA. Not a whit, when it jars so.
HOST. Hark, what fine change is in the music!
JULIA. Ay, that change is the spite.
HOST. You would have them always play but one thing?
JULIA. I would always have one play but one thing.
But, Host, doth this Sir Proteus, that we talk on,
Often resort unto this gentlewoman?
HOST. I tell you what Launce, his man, told me: he lov'd
her out of all nick.
JULIA. Where is Launce?
HOST. Gone to seek his dog, which to-morrow, by his master's command, he must carry for a present to his lady.
JULIA. Peace, stand aside; the company parts.
PROTEUS. Sir Thurio, fear not you; I will so plead
That you shall say my cunning drift excels.
THURIO. Where meet we?
PROTEUS. At Saint Gregory's well.
THURIO. Farewell. _Exeunt_ THURIO _and_ MUSICIANS

Enter SILVIA _above, at her window_

PROTEUS. Madam, good ev'n to your ladyship.
SILVIA. I thank you for your music, gentlemen.

Who is that that spake?

PROTEUS. One, lady, if you knew his pure heart's truth,
You would quickly learn to know him by his voice.

SILVIA. Sir Proteus, as I take it.

PROTEUS. Sir Proteus, gentle lady, and your servant.

SILVIA. What's your will?

PROTEUS. That I may compass yours.

SILVIA. You have your wish; my will is even this,
That presently you hie you home to bed.
Thou subtle, perjur'd, false, disloyal man,
Think'st thou I am so shallow, so conceitless,
To be seduced by thy flattery
That hast deceiv'd so many with thy vows?
Return, return, and make thy love amends.
For me, by this pale queen of night I swear,
I am so far from granting thy request
That I despise thee for thy wrongful suit,
And by and by intend to chide myself
Even for this time I spend in talking to thee.

PROTEUS. I grant, sweet love, that I did love a lady;
But she is dead.

JULIA. [Aside] 'Twere false, if I should speak it;
For I am sure she is not buried.

SILVIA. Say that she be; yet Valentine, thy friend,
Survives, to whom, thyself art witness,
I am betroth'd; and art thou not asham'd
To wrong him with thy importunacy?

PROTEUS. I likewise hear that Valentine is dead.

SILVIA. And so suppose am I; for in his grave
Assure thyself my love is buried.

PROTEUS. Sweet lady, let me rake it from the earth.

SILVIA. Go to thy lady's grave, and call hers thence;
Or, at the least, in hers sepulchre thine.

JULIA. [Aside] He heard not that.

PROTEUS. Madam, if your heart be so obdurate,
Vouchsafe me yet your picture for my love,
The picture that is hanging in your chamber;
To that I'll speak, to that I'll sigh and weep;
For, since the substance of your perfect self
Is else devoted, I am but a shadow;

And to your shadow will I make true love.

JULIA. [*Aside*] If 'twere a substance, you would, sure, deceive it
  And make it but a shadow, as I am.

SILVIA. I am very loath to be your idol, sir;
  But since your falsehood shall become you well
  To worship shadows and adore false shapes,
  Send to me in the morning, and I'll send it;
  And so, good rest.

PROTEUS. As wretches have o'ernight
  That wait for execution in the morn.

Exeunt PROTEUS *and* SILVIA

JULIA. Host, will you go?

HOST. By my halidom, I was fast asleep.

JULIA. Pray you, where lies Sir Proteus?

HOST. Marry, at my house. Trust me, I think 'tis almost day.

JULIA. Not so; but it hath been the longest night
  That e'er I watch'd, and the most heaviest.   *Exeunt*

SCENE 3

Under SILVIA'S *window*

Enter EGLAMOUR

EGLAMOUR. This is the hour that Madam Silvia
  Entreated me to call and know her mind;
  There's some great matter she'd employ me in.
  Madam, madam!

Enter SILVIA *above, at her window*

SILVIA. Who calls?

EGLAMOUR. Your servant and your friend;
  One that attends your ladyship's command.

SILVIA. Sir Eglamour, a thousand times good morrow!

EGLAMOUR. As many, worthy lady, to yourself!
  According to your ladyship's impose,
  I am thus early come to know what service
  It is your pleasure to command me in.

SILVIA. O Eglamour, thou art a gentleman—

Think not I flatter, for I swear I do not—
Valiant, wise, remorseful, well accomplish'd.
Thou art not ignorant what dear good will
I bear unto the banish'd Valentine;
Nor how my father would enforce me marry
Vain Thurio, whom my very soul abhors.
Thyself hast lov'd; and I have heard thee say
No grief did ever come so near thy heart
As when thy lady and thy true love died,
Upon whose grave thou vow'dst pure chastity.
Sir Eglamour, I would to Valentine,
To Mantua, where I hear he makes abode;
And, for the ways are dangerous to pass,
I do desire thy worthy company,
Upon whose faith and honour I repose.
Urge not my father's anger, Eglamour,
But think upon my grief, a lady's grief,
And on the justice of my flying hence
To keep me from a most unholy match,
Which heaven and fortune still rewards with plagues.
I do desire thee, even from a heart
As full of sorrows as the sea of sands,
To bear me company and go with me;
If not, to hide what I have said to thee,
That I may venture to depart alone.

EGLAMOUR. Madam, I pity much your grievances;
    Which since I know they virtuously are plac'd,
    I give consent to go along with you,
    Recking as little what betideth me
    As much I wish all good befortune you.
    When will you go?

SILVIA. This evening coming.

EGLAMOUR. Where shall I meet you?

SILVIA. At Friar Patrick's cell,
    Where I intend holy confession.

EGLAMOUR. I will not fail your ladyship. Good morrow,
    gentle lady.

SILVIA. Good morrow, kind Sir Eglamour.   *Exeunt*

VALENTINE. *All that was mine in Silvia I give thee* (ACT V. SCENE IV)

SCENE 4

Under SILVIA's *window*

Enter LAUNCE, *with his dog*

LAUNCE. When a man's servant shall play the cur with him, look you, it goes hard—one that I brought up of a puppy; one that I sav'd from drowning, when three or four of his blind brothers and sisters went to it. I have taught him, even as one would say precisely 'Thus I would teach a dog.' I was sent to deliver him as a present to Mistress Silvia from my master; and I came no sooner into the dining-chamber, but he steps me to her trencher and steals her capon's leg. O, 'tis a foul thing when a cur cannot keep himself in all companies! I would have, as one should say, one that takes upon him to be a dog indeed, to be, as it were, a dog at all things. If I had not had more wit than he, to take a fault upon me that he did, I think verily he had been hang'd for't; sure as I live, he had suffer'd for't. You shall judge. He thrusts me himself into the company of three or four gentleman-like dogs under the Duke's table; he had not been there, bless the mark, a pissing while but all the chamber smelt him. 'Out with the dog' says one; 'What cur is that?' says another; 'Whip him out' says the third; 'Hang him up' says the Duke. I, having been acquainted with the smell before, knew it was Crab, and goes me to the fellow that whips the dogs. 'Friend,' quoth I 'you mean to whip the dog.' 'Ay, marry do I' quoth he. 'You do him the more wrong,' quoth I; ' 'twas I did the thing you wot of.' He makes me no more ado, but whips me out of the chamber. How many masters would do this for his servant? Nay, I'll be sworn, I have sat in the stock for puddings he hath stol'n, otherwise he had been executed; I have stood on the pillory for geese he hath kill'd, otherwise he had suffer'd for't. Thou think'st not of this now. Nay, I remember the trick you serv'd me when I took my leave of Madam Silvia. Did not I bid thee still mark me and do as I do? When didst thou see me heave

up my leg and make water against a gentlewoman's farthingale? Didst thou ever see me do such a trick?

Enter PROTEUS, *and* JULIA *in boy's clothes*

PROTEUS. Sebastian is thy name? I like thee well,
And will employ thee in some service presently.
JULIA. In what you please; I'll do what I can.
PROTEUS. I hope thou wilt. [*To* LAUNCE] How now, you
   whoreson peasant!
   Where have you been these two days loitering?
LAUNCE. Marry, sir, I carried Mistress Silvia the dog you
   bade me.
PROTEUS. And what says she to my little jewel?
LAUNCE. Marry, she says your dog was a cur, and tells you
   currish thanks is good enough for such a present.
PROTEUS. But she receiv'd my dog?
LAUNCE. No, indeed, did she not; here have I brought him
   back again.
PROTEUS. What, didst thou offer her this from me?
LAUNCE. Ay, sir; the other squirrel was stol'n from me by
   the hangman's boys in the market-place; and then I offer'd
   her mine own, who is a dog as big as ten of yours, and
   therefore the gift the greater.
PROTEUS. Go, get thee hence and find my dog again,
   Or ne'er return again into my sight.
   Away, I say. Stayest thou to vex me here?   *Exit* LAUNCE
   A slave that still an end turns me to shame!
   Sebastian, I have entertained thee
   Partly that I have need of such a youth
   That can with some discretion do my business,
   For 'tis no trusting to yond foolish lout,
   But chiefly for thy face and thy behaviour,
   Which, if my augury deceive me not,
   Witness good bringing up, fortune, and truth;
   Therefore, know thou, for this I entertain thee.
   Go presently, and take this ring with thee,
   Deliver it to Madam Silvia—
   She lov'd me well deliver'd it to me.
JULIA. It seems you lov'd not her, to leave her token.
   She is dead, belike?

PROTEUS. Not so; I think she lives.
JULIA. Alas!
PROTEUS. Why dost thou cry 'Alas'?
JULIA. I cannot choose
  But pity her.
PROTEUS. Wherefore shouldst thou pity her?
JULIA. Because methinks that she lov'd you as well
  As you do love your lady Silvia.
  She dreams on him that has forgot her love:
  You dote on her that cares not for your love.
  'Tis pity love should be so contrary;
  And thinking on it makes me cry 'Alas!'
PROTEUS. Well, give her that ring, and therewithal
  This letter. That's her chamber. Tell my lady
  I claim the promise for her heavenly picture.
  Your message done, hie home unto my chamber,
  Where thou shalt find me sad and solitary.   *Exit* PROTEUS
JULIA. How many women would do such a message?
  Alas, poor Proteus, thou hast entertain'd
  A fox to be the shepherd of thy lambs.
  Alas, poor fool, why do I pity him
  That with his very heart despiseth me?
  Because he loves her, he despiseth me;
  Because I love him, I must pity him.
  This ring I gave him, when he parted from me,
  To bind him to remember my good will;
  And now am I, unhappy messenger,
  To plead for that which I would not obtain,
  To carry that which I would have refus'd,
  To praise his faith, which I would have disprais'd.
  I am my master's true confirmed love,
  But cannot be true servant to my master
  Unless I prove false traitor to myself.
  Yet will I woo for him, but yet so coldly
  As, heaven it knows, I would not have him speed.

Enter SILVIA, *attended*

  Gentlewoman, good day! I pray you be my mean
  To bring me where to speak with Madam Silvia.
SILVIA. What would you with her, if that I be she?

JULIA. If you be she, I do entreat your patience
   To hear me speak the message I am sent on.
SILVIA. From whom?
JULIA. From my master, Sir Proteus, madam.
SILVIA. O, he sends you for a picture?
JULIA. Ay, madam.
SILVIA. Ursula, bring my picture there.
   Go, give your master this. Tell him from me,
   One Julia, that his changing thoughts forget,
   Would better fit his chamber than this shadow.
JULIA. Madam, please you peruse this letter.
   Pardon me, madam; I have unadvis'd
   Deliver'd you a paper that I should not.
   This is the letter to your ladyship.
SILVIA. I pray thee let me look on that again.
JULIA. It may not be; good madam, pardon me.
SILVIA. There, hold!
   I will not look upon your master's lines.
   I know they are stuff'd with protestations,
   And full of new-found oaths, which he will break
   As easily as I do tear his paper.
JULIA. Madam, he sends your ladyship this ring.
SILVIA. The more shame for him that he sends it me;
   For I have heard him say a thousand times
   His Julia gave it him at his departure.
   Though his false finger have profan'd the ring,
   Mine shall not do his Julia so much wrong.
JULIA. She thanks you.
SILVIA. What say'st thou?
JULIA. I thank you, madam, that you tender her.
   Poor gentlewoman, my master wrongs her much.
SILVIA. Dost thou know her?
JULIA. Almost as well as I do know myself.
   To think upon her woes, I do protest
   That I have wept a hundred several times.
SILVIA. Belike she thinks that Proteus hath forsook her.
JULIA. I think she doth, and that's her cause of sorrow.
SILVIA. Is she not passing fair?
JULIA. She hath been fairer, madam, than she is.
   When she did think my master lov'd her well,

She, in my judgment, was as fair as you;
But since she did neglect her looking-glass
And threw her sun-expelling mask away,
The air hath starv'd the roses in her cheeks
And pinch'd the lily-tincture of her face,
That now she is become as black as I.

SILVIA. How tall was she?

JULIA. About my stature; for at Pentecost,
When all our pageants of delight were play'd,
Our youth got me to play the woman's part,
And I was trimm'd in Madam Julia's gown;
Which served me as fit, by all men's judgments,
As if the garment had been made for me;
Therefore I know she is about my height.
And at that time I made her weep agood,
For I did play a lamentable part.
Madam, 'twas Ariadne passioning
For Theseus' perjury and unjust flight;
Which I so lively acted with my tears
That my poor mistress, moved therewithal,
Wept bitterly; and would I might be dead
If I in thought felt not her very sorrow.

SILVIA. She is beholding to thee, gentle youth.
Alas, poor lady, desolate and left!
I weep myself, to think upon thy words.
Here, youth, there is my purse; I give thee this
For thy sweet mistress' sake, because thou lov'st her.
Farewell.   *Exit* SILVIA *with* ATTENDANTS

JULIA. And she shall thank you for't, if e'er you know her.
A virtuous gentlewoman, mild and beautiful!
I hope my master's suit will be but cold,
Since she respects my mistress' love so much.
Alas, how love can trifle with itself!
Here is her picture; let me see. I think,
If I had such a tire, this face of mine
Were full as lovely as is this of hers;
And yet the painter flatter'd her a little,
Unless I flatter with myself too much.
Her hair is auburn, mine is perfect yellow;
If that be all the difference in his love,

I'll get me such a colour'd periwig.
Her eyes are grey as glass, and so are mine;
Ay, but her forehead's low, and mine's as high.
What should it be that he respects in her
But I can make respective in myself,
If this fond Love were not a blinded god?
Come, shadow, come, and take this shadow up,
For 'tis thy rival. O thou senseless form,
Thou shalt be worshipp'd, kiss'd, lov'd, and ador'd!
And were there sense in his idolatry
My substance should be statue in thy stead.
I'll use thee kindly for thy mistress' sake,
That us'd me so; or else, by Jove I vow,
I should have scratch'd out your unseeing eyes,
To make my master out of love with thee.   *Exit*

ACT V. SCENE 1

Milan. An abbey

Enter EGLAMOUR

EGLAMOUR. The sun begins to gild the western sky,
And now it is about the very hour
That Silvia at Friar Patrick's cell should meet me.
She will not fail, for lovers break not hours
Unless it be to come before their time,
So much they spur their expedition.

Enter SILVIA

See where she comes. Lady, a happy evening!
SILVIA. Amen, amen! Go on, good Eglamour,
Out at the postern by the abbey wall;
I fear I am attended by some spies.
EGLAMOUR. Fear not. The forest is not three leagues off;
If we recover that, we are sure enough.   *Exeunt*

SCENE 2

Milan. The DUKE's *palace*

Enter THURIO, PROTEUS, *and* JULIA *as* SEBASTIAN

THURIO. Sir Proteus, what says Silvia to my suit?

PROTEUS. O, sir, I find her milder than she was;
And yet she takes exceptions at your person.

THURIO. What, that my leg is too long?

PROTEUS. No; that it is too little.

THURIO. I'll wear a boot to make it somewhat rounder.

JULIA. [*Aside*] But love will not be spurr'd to what it
loathes.

THURIO. What says she to my face?

PROTEUS. She says it is a fair one.

THURIO. Nay, then, the wanton lies; my face is black.

PROTEUS. But pearls are fair; and the old saying is:
Black men are pearls in beauteous ladies' eyes.

JULIA. [*Aside*] 'Tis true, such pearls as put out ladies' eyes;
For I had rather wink than look on them.

THURIO. How likes she my discourse?

PROTEUS. Ill, when you talk of war.

THURIO. But well when I discourse of love and peace?

JULIA. [*Aside*] But better, indeed, when you hold your
peace.

THURIO. What says she to my valour?

PROTEUS. O, sir, she makes no doubt of that.

JULIA. [*Aside*] She needs not, when she knows it cowardice.

THURIO. What says she to my birth?

PROTEUS. That you are well deriv'd.

JULIA. [*Aside*] True; from a gentleman to a fool.

THURIO. Considers she my possessions?

PROTEUS. O, ay; and pities them.

THURIO. Wherefore?

JULIA. [*Aside*] That such an ass should owe them.

PROTEUS. That they are out by lease.

JULIA. Here comes the Duke.

Enter DUKE

DUKE. How now, Sir Proteus! how now, Thurio!
  Which of you saw Sir Eglamour of late?
THURIO. Not I.
PROTEUS. Nor I.
DUKE. Saw you my daughter?
PROTEUS. Neither.
DUKE. Why then,
  She's fled unto that peasant Valentine;
  And Eglamour is in her company.
  'Tis true; for Friar Lawrence met them both
  As he in penance wander'd through the forest;
  Him he knew well, and guess'd that it was she,
  But, being mask'd, he was not sure of it;
  Besides, she did intend confession
  At Patrick's cell this even; and there she was not.
  These likelihoods confirm her flight from hence;
  Therefore, I pray you, stand not to discourse,
  But mount you presently, and meet with me
  Upon the rising of the mountain foot
  That leads toward Mantua, whither they are fled.
  Dispatch, sweet gentlemen, and follow me.   *Exit*
THURIO. Why, this it is to be a peevish girl
  That flies her fortune when it follows her.
  I'll after, more to be reveng'd on Eglamour
  Than for the love of reckless Silvia.   *Exit*
PROTEUS. And I will follow, more for Silvia's love
  Than hate of Eglamour, that goes with her.   *Exit*
JULIA. And I will follow, more to cross that love
  Than hate for Silvia, that is gone for love.   *Exit*

SCENE 3

The frontiers of Mantua. The forest

Enter OUTLAWS *with* SILVIA

FIRST OUTLAW. Come, come.
  Be patient; we must bring you to our captain.
SILVIA. A thousand more mischances than this one
  Have learn'd me how to brook this patiently.

SECOND OUTLAW. Come, bring her away.
FIRST OUTLAW. Where is the gentleman that was with her?
SECOND OUTLAW. Being nimble-footed, he hath outrun us,
  But Moyses and Valerius follow him.
  Go thou with her to the west end of the wood;
  There is our captain; we'll follow him that's fled.
  The thicket is beset; he cannot 'scape.
FIRST OUTLAW. Come, I must bring you to our captain's
  cave;
  Fear not; he bears an honourable mind,
  And will not use a woman lawlessly.
SILVIA. O Valentine, this I endure for thee!   *Exeunt*

SCENE 4

Another part of the forest

Enter VALENTINE

VALENTINE. How use doth breed a habit in a man!
  This shadowy desert, unfrequented woods,
  I better brook than flourishing peopled towns.
  Here can I sit alone, unseen of any,
  And to the nightingale's complaining notes
  Tune my distresses and record my woes.
  O thou that dost inhabit in my breast,
  Leave not the mansion so long tenantless,
  Lest, growing ruinous, the building fall
  And leave no memory of what it was!
  Repair me with thy presence, Silvia:
  Thou gentle nymph, cherish thy forlorn swain.
  What halloing and what stir is this to-day?
  These are my mates, that make their wills their law,
  Have some unhappy passenger in chase.
  They love me well; yet I have much to do
  To keep them from uncivil outrages.
  Withdraw thee, Valentine. Who's this comes here?
                                        [*Steps aside*]

Enter PROTEUS, SILVIA, *and* JULIA *as Sebastian*

135

PROTEUS. Madam, this service I have done for you,
Though you respect not aught your servant doth,
To hazard life, and rescue you from him
That would have forc'd your honour and your love.
Vouchsafe me, for my meed, but one fair look;
A smaller boon than this I cannot beg,
And less than this, I am sure, you cannot give.
VALENTINE. [*Aside*] How like a dream is this I see and hear!
Love, lend me patience to forbear awhile.
SILVIA. O miserable, unhappy that I am!
PROTEUS. Unhappy were you, madam, ere I came;
But by my coming I have made you happy.
SILVIA. By thy approach thou mak'st me most unhappy.
JULIA. [*Aside*] And me, when he approacheth to your presence.
SILVIA. Had I been seized by a hungry lion,
I would have been a breakfast to the beast
Rather than have false Proteus rescue me.
O, heaven be judge how I love Valentine,
Whose life's as tender to me as my soul!
And full as much, for more there cannot be,
I do detest false, perjur'd Proteus.
Therefore be gone; solicit me no more.
PROTEUS. What dangerous action, stood it next to death,
Would I not undergo for one calm look?
O, 'tis the curse in love, and still approv'd,
When women cannot love where they're belov'd!
SILVIA. When Proteus cannot love where he's belov'd!
Read over Julia's heart, thy first best love,
For whose dear sake thou didst then rend thy faith
Into a thousand oaths; and all those oaths
Descended into perjury, to love me.
Thou hast no faith left now, unless thou'dst two,
And that's far worse than none; better have none
Than plural faith, which is too much by one.
Thou counterfeit to thy true friend!
PROTEUS. In love,
Who respects friend?
SILVIA. All men but Proteus.
PROTEUS. Nay, if the gentle spirit of moving words
Can no way change you to a milder form,

I'll woo you like a soldier, at arms' end,
And love you 'gainst the nature of love—force ye.
SILVIA. O heaven!
PROTEUS. I'll force thee yield to my desire.
VALENTINE. Ruffian! let go that rude uncivil touch;
　Thou friend of an ill fashion!
PROTEUS. Valentine!
VALENTINE. Thou common friend, that's without faith or
　love—
　For such is a friend now; treacherous man,
　Thou hast beguil'd my hopes; nought but mine eye
　Could have persuaded me. Now I dare not say
　I have one friend alive: thou wouldst disprove me.
　Who should be trusted, when one's own right hand
　Is perjured to the bosom? Proteus,
　I am sorry I must never trust thee more,
　But count the world a stranger for thy sake.
　The private wound is deepest. O time most accurst!
　'Mongst all foes that a friend should be the worst!
PROTEUS. My shame and guilt confounds me.
　Forgive me, Valentine; if hearty sorrow
　Be a sufficient ransom for offence,
　I tender 't here; I do as truly suffer
　As e'er I did commit.
VALENTINE. Then I am paid;
　And once again I do receive thee honest.
　Who by repentance is not satisfied
　Is nor of heaven nor earth, for these are pleas'd;
　By penitence th' Eternal's wrath's appeas'd.
　And, that my love may appear plain and free,
　All that was mine in Silvia I give thee.
JULIA. O me unhappy!　　　　　　　　　　　[Swoons]
PROTEUS. Look to the boy.
VALENTINE. Why, boy! why, wag! how now!
　What's the matter? Look up; speak.
JULIA. O good sir, my master charg'd me to deliver a ring
　to Madam Silvia, which, out of my neglect, was never
　done.
PROTEUS. Where is that ring, boy?
JULIA. Here 'tis; this is it.

137

PROTEUS. How! let me see. Why, this is the ring I gave to
    Julia.

JULIA. O, cry you mercy, sir, I have mistook;
    This is the ring you sent to Silvia.

PROTEUS. But how cam'st thou by this ring?
    At my depart I gave this unto Julia.

JULIA. And Julia herself did give it me;
    And Julia herself have brought it hither.

PROTEUS. How! Julia!

JULIA. Behold her that gave aim to all thy oaths,
    And entertain'd 'em deeply in her heart.
    How oft hast thou with perjury cleft the root!
    O Proteus, let this habit make thee blush!
    Be thou asham'd that I have took upon me
    Such an immodest raiment—if shame live
    In a disguise of love.
    It is the lesser blot, modesty finds,
    Women to change their shapes than men their minds.

PROTEUS. Than men their minds! 'tis true. O heaven, were
    man
    But constant, he were perfect! That one error
    Fills him with faults; makes him run through all th' sins:
    Inconstancy falls off ere it begins.
    What is in Silvia's face but I may spy
    More fresh in Julia's with a constant eye?

VALENTINE. Come, come, a hand from either.
    Let me be blest to make this happy close;
    'Twere pity two such friends should be long foes.

PROTEUS. Bear witness, heaven, I have my wish for ever.

JULIA. And I mine.

Enter OUTLAWS, *with* DUKE *and* THURIO

OUTLAW. A prize, a prize, a prize!

VALENTINE. Forbear, forbear, I say; it is my lord the Duke.
    Your Grace is welcome to a man disgrac'd,
    Banished Valentine.

DUKE. Sir Valentine!

THURIO. Yonder is Silvia; and Silvia's mine.

VALENTINE. Thurio, give back, or else embrace thy death;
    Come not within the measure of my wrath;

Do not name Silvia thine; if once again,
Verona shall not hold thee. Here she stands
Take but possession of her with a touch—
I dare thee but to breathe upon my love.

THURIO. Sir Valentine, I care not for her, I;
I hold him but a fool that will endanger
His body for a girl that loves him not.
I claim her not, and therefore she is thine.

DUKE. The more degenerate and base art thou
To make such means for her as thou hast done
And leave her on such slight conditions.
Now, by the honour of my ancestry,
I do applaud thy spirit, Valentine,
And think thee worthy of an empress' love.
Know then, I here forget all former griefs,
Cancel all grudge, repeal thee home again,
Plead a new state in thy unrivall'd merit,
To which I thus subscribe: Sir Valentine,
Thou art a gentleman, and well deriv'd;
Take thou thy Silvia, for thou hast deserv'd her.

VALENTINE. I thank your Grace; the gift hath made me
happy.
I now beseech you, for your daughter's sake,
To grant one boon that I shall ask of you.

DUKE. I grant it for thine own, whate'er it be.

VALENTINE. These banish'd men, that I have kept withal,
Are men endu'd with worthy qualities;
Forgive them what they have committed here,
And let them be recall'd from their exile:
They are reformed, civil, full of good,
And fit for great employment, worthy lord.

DUKE. Thou hast prevail'd; I pardon them, and thee;
Dispose of them as thou know'st their deserts.
Come, let us go; we will include all jars
With triumphs, mirth, and rare solemnity.

VALENTINE. And, as we walk along, I dare be bold
With our discourse to make your Grace to smile.
What think you of this page, my lord?

DUKE. I think the boy hath grace in him; he blushes.

VALENTINE. I warrant you, my lord—more grace than boy.

Duke. What mean you by that saying?
Valentine. Please you, I'll tell you as we pass along,
That you will wonder what hath fortuned.
Come, Proteus, 'tis your penance but to hear
The story of your loves discovered.
That done, our day of marriage shall be yours;
One feast, one house, one mutual happiness!   *Exeunt*

The Merry Wives of Windsor

THE MERRY WIVES OF WINDSOR

S HAKESPEARE's comedies, although they are a distillation of the spirit of England, are generally laid in foreign parts, more often than not in that province Shakespeare added to the world, a country which a French critic has so happily described as *une Italie de l'âme*. The Merry Wives is his only comedy in which the scene is declared to be England; and one might wonder why Shakespeare hit on Windsor for this unique production.

Dr. Hotson, the American scholar, has provided an answer that not only explains Shakespeare's choice of Windsor for his scene but allows us to see more clearly the conditions that dictated the main lines of the plot.

In the final scene the Fairy band led by Sir Hugh Evans disguised as a satyr surround Sir John Falstaff as he lurks in Windsor Park. It is no doubt natural that the fairies should refer to the royal castle in whose shadow they were supposed to be revelling; but the references are peculiarly specific. Puck or Hobgoblin gives the following instructions:

Cricket, to Windsor chimneys shalt thou leap;
Where fires thou find'st unrak'd, and hearths unswept,
There pinch the maids as blue as bilberry;
Our radiant Queen hates sluts and sluttery.

And the Fairy Queen, played by Anne Page, gives these further orders:

Search Windsor castle, elves, within and out;
Strew good luck, ouphes, on every sacred room,
That it may stand till the perpetual doom
In state as wholesome as in state 'tis fit,
Worthy the owner and the owner it.
The several chairs of order look you scour
With juice of balm and every precious flower;
Each fair instalment, coat, and sev'ral crest,
With loyal blazon, evermore be blest!
And nightly, meadow-fairies, look you sing
Like to the Garter's compass, in a ring.

FALSTAFF. *My honest lads, I will tell you what I am about*
(ACT I. SCENE III)

There is nothing out of the way, it may be said, in this further reference to St. George's Chapel and the stalls there assigned to the Knights of the Garter. Still the preparations described for making the castle ready for the sovereign and the chapel for the Knights would be specially appropriate at a performance that had some connection with the social ritual that required these preparations. This occasion, Dr. Hotson has suggested, was the Garter Feast on St. George's day at Greenwich on 23rd April 1597. This feast followed the election of the new Knights and preceded their installation at Windsor.

Two details suggest this particular date. Among those elected on this occasion was the Duke of Württemberg who as Count Mompelgart had gone to Windsor in 1592 to ask his cousin Elizabeth to make him a Knight of the Garter. The Queen obviously found him uninteresting and she conferred the honour on him only in 1597 and then in his absence. This is hinted at in Act IV, Scene 5, where Dr. Caius says to the Host of the Garter Inn,

> it is tell-a me dat you make grand preparation for a Duke de Jamany. By my trot, dere is no duke that the court is know to come . . .

and a few lines earlier we hear of some Germans that have made off with the Host's horses, a reference perhaps to Mompelgart's high-handed dealings in commandeering post-horses during his 1592 visit. Further the Lord Chamberlain, under whose patronage Shakespeare's company played, was elected a member of the Order in 1597 and it would be natural for his company of actors, especially as they were the leading company in the land, to give a private performance to add to the festivities. All this would square with the tradition that Shakespeare wrote *The Merry Wives* at short notice for a command performance: the Queen wished to see Falstaff in love.

The date 23rd April 1597 for the first performance of *The Merry Wives* is probably one of the few dates in the chronology we can be confident about. Accepting it as established, Dr. Hotson has been able to offer an explanation of a passage in the opening scene of the play that has given rise to much dispute. Justice Shallow comes on complaining that Falstaff has robbed his deer park; references to his family's ancient coat of arms introduces the pun on luces which might be the pike-like fish on a coat of arms or the louse that infests old coats of another sort. Sir Thomas Lucy of Charlecote had luces on his arms, and the story that Shakespeare was here trying to pay off old scores on Sir Thomas, who had, so it was affirmed, prosecuted the youthful poet for poaching, was given currency at the very end of the seventeenth century. Dr. Hotson has shown that if Shakespeare had any Justice with luces in his coat in mind in 1597 it may well have been William Gardiner, an unscrupulous Justice whom Shakespeare had at this time very good reason to dislike. Gardiner had married a Frances Lucy and showed the luces of her arms with his own.

In 1602 a piratical publisher issued a garbled version of the play. The version however imperfect which it gives of the final scene suggests that when *The Merry Wives* was played in the public theatre the finale was revised and much appropriate to the Royal performance modified to suit the new audience.

SIR JOHN FALSTAFF
FENTON, *a young gentleman*
SHALLOW, *a country justice*
SLENDER, *cousin to Shallow*
FORD ⎱ *gentlemen of Windsor*
PAGE ⎰
WILLIAM PAGE, *a boy, son to Page*
SIR HUGH EVANS, *a Welsh parson*
DOCTOR CAIUS, *a French physician*
HOST *of the Garter Inn*
BARDOLPH ⎱
PISTOL ⎬ *followers of Falstaff*
NYM ⎰
ROBIN, *page to Falstaff*
SIMPLE, *servant to Slender*
RUGBY, *servant to Doctor Caius*

MISTRESS FORD
MISTRESS PAGE
MISTRESS ANNE PAGE, *her daughter*
MISTRESS QUICKLY, *servant to Doctor Caius*

Servants to *Page, Ford, etc.*

SCENE:

Windsor, and the neighbourhood

The Merry Wives of Windsor

ACT I. SCENE 1

Windsor. Before PAGE'S *house*

Enter JUSTICE SHALLOW, SLENDER, *and* SIR HUGH EVANS

SHALLOW. Sir Hugh, persuade me not; I will make a Star Chamber matter of it; if he were twenty Sir John Falstaffs, he shall not abuse Robert Shallow, esquire.

SLENDER. In the county of Gloucester, Justice of Peace, and Coram.

SHALLOW. Ay, cousin Slender, and Custalorum.

SLENDER. Ay, and Ratolorum too; and a gentleman born, Master Parson, who writes himself 'Armigero' in any bill, warrant, quittance, or obligation—'Armigero.'

SHALLOW. Ay, that I do; and have done any time these three hundred years.

SLENDER. All his successors, gone before him, hath done't; and all his ancestors, that come after him, may: they may give the dozen white luces in their coat.

SHALLOW. It is an old coat.

EVANS. The dozen white louses do become an old coat well; it agrees well, passant; it is a familiar beast to man, and signifies love.

SHALLOW. The luce is the fresh fish; the salt fish is an old coat.

SLENDER. I may quarter, coz.

SHALLOW. You may, by marrying.

EVANS. It is marring indeed, if he quarter it.

SHALLOW. Not a whit.

EVANS. Yes, py'r lady! If he has a quarter of your coat, there is but three skirts for yourself, in my simple conjectures; but that is all one. If Sir John Falstaff have committed disparagements unto you, I am of the church, and will be glad to do my benevolence, to make atonements and compremises between you.

147

SHALLOW. The Council shall hear it; it is a riot.

EVANS. It is not meet the Council hear a riot; there is no fear of Got in a riot; the Council, look you, shall desire to hear the fear of Got, and not to hear a riot; take your vizaments in that.

SHALLOW. Ha! o' my life, if I were young again, the sword should end it.

EVANS. It is petter that friends is the sword and end it; and there is also another device in my prain, which peradventure prings goot discretions with it. There is Anne Page, which is daughter to Master George Page, which is pretty virginity.

SLENDER. Mistress Anne Page? She has brown hair, and speaks small like a woman.

EVANS. It is that fery person for all the orld, as just as you will desire; and seven hundred pounds of moneys, and gold, and silver, is her grandsire upon his death's-bed—Got deliver to a joyful resurrections!—give, when she is able to overtake seventeen years old. It were a goot motion if we leave our pribbles and prabbles, and desire a marriage between Master Abraham and Mistress Anne Page.

SHALLOW. Did her grandsire leave her seven hundred pound?

EVANS. Ay, and her father is make her a petter penny.

SHALLOW. I know the young gentlewoman; she has good gifts.

EVANS. Seven hundred pounds, and possibilities, is goot gifts.

SHALLOW. Well, let us see honest Master Page. Is Falstaff there?

EVANS. Shall I tell you a lie? I do despise a liar as I do despise one that is false; or as I despise one that is not true. The knight Sir John is there; and, I beseech you, be ruled by your well-willers. I will peat the door for Master Page. [*Knocks*] What, hoa! Got pless your house here!

PAGE. [*Within*] Who's there?

Enter PAGE

EVANS. Here is Got's plessing, and your friend, and Justice Shallow; and here young Master Slender, that peradventures shall tell you another tale, if matters grow to your likings.

PAGE. I am glad to see your worships well. I thank you for my venison, Master Shallow.

SHALLOW. Master Page, I am glad to see you; much good do it your good heart! I wish'd your venison better; it was ill kill'd. How doth good Mistress Page?—and I thank you always with my heart, la! with my heart.

PAGE. Sir, I thank you.

SHALLOW. Sir, I thank you; by yea and no, I do.

PAGE. I am glad to see you, good Master Slender.

SLENDER. How does your fallow greyhound, sir? I heard say he was outrun on Cotsall.

PAGE. It could not be judg'd, sir.

SLENDER. You'll not confess, you'll not confess.

SHALLOW. That he will not. 'Tis your fault; 'tis your fault; 'tis a good dog.

PAGE. A cur, sir.

SHALLOW. Sir, he's a good dog, and a fair dog. Can there be more said? He is good, and fair. Is Sir John Falstaff here?

PAGE. Sir, he is within; and I would I could do a good office between you.

EVANS. It is spoke as a Christians ought to speak.

SHALLOW. He hath wrong'd me, Master Page.

PAGE. Sir, he doth in some sort confess it.

SHALLOW. If it be confessed, it is not redressed; is not that so, Master Page? He hath wrong'd me; indeed he hath; at a word, he hath, believe me; Robert Shallow, esquire, saith he is wronged.

PAGE. Here comes Sir John.

Enter SIR JOHN FALSTAFF, BARDOLPH, NYM, *and* PISTOL

FALSTAFF. Now, Master Shallow, you'll complain of me to the King?

SHALLOW. Knight, you have beaten my men, kill'd my deer, and broke open my lodge.

FALSTAFF. But not kiss'd your keeper's daughter.

SHALLOW. Tut, a pin! this shall be answer'd.

FALSTAFF. I will answer it straight: I have done all this. That is now answer'd.

SHALLOW. The Council shall know this.

FALSTAFF. 'Twere better for you if it were known in counsel: you'll be laugh'd at.

EVANS. Pauca verba, Sir John; goot worts.

FALSTAFF. Good worts! good cabbage! Slender, I broke your head; what matter have you against me?

SLENDER. Marry, sir, I have matter in my head against you; and against your cony-catching rascals, Bardolph, Nym, and Pistol. They carried me to the tavern, and made me drunk, and afterwards pick'd my pocket.

BARDOLPH. You Banbury cheese!

SLENDER. Ay, it is no matter.

PISTOL. How now, Mephostophilus!

SLENDER. Ay, it is no matter.

NYM. Slice, I say! pauca, pauca; slice! That's my humour.

SLENDER. Where's Simple, my man? Can you tell, cousin?

EVANS. Peace, I pray you. Now let us understand. There is three umpires in this matter, as I understand: that is, Master Page, fidelicet Master Page; and there is myself, fidelicet myself; and the three party is, lastly and finally, mine host of the Garter.

PAGE. We three to hear it and end it between them.

EVANS. Fery goot. I will make a prief of it in my note-book; and we will afterwards ork upon the cause with as great discreetly as we can.

FALSTAFF. Pistol!

PISTOL. He hears with ears.

EVANS. The tevil and his tam! What phrase is this, 'He hears with ear'? Why, it is affectations.

FALSTAFF. Pistol, did you pick Master Slender's purse?

SLENDER. Ay, by these gloves, did he—or I would I might never come in mine own great chamber again else!—of seven groats in mill-sixpences, and two Edward shovel-boards that cost me two shilling and two pence apiece of Yead Miller, by these gloves.

FALSTAFF. Is this true, Pistol?

EVANS. No, it is false, if it is a pick-purse.

PISTOL. Ha, thou mountain-foreigner! Sir John and master mine,
I combat challenge of this latten bilbo.
Word of denial in thy labras here!

Word of denial! Froth and scum, thou liest.

SLENDER. By these gloves, then, 'twas he.

NYM. Be avis'd, sir, and pass good humours; I will say 'marry trap' with you, if you run the nuthook's humour on me; that is the very note of it.

SLENDER. By this hat, then, he in the red face had it; for though I cannot remember what I did when you made me drunk, yet I am not altogether an ass.

FALSTAFF. What say you, Scarlet and John?

BARDOLPH. Why, sir, for my part, I say the gentleman had drunk himself out of his five sentences.

EVANS. It is his five senses; fie, what the ignorance is!

BARDOLPH. And being fap, sir, was, as they say, cashier'd; and so conclusions pass'd the careers.

SLENDER. Ay, you spake in Latin then too; but 'tis no matter; I'll ne'er be drunk whilst I live again, but in honest, civil, godly company, for this trick. If I be drunk, I'll be drunk with those that have the fear of God, and not with drunken knaves.

EVANS. So Got udge me, that is a virtuous mind.

FALSTAFF. You hear all these matters deni'd, gentlemen; you hear it.

Enter MISTRESS ANNE PAGE *with wine;* MISTRESS
FORD *and* MISTRESS PAGE, *following*

PAGE. Nay, daughter, carry the wine in; we'll drink within.
Exit ANNE PAGE

SLENDER. O heaven! this is Mistress Anne Page.

PAGE. How now, Mistress Ford!

FALSTAFF. Mistress Ford, by my troth, you are very well met; by your leave, good mistress.   [*Kisses her*]

PAGE. Wife, bid these gentlemen welcome. Come, we have a hot venison pasty to dinner; come, gentlemen, I hope we shall drink down all unkindness.
Exeunt all but SHALLOW, SLENDER, *and* EVANS

SLENDER. I had rather than forty shillings I had my Book of Songs and Sonnets here.

Enter SIMPLE

How, Simple! Where have you been? I must wait on myself, must I? You have not the Book of Riddles about you, have you?

SIMPLE. Book of Riddles! Why, did you not lend it to Alice Shortcake upon Allhallowmas last, a fortnight afore Michaelmas?

SHALLOW. Come, coz; come, coz; we stay for you. A word with you, coz; marry, this, coz: there is, as 'twere, a tender, a kind of tender, made afar off by Sir Hugh here. Do you understand me?

SLENDER. Ay, sir, you shall find me reasonable; if it be so, I shall do that that is reason.

SHALLOW. Nay, but understand me.

SLENDER. So I do, sir.

EVANS. Give ear to his motions: Master Slender, I will description the matter to you, if you be capacity of it.

SLENDER. Nay, I will do as my cousin Shallow says; I pray you pardon me; he's a justice of peace in his country, simple though I stand here.

EVANS. But that is not the question. The question is concerning your marriage.

SHALLOW. Ay, there's the point, sir.

EVANS. Marry is it; the very point of it; to Mistress Anne Page.

SLENDER. Why, if it be so, I will marry her upon any reasonable demands.

EVANS. But can you affection the oman? Let us command to know that of your mouth or of your lips; for divers philosophers hold that the lips is parcel of the mouth. Therefore, precisely, can you carry your good will to the maid?

SHALLOW. Cousin Abraham Slender, can you love her?

SLENDER. I hope, sir, I will do as it shall become one that would do reason.

EVANS. Nay, Got's lords and his ladies! you must speak possitable, if you can carry her your desires towards her.

SHALLOW. That you must. Will you, upon good dowry, marry her?

SLENDER. I will do a greater thing than that upon your request, cousin, in any reason.

SHALLOW. Nay, conceive me, conceive me, sweet coz; what I do is to pleasure you, coz. Can you love the maid?

SLENDER. I will marry her, sir, at your request; but if there be no great love in the beginning, yet heaven may decrease it upon better acquaintance, when we are married and have more occasion to know one another. I hope upon familiarity will grow more contempt. But if you say 'marry her,' I will marry her; that I am freely dissolved, and dissolutely.

EVANS. It is a fery discretion answer, save the fall is in the ord 'dissolutely': the ort is, according to our meaning, 'resolutely'; his meaning is good.

SHALLOW. Ay, I think my cousin meant well.

SLENDER. Ay, or else I would I might be hang'd, la!

Re-enter ANNE PAGE

SHALLOW. Here comes fair Mistress Anne. Would I were young for your sake, Mistress Anne!

ANNE. The dinner is on the table; my father desires your worships' company.

SHALLOW. I will wait on him, fair Mistress Anne!

EVANS. Od's plessed will! I will not be absence at the grace.
Exeunt SHALLOW *and* EVANS

ANNE. Will't please your worship to come in, sir?

SLENDER. No, I thank you, forsooth, heartily; I am very well.

ANNE. The dinner attends you, sir.

SLENDER. I am not a-hungry, I thank you, forsooth. Go, sirrah, for all you are my man, go wait upon my cousin Shallow. [*Exit* SIMPLE] A justice of peace sometime may be beholding to his friend for a man. I keep but three men and a boy yet, till my mother be dead. But what though? Yet I live like a poor gentleman born.

ANNE. I may not go in without your worship; they will not sit till you come.

SLENDER. I'faith, I'll eat nothing; I thank you as much as though I did.

ANNE. I pray you, sir, walk in.

SLENDER. I had rather walk here, I thank you. I bruis'd my shin th' other day with playing at sword and dagger with a master of fence—three veneys for a dish of stew'd prunes —and, I with my ward defending my head, he hot my shin, and, by my troth, I cannot abide the smell of hot meat since. Why do your dogs bark so? Be there bears i' th' town?

ANNE. I think there are, sir; I heard them talk'd of.

SLENDER. I love the sport well; but I shall as soon quarrel at it as any man in England. You are afraid, if you see the bear loose, are you not?

ANNE. Ay, indeed, sir.

SLENDER. That's meat and drink to me now. I have seen Sackerson loose twenty times, and have taken him by the chain; but I warrant you, the women have so cried and shriek'd at it that it pass'd; but women, indeed, cannot abide 'em; they are very ill-favour'd rough things.

Re-enter PAGE

PAGE. Come, gentle Master Slender, come; we stay for you.

SLENDER. I'll eat nothing, I thank you, sir.

PAGE. By cock and pie, you shall not choose, sir! Come, come.

SLENDER. Nay, pray you lead the way.

PAGE. Come on, sir.

SLENDER. Mistress Anne, yourself shall go first.

ANNE. Not I, sir; pray you keep on.

SLENDER. Truly, I will not go first; truly, la! I will not do you that wrong.

ANNE. I pray you, sir.

SLENDER. I'll rather be unmannerly than troublesome. You do yourself wrong indeed, la!   *Exeunt*

SCENE 2

Before PAGE's *house*

Enter SIR HUGH EVANS *and* SIMPLE

EVANS. Go your ways, and ask of Doctor Caius' house which is the way; and there dwells one Mistress Quickly, which is in the manner of his nurse, or his dry nurse, or his cook, or his laundry, his washer, and his wringer.

SIMPLE. Well, sir.

EVANS. Nay, it is petter yet. Give her this letter; for it is a oman that altogether's acquaintance with Mistress Anne Page; and the letter is to desire and require her to solicit your master's desires to Mistress Anne Page. I pray you be gone. I will make an end of my dinner; there's pippins and cheese to come. *Exeunt*

SCENE 3

The Garter Inn

Enter FALSTAFF, HOST, BARDOLPH, NYM, PISTOL, *and* ROBIN

FALSTAFF. Mine host of the Garter!

HOST. What says my bully rook? Speak scholarly and wisely.

FALSTAFF. Truly, mine host, I must turn away some of my followers.

HOST. Discard, bully Hercules; cashier; let them wag; trot, trot.

FALSTAFF. I sit at ten pounds a week.

HOST. Thou'rt an emperor—Cæsar, Keiser, and Pheazar. I will entertain Bardolph; he shall draw, he shall tap; said I well, bully Hector?

FALSTAFF. Do so, good mine host.

HOST. I have spoke; let him follow. [*To* BARDOLPH] Let me see thee froth and lime. I am at a word; follow. *Exit* HOST

FALSTAFF. Bardolph, follow him. A tapster is a good trade; an old cloak makes a new jerkin; a wither'd serving-man a fresh tapster. Go; adieu.

BARDOLPH. It is a life that I have desir'd; I will thrive.

PISTOL. O base Hungarian wight! Wilt thou the spigot wield? *Exit* BARDOLPH

NYM. He was gotten in drink. Is not the humour conceited?

FALSTAFF. I am glad I am so acquit of this tinder-box: his thefts were too open; his filching was like an unskilful singer—he kept not time.

NYM. The good humour is to steal at a minute's rest.

PISTOL. 'Convey' the wise it call. 'Steal' foh! A fico for the phrase!

FALSTAFF. Well, sirs, I am almost out at heels.

PISTOL. Why, then, let kibes ensue.

FALSTAFF. There is no remedy; I must cony-catch; I must shift.

PISTOL. Young ravens must have food.

FALSTAFF. Which of you know Ford of this town?

PISTOL. I ken the wight; he is of substance good.

FALSTAFF. My honest lads, I will tell you what I am about.

PISTOL. Two yards, and more.

FALSTAFF. No quips now, Pistol. Indeed, I am in the waist two yards about; but I am now about no waste; I am about thrift. Briefly, I do mean to make love to Ford's wife; I spy entertainment in her; she discourses, she carves, she gives the leer of invitation; I can construe the action of her familiar style; and the hardest voice of her behaviour, to be English'd rightly, is 'I am Sir John Falstaff's.'

PISTOL. He hath studied her well, and translated her will out of honesty into English.

NYM. The anchor is deep; will that humour pass?

FALSTAFF. Now, the report goes she has all the rule of her husband's purse; he hath a legion of angels.

PISTOL. As many devils entertain; and 'To her, boy,' say I.

NYM. The humour rises; it is good; humour me the angels.

FALSTAFF. I have writ me here a letter to her; and here another to Page's wife, who even now gave me good eyes too, examin'd my parts with most judicious œillades; sometimes the beam of her view gilded my foot, sometimes my portly belly.

PISTOL. Then did the sun on dunghill shine.

NYM. I thank thee for that humour.

FALSTAFF. O, she did so course o'er my exteriors with such a greedy intention that the appetite of her eye did seem to scorch me up like a burning-glass! Here's another letter to her. She bears the purse too; she is a region in Guiana, all gold and bounty. I will be cheaters to them both, and they shall be exchequers to me; they shall be my East and West Indies, and I will trade to them both. Go, bear thou this letter to Mistress Page; and thou this to Mistress Ford. We will thrive, lads, we will thrive.

PISTOL. Shall I Sir Pandarus of Troy become,

And by my side wear steel? Then Lucifer take all!

NYM. I will run no base humour. Here, take the humour-letter; I will keep the haviour of reputation.

FALSTAFF. [*To* ROBIN] Hold, sirrah; bear you these letters tightly;

Sail like my pinnace to these golden shores.

Rogues, hence, avaunt! vanish like hailstones, go;

Trudge, plod away i' th' hoof; seek shelter, pack!

Falstaff will learn the humour of the age;

French thrift, you rogues; myself, and skirted page.

Exeunt FALSTAFF *and* ROBIN

PISTOL. Let vultures gripe thy guts! for gourd and fullam holds,

And high and low beguiles the rich and poor;

Tester I'll have in pouch when thou shalt lack,

Base Phrygian Turk!

NYM. I have operations in my head which be humours of revenge.

PISTOL. Wilt thou revenge?

NYM. By welkin and her star!

PISTOL. With wit or steel?

NYM. With both the humours, I.

I will discuss the humour of this love to Page.

PISTOL.   And I to Ford shall eke unfold

How Falstaff, varlet vile,

His dove will prove, his gold will hold,

And his soft couch defile.

NYM. My humour shall not cool; I will incense Page to deal with poison; I will possess him with yellowness; for the revolt of mine is dangerous. That is my true humour.

PISTOL. Thou art the Mars of malcontents; I second thee; troop on.   *Exeunt*

157

SCENE 4

Doctor Caius's *house*

Enter Mistress Quickly, Simple, *and* Rugby

QUICKLY. What, John Rugby! I pray thee go to the casement and see if you can see my master, Master Doctor Caius, coming. If he do, i' faith, and find anybody in the house, here will be an old abusing of God's patience and the King's English.

RUGBY. I'll go watch.

QUICKLY. Go; and we'll have a posset for't soon at night, in faith, at the latter end of a sea-coal fire. [*Exit* RUGBY] An honest, willing, kind fellow, as ever servant shall come in house withal; and, I warrant you, no tell-tale nor no breed-bate; his worst fault is that he is given to prayer; he is something peevish that way; but nobody but has his fault; but let that pass. Peter Simple you say your name is?

SIMPLE. Ay, for fault of a better.

QUICKLY. And Master Slender's your master?

SIMPLE. Ay, forsooth.

QUICKLY. Does he not wear a great round beard, like a glover's paring-knife?

SIMPLE. No, forsooth; he hath but a little whey face, with a little yellow beard, a Cain-colour'd beard.

QUICKLY. A softly-sprighted man, is he not?

SIMPLE. Ay, forsooth; but he is as tall a man of his hands as any is between this and his head; he hath fought with a warrener.

QUICKLY. How say you? O, I should remember him. Does he not hold up his head, as it were, and strut in his gait?

SIMPLE. Yes, indeed, does he.

QUICKLY. Well, heaven send Anne Page no worse fortune! Tell Master Parson Evans I will do what I can for your master. Anne is a good girl, and I wish—

Re-enter RUGBY

RUGBY. Out, alas! here comes my master.

QUICKLY. We shall all be shent. Run in here, good young

man; go into this closet. [*Shuts* SIMPLE *in the closet*] He
will not stay long. What, John Rugby! John! what, John,
I say! Go, John, go inquire for my master; I doubt he be
not well that he comes not home.   [*Singing*]
                And down, down, adown-a, etc.

Enter DOCTOR CAIUS

CAIUS. Vat is you sing? I do not like des toys. Pray you, go
    and vetch me in my closet un boitier vert—a box, a green-a
    box. Do intend vat I speak? A green-a box.
QUICKLY. Ay, forsooth, I'll fetch it you. [*Aside*] I am glad
    he went not in himself; if he had found the young man,
    he would have been horn-mad.
CAIUS. Fe, fe, fe fe! ma foi, il fait fort chaud. Je m'en vais à
    la cour—la grande affaire.
QUICKLY. Is it this, sir?
CAIUS. Oui; mette le au mon pocket: dépêche, quickly. Vere
    is dat knave, Rugby?
QUICKLY. What, John Rugby? John!
RUGBY. Here, sir.
CAIUS. You are John Rugby, and you are Jack Rugby.
    Come, take-a your rapier, and come after my heel to the
    court.
RUGBY. 'Tis ready, sir, here in the porch.
CAIUS. By my trot, I tarry too long. Od's me! Qu'ai j'oublié?
    Dere is some simples in my closet dat I vill not for the
    varld I shall leave behind.
QUICKLY. Ay me, he'll find the young man there, and be
    mad!
CAIUS. O diable, diable! vat is in my closet? Villainy! larron!
    [*Pulling* SIMPLE *out*] Rugby, my rapier!
QUICKLY. Good master, be content.
CAIUS. Wherefore shall I be content-a?
QUICKLY. The young man is an honest man.
CAIUS. What shall de honest man do in my closet? Dere is
    no honest man dat shall come in my closet.
QUICKLY. I beseech you, be not so phlegmatic; hear the
    truth of it. He came of an errand to me from Parson Hugh.
CAIUS. Vell?
SIMPLE. Ay, forsooth, to desire her to—

QUICKLY. Peace, I pray you.

CAIUS. Peace-a your tongue. Speak-a your tale.

SIMPLE. To desire this honest gentlewoman, your maid, to speak a good word to Mistress Anne Page for my master, in the way of marriage.

QUICKLY. This is all, indeed, la! but I'll ne'er put my finger in the fire, and need not.

CAIUS. Sir Hugh send-a you? Rugby, baillez me some paper. Tarry you a little-a-while. [*Writes*]

QUICKLY. [*Aside to* SIMPLE] I am glad he is so quiet; if he had been throughly moved, you should have heard him so loud and so melancholy. But notwithstanding, man, I'll do you your master what good I can; and the very yea and the no is, the French doctor, my master—I may call him my master, look you, for I keep his house; and I wash, wring, brew, bake, scour, dress meat and drink, make the beds, and do all myself—

SIMPLE. [*Aside to* QUICKLY] 'Tis a great charge to come under one body's hand.

QUICKLY. [*Aside to* SIMPLE] Are you avis'd o' that? You shall find it a great charge; and to be up early and down late; but notwithstanding—to tell you in your ear, I would have no words of it—my master himself is in love with Mistress Anne Page; but notwithstanding that, I know Anne's mind—that's neither here nor there.

CAIUS. You jack'nape; give-a this letter to Sir Hugh; by gar, it is a shallenge; I will cut his troat in de park; and I will teach a scurvy jack-a-nape priest to meddle or make. You may be gone; it is not good you tarry here. By gar, I will cut all his two stones; by gar, he shall not have a stone to throw at his dog. *Exit* SIMPLE

QUICKLY. Alas, he speaks but for his friend.

CAIUS. It is no matter-a ver dat. Do not you tell-a me dat I shall have Anne Page for myself? By gar, I vill kill de Jack priest; and I have appointed mine host of de Jarteer to measure our weapon. By gar, I will myself have Anne Page.

QUICKLY. Sir, the maid loves you, and all shall be well. We must give folks leave to prate. What the good-year!

CAIUS. Rugby, come to the court with me. By gar, if I have

not Anne Page, I shall turn your head out of my door.
Follow my heels, Rugby.   *Exeunt* Caius *and* Rugby
Quickly. You shall have—An fool's-head of your own. No,
I know Anne's mind for that; never a woman in Windsor
knows more of Anne's mind than I do; nor can do more
than I do with her, I thank heaven.
Fenton. [*Within*] Who's within there? ho!
Quickly. Who's there, I trow? Come near the house, I pray
you.
Enter Fenton

Fenton. How now, good woman, how dost thou?
Quickly. The better that it pleases your good worship to
ask.
Fenton. What news? How does pretty Mistress Anne?
Quickly. In truth, sir, and she is pretty, and honest, and
gentle; and one that is your friend, I can tell you that by
the way; I praise heaven for it.
Fenton. Shall I do any good, think'st thou? Shall I not lose
my suit?
Quickly. Troth, sir, all is in His hands above; but notwithstanding, Master Fenton, I'll be sworn on a book she loves
you. Have not your worship a wart above your eye?
Fenton. Yes, marry, have I; what of that?
Quickly. Well, thereby hangs a tale; good faith, it is such
another Nan; but, I detest, an honest maid as ever broke
bread. We had an hour's talk of that wart; I shall never
laugh but in that maid's company! But, indeed, she is
given too much to allicholy and musing; but for you—well,
go to.
Fenton. Well, I shall see her to-day. Hold, there's money
for thee; let me have thy voice in my behalf. If thou seest
her before me, commend me.
Quickly. Will I? I'faith, that we will; and I will tell your
worship more of the wart the next time we have confidence; and of other wooers.
Fenton. Well, farewell; I am in great haste now.
Quickly. Farewell to your worship. [*Exit* Fenton] Truly,
an honest gentleman; but Anne loves him not; for I know
Anne's mind as well as another does. Out upon 't, what
have I forgot?   *Exit*

161

ACT II. SCENE 1

Before PAGE'S *house*

Enter MISTRESS PAGE, *with a letter*

MRS. PAGE. What! have I scap'd love-letters in the holiday-time of my beauty, and am I now a subject for them? Let me see.   [*Reads*]

'Ask me no reason why I love you; for though Love use Reason for his precisian, he admits him not for his counsellor. You are not young, no more am I; go to, then, there's sympathy. You are merry, so am I; ha! ha! then there's more sympathy. You love sack, and so do I; would you desire better sympathy? Let it suffice thee, Mistress Page—at the least, if the love of soldier can suffice—that I love thee. I will not say, Pity me: 'tis not a soldier-like phrase; but I say, Love me. By me,

> Thine own true knight,
> By day or night,
> Or any kind of light,
> With all his might,
> For thee to fight,
>   JOHN FALSTAFF.'

What a Herod of Jewry is this! O wicked, wicked world! One that is well-nigh worn to pieces with age to show himself a young gallant! What an unweighed behaviour hath this Flemish drunkard pick'd—with the devil's name! —out of my conversation, that he dares in this manner assay me? Why, he hath not been thrice in my company! What should I say to him? I was then frugal of my mirth. Heaven forgive me! Why, I'll exhibit a bill in the parliament for the putting down of men. How shall I be reveng'd on him? for reveng'd I will be, as sure as his guts are made of puddings.

Enter MISTRESS FORD

MRS. FORD. Mistress Page! trust me, I was going to your house.

MRS. PAGE. And, trust me, I was coming to you. You look very ill.

MRS. FORD. Nay, I'll ne'er believe that; I have to show to the contrary.

MRS. PAGE. Faith, but you do, in my mind.

MRS. FORD. Well, I do, then; yet, I say, I could show you to the contrary. O Mistress Page, give me some counsel.

MRS. PAGE. What's the matter, woman?

MRS. FORD. O woman, if it were not for one trifling respect, I could come to such honour!

MRS. PAGE. Hang the trifle, woman; take the honour. What is it? Dispense with trifles; what is it?

MRS. FORD. If I would but go to hell for an eternal moment or so, I could be knighted.

MRS. PAGE. What? Thou liest. Sir Alice Ford! These knights will hack; and so thou shouldst not alter the article of thy gentry.

MRS. FORD. We burn daylight. Here, read, read; perceive how I might be knighted. I shall think the worse of fat men as long as I have an eye to make difference of men's liking. And yet he would not swear; prais'd women's modesty, and gave such orderly and well-behaved reproof to all uncomeliness that I would have sworn his disposition would have gone to the truth of his words; but they do no more adhere and keep place together than the Hundredth Psalm to the tune of 'Greensleeves.' What tempest, I trow, threw this whale, with so many tuns of oil in his belly, ashore at Windsor? How shall I be revenged on him? I think the best way were to entertain him with hope, till the wicked fire of lust have melted him in his own grease. Did you ever hear the like?

MRS. PAGE. Letter for letter, but that the name of Page and Ford differs. To thy great comfort in this mystery of ill opinions, here's the twin-brother of thy letter; but let thine inherit first, for, I protest, mine never shall. I warrant he hath a thousand of these letters, writ with blank space for different names—sure, more!—and these are of the second edition. He will print them, out of doubt; for he cares not what he puts into the press when he would put us two. I had rather be a giantess and lie under Mount Pelion. Well,

I will find you twenty lascivious turtles ere one chaste
man.

MRS. FORD. Why, this is the very same; the very hand, the
very words. What doth he think of us?

MRS. PAGE. Nay, I know not; it makes me almost ready to
wrangle with mine own honesty. I'll entertain myself like
one that I am not acquainted withal; for, sure, unless he
know some strain in me that I know not myself, he would
never have boarded me in this fury.

MRS. FORD. 'Boarding' call you it? I'll be sure to keep him
above deck.

MRS. PAGE. So will I; if he come under my hatches, I'll never
to sea again. Let's be reveng'd on him; let's appoint him a
meeting, give him a show of comfort in his suit, and lead
him on with a fine-baited delay, till he hath pawn'd his
horses to mine host of the Garter.

MRS. FORD. Nay, I will consent to act any villainy against
him that may not sully the chariness of our honesty. O
that my husband saw this letter! It would give eternal food
to his jealousy.

MRS. PAGE. Why, look where he comes; and my good man
too; he's as far from jealousy as I am from giving him
cause; and that, I hope, is an unmeasurable distance.

MRS. FORD. You are the happier woman.

MRS. PAGE. Let's consult together against this greasy knight.
Come hither. [*They retire*]

Enter FORD *with* PISTOL, *and* PAGE *with* NYM

FORD. Well, I hope it be not so.

PISTOL. Hope is a curtal dog in some affairs.
Sir John affects thy wife.

FORD. Why, sir, my wife is not young.

PISTOL. He woos both high and low, both rich and poor,
Both young and old, one with another, Ford;
He loves the gallimaufry. Ford, perpend.

FORD. Love my wife!

PISTOL. With liver burning hot. Prevent, or go thou,
Like Sir Actæon he, with Ringwood at thy heels.
O, odious is the name!

FORD. What name, sir?

PISTOL. The horn, I say. Farewell.
Take heed, have open eye, for thieves do foot by night;
Take heed, ere summer comes, or cuckoo birds do sing.
Away, Sir Corporal Nym.
Believe it, Page; he speaks sense. *Exit* PISTOL

FORD. [*Aside*] I will be patient; I will find out this.

NYM. [*To* PAGE] And this is true; I like not the humour of lying. He hath wronged me in some humours; I should have borne the humour'd letter to her; but I have a sword, and it shall bite upon my necessity. He loves your wife; there's the short and the long.
My name is Corporal Nym; I speak, and I avouch;
'Tis true. My name is Nym, and Falstaff loves your wife. Adieu! I love not the humour of bread and cheese; and there's the humour of it. Adieu. *Exit* NYM

PAGE. 'The humour of it,' quoth 'a! Here's a fellow frights English out of his wits.

FORD. I will seek out Falstaff.

PAGE. I never heard such a drawling, affecting rogue.

FORD. If I do find it—well.

PAGE. I will not believe such a Cataian though the priest o' th' town commended him for a true man.

FORD. 'Twas a good sensible fellow. Well.

MISTRESS PAGE and MISTRESS FORD *come forward*

PAGE. How now, Meg!

MRS. PAGE. Whither go you, George? Hark you.

MRS. FORD. How now, sweet Frank, why art thou melancholy?

FORD. I melancholy! I am not melancholy. Get you home; go.

MRS. FORD. Faith, thou hast some crotchets in thy head now. Will you go, Mistress Page?

Enter MISTRESS QUICKLY

MRS. PAGE. Have with you. You'll come to dinner, George? [*Aside to* MRS. FORD] Look who comes yonder; she shall be our messenger to this paltry knight.

MRS. FORD. [*Aside to* MRS. PAGE] Trust me, I thought on her; she'll fit it.

MRS. PAGE. You are come to see my daughter Anne?

QUICKLY. Ay, forsooth; and, I pray, how does good Mistress Anne?

MRS. PAGE. Go in with us and see; we have an hour's talk with you.   *Exeunt* MISTRESS PAGE, MISTRESS FORD, *and* MISTRESS QUICKLY

PAGE. How now, Master Ford!

FORD. You heard what this knave told me, did you not?

PAGE. Yes; and you heard what the other told me?

FORD. Do you think there is truth in them?

PAGE. Hang 'em, slaves! I do not think the knight would offer it; but these that accuse him in his intent towards our wives are a yoke of his discarded men; very rogues, now they be out of service.

FORD. Were they his men?

PAGE. Marry, were they.

FORD. I like it never the better for that. Does he lie at the Garter?

PAGE. Ay, marry, does he. If he should intend this voyage toward my wife, I would turn her loose to him; and what he gets more of her than sharp words, let it lie on my head.

FORD. I do not misdoubt my wife; but I would be loath to turn them together. A man may be too confident. I would have nothing lie on my head. I cannot be thus satisfied.

Enter HOST

PAGE. Look where my ranting host of the Garter comes. There is either liquor in his pate or money in his purse when he looks so merrily. How now, mine host!

HOST. How now, bully rook! Thou'rt a gentleman. [*To* SHALLOW *following*] Cavaleiro Justice, I say.

Enter SHALLOW

SHALLOW. I follow, mine host, I follow. Good even and twenty, good Master Page! Master Page, will you go with us? We have sport in hand.

HOST. Tell him, Cavaleiro Justice; tell him, bully rook.

SHALLOW. Sir, there is a fray to be fought between Sir Hugh the Welsh priest and Caius the French doctor.

FORD. Good mine host o' th' Garter, a word with you.

HOST. What say'st thou, my bully rook? [*They go aside*]

SHALLOW. [*To* PAGE] Will you go with us to behold it? My merry host hath had the measuring of their weapons; and, I think, hath appointed them contrary places; for, believe me, I hear the parson is no jester. Hark, I will tell you what our sport shall be. [*They converse apart*]

HOST. Hast thou no suit against my knight, my guest-cavaleiro.

FORD. None, I protest; but I'll give you a pottle of burnt sack to give me recourse to him, and tell him my name is Brook—only for a jest.

HOST. My hand, bully; thou shalt have egress and regress—said I well?—and thy name shall be Brook. It is a merry knight. Will you go, Mynheers?

SHALLOW. Have with you, mine host.

PAGE. I have heard the Frenchman hath good skill in his rapier.

SHALLOW. Tut, sir, I could have told you more. In these times you stand on distance, your passes, stoccadoes, and I know not what. 'Tis the heart, Master Page; 'tis here, 'tis here. I have seen the time with my long sword I would have made you four tall fellows skip like rats.

HOST. Here, boys, here, here! Shall we wag?

PAGE. Have with you. I had rather hear them scold than fight. *Exeunt all but* FORD

FORD. Though Page be a secure fool, and stands so firmly on his wife's frailty, yet I cannot put off my opinion so easily. She was in his company at Page's house, and what they made there I know not. Well, I will look further into 't, and I have a disguise to sound Falstaff. If I find her honest, I lose not my labour; if she be otherwise, 'tis labour well bestowed. *Exit*

SCENE 2

A room in the Garter Inn

Enter FALSTAFF *and* PISTOL

FALSTAFF. I will not lend thee a penny.

PISTOL. I will retort the sum in equipage.

FALSTAFF. Not a penny.

PISTOL. Why, then the world's mine oyster. Which I with sword will open.

FALSTAFF. Not a penny. I have been content, sir, you should lay my countenance to pawn. I have grated upon my good friends for three reprieves for you and your coach-fellow, Nym; or else you had look'd through the grate, like a geminy of baboons. I am damn'd in hell for swearing to gentlemen my friends you were good soldiers and tall fellows; and when Mistress Bridget lost the handle of her fan, I took 't upon mine honour thou hadst it not.

PISTOL. Didst not thou share? Hadst thou not fifteen pence?

FALSTAFF. Reason, you rogue, reason. Think'st thou I'll endanger my soul gratis? At a word, hang no more about me, I am no gibbet for you. Go—a short knife and a throng!— to your manor of Pickt-hatch; go. You'll not bear a letter for me, you rogue! You stand upon your honour! Why, thou unconfinable baseness, it is as much as I can do to keep the terms of my honour precise. I, I, I myself sometimes, leaving the fear of God on the left hand, and hiding mine honour in my necessity, am fain to shuffle, to hedge, and to lurch; and yet you, rogue, will ensconce your rags, your cat-a-mountain looks, your red-lattice phrases, and your bold-beating oaths, under the shelter of your honour! You will not do it, you!

PISTOL. I do relent; what would thou more of man?

Enter ROBIN

ROBIN. Sir, here's a woman would speak with you.

FALSTAFF. Let her approach.

Enter MISTRESS QUICKLY

QUICKLY. Give your worship good morrow.

FALSTAFF. Good morrow, good wife.

QUICKLY. Not so, an't please your worship.

FALSTAFF. Good maid, then.

QUICKLY. I'll be sworn;
As my mother was, the first hour I was born.

FALSTAFF. I do believe the swearer. What with me?

QUICKLY. Shall I vouchsafe your worship a word or two?

FALSTAFF. Two thousand, fair woman; and I'll vouchsafe
thee the hearing.

QUICKLY. There is one Mistress Ford, sir—I pray, come a little nearer this ways. I myself dwell with Master Doctor
Caius.

FALSTAFF. Well, on: Mistress Ford, you say—

QUICKLY. Your worship says very true. I pray your worship
come a little nearer this ways.

FALSTAFF. I warrant thee nobody hears—mine own people,
mine own people.

QUICKLY. Are they so? God bless them, and make them his
servants!

FALSTAFF. Well; Mistress Ford, what of her?

QUICKLY. Why, sir, she's a good creature. Lord, Lord, your
worship's a wanton! Well, heaven forgive you, and all of
us, I pray.

FALSTAFF. Mistress Ford; come, Mistress Ford—

QUICKLY. Marry, this is the short and the long of it: you
have brought her into such a canaries as 'tis wonderful.
The best courtier of them all, when the court lay at Windsor, could never have brought her to such a canary. Yet
there has been knights, and lords, and gentlemen, with
their coaches; I warrant you, coach after coach, letter after
letter, gift after gift; smelling so sweetly, all musk, and so
rushling, I warrant you, in silk and gold; and in such alli-
gant terms; and in such wine and sugar of the best and the
fairest, that would have won any woman's heart; and I
warrant you, they could never get an eye-wink of her.
I had myself twenty angels given me this morning; but I
defy all angels, in any such sort, as they say, but in the
way of honesty; and, I warrant you, they could never get
her so much as sip on a cup with the proudest of them all;
and yet there has been earls, nay, which is more, pensioners; but, I warrant you, all is one with her.

FALSTAFF. But what says she to me? Be brief, my good she-
Mercury.

QUICKLY. Marry, she hath receiv'd your letter; for the
which she thanks you a thousand times; and she gives you

to notify that her husband will be absence from his house between ten and eleven.

FALSTAFF. Ten and eleven?

QUICKLY. Ay, forsooth; and then you may come and see the picture, she says, that you wot of. Master Ford, her husband, will be from home. Alas, the sweet woman leads an ill life with him! He's a very jealousy man; she leads a very frampold life with him, good heart.

FALSTAFF. Ten and eleven. Woman, commend me to her; I will not fail her.

QUICKLY. Why, you say well. But I have another messenger to your worship. Mistress Page hath her hearty commendations to you too; and let me tell you in your ear, she's as fartuous a civil modest wife, and one, I tell you, that will not miss you morning nor evening prayer, as any is in Windsor, whoe'er be the other; and she bade me tell your worship that her husband is seldom from home, but she hopes there will come a time. I never knew a woman so dote upon a man: surely I think you have charms, la! Yes, in truth.

FALSTAFF. Not I, I assure thee; setting the attraction of my good parts aside, I have no other charms.

QUICKLY. Blessing on your heart for 't!

FALSTAFF. But, I pray thee, tell me this: has Ford's wife and Page's wife acquainted each other how they love me?

QUICKLY. That were a jest indeed! They have not so little grace, I hope—that were a trick indeed! But Mistress Page would desire you to send her your little page of all loves. Her husband has a marvellous infection to the little page; and truly Master Page is an honest man. Never a wife in Windsor leads a better life than she does; do what she will, say what she will, take all, pay all, go to bed when she list, rise when she list, all is as she will; and truly she deserves it; for if there be a kind woman in Windsor, she is one. You must send her your page; no remedy.

FALSTAFF. Why, I will.

QUICKLY. Nay, but do so then; and, look you, he may come and go between you both; and in any case have a nayword, that you may know one another's mind, and the boy never need to understand any thing; for 'tis not good that children should know any wickedness. Old folks, you know, have discretion, as they say, and know the world.

FALSTAFF. Fare thee well; commend me to them both. There's my purse; I am yet thy debtor. Boy, go along with this woman. [*Exeunt* QUICKLY *and* ROBIN] This news distracts me.

PISTOL. [*Aside*] This punk is one of Cupid's carriers;
Clap on more sails; pursue; up with your fights;
Give fire; she is my prize, or ocean whelm them all!   *Exit*

FALSTAFF. Say'st thou so, old Jack; go thy ways; I'll make more of thy old body than I have done. Will they yet look after thee? Wilt thou, after the expense of so much money, be now a gainer? Good body, I thank thee. Let them say 'tis grossly done; so it be fairly done, no matter.

Enter BARDOLPH

BARDOLPH. Sir John, there's one Master Brook below would fain speak with you, and be acquainted with you; and hath sent your worship a morning's draught of sack.

FALSTAFF. Brook is his name?

BARDOLPH. Ay, sir.

FALSTAFF. Call him in. [*Exit* BARDOLPH] Such Brooks are welcome to me, that o'erflows such liquor. Ah, ha! Mistress Ford and Mistress Page, have I encompass'd you? Go to; via!

Re-enter BARDOLPH, *with* FORD *disguised*

FORD. Bless you, sir!

FALSTAFF. And you, sir! Would you speak with me?

FORD. I make bold to press with so little preparation upon you.

FALSTAFF. You're welcome. What's your will? Give us leave, drawer.   *Exit* BARDOLPH

FORD. Sir, I am a gentleman that have spent much; my name is Brook.

FALSTAFF. Good Master Brook, I desire more acquaintance of you.

FORD. Good Sir John, I sue for yours—not to charge you; for I must let you understand I think myself in better plight for a lender than you are; the which hath something em-bold'ned me to this unseason'd intrusion; for they say, if money go before, all ways do lie open.

FALSTAFF. Money is a good soldier, sir, and will on.

FORD. Troth, and I have a bag of money here troubles me; if you will help to bear it, Sir John, take all, or half, for easing me of the carriage.

FALSTAFF. Sir, I know not how I may deserve to be your porter.

FORD. I will tell you, sir, if you will give me the hearing.

FALSTAFF. Speak, good Master Brook; I shall be glad to be your servant.

FORD. Sir, I hear you are a scholar—I will be brief with you —and you have been a man long known to me, though I had never so good means as desire to make myself acquainted with you. I shall discover a thing to you, wherein I must very much lay open mine own imperfection; but, good Sir John, as you have one eye upon my follies, as you hear them unfolded, turn another into the register of your own, that I may pass with a reproof the easier, sith you yourself know how easy is it to be such an offender.

FALSTAFF. Very well, sir; proceed.

FORD. There is a gentlewoman in this town, her husband's name is Ford.

FALSTAFF. Well, sir.

FORD. I have long lov'd her, and, I protest to you, bestowed much on her; followed her with a doting observance; engross'd opportunities to meet her; fee'd every slight occasion that could but niggardly give me sight of her; not only bought many presents to give her, but have given largely to many to know what she would have given; briefly, I have pursu'd her as love hath pursued me; which hath been on the wing of all occasions. But whatsoever I have merited, either in my mind or in my means, meed, I am sure, I have received none, unless experience be a jewel; that I have purchased at an infinite rate, and that hath taught me to say this:
'Love like a shadow flies when substance love pursues;
Pursuing that that flies, and flying what pursues.'

FALSTAFF. Have you receiv'd no promise of satisfaction at her hands?

Ford. Never.

Falstaff. Have you importun'd her to such a purpose?

Ford. Never.

Falstaff. Of what quality was your love, then?

Ford. Like a fair house built on another man's ground; so that I have lost my edifice by mistaking the place where I erected it.

Falstaff. To what purpose have you unfolded this to me?

Ford. When I have told you that, I have told you all. Some say that though she appear honest to me, yet in other places she enlargeth her mirth so far that there is shrewd construction made of her. Now, Sir John, here is the heart of my purpose: you are a gentleman of excellent breeding, admirable discourse, of great admittance, authentic in your place and person, generally allow'd for your many war-like, courtlike, and learned preparations.

Falstaff. O, sir!

Ford. Believe it, for you know it. There is money; spend it, spend it; spend more; spend all I have; only give me so much of your time in exchange of it as to lay an amiable siege to the honesty of this Ford's wife; use your art of wooing, win her to consent to you; if any man may, you may as soon as any.

Falstaff. Would it apply well to the vehemency of your affection, that I should win what you would enjoy? Methinks you prescribe to yourself very preposterously.

Ford. O, understand my drift. She dwells so securely on the excellency of her honour that the folly of my soul dares not present itself; she is too bright to be look'd against. Now, could I come to her with any detection in my hand, my desires had instance and argument to commend themselves; I could drive her then from the ward of her purity, her reputation, her marriage vow, and a thousand other her defences, which now are too too strongly embattl'd against me. What say you to't, Sir John?

Falstaff. Master Brook, I will first make bold with your money; next, give me your hand; and last, as I am a gentleman, you shall, if you will, enjoy Ford's wife.

Ford. O good sir!

Falstaff. I say you shall.

FORD. Want no money, Sir John; you shall want none.

FALSTAFF. Want no Mistress Ford, Master Brook; you shall want none. I shall be with her, I may tell you, by her own appointment; even as you came in to me her assistant, or go-between, parted from me; I say I shall be with her between ten and eleven; for at that time the jealous rascally knave, her husband, will be forth. Come you to me at night; you shall know how I speed.

FORD. I am blest in your acquaintance. Do you know Ford, Sir?

FALSTAFF. Hang him, poor cuckoldly knave! I know him not; yet I wrong him to call him poor; they say the jealous wittolly knave hath masses of money; for the which his wife seems to me well-favour'd. I will use her as the key of the cuckoldly rogue's coffer; and there's my harvest-home.

FORD. I would you knew Ford, sir, that you might avoid him if you saw him.

FALSTAFF. Hang him, mechanical salt-butter rogue! I will stare him out of his wits; I will awe him with my cudgel; it shall hang like a meteor o'er the cuckold's horns. Master Brook, thou shalt know I will predominate over the peasant, and thou shalt lie with his wife. Come to me soon at night. Ford's a knave, and I will aggravate his style; thou, Master Brook, shalt know him for knave and cuckold. Come to me soon at night. *Exit*

FORD. What a damn'd Epicurean rascal is this! My heart is ready to crack with impatience. Who says this is improvident jealousy? My wife hath sent to him; the hour is fix'd; the match is made. Would any man have thought this? See the hell of having a false woman! My bed shall be abus'd, my coffers ransack'd, my reputation gnawn at; and I shall not only receive this villainous wrong, but stand under the adoption of abominable terms, and by him that does me this wrong. Terms! names! Amaimon sounds well; Lucifer, well; Barbason, well; yet they are devils' additions, the names of fiends. But cuckold! Wittol! Cuckold! the devil himself hath not such a name. Page is an ass, a secure ass; he will trust his wife; he will not be jealous; I will rather trust a Fleming with my butter, Parson Hugh the Welshman with my

cheese, an Irishman with my aqua-vitæ bottle, or a thief to
walk my ambling gelding, than my wife with herself. Then
she plots, then she ruminates, then she devises; and what
they think in their hearts they may effect, they will break
their hearts but they will effect. God be prais'd for my
jealousy! Eleven o'clock the hour. I will prevent this, detect my wife, be reveng'd on Falstaff, and laugh at Page.
I will about it; better three hours too soon than a minute
too late. Fie, fie, fie! cuckold! cuckold! cuckold! *Exit*

SCENE 3

A field near Windsor

Enter CAIUS *and* RUGBY

CAIUS. Jack Rugby!
RUGBY. Sir?
CAIUS. Vat is de clock, Jack?
RUGBY. 'Tis past the hour, sir, that Sir Hugh promis'd to
meet.
CAIUS. By gar, he has save his soul dat he is no come; he has
pray his Pible well dat he is no come; by gar, Jack Rugby,
he is dead already, if he be come.
RUGBY. He is wise, sir; he knew your worship would kill
him if he came.
CAIUS. By gar, de herring is no dead so as I vill kill him. Take
your rapier, Jack; I vill tell you how I vill kill him.
RUGBY. Alas, sir, I cannot fence!
CAIUS. Villainy, take your rapier.
RUGBY. Forbear; here's company.

Enter HOST, SHALLOW, SLENDER, *and* PAGE

HOST. Bless thee, bully doctor!
SHALLOW. Save you, Master Doctor Caius!
PAGE. Now, good Master Doctor!
SLENDER. Give you good morrow, sir.
CAIUS. Vat be all you, one, two, tree, four, come for?
HOST. To see thee fight, to see thee foin, to see thee traverse;
to see thee here, to see thee there; to see thee pass thy

punto, thy stock, thy reverse, thy distance, thy montant.
Is he dead, my Ethiopian? Is he dead, my Francisco? Ha,
bully! What says my Æsculapius? my Galen? my heart
of elder? Ha! is he dead, bully stale? Is he dead?

CAIUS. By gar, he is de coward Jack priest of de vorld; he is
not show his face.

HOST. Thou art a Castalion-King-Urinal. Hector of Greece,
my boy!

CAIUS. I pray you, bear witness that me have stay six or
seven, two tree hours for him, and he is no come.

SHALLOW. He is the wiser man, Master Doctor: he is a curer
of souls, and you a curer of bodies; if you should fight,
you go against the hair of your professions. Is it not true,
Master Page?

PAGE. Master Shallow, you have yourself been a great fighter,
though now a man of peace.

SHALLOW. Bodykins, Master Page, though I now be old, and
of the peace, if I see a sword out, my finger itches to make
one. Though we are justices, and doctors, and churchmen,
Master Page, we have some salt of our youth in us; we are
the sons of women, Master Page.

PAGE. 'Tis true, Master Shallow.

SHALLOW. It will be found so, Master Page. Master Doctor
Caius, I come to fetch you home. I am sworn of the peace;
you have show'd yourself a wise physician, and Sir Hugh
hath shown himself a wise and patient churchman. You
must go with me, Master Doctor.

HOST. Pardon, Guest Justice. A word, Mounseur Mockwater.

CAIUS. Mock-vater! Vat is dat?

HOST. Mockwater, in our English tongue, is valour, bully.

CAIUS. By gar, then I have as much mockvater as de Englishman. Scurvy jack-dog priest! By gar, me vill cut his ears.

HOST. He will clapper-claw thee tightly, bully.

CAIUS. Clapper-de-claw! Vat is dat?

HOST. That is, he will make thee amends.

CAIUS. By gar, me do look he shall clapper-de-claw me; for,
by gar, me vill have it.

HOST. And I will provoke him to't, or let him wag.

CAIUS. Me tank you for dat.

Host. And, moreover, bully—but first: [*Aside to the others*] Master Guest, and Master Page, and eke Cavaleiro Slender, go you through the town to Frogmore.

Page. [*Aside*] Sir Hugh is there, is he?

Host. [*Aside*] He is there. See what humour he is in; and I will bring the doctor about by the fields. Will it do well?

Shallow. [*Aside*] We will do it.

Page, Shallow, *and* Slender. Adieu, good Master Doctor.

Exeunt Page, Shallow, *and* Slender

Caius. By gar, me vill kill de priest; for he speak for a jack-an-ape to Anne Page.

Host. Let him die. Sheathe thy impatience; throw cold water on thy choler; go about the fields with me through Frogmore; I will bring thee where Mistress Anne Page is, at a farm-house, a-feasting; and thou shalt woo her. Cried game! Said I well?

Caius. By gar, me dank you vor dat; by gar, I love you; and I shall procure-a you de good guest, de earl, de knight, de lords, de gentlemen, my patients.

Host. For the which I will be thy adversary toward Anne Page. Said I well?

Caius. By gar, 'tis good; vell said.

Host. Let us wag, then.

Caius. Come at my heels, Jack Rugby.   *Exeunt*

ACT III. SCENE 1

A field near Frogmore

Enter Sir Hugh Evans *and* Simple

Evans. I pray you now, good Master Slender's serving-man, and friend Simple by your name, which way have you look'd for Master Caius, that calls himself Doctor of Physic?

Simple. Marry, sir, the pittie-ward, the park-ward; every way; old Windsor way, and every way but the town way.

EVANS. I most fehemently desire you you will also look that way.

SIMPLE. I will, sir. *Exit*

EVANS. Pless my soul, how full of chollors I am, and trempling of mind! I shall be glad if he have deceived me. How melancholies I am! I will knog his urinals about his knave's costard when I have goot opportunities for the ork. Pless my soul! *[Sings]*

> To shallow rivers, to whose falls
> Melodious birds sings madrigals;
> There will we make our peds of roses,
> And a thousand fragrant posies.
> To shallow—

Mercy on me! I have a great dispositions to cry. *[Sings]*

> Melodious birds sing madrigals—
> Whenas I sat in Pabylon—
> And a thousand vagram posies.
> To shallow, etc.

Re-enter SIMPLE

SIMPLE. Yonder he is, coming this way, Sir Hugh.

EVANS. He's welcome. *[Sings]*

> To shallow rivers, to whose falls—

Heaven prosper the right! What weapons is he?

SIMPLE. No weapons, sir. There comes my master, Master Shallow, and another gentleman, from Frogmore, over the stile, this way.

EVANS. Pray you give me my gown; or else keep it in your arms. *[Takes out a book]*

Enter PAGE, SHALLOW, *and* SLENDER

SHALLOW. How now, Master Parson! Good morrow, good Sir Hugh. Keep a gamester from the dice, and a good student from his book, and it is wonderful.

SLENDER. *[Aside]* Ah, sweet Anne Page!

PAGE. Save you, good Sir Hugh!

EVANS. Pless you from his mercy sake, all of you!

SHALLOW. What, the sword and the word! Do you study
them both, Master Parson?

PAGE. And youthful still, in your doublet and hose, this raw
rheumatic day!

EVANS. There is reasons and causes for it.

PAGE. We are come to you to do a good office, Master Parson.

EVANS. Fery well; what is it?

PAGE. Yonder is a most reverend gentleman, who, belike having received wrong by some person, is at most odds with
his own gravity and patience that ever you saw.

SHALLOW. I have lived fourscore years and upward; I never
heard a man of his place, gravity, and learning, so wide of
his own respect.

EVANS. What is he?

PAGE. I think you know him: Master Doctor Caius, the renowned French physician.

EVANS. Got's will and his passion of my heart! I had as lief
you would tell me of a mess of porridge.

PAGE. Why?

EVANS. He has no more knowledge in Hibocrates and
Galen, and he is a knave besides—a cowardly knave as you
would desires to be acquainted withal.

PAGE. I warrant you, he's the man should fight with him.

SLENDER. [Aside] O sweet Anne Page!

SHALLOW. It appears so, by his weapons. Keep them asunder;
here comes Doctor Caius.

Enter HOST, CAIUS, *and* RUGBY

PAGE. Nay, good Master Parson, keep in your weapon.

SHALLOW. So do you, good Master Doctor.

HOST. Disarm them, and let them question; let them keep
their limbs whole and hack our English.

CAIUS. I pray you, let-a me speak a word with your ear.
Verefore will you not meet-a me?

EVANS. [Aside to CAIUS] Pray you use your patience; in
good time.

CAIUS. By gar, you are de coward, de Jack dog, John ape.

EVANS. [Aside to CAIUS] Pray you, let us not be laughing-
stocks to other men's humours; I desire you in friendship,

179

and I will one way or other make you amends. [*Aloud*] I will knog your urinals about your knave's cogscomb for missing your meetings and appointments.

CAIUS. Diable! Jack Rugby—mine Host de Jarteer—have I not stay for him to kill him? Have I not, at de place I did appoint?

EVANS. As I am a Christians soul, now, look you, this is the place appointed. I'll be judgment by mine host of the Garter.

HOST. Peace, I say, Gallia and Gaul, French and Welsh, soul-curer and body-curer.

CAIUS. Ay, dat is very good! excellent!

HOST. Peace, I say. Hear mine host of the Garter. Am I politic? am I subtle? am I a Machiavel? Shall I lose my doctor? No; he gives me the potions and the motions. Shall I lose my parson, my priest, my Sir Hugh? No; he gives me the proverbs and the noverbs. Give me thy hand, terrestrial; so. Give me thy hand, celestial; so. Boys of art, I have deceiv'd you both; I have directed you to wrong places; your hearts are mighty, your skins are whole, and let burnt sack be the issue. Come, lay their swords to pawn. Follow me, lads of peace; follow, follow, follow.

SHALLOW. Trust me, a mad host. Follow, gentlemen, follow.

SLENDER. [*Aside*] O sweet Anne Page!

Exeunt all but CAIUS *and* EVANS

CAIUS. Ha, do I perceive dat? Have you make-a de sot of us, ha, ha?

EVANS. This is well; he has made us his vlouting-stog. I desire you that we may be friends; and let us knog our prains together to be revenge on this same scall, scurvy, cogging companion, the host of the Garter.

CAIUS. By gar, with all my heart. He promise to bring me where is Anne Page; by gar, he deceive me too.

EVANS. Well, I will smite his noddles. Pray you follow.

Exeunt

SCENE 2

The street in Windsor

Enter MISTRESS PAGE *and* ROBIN

MRS. PAGE. Nay, keep your way, little gallant; you were wont to be a follower, but now you are a leader. Whether had you rather lead mine eyes, or eye your master's heels?

ROBIN. I had rather, forsooth, go before you like a man than follow him like a dwarf.

MRS. PAGE. O, you are a flattering boy; now I see you'll be a courtier.

Enter FORD

FORD. Well met, Mistress Page. Whither go you?

MRS. PAGE. Truly, sir, to see your wife. Is she at home?

FORD. Ay; and as idle as she may hang together, for want of company. I think, if your husbands were dead, you two would marry.

MRS. PAGE. Be sure of that—two other husbands.

FORD. Where had you this pretty weathercock?

MRS. PAGE. I cannot tell what the dickens his name is my husband had him of. What do you call your knight's name, sirrah?

ROBIN. Sir John Falstaff.

FORD. Sir John Falstaff!

MRS. PAGE. He, he; I can never hit on's name. There is such a league between my good man and he! Is your wife at home indeed?

FORD. Indeed she is.

MRS. PAGE. By your leave, sir. I am sick till I see her.

Exeunt MRS. PAGE *and* ROBIN

FORD. Has Page any brains? Hath he any eyes? Hath he any thinking? Sure, they sleep; he hath no use of them. Why, this boy will carry a letter twenty mile as easy as a cannon will shoot pointblank twelve score. He pieces out his wife's inclination; he gives her folly motion and advantage; and now she's going to my wife, and Falstaff's boy with her. A man may hear this show'r sing in the wind. And Falstaff's boy with her! Good plots! They are laid; and our revolted wives share damnation together. Well; I will take him, then torture my wife, pluck the borrowed veil of modesty from the so seeming Mistress Page, divulge Page himself for a secure and wilful Actæon; and to these violent proceedings all my neighbours shall cry aim. [*Clock strikes*] The clock gives me my cue, and my assurance bids me search; there I shall find Falstaff. I shall be rather prais'd for this than mock'd; for it is as positive as the earth is firm that Falstaff is there. I will go.

Enter PAGE, SHALLOW, SLENDER, HOST, SIR HUGH EVANS, CAIUS, *and* RUGBY

SHALLOW, PAGE, &c. Well met, Master Ford.

FORD. Trust me, a good knot; I have good cheer at home, and I pray you all go with me.

SHALLOW. I must excuse myself, Master Ford.

SLENDER. And so must I, sir; we have appointed to dine with Mistress Anne, and I would not break with her for more money than I'll speak of.

SHALLOW. We have linger'd about a match between Anne Page and my cousin Slender, and this day we shall have our answer.

SLENDER. I hope I have your good will, father Page.

PAGE. You have, Master Slender; I stand wholly for you. But my wife, Master Doctor, is for you altogether.

CAIUS. Ay, be-gar; and de maid is love-a me; my nursh-a Quickly tell me so mush.

HOST. What say you to young Master Fenton? He capers, he dances, he has eyes of youth, he writes verses, he speaks holiday, he smells April and May; he will carry 't, he will carry 't; 'tis in his buttons; he will carry 't.

PAGE. Not by my consent, I promise you. The gentleman is of no having: he kept company with the wild Prince and Poins; he is of too high a region, he knows too much. No, he shall not knit a knot in his fortunes with the finger of my substance; if he take her, let him take her simply; the wealth I have waits on my consent, and my consent goes not that way.

FORD. I beseech you, heartily, some of you go home with me

to dinner: besides your cheer, you shall have sport; I will show you a monster. Master Doctor, you shall go; so shall you, Master Page; and you, Sir Hugh.

SHALLOW. Well, fare you well; we shall have the freer wooing at Master Page's.   *Exeunt* SHALLOW *and* SLENDER

CAIUS. Go home, John Rugby; I come anon.   *Exit* RUGBY

HOST. Farewell, my hearts; I will to my honest knight Falstaff, and drink canary with him.   *Exit* HOST

FORD. [*Aside*] I think I shall drink in pipe-wine first with him. I'll make him dance. Will you go, gentles?

ALL. Have with you to see this monster.   *Exeunt*

SCENE 3

FORD's house

Enter MISTRESS FORD *and* MISTRESS PAGE

MRS. FORD. What, John! what, Robert!

MRS. PAGE. Quickly, quickly! Is the buck-basket—

MRS. FORD. I warrant. What, Robin, I say!

Enter SERVANTS *with a basket*

MRS. PAGE. Come, come, come.

MRS. FORD. Here, set it down.

MRS. PAGE. Give your men the charge; we must be brief.

MRS. FORD. Marry, as I told you before, John and Robert, be ready here hard by in the brew-house; and when I suddenly call you, come forth, and, without any pause or staggering, take this basket on your shoulders. That done, trudge with it in all haste, and carry it among the whitsters in Datchet Mead, and there empty it in the muddy ditch close by the Thames side.

MRS. PAGE. You will do it?

MRS. FORD. I ha' told them over and over; they lack no direction. Be gone, and come when you are call'd.

Exeunt SERVANTS

MRS. PAGE. Here comes little Robin.

Enter ROBIN

MRS. FORD. How now, my eyas-musket, what news with you?

ROBIN. My master Sir John is come in at your back-door, Mistress Ford, and requests your company.

MRS. PAGE. You little Jack-a-Lent, have you been true to us?

ROBIN. Ay, I'll be sworn. My master knows not of your being here, and hath threat'ned to put me into everlasting liberty, if I tell you of it; for he swears he'll turn me away.

MRS. PAGE. Thou 'rt a good boy; this secrecy of thine shall be a tailor to thee, and shall make thee a new doublet and hose. I'll go hide me.

MRS. FORD. Do so. Go tell thy master I am alone. [*Exit* ROBIN] Mistress Page, remember you your cue.

MRS. PAGE. I warrant thee; if I do not act it, hiss me.

Exit MRS. PAGE

MRS. FORD. Go to, then; we'll use this unwholesome humidity, this gross wat'ry pumpion; we'll teach him to know turtles from jays.

Enter FALSTAFF

FALSTAFF. Have I caught thee, my heavenly jewel?
Why, now let me die, for I have liv'd long enough; this is the period of my ambition. O this blessed hour!

MRS. FORD. O sweet Sir John!

FALSTAFF. Mistress Ford, I cannot cog, I cannot prate, Mistress Ford. Now shall I sin in my wish; I would thy husband were dead; I'll speak it before the best lord, I would make thee my lady.

MRS. FORD. I your lady, Sir John? Alas, I should be a pitiful lady.

FALSTAFF. Let the court of France show me such another. I see how thine eye would emulate the diamond; thou hast the right arched beauty of the brow that becomes the ship-tire, the tire-valiant, or any tire of Venetian admittance.

MRS. FORD. A plain kerchief, Sir John; my brows become nothing else, nor that well neither.

FALSTAFF. By the Lord, thou art a tyrant to say so; thou wouldst make an absolute courtier, and the firm fixture of thy foot would give an excellent motion to thy gait in a semi-circled farthingale. I see what thou wert, if Fortune thy foe were, not Nature, thy friend. Come, thou canst not hide it.

MRS. FORD. Believe me, there's no such thing in me.

FALSTAFF. What made me love thee? Let that persuade thee there's something extra-ordinary in thee. Come, I cannot cog, and say thou art this and that, like a many of these lisping hawthorn-buds that come like women in men's apparel, and smell like Bucklersbury in simple time; I cannot; but I love thee, none but thee; and thou deserv'st it.

MRS. FORD. Do not betray me, sir; I fear you love Mistress Page.

FALSTAFF. Thou mightst as well say I love to walk by the Counter-gate, which is as hateful to me as the reek of a lime-kiln.

MRS. FORD. Well, heaven knows how I love you; and you shall one day find it.

FALSTAFF. Keep in that mind; I'll deserve it.

MRS. FORD. Nay, I must tell you, so you do; or else I could not be in that mind.

ROBIN. [*Within*] Mistress Ford, Mistress Ford! here's Mistress Page at the door, sweating and blowing and looking wildly, and would needs speak with you presently.

FALSTAFF. She shall not see me; I will ensconce me behind the arras.

MRS. FORD. Pray you, do so; she's a very tattling woman.

[FALSTAFF *hides himself*]

Re-enter MISTRESS PAGE *and* ROBIN

What's the matter? How now!

MRS. PAGE. O Mistress Ford, what have you done? You're sham'd, y'are overthrown, y'are undone for ever.

MRS. FORD. What's the matter, good Mistress Page?

MRS. PAGE. O well-a-day, Mistress Ford, having an honest man to your husband, to give him such cause of suspicion!

MRS. FORD. What cause of suspicion?

MRS. PAGE. What cause of suspicion? Out upon you, how am I mistook in you!

MRS. FORD. Why, alas, what's the matter?

MRS. PAGE. Your husband's coming hither, woman, with all the officers in Windsor, to search for a gentleman that he says is here now in the house, by your consent, to take an ill advantage of his absence. You are undone.

MRS. FORD. 'Tis not so, I hope.

MRS. PAGE. Pray heaven it be not so that you have such a man here; but 'tis most certain your husband's coming, with half Windsor at his heels, to search for such a one. I come before to tell you. If you know yourself clear, why, I am glad of it; but if you have a friend here, convey, convey him out. Be not amaz'd; call all your senses to you; defend your reputation, or bid farewell to your good life for ever.

MRS. FORD. What shall I do? There is a gentleman, my dear friend; and I fear not mine own shame as much as his peril. I had rather than a thousand pound he were out of the house.

MRS. PAGE. For shame, never stand 'you had rather' and 'you had rather'! Your husband's here at hand; bethink you of some conveyance; in the house you cannot hide him. O, how have you deceiv'd me! Look, here is a basket; if he be of any reasonable stature, he may creep in here; and throw foul linen upon him, as if it were going to bucking, or—it is whiting-time—send him by your two men to Datchet Mead.

MRS. FORD. He's too big to go in there. What shall I do?

FALSTAFF. [Coming forward] Let me see 't, let me see 't. O, let me see 't! I'll in, I'll in; follow your friend's counsel; I'll in.

MRS. PAGE. What, Sir John Falstaff! [Aside to FALSTAFF] Are these your letters, knight?

FALSTAFF. [Aside to MRS. PAGE] I love thee and none but thee; help me away.—Let me creep in here; I'll never—

[Gets into the basket; they cover him with foul linen]

MRS. PAGE. Help to cover your master, boy. Call your men, Mistress Ford. You dissembling knight!

MRS. FORD. What, John! Robert! John!   Exit ROBIN

Re-enter SERVANTS

Go, take up these clothes here, quickly; where's the cowl-staff? Look how you drumble. Carry them to the laundress in Datchet Mead; quickly, come.

Enter FORD, PAGE, CAIUS, *and* SIR HUGH EVANS

FORD. Pray you come near. If I suspect without cause, why then make sport at me, then let me be your jest; I deserve it. How now, whither bear you this?

SERVANT. To the laundress, forsooth.

MRS. FORD. Why, what have you to do whither they bear it? You were best meddle with buck-washing.

FORD. Buck? I would I could wash myself of the buck! Buck, buck, buck! ay, buck! I warrant you, buck; and of the season too, it shall appear. [*Exeunt* SERVANTS *with basket*] Gentlemen, I have dream'd to-night; I'll tell you my dream. Here, here, here be my keys; ascend my chambers, search, seek, find out. I'll warrant we'll unkennel the fox. Let me stop this way first. [*Locking the door*] So, now uncape.

PAGE. Good Master Ford, be contented; you wrong yourself too much.

FORD. True, Master Page. Up, gentlemen, you shall see sport anon; follow me, gentlemen.   *Exit*

EVANS. This is fery fantastical humours and jealousies.

CAIUS. By gar, 'tis no the fashion of France; it is not jealous in France.

PAGE. Nay, follow him, gentlemen; see the issue of his search.   *Exeunt* EVANS, PAGE, *and* CAIUS

MRS. PAGE. Is there not a double excellency in this?

MRS. FORD. I know not which pleases me better, that my husband is deceived, or Sir John.

MRS. PAGE. What a taking was he in when your husband ask'd who was in the basket!

MRS. FORD. I am half afraid he will have need of washing; so throwing him into the water will do him a benefit.

MRS. PAGE. Hang him, dishonest rascal! I would all of the same strain were in the same distress.

MRS. FORD. I think my husband hath some special suspicion of Falstaff's being here, for I never saw him so gross in his jealousy till now.

MRS. PAGE. I will lay a plot to try that, and we will yet have more tricks with Falstaff. His dissolute disease will scarce obey this medicine.

MRS. FORD. Shall we send that foolish carrion, Mistress Quickly, to him, and excuse his throwing into the water, and give him another hope, to betray him to another punishment?

MRS. PAGE. We will do it; let him be sent for to-morrow eight o'clock, to have amends.

Re-enter FORD, PAGE, CAIUS, *and* SIR HUGH EVANS

FORD. I cannot find him; may be the knave bragg'd of that he could not compass.

MRS. PAGE. [*Aside to* MRS. FORD] Heard you that?

MRS. FORD. You use me well, Master Ford, do you?

FORD. Ay, I do so.

MRS. FORD. Heaven make you better than your thoughts!

FORD. Amen.

MRS. PAGE. You do yourself mighty wrong, Master Ford.

FORD. Ay, ay; I must bear it.

EVANS. If there be any pody in the house, and in the chambers, and in the coffers, and in the presses, heaven forgive my sins at the day of judgment!

CAIUS. Be gar, nor I too; there is no bodies.

PAGE. Fie, fie, Master Ford, are you not asham'd? What spirit, what devil suggests this imagination? I would not ha' your distemper in this kind for the wealth of Windsor Castle.

FORD. 'Tis my fault, Master Page; I suffer for it.

EVANS. You suffer for a pad conscience. Your wife is as honest a omans as I will desires among five thousand, and five hundred too.

CAIUS. By gar, I see 'tis an honest woman.

FORD. Well, I promis'd you a dinner. Come, come, walk in the Park. I pray you pardon me; I will hereafter make known to you why I have done this. Come, wife, come, Mistress Page; I pray you pardon me; pray heartly, pardon me.

PAGE. Let's go in, gentlemen; but, trust me, we'll mock him. I do invite you to-morrow morning to my house to breakfast; after, we'll a-birding together; I have a fine hawk for the bush. Shall it be so?

FORD. Any thing.

EVANS. If there is one, I shall make two in the company.
CAIUS. If there be one or two, I shall make-a the turd.
FORD. Pray you go, Master Page.
EVANS. I pray you now, remembrance to-morrow on the
lousy knave, mine host.
CAIUS. Dat is good; by gar, with all my heart.
EVANS. A lousy knave, to have his gibes and his mockeries!

Exeunt

SCENE 4

Before PAGE's *house*

Enter FENTON *and* ANNE PAGE

FENTON. I see I cannot get thy father's love;
  Therefore no more turn me to him, sweet Nan.
ANNE. Alas, how then?
FENTON. Why, thou must be thyself.
  He doth object I am too great of birth;
  And that, my state being gall'd with my expense,
  I seek to heal it only by his wealth.
  Besides these, other bars he lays before me,
  My riots past, my wild societies;
  And tells me 'tis a thing impossible
  I should love thee but as a property.
ANNE. May be he tells you true.
FENTON. No, heaven so speed me in my time to come!
  Albeit I will confess thy father's wealth
  Was the first motive that I woo'd thee, Anne;
  Yet, wooing thee, I found thee of more value
  Than stamps in gold, or sums in sealed bags;
  And 'tis the very riches of thyself
  That now I aim at.
ANNE. Gentle Master Fenton,
  Yet seek my father's love; still seek it, sir.
  If opportunity and humblest suit
  Cannot attain it, why then—hark you hither.

[*They converse apart*]

Enter SHALLOW, SLENDER, *and* MISTRESS QUICKLY

189

SHALLOW. Break their talk, Mistress Quickly; my kinsman shall speak for himself.

SLENDER. I'll make a shaft or a bolt on 't; 'slid, 'tis but venturing.

SHALLOW. Be not dismay'd.

SLENDER. No, she shall not dismay me. I care not for that, but that I am afeard.

QUICKLY. Hark ye, Master Slender would speak a word with you.

ANNE. I come to him. [*Aside*] This is my father's choice.
O, what a world of vile ill-favour'd faults
Looks handsome in three hundred pounds a year!

QUICKLY. And how does good Master Fenton? Pray you, a word with you.

SHALLOW. She's coming; to her, coz. O boy, thou hadst a father!

SLENDER. I had a father, Mistress Anne; my uncle can tell you good jests of him. Pray you, uncle, tell Mistress Anne the jest how my father stole two geese out of a pen, good uncle.

SHALLOW. Mistress Anne, my cousin loves you.

SLENDER. Ay, that I do; as well as I love any woman in Gloucestershire.

SHALLOW. He will maintain you like a gentlewoman.

SLENDER. Ay, that I will come cut and longtail, under the degree of a squire.

SHALLOW. He will make you a hundred and fifty pounds jointure.

ANNE. Good Master Shallow, let him woo for himself.

SHALLOW. Marry, I thank you for it; I thank you for that good comfort. She calls you, coz; I'll leave you.

ANNE. Now, Master Slender—

SLENDER. Now, good Mistress Anne—

ANNE. What is your will?

SLENDER. My will! 'Od's heartlings, that's a pretty jest indeed! I ne'er made my will yet, I thank heaven; I am not such a sickly creature, I give heaven praise.

ANNE. I mean, Master Slender, what would you with me?

SLENDER. Truly, for mine own part I would little or nothing with you. Your father and my uncle hath made motions;

if it be my luck, so; if not, happy man be his dole! They
can tell you how things go better than I can. You may ask
your father; here he comes.

Enter PAGE *and* MISTRESS PAGE

PAGE. Now, Master Slender! Love him, daughter Anne—
Why, how now, what does Master Fenton here?
You wrong me, sir, thus still to haunt my house.
I told you, sir, my daughter is dispos'd of.
FENTON. Nay, Master Page, be not impatient.
MRS. PAGE. Good Master Fenton, come not to my child.
PAGE. She is no match for you.
FENTON. Sir, will you hear me?
PAGE. No, good Master Fenton.
Come, Master Shallow; come, son Slender; in.
Knowing my mind, you wrong me, Master Fenton.
                    Exeunt PAGE, SHALLOW, *and* SLENDER
QUICKLY. Speak to Mistress Page.
FENTON. Good Mistress Page, for that I love your daughter
In such a righteous fashion as I do,
Perforce, against all checks, rebukes, and manners,
I must advance the colours of my love,
And not retire. Let me have your good will.
ANNE. Good mother, do not marry me to yond fool.
MRS. PAGE. I mean it not; I seek you a better husband.
QUICKLY. That's my master, Master Doctor.
ANNE. Alas, I had rather be set quick i' th' earth.
And bowl'd to death with turnips.
MRS. PAGE. Come, trouble not yourself. Good Master Fen-
ton,
I will not be your friend, nor enemy;
My daughter will I question how she loves you,
And as I find her, so am I affected;
Till then, farewell, sir; she must needs go in;
Her father will be angry.
FENTON. Farewell, gentle mistress; farewell, Nan.
                    Exeunt MRS. PAGE *and* ANNE
QUICKLY. This is my doing now: 'Nay,' said I 'will you cast
away your child on a fool, and a physician? Look on Mas-
ter Fenton.' This is my doing.

FENTON. I thank thee; and I pray thee, once to-night
Give my sweet Nan this ring. There's for thy pains.
QUICKLY. Now Heaven send thee good fortune! [*Exit* FEN-
TON] A kind heart he hath; a woman would run through
fire and water for such a kind heart. But yet I would my
master had Mistress Anne; or I would Master Slender had
her; or, in sooth, I would Master Fenton had her; I will
do what I can for them all three, for so I have promis'd,
and I'll be as good as my word; but speciously for Master
Fenton. Well, I must of another errand to Sir John Falstaff
from my two mistresses. What a beast am I to slack it!
Exit

SCENE 5

The Garter Inn

Enter FALSTAFF *and* BARDOLPH

FALSTAFF. Bardolph, I say!
BARDOLPH. Here, sir.
FALSTAFF. Go fetch me a quart of sack; put a toast in 't.
Exit BARDOLPH
Have I liv'd to be carried in a basket, like a barrow of
butcher's offal, and to be thrown in the Thames? Well, if
I be serv'd such another trick, I'll have my brains ta'en out
and butter'd, and give them to a dog for a new-year's gift.
The rogues slighted me into the river with as little remorse
as they would have drown'd a blind bitch's puppies, fifteen
i' th' litter; and you may know by my size that I have a
kind of alacrity in sinking; if the bottom were as deep as
hell I should down. I had been drown'd but that the shore
was shelvy and shallow—a death that I abhor; for the water
swells a man; and what a thing should I have been when I
had been swell'd! I should have been a mountain of
mummy.

Re-enter BARDOLPH, *with sack*

BARDOLPH. Here's Mistress Quickly, sir, to speak with you.
FALSTAFF. Come, let me pour in some sack to the Thames

water; for my belly's as cold as if I had swallow'd snow-
balls for pills to cool the reins. Call her in.

BARDOLPH. Come in, woman.

Enter MISTRESS QUICKLY

QUICKLY. By your leave; I cry you mercy. Give your worship good morrow.

FALSTAFF. Take away these chalices. Go, brew me a pottle
of sack finely.

BARDOLPH. With eggs, sir?

FALSTAFF. Simple of itself; I'll no pullet-sperm in my brew-
age. [*Exit* BARDOLPH] How now!

QUICKLY. Marry, sir, I come to your worship from Mistress
Ford.

FALSTAFF. Mistress Ford! I have had ford enough; I was
thrown into the ford; I have my belly full of ford.

QUICKLY. Alas the day, good heart, that was not her fault!
She does so take on with her men; they mistook their erec-
tion.

FALSTAFF. So did I mine, to build upon a foolish woman's
promise.

QUICKLY. Well, she laments, sir, for it, that it would yearn
your heart to see it. Her husband goes this morning a-birding; she desires you once more to come to her between
eight and nine; I must carry her word quickly. She'll make
you amends, I warrant you.

FALSTAFF. Well, I will visit her. Tell her so; and bid her
think what a man is. Let her consider his frailty, and then
judge of my merit.

QUICKLY. I will tell her.

FALSTAFF. Do so. Between nine and ten, say'st thou?

QUICKLY. Eight and nine, sir.

FALSTAFF. Well, be gone; I will not miss her.

QUICKLY. Peace be with you, sir.   *Exit*

FALSTAFF. I marvel I hear not of Master Brook; he sent me
word to stay within. I like his money well. O, here he
comes.

Enter FORD *disguised*

FORD. Bless you, sir!

193

MISTRESS PAGE. *Help to cover your master, boy* (ACT III. SCENE III)

FALSTAFF. Now, Master Brook, you come to know what hath pass'd between me and Ford's wife?

FORD. That, indeed, Sir John, is my business.

FALSTAFF. Master Brook, I will not lie to you; I was at her house the hour she appointed me.

FORD. And sped you, sir?

FALSTAFF. Very ill-favouredly, Master Brook.

FORD. How so, sir; did she change her determination?

FALSTAFF. No, Master Brook; but the peaking cornuto her husband, Master Brook, dwelling in a continual 'larum of jealousy, comes me in the instant of our encounter, after we had embrac'd, kiss'd, protested, and, as it were, spoke the prologue of our comedy; and at his heels a rabble of his companions, thither provoked and instigated by his distemper, and, forsooth, to search his house for his wife's love.

FORD. What, while you were there?

FALSTAFF. While I was there.

FORD. And did he search for you, and could not find you?

FALSTAFF. You shall hear. As good luck would have it, comes in one Mistress Page, gives intelligence of Ford's approach; and, in her invention and Ford's wife's distraction, they convey'd me into a buck-basket.

FORD. A buck-basket!

FALSTAFF. By the Lord, a buck-basket! Ramm'd me in with foul shirts and smocks, socks, foul stockings, greasy napkins, that, Master Brook, there was the rankest compound of villainous smell that ever offended nostril.

FORD. And how long lay you there?

FALSTAFF. Nay, you shall hear, Master Brook, what I have suffer'd to bring this woman to evil for your good. Being thus cramm'd in the basket, a couple of Ford's knaves, his hinds, were call'd forth by their mistress to carry me in the name of foul clothes to Datchet Lane; they took me on their shoulders; met the jealous knave their master in the door; who ask'd them once or twice what they had in their basket. I quak'd for fear lest the lunatic knave would have search'd it; but Fate, ordaining he should be a cuckold, held his hand. Well, on went he for a search, and away went I for foul clothes. But mark the sequel, Master

195

Brook—I suffered the pangs of three several deaths: first, an intolerable fright to be detected with a jealous rotten bell-wether; next, to be compass'd like a good bilbo in the circumference of a peck, hilt to point, heel to head; and then, to be stopp'd in, like a strong distillation, with stinking clothes that fretted in their own grease. Think of that —a man of my kidney. Think of that—that am as subject to heat as butter; a man of continual dissolution and thaw. It was a miracle to scape suffocation. And in the height of this bath, when I was more than half-stew'd in grease, like a Dutch dish, to be thrown into the Thames, and cool'd, glowing hot, in that surge, like a horse-shoe; think of that —hissing hot. Think of that, Master Brook.

FORD. In good sadness, sir, I am sorry that for my sake you have suffer'd all this. My suit, then, is desperate; you'll undertake her no more.

FALSTAFF. Master Brook, I will be thrown into Etna, as I have been into Thames, ere I will leave her thus. Her husband is this morning gone a-birding; I have received from her another embassy of meeting; 'twixt eight and nine is the hour, Master Brook.

FORD. 'Tis past eight already, sir.

FALSTAFF. Is it? I will then address me to my appointment. Come to me at your convenient leisure, and you shall know how I speed; and the conclusion shall be crowned with your enjoying her. Adieu. You shall have her, Master Brook; Master Brook, you shall cuckold Ford.   *Exit*

FORD. Hum! ha! Is this a vision? Is this a dream? Do I sleep? Master Ford, awake; awake, Master Ford. There's a hole made in your best coat, Master Ford. This 'tis to be married; this 'tis to have linen and buck-baskets! Well, I will proclaim myself what I am; I will now take the lecher; he is at my house. He cannot scape me; 'tis impossible he should; he cannot creep into a halfpenny purse nor into a pepper box. But, lest the devil that guides him should aid him, I will search impossible places. Though what I am I cannot avoid, yet to be what I would not shall not make me tame. If I have horns to make one mad, let the proverb go with me—I'll be horn mad.   *Exit*

ACT IV. SCENE 1

Windsor. A street

Enter MISTRESS PAGE, MISTRESS QUICKLY, *and* WILLIAM

MRS. PAGE. Is he at Master Ford's already, think'st thou?

QUICKLY. Sure he is by this; or will be presently; but truly he is very courageous mad about his throwing into the water. Mistress Ford desires you to come suddenly.

MRS. PAGE. I'll be with her by and by; I'll but bring my young man here to school. Look where his master comes; 'tis a playing day, I see.

Enter SIR HUGH EVANS

How now, Sir Hugh, no school to-day?

EVANS. No; Master Slender is let the boys leave to play.

QUICKLY. Blessing of his heart!

MRS. PAGE. Sir Hugh, my husband says my son profits nothing in the world at his book; I pray you ask him some questions in his accidence.

EVANS. Come hither, William; hold up your head; come.

MRS. PAGE. Come on, sirrah; hold up your head; answer your master; be not afraid.

EVANS. William, how many numbers is in nouns?

WILLIAM. Two.

QUICKLY. Truly, I thought there had been one number more, because they say 'Od's nouns.'

EVANS. Peace your tattlings. What is 'fair,' William?

WILLIAM. Pulcher.

QUICKLY. Polecats! There are fairer things than polecats, sure.

EVANS. You are a very simplicity oman; I pray you, peace. What is 'lapis,' William?

WILLIAM. A stone.

EVANS. And what is 'a stone,' William?

WILLIAM. A pebble.

EVANS. No, it is 'lapis'; I pray you remember in your prain.

WILLIAM. Lapis.

EVANS. That is a good William. What is he, William, that does lend articles?

WILLIAM. Articles are borrowed of the pronoun, and be thus declined: Singulariter, nominativo; hic, hæc, hoc.

EVANS. Nominativo, hig, hag, hog; pray you, mark: genitivo, hujus. Well, what is your accusative case?

WILLIAM. Accusativo, hinc.

EVANS. I pray you, have your remembrance, child. Accusativo, hung, hang, hog.

QUICKLY. 'Hang-hog' is Latin for bacon, I warrant you.

EVANS. Leave your prabbles, oman. What is the focative case, William?

WILLIAM. O—vocativo, O.

EVANS. Remember, William: focative is caret.

QUICKLY. And that's a good root.

EVANS. Oman, forbear.

MRS. PAGE. Peace.

EVANS. What is your genitive case plural, William?

WILLIAM. Genitive case?

EVANS. Ay.

WILLIAM. Genitive: horum, harum, horum.

QUICKLY. Vengeance of Jenny's case; fie on her! Never name her, child, if she be a whore.

EVANS. For shame, oman.

QUICKLY. You do ill to teach the child such words. He teaches him to hick and to hack, which they'll do fast enough of themselves; and to call 'horum'; fie upon you!

EVANS. Oman, art thou lunatics? Hast thou no understandings for thy cases, and the numbers of the genders? Thou art as foolish Christian creatures as I would desires.

MRS. PAGE. Prithee hold thy peace.

EVANS. Show me now, William, some declensions of your pronouns.

WILLIAM. Forsooth, I have forgot.

EVANS. It is qui, quæ, quod; if you forget your qui's, your quæ's, and your quod's, you must be preeches. Go your ways and play; go.

MRS. PAGE. He is a better scholar than I thought he was.

EVANS. He is a good sprag memory. Farewell, Mistress Page.

MRS. PAGE. Adieu, good Sir Hugh.   *Exit* SIR HUGH

Get you home, boy. Come, we stay too long.   *Exeunt*

SCENE 2

FORD'S *house*

Enter FALSTAFF *and* MISTRESS FORD

FALSTAFF. Mistress Ford, your sorrow hath eaten up my sufferance. I see you are obsequious in your love, and I profess requital to a hair's breadth; not only, Mistress Ford, in the simple office of love, but in all the accoutrement, complement, and ceremony of it. But are you sure of your husband now?

MRS. FORD. He's a-birding, sweet Sir John.

MRS. PAGE. [*Within*] What hoa, gossip Ford, what hoa!

MRS. FORD. Step into th' chamber, Sir John. *Exit* FALSTAFF

Enter MISTRESS PAGE

MRS. PAGE. How now, sweetheart, who's at home besides yourself?

MRS. FORD. Why, none but mine own people.

MRS. PAGE. Indeed?

MRS. FORD. No, certainly. [*Aside to her*] Speak louder.

MRS. PAGE. Truly, I am so glad you have nobody here.

MRS. FORD. Why?

MRS. PAGE. Why, woman, your husband is in his old lunes again. He so takes on yonder with my husband; so rails against all married mankind; so curses all Eve's daughters, of what complexion soever; and so buffets himself on the forehead, crying 'Peer-out, peer-out!' that any madness I ever yet beheld seem'd but tameness, civility, and patience, to this his distemper he is in now. I am glad the fat knight is not here.

MRS. FORD. Why, does he talk of him?

MRS. PAGE. Of none but him; and swears he was carried out, the last time he search'd for him, in a basket; protests to my husband he is now here; and hath drawn him and the rest of their company from their sport, to make another experiment of his suspicion. But I am glad the knight is not here; now he shall see his own foolery.

MRS. FORD. How near is he, Mistress Page?

MRS. PAGE. Hard by, at street end; he will be here anon.

MRS. FORD. I am undone: the knight is here.

MRS. PAGE. Why, then, you are utterly sham'd, and he's but a dead man. What a woman are you! Away with him, away with him; better shame than murder.

MRS. FORD. Which way should he go? How should I bestow him? Shall I put him into the basket again?

Re-enter FALSTAFF

FALSTAFF. No, I'll come no more i' th' basket. May I not go out ere he come?

MRS. PAGE. Alas, three of Master Ford's brothers watch the door with pistols, that none shall issue out; otherwise you might slip away ere he came. But what make you here?

FALSTAFF. What shall I do? I'll creep up into the chimney.

MRS. FORD. There they always use to discharge their bird-ing-pieces.

MRS. PAGE. Creep into the kiln-hole.

FALSTAFF. Where is it?

MRS. FORD. He will seek there, on my word. Neither press, coffer, chest, trunk, well, vault, but he hath an abstract for the remembrance of such places, and goes to them by his note. There is no hiding you in the house.

FALSTAFF. I'll go out then.

MRS. PAGE. If you go out in your own semblance, you die, Sir John. Unless you go out disguis'd.

MRS. FORD. How might we disguise him?

MRS. PAGE. Alas the day, I know not! There is no woman's gown big enough for him; otherwise he might put on a hat, a muffler, and a kerchief, and so escape.

FALSTAFF. Good hearts, devise something; any extremity rather than a mischief.

MRS. FORD. My maid's aunt, the fat woman of Brainford, has a gown above.

MRS. PAGE. On my word, it will serve him; she's as big as he is; and there's her thrumm'd hat, and her muffler too. Run up, Sir John.

MRS. FORD. Go, go, sweet Sir John. Mistress Page and I will look some linen for your head.

MRS. PAGE. Quick, quick; we'll come dress you straight. Put

on the gown the while. *Exit* FALSTAFF

MRS. FORD. I would my husband would meet him in this shape; he cannot abide the old woman of Brainford; he swears she's a witch, forbade her my house, and hath threat'ned to beat her.

MRS. PAGE. Heaven guide him to thy husband's cudgel; and the devil guide his cudgel afterwards!

MRS. FORD. But is my husband coming?

MRS. PAGE. Ay, in good sadness is he; and talks of the basket too, howsoever he hath had intelligence.

MRS. FORD. We'll try that; for I'll appoint my men to carry the basket again, to meet him at the door with it as they did last time.

MRS. PAGE. Nay, but he'll be here presently; let's go dress him like the witch of Brainford.

MRS. FORD. I'll first direct my men what they shall do with the basket. Go up; I'll bring linen for him straight. *Exit*

MRS. PAGE. Hang him, dishonest varlet! we cannot misuse him enough.
We'll leave a proof, by that which we will do,
Wives may be merry and yet honest too.
We do not act that often jest and laugh;
'Tis old but true: Still swine eats all the draff. *Exit*

Re-enter MISTRESS FORD, *with two* SERVANTS

MRS. FORD. Go, sirs, take the basket again on your shoulders; your master is hard at door; if he bid you set it down, obey him; quickly, dispatch. *Exit*

FIRST SERVANT. Come, come, take it up.

SECOND SERVANT. Pray heaven it be not full of knight again.

FIRST SERVANT. I hope not; I had lief as bear so much lead.

Enter FORD, PAGE, SHALLOW, CAIUS, *and* SIR HUGH EVANS

FORD. Ay, but if it prove true, Master Page, have you any way then to unfool me again? Set down the basket, villain! Somebody call my wife. Youth in a basket! O you panderly rascals, there's a knot, a ging, a pack, a conspiracy against me. Now shall the devil be sham'd. What, wife, I say! Come, come forth; behold what honest clothes you send forth to bleaching.

PAGE. Why, this passes, Master Ford; you are not to go loose any longer; you must be pinion'd.

EVANS. Why, this is lunatics. This is mad as a mad dog.

SHALLOW. Indeed, Master Ford, this is not well, indeed.

FORD. So say I too, sir.

Re-enter MISTRESS FORD

Come hither, Mistress Ford; Mistress Ford, the honest woman, the modest wife, the virtuous creature, that hath the jealous fool to her husband! I suspect without cause, mistress, do I?

MRS. FORD. Heaven be my witness, you do, if you suspect me in any dishonesty.

FORD. Well said, brazen-face; hold it out. Come forth, sirrah.

[*Pulling clothes out of the basket*]

PAGE. This passes!

MRS. FORD. Are you not asham'd? Let the clothes alone.

FORD. I shall find you anon.

EVANS. 'Tis unreasonable. Will you take up your wife's clothes? Come away.

FORD. Empty the basket, I say.

MRS. FORD. Why, man, why?

FORD. Master Page, as I am a man, there was one convey'd out of my house yesterday in this basket. Why may not he be there again? In my house I am sure he is; my intelligence is true; my jealousy is reasonable. Pluck me out all the linen.

MRS. FORD. If you find a man there, he shall die a flea's death.

PAGE. Here's no man.

SHALLOW. By my fidelity, this is not well, Master Ford; this wrongs you.

EVANS. Master Ford, you must pray, and not follow the imaginations of your own heart; this is jealousies.

FORD. Well, he's not here I seek for.

PAGE. No, nor nowhere else but in your brain.

FORD. Help to search my house this one time. If I find not what I seek, show no colour for my extremity; let me for ever be your table sport; let them say of me 'As jealous as

Ford, that search'd a hollow walnut for his wife's leman.'
Satisfy me once more; once more search with me.

MRS. FORD. What, hoa, Mistress Page! Come you and the old
woman down; my husband will come into the chamber.

FORD. Old woman? what old woman's that?

MRS. FORD. Why, it is my maid's aunt of Brainford.

FORD. A witch, a quean, an old cozening quean! Have I not
forbid her my house? She comes of errands, does she? We
are simple men; we do not know what's brought to pass
under the profession of fortune-telling. She works by
charms, by spells, by th' figure, and such daub'ry as this is,
beyond our element. We know nothing. Come down, you
witch, you hag you; come down, I say.

MRS. FORD. Nay, good sweet husband! Good gentlemen, let
him not strike the old woman.

Re-enter FALSTAFF *in woman's clothes, and* MISTRESS PAGE

MRS. PAGE. Come, Mother Prat; come, give me your hand.

FORD. I'll prat her. [*Beating him*] Out of my door, you
witch, you hag, you baggage, you polecat, you ronyon!
Out, out! I'll conjure you, I'll fortune-tell you.

Exit FALSTAFF

MRS. PAGE. Are you not asham'd? I think you have kill'd the
poor woman.

MRS. FORD. Nay, he will do it. 'Tis a goodly credit for you.

FORD. Hang her, witch!

EVANS. By yea and no, I think the oman is a witch indeed; I
like not when a oman has a great peard; I spy a great peard
under his muffler.

FORD. Will you follow, gentlemen? I beseech you follow;
see but the issue of my jealousy; if I cry out thus upon no
trail, never trust me when I open again.

PAGE. Let's obey his humour a little further. Come, gentlemen.   *Exeunt all but* MRS. FORD *and* MRS. PAGE

MRS. PAGE. Trust me, he beat him most pitifully.

MRS. FORD. Nay, by th' mass, that he did not; he beat him
most unpitifully methought.

MRS. PAGE. I'll have the cudgel hallow'd and hung o'er the
altar; it hath done meritorious service.

MRS. FORD. What think you? May we, with the warrant of

womanhood and the witness of a good conscience, pursue him with any further revenge?

MRS. PAGE. The spirit of wantonness is sure scar'd out of him; if the devil have him not in fee-simple, with fine and recovery, he will never, I think, in the way of waste, attempt us again.

MRS. FORD. Shall we tell our husbands how we have serv'd him?

MRS. PAGE. Yes, by all means; if it be but to scrape the figures out of your husband's brains. If they can find in their hearts the poor unvirtuous fat knight shall be any further afflicted, we two will still be the ministers.

MRS. FORD. I'll warrant they'll have him publicly sham'd; and methinks there would be no period to the jest, should he not be publicly sham'd.

MRS. PAGE. Come, to the forge with it then; shape it. I would not have things cool.   *Exeunt*

SCENE 3

The Garter Inn

Enter HOST *and* BARDOLPH

BARDOLPH. Sir, the Germans desire to have three of your horses; the Duke himself will be to-morrow at court, and they are going to meet him.

HOST. What duke should that be comes so secretly? I hear not of him in the court. Let me speak with the gentlemen; they speak English?

BARDOLPH. Ay, sir; I'll call them to you.

HOST. They shall have my horses, but I'll make them pay; I'll sauce them; they have had my house a week at command; I have turn'd away my other guests. They must come off; I'll sauce them. Come.   *Exeunt*

SCENE 4

FORD's *house*

Enter PAGE, FORD, MISTRESS PAGE, MISTRESS FORD, *and*
SIR HUGH EVANS

EVANS. 'Tis one of the best discretions of a oman as ever I
did look upon.
PAGE. And did he send you both these letters at an instant?
MRS. PAGE. Within a quarter of an hour.
FORD. Pardon me, wife. Henceforth, do what thou wilt;
I rather will suspect the sun with cold
Than thee with wantonness. Now doth thy honour stand,
In him that was of late an heretic,
As firm as faith.
PAGE. 'Tis well, 'tis well; no more.
Be not as extreme in submission as in offence;
But let our plot go forward. Let our wives
Yet once again, to make us public sport,
Appoint a meeting with this old fat fellow,
Where we may take him and disgrace him for it.
FORD. There is no better way than that they spoke of.
PAGE. How? To send him word they'll meet him in the Park
at midnight? Fie, fie! he'll never come!
EVANS. You say he has been thrown in the rivers; and has
been grievously peaten as an old oman; methinks there
should be terrors in him, that he should not come; me-
thinks his flesh is punish'd; he shall have no desires.
PAGE. So think I too.
MRS. FORD. Devise but how you'll use him when he comes,
And let us two devise to bring him thither.
MRS. PAGE. There is an old tale goes that Herne the Hunter,
Sometime a keeper here in Windsor Forest,
Doth all the winter-time, at still midnight,
Walk round about an oak, with great ragg'd horns;
And there he blasts the tree, and takes the cattle,
And makes milch-kine yield blood, and shakes a chain
In a most hideous and dreadful manner.
You have heard of such a spirit, and well you know

The superstitious idle-headed eld
Receiv'd, and did deliver to our age,
This tale of Herne the Hunter for a truth.
PAGE. Why yet there want not many that do fear
In deep of night to walk by this Herne's oak.
But what of this?
MRS. FORD. Marry, this is our device—
That Falstaff at that oak shall meet with us,
Disguis'd, like Herne, with huge horns on his head.
PAGE. Well, let it not be doubted but he'll come,
And in this shape. When you have brought him thither,
What shall be done with him? What is your plot?
MRS. PAGE. That likewise have we thought upon, and
thus:
Nan Page my daughter, and my little son,
And three or four more of their growth, we'll dress
Like urchins, ouphes, and fairies, green and white,
With rounds of waxen tapers on their heads,
And rattles in their hands; upon a sudden,
As Falstaff, she, and I, are newly met,
Let them from forth a sawpit rush at once
With some diffused song; upon their sight
We two in great amazedness will fly.
Then let them all encircle him about,
And fairy-like, to pinch the unclean knight;
And ask him why, that hour of fairy revel,
In their so sacred paths he dares to tread
In shape profane.
MRS. FORD. And till he tell the truth,
Let the supposed fairies pinch him sound,
And burn him with their tapers.
MRS. PAGE. The truth being known,
We'll all present ourselves; dis-horn the spirit,
And mock him home to Windsor.
FORD. The children must
Be practis'd well to this or they'll nev'r do 't.
EVANS. I will teach the children their behaviours; and I will
be like a jack-an-apes also, to burn the knight with my
taber.
FORD. That will be excellent. I'll go buy them vizards.

Mrs. Page. My Nan shall be the Queen of all the Fairies,
Finely attired in a robe of white.
Page. That silk will I go buy. [*Aside*] And in that time
Shall Master Slender steal my Nan away,
And marry her at Eton.—Go, send to Falstaff straight.
Ford. Nay, I'll to him again, in name of Brook;
He'll tell me all his purpose. Sure, he'll come.
Mrs. Page. Fear not you that. Go get us properties
And tricking for our fairies.
Evans. Let us about it. It is admirable pleasures, and fery
honest knaveries.   *Exeunt* Page, Ford, *and* Evans
Mrs. Page. Go, Mistress Ford.
Send Quickly to Sir John to know his mind.
                                        Exit Mrs. Ford
I'll to the Doctor; he hath my good will,
And none but he, to marry with Nan Page.
That Slender, though well landed, is an idiot;
And he my husband best of all affects.
The Doctor is well money'd, and his friends
Potent at court; he, none but he, shall have her,
Though twenty thousand worthier come to crave her.   *Exit*

SCENE 5

The Garter Inn

Enter Host *and* Simple

Host. What wouldst thou have, boor? What, thick-skin?
Speak, breathe, discuss; brief, short, quick, snap.
Simple. Marry, sir, I come to speak with Sir John Falstaff
from Master Slender.
Host. There's his chamber, his house, his castle, his standing-
bed and truckle-bed; 'tis painted about with the story of
the Prodigal, fresh and new. Go, knock and call; he'll
speak like an Anthropophaginian unto thee. Knock, I say.
Simple. There's an old woman, a fat woman, gone up into
his chamber; I'll be so bold as stay, sir, till she come down;
I come to speak with her, indeed.

Host. Ha! a fat woman? The knight may be robb'd. I'll call. Bully knight! Bully Sir John! Speak from thy lungs military. Art thou there? It is thine host, thine Ephesian, calls.

Falstaff. [*Above*] How now, mine host?

Host. Here's a Bohemian-Tartar tarries the coming down of thy fat woman. Let her descend, bully, let her descend; my chambers are honourable. Fie, privacy, fie!

Enter Falstaff

Falstaff. There was, mine host, an old fat woman even now with me; but she's gone.

Simple. Pray you, sir, was't not the wise woman of Brainford?

Falstaff. Ay, marry was it, mussel-shell. What would you with her?

Simple. My master, sir, my Master Slender, sent to her, seeing her go thorough the streets, to know, sir, whether one Nym, sir, that beguil'd him of a chain, had the chain or no.

Falstaff. I spake with the old woman about it.

Simple. And what says she, I pray, sir?

Falstaff. Marry, she says that the very same man that beguil'd Master Slender of his chain cozen'd him of it.

Simple. I would I could have spoken with the woman herself; I had other things to have spoken with her too, from him.

Falstaff. What are they? Let us know.

Host. Ay, come; quick.

Simple. I may not conceal them, sir.

Falstaff. Conceal them, or thou diest.

Simple. Why, sir, they were nothing but about Mistress Anne Page: to know if it were my master's fortune to have her or no.

Falstaff. 'Tis, 'tis his fortune.

Simple. What, sir?

Falstaff. To have her, or no. Go; say the woman told me so.

Simple. May I be bold to say so, sir?

Falstaff. Ay, sir, like who more bold?

Simple. I thank your worship; I shall make my master glad with these tidings.   *Exit* Simple

Host. Thou art clerkly, thou art clerkly, Sir John. Was there a wise woman with thee?

Falstaff. Ay, that there was, mine host; one that hath taught me more wit than ever I learn'd before in my life; and I paid nothing for it neither, but was paid for my learning.

Enter Bardolph

Bardolph. Out, alas, sir, cozenage, mere cozenage!

Host. Where be my horses? Speak well of them, varletto.

Bardolph. Run away with the cozeners; for so soon as I came beyond Eton, they threw me off from behind one of them, in a slough of mire; and set spurs and away, like three German devils, three Doctor Faustuses.

Host. They are gone but to meet the Duke, villain; do not say they be fled. Germans are honest men.

Enter Sir Hugh Evans

Evans. Where is mine host?

Host. What is the matter, sir?

Evans. Have a care of your entertainments. There is a friend of mine come to town tells me there is three cozen-germans that has cozen'd all the hosts of Readins, of Maidenhead, of Colebrook, of horses and money. I tell you for good will, look you; you are wise, and full of gibes and vlouting-stogs, and 'tis not convenient you should be cozened. Fare you well. *Exit*

Enter Doctor Caius

Caius. Vere is mine host de Jarteer?

Host. Here, Master Doctor, in perplexity and doubtful dilemma.

Caius. I cannot tell vat is dat; but it is tell-a me dat you make grand preparation for a Duke de Jamany. By my trot, dere is no duke that the court is know to come; I tell you for good will. Adieu. *Exit*

Host. Hue and cry, villain, go! Assist me, knight; I am undone. Fly, run, hue and cry, villain; I am undone.

Exeunt Host *and* Bardolph

Falstaff. I would all the world might be cozen'd, for I have been cozen'd and beaten too. If it should come to the ear

209

of the court how I have been transformed, and how my transformation hath been wash'd and cudgell'd, they would melt me out of my fat, drop by drop, and liquor fishermen's boots with me; I warrant they would whip me with their fine wits till I were as crestfall'n as a dried pear. I never prosper'd since I forswore myself at primero. Well, if my wind were but long enough to say my prayers, I would repent.

Enter MISTRESS QUICKLY

Now! whence come you?

QUICKLY. From the two parties, forsooth.

FALSTAFF. The devil take one party and his dam the other! And so they shall be both bestowed. I have suffer'd more for their sakes, more than the villainous inconstancy of man's disposition is able to bear.

QUICKLY. And have not they suffer'd? Yes, I warrant; speciously one of them; Mistress Ford, good heart, is beaten black and blue, that you cannot see a white spot about her.

FALSTAFF. What tell'st thou me of black and blue? I was beaten myself into all the colours of the rainbow; and I was like to be apprehended for the witch of Brainford. But that my admirable dexterity of wit, my counterfeiting the action of an old woman, deliver'd me, the knave constable had set me i' th' stocks, i' th' common stocks, for a witch.

QUICKLY. Sir, let me speak with you in your chamber; you shall hear how things go, and, I warrant, to your content. Here is a letter will say somewhat. Good hearts, what ado here is to bring you together! Sure, one of you does not serve heaven well, that you are so cross'd.

FALSTAFF. Come up into my chamber. *Exeunt*

SCENE 6

The Garter Inn

Enter FENTON *and* HOST

HOST. Master Fenton, talk not to me; my mind is heavy; I will give over all.

FENTON. Yet hear me speak. Assist me in my purpose,
  And, as I am a gentleman, I'll give thee
  A hundred pound in gold more than your loss.
HOST. I will hear you, Master Fenton; and I will, at the least,
  keep your counsel.
FENTON. From time to time I have acquainted you
  With the dear love I bear to fair Anne Page;
  Who, mutually, hath answer'd my affection,
  So far forth as herself might be her chooser,
  Even to my wish. I have a letter from her
  Of such contents as you will wonder at;
  The mirth whereof so larded with my matter
  That neither, singly, can be manifested
  Without the show of both. Fat Falstaff
  Hath a great scene. The image of the jest
  I'll show you here at large. Hark, good mine host:
  To-night at Herne's oak, just 'twixt twelve and one,
  Must my sweet Nan present the Fairy Queen—
  The purpose why is here—in which disguise,
  While other jests are something rank on foot,
  Her father hath commanded her to slip
  Away with Slender, and with him at Eton
  Immediately to marry; she hath consented.
  Now, sir,
  Her mother, even strong against that match
  And firm for Doctor Caius, hath appointed
  That he shall likewise shuffle her away
  While other sports are tasking of their minds,
  And at the dean'ry, where a priest attends,
  Straight marry her. To this her mother's plot
  She seemingly obedient likewise hath
  Made promise to the doctor. Now thus it rests:
  Her father means she shall be all in white;
  And in that habit, when Slender sees his time
  To take her by the hand and bid her go,
  She shall go with him; her mother hath intended
  The better to denote her to the doctor—
  For they must all be mask'd and vizarded—
  That quaint in green she shall be loose enrob'd,
  With ribands pendent, flaring 'bout her head;

And when the doctor spies his vantage ripe,
To pinch her by the hand, and, on that token,
The maid hath given consent to go with him.
Host. Which means she to deceive, father or mother?
Fenton. Both, my good host, to go along with me.
And here it rests—that you'll procure the vicar
To stay for me at church, 'twixt twelve and one,
And in the lawful name of marrying,
To give our hearts united ceremony.
Host. Well, husband your device; I'll to the vicar.
Bring you the maid, you shall not lack a priest.
Fenton. So shall I evermore be bound to thee;
Besides, I'll make a present recompense.   *Exeunt*

ACT V. SCENE 1

The Garter Inn

Enter Falstaff *and* Mistress Quickly

Falstaff. Prithee, no more prattling; go. I'll hold. This is
the third time; I hope good luck lies in odd numbers.
Away, go; they say there is divinity in odd numbers, either
in nativity, chance, or death. Away.
Quickly. I'll provide you a chain, and I'll do what I can to
get you a pair of horns.
Falstaff. Away, I say; time wears; hold up your head, and
mince.   *Exit* Mrs. Quickly

Enter Ford, *disguised*

How now, Master Brook. Master Brook, the matter will
be known tonight or never. Be you in the Park about midnight, at Herne's oak, and you shall see wonders.
Ford. Went you not to her yesterday, sir, as you told me
you had appointed?
Falstaff. I went to her, Master Brook, as you see, like a
poor old man; but I came from her, Master Brook, like a
poor old woman. That same knave Ford, her husband, hath

the finest mad devil of jealousy in him, Master Brook, that ever govern'd frenzy. I will tell you—he beat me grievously in the shape of a woman; for in the shape of man, Master Brook, I fear not Goliath with a weaver's beam; because I know also life is a shuttle. I am in haste; go along with me; I'll tell you all, Master Brook. Since I pluck'd geese, play'd truant, and whipp'd top, I knew not what 'twas to be beaten till lately. Follow me. I'll tell you strange things of this knave Ford, on whom to-night I will be revenged, and I will deliver his wife into your hand. Follow. Strange things in hand, Master Brook! Follow. *Exeunt*

SCENE 2

Windsor Park

Enter PAGE, SHALLOW, *and* SLENDER

PAGE. Come, come; we'll couch i' th' Castle ditch till we see the light of our fairies. Remember, son Slender, my daughter.
SLENDER. Ay, forsooth; I have spoke with her, and we have a nay-word how to know one another. I come to her in white and cry 'mum'; she cries 'budget,' and by that we know one another.
SHALLOW. That's good too; but what needs either your mum or her budget? The white will decipher her well enough. It hath struck ten o'clock.
PAGE. The night is dark; light and spirits will become it well. Heaven prosper our sport! No man means evil but the devil, and we shall know him by his horns. Let's away; follow me. *Exeunt*

SCENE 3

A street leading to the Park

Enter MISTRESS PAGE, MISTRESS FORD, *and* DOCTOR CAIUS

MRS. PAGE. Master Doctor, my daughter is in green; when you see your time, take her by the hand, away with her to

213

the deanery, and dispatch it quickly. Go before into the Park; we two must go together.

CAIUS. I know vat I have to do; adieu.

MRS. PAGE. Fare you well, sir. [*Exit* CAIUS] My husband will not rejoice so much at the abuse of Falstaff as he will chafe at the doctor's marrying my daughter; but 'tis no matter; better a little chiding than a great deal of heart-break.

MRS. FORD. Where is Nan now, and her troop of fairies, and the Welsh devil, Hugh?

MRS. PAGE. They are all couch'd in a pit hard by Herne's oak, with obscur'd lights; which, at the very instant of Falstaff's and our meeting, they will at once display to the night.

MRS. FORD. That cannot choose but amaze him.

MRS. PAGE. If he be not amaz'd, he will be mock'd; if he be amaz'd, he will every way be mock'd.

MRS. FORD. We'll betray him finely.

MRS. PAGE. Against such lewdsters and their lechery,
Those that betray them do no treachery.

MRS. FORD. The hour draws on. To the oak, to the oak!
Exeunt

SCENE 4

Windsor Park

Enter SIR HUGH EVANS *like a satyr, with* OTHERS *as fairies*

EVANS. Trib, trib, fairies; come; and remember your parts. Be pold, I pray you; follow me into the pit; and when I give the watch-ords, do as I pid you. Come, come; trib, trib.
Exeunt

SCENE 5

Another part of the Park

Enter FALSTAFF *disguised as* HERNE

FALSTAFF. The Windsor bell hath struck twelve; the minute

214

draws on. Now the hot-blooded gods assist me! Remember, Jove, thou wast a bull for thy Europa; love set on thy horns. O powerful love! that in some respects makes a beast a man; in some other a man a beast. You were also, Jupiter, a swan, for the love of Leda. O omnipotent love! how near the god drew to the complexion of a goose! A fault done first in the form of a beast—O Jove, a beastly fault!—and then another fault in the semblance of a fowl—think on't, Jove, a foul fault! When gods have hot backs what shall poor men do? For me, I am here a Windsor stag; and the fattest, I think, i' th' forest. Send me a cool rut-time, Jove, or who can blame me to piss my tallow? Who comes here? my doe?

Enter Mistress Ford *and* Mistress Page

Mrs. Ford. Sir John! Art thou there, my deer, my male deer.

Falstaff. My doe with the black scut! Let the sky rain potatoes; let it thunder to the tune of Greensleeves, hail kissing-comfits, and snow eringoes; let there come a tempest of provocation, I will shelter me here.   [*Embracing her*]

Mrs. Ford. Mistress Page is come with me, sweetheart.

Falstaff. Divide me like a brib'd buck, each a haunch; I will keep my sides to myself, my shoulders for the fellow of this walk, and my horns I bequeath your husbands. Am I a woodman, ha? Speak I like Herne the Hunter? Why, now is Cupid a child of conscience; he makes restitution. As I am a true spirit, welcome!   [*A noise of horns*]

Mrs. Page. Alas, what noise?

Mrs. Ford. Heaven forgive our sins!

Falstaff. What should this be?

Mrs. Ford.⎫
Mrs. Page.⎭ Away, away.   [*They run off*]

Falstaff. I think the devil will not have me damn'd, lest the oil that's in me should set hell on fire; he would never else cross me thus.

Enter Sir Hugh Evans *like a satyr,* Anne Page *as a fairy, and* Others *as the Fairy Queen, fairies, and Hobgoblin; all with tapers*

Fairy Queen. Fairies, black, grey, green, and white,

You moonshine revellers, and shades of night,
You orphan heirs of fixed destiny,
Attend your office and your quality.
Crier Hobgoblin, make the fairy oyes.

PUCK. Elves, list your names; silence, you airy toys.
Cricket, to Windsor chimneys shalt thou leap;
Where fires thou find'st unrak'd, and hearths unswept,
There pinch the maids as blue as bilberry;
Our radiant Queen hates sluts and sluttery.

FALSTAFF. They are fairies; he that speaks to them shall die.
I'll wink and couch; no man their works must eye.

[Lies down upon his face]

EVANS. Where's Pede? Go you, and where you find a maid
That, ere she sleep, has thrice her prayers said,
Raise up the organs of her fantasy,
Sleep she as sound as careless infancy;
But those as sleep and think not on their sins,
Pinch them, arms, legs, backs, shoulders, sides, and shins.

FAIRY QUEEN. About, about;
Search Windsor castle, elves, within and out;
Strew good luck, ouphes, on every sacred room,
That it may stand till the perpetual doom
In state as wholesome as in state 'tis fit,
Worthy the owner and the owner it.
The several chairs of order look you scour
With juice of balm and every precious flower;
Each fair instalment, coat, and sev'ral crest,
With loyal blazon, evermore be blest!
And nightly, meadow-fairies, look you sing,
Like to the Garter's compass, in a ring;
Th' expressure that it bears, green let it be,
More fertile-fresh than all the field to see;
And 'Honi soit qui mal y pense' write
In em'rald tufts, flow'rs purple, blue and white;
Like sapphire, pearl, and rich embroidery,
Buckled below fair knighthood's bending knee.
Fairies use flow'rs for their charactery.
Away, disperse; but till 'tis one o'clock,
Our dance of custom round about the oak
Of Herne the Hunter let us not forget.

EVANS. Pray you, lock hand in hand; yourselves in order set;
    And twenty glow-worms shall our lanterns be,
    To guide our measure round about the tree.
    But, stay. I smell a man of middle earth.
FALSTAFF. Heavens defend me from that Welsh fairy, lest he
    transform me to a piece of cheese!
PUCK. Vile worm, thou wast o'erlook'd even in thy birth.
FAIRY QUEEN. With trial-fire touch me his finger-end;
    If he be chaste, the flame will back descend,
    And turn him to no pain; but if he start,
    It is the flesh of a corrupted heart.
PUCK. A trial, come.
EVANS. Come, will this wood take fire?
        [*They put the tapers to his fingers, and he starts*]
FALSTAFF. Oh, oh, oh!
FAIRY QUEEN. Corrupt, corrupt, and tainted in desire!
    About him, fairies; sing a scornful rhyme;
    And, as you trip, still pinch him to your time.

THE SONG

    Fie on sinful fantasy!
    Fie on lust and luxury!
    Lust is but a bloody fire,
    Kindled with unchaste desire,
    Fed in heart, whose flames aspire,
    As thoughts do blow them, higher and higher.
    Pinch him, fairies, mutually;
    Pinch him for his villainy;
    Pinch him and burn him and turn him about,
    Till candles and star-light and moonshine be out.

During this song they pinch FALSTAFF. DOCTOR
CAIUS *comes one way, and steals away a fairy in
green;* SLENDER *another way, and takes off a fairy in
white; and* FENTON *steals away* ANNE PAGE. *A noise
of hunting is heard within. All the fairies run away.*
FALSTAFF *pulls off his buck's head, and rises*

Enter PAGE, FORD, MISTRESS PAGE, MISTRESS FORD, *and*
SIR HUGH EVANS

PAGE. Nay, do not fly; I think we have watch'd you now.
Will none but Herne the Hunter serve your turn?

MRS. PAGE. I pray you, come, hold up the jest no higher.
Now, good Sir John, how like you Windsor wives?
See you these, husband? Do not these fair yokes
Become the forest better than the town?

FORD. Now, sir, who's a cuckold now? Master Brook, Falstaff's a knave, a cuckoldly knave; here are his horns, Master Brook; and, Master Brook, he hath enjoyed nothing of
Ford's but his buck-basket, his cudgel, and twenty pounds
of money, which must be paid to Master Brook; his horses
are arrested for it, Master Brook.

MRS. FORD. Sir John, we have had ill luck; we could never
meet. I will never take you for my love again; but I will
always count you my deer.

FALSTAFF. I do begin to perceive that I am made an ass.

FORD. Ay, and an ox too; both the proofs are extant.

FALSTAFF. And these are not fairies? I was three or four
times in the thought they were not fairies; and yet the
guiltiness of my mind, the sudden surprise of my powers,
drove the grossness of the foppery into a receiv'd belief,
in despite of the teeth of all rhyme and reason, that they
were fairies. See now how wit may be made a Jack-a-Lent
when 'tis upon ill employment.

EVANS. Sir John Falstaff, serve Got, and leave your desires,
and fairies will not pinse you.

FORD. Well said, fairy Hugh.

EVANS. And leave you your jealousies too, I pray you.

FORD. I will never mistrust my wife again, till thou art able
to woo her in good English.

FALSTAFF. Have I laid my brain in the sun, and dried it, that
it wants matter to prevent so gross o'er-reaching as this?
Am I ridden with a Welsh goat too? Shall I have a coxcomb of frieze? 'Tis time I were chok'd with a piece of
toasted cheese.

EVANS. Seese is not good to give putter; your belly is all
putter.

FALSTAFF. 'Seese' and 'putter'! Have I liv'd to stand at the
taunt of one that makes fritters of English? This is enough
to be the decay of lust and late-walking through the realm.

Mrs. Page. Why, Sir John, do you think, though we would have thrust virtue out of our hearts by the head and shoulders, and have given ourselves without scruple to hell, that ever the devil could have made you our delight?

Ford. What, a hodge-pudding? a bag of flax?

Mrs. Page. A puff'd man?

Page. Old, cold, wither'd, and of intolerable entrails?

Ford. And one that is as slanderous as Satan?

Page. And as poor as Job?

Ford. And as wicked as his wife?

Evans. And given to fornications, and to taverns, and sack, and wine, and metheglins, and to drinkings, and swearings, and starings, pribbles and prabbles?

Falstaff. Well, I am your theme; you have the start of me; I am dejected; I am not able to answer the Welsh flannel; ignorance itself is a plummet o'er me; use me as you will.

Ford. Marry, sir, we'll bring you to Windsor, to one Master Brook, that you have cozen'd of money, to whom you should have been a pander. Over and above that you have suffer'd, I think to repay that money will be a biting affliction.

Page. Yet be cheerful, knight; thou shalt eat a posset to-night at my house, where I will desire thee to laugh at my wife, that now laughs at thee. Tell her Master Slender hath married her daughter.

Mrs. Page. [Aside] Doctors doubt that; if Anne Page be my daughter, she is, by this, Doctor Caius' wife.

Enter Slender

Slender. Whoa, ho, ho, father Page!

Page. Son, how now! how now, son! Have you dispatch'd?

Slender. Dispatch'd! I'll make the best in Gloucestershire know on't; would I were hang'd, la, else!

Page. Of what, son?

Slender. I came yonder at Eton to marry Mistress Anne Page, and she's a great lubberly boy. If it had not been i' th' church, I would have swing'd him, or he should have swing'd me. If I did not think it had been Anne Page, would I might never stir!—and 'tis a postmaster's boy.

Page. Upon my life, then, you took the wrong.

SLENDER. What need you tell me that? I think so, when I took a boy for a girl. If I had been married to him, for all he was in woman's apparel, I would not have had him.

PAGE. Why, this is your own folly. Did not I tell you how you should know my daughter by her garments?

SLENDER. I went to her in white and cried 'mum' and she cried 'budget' as Anne and I had appointed; and yet it was not Anne, but a postmaster's boy.

MRS. PAGE. Good George, be not angry. I knew of your purpose; turn'd my daughter into green; and, indeed, she is now with the Doctor at the dean'ry, and there married.

Enter CAIUS

CAIUS. Vere is Mistress Page? By gar, I am cozened; I ha' married un garçon, a boy; un paysan, by gar, a boy; it is not Anne Page; by gar, I am cozened.

MRS. PAGE. Why, did you take her in green?

CAIUS. Ay, be gar, and 'tis a boy; be gar, I'll raise all Windsor.   *Exit* CAIUS

FORD. This is strange. Who hath got the right Anne?

PAGE. My heart misgives me; here comes Master Fenton.

Enter FENTON *and* ANNE PAGE

How now, Master Fenton!

ANNE. Pardon, good father. Good my mother, pardon.

PAGE. Now, Mistress, how chance you went not with Master Slender?

MRS. PAGE. Why went you not with Master Doctor, maid?

FENTON. You do amaze her. Hear the truth of it.
You would have married her most shamefully,
Where there was no proportion held in love.
The truth is, she and I, long since contracted,
Are now so sure that nothing can dissolve us.
Th' offence is holy that she hath committed;
And this deceit loses the name of craft,
Of disobedience, or unduteous title,
Since therein she doth evitate and shun
A thousand irreligious cursed hours,
Which forced marriage would have brought upon her.

FORD. Stand not amaz'd; here is no remedy.

In love, the heavens themselves do guide the state;
Money buys lands, and wives are sold by fate.
FALSTAFF. I am glad, though you have ta'en a special stand
to strike at me, that your arrow hath glanc'd.
PAGE. Well, what remedy? Fenton, heaven give thee joy!
What cannot be eschew'd must be embrac'd.
FALSTAFF. When night-dogs run, all sorts of deer are chas'd.
MRS. PAGE. Well, I will muse no further. Master Fenton,
Heaven give you many, many merry days!
Good husband, let us every one go home,
And laugh this sport o'er by a country fire;
Sir John and all.
FORD. Let it be so. Sir John,
To Master Brook you yet shall hold your word;
For he, to-night, shall lie with Mistress Ford.   *Exeunt*

Measure for Measure

MEASURE FOR MEASURE

MEASURE FOR MEASURE is usually regarded as one of Shakespeare's 'problem plays,' a drama in which our sympathies lack direction, so that we are left at the end with no unified impression of the work as a whole. Commentators have ascribed the confusion they feel over the moral issues of the action to a confusion in Shakespeare's own mind which they attribute to some crisis in the dramatist's intellectual or spiritual life. With *Measure for Measure* they group *All's Well that Ends Well* and *Troilus and Cressida*, labelling them 'the dark comedies.'

The treatment of *Measure for Measure* as evidence of some gloomy and even despairing reaction to experience was naturally fashionable as long as critics regarded the *Tragedies* as the poetry of disillusion, for Shakespeare must have written *Measure for Measure* in the middle years of what was called his tragic period. It was performed at Court on 26th December 1604 as an item in the Christmas festivities, and must have been written about the same time as *Othello*. *Othello* was also performed at Court that winter on 1st November, but it must have been on the stage by 1603. We cannot say therefore that *Measure for Measure* was not already by December 1604 known on the public stage. The two plays however are first heard of about the same date, and Shakespeare found his material for both in the same quarry, the *Hecatommithi* of Giraldi Cinthio.

Cinthio, a scholar who had long resided in Ferrara, published in 1565 a collection of tales in imitation of Boccaccio's *Decameron*. There Shakespeare found a story belonging to the type in which a woman has to ransom a man, usually her husband, by complying with the desires of some judge in whose power the man lies. Cinthio makes the man and woman brother and sister. Epitia, his heroine, complies with the judge's request on a half-promise of marriage, only to find that her brother has been executed. She seeks out the Emperor who condemns the judge to death after he has been made to keep his promise of marriage to Epitia. Epitia however now pleads for her husband's life and the Emperor surprised at her magnanimity pardons the offender, who lives happily ever after with his wife. Shakespeare doubtless looked at Cinthio's story but he also knew a dramatised version of it by George Whetstone published in 1578 with the title *Promos and Cassandra*.

Promos and Cassandra is in two parts, each of five Acts, and was never put on the stage. Promos deceives Cassandra as in Cinthio's story but the gaoler releases her brother and sends the judge the head of a man who is already dead. After Promos has been convicted and Cassandra is grieving at the coming execution her brother, Andrugio, reveals himself and the King pardons everyone.

Whetstone's device for softening the story and preserving the brother's life had already been anticipated by Cinthio in his *Epitia*, a later and dramatised version of his story. This drama was not printed till 1583, ten years after the author's death, and can hardly have been seen by Whetstone. The device they both use to preserve the condemned man was one familiar to story-tellers.

Shakespeare may have been influenced by other versions of the theme; Whetstone like Cinthio wrote a second version of the story, but while Cinthio turned his prose narrative into drama Whetstone reduced his drama to narrative for his *Heptameron*, a collection of stories in imitation of Boccaccio and Cinthio, published in 1582. Whatever versions he may have examined Shakespeare's own contribution to the machinery of the plot is Mariana, who is required to save Isabella in her dilemma. In earlier versions the sister's sacrifice to save her brother is made less forbidding by the prospect of a marriage that will restore the decencies. The convention that such a marriage mends all obliterates the inhumanity of the initial proposal; but Shakespeare rejects this solution and insists that Isabella is of such a nature that this compromise is unthinkable. Yet to allow Isabella to retain her principles and nature he has to allow her to be a party to the substitution of Mariana. He rejects one convention as out of keeping with his dramatic purpose but he has to introduce another that is hardly less inconsistent with the heroine's integrity. Shakespeare it is true shifts the conventional accent of the story; the burden is removed from the heroine but she has to see it transferred to another.

Recent attempts have been made to show that Shakespeare is here offering us a great parable of charity and forgiveness; that everything is calculated to that end. But Angelo's repentance is hardly presented to us with more substance than that of Proteus in *The Two Gentlemen of Verona*, and the forgiveness motive here as there is obviously a convenient and popular formula with which to conclude a comedy. The reality of the play does not lie here, though the themes of repentance and forgiveness are undoubtedly developed, but rather in the meeting of those two unusual and uncompromising figures, Isabella and Angelo. It is they who give the play its incandescent core that all the overlay required to present so burning an issue on the stage without a disastrous conclusion cannot wholly conceal.

In his *Promos and Cassandra* Whetstone had added to his main plot, which involves the main characters, doings from his life that also reflect the inhumanity of authority. Shakespeare did not of course need Whetstone to teach him the advantage of combining high and low life, but where Whetstone is content to allow the two streams to run parallel Shakespeare allows them to mingle and reinforce each other. This sense of life and stir in a city provides some sort of excuse for the Duke's perplexity and conduct and gives the duel between Isabella and Angelo, a secret in such a society, an added grimness.

The central situations in *Measure for Measure* are handled with the power and authority characteristic of this period in Shakespeare's artistic life. The hand that had just drawn *Othello* is equally visible here; but the subject did not admit of tragic treatment on the lines Shakespeare was then following. In accommodating it to the conventions of comedy the confusions in the design that have so troubled the critics were inevitable.

ISABELLA. *Peace and prosperity! Who is't that calls?*

(ACT I. SCENE IV)

VINCENTIO, *the Duke*
ANGELO, *the Deputy*
ESCALUS, *an ancient Lord*
CLAUDIO, *a young gentleman*
LUCIO, *a fantastic*
Two other like Gentlemen
VARRIUS, *a gentleman, servant to the Duke*
PROVOST
THOMAS ⎱ *two friars*
PETER ⎰
A JUSTICE
ELBOW, *a simple constable*
FROTH, *a foolish gentleman*
POMPEY, *a clown and servant to Mistress Overdone*
ABHORSON, *an executioner*
BARNARDINE, *a dissolute prisoner*

ISABELLA, *sister to Claudio*
MARIANA, *betrothed to Angelo*
JULIET, *beloved of Claudio*
FRANCISCA, *a nun*
MISTRESS OVERDONE, *a bawd*

Lords, Officers, Citizens, Boy, *and* Attendants

SCENE:
Vienna

Measure for Measure

ACT I. SCENE 1

The DUKE's *palace*

Enter DUKE, ESCALUS, LORDS, *and* ATTENDANTS

DUKE. Escalus!
ESCALUS. My lord.
DUKE. Of government the properties to unfold
  Would seem in me t' affect speech and discourse,
  Since I am put to know that your own science
  Exceeds, in that, the lists of all advice
  My strength can give you; then no more remains
  But that to your sufficiency—as your worth is able—
  And let them work. The nature of our people,
  Our city's institutions, and the terms
  For common justice, y'are as pregnant in
  As art and practice hath enriched any
  That we remember. There is our commission,
  From which we would not have you warp. Call hither,
  I say, bid come before us, Angelo.   *Exit an* ATTENDANT
  What figure of us think you he will bear?
  For you must know we have with special soul
  Elected him our absence to supply;
  Lent him our terror, dress'd him with our love,
  And given his deputation all the organs
  Of our own power. What think you of it?
ESCALUS. If any in Vienna be of worth
  To undergo such ample grace and honour,
  It is Lord Angelo.

Enter ANGELO

DUKE. Look where he comes.
ANGELO. Always obedient to your Grace's will,
  I come to know your pleasure.
DUKE. Angelo,
  There is a kind of character in thy life

That to th' observer doth thy history
Fully unfold. Thyself and thy belongings
Are not thine own so proper as to waste
Thyself upon thy virtues, they on thee.
Heaven doth with us as we with torches do,
Not light them for themselves; for if our virtues
Did not go forth of us, 'twere all alike
As if we had them not. Spirits are not finely touch'd
But to fine issues; nor Nature never lends
The smallest scruple of her excellence
But, like a thrifty goddess, she determines
Herself the glory of a creditor,
Both thanks and use. But I do bend my speech
To one that can my part in him advertise.
Hold, therefore, Angelo—
In our remove be thou at full ourself;
Mortality and mercy in Vienna
Live in thy tongue and heart. Old Escalus,
Though first in question, is thy secondary.
Take thy commission.
ANGELO. Now, good my lord,
Let there be some more test made of my metal,
Before so noble and so great a figure
Be stamp'd upon it.
DUKE. No more evasion!
We have with a leaven'd and prepared choice
Proceeded to you; therefore take your honours.
Our haste from hence is of so quick condition
That it prefers itself, and leaves unquestion'd
Matters of needful value. We shall write to you,
As time and our concernings shall importune,
How it goes with us, and do look to know
What doth befall you here. So, fare you well.
To th' hopeful execution do I leave you .
Of your commissions.
ANGELO. Yet give leave, my lord,
That we may bring you something on the way.
DUKE. My haste may not admit it;
Nor need you, on mine honour, have to do
With any scruple: your scope is as mine own,

So to enforce or qualify the laws
As to your soul seems good. Give me your hand;
I'll privily away. I love the people,
But do not like to stage me to their eyes;
Though it do well, I do not relish well
Their loud applause and Aves vehement;
Nor do I think the man of safe discretion
That does affect it. Once more, fare you well.
ANGELO. The heavens give safety to your purposes!
ESCALUS. Lead forth and bring you back in happiness!
DUKE. I thank you. Fare you well.   *Exit*
ESCALUS. I shall desire you, sir, to give me leave
To have free speech with you; and it concerns me
To look into the bottom of my place:
A pow'r I have, but of what strength and nature
I am not yet instructed.
ANGELO. 'Tis so with me. Let us withdraw together,
And we may soon our satisfaction have
Touching that point.
ESCALUS. I'll wait upon your honour.   *Exeunt*

SCENE 2

A street

Enter LUCIO *and two other* GENTLEMEN

LUCIO. If the Duke, with the other dukes, come not to com-
position with the King of Hungary, why then all the
dukes fall upon the King.
FIRST GENTLEMAN. Heaven grant us its peace, but not the
King of Hungary's!
SECOND GENTLEMAN. Amen.
LUCIO. Thou conclud'st like the sanctimonious pirate that
went to sea with the Ten Commandments, but scrap'd one
out of the table.
SECOND GENTLEMAN. 'Thou shalt not steal'?
LUCIO. Ay, that he raz'd.
FIRST GENTLEMAN. Why, 'twas a commandment to com-
mand the captain and all the rest from their functions: they

put forth to steal. There's not a soldier of us all that, in the thanksgiving before meat, do relish the petition well that prays for peace.

SECOND GENTLEMAN. I never heard any soldier dislike it.

LUCIO. I believe thee; for I think thou never wast where grace was said.

SECOND GENTLEMAN. No? A dozen times at least.

FIRST GENTLEMAN. What, in metre?

LUCIO. In any proportion or in any language.

FIRST GENTLEMAN. I think, or in any religion.

LUCIO. Ay, why not? Grace is grace, despite of all controversy; as, for example, thou thyself art a wicked villain, despite of all grace.

FIRST GENTLEMAN. Well, there went but a pair of shears between us.

LUCIO. I grant; as there may between the lists and the velvet. Thou art the list.

FIRST GENTLEMAN. And thou the velvet; thou art good velvet; thou'rt a three-pil'd piece, I warrant thee. I had as lief be a list of an English kersey as be pil'd, as thou art pil'd, for a French velvet. Do I speak feelingly now?

LUCIO. I think thou dost; and, indeed, with most painful feeling of thy speech. I will, out of thine own confession, learn to begin thy health; but, whilst I live, forget to drink after thee.

FIRST GENTLEMAN. I think I have done myself wrong, have I not?

SECOND GENTLEMAN. Yes, that thou hast, whether thou art tainted or free.

Enter MISTRESS OVERDONE

LUCIO. Behold, behold, where Madam Mitigation comes! I have purchas'd as many diseases under her roof as come to—

SECOND GENTLEMAN. To what, I pray?

FIRST GENTLEMAN. Judge.

SECOND GENTLEMAN. To three thousand dolours a year.

FIRST GENTLEMAN. Ay, and more.

LUCIO. A French crown more.

FIRST GENTLEMAN. Thou art always figuring diseases in me, but thou art full of error; I am sound.

LUCIO. Nay, not, as one would say, healthy; but so sound as things that are hollow: thy bones are hollow; impiety has made a feast of thee.

FIRST GENTLEMAN. How now! which of your hips has the most profound sciatica?

MRS. OVERDONE. Well, well! there's one yonder arrested and carried to prison was worth five thousand of you all.

FIRST GENTLEMAN. Who's that, I pray thee?

MRS. OVERDONE. Marry, sir, that's Claudio, Signior Claudio.

FIRST GENTLEMAN. Claudio to prison? 'Tis not so.

MRS. OVERDONE. Nay, but I know 'tis so: I saw him arrested; saw him carried away; and, which is more, within these three days his head to be chopp'd off.

LUCIO. But, after all this fooling, I would not have it so. Art thou sure of this?

MRS. OVERDONE. I am too sure of it; and it is for getting Madam Julietta with child.

LUCIO. Believe me, this may be; he promis'd to meet me two hours since, and he was ever precise in promise-keeping.

SECOND GENTLEMAN. Besides, you know, it draws something near to the speech we had to such a purpose.

FIRST GENTLEMAN. But most of all agreeing with the proclamation.

LUCIO. Away; let's go learn the truth of it.

Exeunt LUCIO *and* GENTLEMEN

MRS. OVERDONE. Thus, what with the war, what with the sweat, what with the gallows, and what with poverty, I am custom-shrunk.

Enter POMPEY

How now! what's the news with you?

POMPEY. Yonder man is carried to prison.

MRS. OVERDONE. Well, what has he done?

POMPEY. A woman.

MRS. OVERDONE. But what's his offence?

POMPEY. Groping for trouts in a peculiar river.

MRS. OVERDONE. What! is there a maid with child by him?

POMPEY. No; but there's a woman with maid by him. You have not heard of the proclamation, have you?

Mrs. Overdone. What proclamation, man?

Pompey. All houses in the suburbs of Vienna must be pluck'd down.

Mrs. Overdone. And what shall become of those in the city?

Pompey. They shall stand for seed; they had gone down too, but that a wise burgher put in for them.

Mrs. Overdone. But shall all our houses of resort in the suburbs be pull'd down?

Pompey. To the ground, mistress.

Mrs. Overdone. Why, here's a change indeed in the commonwealth! What shall become of me?

Pompey. Come, fear not you: good counsellors lack no clients. Though you change your place you need not change your trade; I'll be your tapster still. Courage, there will be pity taken on you; you that have worn your eyes almost out in the service, you will be considered.

Mrs. Overdone. What's to do here, Thomas Tapster? Let's withdraw.

Pompey. Here comes Signior Claudio, led by the provost to prison; and there's Madam Juliet. *Exeunt*

Enter Provost, Claudio, Juliet, *and* Officers;
Lucio *following*

Claudio. Fellow, why dost thou show me thus to th' world?
Bear me to prison, where I am committed.

Provost. I do it not in evil disposition,
But from Lord Angelo by special charge.

Claudio. Thus can the demigod Authority
Make us pay down for our offence by weight
The words of heaven: on whom it will, it will;
On whom it will not, so; yet still 'tis just.

Lucio. Why, how now, Claudio, whence comes this restraint?

Claudio. From too much liberty, my Lucio, liberty;
As surfeit is the father of much fast,
So every scope by the immoderate use
Turns to restraint. Our natures do pursue,
Like rats that ravin down their proper bane,
A thirsty evil; and when we drink we die.

LUCIO. If I could speak so wisely under an arrest, I would
send for certain of my creditors; and yet, to say the truth,
I had as lief have the foppery of freedom as the morality
of imprisonment. What's thy offence, Claudio?

CLAUDIO. What but to speak of would offend again.

LUCIO. What, is't murder?

CLAUDIO. No.

LUCIO. Lechery?

CLAUDIO. Call it so.

PROVOST. Away, sir; you must go.

CLAUDIO. One word, good friend. Lucio, a word with you.

LUCIO. A hundred, if they'll do you any good. Is lechery so
look'd after?

CLAUDIO. Thus stands it with me: upon a true contract
I got possession of Julietta's bed.
You know the lady; she is fast my wife,
Save that we do the denunciation lack
Of outward order; this we came not to,
Only for propagation of a dow'r
Remaining in the coffer of her friends.
From whom we thought it meet to hide our love
Till time had made them for us. But it chances
The stealth of our most mutual entertainment,
With character too gross, is writ on Juliet.

LUCIO. With child, perhaps?

CLAUDIO. Unhappily, even so.
And the new deputy now for the Duke—
Whether it be the fault and glimpse of newness,
Or whether that the body public be
A horse whereon the governor doth ride,
Who, newly in the seat, that it may know
He can command, lets it straight feel the spur;
Whether the tyranny be in his place,
Or in his eminence that fills it up,
I stagger in. But this new governor
Awakes me all the enrolled penalties
Which have, like unscour'd armour, hung by th' wall
So long that nineteen zodiacs have gone round
And none of them been worn; and, for a name,
Now puts the drowsy and neglected act

Freshly on me. 'Tis surely for a name.

LUCIO. I warrant it is; and thy head stands so tickle on thy shoulders that a milkmaid, if she be in love, may sigh it off. Send after the Duke, and appeal to him.

CLAUDIO. I have done so, but he's not to be found.
I prithee, Lucio, do me this kind service:
This day my sister should the cloister enter,
And there receive her approbation;
Acquaint her with the danger of my state;
Implore her, in my voice, that she make friends
To the strict deputy; bid herself assay him.
I have great hope in that; for in her youth
There is a prone and speechless dialect
Such as move men; beside, she hath prosperous art
When she will play with reason and discourse,
And well she can persuade.

LUCIO. I pray she may; as well for the encouragement of the like, which else would stand under grievous imposition, as for the enjoying of thy life, who I would be sorry should be thus foolishly lost at a game of tick-tack. I'll to her.

CLAUDIO. I thank you, good friend Lucio.

LUCIO. Within two hours.

CLAUDIO. Come, officer, away.   *Exeunt*

SCENE 3

A monastery

Enter DUKE *and* FRIAR THOMAS

DUKE. No, holy father; throw away that thought;
Believe not that the dribbling dart of love
Can pierce a complete bosom. Why I desire thee
To give me secret harbour hath a purpose
More grave and wrinkled than the aims and ends
Of burning youth.

FRIAR. May your Grace speak of it?

DUKE. My holy sir, none better knows than you
How I have ever lov'd the life removed,
And held in idle price to haunt assemblies

Where youth, and cost, a witless bravery keeps.
I have deliver'd to Lord Angelo,
A man of stricture and firm abstinence,
My absolute power and place here in Vienna,
And he supposes me travell'd to Poland;
For so I have strew'd it in the common ear,
And so it is received. Now, pious sir,
You will demand of me why I do this.
FRIAR. Gladly, my lord.
DUKE. We have strict statutes and most biting laws,
The needful bits and curbs to headstrong steeds,
Which for this fourteen years we have let slip;
Even like an o'ergrown lion in a cave,
That goes not out to prey. Now, as fond fathers,
Having bound up the threat'ning twigs of birch,
Only to stick it in their children's sight
For terror, not to use, in time the rod
Becomes more mock'd than fear'd; so our decrees,
Dead to infliction, to themselves are dead;
And liberty plucks justice by the nose;
The baby beats the nurse, and quite athwart
Goes all decorum.
FRIAR. It rested in your Grace
To unloose this tied-up justice when you pleas'd;
And it in you more dreadful would have seem'd
Than in Lord Angelo.
DUKE. I do fear, too dreadful.
Sith 'twas my fault to give the people scope,
'Twould be my tyranny to strike and gall them
For what I bid them do; for we bid this be done,
When evil deeds have their permissive pass
And not the punishment. Therefore, indeed, my father,
I have on Angelo impos'd the office;
Who may, in th' ambush of my name, strike home,
And yet my nature never in the fight
To do in slander. And to behold his sway,
I will, as 'twere a brother of your order,
Visit both prince and people. Therefore, I prithee,
Supply me with the habit, and instruct me
How I may formally in person bear me

237

Like a true friar. Moe reasons for this action
At our more leisure shall I render you.
Only, this one: Lord Angelo is precise;
Stands at a guard with envy; scarce confesses
That his blood flows, or that his appetite
Is more to bread than stone. Hence shall we see,
If power change purpose, what our seemers be.   *Exeunt*

SCENE 4

A nunnery

Enter ISABELLA *and* FRANCISCA

ISABELLA. And have you nuns no farther privileges?
FRANCISCA. Are not these large enough?
ISABELLA. Yes, truly; I speak not as desiring more,
But rather wishing a more strict restraint
Upon the sisterhood, the votarists of Saint Clare.
LUCIO. [*Within*] Ho! Peace be in this place!
ISABELLA. Who's that which calls?
FRANCISCA. It is a man's voice. Gentle Isabella,
Turn you the key, and know his business of him:
You may, I may not; you are yet unsworn;
When you have vow'd, you must not speak with men
But in the presence of the prioress;
Then, if you speak, you must not show your face,
Or, if you show your face, you must not speak.
He calls again; I pray you answer him.   *Exit* FRANCISCA
ISABELLA. Peace and prosperity! Who is't that calls?

Enter LUCIO

LUCIO. Hail, virgin, if you be, as those cheek-roses
Proclaim you are no less. Can you so stead me
As bring me to the sight of Isabella,
A novice of this place, and the fair sister
To her unhappy brother Claudio?
ISABELLA. Why her 'unhappy brother'? Let me ask
The rather, for I now must make you know
I am that Isabella, and his sister.

Lucio. Gentle and fair, your brother kindly greets you.
Not to be weary with you, he's in prison.
Isabella. Woe me! For what?
Lucio. For that which, if myself might be his judge,
He should receive his punishment in thanks:
He hath got his friend with child.
Isabella. Sir, make me not your story.
Lucio. It is true.
I would not—though 'tis my familiar sin
With maids to seem the lapwing, and to jest,
Tongue far from heart—play with all virgins so:
I hold you as a thing enskied and sainted,
By your renouncement an immortal spirit,
And to be talk'd with in sincerity,
As with a saint.
Isabella. You do blaspheme the good in mocking me.
Lucio. Do not believe it. Fewness and truth, 'tis thus:
Your brother and his lover have embrac'd.
As those that feed grow full, as blossoming time
That from the seedness the bare fallow brings
To teeming foison, even so her plenteous womb
Expresseth his full tilth and husbandry.
Isabella. Some one with child by him? My cousin Juliet?
Lucio. Is she your cousin?
Isabella. Adoptedly, as school-maids change their names
By vain though apt affection.
Lucio. She it is.
Isabella. O, let him marry her!
Lucio. This is the point.
The Duke is very strangely gone from hence;
Bore many gentlemen, myself being one,
In hand, and hope of action; but we do learn,
By those that know the very nerves of state,
His givings-out were of an infinite distance
From his true-meant design. Upon his place,
And with full line of his authority,
Governs Lord Angelo, a man whose blood
Is very snow-broth, one who never feels
The wanton stings and motions of the sense,
But doth rebate and blunt his natural edge

With profits of the mind, study and fast.
He—to give fear to use and liberty,
Which have for long run by the hideous law,
As mice by lions—hath pick'd out an act
Under whose heavy sense your brother's life
Falls into forfeit; he arrests him on it,
And follows close the rigour of the statute
To make him an example. All hope is gone,
Unless you have the grace by your fair prayer
To soften Angelo. And that's my pith of business
'Twixt you and your poor brother.

ISABELLA. Doth he so seek his life?

LUCIO. Has censur'd him
Already, and, as I hear, the Provost hath
A warrant for his execution.

ISABELLA. Alas! what poor ability's in me
To do him good?

LUCIO. Assay the pow'r you have.

ISABELLA. My power, alas, I doubt!

LUCIO. Our doubts are traitors,
And make us lose the good we oft might win
By fearing to attempt. Go to Lord Angelo,
And let him learn to know, when maidens sue,
Men give like gods; but when they weep and kneel,
All their petitions are as freely theirs
As they themselves would owe them.

ISABELLA. I'll see what I can do.

LUCIO. But speedily.

ISABELLA. I will about it straight;
No longer staying but to give the Mother
Notice of my affair. I humbly thank you.
Commend me to my brother; soon at night
I'll send him certain word of my success.

LUCIO. I take my leave of you.

ISABELLA. Good sir, adieu.   *Exeunt*

ACT II. SCENE 1

A hall in ANGELO's *house*

Enter ANGELO, ESCALUS, *a* JUSTICE, PROVOST, OFFICERS, *and other* ATTENDANTS

ANGELO. We must not make a scarecrow of the law,
Setting it up to fear the birds of prey,
And let it keep one shape till custom make it
Their perch, and not their terror.
ESCALUS. Ay, but yet
Let us be keen, and rather cut a little
Than fall and bruise to death. Alas! this gentleman,
Whom I would save, had a most noble father.
Let but your honour know,
Whom I believe to be most strait in virtue,
That, in the working of your own affections,
Had time coher'd with place, or place with wishing,
Or that the resolute acting of our blood
Could have attain'd th' effect of your own purpose
Whether you had not sometime in your life
Err'd in this point which now you censure him,
And pull'd the law upon you.
ANGELO. 'Tis one thing to be tempted, Escalus,
Another thing to fall. I not deny
The jury, passing on the prisoner's life,
May in the sworn twelve have a thief or two
Guiltier than him they try. What's open made to justice,
That justice seizes. What knows the laws
That thieves do pass on thieves? 'Tis very pregnant,
The jewel that we find, we stoop and take't,
Because we see it; but what we do not see
We tread upon, and never think of it.
You may not so extenuate his offence
For I have had such faults; but rather tell me,
When I, that censure him, do so offend,
Let mine own judgment pattern out my death,
And nothing come in partial. Sir, he must die.
ESCALUS. Be it as your wisdom will.
ANGELO. Where is the Provost?

PROVOST. Here, if it like your honour.

ANGELO. See that Claudio
Be executed by nine to-morrow morning;
Bring him his confessor; let him be prepar'd;
For that's the utmost of his pilgrimage. *Exit* PROVOST

ESCALUS. [*Aside*] Well, heaven forgive him! and forgive us
all!
Some rise by sin, and some by virtue fall;
Some run from breaks of ice, and answer none,
And some condemned for a fault alone.

Enter ELBOW *and* OFFICERS *with* FROTH *and* POMPEY

ELBOW. Come, bring them away; if these be good people in
a commonweal that do nothing but use their abuses in
common houses, I know no law; bring them away.

ANGELO. How now, sir! What's your name, and what's the
matter?

ELBOW. If it please your honour, I am the poor Duke's constable, and my name is Elbow; I do lean upon justice, sir,
and do bring in here before your good honour two notorious benefactors.

ANGELO. Benefactors! Well—what benefactors are they? Are
they not malefactors?

ELBOW. If it please your honour, I know not well what they
are; but precise villains they are, that I am sure of, and
void of all profanation in the world that good Christians
ought to have.

ESCALUS. This comes off well; here's a wise officer.

ANGELO. Go to; what quality are they of? Elbow is your
name? Why dost thou not speak, Elbow?

POMPEY. He cannot, sir; he's out at elbow.

ANGELO. What are you, sir?

ELBOW. He, sir? A tapster, sir; parcel-bawd; one that serves a
bad woman; whose house, sir, was, as they say, pluck'd
down in the suburbs; and now she professes a hot-house,
which, I think, is a very ill house too.

ESCALUS. How know you that?

ELBOW. My wife, sir, whom I detest before heaven and your
honour—

ESCALUS. How! thy wife!

ELBOW. Ay, sir; whom I thank heaven, is an honest woman—

ESCALUS. Dost thou detest her therefore?

ELBOW. I say, sir, I will detest myself also, as well as she, that this house, if it be not a bawd's house, it is pity of her life, for it is a naughty house.

ESCALUS. How dost thou know that, constable?

ELBOW. Marry, sir, by my wife; who, if she had been a woman cardinally given, might have been accus'd in fornication, adultery, and all uncleanliness there.

ESCALUS. By the woman's means?

ELBOW. Ay, sir, by Mistress Overdone's means; but as she spit in his face, so she defied him.

POMPEY. Sir, if it please your honour, this is not so.

ELBOW. Prove it before these varlets here, thou honourable man, prove it.

ESCALUS. Do you hear how he misplaces?

POMPEY. Sir, she came in great with child; and longing, saving your honour's reverence, for stew'd prunes. Sir, we had but two in the house, which at that very distant time stood, as it were, in a fruit dish, a dish of some three pence; your honours have seen such dishes; they are not China dishes, but very good dishes.

ESCALUS. Go to, go to; no matter for the dish, sir.

POMPEY. No, indeed, sir, not of a pin; you are therein in the right; but to the point. As I say, this Mistress Elbow, being, as I say, with child, and being great-bellied, and longing, as I said, for prunes; and having but two in the dish, as I said, Master Froth here, this very man, having eaten the rest, as I said, and, as I say, paying for them very honestly; for, as you know, Master Froth, I could not give you three pence again—

FROTH. No, indeed.

POMPEY. Very well; you being then, if you be rememb'red, cracking the stones of the foresaid prunes—

FROTH. Ay, so I did indeed.

POMPEY. Why, very well; I telling you then, if you be rememb'red, that such a one and such a one were past cure of the thing you wot of, unless they kept very good diet, as I told you—

FROTH. All this is true.

POMPEY. Why, very well then—

ESCALUS. Come, you are a tedious fool. To the purpose: what was done to Elbow's wife that he hath cause to complain of? Come me to what was done to her.

POMPEY. Sir, your honour cannot come to that yet.

ESCALUS. No, sir, nor I mean it not.

POMPEY. Sir, but you shall come to it, by your honour's leave. And, I beseech you, look into Master Froth here, sir, a man of fourscore pound a year; whose father died at Hallowmas—was't not at Hallowmas, Master Froth?

FROTH. All-hallond eve.

POMPEY. Why, very well; I hope here be truths. He, sir, sitting, as I say, in a lower chair, sir; 'twas in the Bunch of Grapes, where, indeed, you have a delight to sit, have you not?

FROTH. I have so; because it is an open room, and good for winter.

POMPEY. Why, very well then; I hope here be truths.

ANGELO. This will last out a night in Russia,
When nights are longest there; I'll take my leave,
And leave you to the hearing of the cause,
Hoping you'll find good cause to whip them all.

ESCALUS. I think no less. Good morrow to your lordship.
[*Exit* ANGELO] Now, sir, come on; what was done to Elbow's wife, once more?

POMPEY. Once?—sir. There was nothing done to her once.

ELBOW. I beseech you, sir, ask him what this man did to my wife.

POMPEY. I beseech your honour, ask me.

ESCALUS. Well, sir, what did this gentleman to her?

POMPEY. I beseech you, sir, look in this gentleman's face. Good Master Froth, look upon his honour; 'tis for a good purpose. Doth your honour mark his face?

ESCALUS. Ay, sir, very well.

POMPEY. Nay, I beseech you, mark it well.

ESCALUS. Well, I do so.

POMPEY. Doth your honour see any harm in his face?

ESCALUS. Why, no.

POMPEY. I'll be suppos'd upon a book his face is the worst thing about him. Good then; if his face be the worst thing

244

about him, how could Master Froth do the constable's wife any harm? I would know that of your honour.

ESCALUS. He's in the right, constable; what say you to it?

ELBOW. First, an it like you, the house is a respected house; next, this is a respected fellow; and his mistress is a respected woman.

POMPEY. By this hand, sir, his wife is a more respected person than any of us all.

ELBOW. Varlet, thou liest; thou liest, wicket varlet; the time is yet to come that she was ever respected with man, woman, or child.

POMPEY. Sir, she was respected with him before he married with her.

ESCALUS. Which is the wiser here, Justice or Iniquity? Is this true?

ELBOW. O thou caitiff! O thou varlet! O thou wicked Hannibal! I respected with her before I was married to her! If ever I was respected with her, or she with me, let not your worship think me the poor Duke's officer. Prove this, thou wicked Hannibal, or I'll have mine action of batt'ry on thee.

ESCALUS. If he took you a box o' th' ear, you might have your action of slander too.

ELBOW. Marry, I thank your good worship for it. What is't your worship's pleasure I shall do with this wicked caitiff?

ESCALUS. Truly, officer, because he hath some offences in him that thou wouldst discover if thou couldst, let him continue in his courses till thou know'st what they are.

ELBOW. Marry, I thank your worship for it. Thou seest, thou wicked varlet, now, what's come upon thee: thou art to continue now, thou varlet; thou art to continue.

ESCALUS. Where were you born, friend?

FROTH. Here in Vienna, sir.

ESCALUS. Are you of fourscore pounds a year?

FROTH. Yes, an't please you, sir.

ESCALUS. So. What trade are you of, sir?

POMPEY. A tapster, a poor widow's tapster.

ESCALUS. Your mistress' name?

POMPEY. Mistress Overdone.

ESCALUS. Hath she had any more than one husband?

POMPEY. Nine, sir; Overdone by the last.

ESCALUS. Nine! Come hither to me, Master Froth. Master
Froth, I would not have you acquainted with tapsters:
they will draw you, Master Froth, and you will hang
them. Get you gone, and let me hear no more of you.

FROTH. I thank your worship. For mine own part, I never
come into any room in a taphouse but I am drawn in.

ESCALUS. Well, no more of it, Master Froth; farewell. [*Exit*
FROTH] Come you hither to me, Master Tapster; what's
your name, Master Tapster?

POMPEY. Pompey.

ESCALUS. What else?

POMPEY. Bum, sir.

ESCALUS. Troth, and your bum is the greatest thing about
you; so that, in the beastliest sense, you are Pompey the
Great. Pompey, you are partly a bawd, Pompey, howsoever you colour it in being a tapster. Are you not? Come,
tell me true; it shall be the better for you.

POMPEY. Truly, sir, I am a poor fellow that would live.

ESCALUS. How would you live, Pompey—by being a bawd?
What do you think of the trade, Pompey? Is it a lawful
trade?

POMPEY. If the law would allow it, sir.

ESCALUS. But the law will not allow it, Pompey; nor it shall
not be allowed in Vienna.

POMPEY. Does your worship mean to geld and splay all the
youth of the city?

ESCALUS. No, Pompey.

POMPEY. Truly, sir, in my poor opinion, they will to't then.
If your worship will take order for the drabs and the
knaves, you need not to fear the bawds.

ESCALUS. There is pretty orders beginning, I can tell you:
but it is but heading and hanging.

POMPEY. If you head and hang all that offend that way but
for ten year together, you'll be glad to give out a commission for more heads; if this law hold in Vienna ten year,
I'll rent the fairest house in it, after threepence a bay. If
you live to see this come to pass, say Pompey told you so.

ESCALUS. Thank you, good Pompey; and, in requital of
your prophecy, hark you: I advise you, let me not find you

before me again upon any complaint whatsoever—no, not
for dwelling where you do; if I do, Pompey, I shall beat
you to your tent, and prove a shrewd Cæsar to you; in
plain dealing, Pompey, I shall have you whipt. So for this
time, Pompey, fare you well.

POMPEY. I thank your worship for your good counsel;
[*Aside*] but I shall follow it as the flesh and fortune shall
better determine.
Whip me? No, no; let carman whip his jade;
The valiant heart's not whipt out of his trade.   *Exit*

ESCALUS. Come hither to me, Master Elbow; come hither,
Master Constable. How long have you been in this place
of constable?

ELBOW. Seven year and a half, sir.

ESCALUS. I thought, by the readiness in the office, you had
continued in it some time. You say seven years together?

ELBOW. And a half, sir.

ESCALUS. Alas, it hath been great pains to you! They do you
wrong to put you so oft upon't. Are there not men in your
ward sufficient to serve it?

ELBOW. Faith, sir, few of any wit in such matters; as they are
chosen, they are glad to choose me for them; I do it for
some piece of money, and go through with all.

ESCALUS. Look you, bring me in the names of some six or
seven, the most sufficient of your parish.

ELBOW. To your worship's house, sir?

ESCALUS. To my house. Fare you well. [*Exit* ELBOW]
What's o'clock, think you?

JUSTICE. Eleven, sir.

ESCALUS. I pray you home to dinner with me.

JUSTICE. I humbly thank you.

ESCALUS. It grieves me for the death of Claudio;
But there's no remedy.

JUSTICE. Lord Angelo is severe.

ESCALUS. It is but needful:
Mercy is not itself that oft looks so;
Pardon is still the nurse of second woe.
But yet, poor Claudio! There is no remedy.
Come, sir.   *Exeunt*

SCENE 2

Another room in ANGELO'S *house*

Enter PROVOST *and a* SERVANT

SERVANT. He's hearing of a cause; he will come straight.
I'll tell him of you.
PROVOST. Pray you do. [*Exit* SERVANT] I'll know
His pleasure; may be he will relent. Alas,
He hath but as offended in a dream!
All sects, all ages, smack of this vice; and he
To die for 't!

Enter ANGELO

ANGELO. Now, what's the matter, Provost?
PROVOST. Is it your will Claudio shall die to-morrow?
ANGELO. Did not I tell thee yea? Hadst thou not order?
Why dost thou ask again?
PROVOST. Lest I might be too rash;
Under your good correction, I have seen
When, after execution, judgment hath
Repented o'er his doom.
ANGELO. Go to; let that be mine.
Do you your office, or give up your place,
And you shall well be spar'd.
PROVOST. I crave your honour's pardon.
What shall be done, sir, with the groaning Juliet?
She's very near her hour.
ANGELO. Dispose of her
To some more fitter place, and that with speed.

Re-enter SERVANT

SERVANT. Here is the sister of the man condemn'd
Desires access to you.
ANGELO. Hath he a sister?
PROVOST. Ay, my good lord; a very virtuous maid,
And to be shortly of a sisterhood,
If not already.

ANGELO. Well, let her be admitted.   *Exit* SERVANT
  See you the fornicatress be remov'd;
  Let her have needful but not lavish means;
  There shall be order for't.

Enter LUCIO *and* ISABELLA

PROVOST. [*Going*] Save your honour!
ANGELO. Stay a little while. [*To* ISABELLA] Y'are welcome;
  what's your will?
ISABELLA. I am a woeful suitor to your honour,
  Please but your honour hear me.
ANGELO. Well; what's your suit?
ISABELLA. There is a vice that most I do abhor,
  And most desire should meet the blow of justice;
  For which I would not plead, but that I must;
  For which I must not plead, but that I am
  At war 'twixt will and will not.
ANGELO. Well; the matter?
ISABELLA. I have a brother is condemn'd to die;
  I do beseech you, let it be his fault,
  And not my brother.
PROVOST. [*Aside*] Heaven give thee moving graces.
ANGELO. Condemn the fault and not the actor of it!
  Why, every fault's condemn'd ere it be done;
  Mine were the very cipher of a function,
  To fine the faults whose fine stands in record,
  And let go by the actor.
ISABELLA. O just but severe law!
  I had a brother, then. Heaven keep your honour!
LUCIO. [*To* ISABELLA] Give't not o'er so; to him again, en-
  treat him,
  Kneel down before him, hang upon his gown;
  You are too cold: if you should need a pin,
  You could not with more tame a tongue desire it.
  To him, I say.
ISABELLA. Must he needs die?
ANGELO. Maiden, no remedy.
ISABELLA. Yes; I do think that you might pardon him.
  And neither heaven nor man grieve at the mercy.
ANGELO. I will not do't.

Isabella. But can you, if you would?

Angelo. Look, what I will not, that I cannot do.

Isabella. But might you do't, and do the world no wrong,
If so your heart were touch'd with that remorse
As mine is to him?

Angelo. He's sentenc'd; 'tis too late.

Lucio. [To Isabella] You are too cold.

Isabella. Too late? Why, no; I, that do speak a word,
May call it back again. Well, believe this:
No ceremony that to great ones longs,
Not the king's crown nor the deputed sword,
The marshal's truncheon nor the judge's robe,
Become them with one half so good a grace
As mercy does.
If he had been as you, and you as he,
You would have slipp'd like him; but he, like you,
Would not have been so stern.

Angelo. Pray you be gone.

Isabella. I would to heaven I had your potency,
And you were Isabel! Should it then be thus?
No; I would tell what 'twere to be a judge
And what a prisoner.

Lucio. [To Isabella] Ay, touch him; there's the vein.

Angelo. Your brother is a forfeit of the law,
And you but waste your words.

Isabella. Alas! Alas!
Why, all the souls that were were forfeit once;
And He that might the vantage best have took
Found out the remedy. How would you be
If He, which is the top of judgment, should
But judge you as you are? O, think on that;
And mercy then will breathe within your lips,
Like man new made.

Angelo. Be you content, fair maid.
It is the law, not I condemn your brother.
Were he my kinsman, brother, or my son,
It should be thus with him. He must die to-morrow.

Isabella. To-morrow! O, that's sudden! Spare him, spare him.
He's not prepar'd for death. Even for our kitchens

We kill the fowl of season; shall we serve heaven
With less respect than we do minister
To our gross selves? Good, good my lord, bethink you.
Who is it that hath died for this offence?
There's many have committed it.

LUCIO. [*Aside*] Ay, well said.

ANGELO. The law hath not been dead, though it hath slept.
Those many had not dar'd to do that evil
If the first that did th' edict infringe
Had answer'd for his deed. Now 'tis awake,
Takes note of what is done, and, like a prophet,
Looks in a glass that shows what future evils—
Either now or by remissness new conceiv'd,
And so in progress to be hatch'd and born—
Are now to have no successive degrees,
But here they live to end.

ISABELLA. Yet show some pity.

ANGELO. I show it most of all when I show justice;
For then I pity those I do not know,
Which a dismiss'd offence would after gall,
And do him right that, answering one foul wrong,
Lives not to act another. Be satisfied;
Your brother dies to-morrow; be content.

ISABELLA. So you must be the first that gives this sentence,
And he that suffers. O, it is excellent
To have a giant's strength! But it is tyrannous
To use it like a giant.

LUCIO. [*To* ISABELLA] That's well said.

ISABELLA. Could great men thunder
As Jove himself does, Jove would never be quiet,
For every pelting petty officer
Would use his heaven for thunder,
Nothing but thunder. Merciful Heaven,
Thou rather, with thy sharp and sulphurous bolt,
Splits the unwedgeable and gnarled oak
Than the soft myrtle. But man, proud man,
Dress'd in a little brief authority,
Most ignorant of what he's most assur'd,
His glassy essence, like an angry ape,
Plays such fantastic tricks before high heaven

As makes the angels weep; who, with our spleens,
Would all themselves laugh mortal.
LUCIO. [*To* ISABELLA] O, to him, to him, wench! He will
relent;
He's coming; I perceive 't.
PROVOST. [*Aside*] Pray heaven she win him.
ISABELLA. We cannot weigh our brother with ourself.
Great men may jest with saints: 'tis wit in them;
But in the less foul profanation.
LUCIO. [*To* ISABELLA] Thou'rt i' th' right, girl; more o' that.
ISABELLA. That in the captain's but a choleric word
Which in the soldier is flat blasphemy.
LUCIO. [*To* ISABELLA] Art avis'd o' that? More on't.
ANGELO. Why do you put these sayings upon me?
ISABELLA. Because authority, though it err like others,
Hath yet a kind of medicine in itself
That skins the vice o' th' top. Go to your bosom,
Knock there, and ask your heart what it doth know
That's like my brother's fault. If it confess
A natural guiltiness such as is his,
Let it not sound a thought upon your tongue
Against my brother's life.
ANGELO. [*Aside*] She speaks, and 'tis
Such sense that my sense breeds with it.—Fare you well.
ISABELLA. Gentle my lord, turn back.
ANGELO. I will bethink me. Come again to-morrow.
ISABELLA. Hark how I'll bribe you; good my lord, turn back.
ANGELO. How, bribe me?
ISABELLA. Ay, with such gifts that heaven shall share with
you.
LUCIO. [*To* ISABELLA] You had marr'd all else.
ISABELLA. Not with fond sicles of the tested gold,
Or stones, whose rate are either rich or poor
As fancy values them; but with true prayers
That shall be up at heaven and enter there
Ere sun-rise, prayers from preserved souls,
From fasting maids, whose minds are dedicate
To nothing temporal.
ANGELO. Well; come to me to-morrow.
LUCIO. [*To* ISABELLA] Go to; 'tis well; away.

ISABELLA. Heaven keep your honour safe!
ANGELO. [*Aside*] Amen; for I
  Am that way going to temptation
  Where prayers cross.
ISABELLA. At what hour to-morrow
  Shall I attend your lordship?
ANGELO. At any time 'fore noon.
ISABELLA. Save your honour!   *Exeunt all but* ANGELO
ANGELO. From thee; even from thy virtue!
  What's this, what's this? Is this her fault or mine?
  The tempter or the tempted, who sins most?
  Ha!
  Not she; nor doth she tempt; but it is I
  That, lying by the violet in the sun,
  Do as the carrion does, not as the flow'r,
  Corrupt with virtuous season. Can it be
  That modesty may more betray our sense
  Than woman's lightness? Having waste ground enough,
  Shall we desire to raze the sanctuary,
  And pitch our evils there? O, fie, fie, fie!
  What dost thou, or what art thou, Angelo?
  Dost thou desire her foully for those things
  That make her good? O, let her brother live!
  Thieves for their robbery have authority
  When judges steal themselves. What, do I love her,
  That I desire to hear her speak again,
  And feast upon her eyes? What is't I dream on?
  O cunning enemy, that, to catch a saint,
  With saints dost bait thy hook! Most dangerous
  Is that temptation that doth goad us on
  To sin in loving virtue. Never could the strumpet,
  With all her double vigour, art and nature,
  Once stir my temper; but this virtuous maid
  Subdues me quite. Ever till now,
  When men were fond, I smil'd and wond'red how.   *Exit*

SCENE 3

A prison

Enter, severally, DUKE, *disguised as a* FRIAR, *and* PROVOST

DUKE. Hail to you, Provost! so I think you are.
PROVOST. I am the Provost. What's your will, good friar?
DUKE. Bound by my charity and my blest order,
  I come to visit the afflicted spirits
  Here in the prison. Do me the common right
  To let me see them, and to make me know
  The nature of their crimes, that I may minister
  To them accordingly.
PROVOST. I would do more than that, if more were needful.

Enter JULIET

Look, here comes one; a gentlewoman of mine,
Who, falling in the flaws of her own youth,
Hath blister'd her report. She is with child;
And he that got it, sentenc'd—a young man
More fit to do another such offence
Than die for this.
DUKE. When must he die?
PROVOST. As I do think, to-morrow.
  [*To* JULIET] I have provided for you; stay awhile
  And you shall be conducted.
DUKE. Repent you, fair one, of the sin you carry?
JULIET. I do; and bear the shame most patiently.
DUKE. I'll teach you how you shall arraign your conscience,
  And try your penitence, if it be sound
  Or hollowly put on.
JULIET. I'll gladly learn.
DUKE. Love you the man that wrong'd you?
JULIET. Yes, as I love the woman that wrong'd him.
DUKE. So then, it seems, your most offenceful act
  Was mutually committed.
JULIET. Mutually.
DUKE. Then was your sin of heavier kind than his.
JULIET. I do confess it, and repent it, father.

ACT II. SCENE 3

DUKE. 'Tis meet so, daughter; but lest you do repent
  As that the sin hath brought you to this shame,
  Which sorrow is always toward ourselves, not heaven,
  Showing we would not spare heaven as we love it,
  But as we stand in fear—
JULIET. I do repent me as it is an evil,
  And take the shame with joy.
DUKE. There rest.
  Your partner, as I hear, must die to-morrow,
  And I am going with instruction to him.
  Grace go with you! Benedicite!   *Exit*
JULIET. Must die to-morrow! O, injurious law,
  That respites me a life whose very comfort
  Is still a dying horror!
PROVOST. 'Tis pity of him.   *Exeunt*

SCENE 4

ANGELO's house

Enter ANGELO

ANGELO. When I would pray and think, I think and pray
  To several subjects. Heaven hath my empty words,
  Whilst my invention, hearing not my tongue,
  Anchors on Isabel. Heaven in my mouth,
  As if I did but only chew his name,
  And in my heart the strong and swelling evil
  Of my conception. The state whereon I studied
  Is, like a good thing being often read,
  Grown sere and tedious; yea, my gravity,
  Wherein—let no man hear me—I take pride,
  Could I with boot change for an idle plume
  Which the air beats for vain. O place, O form,
  How often dost thou with thy case, thy habit,
  Wrench awe from fools, and tie the wiser souls
  To thy false seeming! Blood, thou art blood.
  Let's write 'good angel' on the devil's horn;
  'Tis not the devil's crest.

Enter SERVANT

How now, who's there?

SERVANT. One Isabel, a sister, desires access to you.

ANGELO. Teach her the way. [*Exit* SERVANT] O heavens!
Why does my blood thus muster to my heart,
Making both it unable for itself
And dispossessing all my other parts
Of necessary fitness?
So play the foolish throngs with one that swoons;
Come all to help him, and so stop the air
By which he should revive; and even so
The general subject to a well-wish'd king
Quit their own part, and in obsequious fondness
Crowd to his presence, where their untaught love
Must needs appear offence.

Enter ISABELLA

How now, fair maid?

ISABELLA. I am come to know your pleasure.

ANGELO. That you might know it would much better please
    me
Than to demand what 'tis. Your brother cannot live.

ISABELLA. Even so! Heaven keep your honour!

ANGELO. Yet may he live awhile, and, it may be,
    As long as you or I; yet he must die.

ISABELLA. Under your sentence?

ANGELO. Yea.

ISABELLA. When? I beseech you; that in his reprieve,
    Longer or shorter, he may be so fitted
    That his soul sicken not.

ANGELO. Ha! Fie, these filthy vices! It were as good
    To pardon him that hath from nature stol'n
    A man already made, as to remit
    Their saucy sweetness that do coin heaven's image
    In stamps that are forbid; 'tis all as easy
    Falsely to take away a life true made
    As to put metal in restrained means
    To make a false one.

ISABELLA. 'Tis set down so in heaven, but not in earth.

ANGELO. Say you so? Then I shall pose you quickly.
  Which had you rather—that the most just law
  Now took your brother's life; or, to redeem him,
  Give up your body to such sweet uncleanness
  As she that he hath stain'd?
ISABELLA. Sir, believe this:
  I had rather give my body than my soul.
ANGELO. I talk not of your soul; our compell'd sins
  Stand more for number than for accompt.
ISABELLA. How say you?
ANGELO. Nay, I'll not warrant that; for I can speak
  Against the thing I say. Answer to this:
  I, now the voice of the recorded law,
  Pronounce a sentence on your brother's life;
  Might there not be a charity in sin
  To save this brother's life?
ISABELLA. Please you to do't,
  I'll take it as a peril to my soul
  It is no sin at all, but charity.
ANGELO. Pleas'd you to do't at peril of your soul,
  Were equal poise of sin and charity.
ISABELLA. That I do beg his life, if it be sin,
  Heaven let me bear it! You granting of my suit,
  If that be sin, I'll make it my morn prayer
  To have it added to the faults of mine,
  And nothing of your answer.
ANGELO. Nay, but hear me;
  Your sense pursues not mine; either you are ignorant
  Or seem so, craftily; and that's not good.
ISABELLA. Let me be ignorant, and in nothing good
  But graciously to know I am no better.
ANGELO. Thus wisdom wishes to appear most bright
  When it doth tax itself; as these black masks
  Proclaim an enshielded beauty ten times louder
  Than beauty could, display'd. But mark me:
  To be received plain, I'll speak more gross—
  Your brother is to die.
ISABELLA. So.
ANGELO. And his offence is so, as it appears,
  Accountant to the law upon that pain.

257

ISABELLA. True.

ANGELO. Admit no other way to save his life,
As I subscribe not that, nor any other,
But, in the loss of question, that you, his sister,
Finding yourself desir'd of such a person
Whose credit with the judge, or own great place,
Could fetch your brother from the manacles
Of the all-binding law; and that there were
No earthly mean to save him but that either
You must lay down the treasures of your body
To this supposed, or else to let him suffer—
What would you do?

ISABELLA. As much for my poor brother as myself;
That is, were I under the terms of death,
Th' impression of keen whips I'd wear as rubies,
And strip myself to death as to a bed
That longing have been sick for, ere I'd yield
My body up to shame.

ANGELO. Then must your brother die.

ISABELLA. And 'twere the cheaper way:
Better it were a brother died at once
Than that a sister, by redeeming him,
Should die for ever.

ANGELO. Were not you, then, as cruel as the sentence
That you have slander'd so?

ISABELLA. Ignominy in ransom and free pardon
Are of two houses: lawful mercy
Is nothing kin to foul redemption.

ANGELO. You seem'd of late to make the law a tyrant;
And rather prov'd the sliding of your brother
A merriment than a vice.

ISABELLA. O, pardon me, my lord! It oft falls out,
To have what we would have, we speak not what we
mean:
I something do excuse the thing I hate
For his advantage that I dearly love.

ANGELO. We are all frail.

ISABELLA. Else let my brother die,
If not a fedary but only he
Owe and succeed thy weakness.

ANGELO. Nay, women are frail too.

ISABELLA. Ay, as the glasses where they view themselves,
Which are as easy broke as they make forms.
Women, help heaven! Men their creation mar
In profiting by them. Nay, call us ten times frail;
For we are soft as our complexions are,
And credulous to false prints.

ANGELO. I think it well;
And from this testimony of your own sex,
Since I suppose we are made to be no stronger
Than faults may shake our frames, let me be bold.
I do arrest your words. Be that you are,
That is, a woman; if you be more, you're none;
If you be one, as you are well express'd
By all external warrants, show it now
By putting on the destin'd livery.

ISABELLA. I have no tongue but one; gentle, my lord,
Let me intreat you speak the former language.

ANGELO. Plainly conceive, I love you.

ISABELLA. My brother did love Juliet,
And you tell me that he shall die for't.

ANGELO. He shall not, Isabel, if you give me love.

ISABELLA. I know your virtue hath a license in't,
Which seems a little fouler than it is,
To pluck on others.

ANGELO. Believe me, on mine honour,
My words express my purpose.

ISABELLA. Ha! little honour to be much believ'd,
And most pernicious purpose! Seeming, seeming!
I will proclaim thee, Angelo, look for't.
Sign me a present pardon for my brother
Or, with an outstretch'd throat, I'll tell the world aloud
What man thou art.

ANGELO. Who will believe thee, Isabel?
My unsoil'd name, th' austereness of my life,
My vouch against you, and my place i' th' state,
Will so your accusation overweigh
That you shall stifle in your own report,
And smell of calumny. I have begun,
And now I give my sensual race the rein:

Fit thy consent to my sharp appetite;
Lay by all nicety and prolixious blushes
That banish what they sue for; redeem thy brother
By yielding up thy body to my will;
Or else he must not only die the death,
But thy unkindness shall his death draw out
To ling'ring sufferance. Answer me to-morrow,
Or, by the affection that now guides me most,
I'll prove a tyrant to him. As for you,
Say what you can: my false o'erweighs your true.   *Exit*
ISABELLA. To whom should I complain? Did I tell this,
Who would believe me? O perilous mouths
That bear in them one and the self-same tongue
Either of condemnation or approof,
Bidding the law make curtsy to their will;
Hooking both right and wrong to th' appetite,
To follow as it draws! I'll to my brother.
Though he hath fall'n by prompture of the blood,
Yet hath he in him such a mind of honour
That, had he twenty heads to tender down
On twenty bloody blocks, he'd yield them up
Before his sister should her body stoop
To such abhorr'd pollution.
Then, Isabel, live chaste, and, brother, die:
More than our brother is our chastity.
I'll tell him yet of Angelo's request,
And fit his mind to death, for his soul's rest.   *Exit*

ACT III. SCENE 1

The prison

Enter DUKE, *disguised as before*, CLAUDIO, *and* PROVOST

DUKE. So, then you hope of pardon from Lord Angelo?
CLAUDIO. The miserable have no other medicine
But only hope:
I have hope to live, and am prepar'd to die.

DUKE. Be absolute for death; either death or life
  Shall thereby be the sweeter. Reason thus with life.
  If I do lose thee, I do lose a thing
  That none but fools would keep. A breath thou art,
  Servile to all the skyey influences,
  That dost this habitation where thou keep'st
  Hourly afflict. Merely, thou art Death's fool;
  For him thou labour'st by thy flight to shun
  And yet run'st toward him still. Thou art not noble;
  For all th' accommodations that thou bear'st
  Are nurs'd by baseness. Thou 'rt by no means valiant;
  For thou dost fear the soft and tender fork
  Of a poor worm. Thy best of rest is sleep,
  And that thou oft provok'st; yet grossly fear'st
  Thy death, which is no more. Thou art not thyself;
  For thou exists on many a thousand grains
  That issue out of dust. Happy thou art not;
  For what thou hast not, still thou striv'st to get,
  And what thou hast, forget'st. Thou art not certain;
  For thy complexion shifts to strange effects,
  After the moon. If thou art rich, thou'rt poor;
  For, like an ass whose back with ingots bows,
  Thou bear'st thy heavy riches but a journey,
  And Death unloads thee. Friend hast thou none;
  For thine own bowels which do call thee sire,
  The mere effusion of thy proper loins,
  Do curse the gout, serpigo, and the rheum,
  For ending thee no sooner. Thou hast nor youth nor age,
  But, as it were, an after-dinner's sleep,
  Dreaming on both; for all thy blessed youth
  Becomes as aged, and doth beg the alms
  Of palsied eld; and when thou art old and rich,
  Thou hast neither heat, affection, limb, nor beauty,
  To make thy riches pleasant. What's yet in this
  That bears the name of life? Yet in this life
  Lie hid moe thousand deaths; yet death we fear,
  That makes these odds all even.
CLAUDIO. I humbly thank you.
  To sue to live, I find I seek to die;
  And, seeking death, find life. Let it come on.

ISABELLA. [*Within*] What, ho! Peace here; grace and good company!

PROVOST. Who's there? Come in; the wish deserves a welcome.

DUKE. Dear sir, ere long I'll visit you again.

CLAUDIO. Most holy sir, I thank you.

Enter ISABELLA

ISABELLA. My business is a word or two with Claudio.

PROVOST. And very welcome. Look, signior, here's your sister.

DUKE. Provost, a word with you.

PROVOST. As many as you please.

DUKE. Bring me to hear them speak, where I may be conceal'd. *Exeunt* DUKE *and* PROVOST

CLAUDIO. Now, sister, what's the comfort?

ISABELLA. Why,
As all comforts are; most good, most good, indeed.
Lord Angelo, having affairs to heaven,
Intends you for his swift ambassador,
Where you shall be an everlasting leiger.
Therefore, your best appointment make with speed;
To-morrow you set on.

CLAUDIO. Is there no remedy?

ISABELLA. None, but such remedy as, to save a head,
To cleave a heart in twain.

CLAUDIO. But is there any?

ISABELLA. Yes, brother, you may live:
There is a devilish mercy in the judge,
If you'll implore it, that will free your life,
But fetter you till death.

CLAUDIO. Perpetual durance?

ISABELLA. Ay, just; perpetual durance, a restraint,
Though all the world's vastidity you had,
To a determin'd scope.

CLAUDIO. But in what nature?

ISABELLA. In such a one as, you consenting to't,
Would bark your honour from that trunk you bear,
And leave you naked.

CLAUDIO. Let me know the point.

ISABELLA. O, I do fear thee, Claudio; and I quake,
 Lest thou a feverous life shouldst entertain,
 And six or seven winters more respect
 Than a perpetual honour. Dar'st thou die?
 The sense of death is most in apprehension;
 And the poor beetle that we tread upon
 In corporal sufferance finds a pang as great
 As when a giant dies.
CLAUDIO. Why give you me this shame?
 Think you I can a resolution fetch
 From flow'ry tenderness? If I must die,
 I will encounter darkness as a bride
 And hug it in mine arms.
ISABELLA. There spake my brother; there my father's grave
 Did utter forth a voice. Yes, thou must die:
 Thou art too noble to conserve a life
 In base appliances. This outward-sainted deputy,
 Whose settled visage and deliberate word
 Nips youth i' th' head, and follies doth enew
 As falcon doth the fowl, is yet a devil;
 His filth within being cast, he would appear
 A pond as deep as hell.
CLAUDIO. The precise Angelo!
ISABELLA. O, 'tis the cunning livery of hell
 The damned'st body to invest and cover
 In precise guards! Dost thou think, Claudio,
 If I would yield him my virginity
 Thou mightst be freed?
CLAUDIO. O heavens! it cannot be.
ISABELLA. Yes, he would give't thee, from this rank offence,
 So to offend him still. This night's the time
 That I should do what I abhor to name,
 Or else thou diest to-morrow.
CLAUDIO. Thou shalt not do't.
ISABELLA. O, were it but my life!
 I'd throw it down for your deliverance
 As frankly as a pin.
CLAUDIO. Thanks, dear Isabel.
ISABELLA. Be ready, Claudio, for your death to-morrow.
CLAUDIO. Yes. Has he affections in him

That thus can make him bite the law by th' nose
When he would force it? Sure it is no sin;
Or of the deadly seven it is the least.

ISABELLA. Which is the least?

CLAUDIO. If it were damnable, he being so wise,
Why would he for the momentary trick
Be perdurably fin'd?—O Isabel!

ISABELLA. What says my brother?

CLAUDIO. Death is a fearful thing.

ISABELLA. And shamed life a hateful.

CLAUDIO. Ay, but to die, and go we know not where;
To lie in cold obstruction, and to rot;
This sensible warm motion to become
A kneaded clod; and the delighted spirit
To bathe in fiery floods or to reside
In thrilling region of thick-ribbed ice;
To be imprison'd in the viewless winds,
And blown with restless violence round about
The pendent world; or to be worse than worst
Of those that lawless and incertain thought
Imagine howling—'tis too horrible.
The weariest and most loathed worldly life
That age, ache, penury, and imprisonment,
Can lay on nature is a paradise
To what we fear of death.

ISABELLA. Alas, alas!

CLAUDIO. Sweet sister, let me live.
What sin you do to save a brother's life,
Nature dispenses with the deed so far
That it becomes a virtue.

ISABELLA. O you beast!
O faithless coward! O dishonest wretch!
Wilt thou be made a man out of my vice?
Is't not a kind of incest to take life
From thine own sister's shame? What should I think?
Heaven shield my mother play'd my father fair!
For such a warped slip of wilderness
Ne'er issu'd from his blood. Take my defiance;
Die; perish. Might but my bending down
Reprieve thee from thy fate, it should proceed.

I'll pray a thousand prayers for thy death,
No word to save thee.

CLAUDIO. Nay, hear me, Isabel.

ISABELLA. O fie, fie, fie!
Thy sin's not accidental, but a trade.
Mercy to thee would prove itself a bawd;
'Tis best that thou diest quickly.

CLAUDIO. O, hear me, Isabella.

Re-enter DUKE

DUKE. Vouchsafe a word, young sister, but one word.

ISABELLA. What is your will?

DUKE. Might you dispense with your leisure, I would by
and by have some speech with you; the satisfaction I
would require is likewise your own benefit.

ISABELLA. I have no superfluous leisure; my stay must be
stolen out of other affairs; but I will attend you awhile.
[Walks apart]

DUKE. Son, I have overheard what hath pass'd between you
and your sister. Angelo had never the purpose to corrupt
her; only he hath made an assay of her virtue to practise
his judgment with the disposition of natures. She, having
the truth of honour in her, hath made him that gracious
denial which he is most glad to receive. I am confessor to
Angelo, and I know this to be true; therefore prepare
yourself to death. Do not satisfy your resolution with
hopes that are fallible; to-morrow you must die; go to
your knees and make ready.

CLAUDIO. Let me ask my sister pardon. I am so out of
love with life that I will sue to be rid of it.

DUKE. Hold you there. Farewell. *[Exit* CLAUDIO] Provost, a
word with you.

Re-enter PROVOST

PROVOST. What's your will, father?

DUKE. That, now you are come, you will be gone. Leave
me a while with the maid; my mind promises with my
habit no loss shall touch her by my company.

PROVOST. In good time.   *Exit* PROVOST

DUKE. The hand that hath made you fair hath made you

good; the goodness that is cheap in beauty makes beauty brief in goodness; but grace, being the soul of your complexion, shall keep the body of it ever fair. The assault that Angelo hath made to you, fortune hath convey'd to my understanding; and, but that frailty hath examples for his falling, I should wonder at Angelo. How will you do to content this substitute, and to save your brother?

ISABELLA. I am now going to resolve him; I had rather my brother die by the law than my son should be unlawfully born. But, O, how much is the good Duke deceiv'd in Angelo! If ever he return, and I can speak to him, I will open my lips in vain, or discover his government.

DUKE. That shall not be much amiss; yet, as the matter now stands, he will avoid your accusation: he made trial of you only. Therefore fasten your ear on my advisings; to the love I have in doing good a remedy presents itself. I do make myself believe that you may most uprighteously do a poor wronged lady a merited benefit; redeem your brother from the angry law; do no stain to your own gracious person; and much please the absent Duke, if peradventure he shall ever return to have hearing of this business.

ISABELLA. Let me hear you speak farther; I have spirit to do anything that appears not foul in the truth of my spirit.

DUKE. Virtue is bold, and goodness never fearful. Have you not heard speak of Mariana, the sister of Frederick, the great soldier who miscarried at sea?

ISABELLA. I have heard of the lady, and good words went with her name.

DUKE. She should this Angelo have married; was affianced to her by oath, and the nuptial appointed; between which time of the contract and limit of the solemnity her brother Frederick was wreck'd at sea, having in that perished vessel the dowry of his sister. But mark how heavily this befell to the poor gentlewoman: there she lost a noble and renowned brother, in his love toward her ever most kind and natural; with him the portion and sinew of her fortune, her marriage-dowry; with both, her combinate husband, this well-seeming Angelo.

ISABELLA. Can this be so? Did Angelo so leave her?

DUKE. Left her in her tears, and dried not one of them with

266

his comfort; swallowed his vows whole, pretending in her discoveries of dishonour; in few, bestow'd her on her own lamentation, which she yet wears for his sake; and he, a marble to her tears, is washed with them, but relents not.

ISABELLA. What a merit were it in death to take this poor maid from the world! What corruption in this life that it will let this man live! But how out of this can she avail?

DUKE. It is a rupture that you may easily heal; and the cure of it not only saves your brother, but keeps you from dishonour in doing it.

ISABELLA. Show me how, good father.

DUKE. This forenamed maid hath yet in her the continuance of her first affection; his unjust unkindness, that in all reason should have quenched her love, hath, like an impediment in the current, made it more violent and unruly. Go you to Angelo; answer his requiring with a plausible obedience; agree with his demands to the point; only refer yourself to this advantage: first, that your stay with him may not be long; that the time may have all shadow and silence in it; and the place answer to convenience. This being granted in course—and now follows all: we shall advise this wronged maid to stead up your appointment, go in your place. If the encounter acknowledge itself hereafter, it may compel him to her recompense; and here, by this, is your brother saved, your honour untainted, the poor Mariana advantaged, and the corrupt deputy scaled. The maid will I frame and make fit for his attempt. If you think well to carry this as you may, the doubleness of the benefit defends the deceit from reproof. What think you of it?

ISABELLA. The image of it gives me content already; and I trust it will grow to a most prosperous perfection.

DUKE. It lies much in your holding up. Haste you speedily to Angelo; if for this night he entreat you to his bed, give him promise of satisfaction. I will presently to Saint Luke's; there, at the moated grange, resides this dejected Mariana. At that place call upon me; and dispatch with Angelo, that it may be quickly.

ISABELLA. I thank you for this comfort. Fare you well, good father. *Exeunt severally*

SCENE 2

The street before the prison

Enter, on one side, DUKE *disguised as before; on the other,* ELBOW, *and* OFFICERS *with* POMPEY

ELBOW. Nay, if there be no remedy for it, but that you will needs buy and sell men and women like beasts, we shall have all the world drink brown and white bastard.

DUKE. O heavens! what stuff is here?

POMPEY. 'Twas never merry world since, of two usuries, the merriest was put down, and the worser allow'd by order of law a furr'd gown to keep him warm; and furr'd with fox on lamb-skins too, to signify that craft, being richer than innocency, stands for the facing.

ELBOW. Come your way, sir. Bless you, good father friar.

DUKE. And you, good brother father. What offence hath this man made you, sir?

ELBOW. Marry, sir, he hath offended the law; and, sir, we take him to be a thief too, sir, for we have found upon him, sir, a strange picklock, which we have sent to the deputy.

DUKE. Fie, sirrah, a bawd, a wicked bawd!
The evil that thou causest to be done,
That is thy means to live. Do thou but think
What 'tis to cram a maw or clothe a back
From such a filthy vice; say to thyself
'From their abominable and beastly touches
I drink, I eat, array myself, and live.'
Canst thou believe thy living is a life,
So stinkingly depending? Go mend, go mend.

POMPEY. Indeed, it does stink in some sort, sir; but yet, sir, I would prove—

DUKE. Nay, if the devil have given thee proofs for sin,
Thou wilt prove his. Take him to prison, officer;
Correction and instruction must both work
Ere this rude beast will profit.

ELBOW. He must before the deputy, sir; he has given him

warning. The deputy cannot abide a whoremaster; if he be a whoremonger, and comes before him, he were as good go a mile on his errand.

DUKE. That we were all, as some would seem to be, From our faults, as his faults from seeming, free.

ELBOW. His neck will come to your waist—a cord, sir.

Enter LUCIO

POMPEY. I spy comfort; I cry bail. Here's a gentleman, and a friend of mine.

LUCIO. How now, noble Pompey! What, at the wheels of Cæsar? Art thou led in triumph? What, is there none of Pygmalion's images, newly made woman, to be had now for putting the hand in the pocket and extracting it clutch'd? What reply, ha? What say'st thou to this tune, matter, and method? Is't not drown'd i' th' last rain, ha? What say'st thou, trot? Is the world as it was, man? Which is the way? Is it sad, and few words? or how? The trick of it?

DUKE. Still thus, and thus; still worse!

LUCIO. How doth my dear morsel, thy mistress? Procures she still, ha?

POMPEY. Troth, sir, she hath eaten up all her beef, and she is herself in the tub.

LUCIO. Why, 'tis good; it is the right of it; it must be so; ever your fresh whore and your powder'd bawd—an un-shunn'd consequence; it must be so. Art going to prison, Pompey?

POMPEY. Yes, faith, sir.

LUCIO. Why, 'tis not amiss, Pompey. Farewell; go, say I sent thee thither. For debt, Pompey—or how?

ELBOW. For being a bawd, for being a bawd.

LUCIO. Well, then, imprison him. If imprisonment be the due of a bawd, why, 'tis his right. Bawd is he doubtless, and of antiquity, too; bawd-born. Farewell, good Pompey. Commend me to the prison, Pompey. You will turn good husband now, Pompey; you will keep the house.

POMPEY. I hope, sir, your good worship will be my bail.

LUCIO. No, indeed, will I not, Pompey; it is not the wear. I will pray, Pompey, to increase your bondage. If you take it not patiently, why, your mettle is the more. Adieu, trusty Pompey. Bless you, friar.

Duke. And you.

Lucio. Does Bridget paint still, Pompey, ha?

Elbow. Come your ways, sir; come.

Pompey. You will not bail me then, sir?

Lucio. Then, Pompey, nor now. What news abroad, friar? what news?

Elbow. Come your ways, sir; come.

Lucio. Go to kennel, Pompey, go.

Exeunt Elbow, Pompey *and* Officers

What news, friar, of the Duke?

Duke. I know none. Can you tell me of any?

Lucio. Some say he is with the Emperor of Russia; other some, he is in Rome; but where is he, think you?

Duke. I know not where; but wheresoever, I wish him well.

Lucio. It was a mad fantastical trick of him to steal from the state and usurp the beggary he was never born to. Lord Angelo dukes it well in his absence; he puts transgression to't.

Duke. He does well in't.

Lucio. A little more lenity to lechery would do no harm in him. Something too crabbed that way, friar.

Duke. It is too general a vice, and severity must cure it.

Lucio. Yes, in good sooth, the vice is of a great kindred; it is well allied; but it is impossible to extirp it quite, friar, till eating and drinking be put down. They say this Angelo was not made by man and woman after this downright way of creation. Is it true, think you?

Duke. How should he be made, then?

Lucio. Some report a sea-maid spawn'd him; some, that he was begot between two stock-fishes. But it is certain that when he makes water his urine is congeal'd ice; that I know to be true. And he is a motion generative; that's infallible.

Duke. You are pleasant, sir, and speak apace.

Lucio. Why, what a ruthless thing is this in him, for the rebellion of a codpiece to take away the life of a man! Would the Duke that is absent have done this? Ere he

would have hang'd a man for the getting a hundred bastards, he would have paid for the nursing a thousand. He
had some feeling of the sport; he knew the service, and
that instructed him to mercy.

DUKE. I never heard the absent Duke much detected for
women; he was not inclin'd that way.

LUCIO. O, sir, you are deceiv'd.

DUKE. 'Tis not possible.

LUCIO. Who—not the Duke? Yes, your beggar of fifty; and
his use was to put a ducat in her clack-dish. The Duke had
crotchets in him. He would be drunk too; that let me inform you.

DUKE. You do him wrong, surely.

LUCIO. Sir, I was an inward of his. A shy fellow was the
Duke; and I believe I know the cause of his withdrawing.

DUKE. What, I prithee, might be the cause?

LUCIO. No, pardon; 'tis a secret must be lock'd within the
teeth and the lips; but this I can let you understand: the
greater file of the subject held the Duke to be wise.

DUKE. Wise? Why, no question but he was.

LUCIO. A very superficial, ignorant, unweighing fellow.

DUKE. Either this is envy in you, folly, or mistaking; the
very stream of his life, and the business he hath helmed,
must, upon a warranted need, give him a better proclamation. Let him be but testimonied in his own bringings-
forth, and he shall appear to the envious a scholar, a statesman, and a soldier. Therefore you speak unskilfully; or, if
your knowledge be more, it is much dark'ned in your
malice.

LUCIO. Sir, I know him, and I love him.

DUKE. Love talks with better knowledge, and knowledge
with dearer love.

LUCIO. Come, sir, I know what I know.

DUKE. I can hardly believe that, since you know not what
you speak. But, if ever the Duke return, as our prayers
are he may, let me desire you to make your answer before
him. If it be honest you have spoke, you have courage to
maintain it; I am bound to call upon you; and I pray you
your name?

LUCIO. Sir, my name is Lucio, well known to the Duke.

DUKE. He shall know you better, sir, if I may live to report you.

LUCIO. I fear you not.

DUKE. O, you hope the Duke will return no more; or you imagine me too unhurtful an opposite. But, indeed, I can do you little harm: you'll forswear this again.

LUCIO. I'll be hang'd first. Thou art deceiv'd in me, friar. But no more of this. Canst thou tell if Claudio die to-morrow or no?

DUKE. Why should he die, sir?

LUCIO. Why? For filling a bottle with a tun-dish. I would the Duke we talk of were return'd again. This ungenitur'd agent will unpeople the province with continency; sparrows must not build in his house-eaves because they are lecherous. The Duke yet would have dark deeds darkly answered; he would never bring them to light. Would he were return'd! Marry, this Claudio is condemned for untrussing. Farewell, good friar; I prithee pray for me. The Duke, I say to thee again, would eat mutton on Fridays. He's not past it yet; and, I say to thee, he would mouth with a beggar though she smelt brown bread and garlic. Say that I said so. Farewell.   *Exit*

DUKE. No might nor greatness in mortality
Can censure scape; back-wounding calumny
The whitest virtue strikes. What king so strong
Can tie the gall up in the slanderous tongue?
But who comes here?

Enter ESCALUS, PROVOST, *and* OFFICERS *with*
MISTRESS OVERDONE

ESCALUS. Go, away with her to prison.

MRS. OVERDONE. Good my lord, be good to me; your honour is accounted a merciful man; good my lord.

ESCALUS. Double and treble admonition, and still forfeit in the same kind! This would make mercy swear and play the tyrant.

PROVOST. A bawd of eleven years' continuance, may it please your honour.

MRS. OVERDONE. My lord, this is one Lucio's information against me. Mistress Kate Keepdown was with child by him in the Duke's time; he promis'd her marriage. His child is a year and a quarter old come Philip and Jacob; I have kept it myself; and see how he goes about to abuse me.

Escalus. That fellow is a fellow of much license. Let him be call'd before us. Away with her to prison. Go to; no more words. [*Exeunt* Officers *with* Mistress Overdone] Provost, my brother Angelo will not be alter'd: Claudio must die to-morrow. Let him be furnish'd with divines, and have all charitable preparation. If my brother wrought by my pity, it should not be so with him.

Provost. So please you, this friar hath been with him, and advis'd him for th' entertainment of death.

Escalus. Good even, good father.

Duke. Bliss and goodness on you!

Escalus. Of whence are you?

Duke. Not of this country, though my chance is now
To use it for my time. I am a brother
Of gracious order, late come from the See
In special business from his Holiness.

Escalus. What news abroad i' th' world?

Duke. None, but that there is so great a fever on goodness that the dissolution of it must cure it. Novelty is only in request; and, as it is, as dangerous to be aged in any kind of course as it is virtuous to be constant in any undertaking. There is scarce truth enough alive to make societies secure; but security enough to make fellowships accurst. Much upon this riddle runs the wisdom of the world. This news is old enough, yet it is every day's news. I pray you, sir, of what disposition was the Duke?

Escalus. One that, above all other strifes, contended especially to know himself.

Duke. What pleasure was he given to?

Escalus. Rather rejoicing to see another merry than merry at anything which profess'd to make him rejoice; a gentleman of all temperance. But leave we him to his events, with a prayer they may prove prosperous; and let me desire to know how you find Claudio prepar'd. I am made to understand that you have lent him visitation.

Duke. He professes to have received no sinister measure

from his judge, but most willingly humbles himself to the determination of justice. Yet had he framed to himself, by the instruction of his frailty, many deceiving promises of life; which I, by my good leisure, have discredited to him, and now he is resolv'd to die.

ESCALUS. You have paid the heavens your function, and the prisoner the very debt of your calling. I have labour'd for the poor gentleman to the extremest shore of my modesty; but my brother justice have I found so severe that he hath forc'd me to tell him he is indeed Justice.

DUKE. If his own life answer the straitness of his proceeding, it shall become him well; wherein if he chance to fail, he hath sentenc'd himself.

ESCALUS. I am going to visit the prisoner. Fare you well.

DUKE. Peace be with you!   *Exeunt* ESCALUS *and* PROVOST

> He who the sword of heaven will bear
> Should be as holy as severe;
> Pattern in himself to know,
> Grace to stand, and virtue go;
> More nor less to others paying
> Than by self-offences weighing.
> Shame to him whose cruel striking
> Kills for faults of his own liking!
> Twice treble shame on Angelo,
> To weed my vice and let his grow!
> O, what may man within him hide,
> Though angel on the outward side!
> How may likeness, made in crimes,
> Make a practice on the times,
> To draw with idle spiders' strings
> Most ponderous and substantial things!
> Craft against vice I must apply.
> With Angelo to-night shall lie
> His old betrothed but despised;
> So disguise shall, by th' disguised,
> Pay with falsehood false exacting,
> And perform an old contracting.   *Exit*

ACT IV. SCENE 1

The moated grange at Saint Luke's

Enter MARIANA; *and* BOY *singing*

SONG

Take, O, take those lips away,
   That so sweetly were forsworn;
And those eyes, the break of day,
   Lights that do mislead the morn;
But my kisses bring again, bring again;
Seals of love, but seal'd in vain, seal'd in vain.

Enter DUKE, *disguised as before*

MARIANA. Break off thy song, and haste thee quick away;
  Here comes a man of comfort, whose advice
  Hath often still'd my brawling discontent.   *Exit* BOY
  I cry you mercy, sir, and well could wish
  You had not found me here so musical.
  Let me excuse me, and believe me so,
  My mirth it much displeas'd, but pleas'd my woe.
DUKE. 'Tis good; though music oft hath such a charm
  To make bad good and good provoke to harm.
  I pray you tell me hath anybody inquir'd for me here to-
  day. Much upon this time have I promis'd here to meet.
MARIANA. You have not been inquir'd after; I have sat here
  all day.

Enter ISABELLA

DUKE. I do constantly believe you. The time is come even
  now. I shall crave your forbearance a little. May be I will
  call upon you anon, for some advantage to yourself.
MARIANA. I am always bound to you.   *Exit*
DUKE. Very well met, and well come.
  What is the news from this good deputy?
ISABELLA. He hath a garden circummur'd with brick,
  Whose western side is with a vineyard back'd;
  And to that vineyard is a planched gate
  That makes his opening with this bigger key;
  This other doth command a little door

275

Which from the vineyard to the garden leads.
There have I made my promise
Upon the heavy middle of the night
To call upon him.
DUKE. But shall you on your knowledge find this way?
ISABELLA. I have ta'en a due and wary note upon't;
  With whispering and most guilty diligence,
  In action all of precept, he did show me
  The way twice o'er.
DUKE. Are there no other tokens
  Between you 'greed concerning her observance?
ISABELLA. No, none, but only a repair i' th' dark;
  And that I have possess'd him my most stay
  Can be but brief; for I have made him know
  I have a servant comes with me along,
  That stays upon me; whose persuasion is
  I come about my brother.
DUKE. 'Tis well borne up.
  I have not yet made known to Mariana
  A word of this. What ho, within! come forth.

Re-enter MARIANA

I pray you be acquainted with this maid;
She comes to do you good.
ISABELLA. I do desire the like.
DUKE. Do you persuade yourself that I respect you?
MARIANA. Good friar, I know you do, and have found it.
DUKE. Take, then, this your companion by the hand,
  Who hath a story ready for your ear.
  I shall attend your leisure; but make haste;
  The vaporous night approaches.
MARIANA. Will't please you walk aside?

                Exeunt MARIANA *and* ISABELLA

DUKE. O place and greatness! Millions of false eyes
  Are stuck upon thee. Volumes of report
  Run with these false, and most contrarious quest
  Upon thy doings. Thousand escapes of wit
  Make thee the father of their idle dream,
  And rack thee in their fancies.

Re-enter MARIANA *and* ISABELLA

Welcome, how agreed?
ISABELLA. She'll take the enterprise upon her, father,
  If you advise it.
DUKE. It is not my consent,
  But my entreaty too.
ISABELLA. Little have you to say,
  When you depart from him, but, soft and low,
  'Remember now my brother.'
MARIANA. Fear me not.
DUKE. Nor, gentle daughter, fear you not at all.
  He is your husband on a pre-contract.
  To bring you thus together 'tis no sin,
  Sith that the justice of your title to him
  Doth flourish the deceit. Come, let us go;
  Our corn's to reap, for yet our tithe's to sow.   *Exeunt*

SCENE 2

The prison

Enter PROVOST *and* POMPEY

PROVOST. Come hither, sirrah. Can you cut off a man's head?
POMPEY. If the man be a bachelor, sir, I can; but if he be a
  married man, he's his wife's head, and I can never cut off
  a woman's head.
PROVOST. Come, sir, leave me your snatches and yield me a
  direct answer. To-morrow morning are to die Claudio and
  Barnardine. Here is in our prison a common executioner,
  who in his office lacks a helper; if you will take it on you
  to assist him, it shall redeem you from your gyves; if not,
  you shall have your full time of imprisonment, and your
  deliverance with an unpitied whipping, for you have been
  a notorious bawd.
POMPEY. Sir, I have been an unlawful bawd time out of
  mind; but yet I will be content to be a lawful hangman.
  I would be glad to receive some instructions from my
  fellow partner.
PROVOST. What ho, Abhorson! Where's Abhorson there?

Enter ABHORSON

277

ABHORSON. Do you call, sir?

PROVOST. Sirrah, here's a fellow will help you to-morrow in your execution. If you think it meet, compound with him by the year, and let him abide here with you; if not, use him for the present, and dismiss him. He cannot plead his estimation with you; he hath been a bawd.

ABHORSON. A bawd, sir? Fie upon him! He will discredit our mystery.

PROVOST. Go to, sir; you weigh equally; a feather will turn the scale. *Exit*

POMPEY. Pray, sir, by your good favour—for surely, sir, a good favour you have but that you have a hanging look— do you call, sir, your occupation a mystery?

ABHORSON. Ay, sir; a mystery.

POMPEY. Painting, sir, I have heard say, is a mystery; and your whores, sir, being members of my occupation, using painting, do prove my occupation a mystery; but what mystery there should be in hanging, if I should be hang'd, I cannot imagine.

ABHORSON. Sir, it is a mystery.

POMPEY. Proof?

ABHORSON. Every true man's apparel fits your thief: if it be too little for your thief, your true man thinks it big enough; if it be too big for your thief, your thief thinks it little enough; so every true man's apparel fits your thief.

Re-enter PROVOST

PROVOST. Are you agreed?

POMPEY. Sir, I will serve him; for I do find your hangman is a more penitent trade than your bawd; he doth oftener ask forgiveness.

PROVOST. You, sirrah, provide your block and your axe to-morrow four o'clock.

ABHORSON. Come on, bawd; I will instruct thee in my trade; follow.

POMPEY. I do desire to learn, sir; and I hope, if you have occasion to use me for your own turn, you shall find me yare; for truly, sir, for your kindness I owe you a good turn.

PROVOST. Call hither Barnardine and Claudio.

Exeunt ABHORSON *and* POMPEY

Th' one has my pity; not a jot the other,
Being a murderer, though he were my brother.

Enter CLAUDIO

Look, here's the warrant, Claudio, for thy death;
'Tis now dead midnight, and by eight to-morrow
Thou must be made immortal. Where's Barnardine?
CLAUDIO. As fast lock'd up in sleep as guiltless labour
When it lies starkly in the traveller's bones.
He will not wake.
PROVOST. Who can do good on him?
Well, go, prepare yourself. [*Knocking within*] But hark,
what noise?
Heaven give your spirits comfort!   *Exit* CLAUDIO
[*Knocking continues*] By and by.
I hope it is some pardon or reprieve
For the most gentle Claudio.

Enter DUKE, *disguised as before*

Welcome, father.
DUKE. The best and wholesom'st spirits of the night
Envelop you, good Provost! Who call'd here of late?
PROVOST. None, since the curfew rung.
DUKE. Not Isabel?
PROVOST. No.
DUKE. They will then, ere't be long.
PROVOST. What comfort is for Claudio?
DUKE. There's some in hope.
PROVOST. It is a bitter deputy.
DUKE. Not so, not so; his life is parallel'd
Even with the stroke and line of his great justice;
He doth with holy abstinence subdue
That in himself which he spurs on his pow'r
To qualify in others. Were he meal'd with that
Which he corrects, then were he tyrannous;
But this being so, he's just. [*Knocking within*] Now are
they come.   *Exit* PROVOST
This is a gentle provost; seldom when
The steeled gaoler is the friend of men. [*Knocking within*]

279

How now, what noise! That spirit's possess'd with haste
That wounds th' unsisting postern with these strokes.

Re-enter PROVOST

PROVOST. There he must stay until the officer
Arise to let him in; he is call'd up.
DUKE. Have you no countermand for Claudio yet
But he must die to-morrow?
PROVOST. None, sir, none.
DUKE. As near the dawning, Provost, as it is,
You shall hear more ere morning.
PROVOST. Happily
You something know; yet I believe there comes
No countermand; no such example have we.
Besides, upon the very siege of justice,
Lord Angelo hath to the public ear
Profess'd the contrary.

Enter a MESSENGER

This is his lordship's man.
DUKE. And here comes Claudio's pardon.
MESSENGER. My lord hath sent you this note; and by me
this further charge, that you swerve not from the smallest
article of it, neither in time, matter, or other circumstance.
Good morrow; for as I take it, it is almost day.
PROVOST. I shall obey him.   *Exit* MESSENGER
DUKE. [*Aside*] This is his pardon, purchas'd by such sin
For which the pardoner himself is in;
Hence hath offence his quick celerity,
When it is borne in high authority.
When vice makes mercy, mercy's so extended
That for the fault's love is th' offender friended.
Now, sir, what news?
PROVOST. I told you: Lord Angelo, belike thinking me remiss
in mine office, awakens me with this unwonted putting-on;
methinks strangely, for he hath not us'd it before.
DUKE. Pray you, let's hear.
PROVOST. [*Reads*] 'Whatsoever you may hear to the con-
trary, let Claudio be executed by four of the clock, and,
in the afternoon, Barnardine. For my better satisfaction, let

me have Claudio's head sent me by five. Let this be duly
performed, with a thought that more depends on it than
we must yet deliver. Thus fail not to do your office, as
you will answer it at your peril.'
What say you to this, sir?

DUKE. What is that Barnardine who is to be executed in th'
afternoon?

PROVOST. A Bohemian born; but here nurs'd up and bred.
One that is a prisoner nine years old.

DUKE. How came it that the absent Duke had not either deliver'd him to his liberty or executed him? I have heard it
was ever his manner to do so.

PROVOST. His friends still wrought reprieves for him; and,
indeed, his fact, till now in the government of Lord Angelo, came not to an undoubted proof.

DUKE. It is now apparent?

PROVOST. Most manifest, and not denied by himself.

DUKE. Hath he borne himself penitently in prison? How
seems he to be touch'd?

PROVOST. A man that apprehends death no more dreadfully
but as a drunken sleep; careless, reckless, and fearless, of
what's past, present, or to come; insensible of mortality and
desperately mortal.

DUKE. He wants advice.

PROVOST. He will hear none. He hath evermore had the
liberty of the prison; give him leave to escape hence, he
would not; drunk many times a day, if not many days entirely drunk. We have very oft awak'd him, as if to carry
him to execution, and show'd him a seeming warrant for
it; it hath not moved him at all.

DUKE. More of him anon. There is written in your brow,
Provost, honesty and constancy. If I read it not truly, my
ancient skill beguiles me; but in the boldness of my cunning I will lay myself in hazard. Claudio, whom here you
have warrant to execute, is no greater forfeit to the law
than Angelo who hath sentenc'd him. To make you understand this in a manifested effect, I crave but four days'
respite; for the which you are to do me both a present and
a dangerous courtesy.

PROVOST. Pray, sir, in what?

DUKE. In the delaying death.

PROVOST. Alack! How may I do it, having the hour limited, and an express command, under penalty, to deliver his head in the view of Angelo? I may make my case as Claudio's, to cross this in the smallest.

DUKE. By the vow of mine order, I warrant you, if my instructions may be your guide. Let this Barnardine be this morning executed, and his head borne to Angelo.

PROVOST. Angelo hath seen them both, and will discover the favour.

DUKE. O, death's a great disguiser; and you may add to it. Shave the head and tie the beard; and say it was the desire of the penitent to be so bar'd before his death. You know the course is common. If anything fall to you upon this more than thanks and good fortune, by the saint whom I profess, I will plead against it with my life.

PROVOST. Pardon me, good father; it is against my oath.

DUKE. Were you sworn to the Duke, or to the deputy?

PROVOST. To him and to his substitutes.

DUKE. You will think you have made no offence if the Duke avouch the justice of your dealing?

PROVOST. But what likelihood is in that?

DUKE. Not a resemblance, but a certainty. Yet since I see you fearful, that neither my coat, integrity, nor persuasion, can with ease attempt you, I will go further than I meant, to pluck all fears out of you. Look you, sir, here is the hand and seal of the Duke. You know the character, I doubt not; and the signet is not strange to you.

PROVOST. I know them both.

DUKE. The contents of this is the return of the Duke; you shall anon over-read it at your pleasure, where you shall find within these two days he will be here. This is a thing that Angelo knows not; for he this very day receives letters of strange tenour, perchance of the Duke's death, perchance entering into some monastery; but, by chance, nothing of what is writ. Look, th' unfolding star calls up the shepherd. Put not yourself into amazement how these things should be: all difficulties are but easy when they are known. Call your executioner, and off with Barnardine's head. I will give him a present shrift, and advise him for a

better place. Yet you are amaz'd, but this shall absolutely
resolve you. Come away; it is almost clear dawn. *Exeunt*

SCENE 3

The prison

Enter POMPEY

POMPEY. I am as well acquainted here as I was in our house
of profession; one would think it were Mistress Overdone's
own house, for here be many of her old customers. First,
here's young Master Rash; he's in for a commodity of
brown paper and old ginger, nine score and seventeen
pounds, of which he made five marks ready money. Marry,
then ginger was not much in request, for the old women
were all dead. Then is there here one Master Caper, at the
suit of Master Threepile the mercer, for some four suits
of peach-colour'd satin, which now peaches him a beggar.
Then have we here young Dizy, and young Master Deep-
vow, and Master Copperspur, and Master Starvelackey, the
rapier and dagger man, and young Dropheir that kill'd
lusty Pudding, and Master Forthlight the tilter, and brave
Master Shootie the great traveller, and wild Halfcan that
stabb'd Pots, and, I think, forty more—all great doers in
our trade, and are now 'for the Lord's sake.'

Enter ABHORSON

ABHORSON. Sirrah, bring Barnardine hither.
POMPEY. Master Barnardine! You must rise and be hang'd,
Master Barnardine!
ABHORSON. What ho, Barnardine!
BARNARDINE. [*Within*] A pox o' your throats! Who makes
that noise there? What are you?
POMPEY. Your friends, sir; the hangman. You must be so
good, sir, to rise and be put to death.
BARNARDINE. [*Within*] Away, you rogue, away; I am sleepy.
ABHORSON. Tell him he must awake, and that quickly too.
POMPEY. Pray, Master Barnardine, awake till you are ex-
ecuted, and sleep afterwards.

ABHORSON. Go in to him, and fetch him out.

POMPEY. He is coming, sir, he is coming; I hear his straw rustle.

Enter BARNARDINE

ABHORSON. Is the axe upon the block, sirrah?

POMPEY. Very ready, sir.

BARNARDINE. How now, Abhorson, what's the news with you?

ABHORSON. Truly, sir, I would desire you to clap into your prayers; for, look you, the warrant's come.

BARNARDINE. You rogue, I have been drinking all night; I am not fitted for't.

POMPEY. O, the better, sir! For he that drinks all night and is hanged betimes in the morning may sleep the sounder all the next day.

Enter DUKE, *disguised as before*

ABHORSON. Look you, sir, here comes your ghostly father. Do we jest now, think you?

DUKE. Sir, induced by my charity, and hearing how hastily you are to depart, I am come to advise you, comfort you, and pray with you.

BARNARDINE. Friar, not I; I have been drinking hard all night, and I will have more time to prepare me, or they shall beat out my brains with billets. I will not consent to die this day, that's certain.

DUKE. O, sir, you must; and therefore I beseech you Look forward on the journey you shall go.

BARNARDINE. I swear I will not die to-day for any man's persuasion.

DUKE. But hear you—

BARNARDINE. Not a word; if you have anything to say to me, come to my ward; for thence will not I to-day.   *Exit*

DUKE. Unfit to live or die. O gravel heart!
After him, fellows; bring him to the block.

Exeunt ABHORSON *and* POMPEY

Enter PROVOST

PROVOST. Now, sir, how do you find the prisoner?

DUKE. A creature unprepar'd, unmeet for death;
And to transport him in the mind he is
Were damnable.
PROVOST. Here in the prison, father,
There died this morning of a cruel fever
One Ragozine, a most notorious pirate,
A man of Claudio's years; his beard and head
Just of his colour. What if we do omit
This reprobate till he were well inclin'd,
And satisfy the deputy with the visage
Of Ragozine, more like to Claudio?
DUKE. O, 'tis an accident that heaven provides!
Dispatch it presently; the hour draws on
Prefix'd by Angelo. See this be done,
And sent according to command; whiles I
Persuade this rude wretch willingly to die.
PROVOST. This shall be done, good father, presently.
But Barnardine must die this afternoon;
And how shall we continue Claudio,
To save me from the danger that might come
If he were known alive?
DUKE. Let this be done:
Put them in secret holds, both Barnardine and Claudio.
Ere twice the sun hath made his journal greeting
To the under generation, you shall find
Your safety manifested.
PROVOST. I am your free dependant.
DUKE. Quick, dispatch, and send the head to Angelo.
Exit PROVOST

Now will I write letters to Angelo—
The Provost, he shall bear them—whose contents
Shall witness to him I am near at home,
And that, by great injunctions, I am bound
To enter publicly. Him I'll desire
To meet me at the consecrated fount,
A league below the city; and from thence,
By cold gradation and well-balanc'd form,
We shall proceed with Angelo.

Re-enter PROVOST

285

PROVOST. Here is the head; I'll carry it myself.
DUKE. Convenient is it. Make a swift return;
For I would commune with you of such things
That want no ear but yours.
PROVOST. I'll make all speed.   *Exit*
ISABELLA. [*Within*] Peace, ho, be here!
DUKE. The tongue of Isabel. She's come to know
If yet her brother's pardon be come hither;
But I will keep her ignorant of her good,
To make her heavenly comforts of despair
When it is least expected.

Enter ISABELLA

ISABELLA. Ho, by your leave!
DUKE. Good morning to you, fair and gracious daughter.
ISABELLA. The better, given me by so holy a man.
Hath yet the deputy sent my brother's pardon?
DUKE. He hath releas'd him, Isabel, from the world.
His head is off and sent to Angelo.
ISABELLA. Nay, but it is not so.
DUKE. It is no other.
Show your wisdom, daughter, in your close patience,
ISABELLA. O, I will to him and pluck out his eyes!
DUKE. You shall not be admitted to his sight.
ISABELLA. Unhappy Claudio! Wretched Isabel!
Injurious world! Most damned Angelo!
DUKE. This nor hurts him nor profits you a jot;
Forbear it, therefore; give your cause to heaven.
Mark what I say, which you shall find
By every syllable a faithful verity.
The Duke comes home to-morrow. Nay, dry your eyes.
One of our covent, and his confessor,
Gives me this instance. Already he hath carried
Notice to Escalus and Angelo,
Who do prepare to meet him at the gates,
There to give up their pow'r. If you can, pace your wis-
dom
In that good path that I would wish it go,
And you shall have your bosom on this wretch,
Grace of the Duke, revenges to your heart,

And general honour.

ISABELLA. I am directed by you.

DUKE. This letter, then, to Friar Peter give;
'Tis that he sent me of the Duke's return.
Say, by this token, I desire his company
At Mariana's house to-night. Her cause and yours
I'll perfect him withal; and he shall bring you
Before the Duke; and to the head of Angelo
Accuse him home and home. For my poor self,
I am combined by a sacred vow,
And shall be absent. Wend you with this letter.
Command these fretting waters from your eyes
With a light heart; trust not my holy order,
If I pervert your course. Who's here?

Enter LUCIO

LUCIO. Good even. Friar, where's the Provost?

DUKE. Not within, sir.

LUCIO. O pretty Isabella, I am pale at mine heart to see thine
eyes so red. Thou must be patient. I am fain to dine and
sup with water and bran; I dare not for my head fill my
belly; one fruitful meal would set me to't. But they say
the Duke will be here to-morrow. By my troth, Isabel, I
lov'd thy brother. If the old fantastical Duke of dark
corners had been at home, he had lived.   *Exit* ISABELLA

DUKE. Sir, the Duke is marvellous little beholding to your
reports; but the best is, he lives not in them.

LUCIO. Friar, thou knowest not the Duke so well as I do;
he's a better woodman than thou tak'st him for.

DUKE. Well, you'll answer this one day. Fare ye well.

LUCIO. Nay, tarry; I'll go along with thee; I can tell thee
pretty tales of the Duke.

DUKE. You have told me too many of him already, sir, if
they be true; if not true, none were enough.

LUCIO. I was once before him for getting a wench with child.

DUKE. Did you such a thing?

LUCIO. Yes, marry, did I; but I was fain to forswear it: they
would else have married me to the rotten medlar.

DUKE. Sir, your company is fairer than honest. Rest you
well.

Lucio. By my troth, I'll go with thee to the lane's end. If bawdy talk offend you, we'll have very little of it. Nay, friar, I am a kind of burr; I shall stick.   *Exeunt*

SCENE 4

ANGELO's *house*

Enter ANGELO *and* ESCALUS

ESCALUS. Every letter he hath writ hath disvouch'd other.

ANGELO. In most uneven and distracted manner. His actions show much like to madness; pray heaven his wisdom be not tainted! And why meet him at the gates, and redeliver our authorities there?

ESCALUS. I guess not.

ANGELO. And why should we proclaim it in an hour before his ent'ring that, if any crave redress of injustice, they should exhibit their petitions in the street?

ESCALUS. He shows his reason for that: to have a dispatch of complaints; and to deliver us from devices hereafter, which shall then have no power to stand against us.

ANGELO. Well, I beseech you, let it be proclaim'd;
Betimes i' th' morn I'll call you at your house;
Give notice to such men of sort and suit
As are to meet him.

ESCALUS. I shall, sir; fare you well.

ANGELO. Good night.   *Exit* ESCALUS
This deed unshapes me quite, makes me unpregnant
And dull to all proceedings. A deflow'red maid!
And by an eminent body that enforc'd
The law against it! But that her tender shame
Will not proclaim against her maiden loss,
How might she tongue me! Yet reason dares her no;
For my authority bears a so credent bulk
That no particular scandal once can touch
But it confounds the breather. He should have liv'd,
Save that his riotous youth, with dangerous sense,
Might in the times to come have ta'en revenge,
By so receiving a dishonour'd life

With ransom of such shame. Would yet he had liv'd!
Alack, when once our grace we have forgot,
Nothing goes right; we would, and we would not.   *Exit*

SCENE 5

Fields without the town

Enter DUKE *in his own habit, and* FRIAR PETER

DUKE. These letters at fit time deliver me.   [*Giving letters*]
The Provost knows our purpose and our plot.
The matter being afoot, keep your instruction
And hold you ever to our special drift;
Though sometimes you do blench from this to that
As cause doth minister. Go, call at Flavius' house,
And tell him where I stay; give the like notice
To Valentinus, Rowland, and to Crassus,
And bid them bring the trumpets to the gate;
But send me Flavius first.
PETER. It shall be speeded well.   *Exit* FRIAR

Enter VARRIUS

DUKE. I thank thee, Varrius; thou hast made good haste.
Come, we will walk. There's other of our friends
Will greet us here anon. My gentle Varrius!   *Exeunt*

SCENE 6

A street near the city gate

Enter ISABELLA *and* MARIANA

ISABELLA. To speak so indirectly I am loath;
I would say the truth; but to accuse him so,
That is your part. Yet I am advis'd to do it;
He says, to veil full purpose.
MARIANA. Be rul'd by him.
ISABELLA. Besides, he tells me that, if peradventure
He speak against me on the adverse side,

I should not think it strange; for 'tis a physic
That's bitter to sweet end.
MARIANA. I would Friar Peter—

Enter FRIAR PETER

ISABELLA. O, peace! the friar is come.
PETER. Come, I have found you out a stand most fit,
Where you may have such vantage on the Duke
He shall not pass you. Twice have the trumpets sounded;
The generous and gravest citizens
Have hent the gates, and very near upon
The Duke is ent'ring; therefore, hence, away.   *Exeunt*

ACT V. SCENE 1

The city gate

Enter at several doors DUKE, VARRIUS, LORDS; ANGELO,
ESCALUS, LUCIO, PROVOST, OFFICERS, *and* CITIZENS

DUKE. My very worthy cousin, fairly met!
Our old and faithful friend, we are glad to see you.
ANGELO, ESCALUS. Happy return be to your royal Grace!
DUKE. Many and hearty thankings to you both.
We have made inquiry of you, and we hear
Such goodness of your justice that our soul
Cannot but yield you forth to public thanks,
Forerunning more requital.
ANGELO. You make my bonds still greater.
DUKE. O, your desert speaks loud; and I should wrong it
To lock it in the wards of covert bosom,
When it deserves, with characters of brass,
A forted residence 'gainst the tooth of time
And razure of oblivion. Give me your hand.
And let the subject see, to make them know
That outward courtesies would fain proclaim
Favours that keep within. Come, Escalus,

You must walk by us on our other hand,
And good supporters are you.

Enter FRIAR PETER *and* ISABELLA

PETER. Now is your time; speak loud, and kneel before him.
ISABELLA. Justice, O royal Duke! Vail your regard
  Upon a wrong'd—I would fain have said a maid!
  O worthy Prince, dishonour not your eye
  By throwing it on any other object
  Till you have heard me in my true complaint,
  And given me justice, justice, justice, justice.
DUKE. Relate your wrongs. In what? By whom? Be brief.
  Here is Lord Angelo shall give you justice;
  Reveal yourself to him.
ISABELLA. O worthy Duke,
  You bid me seek redemption of the devil!
  Hear me yourself; for that which I must speak
  Must either punish me, not being believ'd,
  Or wring redress from you. Hear me, O, hear me, here!
ANGELO. My lord, her wits, I fear me, are not firm;
  She hath been a suitor to me for her brother,
  Cut off by course of justice—
ISABELLA. By course of justice!
ANGELO. And she will speak most bitterly and strange.
ISABELLA. Most strange, but yet most truly, will I speak.
  That Angelo's forsworn, is it not strange?
  That Angelo's a murderer, is't not strange?
  That Angelo is an adulterous thief,
  An hypocrite, a virgin-violator,
  Is it not strange and strange?
DUKE. Nay, it is ten times strange.
ISABELLA. It is not truer he is Angelo
  Than this is all as true as it is strange;
  Nay, it is ten times true; for truth is truth
  To th' end of reck'ning.
DUKE. Away with her. Poor soul,
  She speaks this in th' infirmity of sense.
ISABELLA. O Prince! I conjure thee, as thou believ'st
  There is another comfort than this world,
  That thou neglect me not with that opinion

That I am touch'd with madness. Make not impossible
That which but seems unlike: 'tis not impossible
But one, the wicked'st caitiff on the ground,
May seem as shy, as grave, as just, as absolute,
As Angelo; even so may Angelo,
In all his dressings, characts, titles, forms,
Be an arch-villain. Believe it, royal Prince,
If he be less, he's nothing; but he's more,
Had I more name for badness.

DUKE. By mine honesty,
If she be mad, as I believe no other,
Her madness hath the oddest frame of sense,
Such a dependency of thing on thing,
As e'er I heard in madness.

ISABELLA. O gracious Duke,
Harp not on that; nor do not banish reason
For inequality; but let your reason serve
To make the truth appear where it seems hid,
And hide the false seems true.

DUKE. Many that are not mad
Have, sure, more lack of reason. What would you say?

ISABELLA. I am the sister of one Claudio,
Condemn'd upon the act of fornication
To lose his head; condemn'd by Angelo.
I, in probation of a sisterhood,
Was sent to by my brother; one Lucio
As then the messenger—

LUCIO. That's I, an't like your Grace.
I came to her from Claudio, and desir'd her
To try her gracious fortune with Lord Angelo
For her poor brother's pardon.

ISABELLA. That's he, indeed.

DUKE. You were not bid to speak.

LUCIO. No, my good lord;
Nor wish'd to hold my peace.

DUKE. I wish you now, then;
Pray you take note of it; and when you have
A business for yourself, pray heaven you then
Be perfect.

LUCIO. I warrant your honour.

DUKE. The warrant's for yourself; take heed to't.
ISABELLA. This gentleman told somewhat of my tale.
LUCIO. Right.
DUKE. It may be right; but you are i' the wrong
 To speak before your time. Proceed.
ISABELLA. I went
 To this pernicious caitiff deputy.
DUKE. That's somewhat madly spoken.
ISABELLA. Pardon it;
 The phrase is to the matter.
DUKE. Mended again. The matter—proceed.
ISABELLA. In brief—to set the needless process by,
 How I persuaded, how I pray'd, and kneel'd,
 How he refell'd me, and how I replied,
 For this was of much length—the vile conclusion
 I now begin with grief and shame to utter:
 He would not, but by gift of my chaste body
 To his concupiscible intemperate lust,
 Release my brother; and, after much debatement,
 My sisterly remorse confutes mine honour,
 And I did yield to him. But the next morn betimes,
 His purpose surfeiting, he sends a warrant
 For my poor brother's head.
DUKE. This is most likely!
ISABELLA. O that it were as like as it is true!
DUKE. By heaven, fond wretch, thou know'st not what thou
 speak'st,
 Or else thou art suborn'd against his honour
 In hateful practice. First, his integrity
 Stands without blemish; next, it imports no reason
 That with such vehemency he should pursue
 Faults proper to himself. If he had so offended,
 He would have weigh'd thy brother by himself,
 And not have cut him off. Some one hath set you on;
 Confess the truth, and say by whose advice
 Thou cam'st here to complain.
ISABELLA. And is this all?
 Then, O you blessed ministers above,
 Keep me in patience; and, with ripened time,
 Unfold the evil which is here wrapt up

ISABELLA. *Justice, justice, justice, justice!* (ACT V. SCENE I)

In countenance! Heaven shield your Grace from woe,
As I, thus wrong'd, hence unbelieved go!
DUKE. I know you'd fain be gone. An officer!
To prison with her! Shall we thus permit
A blasting and a scandalous breath to fall
On him so near us? This needs must be a practice.
Who knew of your intent and coming hither?
ISABELLA. One that I would were here, Friar Lodowick.
DUKE. A ghostly father, belike. Who knows that Lodowick?
LUCIO. My lord, I know him; 'tis a meddling friar.
I do not like the man; had he been lay, my lord,
For certain words he spake against your Grace
In your retirement, I had swing'd him soundly.
DUKE. Words against me? This's a good friar, belike!
And to set on this wretched woman here
Against our substitute! Let this friar be found.
LUCIO. But yesternight, my lord, she and that friar,
I saw them at the prison; a saucy friar,
A very scurvy fellow.
PETER. Blessed be your royal Grace!
I have stood by, my lord, and I have heard
Your royal ear abus'd. First, hath this woman
Most wrongfully accus'd your substitute;
Who is as free from touch or soil with her
As she from one ungot.
DUKE. We did believe no less.
Know you that Friar Lodowick that she speaks of?
PETER. I know him for a man divine and holy;
Not scurvy, nor a temporary meddler,
As he's reported by this gentleman;
And, on my trust, a man that never yet
Did, as he vouches, misreport your Grace.
LUCIO. My lord, most villainously; believe it.
PETER. Well, he in time may come to clear himself;
But at this instant he is sick, my lord,
Of a strange fever. Upon his mere request—
Being come to knowledge that there was complaint
Intended 'gainst Lord Angelo—came I hither
To speak, as from his mouth, what he doth know
Is true and false; and what he, with his oath

And all probation, will make up full clear,
Whensoever he's convented. First, for this woman—
To justify this worthy nobleman,
So vulgarly and personally accus'd—
Her shall you hear disproved to her eyes,
Till she herself confess it.

DUKE. Good friar, let's hear it.   *Exit* ISABELLA *guarded*
Do you not smile at this, Lord Angelo?
O heaven, the vanity of wretched fools!
Give us some seats. Come, cousin Angelo;
In this I'll be impartial; be you judge
Of your own cause.

Enter MARIANA *veiled*

Is this the witness, friar?
First let her show her face, and after speak.

MARIANA. Pardon, my lord; I will not show my face
Until my husband bid me.

DUKE. What, are you married?

MARIANA. No, my lord.

DUKE. Are you a maid?

MARIANA. No, my lord.

DUKE. A widow, then?

MARIANA. Neither, my lord.

DUKE. Why, you are nothing then; neither maid, widow,
nor wife.

LUCIO. My lord, she may be a punk; for many of them are
neither maid, widow, nor wife.

DUKE. Silence that fellow. I would he had some cause
To prattle for himself.

LUCIO. Well, my lord.

MARIANA. My lord, I do confess I ne'er was married,
And I confess, besides, I am no maid.
I have known my husband; yet my husband
Knows not that ever he knew me.

LUCIO. He was drunk, then, my lord; it can be no better.

DUKE. For the benefit of silence, would thou wert so too!

LUCIO. Well, my lord.

DUKE. This is no witness for Lord Angelo.

MARIANA. Now I come to't, my lord:

She that accuses him of fornication,
In self-same manner doth accuse my husband;
And charges him, my lord, with such a time
When I'll depose I had him in mine arms,
With all th' effect of love.

ANGELO. Charges she moe than me?

MARIANA. Not that I know.

DUKE. No? You say your husband.

MARIANA. Why, just, my lord, and that is Angelo,
Who thinks he knows that he ne'er knew my body,
But knows he thinks that he knows Isabel's.

ANGELO. This is a strange abuse. Let's see thy face.

MARIANA. My husband bids me; now I will unmask.

[*Unveiling*]

This is that face, thou cruel Angelo,
Which once thou swor'st was worth the looking on;
This is the hand which, with a vow'd contract,
Was fast belock'd in thine; this is the body
That took away the match from Isabel,
And did supply thee at thy garden-house
In her imagin'd person.

DUKE. Know you this woman?

LUCIO. Carnally, she says.

DUKE. Sirrah, no more.

LUCIO. Enough, my lord.

ANGELO. My lord, I must confess I know this woman;
And five years since there was some speech of marriage
Betwixt myself and her; which was broke off,
Partly for that her promised proportions
Came short of composition; but in chief
For that her reputation was disvalued
In levity. Since which time of five years
I never spake with her, saw her, nor heard from her,
Upon my faith and honour.

MARIANA. Noble Prince,
As there comes light from heaven and words from breath,
As there is sense in truth and truth in virtue,
I am affianc'd this man's wife as strongly
As words could make up vows. And, my good lord,
But Tuesday night last gone, in's garden-house,

He knew me as a wife. As this is true,
Let me in safety raise me from my knees,
Or else for ever be confixed here,
A marble monument!

ANGELO. I did but smile till now.
Now, good my lord, give me the scope of justice;
My patience here is touch'd. I do perceive
These poor informal women are no more
But instruments of some more mightier member
That sets them on. Let me have way, my lord,
To find this practice out.

DUKE. Ay, with my heart;
And punish them to your height of pleasure.
Thou foolish friar, and thou pernicious woman,
Compact with her that's gone, think'st thou thy oaths,
Though they would swear down each particular saint,
Were testimonies against his worth and credit,
That's seal'd in approbation? You, Lord Escalus,
Sit with my cousin; lend him your kind pains
To find out this abuse, whence 'tis deriv'd.
There is another friar that set them on;
Let him be sent for.

PETER. Would he were here, my lord! For he indeed
Hath set the women on to this complaint.
Your provost knows the place where he abides,
And he may fetch him.

DUKE. Go, do it instantly. *Exit* PROVOST
And you, my noble and well-warranted cousin,
Whom it concerns to hear this matter forth,
Do with your injuries as seems you best
In any chastisement. I for a while will leave you;
But stir not you till you have well determin'd
Upon these slanderers.

ESCALUS. My lord, we'll do it throughly. *Exit* DUKE
Signior Lucio, did not you say you knew that Friar Lodowick to be a dishonest person?

LUCIO. 'Cucullus non facit monachum': honest in nothing
but in his clothes; and one that hath spoke most villainous
speeches of the Duke.

ESCALUS. We shall entreat you to abide here till he come,

298

and enforce them against him. We shall find this friar a
notable fellow.

LUCIO. As any in Vienna, on my word.

ESCALUS. Call that same Isabel here once again; I would
speak with her. [*Exit an* ATTENDANT] Pray you, my lord,
give me leave to question; you shall see how I'll handle
her.

LUCIO. Not better than he, by her own report.

ESCALUS. Say you?

LUCIO. Marry, sir, I think, if you handled her privately, she
would sooner confess; perchance, publicly, she'll be
asham'd.

Re-enter OFFICERS *with* ISABELLA; *and* PROVOST *with the*
DUKE *in his friar's habit*

ESCALUS. I will go darkly to work with her.

LUCIO. That's the way; for women are light at midnight.

ESCALUS. Come on, mistress; here's a gentlewoman denies all
that you have said.

LUCIO. My lord, here comes the rascal I spoke of, here with
the Provost.

ESCALUS. In very good time. Speak not you to him till we
call upon you.

LUCIO. Mum.

ESCALUS. Come, sir; did you set these women on to slander
Lord Angelo? They have confess'd you did.

DUKE. 'Tis false.

ESCALUS. How! Know you where you are?

DUKE. Respect to your great place! and let the devil
Be sometime honour'd for his burning throne!
Where is the Duke? 'Tis he should hear me speak.

ESCALUS. The Duke's in us; and we will hear you speak;
Look you speak justly.

DUKE. Boldly, at least. But, O, poor souls,
Come you to seek the lamb here of the fox,
Good night to your redress! Is the Duke gone?
Then is your cause gone too. The Duke's unjust
Thus to retort your manifest appeal,
And put your trial in the villain's mouth
Which here you come to accuse.

LUCIO. This is the rascal; this is he I spoke of.

ESCALUS. Why, thou unreverend and unhallowed friar,
  Is't not enough thou hast suborn'd these women
  To accuse this worthy man, but, in foul mouth,
  And in the witness of his proper ear,
  To call him villain; and then to glance from him
  To th' Duke himself, to tax him with injustice?
  Take him hence; to th' rack with him! We'll touze you
  Joint by joint, but we will know his purpose.
  What, 'unjust'!

DUKE. Be not so hot; the Duke
  Dare no more stretch this finger of mine than he
  Dare rack his own; his subject am I not,
  Nor here provincial. My business in this state
  Made me a looker-on here in Vienna,
  Where I have seen corruption boil and bubble
  Till it o'errun the stew: laws for all faults,
  But faults so countenanc'd that the strong statutes
  Stand like the forfeits in a barber's shop,
  As much in mock as mark.

ESCALUS. Slander to th' state! Away with him to prison!

ANGELO. What can you vouch against him, Signior Lucio?
  Is this the man that you did tell us of?

LUCIO. 'Tis he, my lord. Come hither, good-man bald-pate.
  Do you know me?

DUKE. I remember you, sir, by the sound of your voice. I
  met you at the prison, in the absence of the Duke.

LUCIO. O did you so? And do you remember what you said
  of the Duke?

DUKE. Most notedly, sir.

LUCIO. Do you so, sir? And was the Duke a fleshmonger, a
  fool, and a coward, as you then reported him to be?

DUKE. You must, sir, change persons with me ere you make
  that my report; you, indeed, spoke so of him; and much
  more, much worse.

LUCIO. O thou damnable fellow! Did not I pluck thee by the
  nose for thy speeches?

DUKE. I protest I love the Duke as I love myself.

ANGELO. Hark how the villain would close now, after his
  treasonable abuses!

ESCALUS. Such a fellow is not to be talk'd withal. Away
with him to prison! Where is the Provost? Away with him
to prison! Lay bolts enough upon him; let him speak no
more. Away with those giglets too, and with the other
confederate companion!

                        [The PROVOST *lays hands on the* DUKE]

DUKE. Stay, sir; stay awhile.

ANGELO. What, resists he? Help him, Lucio.

LUCIO. Come, sir; come, sir; come, sir; foh, sir! Why, you
bald-pated lying rascal, you must be hooded, must you?
Show your knave's visage, with a pox to you! Show your
sheep-biting face, and be hang'd an hour! Will't not off?

        [Pulls off the FRIAR's *hood and discovers the* DUKE]

DUKE. Thou art the first knave that e'er mad'st a duke.
First, Provost, let me bail these gentle three.
[*To* LUCIO] Sneak not away, sir, for the friar and you
Must have a word anon. Lay hold on him.

LUCIO. This may prove worse than hanging.

DUKE. [*To* ESCALUS] What you have spoke I pardon; sit
you down.
We'll borrow place of him. [*To* ANGELO] Sir, by your
leave.
Hast thou or word, or wit, or impudence,
That yet can do thee office? If thou hast,
Rely upon it till my tale be heard,
And hold no longer out.

ANGELO. O my dread lord,
I should be guiltier than my guiltiness,
To think I can be undiscernible,
When I perceive your Grace, like pow'r divine,
Hath look'd upon my passes. Then, good Prince,
No longer session hold upon my shame,
But let my trial be mine own confession;
Immediate sentence then, and sequent death,
Is all the grace I beg.

DUKE. Come hither, Mariana.
Say, wast thou e'er contracted to this woman?

ANGELO. I was, my lord.

DUKE. Go, take her hence and marry her instantly.
Do you the office, friar; which consummate,

Return him here again. Go with him, Provost.

Exeunt ANGELO, MARIANA, FRIAR PETER, *and* PROVOST

ESCALUS. My lord, I am more amaz'd at his dishonour
Than at the strangeness of it.

DUKE. Come hither, Isabel.
Your friar is now your prince. As I was then
Advertising and holy to your business,
Not changing heart with habit, I am still
Attorney'd at your service.

ISABELLA. O, give me pardon,
That I, your vassal, have employ'd and pain'd
Your unknown sovereignty.

DUKE. You are pardon'd, Isabel.
And now, dear maid, be you as free to us.
Your brother's death, I know, sits at your heart;
And you may marvel why I obscur'd myself,
Labouring to save his life, and would not rather
Make rash remonstrance of my hidden pow'r
Than let him so be lost. O most kind maid,
It was the swift celerity of his death,
Which I did think with slower foot came on,
That brain'd my purpose. But peace be with him!
That life is better life, past fearing death,
Than that which lives to fear. Make it your comfort,
So happy is your brother.

ISABELLA. I do, my lord.

Re-enter ANGELO, MARIANA, FRIAR PETER, *and* PROVOST

DUKE. For this new-married man approaching here,
Whose salt imagination yet hath wrong'd
Your well-defended honour, you must pardon
For Mariana's sake; but as he adjudg'd your brother—
Being criminal in double violation
Of sacred chastity and of promise-breach,
Thereon dependent, for your brother's life—
The very mercy of the law cries out
Most audible, even from his proper tongue,
'An Angelo for Claudio, death for death!'
Haste still pays haste, and leisure answers leisure;
Like doth quit like, and Measure still for Measure.

Then, Angelo, thy fault's thus manifested,
Which, though thou wouldst deny, denies thee vantage.
We do condemn thee to the very block
Where Claudio stoop'd to death, and with like haste.
Away with him!
MARIANA. O my most gracious lord,
I hope you will not mock me with a husband.
DUKE. It is your husband mock'd you with a husband.
Consenting to the safeguard of your honour,
I thought your marriage fit; else imputation,
For that he knew you, might reproach your life,
And choke your good to come. For his possessions,
Although by confiscation they are ours,
We do instate and widow you withal,
To buy you a better husband.
MARIANA. O my dear lord,
I crave no other, nor no better man.
DUKE. Never crave him; we are definitive.
MARIANA. Gentle my liege—   [*Kneeling*]
DUKE. You do but lose your labour.
Away with him to death! [*To* LUCIO] Now, sir, to you.
MARIANA. O my good lord! Sweet Isabel, take my part;
Lend me your knees, and all my life to come
I'll lend you all my life to do you service.
DUKE. Against all sense you do importune her.
Should she kneel down in mercy of this fact,
Her brother's ghost his paved bed would break,
And take her hence in horror.
MARIANA. Isabel,
Sweet Isabel, do yet but kneel by me;
Hold up your hands, say nothing; I'll speak all.
They say best men are moulded out of faults;
And, for the most, become much more the better
For being a little bad; so may my husband.
O Isabel, will you not lend a knee?
DUKE. He dies for Claudio's death.
ISABELLA. [*Kneeling*] Most bounteous sir,
Look, if it please you, on this man condemn'd,
As if my brother liv'd. I partly think
A due sincerity govern'd his deeds

Till he did look on me; since it is so,
Let him not die. My brother had but justice,
In that he did the thing for which he died;
For Angelo,
His act did not o'ertake his bad intent,
And must be buried but as an intent
That perish'd by the way. Thoughts are no subjects;
Intents but merely thoughts.

MARIANA. Merely, my lord.

DUKE. Your suit's unprofitable; stand up, I say.
I have bethought me of another fault.
Provost, how came it Claudio was beheaded
At an unusual hour?

PROVOST. It was commanded so.

DUKE. Had you a special warrant for the deed?

PROVOST. No, my good lord; it was by private message.

DUKE. For which I do discharge you of your office;
Give up your keys.

PROVOST. Pardon me, noble lord;
I thought it was a fault, but knew it not;
Yet did repent me, after more advice;
For testimony whereof, one in the prison,
That should by private order else have died,
I have reserv'd alive.

DUKE. What's he?

PROVOST. His name is Barnardine.

DUKE. I would thou hadst done so by Claudio.
Go fetch him hither; let me look upon him. *Exit* PROVOST

ESCALUS. I am sorry one so learned and so wise
As you, Lord Angelo, have still appear'd,
Should slip so grossly, both in the heat of blood
And lack of temper'd judgment afterward.

ANGELO. I am sorry that such sorrow I procure;
And so deep sticks it in my penitent heart
That I crave death more willingly than mercy;
'Tis my deserving, and I do entreat it.

Re-enter PROVOST, *with* BARNARDINE, CLAUDIO (*muffled*)
and JULIET

DUKE. Which is that Barnardine?

PROVOST. This, my lord.

DUKE. There was a friar told me of this man.
Sirrah, thou art said to have a stubborn soul,
That apprehends no further than this world,
And squar'st thy life according. Thou'rt condemn'd;
But, for those earthly faults, I quit them all,
And pray thee take this mercy to provide
For better times to come. Friar, advise him;
I leave him to your hand. What muffl'd fellow's that?

PROVOST. This is another prisoner that I sav'd,
Who should have died when Claudio lost his head;
As like almost to Claudio as himself. [*Unmuffles* CLAUDIO]

DUKE. [*To* ISABELLA] If he be like your brother, for his
sake
Is he pardon'd; and for your lovely sake,
Give me your hand and say you will be mine,
He is my brother too. But fitter time for that.
By this Lord Angelo perceives he's safe;
Methinks I see a quick'ning in his eye.
Well, Angelo, your evil quits you well.
Look that you love your wife; her worth worth yours.
I find an apt remission in myself;
And yet here's one in place I cannot pardon.
[*To* LUCIO] You, sirrah, that knew me for a fool, a
coward,
One all of luxury, an ass, a madman!
Wherein have I so deserv'd of you
That you extol me thus?

LUCIO. Faith, my lord, I spoke it but according to the trick.
If you will hang me for it, you may; but I had rather it
would please you I might be whipt.

DUKE. Whipt first, sir, and hang'd after.
Proclaim it, Provost, round about the city,
If any woman wrong'd by this lewd fellow—
As I have heard him swear himself there's one
Whom he begot with child, let her appear,
And he shall marry her. The nuptial finish'd,
Let him be whipt and hang'd.

LUCIO. I beseech your Highness, do not marry me to a
whore. Your Highness said even now I made you a duke;

good my lord, do not recompense me in making me a
cuckold.

DUKE. Upon mine honour, thou shalt marry her.
Thy slanders I forgive; and therewithal
Remit thy other forfeits. Take him to prison;
And see our pleasure herein executed.

LUCIO. Marrying a punk, my lord, is pressing to death, whipping, and hanging.

DUKE. Slandering a prince deserves it.

Exeunt OFFICERS *with* LUCIO

She, Claudio, that you wrong'd, look you restore.
Joy to you, Mariana! Love her, Angelo;
I have confess'd her, and I know her virtue.
Thanks, good friend Escalus, for thy much goodness;
There's more behind that is more gratulate.
Thanks, Provost, for thy care and secrecy;
We shall employ thee in a worthier place.
Forgive him, Angelo, that brought you home
The head of Ragozine for Claudio's:
Th' offence pardons itself. Dear Isabel,
I have a motion much imports your good;
Whereto if you'll a willing ear incline,
What's mine is yours, and what is yours is mine.
So, bring us to our palace, where we'll show
What's yet behind that's meet you all should know.

Exeunt

The Comedy of Errors

THE COMEDY OF ERRORS

THE COMEDY OF ERRORS was performed on 28th December 1594 before the members of Gray's Inn. This was part of their elaborate Christmas celebrations for which they had elected a Lord of Misrule. According to the account that has survived of the proceedings the members of the Inner Temple were to join them to witness the performance. The details of accommodation however had been badly miscalculated and the Templars withdrew before the performance; their displeasure at what they regarded as uncivil treatment was however placated by a performance on 3rd January of a *Masque of Proteus* at which everything was carefully ordered for them by heir hosts of Gray's Inn.

The Comedy of Errors was not of course written for this occasion. It must be one of Shakespeare's earliest plays, but it was no doubt regarded as specially suitable for performance before the lawyers at this season because of its classical affinities. Shakespeare had combined features from two plays by Plautus, the *Menaechmi* and the *Amphitruo*. In the *Amphitruo* a master and his servant are locked out by the lady of the house while she entertains in their stead and in all innocence Jupiter and his servant Mercury, disguised as her husband and his servant. Here are identical masters and identical servants. By adding to the *Menaechmi*, where the confusions are caused by a pair of twins, a second pair to act as their servants, Shakespeare was able to include in his mistakings a central scene (like that in the *Amphitruo*) where Adriana entertains Antipholus of Syracuse and his servant, while her husband and his man are fretting in the street.

It is absurd to say as some do that Shakespeare has made the plot more improbable. The probability of the premises is not here the first consideration. The question is, Does Shakespeare use his extra material skilfully and economically? Does he make his addition pay its way? Unfortunately the play is not performed nowadays, but even a reading acquaintance will show that this report of a performance by Charles Armitage Brown, a friend of Keats, is not exaggerated:

308

'Until I saw it on the stage, I had not imagined the extent of the mistakes, the drollery of them, their unabated continuance, till, at the end of the fourth act, they reach their climax, with the assistance of Dr. Pinch, when the audience in their laughter rolled about like waves.'

Shakespeare was obviously early a master in the dexterous contrivance of comic situations.

To the comedy of Plautus Shakespeare has added a touch of romance of his own: Adriana is given a sister Luciana; this adds at first to the confusion, for the wandering twin falls in love with her to the grief of Adriana who thinks her husband is unfaithful; in the end it makes for a neater solution and happy marriage.

In this play Shakespeare strictly observes the Unities of Time and Place. In the first scene it is morning and Aegeon is being led to execution; the last scene is on the evening of the same day, when Aegeon is pardoned and united to his long-lost wife and sons. In short the action takes place between sunrise and sunset. Nor does the place change. The houses are arranged round an open space like a square in Ephesus, the sign of the Phoenix indicating the house of Antipholus, that of the Porpentine the house of the courtesan, with the Priory near by. Those going to or coming from the harbour use one side of the stage for their exits and entrances, the other side is to and from the town—all according to classical convention.

It is unnecessary to wonder how Shakespeare came by the Latin required to read Plautus. A grammar school education would give him that. To suppose that he must have rewritten a play by someone who did know Plautus is to multiply versions without necessity. *The Comedy of Errors* goes naturally with the other 'classical' pieces of his early years, *Titus Andronicus* and *Venus and Adonis*. No one, except those who regard Shakespeare as the ghost of Bacon or Oxford, denies that *Venus and Adonis* is from the poet's own hand. If he could write that poem there seems no good reason why he should not have been able to write *The Comedy of Errors*. Of course it is different from the poem; only here and there has Shakespeare allowed himself lyrical flights, although these, few as they may be, are characteristic of the poet. In the comedy Shakespeare is the dramatist, exploiting the opportunities his stage allowed and developing the possibilities in his plot. He is here the dramatic craftsman rather than the poet; and *The Comedy of Errors* exhibits in a particularly clear way and almost in isolation one of his talents that he was not to neglect and that he was later to combine so profitably with others. Those who suppose that Shakespeare's masterpieces are a series of disconnected scenes rather than the highly organised unities they indeed are should turn back to such an earlier and simpler play as *The Comedy of Errors*, where the liaison between scene and scene is so obvious and essential, and then ask themselves if years of practice really deprived Shakespeare of this early skill. The unity of the later plays is of course subtler and more complicated but it includes the technical mastery already visible in *The Comedy of Errors*.

ANTIPHOLUS OF SYRACUSE. *There, take you that, sir knave*

(ACT I. SCENE II)

SOLINUS, *Duke of Ephesus*
ÆGEON, *a merchant of Syracuse*
ANTIPHOLUS OF EPHESUS ⎱ *twin brothers, and sons to*
ANTIPHOLUS OF SYRACUSE ⎰ *Ægeon and Æmilia*
DROMIO OF EPHESUS ⎱ *twin brothers, and attendants on*
DROMIO OF SYRACUSE ⎰ *the two Antipholuses*
BALTHAZAR, *a merchant*
ANGELO, *a goldsmith*
FIRST MERCHANT, *friend to Antipholus of Syracuse*
SECOND MERCHANT, *to whom Angelo is a debtor*
PINCH, *a schoolmaster*

ÆMILIA, *wife to Ægeon; an abbess at Ephesus*
ADRIANA, *wife to Antipholus of Ephesus*
LUCIANA, *her sister*
LUCE, *servant to Adriana*
A COURTEZAN

Gaoler, Officers, Attendants

SCENE:

Ephesus

The Comedy of Errors

ACT I. SCENE 1

A hall in the DUKE's *palace*

Enter the DUKE OF EPHESUS, ÆGEON, *the Merchant of Syracuse*, GAOLER, OFFICERS, *and other* ATTENDANTS

ÆGEON. Proceed, Solinus, to procure my fall,
  And by the doom of death end woes and all.
DUKE. Merchant of Syracusa, plead no more;
  I am not partial to infringe our laws.
  The enmity and discord which of late
  Sprung from the rancorous outrage of your duke
  To merchants, our well-dealing countrymen,
  Who, wanting guilders to redeem their lives,
  Have seal'd his rigorous statutes with their bloods,
  Excludes all pity from our threat'ning looks.
  For, since the mortal and intestine jars
  'Twixt thy seditious countrymen and us,
  It hath in solemn synods been decreed,
  Both by the Syracusians and ourselves,
  To admit no traffic to our adverse towns;
  Nay, more: if any born at Ephesus
  Be seen at any Syracusian marts and fairs;
  Again, if any Syracusian born
  Come to the bay of Ephesus—he dies,
  His goods confiscate to the Duke's dispose,
  Unless a thousand marks be levied,
  To quit the penalty and to ransom him.
  Thy substance, valued at the highest rate,
  Cannot amount unto a hundred marks;
  Therefore by law thou art condemn'd to die.
ÆGEON. Yet this my comfort: when your words are done,
  My woes end likewise with the evening sun.
DUKE. Well, Syracusian, say in brief the cause
  Why thou departed'st from thy native home,

And for what cause thou cam'st to Ephesus.

ÆGEON. A heavier task could not have been impos'd
Than I to speak my griefs unspeakable;
Yet, that the world may witness that my end
Was wrought by nature, not by vile offence,
I'll utter what my sorrow gives me leave.
In Syracusa was I born, and wed
Unto a woman, happy but for me,
And by me, had not our hap been bad.
With her I liv'd in joy; our wealth increas'd
By prosperous voyages I often made
To Epidamnum; till my factor's death,
And the great care of goods at random left,
Drew me from kind embracements of my spouse:
From whom my absence was not six months old,
Before herself, almost at fainting under
The pleasing punishment that women bear,
Had made provision for her following me,
And soon and safe arrived where I was.
There had she not been long but she became
A joyful mother of two goodly sons;
And, which was strange, the one so like the other
As could not be distinguish'd but by names.
That very hour, and in the self-same inn,
A mean woman was delivered
Of such a burden, male twins, both alike.
Those, for their parents were exceeding poor,
I bought, and brought up to attend my sons.
My wife, not meanly proud of two such boys,
Made daily motions for our home return;
Unwilling, I agreed. Alas! too soon
We came aboard.
A league from Epidamnum had we sail'd
Before the always-wind-obeying deep
Gave any tragic instance of our harm:
But longer did we not retain much hope,
For what obscured light the heavens did grant
Did but convey unto our fearful minds
A doubtful warrant of immediate death;
Which though myself would gladly have embrac'd,

Yet the incessant weepings of my wife,
Weeping before for what she saw must come,
And piteous plainings of the pretty babes,
That mourn'd for fashion, ignorant what to fear,
Forc'd me to seek delays for them and me.
And this it was, for other means was none:
The sailors sought for safety by our boat,
And left the ship, then sinking-ripe, to us;
My wife, more careful for the latter-born,
Had fast'ned him unto a small spare mast,
Such as sea-faring men provide for storms;
To him one of the other twins was bound,
Whilst I had been like heedful of the other.
The children thus dispos'd, my wife and I,
Fixing our eyes on whom our care was fix'd,
Fast'ned ourselves at either end the mast,
And, floating straight, obedient to the stream,
Was carried towards Corinth, as we thought.
At length the sun, gazing upon the earth,
Dispers'd those vapours that offended us;
And, by the benefit of his wished light,
The seas wax'd calm, and we discovered
Two ships from far making amain to us—
Of Corinth that, of Epidaurus this.
But ere they came—O, let me say no more!
Gather the sequel by that went before.
DUKE. Nay, forward, old man, do not break off so;
For we may pity, though not pardon thee.
ÆGEON. O, had the gods done so, I had not now
Worthily term'd them merciless to us!
For, ere the ships could meet by twice five leagues,
We were encount'red by a mighty rock,
Which being violently borne upon,
Our helpful ship was splitted in the midst;
So that, in this unjust divorce of us,
Fortune had left to both of us alike
What to delight in, what to sorrow for.
Her part, poor soul, seeming as burdened
With lesser weight, but not with lesser woe,
Was carried with more speed before the wind;

And in our sight they three were taken up
By fishermen of Corinth, as we thought.
At length another ship had seiz'd on us;
And, knowing whom it was their hap to save,
Gave healthful welcome to their ship-wreck'd guests,
And would have reft the fishers of their prey,
Had not their bark been very slow of sail;
And therefore homeward did they bend their course.
Thus have you heard me sever'd from my bliss,
That by misfortunes was my life prolong'd,
To tell sad stories of my own mishaps.

DUKE. And, for the sake of them thou sorrowest for,
Do me the favour to dilate at full
What have befall'n of them and thee till now.

ÆGEON. My youngest boy, and yet my eldest care,
At eighteen years became inquisitive
After his brother, and importun'd me
That his attendant—so his case was like,
Reft of his brother, but retain'd his name—
Might bear him company in the quest of him;
Whom whilst I laboured of a love to see,
I hazarded the loss of whom I lov'd.
Five summers have I spent in farthest Greece,
Roaming clean through the bounds of Asia,
And, coasting homeward, came to Ephesus;
Hopeless to find, yet loath to leave unsought
Or that or any place that harbours men.
But here must end the story of my life;
And happy were I in my timely death,
Could all my travels warrant me they live.

DUKE. Hapless, Ægeon, whom the fates have mark'd
To bear the extremity of dire mishap!
Now, trust me, were it not against our laws,
Against my crown, my oath, my dignity,
Which princes, would they, may not disannul,
My soul should sue as advocate for thee.
But though thou art adjudged to the death,
And passed sentence may not be recall'd
But to our honour's great disparagement,
Yet will I favour thee in what I can.

316

Therefore, merchant, I'll limit thee this day
To seek thy help by beneficial hap.
Try all the friends thou hast in Ephesus;
Beg thou, or borrow, to make up the sum,
And live; if no, then thou art doom'd to die.
Gaoler, take him to thy custody.
GAOLER. I will, my lord.
ÆGEON. Hopeless and helpless doth Ægeon wend,
But to procrastinate his lifeless end.   *Exeunt*

SCENE 2

The mart

Enter ANTIPHOLUS OF SYRACUSE, DROMIO OF SYRACUSE,
        and FIRST MERCHANT

FIRST MERCHANT. Therefore, give out you are of Epidamnum,
Lest that your goods too soon be confiscate.
This very day a Syracusian merchant
Is apprehended for arrival here;
And, not being able to buy out his life,
According to the statute of the town,
Dies ere the weary sun set in the west.
There is your money that I had to keep.
ANTIPHOLUS OF SYRACUSE. Go bear it to the Centaur, where
    we host.
And stay there, Dromio, till I come to thee.
Within this hour it will be dinner-time;
Till that, I'll view the manners of the town,
Peruse the traders, gaze upon the buildings,
And then return and sleep within mine inn;
For with long travel I am stiff and weary.
Get thee away.
DROMIO OF SYRACUSE. Many a man would take you at your
    word,
And go indeed, having so good a mean.   *Exit*
ANTIPHOLUS OF SYRACUSE. A trusty villain, sir, that very oft,
When I am dull with care and melancholy,

317

Lightens my humour with his merry jests.
What, will you walk with me about the town,
And then go to my inn and dine with me?
FIRST MERCHANT. I am invited, sir, to certain merchants,
Of whom I hope to make much benefit;
I crave your pardon. Soon at five o'clock,
Please you, I'll meet with you upon the mart,
And afterward consort you till bed time.
My present business calls me from you now.
ANTIPHOLUS OF SYRACUSE. Farewell till then. I will go lose
myself,
And wander up and down to view the city.
FIRST MERCHANT. Sir, I commend you to your own content.
Exit FIRST MERCHANT
ANTIPHOLUS OF SYRACUSE. He that commends me to mine
own content
Commends me to the thing I cannot get.
I to the world am like a drop of water
That in the ocean seeks another drop,
Who, falling there to find his fellow forth,
Unseen, inquisitive, confounds himself.
So I, to find a mother and a brother,
In quest of them, unhappy, lose myself.

Enter DROMIO OF EPHESUS

Here comes the almanac of my true date.
What now? How chance thou art return'd so soon?
DROMIO OF EPHESUS. Return'd so soon! rather approach'd
too late.
The capon burns, the pig falls from the spit;
The clock hath strucken twelve upon the bell—
My mistress made it one upon my cheek;
She is so hot because the meat is cold,
The meat is cold because you come not home,
You come not home because you have no stomach,
You have no stomach, having broke your fast;
But we, that know what 'tis to fast and pray,
Are penitent for your default to-day.
ANTIPHOLUS OF SYRACUSE. Stop in your wind, sir; tell me
this, I pray:

318

Where have you left the money that I gave you?

DROMIO OF EPHESUS. O—sixpence that I had a Wednesday last
To pay the saddler for my mistress' crupper?
The saddler had it, sir; I kept it not.

ANTIPHOLUS OF SYRACUSE. I am not in a sportive humour now;
Tell me, and dally not, where is the money?
We being strangers here, how dar'st thou trust
So great a charge from thine own custody?

DROMIO OF EPHESUS. I pray you jest, sir, as you sit at dinner.
I from my mistress come to you in post;
If I return, I shall be post indeed,
For she will score your fault upon my pate.
Methinks your maw, like mine, should be your clock,
And strike you home without a messenger.

ANTIPHOLUS OF SYRACUSE. Come, Dromio, come, these jests are out of season;
Reserve them till a merrier hour than this.
Where is the gold I gave in charge to thee?

DROMIO OF EPHESUS. To me, sir? Why, you gave no gold to me.

ANTIPHOLUS OF SYRACUSE. Come on, sir knave, have done your foolishness,
And tell me how thou hast dispos'd thy charge.

DROMIO OF EPHESUS. My charge was but to fetch you from the mart
Home to your house, the Phœnix, sir, to dinner.
My mistress and her sister stays for you.

ANTIPHOLUS OF SYRACUSE. Now, as I am a Christian, answer me
In what safe place you have bestow'd my money,
Or I shall break that merry sconce of yours,
That stands on tricks when I am undispos'd.
Where is the thousand marks thou hadst of me?

DROMIO OF EPHESUS. I have some marks of yours upon my pate,
Some of my mistress' marks upon my shoulders,
But not a thousand marks between you both.
If I should pay your worship those again,

319

Perchance you will not bear them patiently.

ANTIPHOLUS OF SYRACUSE. Thy mistress' marks! What mistress, slave, hast thou?

DROMIO OF EPHESUS. Your worship's wife, my mistress at the Phœnix;
She that doth fast till you come home to dinner,
And prays that you will hie you home to dinner.

ANTIPHOLUS OF SYRACUSE. What, wilt thou flout me thus unto my face,
Being forbid? There, take you that, sir knave. [*Beats him*]

DROMIO OF EPHESUS. What mean you, sir? For God's sake hold your hands!
Nay, an you will not, sir, I'll take my heels.   *Exit*

ANTIPHOLUS OF SYRACUSE. Upon my life, by some device or other
The villain is o'erraught of all my money.
They say this town is full of cozenage;
As, nimble jugglers that deceive the eye,
Dark-working sorcerers that change the mind,
Soul-killing witches that deform the body,
Disguised cheaters, prating mountebanks,
And many such-like liberties of sin;
If it prove so, I will be gone the sooner.
I'll to the Centaur to go seek this slave.
I greatly fear my money is not safe.   *Exit*

ACT II. SCENE 1

The house of ANTIPHOLUS OF EPHESUS

Enter ADRIANA, *wife to* ANTIPHOLUS OF EPHESUS,
with LUCIANA, *her sister*

ADRIANA. Neither my husband nor the slave return'd
That in such haste I sent to seek his master!
Sure, Luciana, it is two o'clock.

LUCIANA. Perhaps some merchant hath invited him,
And from the mart he's somewhere gone to dinner;

Good sister, let us dine, and never fret.
A man is master of his liberty;
Time is their master, and when they see time,
They'll go or come. If so, be patient, sister.

ADRIANA. Why should their liberty than ours be more?
LUCIANA. Because their business still lies out o' door.
ADRIANA. Look when I serve him so, he takes it ill.
LUCIANA. O, know he is the bridle of your will.
ADRIANA. There's none but asses will be bridled so.
LUCIANA. Why, headstrong liberty is lash'd with woe.
There's nothing situate under heaven's eye
But hath his bound, in earth, in sea, in sky.
The beasts, the fishes, and the winged fowls,
Are their males' subjects, and at their controls.
Man, more divine, the master of all these,
Lord of the wide world and wild wat'ry seas,
Indu'd with intellectual sense and souls,
Of more pre-eminence than fish and fowls,
Are masters to their females, and their lords;
Then let your will attend on their accords.

ADRIANA. This servitude makes you to keep unwed.
LUCIANA. Not this, but troubles of the marriage-bed.
ADRIANA. But, were you wedded, you would bear some sway.
LUCIANA. Ere I learn love, I'll practise to obey.
ADRIANA. How if your husband start some other where?
LUCIANA. Till he come home again, I would forbear.
ADRIANA. Patience unmov'd! no marvel though she pause:
They can be meek that have no other cause.
A wretched soul, bruis'd with adversity,
We bid be quiet when we hear it cry;
But were we burd'ned with like weight of pain,
As much, or more, we should ourselves complain.
So thou, that hast no unkind mate to grieve thee,
With urging helpless patience would relieve me;
But if thou live to see like right bereft,
This fool-begg'd patience in thee will be left.

LUCIANA. Well, I will marry one day, but to try.
Here comes your man, now is your husband nigh.

Enter DROMIO OF EPHESUS

ADRIANA. Say, is your tardy master now at hand?

DROMIO OF EPHESUS. Nay, he's at two hands with me, and
that my two ears can witness.

ADRIANA. Say, didst thou speak with him? Know'st thou his
mind?

DROMIO OF EPHESUS. Ay, ay, he told his mind upon mine
ear.

Beshrew his hand, I scarce could understand it.

LUCIANA. Spake he so doubtfully thou could'st not feel his
meaning?

DROMIO OF EPHESUS. Nay, he struck so plainly I could too
well feel his blows; and withal so doubtfully that I could
scarce understand them.

ADRIANA. But say, I prithee, is he coming home?

It seems he hath great care to please his wife.

DROMIO OF EPHESUS. Why, mistress, sure my master is horn-
mad.

ADRIANA. Horn-mad, thou villain!

DROMIO OF EPHESUS. I mean not cuckold-mad;

But, sure, he is stark mad.

When I desir'd him to come home to dinner,

He ask'd me for a thousand marks in gold.

' 'Tis dinner time' quoth I; 'My gold!' quoth he.

'Your meat doth burn' quoth I; 'My gold!' quoth he.

'Will you come home?' quoth I; 'My gold!' quoth he.

'Where is the thousand marks I gave thee, villain?'

'The pig' quoth I 'is burn'd'; 'My gold!' quoth he.

'My mistress, sir,' quoth I; 'Hang up thy mistress;

I know not thy mistress; out on thy mistress.'

LUCIANA. Quoth who?

DROMIO OF EPHESUS. Quoth my master.

'I know' quoth he 'no house, no wife, no mistress.'

So that my errand, due unto my tongue,

I thank him, I bare home upon my shoulders;

For, in conclusion, he did beat me there.

ADRIANA. Go back again, thou slave, and fetch him home.

DROMIO OF EPHESUS. Go back again, and be new beaten
home?

For God's sake, send some other messenger.

ADRIANA. Back, slave, or I will break thy pate across.

DROMIO OF EPHESUS. And he will bless that cross with other
    beating;
    Between you I shall have a holy head.
ADRIANA. Hence, prating peasant! Fetch thy master home.
DROMIO OF EPHESUS. Am I so round with you, as you with
    me,
    That like a football you do spurn me thus?
    You spurn me hence, and he will spurn me hither;
    If I last in this service, you must case me in leather.   *Exit*
LUCIANA. Fie, how impatience loureth in your face!
ADRIANA. His company must do his minions grace,
    Whilst I at home starve for a merry look.
    Hath homely age th' alluring beauty took
    From my poor cheek? Then he hath wasted it.
    Are my discourses dull? Barren my wit?
    If voluble and sharp discourse be marr'd,
    Unkindness blunts it more than marble hard.
    Do their gay vestments his affections bait?
    That's not my fault; he's master of my state.
    What ruins are in me that can be found
    By him not ruin'd? Then is he the ground
    Of my defeatures. My decayed fair
    A sunny look of his would soon repair.
    But, too unruly deer, he breaks the pale,
    And feeds from home; poor I am but his stale.
LUCIANA. Self-harming jealousy! fie, beat it hence.
ADRIANA. Unfeeling fools can with such wrongs dispense.
    I know his eye doth homage otherwhere;
    Or else what lets it but he would be here?
    Sister, you know he promis'd me a chain;
    Would that alone a love he would detain,
    So he would keep fair quarter with his bed!
    I see the jewel best enamelled
    Will lose his beauty; yet the gold bides still
    That others touch and, often touching, will
    Where gold; and no man that hath a name
    By falsehood and corruption doth it shame.
    Since that my beauty cannot please his eye,
    I'll weep what's left away, and weeping die.
LUCIANA. How many fond fools serve mad jealousy!   *Exeunt*

SCENE 2

The mart

Enter ANTIPHOLUS OF SYRACUSE

ANTIPHOLUS OF SYRACUSE. The gold I gave to Dromio is laid up
Safe at the Centaur, and the heedful slave
Is wand'red forth in care to seek me out.
By computation and mine host's report
I could not speak with Dromio since at first
I sent him from the mart. See, here he comes.

Enter DROMIO OF SYRACUSE

How now, sir, is your merry humour alter'd?
As you love strokes, so jest with me again.
You know no Centaur! You receiv'd no gold!
Your mistress sent to have me home to dinner!
My house was at the Phœnix! Wast thou mad,
That thus so madly thou didst answer me?
DROMIO OF SYRACUSE. What answer, sir? When spake I such
a word?
ANTIPHOLUS OF SYRACUSE. Even now, even here, not half an
hour since.
DROMIO OF SYRACUSE. I did not see you since you sent me
hence,
Home to the Centaur, with the gold you gave me.
ANTIPHOLUS OF SYRACUSE. Villain, thou didst deny the gold's
receipt,
And told'st me of a mistress and a dinner;
For which, I hope, thou felt'st I was displeas'd.
DROMIO OF SYRACUSE. I am glad to see you in this merry vein.
What means this jest? I pray you, master, tell me.
ANTIPHOLUS OF SYRACUSE. Yea, dost thou jeer and flout me
in the teeth?
Think'st thou I jest? Hold, take thou that, and that.
[*Beating him*]
DROMIO OF SYRACUSE. Hold, sir, for God's sake! Now your
jest is earnest.
Upon what bargain do you give it me?

ACT II. SCENE 2

ANTIPHOLUS OF SYRACUSE. Because that I familiarly some-
times
Do use you for my fool and chat with you,
Your sauciness will jest upon my love,
And make a common of my serious hours.
When the sun shines let foolish gnats make sport,
But creep in crannies when he hides his beams.
If you will jest with me, know my aspect,
And fashion your demeanour to my looks,
Or I will beat this method in your sconce.
DROMIO OF SYRACUSE. Sconce, call you it? So you would
leave battering, I had rather have it a head. An you use
these blows long, I must get a sconce for my head, and
insconce it too; or else I shall seek my wit in my shoulders.
But I pray, sir, why am I beaten?
ANTIPHOLUS OF SYRACUSE. Dost thou not know?
DROMIO OF SYRACUSE. Nothing, sir, but that I am beaten.
ANTIPHOLUS OF SYRACUSE. Shall I tell you why?
DROMIO OF SYRACUSE. Ay, sir, and wherefore; for they say
every why hath a wherefore.
ANTIPHOLUS OF SYRACUSE. Why, first for flouting me; and
then wherefore,
For urging it the second time to me.
DROMIO OF SYRACUSE. Was there ever any man thus beaten
out of season,
When in the why and the wherefore is neither rhyme nor
reason?
Well, sir, I thank you.
ANTIPHOLUS OF SYRACUSE. Thank me, sir! for what?
DROMIO OF SYRACUSE. Marry, sir, for this something that
you gave me for nothing.
ANTIPHOLUS OF SYRACUSE. I'll make you amends next, to
give you nothing for something. But say, sir, is it dinner-
time?
DROMIO OF SYRACUSE. No, sir; I think the meat wants that I
have.
ANTIPHOLUS OF SYRACUSE. In good time, sir, what's that?
DROMIO OF SYRACUSE. Basting.
ANTIPHOLUS OF SYRACUSE. Well, sir, then 'twill be dry.
DROMIO OF SYRACUSE. If it be, sir, I pray you eat none of it.

ANTIPHOLUS OF SYRACUSE. Your reason?

DROMIO OF SYRACUSE. Lest it make you choleric, and purchase me another dry basting.

ANTIPHOLUS OF SYRACUSE. Well, sir, learn to jest in good time; there's a time for all things.

DROMIO OF SYRACUSE. I durst have denied that, before you were so choleric.

ANTIPHOLUS OF SYRACUSE. By what rule, sir?

DROMIO OF SYRACUSE. Marry, sir, by a rule as plain as the plain bald pate of Father Time himself.

ANTIPHOLUS OF SYRACUSE. Let's hear it.

DROMIO OF SYRACUSE. There's no time for a man to recover his hair that grows bald by nature.

ANTIPHOLUS OF SYRACUSE. May he not do it by fine and recovery?

DROMIO OF SYRACUSE. Yes, to pay a fine for a periwig, and recover the lost hair of another man.

ANTIPHOLUS OF SYRACUSE. Why is Time such a niggard of hair, being, as it is, so plentiful an excrement?

DROMIO OF SYRACUSE. Because it is a blessing that he bestows on beasts, and what he hath scanted men in hair he hath given them in wit.

ANTIPHOLUS OF SYRACUSE. Why, but there's many a man hath more hair than wit.

DROMIO OF SYRACUSE. Not a man of those but he hath the wit to lose his hair.

ANTIPHOLUS OF SYRACUSE. Why, thou didst conclude hairy men plain dealers without wit.

DROMIO OF SYRACUSE. The plainer dealer, the sooner lost; yet he loseth it in a kind of jollity.

ANTIPHOLUS OF SYRACUSE. For what reason?

DROMIO OF SYRACUSE. For two; and sound ones too.

ANTIPHOLUS OF SYRACUSE. Nay, not sound I pray you.

DROMIO OF SYRACUSE. Sure ones, then.

ANTIPHOLUS OF SYRACUSE. Nay, not sure, in a thing falsing.

DROMIO OF SYRACUSE. Certain ones, then.

ANTIPHOLUS OF SYRACUSE. Name them.

DROMIO OF SYRACUSE. The one, to save the money that he spends in tiring; the other, that at dinner they should not drop in his porridge.

ANTIPHOLUS OF SYRACUSE. You would all this time have
prov'd there is no time for all things.
DROMIO OF SYRACUSE. Marry, and did, sir; namely, no time
to recover hair lost by nature.
ANTIPHOLUS OF SYRACUSE. But your reason was not substantial, why there is no time to recover.
DROMIO OF SYRACUSE. Thus I mend it: Time himself is bald,
and therefore to the world's end will have bald followers.
ANTIPHOLUS OF SYRACUSE. I knew 'twould be a bald conclusion. But, soft, who wafts us yonder?

Enter ADRIANA *and* LUCIANA

ADRIANA. Ay, ay, Antipholus, look strange and frown.
Some other mistress hath thy sweet aspects;
I am not Adriana, nor thy wife.
The time was once when thou unurg'd wouldst vow
That never words were music to thine ear,
That never object pleasing in thine eye,
That never touch well welcome to thy hand,
That never meat sweet-savour'd in thy taste,
Unless I spake, or look'd, or touch'd, or carv'd to thee.
How comes it now, my husband, O, how comes it,
That thou art then estranged from thyself?
Thyself I call it, being strange to me,
That, undividable, incorporate,
Am better than thy dear self's better part.
Ah, do not tear away thyself from me;
For know, my love, as easy mayst thou fall
A drop of water in the breaking gulf,
And take unmingled thence that drop again
Without addition or diminishing,
As take from me thyself, and not me too.
How dearly would it touch thee to the quick,
Shouldst thou but hear I were licentious,
And that this body, consecrate to thee,
By ruffian lust should be contaminate!
Wouldst thou not spit at me and spurn at me,
And hurl the name of husband in my face,
And tear the stain'd skin off my harlot-brow,

And from my false hand cut the wedding-ring,
And break it with a deep-divorcing vow?
I know thou canst, and therefore see thou do it.
I am possess'd with an adulterate blot;
My blood is mingled with the crime of lust;
For if we two be one, and thou play false,
I do digest the poison of thy flesh,
Being strumpeted by thy contagion.
Keep then fair league and truce with thy true bed;
I live dis-stain'd, thou undishonoured.

ANTIPHOLUS OF SYRACUSE. Plead you to me, fair dame? I
know you not:
In Ephesus I am but two hours old,
As strange unto your town as to your talk,
Who, every word by all my wit being scann'd,
Wants wit in all one word to understand.

LUCIANA. Fie, brother, how the world is chang'd with you!
When were you wont to use my sister thus?
She sent for you by Dromio home to dinner.

ANTIPHOLUS OF SYRACUSE. By Dromio?

DROMIO OF SYRACUSE. By me?

ADRIANA. By thee; and this thou didst return from him—
That he did buffet thee, and in his blows
Denied my house for his, me for his wife.

ANTIPHOLUS OF SYRACUSE. Did you converse, sir, with this
gentlewoman?
What is the course and drift of your compact?

DROMIO OF SYRACUSE. I, sir? I never saw her till this time.

ANTIPHOLUS OF SYRACUSE. Villain, thou liest; for even her
very words
Didst thou deliver to me on the mart.

DROMIO OF SYRACUSE. I never spake with her in all my life.

ANTIPHOLUS OF SYRACUSE. How can she thus, then, call us
by our names,
Unless it be by inspiration?

ADRIANA. How ill agrees it with your gravity
To counterfeit thus grossly with your slave,
Abetting him to thwart me in my mood!
Be it my wrong you are from me exempt,
But wrong not that wrong with a more contempt.

Come, I will fasten on this sleeve of thine;
Thou art an elm, my husband, I a vine,
Whose weakness, married to thy stronger state,
Makes me with thy strength to communicate.
If aught possess thee from me, it is dross,
Usurping ivy, brier, or idle moss;
Who all, for want of pruning, with intrusion
Infect thy sap, and live on thy confusion.

ANTIPHOLUS OF SYRACUSE. To me she speaks; she moves me
for her theme.
What, was I married to her in my dream?
Or sleep I now, and think I hear all this?
What error drives our eyes and ears amiss?
Until I know this sure uncertainty,
I'll entertain the offer'd fallacy.

LUCIANA. Dromio, go bid the servants spread for dinner.

DROMIO OF SYRACUSE. O, for my beads! I cross me for a
sinner.
This is the fairy land. O spite of spites!
We talk with goblins, owls, and sprites.
If we obey them not, this will ensue:
They'll suck our breath, or pinch us black and blue.

LUCIANA. Why prat'st thou to thyself, and answer'st not?
Dromio, thou drone, thou snail, thou slug, thou sot!

DROMIO OF SYRACUSE. I am transformed, master, am not I?

ANTIPHOLUS OF SYRACUSE. I think thou art in mind, and so
am I.

DROMIO OF SYRACUSE. Nay, master, both in mind and in my
shape.

ANTIPHOLUS OF SYRACUSE. Thou hast thine own form.

DROMIO OF SYRACUSE. No, I am an ape.

LUCIANA. If thou art chang'd to aught, 'tis to an ass.

DROMIO OF SYRACUSE. 'Tis true; she rides me, and I long for
grass.
'Tis so, I am an ass; else it could never be
But I should know her as well as she knows me.

ADRIANA. Come, come, no longer will I be a fool,
To put the finger in the eye and weep,
Whilst man and master laughs my woes to scorn.
Come, sir, to dinner. Dromio, keep the gate.

Husband, I'll dine above with you to-day,
And shrive you of a thousand idle pranks.
Sirrah, if any ask you for your master,
Say he dines forth, and let no creature enter.
Come, sister. Dromio, play the porter well.
ANTIPHOLUS OF SYRACUSE. Am I in earth, in heaven, or in
hell?
Sleeping or waking, mad or well-advis'd?
Known unto these, and to myself disguis'd!
I'll say as they say, and persever so,
And in this mist at all adventures go.
DROMIO OF SYRACUSE. Master, shall I be porter at the gate?
ADRIANA. Ay; and let none enter, lest I break your pate.
LUCIANA. Come, come, Antipholus, we dine too late. *Exeunt*

ACT III. SCENE 1

Before the house of ANTIPHOLUS OF EPHESUS

Enter ANTIPHOLUS OF EPHESUS, DROMIO OF EPHESUS,
ANGELO, *and* BALTHAZAR

ANTIPHOLUS OF EPHESUS. Good Signior Angelo, you must
excuse us all;
My wife is shrewish when I keep not hours.
Say that I linger'd with you at your shop
To see the making of her carcanet,
And that to-morrow you will bring it home.
But here's a villain that would face me down
He met me on the mart, and that I beat him,
And charg'd him with a thousand marks in gold,
And that I did deny my wife and house.
Thou drunkard, thou, what didst thou mean by this?
DROMIO OF EPHESUS. Say what you will, sir, but I know
what I know.
That you beat me at the mart I have your hand to show;
If the skin were parchment, and the blows you gave were
ink,
Your own handwriting would tell you what I think.

ANTIPHOLUS OF EPHESUS. I think thou art an ass.

DROMIO OF EPHESUS. Marry, so it doth appear
  By the wrongs I suffer and the blows I bear.
  I should kick, being kick'd; and being at that pass,
  You would keep from my heels, and beware of an ass.

ANTIPHOLUS OF EPHESUS. Y'are sad, Signior Balthazar; pray
    God our cheer
  May answer my good will and your good welcome here.

BALTHAZAR. I hold your dainties cheap, sir, and your wel-
    come dear.

ANTIPHOLUS OF EPHESUS. O, Signior Balthazar, either at flesh
    or fish,
  A table full of welcome makes scarce one dainty dish.

BALTHAZAR. Good meat, sir, is common; that every churl
    affords.

ANTIPHOLUS OF EPHESUS. And welcome more common; for
    that's nothing but words.

BALTHAZAR. Small cheer and great welcome makes a merry
    feast.

ANTIPHOLUS OF EPHESUS. Ay, to a niggardly host and more
    sparing guest.
  But though my cates be mean, take them in good part;
  Better cheer may you have, but not with better heart.
  But, soft, my door is lock'd; go bid them let us in.

DROMIO OF EPHESUS. Maud, Bridget, Marian, Cicely, Gillian,
    Ginn!

DROMIO OF SYRACUSE. [*Within*] Mome, malt-horse, capon,
    coxcomb, idiot, patch!
  Either get thee from the door, or sit down at the hatch.
  Dost thou conjure for wenches, that thou call'st for such
    store,
  When one is one too many? Go get thee from the door.

DROMIO OF EPHESUS. What patch is made our porter? My
    master stays in the street.

DROMIO OF SYRACUSE. [*Within*] Let him walk from whence
    he came, lest he catch cold on's feet.

ANTIPHOLUS OF EPHESUS. Who talks within there? Ho, open
    the door!

DROMIO OF SYRACUSE. [*Within*] Right, sir; I'll tell you
    when, an you'll tell me wherefore.

ANTIPHOLUS OF EPHESUS. Wherefore? For my dinner; I have not din'd to-day.

DROMIO OF SYRACUSE. [*Within*] Nor to-day here you must not; come again when you may.

ANTIPHOLUS OF EPHESUS. What art thou that keep'st me out from the house I owe?

DROMIO OF SYRACUSE. [*Within*] The porter for this time, sir, and my name is Dromio.

DROMIO OF EPHESUS. O villain, thou hast stol'n both mine office and my name!
  The one ne'er got me credit, the other mickle blame.
  If thou hadst been Dromio to-day in my place,
  Thou wouldst have chang'd thy face for a name, or thy name for an ass.

Enter LUCE, *within*

LUCE. [*Within*] What a coil is there, Dromio? Who are those at the gate?

DROMIO OF EPHESUS. Let my master in, Luce.

LUCE. [*Within*] Faith, no, he comes too late;
  And so tell your master.

DROMIO OF EPHESUS. O Lord, I must laugh!
  Have at you with a proverb: Shall I set in my staff?

LUCE. [*Within*] Have at you with another: that's—when? can you tell?

DROMIO OF SYRACUSE. [*Within*] If thy name be called Luce
  —Luce, thou hast answer'd him well.

ANTIPHOLUS OF EPHESUS. Do you hear, you minion? You'll let us in, I hope?

LUCE. [*Within*] I thought to have ask'd you.

DROMIO OF SYRACUSE. [*Within*] And you said no.

DROMIO OF EPHESUS. So, come, help: well struck! there was blow for blow.

ANTIPHOLUS OF EPHESUS. Thou baggage, let me in.

LUCE. [*Within*] Can you tell for whose sake?

DROMIO OF EPHESUS. Master, knock the door hard.

LUCE. [*Within*] Let him knock till it ache.

ANTIPHOLUS OF EPHESUS. You'll cry for this, minion, if I beat the door down.

LUCE. [*Within*] What needs all that, and a pair of stocks in the town?

Enter ADRIANA, *within*

ADRIANA. [*Within*] Who is that at the door, that keeps all this noise?

DROMIO OF SYRACUSE. [*Within*] By my troth, your town is troubled with unruly boys.

ANTIPHOLUS OF EPHESUS. Are you there, wife? You might have come before.

ADRIANA. [*Within*] Your wife, sir knave! Go get you from the door.

DROMIO OF EPHESUS. If you went in pain, master, this 'knave' would go sore.

ANGELO. Here is neither cheer, sir, nor welcome; we would fain have either.

BALTHAZAR. In debating which was best, we shall part with neither.

DROMIO OF EPHESUS. They stand at the door, master; bid them welcome hither.

ANTIPHOLUS OF EPHESUS. There is something in the wind, that we cannot get in.

DROMIO OF EPHESUS. You would say so, master, if your garments were thin.
Your cake here is warm within; you stand here in the cold;
It would make a man mad as a buck to be so bought and sold.

ANTIPHOLUS OF EPHESUS. Go fetch me something; I'll break ope the gate.

DROMIO OF SYRACUSE. [*Within*] Break any breaking here, and I'll break your knave's pate.

DROMIO OF EPHESUS. A man may break a word with you, sir; and words are but wind;
Ay, and break it in your face, so he break it not behind.

DROMIO OF SYRACUSE. [*Within*] It seems thou want'st breaking; out upon thee, hind!

DROMIO OF EPHESUS. Here's too much 'out upon thee!' I pray thee let me in.

DROMIO OF SYRACUSE. [*Within*] Ay, when fowls have no
feathers and fish have no fin.

ANTIPHOLUS OF EPHESUS. Well, I'll break in; go borrow me
a crow.

DROMIO OF EPHESUS. A crow without feather? Master, mean
you so?
For a fish without a fin, there's a fowl without a feather;
If a crow help us in, sirrah, we'll pluck a crow together.

ANTIPHOLUS OF EPHESUS. Go get thee gone; fetch me an
iron crow.

BALTHAZAR. Have patience, sir; O, let it not be so!
Herein you war against your reputation,
And draw within the compass of suspect
Th' unviolated honour of your wife.
Once this—your long experience of her wisdom,
Her sober virtue, years, and modesty,
Plead on her part some cause to you unknown;
And doubt not, sir, but she will well excuse
Why at this time the doors are made against you.
Be rul'd by me: depart in patience,
And let us to the Tiger all to dinner;
And, about evening, come yourself alone
To know the reason of this strange restraint.
If by strong hand you offer to break in
Now in the stirring passage of the day,
A vulgar comment will be made of it,
And that supposed by the common rout
Against your yet ungalled estimation
That may with foul intrusion enter in
And dwell upon your grave when you are dead;
For slander lives upon succession,
For ever hous'd where it gets possession.

ANTIPHOLUS OF EPHESUS. You have prevail'd. I will depart in
quiet,
And in despite of mirth mean to be merry.
I know a wench of excellent discourse,
Pretty and witty; wild, and yet, too, gentle;
There will we dine. This woman that I mean,
My wife—but, I protest, without desert—
Hath oftentimes upbraided me withal;

334

To her will we to dinner. [*To* ANGELO] Get you home
And fetch the chain; by this I know 'tis made.
Bring it, I pray you, to the Porpentine;
For there's the house. That chain will I bestow—
Be it for nothing but to spite my wife—
Upon mine hostess there; good sir, make haste.
Since mine own doors refuse to entertain me,
I'll knock elsewhere, to see if they'll disdain me.
ANGELO. I'll meet you at that place some hour hence.
ANTIPHOLUS OF EPHESUS. Do so; this jest shall cost me some
    expense.   *Exeunt*

SCENE 2

Before the house of ANTIPHOLUS OF EPHESUS

Enter LUCIANA *with* ANTIPHOLUS OF SYRACUSE

LUCIANA. And may it be that you have quite forgot
A husband's office? Shall, Antipholus,
Even in the spring of love, thy love-springs rot?
Shall love, in building, grow so ruinous?
If you did wed my sister for her wealth,
Then for her wealth's sake use her with more kindness;
Or, if you like elsewhere, do it by stealth;
Muffle your false love with some show of blindness;
Let not my sister read it in your eye;
Be not thy tongue thy own shame's orator;
Look sweet, speak fair, become disloyalty;
Apparel vice like virtue's harbinger;
Bear a fair presence, though your heart be tainted;
Teach sin the carriage of a holy saint;
Be secret-false. What need she be acquainted?
What simple thief brags of his own attaint?
'Tis double wrong to truant with your bed
And let her read it in thy looks at board;
Shame hath a bastard fame, well managed;
Ill deeds is doubled with an evil word.
Alas, poor women! make us but believe,
Being compact of credit, that you love us;
Though others have the arm, show us the sleeve;

335

We in your motion turn, and you may move us.
Then, gentle brother, get you in again;
Comfort my sister, cheer her, call her wife.
'Tis holy sport to be a little vain
When the sweet breath of flattery conquers strife.
ANTIPHOLUS OF SYRACUSE. Sweet mistress—what your name
is else, I know not,
Nor by what wonder you do hit of mine—
Less in your knowledge and your grace you show not
Than our earth's wonder—more than earth, divine.
Teach me, dear creature, how to think and speak;
Lay open to my earthy-gross conceit,
Smoth'red in errors, feeble, shallow, weak,
The folded meaning of your words' deceit.
Against my soul's pure truth why labour you
To make it wander in an unknown field?
Are you a god? Would you create me new?
Transform me, then, and to your pow'r I'll yield.
But if that I am I, then well I know
Your weeping sister is no wife of mine,
Nor to her bed no homage do I owe;
Far more, far more, to you do I decline.
O, train me not, sweet mermaid, with thy note,
To drown me in thy sister's flood of tears.
Sing, siren, for thyself, and I will dote;
Spread o'er the silver waves thy golden hairs,
And as a bed I'll take them, and there lie;
And in that glorious supposition think
He gains by death that hath such means to die.
Let Love, being light, be drowned if she sink.
LUCIANA. What, are you mad, that you do reason so?
ANTIPHOLUS OF SYRACUSE. Not mad, but mated; how, I do
not know.
LUCIANA. It is a fault that springeth from your eye.
ANTIPHOLUS OF SYRACUSE. For gazing on your beams, fair
sun, being by.
LUCIANA. Gaze where you should, and that will clear your
sight.
ANTIPHOLUS OF SYRACUSE. As good to wink, sweet love, as
look on night.

LUCIANA. Why call you me love? Call my sister so.
ANTIPHOLUS OF SYRACUSE. Thy sister's sister.
LUCIANA. That's my sister.
ANTIPHOLUS OF SYRACUSE. No;
  It is thyself, mine own self's better part;
  Mine eye's clear eye, my dear heart's dearer heart,
  My food, my fortune, and my sweet hope's aim,
  My sole earth's heaven, and my heaven's claim.
LUCIANA. All this my sister is, or else should be.
ANTIPHOLUS OF SYRACUSE. Call thyself sister, sweet, for I
  am thee;
  Thee will I love, and with thee lead my life;
  Thou hast no husband yet, nor I no wife.
  Give me thy hand.
LUCIANA. O, soft, sir, hold you still;
  I'll fetch my sister to get her good will.   *Exit* LUCIANA

Enter DROMIO OF SYRACUSE

ANTIPHOLUS OF SYRACUSE. Why, how now, Dromio! Where
  run'st thou so fast?
DROMIO OF SYRACUSE. Do you know me, sir? Am I Dromio?
  Am I your man? Am I myself?
ANTIPHOLUS OF SYRACUSE. Thou art Dromio, thou art my
  man, thou art thyself.
DROMIO OF SYRACUSE. I am an ass, I am a woman's man, and
  besides myself.
ANTIPHOLUS OF SYRACUSE. What woman's man, and how be-
  sides thyself?
DROMIO OF SYRACUSE. Marry, sir, besides myself, I am due
  to a woman—one that claims me, one that haunts me, one
  that will have me.
ANTIPHOLUS OF SYRACUSE. What claim lays she to thee?
DROMIO OF SYRACUSE. Marry, sir, such claim as you would
  lay to your horse; and she would have me as a beast: not
  that, I being a beast, she would have me; but that she,
  being a very beastly creature, lays claim to me.
ANTIPHOLUS OF SYRACUSE. What is she?
DROMIO OF SYRACUSE. A very reverent body; ay, such a one
  as a man may not speak of without he say 'Sir-reverence.'

I have but lean luck in the match, and yet is she a wondrous fat marriage.

ANTIPHOLUS OF SYRACUSE. How dost thou mean a fat marriage?

DROMIO OF SYRACUSE. Marry, sir, she's the kitchen-wench, and all grease; and I know not what use to put her to but to make a lamp of her and run from her by her own light. I warrant, her rags and the tallow in them will burn a Poland winter. If she lives till doomsday, she'll burn a week longer than the whole world.

ANTIPHOLUS OF SYRACUSE. What complexion is she of?

DROMIO OF SYRACUSE. Swart, like my shoe; but her face nothing like so clean kept; for why, she sweats, a man may go over shoes in the grime of it.

ANTIPHOLUS OF SYRACUSE. That's a fault that water will mend.

DROMIO OF SYRACUSE. No, sir, 'tis in grain; Noah's flood could not do it.

ANTIPHOLUS OF SYRACUSE. What's her name?

DROMIO OF SYRACUSE. Nell, sir; but her name and three quarters, that's an ell and three quarters, will not measure her from hip to hip.

ANTIPHOLUS OF SYRACUSE. Then she bears some breadth?

DROMIO OF SYRACUSE. No longer from head to foot than from hip to hip: she is spherical, like a globe; I could find out countries in her.

ANTIPHOLUS OF SYRACUSE. In what part of her body stands Ireland?

DROMIO OF SYRACUSE. Marry, sir, in her buttocks; I found it out by the bogs.

ANTIPHOLUS OF SYRACUSE. Where Scotland?

DROMIO OF SYRACUSE. I found it by the barrenness, hard in the palm of the hand.

ANTIPHOLUS OF SYRACUSE. Where France?

DROMIO OF SYRACUSE. In her forehead, arm'd and reverted, making war against her heir.

ANTIPHOLUS OF SYRACUSE. Where England?

DROMIO OF SYRACUSE. I look'd for the chalky cliffs, but I could find no whiteness in them; but I guess it stood in her chin, by the salt rheum that ran between France and it.

ACT III. SCENE 2

ANTIPHOLUS OF SYRACUSE. Where Spain?

DROMIO OF SYRACUSE. Faith, I saw it not, but I felt it hot in her breath.

ANTIPHOLUS OF SYRACUSE. Where America, the Indies?

DROMIO OF SYRACUSE. O, sir, upon her nose, all o'er embellished with rubies, carbuncles, sapphires, declining their rich aspect to the hot breath of Spain; who sent whole armadoes of caracks to be ballast at her nose.

ANTIPHOLUS OF SYRACUSE. Where stood Belgia, the Netherlands?

DROMIO OF SYRACUSE. O, sir, I did not look so low. To conclude: this drudge or diviner laid claim to me; call'd me Dromio; swore I was assur'd to her; told me what privy marks I had about me, as, the mark of my shoulder, the mole in my neck, the great wart on my left arm, that I, amaz'd, ran from her as a witch.
And, I think, if my breast had not been made of faith, and my heart of steel,
She had transform'd me to a curtal dog, and made me turn i' th' wheel.

ANTIPHOLUS OF SYRACUSE. Go hie thee presently post to the road;
An if the wind blow any way from shore,
I will not harbour in this town to-night.
If any bark put forth, come to the mart,
Where I will walk till thou return to me.
If every one knows us, and we know none,
'Tis time, I think, to trudge, pack and be gone.

DROMIO OF SYRACUSE. As from a bear a man would run for life,
So fly I from her that would be my wife.   *Exit*

ANTIPHOLUS OF SYRACUSE. There's none but witches do inhabit here,
And therefore 'tis high time that I were hence.
She that doth call me husband, even my soul
Doth for a wife abhor. But her fair sister,
Possess'd with such a gentle sovereign grace,
Of such enchanting presence and discourse,
Hath almost made me traitor to myself;
But, lest myself be guilty to self-wrong,

339

I'll stop mine ears against the mermaid's song.

Enter ANGELO *with the chain*

ANGELO. Master Antipholus!

ANTIPHOLUS OF SYRACUSE. Ay, that's my name.

ANGELO. I know it well, sir. Lo, here is the chain.
I thought to have ta'en you at the Porpentine;
The chain unfinish'd made me stay thus long.

ANTIPHOLUS OF SYRACUSE. What is your will that I shall do
with this?

ANGELO. What please yourself, sir; I have made it for you.

ANTIPHOLUS OF SYRACUSE. Made it for me, sir! I bespoke it
not.

ANGELO. Not once nor twice, but twenty times you have.
Go home with it, and please your wife withal;
And soon at supper-time I'll visit you,
And then receive my money for the chain.

ANTIPHOLUS OF SYRACUSE. I pray you, sir, receive the money
now,
For fear you ne'er see chain nor money more.

ANGELO. You are a merry man, sir; fare you well.   *Exit*

ANTIPHOLUS OF SYRACUSE. What I should think of this I
cannot tell:
But this I think, there's no man is so vain
That would refuse so fair an offer'd chain.
I see a man here needs not live by shifts,
When in the streets he meets such golden gifts.
I'll to the mart, and there for Dromio stay;
If any ship put out, then straight away.   *Exit*

ACT IV. SCENE 1

A public place

Enter SECOND MERCHANT, ANGELO, *and an* OFFICER

SECOND MERCHANT. You know since Pentecost the sum is
due,
And since I have not much importun'd you;

Nor now I had not, but that I am bound
To Persia, and want guilders for my voyage.
Therefore make present satisfaction,
Or I'll attach you by this officer.

ANGELO. Even just the sum that I do owe to you
Is growing to me by Antipholus;
And in the instant that I met with you
He had of me a chain; at five o'clock
I shall receive the money for the same.
Pleaseth you walk with me down to his house,
I will discharge my bond, and thank you too.

Enter ANTIPHOLUS OF EPHESUS, *and* DROMIO OF EPHESUS,
from the COURTEZAN'S

OFFICER. That labour may you save; see where he comes.

ANTIPHOLUS OF EPHESUS. While I go to the goldsmith's
house, go thou
And buy a rope's end; that will I bestow
Among my wife and her confederates,
For locking me out of my doors by day.
But, soft, I see the goldsmith. Get thee gone;
Buy thou a rope, and bring it home to me.

DROMIO OF EPHESUS. I buy a thousand pound a year; I buy
a rope.   *Exit* DROMIO

ANTIPHOLUS OF EPHESUS. A man is well holp up that trusts
to you!
I promised your presence and the chain;
But neither chain nor goldsmith came to me.
Belike you thought our love would last too long,
If it were chain'd together, and therefore came not.

ANGELO. Saving your merry humour, here's the note
How much your chain weighs to the utmost carat,
The fineness of the gold, and chargeful fashion,
Which doth amount to three odd ducats more
Than I stand debted to this gentleman.
I pray you see him presently discharg'd,
For he is bound to sea, and stays but for it.

ANTIPHOLUS OF EPHESUS. I am not furnish'd with the present
money;
Besides, I have some business in the town.

Good signior, take the stranger to my house,
And with you take the chain, and bid my wife
Disburse the sum on the receipt thereof.
Perchance I will be there as soon as you.
ANGELO. Then you will bring the chain to her yourself?
ANTIPHOLUS OF EPHESUS. No; bear it with you, lest I come
not time enough.
ANGELO. Well, sir, I will. Have you the chain about you?
ANTIPHOLUS OF EPHESUS. An if I have not, sir, I hope you
have;
Or else you may return without your money.
ANGELO. Nay, come, I pray you, sir, give me the chain;
Both wind and tide stays for this gentleman,
And I, to blame, have held him here too long.
ANTIPHOLUS OF EPHESUS. Good Lord! you use this dalliance
to excuse
Your breach of promise to the Porpentine;
I should have chid you for not bringing it,
But, like a shrew, you first begin to brawl.
SECOND MERCHANT. The hour steals on; I pray you, sir, dis-
patch.
ANGELO. You hear how he importunes me—the chain!
ANTIPHOLUS OF EPHESUS. Why, give it to my wife, and
fetch your money.
ANGELO. Come, come, you know I gave it you even now.
Either send the chain or send by me some token.
ANTIPHOLUS OF EPHESUS. Fie, now you run this humour out
of breath!
Come, where's the chain? I pray you let me see it.
SECOND MERCHANT. My business cannot brook this dalliance.
Good sir, say whe'r you'll answer me or no;
If not, I'll leave him to the officer.
ANTIPHOLUS OF EPHESUS. I answer you! What should I an-
swer you?
ANGELO. The money that you owe me for the chain.
ANTIPHOLUS OF EPHESUS. I owe you none till I receive the
chain.
ANGELO. You know I gave it you half an hour since.
ANTIPHOLUS OF EPHESUS. You gave me none; you wrong me
much to say so.

ANGELO. You wrong me more, sir, in denying it.
Consider how it stands upon my credit.
SECOND MERCHANT. Well, officer, arrest him at my suit.
OFFICER. I do; and charge you in the Duke's name to obey
me.
ANGELO. This touches me in reputation.
Either consent to pay this sum for me,
Or I attach you by this officer.
ANTIPHOLUS OF EPHESUS. Consent to pay thee that I never
had!
Arrest me, foolish fellow, if thou dar'st.
ANGELO. Here is thy fee; arrest him, officer.
I would not spare my brother in this case,
If he should scorn me so apparently.
OFFICER. I do arrest you, sir; you hear the suit.
ANTIPHOLUS OF EPHESUS. I do obey thee till I give thee bail.
But, sirrah, you shall buy this sport as dear
As all the metal in your shop will answer.
ANGELO. Sir, sir, I shall have law in Ephesus,
To your notorious shame, I doubt it not.

Enter DROMIO OF SYRACUSE, *from the bay*

DROMIO OF SYRACUSE. Master, there's a bark of Epidamnum
That stays but till her owner comes aboard,
And then, sir, she bears away. Our fraughtage, sir,
I have convey'd aboard; and I have bought
The oil, the balsamum, and aqua-vitæ.
The ship is in her trim; the merry wind
Blows fair from land; they stay for nought at all
But for their owner, master, and yourself.
ANTIPHOLUS OF EPHESUS. How now! a madman? Why, thou
peevish sheep,
What ship of Epidamnum stays for me?
DROMIO OF SYRACUSE. A ship you sent me to, to hire
waftage.
ANTIPHOLUS OF EPHESUS. Thou drunken slave! I sent thee
for a rope;
And told thee to what purpose and what end.
DROMIO OF SYRACUSE. You sent me for a rope's end as soon—

You sent me to the bay, sir, for a bark.

ANTIPHOLUS OF EPHESUS. I will debate this matter at more
  leisure,
And teach your ears to list me with more heed.
To Adriana, villain, hie thee straight;
Give her this key, and tell her in the desk
That's cover'd o'er with Turkish tapestry
There is a purse of ducats; let her send it.
Tell her I am arrested in the street,
And that shall bail me; hie thee, slave, be gone.
On, officer, to prison till it come.   *Exeunt all but* DROMIO

DROMIO OF SYRACUSE. To Adriana! that is where we din'd,
Where Dowsabel did claim me for her husband.
She is too big, I hope, for me to compass.
Thither I must, although against my will,
For servants must their masters' minds fulfil.   *Exit*

SCENE 2

The house of ANTIPHOLUS OF EPHESUS

Enter ADRIANA *and* LUCIANA

ADRIANA. Ah, Luciana, did he tempt thee so?
Mightst thou perceive austerely in his eye
That he did plead in earnest? Yea or no?
Look'd he or red or pale, or sad or merrily?
What observation mad'st thou in this case
Of his heart's meteors tilting in his face?
LUCIANA. First he denied you had in him no right.
ADRIANA. He meant he did me none—the more my spite.
LUCIANA. Then swore he that he was a stranger here.
ADRIANA. And true he swore, though yet forsworn he were.
LUCIANA. Then pleaded I for you.
ADRIANA. And what said he?
LUCIANA. That love I begg'd for you he begg'd of me.
ADRIANA. With what persuasion did he tempt thy love?
LUCIANA. With words that in an honest suit might move.
First he did praise my beauty, then my speech.

LUCIANA. *And may it be that you have quite forgot*
A husband's office? (ACT III. SCENE II)

ADRIANA. Didst speak him fair?

LUCIANA. Have patience, I beseech.

ADRIANA. I cannot, nor I will not hold me still;
My tongue, though not my heart, shall have his will.
He is deformed, crooked, old, and sere,
Ill-fac'd, worse bodied, shapeless everywhere;
Vicious, ungentle, foolish, blunt, unkind;
Stigmatical in making, worse in mind.

LUCIANA. Who would be jealous then of such a one?
No evil lost is wail'd when it is gone.

ADRIANA. Ah, but I think him better than I say,
And yet would herein others' eyes were worse.
Far from her nest the lapwing cries away;
My heart prays for him, though my tongue do curse.

Enter DROMIO OF SYRACUSE

DROMIO OF SYRACUSE. Here go—the desk, the purse. Sweet now, make haste.

LUCIANA. How hast thou lost thy breath?

DROMIO OF SYRACUSE. By running fast.

ADRIANA. Where is thy master, Dromio? Is he well?

DROMIO OF SYRACUSE. No, he's in Tartar limbo, worse than hell.
A devil in an everlasting garment hath him;
One whose hard heart is button'd up with steel;
A fiend, a fairy, pitiless and rough;
A wolf, nay worse, a fellow all in buff;
A back-friend, a shoulder-clapper, one that countermands
The passages of alleys, creeks, and narrow lands;
A hound that runs counter, and yet draws dry-foot well;
One that, before the Judgment, carries poor souls to hell.

ADRIANA. Why, man, what is the matter?

DROMIO OF SYRACUSE. I do not know the matter; he is 'rested on the case.

ADRIANA. What, is he arrested? Tell me, at whose suit?

DROMIO OF SYRACUSE. I know not at whose suit he is arrested well;
But he's in a suit of buff which 'rested him, that can I tell.
Will you send him, mistress, redemption, the money in his desk?

ACT IV. SCENE 2

ADRIANA. Go fetch it, sister. [*Exit* LUCIANA] This I wonder
at:
Thus he unknown to me should be in debt.
Tell me, was he arrested on a band?
DROMIO OF SYRACUSE. Not on a band, but on a stronger
thing,
A chain, a chain. Do you not hear it ring?
ADRIANA. What, the chain?
DROMIO OF SYRACUSE. No, no, the bell; 'tis time that I were
gone.
It was two ere I left him, and now the clock strikes one.
ADRIANA. The hours come back! That did I never hear.
DROMIO OF SYRACUSE. O yes. If any hour meet a sergeant,
'a turns back for very fear.
ADRIANA. As if Time were in debt! How fondly dost thou
reason!
DROMIO OF SYRACUSE. Time is a very bankrupt, and owes
more than he's worth to season.
Nay, he's a thief too: have you not heard men say
That Time comes stealing on by night and day?
If 'a be in debt and theft, and a sergeant in the way,
Hath he not reason to turn back an hour in a day?

Re-enter LUCIANA *with a purse*

ADRIANA. Go, Dromio, there's the money; bear it straight,
And bring thy master home immediately.
Come, sister; I am press'd down with conceit—
Conceit, my comfort and my injury.   *Exeunt*

SCENE 3

The mart

Enter ANTIPHOLUS OF SYRACUSE

ANTIPHOLUS OF SYRACUSE. There's not a man I meet but
doth salute me
As if I were their well-acquainted friend;
And every one doth call me by my name.
Some tender money to me, some invite me,

Some other give me thanks for kindnesses,
Some offer me commodities to buy;
Even now a tailor call'd me in his shop,
And show'd me silks that he had bought for me,
And therewithal took measure of my body.
Sure, these are but imaginary wiles,
And Lapland sorcerers inhabit here.

Enter DROMIO OF SYRACUSE

DROMIO OF SYRACUSE. Master, here's the gold you sent me for. What, have you got the picture of old Adam new-apparell'd?

ANTIPHOLUS OF SYRACUSE. What gold is this? What Adam dost thou mean?

DROMIO OF SYRACUSE. Not that Adam that kept the Paradise, but that Adam that keeps the prison; he that goes in the calf's skin that was kill'd for the Prodigal; he that came behind you, sir, like an evil angel, and bid you forsake your liberty.

ANTIPHOLUS OF SYRACUSE. I understand thee not.

DROMIO OF SYRACUSE. No? Why, 'tis a plain case: he that went, like a bass-viol, in a case of leather; the man, sir, that, when gentlemen are tired, gives them a sob, and rests them; he, sir, that takes pity on decayed men, and gives them suits of durance; he that sets up his rest to do more exploits with his mace than a morris-pike.

ANTIPHOLUS OF SYRACUSE. What, thou mean'st an officer?

DROMIO OF SYRACUSE. Ay, sir, the sergeant of the band; he that brings any man to answer it that breaks his band; one that thinks a man always going to bed, and says 'God give you good rest!'

ANTIPHOLUS OF SYRACUSE. Well, sir, there rest in your foolery. Is there any ship puts forth to-night? May we be gone?

DROMIO OF SYRACUSE. Why, sir, I brought you word an hour since that the bark Expedition put forth to-night; and then were you hind'red by the sergeant, to tarry for the hoy Delay. Here are the angels that you sent for to deliver you.

ANTIPHOLUS OF SYRACUSE. The fellow is distract, and so
am I;
And here we wander in illusions.
Some blessed power deliver us from hence!

Enter a COURTEZAN

COURTEZAN. Well met, well met, Master Antipholus.
I see, sir, you have found the goldsmith now.
Is that the chain you promis'd me to-day?
ANTIPHOLUS OF SYRACUSE. Satan, avoid! I charge thee, tempt
me not.
DROMIO OF SYRACUSE. Master, is this Mistress Satan?
ANTIPHOLUS OF SYRACUSE. It is the devil.
DROMIO OF SYRACUSE. Nay, she is worse, she is the devil's
dam, and here she comes in the habit of a light wench; and
thereof comes that the wenches say 'God damn me!' That's
as much to say 'God make me a light wench!' It is written
they appear to men like angels of light; light is an effect
of fire, and fire will burn; ergo, light wenches will burn.
Come not near her.
COURTEZAN. Your man and you are marvellous merry, sir.
Will you go with me? We'll mend our dinner here.
DROMIO OF SYRACUSE. Master, if you do, expect spoon-meat,
or bespeak a long spoon.
ANTIPHOLUS OF SYRACUSE. Why, Dromio?
DROMIO OF SYRACUSE. Marry, he must have a long spoon
that must eat with the devil.
ANTIPHOLUS OF SYRACUSE. Avoid then, fiend! What tell'st
thou me of supping?
Thou art, as you are all, a sorceress;
I conjure thee to leave me and be gone.
COURTEZAN. Give me the ring of mine you had at dinner,
Or, for my diamond, the chain you promis'd,
And I'll be gone, sir, and not trouble you.
DROMIO OF SYRACUSE. Some devils ask but the parings of
one's nail,
A rush, a hair, a drop of blood, a pin,
A nut, a cherry-stone;
But she, more covetous, would have a chain.
Master, be wise; an if you give it her,

The devil will shake her chain, and fright us with it.
COURTEZAN. I pray you, sir, my ring, or else the chain;
I hope you do not mean to cheat me so.
ANTIPHOLUS OF SYRACUSE. Avaunt, thou witch! Come, Dromio, let us go.
DROMIO OF SYRACUSE. 'Fly pride' says the peacock. Mistress, that you know.

Exeunt ANTIPHOLUS OF SYRACUSE *and* DROMIO OF SYRACUSE

COURTEZAN. Now, out of doubt, Antipholus is mad,
Else would he never so demean himself.
A ring he hath of mine worth forty ducats,
And for the same he promis'd me a chain;
Both one and other he denies me now.
The reason that I gather he is mad,
Besides this present instance of his rage,
Is a mad tale he told to-day at dinner
Of his own doors being shut against his entrance.
Belike his wife, acquainted with his fits,
On purpose shut the doors against his way.
My way is now to hie home to his house,
And tell his wife that, being lunatic,
He rush'd into my house and took perforce
My ring away. This course I fittest choose,
For forty ducats is too much to lose. *Exit*

SCENE 4

A street

Enter ANTIPHOLUS OF EPHESUS *with the* OFFICER

ANTIPHOLUS OF EPHESUS. Fear me not, man; I will not break away.
I'll give thee, ere I leave thee, so much money,
To warrant thee, as I am 'rested for.
My wife is in a wayward mood to-day,
And will not lightly trust the messenger.
That I should be attach'd in Ephesus,
I tell you 'twill sound harshly in her ears.

Enter DROMIO OF EPHESUS, *with a rope's-end*

Here comes my man; I think he brings the money.
How now, sir! Have you that I sent you for?
DROMIO OF EPHESUS. Here's that, I warrant you, will pay
them all.
ANTIPHOLUS OF EPHESUS. But where's the money?
DROMIO OF EPHESUS. Why, sir, I gave the money for the
rope.
ANTIPHOLUS OF EPHESUS. Five hundred ducats, villain, for a
rope?
DROMIO OF EPHESUS. I'll serve you, sir, five hundred at the
rate.
ANTIPHOLUS OF EPHESUS. To what end did I bid thee hie
thee home?
DROMIO OF EPHESUS. To a rope's-end, sir; and to that end
am I return'd.
ANTIPHOLUS OF EPHESUS. And to that end, sir, I will wel-
come you. *[Beating him]*
OFFICER. Good sir, be patient.
DROMIO OF EPHESUS. Nay, 'tis for me to be patient; I am in
adversity.
OFFICER. Good now, hold thy tongue.
DROMIO OF EPHESUS. Nay, rather persuade him to hold his
hands.
ANTIPHOLUS OF EPHESUS. Thou whoreson, senseless villain!
DROMIO OF EPHESUS. I would I were senseless, sir, that I
might not feel your blows.
ANTIPHOLUS OF EPHESUS. Thou art sensible in nothing but
blows, and so is an ass.
DROMIO OF EPHESUS. I am an ass indeed; you may prove it
by my long 'ears. I have served him from the hour of my
nativity to this instant, and have nothing at his hands for
my service but blows. When I am cold he heats me with
beating; when I am warm he cools me with beating. I am
wak'd with it when I sleep; rais'd with it when I sit; driven
out of doors with it when I go from home; welcom'd home
with it when I return; nay, I bear it on my shoulders as a
beggar wont her brat; and I think, when he hath lam'd me,
I shall beg with it from door to door.

Enter ADRIANA, LUCIANA, *the* COURTEZAN, *and a*
SCHOOLMASTER *call'd* PINCH

ANTIPHOLUS OF EPHESUS. Come, go along; my wife is coming yonder.

DROMIO OF EPHESUS. Mistress, 'respice finem,' respect your
end; or rather, to prophesy like the parrot, 'Beware the
rope's-end.'

ANTIPHOLUS OF EPHESUS. Wilt thou still talk? [*Beating him*]

COURTEZAN. How say you now? Is not your husband mad?

ADRIANA. His incivility confirms no less.
Good Doctor Pinch, you are a conjurer:
Establish him in his true sense again,
And I will please you what you will demand.

LUCIANA. Alas, how fiery and how sharp he looks!

COURTEZAN. Mark how he trembles in his ecstasy.

PINCH. Give me your hand, and let me feel your pulse.

ANTIPHOLUS OF EPHESUS. There is my hand, and let it feel
your ear.   [*Striking him*]

PINCH. I charge thee, Satan, hous'd within this man,
To yield possession to my holy prayers,
And to thy state of darkness hie thee straight.
I conjure thee by all the saints in heaven.

ANTIPHOLUS OF EPHESUS. Peace, doting wizard, peace! I am
not mad.

ADRIANA. O, that thou wert not, poor distressed soul!

ANTIPHOLUS OF EPHESUS. You minion, you, are these your
customers?
Did this companion with the saffron face
Revel and feast it at my house to-day,
Whilst upon me the guilty doors were shut,
And I denied to enter in my house?

ADRIANA. O husband, God doth know you din'd at home,
Where would you had remain'd until this time,
Free from these slanders and this open shame!

ANTIPHOLUS OF EPHESUS. Din'd at home! Thou villain, what
sayest thou?

DROMIO OF EPHESUS. Sir, sooth to say, you did not dine at
home.

ANTIPHOLUS OF EPHESUS. Were not my doors lock'd up and
I shut out?

DROMIO OF EPHESUS. Perdie, your doors were lock'd and
you shut out.

ANTIPHOLUS OF EPHESUS. And did not she herself revile me
there?

DROMIO OF EPHESUS. Sans fable, she herself revil'd you there.

ANTIPHOLUS OF EPHESUS. Did not her kitchen-maid rail,
taunt, and scorn me?

DROMIO OF EPHESUS. Certes, she did; the kitchen-vestal
scorn'd you.

ANTIPHOLUS OF EPHESUS. And did not I in rage depart from
thence?

DROMIO OF EPHESUS. In verity, you did. My bones bear witness,
That since have felt the vigour of his rage.

ADRIANA. Is't good to soothe him in these contraries?

PINCH. It is no shame; the fellow finds his vein,
And, yielding to him, humours well his frenzy.

ANTIPHOLUS OF EPHESUS. Thou hast suborn'd the goldsmith
to arrest me.

ADRIANA. Alas, I sent you money to redeem you,
By Dromio here, who came in haste for it.

DROMIO OF EPHESUS. Money by me! Heart and goodwill
you might,
But surely, master, not a rag of money.

ANTIPHOLUS OF EPHESUS. Went'st not thou to her for a
purse of ducats?

ADRIANA. He came to me, and I deliver'd it.

LUCIANA. And I am witness with her that she did.

DROMIO OF EPHESUS. God and the rope-maker bear me witness
That I was sent for nothing but a rope!

PINCH. Mistress, both man and master is possess'd;
I know it by their pale and deadly looks.
They must be bound, and laid in some dark room.

ANTIPHOLUS OF EPHESUS. Say, wherefore didst thou lock me
forth to-day?
And why dost thou deny the bag of gold?

ADRIANA. I did not, gentle husband, lock thee forth.

DROMIO OF EPHESUS. And, gentle master, I receiv'd no gold;
But I confess, sir, that we were lock'd out.

ADRIANA. Dissembling villain, thou speak'st false in both.

ANTIPHOLUS OF EPHESUS. Dissembling harlot, thou art false
in all,
And art confederate with a damned pack
To make a loathsome abject scorn of me;
But with these nails I'll pluck out these false eyes
That would behold in me this shameful sport.

ADRIANA. O, bind him, bind him; let him not come near me.

PINCH. More company! The fiend is strong within him.

Enter three or four, and offer to bind him. He strives

LUCIANA. Ay me, poor man, how pale and wan he looks!

ANTIPHOLUS OF EPHESUS. What, will you murder me? Thou
gaoler, thou,
I am thy prisoner. Wilt thou suffer them
To make a rescue?

OFFICER. Masters, let him go;
He is my prisoner, and you shall not have him.

PINCH. Go bind this man, for he is frantic too.

[*They bind* DROMIO]

ADRIANA. What wilt thou do, thou peevish officer?
Hast thou delight to see a wretched man
Do outrage and displeasure to himself?

OFFICER. He is my prisoner; if I let him go,
The debt he owes will be requir'd of me.

ADRIANA. I will discharge thee ere I go from thee;
Bear me forthwith unto his creditor,
And, knowing how the debt grows, I will pay it.
Good Master Doctor, see him safe convey'd
Home to my house. O most unhappy day!

ANTIPHOLUS OF EPHESUS. O most unhappy strumpet!

DROMIO OF EPHESUS. Master, I am here ent'red in bond for
you.

ANTIPHOLUS OF EPHESUS. Out on thee, villain! Wherefore
dost thou mad me?

DROMIO OF EPHESUS. Will you be bound for nothing?
Be mad, good master; cry 'The devil!'

LUCIANA. God help, poor souls, how idly do they talk!

ADRIANA. Go bear him hence. Sister, go you with me.
Exeunt all but ADRIANA, LUCIANA, OFFICERS, *and* COURTEZAN
  Say now, whose suit is he arrested at?
OFFICER. One Angelo, a goldsmith; do you know him?
ADRIANA. I know the man. What is the sum he owes?
OFFICER. Two hundred ducats.
ADRIANA. Say, how grows it due?
OFFICER. Due for a chain your husband had of him.
ADRIANA. He did bespeak a chain for me, but had it not.
COURTEZAN. When as your husband, all in rage, to-day
  Came to my house, and took away my ring—
  The ring I saw upon his finger now—
  Straight after did I meet him with a chain.
ADRIANA. It may be so, but I did never see it.
  Come, gaoler, bring me where the goldsmith is;
  I long to know the truth hereof at large.

Enter ANTIPHOLUS OF SYRACUSE, *with his rapier drawn,*
and DROMIO OF SYRACUSE

LUCIANA. God, for thy mercy! they are loose again.
ADRIANA. And come with naked swords.
  Let's call more help to have them bound again.
OFFICER. Away, they'll kill us!
                Exeunt all but ANTIPHOLUS OF SYRACUSE *and*
      DROMIO OF SYRACUSE *as fast as may be, frighted*
ANTIPHOLUS OF SYRACUSE. I see these witches are afraid of
  swords.
DROMIO OF SYRACUSE. She that would be your wife now ran
  from you.
ANTIPHOLUS OF SYRACUSE. Come to the Centaur; fetch our
  stuff from thence.
  I long that we were safe and sound aboard.
DROMIO OF SYRACUSE. Faith, stay here this night; they will
  surely do us no harm; you saw they speak us fair, give us
  gold; methinks they are such a gentle nation that, but for
  the mountain of mad flesh that claims marriage of me, I
  could find in my heart to stay here still and turn witch.
ANTIPHOLUS OF SYRACUSE. I will not stay to-night for all the
  town;
  Therefore away, to get our stuff aboard.   *Exeunt*

ACT V. SCENE 1

A street before a priory

Enter SECOND MERCHANT *and* ANGELO

ANGELO. I am sorry, sir, that I have hind'red you;
But I protest he had the chain of me,
Though most dishonestly he doth deny it.
SECOND MERCHANT. How is the man esteem'd here in the
city?
ANGELO. Of very reverend reputation, sir,
Of credit infinite, highly belov'd,
Second to none that lives here in the city;
His word might bear my wealth at any time.
SECOND MERCHANT. Speak softly; yonder, as I think, he
walks.

Enter ANTIPHOLUS OF SYRACUSE *and* DROMIO OF SYRACUSE

ANGELO. 'Tis so; and that self chain about his neck
Which he forswore most monstrously to have.
Good sir, draw near to me, I'll speak to him.
Signior Antipholus, I wonder much
That you would put me to this shame and trouble;
And, not without some scandal to yourself,
With circumstance and oaths so to deny
This chain, which now you wear so openly.
Beside the charge, the shame, imprisonment,
You have done wrong to this my honest friend;
Who, but for staying on our controversy,
Had hoisted sail and put to sea to-day.
This chain you had of me; can you deny it?
ANTIPHOLUS OF SYRACUSE. I think I had; I never did deny it.
SECOND MERCHANT. Yes, that you did, sir, and forswore it
too.
ANTIPHOLUS OF SYRACUSE. Who heard me to deny it or for-
swear it?
SECOND MERCHANT. These ears of mine, thou know'st, did
hear thee.
Fie on thee, wretch! 'tis pity that thou liv'st

To walk where any honest men resort.

ANTIPHOLUS OF SYRACUSE. Thou art a villain to impeach me
thus;
I'll prove mine honour and mine honesty
Against thee presently, if thou dar'st stand.

SECOND MERCHANT. I dare, and do defy thee for a villain.

[*They draw*]

Enter ADRIANA, LUCIANA, *the* COURTEZAN, *and* OTHERS

ADRIANA. Hold, hurt him not, for God's sake! He is mad.
Some get within him, take his sword away;
Bind Dromio too, and bear them to my house.

DROMIO OF SYRACUSE. Run, master, run; for God's sake take
a house.
This is some priory. In, or we are spoil'd.

Exeunt ANTIPHOLUS OF SYRACUSE *and* DROMIO OF
SYRACUSE *to the priory*

Enter the LADY ABBESS

ABBESS. Be quiet, people. Wherefore throng you hither?

ADRIANA. To fetch my poor distracted husband hence.
Let us come in, that we may bind him fast,
And bear him home for his recovery.

ANGELO. I knew he was not in his perfect wits.

SECOND MERCHANT. I am sorry now that I did draw on him.

ABBESS. How long hath this possession held the man?

ADRIANA. This week he hath been heavy, sour, sad,
And much different from the man he was;
But till this afternoon his passion
Ne'er brake into extremity of rage.

ABBESS. Hath he not lost much wealth by wreck of sea?
Buried some dear friend? Hath not else his eye
Stray'd his affection in unlawful love?
A sin prevailing much in youthful men
Who give their eyes the liberty of gazing.
Which of these sorrows is he subject to?

ADRIANA. To none of these, except it be the last;
Namely, some love that drew him oft from home.

ABBESS. You should for that have reprehended him.

ADRIANA. Why, so I did.

357

ABBESS. Ay, but not rough enough.
ADRIANA. As roughly as my modesty would let me.
ABBESS. Haply in private.
ADRIANA. And in assemblies too.
ABBESS. Ay, but not enough.
ADRIANA. It was the copy of our conference.
  In bed, he slept not for my urging it;
  At board, he fed not for my urging it;
  Alone, it was the subject of my theme;
  In company, I often glanced it;
  Still did I tell him it was vile and bad.
ABBESS. And thereof came it that the man was mad.
  The venom clamours of a jealous woman
  Poisons more deadly than a mad dog's tooth.
  It seems his sleeps were hind'red by thy railing,
  And thereof comes it that his head is light.
  Thou say'st his meat was sauc'd with thy upbraidings:
  Unquiet meals make ill digestions;
  Thereof the raging fire of fever bred;
  And what's a fever but a fit of madness?
  Thou say'st his sports were hind'red by thy brawls.
  Sweet recreation barr'd, what doth ensue
  But moody and dull melancholy,
  Kinsman to grim and comfortless despair,
  And at her heels a huge infectious troop
  Of pale distemperatures and foes to life?
  In food, in sport, and life-preserving rest,
  To be disturb'd would mad or man or beast.
  The consequence is, then, thy jealous fits
  Hath scar'd thy husband from the use of wits.
LUCIANA. She never reprehended him but mildly,
  When he demean'd himself rough, rude, and wildly.
  Why bear you these rebukes, and answer not?
ADRIANA. She did betray me to my own reproof.
  Good people, enter, and lay hold on him.
ABBESS. No, not a creature enters in my house.
ADRIANA. Then let your servants bring my husband forth.
ABBESS. Neither; he took this place for sanctuary,
  And it shall privilege him from your hands
  Till I have brought him to his wits again,

Or lose my labour in assaying it.

ADRIANA. I will attend my husband, be his nurse,
Diet his sickness, for it is my office,
And will have no attorney but myself;
And therefore let me have him home with me.

ABBESS. Be patient; for I will not let him stir
Till I have us'd the approved means I have,
With wholesome syrups, drugs, and holy prayers,
To make of him a formal man again.
It is a branch and parcel of mine oath,
A charitable duty of my order;
Therefore depart, and leave him here with me.

ADRIANA. I will not hence and leave my husband here;
And ill it doth beseem your holiness
To separate the husband and the wife.

ABBESS. Be quiet, and depart; thou shalt not have him. *Exit*

LUCIANA. Complain unto the Duke of this indignity.

ADRIANA. Come, go; I will fall prostrate at his feet,
And never rise until my tears and prayers
Have won his Grace to come in person hither
And take perforce my husband from the Abbess.

SECOND MERCHANT. By this, I think, the dial points at five;
Anon, I'm sure, the Duke himself in person
Comes this way to the melancholy vale,
The place of death and sorry execution,
Behind the ditches of the abbey here.

ANGELO. Upon what cause?

SECOND MERCHANT. To see a reverend Syracusian merchant,
Who put unluckily into this bay
Against the laws and statutes of this town,
Beheaded publicly for his offence.

ANGELO. See where they come; we will behold his death.

LUCIANA. Kneel to the Duke before he pass the abbey.

Enter the DUKE, *attended;* ÆGEON, *bareheaded; with the*
HEADSMAN *and other* OFFICERS

DUKE. Yet once again proclaim it publicly,
If any friend will pay the sum for him,
He shall not die; so much we tender him.

ADRIANA. Justice, most sacred Duke, against the Abbess!

DUKE. She is a virtuous and a reverend lady;
It cannot be that she hath done thee wrong.
ADRIANA. May it please your Grace, Antipholus, my hus-
band,
Who I made lord of me and all I had
At your important letters—this ill day
A most outrageous fit of madness took him,
That desp'rately he hurried through the street,
With him his bondman all as mad as he,
Doing displeasure to the citizens
By rushing in their houses, bearing thence
Rings, jewels, anything his rage did like.
Once did I get him bound and sent him home,
Whilst to take order for the wrongs I went,
That here and there his fury had committed.
Anon, I wot not by what strong escape,
He broke from those that had the guard of him,
And with his mad attendant and himself,
Each one with ireful passion, with drawn swords,
Met us again and, madly bent on us,
Chas'd us away; till, raising of more aid,
We came again to bind them. Then they fled
Into this abbey, whither we pursu'd them;
And here the Abbess shuts the gates on us,
And will not suffer us to fetch him out,
Nor send him forth that we may bear him hence.
Therefore, most gracious Duke, with thy command
Let him be brought forth and borne hence for help.
DUKE. Long since thy husband serv'd me in my wars,
And I to thee engag'd a prince's word,
When thou didst make him master of thy bed,
To do him all the grace and good I could.
Go, some of you, knock at the abbey gate,
And bid the Lady Abbess come to me,
I will determine this before I stir.

Enter a MESSENGER

MESSENGER. O mistress, mistress, shift and save yourself!
My master and his man are both broke loose,
Beaten the maids a-row and bound the doctor,

Whose beard they have sing'd off with brands of fire;
And ever, as it blaz'd, they threw on him
Great pails of puddled mire to quench the hair.
My master preaches patience to him, and the while
His man with scissors nicks him like a fool;
And sure, unless you send some present help,
Between them they will kill the conjurer.

ADRIANA. Peace, fool! thy master and his man are here,
And that is false thou dost report to us.

MESSENGER. Mistress, upon my life, I tell you true;
I have not breath'd almost since I did see it.
He cries for you, and vows, if he can take you,
To scorch your face, and to disfigure you. [*Cry within*]
Hark, hark, I hear him, mistress; fly, be gone!

DUKE. Come, stand by me; fear nothing. Guard with halberds.

ADRIANA. Ay me, it is my husband! Witness you
That he is borne about invisible.
Even now we hous'd him in the abbey here,
And now he's there, past thought of human reason.

Enter ANTIPHOLUS OF EPHESUS *and* DROMIO OF EPHESUS

ANTIPHOLUS OF EPHESUS. Justice, most gracious Duke; O,
grant me justice!
Even for the service that long since I did thee,
When I bestrid thee in the wars, and took
Deep scars to save thy life; even for the blood
That then I lost for thee, now grant me justice.

ÆGEON. Unless the fear of death doth make me dote,
I see my son Antipholus, and Dromio.

ANTIPHOLUS OF EPHESUS. Justice, sweet Prince, against that
woman there!
She whom thou gav'st to me to be my wife,
That hath abused and dishonoured me
Even in the strength and height of injury.
Beyond imagination is the wrong
That she this day hath shameless thrown on me.

DUKE. Discover how, and thou shalt find me just.

ANTIPHOLUS OF EPHESUS. This day, great Duke, she shut the
doors upon me,

While she with harlots feasted in my house.
DUKE. A grievous fault. Say, woman, didst thou so?
ADRIANA. No, my good lord. Myself, he, and my sister,
   To-day did dine together. So befall my soul
   As this is false he burdens me withal!
LUCIANA. Ne'er may I look on day nor sleep on night
   But she tells to your Highness simple truth!
ANGELO. O perjur'd woman! They are both forsworn.
   In this the madman justly chargeth them.
ANTIPHOLUS OF EPHESUS. My liege, I am advised what I say;
   Neither disturbed with the effect of wine,
   Nor heady-rash, provok'd with raging ire,
   Albeit my wrongs might make one wiser mad.
   This woman lock'd me out this day from dinner;
   That goldsmith there, were he not pack'd with her,
   Could witness it, for he was with me then;
   Who parted with me to go fetch a chain,
   Promising to bring it to the Porpentine,
   Where Balthazar and I did dine together.
   Our dinner done, and he not coming thither,
   I went to seek him. In the street I met him,
   And in his company that gentleman.
   There did this perjur'd goldsmith swear me down
   That I this day of him receiv'd the chain,
   Which, God he knows, I saw not; for the which
   He did arrest me with an officer.
   I did obey, and sent my peasant home
   For certain ducats; he with none return'd.
   Then fairly I bespoke the officer
   To go in person with me to my house.
   By th' way we met my wife, her sister, and a rabble more
   Of vile confederates. Along with them
   They brought one Pinch, a hungry lean-fac'd villain,
   A mere anatomy, a mountebank,
   A threadbare juggler, and a fortune-teller,
   A needy, hollow-ey'd, sharp-looking wretch,
   A living dead man. This pernicious slave,
   Forsooth, took on him as a conjurer,
   And gazing in mine eyes, feeling my pulse,
   And with no face, as 'twere, outfacing me,

Cries out I was possess'd. Then all together
They fell upon me, bound me, bore me thence,
And in a dark and dankish vault at home
There left me and my man, both bound together;
Till, gnawing with my teeth my bonds in sunder,
I gain'd my freedom, and immediately
Ran hither to your Grace; whom I beseech
To give me ample satisfaction
For these deep shames and great indignities.

ANGELO. My lord, in truth, thus far I witness with him,
That he din'd not at home, but was lock'd out.

DUKE. But had he such a chain of thee, or no?

ANGELO. He had, my lord, and when he ran in here,
These people saw the chain about his neck.

SECOND MERCHANT. Besides, I will be sworn these ears of mine
Heard you confess you had the chain of him,
After you first forswore it on the mart;
And thereupon I drew my sword on you,
And then you fled into this abbey here,
From whence, I think, you are come by miracle.

ANTIPHOLUS OF EPHESUS. I never came within these abbey walls,
Nor ever didst thou draw thy sword on me;
I never saw the chain, so help me Heaven!
And this is false you burden me withal.

DUKE. Why, what an intricate impeach is this!
I think you all have drunk of Circe's cup.
If here you hous'd him, here he would have been;
If he were mad, he would not plead so coldly.
You say he din'd at home: the goldsmith here
Denies that saying. Sirrah, what say you?

DROMIO OF EPHESUS. Sir, he din'd with her there, at the Porpentine.

COURTEZAN. He did; and from my finger snatch'd that ring.

ANTIPHOLUS OF EPHESUS. 'Tis true, my liege; this ring I had of her.

DUKE. Saw'st thou him enter at the abbey here?

COURTEZAN. As sure, my liege, as I do see your Grace.

DUKE. Why, this is strange. Go call the Abbess hither.

I think you are all mated or stark mad.

Exit one to the ABBESS

ÆGEON. Most mighty Duke, vouchsafe me speak a word:
Haply I see a friend will save my life
And pay the sum that may deliver me.

DUKE. Speak freely, Syracusian, what thou wilt.

ÆGEON. Is not your name, sir, call'd Antipholus?
And is not that your bondman Dromio?

DROMIO OF EPHESUS. Within this hour I was his bondman, sir,
But he, I thank him, gnaw'd in two my cords
Now am I Dromio and his man unbound.

ÆGEON. I am sure you both of you remember me.

DROMIO OF EPHESUS. Ourselves we do remember, sir, by you;
For lately we were bound as you are now.
You are not Pinch's patient, are you, sir?

ÆGEON. Why look you strange on me? You know me well.

ANTIPHOLUS OF EPHESUS. I never saw you in my life till now.

ÆGEON. O! grief hath chang'd me since you saw me last;
And careful hours with time's deformed hand
Have written strange defeatures in my face.
But tell me yet, dost thou not know my voice?

ANTIPHOLUS OF EPHESUS. Neither.

ÆGEON. Dromio, nor thou?

DROMIO OF EPHESUS. No, trust me, sir, nor I.

ÆGEON. I am sure thou dost.

DROMIO OF EPHESUS. Ay, sir, but I am sure I do not; and
whatsoever a man denies, you are now bound to believe
him.

ÆGEON. Not know my voice! O time's extremity,
Hast thou so crack'd and splitted my poor tongue
In seven short years that here my only son
Knows not my feeble key of untun'd cares?
Though now this grained face of mine be hid
In sap-consuming winter's drizzled snow,
And all the conduits of my blood froze up,
Yet hath my night of life some memory,
My wasting lamps some fading glimmer left,
My dull deaf ears a little use to hear;

All these old witnesses—I cannot err—
Tell me thou art my son Antipholus.
ANTIPHOLUS OF EPHESUS. I never saw my father in my life.
ÆGEON. But seven years since, in Syracusa, boy,
Thou know'st we parted; but perhaps, my son,
Thou sham'st to acknowledge me in misery.
ANTIPHOLUS OF EPHESUS. The Duke and all that know me in
the city
Can witness with me that it is not so:
I ne'er saw Syracusa in my life.
DUKE. I tell thee, Syracusian, twenty years
Have I been patron to Antipholus,
During which time he ne'er saw Syracusa.
I see thy age and dangers make thee dote.

Re-enter the ABBESS, *with* ANTIPHOLUS OF SYRACUSE *and*
DROMIO OF SYRACUSE

ABBESS. Most mighty Duke, behold a man much wrong'd.
[*All gather to see them*]
ADRIANA. I see two husbands, or mine eyes deceive me.
DUKE. One of these men is genius to the other;
And so of these. Which is the natural man,
And which the spirit? Who deciphers them?
DROMIO OF SYRACUSE. I, sir, am Dromio; command him
away.
DROMIO OF EPHESUS. I, sir, am Dromio; pray let me stay.
ANTIPHOLUS OF SYRACUSE. Ægeon, art thou not? or else his
ghost?
DROMIO OF SYRACUSE. O, my old master! who hath bound
him here?
ABBESS. Whoever bound him, I will loose his bonds,
And gain a husband by his liberty.
Speak, old Ægeon, if thou be'st the man
That hadst a wife once call'd Æmilia,
That bore thee at a burden two fair sons.
O, if thou be'st the same Ægeon, speak,
And speak unto the same Æmilia!
ÆGEON. If I dream not, thou art Æmilia.
If thou art she, tell me where is that son
That floated with thee on the fatal raft?

ABBESS. By men of Epidamnum he and I
And the twin Dromio, all were taken up;
But by and by rude fishermen of Corinth
By force took Dromio and my son from them,
And me they left with those of Epidamnum.
What then became of them I cannot tell;
I to this fortune that you see me in.
DUKE. Why, here begins his morning story right.
These two Antipholus', these two so like,
And these two Dromios, one in semblance—
Besides her urging of her wreck at sea—
These are the parents to these children,
Which accidentally are met together.
Antipholus, thou cam'st from Corinth first?
ANTIPHOLUS OF SYRACUSE. No, sir, not I; I came from Syra-
cuse.
DUKE. Stay, stand apart; I know not which is which.
ANTIPHOLUS OF EPHESUS. I came from Corinth, my most
gracious lord.
DROMIO OF EPHESUS. And I with him.
ANTIPHOLUS OF EPHESUS. Brought to this town by that most
famous warrior,
Duke Menaphon, your most renowned uncle.
ADRIANA. Which of you two did dine with me to-day?
ANTIPHOLUS OF SYRACUSE. I, gentle mistress.
ADRIANA. And are not you my husband?
ANTIPHOLUS OF EPHESUS. No; I say nay to that.
ANTIPHOLUS OF SYRACUSE. And so do I, yet did she call me
so;
And this fair gentlewoman, her sister here,
Did call me brother. [*To* LUCIANA] What I told you then,
I hope I shall have leisure to make good;
If this be not a dream I see and hear.
ANGELO. That is the chain, sir, which you had of me.
ANTIPHOLUS OF SYRACUSE. I think it be, sir; I deny it not.
ANTIPHOLUS OF EPHESUS. And you, sir, for this chain ar-
rested me.
ANGELO. I think I did, sir; I deny it not.
ADRIANA. I sent you money, sir, to be your bail,
By Dromio; but I think he brought it not.

DROMIO OF EPHESUS. No, none by me.
ANTIPHOLUS OF SYRACUSE. This purse of ducats I receiv'd
from you,
And Dromio my man did bring them me.
I see we still did meet each other's man,
And I was ta'en for him, and he for me,
And thereupon these ERRORS are arose.
ANTIPHOLUS OF EPHESUS. These ducats pawn I for my father
here.
DUKE. It shall not need; thy father hath his life.
COURTEZAN. Sir, I must have that diamond from you.
ANTIPHOLUS OF EPHESUS. There, take it; and much thanks
for my good cheer.
ABBESS. Renowned Duke, vouchsafe to take the pains
To go with us into the abbey here,
And hear at large discoursed all our fortunes;
And all that are assembled in this place
That by this sympathized one day's error
Have suffer'd wrong, go keep us company,
And we shall make full satisfaction.
Thirty-three years have I but gone in travail
Of you, my sons; and till this present hour
My heavy burden ne'er delivered.
The Duke, my husband, and my children both,
And you the calendars of their nativity,
Go to a gossips' feast, and go with me;
After so long grief, such nativity!
DUKE. With all my heart, I'll gossip at this feast.
Exeunt all but ANTIPHOLUS OF SYRACUSE, ANTIPHOLUS OF
EPHESUS, DROMIO OF SYRACUSE, *and* DROMIO OF EPHESUS
DROMIO OF SYRACUSE. Master, shall I fetch your stuff from
shipboard?
ANTIPHOLUS OF EPHESUS. Dromio, what stuff of mine hast
thou embark'd?
DROMIO OF SYRACUSE. Your goods that lay at host, sir, in the
Centaur.
ANTIPHOLUS OF SYRACUSE. He speaks to me. I am your
master, Dromio.
Come, go with us; we'll look to that anon.
Embrace thy brother there; rejoice with him.

Exeunt ANTIPHOLUS OF SYRACUSE *and* ANTIPHOLUS
OF EPHESUS

DROMIO OF SYRACUSE. There is a fat friend at your master's
house,
That kitchen'd me for you to-day at dinner;
She now shall be my sister, not my wife.
DROMIO OF EPHESUS. Methinks you are my glass, and not my
brother;
I see by you I am a sweet-fac'd youth.
Will you walk in to see their gossiping?
DROMIO OF SYRACUSE. Not I, sir; you are my elder.
DROMIO OF EPHESUS. That's a question; how shall we try it?
DROMIO OF SYRACUSE. We'll draw cuts for the senior; till
then, lead thou first.
DROMIO OF EPHESUS. Nay, then, thus:
We came into the world like brother and brother,
And now let's go hand in hand, not one before another.
Exeunt

Much Ado About Nothing

MUCH ADO ABOUT NOTHING

HERE as in *Twelfth Night* and *As You Like It*, the comedies that group themselves with *Much Ado*, Shakespeare has peopled an old story with a host of characters unknown to the earlier narrator. In Bandello's version of the story King Peter of Arragon having reduced Sicily holds his court at Messina. The daughter of Lionato, a gentleman of the town, attracts the attentions of one of the King's suite. The marriage that is in prospect is however delayed. An intimate friend of the future bridegroom, jealous of his companion's happiness, employs an unscrupulous fellow to slander the lady to her lover, and to offer to provide evidence of her infidelity. On the night fixed for the lady's conviction the accomplices show the deluded lover someone entering an upper window by a ladder as if to an assignation. The lover then causes her father to be informed of his daughter's treachery and breaks off the marriage. The lady all but dies of the accusation, recovers and is concealed by her father who gives out that she is dead, has funeral rites performed and a tomb erected to her memory. Here the false friend eventually confesses his guilt to his companion who spares his life but reveals all to the girl's father. The father is now to select a wife for the repentant lover and gives him his daughter. She has become even more beautiful in the interval and is unrecognised at first by her old lover. His recognition of her identity and a second marriage between the reformed friend and the wronged lady's sister complete the story.

From Bandello or from some version of the Italian story Shakespeare took the main elements in the Hero-Claudio episode. The maid disguising herself as her mistress is a feature in Ariosto's very different version of the story. Ariosto's version seems to have provided at least the groundwork of a play no longer extant but performed in 1583 before the Queen by the pupils of the Merchant Taylor's school under Richard Mulcaster.

It would have been difficult for Shakespeare to make his Claudio a sympathetic figure; Shakespeare did not try, but

370

sacrificed him for the sake of Benedick and Beatrice, knowing that the audience would forgive him for Hero's sake. Claudio has to denounce Hero in public and at the altar so that the most may be made of the indignation of Beatrice and her appeal to Benedick to revenge the wrong on his friend. What was in the original the main figure becomes rather a subsidiary in the extension Shakespeare added. That is why Charles I in his copy of the second Folio added the alternative title 'Benedick and Beatrice' to that of *Much Ado;* and these are the characters mentioned by Leonard Digges as among the public's chief favourites.

Amongst Shakespeare's most successful additions to the company of characters that are drawn together in the plot are Dogberry and Verges. They are dovetailed into the scheme most economically. These charming blunderers discover the plot before it can be brought to a head, and would have made all clear to Leonato had he not been in such haste to the wedding that he could not spare the time to interpret their language. The audience however are consoled in the scene of Hero's repudiation by the knowledge that the plot is already being unravelled by the constabulary.

Dogberry and Verges not only provide the clue to Don John's intrigue, they furnish the student of Shakespeare with most useful evidence about the date of *Much Ado* itself. The first Quarto of *Much Ado* appeared in 1600. That the printer worked from Shakespeare's own manuscript seems clear from various irregularities in the text and stage-directions and above all from the presence of the names of actors standing in place of the characters they were to play. In a prompt-book the actor and the character he presented might stand coupled together for the information and convenience of the prompter; but in *Much Ado* Q1 we have the actor's name by itself, as if the author had actors in view for special parts. This would be natural for a dramatist in Shakespeare's position; he was writing for a closely-knit company and knew all their styles and roles, and he could no more ignore the resources of his company than could Gilbert and Sullivan when they were planning their diversions. When therefore we find the names of Kempe and Cowley in place of Dogberry and Verges we can be sure that Shakespeare as he wrote had these particular actors in his mind for the parts he was creating. We know from other sources that Kempe and Cowley were just the men for the constables.

Will Kempe was the leading clown of his day, having fallen heir to Tarleton's popularity. He left the Chamberlain's men in 1599 about the time of the opening of the Globe Theatre or shortly after, perhaps because he felt that Shakespeare was limiting more strictly, as his prestige with the public and his company grew, the part assigned to the clowns, requiring them, as Hamlet says when he speaks to the players, to 'speak no more than is set down for them.' Kempe unable to submit to such discipline in the interests of the play turned elsewhere to display his talent.

Shakespeare must have written *Much Ado* therefore before Kempe left the company. Meres in his *Palladis Tamia* makes no mention of it; had so popular a play been in the repertory of Shakespeare's company when Meres was writing he could hardly have omitted it. Meres, it is true, has on his list a play called *Love's Labour's Won;* to which of Shakespeare's pieces this refers we cannot be sure, but it does not seem a very likely alternative title for *Much Ado.*

The conjecture that *Much Ado* was written about 1598 or 1599 cannot be far wrong. It continues the sequence of Romantic comedies built round some love intrigue that story-tellers had already used or dramatists turned to account. Perhaps *Much Ado* stands out in the sequence as the play containing the pair of anti-Romantics that give the play its real Romantic interest. Benedick and Beatrice were certainly the characters that found favour with Shakespeare's contemporaries, and they are still the principal, though not the only, attractions of the comedy.

BEATRICE. *What fire is in my ears? Can this be true?*
(ACT III. SCENE I)

DON PEDRO, *Prince of Arragon*
DON JOHN, *his bastard brother*
CLAUDIO, *a young lord of Florence*
BENEDICK, *a young lord of Padua*
LEONATO, *Governor of Messina*
ANTONIO, *his brother*
BALTHASAR, *attendant on Don Pedro*
BORACHIO ⎤
CONRADE ⎦ *followers of Don John*
FRIAR FRANCIS
DOGBERRY, *a constable*
VERGES, *a headborough*
A SEXTON
A BOY

HERO, *daughter to Leonato*
BEATRICE, *niece to Leonato*
MARGARET ⎤
URSULA ⎦ *gentlewomen attending on Hero*

Messengers, Watch, Attendants

SCENE:

Messina

Much Ado About Nothing

ACT I. SCENE 1

Before LEONATO's *house*

Enter LEONATO, HERO, *and* BEATRICE, *with a* MESSENGER

LEONATO. I learn in this letter that Don Pedro of Arragon comes this night to Messina.

MESSENGER. He is very near by this; he was not three leagues off when I left him.

LEONATO. How many gentlemen have you lost in this action?

MESSENGER. But few of any sort, and none of name.

LEONATO. A victory is twice itself when the achiever brings home full numbers. I find here that Don Pedro hath bestowed much honour on a young Florentine called Claudio.

MESSENGER. Much deserv'd on his part, and equally rememb'red by Don Pedro. He hath borne himself beyond the promise of his age, doing, in the figure of a lamb, the feats of a lion; he hath, indeed, better bett'red expectation than you must expect of me to tell you how.

LEONATO. He hath an uncle here in Messina will be very much glad of it.

MESSENGER. I have already delivered him letters, and there appears much joy in him; even so much that joy could not show itself modest enough without a badge of bitterness.

LEONATO. Did he break out into tears?

MESSENGER. In great measure.

LEONATO. A kind overflow of kindness. There are no faces truer than those that are so wash'd. How much better is it to weep at joy than to joy at weeping!

BEATRICE. I pray you, is Signior Mountanto return'd from the wars or no?

MESSENGER. I know none of that name, lady; there was none such in the army of any sort.

LEONATO. What is he that you ask for, niece?

HERO. My cousin means Signior Benedick of Padua.

MESSENGER. O, he's return'd, and as pleasant as ever he was.

BEATRICE. He set up his bills here in Messina, and challeng'd Cupid at the flight; and my uncle's fool, reading the challenge, subscrib'd for Cupid, and challeng'd him at the birdbolt. I pray you, how many hath he kill'd and eaten in these wars? But how many hath he kill'd? For, indeed, I promised to eat all of his killing.

LEONATO. Faith, niece, you tax Signior Benedick too much; but he'll be meet with you, I doubt it not.

MESSENGER. He hath done good service, lady, in these wars.

BEATRICE. You had musty victual, and he hath holp to eat it; he is a very valiant trencherman; he hath an excellent stomach.

MESSENGER. And a good soldier too, lady.

BEATRICE. And a good soldier to a lady; but what is he to a lord?

MESSENGER. A lord to a lord, a man to a man; stuff'd with all honourable virtues.

BEATRICE. It is so, indeed; he is no less than a stuff'd man; but for the stuffing—well, we are all mortal.

LEONATO. You must not, sir, mistake my niece: there is a kind of merry war betwixt Signior Benedick and her; they never meet but there's a skirmish of wit between them.

BEATRICE. Alas, he gets nothing by that. In our last conflict four of his five wits went halting off, and now is the whole man govern'd with one; so that if he have wit enough to keep himself warm, let him bear it for a difference between himself and his horse; for it is all the wealth that he hath left, to be known a reasonable creature. Who is his companion now? He hath every month a new sworn brother.

MESSENGER. Is't possible?

BEATRICE. Very easily possible: he wears his faith but as the fashion of his hat; it ever changes with the next block.

MESSENGER. I see, lady, the gentleman is not in your books.

BEATRICE. No; an he were, I would burn my study. But, I pray you, who is his companion? Is there no young squarer now that will make a voyage with him to the devil?

MESSENGER. He is most in the company of the right noble Claudio.

BEATRICE. O Lord! he will hang upon him like a disease; he is sooner caught than the pestilence, and the taker runs presently mad. God help the noble Claudio! If he have caught the Benedick, it will cost him a thousand pound ere 'a be cured.

MESSENGER. I will hold friends with you, lady.

BEATRICE. Do, good friend.

LEONATO. You will never run mad, niece.

BEATRICE. No, not till a hot January.

MESSENGER. Don Pedro is approach'd.

Enter DON PEDRO, CLAUDIO, BENEDICK, BALTHASAR,
and JOHN the Bastard

DON PEDRO. Good Signior Leonato, are you come to meet your trouble? The fashion of the world is to avoid cost, and you encounter it.

LEONATO. Never came trouble to my house in the likeness of your Grace; for trouble being gone comfort should remain; but when you depart from me sorrow abides, and happiness takes his leave.

DON PEDRO. You embrace your charge too willingly. I think this is your daughter.

LEONATO. Her mother hath many times told me so.

BENEDICK. Were you in doubt, sir, that you ask'd her?

LEONATO. Signior Benedick, no; for then were you a child.

DON PEDRO. You have it full, Benedick; we may guess by this what you are, being a man. Truly, the lady fathers herself. Be happy, lady, for you are like an honourable father.

BENEDICK. If Signior Leonato be her father, she would not have his head on her shoulders for all Messina, as like him as she is.

BEATRICE. I wonder that you will still be talking, Signior Benedick; nobody marks you.

BENEDICK. What, my dear Lady Disdain! Are you yet living?

BEATRICE. Is it possible disdain should die while she hath such meet food to feed it as Signior Benedick? Courtesy itself must convert to disdain if you come in her presence.

BENEDICK. Then is courtesy a turncoat. But it is certain I am loved of all ladies, only you excepted; and I would I could find in my heart that I had not a hard heart, for, truly, I love none.

BEATRICE. A dear happiness to women! They would else have been troubled with a pernicious suitor. I thank God, and my cold blood, I am of your humour for that: I had rather hear my dog bark at a crow than a man swear he loves me.

BENEDICK. God keep your ladyship still in that mind! So some gentleman or other shall scrape a predestinate scratch'd face.

BEATRICE. Scratching could not make it worse, and 'twere such a face as yours were.

BENEDICK. Well, you are a rare parrot-teacher.

BEATRICE. A bird of my tongue is better than a beast of yours.

BENEDICK. I would my horse had the speed of your tongue, and so good a continuer. But keep your way a God's name, I have done.

BEATRICE. You always end with a jade's trick; I know you of old.

DON PEDRO. That is the sum of all, Leonato. Signior Claudio and Signior Benedick, my dear friend Leonato hath invited you all. I tell him we shall stay here at the least a month; and he heartily prays some occasion may detain us longer. I dare swear he is no hypocrite, but prays from his heart.

LEONATO. If you swear, my lord, you shall not be forsworn. [*To* DON JOHN] Let me bid you welcome, my lord—being reconciled to the Prince your brother, I owe you all duty.

DON JOHN. I thank you; I am not of many words, but I thank you.

LEONATO. Please it your Grace lead on?

DON PEDRO. Your hand, Leonato; we will go together.

Exeunt all but BENEDICK *and* CLAUDIO

CLAUDIO. Benedick, didst thou note the daughter of Signior Leonato?

BENEDICK. I noted her not, but I look'd on her.

CLAUDIO. Is she not a modest young lady?

BENEDICK. Do you question me, as an honest man should do, for my simple true judgment; or would you have me speak after my custom, as being a professed tyrant to their sex?

CLAUDIO. No, I pray thee speak in sober judgment.

BENEDICK. Why, i' faith, methinks she's too low for a high praise, too brown for a fair praise, and too little for a great praise; only this commendation I can afford her, that were she other than she is, she were unhandsome, and being no other but as she is, I do not like her.

CLAUDIO. Thou thinkest I am in sport; I pray thee tell me truly how thou lik'st her.

BENEDICK. Would you buy her, that you inquire after her?

CLAUDIO. Can the world buy such a jewel?

BENEDICK. Yea, and a case to put it into. But speak you this with a sad brow, or do you play the flouting Jack, to tell us Cupid is a good hare-finder, and Vulcan a rare carpenter? Come, in what key shall a man take you to go in the song?

CLAUDIO. In mine eye she is the sweetest lady that ever I look'd on.

BENEDICK. I can see yet without spectacles, and I see no such matter; there's her cousin, an she were not possess'd with a fury, exceeds her as much in beauty as the first of May doth the last of December. But I hope you have no intent to turn husband, have you?

CLAUDIO. I would scarce trust myself, though I had sworn the contrary, if Hero would be my wife.

BENEDICK. Is't come to this? In faith, hath not the world one man but he will wear his cap with suspicion? Shall I never see a bachelor of threescore again? Go to, i' faith; an thou wilt needs thrust thy neck into a yoke, wear the print of it, and sigh away Sundays. Look, Don Pedro is returned to seek you.

Re-enter DON PEDRO

DON PEDRO. What secret hath held you here, that you followed not to Leonato's?

BENEDICK. I would your Grace would constrain me to tell.

DON PEDRO. I charge thee on thy allegiance.

BENEDICK. You hear, Count Claudio; I can be secret as a dumb man, I would have you think so; but on my allegiance, mark you this, on my allegiance—he is in love.

With who? now that is your Grace's part. Mark how short his answer is: with Hero, Leonato's short daughter.

CLAUDIO. . If this were so, so were it utt'red.

BENEDICK. Like the old tale, my lord: 'It is not so, nor 'twas not so; but, indeed, God forbid it should be so!'

CLAUDIO. If my passion change not shortly, God forbid it should be otherwise!

DON PEDRO. Amen, if you love her; for the lady is very well worthy.

CLAUDIO. You speak this to fetch me in, my lord?

DON PEDRO. By my troth, I speak my thought.

CLAUDIO. And, in faith, my lord, I spoke mine.

BENEDICK. And, by my two faiths and troths, my lord, I spoke mine.

CLAUDIO. That I love her, I feel.

DON PEDRO. That she is worthy, I know.

BENEDICK. That I neither feel how she should be loved, nor know how she should be worthy, is the opinion that fire cannot melt out of me; I will die in it at the stake.

DON PEDRO. Thou wast ever an obstinate heretic in the despite of beauty.

CLAUDIO. And never could maintain his part but in the force of his will.

BENEDICK. That a woman conceived me, I thank her; that she brought me up, I likewise give her most humble thanks; but that I will have a recheat winded in my forehead, or hang my bugle in an invisible baldrick, all women shall pardon me. Because I will not do them the wrong to mistrust any, I will do myself the right to trust none; and the fine is, for the which I may go the finer, I will live a bachelor.

DON PEDRO. I shall see thee, ere I die, look pale with love.

BENEDICK. With anger, with sickness, or with hunger, my lord; not with love. Prove that ever I lose more blood with love than I will get again with drinking, pick out mine eyes with a ballad-maker's pen, and hang me up at the door of a brothel-house for the sign of blind Cupid.

DON PEDRO. Well, if ever thou dost fall from this faith, thou wilt prove a notable argument.

BENEDICK. If I do, hang me in a bottle like a cat, and shoot at me; and he that hits me, let him be clapp'd on the shoulder and call'd Adam.

DON PEDRO. Well, as time shall try.
'In time the savage bull doth bear the yoke.'

BENEDICK. The savage bull may; but if ever the sensible Benedick bear it, pluck off the bull's horns and set them in my forehead, and let me be vilely painted; and in such great letters as they write 'Here is good horse to hire' let them signify under my sign 'Here you may see Benedick the married man.'

CLAUDIO. If this should ever happen, thou wouldst be horn-mad.

DON PEDRO. Nay, if Cupid have not spent all his quiver in Venice, thou wilt quake for this shortly.

BENEDICK. I look for an earthquake too, then.

DON PEDRO. Well, you will temporize with the hours. In the meantime, good Signior Benedick, repair to Leonato's; commend me to him, and tell him I will not fail him at supper; for, indeed, he hath made great preparation.

BENEDICK. I have almost matter enough in me for such an embassage; and so I commit you—

CLAUDIO. To the tuition of God. From my house—if I had it—

DON PEDRO. The sixth of July. Your loving friend, Benedick.

BENEDICK. Nay, mock not, mock not. The body of your discourse is sometime guarded with fragments, and the guards are but slightly basted on neither; ere you flout old ends any further, examine your conscience; and so I leave you.   *Exit* BENEDICK

CLAUDIO. My liege, your Highness now may do me good.

DON PEDRO. My love is thine to teach; teach it but how,
And thou shalt see how apt it is to learn
Any hard lesson that may do thee good.

CLAUDIO. Hath Leonato any son, my lord?

DON PEDRO. No child but Hero; she's his only heir.
Dost thou affect her, Claudio?

CLAUDIO. O, my lord,
When you went onward on this ended action,
I look'd upon her with a soldier's eye,
That lik'd, but had a rougher task in hand

Than to drive liking to the name of love;
But now I am return'd, and that war-thoughts
Have left their places vacant, in their rooms
Come thronging soft and delicate desires,
All prompting me how fair young Hero is,
Saying I lik'd her ere I went to wars.

DON PEDRO. Thou wilt be like a lover presently,
And tire the hearer with a book of words.
If thou dost love fair Hero, cherish it;
And I will break with her, and with her father,
And thou shalt have her. Was't not to this end
That thou began'st to twist so fine a story?

CLAUDIO. How sweetly you do minister to love,
That know love's grief by his complexion!
But lest my liking might too sudden seem,
I would have salv'd it with a longer treatise.

DON PEDRO. What need the bridge much broader than the
flood?
The fairest grant is the necessity.
Look what will serve is fit. 'Tis once, thou lovest;
And I will fit thee with the remedy.
I know we shall have revelling to-night;
I will assume thy part in some disguise,
And tell fair Hero I am Claudio;
And in her bosom I'll unclasp my heart,
And take her hearing prisoner with the force
And strong encounter of my amorous tale.
Then, after, to her father will I break;
And the conclusion is she shall be thine.
In practice let us put it presently.   *Exeunt*

SCENE 2

LEONATO's *house*

Enter, severally, LEONATO *and* ANTONIO

LEONATO. How now, brother! Where is my cousin, your
son? Hath he provided this music?

382

ANTONIO. He is very busy about it. But, brother, I can tell you strange news that you yet dreamt not of.

LEONATO. Are they good?

ANTONIO. As the event stamps them; but they have a good cover; they show well outward. The Prince and Count Claudio, walking in a thick-pleached alley in mine orchard, were thus much overheard by a man of mine: the Prince discovered to Claudio that he loved my niece your daughter, and meant to acknowledge it this night in a dance; and, if he found her accordant, he meant to take the present time by the top, and instantly break with you of it.

LEONATO. Hath the fellow any wit that told you this?

ANTONIO. A good sharp fellow; I will send for him, and question him yourself.

LEONATO. No, no; we will hold it as a dream, till it appear itself; but I will acquaint my daughter withal, that she may be the better prepared for an answer, if peradventure this be true. Go you and tell her of it. [*Several persons cross the stage*] Cousins, you know what you have to do. O, I cry you mercy, friend; go with me, and I will use your skill. Good cousin, have a care this busy time.   *Exeunt*

SCENE 3

LEONATO'S *house*

Enter DON JOHN *and* CONRADE

CONRADE. What the good-year, my lord! Why are you thus out of measure sad?

DON JOHN. There is no measure in the occasion that breeds; therefore the sadness is without limit.

CONRADE. You should hear reason.

DON JOHN. And when I have heard it, what blessing brings it?

CONRADE. If not a present remedy, at least a patient sufferance.

DON JOHN. I wonder that thou, being, as thou say'st thou art, born under Saturn, goest about to apply a moral medicine to a mortifying mischief. I cannot hide what I am; I must be sad when I have cause, and smile at no man's jests; eat when I have stomach, and wait for no man's leisure; sleep when I am drowsy, and tend on no man's business; laugh when I am merry, and claw no man in his humour.

CONRADE. Yea, but you must not make the full show of this till you may do it without controlment. You have of late stood out against your brother, and he hath ta'en you newly into his grace; where it is impossible you should take true root but by the fair weather that you make yourself; it is needful that you frame the season for your own harvest.

DON JOHN. I had rather be a canker in a hedge than a rose in his grace; and it better fits my blood to be disdain'd of all than to fashion a carriage to rob love from any. In this, though I cannot be said to be a flattering honest man, it must not be denied but I am a plain-dealing villain. I am trusted with a muzzle and enfranchis'd with a clog; therefore I have decreed not to sing in my cage. If I had my mouth, I would bite; if I had my liberty, I would do my liking; in the meantime let me be that I am, and seek not to alter me.

CONRADE. Can you make no use of your discontent?

DON JOHN. I make all use of it, for I use it only. Who comes here?

Enter BORACHIO

What news, Borachio?

BORACHIO. I came yonder from a great supper. The Prince, your brother, is royally entertain'd by Leonato; and I can give you intelligence of an intended marriage.

DON JOHN. Will it serve for any model to build mischief on? What is he for a fool that betroths himself to unquietness?

BORACHIO. Marry, it is your brother's right hand.

DON JOHN. Who? The most exquisite Claudio?

BORACHIO. Even he.

DON JOHN. A proper squire! And who, and who? Which way looks he?

BORACHIO. Marry, on Hero, the daughter and heir of Leonato.

Don John. A very forward March-chick! How came you to this?

Borachio. Being entertain'd for a perfumer, as I was smoking a musty room, comes me the Prince and Claudio hand in hand, in sad conference. I whipt me behind the arras, and there heard it agreed upon that the Prince should woo Hero for himself, and, having obtain'd her, give her to Count Claudio.

Don John. Come, come, let us thither; this may prove food to my displeasure; that young start-up hath all the glory of my overthrow. If I can cross him any way, I bless myself every way. You are both sure, and will assist me?

Conrade. To the death, my lord.

Don John. Let us to the great supper; their cheer is the greater that I am subdued. Would the cook were o' my mind! Shall we go prove what's to be done?

Borachio. We'll wait upon your lordship.   *Exeunt*

ACT II. SCENE 1

A hall in Leonato's *house*

Enter Leonato, Antonio, Hero, Beatrice, Margaret, Ursula, *and* Others

Leonato. Was not Count John here at supper?

Antonio. I saw him not.

Beatrice. How tartly that gentleman looks! I never can see him but I am heart-burn'd an hour after.

Hero. He is of a very melancholy disposition.

Beatrice. He were an excellent man that were made just in the mid-way between him and Benedick: the one is too like an image and says nothing, and the other too like my lady's eldest son, evermore tattling.

Leonato. Then half Signior Benedick's tongue in Count John's mouth, and half Count John's melancholy in Signior Benedick's face—

Beatrice. With a good leg and a good foot, uncle, and

money enough in his purse, such a man would win any woman in the world, if 'a could get her good-will.

LEONATO. By my troth, niece, thou wilt never get thee a husband if thou be so shrewd of thy tongue.

ANTONIO. In faith, she's too curst.

BEATRICE. Too curst is more than curst. I shall lessen God's sending that way; for it is said 'God sends a curst cow short horns'; but to a cow too curst he sends none.

LEONATO. So, by being too curst, God will send you no horns.

BEATRICE. Just, if he send me no husband; for the which blessing I am at him upon my knees every morning and evening. Lord! I could not endure a husband with a beard on his face; I had rather lie in the woollen.

LEONATO. You may light on a husband that hath no beard.

BEATRICE. What should I do with him? Dress him in my apparel, and make him my waiting gentlewoman? He that hath a beard is more than a youth, and he that hath no beard is less than a man; and he that is more than a youth is not for me, and he that is less than a man I am not for him; therefore I will even take sixpence in earnest of the berrord, and lead his apes into hell.

LEONATO. Well then, go you into hell?

BEATRICE. No; but to the gate, and there will the devil meet me, like an old cuckold, with horns on his head, and say 'Get you to heaven, Beatrice, get you to heaven; here's no place for you maids.' So deliver I up my apes and away to Saint Peter for the heavens; he shows me where the bachelors sit, and there live we as merry as the day is long.

ANTONIO. [*To* HERO] Well, niece, I trust you will be rul'd by your father.

BEATRICE. Yes, faith; it is my cousin's duty to make curtsy, and say 'Father, as it please you.' But yet for all that, cousin, let him be a handsome fellow, or else make another curtsy and say 'Father, as it please me.'

LEONATO. Well, niece, I hope to see you one day fitted with a husband.

BEATRICE. Not till God make men of some other metal than earth. Would it not grieve a woman to be over-master'd with a piece of valiant dust, to make an account of her life to a clod of wayward marl? No, uncle, I'll none: Adam's sons are my brethren; and, truly, I hold it a sin to match in my kindred.

LEONATO. Daughter, remember what I told you: if the Prince do solicit you in that kind, you know your answer.

BEATRICE. The fault will be in the music, cousin, if you be not wooed in good time. If the Prince be too important, tell him there is measure in every thing, and so dance out the answer. For, hear me, Hero; wooing, wedding, and repenting, is as a Scotch jig, a measure, and a cinquepace; the first suit is hot and tasty, like a Scotch jig, and full as fantastical; the wedding, mannerly modest, as a measure, full of state and ancientry; and then comes repentance, and, with his bad legs, falls into the cinquepace faster and faster, till he sink into his grave.

LEONATO. Cousin, you apprehend passing shrewdly.

BEATRICE. I have a good eye, uncle; I can see a church by daylight.

LEONATO. The revellers are ent'ring, brother; make good room.   [ANTONIO *masks*]

Enter DON PEDRO, CLAUDIO, BENEDICK, BALTHASAR, DON JOHN, *and* BORACHIO, *as maskers, with a drum*

DON PEDRO. Lady, will you walk about with your friend?

HERO. So you walk softly, and look sweetly, and say nothing, I am yours for the walk; and, especially, when I walk away.

DON PEDRO. With me in your company?

HERO. I may say so, when I please.

DON PEDRO. And when please you to say so?

HERO. When I like your favour; for God defend the lute should be like the case!

DON PEDRO. My visor is Philemon's roof; within the house is Jove.

HERO. Why, then, your visor should be thatch'd.

DON PEDRO. Speak low, if you speak love.   [*Takes her aside*]

BALTHASAR. Well, I would you did like me.

MARGARET. So would not I, for your own sake; for I have many ill qualities.

BALTHASAR. Which is one?

387

MARGARET. I say my prayers aloud.

BALTHASAR. I love you the better; the hearers may cry Amen.

MARGARET. God match me with a good dancer!

BALTHASAR. Amen.

MARGARET. And God keep him out of my sight when the dance is done! Answer, clerk.

BALTHASAR. No more words; the clerk is answered.

URSULA. I know you well enough; you are Signior Antonio.

ANTONIO. At a word, I am not.

URSULA. I know you by the waggling of your head.

ANTONIO. To tell you true, I counterfeit him.

URSULA. You could never do him so ill-well unless you were the very man. Here's his dry hand up and down; you are he, you are he.

ANTONIO. At a word, I am not.

URSULA. Come, come; do you think I do not know you by your excellent wit? Can virtue hide itself? Go to; mum; you are he; graces will appear, and there's an end.

BEATRICE. Will you not tell me who told you so?

BENEDICK. No, you shall pardon me.

BEATRICE. Nor will you not tell me who you are?

BENEDICK. Not now.

BEATRICE. That I was disdainful, and that I had my good wit out of the 'Hundred Merry Tales'—well, this was Signior Benedick that said so.

BENEDICK. What's he?

BEATRICE. I am sure you know him well enough.

BENEDICK. Not I, believe me.

BEATRICE. Did he never make you laugh?

BENEDICK. I pray you, what is he?

BEATRICE. Why, he is the Prince's jester, a very dull fool; only his gift is in devising impossible slanders; none but libertines delight in him, and the commendation is not in his wit but in his villainy; for he both pleases men and angers them, and then they laugh at him and beat him. I am sure he is in the fleet; I would he had boarded me.

BENEDICK. When I know the gentleman, I'll tell him what you say.

BEATRICE. Do, do; he'll but break a comparison or two on

me; which, peradventure, not mark'd, or not laugh'd at,
strikes him into melancholy; and then there's a partridge
wing saved, for the fool will eat no supper that night.
[*Music*] We must follow the leaders.

BENEDICK. In every good thing.

BEATRICE. Nay, if they lead to any ill, I will leave them at
the next turning.

> [*Dance. Then exeunt all but* DON JOHN, BORACHIO,
> *and* CLAUDIO]

DON JOHN. Sure, my brother is amorous on Hero, and hath
withdrawn her father to break with him about it. The
ladies follow her, and but one visor remains.

BORACHIO. And that is Claudio; I know him by his bearing.

DON JOHN. Are not you Signior Benedick?

CLAUDIO. You know me well; I am he.

DON JOHN. Signior, you are very near my brother in his
love; he is enamour'd on Hero; I pray you dissuade him
from her; she is no equal for his birth. You may do the
part of an honest man in it.

CLAUDIO. How know you he loves her?

DON JOHN. I heard him swear his affection.

BORACHIO. So did I too; and he swore he would marry her
to-night.

DON JOHN. Come, let us to the banquet.

> *Exeunt* DON JOHN *and* BORACHIO

CLAUDIO. Thus answer I in name of Benedick,
But hear these ill news with the ears of Claudio.
'Tis certain so: the Prince woos for himself.
Friendship is constant in all other things
Save in the office and affairs of love;
Therefore all hearts in love use their own tongues.
Let every eye negotiate for itself,
And trust no agent: for beauty is a witch
Against whose charms faith melteth into blood.
This is an accident of hourly proof,
Which I mistrusted not. Farewell, therefore, Hero.

> *Re-enter* BENEDICK

BENEDICK. Count Claudio?

CLAUDIO. Yea, the same.

BENEDICK. Come, will you go with me?

CLAUDIO. Whither?

BENEDICK. Even to the next willow, about your own business, County. What fashion will you wear the garland of? About your neck, like an usurer's chain, or under your arm, like a lieutenant's scarf? You must wear it one way, for the Prince hath got your Hero.

CLAUDIO. I wish him joy of her.

BENEDICK. Why, that's spoken like an honest drovier; so they sell bullocks. But did you think the Prince would have served you thus?

CLAUDIO. I pray you leave me.

BENEDICK. Ho! now you strike like the blind man; 'twas the boy that stole your meat, and you'll beat the post.

CLAUDIO. If it will not be, I'll leave you.   *Exit*

BENEDICK. Alas, poor hurt fowl! Now will he creep into sedges. But that my Lady Beatrice should know me, and not know me! The Prince's fool! Ha! It may be I go under that title because I am merry. Yea, but so I am apt to do myself wrong; I am not so reputed; it is the base, though bitter, disposition of Beatrice that puts the world into her person, and so gives me out. Well, I'll be revenged as I may.

Re-enter DON PEDRO

DON PEDRO. Now, signior, where's the Count? Did you see him?

BENEDICK. Troth, my lord, I have played the part of Lady Fame. I found him here as melancholy as a lodge in a warren; I told him, and I think I told him true, that your Grace had got the good will of this young lady; and I off'red him my company to a willow tree, either to make him a garland, as being forsaken, or to bind him up a rod, as being worthy to be whipt.

DON PEDRO. To be whipt! What's his fault?

BENEDICK. The flat transgression of a schoolboy, who, being overjoyed with finding a bird's nest, shows it his companion, and he steals it.

DON PEDRO. Wilt thou make a trust a transgression? The transgression is in the stealer.

BENEDICK. Yet it had not been amiss the rod had been made, and the garland too; for the garland he might have worn himself, and the rod he might have bestowed on you, who, as I take it, have stol'n his bird's nest.

DON PEDRO. I will but teach them to sing, and restore them to the owner.

BENEDICK. If their singing answer your saying, by my faith, you say honestly.

DON PEDRO. The Lady Beatrice hath a quarrel to you; the gentleman that danc'd with her told her she is much wrong'd by you.

BENEDICK. O, she misus'd me past the endurance of a block; an oak but with one green leaf on it would have answered her; my very visor began to assume life and scold with her. She told me, not thinking I had been myself, that I was the Prince's jester, that I was duller than a great thaw; huddling jest upon jest with such impossible conveyance upon me that I stood like a man at a mark, with a whole army shooting at me. She speaks poniards, and every word stabs; if her breath were as terrible as her terminations, there were no living near her; she would infect to the north star. I would not marry her though she were endowed with all that Adam had left him before he transgress'd; she would have made Hercules have turn'd spit, yea, and have cleft his club to make the fire too. Come, talk not of her; you shall find her the infernal Ate in good apparel. I would to God some scholar would conjure her; for certainly, while she is here, a man may live as quiet in hell as in a sanctuary; and people sin upon purpose, because they would go thither; so, indeed, all disquiet, horror, and perturbation, follows her.

Re-enter CLAUDIO *and* BEATRICE, LEONATO *and* HERO

DON PEDRO. Look, here she comes.

BENEDICK. Will your Grace command me any service to the world's end? I will go on the slightest errand now to the Antipodes that you can devise to send me on; I will fetch you a toothpicker now from the furthest inch of Asia; bring you the length of Prester John's foot; fetch you a hair off the great Cham's beard; do you any embassage to the Pigmies—rather than hold three words' conference with this harpy. You have no employment for me?

DON PEDRO. None, but to desire your good company.

BENEDICK. O God, sir, here's a dish I love not; I cannot endure my Lady Tongue. *Exit*

DON PEDRO. Come, lady, come; you have lost the heart of Signior Benedick.

BEATRICE. Indeed, my lord, he lent it me awhile; and I gave him use for it, a double heart for his single one; marry, once before he won it of me with false dice, therefore your Grace may well say I have lost it.

DON PEDRO. You have put him down, lady, you have put him down.

BEATRICE. So I would not he should do me, my lord, lest I should prove the mother of fools. I have brought Count Claudio, whom you sent me to seek.

DON PEDRO. Why, how now, Count! Wherefore are you sad?

CLAUDIO. Not sad, my lord.

DON PEDRO. How then, sick?

CLAUDIO. Neither, my lord.

BEATRICE. The Count is neither sad, nor sick, nor merry, nor well; but civil count—civil as an orange, and something of that jealous complexion.

DON PEDRO. I' faith, lady, I think your blazon to be true, though I'll be sworn, if he be so, his conceit is false. Here, Claudio, I have wooed in thy name, and fair Hero is won. I have broke with her father, and his good will obtained. Name the day of marriage, and God give thee joy!

LEONATO. Count, take of me my daughter, and with her my fortunes; his Grace hath made the match, and all grace say Amen to it!

BEATRICE. Speak, Count, 'tis your cue.

CLAUDIO. Silence is the perfectest herald of joy: I were but little happy if I could say how much. Lady, as you are mine, I am yours; I give away myself for you, and dote upon the exchange.

BEATRICE. Speak, cousin; or, if you cannot, stop his mouth with a kiss, and let not him speak neither.

DON PEDRO. In faith, lady, you have a merry heart.

BEATRICE. Yea, my lord; I thank it, poor fool, it keeps on the windy side of care. My cousin tells him in his ear that he is in her heart.

CLAUDIO. And so she doth, cousin.

BEATRICE. Good Lord, for alliance! Thus goes every one to the world but I, and I am sunburnt; I may sit in a corner and cry 'Heigh-ho for a husband!'

DON PEDRO. Lady Beatrice, I will get you one.

BEATRICE. I would rather have one of your father's getting. Hath your Grace ne'er a brother like you? Your father got excellent husbands, if a maid could come by them.

DON PEDRO. Will you have me, lady?

BEATRICE. No, my lord, unless I might have another for working-days; your Grace is too costly to wear every day. But, I beseech your Grace, pardon me; I was born to speak all mirth and no matter.

DON PEDRO. Your silence most offends me, and to be merry best becomes you; for, out o' question, you were born in a merry hour.

BEATRICE. No, sure, my lord, my mother cried; but then there was a star danc'd, and under that was I born. Cousins, God give you joy!

LEONATO. Niece, you will look to those things I told you of?

BEATRICE. I cry your mercy, uncle. By your Grace's pardon.

Exit BEATRICE

DON PEDRO. By my troth, a pleasant-spirited lady.

LEONATO. There's little of the melancholy element in her, my lord; she is never sad but when she sleeps, and not ever sad then; for I have heard my daughter say she hath often dreamt of unhappiness, and wak'd herself with laughing.

DON PEDRO. She cannot endure to hear tell of a husband.

LEONATO. O, by no means; she mocks all her wooers out of suit.

DON PEDRO. She were an excellent wife for Benedick.

LEONATO. O Lord, my lord, if they were but a week married, they would talk themselves mad.

DON PEDRO. County Claudio, when mean you to go to church?

CLAUDIO. To-morrow, my lord. Time goes on crutches till love have all his rites.

LEONATO. Not till Monday, my dear son, which is hence a just seven-night; and a time too brief, too, to have all things answer my mind.

DON PEDRO. Come, you shake the head at so long a breathing; but I warrant thee, Claudio, the time shall not go dully by us. I will in the interim undertake one of Hercules' labours; which is, to bring Signior Benedick and the Lady Beatrice into a mountain of affection th' one with th' other. I would fain have it a match; and I doubt not but to fashion it if you three will but minister such assistance as I shall give you direction.

LEONATO. My lord, I am for you, though it cost me ten nights' watchings.

CLAUDIO. And I, my lord.

DON PEDRO. And you too, gentle Hero?

HERO. I will do any modest office, my lord, to help my cousin to a good husband.

DON PEDRO. And Benedick is not the unhopefullest husband that I know. Thus far can I praise him: he is of a noble strain, of approved valour, and confirm'd honesty. I will teach you how to humour your cousin that she shall fall in love with Benedick; and I, with your two helps, will so practise on Benedick that, in despite of his quick wit and his queasy stomach, he shall fall in love with Beatrice. If we can do this, Cupid is no longer an archer; his glory shall be ours, for we are the only love-gods. Go in with me, and I will tell you my drift.   *Exeunt*

SCENE 2

LEONATO's *house*

Enter DON JOHN *and* BORACHIO

DON JOHN. It is so; the Count Claudio shall marry the daughter of Leonato.

BORACHIO. Yea, my lord, but I can cross it.

DON JOHN. Any bar, any cross, any impediment, will be med'cinable to me. I am sick in displeasure to him; and whatsoever comes athwart his affection ranges evenly with mine. How canst thou cross this marriage?

BORACHIO. Not honestly, my lord; but so covertly that no dishonesty shall appear in me.

DON JOHN. Show me briefly how.

BORACHIO. I think I told your lordship a year since how much I am in the favour of Margaret, the waiting gentle-woman to Hero.

DON JOHN. I remember.

BORACHIO. I can at any unseasonable instant of the night appoint her to look out at her lady's chamber window.

DON JOHN. What life is in that, to be the death of this marriage?

BORACHIO. The poison of that lies in you to temper. Go you to the Prince your brother; spare not to tell him that he hath wronged his honour in marrying the renowned Claudio—whose estimation do you mightily hold up—to a contaminated stale, such a one as Hero.

DON JOHN. What proof shall I make of that?

BORACHIO. Proof enough to misuse the Prince, to vex Claudio, to undo Hero, and kill Leonato. Look you for any other issue?

DON JOHN. Only to despite them I will endeavour anything.

BORACHIO. Go, then; find me a meet hour to draw Don Pedro and the Count Claudio alone; tell them that you know that Hero loves me; intend a kind of zeal both to the Prince and Claudio—as in love of your brother's honour, who hath made this match, and his friend's reputation, who is thus like to be cozen'd with the semblance of a maid—that you have discover'd thus. They will scarcely believe this without trial; offer them instances; which shall bear no less likelihood than to see me at her chamber window; hear me call Margaret Hero; hear Margaret term me Borachio; and bring them to see this the very night before the intended wedding—for in the meantime I will so fashion the matter that Hero shall be absent—and there shall appear such seeming truth of Hero's disloyalty that jealousy shall be call'd assurance, and all the preparation overthrown.

DON JOHN. Grow this to what adverse issue it can, I will

put it in practice. Be cunning in the working this, and thy fee is a thousand ducats.

BORACHIO. Be you constant in the accusation, and my cunning shall not shame me.

DON JOHN. I will presently go learn their day of marriage.

Exeunt

SCENE 3

LEONATO'S *orchard*

Enter BENEDICK, *alone*

BENEDICK. Boy!

BOY. [*Within*] Signior?

BENEDICK. In my chamber-window lies a book; bring it hither to me in the orchard.

BOY. [*Above, at chamber window*] I am here already, sir.

BENEDICK. I know that; but I would have thee hence and here again. [BOY *brings book; exit*] I do much wonder that one man, seeing how much another man is a fool when he dedicates his behaviours to love, will, after he hath laugh'd at such shallow follies in others, become the argument of his own scorn by falling in love; and such a man is Claudio. I have known when there was no music with him but the drum and the fife, and now had he rather hear the tabor and the pipe; I have known when he would have walk'd ten mile afoot to see a good armour, and now will he lie ten nights awake carving the fashion of a new doublet. He was wont to speak plain and to the purpose, like an honest man and a soldier, and now is he turn'd orthography; his words are a very fantastical banquet, just so many strange dishes. May I be so converted, and see with these eyes? I cannot tell; I think not. I will not be sworn but love may transform me to an oyster; but I'll take my oath on it, till he have made an oyster of me he shall never make me such a fool. One woman is fair, yet I am well; another is wise, yet I am well; another virtuous, yet I am well; but till all graces be in one woman, one woman shall not come in my grace. Rich she shall be, that's certain; wise, or I'll none; virtuous, or I'll never cheapen

her; fair, or I'll never look on her; mild, or come not near
me; noble, or not I for an angel; of good discourse, an excellent musician, and her hair shall be of what colour it
please God. Ha! the Prince and Monsieur Love! I will hide
me in the arbour.   [*Withdraws*]

Enter DON PEDRO, LEONATO, *and* CLAUDIO

DON PEDRO. Come, shall we hear this music?
CLAUDIO. Yea, my good lord. How still the evening is,
  As hush'd on purpose to grace harmony!
DON PEDRO. See you where Benedick hath hid himself?
CLAUDIO. O, very well, my lord; the music ended,
  We'll fit the kid-fox with a pennyworth.

Enter BALTHASAR, *with music*

DON PEDRO. Come, Balthasar, we'll hear that song again.
BALTHASAR. O, good my lord, tax not so bad a voice
  To slander music any more than once.
DON PEDRO. It is the witness still of excellency
  To put a strange face on his own perfection.
  I pray thee sing, and let me woo no more.
BALTHASAR. Because you talk of wooing, I will sing,
  Since many a wooer doth commence his suit
  To her he thinks not worthy; yet he woos;
  Yet will he swear he loves.
DON PEDRO. Nay, pray thee, come;
  Or if thou wilt hold longer argument,
  Do it in notes.
BALTHASAR. Note this before my notes:
  There's not a note of mine that's worth the noting.
DON PEDRO. Why, these are very crotchets that he speaks;
  Note notes, forsooth, and nothing!   [*Music*]
BENEDICK. Now, divine air! now is his soul ravish'd. Is it not
  strange that sheeps' guts should hale souls out of men's
  bodies? Well, a horn for my money, when all's done.

BALTHASAR *sings*

Sigh no more, ladies, sigh no more,
  Men were deceivers ever,
One foot in sea and one on shore,

397

To one thing constant never.
Then sigh not so, but let them go,
And be you blithe and bonny;
Converting all your sounds of woe
Into Hey nonny nonny.

Sing no more ditties, sing no moe
Of dumps so dull and heavy;
The fraud of men was ever so,
Since summer first was leavy.
Then sigh not so, &c.

DON PEDRO. By my troth, a good song.

BALTHASAR. And an ill singer, my lord.

CLAUDIO. Ha, no; no, faith; thou sing'st well enough for a shift.

BENEDICK. An he had been a dog that should have howl'd thus, they would have hang'd him; and I pray God his bad voice bode no mischief. I had as lief have heard the night-raven, come what plague could have come after it.

DON PEDRO. Yea, marry; dost thou hear, Balthasar? I pray thee get us some excellent music; for to-morrow night we would have it at the Lady Hero's chamber window.

BALTHASAR. The best I can, my lord.

DON PEDRO. Do so; farewell. [*Exit* BALTHASAR] Come hither, Leonato. What was it you told me of to-day—that your niece Beatrice was in love with Signior Benedick?

CLAUDIO. O ay; stalk on, stalk on; the fowl sits. I did never think that lady would have loved any man.

LEONATO. No, nor I neither; but most wonderful that she should so dote on Signior Benedick, whom she hath in all outward behaviours seem'd ever to abhor.

BENEDICK. Is't possible? Sits the wind in that corner?

LEONATO. By my troth, my lord, I cannot tell what to think of it; but that she loves him with an enraged affection—it is past the infinite of thought.

DON PEDRO. May be she doth but counterfeit.

CLAUDIO. Faith, like enough.

LEONATO. O God, counterfeit! There was never counterfeit of passion came so near the life of passion as she discovers it.

DON PEDRO. Why, what effects of passion shows she?

CLAUDIO. Bait the hook well; this fish will bite.

LEONATO. What effects, my lord? She will sit you—you heard my daughter tell you how.

CLAUDIO. She did, indeed.

DON PEDRO. How, how, I pray you? You amaze me; I would have thought her spirit had been invincible against all assaults of affection.

LEONATO. I would have sworn it had, my lord; especially against Benedick.

BENEDICK. I should think this a gull, but that the white-bearded fellow speaks it; knavery cannot, sure, hide himself in such reverence.

CLAUDIO. He hath ta'en th' infection; hold it up.

DON PEDRO. Hath she made her affection known to Benedick?

LEONATO. No; and swears she never will; that's her torment.

CLAUDIO. 'Tis true, indeed; so your daughter says. 'Shall I,' says she 'that have so oft encount'red him with scorn, write to him that I love him?'

LEONATO. This says she now, when she is beginning to write to him; for she'll be up twenty times a night; and there will she sit in her smock till she have writ a sheet of paper. My daughter tells us all.

CLAUDIO. Now you talk of a sheet of paper, I remember a pretty jest your daughter told us of.

LEONATO. O, when she had writ it, and was reading it over, she found 'Benedick' and 'Beatrice' between the sheet!

CLAUDIO. That.

LEONATO. O, she tore the letter into a thousand halfpence; rail'd at herself that she should be so immodest to write to one that she knew would flout her. 'I measure him' says she 'by my own spirit; for I should flout him if he writ to me; yea, though I love him, I should.'

CLAUDIO. Then down upon her knees she falls, weeps, sobs, beats her heart, tears her hair, prays, curses—'O sweet Benedick! God give me patience!'

LEONATO. She doth indeed; my daughter says so; and the ecstasy hath so much overborne her that my daughter is sometime afeard she will do a desperate outrage to herself. It is very true.

Don Pedro. It were good that Benedick knew of it by some other, if she will not discover it.

Claudio. To what end? He would make but a sport of it, and torment the poor lady worse.

Don Pedro. An he should, it were an alms to hang him. She's an excellent sweet lady, and, out of all suspicion, she is virtuous.

Claudio. And she is exceeding wise.

Don Pedro. In everything but in loving Benedick.

Leonato. O my lord, wisdom and blood combating in so tender a body, we have ten proofs to one that blood hath the victory. I am sorry for her, as I have just cause, being her uncle and her guardian.

Don Pedro. I would she had bestowed this dotage on me; I would have daff'd all other respects and made her half myself. I pray you, tell Benedick of it, and hear what 'a will say.

Leonato. Were it good, think you?

Claudio. Hero thinks surely she will die; for she says she will die if he love her not; and she will die ere she make her love known; and she will die if he woo her, rather than she will bate one breath of her accustomed crossness.

Don Pedro. She doth well; if she should make tender of her love, 'tis very possible he'll scorn it; for the man, as you know all, hath a contemptible spirit.

Claudio. He is a very proper man.

Don Pedro. He hath, indeed, a good outward happiness.

Claudio. Before God, and in my mind, very wise!

Don Pedro. He doth, indeed, show some sparks that are like wit.

Leonato. And I take him to be valiant.

Don Pedro. As Hector, I assure you; and in the managing of quarrels you may say he is wise, for either he avoids them with great discretion, or undertakes them with a most Christian-like fear.

Leonato. If he do fear God, 'a must necessarily keep peace; if he break the peace, he ought to enter into a quarrel with fear and trembling.

Don Pedro. And so will he do; for the man doth fear God, howsoever it seems not in him by some large jests he will

make. Well, I am sorry for your niece. Shall we go seek
Benedick, and tell him of her love?

CLAUDIO. Never tell him, my lord; let her wear it out with
good counsel.

LEONATO. Nay, that's impossible; she may wear her heart out
first.

DON PEDRO. Well, we will hear further of it by your daughter; let it cool the while. I love Benedick well; and I could
wish he would modestly examine himself, to see how much
he is unworthy so good a lady.

LEONATO. My lord, will you walk? Dinner is ready.

CLAUDIO. If he do not dote on her upon this, I will never
trust my expectation.

DON PEDRO. Let there be the same net spread for her; and
that must your daughter and her gentlewomen carry. The
sport will be when they hold one an opinion of another's
dotage, and no such matter; that's the scene that I would
see, which will be merely a dumb show. Let us send her
to call him in to dinner.

Exeunt DON PEDRO, CLAUDIO, *and* LEONATO

BENEDICK. [*Coming forward*] This can be no trick: the conference was sadly borne; they have the truth of this from
Hero; they seem to pity the lady; it seems her affections
have their full bent. Love me! Why, it must be requited.
I hear how I am censur'd: they say I will bear myself
proudly if I perceive the love come from her; they say,
too, that she will rather die than give any sign of affection.
I did never think to marry. I must not seem proud; happy
are they that hear their detractions and can put them to
mending. They say the lady is fair; 'tis a truth, I can bear
them witness; and virtuous; 'tis so, I cannot reprove it; and
wise, but for loving me. By my troth, it is no addition to
her wit; nor no great argument of her folly, for I will be
horribly in love with her. I may chance have some odd
quirks and remnants of wit broken on me because I have
railed so long against marriage; but doth not the appetite
alter? A man loves the meat in his youth that he cannot
endure in his age. Shall quips, and sentences, and these
paper bullets of the brain, awe a man from the career of
his humour? No; the world must be peopled. When I said

I would die a bachelor, I did not think I should live till I were married. Here comes Beatrice. By this day, she's a fair lady; I do spy some marks of love in her.

Enter BEATRICE

BEATRICE. Against my will I am sent to bid you come in to dinner.

BENEDICK. Fair Beatrice, I thank you for your pains.

BEATRICE. I took no more pains for those thanks than you take pains to thank me; if it had been painful, I would not have come.

BENEDICK. You take pleasure, then, in the message?

BEATRICE. Yea, just so much as you may take upon a knife's point, and choke a daw withal. You have no stomach, signior; fare you well. *Exit*

BENEDICK. Ha! 'Against my will I am sent to bid you come in to dinner'—there's a double meaning in that. 'I took no more pains for those thanks than you took pains to thank me'—that's as much as to say 'Any pains that I take for you is as easy as thanks.' If I do not take pity of her, I am a villain; if I do not love her, I am a Jew. I will go get her picture. *Exit*

ACT III. SCENE 1

LEONATO'S *orchard*

Enter HERO, MARGARET, *and* URSULA

HERO. Good Margaret, run thee to the parlour;
There shalt thou find my cousin Beatrice
Proposing with the Prince and Claudio.
Whisper her ear, and tell her I and Ursula
Walk in the orchard, and our whole discourse
Is all of her; say that thou overheard'st us;
And bid her steal into the pleached bower,
Where honeysuckles, ripened by the sun,
Forbid the sun to enter—like favourites,
Made proud by princes, that advance their pride

Against that power that bred it. There will she hide her
To listen our propose. This is thy office;
Bear thee well in it, and leave us alone.

MARGARET. I'll make her come, I warrant you, presently.

Exit

HERO. Now, Ursula, when Beatrice doth come,
As we do trace this alley up and down,
Our talk must only be of Benedick.
When I do name him, let it be thy part
To praise him more than ever man did merit;
My talk to thee must be how Benedick
Is sick in love with Beatrice. Of this matter
Is little Cupid's crafty arrow made,
That only wounds by hearsay. Now begin;

Enter BEATRICE, *behind*

For look where Beatrice, like a lapwing, runs
Close by the ground, to hear our conference.

URSULA. The pleasant'st angling is to see the fish
Cut with her golden oars the silver stream,
And greedily devour the treacherous bait.
So angle we for Beatrice; who even now
Is couched in the woodbine coverture.
Fear you not my part of the dialogue.

HERO. Then go we near her, that her ear lose nothing
Of the false sweet bait that we lay for it.

[*They advance to the bower*]

No, truly, Ursula, she is too disdainful;
I know her spirits are as coy and wild
As haggards of the rock.

URSULA. But are you sure
That Benedick loves Beatrice so entirely?

HERO. So says the Prince and my new-trothed lord.

URSULA. And did they bid you tell her of it, madam?

HERO. They did entreat me to acquaint her of it;
But I persuaded them, if they lov'd Benedick,
To wish him wrestle with affection,
And never to let Beatrice know of it.

URSULA. Why did you so? Doth not the gentleman
Deserve as full as fortunate a bed

403

As ever Beatrice shall couch upon?

HERO. O god of love! I know he doth deserve
As much as may be yielded to a man;
But nature never fram'd a woman's heart
Of prouder stuff than that of Beatrice.
Disdain and scorn ride sparkling in her eyes,
Misprising what they look on; and her wit
Values itself so highly that to her
All matter else seems weak. She cannot love,
Nor take no shape nor project of affection,
She is so self-endeared.

URSULA. Sure, I think so;
And therefore, certainly, it were not good
She knew his love, lest she'll make sport at it.

HERO. Why, you speak truth. I never yet saw man,
How wise, how noble, young, how rarely featur'd,
But she would spell him backward. If fair-fac'd,
She would swear the gentleman should be her sister;
If black, why, Nature, drawing of an antic,
Made a foul blot; if tall, a lance ill-headed;
If low, an agate very vilely cut;
If speaking, why, a vane blown with all winds;
If silent, why, a block moved with none.
So turns she every man the wrong side out,
And never gives to truth and virtue that
Which simpleness and merit purchaseth.

URSULA. Sure, sure, such carping is not commendable.

HERO. No; not to be so odd and from all fashions,
As Beatrice is, cannot be commendable;
But who dare tell her so? If I should speak,
She would mock me into air; O, she would laugh me
Out of myself, press me to death with wit!
Therefore let Benedick, like cover'd fire,
Consume away in sighs, waste inwardly.
It were a better death than die with mocks,
Which is as bad as die with tickling.

URSULA. Yet tell her of it; hear what she will say.

HERO. No; rather I will go to Benedick
And counsel him to fight against his passion;
And, truly, I'll devise some honest slanders

To stain my cousin with. One doth not know
How much an ill word may empoison liking.
URSULA. O, do not do your cousin such a wrong!
She cannot be so much without true judgment—
Having so swift and excellent a wit
As she is priz'd to have—as to refuse
So rare a gentleman as Signior Benedick.
HERO. He is the only man of Italy,
Always excepted my dear Claudio.
URSULA. I pray you be not angry with me, madam,
Speaking my fancy: Signior Benedick,
For shape, for bearing, argument, and valour,
Goes foremost in report through Italy.
HERO. Indeed, he hath an excellent good name.
URSULA. His excellence did earn it ere he had it.
When are you married, madam?
HERO. Why, every day—to-morrow. Come, go in;
I'll show thee some attires, and have thy counsel
Which is the best to furnish me to-morrow.
URSULA. She's lim'd, I warrant you; we have caught her,
madam.
HERO. If it proves so, then loving goes by haps:
Some Cupid kills with arrows, some with traps.
                              Exeunt HERO *and* URSULA
BEATRICE. [*Coming forward*] What fire is in mine ears? Can
this be true?
Stand I condemn'd for pride and scorn so much?
Contempt, farewell! and maiden pride, adieu!
No glory lives behind the back of such.
And, Benedick, love on; I will requite thee,
Taming my wild heart to thy loving hand;
If thou dost love, my kindness shall incite thee
To bind our loves up in a holy band;
For others say thou dost deserve, and I
Believe it better than reportingly.   *Exit*

SCENE 2

LEONATO's *house*

Enter DON PEDRO, CLAUDIO, BENEDICK, *and* LEONATO

DON PEDRO. I do but stay till your marriage be consummate, and then go I toward Arragon.

CLAUDIO. I'll bring you thither, my lord, if you'll vouchsafe me.

DON PEDRO. Nay, that would be as great a soil in the new gloss of your marriage as to show a child his new coat, and forbid him to wear it. I will only be bold with Benedick for his company; for, from the crown of his head to the sole of his foot, he is all mirth; he hath twice or thrice cut Cupid's bow-string, and the little hangman dare not shoot at him; he hath a heart as sound as a bell, and his tongue is the clapper; for what his heart thinks, his tongue speaks.

BENEDICK. Gallants, I am not as I have been.

LEONATO. So say I; methinks you are sadder.

CLAUDIO. I hope he be in love.

DON PEDRO. Hang him, truant! There's no true drop of blood in him to be truly touch'd with love; if he be sad, he wants money.

BENEDICK. I have the toothache.

DON PEDRO. Draw it.

BENEDICK. Hang it!

CLAUDIO. You must hang it first and draw it afterwards.

DON PEDRO. What! sigh for the toothache?

LEONATO. Where is but a humour or a worm.

BENEDICK. Well, every one can master a grief but he that has it.

CLAUDIO. Yet, say I, he is in love.

DON PEDRO. There is no appearance of fancy in him, unless it be a fancy that he hath to strange disguises; as to be a Dutchman to-day, a Frenchman to-morrow; or in the shape of two countries at once, as a German from the waist downward, all slops, and a Spaniard from the hip upward, no doublet. Unless he have a fancy to this foolery, as it appears he hath, he is no fool for fancy, as you would have it appear he is.

CLAUDIO. If he be not in love with some woman, there is no believing old signs: 'a brushes his hat o' mornings; what should that bode?

DON PEDRO. Hath any man seen him at the barber's?

CLAUDIO. No, but the barber's man hath been seen with him; and the old ornament of his cheek hath already stuff'd tennis-balls.

LEONATO. Indeed, he looks younger than he did, by the loss of a beard.

DON PEDRO. Nay, 'a rubs himself with civet. Can you smell him out by that?

CLAUDIO. That's as much as to say the sweet youth's in love.

DON PEDRO. The greatest note of it is his melancholy.

CLAUDIO. And when was he wont to wash his face?

DON PEDRO. Yea, or to paint himself? For the which I hear what they say of him.

CLAUDIO. Nay, but his jesting spirit, which is now crept into a lute-string, and now govern'd by stops.

DON PEDRO. Indeed, that tells a heavy tale for him; conclude, conclude, he is in love.

CLAUDIO. Nay, but I know who loves him.

DON PEDRO. That would I know too; I warrant, one that knows him not.

CLAUDIO. Yes, and his ill conditions; and, in despite of all, dies for him.

DON PEDRO. She shall be buried with her face upwards.

BENEDICK. Yet is this no charm for the toothache. Old signior, walk aside with me; I have studied eight or nine wise words to speak to you, which these hobby-horses must not hear. *Exeunt* BENEDICK *and* LEONATO

DON PEDRO. For my life, to break with him about Beatrice.

CLAUDIO. 'Tis even so. Hero and Margaret have by this played their parts with Beatrice; and then the two bears will not bite one another when they meet.

Enter DON JOHN

DON JOHN. My lord and brother, God save you!

407

Don Pedro. Good den, brother.

Don John. If your leisure serv'd, I would speak with you.

Don Pedro. In private?

Don John. If it please you; yet Count Claudio may hear, for what I would speak of concerns him.

Don Pedro. What's the matter?

Don John. [*To* Claudio] Means your lordship to be married to-morrow?

Don Pedro. You know he does.

Don John. I know not that, when he knows what I know.

Claudio. If there be any impediment, I pray you discover it.

Don John. You may think I love you not; let that appear hereafter, and aim better at me by that I now will manifest. For my brother, I think he holds you well, and in dearness of heart hath holp to effect your ensuing marriage —surely suit ill spent, and labour ill bestowed.

Don Pedro. Why, what's the matter?

Don John. I came hither to tell you; and, circumstances short'ned, for she has been too long a talking of, the lady is disloyal.

Claudio. Who? Hero?

Don John. Even she—Leonato's Hero, your Hero, every man's Hero.

Claudio. Disloyal?

Don John. The word is too good to paint out her wickedness; I could say she were worse; think you of a worse title, and I will fit her to it. Wonder not till further warrant; go but with me to-night, you shall see her chamber window ent'red, even the night before her wedding-day. If you love her then, to-morrow wed her; but it would better fit your honour to change your mind.

Claudio. May this be so?

Don Pedro. I will not think it.

Don John. If you dare not trust that you see, confess not that you know. If you will follow me, I will show you enough; and when you have seen more, and heard more, proceed accordingly.

Claudio. If I see anything to-night why I should not marry her, to-morrow in the congregation where I should wed, there will I shame her.

DON PEDRO. And, as I wooed for thee to obtain her, I will join with thee to disgrace her.

DON JOHN. I will disparage her no farther till you are my witnesses; bear it coldly but till midnight, and let the issue show itself.

DON PEDRO. O day untowardly turned!

CLAUDIO. O mischief strangely thwarting!

DON JOHN. O plague right well prevented! So will you say when you have seen the sequel. *Exeunt*

SCENE 3

A street

Enter DOGBERRY *and his compartner* VERGES, *with the* WATCH

DOGBERRY. Are you good men and true?

VERGES. Yea, or else it were pity but they should suffer salvation, body and soul.

DOGBERRY. Nay, that were a punishment too good for them, if they should have any allegiance in them, being chosen for the Prince's watch.

VERGES. Well, give them their charge, neighbour Dogberry.

DOGBERRY. First, who think you the most desartless man to be constable?

FIRST WATCH. Hugh Oatcake, sir, or George Seacoal; for they can write and read.

DOGBERRY. Come hither, neighbour Seacoal. God hath bless'd you with a good name. To be a well-favoured man is the gift of fortune; but to write and read comes by nature.

SECOND WATCH. Both which, Master Constable—

DOGBERRY. You have; I knew it would be your answer. Well, for your favour, sir; why, give God thanks, and make no boast of it; and for your writing and reading, let that appear when there is no need of such vanity. You are thought here to be the most senseless and fit man for the constable of the watch; therefore bear you the lantern. This is your charge: you shall comprehend all vagrom men; you are to bid any man stand, in the Prince's name.

SECOND WATCH. How if 'a will not stand?

DOGBERRY. Why, then, take no note of him, but let him go; and presently call the rest of the watch together, and thank God you are rid of a knave.

VERGES. If he will not stand when he is bidden, he is none of the Prince's subjects.

DOGBERRY. True, and they are to meddle with none but the Prince's subjects. You shall also make no noise in the streets; for for the watch to babble and to talk is most tolerable and not to be endured.

SECOND WATCH. We will rather sleep than talk; we know what belongs to a watch.

DOGBERRY. Why, you speak like an ancient and most quiet watchman, for I cannot see how sleeping should offend; only, have a care that your bills be not stol'n. Well, you are to call at all the alehouses, and bid those that are drunk get them to bed.

SECOND WATCH. How if they will not?

DOGBERRY. Why, then, let them alone till they are sober; if they make you not then the better answer, you may say they are not the men you took them for.

SECOND WATCH. Well, sir.

DOGBERRY. If you meet a thief, you may suspect him, by virtue of your office, to be no true man; and, for such kind of men, the less you meddle or make with them, why, the more is for your honesty.

SECOND WATCH. If we know him to be a thief, shall we not lay hands on him?

DOGBERRY. Truly, by your office you may, but I think they that touch pitch will be defil'd; the most peaceable way for you, if you do take a thief, is to let him show himself what he is, and steal out of your company.

VERGES. You have been always called a merciful man, partner.

DOGBERRY. Truly, I would not hang a dog by my will, much more a man who hath any honesty in him.

VERGES. If you hear a child cry in the night, you must call to the nurse and bid her still it.

SECOND WATCH. How if the nurse be asleep and will not hear us?

DOGBERRY. Why, then, depart in peace, and let the child wake her with crying; for the ewe that will not hear her lamb when it baes will never answer a calf when he bleats.
VERGES. 'Tis very true.
DOGBERRY. This is the end of the charge: you, constable, are to present the Prince's own person; if you meet the Prince in the night, you may stay him.
VERGES. Nay, by'r lady, that I think 'a cannot.
DOGBERRY. Five shillings to one on't, with any man that knows the statues, he may stay him; marry, not without the Prince be willing; for, indeed, the watch ought to offend no man, and it is an offence to stay a man against his will.
VERGES. By'r lady, I think it be so.
DOGBERRY. Ha, ah, ha! Well, masters, good night; an there be any matter of weight chances, call up me; keep your fellows' counsels and your own, and good night. Come, neighbour.
SECOND WATCH. Well, masters, we hear our charge; let us go sit here upon the church bench till two, and then all to bed.
DOGBERRY. One word more, honest neighbours: I pray you watch about Signior Leonato's door; for the wedding being there to-morrow, there is a great coil to-night. Adieu; be vigilant, I beseech you.

Exeunt DOGBERRY *and* VERGES

Enter BORACHIO *and* CONRADE

BORACHIO. What, Conrade!
SECOND WATCH. [*Aside*] Peace, stir not.
BORACHIO. Conrade, I say!
CONRADE. Here, man, I am at thy elbow.
BORACHIO. Mass, and my elbow itch'd; I thought there would a scab follow.
CONRADE. I will owe thee an answer for that; and now forward with thy tale.
BORACHIO. Stand thee close then under this penthouse, for it drizzles rain; and I will, like a true drunkard, utter all to thee.

SECOND WATCH. [*Aside*] Some treason, masters; yet stand close.

BORACHIO. Therefore know I have earned of Don John a thousand ducats.

CONRADE. Is it possible that any villainy should be so dear?

BORACHIO. Thou shouldst rather ask if it were possible any villainy should be so rich; for when rich villains have need of poor ones, poor ones may make what price they will.

CONRADE. I wonder at it.

BORACHIO. That shows thou art unconfirm'd. Thou knowest that the fashion of a doublet, or a hat, or a cloak, is nothing to a man.

CONRADE. Yes, it is apparel.

BORACHIO. I mean the fashion.

CONRADE. Yes, the fashion is the fashion.

BORACHIO. Tush! I may as well say the fool's the fool. But seest thou not what a deformed thief this fashion is?

SECOND WATCH. [*Aside*] I know that Deformed; 'a has been a vile thief this seven year; 'a goes up and down like a gentleman; I remember his name.

BORACHIO. Didst thou not hear somebody?

CONRADE. No; 'twas the vane on the house.

BORACHIO. Seest thou not, I say, what a deformed thief this fashion is, how giddily 'a turns about all the hot bloods between fourteen and five and thirty, sometimes fashioning them like Pharaoh's soldiers in the reechy painting, sometime like god Bel's priests in the old church-window, sometime like the shaven Hercules in the smirch'd worm-eaten tapestry, where his codpiece seems as massy as his club?

CONRADE. All this I see; and I see that the fashion wears out more apparel than the man. But art not thou thyself giddy with the fashion too, that thou hast shifted out of thy tale into telling me of the fashion?

BORACHIO. Not so neither; but know that I have to-night wooed Margaret, the Lady Hero's gentlewoman, by the name of Hero; she leans me out at her mistress' chamber-window, bids me a thousand times good night—I tell this tale vilely. I should first tell thee how the Prince, Claudio, and my master, planted and placed and possessed by my master Don John, saw afar off in the orchard this amiable encounter.

CONRADE. And thought they Margaret was Hero?

BORACHIO. Two of them did, the Prince and Claudio; but the devil my master knew she was Margaret; and partly by his oaths, which first possess'd them, partly by the dark night, which did deceive them, but chiefly by my villainy, which did confirm any slander that Don John had made, away went Claudio enrag'd; swore he would meet her, as he was appointed, next morning at the temple, and there, before the whole congregation, shame her with what he saw o'er night, and send her home again without a husband.

SECOND WATCH. We charge you in the Prince's name, stand.

FIRST WATCH. Call up the right Master Constable; we have here recover'd the most dangerous piece of lechery that ever was known in the commonwealth.

SECOND WATCH. And one Deformed is one of them; I know him, 'a wears a lock.

CONRADE. Masters, masters!

SECOND WATCH. You'll be made bring Deformed forth, I warrant you.

CONRADE. Masters—

FIRST WATCH. Never speak, we charge you; let us obey you to go with us.

BORACHIO. We are like to prove a goodly commodity, being taken up of these men's bills.

CONRADE. A commodity in question, I warrant you. Come, we'll obey you. *Exeunt*

SCENE 4

HERO'S *apartment*

Enter HERO, MARGARET, *and* URSULA

HERO. Good Ursula, wake my cousin Beatrice, and desire her to rise.

URSULA. I will, lady.

HERO. And bid her come hither.

413

URSULA. Well. *Exit* URSULA

MARGARET. Troth, I think your other rabato were better.

HERO. No, pray thee, good Meg, I'll wear this.

MARGARET. By my troth's not so good; and I warrant your cousin will say so.

HERO. My cousin's a fool, and thou art another; I'll wear none but this.

MARGARET. I like the new tire within excellently, if the hair were a thought browner; and your gown's a most rare fashion, i' faith. I saw the Duchess of Milan's gown that they praise so.

HERO. O, that exceeds, they say.

MARGARET. By my troth's but a night-gown in respect of yours—cloth o' gold, and cuts, and lac'd with silver, set with pearls, down sleeves, side sleeves, and skirts, round underborne with a bluish tinsel; but for a fine, quaint, graceful, and excellent fashion, yours is worth ten on't.

HERO. God give me joy to wear it, for my heart is exceeding heavy.

MARGARET. 'Twill be heavier soon, by the weight of a man.

HERO. Fie upon thee! art not ashamed?

MARGARET. O what, lady, of speaking honourably? Is not marriage honourable in a beggar? Is not your lord honourable without marriage? I think you would have me say 'saving your reverence, a husband'; an bad thinking do not wrest true speaking I'll offend nobody. Is there any harm in 'the heavier for a husband'? None, I think, an it be the right husband and the right wife; otherwise 'tis light, and not heavy. Ask my Lady Beatrice else; here she comes.

Enter BEATRICE

HERO. Good morrow, coz.

BEATRICE. Good morrow, sweet Hero.

HERO. Why, how now! do you speak in the sick tune?

BEATRICE. I am out of all other tune, methinks.

MARGARET. Clap's into 'Light o' love'; that goes without a burden. Do you sing it, and I'll dance it.

BEATRICE. Ye light o' love with your heels! Then if your husband have stables enough, you'll see he shall lack no barnes.

MARGARET. O illegitimate construction! I scorn that with my heels.

BEATRICE. 'Tis almost five o'clock, cousin; 'tis time you were ready. By my troth, I am exceeding ill. Heigh-ho!

MARGARET. For a hawk, a horse, or a husband?

BEATRICE. For the letter that begins them all—H.

MARGARET. Well, an you be not turn'd Turk, there's no more sailing by the star.

BEATRICE. What means the fool, trow?

MARGARET. Nothing I; but God send every one their heart's desire!

HERO. These gloves the Count sent me; they are an excellent perfume.

BEATRICE. I am stuff'd, cousin, I cannot smell.

MARGARET. A maid and stuff'd! There's goodly catching of cold.

BEATRICE. O, God help me! God help me! How long have you profess'd apprehension?

MARGARET. Ever since you left it. Doth not my wit become me rarely?

BEATRICE. It is not seen enough; you should wear it in your cap. By my troth, I am sick.

MARGARET. Get you some of this distill'd Carduus Benedictus, and lay it to your heart; it is the only thing for a qualm.

HERO. There thou prick'st her with a thistle.

BEATRICE. Benedictus! why Benedictus? You have some moral in this 'Benedictus.'

MARGARET. Moral? No, by my troth, I have no moral meaning; I meant plain holy-thistle. You may think, perchance, that I think you are in love. Nay, by'r lady, I am not such a fool to think what I list; nor I list not to think what I can; nor, indeed, I cannot think, if I would think my heart out of thinking, that you are in love, or that you will be in love, or that you can be in love. Yet Benedick was such another, and now is he become a man; he swore he would never marry, and yet now, in despite of his heart, he eats his meat without grudging. And how you may be converted I know not; but methinks you look with your eyes as other women do.

BEATRICE. What pace is this that thy tongue keeps?
MARGARET. Not a false gallop.

Re-enter URSULA

URSULA. Madam, withdraw; the Prince, the Count, Signior
Benedick, Don John, and all the gallants of the town, are
come to fetch you to church.
HERO. Help to dress me, good coz, good Meg, good Ursula.

Exeunt

SCENE 5

LEONATO's *house*

Enter LEONATO, *with* DOGBERRY *and* VERGES

LEONATO. What would you with me, honest neighbour?
DOGBERRY. Marry, sir, I would have some confidence with
you that decerns you nearly.
LEONATO. Brief, I pray you; for you see it is a busy time with
me.
DOGBERRY. Marry, this it is, sir.
VERGES. Yes, in truth it is, sir.
LEONATO. What is it, my good friends?
DOGBERRY. Goodman Verges, sir, speaks a little off the mat-
ter—an old man, sir, and his wits are not so blunt as, God
help, I would desire they were; but, in faith, honest as the
skin between his brows.
VERGES. Yes, I thank God I am as honest as any man living
that is an old man and no honester than I.
DOGBERRY. Comparisons are odorous; palabras, neighbour
Verges.
LEONATO. Neighbours, you are tedious.
DOGBERRY. It pleases your worship to say so, but we are the
poor Duke's officers; but, truly, for mine own part, if I
were as tedious as a king, I could find in my heart to bestow it all of your worship.
LEONATO. All thy tediousness on me, ah?
DOGBERRY. Yea, an 'twere a thousand pound more than 'tis;
for I hear as good exclamation on your worship as of any

man in the city; and though I be but a poor man, I am
glad to hear it.

VERGES. And so am I.

LEONATO. I would fain know what you have to say.

VERGES. Marry, sir, our watch to-night, excepting your worship's presence, ha' ta'en a couple of as arrant knaves as
any in Messina.

DOGBERRY. A good old man, sir, he will be talking; as they
say 'When the age is in the wit is out.' God help us, it is
a world to see! Well said, i' faith, neighbour Verges; well,
God's a good man; an two men ride of a horse, one must
ride behind. An honest soul, i' faith, sir, by my troth he is,
as ever broke bread; but God is to be worshipp'd; all men
are not alike; alas, good neighbour!

LEONATO. Indeed, neighbour, he comes too short of you.

DOGBERRY. Gifts that God gives.

LEONATO. I must leave you.

DOGBERRY. One word, sir: our watch, sir, have indeed com-
prehended two aspicious persons, and we would have them
this morning examined before your worship.

LEONATO. Take their examination yourself, and bring it me;
I am now in great haste, as it may appear unto you.

DOGBERRY. It shall be suffigance.

LEONATO. Drink some wine ere you go; fare you well.

Enter a MESSENGER

MESSENGER. My lord, they stay for you to give your daughter to her husband.

LEONATO. I'll wait upon them; I am ready.

Exeunt LEONATO *and* MESSENGER

DOGBERRY. Go, good partner, go, get you to Francis Seacoal;
bid him bring his pen and inkhorn to the gaol; we are now
to examination these men.

VERGES. And we must do it wisely.

DOGBERRY. We will spare for no wit, I warrant you; here's
that shall drive some of them to a non-come; only get the
learned writer to set down our excommunication, and meet
me at the gaol.   *Exeunt*

ACT IV. SCENE 1

A church

Enter Don Pedro, Don John, Leonato, Friar Francis, Claudio, Benedick, Hero, Beatrice, *and* Attendants

Leonato. Come, Friar Francis, be brief; only to the plain form of marriage, and you shall recount their particular duties afterwards.

Friar. You come hither, my lord, to marry this lady?

Claudio. No.

Leonato. To be married to her, friar! You come to marry her.

Friar. Lady, you come hither to be married to this count?

Hero. I do.

Friar. If either of you know any inward impediment why you should not be conjoined, I charge you, on your souls, to utter it.

Claudio. Know you any, Hero?

Hero. None, my lord.

Friar. Know you any, Count?

Leonato. I dare make his answer, None.

Claudio. O, what men dare do! What men may do! What men daily do, not knowing what they do!

Benedick. How now! Interjections? Why, then, some be of laughing, as, ah, ha, he!

Claudio. Stand thee by, friar. Father, by your leave:
Will you with free and unconstrained soul
Give me this maid, your daughter?

Leonato. As freely, son, as God did give her me.

Claudio. And what have I to give you back whose worth
May counterpoise this rich and precious gift?

Don Pedro. Nothing, unless you render her again.

Claudio. Sweet Prince, you learn me noble thankfulness.
There, Leonato, take her back again;
Give not this rotten orange to your friend;
She's but the sign and semblance of her honour.
Behold how like a maid she blushes here.

418

O, what authority and show of truth
Can cunning sin cover itself withal!
Comes not that blood as modest evidence
To witness simple virtue? Would you not swear,
All you that see her, that she were a maid
By these exterior shows? But she is none:
She knows the heat of a luxurious bed;
Her blush is guiltiness, not modesty.
LEONATO. What do you mean, my lord?
CLAUDIO. Not to be married,
Not to knit my soul to an approved wanton.
LEONATO. Dear, my lord, if you, in your own proof,
Have vanquish'd the resistance of her youth,
And made defeat of her virginity—
CLAUDIO. I know what you would say. If I have known her,
You will say she did embrace me as a husband,
And so extenuate the 'forehand sin.
No, Leonato,
I never tempted her with word too large
But, as a brother to his sister, show'd
Bashful sincerity and comely love.
HERO. And seem'd I ever otherwise to you?
CLAUDIO. Out on thee! Seeming! I will write against it.
You seem to me as Dian in her orb,
As chaste as is the bud ere it be blown;
But you are more intemperate in your blood
Than Venus, or those pamp'red animals
That rage in savage sensuality.
HERO. Is my lord well, that he doth speak so wide?
LEONATO. Sweet Prince, why speak not you?
DON PEDRO. What should I speak?
I stand dishonour'd that have gone about
To link my dear friend to a common stale.
LEONATO. Are these things spoken, or do I but dream?
DON JOHN. Sir, they are spoken, and these things are true.
BENEDICK. This looks not like a nuptial.
HERO. True! O God.
CLAUDIO. Leonato, stand I here?
Is this the Prince? Is this the Prince's brother?
Is this face Hero's? Are our eyes our own?

LEONATO. All this is so, but what of this, my lord?
CLAUDIO. Let me but move one question to your daughter;
  And, by that fatherly and kindly power
  That you have in her, bid her answer truly.
LEONATO. I charge thee do so, as thou art my child.
HERO. O, God defend me! how am I beset!
  What kind of catechising call you this?
CLAUDIO. To make you answer truly to your name.
HERO. Is it not Hero? Who can blot that name
  With any just reproach?
CLAUDIO. Marry, that can Hero;
  Hero itself can blot out Hero's virtue.
  What man was he talk'd with you yesternight
  Out at your window, betwixt twelve and one?
  Now, if you are a maid, answer to this.
HERO. I talk'd with no man at that hour, my lord.
DON PEDRO. Why, then are you no maiden. Leonato,
  I am sorry you must hear: upon mine honour,
  Myself, my brother, and this grieved Count,
  Did see her, hear her, at that hour last night,
  Talk with a ruffian at her chamber window;
  Who hath, indeed, most like a liberal villain,
  Confess'd the vile encounters they have had
  A thousand times in secret.
DON JOHN. Fie, fie! they are not to be nam'd, my lord,
  Not to be spoke of;
  There is not chastity enough in language
  Without offence to utter them. Thus, pretty lady,
  I am sorry for thy much misgovernment.
CLAUDIO. O Hero, what a Hero hadst thou been,
  If half thy outward graces had been placed
  About thy thoughts and counsels of thy heart!
  But fare thee well, most foul, most fair! Farewell,
  Thou pure impiety and impious purity!
  For thee I'll lock up all the gates of love,
  And on my eyelids shall conjecture hang,
  To turn all beauty into thoughts of harm,
  And never shall it more be gracious.
LEONATO. Hath no man's dagger here a point for me?
                          [HERO *swoons*]

BEATRICE. Why, how now, cousin! Wherefore sink you
 down?
DON JOHN. Come, let us go. These things, come thus to light,
 Smother her spirits up.
                    Exeunt DON PEDRO, DON JOHN, *and* CLAUDIO
BENEDICK. How doth the lady?
BEATRICE. Dead, I think. Help, uncle!
 Hero, why, Hero! Uncle! Signior Benedick! Friar!
LEONATO. O Fate, take not away thy heavy hand!
 Death is the fairest cover for her shame
 That may be wish'd for.
BEATRICE. How now, cousin Hero!
FRIAR. Have comfort, lady.
LEONATO. Dost thou look up?
FRIAR. Yea; wherefore should she not?
LEONATO. Wherefore! Why, doth not every earthly thing
 Cry shame upon her? Could she here deny
 The story that is printed in her blood?
 Do not live, Hero; do not ope thine eyes;
 For, did I think thou wouldst not quickly die,
 Thought I thy spirits were stronger than thy shames,
 Myself would, on the rearward of reproaches,
 Strike at thy life. Griev'd I, I had but one?
 Chid I for that at frugal nature's frame?
 O, one too much by thee! Why had I one?
 Why ever wast thou lovely in my eyes?
 Why had I not, with charitable hand,
 Took up a beggar's issue at my gates,
 Who smirched thus and mir'd with infamy,
 I might have said 'No part of it is mine;
 This shame derives itself from unknown loins'?
 But mine, and mine I lov'd, and mine I prais'd,
 And mine that I was proud on; mine so much
 That I myself was to myself not mine,
 Valuing of her—why, she, O, she is fall'n
 Into a pit of ink, that the wide sea
 Hath drops too few to wash her clean again,
 And salt too little which may season give
 To her foul tainted flesh!
BENEDICK. Sir, sir, be patient.

For my part, I am so attir'd in wonder,
I know not what to say.
BEATRICE. O, on my soul, my cousin is belied!
BENEDICK. Lady, were you her bedfellow last night?
BEATRICE. No, truly not; although, until last night,
I have this twelvemonth been her bedfellow.
LEONATO. Confirm'd, confirm'd! O, that is stronger made
Which was before barr'd up with ribs of iron!
Would the two princes lie; and Claudio lie,
Who lov'd her so, that, speaking of her foulness,
Wash'd it with tears? Hence from her! let her die.
FRIAR. Hear me a little;
For I have only been silent so long,
And given way unto this course of fortune,
By noting of the lady: I have mark'd
A thousand blushing apparitions
To start into her face, a thousand innocent shames
In angel whiteness beat away those blushes;
And in her eye there hath appear'd a fire
To burn the errors that these princes hold
Against her maiden truth. Call me a fool;
Trust not my reading nor my observations,
Which with experimental seal doth warrant
The tenour of my book; trust not my age,
My reverence, calling, nor divinity,
If this sweet lady lie not guiltless here
Under some biting error.
LEONATO. Friar, it cannot be.
Thou seest that all the grace that she hath left
Is that she will not add to her damnation
A sin of perjury; she not denies it.
Why seek'st thou then to cover with excuse
That which appears in proper nakedness?
FRIAR. Lady, what man is he you are accus'd of?
HERO. They know that do accuse me; I know none.
If I know more of any man alive
Than that which maiden modesty doth warrant,
Let all my sins lack mercy! O my father,
Prove you that any man with me convers'd
At hours unmeet, or that I yesternight

Maintain'd the change of words with any creature,
Refuse me, hate me, torture me to death.
FRIAR. There is some strange misprision in the princes.
BENEDICK. Two of them have the very bent of honour;
And if their wisdoms be misled in this,
The practice of it lives in John the bastard,
Whose spirits toil in frame of villainies.
LEONATO. I know not. If they speak but truth of her,
These hands shall tear her; if they wrong her honour,
The proudest of them shall well hear of it.
Time hath not yet so dried this blood of mine,
Nor age so eat up my invention,
Nor fortune made such havoc of my means,
Nor my bad life reft me so much of friends,
But they shall find awak'd in such a kind
Both strength of limb and policy of mind,
Ability in means and choice of friends,
To quit me of them throughly.
FRIAR. Pause awhile,
And let my counsel sway you in this case.
Your daughter here the princes left for dead;
Let her awhile be secretly kept in,
And publish it that she is dead indeed;
Maintain a mourning ostentation,
And on your family's old monument
Hang mournful epitaphs, and do all rites
That appertain unto a burial.
LEONATO. What shall become of this? What will this do?
FRIAR. Marry, this, well carried, shall on her behalf
Change slander to remorse; that is some good.
But not for that dream I on this strange course,
But on this travail look for greater birth.
She dying, as it must be so maintain'd,
Upon the instant that she was accus'd,
Shall be lamented, pitied, and excus'd,
Of every hearer; for it so falls out
That what we have we prize not to the worth
Whiles we enjoy it, but being lack'd and lost,
Why, then we rack the value, then we find
The virtue that possession would not show us

Whiles it was ours. So will it fare with Claudio.
When he shall hear she died upon his words,
Th' idea of her life shall sweetly creep
Into his study of imagination,
And every lovely organ of her life
Shall come apparell'd in more precious habit,
More moving, delicate, and full of life,
Into the eye and prospect of his soul,
Than when she liv'd indeed. Then shall he mourn,
If ever love had interest in his liver,
And wish he had not so accused her—
No, though he thought his accusation true.
Let this be so, and doubt not but success
Will fashion the event in better shape
Than I can lay it down in likelihood.
But if all aim but this be levell'd false,
The supposition of the lady's death
Will quench the wonder of her infamy.
And if it sort not well, you may conceal her,
As best befits her wounded reputation,
In some reclusive and religious life,
Out of all eyes, tongues, minds, and injuries.
BENEDICK. Signior Leonato, let the friar advise you;
And though you know my inwardness and love
Is very much unto the Prince and Claudio,
Yet, by mine honour, I will deal in this
As secretly and justly as your soul
Should with your body.
LEONATO. Being that I flow in grief
The smallest twine may lead me.
FRIAR. 'Tis well consented. Presently away;
For to strange sores strangely they strain the cure.
Come, lady, die to live; this wedding day
Perhaps is but prolong'd; have patience and endure.
Exeunt all but BENEDICK *and* BEATRICE
BENEDICK. Lady Beatrice, have you wept all this while?
BEATRICE. Yea, and I will weep a while longer.
BENEDICK. I will not desire that.
BEATRICE. You have no reason; I do it freely.
BENEDICK. Surely I do believe your fair cousin is wronged.

BEATRICE. Ah, how much might the man deserve of me that would right her!

BENEDICK. Is there any way to show such friendship?

BEATRICE. A very even way, but no such friend.

BENEDICK. May a man do it?

BEATRICE. It is a man's office, but not yours.

BENEDICK. I do love nothing in the world so well as you. Is not that strange?

BEATRICE. As strange as the thing I know not. It were as possible for me to say I lov'd nothing so well as you; but believe me not, and yet I lie not; I confess nothing, nor I deny nothing. I am sorry for my cousin.

BENEDICK. By my sword, Beatrice, thou lovest me.

BEATRICE. Do not swear, and eat it.

BENEDICK. I will swear by it that you love me; and I will make him eat it that says I love not you.

BEATRICE. Will you not eat your word?

BENEDICK. With no sauce that can be devised to it; I protest I love thee.

BEATRICE. Why, then, God forgive me!

BENEDICK. What offence, sweet Beatrice?

BEATRICE. You have stayed me in a happy hour; I was about to protest I loved you.

BENEDICK. And do it with all thy heart?

BEATRICE. I love you with so much of my heart that none is left to protest.

BENEDICK. Come, bid me do anything for thee.

BEATRICE. Kill Claudio.

BENEDICK. Ha! not for the wide world.

BEATRICE. You kill me to deny it. Farewell.

BENEDICK. Tarry, sweet Beatrice.

BEATRICE. I am gone though I am here; there is no love in you; nay, I pray you, let me go.

BENEDICK. Beatrice—

BEATRICE. In faith, I will go.

BENEDICK. We'll be friends first.

BEATRICE. You dare easier be friends with me than fight with mine enemy.

BENEDICK. Is Claudio thine enemy?

BEATRICE. Is 'a not approved in the height a villain that hath

slandered, scorned, dishonoured, my kinswoman? O that I
were a man! What! bear her in hand until they come to
take hands, and then with public accusation, uncover'd
slander, unmitigated rancour—O God, that I were a man!
I would eat his heart in the market-place.

BENEDICK. Hear me, Beatrice.

BEATRICE. Talk with a man out a window! A proper saying!

BENEDICK. Nay, but, Beatrice—

BEATRICE. Sweet Hero! She is wrong'd, she is sland'red, she
is undone.

BENEDICK. Beat—

BEATRICE. Princes and Counties! Surely, a princely testimony,
a goodly count, Count Comfect; a sweet gallant, surely!
O that I were a man for his sake! or that I had any friend
would be a man for my sake! But manhood is melted into
curtsies, valour into compliment, and men are only turn'd
into tongue, and trim ones too. He is now as valiant as
Hercules that only tells a lie and swears it. I cannot be a
man with wishing, therefore I will die a woman with grieving.

BENEDICK. Tarry, good Beatrice. By this hand, I love thee.

BEATRICE. Use it for my love some other way than swearing
by it.

BENEDICK. Think you in your soul the Count Claudio hath
wrong'd Hero?

BEATRICE. Yea, as sure as I have a thought or a soul.

BENEDICK. Enough, I am engag'd; I will challenge him; I
will kiss your hand, and so I leave you. By this hand,
Claudio shall render me a dear account. As you hear of
me, so think of me. Go comfort your cousin; I must say
she is dead; and so, farewell. *Exeunt*

SCENE 2

A prison

Enter DOGBERRY, VERGES, *and* SEXTON, *in gowns; and the*
WATCH, *with* CONRADE *and* BORACHIO

DOGBERRY. Is our whole dissembly appear'd?

VERGES. O, a stool and a cushion for the sexton!

SEXTON. Which be the malefactors?

DOGBERRY. Marry, that am I and my partner.

VERGES. Nay, that's certain; we have the exhibition to examine.

SEXTON. But which are the offenders that are to be examin'd? Let them come before Master Constable.

DOGBERRY. Yea, marry, let them come before me. What is your name, friend?

BORACHIO. Borachio.

DOGBERRY. Pray write down Borachio. Yours, sirrah?

CONRADE. I am a gentleman, sir, and my name is Conrade.

DOGBERRY. Write down Master Gentleman Conrade. Masters, do you serve God?

CONRADE. ⎫
BORACHIO. ⎬ Yea, sir, we hope.

DOGBERRY. Write down that they hope they serve God; and write God first; for God defend but God should go before such villains! Masters, it is proved already that you are little better than false knaves, and it will go near to be thought so shortly. How answer you for yourselves?

CONRADE. Marry, sir, we say we are none.

DOGBERRY. A marvellous witty fellow, I assure you; but I will go about with him. Come you hither, sirrah; a word in your ear: sir, I say to you it is thought you are false knaves.

BORACHIO. Sir, I say to you we are none.

DOGBERRY. Well, stand aside. Fore God, they are both in a tale. Have you writ down that they are none?

SEXTON. Master Constable, you go not the way to examine; you must call forth the watch that are their accusers.

DOGBERRY. Yea, marry, that's the eftest way. Let the watch come forth. Masters, I charge you in the Prince's name, accuse these men.

FIRST WATCHMAN. This man said, sir, that Don John, the Prince's brother, was a villain.

DOGBERRY. Write down Prince John a villain. Why, this is flat perjury, to call a prince's brother villain.

BORACHIO. Master Constable—

427

DOGBERRY. Pray thee, fellow, peace; I do not like thy look, I promise thee.

SEXTON. What heard you him say else?

SECOND WATCHMAN. Marry, that he had received a thousand ducats of Don John for accusing the Lady Hero wrongfully.

DOGBERRY. Flat burglary as ever was committed.

VERGES. Yea, by mass, that it is.

SEXTON. What else, fellow?

FIRST WATCHMAN. And that Count Claudio did mean, upon his words, to disgrace Hero before the whole assembly, and not marry her.

DOGBERRY. O villain! thou wilt be condemn'd into everlasting redemption for this.

SEXTON. What else?

SECOND WATCHMAN. This is all.

SEXTON. And this is more, masters, than you can deny. Prince John is this morning secretly stol'n away; Hero was in this manner accus'd, in this very manner refus'd, and upon the grief of this suddenly died. Master Constable, let these men be bound and brought to Leonato's; I will go before and show him their examination.

Exit SEXTON

DOGBERRY. Come, let them be opinion'd.

VERGES. Let them be in the hands.

CONRADE. Off, coxcomb.

DOGBERRY. God's my life, where's the sexton? Let him write down the Prince's officer coxcomb. Come, bind them. Thou naughty varlet!

CONRADE. Away! you are an ass, you are an ass.

DOGBERRY. Dost thou not suspect my place? Dost thou not suspect my years? O that he were here to write me down an ass! But, masters, remember that I am an ass; though it be not written down, yet forget not that I am an ass. No, thou villain, thou art full of piety, as shall be prov'd upon thee by good witness. I am a wise fellow; and, which is more, an officer; and, which is more, a householder; and, which is more, as pretty a piece of flesh as any is in Messina; and one that knows the law, go to; and a rich fellow enough, go to; and a fellow that hath had losses; and one

that hath two gowns, and everything handsome about him.
Bring him away. O that I had been writ down an ass!

Exeunt

ACT V. SCENE 1

Before LEONATO's *house*

Enter LEONATO *and* ANTONIO

ANTONIO. If you go on thus, you will kill yourself,
And 'tis not wisdom thus to second grief
Against yourself.
LEONATO. I pray thee cease thy counsel,
Which falls into mine ears as profitless
As water in a sieve. Give not me counsel;
Nor let no comforter delight mine ear
But such a one whose wrongs do suit with mine.
Bring me a father that so lov'd his child,
Whose joy of her is overwhelm'd like mine,
And bid him speak of patience;
Measure his woe the length and breadth of mine,
And let it answer every strain for strain;
As thus for thus, and such a grief for such,
In every lineament, branch, shape, and form.
If such a one will smile and stroke his beard,
And sorrow wag, cry 'hem!' when he should groan,
Patch grief with proverbs, make misfortune drunk
With candle-wasters—bring him yet to me,
And I of him will gather patience.
But there is no such man; for, brother, men
Can counsel and speak comfort to that grief
Which they themselves not feel; but, tasting it,
Their counsel turns to passion, which before
Would give preceptial medicine to rage,
Fetter strong madness in a silken thread,
Charm ache with air and agony with words.
No, no; 'tis all men's office to speak patience

To those that wring under the load of sorrow,
But no man's virtue nor sufficiency
To be so moral when he shall endure
The like himself. Therefore, give me no counsel;
My griefs cry louder than advertisement.

ANTONIO. Therein do men from children nothing differ.

LEONATO. I pray thee peace; I will be flesh and blood;
For there was never yet philosopher
That could endure the toothache patiently,
However they have writ the style of gods,
And made a push at chance and sufferance.

ANTONIO. Yet bend not all the harm upon yourself;
Make those that do offend you suffer too.

LEONATO. There thou speak'st reason; nay, I will do so.
My soul doth tell me Hero is belied;
And that shall Claudio know; so shall the Prince,
And all of them that thus dishonour her.

ANTONIO. Here comes the Prince and Claudio hastily.

Enter DON PEDRO *and* CLAUDIO

DON PEDRO. Good den, good den.

CLAUDIO. Good day to both of you.

LEONATO. Hear you, my lords!

DON PEDRO. We have some haste, Leonato.

LEONATO. Some haste, my lord! Well, fare you well, my
lord.
Are you so hasty now? Well, all is one.

DON PEDRO. Nay, do not quarrel with us, good old man.

ANTONIO. If he could right himself with quarrelling,
Some of us would lie low.

CLAUDIO. Who wrongs him?

LEONATO. Marry, thou dost wrong me; thou dissembler,
thou!
Nay, never lay thy hand upon thy sword;
I fear thee not.

CLAUDIO. Marry, beshrew my hand
If it should give your age such cause of fear!
In faith, my hand meant nothing to my sword.

LEONATO. Tush, tush, man; never fleer and jest at me;
I speak not like a dotard nor a fool,

As under privilege of age to brag
What I have done being young, or what would do
Were I not old. Know, Claudio, to thy head,
Thou hast so wrong'd mine innocent child and me
That I am forc'd to lay my reverence by,
And with grey hairs and bruise of many days
Do challenge thee to trial of a man.
I say thou hast belied mine innocent child;
Thy slander hath gone through and through her heart,
And she lies buried with her ancestors—
O! in a tomb where never scandal slept,
Save this of hers, fram'd by thy villainy.

CLAUDIO. My villainy!

LEONATO. Thine, Claudio; thine, I say.

DON PEDRO. You say not right, old man.

LEONATO. My lord, my lord,
I'll prove it on his body if he dare,
Despite his nice fence and his active practice,
His May of youth and bloom of lustihood.

CLAUDIO. Away! I will not have to do with you.

LEONATO. Canst thou so daff me? Thou hast kill'd my child;
If thou kill'st me, boy, thou shalt kill a man.

ANTONIO. He shall kill two of us, and men indeed;
But that's no matter; let him kill one first.
Win me and wear me; let him answer me.
Come, follow me, boy; come, sir boy, come follow me;
Sir boy, I'll whip you from your foining fence;
Nay, as I am a gentleman, I will.

LEONATO. Brother—

ANTONIO. Content yourself. God knows I lov'd my niece;
And she is dead, slander'd to death by villains,
That dare as well answer a man indeed
As I dare take a serpent by the tongue.
Boys, apes, braggarts, Jacks, milksops!

LEONATO. Brother Antony—

ANTONIO. Hold you content. What, man! I know them, yea,
And what they weigh, even to the utmost scruple—
Scambling, out-facing, fashion-monging boys,
That lie and cog and flout, deprave and slander,
Go anticly, and show outward hideousness,

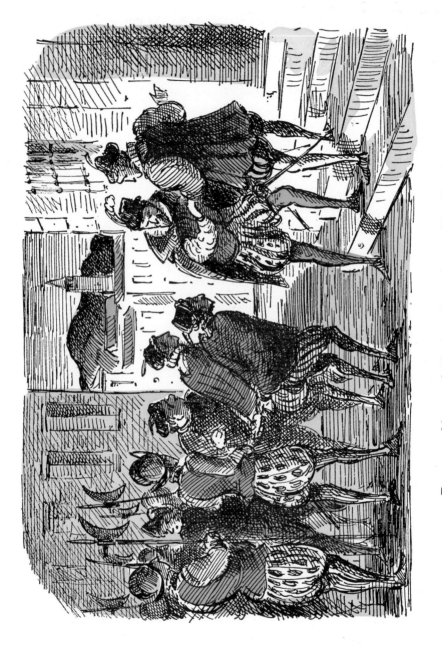

DON PEDRO. *Runs not this speech like iron through your blood?* (ACT V. SCENE I)

And speak off half a dozen dang'rous words,
How they might hurt their enemies, if they durst;
And this is all.

LEONATO. But, brother Antony—

ANTONIO. Come, 'tis no matter;
Do not you meddle; let me deal in this.

DON PEDRO. Gentlemen both, we will not wake your patience.
My heart is sorry for your daughter's death;
But, on my honour, she was charg'd with nothing
But what was true, and very full of proof.

LEONATO. My lord, my lord—

DON PEDRO. I will not hear you.

LEONATO. No?
Come, brother, away. I will be heard.

ANTONIO. And shall, or some of us will smart for it.

Exeunt LEONATO *and* ANTONIO

DON PEDRO. See, see; here comes the man we went to seek.

Enter BENEDICK

CLAUDIO. Now, signior, what news?

BENEDICK. Good day, my lord.

DON PEDRO. Welcome, signior; you are almost come to part almost a fray.

CLAUDIO. We had lik'd to have had our two noses snapp'd off with two old men without teeth.

DON PEDRO. Leonato and his brother. What think'st thou? Had we fought, I doubt we should have been too young for them.

BENEDICK. In a false quarrel there is no true valour. I came to seek you both.

CLAUDIO. We have been up and down to seek thee; for we are high-proof melancholy, and would fain have it beaten away. Wilt thou use thy wit?

BENEDICK. It is in my scabbard; shall I draw it?

DON PEDRO. Dost thou wear thy wit by thy side?

CLAUDIO. Never any did so, though very many have been beside their wit. I will bid thee draw, as we do the minstrels—draw to pleasure us.

Don Pedro. As I am an honest man, he looks pale. Art thou sick or angry?

Claudio. What, courage, man! What though care kill'd a cat, thou hast mettle enough in thee to kill care.

Benedick. Sir, I shall meet your wit in the career, an you charge it against me. I pray you choose another subject.

Claudio. Nay, then, give him another staff; this last was broke cross.

Don Pedro. By this light, he changes more and more; I think he be angry indeed.

Claudio. If he be, he knows how to turn his girdle.

Benedick. Shall I speak a word in your ear?

Claudio. God bless me from a challenge!

Benedick. [*Aside to* Claudio] You are a villain; I jest not; I will make it good how you dare, with what you dare, and when you dare. Do me right, or I will protest your cowardice. You have kill'd a sweet lady, and her death shall fall heavy on you. Let me hear from you.

Claudio. Well, I will meet you, so I may have good cheer.

Don Pedro. What, a feast? a feast?

Claudio. I' faith, I thank him; he hath bid me to a calf's head and a capon, the which if I do not carve most curiously, say my knife's naught. Shall I not find a woodcock too?

Benedick. Sir, your wit ambles well; it goes easily.

Don Pedro. I'll tell thee how Beatrice prais'd thy wit the other day. I said thou hadst a fine wit. 'True,' said she, 'a fine little one.' 'No,' said I, 'a great wit.' 'Right,' says she, 'a great gross one.' 'Nay,' said I, 'a good wit.' 'Just,' said she, 'it hurts nobody.' 'Nay,' said I, 'the gentleman is wise.' 'Certain,' said she, 'a wise gentleman.' 'Nay,' said I, 'he hath the tongues.' 'That I believe,' said she 'for he swore a thing to me on Monday night, which he forswore on Tuesday morning. There's a double tongue; there's two tongues.' Thus did she, an hour together, trans-shape thy particular virtues; yet, at last, she concluded, with a sigh, thou wast the proper'st man in Italy.

Claudio. For the which she wept heartily, and said she cared not.

Don Pedro. Yea, that she did; but yet, for all that, an if she did not hate him deadly, she would love him dearly. The old man's daughter told us all.

CLAUDIO. All, all; and, moreover, 'God saw him when he was hid in the garden.'

DON PEDRO. But when shall we set the savage bull's horns on the sensible Benedick's head?

CLAUDIO. Yea, and text underneath, 'Here dwells Benedick the married man'?

BENEDICK. Fare you well, boy; you know my mind. I will leave you now to your gossip-like humour; you break jests as braggarts do their blades, which, God be thanked, hurt not. My lord, for your many courtesies I thank you. I must discontinue your company. Your brother the bastard is fled from Messina. You have among you kill'd a sweet and innocent lady. For my Lord Lackbeard there, he and I shall meet; and till then, peace be with him.   *Exit*

DON PEDRO. He is in earnest.

CLAUDIO. In most profound earnest; and I'll warrant you for the love of Beatrice.

DON PEDRO. And hath challeng'd thee?

CLAUDIO. Most sincerely.

DON PEDRO. What a pretty thing man is when he goes in his doublet and hose and leaves off his wit!

CLAUDIO. He is then a giant to an ape; but then is an ape a doctor to such a man.

DON PEDRO. But, soft you, let me be; pluck up, my heart, and be sad. Did he not say my brother was fled?

Enter DOGBERRY, VERGES, *and the* WATCH, *with*
CONRADE *and* BORACHIO

DOGBERRY. Come you, sir; if justice cannot tame you, she shall ne'er weigh more reasons in her balance; nay, an you be a cursing hypocrite once, you must be look'd to.

DON PEDRO. How now! two of my brother's men bound—Borachio one.

CLAUDIO. Hearken after their offence, my lord.

DON PEDRO. Officers, what offence have these men done?

DOGBERRY. Marry, sir, they have committed false report; moreover, they have spoken untruths; secondarily, they are slanders; sixth and lastly, they have belied a lady; thirdly,

they have verified unjust things; and to conclude, they are
lying knaves.

Don Pedro. First, I ask thee what they have done; thirdly, I
ask thee what's their offence; sixth and lastly, why they are
committed; and to conclude, what you lay to their charge.

Claudio. Rightly reasoned, and in his own division; and, by
my troth, there's one meaning well suited.

Don Pedro. Who have you offended, masters, that you are
thus bound to your answer? This learned constable is too
cunning to be understood. What's your offence?

Borachio. Sweet Prince, let me go no farther to mine answer; do you hear me, and let this Count kill me. I have
deceived even your very eyes. What your wisdoms could
not discover, these shallow fools have brought to light;
who, in the night, overheard me confessing to this man
how Don John your brother incensed me to slander the
Lady Hero; how you were brought into the orchard, and
saw me court Margaret in Hero's garments; how you disgrac'd her, when you should marry her. My villainy they
have upon record; which I had rather seal with my death
than repeat over to my shame. The lady is dead upon mine
and my master's false accusation; and, briefly, I desire
nothing but the reward of a villain.

Don Pedro. Runs not this speech like iron through your
blood?

Claudio. I have drunk poison whiles he utter'd it.

Don Pedro. But did my brother set thee on to this?

Borachio. Yea, and paid me richly for the practice of it.

Don Pedro. He is compos'd and fram'd of treachery,
And fled he is upon this villainy.

Claudio. Sweet Hero, now thy image doth appear
In the rare semblance that I lov'd it first.

Dogberry. Come, bring away the plaintiffs; by this time our
sexton hath reformed Signior Leonato of the matter. And,
masters, do not forget to specify, when time and place
shall serve, that I am an ass.

Verges. Here, here comes Master Signior Leonato and the
sexton too.

Re-enter Leonato *and* Antonio, *with the* Sexton

LEONATO. Which is the villain? Let me see his eyes,
That when I note another man like him
I may avoid him. Which of these is he?
BORACHIO. If you would know your wronger, look on me.
LEONATO. Art thou the slave that with thy breath hast kill'd
Mine innocent child?
BORACHIO. Yea, even I alone.
LEONATO. No, not so, villain; thou beliest thyself;
Here stand a pair of honourable men,
A third is fled, that had a hand in it.
I thank you, princes, for my daughter's death;
Record it with your high and worthy deeds;
'Twas bravely done, if you bethink you of it.
CLAUDIO. I know not how to pray your patience,
Yet I must speak. Choose your revenge yourself;
Impose me to what penance your invention
Can lay upon my sin; yet sinn'd I not
But in mistaking.
DON PEDRO. By my soul, nor I;
And yet, to satisfy this good old man,
I would bend under any heavy weight
That he'll enjoin me to.
LEONATO. I cannot bid you bid my daughter live—
That were impossible; but, I pray you both,
Possess the people in Messina here
How innocent she died; and, if your love
Can labour aught in sad invention,
Hang her an epitaph upon her tomb,
And sing it to her bones; sing it to-night.
To-morrow morning come you to my house;
And since you could not be my son-in-law,
Be yet my nephew. My brother hath a daughter,
Almost the copy of my child that's dead;
And she alone is heir to both of us.
Give her the right you should have giv'n her cousin,
And so dies my revenge.
CLAUDIO. O noble sir!
Your over-kindness doth wring tears from me.
I do embrace your offer; and dispose
For henceforth of poor Claudio.

LEONATO. To-morrow, then, I will expect your coming;
To-night I take my leave. This naughty man
Shall face to face be brought to Margaret,
Who, I believe, was pack'd in all this wrong,
Hir'd to it by your brother.

BORACHIO. No, by my soul, she was not;
Nor knew not what she did when she spoke to me;
But always hath been just and virtuous
In anything that I do know by her.

DOGBERRY. Moreover, sir, which indeed is not under white
and black, this plaintiff here, the offender, did call me ass;
I beseech you, let it be rememb'red in his punishment. And
also, the watch heard them talk of one Deformed; they say
he wears a key in his ear and a lock hanging by it, and borrows money in God's name; the which he hath us'd so
long, and never paid, that now men grow hard-hearted,
and will lend nothing for God's sake. Pray you examine
him upon that point.

LEONATO. I thank thee for thy care and honest pains.

DOGBERRY. Your worship speaks like a most thankful and
reverend youth, and I praise God for you.

LEONATO. There's for thy pains.

DOGBERRY. God save the foundation!

LEONATO. Go; I discharge thee of thy prisoner, and I thank
thee.

DOGBERRY. I leave an arrant knave with your worship; which
I beseech your worship to correct yourself, for the example of others. God keep your worship! I wish your
worship well; God restore you to health! I humbly give
you leave to depart; and if a merry meeting may be wish'd,
God prohibit it! Come, neighbour.   *Exit with* VERGES

LEONATO. Until to-morrow morning, lords, farewell.

ANTONIO. Farewell, my lords; we look for you to-morrow.

DON PEDRO. We will not fail.

CLAUDIO. To-night I'll mourn with Hero.
Exeunt DON PEDRO *and* CLAUDIO

LEONATO. [*To the* WATCH] Bring you these fellows on.
We'll talk with Margaret
How her acquaintance grew with this lewd fellow.
Exeunt severally

SCENE 2

LEONATO'S *orchard*

Enter BENEDICK *and* MARGARET, *meeting*

BENEDICK. Pray thee, sweet Mistress Margaret, deserve well at my hands by helping me to the speech of Beatrice.
MARGARET. Will you then write me a sonnet in praise of my beauty?
BENEDICK. In so high a style, Margaret, that no man living shall come over it; for, in most comely truth, thou deservest it.
MARGARET. To have no man come over me! Why, shall I always keep below stairs?
BENEDICK. Thy wit is as quick as the greyhound's mouth; it catches.
MARGARET. And yours as blunt as the fencer's foils, which hit, but hurt not.
BENEDICK. A most manly wit, Margaret; it will not hurt a woman; and so, I pray thee, call Beatrice. I give thee the bucklers.
MARGARET. Give us the swords; we have bucklers of our own.
BENEDICK. If you use them, Margaret, you must put in the pikes with a vice; and they are dangerous weapons for maids.
MARGARET. Well, I will call Beatrice to you, who, I think, hath legs. *Exit*
BENEDICK. And therefore will come. [*Sings*]

The god of love,
That sits above,
And knows me, and knows me,
How pitiful I deserve—

I mean in singing; but in loving—Leander the good swimmer, Troilus the first employer of panders, and a whole bookful of these quondam carpet-mongers, whose names yet run smoothly in the even road of a blank verse, why, they were never so truly turn'd over and over as my poor

self in love. Marry, I cannot show it in rhyme; I have
tried; I can find out no rhyme to 'lady' but 'baby'—an innocent rhyme; for 'scorn,' 'horn'—a hard rhyme; for 'school,'
'fool'—a babbling rhyme; very ominous endings. No, I was
not born under a rhyming planet, nor I cannot woo in festival terms.

Enter BEATRICE

Sweet Beatrice, wouldst thou come when I call'd thee?
BEATRICE. Yea, signior, and depart when you bid me.
BENEDICK. O, stay but till then!
BEATRICE. 'Then' is spoken; fare you well now. And yet, ere
I go, let me go with that I came, which is, with knowing
what hath pass'd between you and Claudio.
BENEDICK. Only foul words; and thereupon I will kiss thee.
BEATRICE. Foul words is but foul wind, and foul wind is but
foul breath, and foul breath is noisome; therefore I will depart unkiss'd.
BENEDICK. Thou hast frighted the word out of his right
sense, so forcible is thy wit. But, I must tell thee plainly,
Claudio undergoes my challenge; and either I must shortly
hear from him, or I will subscribe him a coward. And, I
pray thee now, tell me for which of my bad parts didst
thou first fall in love with me?
BEATRICE. For them all together; which maintain'd so politic
a state of evil that they will not admit any good part to
intermingle with them. But for which of my good parts
did you first suffer love for me?
BENEDICK. Suffer love—a good epithet! I do suffer love indeed, for I love thee against my will.
BEATRICE. In spite of your heart, I think; alas, poor heart! If
you spite it for my sake, I will spite it for yours; for I will
never love that which my friend hates.
BENEDICK. Thou and I are too wise to woo peaceably.
BEATRICE. It appears not in this confession: there's not one
wise man among twenty that will praise himself.
BENEDICK. An old, an old instance, Beatrice, that liv'd in the
time of good neighbours; if a man do not erect in this age
his own tomb ere he dies, he shall live no longer in monument than the bell rings and the widow weeps.

440

BEATRICE. And how long is that, think you?

BENEDICK. Question: why, an hour in clamour, and a quarter in rheum. Therefore is it most expedient for the wise, if Don Worm, his conscience, find no impediment to the contrary, to be the trumpet of his own virtues, as I am to myself. So much for praising myself, who, I myself will bear witness, is praiseworthy. And now tell me, how doth your cousin?

BEATRICE. Very ill.

BENEDICK. And how do you?

BEATRICE. Very ill too.

BENEDICK. Serve God, love me, and mend; there will I leave you too, for here comes one in haste.

Enter URSULA

URSULA. Madam, you must come to your uncle. Yonder's old coil at home. It is proved my Lady Hero hath been falsely accus'd, the Prince and Claudio mightily abus'd; and Don John is the author of all, who is fled and gone. Will you come presently?

BEATRICE. Will you go hear this news, signior?

BENEDICK. I will live in thy heart, die in thy lap, and be buried in thy eyes; and, moreover, I will go with thee to thy uncle's.   *Exeunt*

SCENE 3

A churchyard

Enter DON PEDRO, CLAUDIO, *and three or four with tapers*

CLAUDIO. Is this the monument of Leonato?

A LORD. It is, my lord.

CLAUDIO. [*Reads from a scroll*]

EPITAPH

'Done to death by slanderous tongues
Was the Hero that here lies;
Death, in guerdon of her wrongs,
Gives her fame which never dies.
So the life that died with shame

441

Lives in death with glorious fame.'
Hang thou there upon the tomb,
Praising her when I am dumb.
Now, music, sound, and sing your solemn hymn.

SONG

Pardon, goddess of the night,
Those that slew thy virgin knight;
For the which, with songs of woe,
Round about her tomb they go.
    Midnight, assist our moan;
    Help us to sigh and groan,
        Heavily, heavily.
    Graves, yawn, and yield your dead,
    Till death be uttered,
        Heavily, heavily.

CLAUDIO. Now, unto thy bones good night.
    Yearly will I do this rite.
DON PEDRO. Good morrow, masters; put your torches out;
    The wolves have prey'd; and look, the gentle day,
    Before the wheels of Phœbus, round about
    Dapples the drowsy east with spots of grey.
    Thanks to you all, and leave us. Fare you well.
CLAUDIO. Good morrow, masters; each his several way.
DON PEDRO. Come, let us hence, and put on other weeds;
    And then to Leonato's we will go.
CLAUDIO. And Hymen now with luckier issue speed's
    Than this for whom we rend'red up this woe.   *Exeunt*

SCENE 4

LEONATO's *house*

Enter LEONATO, ANTONIO, BENEDICK, BEATRICE, MARGARET,
    URSULA, FRIAR FRANCIS, *and* HERO

FRIAR. Did I not tell you she was innocent?
LEONATO. So are the Prince and Claudio, who accus'd her

Upon the error that you heard debated.
But Margaret was in some fault for this,
Although against her will, as it appears
In the true course of all the question.

ANTONIO. Well, I am glad that all things sorts so well.

BENEDICK. And so am I, being else by faith enforc'd
To call young Claudio to a reckoning for it.

LEONATO. Well, daughter, and you gentlewomen all,
Withdraw into a chamber by yourselves;
And when I send for you, come hither mask'd.
The Prince and Claudio promis'd by this hour
To visit me. You know your office, brother:
You must be father to your brother's daughter,
And give her to young Claudio.   *Exeunt* LADIES

ANTONIO. Which I will do with confirm'd countenance.

BENEDICK. Friar, I must entreat your pains, I think.

FRIAR. To do what, signior?

BENEDICK. To bind me, or undo me—one of them.
Signior Leonato, truth it is, good signior,
Your niece regards me with an eye of favour.

LEONATO. That eye my daughter lent her.
'Tis most true.

BENEDICK. And I do with an eye of love requite her.

LEONATO. The sight whereof, I think, you had from me,
From Claudio, and the Prince. But what's your will?

BENEDICK. Your answer, sir, is enigmatical.
But, for my will, my will is your good will
May stand with ours, this day to be conjoin'd
In the state of honourable marriage:
In which, good friar, I shall desire your help.

LEONATO. My heart is with your liking.

FRIAR. And my help.
Here comes the Prince and Claudio.

Enter DON PEDRO *and* CLAUDIO, *with* ATTENDANTS

DON PEDRO. Good morrow to this fair assembly.

LEONATO. Good morrow, Prince; good morrow, Claudio;
We here attend you. Are you yet determin'd
To-day to marry with my brother's daughter?

CLAUDIO. I'll hold my mind were she an Ethiope.

LEONATO. Call her forth, brother; here's the friar ready.

Exit ANTONIO

DON PEDRO. Good morrow, Benedick. Why, what's the matter
That you have such a February face,
So full of frost, of storm, and cloudiness?
CLAUDIO. I think he thinks upon the savage bull.
Tush, fear not, man; we'll tip thy horns with gold,
And all Europa shall rejoice at thee,
As once Europa did at lusty Jove,
When he would play the noble beast in love.
BENEDICK. Bull Jove, sir, had an amiable low;
And some such strange bull leap'd your father's cow,
And got a calf in that same noble feat
Much like to you, for you have just his bleat.

Re-enter ANTONIO, *with the* LADIES *masked*

CLAUDIO. For this I owe you. Here comes other reck'nings.
Which is the lady I must seize upon?
ANTONIO. This same is she, and I do give you her.
CLAUDIO. Why, then she's mine. Sweet, let me see your face.
LEONATO. No, that you shall not, till you take her hand
Before this friar, and swear to marry her.
CLAUDIO. Give me your hand; before this holy friar
I am your husband, if you like of me.
HERO. And when I liv'd I was your other wife;   [*Unmasking*]
And when you lov'd you were my other husband.
CLAUDIO. Another Hero!
HERO. Nothing certainer.
One Hero died defil'd; but I do live,
And, surely as I live, I am a maid.
DON PEDRO. The former Hero! Hero that is dead!
LEONATO. She died, my lord, but whiles her slander liv'd.
FRIAR. All this amazement can I qualify,
When, after that the holy rites are ended,
I'll tell you largely of fair Hero's death.
Meantime let wonder seem familiar,
And to the chapel let us presently.
BENEDICK. Soft and fair, friar. Which is Beatrice?
BEATRICE. I answer to that name.   [*Unmasking*]
What is your will?

444

BENEDICK. Do not you love me?

BEATRICE. Why no, no more than reason.

BENEDICK. Why, then your uncle, and the Prince, and Claudio,
Have been deceived: they swore you did.

BEATRICE. Do not you love me?

BENEDICK. Troth no, no more than reason.

BEATRICE. Why, then my cousin, Margaret, and Ursula,
Are much deceiv'd; for they did swear you did.

BENEDICK. They swore that you were almost sick for me.

BEATRICE. They swore that you were well-nigh dead for me.

BENEDICK. 'Tis no such matter. Then you do not love me?

BEATRICE. No, truly, but in friendly recompense.

LEONATO. Come, cousin, I am sure you love the gentleman.

CLAUDIO. And I'll be sworn upon't that he loves her;
For here's a paper written in his hand,
A halting sonnet of his own pure brain,
Fashion'd to Beatrice.

HERO. And here's another,
Writ in my cousin's hand, stol'n from her pocket,
Containing her affection unto Benedick.

BENEDICK. A miracle! here's our own hands against our hearts. Come, I will have thee; but, by this light, I take thee for pity.

BEATRICE. I would not deny you; but, by this good day, I yield upon great persuasion; and partly to save your life, for I was told you were in a consumption.

BENEDICK. Peace; I will stop your mouth.   [Kissing her]

DON PEDRO. How dost thou, Benedick the married man?

BENEDICK. I'll tell thee what, Prince: a college of wit-crackers cannot flout me out of my humour. Dost thou think I care for a satire or an epigram? No. If a man will be beaten with brains, 'a shall wear nothing handsome about him. In brief, since I do purpose to marry, I will think nothing to any purpose that the world can say against it; and therefore never flout at me for what I have said against it; for man is a giddy thing, and this is my conclusion. For thy part, Claudio, I did think to have beaten thee; but in that thou art like to be my kinsman, live unbruis'd, and love my cousin.

CLAUDIO. I had well hop'd thou wouldst have denied Beatrice, that I might have cudgell'd thee out of thy single life, to make thee a double dealer; which out of question thou wilt be, if my cousin do not look exceeding narrowly to thee.

BENEDICK. Come, come, we are friends. Let's have a dance ere we are married, that we may lighten our own hearts and our wives' heels.

LEONATO. We'll have dancing afterward.

BENEDICK. First, of my word; therefore play, music. Prince, thou art sad; get thee a wife, get thee a wife. There is no staff more reverend than one tipp'd with horn.

Enter a MESSENGER

MESSENGER. My lord, your brother John is ta'en in flight,
And brought with armed men back to Messina.

BENEDICK. Think not on him till tomorrow. I'll devise thee brave punishments for him. Strike up, pipers.   [*Dance*]
Exeunt

Love's Labour's Lost

LOVE'S LABOUR'S LOST

IN EARLIER days when verse tests were interpreted more mechanically than now it was customary to regard *Love's Labour's Lost* as Shakespeare's first play—it contained more rhyming lines than any other, and rhyme was regarded as the mark of immaturity. How Shakespeare's first attempt happened to be in so sophisticated a manner as this comedy and to exhibit so easy a familiarity not merely with the literary feuds and personalities of the town but with an aristocratic circle to which the dramatist could hardly have had direct and immediate access from the provinces—all this was left unexplained. All these features however become immediately intelligible if we suppose that Shakespeare's earlier success on the stage had gained for him the attention of an aristocratic following and that with his dedication of *Venus and Adonis* to the Earl of Southampton the dramatist entered a courtly circle in which his lordship was a prominent and popular figure.

The question set by the situation in the play to the King and his associates is 'Love or Learning?' And in the debate that follows Shakespeare finds occasion to glance at some of his well-known contemporaries who were carrying on not without acrimony an actual dispute on this and allied topics. The quarrel between Gabriel Harvey and Thomas Nashe which Whitgift, the Archbishop of Canterbury, brought to an end by ordering the pamphlets they printed against each other to be burnt by the common hangman, touches one aspect of the question. Gabriel Harvey, the Cambridge scholar, stood for Learning, and also, Nashe declared, for pedantry and conceit: Nashe, the Cambridge graduate and satirist, regarded himself as the man of worldly experience as opposed to the mere plodder in books. The opposing parties fought under names that now require some translating: those who stood for scholarship were known as the Artists; those who preferred experience as their teacher called themselves Villainists, Nashe the protagonist of the Villainists professing to regard the debtors' prison, which he had known,

Don Adriano de Armado *and* Moth   (ACT I. SCENE II)

as a more instructive centre for an author than a college. Worldly experience was of course incomplete without love. Although Moth in the play is not to be regarded as a portrait of Nashe, the quips against the learned given to the stage-character do echo the thrusts of Nashe at Harvey. Nashe and Harvey however stand not only for two opposed attitudes to life, their styles are naturally as different, and *Love's Labour's Lost* is much concerned with the exhibition and criticism of style and expression. Nashe and Harvey are however only one pair of many such opposites.

Florio, known to-day as the translator of Montaigne, stands like Harvey among the Artists, and although Holofernes is not to be taken as a deliberate portrait, there can be little doubt that the dramatist meant his audience to think of the scholar and his writings as they listened to the character whose name is almost an anagram on John Florio. Florio, born in London of Italian parents, made his reputation as a teacher of Italian by publishing two manuals designed to provide instruction in that language. These known from their titles as his *First Fruits* and his *Second Fruits* provided an Englishman, who regarded foreigners teaching their own languages in England in no very friendly light, with the title of his satirical counter-blast *Eliot's Fruits for the French*. This was part of the title of *Ortho-epia Gallica*, a manual for teaching French, but providing as part of its material a running satirical commentary on the ways of the foreigners. Eliot plays the villainist to Florio's artist, and is reported as observing of the Nashe-Harvey controversy:

> The Book-woorme was never but a pick-goose; it is the Multiplying spirit, not of the Alchimist, but of the villain-ist, that knocketh the naile one the head, and spurreth cutt farther in a day, than the quickest Artist in a weeke.

Shakespeare knew the manuals of both Florio and Eliot and uses this knowledge to season the dialogue of his disputants.

The dispute between Love and Learning Florio had carried back half a generation in the last of his *Second Fruits*, a discourse on the subject of love and women, by recalling the views on this subject of the celebrated Italian philosopher Giordano Bruno. During his wanderings Bruno stayed some years in England, where he found leisure to write his best-known works. Dedicating one of these to Sir Philip Sidney, with whom he was on intimate terms, Bruno exhorts his friend to forsake the love of women for pursuits worthy of his intellect—the implication being that Sidney should give up writing sonnets to Stella and study instead the stars and their motions as explained by Copernicus; for Bruno was an enthusiastic propagator of the new astronomical theories, and it was these and other unfamiliar speculations that were to lead to his being burned to death in Rome by the Inquisition in 1600. Shakespeare turned this opposition between the astronomer and the lover to account in his play; for the King and his courtiers, as Berowne suggests, begin as students of astronomy, although they are attracted from their studies by the starry eyes of the Princess and her ladies. All these references and allusions would of course be obvious to any courtly audience that would be found gathered round Essex, for Sidney's Stella was Penelope Devereux the sister of Essex himself.

One final aspect of the opposition between lovers and astronomers may be mentioned, although Shakespeare does not stress it in his play. In opposition to Essex and his party there stood a rival political group with Raleigh as a central figure—a rivalry that was to bring both Essex and Raleigh to the block. Raleigh and his friends were students of the new astronomy and had as their teacher Thomas Hariot, a scientist of original genius, himself a student of Bruno. Hariot was particularly interested in optics and devised an early form of telescope for observing the heavens, and it may have been this astronomical bent that fastened on Raleigh and his coterie the nickname 'School of Night.' Such at least is the explanation that has been given of the cryptic reference in the play in Act IV, Scene 3 to 'the School of Night.'

FERDINAND, *King of Navarre*
BEROWNE ⎫
LONGAVILLE ⎬ *lords attending on the King*
DUMAIN ⎭

BOYET ⎫ *lords attending on the Princess of France*
MARCADE ⎭

DON ADRIANO DE ARMADO, *a fantastical Spaniard*
SIR NATHANIEL, *a curate*
HOLOFERNES, *a schoolmaster*
DULL, *a constable*
COSTARD, *a clown*
MOTH, *page to Armado*
A FORESTER

THE PRINCESS OF FRANCE
ROSALINE ⎫
MARIA ⎬ *ladies attending on the Princess*
KATHARINE ⎭
JAQUENETTA, *a country wench*

Lords, Attendants, etc.

SCENE:

Navarre

Love's Labour's Lost

ACT I. SCENE 1

Navarre. The KING's *park*

Enter the KING, BEROWNE, LONGAVILLE, *and* DUMAIN

KING. Let fame, that all hunt after in their lives,
Live regist'red upon our brazen tombs,
And then grace us in the disgrace of death;
When, spite of cormorant devouring Time,
Th' endeavour of this present breath may buy
That honour which shall bate his scythe's keen edge,
And make us heirs of all eternity.
Therefore, brave conquerors—for so you are
That war against your own affections
And the huge army of the world's desires—
Our late edict shall strongly stand in force:
Navarre shall be the wonder of the world;
Our court shall be a little Academe,
Still and contemplative in living art.
You three, Berowne, Dumain, and Longaville,
Have sworn for three years' term to live with me
My fellow-scholars, and to keep those statutes
That are recorded in this schedule here.
Your oaths are pass'd; and now subscribe your names,
That his own hand may strike his honour down
That violates the smallest branch herein.
If you are arm'd to do as sworn to do,
Subscribe to your deep oaths, and keep it too.
LONGAVILLE. I am resolv'd; 'tis but a three years' fast.
The mind shall banquet, though the body pine.
Fat paunches have lean pates; and dainty bits
Make rich the ribs, but bankrupt quite the wits.
DUMAIN. My loving lord, Dumain is mortified.
The grosser manner of these world's delights
He throws upon the gross world's baser slaves;

453

To love, to wealth, to pomp, I pine and die,
With all these living in philosophy.
BEROWNE. I can but say their protestation over;
So much, dear liege, I have already sworn,
That is, to live and study here three years.
But there are other strict observances,
As: not to see a woman in that term,
Which I hope well is not enrolled there;
And one day in a week to touch no food,
And but one meal on every day beside,
The which I hope is not enrolled there;
And then to sleep but three hours in the night
And not be seen to wink of all the day—
When I was wont to think no harm all night,
And make a dark night too of half the day—
Which I hope well is not enrolled there.
O, these are barren tasks, too hard to keep,
Not to see ladies, study, fast, not sleep!
KING. Your oath is pass'd to pass away from these.
BEROWNE. Let me say no, my liege, an if you please:
I only swore to study with your Grace,
And stay here in your court for three years' space.
LONGAVILLE. You swore to that, Berowne, and to the rest.
BEROWNE. By yea and nay, sir, then I swore in jest.
What is the end of study, let me know.
KING. Why, that to know which else we should not know.
BEROWNE. Things hid and barr'd, you mean, from common
sense?
KING. Ay, that is study's god-like recompense.
BEROWNE. Come on, then; I will swear to study so,
To know the thing I am forbid to know,
As thus: to study where I well may dine,
When I to feast expressly am forbid;
Or study where to meet some mistress fine,
When mistresses from common sense are hid;
Or, having sworn too hard-a-keeping oath,
Study to break it, and not break my troth.
If study's gain be thus, and this be so,
Study knows that which yet it doth not know.
Swear me to this, and I will ne'er say no.

KING. These be the stops that hinder study quite,
And train our intellects to vain delight.
BEROWNE. Why, all delights are vain; but that most vain
Which, with pain purchas'd, doth inherit pain,
As painfully to pore upon a book
To seek the light of truth; while truth the while
Doth falsely blind the eyesight of his look.
Light, seeking light, doth light of light beguile;
So, ere you find where light in darkness lies,
Your light grows dark by losing of your eyes.
Study me how to please the eye indeed,
By fixing it upon a fairer eye;
Who dazzling so, that eye shall be his heed,
And give him light that it was blinded by.
Study is like the heaven's glorious sun,
That will not be deep-search'd with saucy looks;
Small have continual plodders ever won,
Save base authority from others' books.
These earthly godfathers of heaven's lights
That give a name to every fixed star
Have no more profit of their shining nights
Than those that walk and wot not what they are.
Too much to know is to know nought but fame;
And every godfather can give a name.
KING. How well he's read, to reason against reading!
DUMAIN. Proceeded well, to stop all good proceeding!
LONGAVILLE. He weeds the corn, and still lets grow the
weeding.
BEROWNE. The spring is near, when green geese are a-breeding.
DUMAIN. How follows that?
BEROWNE. Fit in his place and time.
DUMAIN. In reason nothing.
BEROWNE. Something then in rhyme.
LONGAVILLE. Berowne is like an envious sneaping frost
That bites the first-born infants of the spring.
BEROWNE. Well, say I am; why should proud summer boast
Before the birds have any cause to sing?
Why should I joy in any abortive birth?
At Christmas I no more desire a rose
Than wish a snow in May's new-fangled shows;

But like of each thing that in season grows;
So you, to study now it is too late,
Climb o'er the house to unlock the little gate.

KING. Well, sit you out; go home, Berowne; adieu.

BEROWNE. No, my good lord; I have sworn to stay with you;
And though I have for barbarism spoke more
Than for that angel knowledge you can say,
Yet confident I'll keep what I have swore,
And bide the penance of each three years' day.
Give me the paper; let me read the same;
And to the strictest decrees I'll write my name.

KING. How well this yielding rescues thee from shame!

BEROWNE. [*Reads*] 'Item. That no woman shall come within
a mile of my court'—Hath this been proclaimed?

LONGAVILLE. Four days ago.

BEROWNE. Let's see the penalty. [*Reads*] '—on pain of losing
her tongue.' Who devis'd this penalty?

LONGAVILLE. Marry, that did I.

BEROWNE. Sweet lord, and why?

LONGAVILLE. To fright them hence with that dread penalty.

BEROWNE. A dangerous law against gentility.
[*Reads*] 'Item. If any man be seen to talk with a woman
within the term of three years, he shall endure such public
shame as the rest of the court can possibly devise.'
This article, my liege, yourself must break;
For well you know here comes in embassy
The French king's daughter, with yourself to speak—
A maid of grace and complete majesty—
About surrender up of Aquitaine
To her decrepit, sick, and bedrid father;
Therefore this article is made in vain,
Or vainly comes th' admired princess hither.

KING. What say you, lords? Why, this was quite forgot.

BEROWNE. So study evermore is over-shot.
While it doth study to have what it would,
It doth forget to do the thing it should;
And when it hath the thing it hunteth most,
'Tis won as towns with fire—so won, so lost.

KING. We must of force dispense with this decree;
She must lie here on mere necessity.

BEROWNE. Necessity will make us all forsworn
　Three thousand times within this three years' space;
　For every man with his affects is born,
　Not by might mast'red, but by special grace.
　If I break faith, this word shall speak for me:
　I am forsworn on mere necessity.
　So to the laws at large I write my name;　　[*Subscribes*]
　And he that breaks them in the least degree
　Stands in attainder of eternal shame.
　Suggestions are to other as to me;
　But I believe, although I seem so loath,
　I am the last that will last keep his oath.
　But is there no quick recreation granted?
KING. Ay, that there is. Our court, you know, is haunted
　With a refined traveller of Spain,
　A man in all the world's new fashion planted,
　That hath a mint of phrases in his brain;
　One who the music of his own vain tongue
　Doth ravish like enchanting harmony;
　A man of complements, whom right and wrong
　Have chose as umpire of their mutiny.
　This child of fancy, that Armado hight,
　For interim to our studies shall relate,
　In high-born words, the worth of many a knight
　From tawny Spain lost in the world's debate.
　How you delight, my lords, I know not, I;
　But I protest I love to hear him lie,
　And I will use him for my minstrelsy.
BEROWNE. Armado is a most illustrious wight,
　A man of fire-new words, fashion's own knight.
LONGAVILLE. Costard the swain and he shall be our sport;
　And so to study three years is but short.

　　Enter DULL, *a constable, with a letter, and* COSTARD

DULL. Which is the Duke's own person?
BEROWNE. This, fellow. What wouldst?
DULL. I myself reprehend his own person, for I am his
　Grace's farborough; but I would see his own person in
　flesh and blood.
BEROWNE. This is he.

DULL. Signior Arme—Arme—commends you. There's villainy abroad; this letter will tell you more.

COSTARD. Sir, the contempts thereof are as touching me.

KING. A letter from the magnificent Armado.

BEROWNE. How low soever the matter, I hope in God for high words.

LONGAVILLE. A high hope for a low heaven. God grant us patience!

BEROWNE. To hear, or forbear hearing?

LONGAVILLE. To hear meekly, sir, and to laugh moderately; or, to forbear both.

BEROWNE. Well, sir, be it as the style shall give us cause to climb in the merriness.

COSTARD. The matter is to me, sir, as concerning Jaquenetta. The manner of it is, I was taken with the manner.

BEROWNE. In what manner?

COSTARD. In manner and form following, sir; all those three: I was seen with her in the manor-house, sitting with her upon the form, and taken following her into the park; which, put together, is in manner and form following. Now, sir, for the manner—it is the manner of a man to speak to a woman. For the form—in some form.

BEROWNE. For the following, sir?

COSTARD. As it shall follow in my correction; and God defend the right!

KING. Will you hear this letter with attention?

BEROWNE. As we would hear an oracle.

COSTARD. Such is the simplicity of man to hearken after the flesh.

KING. [Reads] 'Great deputy, the welkin's vicegerent and sole dominator of Navarre, my soul's earth's god and body's fost'ring patron'—

COSTARD. Not a word of Costard yet.

KING. [Reads] 'So it is'—

COSTARD. It may be so; but if he say it is so, he is, in telling true, but so.

KING. Peace!

COSTARD. Be to me, and every man that dares not fight!

KING. No words!

COSTARD. Of other men's secrets, I beseech you.

KING. [*Reads*] 'So it is, besieged with sable-coloured melancholy, I did commend the black oppressing humour to the
most wholesome physic of thy health-giving air; and, as I
am a gentleman, betook myself to walk. The time When?
About the sixth hour; when beasts most graze, birds best
peck, and men sit down to that nourishment which is called
supper. So much for the time When. Now for the ground
Which? which, I mean, I walk'd upon; it is ycleped thy
park. Then for the place Where? where, I mean, I did
encounter that obscene and most prepost'rous event that
draweth from my snow-white pen the ebon-coloured ink
which here thou viewest, beholdest, surveyest, or seest.
But to the place Where? It standeth north-north-east and
by east from the west corner of thy curious-knotted gar-
den. There did I see that low-spirited swain, that base min-
now of thy mirth,'
COSTARD. Me?
KING. 'that unlettered small-knowing soul,'
COSTARD. Me?
KING. 'that shallow vassal,'
COSTARD. Still me?
KING. 'which, as I remember, hight Costard,'
COSTARD. O, me!
KING. 'sorted and consorted, contrary to thy established pro-
claimed edict and continent canon; which, with, O, with—
but with this I passion to say wherewith—'
COSTARD. With a wench.
KING. 'with a child of our grandmother Eve, a female; or,
for thy more sweet understanding, a woman. Him I, as my
ever-esteemed duty pricks me on, have sent to thee, to re-
ceive the meed of punishment, by thy sweet Grace's officer,
Antony Dull, a man of good repute, carriage, bearing, and
estimation.'
DULL. Me, an't shall please you; I am Antony Dull.
KING. 'For Jaquenetta—so is the weaker vessel called, which
I apprehended with the aforesaid swain—I keep her as a
vessel of thy law's fury; and shall, at the least of thy sweet
notice, bring her to trial. Thine, in all compliments of devoted and heart-burning heat of duty,
                    DON ADRIANO DE ARMADO.'

459

BEROWNE. This is not so well as I look'd for, but the best that ever I heard.

KING. Ay, the best for the worst. But, sirrah, what say you to this?

COSTARD. Sir, I confess the wench.

KING. Did you hear the proclamation?

COSTARD. I do confess much of the hearing it, but little of the marking of it.

KING. It was proclaimed a year's imprisonment to be taken with a wench.

COSTARD. I was taken with none, sir; I was taken with a damsel.

KING. Well, it was proclaimed damsel.

COSTARD. This was no damsel neither, sir; she was a virgin.

KING. It is so varied too, for it was proclaimed virgin.

COSTARD. If it were, I deny her virginity; I was taken with a maid.

KING. This 'maid' will not serve your turn, sir.

COSTARD. This maid will serve my turn, sir.

KING. Sir, I will pronounce your sentence: you shall fast a week with bran and water.

COSTARD. I had rather pray a month with mutton and porridge.

KING. And Don Armado shall be your keeper.
My Lord Berowne, see him delivered o'er;
And go we, lords, to put in practice that
Which each to other hath so strongly sworn.
                    Exeunt KING, LONGAVILLE, *and* DUMAIN

BEROWNE. I'll lay my head to any good man's hat
These oaths and laws will prove an idle scorn.
Sirrah, come on.

COSTARD. I suffer for the truth, sir; for true it is I was taken with Jaquenetta, and Jaquenetta is a true girl; and therefore welcome the sour cup of prosperity! Affliction may one day smile again; and till then, sit thee down, sorrow.
                                        Exeunt

SCENE 2

The park

Enter ARMADO *and* MOTH, *his page*

ARMADO. Boy, what sign is it when a man of great spirit grows melancholy?

MOTH. A great sign, sir, that he will look sad.

ARMADO. Why, sadness is one and the self-same thing, dear imp.

MOTH. No, no; O Lord, sir, no!

ARMADO. How canst thou part sadness and melancholy, my tender juvenal?

MOTH. By a familiar demonstration of the working, my tough signior.

ARMADO. Why tough signior? Why tough signior?

MOTH. Why tender juvenal? Why tender juvenal?

ARMADO. I spoke it, tender juvenal, as a congruent epitheton appertaining to thy young days, which we may nominate tender.

MOTH. And I, tough signior, as an appertinent title to your old time, which we may name tough.

ARMADO. Pretty and apt.

MOTH. How mean you, sir? I pretty, and my saying apt? or I apt, and my saying pretty?

ARMADO. Thou pretty, because little.

MOTH. Little pretty, because little. Wherefore apt?

ARMADO. And therefore apt, because quick.

MOTH. Speak you this in my praise, master?

ARMADO. In thy condign praise.

MOTH. I will praise an eel with the same praise.

ARMADO. What, that an eel is ingenious?

MOTH. That an eel is quick.

ARMADO. I do say thou art quick in answers; thou heat'st my blood.

MOTH. I am answer'd, sir.

ARMADO. I love not to be cross'd.

MOTH. [*Aside*] He speaks the mere contrary: crosses love not him.

461

ARMADO. I have promised to study three years with the
Duke.

MOTH. You may do it in an hour, sir.

ARMADO. Impossible.

MOTH. How many is one thrice told?

ARMADO. I am ill at reck'ning; it fitteth the spirit of a tapster.

MOTH. You are a gentleman and a gamester, sir.

ARMADO. I confess both; they are both the varnish of a complete man.

MOTH. Then I am sure you know how much the gross sum
of deuce-ace amounts to.

ARMADO. It doth amount to one more than two.

MOTH. Which the base vulgar do call three.

ARMADO. True.

MOTH. Why, sir, is this such a piece of study? Now here is
three studied ere ye'll thrice wink; and how easy it is to
put 'years' to the word 'three,' and study three years in
two words, the dancing horse will tell you.

ARMADO. A most fine figure!

MOTH. [Aside] To prove you a cipher.

ARMADO. I will hereupon confess I am in love. And as it is
base for a soldier to love, so am I in love with a base
wench. If drawing my sword against the humour of affection would deliver me from the reprobate thought of it, I
would take Desire prisoner, and ransom him to any French
courtier for a new-devis'd curtsy. I think scorn to sigh;
methinks I should out-swear Cupid. Comfort me, boy;
what great men have been in love?

MOTH. Hercules, master.

ARMADO. Most sweet Hercules! More authority, dear boy,
name more; and, sweet my child, let them be men of good
repute and carriage.

MOTH. Samson, master; he was a man of good carriage, great
carriage, for he carried the town gates on his back like a
porter; and he was in love.

ARMADO. O well-knit Samson! strong-jointed Samson! I do
excel thee in my rapier as much as thou didst me in carrying gates. I am in love too. Who was Samson's love, my
dear Moth?

MOTH. A woman, master.

462

ARMADO. Of what complexion?

MOTH. Of all the four, or the three, or the two, or one of the four.

ARMADO. Tell me precisely of what complexion.

MOTH. Of the sea-water green, sir.

ARMADO. Is that one of the four complexions?

MOTH. As I have read, sir; and the best of them too.

ARMADO. Green, indeed, is the colour of lovers; but to have a love of that colour, methinks Samson had small reason for it. He surely affected her for her wit.

MOTH. It was so, sir; for she had a green wit.

ARMADO. My love is most immaculate white and red.

MOTH. Most maculate thoughts, master, are mask'd under such colours.

ARMADO. Define, define, well-educated infant.

MOTH. My father's wit and my mother's tongue assist me!

ARMADO. Sweet invocation of a child; most pretty, and pathetical!

MOTH.   If she be made of white and red,
              Her faults will ne'er be known;
          For blushing cheeks by faults are bred,
              And fears by pale white shown.
          Then if she fear, or be to blame,
              By this you shall not know;
          For still her cheeks possess the same
              Which native she doth owe.

A dangerous rhyme, master, against the reason of white and red.

ARMADO. Is there not a ballad, boy, of the King and the Beggar?

MOTH. The world was very guilty of such a ballad some three ages since; but I think now 'tis not to be found; or if it were, it would neither serve for the writing nor the tune.

ARMADO. I will have that subject newly writ o'er, that I may example my digression by some mighty precedent. Boy, I do love that country girl that I took in the park with the rational hind Costard; she deserves well.

MOTH. [*Aside*] To be whipt; and yet a better love than my master.

ARMADO. Sing, boy; my spirit grows heavy in love.
MOTH. And that's great marvel, loving a light wench.
ARMADO. I say, sing.
MOTH. Forbear till this company be past.

Enter DULL, COSTARD, *and* JAQUENETTA

DULL. Sir, the Duke's pleasure is that you keep Costard safe; and you must suffer him to take no delight nor no penance; but 'a must fast three days a week. For this damsel, I must keep her at the park; she is allow'd for the day-woman. Fare you well.
ARMADO. I do betray myself with blushing. Maid!
JAQUENETTA. Man!
ARMADO. I will visit thee at the lodge.
JAQUENETTA. That's hereby.
ARMADO. I know where it is situate.
JAQUENETTA. Lord, how wise you are!
ARMADO. I will tell thee wonders.
JAQUENETTA. With that face?
ARMADO. I love thee.
JAQUENETTA. So I heard you say.
ARMADO. And so, farewell.
JAQUENETTA. Fair weather after you!
DULL. Come, Jaquenetta, away.   *Exit with* JAQUENETTA
ARMADO. Villain, thou shalt fast for thy offences ere thou be pardoned.
COSTARD. Well, sir, I hope when I do it I shall do it on a full stomach.
ARMADO. Thou shalt be heavily punished.
COSTARD. I am more bound to you than your fellows, for they are but lightly rewarded.
ARMADO. Take away this villain; shut him up.
MOTH. Come, you transgressing slave, away.
COSTARD. Let me not be pent up, sir; I will fast, being loose.
MOTH. No, sir; that were fast, and loose. Thou shalt to prison.
COSTARD. Well, if ever I do see the merry days of desolation that I have seen, some shall see.
MOTH. What shall some see?
COSTARD. Nay, nothing, Master Moth, but what they look

upon. It is not for prisoners to be too silent in their words, and therefore I will say nothing. I thank God I have as little patience as another man, and therefore I can be quiet.

Exeunt MOTH *and* COSTARD

ARMADO. I do affect the very ground, which is base, where her shoe, which is baser, guided by her foot, which is basest, doth tread. I shall be forsworn—which is a great argument of falsehood—if I love. And how can that be true love which is falsely attempted? Love is a familiar; Love is a devil. There is no evil angel but Love. Yet was Samson so tempted, and he had an excellent strength; yet was Solomon so seduced, and he had a very good wit. Cupid's butt-shaft is too hard for Hercules' club, and therefore too much odds for a Spaniard's rapier. The first and second cause will not serve my turn; the passado he respects not, the duello he regards not; his disgrace is to be called boy, but his glory is to subdue men. Adieu, valour; rust, rapier; be still, drum; for your manager is in love; yea, he loveth. Assist me, some extemporal god of rhyme, for I am sure I shall turn sonnet. Devise, wit; write, pen; for I am for whole volumes in folio. *Exit*

ACT II. SCENE 1

The park

Enter the PRINCESS OF FRANCE, *with three attending ladies,* ROSALINE, MARIA, KATHARINE, BOYET, *and two other* LORDS

BOYET. Now, madam, summon up your dearest spirits.
Consider who the King your father sends,
To whom he sends, and what's his embassy:
Yourself, held precious in the world's esteem,
To parley with the sole inheritor
Of all perfections that a man may owe,
Matchless Navarre; the plea of no less weight
Than Aquitaine, a dowry for a queen.
Be now as prodigal of all dear grace

As Nature was in making graces dear,
When she did starve the general world beside
And prodigally gave them all to you.
PRINCESS OF FRANCE. Good Lord Boyet, my beauty, though
but mean,
Needs not the painted flourish of your praise.
Beauty is bought by judgment of the eye,
Not utt'red by base sale of chapmen's tongues;
I am less proud to hear you tell my worth
Than you much willing to be counted wise
In spending your wit in the praise of mine.
But now to task the tasker: good Boyet,
You are not ignorant all-telling fame
Doth noise abroad Navarre hath made a vow,
Till painful study shall outwear three years,
No woman may approach his silent court.
Therefore to's seemeth it a needful course,
Before we enter his forbidden gates,
To know his pleasure; and in that behalf,
Bold of your worthiness, we single you
As our best-moving fair solicitor.
Tell him the daughter of the King of France,
On serious business, craving quick dispatch,
Importunes personal conference with his Grace.
Haste, signify so much; while we attend,
Like humble-visag'd suitors, his high will.
BOYET. Proud of employment, willingly I go.
PRINCESS OF FRANCE. All pride is willing pride, and yours is
so.   *Exit* BOYET
Who are the votaries, my loving lords,
That are vow-fellows with this virtuous duke?
FIRST LORD. Lord Longaville is one.
PRINCESS OF FRANCE. Know you the man?
MARIA. I know him, madam; at a marriage feast,
Between Lord Perigort and the beauteous heir
Of Jaques Falconbridge, solemnized
In Normandy, saw I this Longaville.
A man of sovereign parts, peerless esteem'd,
Well fitted in arts, glorious in arms;
Nothing becomes him ill that he would well.

The only soil of his fair virtue's gloss,
If virtue's gloss will stain with any soil,
Is a sharp wit match'd with too blunt a will,
Whose edge hath power to cut, whose will still wills
It should none spare that come within his power.

PRINCESS OF FRANCE. Some merry mocking lord, belike; is't
    so?

MARIA. They say so most that most his humours know.

PRINCESS OF FRANCE. Such short-liv'd wits do wither as they
    grow.
    Who are the rest?

KATHARINE. The young Dumain, a well-accomplish'd youth,
    Of all that virtue love for virtue loved;
    Most power to do most harm, least knowing ill,
    For he hath wit to make an ill shape good,
    And shape to win grace though he had no wit.
    I saw him at the Duke Alençon's once;
    And much too little of that good I saw
    Is my report to his great worthiness.

ROSALINE. Another of these students at that time
    Was there with him, if I have heard a truth.
    Berowne they call him; but a merrier man,
    Within the limit of becoming mirth,
    I never spent an hour's talk withal.
    His eye begets occasion for his wit,
    For every object that the one doth catch
    The other turns to a mirth-moving jest,
    Which his fair tongue, conceit's expositor,
    Delivers in such apt and gracious words
    That aged ears play truant at his tales,
    And younger hearings are quite ravished;
    So sweet and voluble is his discourse.

PRINCESS OF FRANCE. God bless my ladies! Are they all in
    love,
    That every one her own hath garnished
    With such bedecking ornaments of praise?

FIRST LORD. Here comes Boyet.

Re-enter BOYET

PRINCESS OF FRANCE. Now, what admittance, lord?

BOYET. Navarre had notice of your fair approach,
And he and his competitors in oath
Were all address'd to meet you, gentle lady,
Before I came. Marry, thus much I have learnt:
He rather means to lodge you in the field,
Like one that comes here to besiege his court,
Than seek a dispensation for his oath,
To let you enter his unpeopled house.

> [*The* LADIES-IN-WAITING *mask*]

Enter KING, LONGAVILLE, DUMAIN, BEROWNE,
and ATTENDANTS

Here comes Navarre.

KING. Fair Princess, welcome to the court of Navarre.

PRINCESS OF FRANCE. 'Fair' I give you back again; and 'welcome' I have not yet. The roof of this court is too high to be yours, and welcome to the wide fields too base to be mine.

KING. You shall be welcome, madam, to my court.

PRINCESS OF FRANCE. I will be welcome then; conduct me thither.

KING. Hear me, dear lady: I have sworn an oath—

PRINCESS OF FRANCE. Our Lady help my lord! He'll be forsworn.

KING. Not for the world, fair madam, by my will.

PRINCESS OF FRANCE. Why, will shall break it; will, and nothing else.

KING. Your ladyship is ignorant what it is.

PRINCESS OF FRANCE. Were my lord so, his ignorance were wise,
Where now his knowledge must prove ignorance.
I hear your Grace hath sworn out house-keeping.
'Tis deadly sin to keep that oath, my lord,
And sin to break it.
But pardon me, I am too sudden bold;
To teach a teacher ill beseemeth me.
Vouchsafe to read the purpose of my coming,
And suddenly resolve me in my suit. [*Giving a paper*]

KING. Madam, I will, if suddenly I may.

PRINCESS OF FRANCE. You will the sooner that I were away,
  For you'll prove perjur'd if you make me stay.
BEROWNE. Did not I dance with you in Brabant once?
KATHARINE. Did not I dance with you in Brabant once?
BEROWNE. I know you did.
KATHARINE. How needless was it then to ask the question!
BEROWNE. You must not be so quick.
KATHARINE. 'Tis long of you, that spur me with such ques-
  tions.
BEROWNE. Your wit 's too hot, it speeds too fast, 'twill tire.
KATHARINE. Not till it leave the rider in the mire.
BEROWNE. What time o' day?
KATHARINE. The hour that fools should ask.
BEROWNE. Now fair befall your mask!
KATHARINE. Fair fall the face it covers!
BEROWNE. And send you many lovers!
KATHARINE. Amen, so you be none.
BEROWNE. Nay, then will I be gone.
KING. Madam, your father here doth intimate
  The payment of a hundred thousand crowns;
  Being but the one half of an entire sum
  Disbursed by my father in his wars.
  But say that he or we, as neither have,
  Receiv'd that sum, yet there remains unpaid
  A hundred thousand more, in surety of the which,
  One part of Aquitaine is bound to us,
  Although not valued to the money's worth.
  If then the King your father will restore
  But that one half which is unsatisfied,
  We will give up our right in Aquitaine,
  And hold fair friendship with his Majesty.
  But that, it seems, he little purposeth,
  For here he doth demand to have repaid
  A hundred thousand crowns; and not demands,
  On payment of a hundred thousand crowns,
  To have his title live in Aquitaine;
  Which we much rather had depart withal,
  And have the money by our father lent,
  Than Aquitaine so gelded as it is.
  Dear Princess, were not his requests so far

From reason's yielding, your fair self should make
A yielding 'gainst some reason in my breast,
And go well satisfied to France again.
PRINCESS OF FRANCE. You do the King my father too much
    wrong,
And wrong the reputation of your name,
In so unseeming to confess receipt
Of that which hath so faithfully been paid.
KING. I do protest I never heard of it;
    And, if you prove it, I'll repay it back
Or yield up Aquitaine.
PRINCESS OF FRANCE. We arrest your word.
    Boyet, you can produce acquittances
For such a sum from special officers
Of Charles his father.
KING. Satisfy me so.
BOYET. So please your Grace, the packet is not come,
    Where that and other specialties are bound;
To-morrow you shall have a sight of them.
KING. It shall suffice me; at which interview
    All liberal reason I will yield unto.
Meantime receive such welcome at my hand
As honour, without breach of honour, may
Make tender of to thy true worthiness.
You may not come, fair Princess, within my gates;
But here without you shall be so receiv'd
As you shall deem yourself lodg'd in my heart,
Though so denied fair harbour in my house.
Your own good thoughts excuse me, and farewell.
To-morrow shall we visit you again.
PRINCESS OF FRANCE. Sweet health and fair desires consort
    your Grace!
KING. Thy own wish wish I thee in every place.

                          Exit with attendants
BEROWNE. Lady, I will commend you to mine own heart.
ROSALINE. Pray you, do my commendations;
    I would be glad to see it.
BEROWNE. I would you heard it groan.
ROSALINE. Is the fool sick?
BEROWNE. Sick at the heart.

ROSALINE. Alack, let it blood.
BEROWNE. Would that do it good?
ROSALINE. My physic says 'ay.'
BEROWNE. Will you prick't with your eye?
ROSALINE. No point, with my knife.
BEROWNE. Now, God save thy life!
ROSALINE. And yours from long living!
BEROWNE. I cannot stay thanksgiving.   [*Retiring*]
DUMAIN. Sir, I pray you, a word: what lady is that same?
BOYET. The heir of Alençon, Katharine her name.
DUMAIN. A gallant lady! Monsieur, fare you well.   *Exit*
LONGAVILLE. I beseech you a word: what is she in the white?
BOYET. A woman sometimes, an you saw her in the light.
LONGAVILLE. Perchance light in the light. I desire her name.
BOYET. She hath but one for herself; to desire that were a
    shame.
LONGAVILLE. Pray you, sir, whose daughter?
BOYET. Her mother's, I have heard.
LONGAVILLE. God's blessing on your beard!
BOYET. Good sir, be not offended;
    She is an heir of Falconbridge.
LONGAVILLE. Nay, my choler is ended.
    She is a most sweet lady.
BOYET. Not unlike, sir; that may be.   *Exit* LONGAVILLE
BEROWNE. What's her name in the cap?
BOYET. Rosaline, by good hap.
BEROWNE. Is she wedded or no?
BOYET. To her will, sir, or so.
BEROWNE. You are welcome, sir; adieu!
BOYET. Farewell to me, sir, and welcome to you.
                              Exit BEROWNE. LADIES *unmask*
MARIA. That last is Berowne, the merry mad-cap lord;
    Not a word with him but a jest.
BOYET. And every jest but a word.
PRINCESS OF FRANCE. It was well done of you to take him at
    his word.
BOYET. I was as willing to grapple as he was to board.
KATHARINE. Two hot sheeps, marry!
BOYET. And wherefore not ships?
    No sheep, sweet lamb, unless we feed on your lips.

KATHARINE. You sheep and I pasture—shall that finish the jest?

BOYET. So you grant pasture for me. *[Offering to kiss her]*

KATHARINE. Not so, gentle beast;
My lips are no common, though several they be.

BOYET. Belonging to whom?

KATHARINE. To my fortunes and me.

PRINCESS OF FRANCE. Good wits will be jangling; but, gentles, agree;
This civil war of wits were much better used
On Navarre and his book-men, for here 'tis abused.

BOYET. If my observation, which very seldom lies,
By the heart's still rhetoric disclosed with eyes,
Deceive me not now, Navarre is infected.

PRINCESS OF FRANCE. With what?

BOYET. With that which we lovers entitle 'affected.'

PRINCESS OF FRANCE. Your reason?

BOYET. Why, all his behaviours did make their retire
To the court of his eye, peeping thorough desire.
His heart, like an agate, with your print impressed,
Proud with his form, in his eye pride expressed;
His tongue, all impatient to speak and not see,
Did stumble with haste in his eyesight to be;
All senses to that sense did make their repair,
To feel only looking on fairest of fair.
Methought all his senses were lock'd in his eye,
As jewels in crystal for some prince to buy;
Who, tend'ring their own worth from where they were glass'd,
Did point you to buy them, along as you pass'd.
His face's own margent did quote such amazes
That all eyes saw his eyes enchanted with gazes.
I'll give you Aquitaine and all that is his,
An you give him for my sake but one loving kiss.

PRINCESS OF FRANCE. Come, to our pavilion. Boyet is dispos'd.

BOYET. But to speak that in words which his eye hath disclos'd;
I only have made a mouth of his eye,
By adding a tongue which I know will not lie.

MARIA. Thou art an old love-monger, and speakest skil-
fully.
KATHARINE. He is Cupid's grandfather, and learns news of
him.
ROSALINE. Then was Venus like her mother; for her father is
but grim.
BOYET. Do you hear, my mad wenches?
MARIA. No.
BOYET. What, then; do you see?
MARIA. Ay, our way to be gone.
BOYET. You are too hard for me.   *Exeunt*

ACT III. SCENE 1

The park

Enter ARMADO *and* MOTH

ARMADO. Warble, child; make passionate my sense of hearing.
                              [MOTH *sings* Concolinel]
ARMADO. Sweet air! Go, tenderness of years, take this key,
give enlargement to the swain, bring him festinately hither;
I must employ him in a letter to my love.
MOTH. Master, will you win your love with a French brawl?
ARMADO. How meanest thou? Brawling in French?
MOTH. No, my complete master; but to jig off a tune at the
tongue's end, canary to it with your feet, humour it
with turning up your eyelids, sigh a note and sing a note,
sometime through the throat, as if you swallowed love
with singing love, sometime through the nose, as if you
snuff'd up love by smelling love, with your hat penthouse-
like o'er the shop of your eyes, with your arms cross'd on
your thin-belly doublet, like a rabbit on a spit, or your
hands in your pocket, like a man after the old painting;
and keep not too long in one tune, but a snip and away.
These are complements, these are humours; these betray
nice wenches, that would be betrayed without these; and

473

make them men of note—do you note me?—that most are affected to these.

ARMADO. How hast thou purchased this experience?

MOTH. By my penny of observation.

ARMADO. But O—but O—

MOTH. The hobby-horse is forgot.

ARMADO. Call'st thou my love 'hobby-horse'?

MOTH. No, master; the hobby-horse is but a colt, and your love perhaps a hackney. But have you forgot your love?

ARMADO. Almost I had.

MOTH. Negligent student! learn her by heart.

ARMADO. By heart and in heart, boy.

MOTH. And out of heart, master; all those three I will prove.

ARMADO. What wilt thou prove?

MOTH. A man, if I live; and this, by, in, and without, upon the instant. By heart you love her, because your heart cannot come by her; in heart you love her, because your heart is in love with her; and out of heart you love her, being out of heart that you cannot enjoy her.

ARMADO. I am all these three.

MOTH. And three times as much more, and yet nothing at all.

ARMADO. Fetch hither the swain; he must carry me a letter.

MOTH. A message well sympathiz'd—a horse to be ambassador for an ass.

ARMADO. Ha, ha, what sayest thou?

MOTH. Marry, sir, you must send the ass upon the horse, for he is very slow-gaited. But I go.

ARMADO. The way is but short; away.

MOTH. As swift as lead, sir.

ARMADO. The meaning, pretty ingenious?
Is not lead a metal heavy, dull, and slow?

MOTH. Minime, honest master; or rather, master, no.

ARMADO. I say lead is slow.

MOTH. You are too swift, sir, to say so:
Is that lead slow which is fir'd from a gun?

ARMADO. Sweet smoke of rhetoric!
He reputes me a cannon; and the bullet, that's he;
I shoot thee at the swain.

MOTH. Thump, then, and I flee. *Exit*

ARMADO. A most acute juvenal; volable and free of grace!

By thy favour, sweet welkin, I must sigh in thy face;
Most rude melancholy, valour gives thee place.
My herald is return'd.

Re-enter MOTH *with* COSTARD

MOTH. A wonder, master! here's a costard broken in a shin.

ARMADO. Some enigma, some riddle; come, thy l'envoy; begin.

COSTARD. No egma, no riddle, no l'envoy; no salve in the mail, sir. O, sir, plantain, a plain plantain; no l'envoy, no l'envoy; no salve, sir, but a plantain!

ARMADO. By virtue thou enforcest laughter; thy silly thought, my spleen; the heaving of my lungs provokes me to ridiculous smiling. O, pardon me, my stars! Doth the inconsiderate take salve for l'envoy, and the word 'l'envoy' for a salve?

MOTH. Do the wise think them other? Is not l'envoy a salve?

ARMADO. No, page; it is an epilogue or discourse to make plain
Some obscure precedence that hath tofore been sain.
I will example it:
> The fox, the ape, and the humble-bee,
> Were still at odds, being but three.
There's the moral. Now the l'envoy.

MOTH. I will add the l'envoy. Say the moral again.

ARMADO. The fox, the ape, and the humble-bee,
> Were still at odds, being but three.

MOTH. Until the goose came out of door,
> And stay'd the odds by adding four.
Now will I begin your moral, and do you follow with my l'envoy.
> The fox, the ape, and the humble-bee,
> Were still at odds, being but three.

ARMADO. Until the goose came out of door,
> Staying the odds by adding four.

MOTH. A good l'envoy, ending in the goose; would you desire more?

COSTARD. The boy hath sold him a bargain, a goose, that's flat.

475

Sir, your pennyworth is good, an your goose be fat.
To sell a bargain well is as cunning as fast and loose;
Let me see: a fat l'envoy; ay, that's a fat goose.

ARMADO. Come hither, come hither. How did this argument begin?

MOTH. By saying that a costard was broken in a shin.
Then call'd you for the l'envoy.

COSTARD. True, and I for a plantain. Thus came your argument in;
Then the boy's fat l'envoy, the goose that you bought;
And he ended the market.

ARMADO. But tell me: how was there a costard broken in a shin?

MOTH. I will tell you sensibly.

COSTARD. Thou hast no feeling of it, Moth; I will speak that l'envoy.
I, Costard, running out, that was safely within,
Fell over the threshold and broke my shin.

ARMADO. We will talk no more of this matter.

COSTARD. Till there be more matter in the shin.

ARMADO. Sirrah Costard. I will enfranchise thee.

COSTARD. O, marry me to one Frances! I smell some l'envoy, some goose, in this.

ARMADO. By my sweet soul, I mean setting thee at liberty, enfreedoming thy person; thou wert immured, restrained, captivated, bound.

COSTARD. True, true; and now you will be my purgation, and let me loose.

ARMADO. I give thee thy liberty, set thee from durance; and, in lieu thereof, impose on thee nothing but this: bear this significant [*giving a letter*] to the country maid Jaquenetta; there is remuneration; for the best ward of mine honour is rewarding my dependents. Moth, follow.   *Exit*

MOTH. Like the sequel, I. Signior Costard, adieu.

COSTARD. My sweet ounce of man's flesh, my incony Jew!
Exit MOTH

Now will I look to his remuneration. Remuneration! O, that's the Latin word for three farthings. Three farthings —remuneration. 'What's the price of this inkle?'—'One penny.'—'No, I'll give you a remuneration.' Why, it carries

476

it. Remuneration! Why, it is a fairer name than French crown. I will never buy and sell out of this word.

Enter BEROWNE

BEROWNE. My good knave Costard, exceedingly well met!
COSTARD. Pray you, sir, how much carnation ribbon may a man buy for a remuneration?
BEROWNE. What is a remuneration?
COSTARD. Marry, sir, halfpenny farthing.
BEROWNE. Why, then, three-farthing worth of silk.
COSTARD. I thank your worship. God be wi' you!
BEROWNE. Stay, slave; I must employ thee.
 As thou wilt win my favour, good my knave,
 Do one thing for me that I shall entreat.
COSTARD. When would you have it done, sir?
BEROWNE. This afternoon.
COSTARD. Well, I will do it, sir; fare you well.
BEROWNE. Thou knowest not what it is.
COSTARD. I shall know, sir, when I have done it.
BEROWNE. Why, villain, thou must know first.
COSTARD. I will come to your worship to-morrow morning.
BEROWNE. It must be done this afternoon.
 Hark, slave, it is but this:
 The Princess comes to hunt here in the park,
 And in her train there is a gentle lady;
 When tongues speak sweetly, then they name her name,
 And Rosaline they call her. Ask for her,
 And to her white hand see thou do commend
 This seal'd-up counsel. There's thy guerdon; go.
       [Giving him a shilling]
COSTARD. Gardon, O sweet gardon! better than remuneration; a 'leven-pence farthing better; most sweet gardon! I will do it, sir, in print. Gardon—remuneration! *Exit*
BEROWNE. And I, forsooth, in love; I, that have been love's whip;
 A very beadle to a humorous sigh;
 A critic, nay, a night-watch constable;
 A domineering pedant o'er the boy,
 Than whom no mortal so magnificent!
 This wimpled, whining, purblind, wayward boy,

This senior-junior, giant-dwarf, Dan Cupid;
Regent of love-rhymes, lord of folded arms,
Th' anointed sovereign of sighs and groans,
Liege of all loiterers and malcontents,
Dread prince of plackets, king of codpieces,
Sole imperator, and great general
Of trotting paritors. O my little heart!
And I to be a corporal of his field,
And wear his colours like a tumbler's hoop!
What! I love, I sue, I seek a wife—
A woman, that is like a German clock,
Still a-repairing, ever out of frame,
And never going aright, being a watch,
But being watch'd that it may still go right!
Nay, to be perjur'd, which is worst of all;
And, among three, to love the worst of all,
A whitely wanton with a velvet brow,
With two pitch balls stuck in her face for eyes;
Ay, and, by heaven, one that will do the deed,
Though Argus were her eunuch and her guard.
And I to sigh for her! to watch for her!
To pray for her! Go to; it is a plague
That Cupid will impose for my neglect
Of his almighty dreadful little might.
Well, I will love, write, sigh, pray, sue, and groan:
Some men must love my lady, and some Joan.   *Exit*

ACT IV. SCENE 1

The park

Enter the PRINCESS, ROSALINE, MARIA, KATHARINE, BOYET,
LORDS, ATTENDANTS, *and a* FORESTER

PRINCESS OF FRANCE. Was that the King that spurr'd his
horse so hard
Against the steep uprising of the hill?
BOYET. I know not; but I think it was not he.

PRINCESS OF FRANCE. Whoe'er 'a was, 'a show'd a mounting
    mind.
    Well, lords, to-day we shall have our dispatch;
    On Saturday we will return to France.
    Then, forester, my friend, where is the bush
    That we must stand and play the murderer in?
FORESTER. Hereby, upon the edge of yonder coppice;
    A stand where you may make the fairest shoot.
PRINCESS OF FRANCE. I thank my beauty I am fair that shoot,
    And thereupon thou speak'st the fairest shoot.
FORESTER. Pardon me, madam, for I meant not so.
PRINCESS OF FRANCE. What, what? First praise me, and again
    say no?
    O short-liv'd pride! Not fair? Alack for woe!
FORESTER. Yes, madam, fair.
PRINCESS OF FRANCE. Nay, never paint me now;
    Where fair is not, praise cannot mend the brow.
    Here, good my glass, take this for telling true:
                                   [*Giving him money*]
    Fair payment for foul words is more than due.
FORESTER. Nothing but fair is that which you inherit.
PRINCESS OF FRANCE. See, see, my beauty will be sav'd by
    merit.
    O heresy in fair, fit for these days!
    A giving hand, though foul, shall have fair praise.
    But come, the bow. Now mercy goes to kill,
    And shooting well is then accounted ill;
    Thus will I save my credit in the shoot:
    Not wounding, pity would not let me do't;
    If wounding, then it was to show my skill,
    That more for praise than purpose meant to kill.
    And, out of question, so it is sometimes:
    Glory grows guilty of detested crimes,
    When, for fame's sake, for praise, an outward part,
    We bend to that the working of the heart;
    As I for praise alone now seek to spill
    The poor deer's blood that my heart means no ill.
BOYET. Do not curst wives hold that self-sovereignty
    Only for praise sake, when they strive to be
    Lords o'er their lords?

PRINCESS OF FRANCE. Only for praise; and praise we may afford
To any lady that subdues a lord.

Enter COSTARD

BOYET. Here comes a member of the commonwealth.

COSTARD. God dig-you-den all! Pray you, which is the head lady?

PRINCESS OF FRANCE. Thou shalt know her, fellow, by the rest that have no heads.

COSTARD. Which is the greatest lady, the highest?

PRINCESS OF FRANCE. The thickest and the tallest.

COSTARD. The thickest and the tallest! It is so; truth is truth.
An your waist, mistress, were as slender as my wit,
One o' these maids' girdles for your waist should be fit.
Are not you the chief woman? You are the thickest here.

PRINCESS OF FRANCE. What's your will, sir? What's your will?

COSTARD. I have a letter from Monsieur Berowne to one Lady Rosaline.

PRINCESS OF FRANCE. O, thy letter, thy letter! He's a good friend of mine.
Stand aside, good bearer. Boyet, you can carve.
Break up this capon.

BOYET. I am bound to serve.
This letter is mistook; it importeth none here.
It is writ to Jaquenetta.

PRINCESS OF FRANCE. We will read it, I swear.
Break the neck of the wax, and every one give ear.

BOYET. [*Reads*] 'By heaven, that thou art fair is most infallible; true that thou art beauteous; truth itself that thou art lovely. More fairer than fair, beautiful than beauteous, truer than truth itself, have commiseration on thy heroical vassal. The magnanimous and most illustrate king Cophetua set eye upon the pernicious and indubitate beggar Zenelophon; and he it was that might rightly say, 'Veni, vidi, vici'; which to annothanize in the vulgar,—O base and obscure vulgar!—videlicet, He came, saw, and overcame. He came, one; saw, two; overcame, three. Who came?—the king. Why did he come?—to see. Why did he see?—to overcome. To whom came he?—to the beggar. What saw he?—the beggar. Who overcame he?—the beggar. The conclusion is victory; on whose side?—the king's. The captive is enrich'd; on whose side?—the beggar's. The catastrophe is a nuptial; on whose side?—the king's. No, on both in one, or one in both. I am the king, for so stands the comparison; thou the beggar, for so witnesseth thy lowliness. Shall I command thy love? I may. Shall I enforce thy love? I could. Shall I entreat thy love? I will. What shalt thou exchange for rags?—robes, for tittles?—titles, for thyself? —me. Thus expecting thy reply, I profane my lips on thy foot, my eyes on thy picture, and my heart on thy every part.

> Thine in the dearest design of industry,
>> DON ADRIANO DE ARMADO.

'Thus dost thou hear the Nemean lion roar
'Gainst thee, thou lamb, that standest as his prey;
Submissive fall his princely feet before,
And he from forage will incline to play.
But if thou strive, poor soul, what are thou then?
Food for his rage, repasture for his den.'

PRINCESS OF FRANCE. What plume of feathers is he that indited this letter?
What vane? What weathercock? Did you ever hear better?
BOYET. I am much deceived but I remember the style.
PRINCESS OF FRANCE. Else your memory is bad, going o'er it erewhile.
BOYET. This Armado is a Spaniard, that keeps here in court;
A phantasime, a Monarcho, and one that makes sport
To the Prince and his book-mates.
PRINCESS OF FRANCE. Thou fellow, a word.
Who gave thee this letter?
COSTARD. I told you: my lord.
PRINCESS OF FRANCE. To whom shouldst thou give it?
COSTARD. From my lord to my lady.
PRINCESS OF FRANCE. From which lord to which lady?
COSTARD. From my Lord Berowne, a good master of mine,
To a lady of France that he call'd Rosaline.
PRINCESS OF FRANCE. Thou hast mistaken his letter. Come, lords, away.

[*To* ROSALINE] Here, sweet, put up this; 'twill be thine
another day.   *Exeunt* PRINCESS *and* TRAIN
BOYET. Who is the shooter? who is the shooter?
ROSALINE. Shall I teach you to know?
BOYET. Ay, my continent of beauty.
ROSALINE. Why, she that bears the bow.
  Finely put off!
BOYET. My lady goes to kill horns; but, if thou marry,
Hang me by the neck, if horns that year miscarry.
  Finely put on!
ROSALINE. Well then, I am the shooter.
BOYET. And who is your deer?
ROSALINE. If we choose by the horns, yourself come not
  near.
  Finely put on indeed!
MARIA. You still wrangle with her, Boyet, and she strikes
  at the brow.
BOYET. But she herself is hit lower. Have I hit her now?
ROSALINE. Shall I come upon thee with an old saying, that
  was a man when King Pepin of France was a little boy, as
  touching the hit it?
BOYET. So I may answer thee with one as old, that was a
  woman when Queen Guinever of Britain was a little
  wench, as touching the hit it.
ROSALINE. [*Singing*]
      Thou canst not hit it, hit it, hit it,
      Thou canst not hit it, my good man.
BOYET.   An I cannot, cannot, cannot,
      An I cannot, another can.
               Exeunt ROSALINE *and* KATHARINE
COSTARD. By my troth, most pleasant! How both did fit it!
MARIA. A mark marvellous well shot; for they both did
  hit it.
BOYET. A mark! O, mark but that mark! A mark, says my
  lady!
  Let the mark have a prick in't, to mete at, if it may be.
MARIA. Wide o' the bow-hand! I' faith, your hand is out.
COSTARD. Indeed, 'a must shoot nearer, or he'll ne'er hit the
  clout.
BOYET. An if my hand be out, then belike your hand is in.

COSTARD. Then will she get the upshoot by cleaving the pin.
MARIA. Come, come, you talk greasily; your lips grow foul.
COSTARD. She's too hard for you at pricks, sir; challenge her
to bowl.
BOYET. I fear too much rubbing; good-night, my good owl.
Exeunt BOYET *and* MARIA
COSTARD. By my soul, a swain, a most simple clown!
Lord, Lord! how the ladies and I have put him down!
O' my troth, most sweet jests, most incony vulgar wit!
When it comes so smoothly off, so obscenely, as it were,
so fit.
Armado a th' t'one side—O, a most dainty man!
To see him walk before a lady and to bear her fan!
To see him kiss his hand, and how most sweetly 'a will
swear!
And his page a t' other side, that handful of wit!
Ah, heavens, it is a most pathetical nit!
Sola, sola!
Exit COSTARD

SCENE 2

The park

From the shooting within, enter HOLOFERNES,
SIR NATHANIEL, *and* DULL

NATHANIEL. Very reverent sport, truly; and done in the
testimony of a good conscience.
HOLOFERNES. The deer was, as you know, sanguis, in blood;
ripe as the pomewater, who now hangeth like a jewel in
the ear of caelo, the sky, the welkin, the heaven; and anon
falleth like a crab on the face of terra, the soil, the land,
the earth.
NATHANIEL. Truly, Master Holofernes, the epithets are
sweetly varied, like a scholar at the least; but, sir, I assure
ye it was a buck of the first head.
HOLOFERNES. Sir Nathaniel, haud credo.
DULL. 'Twas not a haud credo; 'twas a pricket.
HOLOFERNES. Most barbarous intimation! yet a kind of in-
sinuation, as it were, in via, in way, of explication; facere,

as it were, replication, or rather, ostentare, to show, as it were, his inclination, after his undressed, unpolished, uneducated, unpruned, untrained, or rather unlettered, or ratherest unconfirmed fashion, to insert again my haud credo for a deer.

DULL. I said the deer was not a haud credo; 'twas a pricket.

HOLOFERNES. Twice-sod simplicity, bis coctus!
O thou monster Ignorance, how deformed dost thou look!

NATHANIEL. Sir, he hath never fed of the dainties that are
    bred in a book;
He hath not eat paper, as it were; he hath not drunk ink;
his intellect is not replenished; he is only an animal, only
sensible in the duller parts;
And such barren plants are set before us that we thankful
    should be—
Which we of taste and feeling are—for those parts that do
    fructify in us more than he.
For as it would ill become me to be vain, indiscreet, or a
    fool,
So, were there a patch set on learning, to see him in a
    school.
But, omne bene, say I, being of an old father's mind:
Many can brook the weather that love not the wind.

DULL. You two are book-men: can you tell me by your wit
What was a month old at Cain's birth that's not five weeks
    old as yet?

HOLOFERNES. Dictynna, goodman Dull; Dictynna, goodman
Dull.

DULL. What is Dictynna?

NATHANIEL. A title to Phœbe, to Luna, to the moon.

HOLOFERNES. The moon was a month old when Adam was
    no more,
And raught not to five weeks when he came to five-score.
Th' allusion holds in the exchange.

DULL. 'Tis true, indeed; the collusion holds in the exchange.

HOLOFERNES. God comfort thy capacity! I say th' allusion
holds in the exchange.

DULL. And I say the polusion holds in the exchange; for the
moon is never but a month old; and I say, beside, that 'twas
a pricket that the Princess kill'd.

HOLOFERNES. Sir Nathaniel, will you hear an extemporal epitaph on the death of the deer? And, to humour the ignorant, call the deer the Princess kill'd a pricket.

NATHANIEL. Perge, good Master Holofernes, perge, so it shall please you to abrogate scurrility.

HOLOFERNES. I will something affect the letter, for it argues facility.

The preyful Princess pierc'd and prick'd a pretty pleasing pricket.
Some say a sore; but not a sore till now made sore with shooting.
The dogs did yell; put el to sore, then sorel jumps from thicket—
Or pricket sore, or else sorel; the people fall a-hooting.
If sore be sore, then L to sore makes fifty sores o' sorel.
Of one sore I an hundred make by adding but one more L.

NATHANIEL. A rare talent!

DULL. [*Aside*] If a talent be a claw, look how he claws him with a talent.

HOLOFERNES. This is a gift that I have, simple, simple; a foolish extravagant spirit, full of forms, figures, shapes, objects, ideas, apprehensions, motions, revolutions. These are begot in the ventricle of memory, nourish'd in the womb of pia mater, and delivered upon the mellowing of occasion. But the gift is good in those in whom it is acute, and I am thankful for it.

NATHANIEL. Sir, I praise the Lord for you, and so may my parishioners; for their sons are well tutor'd by you, and their daughters profit very greatly under you. You are a good member of the commonwealth.

HOLOFERNES. Mehercle, if their sons be ingenious, they shall want no instruction; if their daughters be capable, I will put it to them; but, vir sapit qui pauca loquitur. A soul feminine saluteth us.

Enter JAQUENETTA *and* COSTARD

JAQUENETTA. God give you good morrow, Master Person.

HOLOFERNES. Master Person, quasi pers-one. And if one should be pierc'd which is the one?

Costard. Marry, Master Schoolmaster, he that is likest to a hogshead.

Holofernes. Piercing a hogshead! A good lustre of conceit in a turf of earth; fire enough for a flint, pearl enough for a swine; 'tis pretty; it is well.

Jaquenetta. Good Master Parson, be so good as read me this letter; it was given me by Costard, and sent me from Don Armado. I beseech you read it.

Holofernes. Fauste, precor gelida quando pecus omne sub umbra
Ruminat—
and so forth. Ah, good old Mantuan! I may speak of thee as the traveller doth of Venice:
      Venetia, Venetia,
      Chi non ti vede, non ti pretia.
Old Mantuan, old Mantuan! Who understandeth thee not, loves thee not—
      Ut, re, sol, la, mi, fa.
Under pardon, sir, what are the contents? or rather as Horace says in his—What, my soul, verses?

Nathaniel. Ay, sir, and very learned.

Holofernes. Let me hear a staff, a stanze, a verse; lege, domine.

Nathaniel. [Reads] 'If love make me forsworn, how shall I swear to love?
Ah, never faith could hold, if not to beauty vowed!
Though to myself forsworn, to thee I'll faithful prove;
Those thoughts to me were oaks, to thee like osiers bowed.
Study his bias leaves, and makes his book thine eyes,
Where all those pleasures live that art would comprehend.
If knowledge be the mark, to know thee shall suffice;
Well learned is that tongue that well can thee commend;
All ignorant that soul that sees thee without wonder;
Which is to me some praise that I thy parts admire.
Thy eye Jove's lightning bears, thy voice his dreadful thunder,
Which, not to anger bent, is music and sweet fire.
Celestial as thou art, O, pardon love this wrong,
That singes heaven's praise with such an earthly tongue.'

Holofernes. You find not the apostrophas, and so miss the

accent: let me supervise the canzonet. Here are only numbers ratified; but, for the elegancy, facility, and golden cadence of poesy, caret. Ovidius Naso was the man. And why, indeed, 'Naso' but for smelling out the odoriferous flowers of fancy, the jerks of invention? Imitari is nothing: so doth the hound his master, the ape his keeper, the tired horse his rider. But, damosella virgin, was this directed to you?

JAQUENETTA. Ay, sir, from one Monsieur Berowne, one of the strange queen's lords.

HOLOFERNES. I will overglance the superscript: 'To the snow-white hand of the most beauteous Lady Rosaline.' I will look again on the intellect of the letter, for the nomination of the party writing to the person written unto: 'Your Ladyship's in all desired employment, Berowne.' Sir Nathaniel, this Berowne is one of the votaries with the King; and here he hath framed a letter to a sequent of the stranger queen's which accidentally, or by the way of progression, hath miscarried. Trip and go, my sweet; deliver this paper into the royal hand of the King; it may concern much. Stay not thy compliment; I forgive thy duty. Adieu.

JAQUENETTA. Good Costard, go with me. Sir, God save your life!

COSTARD. Have with thee, my girl.

Exeunt COSTARD *and* JAQUENETTA

NATHANIEL. Sir, you have done this in the fear of God, very religiously; and, as a certain father saith—

HOLOFERNES. Sir, tell not me of the father; I do fear colourable colours. But to return to the verses: did they please you, Sir Nathaniel?

NATHANIEL. Marvellous well for the pen.

HOLOFERNES. I do dine to-day at the father's of a certain pupil of mine; where, if, before repast, it shall please you to gratify the table with a grace, I will, on my privilege I have with the parents of the foresaid child or pupil, undertake your ben venuto; where I will prove those verses to be very unlearned, neither savouring of poetry, wit, nor invention. I beseech your society.

NATHANIEL. And thank you too; for society, saith the text, is the happiness of life.

HOLOFERNES. And certes, the text most infallibly concludes it. [*To* DULL] Sir, I do invite you too; you shall not say me nay: pauca verba. Away; the gentles are at their game, and we will to our recreation. *Exeunt*

SCENE 3

The park

Enter BEROWNE, *with a paper in his hand, alone*

BEROWNE. The King he is hunting the deer: I am coursing myself. They have pitch'd a toil: I am toiling in a pitch—pitch that defiles. Defile! a foul word. Well, 'set thee down, sorrow!' for so they say the fool said, and so say I, and I am the fool. Well proved, wit. By the Lord, this love is as mad as Ajax: it kills sheep; it kills me—I a sheep. Well proved again o' my side. I will not love; if I do, hang me. I' faith, I will not. O, but her eye! By this light, but for her eye, I would not love her—yes, for her two eyes. Well, I do nothing in the world but lie, and lie in my throat. By heaven, I do love; and it hath taught me to rhyme, and to be melancholy; and here is part of my rhyme, and here my melancholy. Well, she hath one o' my sonnets already; the clown bore it, the fool sent it, and the lady hath it: sweet clown, sweeter fool, sweetest lady! By the world, I would not care a pin if the other three were in. Here comes one with a paper; God give him grace to groan!

[Climbs into a tree]

Enter the KING, *with a paper*

KING. Ay me!
BEROWNE. Shot, by heaven! Proceed, sweet Cupid; thou hast thump'd him with thy bird-bolt under the left pap. In faith, secrets!
KING. [*Reads*]
'So sweet a kiss the golden sun gives not
To those fresh morning drops upon the rose,
As thy eye-beams, when their fresh rays have smote
The night of dew that on my cheeks down flows;

Nor shines the silver moon one half so bright
Through the transparent bosom of the deep,
As doth thy face through tears of mine give light.
Thou shin'st in every tear that I do weep;
No drop but as a coach doth carry thee;
So ridest thou triumphing in my woe.
Do but behold the tears that swell in me,
And they thy glory through my grief will show.
But do not love thyself; then thou wilt keep
My tears for glasses, and still make me weep.
O queen of queens! how far dost thou excel
No thought can think nor tongue of mortal tell.'
How shall she know my griefs? I'll drop the paper—
Sweet leaves, shade folly. Who is he comes here?
                                                    [*Steps aside*]

          Enter LONGAVILLE, *with a paper*

What, Longaville, and reading! Listen, ear.
BEROWNE. Now, in thy likeness, one more fool appear!
LONGAVILLE. Ay me, I am forsworn!
BEROWNE. Why, he comes in like a perjure, wearing papers.
KING. In love, I hope; sweet fellowship in shame!
BEROWNE. One drunkard loves another of the name.
LONGAVILLE. Am I the first that have been perjur'd so?
BEROWNE. I could put thee in comfort: not by two that I
     know;
     Thou makest the triumviry, the corner-cap of society,
     The shape of Love's Tyburn that hangs up simplicity.
LONGAVILLE. I fear these stubborn lines lack power to move.
     O sweet Maria, empress of my love!
     These numbers will I tear, and write in prose.
BEROWNE. O, rhymes are guards on wanton Cupid's hose:
     Disfigure not his slop.
LONGAVILLE. This same shall go.   [*He reads the sonnet*]
     'Did not the heavenly rhetoric of thine eye,
     'Gainst whom the world cannot hold argument,
     Persuade my heart to this false perjury?
     Vows for thee broke deserve not punishment.
     A woman I forswore; but I will prove,
     Thou being a goddess, I forswore not thee:

My vow was earthly, thou a heavenly love;
Thy grace being gain'd cures all disgrace in me.
Vows are but breath, and breath a vapour is;
Then thou, fair sun, which on my earth dost shine,
Exhal'st this vapour-vow; in thee it is.
If broken, then it is no fault of mine;
If by me broke, what fool is not so wise
To lose an oath to win a paradise?'
BEROWNE. This is the liver-vein, which makes flesh a deity,
A green goose a goddess—pure, pure idolatry.
God amend us, God amend! We are much out o' th' way.

Enter DUMAIN, *with a paper*

LONGAVILLE. By whom shall I send this?—Company! Stay.
[*Steps aside*]
BEROWNE. 'All hid, all hid'—an old infant play.
Like a demigod here sit I in the sky,
And wretched fools' secrets heedfully o'er-eye.
More sacks to the mill! O heavens, I have my wish!
Dumain transformed! Four woodcocks in a dish!
DUMAIN. O most divine Kate!
BEROWNE. O most profane coxcomb!
DUMAIN. By heaven, the wonder in a mortal eye!
BEROWNE. By earth, she is not, corporal: there you lie.
DUMAIN. Her amber hairs for foul hath amber quoted.
BEROWNE. An amber-colour'd raven was well noted.
DUMAIN. As upright as the cedar.
BEROWNE. Stoop, I say;
Her shoulder is with child.
DUMAIN. As fair as day.
BEROWNE. Ay, as some days; but then no sun must shine.
DUMAIN. O that I had my wish!
LONGAVILLE. And I had mine!
KING. And I mine too, good Lord!
BEROWNE. Amen, so I had mine! Is not that a good word?
DUMAIN. I would forget her; but a fever she
Reigns in my blood, and will rememb'red be.
BEROWNE. A fever in your blood? Why, then incision
Would let her out in saucers. Sweet misprision!

490

DUMAIN. Once more I'll read the ode that I have writ.
BEROWNE. Once more I'll mark how love can vary wit.
DUMAIN. [*Reads*]
       'On a day—alack the day!—
       Love, whose month is ever May,
       Spied a blossom passing fair
       Playing in the wanton air.
       Through the velvet leaves the wind,
       All unseen, can passage find;
       That the lover, sick to death,
       Wish'd himself the heaven's breath.
       "Air," quoth he "thy cheeks may blow;
       Air, would I might triumph so!
       But, alack, my hand is sworn
       Ne'er to pluck thee from thy thorn;
       Vow, alack, for youth unmeet,
       Youth so apt to pluck a sweet.
       Do not call it sin in me
       That I am forsworn for thee;
       Thou for whom Jove would swear
       Juno but an Ethiope were;
       And deny himself for Jove,
       Turning mortal for thy love." '
This will I send; and something else more plain
That shall express my true love's fasting pain.
O, would the King, Berowne and Longaville,
Were lovers too! Ill, to example ill,
Would from my forehead wipe a perjur'd note;
For none offend where all alike do dote.
LONGAVILLE. [*Advancing*] Dumain, thy love is far from
    charity,
    That in love's grief desir'st society;
    You may look pale, but I should blush, I know,
    To be o'erheard and taken napping so.
KING. [*Advancing*] Come, sir, you blush; as his, your case
    is such.
    You chide at him, offending twice as much:
    You do not love Maria! Longaville
    Did never sonnet for her sake compile;
    Nor never lay his wreathed arms athwart

MOTH. *All hail, the richest beauties on the earth!* (ACT V. SCENE II)

His loving bosom, to keep down his heart.
I have been closely shrouded in this bush,
And mark'd you both, and for you both did blush.
I heard your guilty rhymes, observ'd your fashion,
Saw sighs reek from you, noted well your passion.
'Ay me!' says one. 'O Jove!' the other cries.
One, her hairs were gold; crystal the other's eyes.
[*To* LONGAVILLE] You would for paradise break faith and
    troth;
[*To* DUMAIN] And Jove for your love would infringe an
    oath.
What will Berowne say when that he shall hear
Faith infringed which such zeal did swear?
How will he scorn, how will he spend his wit!
How will he triumph, leap, and laugh at it!
For all the wealth that ever I did see,
I would not have him know so much by me.
BEROWNE. . [*Descending*] Now step I forth to whip hypocrisy.
    Ah, good my liege, I pray thee pardon me.
Good heart, what grace hast thou thus to reprove
These worms for loving, that art most in love?
Your eyes do make no coaches; in your tears
There is no certain princess that appears;
You'll not be perjur'd; 'tis a hateful thing;
Tush, none but minstrels like of sonneting.
But are you not ashamed? Nay, are you not,
All three of you, to be thus much o'ershot?
You found his mote; the King your mote did see;
But I a beam do find in each of three.
O, what a scene of fool'ry have I seen,
Of sighs, of groans, of sorrow, and of teen!
O me, with what strict patience have I sat,
To see a king transformed to a gnat!
To see great Hercules whipping a gig,
And profound Solomon to tune a jig,
And Nestor play at push-pin with the boys,
And critic Timon laugh at idle toys!
Where lies thy grief, O, tell me, good Dumain?
And, gentle Longaville, where lies thy pain?
And where my liege's? All about the breast.

A caudle, ho!
KING. Too bitter is thy jest.
Are we betrayed thus to thy over-view?
BEROWNE. Not you by me, but I betrayed to you.
I that am honest, I that hold it sin
To break the vow I am engaged in;
I am betrayed by keeping company
With men like you, men of inconstancy.
When shall you see me write a thing in rhyme?
Or groan for Joan? or spend a minute's time
In pruning me? When shall you hear that I
Will praise a hand, a foot, a face, an eye,
A gait, a state, a brow, a breast, a waist,
A leg, a limb—
KING. Soft! whither away so fast?
A true man or a thief that gallops so?
BEROWNE. I post from love; good lover, let me go.

Enter JAQUENETTA *and* COSTARD

JAQUENETTA. God bless the King!
KING. What present hast thou there?
COSTARD. Some certain treason.
KING. What makes treason here?
COSTARD. Nay, it makes nothing, sir.
KING. If it mar nothing neither,
The treason and you go in peace away together.
JAQUENETTA. I beseech your Grace, let this letter be read;
Our person misdoubts it: 'twas treason, he said.
KING. Berowne, read it over. [BEROWNE *reads the letter*]
Where hadst thou it?
JAQUENETTA. Of Costard.
KING. Where hadst thou it?
COSTARD. Of Dun Adramadio, Dun Adramadio.
[BEROWNE *tears the letter*]
KING. How now! What is in you? Why dost thou tear it?
BEROWNE. A toy, my liege, a toy! Your Grace needs not fear
it.
LONGAVILLE. It did move him to passion, and therefore let's
hear it.

494

DUMAIN. It is Berowne's writing, and here is his name.
                              [*Gathering up the pieces*]
BEROWNE. [*To* COSTARD] Ah, you whoreson loggerhead, you
    were born to do me shame.
    Guilty, my lord, guilty! I confess, I confess.
KING. What?
BEROWNE. That you three fools lack'd me fool to make up
    the mess;
    He, he, and you—and you, my liege!—and I
    Are pick-purses in love, and we deserve to die.
    O, dismiss this audience, and I shall tell you more.
DUMAIN. Now the number is even.
BEROWNE. True, true, we are four.
    Will these turtles be gone?
KING. Hence, sirs, away.
COSTARD. Walk aside the true folk, and let the traitors stay.
                       Exeunt COSTARD *and* JAQUENETTA
BEROWNE. Sweet lords, sweet lovers, O, let us embrace!
    As true we are as flesh and blood can be.
    The sea will ebb and flow, heaven show his face;
    Young blood doth not obey an old decree.
    We cannot cross the cause why we were born,
    Therefore of all hands must we be forsworn.
KING. What, did these rent lines show some love of thine?
BEROWNE. 'Did they?' quoth you. Who sees the heavenly
    Rosaline
    That, like a rude and savage man of Inde
    At the first op'ning of the gorgeous east,
    Bows not his vassal head and, strucken blind,
    Kisses the base ground with obedient breast?
    What peremptory eagle-sighted eye
    Dares look upon the heaven of her brow
    That is not blinded by her majesty?
KING. What zeal, what fury hath inspir'd thee now?
    My love, her mistress, is a gracious moon;
    She, an attending star, scarce seen a light.
BEROWNE. My eyes are then no eyes, nor I Berowne.
    O, but for my love, day would turn to night!
    Of all complexions the cull'd sovereignty
    Do meet, as at a fair, in her fair cheek,

Where several worthies make one dignity,
Where nothing wants that want itself doth seek.
Lend me the flourish of all gentle tongues—
Fie, painted rhetoric! O, she needs it not!
To things of sale a seller's praise belongs:
She passes praise; then praise too short doth blot.
A wither'd hermit, five-score winters worn,
Might shake off fifty, looking in her eye.
Beauty doth varnish age, as if new-born,
And gives the crutch the cradle's infancy.
O, 'tis the sun that maketh all things shine!
KING. By heaven, thy love is black as ebony.
BEROWNE. Is ebony like her? O wood divine!
A wife of such wood were felicity.
O, who can give an oath? Where is a book?
That I may swear beauty doth beauty lack,
If that she learn not of her eye to look.
No face is fair that is not full so black.
KING. O paradox! Black is the badge of hell,
The hue of dungeons, and the school of night;
And beauty's crest becomes the heavens well.
BEROWNE. Devils soonest tempt, resembling spirits of light.
O, if in black my lady's brows be deckt,
It mourns that painting and usurping hair
Should ravish doters with a false aspect;
And therefore is she born to make black fair.
Her favour turns the fashion of the days;
For native blood is counted painting now;
And therefore red that would avoid dispraise
Paints itself black, to imitate her brow.
DUMAIN. To look like her are chimney-sweepers black.
LONGAVILLE. And since her time are colliers counted bright.
KING. And Ethiopes of their sweet complexion crack.
DUMAIN. Dark needs no candles now, for dark is light.
BEROWNE. Your mistresses dare never come in rain
For fear their colours should be wash'd away.
KING. 'Twere good yours did; for, sir, to tell you plain,
I'll find a fairer face not wash'd to-day.
BEROWNE. I'll prove her fair, or talk till doomsday here.
KING. No devil will fright thee then so much as she.

DUMAIN. I never knew man hold vile stuff so dear.
LONGAVILLE. Look, here's thy love: my foot and her face
  see.   [*Showing his shoe*]
BEROWNE. O, if the streets were paved with thine eyes,
  Her feet were much too dainty for such tread!
DUMAIN. O vile! Then, as she goes, what upward lies
  The street should see as she walk'd overhead.
KING. But what of this? Are we not all in love?
BEROWNE. Nothing so sure; and thereby all forsworn.
KING. Then leave this chat; and, good Berowne, now prove
  Our loving lawful, and our faith not torn.
DUMAIN. Ay, marry, there; some flattery for this evil.
LONGAVILLE. O, some authority how to proceed;
  Some tricks, some quillets, how to cheat the devil!
DUMAIN. Some salve for perjury.
BEROWNE. 'Tis more than need.
  Have at you, then, affection's men-at-arms.
  Consider what you first did swear unto:
  To fast, to study, and to see no woman—
  Flat treason 'gainst the kingly state of youth.
  Say, can you fast? Your stomachs are too young,
  And abstinence engenders maladies.
  And where that you have vow'd to study, lords,
  In that each of you have forsworn his book,
  Can you still dream, and pore, and thereon look?
  For when would you, my lord, or you, or you,
  Have found the ground of study's excellence
  Without the beauty of a woman's face?
  From women's eyes this doctrine I derive:
  They are the ground, the books, the academes,
  From whence doth spring the true Promethean fire.
  Why, universal plodding poisons up
  The nimble spirits in the arteries,
  As motion and long-during action tires
  The sinewy vigour of the traveller.
  Now, for not looking on a woman's face,
  You have in that forsworn the use of eyes,
  And study too, the causer of your vow;
  For where is any author in the world
  Teaches such beauty as a woman's eye?

Learning is but an adjunct to ourself,
And where we are our learning likewise is;
Then when ourselves we see in ladies' eyes,
With ourselves.
Do we not likewise see our learning there?
O, we have made a vow to study, lords,
And in that vow we have forsworn our books.
For when would you, my liege, or you, or you,
In leaden contemplation have found out
Such fiery numbers as the prompting eyes
Of beauty's tutors have enrich'd you with?
Other slow arts entirely keep the brain;
And therefore, finding barren practisers,
Scarce show a harvest of their heavy toil;
But love, first learned in a lady's eyes,
Lives not alone immured in the brain,
But with the motion of all elements
Courses as swift as thought in every power,
And gives to every power a double power,
Above their functions and their offices.
It adds a precious seeing to the eye:
A lover's eyes will gaze an eagle blind.
A lover's ear will hear the lowest sound,
When the suspicious head of theft is stopp'd.
Love's feeling is more soft and sensible
Than are the tender horns of cockled snails:
Love's tongue proves dainty Bacchus gross in taste.
For valour, is not Love a Hercules,
Still climbing trees in the Hesperides?
Subtle as Sphinx; as sweet and musical
As bright Apollo's lute, strung with his hair.
And when Love speaks, the voice of all the gods
Make heaven drowsy with the harmony.
Never durst poet touch a pen to write
Until his ink were temp'red with Love's sighs;
O, then his lines would ravish savage ears,
And plant in tyrants mild humility.
From women's eyes this doctrine I derive.
They sparkle still the right Promethean fire;
They are the books, the arts, the academes,

That show, contain, and nourish, all the world,
Else none at all in aught proves excellent.
Then fools you were these women to forswear;
Or, keeping what is sworn, you will prove fools.
For wisdom's sake, a word that all men love;
Or for Love's sake, a word that loves all men;
Or for men's sake, the authors of these women;
Or women's sake, by whom we men are men—
Let us once lose our oaths to find ourselves,
Or else we lose ourselves to keep our oaths.
It is religion to be thus forsworn;
For charity itself fulfils the law,
And who can sever love from charity?
KING. Saint Cupid, then! and, soldiers, to the field!
BEROWNE. Advance your standards, and upon them, lords;
Pell-mell, down with them! But be first advis'd,
In conflict, that you get the sun of them.
LONGAVILLE. Now to plain-dealing; lay these glozes by.
Shall we resolve to woo these girls of France?
KING. And win them too; therefore let us devise
Some entertainment for them in their tents.
BEROWNE. First, from the park let us conduct them thither;
Then homeward every man attach the hand
Of his fair mistress. In the afternoon
We will with some strange pastime solace them,
Such as the shortness of the time can shape;
For revels, dances, masks, and merry hours,
Forerun fair Love, strewing her way with flowers.
KING. Away, away! No time shall be omitted
That will betime, and may by us be fitted.
BEROWNE. Allons! allons! Sow'd cockle reap'd no corn,
And justice always whirls in equal measure.
Light wenches may prove plagues to men forsworn;
If so, our copper buys no better treasure.   *Exeunt*

ACT V. SCENE 1

The park

Enter HOLOFERNES, SIR NATHANIEL, *and* DULL

HOLOFERNES. Satis quod sufficit.

NATHANIEL. I praise God for you, sir. Your reasons at dinner have been sharp and sententious; pleasant without scurrility, witty without affection, audacious without impudency, learned without opinion, and strange without heresy. I did converse this quondam day with a companion of the King's who is intituled, nominated, or called, Don Adriano de Armado.

HOLOFERNES. Novi hominem tanquam te. His humour is lofty, his discourse peremptory, his tongue filed, his eye ambitious, his gait majestical and his general behaviour vain, ridiculous, and thrasonical. He is too picked, too spruce, too affected, too odd, as it were, too peregrinate, as I may call it.

NATHANIEL. A most singular and choice epithet.

[*Draws out his table-book*]

HOLOFERNES. He draweth out the thread of his verbosity finer than the staple of his argument. I abhor such fanatical phantasimes, such insociable and point-devise companions; such rackers of orthography, as to speak 'dout' fine, when he should say 'doubt'; 'det' when he should pronounce 'debt'—d, e, b, t, not d, e, t. He clepeth a calf 'cauf,' half 'hauf'; neighbour vocatur 'nebour'; 'neigh' abbreviated 'ne.' This is abhominable—which he would call 'abbominable.' It insinuateth me of insanie: ne intelligis, domine? to make frantic, lunatic.

NATHANIEL. Laus Deo, bone intelligo.

HOLOFERNES. 'Bone'?—'bone' for 'bene.' Priscian a little scratch'd; 'twill serve.

Enter ARMADO, MOTH, *and* COSTARD

NATHANIEL. Videsne quis venit?

HOLOFERNES. Video, et gaudeo.

ARMADO. [*To* MOTH] Chirrah!

HOLOFERNES. Quare 'chirrah,' not 'sirrah'?

ARMADO. Men of peace, well encount'red.

HOLOFERNES. Most military sir, salutation.

MOTH. [*Aside to* COSTARD] They have been at a great feast of languages and stol'n the scraps.

COSTARD. O, they have liv'd long on the alms-basket of words. I marvel thy master hath not eaten thee for a word, for thou are not so long by the head as honorificabilitudinitatibus; thou art easier swallowed than a flap-dragon.

MOTH. Peace! the peal begins.

ARMADO. [*To* HOLOFERNES] Monsieur, are you not lett'red?

MOTH. Yes, yes; he teaches boys the hornbook. What is a, b, spelt backward with the horn on his head?

HOLOFERNES. Ba, pueritia, with a horn added.

MOTH. Ba, most silly sheep with a horn. You hear his learning.

HOLOFERNES. Quis, quis, thou consonant?

MOTH. The third of the five vowels, if You repeat them; or the fifth, if I.

HOLOFERNES. I will repeat them: a, e, I—

MOTH. The sheep; the other two concludes it: o, U.

ARMADO. Now, by the salt wave of the Mediterraneum, a sweet touch, a quick venue of wit—snip, snap, quick and home. It rejoiceth my intellect. True wit!

MOTH. Offer'd by a child to an old man; which is wit-old.

HOLOFERNES. What is the figure? What is the figure?

MOTH. Horns.

HOLOFERNES. Thou disputes like an infant; go whip thy gig.

MOTH. Lend me your horn to make one, and I will whip about your infamy circum circa—a gig of a cuckold's horn.

COSTARD. An I had but one penny in the world, thou shouldst have it to buy ginger-bread. Hold, there is the very remuneration I had of thy master, thou halfpenny purse of wit, thou pigeon-egg of discretion. O, an the heavens were so pleased that thou wert but my bastard, what a joyful father wouldst thou make me! Go to; thou hast it ad dunghill, at the fingers' ends, as they say.

HOLOFERNES. O, I smell false Latin; 'dunghill' for unguem.

ARMADO. Arts-man, preambulate; we will be singuled from the barbarous. Do you not educate youth at the charge-house on the top of the mountain?

HOLOFERNES. Or mons, the hill.

ARMADO. At your sweet pleasure, for the mountain.

HOLOFERNES. I do, sans question.

ARMADO. Sir, it is the King's most sweet pleasure and affection to congratulate the Princess at her pavilion, in the posteriors of this day; which the rude multitude call the afternoon.

HOLOFERNES. The posterior of the day, most generous sir, is liable, congruent, and measurable, for the afternoon. The word is well cull'd, chose, sweet, and apt, I do assure you, sir, I do assure.

ARMADO. Sir, the King is a noble gentleman, and my familiar, I do assure ye, very good friend. For what is inward between us, let it pass. I do beseech thee, remember thy courtesy. I beseech thee, apparel thy head. And among other importunate and most serious designs, and of great import indeed, too—but let that pass; for I must tell thee it will please his Grace, by the world, sometime to lean upon my poor shoulder, and with his royal finger thus dally with my excrement, with my mustachio; but, sweet heart, let that pass. By the world, I recount no fable: some certain special honours it pleaseth his greatness to impart to Armado, a soldier, a man of travel, that hath seen the world; but let that pass. The very all of all is—but, sweet heart, I do implore secrecy—that the King would have me present the Princess, sweet chuck, with some delightful ostentation, or show, or pageant, or antic, or firework. Now, understanding that the curate and your sweet self are good at such eruptions and sudden breaking-out of mirth, as it were, I have acquainted you withal, to the end to crave your assistance.

HOLOFERNES. Sir, you shall present before her the Nine Worthies. Sir Nathaniel, as concerning some entertainment of time, some show in the posterior of this day, to be rend'red by our assistance, the King's command, and this most gallant, illustrate, and learned gentleman, before the Princess—I say none so fit as to present the Nine Worthies.

NATHANIEL. Where will you find men worthy enough to present them?

HOLOFERNES. Joshua, yourself; myself, Alexander; this gallant gentleman, Judas Maccabæus; this swain, because of his great limb or joint, shall pass Pompey the Great; the page, Hercules.

ARMADO. Pardon, sir; error: he is not quantity enough for that Worthy's thumb; he is not so big as the end of his club.

HOLOFERNES. Shall I have audience? He shall present Hercules in minority: his enter and exit shall be strangling a snake; and I will have an apology for that purpose.

MOTH. An excellent device! So, if any of the audience hiss, you may cry 'Well done, Hercules; now thou crushest the snake!' That is the way to make an offence gracious, though few have the grace to do it.

ARMADO. For the rest of the Worthies?

HOLOFERNES. I will play three myself.

MOTH. Thrice-worthy gentleman!

ARMADO. Shall I tell you a thing?

HOLOFERNES. We attend.

ARMADO. We will have, if this fadge not, an antic. I beseech you, follow.

HOLOFERNES. Via, goodman Dull! Thou has spoken no word all this while.

DULL. Nor understood none neither, sir.

HOLOFERNES. Allons! we will employ thee.

DULL. I'll make one in a dance, or so, or I will play
On the tabor to the Worthies, and let them dance the hay.

HOLOFERNES. Most dull, honest Dull! To our sport, away.

Exeunt

SCENE 2

The park

Enter the PRINCESS, MARIA, KATHARINE, *and* ROSALINE

PRINCESS OF FRANCE. Sweet hearts, we shall be rich ere we depart,
If fairings come thus plentifully in.
A lady wall'd about with diamonds!
Look you what I have from the loving King.

ROSALINE. Madam, came nothing else along with that?

PRINCESS OF FRANCE. Nothing but this! Yes, as much love in rhyme

As would be cramm'd up in a sheet of paper
Writ o' both sides the leaf, margent and all,
That he was fain to seal on Cupid's name.
ROSALINE. That was the way to make his godhead wax;
For he hath been five thousand year a boy.
KATHARINE. Ay, and a shrewd unhappy gallows too.
ROSALINE. You'll ne'er be friends with him: 'a kill'd your
sister.
KATHARINE. He made her melancholy, sad, and heavy;
And so she died. Had she been light, like you,
Of such a merry, nimble, stirring spirit,
She might 'a been a grandam ere she died.
And so may you; for a light heart lives long.
ROSALINE. What's your dark meaning, mouse, of this light
word?
KATHARINE. A light condition in a beauty dark.
ROSALINE. We need more light to find your meaning out.
KATHARINE. You'll mar the light by taking it in snuff;
Therefore I'll darkly end the argument.
ROSALINE. Look what you do, you do it still i' th' dark.
KATHARINE. So do not you; for you are a light wench.
ROSALINE. Indeed, I weigh not you; and therefore light.
KATHARINE. You weigh me not? O, that's you care not for
me.
ROSALINE. Great reason; for 'past cure is still past care.'
PRINCESS OF FRANCE. Well bandied both; a set of wit well
play'd.
But, Rosaline, you have a favour too?
Who sent it? and what is it?
ROSALINE. I would you knew.
An if my face were but as fair as yours,
My favour were as great: be witness this.
Nay, I have verses too, I thank Berowne;
The numbers true, and, were the numb'ring too,
I were the fairest goddess on the ground.
I am compar'd to twenty thousand fairs.
O, he hath drawn my picture in his letter!
PRINCESS OF FRANCE. Anything like?
ROSALINE. Much in the letters; nothing in the praise.
PRINCESS OF FRANCE. Beauteous as ink—a good conclusion.

KATHARINE. Fair as a text B in a copy-book.

ROSALINE. Ware pencils, ho! Let me not die your debtor,
My red dominical, my golden letter:
O that your face were not so full of O's!

KATHARINE. A pox of that jest! and I beshrew all shrows!

PRINCESS OF FRANCE. But, Katharine, what was sent to you
from fair Dumain?

KATHARINE. Madam, this glove.

PRINCESS OF FRANCE. Did he not send you twain?

KATHARINE. Yes, madam; and, moreover,
Some thousand verses of a faithful lover;
A huge translation of hypocrisy,
Vilely compil'd, profound simplicity.

MARIA. This, and these pearl, to me sent Longaville;
The letter is too long by half a mile.

PRINCESS OF FRANCE. I think no less. Dost thou not wish in
heart
The chain were longer and the letter short?

MARIA. Ay, or I would these hands might never part.

PRINCESS OF FRANCE. We are wise girls to mock our lovers
so.

ROSALINE. They are worse fools to purchase mocking so.
That same Berowne I'll torture ere I go.
O that I knew he were but in by th' week!
How I would make him fawn, and beg, and seek,
And wait the season, and observe the times,
And spend his prodigal wits in bootless rhymes,
And shape his service wholly to my hests,
And make him proud to make me proud that jests!
So pertaunt-like would I o'ersway his state
That he should be my fool, and I his fate.

PRINCESS OF FRANCE. None are so surely caught, when they
are catch'd,
As wit turn'd fool; folly, in wisdom hatch'd,
Hath wisdom's warrant and the help of school,
And wit's own grace to grace a learned fool.

ROSALINE. The blood of youth burns not with such excess
As gravity's revolt to wantonness.

MARIA. Folly in fools bears not so strong a note
As fool'ry in the wise when wit doth dote,

Since all the power thereof it doth apply
To prove, by wit, worth in simplicity.

Enter BOYET

PRINCESS OF FRANCE. Here comes Boyet, and mirth is in his
    face.
BOYET. O, I am stabb'd with laughter! Where's her Grace?
PRINCESS OF FRANCE. Thy news, Boyet?
BOYET. Prepare, madam, prepare!
    Arm, wenches, arm! Encounters mounted are
    Against your peace. Love doth approach disguis'd,
    Armed in arguments; you'll be surpris'd.
    Muster your wits; stand in your own defence;
    Or hide your heads like cowards, and fly hence.
PRINCESS OF FRANCE. Saint Dennis to Saint Cupid! What are
    they
    That charge their breath against us? Say, scout, say.
BOYET. Under the cool shade of a sycamore
    I thought to close mine eyes some half an hour;
    When, lo, to interrupt my purpos'd rest,
    Toward that shade I might behold addrest
    The King and his companions; warily
    I stole into a neighbour thicket by,
    And overheard what you shall overhear—
    That, by and by, disguis'd they will be here.
    Their herald is a pretty knavish page,
    That well by heart hath conn'd his embassage.
    Action and accent did they teach him there:
    'Thus must thou speak' and 'thus thy body bear,'
    And ever and anon they made a doubt
    Presence majestical would put him out;
    'For' quoth the King 'an angel shalt thou see;
    Yet fear not thou, but speak audaciously.'
    The boy replied 'An angel is not evil;
    I should have fear'd her had she been a devil.'
    With that all laugh'd, and clapp'd him on the shoulder,
    Making the bold wag by their praises bolder.
    One rubb'd his elbow, thus, and fleer'd, and swore
    A better speech was never spoke before.
    Another with his finger and his thumb

Cried 'Via! we will do't, come what will come.'
The third he caper'd, and cried 'All goes well.'
The fourth turn'd on the toe, and down he fell.
With that they all did tumble on the ground,
With such a zealous laughter, so profound,
That in this spleen ridiculous appears,
To check their folly, passion's solemn tears.

PRINCESS OF FRANCE. But what, but what, come they to visit
 us?

BOYET. They do, they do, and are apparell'd thus,
Like Muscovites or Russians, as I guess.
Their purpose is to parley, court, and dance;
And every one his love-feat will advance
Unto his several mistress; which they'll know
By favours several which they did bestow.

PRINCESS OF FRANCE. And will they so? The gallants shall be
 task'd,
For, ladies, we will every one be mask'd;
And not a man of them shall have the grace,
Despite of suit, to see a lady's face.
Hold, Rosaline, this favour thou shalt wear,
And then the King will court thee for his dear;
Hold, take thou this, my sweet, and give me thine,
So shall Berowne take me for Rosaline.
And change you favours too; so shall your loves
Woo contrary, deceiv'd by these removes.

ROSALINE. Come on, then, wear the favours most in sight.

KATHARINE. But, in this changing, what is your intent?

PRINCESS OF FRANCE. The effect of my intent is to cross
 theirs.
They do it but in mocking merriment,
And mock for mock is only my intent.
Their several counsels they unbosom shall
To loves mistook, and so be mock'd withal
Upon the next occasion that we meet
With visages display'd to talk and greet.

ROSALINE. But shall we dance, if they desire us to't?

PRINCESS OF FRANCE. No, to the death, we will not move a
 foot,
Nor to their penn'd speech render we no grace;

But while 'tis spoke each turn away her face.
BOYET. Why, that contempt will kill the speaker's heart,
And quite divorce his memory from his part.
PRINCESS OF FRANCE. Therefore I do it; and I make no doubt
The rest will ne'er come in, if he be out.
There's no such sport as sport by sport o'erthrown,
To make theirs ours, and ours none but our own;
So shall we stay, mocking intended game,
And they well mock'd depart away with shame.
[*Trumpet sounds within*]
BOYET. The trumpet sounds; be mask'd; the maskers come.
[*The* LADIES *mask*]

Enter BLACKAMOORS *with music,* MOTH *as Prologue, the*
KING *and his* LORDS *as maskers, in the guise of Russians*

MOTH. *All hail, the richest beauties on the earth!*
BOYET. Beauties no richer than rich taffeta.
MOTH. *A holy parcel of the fairest dames*
[*The* LADIES *turn their backs to him*]
That ever turn'd their—backs—to mortal views!
BEROWNE. *Their eyes,* villain, *their eyes.*
MOTH. *That ever turn'd their eyes to mortal views!*
Out—
BOYET. True; *out* indeed.
MOTH. *Out of your favours, heavenly spirits, vouchsafe*
Not to behold—
BEROWNE. *Once to behold,* rogue.
MOTH. *Once to behold with your sun-beamed eyes—with*
your sun-beamed eyes—
BOYET. They will not answer to that epithet;
You were best call it 'daughter-beamed eyes.'
MOTH. They do not mark me, and that brings me out.
BEROWNE. Is this your perfectness? Be gone, you rogue.
Exit MOTH
ROSALINE. What would these strangers? Know their minds,
Boyet.
If they do speak our language, 'tis our will
That some plain man recount their purposes.
Know what they would.
BOYET. What would you with the Princess?

BEROWNE. Nothing but peace and gentle visitation.

ROSALINE. What would they, say they?

BOYET. Nothing but peace and gentle visitation.

ROSALINE. Why, that they have; and bid them so be gone.

BOYET. She says you have it, and you may be gone.

KING. Say to her we have measur'd many miles
    To tread a measure with her on this grass.

BOYET. They say that they have measur'd many a mile
    To tread a measure with you on this grass.

ROSALINE. It is not so. Ask them how many inches
    Is in one mile? If they have measured many,
    The measure, then, of one is eas'ly told.

BOYET. If to come hither you have measur'd miles,
    And many miles, the Princess bids you tell
    How many inches doth fill up one mile.

BEROWNE. Tell her we measure them by weary steps.

BOYET. She hears herself.

ROSALINE. How many weary steps
    Of many weary miles you have o'ergone
    Are numb'red in the travel of one mile?

BEROWNE. We number nothing that we spend for you;
    Our duty is so rich, so infinite,
    That we may do it still without accompt.
    Vouchsafe to show the sunshine of your face,
    That we, like savages, may worship it.

ROSALINE. My face is but a moon, and clouded too.

KING. Blessed are clouds, to do as such clouds do.
    Vouchsafe, bright moon, and these thy stars, to shine,
    Those clouds removed, upon our watery eyne.

ROSALINE. O vain petitioner! beg a greater matter;
    Thou now requests but moonshine in the water.

KING. Then in our measure do but vouchsafe one change.
    Thou bid'st me beg; this begging is not strange.

ROSALINE. Play, music, then. Nay, you must do it soon.
    Not yet? No dance! Thus change I like the moon.

KING. Will you not dance? How come you thus estranged?

ROSALINE. You took the moon at full; but now she's changed.

KING. Yet still she is the Moon, and I the Man.
    The music plays; vouchsafe some motion to it.

ROSALINE. Our ears vouchsafe it.

KING. But your legs should do it.

ROSALINE. Since you are strangers, and come here by chance,
We'll not be nice; take hands. We will not dance.

KING. Why take we hands then?

ROSALINE. Only to part friends.
Curtsy, sweet hearts; and so the measure ends.

KING. More measure of this measure; be not nice.

ROSALINE. We can afford no more at such a price.

KING. Price you yourselves. What buys your company?

ROSALINE. Your absence only.

KING. That can never be.

ROSALINE. Then cannot we be bought; and so adieu—
Twice to your visor and half once to you.

KING. If you deny to dance, let's hold more chat.

ROSALINE. In private then.

KING. I am best pleas'd with that.   [*They converse apart*]

BEROWNE. White-handed mistress, one sweet word with thee.

PRINCESS OF FRANCE. Honey, and milk, and sugar; there is three.

BEROWNE. Nay, then, two treys, an if you grow so nice,
Metheglin, wort, and malmsey; well run dice!
There's half a dozen sweets.

PRINCESS OF FRANCE. Seventh sweet, adieu!
Since you can cog, I'll play no more with you.

BEROWNE. One word in secret.

PRINCESS OF FRANCE. Let it not be sweet.

BEROWNE. Thou grievest my gall.

PRINCESS OF FRANCE. Gall! bitter.

BEROWNE. Therefore meet.   [*They converse apart*]

DUMAIN. Will you vouchsafe with me to change a word?

MARIA. Name it.

DUMAIN. Fair lady—

MARIA. Say you so? Fair lord—
Take that for your fair lady.

DUMAIN. Please it you,
As much in private, and I'll bid adieu.

[*They converse apart*]

KATHARINE. What, was your vizard made without a tongue?

LONGAVILLE. I know the reason, lady, why you ask.

KATHARINE. O for your reason! Quickly, sir; I long.

LONGAVILLE. You have a double tongue within your mask,
And would afford my speechless vizard half.

KATHARINE. 'Veal' quoth the Dutchman. Is not 'veal' a calf?

LONGAVILLE. A calf, fair lady!

KATHARINE. No, a fair lord calf.

LONGAVILLE. Let's part the word.

KATHARINE. No, I'll not be your half.
Take all and wean it; it may prove an ox.

LONGAVILLE. Look how you butt yourself in these sharp
mocks!
Will you give horns, chaste lady? Do not so.

KATHARINE. Then die a calf, before your horns do grow.

LONGAVILLE. One word in private with you ere I die.

KATHARINE. Bleat softly, then; the butcher hears you cry.
[They converse apart]

BOYET. The tongues of mocking wenches are as keen
As is the razor's edge invisible,
Cutting a smaller hair than may be seen,
Above the sense of sense; so sensible
Seemeth their conference; their conceits have wings,
Fleeter than arrows, bullets, wind, thought, swifter things.

ROSALINE. Not one word more, my maids; break off, break
off.

BEROWNE. By heaven, all dry-beaten with pure scoff!

KING. Farewell, mad wenches; you have simple wits.
Exeunt KING, LORDS, *and* BLACKAMOORS

PRINCESS OF FRANCE. Twenty adieus, my frozen Muscovits.
Are these the breed of wits so wondered at?

BOYET. Tapers they are, with your sweet breaths puff'd out.

ROSALINE. Well-liking wits they have; gross, gross; fat, fat.

PRINCESS OF FRANCE. O poverty in wit, kingly-poor flout!
Will they not, think you, hang themselves to-night?
Or ever but in vizards show their faces?
This pert Berowne was out of count'nance quite.

ROSALINE. They were all in lamentable cases!
The King was weeping-ripe for a good word.

PRINCESS OF FRANCE. Berowne did swear himself out of all
suit.

MARIA. Dumain was at my service, and his sword.

'No point' quoth I; my servant straight was mute.

KATHARINE. Lord Longaville said I came o'er his heart;
And trow you what he call'd me?

PRINCESS OF FRANCE. Qualm, perhaps.

KATHARINE. Yes, in good faith.

PRINCESS OF FRANCE. Go, sickness as thou art!

ROSALINE. Well, better wits have worn plain statute-caps.
But will you hear? The King is my love sworn.

PRINCESS OF FRANCE. And quick Berowne hath plighted faith
to me.

KATHARINE. And Longaville was for my service born.

MARIA. Dumain is mine, as sure as bark on tree.

BOYET. Madam, and pretty mistresses, give ear:
Immediately they will again be here
In their own shapes; for it can never be
They will digest this harsh indignity.

PRINCESS OF FRANCE. Will they return?

BOYET. They will, they will, God knows,
And leap for joy, though they are lame with blows;
Therefore, change favours; and, when they repair,
Blow like sweet roses in this summer air.

PRINCESS OF FRANCE. How blow? how blow? Speak to be
understood.

BOYET. Fair ladies mask'd are roses in their bud:
Dismask'd, their damask sweet commixture shown,
Are angels vailing clouds, or roses blown.

PRINCESS OF FRANCE. Avaunt, perplexity! What shall we do
If they return in their own shapes to woo?

ROSALINE. Good madam, if by me you'll be advis'd,
Let's mock them still, as well known as disguis'd.
Let us complain to them what fools were here,
Disguis'd like Muscovites, in shapeless gear;
And wonder what they were, and to what end
Their shallow shows and prologue vilely penn'd,
And their rough carriage so ridiculous,
Should be presented at our tent to us.

BOYET. Ladies, withdraw; the gallants are at hand.

PRINCESS OF FRANCE. Whip to our tents, as roes run o'er
land.

Exeunt PRINCESS, ROSALINE, KATHARINE, *and* MARIA

ACT V. SCENE 2

Re-enter the KING, BEROWNE, LONGAVILLE, *and* DUMAIN,
in their proper habits

KING. Fair sir, God save you! Where's the Princess?
BOYET. Gone to her tent. Please it your Majesty
  Command me any service to her thither?
KING. That she vouchsafe me audience for one word.
BOYET. I will; and so will she, I know, my lord.   *Exit*
BEROWNE. This fellow pecks up wit as pigeons pease,
  And utters it again when God doth please.
  He is wit's pedlar, and retails his wares
  At wakes, and wassails, meetings, markets, fairs;
  And we that sell by gross, the Lord doth know,
  Have not the grace to grace it with such show.
  This gallant pins the wenches on his sleeve;
  Had he been Adam, he had tempted Eve.
  'A can carve too, and lisp; why this is he
  That kiss'd his hand away in courtesy;
  This is the ape of form, Monsieur the Nice,
  That, when he plays at tables, chides the dice
  In honourable terms; nay, he can sing
  A mean most meanly; and in ushering,
  Mend him who can. The ladies call him sweet;
  The stairs, as he treads on them, kiss his feet.
  This is the flow'r that smiles on every one,
  To show his teeth as white as whales-bone;
  And consciences that will not die in debt
  Pay him the due of 'honey-tongued Boyet.'
KING. A blister on his sweet tongue, with my heart,
  That put Armado's page out of his part!

Re-enter the PRINCESS, *ushered by* BOYET; ROSALINE,
MARIA, *and* KATHARINE

BEROWNE. See where it comes! Behaviour, what wert thou
  Till this man show'd thee? And what art thou now?
KING. All hail, sweet madam, and fair time of day!
PRINCESS OF FRANCE. 'Fair' in 'all hail' is foul, as I conceive.
KING. Construe my speeches better, if you may.
PRINCESS OF FRANCE. Then wish me better; I will give you
  leave.
KING. We came to visit you, and purpose now

To lead you to our court; vouchsafe it then.
PRINCESS OF FRANCE. This field shall hold me, and so hold
    your vow:
Nor God, nor I, delights in perjur'd men.
KING. Rebuke me not for that which you provoke.
The virtue of your eye must break my oath.
PRINCESS OF FRANCE. You nickname virtue: vice you should
    have spoke;
    For virtue's office never breaks men's troth.
Now by my maiden honour, yet as pure
As the unsullied lily, I protest,
A world of torments though I should endure,
I would not yield to be your house's guest;
So much I hate a breaking cause to be
Of heavenly oaths, vowed with integrity.
KING. O, you have liv'd in desolation here,
    Unseen, unvisited, much to our shame.
PRINCESS OF FRANCE. Not so, my lord; it is not so, I swear;
    We have had pastimes here, and pleasant game;
    A mess of Russians left us but of late.
KING. How, madam! Russians!
PRINCESS OF FRANCE. Ay, in truth, my lord;
    Trim gallants, full of courtship and of state.
ROSALINE. Madam, speak true. It is not so, my lord.
My lady, to the manner of the days,
In courtesy gives undeserving praise.
We four indeed confronted were with four
In Russian habit; here they stayed an hour
And talk'd apace; and in that hour, my lord,
They did not bless us with one happy word.
I dare not call them fools; but this I think,
When they are thirsty, fools would fain have drink.
BEROWNE. This jest is dry to me. Fair gentle sweet,
Your wit makes wise things foolish; when we greet,
With eyes best seeing, heaven's fiery eye,
By light we lose light; your capacity
Is of that nature that to your huge store
Wise things seem foolish and rich things but poor.
ROSALINE. This proves you wise and rich, for in my eye—
BEROWNE. I am a fool, and full of poverty.

ROSALINE. But that you take what doth to you belong,
It were a fault to snatch words from my tongue.
BEROWNE. O, I am yours, and all that I possess.
ROSALINE. All the fool mine?
BEROWNE. I cannot give you less.
ROSALINE. Which of the vizards was it that you wore?
BEROWNE. Where? when? what vizard? Why demand you
this?
ROSALINE. There, then, that vizard; that superfluous case
That hid the worse and show'd the better face.
KING. We were descried; they'll mock us now downright.
DUMAIN. Let us confess, and turn it to a jest.
PRINCESS OF FRANCE. Amaz'd, my lord? Why looks your
Highness sad?
ROSALINE. Help, hold his brows! he'll swoon! Why look you
pale?
Sea-sick, I think, coming from Muscovy.
BEROWNE. Thus pour the stars down plagues for perjury.
Can any face of brass hold longer out?
Here stand I, lady—dart thy skill at me,
Bruise me with scorn, confound me with a flout,
Thrust thy sharp wit quite through my ignorance,
Cut me to pieces with thy keen conceit;
And I will wish thee never more to dance,
Nor never more in Russian habit wait.
O, never will I trust to speeches penn'd,
Nor to the motion of a school-boy's tongue,
Nor never come in vizard to my friend,
Nor woo in rhyme, like a blind harper's song.
Taffeta phrases, silken terms precise,
Three-pil'd hyperboles, spruce affectation,
Figures pedantical—these summer-flies
Have blown me full of maggot ostentation.
I do forswear them; and I here protest,
By this white glove—how white the hand, God knows!—
Henceforth my wooing mind shall be express'd
In russet yeas, and honest kersey noes.
And, to begin, wench—so God help me, law!—
My love to thee is sound, sans crack or flaw.
ROSALINE. Sans 'sans,' I pray you.

BEROWNE. Yet I have a trick
Of the old rage; bear with me, I am sick;
I'll leave it by degrees. Soft, let us see—
Write 'Lord have mercy on us' on those three;
They are infected; in their hearts it lies;
They have the plague, and caught it of your eyes.
These lords are visited; you are not free,
For the Lord's tokens on you do I see.
PRINCESS OF FRANCE. No, they are free that gave these
tokens to us.
BEROWNE. Our states are forfeit; seek not to undo us.
ROSALINE. It is not so; for how can this be true,
That you stand forfeit, being those that sue?
BEROWNE. Peace; for I will not have to do with you.
ROSALINE. Nor shall not, if I do as I intend.
BEROWNE. Speak for yourselves; my wit is at an end.
KING. Teach us, sweet madam, for our rude transgression
Some fair excuse.
PRINCESS OF FRANCE. The fairest is confession.
Were not you here but even now, disguis'd?
KING. Madam, I was.
PRINCESS OF FRANCE. And were you well advis'd?
KING. I was, fair madam.
PRINCESS OF FRANCE. When you then were here,
What did you whisper in your lady's ear?
KING. That more than all the world I did respect her.
PRINCESS OF FRANCE. When she shall challenge this, you will
reject her.
KING. Upon mine honour, no.
PRINCESS OF FRANCE. Peace, peace, forbear;
Your oath once broke, you force not to forswear.
KING. Despise me when I break this oath of mine.
PRINCESS OF FRANCE. I will; and therefore keep it. Rosaline,
What did the Russian whisper in your ear?
ROSALINE. Madam, he swore that he did hold me dear
As precious eyesight, and did value me
Above this world; adding thereto, moreover,
That he would wed me, or else die my lover.
PRINCESS OF FRANCE. God give thee joy of him! The noble
lord

Most honourably doth uphold his word.

KING. What mean you, madam? By my life, my troth,
  I never swore this lady such an oath.

ROSALINE. By heaven, you did; and, to confirm it plain,
  You gave me this; but take it, sir, again.

KING. My faith and this the Princess I did give;
  I knew her by this jewel on her sleeve.

PRINCESS OF FRANCE. Pardon me, sir, this jewel did she wear;
  And Lord Berowne, I thank him, is my dear.
  What, will you have me, or your pearl again?

BEROWNE. Neither of either; I remit both twain.
  I see the trick on't: here was a consent,
  Knowing aforehand of our merriment,
  To dash it like a Christmas comedy.
  Some carry-tale, some please-man, some slight zany,
  Some mumble-news, some trencher-knight, some Dick,
  That smiles his cheek in years and knows the trick
  To make my lady laugh when she's dispos'd,
  Told our intents before; which once disclos'd,
  The ladies did change favours; and then we,
  Following the signs, woo'd but the sign of she.
  Now, to our perjury to add more terror,
  We are again forsworn in will and error.
  Much upon this it is; [To BOYET] and might not you
  Forestall our sport, to make us thus untrue?
  Do not you know my lady's foot by th' squier,
  And laugh upon the apple of her eye?
  And stand between her back, sir, and the fire,
  Holding a trencher, jesting merrily?
  You put our page out. Go, you are allow'd;
  Die when you will, a smock shall be your shroud.
  You leer upon me, do you? There's an eye
  Wounds like a leaden sword.

BOYET. Full merrily
  Hath this brave manage, this career, been run.

BEROWNE. Lo, he is tilting straight! Peace; I have done.

Enter COSTARD

Welcome, pure wit! Thou part'st a fair fray.

COSTARD. O Lord, sir, they would know

517

Whether the three Worthies shall come in or no?

BEROWNE. What, are there but three?

COSTARD. No, sir; but it is vara fine,
For every one pursents three.

BEROWNE. And three times thrice is nine.

COSTARD. Not so, sir; under correction, sir,
I hope it is not so.
You cannot beg us, sir, I can assure you, sir; we know
what we know;
I hope, sir, three times thrice, sir—

BEROWNE. Is not nine.

COSTARD. Under correction, sir, we know whereuntil it doth
amount.

BEROWNE. By Jove, I always took three threes for nine.

COSTARD. O Lord, sir, it were pity you should get your living by reck'ning, sir.

BEROWNE. How much is it?

COSTARD. O Lord, sir, the parties themselves, the actors, sir,
will show whereuntil it doth amount. For mine own part,
I am, as they say, but to parfect one man in one poor man,
Pompion the Great, sir.

BEROWNE. Art thou one of the Worthies?

COSTARD. It pleased them to think me worthy of Pompey
the Great; for mine own part, I know not the degree of
the Worthy; but I am to stand for him.

BEROWNE. Go, bid them prepare.

COSTARD. We will turn it finely off, sir; we will take some
care.   *Exit* COSTARD

KING. Berowne, they will shame us; let them not approach.

BEROWNE. We are shame-proof, my lord, and 'tis some
policy
To have one show worse than the King's and his company.

KING. I say they shall not come.

PRINCESS OF FRANCE. Nay, my good lord, let me o'errule
you now.
That sport best pleases that doth least know how;
Where zeal strives to content, and the contents
Dies in the zeal of that which it presents.
Their form confounded makes most form in mirth,
When great things labouring perish in their birth.

BEROWNE. A right description of our sport, my lord.

Enter ARMADO

ARMADO. Anointed, I implore so much expense of thy royal
sweet breath as will utter a brace of words.
    [*Converses apart with the* KING, *and delivers a paper*]
PRINCESS OF FRANCE. Doth this man serve God?
BEROWNE. Why ask you?
PRINCESS OF FRANCE. 'A speaks not like a man of God his
    making.
ARMADO. That is all one, my fair, sweet, honey monarch;
    for, I protest, the schoolmaster is exceeding fantastical; too
    too vain, too too vain; but we will put it, as they say, to
    fortuna de la guerra. I wish you the peace of mind, most
    royal couplement!   *Exit* ARMADO
KING. Here is like to be a good presence of Worthies. He
    presents Hector of Troy; the swain, Pompey the Great;
    the parish curate, Alexander; Armado's page, Hercules; the
    pedant, Judas Maccabæus.
    And if these four Worthies in their first show thrive,
    These four will change habits and present the other five.
BEROWNE. There is five in the first show.
KING. You are deceived, 'tis not so.
BEROWNE. The pedant, the braggart, the hedge-priest, the
    fool, and the boy:
    Abate throw at novum, and the whole world again
    Cannot pick out five such, take each one in his vein.
KING. The ship is under sail, and here she comes amain.

Enter COSTARD, *armed for* POMPEY

COSTARD. *I Pompey am—*
BEROWNE. You lie, you are not he.
COSTARD. *I Pompey am—*
BOYET. With libbard's head on knee.
BEROWNE. Well said, old mocker; I must needs be friends
    with thee.
COSTARD. *I Pompey am, Pompey surnam'd the Big—*
DUMAIN. The *Great.*
COSTARD. It is *Great,* sir.
    Pompey surnam'd the Great,

*That oft in field, with targe and shield, did make my foe
to sweat;
And travelling along this coast, I here am come by chance,
And lay my arms before the legs of this sweet lass of
France.*

If your ladyship would say 'Thanks, Pompey,' I had done.
PRINCESS OF FRANCE. Great thanks, great Pompey.
COSTARD. 'Tis not so much worth; but I hope I was perfect.
I made a little fault in *Great*.
BEROWNE. My hat to a halfpenny, Pompey proves the best
Worthy.

Enter SIR NATHANIEL, *for* ALEXANDER

NATHANIEL. *When in the world I liv'd, I was the world's
commander;
By east, west, north, and south, I spread my conquering
might.
My scutcheon plain declares that I am Alisander—*
BOYET. Your nose says, no, you are not; for it stands too
right.
BEROWNE. Your nose smells 'no' in this, most tender-smelling
knight.
PRINCESS OF FRANCE. The conqueror is dismay'd. Proceed,
good Alexander.
NATHANIEL. *When in the world I liv'd, I was the world's
commander—*
BOYET. Most true, 'tis right, you were so, Alisander.
BEROWNE. Pompey the Great!
COSTARD. Your servant, and Costard.
BEROWNE. Take away the conqueror, take away Alisander.
COSTARD. [*To* SIR NATHANIEL] O, sir, you have overthrown
Alisander the conqueror! You will be scrap'd out of the
painted cloth for this. Your lion, that holds his poleaxe sitting on a close-stool, will be given to Ajax. He will be the
ninth Worthy. A conqueror and afeard to speak! Run
away for shame, Alisander. [SIR NATHANIEL *retires*]
There, an't shall please you, a foolish mild man; an honest
man, look you, and soon dash'd. He is a marvellous good
neighbour, faith, and a very good bowler; but for Ali-

sander—alas! you see how 'tis—a little o'erparted. But there are Worthies a-coming will speak their mind in some other sort.

PRINCESS OF FRANCE. Stand aside, good Pompey.

Enter HOLOFERNES, *for* JUDAS; *and* MOTH, *for* HERCULES

HOLOFERNES. *Great Hercules is presented by this imp,*
   Whose club kill'd Cerberus, that three-headed canus;
   And when he was a babe, a child, a shrimp,
   Thus did he strangle serpents in his manus.
   Quoniam he seemeth in minority,
   Ergo I come with this apology.
   Keep some state in thy exit, and vanish.   [MOTH *retires*]
   Judas I am—
DUMAIN. A Judas!
HOLOFERNES. Not Iscariot, sir.
   Judas I am, ycliped Maccabæus.
DUMAIN. Judas Maccabæus clipt is plain Judas.
BEROWNE. A kissing traitor. How art thou prov'd Judas?
HOLOFERNES. *Judas I am—*
DUMAIN. The more shame for you, Judas!
HOLOFERNES. What mean you, sir?
BOYET. To make Judas hang himself.
HOLOFERNES. Begin, sir; you are my elder.
BEROWNE. Well followed: Judas was hanged on an elder.
HOLOFERNES. I will not be put out of countenance.
BEROWNE. Because thou hast no face.
HOLOFERNES. What is this?
BOYET. A cittern-head.
DUMAIN. The head of a bodkin.
BEROWNE. A death's face in a ring.
LONGAVILLE. The face of an old Roman coin, scarce seen.
BOYET. The pommel of Cæsar's falchion.
DUMAIN. The carv'd-bone face on a flask.
BEROWNE. Saint George's half-cheek in a brooch.
DUMAIN. Ay, and in a brooch of lead.
BEROWNE. Ay, and worn in the cap of a tooth-drawer. And
   now, forward; for we have put thee in countenance.
HOLOFERNES. You have put me out of countenance.
BEROWNE. False: we have given thee faces.

HOLOFERNES. But you have outfac'd them all.

BEROWNE. An thou wert a lion we would do so.

BOYET. Therefore, as he is an ass, let him go.
And so adieu, sweet Jude! Nay, why dost thou stay?

DUMAIN. For the latter end of his name.

BEROWNE. For the ass to the Jude; give it him—Jud-as, away.

HOLOFERNES. This is not generous, not gentle, not humble.

BOYET. A light for Monsieur Judas! It grows dark, he may
stumble.   [HOLOFERNES *retires*]

PRINCESS OF FRANCE. Alas, poor Maccabæus, how hath he
been baited!

Enter ARMADO, *for* HECTOR

BEROWNE. Hide thy head, Achilles; here comes Hector in
arms.

DUMAIN. Though my mocks come home by me, I will now
be merry.

KING. Hector was but a Troyan in respect of this.

BOYET. But is this Hector?

DUMAIN. I think Hector was not so clean-timber'd.

LONGAVILLE. His leg is too big for Hector's.

DUMAIN. More calf, certain.

BOYET. No; he is best indued in the small.

BEROWNE. This cannot be Hector.

DUMAIN. He's a god or a painter, for he makes faces.

ARMADO. *The armipotent Mars, of lances the almighty,*
Gave Hector a gift—

DUMAIN. A gilt nutmeg.

BEROWNE. A lemon.

LONGAVILLE. Stuck with cloves.

DUMAIN. No, cloven.

ARMADO. Peace!
The armipotent Mars, of lances the almighty,
Gave Hector a gift, the heir of Ilion;
A man so breathed that certain he would fight ye,
From morn till night out of his pavilion.
I am that flower—

DUMAIN. That mint.

LONGAVILLE. That columbine.

ARMADO. Sweet Lord Longaville, rein thy tongue.

LONGAVILLE. I must rather give it the rein, for it runs against Hector.

DUMAIN. Ay, and Hector's a greyhound.

ARMADO. The sweet war-man is dead and rotten; sweet chucks, beat not the bones of the buried; when he breathed, he was a man. But I will forward with my device. [*To the* PRINCESS] Sweet royalty, bestow on me the sense of hearing.

[BEROWNE *steps forth, and speaks to* COSTARD]

PRINCESS OF FRANCE. Speak, brave Hector; we are much delighted.

ARMADO. I do adore thy sweet Grace's slipper.

BOYET. [*Aside to* DUMAIN] Loves her by the foot.

DUMAIN. [*Aside to* BOYET] He may not by the yard.

ARMADO. *This Hector far surmounted Hannibal—*

COSTARD. The party is gone, fellow Hector, she is gone; she is two months on her way.

ARMADO. What meanest thou?

COSTARD. Faith, unless you play the honest Troyan, the poor wench is cast away. She's quick; the child brags in her belly already; 'tis yours.

ARMADO. Dost thou infamonize me among potentates? Thou shalt die.

COSTARD. Then shall Hector be whipt for Jaquenetta that is quick by him, and hang'd for Pompey that is dead by him.

DUMAIN. Most rare Pompey!

BOYET. Renowned Pompey!

BEROWNE. Greater than Great! Great, great, great Pompey! Pompey the Huge!

DUMAIN. Hector trembles.

BEROWNE. Pompey is moved. More Ates, more Ates! Stir them on! stir them on!

DUMAIN. Hector will challenge him.

BEROWNE. Ay, if 'a have no more man's blood in his belly than will sup a flea.

ARMADO. By the North Pole, I do challenge thee.

COSTARD. I will not fight with a pole, like a Northern man; I'll slash; I'll do it by the sword. I bepray you, let me borrow my arms again.

DUMAIN. Room for the incensed Worthies!

COSTARD. I'll do it in my shirt.

DUMAIN. Most resolute Pompey!

MOTH. Master, let me take you a buttonhole lower. Do you not see Pompey is uncasing for the combat? What mean you? You will lose your reputation.

ARMADO. Gentlemen and soldiers, pardon me; I will not combat in my shirt.

DUMAIN. You may not deny it: Pompey hath made the challenge.

ARMADO. Sweet bloods, I both may and will.

BEROWNE. What reason have you for 't?

ARMADO. The naked truth of it is: I have no shirt; I go woolward for penance.

BOYET. True, and it was enjoined him in Rome for want of linen; since when, I'll be sworn, he wore none but a dishclout of Jaquenetta's, and that 'a wears next his heart for a favour.

Enter as messenger, MONSIEUR MARCADE

MARCADE. God save you, madam!

PRINCESS OF FRANCE. Welcome, Marcade;
But that thou interruptest our merriment.

MARCADE. I am sorry, madam; for the news I bring
Is heavy in my tongue. The King your father—

PRINCESS OF FRANCE. Dead, for my life!

MARCADE. Even so; my tale is told.

BEROWNE. Worthies away; the scene begins to cloud.

ARMADO. For mine own part, I breathe free breath. I have seen the day of wrong through the little hole of discretion, and I will right myself like a soldier. *Exeunt* WORTHIES

KING. How fares your Majesty?

PRINCESS OF FRANCE. Boyet, prepare; I will away to-night.

KING. Madam, not so; I do beseech you stay.

PRINCESS OF FRANCE. Prepare, I say. I thank you, gracious lords,
For all your fair endeavours, and entreat,
Out of a new-sad soul, that you vouchsafe
In your rich wisdom to excuse or hide
The liberal opposition of our spirits,
If over-boldly we have borne ourselves

In the converse of breath—your gentleness
Was guilty of it. Farewell, worthy lord.
A heavy heart bears not a nimble tongue.
Excuse me so, coming too short of thanks
For my great suit so easily obtain'd.

KING. The extreme parts of time extremely forms
All causes to the purpose of his speed;
And often at his very loose decides
That which long process could not arbitrate.
And though the mourning brow of progeny
Forbid the smiling courtesy of love
The holy suit which fain it would convince,
Yet, since love's argument was first on foot,
Let not the cloud of sorrow justle it
From what it purpos'd; since to wail friends lost
Is not by much so wholesome-profitable
As to rejoice at friends but newly found.

PRINCESS OF FRANCE. I understand you not; my griefs are
double.

BEROWNE. Honest plain words best pierce the ear of grief;
And by these badges understand the King.
For your fair sakes have we neglected time,
Play'd foul play with our oaths; your beauty, ladies,
Hath much deformed us, fashioning our humours
Even to the opposed end of our intents;
And what in us hath seem'd ridiculous,
As love is full of unbefitting strains,
All wanton as a child, skipping and vain;
Form'd by the eye and therefore, like the eye,
Full of strange shapes, of habits, and of forms,
Varying in subjects as the eye doth roll
To every varied object in his glance;
Which parti-coated presence of loose love
Put on by us, if in your heavenly eyes
Have misbecom'd our oaths and gravities,
Those heavenly eyes that look into these faults
Suggested us to make. Therefore, ladies,
Our love being yours, the error that love makes
Is likewise yours. We to ourselves prove false,
By being once false for ever to be true

To those that make us both—fair ladies, you;
And even that falsehood, in itself a sin,
Thus purifies itself and turns to grace.
PRINCESS OF FRANCE. We have receiv'd your letters, full of
 love;
Your favours, the ambassadors of love;
And, in our maiden council, rated them
At courtship, pleasant jest, and courtesy,
As bombast and as lining to the time;
But more devout than this in our respects
Have we not been; and therefore met your loves
In their own fashion, like a merriment.
DUMAIN. Our letters, madam, show'd much more than jest.
LONGAVILLE. So did our looks.
ROSALINE. We did not quote them so.
KING. Now, at the latest minute of the hour,
Grant us your loves.
PRINCESS OF FRANCE. A time, methinks, too short
To make a world-without-end bargain in.
No, no, my lord, your Grace is perjur'd much,
Full of dear guiltiness; and therefore this,
If for my love, as there is no such cause,
You will do aught—this shall you do for me:
Your oath I will not trust; but go with speed
To some forlorn and naked hermitage,
Remote from all the pleasures of the world;
There stay until the twelve celestial signs
Have brought about the annual reckoning.
If this austere insociable life
Change not your offer made in heat of blood,
If frosts and fasts, hard lodging and thin weeds,
Nip not the gaudy blossoms of your love,
But that it bear this trial, and last love,
Then, at the expiration of the year,
Come, challenge me, challenge me by these deserts;
And, by this virgin palm now kissing thine,
I will be thine; and, till that instant, shut
My woeful self up in a mournful house,
Raining the tears of lamentation
For the remembrance of my father's death.

If this thou do deny, let our hands part,
Neither intitled in the other's heart.
KING. If this, or more than this, I would deny,
To flatter up these powers of mine with rest,
The sudden hand of death close up mine eye!
Hence hermit then, my heart is in thy breast.
BEROWNE. *And what to me, my love? and what to me?*
ROSALINE. *You must be purged too, your sins are rack'd;*
You are attaint with faults and perjury;
Therefore, if you my favour mean to get,
A twelvemonth shall you spend, and never rest,
But seek the weary beds of people sick.
DUMAIN. But what to me, my love? but what to me?
A wife?
KATHARINE. A beard, fair health, and honesty;
With threefold love I wish you all these three.
DUMAIN. O, shall I say I thank you, gentle wife?
KATHARINE. No so, my lord; a twelvemonth and a day
I'll mark no words that smooth-fac'd wooers say.
Come when the King doth to my lady come;
Then, if I have much love, I'll give you some.
DUMAIN. I'll serve thee true and faithfully till then.
KATHARINE. Yet swear not, lest ye be forsworn again.
LONGAVILLE. What says Maria?
MARIA. At the twelvemonth's end
I'll change my black gown for a faithful friend.
LONGAVILLE. I'll stay with patience; but the time is long.
MARIA. The liker you; few taller are so young.
BEROWNE. Studies my lady? Mistress, look on me;
Behold the window of my heart, mine eye,
What humble suit attends thy answer there.
Impose some service on me for thy love.
ROSALINE. Oft have I heard of you, my Lord Berowne,
Before I saw you; and the world's large tongue
Proclaims you for a man replete with mocks,
Full of comparisons and wounding flouts,
Which you on all estates will execute
That lie within the mercy of your wit.
To weed this wormwood from your fruitful brain,
And therewithal to win me, if you please,

Without the which I am not to be won,
You shall this twelvemonth term from day to day
Visit the speechless sick, and still converse
With groaning wretches; and your task shall be,
With all the fierce endeavour of your wit,
To enforce the pained impotent to smile.
BEROWNE. To move wild laughter in the throat of death?
It cannot be; it is impossible;
Mirth cannot move a soul in agony.
ROSALINE. Why, that's the way to choke a gibing spirit,
Whose influence is begot of that loose grace
Which shallow laughing hearers give to fools.
A jest's prosperity lies in the ear
Of him that hears it, never in the tongue
Of him that makes it; then, if sickly ears,
Deaf'd with the clamours of their own dear groans,
Will hear your idle scorns, continue then,
And I will have you and that fault withal.
But if they will not, throw away that spirit,
And I shall find you empty of that fault,
Right joyful of your reformation.
BEROWNE. A twelvemonth? Well, befall what will befall,
I'll jest a twelvemonth in an hospital.
PRINCESS OF FRANCE. [*To the* KING] Ay, sweet my lord, and
so I take my leave.
KING. No, madam; we will bring you on your way.
BEROWNE. Our wooing doth not end like an old play:
Jack hath not Jill. These ladies' courtesy
Might well have made our sport a comedy.
KING. Come, sir, it wants a twelvemonth an' a day,
And then 'twill end.
BEROWNE. That's too long for a play.

Re-enter ARMADO

ARMADO. Sweet Majesty, vouchsafe me—
PRINCESS OF FRANCE. Was not that Hector?
DUMAIN. The worthy knight of Troy.
ARMADO. I will kiss thy royal finger, and take leave. I am
a votary: I have vow'd to Jaquenetta to hold the plough
for her sweet love three year. But, most esteemed great-

ness, will you hear the dialogue that the two learned men have compiled in praise of the Owl and the Cuckoo? It should have followed in the end of our show.

KING. Call them forth quickly; we will do so.

ARMADO. Holla! approach.

Enter All

This side is Hiems, Winter; this Ver, the Spring—the one maintained by the Owl, th' other by the Cuckoo. Ver, begin.

SPRING

When daisies pied and violets blue
And lady-smocks all silver-white
And cuckoo-buds of yellow hue
Do paint the meadows with delight,
The cuckoo then on every tree
Mocks married men, for thus sings he:
 'Cuckoo;
Cuckoo, cuckoo'—O word of fear,
Unpleasing to a married ear!

When shepherds pipe on oaten straws,
And merry larks are ploughmen's clocks;
When turtles tread, and rooks and daws,
And maidens bleach their summer smocks;
The cuckoo then on every tree
Mocks married men, for thus sings he:
 'Cuckoo;
Cuckoo, cuckoo'—O word of fear,
Unpleasing to a married ear!

WINTER

When icicles hang by the wall,
And Dick the shepherd blows his nail,
And Tom bears logs into the hall,
And milk comes frozen home in pail,
When blood is nipp'd, and ways be foul,
Then nightly sings the staring owl:
 'Tu-who;

Tu-whit, Tu-who'—A merry note,
While greasy Joan doth keel the pot.

When all aloud the wind doth blow,
And coughing drowns the parson's saw,
And birds sit brooding in the snow,
And Marian's nose looks red and raw,
When roasted crabs hiss in the bowl,
Then nightly sings the staring owl:
　　'Tu-who;
Tu-whit, To-who'—A merry note,
While greasy Joan doth keel the pot.

ARMADO. The words of Mercury are harsh after the songs
of Apollo. You that way: we this way.　　　　*Exeunt*

A Midsummer Night's Dream

A MIDSUMMER NIGHT'S DREAM

IN AN EARLY play like *The Comedy of Errors* the ingenuity in the management of the plot is so obvious that we must recognise that from the beginning of his career Shakespeare revealed exceptional gifts as a dramatic craftsman. In *A Midsummer Night's Dream* however the poetry invests it all with a charm like the enchantment that moonlight casts over a familiar scene; yet the lines on which the action is constructed are as firm and carefully designed as ever, though less obtrusive now in a drama with a more developed body of character and greater variety of interest.

So natural does it all seem that it is only on reflection that we wonder how we can without a sense of incongruity see characters from Greek mythology consorting with craftsmen from Elizabethan England, and find a wood outside Athens alive with English fairies. Titania, it is true, has a classical pedigree, her name having been used by Ovid as an alternative for Diana, and it is clear from Act V, Scene 1—

> And we fairies that do run
> By the triple Hecate's team

that Shakespeare had in mind the threefold name of the moon goddess, who is Diana, Phœbe, Hecate, in earth, heaven, and hell, respectively. Oberon however has a more northern ancestry than his queen, and Robin Goodfellow or Puck had no doubt long enjoyed an English domicile. Shakespeare's fairy world, like the play as a whole, is of diverse strands yet completely naturalised and English.

It has been surmised that the scheme which links all the diversity together may have been suggested to Shakespeare by the occasion of some marriage for which the dramatist was expected to devise an entertainment. And certainly *A Midsummer Night's Dream* would have been ideal for such a celebration. Still it is difficult to insist without further evidence that there may have been three marriages celebrated in some great house and that the Queen herself graced the occasion. The Queen's presence would explain the famous refer-

PUCK. *Churl, upon thy eyes I throw*
All the power this charm doth owe
(ACT II. SCENE II)

ence to her as 'the fair vestal throned in the west.' Yet the
entrance, at the end, of the fairy band seems to provide an
unnecessarily elaborate finale if Oberon and his troupe are directing the attention of the audience only to marriages in a
play and not to ceremonies that had just been celebrated in
the house they were now to bless. The other play that introduces a fairy spectacle, *The Merry Wives of Windsor*, was
almost certainly written at the request of the Lord Chamberlain, the company's patron. The choir boys of his chapel
would provide the fairy band. That *A Midsummer Night's
Dream* was first designed for some private occasion when
boys would be available as fairies seems at least a reasonable
conjecture.

Quite independently of such speculations, the marriage of
Theseus and Hippolyta provides the hub on which the action
turns. In a few touches Shakespeare puts the aristocratic pair
before us, with their easy and gracious acceptance of the position of authority that they have the power, if necessary, to
maintain; they provide the centre of repose in which the
often bewildering and fantastic lines of the composition are
anchored. The Duke is not at all disturbed by the reports of
what has been happening in the wood near Athens; the business whatever it was does not call for action on his part. He
has more to do than disturb himself, as he explains, with the
imaginings of lunatics, lovers and poets. He is equally at ease
in the Interlude presented by Bottom and his colleagues.
Hippolyta feels she may have to blush for the performers:

> I love not to see wretchedness o'ercharg'd
> And duty in his service perishing

and she has to be reassured by the Duke that she will see no
such thing. Several times during the performance he reminds
her that she need not distress herself; all one has to do is to
receive such service courteously; what does it matter as long
as simpleness and duty tender it, since the best in this kind—
dramatic entertainment, the poet's frenzy—are but shadows,
and the worst are no worse, if imagination amend them.

It is impossible to suppose that Shakespeare had not met
the type of man he embodies in Theseus, or that the dramatist had not himself played before great personages who re-

garded his art with the condescension the Duke extended to Bottom and his fellow enthusiasts. Shakespeare was of course far too much a humorist to resent such an attitude and his sketch of Theseus, though slight compared with his great portraits, is attractive and free from malice.

In contrast to the indifference to artistic nuance shown by the Duke is the solicitude for theatric detail revealed by Bottom. Bottom has been called Shakespeare's first outstanding dramatic creation, and Dr. Johnson thought that into this character Shakespeare had distilled much of his own observation of actors:

> Bottom, who is generally acknowledged the principal Actor, declares his inclination to be a tyrant, for a part of fury, tumult, and noise, such as every young man wants to perform when he first steps upon the Stage.

Whatever detail one examines in the play seems admirably in keeping with the total effect, not least the poetry of the piece which such masters as the youthful Milton and after him Keats were moved to admire and imitate.

THESEUS, *Duke of Athens*
EGEUS, *father to Hermia*
LYSANDER ⎱ *in love with Hermia*
DEMETRIUS ⎰
PHILOSTRATE, *Master of the Revels to Theseus*
QUINCE, *a carpenter*
SNUG, *a joiner*
BOTTOM, *a weaver*
FLUTE, *a bellows-mender*
SNOUT, *a tinker*
STARVELING, *a tailor*

HIPPOLYTA, *Queen of the Amazons, betrothed to Theseus*
HERMIA, *daughter to Egeus, in love with Lysander*
HELENA, *in love with Demetrius*

OBERON, *King of the Fairies*
TITANIA, *Queen of the Fairies*
PUCK, *or* ROBIN GOODFELLOW
PEASEBLOSSOM ⎤
COBWEB ⎟ *fairies*
MOTH ⎟
MUSTARDSEED ⎦

PROLOGUE ⎤   ⎡ QUINCE
PYRAMUS ⎟   ⎟ BOTTOM
THISBY ⎟ *presented by* ⎟ FLUTE
WALL ⎟   ⎟ SNOUT
MOONSHINE ⎟   ⎟ STARVELING
LION ⎦   ⎣ SNUG

Other Fairies *attending their King and Queen*
Attendants *on Theseus and Hippolyta*

SCENE:
Athens and a wood near it

A Midsummer Night's Dream

ACT I. SCENE 1

Athens. The palace of THESEUS

Enter THESEUS, HIPPOLYTA, PHILOSTRATE, *and* ATTENDANTS

THESEUS. Now, fair Hippolyta, our nuptial hour
Draws on apace; four happy days bring in
Another moon; but, O, methinks, how slow
This old moon wanes! She lingers my desires,
Like to a step-dame or a dowager,
Long withering out a young man's revenue.
HIPPOLYTA. Four days will quickly steep themselves in night;
Four nights will quickly dream away the time;
And then the moon, like to a silver bow
New-bent in heaven, shall behold the night
Of our solemnities.
THESEUS. Go, Philostrate,
Stir up the Athenian youth to merriments;
Awake the pert and nimble spirit of mirth;
Turn melancholy forth to funerals;
The pale companion is not for our pomp. *Exit* PHILOSTRATE
Hippolyta, I woo'd thee with my sword,
And won thy love doing thee injuries;
But I will wed thee in another key,
With pomp, with triumph, and with revelling.

Enter EGEUS, *and his daughter* HERMIA, LYSANDER,
and DEMETRIUS

EGEUS. Happy be Theseus, our renowned Duke!
THESEUS. Thanks, good Egeus; what's the news with thee?
EGEUS. Full of vexation come I, with complaint
Against my child, my daughter Hermia.
Stand forth, Demetrius. My noble lord,
This man hath my consent to marry her.
Stand forth, Lysander. And, my gracious Duke,
This man hath bewitch'd the bosom of my child.

537

Thou, thou, Lysander, thou hast given her rhymes,
And interchang'd love-tokens with my child;
Thou hast by moonlight at her window sung,
With feigning voice, verses of feigning love,
And stol'n the impression of her fantasy
With bracelets of thy hair, rings, gawds, conceits,
Knacks, trifles, nosegays, sweetmeats—messengers
Of strong prevailment in unhardened youth;
With cunning hast thou filch'd my daughter's heart;
Turn'd her obedience, which is due to me,
To stubborn harshness. And, my gracious Duke,
Be it so she will not here before your Grace
Consent to marry with Demetrius,
I beg the ancient privilege of Athens:
As she is mine I may dispose of her;
Which shall be either to this gentleman
Or to her death, according to our law
Immediately provided in that case.

THESEUS. What say you, Hermia? Be advis'd, fair maid.
To you your father should be as a god;
One that compos'd your beauties; yea, and one
To whom you are but as a form in wax,
By him imprinted, and within his power
To leave the figure, or disfigure it.
Demetrius is a worthy gentleman.

HERMIA. So is Lysander.

THESEUS. In himself he is;
But, in this kind, wanting your father's voice,
The other must be held the worthier.

HERMIA. I would my father look'd but with my eyes.

THESEUS. Rather your eyes must with his judgment look.

HERMIA. I do entreat your Grace to pardon me.
I know not by what power I am made bold,
Nor how it may concern my modesty
In such a presence here to plead my thoughts;
But I beseech your Grace that I may know
The worst that may befall me in this case,
If I refuse to wed Demetrius.

THESEUS. Either to die the death, or to abjure
For ever the society of men.

Therefore, fair Hermia, question your desires,
Know of your youth, examine well your blood,
Whether, if you yield not to your father's choice,
You can endure the livery of a nun,
For aye to be in shady cloister mew'd,
To live a barren sister all your life,
Chanting faint hymns to the cold fruitless moon.
Thrice-blessed they that master so their blood
To undergo such maiden pilgrimage;
But earthlier happy is the rose distill'd
Than that which withering on the virgin thorn
Grows, lives, and dies, in single blessedness.
HERMIA. So will I grow, so live, so die, my lord,
Ere I will yield my virgin patent up
Unto his lordship, whose unwished yoke
My soul consents not to give sovereignty.
THESEUS. Take time to pause; and by the next new moon—
The sealing-day betwixt my love and me
For everlasting bond of fellowship—
Upon that day either prepare to die
For disobedience to your father's will,
Or else to wed Demetrius, as he would,
Or on Diana's altar to protest
For aye austerity and single life.
DEMETRIUS. Relent, sweet Hermia; and, Lysander, yield
Thy crazed title to my certain right.
LYSANDER. You have her father's love, Demetrius;
Let me have Hermia's; do you marry him.
EGEUS. Scornful Lysander, true, he hath my love;
And what is mine my love shall render him;
And she is mine; and all my right of her
I do estate unto Demetrius.
LYSANDER. I am, my lord, as well deriv'd as he,
As well possess'd; my love is more than his;
My fortunes every way as fairly rank'd,
If not with vantage, as Demetrius';
And, which is more than all these boasts can be,
I am belov'd of beauteous Hermia.
Why should not I then prosecute my right?
Demetrius, I'll avouch it to his head,

Made love to Nedar's daughter, Helena,
And won her soul; and she, sweet lady, dotes,
Devoutly dotes, dotes in idolatry,
Upon this spotted and inconstant man.
THESEUS. I must confess that I have heard so much,
And with Demetrius thought to have spoke thereof;
But, being over-full of self-affairs,
My mind did lose it. But, Demetrius, come;
And come, Egeus; you shall go with me;
I have some private schooling for you both.
For you, fair Hermia, look you arm yourself
To fit your fancies to your father's will,
Or else the law of Athens yields you up—
Which by no means we may extenuate—
To death, or to a vow of single life.
Come, my Hippolyta; what cheer, my love?
Demetrius, and Egeus, go along;
I must employ you in some business
Against our nuptial, and confer with you
Of something nearly that concerns yourselves.
EGEUS. With duty and desire we follow you.
                    Exeunt all but LYSANDER *and* HERMIA
LYSANDER. How now, my love! Why is your cheek so pale?
How chance the roses there do fade so fast?
HERMIA. Belike for want of rain, which I could well
Beteem them from the tempest of my eyes.
LYSANDER. Ay me! for aught that I could ever read,
Could ever hear by tale or history,
The course of true love never did run smooth;
But either it was different in blood—
HERMIA. O cross! too high to be enthrall'd to low.
LYSANDER. Or else misgraffed in respect of years—
HERMIA. O spite! too old to be engag'd to young.
LYSANDER. Or else it stood upon the choice of friends—
HERMIA. O hell! to choose love by another's eyes.
LYSANDER. Or, if there were a sympathy in choice,
War, death, or sickness, did lay siege to it,
Making it momentary as a sound,
Swift as a shadow, short as any dream,
Brief as the lightning in the collied night

That, in a spleen, unfolds both heaven and earth,
And ere a man hath power to say 'Behold!'
The jaws of darkness do devour it up;
So quick bright things come to confusion.
HERMIA. If then true lovers have been ever cross'd,
It stands as an edict in destiny.
Then let us teach our trial patience,
Because it is a customary cross,
As due to love as thoughts and dreams and sighs,
Wishes and tears, poor Fancy's followers.
LYSANDER. A good persuasion; therefore, hear me, Hermia.
I have a widow aunt, a dowager
Of great revenue, and she hath no child—
From Athens is her house remote seven leagues—
And she respects me as her only son.
There, gentle Hermia, may I marry thee;
And to that place the sharp Athenian law
Cannot pursue us. If thou lovest me then,
Steal forth thy father's house to-morrow night;
And in the wood, a league without the town,
Where I did meet thee once with Helena
To do observance to a morn of May,
There will I stay for thee.
HERMIA. My good Lysander!
I swear to thee by Cupid's strongest bow,
By his best arrow, with the golden head,
By the simplicity of Venus' doves,
By that which knitteth souls and prospers loves,
And by that fire which burn'd the Carthage Queen,
When the false Troyan under sail was seen,
By all the vows that ever men have broke,
In number more than ever women spoke,
In that same place thou hast appointed me,
To-morrow truly will I meet with thee.
LYSANDER. Keep promise, love. Look, here comes Helena.

Enter HELENA

HERMIA. God speed fair Helena! Whither away?
HELENA. Call you me fair? That fair again unsay.
Demetrius loves your fair. O happy fair!

Your eyes are lode-stars and your tongue's sweet air
More tuneable than lark to shepherd's ear,
When wheat is green, when hawthorn buds appear.
Sickness is catching; O, were favour so,
Yours would I catch, fair Hermia, ere I go!
My ear should catch your voice, my eye your eye,
My tongue should catch your tongue's sweet melody.
Were the world mine, Demetrius being bated,
The rest I'd give to be to you translated.
O, teach me how you look, and with what art
You sway the motion of Demetrius' heart!

HERMIA. I frown upon him, yet he loves me still.

HELENA. O that your frowns would teach my smiles such
skill!

HERMIA. I give him curses, yet he gives me love.

HELENA. O that my prayers could such affection move!

HERMIA. The more I hate, the more he follows me.

HELENA. The more I love, the more he hateth me.

HERMIA. His folly, Helena, is no fault of mine.

HELENA. None, but your beauty; would that fault were
mine!

HERMIA. Take comfort: he no more shall see my face;
Lysander and myself will fly this place.
Before the time I did Lysander see,
Seem'd Athens as a paradise to me.
O, then, what graces in my love do dwell,
That he hath turn'd a heaven unto a hell!

LYSANDER. Helen, to you our minds we will unfold:
To-morrow night, when Phœbe doth behold
Her silver visage in the wat'ry glass,
Decking with liquid pearl the bladed grass,
A time that lovers' flights doth still conceal,
Through Athens' gates have we devis'd to steal.

HERMIA. And in the wood where often you and I
Upon faint primrose beds were wont to lie,
Emptying our bosoms of their counsel sweet,
There my Lysander and myself shall meet;
And thence from Athens turn away our eyes,
To seek new friends and stranger companies.
Farewell, sweet playfellow; pray thou for us,

And good luck grant thee thy Demetrius!
Keep word, Lysander; we must starve our sight
From lovers' food till morrow deep midnight.
LYSANDER. I will, my Hermia. [*Exit* HERMIA] Helena, adieu;
  As you on him, Demetrius dote on you.   *Exit*
HELENA. How happy some o'er other some can be!
  Through Athens I am thought as fair as she.
  But what of that? Demetrius thinks not so;
  He will not know what all but he do know.
  And as he errs, doting on Hermia's eyes,
  So I, admiring of his qualities.
  Things base and vile, holding no quantity,
  Love can transpose to form and dignity.
  Love looks not with the eyes, but with the mind;
  And therefore is wing'd Cupid painted blind.
  Nor hath Love's mind of any judgment taste;
  Wings and no eyes figure unheedy haste;
  And therefore is Love said to be a child,
  Because in choice he is so oft beguil'd.
  As waggish boys in game themselves forswear,
  So the boy Love is perjur'd everywhere;
  For ere Demetrius look'd on Hermia's eyne,
  He hail'd down oaths that he was only mine;
  And when this hail some heat from Hermia felt,
  So he dissolv'd, and show'rs of oaths did melt.
  I will go tell him of fair Hermia's flight;
  Then to the wood will he to-morrow night
  Pursue her; and for this intelligence
  If I have thanks, it is a dear expense.
  But herein mean I to enrich my pain,
  To have his sight thither and back again.   *Exit*

SCENE 2

Athens. QUINCE's *house*

Enter QUINCE, SNUG, BOTTOM, FLUTE, SNOUT,
and STARVELING

QUINCE. Is all our company here?

BOTTOM. You were best to call them generally, man by man, according to the scrip.

QUINCE. Here is the scroll of every man's name which is thought fit, through all Athens, to play in our interlude before the Duke and the Duchess on his wedding-day at night.

BOTTOM. First, good Peter Quince, say what the play treats on; then read the names of the actors; and so grow to a point.

QUINCE. Marry, our play is 'The most Lamentable Comedy and most Cruel Death of Pyramus and Thisby.'

BOTTOM. A very good piece of work, I assure you, and a merry. Now, good Peter Quince, call forth your actors by the scroll. Masters, spread yourselves.

QUINCE. Answer, as I call you. Nick Bottom, the weaver.

BOTTOM. Ready. Name what part I am for, and proceed.

QUINCE. You, Nick Bottom, are set down for Pyramus.

BOTTOM. What is Pyramus? A lover, or a tyrant?

QUINCE. A lover, that kills himself most gallant for love.

BOTTOM. That will ask some tears in the true performing of it. If I do it, let the audience look to their eyes; I will move storms; I will condole in some measure. To the rest—yet my chief humour is for a tyrant. I could play Ercles rarely, or a part to tear a cat in, to make all split.

'The raging rocks
And shivering shocks
Shall break the locks
 Of prison gates;

And Phibbus' car
Shall shine from far,
And make and mar
The foolish Fates.'

This was lofty. Now name the rest of the players. This is Ercles' vein, a tyrant's vein: a lover is more condoling.

QUINCE. Francis Flute, the bellows-mender.

FLUTE. Here, Peter Quince.

QUINCE. Flute, you must take Thisby on you.

FLUTE. What is Thisby? A wand'ring knight?

QUINCE. It is the lady that Pyramus must love.

FLUTE. Nay, faith, let not me play a woman; I have a beard coming.

QUINCE. That's all one; you shall play it in a mask, and you may speak as small as you will.

BOTTOM. An I may hide my face, let me play Thisby too. I'll speak in a monstrous little voice: 'Thisne, Thisne!' [*Then speaking small*] 'Ah Pyramus, my lover dear! Thy Thisby dear, and lady dear!'

QUINCE. No, no, you must play Pyramus; and, Flute, you Thisby.

BOTTOM. Well, proceed.

QUINCE. Robin Starveling, the tailor.

STARVELING. Here, Peter Quince.

QUINCE. Robin Starveling, you must play Thisby's mother. Tom Snout, the tinker.

SNOUT. Here, Peter Quince.

QUINCE. You, Pyramus' father; myself, Thisby's father; Snug, the joiner, you, the lion's part. And, I hope, here is a play fitted.

SNUG. Have you the lion's part written? Pray you, if it be, give it me, for I am slow of study.

QUINCE. You may do it extempore, for it is nothing but roaring.

BOTTOM. Let me play the lion too. I will roar that I will do any man's heart good to hear me; I will roar that I will make the Duke say 'Let him roar again, let him roar again.'

QUINCE. An you should do it too terribly, you would fright the Duchess and the ladies, that they would shriek; and that were enough to hang us all.

ALL. That would hang us, every mother's son.

BOTTOM. I grant you, friends, if you should fright the ladies out of their wits, they would have no more discretion but to hang us; but I will aggravate my voice so, that I will roar you as gently as any sucking dove; I will roar you an 'twere any nightingale.

QUINCE. You can play no part but Pyramus; for Pyramus is a sweet-fac'd man; a proper man, as one shall see in a summer's day; a most lovely gentleman-like man; therefore you must needs play Pyramus.

BOTTOM. Well, I will undertake it. What beard were I best to play it in?

QUINCE. Why, what you will.

BOTTOM. I will discharge it in either your straw-colour beard, your orange-tawny beard, your purple-in-grain beard, or your French-crown-colour beard, your perfect yellow.

QUINCE. Some of your French crowns have no hair at all, and then you will play bare-fac'd. But, masters, here are your parts; and I am to entreat you, request you, and desire you, to con them by to-morrow night; and meet me in the palace wood, a mile without the town, by moonlight; there will we rehearse; for if we meet in the city, we shall be dogg'd with company, and our devices known. In the meantime I will draw a bill of properties, such as our play wants. I pray you, fail me not.

BOTTOM. We will meet; and there we may rehearse most obscenely and courageously. Take pains; be perfect; adieu.

QUINCE. At the Duke's oak we meet.

BOTTOM. Enough; hold, or cut bow-strings.   *Exeunt*

ACT II. SCENE 1

A wood near Athens

Enter a FAIRY *at one door, and* PUCK *at another*

PUCK. How now, spirit! whither wander you?

FAIRY.   Over hill, over dale,
   Thorough bush, thorough brier,
  Over park, over pale,
   Thorough flood, thorough fire,
  I do wander every where,
  Swifter than the moon's sphere;
  And I serve the Fairy Queen,
  To dew her orbs upon the green.
  The cowslips tall her pensioners be;
  In their gold coats spots you see;
  Those be rubies, fairy favours,
  In those freckles live their savours.

I must go seek some dewdrops here,
And hang a pearl in every cowslip's ear.
Farewell, thou lob of spirits; I'll be gone.
Our Queen and all her elves come here anon.

Puck. The King doth keep his revels here to-night;
Take heed the Queen come not within his sight;
For Oberon is passing fell and wrath,
Because that she as her attendant hath
A lovely boy, stolen from an Indian king.
She never had so sweet a changeling;
And jealous Oberon would have the child
Knight of his train, to trace the forests wild;
But she perforce withholds the loved boy,
Crowns him with flowers, and makes him all her joy.
And now they never meet in grove or green,
By fountain clear, or spangled starlight sheen,
But they do square, that all their elves for fear
Creep into acorn cups and hide them there.

Fairy. Either I mistake your shape and making quite,
Or else you are that shrewd and knavish sprite
Call'd Robin Goodfellow. Are not you he
That frights the maidens of the villagery,
Skim milk, and sometimes labour in the quern,
And bootless make the breathless housewife churn,
And sometime make the drink to bear no barm,
Mislead night-wanderers, laughing at their harm?
Those that Hobgoblin call you, and sweet Puck,
You do their work, and they shall have good luck.
Are not you he?

Puck. Thou speakest aright:
I am that merry wanderer of the night.
I jest to Oberon, and make him smile
When I a fat and bean-fed horse beguile,
Neighing in likeness of a filly foal;
And sometime lurk I in a gossip's bowl
In very likeness of a roasted crab,
And, when she drinks, against her lips I bob,
And on her withered dewlap pour the ale.
The wisest aunt, telling the saddest tale,
Sometime for three-foot stool mistaketh me;

Then slip I from her bum, down topples she,
And 'tailor' cries, and falls into a cough;
And then the whole quire hold their hips and laugh,
And waxen in their mirth, and neeze, and swear
A merrier hour was never wasted there.
But room, fairy, here comes Oberon.
FAIRY. And here my mistress. Would that he were gone!

Enter OBERON *at one door, with his* TRAIN, *and* TITANIA,
at another, with hers

OBERON. Ill met by moonlight, proud Titania.
TITANIA. What, jealous Oberon! Fairies, skip hence;
I have forsworn his bed and company.
OBERON. Tarry, rash wanton; am not I thy lord?
TITANIA. Then I must be thy lady; but I know
When thou hast stolen away from fairy land,
And in the shape of Corin sat all day,
Playing on pipes of corn, and versing love
To amorous Phillida. Why art thou here,
Come from the farthest steep of India,
But that, forsooth, the bouncing Amazon,
Your buskin'd mistress and your warrior love,
To Theseus must be wedded, and you come
To give their bed joy and prosperity?
OBERON. How canst thou thus, for shame, Titania,
Glance at my credit with Hippolyta,
Knowing I know thy love to Theseus?
Didst not thou lead him through the glimmering night
From Perigouna, whom he ravished?
And make him with fair Ægles break his faith,
With Ariadne and Antiopa?
TITANIA. These are the forgeries of jealousy;
And never, since the middle summer's spring,
Met we on hill, in dale, forest, or mead,
By paved fountain, or by rushy brook,
Or in the beached margent of the sea,
To dance our ringlets to the whistling wind,
But with thy brawls thou hast disturb'd our sport.
Therefore the winds, piping to us in vain,
As in revenge, have suck'd up from the sea

Contagious fogs; which, falling in the land,
Hath every pelting river made so proud
That they have overborne their continents.
The ox hath therefore stretch'd his yoke in vain,
The ploughman lost his sweat, and the green corn
Hath rotted ere his youth attain'd a beard;
The fold stands empty in the drowned field,
And crows are fatted with the murrion flock;
The nine men's morris is fill'd up with mud,
And the quaint mazes in the wanton green,
For lack of tread, are undistinguishable.
The human mortals want their winter here;
No night is now with hymn or carol blest;
Therefore the moon, the governess of floods,
Pale in her anger, washes all the air,
That rheumatic diseases do abound.
And thorough this distemperature we see
The seasons alter: hoary-headed frosts
Fall in the fresh lap of the crimson rose;
And on old Hiems' thin and icy crown
An odorous chaplet of sweet summer buds
Is, as in mockery, set. The spring, the summer,
The childing autumn, angry winter, change
Their wonted liveries; and the mazed world,
By their increase, now knows not which is which.
And this same progeny of evils comes
From our debate, from our dissension;
We are their parents and original.
OBERON. Do you amend it, then; it lies in you.
Why should Titania cross her Oberon?
I do but beg a little changeling boy
To be my henchman.
TITANIA. Set your heart at rest;
The fairy land buys not the child of me.
His mother was a vot'ress of my order;
And, in the spiced Indian air, by night,
Full often hath she gossip'd by my side;
And sat with me on Neptune's yellow sands,
Marking th' embarked traders on the flood;
When we have laugh'd to see the sails conceive,

And grow big-bellied with the wanton wind;
Which she, with pretty and with swimming gait
Following—her womb then rich with my young squire—
Would imitate, and sail upon the land,
To fetch me trifles, and return again,
As from a voyage, rich with merchandise.
But she, being mortal, of that boy did die;
And for her sake do I rear up her boy;
And for her sake I will not part with him.
OBERON. How long within this wood intend you stay?
TITANIA. Perchance till after Theseus' wedding-day.
If you will patiently dance in our round,
And see our moonlight revels, go with us;
If not, shun me, and I will spare your haunts.
OBERON. Give me that boy and I will go with thee.
TITANIA. Not for thy fairy kingdom. Fairies, away.
We shall chide downright if I longer stay.

Exit TITANIA *with her train*

OBERON. Well, go thy way; thou shalt not from this grove
Till I torment thee for this injury.
My gentle Puck, come hither. Thou rememb'rest
Since once I sat upon a promontory,
And heard a mermaid on a dolphin's back
Uttering such dulcet and harmonious breath
That the rude sea grew civil at her song,
And certain stars shot madly from their spheres
To hear the sea-maid's music.
PUCK. I remember.
OBERON. That very time I saw, but thou couldst not,
Flying between the cold moon and the earth
Cupid, all arm'd; a certain aim he took
At a fair vestal, throned by the west,
And loos'd his love-shaft smartly from his bow,
As it should pierce a hundred thousand hearts;
But I might see young Cupid's fiery shaft
Quench'd in the chaste beams of the wat'ry moon;
And the imperial vot'ress passed on,
In maiden meditation, fancy-free.
Yet mark'd I where the bolt of Cupid fell.
It fell upon a little western flower,

Before milk-white, now purple with love's wound,
And maidens call it Love-in-idleness.
Fetch me that flow'r, the herb I showed thee once.
The juice of it on sleeping eyelids laid
Will make or man or woman madly dote
Upon the next live creature that it sees.
Fetch me this herb, and be thou here again
Ere the leviathan can swim a league.
PUCK. I'll put a girdle round about the earth
   In forty minutes.   *Exit* PUCK
OBERON. Having once this juice,
   I'll watch Titania when she is asleep,
   And drop the liquor of it in her eyes;
   The next thing then she waking looks upon,
   Be it on lion, bear, or wolf, or bull,
   On meddling monkey, or on busy ape,
   She shall pursue it with the soul of love.
   And ere I take this charm from off her sight,
   As I can take it with another herb,
   I'll make her render up her page to me.
   But who comes here? I am invisible;
   And I will overhear their conference.

          Enter DEMETRIUS, HELENA *following him*

DEMETRIUS. I love thee not, therefore pursue me not.
   Where is Lysander and fair Hermia?
   The one I'll slay, the other slayeth me.
   Thou told'st me they were stol'n unto this wood,
   And here am I, and wood within this wood,
   Because I cannot meet my Hermia.
   Hence, get thee gone, and follow me no more.
HELENA. You draw me, you hard-hearted adamant;
   But yet you draw not iron, for my heart
   Is true as steel. Leave you your power to draw,
   And I shall have no power to follow you.
DEMETRIUS. Do I entice you? Do I speak you fair?
   Or, rather, do I not in plainest truth
   Tell you I do not nor I cannot love you?
HELENA. And even for that do I love you the more.
   I am your spaniel; and, Demetrius,

551

The more you beat me, I will fawn on you.
Use me but as your spaniel, spurn me, strike me,
Neglect me, lose me; only give me leave,
Unworthy as I am, to follow you.
What worser place can I beg in your love,
And yet a place of high respect with me,
Than to be used as you use your dog?
DEMETRIUS. Tempt not too much the hatred of my spirit;
For I am sick when I do look on thee.
HELENA. And I am sick when I look not on you.
DEMETRIUS. You do impeach your modesty too much
To leave the city and commit yourself
Into the hands of one that loves you not;
To trust the opportunity of night,
And the ill counsel of a desert place,
With the rich worth of your virginity.
HELENA. Your virtue is my privilege for that:
It is not night when I do see your face,
Therefore I think I am not in the night;
Nor doth this wood lack worlds of company,
For you, in my respect, are all the world.
Then how can it be said I am alone
When all the world is here to look on me?
DEMETRIUS. I'll run from thee and hide me in the brakes,
And leave thee to the mercy of wild beasts.
HELENA. The wildest hath not such a heart as you.
Run when you will; the story shall be chang'd:
Apollo flies, and Daphne holds the chase;
The dove pursues the griffin; the mild hind
Makes speed to catch the tiger—bootless speed,
When cowardice pursues and valour flies.
DEMETRIUS. I will not stay thy questions; let me go;
Or, if thou follow me, do not believe
But I shall do thee mischief in the wood.
HELENA. Ay, in the temple, in the town, the field,
You do me mischief. Fie, Demetrius!
Your wrongs do set a scandal on my sex.
We cannot fight for love as men may do;
We should be woo'd, and were not made to woo.

Exit DEMETRIUS

I'll follow thee, and make a heaven of hell,
To die upon the hand I love so well.   *Exit* Helena
Oberon. Fare thee well, nymph; ere he do leave this grove,
Thou shalt fly him, and he shall seek thy love.

Re-enter Puck

Hast thou the flower there? Welcome, wanderer.
Puck. Ay, there it is.
Oberon. I pray thee give it me.
I know a bank where the wild thyme blows,
Where oxlips and the nodding violet grows,
Quite over-canopied with luscious woodbine,
With sweet musk-roses, and with eglantine;
There sleeps Titania sometime of the night,
Lull'd in these flowers with dances and delight;
And there the snake throws her enamell'd skin,
Weed wide enough to wrap a fairy in;
And with the juice of this I'll streak her eyes,
And make her full of hateful fantasies.
Take thou some of it, and seek through this grove:
A sweet Athenian lady is in love
With a disdainful youth; anoint his eyes;
But do it when the next thing he espies
May be the lady. Thou shalt know the man
By the Athenian garments he hath on.
Effect it with some care, that he may prove
More fond on her than she upon her love.
And look thou meet me ere the first cock crow.
Puck. Fear not, my lord; your servant shall do so.   *Exeunt*

SCENE 2

Another part of the wood

Enter Titania, *with her train*

Titania. Come now, a roundel and a fairy song;
Then, for the third part of a minute, hence:
Some to kill cankers in the musk-rose buds;
Some war with rere-mice for their leathern wings,

To make my small elves coats; and some keep back
The clamorous owl that nightly hoots and wonders
At our quaint spirits. Sing me now asleep;
Then to your offices, and let me rest.

The FAIRIES *sing*

FIRST FAIRY. You spotted snakes with double tongue,
    Thorny hedgehogs, be not seen;
    Newts and blind-worms, do no wrong,
    Come not near our fairy Queen.
CHORUS. Philomel with melody
    Sing in our sweet lullaby.
    Lulla, lulla, lullaby; lulla, lulla, lullaby.
    Never harm
    Nor spell nor charm
    Come our lovely lady nigh.
    So good night, with lullaby.
SECOND FAIRY. Weaving spiders, come not here;
    Hence, you long-legg'd spinners, hence.
    Beetles black, approach not near;
    Worm nor snail do no offence.
CHORUS. Philomel with melody, etc. [TITANIA *sleeps*]
FIRST FAIRY. Hence away; now all is well.
    One aloof stand sentinel. *Exeunt* FAIRIES

Enter OBERON *and squeezes the flower on* TITANIA's *eyelids*

OBERON. What thou seest when thou dost wake,
 Do it for thy true-love take;
 Love and languish for his sake.
 Be it ounce, or cat, or bear,
 Pard, or boar with bristled hair,
 In thy eye that shall appear
 When thou wak'st, it is thy dear.
 Wake when some vile thing is near.   *Exit*

Enter LYSANDER *and* HERMIA

LYSANDER. Fair love, you faint with wand'ring in the wood;
 And, to speak troth, I have forgot our way;
 We'll rest us, Hermia, if you think it good,
 And tarry for the comfort of the day.

HERMIA. Be it so, Lysander: find you out a bed,
For I upon this bank will rest my head.
LYSANDER. One turf shall serve as pillow for us both;
One heart, one bed, two bosoms, and one troth.
HERMIA. Nay, good Lysander; for my sake, my dear,
Lie further off yet; do not lie so near.
LYSANDER. O, take the sense, sweet, of my innocence!
Love takes the meaning in love's conference.
I mean that my heart unto yours is knit,
So that but one heart we can make of it;
Two bosoms interchained with an oath,
So then two bosoms and a single troth.
Then by your side no bed-room me deny,
For lying so, Hermia, I do not lie.
HERMIA. Lysander riddles very prettily.
Now much beshrew my manners and my pride,
If Hermia meant to say Lysander lied!
But, gentle friend, for love and courtesy
Lie further off, in human modesty;
Such separation as may well be said
Becomes a virtuous bachelor and a maid,
So far be distant; and good night, sweet friend.
Thy love ne'er alter till thy sweet life end!
LYSANDER. Amen, amen, to that fair prayer say I;
And then end life when I end loyalty!
Here is my bed; sleep give thee all his rest!
HERMIA. With half that wish the wisher's eyes be press'd!

[*They sleep*]

Enter PUCK

PUCK. Through the forest have I gone,
But Athenian found I none
On whose eyes I might approve
This flower's force in stirring love.
Night and silence—Who is here?
Weeds of Athens he doth wear:
This is he, my master said,
Despised the Athenian maid;
And here the maiden, sleeping sound,
On the dank and dirty ground.

Pretty soul! she durst not lie
Near this lack-love, this kill-courtesy.
Churl, upon thy eyes I throw
All the power this charm doth owe:
When thou wak'st let love forbid
Sleep his seat on thy eyelid.
So awake when I am gone;
For I must now to Oberon. *Exit*

Enter DEMETRIUS *and* HELENA, *running*

HELENA. Stay, though thou kill me, sweet Demetrius.
DEMETRIUS. I charge thee, hence, and do not haunt me thus.
HELENA. O, wilt thou darkling leave me? Do not so.
DEMETRIUS. Stay on thy peril; I alone will go. *Exit*
HELENA. O, I am out of breath in this fond chase!
The more my prayer, the lesser is my grace.
Happy is Hermia, wheresoe'er she lies,
For she hath blessed and attractive eyes.
How came her eyes so bright? Not with salt tears;
If so, my eyes are oft'ner wash'd than hers.
No, no, I am as ugly as a bear,
For beasts that meet me run away for fear;
Therefore no marvel though Demetrius
Do, as a monster, fly my presence thus.
What wicked and dissembling glass of mine
Made me compare with Hermia's sphery eyne?
But who is here? Lysander! on the ground!
Dead, or asleep? I see no blood, no wound.
Lysander, if you live, good sir, awake.
LYSANDER. [*Waking*] And run through fire I will for thy
sweet sake.
Transparent Helena! Nature shows art,
That through thy bosom makes me see thy heart.
Where is Demetrius? O, how fit a word
Is that vile name to perish on my sword!
HELENA. Do not say so, Lysander; say not so.
What though he love your Hermia? Lord, what though?
Yet Hermia still loves you; then be content.
LYSANDER. Content with Hermia! No: I do repent
The tedious minutes I with her have spent.

Not Hermia but Helena I love:
Who will not change a raven for a dove?
The will of man is by his reason sway'd,
And reason says you are the worthier maid.
Things growing are not ripe until their season;
So I, being young, till now ripe not to reason;
And touching now the point of human skill,
Reason becomes the marshal to my will,
And leads me to your eyes, where I o'erlook
Love's stories, written in Love's richest book.

HELENA. Wherefore was I to this keen mockery born?
When at your hands did I deserve this scorn?
Is't not enough, is't not enough, young man,
That I did never, no, nor never can,
Deserve a sweet look from Demetrius' eye,
But you must flout my insufficiency?
Good troth, you do me wrong, good sooth, you do,
In such disdainful manner me to woo.
But fare you well; perforce I must confess
I thought you lord of more true gentleness.
O, that a lady of one man refus'd
Should of another therefore be abus'd! *Exit*

LYSANDER. She sees not Hermia. Hermia, sleep thou there;
And never mayst thou come Lysander near!
For, as a surfeit of the sweetest things
The deepest loathing to the stomach brings,
Or as the heresies that men do leave
Are hated most of those they did deceive,
So thou, my surfeit and my heresy,
Of all be hated, but the most of me!
And, all my powers, address your love and might
To honour Helen, and to be her knight! *Exit*

HERMIA. [*Starting*] Help me, Lysander, help me; do thy
best
To pluck this crawling serpent from my breast.
Ay me, for pity! What a dream was here!
Lysander, look how I do quake with fear.
Methought a serpent eat my heart away,
And you sat smiling at his cruel prey.
Lysander! What, remov'd? Lysander! lord!

What, out of hearing gone? No sound, no word?
Alack, where are you? Speak, an if you hear;
Speak, of all loves! I swoon almost with fear.
No? Then I well perceive you are not nigh.
Either death or you I'll find immediately.   *Exit*

ACT III. SCENE 1

The wood. TITANIA *lying asleep*

Enter QUINCE, SNUG, BOTTOM, FLUTE, SNOUT,
and STARVELING

BOTTOM. Are we all met?

QUINCE. Pat, pat; and here's a marvellous convenient place
for our rehearsal. This green plot shall be our stage, this
hawthorn brake our tiring-house; and we will do it in action, as we will do it before the Duke.

BOTTOM. Peter Quince!

QUINCE. What sayest thou, bully Bottom?

BOTTOM. There are things in this comedy of Pyramus and
Thisby that will never please. First, Pyramus must draw
a sword to kill himself; which the ladies cannot abide.
How answer you that?

SNOUT. By'r lakin, a parlous fear.

STARVELING. I believe we must leave the killing out, when all
is done.

BOTTOM. Not a whit; I have a device to make all well. Write
me a prologue; and let the prologue seem to say we will
do no harm with our swords, and that Pyramus is not kill'd
indeed; and for the more better assurance, tell them that
I Pyramus am not Pyramus but Bottom the weaver. This
will put them out of fear.

QUINCE. Well, we will have such a prologue; and it shall be
written in eight and six.

BOTTOM. No, make it two more; let it be written in eight
and eight.

SNOUT. Will not the ladies be afeard of the lion?

STARVELING. I fear it, I promise you.

BOTTOM. Masters, you ought to consider with yourself to bring in—God shield us!—a lion among ladies is a most dreadful thing; for there is not a more fearful wild-fowl than your lion living; and we ought to look to't.

SNOUT. Therefore another prologue must tell he is not a lion.

BOTTOM. Nay, you must name his name, and half his face must be seen through the lion's neck; and he himself must speak through, saying thus, or to the same defect: 'Ladies,' or 'Fair ladies, I would wish you' or 'I would request you' or 'I would entreat you not to fear, not to tremble. My life for yours! If you think I come hither as a lion, it were pity of my life. No, I am no such thing; I am a man as other men are.' And there, indeed, let him name his name, and tell them plainly he is Snug the joiner.

QUINCE. Well, it shall be so. But there is two hard things— that is, to bring the moonlight into a chamber; for, you know, Pyramus and Thisby meet by moonlight.

SNOUT. Doth the moon shine that night we play our play?

BOTTOM. A calendar, a calendar! Look in the almanack; find out moonshine, find out moonshine.

QUINCE. Yes, it doth shine that night.

BOTTOM. Why, then may you leave a casement of the great chamber window, where we play, open; and the moon may shine in at the casement.

QUINCE. Ay; or else one must come in with a bush of thorns and a lantern, and say he comes to disfigure or to present the person of Moonshine. Then there is another thing: we must have a wall in the great chamber; for Pyramus and Thisby, says the story, did talk through the chink of a wall.

SNOUT. You can never bring in a wall. What say you, Bottom?

BOTTOM. Some man or other must present Wall; and let him have some plaster, or some loam, or some rough-cast about him, to signify wall; and let him hold his fingers thus, and through that cranny shall Pyramus and Thisby whisper.

QUINCE. If that may be, then all is well. Come, sit down, every mother's son, and rehearse your parts. Pyramus, you begin; when you have spoken your speech, enter into that brake; and so every one according to his cue.

Enter PUCK *behind*

PUCK. What hempen homespuns have we swagg'ring here,
So near the cradle of the Fairy Queen?
What, a play toward! I'll be an auditor;
An actor too perhaps, if I see cause.

QUINCE. Speak, Pyramus. Thisby, stand forth.

BOTTOM. *Thisby, the flowers of odious savours sweet—*

QUINCE. 'Odious'—odorous!

BOTTOM. ——*odours savours sweet;*
So hath thy breath, my dearest Thisby dear.
But hark, a voice! Stay thou but here awhile,
And by and by I will to thee appear.   *Exit*

PUCK. A stranger Pyramus than e'er played here!   *Exit*

FLUTE. Must I speak now?

QUINCE. Ay, marry, must you; for you must understand he
goes but to see a noise that he heard, and is to come again.

FLUTE. *Most radiant Pyramus, most lily-white of hue,*
Of colour like the red rose on triumphant brier,
Most brisky juvenal, and eke most lovely Jew,
As true as truest horse, that yet would never tire,
I'll meet thee, Pyramus, at Ninny's tomb.

QUINCE. 'Ninus' tomb,' man! Why, you must not speak that
yet; that you answer to Pyramus. You speak all your
part at once, cues, and all. Pyramus enter: your cue is
past; it is 'never tire.'

FLUTE. O—*As true as truest horse, that yet would never tire.*

Re-enter PUCK, *and* BOTTOM *with an ass's head*

BOTTOM. *If I were fair, Thisby, I were only thine.*

QUINCE. O monstrous! O strange! We are haunted. Pray,
masters! fly, masters! Help!

Exeunt all but BOTTOM *and* PUCK

PUCK. I'll follow you; I'll lead you about a round,
Through bog, through bush, through brake, through brier;
Sometime a horse I'll be, sometime a hound,
A hog, a headless bear, sometime a fire;
And neigh, and bark, and grunt, and roar, and burn,
Like horse, hound, hog, bear, fire, at every turn.   *Exit*

BOTTOM. Why do they run away? This is a knavery of them
to make me afeard.

Re-enter SNOUT

SNOUT. O Bottom, thou art chang'd! What do I see on thee?

BOTTOM. What do you see? You see an ass-head of your own, do you? *Exit* SNOUT

Re-enter QUINCE

QUINCE. Bless thee, Bottom, bless thee! Thou art translated. *Exit*

BOTTOM. I see their knavery: this is to make an ass of me; to fright me, if they could. But I will not stir from this place, do what they can; I will walk up and down here, and I will sing, that they shall hear I am not afraid.   [*Sings*]

> The ousel cock, so black of hue,
>   With orange-tawny bill,
> The throstle with his note so true,
>   The wren with little quill.

TITANIA. What angel wakes me from my flow'ry bed?

BOTTOM. [*Sings*]

> The finch, the sparrow, and the lark,
>   The plain-song cuckoo grey,
> Whose note full many a man doth mark,
>   And dares not answer nay—

for, indeed, who would set his wit to so foolish a bird? Who would give a bird the lie, though he cry 'cuckoo' never so?

TITANIA. I pray thee, gentle mortal, sing again.
Mine ear is much enamoured of thy note;
So is mine eye enthralled to thy shape;
And thy fair virtue's force perforce doth move me,
On the first view, to say, to swear, I love thee.

BOTTOM. Methinks, mistress, you should have little reason for that. And yet, to say the truth, reason and love keep little company together now-a-days. The more the pity that some honest neighbours will not make them friends. Nay, I can gleek upon occasion.

TITANIA. Thou art as wise as thou art beautiful.

BOTTOM. Not so, neither; but if I had wit enough to get out of this wood, I have enough to serve mine own turn.

TITANIA. Out of this wood do not desire to go;
Thou shalt remain here whether thou wilt or no.

I am a spirit of no common rate;
The summer still doth tend upon my state;
And I do love thee; therefore, go with me.
I'll give thee fairies to attend on thee;
And they shall fetch thee jewels from the deep,
And sing, while thou on pressed flowers dost sleep;
And I will purge thy mortal grossness so
That thou shalt like an airy spirit go.
Peaseblossom! Cobweb! Moth! and Mustardseed!

Enter PEASEBLOSSOM, COBWEB, MOTH, *and* MUSTARDSEED

PEASEBLOSSOM. Ready.
COBWEB. And I.
MOTH. And I.
MUSTARDSEED. And I.
ALL. Where shall we go?
TITANIA. Be kind and courteous to this gentleman;
Hop in his walks and gambol in his eyes;
Feed him with apricocks and dewberries,
With purple grapes, green figs, and mulberries;
The honey bags steal from the humble-bees,
And for night-tapers crop their waxen thighs,
And light them at the fiery glow-worm's eyes,
To have my love to bed and to arise;
And pluck the wings from painted butterflies,
To fan the moonbeams from his sleeping eyes.
Nod to him, elves, and do him courtesies.
PEASEBLOSSOM. Hail, mortal!
COBWEB. Hail!
MOTH. Hail!
MUSTARDSEED. Hail!
BOTTOM. I cry your worships mercy, heartily; I beseech your
worship's name.
COBWEB. Cobweb.
BOTTOM. I shall desire you of more acquaintance, good Mas-
ter Cobweb. If I cut my finger, I shall make bold with
you. Your name, honest gentleman?
PEASEBLOSSOM. Peaseblossom.
BOTTOM. I pray you, commend me to Mistress Squash, your
mother, and to Master Peascod, your father. Good Mas-

ter Peaseblossom, I shall desire you of more acquaintance
too. Your name, I beseech you, sir?

MUSTARDSEED. Mustardseed.

BOTTOM. Good Master Mustardseed, I know your patience
well. That same cowardly giant-like ox-beef hath devour'd many a gentleman of your house. I promise you
your kindred hath made my eyes water ere now. I desire
you of more acquaintance, good Master Mustardseed.

TITANIA. Come, wait upon him; lead him to my bower.
The moon, methinks, looks with a wat'ry eye;
And when she weeps, weeps every little flower;
Lamenting some enforced chastity.
Tie up my love's tongue, bring him silently. *Exeunt*

SCENE 2

Another part of the wood

Enter OBERON

OBERON. I wonder if Titania be awak'd;
Then, what it was that next came in her eye,
Which she must dote on in extremity.

Enter PUCK

Here comes my messenger. How now, mad spirit!
What night-rule now about this haunted grove?

PUCK. My mistress with a monster is in love.
Near to her close and consecrated bower,
While she was in her dull and sleeping hour,
A crew of patches, rude mechanicals,
That work for bread upon Athenian stalls,
Were met together to rehearse a play
Intended for great Theseus' nuptial day.
The shallowest thickskin of that barren sort,
Who Pyramus presented, in their sport
Forsook his scene and ent'red in a brake;
When I did him at this advantage take,
An ass's nole I fixed on his head.
Anon his Thisby must be answered,

And forth my mimic comes. When they him spy,
As wild geese that the creeping fowler eye,
Or russet-pated choughs, many in sort,
Rising and cawing at the gun's report,
Sever themselves and madly sweep the sky,
So at his sight away his fellows fly;
And at our stamp here, o'er and o'er one falls;
He murder cries, and help from Athens calls.
Their sense thus weak, lost with their fears thus strong,
Made senseless things begin to do them wrong,
For briers and thorns at their apparel snatch;
Some sleeves, some hats, from yielders all things catch.
I led them on in this distracted fear,
And left sweet Pyramus translated there;
When in that moment, so it came to pass,
Titania wak'd, and straightway lov'd an ass.
OBERON. This falls out better than I could devise.
But hast thou yet latch'd the Athenian's eyes
With the love-juice, as I did bid thee do?
PUCK. I took him sleeping—that is finish'd too—
And the Athenian woman by his side;
That, when he wak'd, of force she must be ey'd.

Enter DEMETRIUS *and* HERMIA

OBERON. Stand close; this is the same Athenian.
PUCK. This is the woman, but not this the man.
DEMETRIUS. O, why rebuke you him that loves you so?
Lay breath so bitter on your bitter foe.
HERMIA. Now I but chide, but I should use thee worse,
For thou, I fear, hast given me cause to curse.
If thou hast slain Lysander in his sleep,
Being o'er shoes in blood, plunge in the deep,
And kill me too.
The sun was not so true unto the day
As he to me. Would he have stolen away
From sleeping Hermia? I'll believe as soon
This whole earth may be bor'd, and that the moon
May through the centre creep and so displease
Her brother's noontide with th' Antipodes.
It cannot be but thou hast murd'red him;

So should a murderer look—so dead, so grim.
DEMETRIUS. So should the murdered look; and so should I,
  Pierc'd through the heart with your stern cruelty;
  Yet you, the murderer, look as bright, as clear,
  As yonder Venus in her glimmering sphere.
HERMIA. What's this to my Lysander? Where is he?
  Ah, good Demetrius, wilt thou give him me?
DEMETRIUS. I had rather give his carcass to my hounds.
HERMIA. Out, dog! out, cur! Thou driv'st me past the
    bounds
  Of maiden's patience. Hast thou slain him, then?
  Henceforth be never numb'red among men!
  O, once tell true; tell true, even for my sake!
  Durst thou have look'd upon him being awake,
  And hast thou kill'd him sleeping? O brave touch!
  Could not a worm, an adder, do so much?
  An adder did it; for with doubler tongue
  Than thine, thou serpent, never adder stung.
DEMETRIUS. You spend your passion on a mispris'd mood:
  I am not guilty of Lysander's blood;
  Nor is he dead, for aught that I can tell.
HERMIA. I pray thee, tell me then that he is well.
DEMETRIUS. An if I could, what should I get therefore?
HERMIA. A privilege never to see me more.
  And from thy hated presence part I so;
  See me no more whether he be dead or no.   *Exit*
DEMETRIUS. There is no following her in this fierce vein;
  Here, therefore, for a while I will remain.
  So sorrow's heaviness doth heavier grow
  For debt that bankrupt sleep doth sorrow owe;
  Which now in some slight measure it will pay,
  If for his tender here I make some stay.   [*Lies down*]
OBERON. What hast thou done? Thou hast mistaken quite,
  And laid the love-juice on some true-love's sight.
  Of thy misprision must perforce ensue
  Some true love turn'd, and not a false turn'd true.
PUCK. Then fate o'er-rules, that, one man holding troth,
  A million fail, confounding oath on oath.
OBERON. About the wood go swifter than the wind,
  And Helena of Athens look thou find;

All fancy-sick she is and pale of cheer,
With sighs of love that costs the fresh blood dear.
By some illusion see thou bring her here;
I'll charm his eyes against she do appear.
PUCK. I go, I go; look how I go,
    Swifter than arrow from the Tartar's bow.   *Exit*
OBERON.   Flower of this purple dye,
    Hit with Cupid's archery,
    Sink in apple of his eye.
    When his love he doth espy,
    Let her shine as gloriously
    As the Venus of the sky.
    When thou wak'st, if she be by,
    Beg of her for remedy.

Re-enter PUCK

PUCK.   Captain of our fairy band,
    Helena is here at hand,
    And the youth mistook by me
    Pleading for a lover's fee;
    Shall we their fond pageant see?
    Lord, what fools these mortals be!
OBERON.   Stand aside. The noise they make
    Will cause Demetrius to awake.
PUCK.   Then will two at once woo one.
    That must needs be sport alone;
    And those things do best please me
    That befall prepost'rously.

Enter LYSANDER *and* HELENA

LYSANDER. Why should you think that I should woo in
    scorn?
Scorn and derision never come in tears.
Look when I vow, I weep; and vows so born,
In their nativity all truth appears.
How can these things in me seem scorn to you,
Bearing the badge of faith, to prove them true?
HELENA. You do advance your cunning more and more.
When truth kills truth, O devilish-holy fray!
These vows are Hermia's. Will you give her o'er?

Weigh oath with oath, and you will nothing weigh:
Your vows to her and me, put in two scales,
Will even weigh; and both as light as tales.

LYSANDER. I had no judgment when to her I swore.

HELENA. Nor none, in my mind, now you give her o'er.

LYSANDER. Demetrius loves her, and he loves not you.

DEMETRIUS. [*Awaking*] O Helen, goddess, nymph, perfect,
    divine!
To what, my love, shall I compare thine eyne?
Crystal is muddy. O, how ripe in show
Thy lips, those kissing cherries, tempting grow!
That pure congealed white, high Taurus' snow,
Fann'd with the eastern wind, turns to a crow
When thou hold'st up thy hand. O, let me kiss
This princess of pure white, this seal of bliss!

HELENA. O spite! O hell! I see you all are bent
To set against me for your merriment.
If you were civil and knew courtesy,
You would not do me thus much injury.
Can you not hate me, as I know you do,
But you must join in souls to mock me too?
If you were men, as men you are in show,
You would not use a gentle lady so:
To vow, and swear, and superpraise my parts,
When I am sure you hate me with your hearts.
You both are rivals, and love Hermia;
And now both rivals, to mock Helena.
A trim exploit, a manly enterprise,
To conjure tears up in a poor maid's eyes
With your derision! None of noble sort
Would so offend a virgin, and extort
A poor soul's patience, all to make you sport.

LYSANDER. You are unkind, Demetrius; be not so;
For you love Hermia. This you know I know;
And here, with all good will, with all my heart,
In Hermia's love I yield you up my part;
And yours of Helena to me bequeath,
Whom I do love and will do till my death.

HELENA. Never did mockers waste more idle breath.

DEMETRIUS. Lysander, keep thy Hermia; I will none.

TITANIA. *Sleep thou, and I will wind thee in my arms* (ACT IV. SCENE I)

If e'er I lov'd her, all that love is gone.
My heart to her but as guest-wise sojourn'd,
And now to Helen is it home return'd,
There to remain.
LYSANDER. Helen, it is not so.
DEMETRIUS. Disparage not the faith thou dost not know,
Lest, to thy peril, thou aby it dear.
Look where thy love comes; yonder is thy dear.

Enter HERMIA

HERMIA. Dark night, that from the eye his function takes,
The ear more quick of apprehension makes;
Wherein it doth impair the seeing sense,
It pays the hearing double recompense.
Thou art not by mine eye, Lysander, found;
Mine ear, I thank it, brought me to thy sound.
But why unkindly didst thou leave me so?
LYSANDER. Why should he stay whom love doth press to go?
HERMIA. What love could press Lysander from my side?
LYSANDER. Lysander's love, that would not let him bide—
Fair Helena, who more engilds the night
Than all yon fiery oes and eyes of light.
Why seek'st thou me? Could not this make thee know
The hate I bare thee made me leave thee so?
HERMIA. You speak not as you think; it cannot be.
HELENA. Lo, she is one of this confederacy!
Now I perceive they have conjoin'd all three
To fashion this false sport in spite of me.
Injurious Hermia! most ungrateful maid!
Have you conspir'd, have you with these contriv'd,
To bait me with this foul derision?
Is all the counsel that we two have shar'd,
The sisters' vows, the hours that we have spent,
When we have chid the hasty-footed time
For parting us—O, is all forgot?
All school-days' friendship, childhood innocence?
We, Hermia, like two artificial gods,
Have with our needles created both one flower,
Both on one sampler, sitting on one cushion,
Both warbling of one song, both in one key;

As if our hands, our sides, voices, and minds,
Had been incorporate. So we grew together,
Like to a double cherry, seeming parted,
But yet an union in partition,
Two lovely berries moulded on one stem;
So, with two seeming bodies, but one heart;
Two of the first, like coats in heraldry,
Due but to one, and crowned with one crest.
And will you rent our ancient love asunder,
To join with men in scorning your poor friend?
It is not friendly, 'tis not maidenly;
Our sex, as well as I, may chide you for it,
Though I alone do feel the injury.
HERMIA. I am amazed at your passionate words;
I scorn you not; it seems that you scorn me.
HELENA. Have you not set Lysander, as in scorn,
To follow me and praise my eyes and face?
And made your other love, Demetrius,
Who even but now did spurn me with his foot,
To call me goddess, nymph, divine, and rare,
Precious, celestial? Wherefore speaks he this
To her he hates? And wherefore doth Lysander
Deny your love, so rich within his soul,
And tender me, forsooth, affection,
But by your setting on, by your consent?
What though I be not so in grace as you,
So hung upon with love, so fortunate,
But miserable most, to love unlov'd?
This you should pity rather than despise.
HERMIA. I understand not what you mean by this.
HELENA. Ay, do—persever, counterfeit sad looks,
Make mouths upon me when I turn my back,
Wink each at other; hold the sweet jest up;
This sport, well carried, shall be chronicled.
If you have any pity, grace, or manners,
You would not make me such an argument.
But fare ye well; 'tis partly my own fault,
Which death, or absence, soon shall remedy.
LYSANDER. Stay, gentle Helena; hear my excuse;
My love, my life, my soul, fair Helena!

HELENA. O excellent!

HERMIA. Sweet, do not scorn her so.

DEMETRIUS. If she cannot entreat, I can compel.

LYSANDER. Thou canst compel no more than she entreat;
Thy threats have no more strength than her weak prayers.
Helen, I love thee, by my life I do;
I swear by that which I will lose for thee
To prove him false that says I love thee not.

DEMETRIUS. I say I love thee more than he can do.

LYSANDER. If thou say so, withdraw, and prove it too.

DEMETRIUS. Quick, come.

HERMIA. Lysander, whereto tends all this?

LYSANDER. Away, you Ethiope!

DEMETRIUS. No, no, he will
Seem to break loose—take on as you would follow,
But yet come not. You are a tame man; go!

LYSANDER. Hang off, thou cat, thou burr; vile thing, let
loose,
Or I will shake thee from me like a serpent.

HERMIA. Why are you grown so rude? What change is this,
Sweet love?

LYSANDER. Thy love! Out, tawny Tartar, out!
Out, loathed med'cine! O hated potion, hence!

HERMIA. Do you not jest?

HELENA. Yes, sooth; and so do you.

LYSANDER. Demetrius, I will keep my word with thee.

DEMETRIUS. I would I had your bond; for I perceive
A weak bond holds you; I'll not trust your word.

LYSANDER. What, should I hurt her, strike her, kill her dead?
Although I hate her, I'll not harm her so.

HERMIA. What! Can you do me greater harm than hate?
Hate me! wherefore? O me! what news, my love?
Am not I Hermia? Are not you Lysander?
I am as fair now as I was erewhile.
Since night you lov'd me; yet since night you left me.
Why then, you left me—O, the gods forbid!—
In earnest, shall I say?

LYSANDER. Ay, by my life!
And never did desire to see thee more.
Therefore be out of hope, of question, of doubt;

Be certain, nothing truer; 'tis no jest
That I do hate thee and love Helena.
HERMIA. O me! you juggler! you cankerblossom!
You thief of love! What! Have you come by night,
And stol'n my love's heart from him?
HELENA. Fine, i' faith!
Have you no modesty, no maiden shame,
No touch of bashfulness? What! Will you tear
Impatient answers from my gentle tongue?
Fie, fie! you counterfeit, you puppet you!
HERMIA. 'Puppet!' why so? Ay, that way goes the game.
Now I perceive that she hath made compare
Between our statures; she hath urg'd her height;
And with her personage, her tall personage,
Her height, forsooth, she hath prevail'd with him.
And are you grown so high in his esteem
Because I am so dwarfish and so low?
How low am I, thou painted maypole? Speak.
How low am I? I am not yet so low
But that my nails can reach unto thine eyes.
HELENA. I pray you, though you mock me, gentlemen,
Let her not hurt me. I was never curst;
I have no gift at all in shrewishness;
I am a right maid for my cowardice;
Let her not strike me. You perhaps may think,
Because she is something lower than myself,
That I can match her.
HERMIA. 'Lower' hark, again.
HELENA. Good Hermia, do not be so bitter with me.
I evermore did love you, Hermia,
Did ever keep your counsels, never wrong'd you;
Save that, in love unto Demetrius,
I told him of your stealth unto this wood.
He followed you; for love I followed him;
But he hath chid me hence, and threat'ned me
To strike me, spurn me, nay, to kill me too;
And now, so you will let me quiet go,
To Athens will I bear my folly back,
And follow you no further. Let me go.
You see how simple and how fond I am.

HERMIA. Why, get you gone! Who is't that hinders you?
HELENA. A foolish heart that I leave here behind.
HERMIA. What! with Lysander?
HELENA. With Demetrius.
LYSANDER. Be not afraid; she shall not harm thee, Helena.
DEMETRIUS. No, sir, she shall not, though you take her part.
HELENA. O, when she is angry, she is keen and shrewd;
    She was a vixen when she went to school;
    And, though she be but little, she is fierce.
HERMIA. 'Little' again! Nothing but 'low' and 'little'!
    Why will you suffer her to flout me thus?
    Let me come to her.
LYSANDER. Get you gone, you dwarf;
    You minimus, of hind'ring knot-grass made;
    You bead, you acorn.
DEMETRIUS. You are too officious
    In her behalf that scorns your services.
    Let her alone; speak not of Helena;
    Take not her part; for if thou dost intend
    Never so little show of love to her,
    Thou shalt aby it.
LYSANDER. Now she holds me not.
    Now follow, if thou dar'st, to try whose right,
    Of thine or mine, is most in Helena.
DEMETRIUS. Follow! Nay, I'll go with thee, cheek by jowl.
                    Exeunt LYSANDER *and* DEMETRIUS
HERMIA. You, mistress, all this coil is long of you.
    Nay, go not back.
HELENA. I will not trust you, I;
    Nor longer stay in your curst company.
    Your hands than mine are quicker for a fray;
    My legs are longer though, to run away.   *Exit*
HERMIA. I am amaz'd, and know not what to say.   *Exit*
OBERON. This is thy negligence. Still thou mistak'st,
    Or else committ'st thy knaveries wilfully.
PUCK. Believe me, king of shadows, I mistook.
    Did not you tell me I should know the man
    By the Athenian garments he had on?
    And so far blameless proves my enterprise
    That I have 'nointed an Athenian's eyes;

And so far am I glad it so did sort,
As this their jangling I esteem a sport.
OBERON. Thou seest these lovers seek a place to fight.
Hie therefore, Robin, overcast the night;
The starry welkin cover thou anon
With drooping fog as black as Acheron,
And lead these testy rivals so astray
As one come not within another's way.
Like to Lysander sometime frame thy tongue,
Then stir Demetrius up with bitter wrong;
And sometime rail thou like Demetrius;
And from each other look thou lead them thus,
Till o'er their brows death-counterfeiting sleep
With leaden legs and batty wings doth creep.
Then crush this herb into Lysander's eye;
Whose liquor hath this virtuous property,
To take from thence all error with his might
And make his eyeballs roll with wonted sight.
When they next wake, all this derision
Shall seem a dream and fruitless vision;
And back to Athens shall the lovers wend
With league whose date till death shall never end.
Whiles I in this affair do thee employ,
I'll to my queen, and beg her Indian boy;
And then I will her charmed eye release
From monster's view, and all things shall be peace.
PUCK. My fairy lord, this must be done with haste,
For night's swift dragons cut the clouds full fast;
And yonder shines Aurora's harbinger,
At whose approach ghosts, wand'ring here and there,
Troop home to churchyards. Damned spirits all,
That in cross-ways and floods have burial,
Already to their wormy beds are gone,
For fear lest day should look their shames upon;
They wilfully themselves exil'd from light,
And must for aye consort with black-brow'd night.
OBERON. But we are spirits of another sort:
I with the Morning's love have oft made sport;
And, like a forester, the groves may tread
Even till the eastern gate, all fiery red,

Opening on Neptune with fair blessed beams,
Turns into yellow gold his salt green streams.
But, notwithstanding, haste, make no delay;
We may effect this business yet ere day.　　*Exit* OBERON
PUCK.　　　　Up and down, up and down,
I will lead them up and down.
I am fear'd in field and town.
Goblin, lead them up and down.
Here comes one.

Enter LYSANDER

LYSANDER. Where art thou, proud Demetrius? Speak thou now.
PUCK. Here, villain, drawn and ready. Where art thou?
LYSANDER. I will be with thee straight.
PUCK. Follow me, then,
To plainer ground.　　*Exit* LYSANDER *as following the voice*

Enter DEMETRIUS

DEMETRIUS. Lysander, speak again.
Thou runaway, thou coward, art thou fled?
Speak! In some bush? Where dost thou hide thy head?
PUCK. Thou coward, art thou bragging to the stars,
Telling the bushes that thou look'st for wars,
And wilt not come? Come, recreant, come, thou child;
I'll whip thee with a rod. He is defil'd
That draws a sword on thee.
DEMETRIUS. Yea, art thou there?
PUCK. Follow my voice; we'll try no manhood here.　　*Exeunt*

Re-enter LYSANDER

LYSANDER. He goes before me, and still dares me on;
When I come where he calls, then he is gone.
The villain is much lighter heel'd than I.
I followed fast, but faster he did fly,
That fallen am I in dark uneven way,
And here will rest me. [*Lies down*] Come, thou gentle day.
For if but once thou show me thy grey light,
I'll find Demetrius, and revenge this spite.　　[*Sleeps*]

575

Re-enter PUCK *and* DEMETRIUS

PUCK. Ho, ho, ho! Coward, why com'st thou not?
DEMETRIUS. Abide me, if thou dar'st; for well I wot
  Thou run'st before me, shifting every place,
  And dar'st not stand, nor look me in the face.
  Where art thou now?
PUCK. Come hither; I am here.
DEMETRIUS. Nay, then, thou mock'st me. Thou shalt buy
  this dear,
  If ever I thy face by daylight see;
  Now, go thy way. Faintness constraineth me
  To measure out my length on this cold bed.
  By day's approach look to be visited.
                              [Lies down and sleeps]

Enter HELENA

HELENA. O weary night, O long and tedious night,
  Abate thy hours! Shine comforts from the east,
  That I may back to Athens by daylight,
  From these that my poor company detest.
  And sleep, that sometimes shuts up sorrow's eye,
  Steal me awhile from mine own company.   *[Sleeps]*
PUCK.   Yet but three? Come one more;
        Two of both kinds makes up four.
        Here she comes, curst and sad.
        Cupid is a knavish lad,
        Thus to make poor females mad.

Enter HERMIA

HERMIA. Never so weary, never so in woe,
  Bedabbled with the dew, and torn with briers,
  I can no further crawl, no further go;
  My legs can keep no pace with my desires.
  Here will I rest me till the break of day.
  Heavens shield Lysander, if they mean a fray!
                              [Lies down and sleeps]
PUCK.   On the ground
        Sleep sound;
        I'll apply
        To your eye,

Gentle lover, remedy.
 [*Squeezing the juice on* LYSANDER'S *eyes*]
 When thou wak'st,
 Thou tak'st
 True delight
 In the sight
 Of thy former lady's eye;
 And the country proverb known,
 That every man should take his own,
 In your waking shall be shown:
 Jack shall have Jill;
 Nought shall go ill;
The man shall have his mare again, and all shall be well.
 Exit

ACT IV. SCENE 1

The wood. LYSANDER, DEMETRIUS, HELENA, *and*
 HERMIA, *lying asleep*

Enter TITANIA *and* BOTTOM; PEASEBLOSSOM, COB-
WEB, MOTH, MUSTARDSEED, *and other* FAIRIES *at-*
tending; OBERON *behind, unseen*

TITANIA. Come, sit thee down upon this flow'ry bed,
 While I thy amiable cheeks do coy,
 And stick musk-roses in thy sleek smooth head,
 And kiss thy fair large ears, my gentle joy.
BOTTOM. Where's Peaseblossom?
PEASEBLOSSOM. Ready.
BOTTOM. Scratch my head, Peaseblossom.
 Where's Mounsieur Cobweb?
COBWEB. Ready.
BOTTOM. Mounsieur Cobweb; good mounsieur, get you your
 weapons in your hand and kill me a red-hipp'd humble-bee
 on the top of a thistle; and, good mounsieur, bring me the
 honey-bag. Do not fret yourself too much in the action,
 mounsieur; and, good mounsieur, have a care the honey-

bag break not; I would be loath to have you overflown
with a honey-bag, signior. Where's Mounsieur Mustardseed?

MUSTARDSEED. Ready.

BOTTOM. Give me your neaf, Mounsieur Mustardseed. Pray
you, leave your curtsy, good mounsieur.

MUSTARDSEED. What's your will?

BOTTOM. Nothing, good mounsieur, but to help Cavalery
Cobweb to scratch. I must to the barber's, mounsieur; for
methinks I am marvellous hairy about the face; and I am
such a tender ass, if my hair do but tickle me I must
scratch.

TITANIA. What, wilt thou hear some music, my sweet love?

BOTTOM. I have a reasonable good ear in music. Let's have
the tongs and the bones.

TITANIA. Or say, sweet love, what thou desirest to eat.

BOTTOM. Truly, a peck of provender; I could munch your
good dry oats. Methinks I have a great desire to a bottle
of hay. Good hay, sweet hay, hath no fellow.

TITANIA. I have a venturous fairy that shall seek
The squirrel's hoard, and fetch thee new nuts.

BOTTOM. I had rather have a handful or two of dried peas.
But, I pray you, let none of your people stir me; I have an
exposition of sleep come upon me.

TITANIA. Sleep thou, and I will wind thee in my arms.
Fairies, be gone, and be all ways away.   *Exeunt* FAIRIES
So doth the woodbine the sweet honeysuckle
Gently entwist; the female ivy so
Enrings the barky fingers of the elm.
O, how I love thee! how I dote on thee!   [*They sleep*]

Enter PUCK

OBERON. [*Advancing*] Welcome, good Robin. Seest thou
this sweet sight?
Her dotage now I do begin to pity;
For, meeting her of late behind the wood,
Seeking sweet favours for this hateful fool,
I did upbraid her and fall out with her.
For she his hairy temples then had rounded
With coronet of fresh and fragrant flowers;

And that same dew which sometime on the buds
Was wont to swell like round and orient pearls
Stood now within the pretty flowerets' eyes,
Like tears that did their own disgrace bewail.
When I had at my pleasure taunted her,
And she in mild terms begg'd my patience,
I then did ask of her her changeling child;
Which straight she gave me, and her fairy sent
To bear him to my bower in fairy land.
And now I have the boy, I will undo
This hateful imperfection of her eyes.
And, gentle Puck, take this transformed scalp
From off the head of this Athenian swain,
That he awaking when the other do
May all to Athens back again repair,
And think no more of this night's accidents
But as the fierce vexation of a dream.
But first I will release the Fairy Queen.

                                                               [*Touching her eyes*]

                Be as thou wast wont to be;
                See as thou was wont to see.
                Dian's bud o'er Cupid's flower
                Hath such force and blessed power.
Now, my Titania; wake you, my sweet queen.
TITANIA. My Oberon! What visions have I seen!
Methought I was enamour'd of an ass.
OBERON. There lies your love.
TITANIA. How came these things to pass?
O, how mine eyes do loathe his visage now!
OBERON. Silence awhile. Robin, take off this head.
Titania, music call; and strike more dead
Than common sleep of all these five the sense.
TITANIA. Music, ho, music, such as charmeth sleep!
PUCK. Now when thou wak'st with thine own fool's eyes
   peep.
OBERON. Sound, music. Come, my Queen, take hands with
   me,   [*Music*]
And rock the ground whereon these sleepers be.
Now thou and I are new in amity,
And will to-morrow midnight solemnly

Dance in Duke Theseus' house triumphantly,
And bless it to all fair prosperity.
There shall the pairs of faithful lovers be
Wedded, with Theseus, all in jollity.

PUCK. Fairy King, attend and mark;
I do hear the morning lark.

OBERON. Then, my Queen, in silence sad,
Trip we after night's shade.
We the globe can compass soon,
Swifter than the wand'ring moon.

TITANIA. Come, my lord; and in our flight,
Tell me how it came this night
That I sleeping here was found
With these mortals on the ground. *Exeunt*

To the winding of horns, enter THESEUS, HIPPOLYTA,
EGEUS, *and train*

THESEUS. Go, one of you, find out the forester;
For now our observation is perform'd,
And since we have the vaward of the day,
My love shall hear the music of my hounds.
Uncouple in the western valley; let them go.
Dispatch, I say, and find the forester. *Exit an* ATTENDANT
We will, fair Queen, up to the mountain's top,
And mark the musical confusion
Of hounds and echo in conjunction.

HIPPOLYTA. I was with Hercules and Cadmus once
When in a wood of Crete they bay'd the bear
With hounds of Sparta; never did I hear
Such gallant chiding, for, besides the groves,
The skies, the fountains, every region near
Seem'd all one mutual cry. I never heard
So musical a discord, such sweet thunder.

THESEUS. My hounds are bred out of the Spartan kind,
So flew'd, so sanded; and their heads are hung
With ears that sweep away the morning dew;
Crook-knee'd and dew-lapp'd like Thessalian bulls;
Slow in pursuit, but match'd in mouth like bells,
Each under each. A cry more tuneable
Was never holla'd to, nor cheer'd with horn,

In Crete, in Sparta, nor in Thessaly.
Judge when you hear. But, soft, what nymphs are these?
EGEUS. My lord, this is my daughter here asleep,
  And this Lysander, this Demetrius is,
  This Helena, old Nedar's Helena.
  I wonder of their being here together.
THESEUS. No doubt they rose up early to observe
  The rite of May; and, hearing our intent,
  Came here in grace of our solemnity.
  But speak, Egeus; is not this the day
  That Hermia should give answer of her choice?
EGEUS. It is, my lord.
THESEUS. Go, bid the huntsmen wake them with their horns.
        [*Horns and shout within. The sleepers
              awake and kneel to* THESEUS]
  Good-morrow, friends. Saint Valentine is past;
  Begin these wood-birds but to couple now?
LYSANDER. Pardon, my lord.
THESEUS. I pray you all, stand up.
  I know you two are rival enemies;
  How comes this gentle concord in the world
  That hatred is so far from jealousy
  To sleep by hate, and fear no enmity?
LYSANDER. My lord, I shall reply amazedly,
  Half sleep, half waking; but as yet, I swear,
  I cannot truly say how I came here,
  But, as I think—for truly would I speak,
  And now I do bethink me, so it is—
  I came with Hermia hither. Our intent
  Was to be gone from Athens, where we might,
  Without the peril of the Athenian law—
EGEUS. Enough, enough, my Lord; you have enough;
  I beg the law, the law upon his head.
  They would have stol'n away, they would, Demetrius,
  Thereby to have defeated you and me:
  You of your wife, and me of my consent,
  Of my consent that she should be your wife.
DEMETRIUS. My lord, fair Helen told me of their stealth,
  Of this their purpose hither to this wood;
  And I in fury hither followed them,

Fair Helena in fancy following me.
But, my good lord, I wot not by what power—
But by some power it is—my love to Hermia,
Melted as the snow, seems to me now
As the remembrance of an idle gaud
Which in my childhood I did dote upon;
And all the faith, the virtue of my heart,
The object and the pleasure of mine eye,
Is only Helena. To her, my lord,
Was I betroth'd ere I saw Hermia.
But, like a sickness, did I loathe this food;
But, as in health, come to my natural taste,
Now I do wish it, love it, long for it,
And will for evermore be true to it.
THESEUS. Fair lovers, you are fortunately met;
Of this discourse we more will hear anon.
Egeus, I will overbear your will;
For in the temple, by and by, with us
These couples shall eternally be knit.
And, for the morning now is something worn,
Our purpos'd hunting shall be set aside.
Away with us to Athens, three and three;
We'll hold a feast in great solemnity.
Come, Hippolyta.
                    Exeunt THESEUS, HIPPOLYTA, EGEUS, *and train*
DEMETRIUS. These things seem small and undistinguishable,
Like far-off mountains turned into clouds.
HERMIA. Methinks I see these things with parted eye,
When every thing seems double.
HELENA. So methinks;
And I have found Demetrius like a jewel,
Mine own, and not mine own.
DEMETRIUS. Are you sure
That we are awake? It seems to me
That yet we sleep, we dream. Do not you think
The Duke was here, and bid us follow him?
HERMIA. Yea, and my father.
HELENA. And Hippolyta.
LYSANDER. And he did bid us follow to the temple.
DEMETRIUS. Why, then, we are awake; let's follow him;

And by the way let us recount our dreams.   *Exeunt*

BOTTOM. [*Awaking*] When my cue comes, call me, and I will answer. My next is 'Most fair Pyramus.' Heigh-ho! Peter Quince! Flute, the bellows-mender! Snout, the tinker! Starveling! God's my life, stol'n hence, and left me asleep! I have had a most rare vision. I have had a dream, past the wit of man to say what dream it was. Man is but an ass if he go about to expound this dream. Methought I was—there is no man can tell what. Methought I was, and methought I had, but man is but a patch'd fool, if he will offer to say what methought I had. The eye of man hath not heard, the ear of man hath not seen, man's hand is not able to taste, his tongue to conceive, nor his heart to report, what my dream was. I will get Peter Quince to write a ballad of this dream. It shall be call'd 'Bottom's Dream,' because it hath no bottom; and I will sing it in the latter end of a play, before the Duke. Peradventure, to make it the more gracious, I shall sing it at her death.   *Exit*

SCENE 2

Athens. QUINCE'S *house*

Enter QUINCE, FLUTE, SNOUT, *and* STARVELING

QUINCE. Have you sent to Bottom's house? Is he come home yet?

STARVELING. He cannot be heard of. Out of doubt he is transported.

FLUTE. If he come not, then the play is marr'd; it goes not forward, doth it?

QUINCE. It is not possible. You have not a man in all Athens able to discharge Pyramus but he.

FLUTE. No; he hath simply the best wit of any handicraft man in Athens.

QUINCE. Yea, and the best person too; and he is a very paramour for a sweet voice.

FLUTE. You must say 'paragon.' A paramour is—God bless us!—a thing of naught.

Enter SNUG

SNUG. Masters, the Duke is coming from the temple; and there is two or three lords and ladies more married. If our sport had gone forward, we had all been made men.

FLUTE. O sweet bully Bottom! Thus hath he lost sixpence a day during his life; he could not have scaped sixpence a day. An the Duke had not given him sixpence a day for playing Pyramus, I'll be hanged. He would have deserved it: sixpence a day in Pyramus, or nothing.

Enter BOTTOM

BOTTOM. Where are these lads? Where are these hearts?

QUINCE. Bottom! O most courageous day! O most happy hour!

BOTTOM. Masters, I am to discourse wonders; but ask me not what; for if I tell you, I am not true Athenian. I will tell you everything, right as it fell out.

QUINCE. Let us hear, sweet Bottom.

BOTTOM. Not a word of me. All that I will tell you is, that the Duke hath dined. Get your apparel together; good strings to your beards, new ribbons to your pumps; meet presently at the palace; every man look o'er his part; for the short and the long is, our play is preferr'd. In any case, let Thisby have clean linen; and let not him that plays the lion pare his nails, for they shall hang out for the lion's claws. And, most dear actors, eat no onions nor garlic, for we are to utter sweet breath; and I do not doubt but to hear them say it is a sweet comedy. No more words. Away, go, away!   *Exeunt*

ACT V. SCENE 1

Athens. The palace of THESEUS

Enter THESEUS, HIPPOLYTA, PHILOSTRATE, LORDS,
and ATTENDANTS

HIPPOLYTA. 'Tis strange, my Theseus, that these lovers speak of.

THESEUS. More strange than true. I never may believe
  These antique fables, nor these fairy toys.
  Lovers and madmen have such seething brains,
  Such shaping fantasies, that apprehend
  More than cool reason ever comprehends.
  The lunatic, the lover, and the poet,
  Are of imagination all compact.
  One sees more devils than vast hell can hold;
  That is the madman. The lover, all as frantic,
  Sees Helen's beauty in a brow of Egypt.
  The poet's eye, in a fine frenzy rolling,
  Doth glance from heaven to earth, from earth to heaven;
  And as imagination bodies forth
  The forms of things unknown, the poet's pen
  Turns them to shapes, and gives to airy nothing
  A local habitation and a name.
  Such tricks hath strong imagination
  That, if it would but apprehend some joy,
  It comprehends some bringer of that joy;
  Or in the night, imagining some fear,
  How easy is a bush suppos'd a bear?
HIPPOLYTA. But all the story of the night told over,
  And all their minds transfigur'd so together,
  More witnesseth than fancy's images,
  And grows to something of great constancy,
  But howsoever strange and admirable.

Enter LYSANDER, DEMETRIUS, HERMIA, *and* HELENA

THESEUS. Here come the lovers, full of joy and mirth.
  Joy, gentle friends, joy and fresh days of love
  Accompany your hearts!
LYSANDER. More than to us
  Wait in your royal walks, your board, your bed!
THESEUS. Come now; what masques, what dances shall we
    have,
  To wear away this long age of three hours
  Between our after-supper and bed-time?
  Where is our usual manager of mirth?
  What revels are in hand? Is there no play
  To ease the anguish of a torturing hour?

Call Philostrate.

PHILOSTRATE. Here, mighty Theseus.

THESEUS. Say, what abridgment have you for this evening?
What masque? what music? How shall we beguile
The lazy time, if not with some delight?

PHILOSTRATE. There is a brief how many sports are ripe;
Make choice of which your Highness will see first.

[*Giving a paper*]

THESEUS. 'The battle with the Centaurs, to be sung
By an Athenian eunuch to the harp.'
We'll none of that: that have I told my love,
In glory of my kinsman Hercules.
'The riot of the tipsy Bacchanals,
Tearing the Thracian singer in their rage.'
That is an old device, and it was play'd
When I from Thebes came last a conqueror.
'The thrice three Muses mourning for the death
Of Learning, late deceas'd in beggary.'
That is some satire, keen and critical,
Not sorting with a nuptial ceremony.
'A tedious brief scene of young Pyramus
And his love Thisby; very tragical mirth.'
Merry and tragical! tedious and brief!
That is hot ice and wondrous strange snow.
How shall we find the concord of this discord?

PHILOSTRATE. A play there is, my lord, some ten words long,
Which is as brief as I have known a play;
But by ten words, my lord, it is too long,
Which makes it tedious; for in all the play
There is not one word apt, one player fitted.
And tragical, my noble lord, it is;
For Pyramus therein doth kill himself.
Which when I saw rehears'd, I must confess,
Made mine eyes water; but more merry tears
The passion of loud laughter never shed.

THESEUS. What are they that do play it?

PHILOSTRATE. Hard-handed men that work in Athens here,
Which never labour'd in their minds till now;
And now have toil'd their unbreathed memories
With this same play against your nuptial.

THESEUS. And we will hear it.
PHILOSTRATE. No, my noble lord,
  It is not for you. I have heard it over,
  And it is nothing, nothing in the world;
  Unless you can find sport in their intents,
  Extremely stretch'd and conn'd with cruel pain,
  To do you service.
THESEUS. I will hear that play;
  For never anything can be amiss
  When simpleness and duty tender it.
  Go, bring them in; and take your places, ladies.
                                    Exit PHILOSTRATE
HIPPOLYTA. I love not to see wretchedness o'er-charged,
  And duty in his service perishing.
THESEUS. Why, gentle sweet, you shall see no such thing.
HIPPOLYTA. He says they can do nothing in this kind.
THESEUS. The kinder we, to give them thanks for nothing.
  Our sport shall be to take what they mistake;
  And what poor duty cannot do, noble respect
  Takes it in might, not merit.
  Where I have come, great clerks have purposed
  To greet me with premeditated welcomes;
  Where I have seen them shiver and look pale,
  Make periods in the midst of sentences,
  Throttle their practis'd accent in their fears,
  And, in conclusion, dumbly have broke off,
  Not paying me a welcome. Trust me, sweet,
  Out of this silence yet I pick'd a welcome;
  And in the modesty of fearful duty
  I read as much as from the rattling tongue
  Of saucy and audacious eloquence.
  Love, therefore, and tongue-tied simplicity
  In least speak most to my capacity.

Re-enter PHILOSTRATE

PHILOSTRATE. So please your Grace, the Prologue is address'd.
THESEUS. Let him approach.   *[Flourish of trumpets]*

Enter QUINCE *as the* PROLOGUE

587

A MIDSUMMER NIGHT'S DREAM

PROLOGUE. *If we offend, it is with our good will.*
That you should think, we come not to offend,
But with good will. To show our simple skill,
That is the true beginning of our end.
Consider then, we come but in despite.
We do not come, as minding to content you,
Our true intent is. All for your delight
We are not here. That you should here repent you,
The actors are at hand; and, by their show,
You shall know all, that you are like to know,
THESEUS. This fellow doth not stand upon points.
LYSANDER. He hath rid his prologue like a rough colt; he knows not the stop. A good moral, my lord: it is not enough to speak, but to speak true.
HIPPOLYTA. Indeed he hath play'd on this prologue like a child on a recorder—a sound, but not in government.
THESEUS. His speech was like a tangled chain; nothing impaired, but all disordered. Who is next?

Enter, with a trumpet before them, as in dumb show,
PYRAMUS *and* THISBY, WALL, MOONSHINE, *and* LION

PROLOGUE. *Gentles, perchance you wonder at this show;*
But wonder on, till truth make all things plain.
This man is Pyramus, if you would know;
This beauteous lady Thisby is certain.
This man, with lime and rough-cast, doth present
Wall, that vile Wall which did these lovers sunder;
And through Wall's chink, poor souls, they are content
To whisper. At the which let no man wonder.
This man, with lanthorn, dog, and bush of thorn,
Presenteth Moonshine; for, if you will know,
By moonshine did these lovers think no scorn
To meet at Ninus' tomb, there, there to woo.
This grisly beast, which Lion hight by name,
The trusty Thisby, coming first by night,
Did scare away, or rather did affright;
And as she fled, her mantle she did fall;
Which Lion vile with bloody mouth did stain.
Anon comes Pyramus, sweet youth and tall,
And finds his trusty Thisby's mantle slain;

588

Whereat with blade, with bloody blameful blade,
He bravely broach'd his boiling bloody breast;
And Thisby, tarrying in mulberry shade,
His dagger drew, and died. For all the rest,
Let Lion, Moonshine, Wall, and lovers twain,
At large discourse while here they do remain.
                    Exeunt PROLOGUE, PYRAMUS, THISBY,
                                LION, *and* MOONSHINE

THESEUS. I wonder if the lion be to speak.

DEMETRIUS. No wonder, my lord: one lion may, when many asses do.

WALL. *In this same interlude it doth befall*
That I, one Snout by name, present a wall;
And such a wall as I would have you think
That had in it a crannied hole or chink,
Through which the lovers, Pyramus and Thisby,
Did whisper often very secretly.
This loam, this rough-cast, and this stone, doth show
That I am that same wall; the truth is so;
And this the cranny is, right and sinister,
Through which the fearful lovers are to whisper.

THESEUS. Would you desire lime and hair to speak better?

DEMETRIUS. It is the wittiest partition that ever I heard discourse, my lord.

Enter PYRAMUS

THESEUS. Pyramus draws near the wall; silence.

PYRAMUS. *O grim-look'd night! O night with hue so black!*
O night, which ever art when day is not!
O night, O night, alack, alack, alack,
I fear my Thisby's promise is forgot!
And thou, O wall, O sweet, O lovely wall,
That stand'st between her father's ground and mine;
Thou wall, O wall, O sweet and lovely wall,
Show me thy chink, to blink through with mine eyne.
                              [WALL *holds up his fingers*]
Thanks, courteous wall. Jove shield thee well for this!
But what see I? No Thisby do I see.
O wicked wall, through whom I see no bliss;
Curs'd be thy stones for thus deceiving me!

THESEUS. The wall, methinks, being sensible, should curse again.

PYRAMUS. No, in truth, sir, he should not. *Deceiving me* is Thisby's cue. She is to enter now, and I am to spy her through the wall. You shall see it will fall pat as I told you; yonder she comes.

Enter THISBY

THISBY. *O wall, full often hast thou heard my moans,*
For parting my fair Pyramus and me!
My cherry lips have often kiss'd thy stones,
Thy stones with lime and hair knit up in thee.

PYRAMUS. *I see a voice; now will I to the chink,*
To spy an I can hear my Thisby's face.
Thisby!

THISBY. *My love! thou art my love, I think.*

PYRAMUS. *Think what thou wilt, I am thy lover's grace;*
And like Limander am I trusty still.

THISBY. *And I like Helen, till the Fates me kill.*

PYRAMUS. *Not Shafalus to Procrus was so true.*

THISBY. *As Shafalus to Procrus, I to you.*

PYRAMUS. *O, kiss me through the hole of this vile wall.*

THISBY. *I kiss the wall's hole, not your lips at all.*

PYRAMUS. *Wilt thou at Ninny's tomb meet me straightway?*

THISBY. *Tide life, tide death, I come without delay.*

Exeunt PYRAMUS *and* THISBY

WALL. *Thus have I, Wall, my part discharged so;*
And, being done, thus Wall away doth go. *Exit* WALL

THESEUS. Now is the moon used between the two neighbours.

DEMETRIUS. No remedy, my lord, when walls are so wilful to hear without warning.

HIPPOLYTA. This is the silliest stuff that ever I heard.

THESEUS. The best in this kind are but shadows; and the worst are no worse, if imagination amend them.

HIPPOLYTA. It must be your imagination then, and not theirs.

THESEUS. If we imagine no worse of them than they of themselves, they may pass for excellent men. Here come two noble beasts in, a man and a lion.

Enter LION *and* MOONSHINE

LION. *You, ladies, you, whose gentle hearts do fear*
The smallest monstrous mouse that creeps on floor,
May now, perchance, both quake and tremble here,
  When lion rough in wildest rage doth roar.
Then know that I as Snug the joiner am
A lion fell, nor else no lion's dam;
  For, if I should as lion come in strife
  Into this place, 'twere pity on my life.
THESEUS. A very gentle beast, and of a good conscience.
DEMETRIUS. The very best at a beast, my lord, that e'er I saw.
LYSANDER. This lion is a very fox for his valour.
THESEUS. True; and a goose for his discretion.
DEMETRIUS. Not so, my lord; for his valour cannot carry his discretion, and the fox carries the goose.
THESEUS. His discretion, I am sure, cannot carry his valour; for the goose carries not the fox. It is well. Leave it to his discretion, and let us listen to the Moon.
MOONSHINE. *This lanthorn doth the horned moon present—*
DEMETRIUS. He should have worn the horns on his head.
THESEUS. He is no crescent, and his horns are invisible within the circumference.
MOONSHINE. *This lanthorn doth the horned moon present;*
Myself the Man i' th' Moon do seem to be.
THESEUS. This is the greatest error of all the rest; the man should be put into the lantern. How is it else the man i' th' moon?
DEMETRIUS. He dares not come there for the candle; for, you see, it is already in snuff.
HIPPOLYTA. I am aweary of this moon. Would he would change!
THESEUS. It appears, by his small light of discretion, that he is in the wane; but yet, in courtesy, in all reason, we must stay the time.
LYSANDER. Proceed, Moon.
MOON. All that I have to say is to tell you that the lanthorn is the moon; I, the Man i' th' Moon; this thorn-bush, my thorn-bush; and this dog, my dog.

DEMETRIUS. Why, all these should be in the lantern; for all
these are in the moon. But silence; here comes Thisby.

Re-enter THISBY

THISBY. *This is old Ninny's tomb. Where is my love?*
LION. [*Roaring*] *O*— [THISBY *runs off*]
DEMETRIUS. Well roar'd, Lion.
THESEUS. Well run, Thisby.
HIPPOLYTA. Well shone, Moon. Truly, the moon shines with
a good grace. [*The* LION *tears* THISBY'S *mantle, and exit*]
THESEUS. Well mous'd, Lion.

Re-enter PYRAMUS

DEMETRIUS. And then came Pyramus.
LYSANDER. And so the lion vanish'd.
PYRAMUS. *Sweet Moon, I thank thee for thy sunny beams;*
I thank thee, Moon, for shining now so bright;
For, by thy gracious golden, glittering gleams,
I trust to take of truest Thisby sight.
   But stay, O spite!
   But mark, poor knight,
  What dreadful dole is here!
   Eyes, do you see?
   How can it be?
  O dainty duck! O dear!
   Thy mantle good,
  What! stain'd with blood?
  Approach, ye Furies fell.
  O Fates! come, come;
  Cut thread and thrum;
  Quail, crush, conclude, and quell.
THESEUS. This passion, and the death of a dear friend, would
go near to make a man look sad.
HIPPOLYTA. Beshrew my heart, but I pity the man.
PYRAMUS. *O wherefore, Nature, didst thou lions frame?*
Since lion vile hath here deflower'd my dear;
Which is—no, no—which was the fairest dame
That liv'd, that lov'd, that lik'd, that look'd with cheer.
  Come, tears, confound;
  Out, sword, and wound

The pap of Pyramus;
   Ay, that left pap,
   Where heart doth hop.   *[Stabs himself]*
Thus die I, thus, thus, thus.
   Now am I dead,
   Now am I fled;
My soul is in the sky.
   Tongue, lose thy light;
   Moon, take thy flight.   *[Exit* MOONSHINE*]*
Now die, die, die, die, die.   *[Dies]*

DEMETRIUS. No die, but an ace, for him; for he is but one.

LYSANDER. Less than an ace, man; for he is dead; he is nothing.

THESEUS. With the help of a surgeon he might yet recover and yet prove an ass.

HIPPOLYTA. How chance Moonshine is gone before Thisby comes back and finds her lover?

Re-enter THISBY

THESEUS. She will find him by starlight. Here she comes; and her passion ends the play.

HIPPOLYTA. Methinks she should not use a long one for such a Pyramus; I hope she will be brief.

DEMETRIUS. A mote will turn the balance, which Pyramus, which Thisby, is the better—he for a man, God warrant us: she for a woman, God bless us!

LYSANDER. She hath spied him already with those sweet eyes.

DEMETRIUS. And thus she moans, videlicet:—

THISBY.   *Asleep, my love?*
     What, dead, my dove?
O Pyramus, arise,
   Speak, speak. Quite dumb?
   Dead, dead? A tomb
Must cover thy sweet eyes.
   These lily lips,
   This cherry nose,
These yellow cowslip cheeks,
   Are gone, are gone;
   Lovers, make moan;
His eyes were green as leeks.

O Sisters Three,
Come, come to me,
With hands as pale as milk;
Lay them in gore,
Since you have shore
With shears his thread of silk.
Tongue, not a word.
Come, trusty sword;
Come, blade, my breast imbrue.
           [Stabs herself]
And farewell, friends;
Thus Thisby ends;
Adieu, adieu, adieu.   *[Dies]*

THESEUS. Moonshine and Lion are left to bury the dead.
DEMETRIUS. Ay, and Wall too.
BOTTOM. [*Starting up*] No, I assure you; the wall is down that parted their fathers. Will it please you to see the Epilogue, or to hear a Bergomask dance between two of our company?
THESEUS. No epilogue, I pray you; for your play needs no excuse. Never excuse; for when the players are all dead there need none to be blamed. Marry, if he that writ it had played Pyramus, and hang'd himself in Thisby's garter, it would have been a fine tragedy. And so it is, truly; and very notably discharg'd. But come, your Bergomask; let your epilogue alone.   [*A dance*]
The iron tongue of midnight hath told twelve.
Lovers, to bed; 'tis almost fairy time.
I fear we shall out-sleep the coming morn,
As much as we this night have overwatch'd.
This palpable-gross play hath well beguil'd
The heavy gait of night. Sweet friends, to bed.
A fortnight hold we this solemnity,
In nightly revels and new jollity.   *Exeunt*

Enter PUCK *with a broom*

PUCK. Now the hungry lion roars,
And the wolf behowls the moon;
Whilst the heavy ploughman snores,
All with weary task fordone.

Now the wasted brands do glow,
Whilst the screech-owl, screeching loud,
Puts the wretch that lies in woe
In remembrance of a shroud.
Now it is the time of night
That the graves, all gaping wide,
Every one lets forth his sprite,
In the church-way paths to glide.
And we fairies, that do run
By the triple Hecate's team
From the presence of the sun,
Following darkness like a dream,
Now are frolic. Not a mouse
Shall disturb this hallowed house.
I am sent with broom before,
To sweep the dust behind the door.

Enter OBERON *and* TITANIA, *with all their train*

OBERON. Through the house give glimmering light,
By the dead and drowsy fire;
Every elf and fairy sprite
Hop as light as bird from brier;
And this ditty, after me,
Sing and dance it trippingly.
TITANIA.   First, rehearse your song by rote,
To each word a warbling note;
Hand in hand, with fairy grace,
Will we sing, and bless this place.

[OBERON *leading, the* FAIRIES *sing and dance*]

OBERON. Now, until the break of day,
Through this house each fairy stray.
To the best bride-bed will we,
Which by us shall blessed be;
And the issue there create
Ever shall be fortunate.
So shall all the couples three
Ever true in loving be;
And the blots of Nature's hand
Shall not in their issue stand;

595

Never mole, hare-lip, nor scar,
Nor mark prodigious, such as are
Despised in nativity,
Shall upon their children be.
With this field-dew consecrate,
Every fairy take his gait,
And each several chamber bless,
Through this palace, with sweet peace;
And the owner of it blest
Ever shall in safety rest.
Trip away; make no stay;
Meet me all by break of day. *Exeunt all but* PUCK

PUCK. If we shadows have offended,
Think but this, and all is mended,
That you have but slumb'red here
While these visions did appear.
And this weak and idle theme,
No more yielding but a dream,
Gentles, do not reprehend.
If you pardon, we will mend.
And, as I am an honest Puck,
If we have unearned luck
Now to scape the serpent's tongue,
We will make amends ere long;
Else the Puck a liar call.
So, good night unto you all.
Give me your hands, if we be friends,
And Robin shall restore amends. *Exit*

The Merchant of Venice

THE MERCHANT OF VENICE

LOOKED at from the outside as it were *The Merchant of Venice* seems built on two improbabilities that could hardly be expected to sustain a popular play. The bond that carried a forfeit of a pound of flesh, and the fate of an heiress depending on a choice of caskets, seem so unlikely and indeed preposterous that one may wonder how *The Merchant of Venice* is still so welcome on the stage and indeed one of Shakespeare's best known plays.

The answer that Shakespeare has covered the improbabilities with a trellis-work of fine poetry is not adequate. Of course part of the charm of the play lies in its poetry; but fine verse would not by itself be sufficient to enlist and sustain the interest of the audience, did the hearer or reader not feel that the poetry was the natural vehicle for the significance of the action, that the words make explicit what was only shadowed forth in the episodes of the plot. We are for example meant to feel that Bassanio is guided in his choice of casket by a sensibility beyond that possessed by such rivals as Morocco or Arragon. That he is at once less wealthy and less certain of his claims to success is meant to be part of Bassanio's claim on our sympathies. And undoubtedly these are elements in our reaction: we feel that Bassanio does love Portia as the others do not. Nor can this feeling be banished by the critic who points out that Bassanio has had to borrow the money that provides the very finery in which he and his followers are dressed, and that he has come to mend his rather broken fortunes by marriage with an heiress. For it is clear that whatever his apparent disabilities the right choice discovers the true lover: the caskets cannot be mistaken. That Portia agrees with the caskets makes our assurance doubly sure.

In the Bassanio-Portia part of the play the author's intentions and our sympathies run so easily together that Shakespeare has no difficulty in carrying us with him over the impossibilities of the ordeal by caskets; the bond between Antonio and Shylock however raises more serious obstacles in the way of plain acceptance.

INTRODUCTION

To Jews the England of Shakespeare's time was less hospitable than the London of to-day. There were however Jews in Elizabeth's London and the Queen had for a time a Jewish physician Roderigo Lopez. This unfortunate man was executed in June 1594 on being found guilty, with what justice it seems impossible to say, of attempting to poison the Queen. Whether this event suggested to Shakespeare that a play with a Jewish character would be topical we cannot say; what is clear however is that the medieval type of story in which a Jew might figure as the villain would not have seemed in any way unnatural to Shakespeare's audience. Shakespeare's play is based on such a story, written late in the fourteenth century but not printed till 1558. This story in the collection made by Ser Giovanni of Florence entitled *Il Pecorone* tells how a youthful Venetian trading to Alexandria is tempted to anchor at Belmonte in the hope of winning the lady there and fails twice to survive the ordeal to which her lovers are subjected. The lady drugs the cup she offers them in entertainment and falling asleep they forfeit the property they have given her as pledge of their faith. On his third voyage however the young man is warned and wins the lady; he forgets however that the third voyage was made possible by a friend's borrowing from a Jew; who can have a pound of the borrower's flesh if he is behindhand with the money. The borrower is about to forfeit his flesh when the young man turns up with ten times the money due—for if the Lady of Belmonte seems an avaricious siren when seizing on the property of her defeated suitors, she is generosity itself in this crisis. The Jew however is obdurate and the Lady of Belmonte has to deliver her husband's friend as Portia rescues Antonio. The story concludes with the ring episode as in Shakespeare's play.

Shakespeare had to modify the story for the stage by changing the ordeal to that by choice of caskets. It is possible that an earlier play called *The Jew* may have suggested this change to Shakespeare. Stephen Gosson in his tirade *The Schoole of Abuse* (1579) against the stage allows that *The Jew* may warn us against 'the greediness of worldly chusers and the bloody mind of Usurers.' It may be that the 'worldly chusers' are those who try to pick the winning casket; it is

599

clear that the Jew is the usurer. Though Shakespeare had to modify one part of the original story he was free to take over the Jew with all the villainies that the ages had heaped on the usurer.

Shylock's role is indicated by Shakespeare's source and dictated by his part in the action. He is not meant to be a good man who puts the Christians to shame; he is at the end an obstacle in the way of happiness and peace and has to be removed. But as a man who takes up a challenge flung at him by those who treat him as an enemy and has to play a lone hand he naturally holds our attention and makes us feel his passion. The character is undoubtedly one of Shakespeare's triumphs: Shylock as an observer of the law feels entitled to all the law allows; his Judaism is uncompromising; and, although despised by the gentiles round him, he feels himself one of a peculiar people.

The bond then allows Shakespeare to interest us in a question that has, as well as a bearing on the happy ending we require, an interest of its own. Shylock is for the letter of the law, Portia for the spirit in which law should be interpreted. And if it be objected that the story as a whole is too flimsy and fairy-tale-like to carry such serious issues it must be admitted that it is the development of these issues that gives the play the vitality that the original story lacks.

The lines on which Shakespeare has developed his original show that he had no intention of representing Bassanio as a sponger because he borrowed money from Antonio, or of holding up Portia as a Jew-baiter because she delivers her husband's friend from Shylock. Shakespeare had no need to fear that the audience at The Theatre or The Globe would so distort his intentions; only a hypercritical reading of the comedy has suggested such modern aberrations.

SHYLOCK. *I am debating of my present store*
(ACT I. SCENE III)

THE DUKE OF VENICE
THE PRINCE OF MOROCCO ⎱
THE PRINCE OF ARRAGON ⎰ *suitors to Portia*
ANTONIO, *a merchant of Venice*
BASSANIO, *his friend, suitor to Portia*
SOLANIO ⎱
SALERIO ⎬ *friends to Antonio and Bassanio*
GRATIANO ⎰
LORENZO, *in love with Jessica*
SHYLOCK, *a rich Jew*
TUBAL, *a Jew, his friend*
LAUNCELOT GOBBO, *a clown, servant to Shylock*
OLD GOBBO, *father to Launcelot*
LEONARDO, *servant to Bassanio*
BALTHASAR ⎱
STEPHANO ⎰ *servants to Portia*

PORTIA, *a rich heiress*
NERISSA, *her waiting-maid*
JESSICA, *daughter to Shylock*

Magnificoes of Venice, Officers of the Court of Justice, Gaoler, Servants, *and other* Attendants

SCENE:

Venice, and PORTIA's *house at Belmont*

The Merchant of Venice

ACT I. SCENE 1

Venice. A street

Enter ANTONIO, SALERIO, *and* SOLANIO

ANTONIO. In sooth, I know not why I am so sad.
It wearies me; you say it wearies you;
But how I caught it, found it, or came by it,
What stuff 'tis made of, whereof it is born,
I am to learn;
And such a want-wit sadness makes of me
That I have much ado to know myself.

SALERIO. Your mind is tossing on the ocean;
There where your argosies, with portly sail—
Like signiors and rich burghers on the flood,
Or as it were the pageants of the sea—
Do overpeer the petty traffickers,
That curtsy to them, do them reverence,
As they fly by them with their woven wings.

SOLANIO. Believe me, sir, had I such venture forth,
The better part of my affections would
Be with my hopes abroad. I should be still
Plucking the grass to know where sits the wind,
Peering in maps for ports, and piers, and roads;
And every object that might make me fear
Misfortune to my ventures, out of doubt,
Would make me sad.

SALERIO. My wind, cooling my broth,
Would blow me to an ague when I thought
What harm a wind too great might do at sea.
I should not see the sandy hour-glass run
But I should think of shallows and of flats,
And see my wealthy Andrew dock'd in sand,
Vailing her high top lower than her ribs
To kiss her burial. Should I go to church
And see the holy edifice of stone,

And not bethink me straight of dangerous rocks,
Which, touching but my gentle vessel's side,
Would scatter all her spices on the stream,
Enrobe the roaring waters with my silks,
And, in a word, but even now worth this,
And now worth nothing? Shall I have the thought
To think on this, and shall I lack the thought
That such a thing bechanc'd would make me sad?
But tell not me; I know Antonio
Is sad to think upon his merchandise.

ANTONIO. Believe me, no; I thank my fortune for it,
My ventures are not in one bottom trusted,
Nor to one place; nor is my whole estate
Upon the fortune of this present year;
Therefore my merchandise makes me not sad.

SOLANIO. Why then you are in love.

ANTONIO. Fie, fie!

SOLANIO. Not in love neither? Then let us say you are sad
Because you are not merry; and 'twere as easy
For you to laugh and leap and say you are merry,
Because you are not sad. Now, by two-headed Janus,
Nature hath fram'd strange fellows in her time:
Some that will evermore peep through their eyes,
And laugh like parrots at a bag-piper;
And other of such vinegar aspect
That they'll not show their teeth in way of smile
Though Nestor swear the jest be laughable.

Enter BASSANIO, LORENZO, *and* GRATIANO

Here comes Bassanio, your most noble kinsman,
Gratiano and Lorenzo. Fare ye well;
We leave you now with better company.

SALERIO. I would have stay'd till I had made you merry,
If worthier friends had not prevented me.

ANTONIO. Your worth is very dear in my regard.
I take it your own business calls on you,
And you embrace th' occasion to depart.

SALERIO. Good morrow, my good lords.

BASSANIO. Good signiors both, when shall we laugh? Say when.

You grow exceeding strange; must it be so?
SALERIO. We'll make our leisures to attend on yours.

Exeunt SALERIO *and* SOLANIO

LORENZO. My Lord Bassanio, since you have found Antonio,
We two will leave you; but at dinner-time,
I pray you, have in mind where we must meet.
BASSANIO. I will not fail you.
GRATIANO. You look not well, Signior Antonio;
You have too much respect upon the world;
They lose it that do buy it with much care.
Believe me, you are marvellously chang'd.
ANTONIO. I hold the world but as the world, Gratiano—
A stage, where every man must play a part,
And mine a sad one.
GRATIANO. Let me play the fool.
With mirth and laughter let old wrinkles come;
And let my liver rather heat with wine
Than my heart cool with mortifying groans.
Why should a man whose blood is warm within
Sit like his grandsire cut in alabaster,
Sleep when he wakes, and creep into the jaundice
By being peevish? I tell thee what, Antonio—
I love thee, and 'tis my love that speaks—
There are a sort of men whose visages
Do cream and mantle like a standing pond,
And do a wilful stillness entertain,
With purpose to be dress'd in an opinion
Of wisdom, gravity, profound conceit;
As who should say 'I am Sir Oracle,
And when I ope my lips let no dog bark.'
O my Antonio, I do know of these
That therefore only are reputed wise
For saying nothing; when, I am very sure,
If they should speak, would almost damn those ears
Which, hearing them, would call their brothers fools.
I'll tell thee more of this another time.
But fish not with this melancholy bait
For this fool gudgeon, this opinion.
Come, good Lorenzo. Fare ye well awhile;
I'll end my exhortation after dinner.

605

LORENZO. Well, we will leave you then till dinner-time.
I must be one of these same dumb wise men,
For Gratiano never lets me speak.
GRATIANO. Well, keep me company but two years moe,
Thou shalt not know the sound of thine own tongue.
ANTONIO. Fare you well; I'll grow a talker for this gear.
GRATIANO. Thanks, i' faith, for silence is only commendable
In a neat's tongue dried, and a maid not vendible.

Exeunt GRATIANO *and* LORENZO

ANTONIO. Is that anything now?
BASSANIO. Gratiano speaks an infinite deal of nothing, more
than any man in all Venice. His reasons are as two grains
of wheat hid in two bushels of chaff: you shall seek all day
ere you find them, and when you have them they are not
worth the search.
ANTONIO. Well; tell me now what lady is the same
To whom you swore a secret pilgrimage,
That you to-day promis'd to tell me of?
BASSANIO. 'Tis not unknown to you, Antonio,
How much I have disabled mine estate
By something showing a more swelling port
Than my faint means would grant continuance;
Nor do I now make moan to be abridg'd
From such a noble rate; but my chief care
Is to come fairly off from the great debts
Wherein my time, something too prodigal,
Hath left me gag'd. To you, Antonio,
I owe the most, in money and in love;
And from your love I have a warranty
To unburden all my plots and purposes
How to get clear of all the debts I owe.
ANTONIO. I pray you, good Bassanio, let me know it;
And if it stand, as you yourself still do,
Within the eye of honour, be assur'd
My purse, my person, my extremest means,
Lie all unlock'd to your occasions.
BASSANIO. In my school-days, when I had lost one shaft,
I shot his fellow of the self-same flight
The self-same way, with more advised watch,
To find the other forth; and by adventuring both

I oft found both. I urge this childhood proof,
Because what follows is pure innocence.
I owe you much; and, like a wilful youth,
That which I owe is lost; but if you please
To shoot another arrow that self way
Which you did shoot the first, I do not doubt,
As I will watch the aim, or to find both,
Or bring your latter hazard back again
And thankfully rest debtor for the first.

ANTONIO. You know me well, and herein spend but time
To wind about my love with circumstance;
And out of doubt you do me now more wrong
In making question of my uttermost
Than if you had made waste of all I have.
Then do but say to me what I should do
That in your knowledge may by me be done,
And I am prest unto it; therefore, speak.

BASSANIO. In Belmont is a lady richly left,
And she is fair and, fairer than that word,
Of wondrous virtues. Sometimes from her eyes
I did receive fair speechless messages.
Her name is Portia—nothing undervalu'd
To Cato's daughter, Brutus' Portia.
Nor is the wide world ignorant of her worth;
For the four winds blow in from every coast
Renowned suitors, and her sunny locks
Hang on her temples like a golden fleece,
Which makes her seat of Belmont Colchos' strond,
And many Jasons come in quest of her.
O my Antonio, had I but the means
To hold a rival place with one of them,
I have a mind presages me such thrift
That I should questionless be fortunate.

ANTONIO. Thou know'st that all my fortunes are at sea;
Neither have I money nor commodity
To raise a present sum; therefore go forth,
Try what my credit can in Venice do;
That shall be rack'd, even to the uttermost,
To furnish thee to Belmont to fair Portia.
Go presently inquire, and so will I,

Where money is; and I no question make
To have it of my trust or for my sake.　　　　*Exeunt*

SCENE 2

Belmont. PORTIA's *house*

Enter PORTIA *with her waiting-woman*, NERISSA

PORTIA. By my troth, Nerissa, my little body is aweary of this great world.

NERISSA. You would be, sweet madam, if your miseries were in the same abundance as your good fortunes are; and yet, for aught I see, they are as sick that surfeit with too much as they that starve with nothing. It is no mean happiness, therefore, to be seated in the mean: superfluity comes sooner by white hairs, but competency lives longer.

PORTIA. Good sentences, and well pronounc'd.

NERISSA. They would be better, if well followed.

PORTIA. If to do were as easy as to know what were good to do, chapels had been churches, and poor men's cottages princes' palaces. It is a good divine that follows his own instructions; I can easier teach twenty what were good to be done than to be one of the twenty to follow mine own teaching. The brain may devise laws for the blood, but a hot temper leaps o'er a cold decree; such a hare is madness the youth, to skip o'er the meshes of good counsel the cripple. But this reasoning is not in the fashion to choose me a husband. O me, the word 'choose'! I may neither choose who I would nor refuse who I dislike; so is the will of a living daughter curb'd by the will of a dead father. Is it not hard, Nerissa, that I cannot choose one, nor refuse none?

NERISSA. Your father was ever virtuous, and holy men at their death have good inspirations; therefore the lott'ry that he hath devised in these three chests, of gold, silver, and lead—whereof who chooses his meaning chooses you —will no doubt never be chosen by any rightly but one who you shall rightly love. But what warmth is there in

your affection towards any of these princely suitors that
are already come?

PORTIA. I pray thee over-name them; and as thou namest
them, I will describe them; and according to my description, level at my affection.

NERISSA. First, there is the Neapolitan prince.

PORTIA. Ay, that's a colt indeed, for he doth nothing but talk
of his horse; and he makes it a great appropriation to his
own good parts that he can shoe him himself; I am much
afear'd my lady his mother play'd false with a smith.

NERISSA. Then is there the County Palatine.

PORTIA. He doth nothing but frown, as who should say 'An
you will not have me, choose.' He hears merry tales and
smiles not. I fear he will prove the weeping philosopher
when he grows old, being so full of unmannerly sadness
in his youth. I had rather be married to a death's-head with
a bone in his mouth than to either of these. God defend
me from these two!

NERISSA. How say you by the French lord, Monsieur Le
Bon?

PORTIA. God made him, and therefore let him pass for a man.
In truth, I know it is a sin to be a mocker, but he—why, he
hath a horse better than the Neapolitan's, a better bad
habit of frowning than the Count Palatine; he is every man
in no man. If a throstle sing he falls straight a-cap'ring; he
will fence with his own shadow; if I should marry him, I
should marry twenty husbands. If he would despise me, I
would forgive him; for if he love me to madness, I shall
never requite him.

NERISSA. What say you then to Falconbridge, the young
baron of England?

PORTIA. You know I say nothing to him, for he understands
not me, nor I him: he hath neither Latin, French, nor
Italian, and you will come into the court and swear that I
have a poor pennyworth in the English. He is a proper
man's picture; but alas, who can converse with a dumb-
show? How oddly he is suited! I think he bought his
doublet in Italy, his round hose in France, his bonnet in
Germany, and his behaviour everywhere.

NERISSA. What think you of the Scottish lord, his neighbour?

PORTIA. That he hath a neighbourly charity in him, for he borrowed a box of the ear of the Englishman, and swore he would pay him again when he was able; I think the Frenchman became his surety, and seal'd under for another.

NERISSA. How like you the young German, the Duke of Saxony's nephew?

PORTIA. Very vilely in the morning when he is sober; and most vilely in the afternoon when he is drunk. When he is best, he is a little worse than a man, and when he is worst, he is little better than a beast. An the worst fall that ever fell, I hope I shall make shift to go without him.

NERISSA. If he should offer to choose, and choose the right casket, you should refuse to perform your father's will, if you should refuse to accept him.

PORTIA. Therefore, for fear of the worst, I pray thee set a deep glass of Rhenish wine on the contrary casket; for if the devil be within and that temptation without, I know he will choose it. I will do anything, Nerissa, ere I will be married to a sponge.

NERISSA. You need not fear, lady, the having any of these lords; they have acquainted me with their determinations, which is indeed to return to their home, and to trouble you with no more suit, unless you may be won by some other sort than your father's imposition, depending on the caskets.

PORTIA. If I live to be as old as Sibylla, I will die as chaste as Diana, unless I be obtained by the manner of my father's will. I am glad this parcel of wooers are so reasonable; for there is not one among them but I dote on his very absence, and I pray God grant them a fair departure.

NERISSA. Do you not remember, lady, in your father's time, a Venetian, a scholar and a soldier, that came hither in company of the Marquis of Montferrat?

PORTIA. Yes, yes, it was Bassanio; as I think, so was he call'd.

NERISSA. True, madam; he, of all the men that ever my foolish eyes look'd upon, was the best deserving a fair lady.

PORTIA. I remember him well, and I remember him worthy of thy praise.

Enter a SERVINGMAN

How now! what news?

SERVINGMAN. The four strangers seek for you, madam, to take their leave; and there is a forerunner come from a fifth, the Prince of Morocco, who brings word the Prince his master will be here to-night.

PORTIA. If I could bid the fifth welcome with so good heart as I can bid the other four farewell, I should be glad of his approach; if he have the condition of a saint and the complexion of a devil, I had rather he should shrive me than wive me.

Come, Nerissa. Sirrah, go before.

Whiles we shut the gate upon one wooer, another knocks at the door.   *Exeunt*

SCENE 3

Venice. A public place

Enter BASSANIO *with* SHYLOCK *the Jew*

SHYLOCK. Three thousand ducats—well.

BASSANIO. Ay, sir, for three months.

SHYLOCK. For three months—well.

BASSANIO. For the which, as I told you, Antonio shall be bound.

SHYLOCK. Antonio shall become bound—well.

BASSANIO. May you stead me? Will you pleasure me? Shall I know your answer?

SHYLOCK. Three thousand ducats for three months, and Antonio bound.

BASSANIO. Your answer to that.

SHYLOCK. Antonio is a good man.

BASSANIO. Have you heard any imputation to the contrary?

SHYLOCK. Ho, no, no, no, no; my meaning in saying he is a good man is to have you understand me that he is sufficient; yet his means are in supposition: he hath an argosy bound to Tripolis, another to the Indies; I understand, moreover, upon the Rialto, he hath a third at Mexico, a fourth for England—and other ventures he hath, squand'red abroad. But ships are but boards, sailors but men; there be land-rats and water-rats, water-thieves and land-thieves—I mean pirates; and then there is the peril of waters, winds, and rocks. The man is, notwithstanding, sufficient. Three thousand ducats—I think I may take his bond.

BASSANIO. Be assur'd you may.

SHYLOCK. I will be assur'd I may; and, that I may be assured, I will bethink me. May I speak with Antonio?

BASSANIO. If it please you to dine with us.

SHYLOCK. Yes, to smell pork, to eat of the habitation which your prophet, the Nazarite, conjured the devil into! I will buy with you, sell with you, talk with you, walk with you, and so following; but I will not eat with you, drink with you, nor pray with you. What news on the Rialto? Who is he comes here?

Enter ANTONIO

BASSANIO. This is Signior Antonio.

SHYLOCK. [*Aside*] How like a fawning publican he looks!
I hate him for he is a Christian;
But more for that in low simplicity
He lends out money gratis, and brings down
The rate of usance here with us in Venice.
If I can catch him once upon the hip,
I will feed fat the ancient grudge I bear him.
He hates our sacred nation; and he rails,
Even there where merchants most do congregate,
On me, my bargains, and my well-won thrift,
Which he calls interest. Cursed be my tribe
If I forgive him!

BASSANIO. Shylock, do you hear?

SHYLOCK. I am debating of my present store,
And, by the near guess of my memory,
I cannot instantly raise up the gross
Of full three thousand ducats. What of that?
Tubal, a wealthy Hebrew of my tribe,
Will furnish me. But soft! how many months
Do you desire? [*To* ANTONIO] Rest you fair, good signior;
Your worship was the last man in our mouths.

ANTONIO. Shylock, albeit I neither lend nor borrow
By taking nor by giving of excess,

Yet, to supply the ripe wants of my friend,
I'll break a custom. [*To* BASSANIO] Is he yet possess'd
How much ye would?
SHYLOCK. Ay, ay, three thousand ducats.
ANTONIO. And for three months.
SHYLOCK. I had forgot—three months; you told me so.
Well then, your bond; and, let me see—but hear you,
Methoughts you said you neither lend nor borrow
Upon advantage.
ANTONIO. I do never use it.
SHYLOCK. When Jacob graz'd his uncle Laban's sheep—
This Jacob from our holy Abram was,
As his wise mother wrought in his behalf,
The third possessor; ay, he was the third—
ANTONIO. And what of him? Did he take interest?
SHYLOCK. No, not take interest; not, as you would say,
Directly int'rest; mark what Jacob did:
When Laban and himself were compromis'd
That all the eanlings which were streak'd and pied
Should fall as Jacob's hire, the ewes, being rank,
In end of autumn turned to the rams;
And when the work of generation was
Between these woolly breeders in the act,
The skilful shepherd pill'd me certain wands,
And, in the doing of the deed of kind,
He stuck them up before the fulsome ewes,
Who, then conceiving, did in eaning time
Fall parti-colour'd lambs, and those were Jacob's.
This was a way to thrive, and he was blest;
And thrift is blessing, if men steal it not.
ANTONIO. This was a venture, sir, that Jacob serv'd for;
A thing not in his power to bring to pass,
But sway'd and fashion'd by the hand of heaven.
Was this inserted to make interest good?
Or is your gold and silver ewes and rams?
SHYLOCK. I cannot tell; I make it breed as fast.
But note me, signior.
ANTONIO. [*Aside*] Mark you this, Bassanio,
The devil can cite Scripture for his purpose.
An evil soul producing holy witness

Is like a villain with a smiling cheek,
A goodly apple rotten at the heart.
O, what a goodly outside falsehood hath!
SHYLOCK. Three thousand ducats—'tis a good round sum.
Three months from twelve; then let me see, the rate—
ANTONIO. Well, Shylock, shall we be beholding to you?
SHYLOCK. Signior Antonio, many a time and oft
In the Rialto you have rated me
About my moneys and my usances;
Still have I borne it with a patient shrug,
For suff'rance is the badge of all our tribe;
You call me misbeliever, cut-throat dog,
And spit upon my Jewish gaberdine,
And all for use of that which is mine own.
Well then, it now appears you need my help;
Go to, then; you come to me, and you say
'Shylock, we would have moneys.' You say so—
You that did void your rheum upon my beard
And foot me as you spurn a stranger cur
Over your threshold; moneys is your suit.
What should I say to you? Should I not say
'Hath a dog money? Is it possible
A cur can lend three thousand ducats?' Or
Shall I bend low and, in a bondman's key,
With bated breath and whisp'ring humbleness,
Say this:
'Fair sir, you spit on me on Wednesday last,
You spurn'd me such a day; another time
You call'd me dog; and for these courtesies
I'll lend you thus much moneys'?
ANTONIO. I am as like to call thee so again,
To spit on thee again, to spurn thee too.
If thou wilt lend this money, lend it not
As to thy friends—for when did friendship take
A breed for barren metal of his friend?—
But lend it rather to thine enemy,
Who if he break thou mayst with better face
Exact the penalty.
SHYLOCK. Why, look you, how you storm!
I would be friends with you, and have your love,

Forget the shames that you have stain'd me with,
Supply your present wants, and take no doit
Of usance for my moneys, and you'll not hear me.
This is kind I offer.

BASSANIO. This were kindness.

SHYLOCK. This kindness will I show.
Go with me to a notary, seal me there
Your single bond, and, in a merry sport,
If you repay me not on such a day,
In such a place, such sum or sums as are
Express'd in the condition, let the forfeit
Be nominated for an equal pound
Of your fair flesh, to be cut off and taken
In what part of your body pleaseth me.

ANTONIO. Content, in faith; I'll seal to such a bond,
And say there is much kindness in the Jew.

BASSANIO. You shall not seal to such a bond for me;
I'll rather dwell in my necessity.

ANTONIO. Why, fear not, man; I will not forfeit it;
Within these two months—that's a month before
This bond expires—I do expect return
Of thrice three times the value of this bond.

SHYLOCK. O father Abram, what these Christians are,
Whose own hard dealings teaches them suspect
The thoughts of others! Pray you, tell me this:
If he should break his day, what should I gain
By the exaction of the forfeiture?
A pound of man's flesh taken from a man
Is not so estimable, profitable neither,
As flesh of muttons, beefs, or goats. I say,
To buy his favour, I extend this friendship;
If he will take it, so; if not, adieu;
And, for my love, I pray you wrong me not.

ANTONIO. Yes, Shylock, I will seal unto this bond.

SHYLOCK. Then meet me forthwith at the notary's;
Give him direction for this merry bond,
And I will go and purse the ducats straight,
See to my house, left in the fearful guard
Of an unthrifty knave, and presently
I'll be with you.

ANTONIO. Hie thee, gentle Jew. *Exit* SHYLOCK
The Hebrew will turn Christian: he grows kind.
BASSANIO. I like not fair terms and a villain's mind.
ANTONIO. Come on; in this there can be no dismay;
My ships come home a month before the day. *Exeunt*

ACT II. SCENE 1

Belmont. PORTIA'S *house*

Flourish of cornets. Enter the PRINCE OF MOROCCO, *a tawny Moor all in white, and three or four* FOLLOWERS *accordingly, with* PORTIA, NERISSA, *and train*

PRINCE OF MOROCCO. Mislike me not for my complexion,
The shadowed livery of the burnish'd sun,
To whom I am a neighbour, and near bred.
Bring me the fairest creature northward born,
Where Phœbus' fire scarce thaws the icicles,
And let us make incision for your love
To prove whose blood is reddest, his or mine.
I tell thee, lady, this aspect of mine
Hath fear'd the valiant; by my love, I swear
The best-regarded virgins of our clime
Have lov'd it too. I would not change this hue,
Except to steal your thoughts, my gentle queen.
PORTIA. In terms of choice I am not solely led
By nice direction of a maiden's eyes;
Besides, the lott'ry of my destiny
Bars me the right of voluntary choosing.
But, if my father had not scanted me,
And hedg'd me by his wit to yield myself
His wife who wins me by that means I told you,
Yourself, renowned Prince, then stood as fair
As any comer I have look'd on yet
For my affection.
PRINCE OF MOROCCO. Even for that I thank you.

Therefore, I pray you, lead me to the caskets
To try my fortune. By this scimitar,
That slew the Sophy and a Persian prince,
That won three fields of Sultan Solyman,
I would o'erstare the sternest eyes that look,
Outbrave the heart most daring on the earth,
Pluck the young sucking cubs from the she-bear,
Yea, mock the lion when 'a roars for prey,
To win thee, lady. But, alas the while!
If Hercules and Lichas play at dice
Which is the better man, the greater throw
May turn by fortune from the weaker hand.
So is Alcides beaten by his page;
And so may I, blind Fortune leading me,
Miss that which one unworthier may attain,
And die with grieving.
PORTIA. You must take your chance,
And either not attempt to choose at all,
Or swear before you choose, if you choose wrong,
Never to speak to lady afterward
In way of marriage; therefore be advis'd.
PRINCE OF MOROCCO. Nor will not; come, bring me unto my
chance.
PORTIA. First, forward to the temple. After dinner
Your hazard shall be made.
PRINCE OF MOROCCO. Good fortune then,
To make me blest or cursed'st among men!
[Cornets, and exeunt]

SCENE 2

Venice. A street

Enter LAUNCELOT GOBBO

LAUNCELOT. Certainly my conscience will serve me to run
from this Jew my master. The fiend is at mine elbow and
tempts me, saying to me 'Gobbo, Launcelot Gobbo, good
Launcelot' or 'good Gobbo' or 'good Launcelot Gobbo,
use your legs, take the start, run away.' My conscience

says 'No; take heed, honest Launcelot, take heed, honest Gobbo' or, as aforesaid, 'honest Launcelot Gobbo, do not run; scorn running with thy heels.' Well, the most courageous fiend bids me pack. 'Via!' says the fiend; 'away!' says the fiend. 'For the heavens, rouse up a brave mind' says the fiend 'and run.' Well, my conscience, hanging about the neck of my heart, says very wisely to me 'My honest friend Launcelot, being an honest man's son' or rather 'an honest woman's son'; for indeed my father did something smack, something grow to, he had a kind of taste—well, my conscience says 'Launcelot, budge not.' 'Budge,' says the fiend. 'Budge not," says my conscience. 'Conscience," say I, 'you counsel well.' 'Fiend,' say I, 'you counsel well.' To be rul'd by my conscience, I should stay with the Jew my master, who—God bless the mark!—is a kind of devil; and, to run away from the Jew, I should be ruled by the fiend, who—saving your reverence!—is the devil himself. Certainly the Jew is the very devil incarnation; and, in my conscience, my conscience is but a kind of hard conscience to offer to counsel me to stay with the Jew. The fiend gives the more friendly counsel. I will run, fiend; my heels are at your commandment; I will run.

Enter OLD GOBBO, *with a basket*

GOBBO. Master young man, you, I pray you, which is the way to master Jew's?

LAUNCELOT. [*Aside*] O heavens! This is my true-begotten father, who, being more than sand-blind, high-gravel blind, knows me not. I will try confusions with him.

GOBBO. Master young gentleman, I pray you, which is the way to master Jew's?

LAUNCELOT. Turn up on your right hand at the next turning, but, at the next turning of all, on your left; marry, at the very next turning, turn of no hand, but turn down indirectly to the Jew's house.

GOBBO. Be God's sonties, 'twill be a hard way to hit! Can you tell me whether one Launcelot, that dwells with him, dwell with him or no?

LAUNCELOT. Talk you of young Master Launcelot? [*Aside*]

Mark me now; now will I raise the waters.—Talk you of young Master Launcelot?

GOBBO. No master, sir, but a poor man's son; his father, though I say't, is an honest exceeding poor man, and, God be thanked, well to live.

LAUNCELOT. Well, let his father be what 'a will, we talk of young Master Launcelot.

GOBBO. Your worship's friend, and Launcelot, sir.

LAUNCELOT. But I pray you, ergo, old man, ergo, I beseech you, talk you of young Master Launcelot?

GOBBO. Of Launcelot, an't please your mastership.

LAUNCELOT. Ergo, Master Launcelot. Talk not of Master Launcelot, father; for the young gentleman, according to Fates and Destinies and such odd sayings, the Sisters Three and such branches of learning, is indeed deceased; or, as you would say in plain terms, gone to heaven.

GOBBO. Marry, God forbid! The boy was the very staff of my age, my very prop.

LAUNCELOT. Do I look like a cudgel or a hovel-post, a staff or a prop? Do you know me, father?

GOBBO. Alack the day, I know you not, young gentleman; but I pray you tell me, is my boy—God rest his soul!—alive or dead?

LAUNCELOT. Do you not know me, father?

GOBBO. Alack, sir, I am sand-blind; I know you not.

LAUNCELOT. Nay, indeed, if you had your eyes, you might fail of the knowing me: it is a wise father that knows his own child. Well, old man, I will tell you news of your son. Give me your blessing; truth will come to light; murder cannot be hid long; a man's son may, but in the end truth will out.

GOBBO. Pray you, sir, stand up; I am sure you are not Launcelot my boy.

LAUNCELOT. Pray you, let's have no more fooling about it, but give me your blessing; I am Launcelot, your boy that was, your son that is, your child that shall be.

GOBBO. I cannot think you are my son.

LAUNCELOT. I know not what I shall think of that; but I am Launcelot, the Jew's man, and I am sure Margery your wife is my mother.

GOBBO. Her name is Margery, indeed. I'll be sworn, if thou be Launcelot, thou art mine own flesh and blood. Lord worshipp'd might he be, what a beard hast thou got! Thou hast got more hair on thy chin than Dobbin my fill-horse has on his tail.

LAUNCELOT. It should seem, then, that Dobbin's tail grows backward; I am sure he had more hair of his tail than I have of my face when I last saw him.

GOBBO. Lord, how art thou chang'd! How dost thou and thy master agree? I have brought him a present. How 'gree you now?

LAUNCELOT. Well, well; but, for mine own part, as I have set up my rest to run away, so I will not rest till I have run some ground. My master's a very Jew. Give him a present! Give him a halter. I am famish'd in his service; you may tell every finger I have with my ribs. Father, I am glad you are come; give me your present to one Master Bassanio, who indeed gives rare new liveries; if I serve not him, I will run as far as God has any ground. O rare fortune! Here comes the man. To him, father, for I am a Jew, if I serve the Jew any longer.

Enter BASSANIO, *with* LEONARDO, *with a* FOLLOWER *or two*

BASSANIO. You may do so; but let it be so hasted that supper be ready at the farthest by five of the clock. See these letters delivered, put the liveries to making, and desire Gratiano to come anon to my lodging.   *Exit a* SERVANT

LAUNCELOT. To him, father.

GOBBO. God bless your worship!

BASSANIO. Gramercy; wouldst thou aught with me?

GOBBO. Here's my son, sir, a poor boy—

LAUNCELOT. Not a poor boy, sir, but the rich Jew's man, that would, sir, as my father shall specify—

GOBBO. He hath a great infection, sir, as one would say, to serve—

LAUNCELOT. Indeed the short and the long is, I serve the Jew, and have a desire, as my father shall specify—

GOBBO. His master and he, saving your worship's reverence, are scarce cater-cousins—

LAUNCELOT. To be brief, the very truth is that the Jew, hav-

ing done me wrong, doth cause me, as my father, being I
hope an old man, shall frutify unto you—

GOBBO. I have here a dish of doves that I would bestow upon
your worship; and my suit is—

LAUNCELOT. In very brief, the suit is impertinent to myself,
as your worship shall know by this honest old man; and,
though I say it, though old man, yet poor man, my father.

BASSANIO. One speak for both. What would you?

LAUNCELOT. Serve you, sir.

GOBBO. That is the very defect of the matter, sir.

BASSANIO. I know thee well; thou hast obtain'd thy suit.
Shylock thy master spoke with me this day,
And hath preferr'd thee, if it be preferment
To leave a rich Jew's service to become
The follower of so poor a gentleman.

LAUNCELOT. The old proverb is very well parted between
my master Shylock and you, sir: you have the grace of
God, sir, and he hath enough.

BASSANIO. Thou speak'st it well. Go, father, with thy son.
Take leave of thy old master, and inquire
My lodging out. [*To a* SERVANT] Give him a livery
More guarded than his fellows'; see it done.

LAUNCELOT. Father, in. I cannot get a service, no! I have
ne'er a tongue in my head! [*Looking on his palm*] Well;
if any man in Italy have a fairer table which doth offer to
swear upon a book—I shall have good fortune. Go to,
here's a simple line of life; here's a small trifle of wives;
alas, fifteen wives is nothing; a'leven widows and nine
maids is a simple coming-in for one man. And then to
scape drowning thrice, and to be in peril of my life with
the edge of a feather-bed—here are simple scapes. Well, if
Fortune be a woman, she's a good wench for this gear.
Father, come; I'll take my leave of the Jew in the twinkling.   *Exeunt* LAUNCELOT *and* OLD GOBBO

BASSANIO. I pray thee, good Leonardo, think on this.
These things being bought and orderly bestowed,
Return in haste, for I do feast to-night
My best esteem'd acquaintance; hie thee, go.

LEONARDO. My best endeavours shall be done herein.

Enter GRATIANO

GRATIANO. Where's your master?

LEONARDO. Yonder, sir, he walks. *Exit*

GRATIANO. Signior Bassanio!

BASSANIO. Gratiano!

GRATIANO. I have suit to you.

BASSANIO. You have obtain'd it.

GRATIANO. You must not deny me: I must go with you to
Belmont.

BASSANIO. Why, then you must. But hear thee, Gratiano:
Thou art too wild, too rude, and bold of voice—
Parts that become thee happily enough,
And in such eyes as ours appear not faults;
But where thou art not known, why there they show
Something too liberal. Pray thee, take pain
To allay with some cold drops of modesty
Thy skipping spirit; lest through thy wild behaviour
I be misconst'red in the place I go to
And lose my hopes.

GRATIANO. Signior Bassanio, hear me:
If I do not put on a sober habit,
Talk with respect, and swear but now and then,
Wear prayer-books in my pocket, look demurely,
Nay more, while grace is saying hood mine eyes
Thus with my hat, and sigh, and say amen,
Use all the observance of civility
Like one well studied in a sad ostent
To please his grandam, never trust me more.

BASSANIO. Well, we shall see your bearing.

GRATIANO. Nay, but I bar to-night; you shall not gauge me
By what we do to-night.

BASSANIO. No, that were pity;
I would entreat you rather to put on
Your boldest suit of mirth, for we have friends
That purpose merriment. But fare you well;
I have some business.

GRATIANO. And I must to Lorenzo and the rest;
But we will visit you at supper-time. *Exeunt*

SCENE 3

Venice. SHYLOCK'S *house*

Enter JESSICA *and* LAUNCELOT

JESSICA. I am sorry thou wilt leave my father so.
Our house is hell; and thou, a merry devil,
Didst rob it of some taste of tediousness.
But fare thee well; there is a ducat for thee;
And, Launcelot, soon at supper shalt thou see
Lorenzo, who is thy new master's guest.
Give him this letter; do it secretly.
And so farewell. I would not have my father
See me in talk with thee.
LAUNCELOT. Adieu! tears exhibit my tongue. Most beautiful
pagan, most sweet Jew! If a Christian do not play the
knave and get thee, I am much deceived. But, adieu! these
foolish drops do something drown my manly spirit; adieu!
JESSICA. Farewell, good Launcelot.   *Exit* LAUNCELOT
Alack, what heinous sin is it in me
To be asham'd to be my father's child!
But though I am a daughter to his blood,
I am not to his manners. O Lorenzo,
If thou keep promise, I shall end this strife,
Become a Christian and thy loving wife.   *Exit*

SCENE 4

Venice. A street

Enter GRATIANO, LORENZO, SALERIO, *and* SOLANIO

LORENZO. Nay, we will slink away in suppertime,
Disguise us at my lodging, and return
All in an hour.
GRATIANO. We have not made good preparation.
SALERIO. We have not spoke us yet of torch-bearers.
SOLANIO. 'Tis vile, unless it may be quaintly ordered;
And better in my mind not undertook.

LORENZO. 'Tis now but four o'clock; we have two hours
To furnish us.

Enter LAUNCELOT, *with a letter*

Friend Launcelot, what's the news?
LAUNCELOT. An it shall please you to break up this, it shall
seem to signify.
LORENZO. I know the hand; in faith, 'tis a fair hand,
And whiter than the paper it writ on
Is the fair hand that writ.
GRATIANO. Love-news, in faith!
LAUNCELOT. By your leave, sir.
LORENZO. Whither goest thou?
LAUNCELOT. Marry, sir, to bid my old master, the Jew, to
sup to-night with my new master, the Christian.
LORENZO. Hold, here, take this. Tell gentle Jessica
I will not fail her; speak it privately.
Go, gentlemen,   *Exit* LAUNCELOT
Will you prepare you for this masque to-night?
I am provided of a torch-bearer.
SALERIO. Ay, marry, I'll be gone about it straight.
SOLANIO. And so will I.
LORENZO. Meet me and Gratiano
At Gratiano's lodging some hour hence.
SALERIO. 'Tis good we do so.   *Exeunt* SALERIO *and* SOLANIO
GRATIANO. Was not that letter from fair Jessica?
LORENZO. I must needs tell thee all. She hath directed
How I shall take her from her father's house;
What gold and jewels she is furnish'd with;
What page's suit she hath in readiness.
If e'er the Jew her father come to heaven,
It will be for his gentle daughter's sake;
And never dare misfortune cross her foot,
Unless she do it under this excuse,
That she is issue to a faithless Jew.
Come, go with me, peruse this as thou goest;
Fair Jessica shall be my torch-bearer.   *Exeunt*

SCENE 5

Venice. Before SHYLOCK's *house*

Enter SHYLOCK *and* LAUNCELOT

SHYLOCK. Well, thou shalt see; thy eyes shall be thy judge,
The difference of old Shylock and Bassanio.—
What, Jessica!—Thou shalt not gormandize
As thou hast done with me—What, Jessica!—
And sleep and snore, and rend apparel out—
Why, Jessica, I say!
LAUNCELOT. Why, Jessica!
SHYLOCK. Who bids thee call? I do not bid thee call.
LAUNCELOT. Your worship was wont to tell me I could do
nothing without bidding.

Enter JESSICA

JESSICA. Call you? What is your will?
SHYLOCK. I am bid forth to supper, Jessica;
There are my keys. But wherefore should I go?
I am not bid for love; they flatter me;
But yet I'll go in hate, to feed upon
The prodigal Christian. Jessica, my girl,
Look to my house. I am right loath to go;
There is some ill a-brewing towards my rest,
For I did dream of money-bags to-night.
LAUNCELOT. I beseech you, sir, go; my young master doth
expect your reproach.
SHYLOCK. So do I his.
LAUNCELOT. And they have conspired together; I will not
say you shall see a masque, but if you do, then it was not
for nothing that my nose fell a-bleeding on Black Monday
last at six o'clock i' th' morning, falling out that year on
Ash Wednesday was four year, in th' afternoon.
SHYLOCK. What, are there masques? Hear you me, Jessica:
Lock up my doors, and when you hear the drum,
And the vile squealing of the wry-neck'd fife,
Clamber not you up to the casements then,
Nor thrust your head into the public street

To gaze on Christian fools with varnish'd faces;
But stop my house's ears—I mean my casements;
Let not the sound of shallow fopp'ry enter
My sober house. By Jacob's staff, I swear
I have no mind of feasting forth to-night;
But I will go. Go you before me, sirrah;
Say I will come.

LAUNCELOT. I will go before, sir. Mistress, look out at window for all this.
    There will come a Christian by
    Will be worth a Jewess' eye.   *Exit*

SHYLOCK. What says that fool of Hagar's offspring, ha?

JESSICA. His words were 'Farewell, mistress'; nothing else.

SHYLOCK. The patch is kind enough, but a huge feeder,
Snail-slow in profit, and he sleeps by day
More than the wild-cat; drones hive not with me,
Therefore I part with him; and part with him
To one that I would have him help to waste
His borrowed purse. Well, Jessica, go in;
Perhaps I will return immediately.
Do as I bid you, shut doors after you.
Fast bind, fast find—
A proverb never stale in thrifty mind.   *Exit*

JESSICA. Farewell; and if my fortune be not crost,
I have a father, you a daughter, lost.   *Exit*

SCENE 6

Venice. Before SHYLOCK's *house*

Enter the maskers, GRATIANO *and* SALERIO

GRATIANO. This is the pent-house under which Lorenzo
Desired us to make stand.

SALERIO. His hour is almost past.

GRATIANO. And it is marvel he out-dwells his hour,
For lovers ever run before the clock.

SALERIO. O, ten times faster Venus' pigeons fly
To seal love's bonds new made than they are wont
To keep obliged faith unforfeited!

GRATIANO. That ever holds: who riseth from a feast

With that keen appetite that he sits down?
Where is the horse that doth untread again
His tedious measures with the unbated fire
That he did pace them first? All things that are
Are with more spirit chased than enjoyed.
How like a younker or a prodigal
The scarfed bark puts from her native bay,
Hugg'd and embraced by the strumpet wind;
How like the prodigal doth she return,
With over-weather'd ribs and ragged sails,
Lean, rent, and beggar'd by the strumpet wind!

Enter LORENZO

SALERIO. Here comes Lorenzo; more of this hereafter.
LORENZO. Sweet friends, your patience for my long abode!
Not I, but my affairs, have made you wait.
When you shall please to play the thieves for wives,
I'll watch as long for you then. Approach;
Here dwells my father Jew. Ho! who's within?

Enter JESSICA, *above, in boy's clothes*

JESSICA. Who are you? Tell me, for more certainty,
Albeit I'll swear that I do know your tongue.
LORENZO. Lorenzo, and thy love.
JESSICA. Lorenzo, certain; and my love indeed;
For who love I so much? And now who knows
But you, Lorenzo, whether I am yours?
LORENZO. Heaven and thy thoughts are witness that thou art.
JESSICA. Here, catch this casket; it is worth the pains.
I am glad 'tis night, you do not look on me,
For I am much asham'd of my exchange;
But love is blind, and lovers cannot see
The pretty follies that themselves commit,
For, if they could, Cupid himself would blush
To see me thus transformed to a boy.
LORENZO. Descend, for you must be my torch-bearer.
JESSICA. What! must I hold a candle to my shames?
They in themselves, good sooth, are too too light.
Why, 'tis an office of discovery, love,
And I should be obscur'd.

LORENZO. So are you, sweet,
Even in the lovely garnish of a boy.
But come at once,
For the close night doth play the runaway,
And we are stay'd for at Bassanio's feast.
JESSICA. I will make fast the doors, and gild myself
With some moe ducats, and be with you straight.

Exit above

GRATIANO. Now, by my hood, a gentle, and no Jew.
LORENZO. Beshrew me, but I love her heartily,
For she is wise, if I can judge of her,
And fair she is, if that mine eyes be true,
And true she is, as she hath prov'd herself;
And therefore, like herself, wise, fair, and true,
Shall she be placed in my constant soul.

Enter JESSICA, *below*

What, art thou come? On, gentlemen, away;
Our masquing mates by this time for us stay.

Exit with JESSICA *and* SALERIO

Enter ANTONIO

ANTONIO. Who's there?
GRATIANO. Signior Antonio?
ANTONIO. Fie, fie, Gratiano, where are all the rest?
'Tis nine o'clock; our friends all stay for you;
No masque to-night; the wind is come about;
Bassanio presently will go aboard;
I have sent twenty out to seek for you.
GRATIANO. I am glad on't; I desire no more delight
Than to be under sail and gone to-night.   *Exeunt*

SCENE 7

Belmont. PORTIA's *house*

Flourish of cornets. Enter PORTIA, *with the* PRINCE OF
MOROCCO, *and their trains*

PORTIA. Go draw aside the curtains and discover

The several caskets to this noble Prince.
Now make your choice.
PRINCE OF MOROCCO. The first, of gold, who this inscription
    bears:
'Who chooseth me shall gain what many men desire.'
The second, silver, which this promise carries:
'Who chooseth me shall get as much as he deserves.'
This third, dull lead, with warning all as blunt:
'Who chooseth me must give and hazard all he hath.'
How shall I know if I do choose the right?
PORTIA. The one of them contains my picture, Prince;
    If you choose that, then I am yours withal.
PRINCE OF MOROCCO. Some god direct my judgment! Let
    me see;
I will survey th' inscriptions back again.
What says this leaden casket?
'Who chooseth me must give and hazard all he hath.'
Must give—for what? For lead? Hazard for lead!
This casket threatens; men that hazard all
Do it in hope of fair advantages.
A golden mind stoops not to shows of dross;
I'll then nor give nor hazard aught for lead.
What says the silver with her virgin hue?
'Who chooseth me shall get as much as he deserves.'
As much as he deserves! Pause there, Morocco,
And weigh thy value with an even hand.
If thou beest rated by thy estimation,
Thou dost deserve enough, and yet enough
May not extend so far as to the lady;
And yet to be afeard of my deserving
Were but a weak disabling of myself.
As much as I deserve? Why, that's the lady!
I do in birth deserve her, and in fortunes,
In graces, and in qualities of breeding;
But more than these, in love I do deserve.
What if I stray'd no farther, but chose here?
Let's see once more this saying grav'd in gold:
'Who chooseth me shall gain what many men desire.'
Why, that's the lady! All the world desires her;
From the four corners of the earth they come

To kiss this shrine, this mortal-breathing saint.
The Hyrcanian deserts and the vasty wilds
Of wide Arabia are as throughfares now
For princes to come view fair Portia.
The watery kingdom, whose ambitious head
Spits in the face of heaven, is no bar
To stop the foreign spirits, but they come
As o'er a brook to see fair Portia.
One of these three contains her heavenly picture.
Is't like that lead contains her? 'Twere damnation
To think so base a thought; it were too gross
To rib her cerecloth in the obscure grave.
Or shall I think in silver she's immur'd,
Being ten times undervalued to tried gold?
O sinful thought! Never so rich a gem
Was set in worse than gold. They have in England
A coin that bears the figure of an angel
Stamp'd in gold; but that's insculp'd upon.
But here an angel in a golden bed
Lies all within. Deliver me the key;
Here do I choose, and thrive I as I may!

PORTIA. There, take it, Prince, and if my form lie there,
  Then I am yours.   [*He opens the golden casket*]

PRINCE OF MOROCCO. O hell! what have we here?
A carrion Death, within whose empty eye
There is a written scroll! I'll read the writing.
          'All that glisters is not gold,
          Often have you heard that told;
          Many a man his life hath sold
          But my outside to behold.
          Gilded tombs do worms infold.
          Had you been as wise as bold,
          Young in limbs, in judgment old,
          Your answer had not been inscroll'd.
          Fare you well, your suit is cold.'
    Cold indeed, and labour lost,
      Then farewell, heat, and welcome, frost.
    Portia, adieu! I have too griev'd a heart
    To take a tedious leave; thus losers part.

                    Exit with his train. Flourish of cornets

PORTIA. A gentle riddance. Draw the curtains, go.
Let all of his complexion choose me so.   *Exeunt*

SCENE 8

Venice. A street

Enter SALERIO *and* SOLANIO

SALERIO. Why, man, I saw Bassanio under sail;
  With him is Gratiano gone along;
  And in their ship I am sure Lorenzo is not.
SOLANIO. The villain Jew with outcries rais'd the Duke,
  Who went with him to search Bassanio's ship.
SALERIO. He came too late, the ship was under sail;
  But there the Duke was given to understand
  That in a gondola were seen together
  Lorenzo and his amorous Jessica;
  Besides, Antonio certified the Duke
  They were not with Bassanio in his ship.
SOLANIO. I never heard a passion so confus'd,
  So strange, outrageous, and so variable,
  As the dog Jew did utter in the streets.
  'My daughter! O my ducats! O my daughter!
  Fled with a Christian! O my Christian ducats!
  Justice! the law! My ducats and my daughter!
  A sealed bag, two sealed bags of ducats,
  Of double ducats, stol'n from me by my daughter!
  And jewels—two stones, two rich and precious stones,
  Stol'n by my daughter! Justice! Find the girl;
  She hath the stones upon her and the ducats.'
SALERIO. Why, all the boys in Venice follow him,
  Crying, his stones, his daughter, and his ducats.
SOLANIO. Let good Antonio look he keep his day,
  Or he shall pay for this.
SALERIO. Marry, well rememb'red;
  I reason'd with a Frenchman yesterday,
  Who told me, in the narrow seas that part
  The French and English, there miscarried
  A vessel of our country richly fraught.

I thought upon Antonio when he told me,
And wish'd in silence that it were not his.
SOLANIO. You were best to tell Antonio what you hear;
Yet do not suddenly, for it may grieve him.
SALERIO. A kinder gentleman treads not the earth.
I saw Bassanio and Antonio part.
Bassanio told him he would make some speed
Of his return. He answered 'Do not so;
Slubber not business for my sake, Bassanio,
But stay the very riping of the time;
And for the Jew's bond which he hath of me,
Let it not enter in your mind of love;
Be merry, and employ your chiefest thoughts
To courtship, and such fair ostents of love
As shall conveniently become you there.'
And even there, his eye being big with tears,
Turning his face, he put his hand behind him,
And with affection wondrous sensible
He wrung Bassanio's hand; and so they parted.
SOLANIO. I think he only loves the world for him.
I pray thee, let us go and find him out,
And quicken his embraced heaviness
With some delight or other.
SALERIO. Do we so.   *Exeunt*

SCENE 9

Belmont. PORTIA's *house*

Enter NERISSA, *and a* SERVITOR

NERISSA. Quick, quick, I pray thee, draw the curtain straight;
The Prince of Arragon hath ta'en his oath,
And comes to his election presently.

Flourish of cornets. Enter the PRINCE OF ARRAGON,
PORTIA, *and their trains*

PORTIA. Behold, there stand the caskets, noble Prince.
If you choose that wherein I am contain'd,
Straight shall our nuptial rites be solemniz'd;

But if you fail, without more speech, my lord,
You must be gone from hence immediately.
ARRAGON. I am enjoin'd by oath to observe three things:
First, never to unfold to any one
Which casket 'twas I chose; next, if I fail
Of the right casket, never in my life
To woo a maid in way of marriage;
Lastly,
If I do fail in fortune of my choice,
Immediately to leave you and be gone.
PORTIA. To these injunctions every one doth swear
That comes to hazard for my worthless self.
ARRAGON. And so have I address'd me. Fortune now
To my heart's hope! Gold, silver, and base lead.
'Who chooseth me must give and hazard all he hath.'
You shall look fairer ere I give or hazard.
What says the golden chest? Ha! let me see:
'Who chooseth me shall gain what many men desire.'
What many men desire—that 'many' may be meant
By the fool multitude, that choose by show,
Not learning more than the fond eye doth teach;
Which pries not to th' interior, but, like the martlet,
Builds in the weather on the outward wall,
Even in the force and road of casualty.
I will not choose what many men desire,
Because I will not jump with common spirits
And rank me with the barbarous multitudes.
Why, then to thee, thou silver treasure-house!
Tell me once more what title thou dost bear.
'Who chooseth me shall get as much as he deserves.'
And well said too; for who shall go about
To cozen fortune, and be honourable
Without the stamp of merit? Let none presume
To wear an undeserved dignity.
O that estates, degrees, and offices,
Were not deriv'd corruptly, and that clear honour
Were purchas'd by the merit of the wearer!
How many then should cover that stand bare!
How many be commanded that command!
How much low peasantry would then be gleaned

From the true seed of honour! and how much honour
Pick'd from the chaff and ruin of the times,
To be new varnish'd! Well, but to my choice.
'Who chooseth me shall get as much as he deserves.'
I will assume desert. Give me a key for this,
And instantly unlock my fortunes here.

[He opens the silver casket]

PORTIA. *[Aside]* Too long a pause for that which you find
there.
ARRAGON. What's here? The portrait of a blinking idiot
Presenting me a schedule! I will read it.
How much unlike art thou to Portia!
How much unlike my hopes and my deservings!
'Who chooseth me shall have as much as he deserves.'
Did I deserve no more than a fool's head?
Is that my prize? Are my deserts no better?
PORTIA. To offend and judge are distinct offices
And of opposed natures.
ARRAGON. What is here? *[Reads]*

'The fire seven times tried this;
Seven times tried that judgment is
That did never choose amiss.
Some there be that shadows kiss,
Such have but a shadow's bliss.
There be fools alive iwis
Silver'd o'er, and so was this.
Take what wife you will to bed,
I will ever be your head.
So be gone; you are sped.'

Still more fool I shall appear
By the time I linger here.
With one fool's head I came to woo,
But I go away with two.
Sweet, adieu! I'll keep my oath,
Patiently to bear my wroth. *Exit with his train*

PORTIA. Thus hath the candle sing'd the moth.
O, these deliberate fools! When they do choose,
They have the wisdom by their wit to lose.
NERISSA. The ancient saying is no heresy:

ACT II. SCENE 9

Hanging and wiving goes by destiny.

PORTIA. Come, draw the curtain, Nerissa.

Enter a SERVANT

SERVANT. Where is my lady?

PORTIA. Here; what would my lord?

SERVANT. Madam, there is alighted at your gate
A young Venetian, one that comes before
To signify th' approaching of his lord,
From whom he bringeth sensible regreets;
To wit, besides commends and courteous breath,
Gifts of rich value. Yet I have not seen
So likely an ambassador of love.
A day in April never came so sweet
To show how costly summer was at hand
As this fore-spurrer comes before his lord.

PORTIA. No more, I pray thee; I am half afeard
Thou wilt say anon he is some kin to thee,
Thou spend'st such high-day wit in praising him.
Come, come, Nerissa, for I long to see
Quick Cupid's post that comes so mannerly.

NERISSA. Bassanio, Lord Love, if thy will it be!   *Exeunt*

ACT III. SCENE 1

Venice. A street

Enter SOLANIO *and* SALERIO

SOLANIO. Now, what news on the Rialto?

SALERIO. Why, yet it lives there uncheck'd that Antonio hath
a ship of rich lading wreck'd on the narrow seas; the
Goodwins I think they call the place, a very dangerous flat
and fatal, where the carcases of many a tall ship lie buried,
as they say, if my gossip Report be an honest woman of
her word.

SOLANIO. I would she were as lying a gossip in that as ever
knapp'd ginger or made her neighbours believe she wept

for the death of a third husband. But it is true, without any slips of prolixity or crossing the plain highway of talk, that the good Antonio, the honest Antonio——O that I had a title good enough to keep his name company!—

SALERIO. Come, the full stop.

SOLANIO. Ha! What sayest thou? Why, the end is, he hath lost a ship.

SALERIO. I would it might prove the end of his losses.

SOLANIO. Let me say amen betimes, lest the devil cross my prayer, for here he comes in the likeness of a Jew.

Enter SHYLOCK

How now, Shylock? What news among the merchants?

SHYLOCK. You knew, none so well, none so well as you, of my daughter's flight.

SALERIO. That's certain; I, for my part, knew the tailor that made the wings she flew withal.

SOLANIO. And Shylock, for his own part, knew the bird was flidge; and then it is the complexion of them all to leave the dam.

SHYLOCK. She is damn'd for it.

SALERIO. That's certain, if the devil may be her judge.

SHYLOCK. My own flesh and blood to rebel!

SOLANIO. Out upon it, old carrion! Rebels it at these years?

SHYLOCK. I say my daughter is my flesh and my blood.

SALERIO. There is more difference between thy flesh and hers than between jet and ivory; more between your bloods than there is between red wine and Rhenish. But tell us, do you hear whether Antonio have had any loss at sea or no?

SHYLOCK. There I have another bad match: a bankrupt, a prodigal, who dare scarce show his head on the Rialto; a beggar, that was us'd to come so smug upon the mart. Let him look to his bond. He was wont to call me usurer; let him look to his bond. He was wont to lend money for a Christian courtesy; let him look to his bond.

SALERIO. Why, I am sure, if he forfeit, thou wilt not take his flesh. What's that good for?

SHYLOCK. To bait fish withal. If it will feed nothing else, it will feed my revenge. He hath disgrac'd me and hind'red me half a million; laugh'd at my losses, mock'd at my gains,

scorned my nation, thwarted my bargains, cooled my
friends, heated mine enemies. And what's his reason? I am
a Jew. Hath not a Jew eyes? Hath not a Jew hands, organs,
dimensions, senses, affections, passions, fed with the same
food, hurt with the same weapons, subject to the same
diseases, healed by the same means, warmed and cooled by
the same winter and summer, as a Christian is? If you prick
us, do we not bleed? If you tickle us, do we not laugh?
If you poison us, do we not die? And if you wrong us,
shall we not revenge? If we are like you in the rest, we
will resemble you in that. If a Jew wrong a Christian, what
is his humility? Revenge. If a Christian wrong a Jew, what
should his sufferance be by Christian example? Why, revenge. The villainy you teach me I will execute; and it
shall go hard but I will better the instruction.

Enter a MAN *from* ANTONIO

MAN. Gentlemen, my master Antonio is at his house, and
desires to speak with you both.
SALERIO. We have been up and down to seek him.

Enter TUBAL

SOLANIO. Here comes another of the tribe; a third cannot be
match'd, unless the devil himself turn Jew.
                     Exeunt SOLANIO, SALERIO, *and* MAN
SHYLOCK. How now, Tubal, what news from Genoa? Hast
thou found my daughter?
TUBAL. I often came where I did hear of her, but cannot
find her.
SHYLOCK. Why there, there, there, there! A diamond gone,
cost me two thousand ducats in Frankfort! The curse
never fell upon our nation till now; I never felt it till now.
Two thousand ducats in that, and other precious, precious
jewels. I would my daughter were dead at my foot, and
the jewels in her ear; would she were hears'd at my foot,
and the ducats in her coffin! No news of them? Why, so—
and I know not what's spent in the search. Why, thou—
loss upon loss! The thief gone with so much, and so much
to find the thief; and no satisfaction, no revenge; nor no ill

luck stirring but what lights o' my shoulders; no sighs but o' my breathing; no tears but o' my shedding!

TUBAL. Yes, other men have ill luck too: Antonio, as I heard in Genoa—

SHYLOCK. What, what, what? Ill luck, ill luck?

TUBAL. Hath an argosy cast away coming from Tripolis.

SHYLOCK. I thank God, I thank God. Is it true, is it true?

TUBAL. I spoke with some of the sailors that escaped the wreck.

SHYLOCK. I thank thee, good Tubal. Good news, good news —ha, ha!—heard in Genoa.

TUBAL. Your daughter spent in Genoa, as I heard, one night, fourscore ducats.

SHYLOCK. Thou stick'st a dagger in me—I shall never see my gold again. Fourscore ducats at a sitting! Fourscore ducats!

TUBAL. There came divers of Antonio's creditors in my company to Venice that swear he cannot choose but break.

SHYLOCK. I am very glad of it; I'll plague him, I'll torture him; I am glad of it.

TUBAL. One of them showed me a ring that he had of your daughter for a monkey.

SHYLOCK. Out upon her! Thou torturest me, Tubal. It was my turquoise; I had it of Leah when I was a bachelor; I would not have given it for a wilderness of monkeys.

TUBAL. But Antonio is certainly undone.

SHYLOCK. Nay, that's true; that's very true. Go, Tubal, fee me an officer; bespeak him a fortnight before. I will have the heart of him, if he forfeit; for, were he out of Venice, I can make what merchandise I will. Go, Tubal, and meet me at our synagogue; go, good Tubal; at our synagogue, Tubal.   *Exeunt*

SCENE 2

Belmont. PORTIA's *house*

Enter BASSANIO, PORTIA, GRATIANO, NERISSA, *and all their trains*

PORTIA. I pray you tarry; pause a day or two

Before you hazard; for, in choosing wrong,
I lose your company; therefore forbear a while.
There's something tells me—but it is not love—
I would not lose you; and you know yourself
Hate counsels not in such a quality.
But lest you should not understand me well—
And yet a maiden hath no tongue but thought—
I would detain you here some month or two
Before you venture for me. I could teach you
How to choose right, but then I am forsworn;
So will I never be; so may you miss me;
But if you do, you'll make me wish a sin,
That I had been forsworn. Beshrew your eyes!
They have o'erlook'd me and divided me;
One half of me is yours, the other half yours—
Mine own, I would say; but if mine, then yours,
And so all yours. O! these naughty times
Puts bars between the owners and their rights;
And so, though yours, not yours. Prove it so,
Let fortune go to hell for it, not I.
I speak too long, but 'tis to peize the time,
To eke it, and to draw it out in length,
To stay you from election.
BASSANIO. Let me choose;
    For as I am, I live upon the rack.
PORTIA. Upon the rack, Bassanio? Then confess
    What treason there is mingled with your love.
BASSANIO. None but that ugly treason of mistrust
    Which makes me fear th' enjoying of my love;
    There may as well be amity and life
    'Tween snow and fire as treason and my love.
PORTIA. Ay, but I fear you speak upon the rack,
    Where men enforced do speak anything.
BASSANIO. Promise me life, and I'll confess the truth.
PORTIA. Well then, confess and live.
BASSANIO. 'Confess' and 'love'
    Had been the very sum of my confession.
    O happy torment, when my torturer
    Doth teach me answers for deliverance!
    But let me to my fortune and the caskets.

PORTIA. Away, then; I am lock'd in one of them.
If you do love me, you will find me out.
Nerissa and the rest, stand all aloof;
Let music sound while he doth make his choice;
Then, if he lose, he makes a swan-like end,
Fading in music. That the comparison
May stand more proper, my eye shall be the stream
And wat'ry death-bed for him. He may win;
And what is music then? Then music is
Even as the flourish when true subjects bow
To a new-crowned monarch; such it is
As are those dulcet sounds in break of day
That creep into the dreaming bridegroom's ear
And summon him to marriage. Now he goes,
With no less presence, but with much more love,
Than young Alcides when he did redeem
The virgin tribute paid by howling Troy
To the sea-monster. I stand for sacrifice;
The rest aloof are the Dardanian wives,
With bleared visages come forth to view
The issue of th' exploit. Go, Hercules!
Live thou, I live. With much much more dismay
I view the fight than thou that mak'st the fray.

A SONG

the whilst BASSANIO *comments on the caskets to himself*

Tell me where is fancy bred,
Or in the heart or in the head,
How begot, how nourished?
    Reply, reply.
It is engend'red in the eyes,
With gazing fed; and fancy dies
In the cradle where it lies.
    Let us all ring fancy's knell:
    I'll begin it—Ding, dong, bell.

ALL.   Ding, dong, bell.

BASSANIO. So may the outward shows be least themselves;
The world is still deceiv'd with ornament.
In law, what plea so tainted and corrupt

But, being season'd with a gracious voice,
Obscures the show of evil? In religion,
What damned error but some sober brow
Will bless it, and approve it with a text,
Hiding the grossness with fair ornament?
There is no vice so simple but assumes
Some mark of virtue on his outward parts.
How many cowards, whose hearts are all as false
As stairs of sand, wear yet upon their chins
The beards of Hercules and frowning Mars;
Who, inward search'd, have livers white as milk!
And these assume but valour's excrement
To render them redoubted. Look on beauty
And you shall see 'tis purchas'd by the weight,
Which therein works a miracle in nature,
Making them lightest that wear most of it;
So are those crisped snaky golden locks
Which make such wanton gambols with the wind
Upon supposed fairness often known
To be the dowry of a second head—
The skull that bred them in the sepulchre.
Thus ornament is but the guiled shore
To a most dangerous sea; the beauteous scarf
Veiling an Indian beauty; in a word,
The seeming truth which cunning times put on
To entrap the wisest. Therefore, thou gaudy gold,
Hard food for Midas, I will none of thee;
Nor none of thee, thou pale and common drudge
'Tween man and man; but thou, thou meagre lead,
Which rather threaten'st than dost promise aught,
Thy plainness moves me more than eloquence,
And here choose I. Joy be the consequence!
PORTIA. [*Aside*] How all the other passions fleet to air,
As doubtful thoughts, and rash-embrac'd despair,
And shudd'ring fear, and green-ey'd jealousy!
O love, be moderate, allay thy ecstasy,
In measure rain thy joy, scant this excess!
I feel too much thy blessing. Make it less,
For fear I surfeit.
BASSANIO. [*Opening the leaden casket*] What find I here?

Fair Portia's counterfeit! What demi-god
Hath come so near creation? Move these eyes?
Or whether riding on the balls of mine
Seem they in motion? Here are sever'd lips,
Parted with sugar breath; so sweet a bar
Should sunder such sweet friends. Here in her hairs
The painter plays the spider, and hath woven
A golden mesh t' entrap the hearts of men
Faster than gnats in cobwebs. But her eyes—
How could he see to do them? Having made one,
Methinks it should have power to steal both his,
And leave itself unfurnish'd. Yet look how far
The substance of my praise doth wrong this shadow
In underprizing it, so far this shadow
Doth limp behind the substance. Here's the scroll,
The continent and summary of my fortune.
   'You that choose not by the view,
   Chance as fair and choose as true!
   Since this fortune falls to you,
   Be content and seek no new.
   If you be well pleas'd with this,
   And hold your fortune for your bliss,
   Turn to where your lady is
   And claim her with a loving kiss.'
A gentle scroll. Fair lady, by your leave;
I come by note, to give and to receive.
Like one of two contending in a prize,
That thinks he hath done well in people's eyes,
Hearing applause and universal shout,
Giddy in spirit, still gazing in a doubt
Whether those peals of praise be his or no;
So, thrice-fair lady, stand I even so,
As doubtful whether what I see be true,
Until confirm'd, sign'd, ratified by you.
PORTIA. You see me, Lord Bassanio, where I stand,
Such as I am. Though for myself alone
I would not be ambitious in my wish
To wish myself much better, yet for you
I would be trebled twenty times myself,
A thousand times more fair, ten thousand times more rich,

PORTIA. *Tarry a little; there is something else* (ACT IV. SCENE I)

That only to stand high in your account
I might in virtues, beauties, livings, friends,
Exceed account. But the full sum of me
Is sum of something which, to term in gross,
Is an unlesson'd girl, unschool'd, unpractis'd;
Happy in this, she is not yet so old
But she may learn; happier than this,
She is not bred so dull but she can learn;
Happiest of all is that her gentle spirit
Commits itself to yours to be directed,
As from her lord, her governor, her king.
Myself and what is mine to you and yours
Is now converted. But now I was the lord
Of this fair mansion, master of my servants,
Queen o'er myself; and even now, but now,
This house, these servants, and this same myself,
Are yours—my lord's. I give them with this ring,
Which when you part from, lose, or give away,
Let it presage the ruin of your love,
And be my vantage to exclaim on you.
BASSANIO. Madam, you have bereft me of all words;
Only my blood speaks to you in my veins;
And there is such confusion in my powers
As, after some oration fairly spoke
By a beloved prince, there doth appear
Among the buzzing pleased multitude,
Where every something, being blent together,
Turns to a wild of nothing, save of joy
Express'd and not express'd. But when this ring
Parts from this finger, then parts life from hence;
O, then be bold to say Bassanio's dead!
NERISSA. My lord and lady, it is now our time
That have stood by and seen our wishes prosper
To cry 'Good joy.' Good joy, my lord and lady!
GRATIANO. My Lord Bassanio, and my gentle lady,
I wish you all the joy that you can wish,
For I am sure you can wish none from me;
And, when your honours mean to solemnize
The bargain of your faith, I do beseech you
Even at that time I may be married too.

BASSANIO. With all my heart, so thou canst get a wife.
GRATIANO. I thank your lordship, you have got me one.
   My eyes, my lord, can look as swift as yours:
   You saw the mistress, I beheld the maid;
   You lov'd, I lov'd; for intermission
   No more pertains to me, my lord, than you.
   Your fortune stood upon the caskets there,
   And so did mine too, as the matter falls;
   For wooing here until I sweat again,
   And swearing till my very roof was dry
   With oaths of love, at last—if promise last—
   I got a promise of this fair one here
   To have her love, provided that your fortune
   Achiev'd her mistress.
PORTIA. Is this true, Nerissa?
NERISSA. Madam, it is, so you stand pleas'd withal.
BASSANIO. And do you, Gratiano, mean good faith?
GRATIANO. Yes, faith, my lord.
BASSANIO. Our feast shall be much honoured in your mar-
   riage.
GRATIANO. We'll play with them: the first boy for a thou-
   sand ducats.
NERISSA. What, and stake down?
GRATIANO. No; we shall ne'er win at that sport, and stake
   down—
   But who comes here? Lorenzo and his infidel?
   What, and my old Venetian friend, Salerio!

     Enter LORENZO, JESSICA, *and* SALERIO, *a messenger*
              from Venice

BASSANIO. Lorenzo and Salerio, welcome hither,
   If that the youth of my new int'rest here
   Have power to bid you welcome. By your leave,
   I bid my very friends and countrymen,
   Sweet Portia, welcome.
PORTIA. So do I, my lord;
   They are entirely welcome.
LORENZO. I thank your honour. For my part, my lord,
   My purpose was not to have seen you here;
   But meeting with Salerio by the way,

He did entreat me, past all saying nay,
To come with him along.
SALERIO. I did, my lord,
And I have reason for it. Signior Antonio
Commends him to you.   [*Gives* BASSANIO *a letter*]
BASSANIO. Ere I ope his letter,
I pray you tell me how my good friend doth.
SALERIO. Not sick, my lord, unless it be in mind;
Nor well, unless in mind; his letter there
Will show you his estate.   [BASSANIO *opens the letter*]
GRATIANO. Nerissa, cheer yond stranger; bid her welcome.
Your hand, Salerio. What's the news from Venice?
How doth that royal merchant, good Antonio?
I know he will be glad of our success:
We are the Jasons, we have won the fleece.
SALERIO. I would you had won the fleece that he hath lost.
PORTIA. There are some shrewd contents in yond same paper
That steals the colour from Bassanio's cheek:
Some dear friend dead, else nothing in the world
Could turn so much the constitution
Of any constant man. What, worse and worse!
With leave, Bassanio: I am half yourself,
And I must freely have the half of anything
That this same paper brings you.
BASSANIO. O sweet Portia,
Here are a few of the unpleasant'st words
That ever blotted paper! Gentle lady,
When I did first impart my love to you,
I freely told you all the wealth I had
Ran in my veins—I was a gentleman;
And then I told you true. And yet, dear lady,
Rating myself at nothing, you shall see
How much I was a braggart. When I told you
My state was nothing, I should then have told you
That I was worse than nothing; for indeed
I have engag'd myself to a dear friend,
Engag'd my friend to his mere enemy,
To feed my means. Here is a letter, lady,
The paper as the body of my friend,
And every word in it a gaping wound

Issuing life-blood. But is it true, Salerio?
Hath all his ventures fail'd? What, not one hit?
From Tripolis, from Mexico, and England,
From Lisbon, Barbary, and India,
And not one vessel scape the dreadful touch
Of merchant-marring rocks?
SALERIO. Not one, my lord.
  Besides, it should appear that, if he had
The present money to discharge the Jew,
He would not take it. Never did I know
A creature that did bear the shape of man
So keen and greedy to confound a man.
He plies the Duke at morning and at night,
And doth impeach the freedom of the state,
If they deny him justice. Twenty merchants,
The Duke himself, and the magnificoes
Of greatest port, have all persuaded with him;
But none can drive him from the envious plea
Of forfeiture, of justice, and his bond.
JESSICA. When I was with him, I have heard him swear
To Tubal and to Chus, his countrymen,
That he would rather have Antonio's flesh
Than twenty times the value of the sum
That he did owe him; and I know, my lord,
If law, authority, and power, deny not,
It will go hard with poor Antonio.
PORTIA. Is it your dear friend that is thus in trouble?
BASSANIO. The dearest friend to me, the kindest man,
The best condition'd and unwearied spirit
In doing courtesies; and one in whom
The ancient Roman honour more appears
Than any that draws breath in Italy.
PORTIA. What sum owes he the Jew?
BASSANIO. For me, three thousand ducats.
PORTIA. What! no more?
  Pay him six thousand, and deface the bond;
Double six thousand, and then treble that,
Before a friend of this description
Shall lose a hair through Bassanio's fault.
First go with me to church and call me wife,

And then away to Venice to your friend;
For never shall you lie by Portia's side
With an unquiet soul. You shall have gold
To pay the petty debt twenty times over.
When it is paid, bring your true friend along.
My maid Nerissa and myself meantime
Will live as maids and widows. Come, away;
For you shall hence upon your wedding day.
Bid your friends welcome, show a merry cheer;
Since you are dear bought, I will love you dear.
But let me hear the letter of your friend.

BASSANIO. [*Reads*] 'Sweet Bassanio, my ships have all miscarried, my creditors grow cruel, my estate is very low,
my bond to the Jew is forfeit; and since, in paying it, it is
impossible I should live, all debts are clear'd between you
and I, if I might but see you at my death. Notwithstanding, use your pleasure; if your love do not persuade you
to come, let not my letter.'

PORTIA. O love, dispatch all business and be gone!

BASSANIO. Since I have your good leave to go away,
I will make haste; but, till I come again,
No bed shall e'er be guilty of my stay,
Nor rest be interposer 'twixt us twain.   *Exeunt*

SCENE 3

Venice. A street

Enter SHYLOCK, SOLANIO, ANTONIO, *and* GAOLER

SHYLOCK. Gaoler, look to him. Tell not me of mercy—
This is the fool that lent out money gratis.
Gaoler, look to him.

ANTONIO. Hear me yet, good Shylock.

SHYLOCK. I'll have my bond; speak not against my bond.
I have sworn an oath that I will have my bond.
Thou call'dst me dog before thou hadst a cause,
But, since I am a dog, beware my fangs;
The Duke shall grant me justice. I do wonder,
Thou naughty gaoler, that thou art so fond

To come abroad with him at his request.
ANTONIO. I pray thee hear me speak.
SHYLOCK. I'll have my bond. I will not hear thee speak;
　I'll have my bond; and therefore speak no more.
　I'll not be made a soft and dull-ey'd fool,
　To shake the head, relent, and sigh, and yield,
　To Christian intercessors. Follow not;
　I'll have no speaking; I will have my bond.　　　*Exit*
SOLANIO. It is the most impenetrable cur
　That ever kept with men.
ANTONIO. Let him alone;
　I'll follow him no more with bootless prayers.
　He seeks my life; his reason well I know:
　I oft deliver'd from his forfeitures
　Many that have at times made moan to me;
　Therefore he hates me.
SOLANIO. I am sure the Duke
　Will never grant this forfeiture to hold.
ANTONIO. The Duke cannot deny the course of law;
　For the commodity that strangers have
　With us in Venice, if it be denied,
　Will much impeach the justice of the state,
　Since that the trade and profit of the city
　Consisteth of all nations. Therefore, go;
　These griefs and losses have so bated me
　That I shall hardly spare a pound of flesh
　To-morrow to my bloody creditor.
　Well, gaoler, on; pray God Bassanio come
　To see me pay his debt, and then I care not.　　*Exeunt*

SCENE 4

Belmont. PORTIA's *house*

Enter PORTIA, NERISSA, LORENZO, JESSICA, *and* BALTHASAR

LORENZO. Madam, although I speak it in your presence,
　You have a noble and a true conceit
　Of godlike amity, which appears most strongly
　In bearing thus the absence of your lord.

But if you knew to whom you show this honour,
How true a gentleman you send relief,
How dear a lover of my lord your husband,
I know you would be prouder of the work
Than customary bounty can enforce you.
PORTIA. I never did repent for doing good,
Nor shall not now; for in companions
That do converse and waste the time together,
Whose souls do bear an equal yoke of love,
There must be needs a like proportion
Of lineaments, of manners, and of spirit,
Which makes me think that this Antonio,
Being the bosom lover of my lord,
Must needs be like my lord. If it be so,
How little is the cost I have bestowed
In purchasing the semblance of my soul
From out the state of hellish cruelty!
This comes too near the praising of myself;
Therefore, no more of it; hear other things.
Lorenzo, I commit into your hands
The husbandry and manage of my house
Until my lord's return; for mine own part,
I have toward heaven breath'd a secret vow
To live in prayer and contemplation,
Only attended by Nerissa here,
Until her husband and my lord's return.
There is a monastery two miles off,
And there we will abide. I do desire you
Not to deny this imposition,
The which my love and some necessity
Now lays upon you.
LORENZO. Madam, with all my heart
I shall obey you in all fair commands.
PORTIA. My people do already know my mind,
And will acknowledge you and Jessica
In place of Lord Bassanio and myself.
So fare you well till we shall meet again.
LORENZO. Fair thoughts and happy hours attend on you!
JESSICA. I wish your ladyship all heart's content.
PORTIA. I thank you for your wish, and am well pleas'd

To wish it back on you. Fare you well, Jessica.
Exeunt JESSICA *and* LORENZO
Now, Balthasar,
As I have ever found thee honest-true,
So let me find thee still. Take this same letter,
And use thou all th' endeavour of a man
In speed to Padua; see thou render this
Into my cousin's hands, Doctor Bellario;
And look what notes and garments he doth give thee,
Bring them, I pray thee, with imagin'd speed
Unto the traject, to the common ferry
Which trades to Venice. Waste no time in words,
But get thee gone; I shall be there before thee.
BALTHASAR. Madam, I go with all convenient speed.   *Exit*
PORTIA. Come on, Nerissa, I have work in hand
That you yet know not of; we'll see our husbands
Before they think of us.
NERISSA. Shall they see us?
PORTIA. They shall, Nerissa; but in such a habit
That they shall think we are accomplished
With that we lack. I'll hold thee any wager,
When we are both accoutred like young men,
I'll prove the prettier fellow of the two,
And wear my dagger with the braver grace,
And speak between the change of man and boy
With a reed voice; and turn two mincing steps
Into a manly stride; and speak of frays
Like a fine bragging youth; and tell quaint lies,
How honourable ladies sought my love,
Which I denying, they fell sick and died—
I could not do withal. Then I'll repent,
And wish for all that, that I had not kill'd them.
And twenty of these puny lies I'll tell,
That men shall swear I have discontinued school
About a twelvemonth. I have within my mind
A thousand raw tricks of these bragging Jacks,
Which I will practise.
NERISSA. Why, shall we turn to men?
PORTIA. Fie, what a question's that,
If thou wert near a lewd interpreter!

651

But come, I'll tell thee all my whole device
When I am in my coach, which stays for us
At the park gate; and therefore haste away,
For we must measure twenty miles to-day.   *Exeunt*

SCENE 5

Belmont. The garden

Enter LAUNCELOT *and* JESSICA

LAUNCELOT. Yes, truly; for, look you, the sins of the father
are to be laid upon the children; therefore, I promise you, I
fear you. I was always plain with you, and so now I speak
my agitation of the matter; therefore be o' good cheer, for
truly I think you are damn'd. There is but one hope in it
that can do you any good, and that is but a kind of bastard
hope, neither.

JESSICA. And what hope is that, I pray thee?

LAUNCELOT. Marry, you may partly hope that your father
got you not—that you are not the Jew's daughter.

JESSICA. That were a kind of bastard hope indeed; so the sins
of my mother should be visited upon me.

LAUNCELOT. Truly then I fear you are damn'd both by
father and mother; thus when I shun Scylla, your father, I
fall into Charybdis, your mother; well, you are gone both
ways.

JESSICA. I shall be sav'd by my husband; he hath made me a
Christian.

LAUNCELOT. Truly, the more to blame he; we were Christians enow before, e'en as many as could well live one by
another. This making of Christians will raise the price of
hogs; if we grow all to be pork-eaters, we shall not shortly
have a rasher on the coals for money.

Enter LORENZO

JESSICA. I'll tell my husband, Launcelot, what you say; here
he comes.

LORENZO. I shall grow jealous of you shortly, Launcelot, if
you thus get my wife into corners.

JESSICA. Nay, you need nor fear us, Lorenzo; Launcelot and
I are out; he tells me flatly there's no mercy for me in
heaven, because I am a Jew's daughter; and he says you are
no good member of the commonwealth, for in converting
Jews to Christians you raise the price of pork.

LORENZO. I shall answer that better to the commonwealth
than you can the getting up of the negro's belly; the Moor
is with child by you, Launcelot.

LAUNCELOT. It is much that the Moor should be more than
reason; but if she be less than an honest woman, she is indeed more than I took her for.

LORENZO. How every fool can play upon the word! I think
the best grace of wit will shortly turn into silence, and discourse grow commendable in none only but parrots. Go
in, sirrah; bid them prepare for dinner.

LAUNCELOT. That is done, sir; they have all stomachs.

LORENZO. Goodly Lord, what a wit-snapper are you! Then
bid them prepare dinner.

LAUNCELOT. That is done too, sir, only 'cover' is the word.

LORENZO. Will you cover, then, sir?

LAUNCELOT. Not so, sir, neither; I know my duty.

LORENZO. Yet more quarrelling with occasion! Wilt thou
show the whole wealth of thy wit in an instant? I pray
thee understand a plain man in his plain meaning: go to
thy fellows, bid them cover the table, serve in the meat,
and we will come in to dinner.

LAUNCELOT. For the table, sir, it shall be serv'd in; for the
meat, sir, it shall be cover'd; for your coming in to dinner,
sir, why, let it be as humours and conceits shall govern.

Exit

LORENZO. O dear discretion, how his words are suited!
The fool hath planted in his memory
An army of good words; and I do know
A many fools that stand in better place,
Garnish'd like him, that for a tricksy word
Defy the matter. How cheer'st thou, Jessica?
And now, good sweet, say thy opinion,
How dost thou like the Lord Bassanio's wife?

JESSICA. Past all expressing. It is very meet
The Lord Bassanio live an upright life,

For, having such a blessing in his lady,
He finds the joys of heaven here on earth;
And if on earth he do not merit it,
In reason he should never come to heaven.
Why, if two gods should play some heavenly match,
And on the wager lay two earthly women,
And Portia one, there must be something else
Pawn'd with the other; for the poor rude world
Hath not her fellow.

LORENZO. Even such a husband
Hast thou of me as she is for a wife.

JESSICA. Nay, but ask my opinion too of that.

LORENZO. I will anon; first let us go to dinner.

JESSICA. Nay, let me praise you while I have a stomach.

LORENZO. No, pray thee, let it serve for table-talk;
Then howsome'er thou speak'st, 'mong other things
I shall digest it.

JESSICA. Well, I'll set you forth.   *Exeunt*

ACT IV. SCENE 1

Venice. The court of justice

Enter the DUKE, *the* MAGNIFICOES, ANTONIO, BASSANIO,
GRATIANO, SALERIO, *and* OTHERS

DUKE OF VENICE. What, is Antonio here?

ANTONIO. Ready, so please your Grace.

DUKE OF VENICE. I am sorry for thee; thou art come to
answer
A stony adversary, an inhuman wretch,
Uncapable of pity, void and empty
From any dram of mercy.

ANTONIO. I have heard
Your Grace hath ta'en great pains to qualify
His rigorous course; but since he stands obdurate,
And that no lawful means can carry me
Out of his envy's reach, I do oppose

My patience to his fury, and am arm'd
To suffer with a quietness of spirit
The very tyranny and rage of his.
DUKE OF VENICE. Go one, and call the Jew into the court.
SALERIO. He is ready at the door; he comes, my lord.

Enter SHYLOCK

DUKE OF VENICE. Make room, and let him stand before our
    face.
Shylock, the world thinks, and I think so too,
That thou but leadest this fashion of thy malice
To the last hour of act; and then, 'tis thought,
Thou'lt show thy mercy and remorse, more strange
Than is thy strange apparent cruelty;
And where thou now exacts the penalty,
Which is a pound of this poor merchant's flesh,
Thou wilt not only loose the forfeiture,
But, touch'd with human gentleness and love,
Forgive a moiety of the principal,
Glancing an eye of pity on his losses,
That have of late so huddled on his back—
Enow to press a royal merchant down,
And pluck commiseration of his state
From brassy bosoms and rough hearts of flint,
From stubborn Turks and Tartars, never train'd
To offices of tender courtesy.
We all expect a gentle answer, Jew.
SHYLOCK. I have possess'd your Grace of what I purpose,
And by our holy Sabbath have I sworn
To have the due and forfeit of my bond.
If you deny it, let the danger light
Upon your charter and your city's freedom.
You'll ask me why I rather choose to have
A weight of carrion flesh than to receive
Three thousand ducats. I'll not answer that,
But say it is my humour—is it answer'd?
What if my house be troubled with a rat,
And I be pleas'd to give ten thousand ducats
To have it ban'd? What, are you answer'd yet?
Some men there are love not a gaping pig;

Some that are mad if they behold a cat;
And others, when the bagpipe sings i' th' nose,
Cannot contain their urine; for affection,
Mistress of passion, sways it to the mood
Of what it likes or loathes. Now, for your answer:
As there is no firm reason to be rend'red
Why he cannot abide a gaping pig;
Why he, a harmless necessary cat;
Why he, a woollen bagpipe, but of force
Must yield to such inevitable shame
As to offend, himself being offended;
So can I give no reason, nor I will not,
More than a lodg'd hate and a certain loathing
I bear Antonio, that I follow thus
A losing suit against him. Are you answered?
BASSANIO. This is no answer, thou unfeeling man,
To excuse the current of thy cruelty.
SHYLOCK. I am not bound to please thee with my answers.
BASSANIO. Do all men kill the things they do not love?
SHYLOCK. Hates any man the thing he would not kill?
BASSANIO. Every offence is not a hate at first.
SHYLOCK. What, wouldst thou have a serpent sting thee
    twice?
ANTONIO. I pray you, think you question with the Jew.
You may as well go stand upon the beach
And bid the main flood bate his usual height;
You may as well use question with the wolf,
Why he hath made the ewe bleat for the lamb;
You may as well forbid the mountain pines
To wag their high tops and to make no noise
When they are fretten with the gusts of heaven;
You may as well do anything most hard
As seek to soften that—than which what's harder?—
His Jewish heart. Therefore, I do beseech you,
Make no moe offers, use no farther means,
But with all brief and plain conveniency
Let me have judgment, and the Jew his will.
BASSANIO. For thy three thousand ducats here is six.
SHYLOCK. If every ducat in six thousand ducats
Were in six parts, and every part a ducat,

I would not draw them; I would have my bond.

DUKE OF VENICE. How shalt thou hope for mercy, rend'ring
  none?

SHYLOCK. What judgment shall I dread, doing no wrong?
  You have among you many a purchas'd slave,
  Which, like your asses and your dogs and mules,
  You use in abject and in slavish parts,
  Because you bought them; shall I say to you
  'Let them be free, marry them to your heirs—
  Why sweat they under burdens?—let their beds
  Be made as soft as yours, and let their palates
  Be season'd with such viands'? You will answer
  'The slaves are ours.' So do I answer you:
  The pound of flesh which I demand of him
  Is dearly bought, 'tis mine, and I will have it.
  If you deny me, fie upon your law!
  There is no force in the decrees of Venice.
  I stand for judgment; answer; shall I have it?

DUKE OF VENICE. Upon my power I may dismiss this court,
  Unless Bellario, a learned doctor,
  Whom I have sent for to determine this,
  Come here to-day.

SALERIO. My lord, here stays without
  A messenger with letters from the doctor,
  New come from Padua.

DUKE OF VENICE. Bring us the letters; call the messenger.

BASSANIO. Good cheer, Antonio! What, man, courage yet!
  The Jew shall have my flesh, blood, bones, and all,
  Ere thou shalt lose for me one drop of blood.

ANTONIO. I am a tainted wether of the flock,
  Meetest for death; the weakest kind of fruit
  Drops earliest to the ground, and so let me.
  You cannot better be employ'd, Bassanio,
  Than to live still, and write mine epitaph.

Enter NERISSA, *dressed like a lawyer's clerk*

DUKE OF VENICE. Came you from Padua, from Bellario?

NERISSA. From both, my lord. Bellario greets your Grace.
                                        [*Presents a letter*]

BASSANIO. Why dost thou whet thy knife so earnestly?

SHYLOCK. To cut the forfeiture from that bankrupt there.
GRATIANO. Not on thy sole, but on thy soul, harsh Jew,
Thou mak'st thy knife keen; but no metal can,
No, not the hangman's axe, bear half the keenness
Of thy sharp envy. Can no prayers pierce thee?
SHYLOCK. No, none that thou hast wit enough to make.
GRATIANO. O, be thou damn'd, inexecrable dog!
And for thy life let justice be accus'd.
Thou almost mak'st me waver in my faith,
To hold opinion with Pythagoras
That souls of animals infuse themselves
Into the trunks of men. Thy currish spirit
Govern'd a wolf who, hang'd for human slaughter,
Even from the gallows did his fell soul fleet,
And, whilst thou layest in thy unhallowed dam,
Infus'd itself in thee; for thy desires
Are wolfish, bloody, starv'd and ravenous.
SHYLOCK. Till thou canst rail the seal from off my bond,
Thou but offend'st thy lungs to speak so loud;
Repair thy wit, good youth, or it will fall
To cureless ruin. I stand here for law.
DUKE OF VENICE. This letter from Bellario doth commend
A young and learned doctor to our court.
Where is he?
NERISSA. He attendeth here hard by
To know your answer, whether you'll admit him.
DUKE OF VENICE. With all my heart. Some three or four of
you
Go give him courteous conduct to this place.
Meantime, the court shall hear Bellario's letter.
CLERK. [Reads] 'Your Grace shall understand that at the
receipt of your letter I am very sick; but in the instant that
your messenger came, in loving visitation was with me a
young doctor of Rome—his name is Balthazar. I acquainted
him with the cause in controversy between the Jew and
Antonio the merchant; we turn'd o'er many books together; he is furnished with my opinion which, bettered
with his own learning—the greatness whereof I cannot
enough commend—comes with him at my importunity to
fill up your Grace's request in my stead. I beseech you let

his lack of years be no impediment to let him lack a reverend estimation, for I never knew so young a body with
so old a head. I leave him to your gracious acceptance,
whose trial shall better publish his commendation.'

Enter PORTIA *for* BALTHAZAR, *dressed like a Doctor of Laws*

DUKE OF VENICE. You hear the learn'd Bellario, what he
writes;
And here, I take it, is the doctor come.
Give me your hand; come you from old Bellario?
PORTIA. I did, my lord.
DUKE OF VENICE. You are welcome; take your place.
Are you acquainted with the difference
That holds this present question in the court?
PORTIA. I am informed throughly of the cause.
Which is the merchant here, and which the Jew?
DUKE OF VENICE. Antonio and old Shylock, both stand
forth.
PORTIA. Is your name Shylock?
SHYLOCK. Shylock is my name.
PORTIA. Of a strange nature is the suit you follow;
Yet in such rule that the Venetian law
Cannot impugn you as you do proceed.
You stand within his danger, do you not?
ANTONIO. Ay, so he says.
PORTIA. Do you confess the bond?
ANTONIO. I do.
PORTIA. Then must the Jew be merciful.
SHYLOCK. On what compulsion must I? Tell me that.
PORTIA. The quality of mercy is not strain'd;
It droppeth as the gentle rain from heaven
Upon the place beneath. It is twice blest:
It blesseth him that gives and him that takes.
'Tis mightiest in the mightiest; it becomes
The throned monarch better than his crown;
His sceptre shows the force of temporal power,
The attribute to awe and majesty,
Wherein doth sit the dread and fear of kings;
But mercy is above this sceptred sway,
It is enthroned in the hearts of kings,

It is an attribute to God himself;
And earthly power doth then show likest God's
When mercy seasons justice. Therefore, Jew,
Though justice be thy plea, consider this—
That in the course of justice none of us
Should see salvation; we do pray for mercy,
And that same prayer doth teach us all to render
The deeds of mercy. I have spoke thus much
To mitigate the justice of thy plea,
Which if thou follow, this strict court of Venice
Must needs give sentence 'gainst the merchant there.
SHYLOCK. My deeds upon my head! I crave the law,
The penalty and forfeit of my bond.
PORTIA. Is he not able to discharge the money?
BASSANIO. Yes; here I tender it for him in the court;
Yea, twice the sum; if that will not suffice,
I will be bound to pay it ten times o'er
On forfeit of my hands, my head, my heart;
If this will not suffice, it must appear
That malice bears down truth. And, I beseech you,
Wrest once the law to your authority;
To do a great right do a little wrong,
And curb this cruel devil of his will.
PORTIA. It must not be; there is no power in Venice
Can alter a decree established;
'Twill be recorded for a precedent,
And many an error, by the same example,
Will rush into the state; it cannot be.
SHYLOCK. A Daniel come to judgment! Yea, a Daniel!
O wise young judge, how I do honour thee!
PORTIA. I pray you, let me look upon the bond.
SHYLOCK. Here 'tis, most reverend Doctor; here it is.
PORTIA. Shylock, there's thrice thy money off'red thee.
SHYLOCK. An oath, an oath! I have an oath in heaven.
Shall I lay perjury upon my soul?
No, not for Venice.
PORTIA. Why, this bond is forfeit;
And lawfully by this the Jew may claim
A pound of flesh, to be by him cut off
Nearest the merchant's heart. Be merciful.

Take thrice thy money; bid me tear the bond.
SHYLOCK. When it is paid according to the tenour.
  It doth appear you are a worthy judge;
  You know the law; your exposition
  Hath been most sound; I charge you by the law,
  Whereof you are a well-deserving pillar,
  Proceed to judgment. By my soul I swear
  There is no power in the tongue of man
  To alter me. I stay here on my bond.
ANTONIO. Most heartily I do beseech the court
  To give the judgment.
PORTIA. Why then, thus it is:
  You must prepare your bosom for his knife.
SHYLOCK. O noble judge! O excellent young man!
PORTIA. For the intent and purpose of the law
  Hath full relation to the penalty,
  Which here appeareth due upon the bond.
SHYLOCK. 'Tis very true. O wise and upright judge,
  How much more elder art thou than thy looks!
PORTIA. Therefore, lay bare your bosom.
SHYLOCK. Ay, his breast—
  So says the bond; doth it not, noble judge?
  'Nearest his heart,' those are the very words.
PORTIA. It is so. Are there balance here to weigh
  The flesh?
SHYLOCK. I have them ready.
PORTIA. Have by some surgeon, Shylock, on your charge,
  To stop his wounds, lest he do bleed to death.
SHYLOCK. Is it so nominated in the bond?
PORTIA. It is not so express'd, but what of that?
  'Twere good you do so much for charity.
SHYLOCK. I cannot find it; 'tis not in the bond.
PORTIA. You, merchant, have you anything to say?
ANTONIO. But little: I am arm'd and well prepar'd.
  Give me your hand, Bassanio; fare you well.
  Grieve not that I am fall'n to this for you,
  For herein Fortune shows herself more kind
  Than is her custom. It is still her use
  To let the wretched man outlive his wealth,
  To view with hollow eye and wrinkled brow

An age of poverty; from which ling'ring penance
Of such misery doth she cut me off.
Commend me to your honourable wife;
Tell her the process of Antonio's end;
Say how I lov'd you; speak me fair in death;
And, when the tale is told, bid her be judge
Whether Bassanio had not once a love.
Repent but you that you shall lose your friend,
And he repents not that he pays your debt;
For if the Jew do cut but deep enough,
I'll pay it instantly with all my heart.

BASSANIO. Antonio, I am married to a wife
Which is as dear to me as life itself;
But life itself, my wife, and all the world,
Are not with me esteem'd above thy life;
I would lose all, ay, sacrifice them all
Here to this devil, to deliver you.

PORTIA. Your wife would give you little thanks for that,
If she were by to hear you make the offer.

GRATIANO. I have a wife who I protest I love;
I would she were in heaven, so she could
Entreat some power to change this currish Jew.

NERISSA. 'Tis well you offer it behind her back;
The wish would make else an unquiet house.

SHYLOCK. [Aside] These be the Christian husbands! I have a
    daughter—
Would any of the stock of Barrabas
Had been her husband, rather than a Christian!—
We trifle time; I pray thee pursue sentence.

PORTIA. A pound of that same merchant's flesh is thine.
The court awards it and the law doth give it.

SHYLOCK. Most rightful judge!

PORTIA. And you must cut this flesh from off his breast.
The law allows it and the court awards it.

SHYLOCK. Most learned judge! A sentence! Come, prepare.

PORTIA. Tarry a little; there is something else.
This bond doth give thee here no jot of blood:
The words expressly are 'a pound of flesh.'
Take then thy bond, take thou thy pound of flesh;
But, in the cutting it, if thou dost shed

One drop of Christian blood, thy lands and goods
Are, by the laws of Venice, confiscate
Unto the state of Venice.

GRATIANO. O upright judge! Mark, Jew. O learned judge!

SHYLOCK. Is that the law?

PORTIA. Thyself shalt see the act;
For, as thou urgest justice, be assur'd
Thou shalt have justice, more than thou desir'st.

GRATIANO. O learned judge! Mark, Jew. A learned judge!

SHYLOCK. I take this offer then: pay the bond thrice,
And let the Christian go.

BASSANIO. Here is the money.

PORTIA. Soft!
The Jew shall have all justice. Soft! No haste.
He shall have nothing but the penalty.

GRATIANO. O Jew! an upright judge, a learned judge!

PORTIA. Therefore, prepare thee to cut off the flesh.
Shed thou no blood, nor cut thou less nor more
But just a pound of flesh; if thou tak'st more
Or less than a just pound—be it but so much
As makes it light or heavy in the substance,
Or the division of the twentieth part
Of one poor scruple; nay, if the scale do turn
But in the estimation of a hair—
Thou diest, and all thy goods are confiscate.

GRATIANO. A second Daniel, a Daniel, Jew!
Now, infidel, I have you on the hip.

PORTIA. Why doth the Jew pause? Take thy forfeiture.

SHYLOCK. Give me my principal, and let me go.

BASSANIO. I have it ready for thee; here it is.

PORTIA. He hath refus'd it in the open court;
He shall have merely justice, and his bond.

GRATIANO. A Daniel still say I, a second Daniel!
I thank thee, Jew, for teaching me that word.

SHYLOCK. Shall I not have barely my principal?

PORTIA. Thou shalt have nothing but the forfeiture
To be so taken at thy peril, Jew.

SHYLOCK. Why, then the devil give him good of it!
I'll stay no longer question.

PORTIA. Tarry, Jew.

The law hath yet another hold on you.
It is enacted in the laws of Venice,
If it be proved against an alien
That by direct or indirect attempts
He seek the life of any citizen,
The party 'gainst the which he doth contrive
Shall seize one half his goods; the other half
Comes to the privy coffer of the state;
And the offender's life lies in the mercy
Of the Duke only, 'gainst all other voice.
In which predicament, I say, thou stand'st;
For it appears by manifest proceeding
That indirectly, and directly too,
Thou hast contrived against the very life
Of the defendant; and thou hast incurr'd
The danger formerly by me rehears'd.
Down, therefore, and beg mercy of the Duke.

GRATIANO. Beg that thou mayst have leave to hang thyself;
And yet, thy wealth being forfeit to the state,
Thou hast not left the value of a cord;
Therefore thou must be hang'd at the state's charge.

DUKE OF VENICE. That thou shalt see the difference of our
spirit,
I pardon thee thy life before thou ask it.
For half thy wealth, it is Antonio's;
The other half comes to the general state,
Which humbleness may drive unto a fine.

PORTIA. Ay, for the state; not for Antonio.

SHYLOCK. Nay, take my life and all, pardon not that.
You take my house when you do take the prop
That doth sustain my house; you take my life
When you do take the means whereby I live.

PORTIA. What mercy can you render him, Antonio?

GRATIANO. A halter gratis; nothing else, for God's sake!

ANTONIO. So please my lord the Duke and all the court
To quit the fine for one half of his goods;
I am content, so he will let me have
The other half in use, to render it
Upon his death unto the gentleman
That lately stole his daughter—

Two things provided more; that, for this favour,
He presently become a Christian;
The other, that he do record a gift,
Here in the court, of all he dies possess'd
Unto his son Lorenzo and his daughter.
DUKE OF VENICE. He shall do this, or else I do recant
The pardon that I late pronounced here.
PORTIA. Art thou contented, Jew? What dost thou say?
SHYLOCK. I am content.
PORTIA. Clerk, draw a deed of gift.
SHYLOCK. I pray you, give me leave to go from hence;
I am not well; send the deed after me
And I will sign it.
DUKE OF VENICE. Get thee gone, but do it.
GRATIANO. In christ'ning shalt thou have two god-fathers;
Had I been judge, thou shouldst have had ten more,
To bring thee to the gallows, not to the font.

Exit SHYLOCK

DUKE OF VENICE. Sir, I entreat you home with me to dinner.
PORTIA. I humbly do desire your Grace of pardon;
I must away this night toward Padua,
And it is meet I presently set forth.
DUKE OF VENICE. I am sorry that your leisure serves you
not.
Antonio, gratify this gentleman,
For in my mind you are much bound to him.

Exeunt DUKE, MAGNIFICOES, *and train*

BASSANIO. Most worthy gentleman, I and my friend
Have by your wisdom been this day acquitted
Of grievous penalties; in lieu whereof
Three thousand ducats, due unto the Jew,
We freely cope your courteous pains withal.
ANTONIO. And stand indebted, over and above,
In love and service to you evermore.
PORTIA. He is well paid that is well satisfied,
And I, delivering you, am satisfied,
And therein do account myself well paid.
My mind was never yet more mercenary.
I pray you, know me when we meet again;
I wish you well, and so I take my leave.

BASSANIO. Dear sir, of force I must attempt you further;
Take some remembrance of us, as a tribute,
Not as fee. Grant me two things, I pray you,
Not to deny me, and to pardon me.

PORTIA. You press me far, and therefore I will yield.
[*To* ANTONIO] Give me your gloves, I'll wear them for
your sake.
[*To* BASSANIO] And, for your love, I'll take this ring from
you.
Do not draw back your hand; I'll take no more,
And you in love shall not deny me this.

BASSANIO. This ring, good sir—alas, it is a trifle;
I will not shame myself to give you this.

PORTIA. I will have nothing else but only this;
And now, methinks, I have a mind to it.

BASSANIO.. There's more depends on this than on the value.
The dearest ring in Venice will I give you,
And find it out by proclamation;
Only for this, I pray you, pardon me.

PORTIA. I see, sir, you are liberal in offers;
You taught me first to beg, and now, methinks,
You teach me how a beggar should be answer'd.

BASSANIO. Good sir, this ring was given me by my wife;
And, when she put it on, she made me vow
That I should neither sell, nor give, nor lose it.

PORTIA. That 'scuse serves many men to save their gifts.
And if your wife be not a mad woman,
And know how well I have deserv'd this ring,
She would not hold out enemy for ever
For giving it to me. Well, peace be with you!
Exeunt PORTIA *and* NERISSA

ANTONIO. My Lord Bassanio, let him have the ring.
Let his deservings, and my love withal,
Be valued 'gainst your wife's commandment.

BASSANIO. Go, Gratiano, run and overtake him;
Give him the ring, and bring him, if thou canst,
Unto Antonio's house. Away, make haste. *Exit* GRATIANO
Come, you and I will thither presently;
And in the morning early will we both
Fly toward Belmont. Come, Antonio. *Exeunt*

SCENE 2

Venice. A street

Enter PORTIA *and* NERISSA

PORTIA. Inquire the Jew's house out, give him this deed,
And let him sign it; we'll away tonight,
And be a day before our husbands home.
This deed will be well welcome to Lorenzo.

Enter GRATIANO

GRATIANO. Fair sir, you are well o'erta'en.
My Lord Bassanio, upon more advice,
Hath sent you here this ring, and doth entreat
Your company at dinner.
PORTIA. That cannot be.
His ring I do accept most thankfully,
And so, I pray you, tell him. Furthermore,
I pray you show my youth old Shylock's house.
GRATIANO. That will I do.
NERISSA. Sir, I would speak with you.
[*Aside to* PORTIA] I'll see if I can get my husband's ring,
Which I did make him swear to keep for ever.
PORTIA. [*To* NERISSA] Thou mayst, I warrant. We shall
have old swearing
That they did give the rings away to men;
But we'll outface them, and outswear them too.
[*Aloud*] Away, make haste, thou know'st where I will
tarry.
NERISSA. Come, good sir, will you show me to this house?
Exeunt

ACT V. SCENE 1

Belmont. The garden before PORTIA'S *house*

Enter LORENZO *and* JESSICA

LORENZO. The moon shines bright. In such a night as this,
When the sweet wind did gently kiss the trees,

And they did make no noise—in such a night,
Troilus methinks mounted the Troyan walls,
And sigh'd his soul toward the Grecian tents,
Where Cressid lay that night.

JESSICA. In such a night
Did Thisby fearfully o'ertrip the dew,
And saw the lion's shadow ere himself,
And ran dismayed away.

LORENZO. In such a night
Stood Dido with a willow in her hand
Upon the wild sea-banks, and waft her love
To come again to Carthage.

JESSICA. In such a night
Medea gathered the enchanted herbs
That did renew old Æson.

LORENZO. In such a night
Did Jessica steal from the wealthy Jew,
And with an unthrift love did run from Venice
As far as Belmont.

JESSICA. In such a night
Did young Lorenzo swear he lov'd her well,
Stealing her soul with many vows of faith,
And ne'er a true one.

LORENZO. In such a night
Did pretty Jessica, like a little shrew,
Slander her love, and he forgave it her.

JESSICA. I would out-night you, did no body come;
But, hark, I hear the footing of a man.

Enter STEPHANO

LORENZO. Who comes so fast in silence of the night?

STEPHANO. A friend.

LORENZO. A friend! What friend? Your name, I pray you,
friend?

STEPHANO. Stephano is my name, and I bring word
My mistress will before the break of day
Be here at Belmont; she doth stray about
By holy crosses, where she kneels and prays
For happy wedlock hours.

LORENZO. Who comes with her?

STEPHANO. None but a holy hermit and her maid.
I pray you, is my master yet return'd?
LORENZO. He is not, nor we have not heard from him.
But go we in, I pray thee, Jessica,
And ceremoniously let us prepare
Some welcome for the mistress of the house.

Enter LAUNCELOT

LAUNCELOT. Sola, sola! wo ha, ho! sola, sola!
LORENZO. Who calls?
LAUNCELOT. Sola! Did you see Master Lorenzo? Master
Lorenzo! Sola, sola!
LORENZO. Leave holloaing, man. Here!
LAUNCELOT. Sola! Where, where?
LORENZO. Here!
LAUNCELOT. Tell him there's a post come from my master
with his horn full of good news; my master will be here
ere morning. *Exit*
LORENZO. Sweet soul, let's in, and there expect their coming.
And yet no matter—why should we go in?
My friend Stephano, signify, I pray you,
Within the house, your mistress is at hand;
And bring your music forth into the air. *Exit* STEPHANO
How sweet the moonlight sleeps upon this bank!
Here will we sit and let the sounds of music
Creep in our ears; soft stillness and the night
Become the touches of sweet harmony.
Sit, Jessica. Look how the floor of heaven
Is thick inlaid with patines of bright gold;
There's not the smallest orb which thou behold'st
But in his motion like an angel sings,
Still quiring to the young-ey'd cherubins;
Such harmony is in immortal souls,
But whilst this muddy vesture of decay
Doth grossly close it in, we cannot hear it.

Enter MUSICIANS

Come, ho, and wake Diana with a hymn;
With sweetest touches pierce your mistress' ear.
And draw her home with music. [*Music*]

JESSICA. I am never merry when I hear sweet music.
LORENZO. The reason is your spirits are attentive;
  For do but note a wild and wanton herd,
  Or race of youthful and unhandled colts,
  Fetching mad bounds, bellowing and neighing loud,
  Which is the hot condition of their blood—
  If they but hear perchance a trumpet sound,
  Or any air of music touch their ears,
  You shall perceive them make a mutual stand,
  Their savage eyes turn'd to a modest gaze
  By the sweet power of music. Therefore the poet
  Did feign that Orpheus drew trees, stones, and floods;
  Since nought so stockish, hard, and full of rage,
  But music for the time doth change his nature.
  The man that hath no music in himself,
  Nor is not mov'd with concord of sweet sounds,
  Is fit for treasons, stratagems, and spoils;
  The motions of his spirit are dull as night,
  And his affections dark as Erebus.
  Let no such man be trusted. Mark the music.

Enter PORTIA *and* NERISSA

PORTIA. That light we see is burning in my hall.
  How far that little candle throws his beams!
  So shines a good deed in a naughty world.
NERISSA. When the moon shone, we did not see the candle.
PORTIA. So doth the greater glory dim the less:
  A substitute shines brightly as a king
  Until a king be by, and then his state
  Empties itself, as doth an inland brook
  Into the main of waters. Music! hark!
NERISSA. It is your music, madam, of the house.
PORTIA. Nothing is good, I see, without respect;
  Methinks it sounds much sweeter than by day.
NERISSA. Silence bestows that virtue on it, madam.
PORTIA. The crow doth sing as sweetly as the lark
  When neither is attended; and I think
  The nightingale, if she should sing by day,
  When every goose is cackling, would be thought
  No better a musician than the wren.

How many things by season season'd are
To their right praise and true perfection!
Peace, ho! The moon sleeps with Endymion,
And would not be awak'd.   [*Music ceases*]
LORENZO. That is the voice,
Or I am much deceiv'd, of Portia.
PORTIA. He knows me as the blind man knows the cuckoo,
By the bad voice.
LORENZO. Dear lady, welcome home.
PORTIA. We have been praying for our husbands' welfare,
Which speed, we hope, the better for our words.
Are they return'd?
LORENZO. Madam, they are not yet;
But there is come a messenger before,
To signify their coming.
PORTIA. Go in, Nerissa;
Give order to my servants that they take
No note at all of our being absent hence;
Nor you, Lorenzo; Jessica, nor you.   [*A tucket sounds*]
LORENZO. Your husband is at hand; I hear his trumpet.
We are no tell-tales, madam, fear you not.
PORTIA. This night methinks is but the daylight sick;
It looks a little paler; 'tis a day
Such as the day is when the sun is hid.

Enter BASSANIO, ANTONIO, GRATIANO, *and their followers*

BASSANIO. We should hold day with the Antipodes,
If you would walk in absence of the sun.
PORTIA. Let me give light, but let me not be light,
For a light wife doth make a heavy husband,
And never be Bassanio so for me;
But God sort all! You are welcome home, my lord.
BASSANIO. I thank you, madam; give welcome to my friend.
This is the man, this is Antonio,
To whom I am so infinitely bound.
PORTIA. You should in all sense be much bound to him,
For, as I hear, he was much bound for you.
ANTONIO. No more than I am well acquitted of.
PORTIA. Sir, you are very welcome to our house.
It must appear in other ways than words,

671

Therefore I scant this breathing courtesy.

GRATIANO. [*To* NERISSA] By yonder moon I swear you do
    me wrong;
    In faith, I gave it to the judge's clerk.
    Would he were gelt that had it, for my part,
    Since you do take it, love, so much at heart.

PORTIA. A quarrel, ho, already! What's the matter?

GRATIANO. About a hoop of gold, a paltry ring
    That she did give me, whose posy was
    For all the world like cutler's poetry
    Upon a knife, 'Love me, and leave me not.'

NERISSA. What talk you of the posy or the value?
    You swore to me, when I did give it you,
    That you would wear it till your hour of death,
    And that it should lie with you in your grave;
    Though not for me, yet for your vehement oaths,
    You should have been respective and have kept it.
    Gave it a judge's clerk! No, God's my judge,
    The clerk will ne'er wear hair on's face that had it.

GRATIANO. He will, an if he live to be a man.

NERISSA. Ay, if a woman live to be a man.

GRATIANO. Now by this hand I gave it to a youth,
    A kind of boy, a little scrubbed boy
    No higher than thyself, the judge's clerk;
    A prating boy that begg'd it as a fee;
    I could not for my heart deny it him.

PORTIA. You were to blame, I must be plain with you,
    To part so slightly with your wife's first gift,
    A thing stuck on with oaths upon your finger
    And so riveted with faith unto your flesh.
    I gave my love a ring, and made him swear
    Never to part with it, and here he stands;
    I dare be sworn for him he would not leave it
    Nor pluck it from his finger for the wealth
    That the world masters. Now, in faith, Gratiano,
    You give your wife too unkind a cause of grief;
    An 'twere to me, I should be mad at it.

BASSANIO. [*Aside*] Why, I were best to cut my left hand off,
    And swear I lost the ring defending it.

GRATIANO. My Lord Bassanio gave his ring away

Unto the judge that begg'd it, and indeed
Deserv'd it too; and then the boy, his clerk,
That took some pains in writing, he begg'd mine;
And neither man nor master would take aught
But the two rings.

PORTIA. What ring gave you, my lord?
Not that, I hope, which you receiv'd of me.

BASSANIO. If I could add a lie unto a fault,
I would deny it; but you see my finger
Hath not the ring upon it; it is gone.

PORTIA. Even so void is your false heart of truth;
By heaven, I will ne'er come in your bed
Until I see the ring.

NERISSA. Nor I in yours
Till I again see mine.

BASSANIO. Sweet Portia,
If you did know to whom I gave the ring,
If you did know for whom I gave the ring,
And would conceive for what I gave the ring,
And how unwillingly I left the ring,
When nought would be accepted but the ring,
You would abate the strength of your displeasure.

PORTIA. If you had known the virtue of the ring,
Or half her worthiness that gave the ring,
Or your own honour to contain the ring,
You would not then have parted with the ring.
What man is there so much unreasonable,
If you had pleas'd to have defended it
With any terms of zeal, wanted the modesty
To urge the thing held as a ceremony?
Nerissa teaches me what to believe:
I'll die for't but some woman had the ring.

BASSANIO. No, by my honour, madam, by my soul,
No woman had it, but a civil doctor,
Which did refuse three thousand ducats of me,
And begg'd the ring; the which I did deny him,
And suffer'd him to go displeas'd away—
Even he that had held up the very life
Of my dear friend. What should I say, sweet lady?
I was enforc'd to send it after him;

I was beset with shame and courtesy;
My honour would not let ingratitude
So much besmear it. Pardon me, good lady;
For by these blessed candles of the night,
Had you been there, I think you would have begg'd
The ring of me to give the worthy doctor.
PORTIA. Let not that doctor e'er come near my house;
Since he hath got the jewel that I loved,
And that which you did swear to keep for me,
I will become as liberal as you;
I'll not deny him anything I have,
No, not my body, nor my husband's bed.
Know him I shall, I am well sure of it.
Lie not a night from home; watch me like Argus;
If you do not, if I be left alone,
Now, by mine honour which is yet mine own,
I'll have that doctor for mine bedfellow.
NERISSA. And I his clerk; therefore be well advis'd
How you do leave me to mine own protection.
GRATIANO. Well, do you so, let not me take him then;
For, if I do, I'll mar the young clerk's pen.
ANTONIO. I am th' unhappy subject of these quarrels.
PORTIA. Sir, grieve not you; you are welcome notwithstand-
ing.
BASSANIO. Portia, forgive me this enforced wrong;
And in the hearing of these many friends
I swear to thee, even by thine own fair eyes,
Wherein I see myself—
PORTIA. Mark you but that!
In both my eyes he doubly sees himself,
In each eye one; swear by your double self,
And there's an oath of credit.
BASSANIO. Nay, but hear me.
Pardon this fault, and by my soul I swear
I never more will break an oath with thee.
ANTONIO. I once did lend my body for his wealth,
Which, but for him that had your husband's ring,
Had quite miscarried; I dare be bound again,
My soul upon the forfeit, that your lord
Will never more break faith advisedly.

674

PORTIA. Then you shall be his surety. Give him this,
  And bid him keep it better than the other.
ANTONIO. Here, Lord Bassanio, swear to keep this ring.
BASSANIO. By heaven, it is the same I gave the doctor!
PORTIA. I had it of him. Pardon me, Bassanio,
  For, by this ring, the doctor lay with me.
NERISSA. And pardon me, my gentle Gratiano,
  For that same scrubbed boy, the doctor's clerk,
  In lieu of this, last night did lie with me.
GRATIANO. Why, this is like the mending of highways
  In summer, where the ways are fair enough.
  What, are we cuckolds ere we have deserv'd it?
PORTIA. Speak not so grossly. You are all amaz'd.
  Here is a letter; read it at your leisure;
  It comes from Padua, from Bellario;
  There you shall find that Portia was the doctor,
  Nerissa there her clerk. Lorenzo here
  Shall witness I set forth as soon as you,
  And even but now return'd; I have not yet
  Enter'd my house. Antonio, you are welcome;
  And I have better news in store for you
  Than you expect. Unseal this letter soon;
  There you shall find three of your argosies
  Are richly come to harbour suddenly.
  You shall not know by what strange accident
  I chanced on this letter.
ANTONIO. I am dumb.
BASSANIO. Were you the doctor, and I knew you not?
GRATIANO. Were you the clerk that is to make me cuckold?
NERISSA. Ay, but the clerk that never means to do it,
  Unless he live until he be a man.
BASSANIO. Sweet doctor, you shall be my bedfellow;
  When I am absent, then lie with my wife.
ANTONIO. Sweet lady, you have given me life and living;
  For here I read for certain that my ships
  Are safely come to road.
PORTIA. How now, Lorenzo!
  My clerk hath some good comforts too for you.
NERISSA. Ay, and I'll give them him without a fee.
  There do I give to you and Jessica,

675

From the rich Jew, a special deed of gift,
After his death, of all he dies possess'd of.
LORENZO. Fair ladies, you drop manna in the way
Of starved people.
PORTIA. It is almost morning,
And yet I am sure you are not satisfied
Of these events at full. Let us go in,
And charge us there upon inter'gatories,
And we will answer all things faithfully.
GRATIANO. Let it be so. The first inter'gatory
That my Nerissa shall be sworn on is,
Whether till the next night she had rather stay,
Or go to bed now, being two hours to day.
But were the day come, I should wish it dark,
Till I were couching with the doctor's clerk.
Well, while I live, I'll fear no other thing
So sore as keeping safe Nerissa's ring.   *Exeunt*

As You Like It

ROSALIND. *O Jupiter, how weary are my spirits!*

(ACT II. SCENE IV)

AS YOU LIKE IT

As you like it may safely be dated after 1598, for Meres does not include it in his list, and before August 1600, when it is mentioned in the Stationers' Register. This was a special entry made not with a view to publication but with the intention of preventing some pirate's publishing an unauthorised text; the piece was printed only in 1623 in the First Folio. In date, style, and temper, it goes with *Much Ado About Nothing*.

A date close to 1598 is also suggested by Shakespeare's reference to Marlowe. In his *Hero and Leander* Marlowe had written:

> Where both deliberate, the love is slight;
> Who ever loved that loved not at first sight?

Hero and Leander was printed for the first time in 1598, and the lines Shakespeare gives to Phebe (III, 5) refer to and quote from Marlowe:

> Dead Shepherd, now I find thy saw of might:
> 'Who ever loved that loved not at first sight?'

Of course many had seen *Hero and Leander* in manuscript; there are reasons for thinking Shakespeare was of this number; the quotation is therefore not decisive, and there are other references to Marlowe that have suggested that *As You Like It* may have been shaped in some form soon after Marlowe's death. Marlowe, the 'Dead Shepherd,' was murdered or at least stabbed to death on 30th May 1593 in an inn at Deptford. At the inquest of the affair it was stated that a certain Ingram Frysar quarrelled with Marlowe over the reckoning, that daggers were drawn, and that Marlowe received a fatal blow. The discovery of these facts by Dr. Hotson has thrown a new light on a passage in Act III, Scene 3:

> When a man's verses cannot be understood, nor a man's good wit seconded with the forward child understanding, it strikes a man more dead than a great reckoning in a little room.

This seems to echo a line from Marlowe's *Jew of Malta:*

Infinite riches in a little room

and to refer to the circumstances of Marlowe's death and the quarrel over the reckoning. Such reflections however might well have been provoked by the publication of the dead poet's *Hero and Leander;* and since Meres makes no mention of *As You Like It,* it is safe to say, for style and characterisation support the conclusion, that the play in the form in which we have it was shaped between 1598 and 1600.

The story on which Shakespeare built his plot he found in *Rosalynde: Euphues Golden Legacie,* a novel by Thomas Lodge, published in 1590. Lodge wrote it, he tells the "Gentlemen Readers," to pass the time on his voyage with Captain Clarke to the Canaries:

> To bee briefe, gentlemen, roome for a souldier and a sailer, thet gives you the fruits of his labors that he wrote in the ocean, when everie line was wet with a surge, and every humorous passion countercheckt with a storme. If you like it, so.

These last words gave Shakespeare his title *As You Like It* and Lodge's romance provides the main episodes in the play although not such characters as Jaques, Touchstone or Audrey. As in Shakespeare there are three brothers in Lodge's story: Saladyne, Fernandine, and Rosader, who became Oliver, Jaques de Boys, and Orlando, in Shakespeare. The encounters between Saladyne and Rosader are more violent than those in *As You Like It* and end in the flight of the younger brother with Adam to the forest of Arden. Torismond the usurper has no animus against Rosader, as he has in the play against Orlando, at the wrestling match; he banishes his own daughter Alinda however when she defends Rosalynd. There are other slight differences. Alinda, alias Aliena, falls in love with Saladyne after he saves her from some robbers who have wounded Rosader. In the end Fernandine brings the news that the peers of France have risen against Torismond. Gerismond the banished king, with Rosader and Saladyne, joins the peers. Torismond is defeated and slain.

INTRODUCTION

As can be seen even from so imperfect a summary of Lodge's word, Shakespeare was quite indifferent to explaining the happenings it suited him to introduce. He had no room or need for an episode to explain Celia's love for Oliver, nor could he delay the finish to tell us about the usurper's defeat. His withdrawal to a religious life is sufficient warrant for Duke Senior and his band to leave the audience with the comfortable assurance that the exiles are returning to happiness.

As You Like It will always be a popular play on the stage: it provides an excellent range of contrasted parts and, in addition to its lively dialogue, a number of famous set pieces such as that on the seven ages. But over it all Shakespeare has cast a pastoral charm that gives the play its peculiar appeal. Raleigh has commented most brilliantly on this aspect of the play:

> The scene is laid, for the most part, in the forest of Arden. A minute examination of the play has given a curious result. No single bird, or insect, or flower, is mentioned by name. The words "flower" and "leaf" do not occur. The trees of the forest are the oak, the hawthorn, the palm-tree, and the olive. For animals, there are the deer, one lioness, and one green and gilded snake. The season is not easy to determine; perhaps it is summer; we hear only of the biting cold and the wintry wind. "But these are all lies" as Rosalind would say, and the dramatic truth has been expressed by those critics who speak of "the leafy solitudes sweet with the song of birds."

It would be difficult to show more clearly what the alliance of poetry with the drama can achieve.

DUKE, *living in exile*
FREDERICK, *his brother, and usurper of his dominions*
AMIENS ⎱ *lords attending on the banished Duke*
JAQUES ⎰
LE BEAU, *a courtier attending upon Frederick*
CHARLES, *wrestler to Frederick*
OLIVER ⎱
JAQUES ⎰ *sons of Sir Rowland de Boys*
ORLANDO
ADAM ⎱ *servants to Oliver*
DENNIS ⎰
TOUCHSTONE, *the court jester*
SIR OLIVER MARTEXT, *a vicar*
CORIN ⎱ *shepherds*
SILVIUS ⎰
WILLIAM, *a country fellow, in love with Audrey*
A person representing HYMEN

ROSALIND, *daughter to the banished Duke*
CELIA, *daughter to Frederick*
PHEBE, *a shepherdess*
AUDREY, *a country wench*

Lords, Pages, Foresters, *and* Attendants

SCENE:

OLIVER'S *house;* FREDERICK'S *court; and the Forest of Arden*

As You Like It

ACT I. SCENE 1

Orchard of OLIVER's *house*

Enter ORLANDO *and* ADAM

ORLANDO. As I remember, Adam, it was upon this fashion bequeathed me by will but poor a thousand crowns, and, as thou say'st, charged my brother, on his blessing, to breed me well; and there begins my sadness. My brother Jaques he keeps at school, and report speaks goldenly of his profit. For my part, he keeps me rustically at home, or, to speak more properly, stays me here at home unkept; for call you that keeping for a gentleman of my birth that differs not from the stalling of an ox? His horses are bred better; for, besides that they are fair with their feeding, they are taught their manage, and to that end riders dearly hir'd; but I, his brother, gain nothing under him but growth; for the which his animals on his dunghills are as much bound to him as I. Besides this nothing that he so plentifully gives me, the something that nature gave me his countenance seems to take from me. He lets me feed with his hinds, bars me the place of a brother, and as much as in him lies, mines my gentility with my education. This is it, Adam, that grieves me; and the spirit of my father, which I think is within me, begins to mutiny against this servitude. I will no longer endure it, though yet I know no wise remedy how to avoid it.

Enter OLIVER

ADAM. Yonder comes my master, your brother.
ORLANDO. Go apart, Adam, and thou shalt hear how he will shake me up. [ADAM *retires*]
OLIVER. Now, sir! what make you here?
ORLANDO. Nothing; I am not taught to make any thing.
OLIVER. What mar you then, sir?

ORLANDO. Marry, sir, I am helping you to mar that which God made, a poor unworthy brother of yours, with idleness.

OLIVER. Marry, sir, be better employed, and be nought awhile.

ORLANDO. Shall I keep your hogs, and eat husks with them? What prodigal portion have I spent that I should come to such penury?

OLIVER. Know you where you are, sir?

ORLANDO. O, sir, very well; here in your orchard.

OLIVER. Know you before whom, sir?

ORLANDO. Ay, better than him I am before knows me. I know you are my eldest brother; and in the gentle condition of blood, you should so know me. The courtesy of nations allows you my better in that you are the first-born; but the same tradition takes not away my blood, were there twenty brothers betwixt us. I have as much of my father in me as you, albeit I confess your coming before me is nearer to his reverence.

OLIVER. What, boy!   [*Strikes him*]

ORLANDO. Come, come, elder brother, you are too young in this.

OLIVER. Wilt thou lay hands on me, villain?

ORLANDO. I am no villain; I am the youngest son of Sir Rowland de Boys. He was my father; and he is thrice a villain that says such a father begot villains. Wert thou not my brother, I would not take this hand from thy throat till this other had pull'd out thy tongue for saying so. Thou has rail'd on thyself.

ADAM. [*Coming forward*] Sweet masters, be patient; for your father's remembrance, be at accord.

OLIVER. Let me go, I say.

ORLANDO. I will not, till I please; you shall hear me. My father charg'd you in his will to give me good education: you have train'd me like a peasant, obscuring and hiding from me all gentleman-like qualities. The spirit of my father grows strong in me, and I will no longer endure it; therefore allow me such exercises as may become a gentleman, or give me the poor allottery my father left me by testament; with that I will go buy my fortunes.

OLIVER. And what wilt thou do? Beg, when that is spent?

Well, sir, get you in. I will not long be troubled with you;
you shall have some part of your will. I pray you leave me.
ORLANDO. I will no further offend you than becomes me for
my good.
OLIVER. Get you with him, you old dog.
ADAM. Is 'old dog' my reward? Most true, I have lost my
teeth in your service. God be with my old master! He
would not have spoke such a word.

Exeunt ORLANDO *and* ADAM

OLIVER. Is it even so? Begin you to grow upon me? I will
physic your rankness, and yet give no thousand crowns
neither. Holla, Dennis!

Enter DENNIS

DENNIS. Calls your worship?
OLIVER. Was not Charles, the Duke's wrestler, here to speak
with me?
DENNIS. So please you, he is here at the door and importunes
access to you.
OLIVER. Call him in. [*Exit* DENNIS] 'Twill be a good way;
and to-morrow the wrestling is.

Enter CHARLES

CHARLES. Good morrow to your worship.
OLIVER. Good Monsieur Charles! What's the new news at
the new court?
CHARLES. There's no news at the court, sir, but the old news;
that is, the old Duke is banished by his younger brother
the new Duke; and three or four loving lords have put
themselves into voluntary exile with him, whose lands and
revenues enrich the new Duke; therefore he gives them
good leave to wander.
OLIVER. Can you tell if Rosalind, the Duke's daughter, be
banished with her father?
CHARLES. O, no; for the Duke's daughter, her cousin, so
loves her, being ever from their cradles bred together, that
she would have followed her exile, or have died to stay
behind her. She is at the court, and no less beloved of her
uncle than his own daughter; and never two ladies loved as
they do.

OLIVER. Where will the old Duke live?

CHARLES. They say he is already in the Forest of Arden, and a many merry men with him; and there they live like the old Robin Hood of England. They say many young gentlemen flock to him every day, and fleet the time carelessly, as they did in the golden world.

OLIVER. What, you wrestle to-morrow before the new Duke?

CHARLES. Marry, do I, sir; and I came to acquaint you with a matter. I am given, sir, secretly to understand that your younger brother, Orlando, hath a disposition to come in disguis'd against me to try a fall. To-morrow, sir, I wrestle for my credit; and he that escapes me without some broken limb shall acquit him well. Your brother is but young and tender; and, for your love, I would be loath to foil him, as I must, for my own honour, if he come in; therefore, out of my love to you, I came hither to acquaint you withal, that either you might stay him from his intendment, or brook such disgrace well as he shall run into, in that it is a thing of his own search and altogether against my will.

OLIVER. Charles, I thank thee for thy love to me, which thou shalt find I will most kindly requite. I had myself notice of my brother's purpose herein, and have by underhand means laboured to dissuade him from it; but he is resolute. I'll tell thee, Charles, it is the stubbornest young fellow of France; full of ambition, an envious emulator of every man's good parts, a secret and villainous contriver against me his natural brother. Therefore use thy discretion: I had as lief thou didst break his neck as his finger. And thou wert best look to't; for if thou dost him any slight disgrace, or if he do not mightily grace himself on thee, he will practise against thee by poison, entrap thee by some treacherous device, and never leave thee till he hath ta'en thy life by some indirect means or other; for, I assure thee, and almost with tears I speak it, there is not one so young and so villainous this day living. I speak but brotherly of him; but should I anatomize him to thee as he is, I must blush and weep, and thou must look pale and wonder.

CHARLES. I am heartily glad I came hither to you. If he come to-morrow I'll give him his payment. If ever he go alone

again, I'll never wrestle for prize more. And so, God keep
your worship! *Exit*

OLIVER. Farewell, good Charles. Now will I stir this gamester. I hope I shall see an end of him; for my soul, yet I
know not why, hates nothing more than he. Yet he's
gentle; never school'd and yet learned; full of noble device;
of all sorts enchantingly beloved; and, indeed, so much in
the heart of the world, and especially of my own people,
who best know him, that I am altogether misprised. But it
shall not be so long; this wrestler shall clear all. Nothing
remains but that I kindle the boy thither, which now I'll
go about. *Exit*

SCENE 2

A lawn before the DUKE'S *palace*

Enter ROSALIND *and* CELIA

CELIA. I pray thee, Rosalind, sweet my coz, be merry.

ROSALIND. Dear Celia, I show more mirth than I am mistress
of; and would you yet I were merrier? Unless you could
teach me to forget a banished father, you must not learn
me how to remember any extraordinary pleasure.

CELIA. Herein I see thou lov'st me not with the full weight
that I love thee. If my uncle, thy banished father, had banished thy uncle, the Duke my father, so thou hadst been
still with me, I could have taught my love to take thy
father for mine; so wouldst thou, if the truth of thy love to
me were so righteously temper'd as mine is to thee.

ROSALIND. Well, I will forget the condition of my estate, to
rejoice in yours.

CELIA. You know my father hath no child but I, nor none is
like to have; and, truly, when he dies thou shalt be his heir;
for what he hath taken away from thy father perforce, I
will render thee again in affection. By mine honour, I will;
and when I break that oath, let me turn monster; therefore,
my sweet Rose, my dear Rose, be merry.

ROSALIND. From henceforth I will, coz, and devise sports.
Let me see; what think you of falling in love?

CELIA. Marry, I prithee, do, to make sport withal; but love no man in good earnest, nor no further in sport neither than with safety of a pure blush thou mayst in honour come off again.

ROSALIND. What shall be our sport, then?

CELIA. Let us sit and mock the good housewife Fortune from her wheel, that her gifts may henceforth be bestowed equally.

ROSALIND. I would we could do so; for her benefits are mightily misplaced; and the bountiful blind woman doth most mistake in her gifts to women.

CELIA. 'Tis true; for those that she makes fair she scarce makes honest; and those that she makes honest she makes very ill-favouredly.

ROSALIND. Nay; now thou goest from Fortune's office to Nature's: Fortune reigns in gifts of the world, not in the lineaments of Nature.

Enter TOUCHSTONE

CELIA. No; when Nature hath made a fair creature, may she not by Fortune fall into the fire? Though Nature hath given us wit to flout at Fortune, hath not Fortune sent in this fool to cut off the argument?

ROSALIND. Indeed, there is Fortune too hard for Nature, when Fortune makes Nature's natural the cutter-off of Nature's wit.

CELIA. Peradventure this is not Fortune's work neither, but Nature's, who perceiveth our natural wits too dull to reason of such goddesses, and hath sent this natural for our whetstone; for always the dullness of the fool is the whetstone of the wits. How now, wit! Whither wander you?

TOUCHSTONE. Mistress, you must come away to your father.

CELIA. Were you made the messenger?

TOUCHSTONE. No, by mine honour; but I was bid to come for you.

ROSALIND. Where learned you that oath, fool?

TOUCHSTONE. Of a certain knight that swore by his honour they were good pancakes, and swore by his honour the mustard was naught. Now I'll stand to it, the pancakes were naught and the mustard was good, and yet was not the knight forsworn.

CELIA. How prove you that, in the great heap of your knowledge?

ROSALIND. Ay, marry, now unmuzzle your wisdom.

TOUCHSTONE. Stand you both forth now: stroke your chins, and swear by your beards that I am a knave.

CELIA. By our beards, if we had them, thou art.

TOUCHSTONE. By my knavery, if I had it, then I were. But if you swear by that that is not, you are not forsworn; no more was this knight, swearing by his honour, for he never had any; or if he had, he had sworn it away before ever he saw those pancackes or that mustard.

CELIA. Prithee, who is't that thou mean'st?

TOUCHSTONE. One that old Frederick, your father, loves.

CELIA. My father's love is enough to honour him. Enough, speak no more of him; you'll be whipt for taxation one of these days.

TOUCHSTONE. The more pity that fools may not speak wisely what wise men do foolishly.

CELIA. By my troth, thou sayest true; for since the little wit that fools have was silenced, the little foolery that wise men have makes a great show. Here comes Monsieur Le Beau.

Enter LE BEAU

ROSALIND. With his mouth full of news.

CELIA. Which he will put on us as pigeons feed their young.

ROSALIND. Then shall we be news-cramm'd.

CELIA. All the better; we shall be the more marketable. Bon jour, Monsieur Le Beau. What's the news?

LE BEAU. Fair Princess, you have lost much good sport.

CELIA. Sport! of what colour?

LE BEAU. What colour, madam? How shall I answer you?

ROSALIND. As wit and fortune will.

TOUCHSTONE. Or as the Destinies decrees.

CELIA. Well said; that was laid on with a trowel.

TOUCHSTONE. Nay, if I keep not my rank—

ROSALIND. Thou losest thy old smell.

LE BEAU. You amaze me, ladies. I would have told you of good wrestling, which you have lost the sight of.

ROSALIND. Yet tell us the manner of the wrestling.

LE BEAU. I will tell you the beginning, and, if it please your ladyships, you may see the end; for the best is yet to do; and here, where you are, they are coming to perform it.

CELIA. Well, the beginning that is dead and buried.

LE BEAU. There comes an old man and his three sons—

CELIA. I could match this beginning with an old tale.

LE BEAU. Three proper young men, of excellent growth and presence.

ROSALIND. With bills on their necks: 'Be it known unto all men by these presents'—

LE BEAU. The eldest of the three wrestled with Charles, the Duke's wrestler; which Charles in a moment threw him, and broke three of his ribs, that there is little hope of life in him. So he serv'd the second, and so the third. Yonder they lie; the poor old man, their father, making such pitiful dole over them that all the beholders take his part with weeping.

ROSALIND. Alas!

TOUCHSTONE. But what is the sport, monsieur, that the ladies have lost?

LE BEAU. Why, this that I speak of.

TOUCHSTONE. Thus men may grow wiser every day. It is the first time that ever I heard breaking of ribs was sport for ladies.

CELIA. Or I, I promise thee.

ROSALIND. But is there any else longs to see this broken music in his sides? Is there yet another dotes upon ribbreaking? Shall we see this wrestling, cousin?

LE BEAU. You must, if you stay here; for here is the place appointed for the wrestling, and they are ready to perform it.

CELIA. Yonder, sure, they are coming. Let us now stay and see it.

Flourish. Enter DUKE FREDERICK, LORDS, ORLANDO, CHARLES, *and* ATTENDANTS

FREDERICK. Come on; since the youth will not be entreated, his own peril on his forwardness.

ROSALIND. Is yonder the man?

LE BEAU. Even he, madam.

CELIA. Alas, he is too young; yet he looks successfully.

FREDERICK. How now, daughter and cousin! Are you crept hither to see the wrestling?

ROSALIND. Ay, my liege; so please you give us leave.

FREDERICK. You will take little delight in it, I can tell you, there is such odds in the man. In pity of the challenger's youth I would fain dissuade him, but he will not be entreated. Speak to him, ladies; see if you can move him.

CELIA. Call him hither, good Monsieur Le Beau.

FREDERICK. Do so; I'll not be by.

[DUKE FREDERICK *goes apart*]

LE BEAU. Monsieur the Challenger, the Princess calls for you.

ORLANDO. I attend them with all respect and duty.

ROSALIND. Young man, have you challeng'd Charles the wrestler?

ORLANDO. No, fair Princess; he is the general challenger. I come but in, as others do, to try with him the strength of my youth.

CELIA. Young gentleman, your spirits are too bold for your years. You have seen cruel proof of this man's strength; if you saw yourself with your eyes, or knew yourself with your judgment, the fear of your adventure would counsel you to a more equal enterprise. We pray you, for your own sake, to embrace your own safety and give over this attempt.

ROSALIND. Do, young sir; your reputation shall not therefore be misprised: we will make it our suit to the Duke that the wrestling might not go forward.

ORLANDO. I beseech you, punish me not with your hard thoughts, wherein I confess me much guilty to deny so fair and excellent ladies any thing. But let your fair eyes and gentle wishes go with me to my trial; wherein if I be foil'd there is but one sham'd that was never gracious; if kill'd, but one dead that is willing to be so. I shall do my friends no wrong, for I have none to lament me; the world no injury, for in it I have nothing; only in the world I fill up a place, which may be better supplied when I have made it empty.

ROSALIND. The little strength that I have, I would it were with you.

CELIA. And mine to eke out hers.

ROSALIND. Fare you well. Pray heaven I be deceiv'd in you!

CELIA. Your heart's desires be with you!

CHARLES. Come, where is this young gallant that is so desirous to lie with his mother earth?

ORLANDO. Ready, sir; but his will hath in it a more modest working.

FREDERICK. You shall try but one fall.

CHARLES. No, I warrant your Grace, you shall not entreat him to a second, that have so mightily persuaded him from a first.

ORLANDO. You mean to mock me after; you should not have mock'd me before; but come your ways.

ROSALIND. Now, Hercules be thy speed, young man!

CELIA. I would I were invisible, to catch the strong fellow by the leg.   [*They wrestle*]

ROSALIND. O excellent young man!

CELIA. If I had a thunderbolt in mine eye, I can tell who should down.

[CHARLES *is thrown. Shout*]

FREDERICK. No more, no more.

ORLANDO. Yes, I beseech your Grace; I am not yet well breath'd.

FREDERICK. How dost thou, Charles?

LE BEAU. He cannot speak, my lord.

FREDERICK. Bear him away. What is thy name, young man?

ORLANDO. Orlando, my liege; the youngest son of Sir Rowland de Boys.

FREDERICK. I would thou hadst been son to some man else.
The world esteem'd thy father honourable,
But I did find him still mine enemy.
Thou shouldst have better pleas'd me with this deed,
Hadst thou descended from another house.
But fare thee well; thou art a gallant youth;
I would thou hadst told me of another father.

Exeunt DUKE, *train, and* LE BEAU

CELIA. Were I my father, coz, would I do this?

ORLANDO. I am more proud to be Sir Rowland's son,

His youngest son—and would not change that calling
To be adopted heir to Frederick.

ROSALIND. My father lov'd Sir Rowland as his soul,
And all the world was of my father's mind;
Had I before known this young man his son,
I should have given him tears unto entreaties
Ere he should thus have ventur'd.

CELIA. Gentle cousin,
Let us go thank him, and encourage him;
My father's rough and envious disposition
Sticks me at heart. Sir, you have well deserv'd;
If you do keep your promises in love
But justly as you have exceeded all promise,
Your mistress shall be happy.

ROSALIND. Gentleman,   [*Giving him a chain from her neck*]
Wear this for me; one out of suits with fortune,
That could give more, but that her hand lacks means.
Shall we go, coz?

CELIA. Ay. Fare you well, fair gentleman.

ORLANDO. Can I not say 'I thank you'? My better parts
Are all thrown down; and that which here stands up
Is but a quintain, a mere lifeless block.

ROSALIND. He calls us back. My pride fell with my fortunes;
I'll ask him what he would. Did you call, sir?
Sir, you have wrestled well, and overthrown
More than your enemies.

CELIA. Will you go, coz?

ROSALIND. Have with you. Fare you well.

Exeunt ROSALIND *and* CELIA

ORLANDO. What passion hangs these weights upon my
tongue?
I cannot speak to her, yet she urg'd conference.
O poor Orlando, thou art overthrown!
Or Charles or something weaker masters thee.

Re-enter LE BEAU

LE BEAU. Good sir, I do in friendship counsel you
To leave this place. Albeit you have deserv'd
High commendation, true applause, and love,
Yet such is now the Duke's condition

That he misconstrues all that you have done.
The Duke is humorous; what he is, indeed,
More suits you to conceive than I to speak of.

ORLANDO. I thank you, sir; and pray you tell me this:
Which of the two was daughter of the Duke
That here was at the wrestling?

LE BEAU. Neither his daughter, if we judge by manners;
But yet, indeed, the smaller is his daughter;
The other is daughter to the banish'd Duke,
And here detain'd by her usurping uncle,
To keep his daughter company; whose loves
Are dearer than the natural bond of sisters.
But I can tell you that of late this Duke
Hath ta'en displeasure 'gainst his gentle niece,
Grounded upon no other argument
But that the people praise her for her virtues
And pity her for her good father's sake;
And, on my life, his malice 'gainst the lady
Will suddenly break forth. Sir, fare you well.
Hereafter, in a better world than this,
I shall desire more love and knowledge of you.

ORLANDO. I rest much bounden to you; fare you well.

Exit LE BEAU

Thus must I from the smoke into the smother;
From tyrant Duke unto a tyrant brother.
But heavenly Rosalind!   *Exit*

SCENE 3

The DUKE'S *palace*

Enter CELIA *and* ROSALIND

CELIA. Why, cousin! why, Rosalind! Cupid have mercy!
Not a word?

ROSALIND. Not one to throw at a dog.

CELIA. No, thy words are too precious to be cast away upon
curs; throw some of them at me; come, lame me with
reasons.

ROSALIND. Then there were two cousins laid up, when the one should be lam'd with reasons and the other mad without any.

CELIA. But is all this for your father?

ROSALIND. No, some of it is for my child's father. O, how full of briers is this working-day world!

CELIA. They are but burs, cousin, thrown upon thee in holiday foolery; if we walk not in the trodden paths, our very petticoats will catch them.

ROSALIND. I could shake them off my coat: these burs are in my heart.

CELIA. Hem them away.

ROSALIND. I would try, if I could cry 'hem' and have him.

CELIA. Come, come, wrestle with thy affections.

ROSALIND. O, they take the part of a better wrestler than myself.

CELIA. O, a good wish upon you! You will try in time, in despite of a fall. But, turning these jests out of service, let us talk in good earnest. Is it possible, on such a sudden, you should fall into so strong a liking with old Sir Rowland's youngest son?

ROSALIND. The Duke my father lov'd his father dearly.

CELIA. Doth it therefore ensue that you should love his son dearly? By this kind of chase I should hate him, for my father hated his father dearly; yet I hate not Orlando.

ROSALIND. No, faith, hate him not, for my sake.

CELIA. Why should I not? Doth he not deserve well?

Enter DUKE FREDERICK, *with* LORDS

ROSALIND. Let me love him for that; and do you love him because I do. Look, here comes the Duke.

CELIA. With his eyes full of anger.

FREDERICK. Mistress, dispatch you with your safest haste,
    And get you from our court.

ROSALIND. Me, uncle?

FREDERICK. You, cousin.
    Within these ten days if that thou beest found
    So near our public court as twenty miles,
    Thou diest for it.

ROSALIND. I do beseech your Grace,

Let me the knowledge of my fault bear with me.
If with myself I hold intelligence,
Or have acquaintance with mine own desires;
If that I do not dream, or be not frantic—
As I do trust I am not—then, dear uncle,
Never so much as in a thought unborn
Did I offend your Highness.
FREDERICK. Thus do all traitors;
If their purgation did consist in words,
They are as innocent as grace itself.
Let it suffice thee that I trust thee not.
ROSALIND. Yet your mistrust cannot make me a traitor.
Tell me whereon the likelihood depends.
FREDERICK. Thou art thy father's daughter; there's enough.
ROSALIND. So was I when your Highness took his dukedom;
So was I when your Highness banish'd him.
Treason is not inherited, my lord;
Or, if we did derive it from our friends,
What's that to me? My father was no traitor.
Then, good my liege, mistake me not so much
To think my poverty is treacherous.
CELIA. Dear sovereign, hear me speak.
FREDERICK. Ay, Celia; we stay'd her for your sake,
Else had she with her father rang'd along.
CELIA. I did not then entreat to have her stay;
It was your pleasure, and your own remorse;
I was too young that time to value her,
But now I know her. If she be a traitor,
Why so am I: we still have slept together,
Rose at an instant, learn'd, play'd, eat together;
And wheresoe'er we went, like Juno's swans,
Still we went coupled and inseparable.
FREDERICK. She is too subtle for thee; and her smoothness,
Her very silence and her patience,
Speak to the people, and they pity her.
Thou art a fool. She robs thee of thy name;
And thou wilt show more bright and seem more virtuous
When she is gone. Then open not thy lips.
Firm and irrevocable is my doom
Which I have pass'd upon her; she is banish'd.

CELIA. Pronounce that sentence, then, on me, my liege;
  I cannot live out of her company.
FREDERICK. You are a fool. You, niece, provide yourself.
  If you outstay the time, upon mine honour,
  And in the greatness of my word, you die.
                          Exeunt DUKE *and* LORDS
CELIA. O my poor Rosalind! Whither wilt thou go?
  Wilt thou change fathers? I will give thee mine.
  I charge thee be not thou more griev'd than I am.
ROSALIND. I have more cause.
CELIA. Thou hast not, cousin.
  Prithee be cheerful. Know'st thou not the Duke
  Hath banish'd me, his daughter?
ROSALIND. That he hath not.
CELIA. No, hath not? Rosalind lacks, then, the love
  Which teacheth thee that thou and I am one.
  Shall we be sund'red? Shall we part, sweet girl?
  No; let my father seek another heir.
  Therefore devise with me how we may fly,
  Whither to go, and what to bear with us;
  And do not seek to take your charge upon you,
  To bear your griefs yourself, and leave me out;
  For, by this heaven, now at our sorrows pale,
  Say what thou canst, I'll go along with thee.
ROSALIND. Why, whither shall we go?
CELIA. To seek my uncle in the Forest of Arden.
ROSALIND. Alas, what danger will it be to us,
  Maids as we are, to travel forth so far!
  Beauty provoketh thieves sooner than gold.
CELIA. I'll put myself in poor and mean attire,
  And with a kind of umber smirch my face;
  The like do you; so shall we pass along,
  And never stir assailants.
ROSALIND. Were it not better,
  Because that I am more than common tall,
  That I did suit me all points like a man?
  A gallant curtle-axe upon my thigh,
  A boar spear in my hand; and—in my heart
  Lie there what hidden woman's fear there will—
  We'll have a swashing and a martial outside,

As many other mannish cowards have
That do outface it with their semblances.
CELIA. What shall I call thee when thou art a man?
ROSALIND. I'll have no worse a name than Jove's own page,
And therefore look you call me Ganymede.
But what will you be call'd?
CELIA. Something that hath a reference to my state:
No longer Celia, but Aliena.
ROSALIND. But, cousin, what if we assay'd to steal
The clownish fool out of your father's court?
Would he not be a comfort to our travel?
CELIA. He'll go along o'er the wide world with me;
Leave me alone to woo him. Let's away,
And get our jewels and our wealth together;
Devise the fittest time and safest way
To hide us from pursuit that will be made
After my flight. Now go we in content
To liberty, and not to banishment.   *Exeunt*

ACT II. SCENE 1

The Forest of Arden

Enter DUKE SENIOR, AMIENS, *and two or three* LORDS,
like foresters

DUKE SENIOR. Now, my co-mates and brothers in exile,
Hath not old custom made this life more sweet
Than that of painted pomp? Are not these woods
More free from peril than the envious court?
Here feel we not the penalty of Adam,
The seasons' difference; as the icy fang
And churlish chiding of the winter's wind,
Which when it bites and blows upon my body,
Even till I shrink with cold, I smile and say
'This is no flattery; these are counsellors
That feelingly persuade me what I am.'
Sweet are the uses of adversity,

Which, like the toad, ugly and venomous,
Wears yet a precious jewel in his head;
And this our life, exempt from public haunt,
Finds tongues in trees, books in the running brooks,
Sermons in stones, and good in everything.
I would not change it.
AMIENS. Happy is your Grace,
That can translate the stubbornness of fortune
Into so quiet and so sweet a style.
DUKE SENIOR. Come, shall we go and kill us venison?
And yet it irks me the poor dappled fools,
Being native burghers of this desert city,
Should, in their own confines, with forked heads
Have their round haunches gor'd.
FIRST LORD. Indeed, my lord,
The melancholy Jaques grieves at that;
And, in that kind, swears you do more usurp
Than doth your brother that hath banish'd you.
To-day my Lord of Amiens and myself
Did steal behind him as he lay along
Under an oak whose antique root peeps out
Upon the brook that brawls along this wood!
To the which place a poor sequest'red stag,
That from the hunter's aim had ta'en a hurt,
Did come to languish; and, indeed, my lord,
The wretched animal heav'd forth such groans
That their discharge did stretch his leathern coat
Almost to bursting; and the big round tears
Cours'd one another down his innocent nose
In piteous chase; and thus the hairy fool,
Much marked of the melancholy Jaques,
Stood on th' extremest verge of the swift brook,
Augmenting it with tears.
DUKE SENIOR. But what said Jaques?
Did he not moralize this spectacle?
FIRST LORD. O, yes, into a thousand similes.
First, for his weeping into the needless stream:
'Poor deer,' quoth he 'thou mak'st a testament
As worldlings do, giving thy sum of more
To that which had too much.' Then, being there alone,

Left and abandoned of his velvet friends:
' 'Tis right'; quoth he 'thus misery doth part
The flux of company.' Anon, a careless herd,
Full of the pasture, jumps along by him
And never stays to greet him. 'Ay,' quoth Jaques
'Sweep on, you fat and greasy citizens;
'Tis just the fashion. Wherefore do you look
Upon that poor and broken bankrupt there?'
Thus most invectively he pierceth through
The body of the country, city, court,
Yea, and of this our life; swearing that we
Are mere usurpers, tyrants, and what's worse,
To fright the animals, and to kill them up
In their assign'd and native dwelling-place.
DUKE SENIOR. And did you leave him in this contemplation?
SECOND LORD. We did, my lord, weeping and commenting
Upon the sobbing deer.
DUKE SENIOR. Show me the place;
I love to cope him in these sullen fits,
For then he's full of matter.
FIRST LORD. I'll bring you to him straight.   *Exeunt*

SCENE 2

The DUKE'S *palace*

Enter DUKE FREDERICK, *with* LORDS

FREDERICK. Can it be possible that no man saw them?
It cannot be; some villains of my court
Are of consent and sufferance in this.
FIRST LORD. I cannot hear of any that did see her.
The ladies, her attendants of her chamber,
Saw her abed, and in the morning early
They found the bed untreasur'd of their mistress.
SECOND LORD. My lord, the roynish clown, at whom so oft
Your Grace was wont to laugh, is also missing.
Hisperia, the Princess' gentlewoman,
Confesses that she secretly o'erheard
Your daughter and her cousin much commend

The parts and graces of the wrestler
That did but lately foil the sinewy Charles;
And she believes, wherever they are gone,
That youth is surely in their company.
FREDERICK. Send to his brother; fetch that gallant hither.
  If he be absent, bring his brother to me;
  I'll make him find him. Do this suddenly;
  And let not search and inquisition quail
  To bring again these foolish runaways.   *Exeunt*

SCENE 3

Before OLIVER's *house*

Enter ORLANDO *and* ADAM, *meeting*

ORLANDO. Who's there?
ADAM. What, my young master? O my gentle master!
  O my sweet master! O you memory
  Of old Sir Rowland! Why, what make you here?
  Why are you virtuous? Why do people love you?
  And wherefore are you gentle, strong, and valiant?
  Why would you be so fond to overcome
  The bonny prizer of the humorous Duke?
  Your praise is come too swiftly home before you.
  Know you not, master, to some kind of men
  Their graces serve them but as enemies?
  No more do yours. Your virtues, gentle master,
  Are sanctified and holy traitors to you.
  O, what a world is this, when what is comely
  Envenoms him that bears it!
ORLANDO. Why, what's the matter?
ADAM. O unhappy youth!
  Come not within these doors; within this roof
  The enemy of all your graces lives.
  Your brother—no, no brother; yet the son—
  Yet not the son; I will not call him son
  Of him I was about to call his father—
  Hath heard your praises; and this night he means
  To burn the lodging where you use to lie,

And you within it. If he fail of that,
He will have other means to cut you off;
I overheard him and his practices.
This is no place; this house is but a butchery;
Abhor it, fear it, do not enter it.
ORLANDO. Why, whither, Adam, wouldst thou have me go?
ADAM. No matter whither, so you come not here.
ORLANDO. What, wouldst thou have me go and beg my food,
    Or with a base and boist'rous sword enforce
    A thievish living on the common road?
    This I must do, or know not what to do;
    Yet this I will not do, do how I can.
    I rather will subject me to the malice
    Of a diverted blood and bloody brother.
ADAM. But do not so. I have five hundred crowns,
    The thrifty hire I sav'd under your father,
    Which I did store to be my foster-nurse,
    When service should in my old limbs lie lame,
    And unregarded age in corners thrown.
    Take that, and He that doth the ravens feed,
    Yea, providently caters for the sparrow,
    Be comfort to my age! Here is the gold;
    All this I give you. Let me be your servant;
    Though I look old, yet I am strong and lusty;
    For in my youth I never did apply
    Hot and rebellious liquors in my blood,
    Nor did not with unbashful forehead woo
    The means of weakness and debility;
    Therefore my age is as a lusty winter,
    Frosty, but kindly. Let me go with you;
    I'll do the service of a younger man
    In all your business and necessities.
ORLANDO. O good old man, how well in thee appears
    The constant service of the antique world,
    When service sweat for duty, not for meed!
    Thou art not for the fashion of these times,
    Where none will sweat but for promotion,
    And having that do choke their service up
    Even with the having; it is not so with thee.
    But, poor old man, thou prun'st a rotten tree

That cannot so much as a blossom yield
In lieu of all thy pains and husbandry.
But come thy ways, we'll go along together,
And ere we have thy youthful wages spent
We'll light upon some settled low content.
ADAM. Master, go on; and I will follow thee
To the last gasp, with truth and loyalty.
From seventeen years till now almost four-score
Here lived I, but now live here no more.
At seventeen years many their fortunes seek,
But at fourscore it is too late a week;
Yet fortune cannot recompense me better
Than to die well and not my master's debtor.   *Exeunt*

SCENE 4

The Forest of Arden

Enter ROSALIND *for* GANYMEDE, CELIA *for* ALIENA,
and CLOWN *alias* TOUCHSTONE

ROSALIND. O Jupiter, how weary are my spirits!
TOUCHSTONE. I care not for my spirits, if my legs were not
weary.
ROSALIND. I could find in my heart to disgrace my man's ap-
parel, and to cry like a woman; but I must comfort the
weaker vessel, as doublet and hose ought to show itself
courageous to petticoat; therefore, courage, good Aliena.
CELIA. I pray you bear with me; I cannot go no further.
TOUCHSTONE. For my part, I had rather bear with you than
bear you; yet I should bear no cross if I did bear you; for
I think you have no money in your purse.
ROSALIND. Well, this is the Forest of Arden.
TOUCHSTONE. Ay, now am I in Arden; the more fool I; when
I was at home I was in a better place; but travellers must
be content.

Enter CORIN *and* SILVIUS

ROSALIND. Ay, be so, good Touchstone. Look you, who

comes here, a young man and an old in solemn talk.

CORIN. That is the way to make her scorn you still.

SILVIUS. O Corin, that thou knew'st how I do love her!

CORIN. I partly guess; for I have lov'd ere now.

SILVIUS. No, Corin, being old, thou canst not guess,
Though in thy youth thou wast as true a lover
As ever sigh'd upon a midnight pillow.
But if thy love were ever like to mine,
As sure I think did never man love so,
How many actions most ridiculous
Hast thou been drawn to by thy fantasy?

CORIN. Into a thousand that I have forgotten.

SILVIUS. O, thou didst then never love so heartily!
If thou rememb'rest not the slightest folly
That ever love did make thee run into,
Thou hast not lov'd;
Or if thou hast not sat as I do now,
Wearing thy hearer in thy mistress' praise,
Thou hast not lov'd;
Or if thou hast not broke from company
Abruptly, as my passion now makes me,
Thou hast not lov'd.

O Phebe, Phebe, Phebe! *Exit* SILVIUS

ROSALIND. Alas, poor shepherd! searching of thy wound,
I have by hard adventure found mine own.

TOUCHSTONE. And I mine. I remember, when I was in love, I broke my sword upon a stone, and bid him take that for coming a-night to Jane Smile; and I remember the kissing of her batler, and the cow's dugs that her pretty chopt hands had milk'd; and I remember the wooing of a peascod instead of her; from whom I took two cods, and giving her them again, said with weeping tears 'Wear these for my sake.' We that are true lovers run into strange capers; but as all is mortal in nature, so is all nature in love mortal in folly.

ROSALIND. Thou speak'st wiser than thou art ware of.

TOUCHSTONE. Nay, I shall ne'er be ware of mine own wit till I break my shins against it.

ROSALIND. Jove, Jove! this shepherd's passion
Is much upon my fashion.

TOUCHSTONE. And mine; but it grows something stale with
me.

CELIA. I pray you, one of you question yond man
If he for gold will give us any food;
I faint almost to death.

TOUCHSTONE. Holla, you clown!

ROSALIND. Peace, fool; he's not thy kinsman.

CORIN. Who calls?

TOUCHSTONE. Your betters, sir.

CORIN. Else are they very wretched.

ROSALIND. Peace, I say. Good even to you, friend.

CORIN. And to you, gentle sir, and to you all.

ROSALIND. I prithee, shepherd, if that love or gold
Can in this desert place buy entertainment,
Bring us where we may rest ourselves and feed.
Here's a young maid with travel much oppress'd,
And faints for succour.

CORIN. Fair sir, I pity her,
And wish, for her sake more than for mine own,
My fortunes were more able to relieve her;
But I am shepherd to another man,
And do not shear the fleeces that I graze.
My master is of churlish disposition,
And little recks to find the way to heaven
By doing deeds of hospitality.
Besides, his cote, his flocks, and bounds of feed,
Are now on sale; and at our sheepcote now,
By reason of his absence, there is nothing
That you will feed on; but what is, come see,
And in my voice most welcome shall you be.

ROSALIND. What is he that shall buy his flock and pasture?

CORIN. That young swain that you saw here but erewhile,
That little cares for buying any thing.

ROSALIND. I pray thee, if it stand with honesty,
Buy thou the cottage, pasture, and the flock,
And thou shalt have to pay for it of us.

CELIA. And we will mend thy wages. I like this place,
And willingly could waste my time in it.

CORIN. Assuredly the thing is to be sold.
Go with me; if you like upon report

The soil, the profit, and this kind of life,
I will your very faithful feeder be,
And buy it with your gold right suddenly.   *Exeunt*

SCENE 5

Another part of the forest

Enter AMIENS, JAQUES, *and* OTHERS

SONG

AMIENS.   Under the greenwood tree
Who loves to lie with me,
And turn his merry note
Unto the sweet bird's throat,
Come hither, come hither, come hither.
Here shall he see
No enemy
But winter and rough weather.

JAQUES. More, more, I prithee, more.
AMIENS. It will make you melancholy, Monsieur Jaques.
JAQUES. I thank it. More, I prithee, more. I can suck melancholy out of a song, as a weasel sucks eggs. More, I prithee, more.
AMIENS. My voice is ragged; I know I cannot please you.
JAQUES. I do not desire you to please me; I do desire you to sing. Come, more; another stanzo. Call you 'em stanzos?
AMIENS. What you will, Monsieur Jaques.
JAQUES. Nay, I care not for their names; they owe me nothing. Will you sing?
AMIENS. More at your request than to please myself.
JAQUES. Well then, if ever I thank any man, I'll thank you; but that they call compliment is like th' encounter of two dog-apes; and when a man thanks me heartily, methinks I have given him a penny, and he renders me the beggarly thanks. Come, sing; and you that will not, hold your tongues.
AMIENS. Well, I'll end the song. Sirs, cover the while; the

Duke will drink under this tree. He hath been all this day
to look you.

JAQUES. And I have been all this day to avoid him. He is too
disputable for my company. I think of as many matters as
he; but I give heaven thanks, and make no boast of them.
Come, warble, come.

SONG

[All together here]

Who doth ambition shun,
And loves to live i' th' sun,
Seeking the food he eats,
And pleas'd with what he gets,
Come hither, come hither, come hither.
Here shall he see
No enemy
But winter and rough weather.

JAQUES. I'll give you a verse to this note that I made yester-
day in despite of my invention.
AMIENS. And I'll sing it.
JAQUES. Thus it goes:

If it do come to pass
That any man turn ass,
Leaving his wealth and ease
A stubborn will to please,
Ducdame, ducdame, ducdame;
Here shall he see
Gross fools as he,
An if he will come to me.

AMIENS. What's that 'ducdame'?
JAQUES. 'Tis a Greek invocation, to call fools into a circle.
I'll go sleep, if I can; if I cannot, I'll rail against all the
first-born of Egypt.
AMIENS. And I'll go seek the Duke; his banquet is prepar'd.
Exeunt severally

AS YOU LIKE IT

SCENE 6

The forest

Enter ORLANDO *and* ADAM

ADAM. Dear master, I can go no further. O, I die for food! Here lie I down, and measure out my grave. Farewell, kind master.

ORLANDO. Why, how now, Adam! No greater heart in thee? Live a little; comfort a little; cheer thyself a little. If this uncouth forest yield anything savage, I will either be food for it or bring it for food to thee. Thy conceit is nearer death than thy powers. For my sake be comfortable; hold death awhile at the arm's end. I will here be with thee presently; and if I bring thee not something to eat, I will give thee leave to die; but if thou diest before I come, thou art a mocker of my labour. Well said! thou look'st cheerly; and I'll be with thee quickly. Yet thou liest in the bleak air. Come, I will bear thee to some shelter; and thou shalt not die for lack of a dinner, if there live anything in this desert. Cheerly, good Adam! *Exeunt*

SCENE 7

The forest

A table set out. Enter DUKE SENIOR, AMIENS, *and* LORDS, *like outlaws*

DUKE SENIOR. I think he be transform'd into a beast;
For I can nowhere find him like a man.

FIRST LORD. My lord, he is but even now gone hence;
Here was he merry, hearing of a song.

DUKE SENIOR. If he, compact of jars, grow musical,
We shall have shortly discord in the spheres.
Go seek him; tell him I would speak with him.

Enter JAQUES

FIRST LORD. He saves my labour by his own approach.

DUKE SENIOR. Why, how now, monsieur! what a life is this,
That your poor friends must woo your company?

708

What, you look merrily!

JAQUES. A fool, a fool! I met a fool i' th' forest,
A motley fool. A miserable world!
As I do live by food, I met a fool,
Who laid him down and bask'd him in the sun,
And rail'd on Lady Fortune in good terms,
In good set terms—and yet a motley fool.
'Good morrow, fool,' quoth I; 'No, sir,' quoth he,
'Call me not fool till heaven hath sent me fortune.'
And then he drew a dial from his poke,
And, looking on it with lack-lustre eye,
Says very wisely, 'It is ten o'clock;
Thus we may see,' quoth he, 'how the world wags;
'Tis but an hour ago since it was nine;
And after one hour more 'twill be eleven;
And so, from hour to hour, we ripe and ripe,
And then, from hour to hour, we rot and rot;
And thereby hangs a tale.' When I did hear
The motley fool thus moral on the time,
My lungs began to crow like chanticleer
That fools should be so deep contemplative;
And I did laugh sans intermission
An hour by his dial. O noble fool!
A worthy fool! Motley's the only wear.

DUKE SENIOR. What fool is this?

JAQUES. O worthy fool! One that hath been a courtier,
And says, if ladies be but young and fair,
They have the gift to know it; and in his brain,
Which is as dry as the remainder biscuit
After a voyage, he hath strange places cramm'd
With observation, the which he vents
In mangled forms. O that I were a fool!
I am ambitious for a motley coat.

DUKE SENIOR. Thou shalt have one.

JAQUES. It is my only suit,
Provided that you weed your better judgments
Of all opinion that grows rank in them
That I am wise. I must have liberty
Withal, as large a charter as the wind,
To blow on whom I please, for so fools have;

And they that are most galled with my folly,
They most must laugh. And why, sir, must they so?
The why is plain as way to parish church:
He that a fool doth very wisely hit
Doth very foolishly, although he smart,
Not to seem senseless of the bob; if not,
The wise man's folly is anatomiz'd
Even by the squand'ring glances of the fool.
Invest me in my motley; give me leave
To speak my mind, and I will through and through
Cleanse the foul body of th' infected world,
If they will patiently receive my medicine.
DUKE SENIOR. Fie on thee! I can tell what thou wouldst do.
JAQUES. What, for a counter, would I do but good?
DUKE SENIOR. Most mischievous foul sin, in chiding sin;
For thou thyself hast been a libertine,
As sensual as the brutish sting itself;
And all th' embossed sores and headed evils
That thou with license of free foot hast caught
Wouldst thou disgorge into the general world.
JAQUES. Why, who cries out on pride
That can therein tax any private party?
Doth it not flow as hugely as the sea,
Till that the wearer's very means do ebb?
What woman in the city do I name
When that I say the city-woman bears
The cost of princes on unworthy shoulders?
Who can come in and say that I mean her,
When such a one as she such is her neighbour?
Or what is he of basest function
That says his bravery is not on my cost,
Thinking that I mean him, but therein suits
His folly to the mettle of my speech?
There then! how then? what then? Let me see wherein
My tongue hath wrong'd him: if it do him right,
Then he hath wrong'd himself; if he be free,
Why then my taxing like a wild-goose flies,
Unclaim'd of any man. But who comes here?

Enter ORLANDO, *with his sword drawn*

ORLANDO. Forbear, and eat no more.
JAQUES. Why, I have eat none yet.
ORLANDO. Nor shalt not, till necessity be serv'd.
JAQUES. Of what kind should this cock come of?
DUKE SENIOR. Art thou thus bolden'd, man, by thy distress?
  Or else a rude despiser of good manners,
  That in civility thou seem'st so empty?
ORLANDO. You touch'd my vein at first: the thorny point
  Of bare distress hath ta'en from me the show
  Of smooth civility; yet am I inland bred,
  And know some nurture. But forbear, I say;
  He dies that touches any of this fruit
  Till I and my affairs are answered.
JAQUES. An you will not be answer'd with reason, I must die.
DUKE SENIOR. What would you have? Your gentleness shall force
  More than your force move us to gentleness.
ORLANDO. I almost die for food, and let me have it.
DUKE SENIOR. Sit down and feed, and welcome to our table.
ORLANDO. Speak you so gently? Pardon me, I pray you;
  I thought that all things had been savage here,
  And therefore put I on the countenance
  Of stern commandment. But whate'er you are
  That in this desert inaccessible,
  Under the shade of melancholy boughs,
  Lose and neglect the creeping hours of time;
  If ever you have look'd on better days,
  If ever been where bells have knoll'd to church,
  If ever sat at any good man's feast,
  If ever from your eyelids wip'd a tear,
  And know what 'tis to pity and be pitied,
  Let gentleness my strong enforcement be;
  In the which hope I blush, and hide my sword.
DUKE SENIOR. True is it that we have seen better days,
  And have with holy bell been knoll'd to church,
  And sat at good men's feasts, and wip'd our eyes
  Of drops that sacred pity hath engend'red;
  And therefore sit you down in gentleness,
  And take upon command what help we have
  That to your wanting may be minist'red.

ORLANDO. Then but forbear your food a little while,
Whiles, like a doe, I go to find my fawn,
And give it food. There is an old poor man
Who after me hath many a weary step
Limp'd in pure love; till he be first suffic'd,
Oppress'd with two weak evils, age and hunger,
I will not touch a bit.
DUKE SENIOR. Go find him out.
And we will nothing waste till you return.
ORLANDO. I thank ye; and be blest for your good comfort!
Exit

DUKE SENIOR. Thou seest we are not all alone unhappy:
This wide and universal theatre
Presents more woeful pageants than the scene
Wherein we play in.
JAQUES. All the world's a stage,
And all the men and women merely players;
They have their exits and their entrances;
And one man in his time plays many parts,
His acts being seven ages. At first the infant,
Mewling and puking in the nurse's arms;
Then the whining school-boy, with his satchel
And shining morning face, creeping like snail
Unwillingly to school. And then the lover,
Sighing like furnace, with a woeful ballad
Made to his mistress' eyebrow. Then a soldier,
Full of strange oaths, and bearded like the pard,
Jealous in honour, sudden and quick in quarrel,
Seeking the bubble reputation
Even in the cannon's mouth. And then the justice,
In fair round belly with good capon lin'd,
With eyes severe and beard of formal cut,
Full of wise saws and modern instances;
And so he plays his part. The sixth age shifts
Into the lean and slipper'd pantaloon,
With spectacles on nose and pouch on side,
His youthful hose, well sav'd, a world too wide
For his shrunk shank; and his big manly voice,
Turning again toward childish treble, pipes
And whistles in his sound. Last scene of all,

That ends this strange eventful history,
Is second childishness and mere oblivion;
Sans teeth, sans eyes, sans taste, sans every thing.

Re-enter ORLANDO *with* ADAM

DUKE SENIOR. Welcome. Set down your venerable burden.
And let him feed.
ORLANDO. I thank you most for him.
ADAM. So had you need;
I scarce can speak to thank you for myself.
DUKE SENIOR. Welcome; fall to. I will not trouble you
As yet to question you about your fortunes.
Give us some music; and, good cousin, sing.

SONG

Blow, blow, thou winter wind,
Thou art not so unkind
As man's ingratitude;
Thy tooth is not so keen,
Because thou art not seen,
Although thy breath be rude.
Heigh-ho! sing heigh-ho! unto the green holly.
Most friendship is feigning, most loving mere folly.
Then, heigh-ho, the holly!
This life is most jolly.

Freeze, freeze, thou bitter sky,
That dost not bite so nigh
As benefits forgot;
Though thou the waters warp,
Thy sting is not so sharp
As friend rememb'red not.
Heigh-ho! sing, &c.

DUKE SENIOR. If that you were the good Sir Rowland's son,
As you have whisper'd faithfully you were,
And as mine eye doth his effigies witness
Most truly limn'd and living in your face,
Be truly welcome hither. I am the Duke
That lov'd your father. The residue of your fortune,
Go to my cave and tell me. Good old man,

713

Thou art right welcome as thy master is.
Support him by the arm. Give me your hand,
And let me all your fortunes understand. *Exeunt*

ACT III. SCENE 1

The palace

Enter DUKE FREDERICK, OLIVER, *and* LORDS

FREDERICK. Not see him since! Sir, sir, that cannot be.
But were I not the better part made mercy,
I should not seek an absent argument
Of my revenge, thou present. But look to it:
Find out thy brother wheresoe'er he is;
Seek him with candle; bring him dead or living
Within this twelvemonth, or turn thou no more
To seek a living in our territory.
Thy lands and all things that thou dost call thine
Worth seizure do we seize into our hands,
Till thou canst quit thee by thy brother's mouth
Of what we think against thee.
OLIVER. O that your Highness knew my heart in this!
I never lov'd my brother in my life.
FREDERICK. More villain thou. Well, push him out of doors;
And let my officers of such a nature
Make an extent upon his house and lands.
Do this expediently, and turn him going. *Exeunt*

SCENE 2

The forest

Enter ORLANDO, *with a paper*

ORLANDO. Hang there, my verse, in witness of my love;
And thou, thrice-crowned Queen of Night, survey
With thy chaste eye, from thy pale sphere above,

Thy huntress' name that my full life doth sway.
O Rosalind! these trees shall be my books,
And in their barks my thoughts I'll character,
That every eye which in this forest looks
Shall see thy virtue witness'd every where.
Run, run, Orlando; carve on every tree,
The fair, the chaste, and unexpressive she.   *Exit*

Enter CORIN *and* TOUCHSTONE

CORIN. And how like you this shepherd's life, Master Touchstone?

TOUCHSTONE. Truly, shepherd, in respect of itself, it is a
good life; but in respect that it is a shepherd's life, it is
nought. In respect that it is solitary, I like it very well;
but in respect that it is private, it is a very vile life. Now
in respect it is in the fields, it pleaseth me well; but in respect it is not in the court, it is tedious. As it is a spare life,
look you, it fits my humour well; but as there is no more
plenty in it, it goes much against my stomach. Hast any
philosophy in thee, shepherd?

CORIN. No more but that I know the more one sickens the
worse at ease he is; and that he that wants money, means,
and content, is without three good friends; that the property of rain is to wet, and fire to burn; that good pasture
makes fat sheep; and that a great cause of the night is lack
of the sun; that he that hath learned no wit by nature nor
art may complain of good breeding, or comes of a very
dull kindred.

TOUCHSTONE. Such a one is a natural philosopher. Wast ever
in court, shepherd?

CORIN. No, truly.

TOUCHSTONE. Then thou art damn'd.

CORIN. Nay, I hope.

TOUCHSTONE. Truly, thou art damn'd, like an ill-roasted egg,
all on one side.

CORIN. For not being at court? Your reason.

TOUCHSTONE. Why, if thou never wast at court thou never
saw'st good manners; if thou never saw'st good manners,
then thy manners must be wicked; and wickedness is sin,
and sin is damnation. Thou art in a parlous state, shepherd.

CORIN. Not a whit, Touchstone. Those that are good manners at the court are as ridiculous in the country as the behaviour of the country is most mockable at the court. You told me you salute not at the court, but you kiss your hands; that courtesy would be uncleanly if courtiers were shepherds.

TOUCHSTONE. Instance, briefly; come, instance.

CORIN. Why, we are still handling our ewes; and their fells, you know, are greasy.

TOUCHSTONE. Why, do not your courtier's hands sweat? And is not the grease of a mutton as wholesome as the sweat of a man? Shallow, shallow. A better instance, I say; come.

CORIN. Besides, our hands are hard.

TOUCHSTONE. Your lips will feel them the sooner. Shallow again. A more sounder instance; come.

CORIN. And they are often tarr'd over with the surgery of our sheep; and would you have us kiss tar? The courtier's hands are perfum'd with civet.

TOUCHSTONE. Most shallow man! thou worm's meat in respect of a good piece of flesh indeed! Learn of the wise, and perpend: civet is of a baser birth than tar—the very uncleanly flux of a cat. Mend the instance, shepherd.

CORIN. You have too courtly a wit for me; I'll rest.

TOUCHSTONE. Wilt thou rest damn'd? God help thee, shallow man! God make incision in thee! thou art raw.

CORIN. Sir, I am a true labourer: I earn that I eat, get that I wear; owe no man hate, envy no man's happiness; glad of other men's good, content with my harm; and the greatest of my pride is to see my ewes graze and my lambs suck.

TOUCHSTONE. That is another simple sin in you: to bring the ewes and the rams together, and to offer to get your living by the copulation of cattle; to be bawd to a bell-wether, and to betray a she-lamb of a twelvemonth to a crooked-pated, old, cuckoldly ram, out of all reasonable match. If thou beest not damn'd for this, the devil himself will have no shepherds; I cannot see else how thou shouldst scape.

CORIN. Here comes young Master Ganymede, my new mistress's brother.

ACT III. SCENE 2

Enter ROSALIND, *reading a paper*

ROSALIND. 'From the east to western Inde,
No jewel is like Rosalinde.
Her worth, being mounted on the wind,
Through all the world bears Rosalinde.
All the pictures fairest lin'd
Are but black to Rosalinde.
Let no face be kept in mind
But the fair of Rosalinde.'

TOUCHSTONE. I'll rhyme you so eight years together, dinners, and suppers, and sleeping hours, excepted. It is the right butter-women's rank to market.

ROSALIND. Out, fool!

TOUCHSTONE. For a taste:
If a hart do lack a hind,
Let him seek out Rosalinde.
If the cat will after kind,
So be sure will Rosalinde.
Winter garments must be lin'd,
So must slender Rosalinde.
They that reap must sheaf and bind,
Then to cart with Rosalinde.
Sweetest nut hath sourest rind,
Such a nut is Rosalinde.
He that sweetest rose will find
Must find love's prick and Rosalinde.

This is the very false gallop of verses; why do you infect yourself with them?

ROSALIND. Peace, you dull fool! I found them on a tree.

TOUCHSTONE. Truly, the tree yields bad fruit.

ROSALIND. I'll graff it with you, and then I shall graff it with a medlar. Then it will be the earliest fruit i' th' country; for you'll be rotten ere you be half ripe, and that's the right virtue of the medlar.

TOUCHSTONE. You have said; but whether wisely or no, let the forest judge.

Enter CELIA, *with a writing*

ROSALIND. Peace!

717

Here comes my sister, reading; stand aside.

CELIA. 'Why should this a desert be?
    For it is unpeopled? No;
Tongues I'll hang on every tree
    That shall civil sayings show.
Some, how brief the life of man
    Runs his erring pilgrimage,
That the streching of a span
    Buckles in his sum of age;
Some, of violated vows
    'Twixt the souls of friend and friend;
But upon the fairest boughs,
    Or at every sentence end,
Will I Rosalinda write,
    Teaching all that read to know
The quintessence of every sprite
    Heaven would in little show.
Therefore heaven Nature charg'd
    That one body should be fill'd
With all graces wide-enlarg'd.
    Nature presently distill'd
Helen's cheek, but not her heart,
    Cleopatra's majesty,
Atalanta's better part,
    Sad Lucretia's modesty.
Thus Rosalinde of many parts
    By heavenly synod was devis'd,
Of many faces, eyes, and hearts,
    To have the touches dearest priz'd.
Heaven would that she these gifts should have,
    And I to live and die her slave.'

ROSALIND. O most gentle pulpiter! What tedious homily of love have you wearied your parishioners withal, and never cried 'Have patience, good people.'

CELIA. How now! Back, friends; shepherd, go off a little; go with him, sirrah.

TOUCHSTONE. Come, shepherd, let us make an honourable retreat; though not with bag and baggage, yet with scrip and scrippage.

Exeunt CORIN *and* TOUCHSTONE

718

CELIA. Didst thou hear these verses?

ROSALIND. O, yes, I heard them all, and more too; for some of them had in them more feet than the verses would bear.

CELIA. That's no matter; the feet might bear the verses.

ROSALIND. Ay, but the feet were lame, and could not bear themselves without the verse, and therefore stood lamely in the verse.

CELIA. But didst thou hear without wondering how thy name should be hang'd and carved upon these trees?

ROSALIND. I was seven of the nine days out of the wonder before you came; for look here what I found on a palm-tree. I was never so berhym'd since Pythagoras' time that I was an Irish rat, which I can hardly remember.

CELIA. Trow you who hath done this?

ROSALIND. Is it a man?

CELIA. And a chain, that you once wore, about his neck. Change you colour?

ROSALIND. I prithee, who?

CELIA. O Lord, Lord! it is a hard matter for friends to meet; but mountains may be remov'd with earthquakes, and so encounter.

ROSALIND. Nay, but who is it?

CELIA. Is it possible?

ROSALIND. Nay, I prithee now, with most petitionary vehemence, tell me who it is.

CELIA. O wonderful, wonderful, and most wonderful wonderful, and yet again wonderful, and after that, out of all whooping!

ROSALIND. Good my complexion! dost thou think, though I am caparison'd like a man, I have a doublet and hose in my disposition? One inch of delay more is a South Sea of discovery. I prithee tell me who is it quickly, and speak apace. I would thou could'st stammer, that thou mightst pour this conceal'd man out of thy mouth, as wine comes out of a narrow-mouth'd bottle—either too much at once or none at all. I prithee take the cork out of thy mouth that I may drink thy tidings.

CELIA. So you may put a man in your belly.

ROSALIND. Is he of God's making? What manner of man? Is his head worth a hat or his chin worth a beard?

CELIA. Nay, he hath but a little beard.

ROSALIND. Why, God will send more if the man will be thankful. Let me stay the growth of his beard, if thou delay me not the knowledge of his chin.

CELIA. It is young Orlando, that tripp'd up the wrestler's heels and your heart both in an instant.

ROSALIND. Nay, but the devil take mocking! Speak sad brow and true maid.

CELIA. I' faith, coz, 'tis he.

ROSALIND. Orlando?

CELIA. Orlando.

ROSALIND. Alas the day! what shall I do with my doublet and hose? What did he when thou saw'st him? What said he? How look'd he? Wherein went he? What makes he here? Did he ask for me? Where remains he? How parted he with thee? And when shalt thou see him again? Answer me in one word.

CELIA. You must borrow me Gargantua's mouth first; 'tis a word too great for any mouth of this age's size. To say ay and no to these particulars is more than to answer in a catechism.

ROSALIND. But doth he know that I am in this forest, and in man's apparel? Looks he as freshly as he did the day he wrestled?

CELIA. It is as easy to count atomies as to resolve the propositions of a lover; but take a taste of my finding him, and relish it with good observance. I found him under a tree, like a dropp'd acorn.

ROSALIND. It may well be call'd Jove's tree, when it drops forth such fruit.

CELIA. Give me audience, good madam.

ROSALIND. Proceed.

CELIA. There lay he, stretch'd along like a wounded knight.

ROSALIND. Though it be pity to see such a sight, it well becomes the ground.

CELIA. Cry 'Holla' to thy tongue, I prithee; it curvets unseasonably. He was furnish'd like a hunter.

ROSALIND. O, ominous! he comes to kill my heart.

CELIA. I would sing my song without a burden; thou bring'st me out of tune.

ROSALIND. Do you not know I am a woman? When I think, I must speak. Sweet, say on.

CELIA. You bring me out. Soft! comes he not here?

Enter ORLANDO *and* JAQUES

ROSALIND. 'Tis he; slink by, and note him.

JAQUES. I thank you for your company; but, good faith, I had as lief have been myself alone.

ORLANDO. And so had I; but yet, for fashion sake, I thank you too for your society.

JAQUES. God buy you; let's meet as little as we can.

ORLANDO. I do desire we may be better strangers.

JAQUES. I pray you mar no more trees with writing love songs in their barks.

ORLANDO. I pray you mar no more of my verses with reading them ill-favouredly.

JAQUES. Rosalind is your love's name?

ORLANDO. Yes, just.

JAQUES. I do not like her name.

ORLANDO. There was no thought of pleasing you when she was christen'd.

JAQUES. What stature is she of?

ORLANDO. Just as high as my heart.

JAQUES. You are full of pretty answers. Have you not been acquainted with goldsmiths' wives, and conn'd them out of rings?

ORLANDO. Not so; but I answer you right painted cloth, from whence you have studied your questions.

JAQUES. You have a nimble wit; I think 'twas made of Atalanta's heels. Will you sit down with me? and we two will rail against our mistress the world, and all our misery.

ORLANDO. I will chide no breather in the world but myself, against whom I know most faults.

JAQUES. The worst fault you have is to be in love.

ORLANDO. 'Tis a fault I will not change for your best virtue. I am weary of you.

JAQUES. By my troth, I was seeking for a fool when I found you.

ORLANDO. He is drown'd in the brook; look but in, and you shall see him.

JAQUES. There I shall see mine own figure.

ORLANDO. Which I take to be either a fool or a cipher.

JAQUES. I'll tarry no longer with you; farewell, good Signior Love.

ORLANDO. I am glad of your departure; adieu, good Monsieur Melancholy.

Exit JAQUES

ROSALIND. [*Aside to* CELIA] I will speak to him like a saucy lackey, and under that habit play the knave with him.—Do you hear, forester?

ORLANDO. Very well; what would you?

ROSALIND. I pray you, what is't o'clock?

ORLANDO. You should ask me what time o' day; there's no clock in the forest.

ROSALIND. Then there is no true lover in the forest, else sighing every minute and groaning every hour would detect the lazy foot of Time as well as a clock.

ORLANDO. And why not the swift foot of Time? Had not that been as proper?

ROSALIND. By no means, sir. Time travels in divers paces with divers persons. I'll tell you who Time ambles withal, who Time trots withal, who Time gallops withal, and who he stands still withal.

ORLANDO. I prithee, who doth he trot withal?

ROSALIND. Marry, he trots hard with a young maid between the contract of her marriage and the day it is solemniz'd; if the interim be but a se'nnight, Time's pace is so hard that it seems the length of seven year.

ORLANDO. Who ambles Time withal?

ROSALIND. With a priest that lacks Latin and a rich man that hath not the gout; for the one sleeps easily because he cannot study, and the other lives merrily because he feels no pain; the one lacking the burden of lean and wasteful learning, the other knowing no burden of heavy tedious penury. These Time ambles withal.

ORLANDO. Who doth he gallop withal?

ROSALIND. With a thief to the gallows; for though he go as softly as foot can fall, he thinks himself too soon there.

ORLANDO. Who stays it still withal?

ROSALIND. With lawyers in the vacation; for they sleep between term and term, and then they perceive not how Time moves.

ORLANDO. Where dwell you, pretty youth?

ROSALIND. With this shepherdess, my sister; here in the skirts of the forest, like fringe upon a petticoat.

ORLANDO. Are you native of this place?

ROSALIND. As the coney that you see dwell where she is kindled.

ORLANDO. Your accent is something finer than you could purchase in so removed a dwelling.

ROSALIND. I have been told so of many; but indeed an old religious uncle of mine taught me to speak, who was in his youth an inland man; one that knew courtship too well, for there he fell in love. I have heard him read many lectures against it; and I thank God I am not a woman, to be touch'd with so many giddy offences as he hath generally tax'd their whole sex withal.

ORLANDO. Can you remember any of the principal evils that he laid to the charge of women?

ROSALIND. There were none principal; they were all like one another as halfpence are; every one fault seeming monstrous till his fellow-fault came to match it.

ORLANDO. I prithee recount some of them.

ROSALIND. No; I will not cast away my physic but on those that are sick. There is a man haunts the forest that abuses our young plants with carving 'Rosalind' on their barks; hangs odes upon hawthorns and elegies on brambles; all, forsooth, deifying the name of Rosalind. If I could meet that fancy-monger, I would give him some good counsel, for he seems to have the quotidian of love upon him.

ORLANDO. I am he that is so love-shak'd; I pray you tell me your remedy.

ROSALIND. There is none of my uncle's marks upon you; he taught me how to know a man in love; in which cage of rushes I am sure you are not prisoner.

ORLANDO. What were his marks?

ROSALIND. A lean cheek, which you have not; a blue eye and sunken, which you have not; an unquestionable spirit, which you have not; a beard neglected, which you have not; but I pardon you for that, for simply your having in beard is a younger brother's revenue. Then your hose should be ungarter'd, your bonnet unbanded, your sleeve unbutton'd, your shoe untied, and every thing about you demonstrating a careless desolation. But you are no such man; you are rather point-device in your accoutrements, as loving yourself than seeming the lover of any other.

ORLANDO. Fair youth, I would I could make thee believe I love.

ROSALIND. Me believe it! You may as soon make her that you love believe it; which, I warrant, she is apter to do than to confess she does. That is one of the points in the which women still give the lie to their consciences. But, in good sooth, are you he that hangs the verses on the trees wherein Rosalind is so admired?

ORLANDO. I swear to thee, youth, by the white hand of Rosalind, I am that he, that unfortunate he.

ROSALIND. But are you so much in love as your rhymes speak?

ORLANDO. Neither rhyme nor reason can express how much.

ROSALIND. Love is merely a madness; and, I tell you, deserves as well a dark house and a whip as madmen do; and the reason why they are not so punish'd and cured is that the lunacy is so ordinary that the whippers are in love too. Yet I profess curing it by counsel.

ORLANDO. Did you ever cure any so?

ROSALIND. Yes, one; and in this manner. He was to imagine me his love, his mistress; and I set him every day to woo me; at which time would I, being but a moonish youth, grieve, be effeminate, changeable, longing and liking, proud, fantastical, apish, shallow, inconstant, full of tears, full of smiles; for every passion something and for no passion truly anything, as boys and women are for the most part cattle of this colour; would now like him, now loathe him; then entertain him, then forswear him; now weep for him, then spit at him; that I drave my suitor from his mad humour of love to a living humour of madness; which was, to forswear the full stream of the world and to live in a nook merely monastic. And thus I cur'd him; and this way will I take upon me to wash your liver as clean as a sound sheep's heart, that there shall not be one spot of love in 't.

ACT III. SCENE 2

ORLANDO. I would not be cured, youth.

ROSALIND. I would cure you, if you would but call me Rosalind, and come every day to my cote and woo me.

ORLANDO. Now, by the faith of my love, I will. Tell me where it is.

ROSALIND. Go with me to it, and I'll show it you; and, by the way, you shall tell me where in the forest you live. Will you go?

ORLANDO. With all my heart, good youth.

ROSALIND. Nay, you must call me Rosalind. Come, sister, will you go? *Exeunt*

SCENE 3

The forest

Enter TOUCHSTONE *and* AUDREY; JAQUES *behind*

TOUCHSTONE. Come apace, good Audrey; I will fetch up your goats, Audrey. And how, Audrey, am I the man yet? Doth my simple feature content you?

AUDREY. Your features! Lord warrant us! What features?

TOUCHSTONE. I am here with thee and thy goats, as the most capricious poet, honest Ovid, was among the Goths.

JAQUES. [*Aside*] O knowledge ill-inhabited, worse than Jove in a thatch'd house!

TOUCHSTONE. When a man's verses cannot be understood, nor a man's good wit seconded with the forward child understanding, it strikes a man more dead than a great reckoning in a little room. Truly, I would the gods had made thee poetical.

AUDREY. I do not know what 'poetical' is. Is it honest in deed and word? Is it a true thing?

TOUCHSTONE. No, truly; for the truest poetry is the most feigning, and lovers are given to poetry; and what they swear in poetry may be said as lovers they do feign.

AUDREY. Do you wish, then, that the gods had made me poetical?

TOUCHSTONE. I do, truly, for thou swear'st to me thou art

725

honest; now, if thou wert a poet, I might have some hope thou didst feign.

AUDREY. Would you not have me honest?

TOUCHSTONE. No, truly, unless thou wert hard-favour'd; for honesty coupled to beauty is to have honey a sauce to sugar.

JAQUES. [*Aside*] A material fool!

AUDREY. Well, I am not fair; and therefore I pray the gods make me honest.

TOUCHSTONE. Truly, and to cast away honesty upon a foul slut were to put good meat into an unclean dish.

AUDREY. I am not a slut, though I thank the gods I am foul.

TOUCHSTONE. Well, praised be the gods for thy foulness; sluttishness may come hereafter. But be it as it may be, I will marry thee; and to that end I have been with Sir Oliver Martext, the vicar of the next village, who hath promis'd to meet me in this place of the forest, and to couple us.

JAQUES. [*Aside*] I would fain see this meeting.

AUDREY. Well, the gods give us joy!

TOUCHSTONE. Amen. A man may, if he were of a fearful heart, stagger in this attempt; for here we have no temple but the wood, no assembly but horn-beasts. But what though? Courage! As horns are odious, they are necessary. It is said: 'Many a man knows no end of his goods.' Right! Many a man has good horns and knows no end of them. Well, that is the dowry of his wife; 'tis none of his own getting. Horns? Even so. Poor men alone? No, no; the noblest deer hath them as huge as the rascal. Is the single man therefore blessed? No; as a wall'd town is more worthier than a village, so is the forehead of a married man more honourable than the bare brow of a bachelor; and by how much defence is better than no skill, by so much is a horn more precious than to want. Here comes Sir Oliver.

Enter SIR OLIVER MARTEXT

Sir Oliver Martext, you are well met. Will you dispatch us here under this tree, or shall we go with you to your chapel?

MARTEXT. Is there none here to give the woman?

TOUCHSTONE. I will not take her on gift of any man.

MARTEXT. Truly, she must be given, or the marriage is not lawful.

JAQUES. [*Discovering himself*] Proceed, proceed; I'll give her.

TOUCHSTONE. Good even, good Master What-ye-call't; how do you, sir? You are very well met. Goddild you for your last company. I am very glad to see you. Even a toy in hand here, sir. Nay; pray be cover'd.

JAQUES. Will you be married, motley?

TOUCHSTONE. As the ox hath his bow, sir, the horse his curb, and the falcon her bells, so man hath his desires; and as pigeons bill, so wedlock would be nibbling.

JAQUES. And will you, being a man of your breeding, be married under a bush, like a beggar? Get you to church and have a good priest that can tell you what marriage is; this fellow will but join you together as they join wainscot; then one of you will prove a shrunk panel, and like green timber warp, warp.

TOUCHSTONE. [*Aside*] I am not in the mind but I were better to be married of him than of another; for he is not like to marry me well; and not being well married, it will be a good excuse for me hereafter to leave my wife.

JAQUES. Go thou with me, and let me counsel thee.

TOUCHSTONE. Come, sweet Audrey;
We must be married or we must live in bawdry.
Farewell, good Master Oliver. Not—
          O sweet Oliver,
          O brave Oliver,
     Leave me not behind thee.
But—
          Wind away,
          Begone, I say,
   I will not to wedding with thee.
          Exeunt JAQUES, TOUCHSTONE, *and* AUDREY

MARTEXT. 'Tis no matter; ne'er a fantastical knave of them all shall flout me out of my calling.   *Exit*

SCENE 4

The forest

Enter ROSALIND *and* CELIA

ROSALIND. Never talk to me; I will weep.

CELIA. Do, I prithee; but yet have the grace to consider that tears do not become a man.

ROSALIND. But have I not cause to weep?

CELIA. As good cause as one would desire; therefore weep.

ROSALIND. His very hair is of the dissembling colour.

CELIA. Something browner than Judas's. Marry, his kisses are Judas's own children.

ROSALIND. I'faith, his hair is of a good colour.

CELIA. An excellent colour: your chestnut was ever the only colour.

ROSALIND. And his kissing is as full of sanctity as the touch of holy bread.

CELIA. He hath bought a pair of cast lips of Diana. A nun of winter's sisterhood kisses not more religiously; the very ice of chastity is in them.

ROSALIND. But why did he swear he would come this morning, and comes not?

CELIA. Nay, certainly, there is no truth in him.

ROSALIND. Do you think so?

CELIA. Yes; I think he is not a pick-purse nor a horse-stealer; but for his verity in love, I do think him as concave as a covered goblet or a worm-eaten nut.

ROSALIND. Not true in love?

CELIA. Yes, when he is in; but I think he is not in.

ROSALIND. You have heard him swear downright he was.

CELIA. 'Was' is not 'is'; besides, the oath of a lover is no stronger than the word of a tapster; they are both the confirmer of false reckonings. He attends here in the forest on the Duke, your father.

ROSALIND. I met the Duke yesterday, and had much question with him. He asked me of what parentage I was; I told him, of as good as he; so he laugh'd and let me go. But

what talk we of fathers when there is such a man as Orlando?

CELIA. O, that's a brave man! He writes brave verses, speaks
brave words, swears brave oaths, and breaks them bravely,
quite traverse, athwart the heart of his lover; as a puny
tilter, that spurs his horse but on one side, breaks his staff
like a noble goose. But all's brave that youth mounts and
folly guides. Who comes here?

Enter CORIN

CORIN. Mistress and master, you have oft enquired
After the shepherd that complain'd of love,
Who you saw sitting by me on the turf,
Praising the proud disdainful shepherdess
That was his mistress.

CELIA. Well, and what of him?

CORIN. If you will see a pageant truly play'd
Between the pale complexion of true love
And the red glow of scorn and proud disdain,
Go hence a little, and I shall conduct you,
If you will mark it.

ROSALIND. O, come, let us remove!
The sight of lovers feedeth those in love.
Bring us to this sight, and you shall say
I'll prove a busy actor in their play. *Exeunt*

SCENE 5

Another part of the forest

Enter SILVIUS *and* PHEBE

SILVIUS. Sweet Phebe, do not scorn me; do not, Phebe.
Say that you love me not; but say not so
In bitterness. The common executioner,
Whose heart th' accustom'd sight of death makes hard,
Falls not the axe upon the humbled neck
But first begs pardon. Will you sterner be
Than he that dies and lives by bloody drops?

Enter Rosalind, Celia, *and* Corin, *at a distance*

PHEBE. I would not be thy executioner;
I fly thee, for I would not injure thee.
Thou tell'st me there is murder in mine eye.
'Tis pretty, sure, and very probable,
That eyes, that are the frail'st and softest things,
Who shut their coward gates on atomies,
Should be call'd tyrants, butchers, murderers!
Now I do frown on thee with all my heart;
And if mine eyes can wound, now let them kill thee.
Now counterfeit to swoon; why, now fall down;
Or, if thou canst not, O, for shame, for shame,
Lie not, to say mine eyes are murderers.
Now show the wound mine eye hath made in thee.
Scratch thee but with a pin, and there remains
Some scar of it; lean upon a rush,
The cicatrice and capable impressure
Thy palm some moment keeps; but now mine eyes,
Which I have darted at thee, hurt thee not;
Nor, I am sure, there is not force in eyes
That can do hurt.
SILVIUS. O dear Phebe,
If ever—as that ever may be near—
You meet in some fresh cheek the power of fancy,
Then shall you know the wounds invisible
That love's keen arrows make.
PHEBE. But till that time
Come not thou near me; and when that time comes,
Afflict me with thy mocks, pity me not;
As till that time I shall not pity thee.
ROSALIND. [*Advancing*] And why, I pray you? Who might
be your mother,
That you insult, exult, and all at once,
Over the wretched? What though you have no beauty—
As, by my faith, I see no more in you
Than without candle may go dark to bed—
Must you be therefore proud and pitiless?
Why, what means this? Why do you look on me?
I see no more in you than in the ordinary

Of nature's sale-work. 'Od's my little life,
I think she means to tangle my eyes too!
No faith, proud mistress, hope not after it;
'Tis not your inky brows, your black silk hair,
Your bugle eyeballs, nor your cheek of cream,
That can entame my spirits to your worship.
You foolish shepherd, wherefore do you follow her,
Like foggy south, puffing with wind and rain?
You are a thousand times a properer man
Than she a woman. 'Tis such fools as you
That makes the world full of ill-favour'd children.
'Tis not her glass, but you, that flatters her;
And out of you she sees herself more proper
Than any of her lineaments can show her.
But, mistress, know yourself. Down on your knees,
And thank heaven, fasting, for a good man's love;
For I must tell you friendly in your ear:
Sell when you can; you are not for all markets.
Cry the man mercy, love him, take his offer;
Foul is most foul, being foul to be a scoffer.
So take her to thee, shepherd. Fare you well.
PHEBE. Sweet youth, I pray you chide a year together;
    I had rather hear you chide than this man woo.
ROSALIND. He's fall'n in love with your foulness, and she'll
    fall in love with my anger. If it be so, as fast as she answers
    thee with frowning looks, I'll sauce her with bitter words.
    Why look you so upon me?
PHEBE. For no ill will I bear you.
ROSALIND. I pray you do not fall in love with me,
    For I am falser than vows made in wine;
    Besides, I like you not. If you will know my house,
    'Tis at the tuft of olives here hard by.
    Will you go, sister? Shepherd, ply her hard.
    Come, sister. Shepherdess, look on him better,
    And be not proud; though all the world could see,
    None could be so abus'd in sight as he.
    Come, to our flock.   *Exeunt* ROSALIND, CELIA, *and* CORIN
PHEBE. Dead shepherd, now I find thy saw of might:
    'Who ever lov'd that lov'd not at first sight?'
SILVIUS. Sweet Phebe.

PHEBE. Ha! what say'st thou, Silvius?
SILVIUS. Sweet Phebe, pity me.
PHEBE. Why, I am sorry for thee, gentle Silvius.
SILVIUS. Wherever sorrow is, relief would be.
    If you do sorrow at my grief in love,
    By giving love, your sorrow and my grief
    Were both extermin'd.
PHEBE. Thou hast my love; is not that neighbourly?
SILVIUS. I would have you.
PHEBE. Why, that were covetousness.
    Silvius, the time was that I hated thee;
    And yet it is not that I bear thee love;
    But since that thou canst talk of love so well,
    Thy company, which erst was irksome to me,
    I will endure; and I'll employ thee too.
    But do not look for further recompense
    Than thine own gladness that thou art employ'd.
SILVIUS. So holy and so perfect is my love,
    And I in such a poverty of grace,
    That I shall think it a most plenteous crop
    To glean the broken ears after the man
    That the main harvest reaps; loose now and then
    A scatt'red smile, and that I'll live upon.
PHEBE. Know'st thou the youth that spoke to me erewhile?
SILVIUS. Not very well; but I have met him oft;
    And he hath bought the cottage and the bounds
    That the old carlot once was master of.
PHEBE. Think not I love him, though I ask for him;
    'Tis but a peevish boy; yet he talks well.
    But what care I for words? Yet words do well
    When he that speaks them pleases those that hear.
    It is a pretty youth—not very pretty;
    But, sure, he's proud; and yet his pride becomes him.
    He'll make a proper man. The best thing in him
    Is his complexion; and faster than his tongue
    Did make offence, his eye did heal it up.
    He is not very tall; yet for his years he's tall;
    His leg is but so-so; and yet 'tis well.
    There was a pretty redness in his lip,
    A little riper and more lusty red

Than that mix'd in his cheek; 'twas just the difference
Betwixt the constant red and mingled damask.
There be some women, Silvius, had they mark'd him
In parcels as I did, would have gone near
To fall in love with him; but, for my part,
I love him not, nor hate him not; and yet
I have more cause to hate him than to love him;
For what had he to do to chide at me?
He said mine eyes were black, and my hair black,
And, now I am rememb'red, scorn'd at me.
I marvel why I answer'd not again;
But that's all one: omittance is no quittance.
I'll write to him a very taunting letter,
And thou shalt bear it; wilt thou, Silvius?
SILVIUS. Phebe, with all my heart.
PHEBE. I'll write it straight;
The matter's in my head and in my heart;
I will be bitter with him and passing short.
Go with me, Silvius.   *Exeunt*

ACT IV. SCENE 1

The forest

Enter ROSALIND, CELIA, *and* JAQUES

JAQUES. I prithee, pretty youth, let me be better acquainted
with thee.
ROSALIND. They say you are a melancholy fellow.
JAQUES. I am so; I do love it better than laughing.
ROSALIND. Those that are in extremity of either are abominable fellows, and betray themselves to every modern censure worse than drunkards.
JAQUES. Why, 'tis good to be sad and say nothing.
ROSALIND. Why then, 'tis good to be a post.
JAQUES. I have neither the scholar's melancholy, which is
emulation; nor the musician's, which is fantastical; nor the

courtier's, which is proud; nor the soldier's, which is ambitious; nor the lawyer's, which is politic; nor the lady's, which is nice; nor the lover's, which is all these; but it is a melancholy of mine own, compounded of many simples, extracted from many objects, and, indeed, the sundry contemplation of my travels; in which my often rumination wraps me in a most humorous sadness.

ROSALIND. A traveller! By my faith, you have great reason to be sad. I fear you have sold your own lands to see other men's; then to have seen much and to have nothing is to have rich eyes and poor hands.

JAQUES. Yes, I have gain'd my experience.

Enter ORLANDO

ROSALIND. And your experience makes you sad. I had rather have a fool to make me merry than experience to make me sad—and to travel for it too.

ORLANDO. Good day, and happiness, dear Rosalind!

JAQUES. Nay, then, God buy you, an you talk in blank verse.

ROSALIND. Farewell, Monsieur Traveller; look you lisp and wear strange suits, disable all the benefits of your own country, be out of love with your nativity, and almost chide God for making you that countenance you are; or I will scarce think you have swam in a gondola. [*Exit* JAQUES] Why, how now, Orlando! where have you been all this while? You a lover! An you serve me such another trick, never come in my sight more.

ORLANDO. My fair Rosalind, I come within an hour of my promise.

ROSALIND. Break an hour's promise in love! He that will divide a minute into a thousand parts, and break but a part of the thousand part of a minute in the affairs of love, it may be said of him that Cupid hath clapp'd him o' th' shoulder, but I'll warrant him heart-whole.

ORLANDO. Pardon me, dear Rosalind.

ROSALIND. Nay, an you be so tardy, come no more in my sight. I had as lief be woo'd of a snail.

ORLANDO. Of a snail!

ROSALIND. Ay, of a snail; for though he comes slowly, he carries his house on his head—a better jointure, I think, than you make a woman; besides, he brings his destiny with him.

ORLANDO. What's that?

ROSALIND. Why, horns; which such as you are fain to be beholding to your wives for; but he comes armed in his fortune, and prevents the slander of his wife.

ORLANDO. Virtue is no horn-maker; and my Rosalind is virtuous.

ROSALIND. And I am your Rosalind.

CELIA. It pleases him to call you so; but he hath a Rosalind of a better leer than you.

ROSALIND. Come, woo me, woo me; for now I am in a holiday humour, and like enough to consent. What would you say to me now, an I were your very very Rosalind?

ORLANDO. I would kiss before I spoke.

ROSALIND. Nay, you were better speak first; and when you were gravell'd for lack of matter, you might take occasion to kiss. Very good orators, when they are out, they will spit; and for lovers lacking—God warn us!—matter, the cleanliest shift is to kiss.

ORLANDO. How if the kiss be denied?

ROSALIND. Then she puts you to entreaty, and there begins new matter.

ORLANDO. Who could be out, being before his beloved mistress?

ROSALIND. Marry, that should you, if I were your mistress; or I should think my honesty ranker than my wit.

ORLANDO. What, of my suit?

ROSALIND. Not out of your apparel, and yet out of your suit. Am not I your Rosalind?

ORLANDO. I take some joy to say you are, because I would be talking of her.

ROSALIND. Well, in her person, I say I will not have you.

ORLANDO. Then, in mine own person, I die.

ROSALIND. No, faith, die by attorney. The poor world is almost six thousand years old, and in all this time there was not any man died in his own person, videlicet, in a love-cause. Troilus had his brains dash'd out with a Grecian club; yet he did what he could to die before, and he is one of the patterns of love. Leander, he would have liv'd many

735

a fair year, though Hero had turn'd nun, if it had not been for a hot midsummer night; for, good youth, he went but forth to wash him in the Hellespont, and, being taken with the cramp, was drown'd; and the foolish chroniclers of that age found it was—Hero of Sestos. But these are all lies: men have died from time to time, and worms have eaten them, but not for love.

ORLANDO. I would not have my right Rosalind of this mind; for, I protest, her frown might kill me.

ROSALIND. By this hand, it will not kill a fly. But come, now I will be your Rosalind in a more coming-on disposition; and ask me what you will, I will grant it.

ORLANDO. Then love me, Rosalind.

ROSALIND. Yes, faith, will I, Fridays and Saturdays, and all.

ORLANDO. And wilt thou have me?

ROSALIND. Ay, and twenty such.

ORLANDO. What sayest thou?

ROSALIND. Are you not good?

ORLANDO. I hope so.

ROSALIND. Why then, can one desire too much of a good thing? Come, sister, you shall be the priest, and marry us. Give me your hand, Orlando. What do you say, sister?

ORLANDO. Pray thee, marry us.

CELIA. I cannot say the words.

ROSALIND. You must begin 'Will you, Orlando'—

CELIA. Go to. Will you, Orlando, have to wife this Rosalind?

ORLANDO. I will.

ROSALIND. Ay, but when?

ORLANDO. Why, now; as fast as she can marry us.

ROSALIND. Then you must say 'I take thee, Rosalind, for wife.'

ORLANDO. I take thee, Rosalind, for wife.

ROSALIND. I might ask you for your commission; but—I do take thee, Orlando, for my husband. There's a girl goes before the priest; and, certainly, a woman's thought runs before her actions.

ORLANDO. So do all thoughts; they are wing'd.

ROSALIND. Now tell me how long you would have her, after you have possess'd her.

ORLANDO. For ever and a day.

ROSALIND. Say 'a day' without the 'ever.' No, no, Orlando; men are April when they woo, December when they wed: maids are May when they are maids, but the sky changes when they are wives. I will be more jealous of thee than a Barbary cock-pigeon over his hen, more clamorous than a parrot against rain, more new-fangled than an ape, more giddy in my desires than a monkey. I will weep for nothing, like Diana in the fountain, and I will do that when you are dispos'd to be merry; I will laugh like a hyen, and that when thou are inclin'd to sleep.

ORLANDO. But will my Rosalind do so?

ROSALIND. By my life, she will do as I do.

ORLANDO. O, but she is wise.

ROSALIND. Or else she could not have the wit to do this. The wiser, the waywarder. Make the doors upon a woman's wit, and it will out at the casement; shut that, and 'twill out at the key-hole; stop that, 'twill fly with the smoke out at the chimney.

ORLANDO. A man that had a wife with such a wit, he might say 'Wit, whither wilt?'

ROSALIND. Nay, you might keep that check for it, till you met your wife's wit going to your neighbour's bed.

ORLANDO. And what wit could wit have to excuse that?

ROSALIND. Marry, to say she came to seek you there. You shall never take her without her answer, unless you take her without her tongue. O, that woman that cannot make her fault her husband's occasion, let her never nurse her child herself, for she will breed it like a fool!

ORLANDO. For these two hours, Rosalind, I will leave thee.

ROSALIND. Alas, dear love, I cannot lack thee two hours!

ORLANDO. I must attend the Duke at dinner; by two o'clock I will be with thee again.

ROSALIND. Ay, go your ways, go your ways. I knew what you would prove; my friends told me as much, and I thought no less. That flattering tongue of yours won me. 'Tis but one cast away, and so, come death! Two o'clock is your hour?

ORLANDO. Ay, sweet Rosalind.

ROSALIND. By my troth, and in good earnest, and so God mend me, and by all pretty oaths that are not dangerous, if you break one jot of your promise, or come one minute behind your hour, I will think you the most pathetical break-promise, and the most hollow lover, and the most unworthy of her you call Rosalind, that may be chosen out of the gross band of the unfaithful. Therefore beware my censure, and keep your promise.

ORLANDO. With no less religion than if thou wert indeed my Rosalind; so, adieu.

ROSALIND. Well, Time is the old justice that examines all such offenders, and let Time try. Adieu.   *Exit* ORLANDO

CELIA. You have simply misus'd our sex in your love-prate. We must have your doublet and hose pluck'd over your head, and show the world what the bird hath done to her own nest.

ROSALIND. O coz, coz, coz, my pretty little coz, that thou didst know how many fathom deep I am in love! But it cannot be sounded; my affection hath an unknown bottom, like the Bay of Portugal.

CELIA. Or rather, bottomless; that as fast as you pour affection in, it runs out.

ROSALIND. No; that same wicked bastard of Venus, that was begot of thought, conceiv'd of spleen, and born of madness; that blind rascally boy, that abuses every one's eyes, because his own are out—let him be judge how deep I am in love. I'll tell thee, Aliena, I cannot be out of the sight of Orlando. I'll go find a shadow, and sigh till he come.

CELIA. And I'll sleep.   *Exeunt*

SCENE 2

The forest

Enter JAQUES *and* LORDS, *in the habit of foresters*

JAQUES. Which is he that killed the deer?

LORD. Sir, it was I.

JAQUES. Let's present him to the Duke, like a Roman conqueror; and it would do well to set the deer's horns upon his head for a branch of victory. Have you no song, forester, for this purpose?

LORD. Yes, sir.

JAQUES. Sing it; 'tis no matter how it be in tune, so it make noise enough.

SONG

What shall he have that kill'd the deer?
His leather skin and horns to wear.
           [*The rest shall bear this burden:*]
    Then sing him home.

Take thou no scorn to wear the horn;
It was a crest ere thou wast born.
    Thy father's father wore it;
    And thy father bore it.
The horn, the horn, the lusty horn,
Is not a thing to laugh to scorn.   *Exeunt*

SCENE 3

The forest

Enter ROSALIND *and* CELIA

ROSALIND. How say you now? Is it not past two o'clock?
  And here much Orlando!

CELIA. I warrant you, with pure love and troubled brain, he
  hath ta'en his bow and arrows, and is gone forth—to sleep.
  Look, who comes here.

Enter SILVIUS

SILVIUS. My errand is to you, fair youth;
  My gentle Phebe did bid me give you this.
  I know not the contents; but, as I guess
  By the stern brow and waspish action
  Which she did use as she was writing of it,
  It bears an angry tenour. Pardon me,
  I am but as a guiltless messenger.

ROSALIND. Patience herself would startle at this letter,
  And play the swaggerer. Bear this, bear all.
  She says I am not fair, that I lack manners;
  She calls me proud, and that she could not love me,

Were man as rare as Phœnix. 'Od's my will!
Her love is not the hare that I do hunt;
Why writes she so to me? Well, shepherd, well,
This is a letter of your own device.
SILVIUS. No, I protest, I know not the contents;
Phebe did write it.
ROSALIND. Come, come, you are a fool,
And turn'd into the extremity of love.
I saw her hand; she has a leathern hand,
A freestone-colour'd hand; I verily did think
That her old gloves were on, but 'twas her hands;
She has a huswife's hand—but that's no matter.
I say she never did invent this letter:
This is a man's invention, and his hand.
SILVIUS. Sure, it is hers.
ROSALIND. Why, 'tis a boisterous and a cruel style;
A style for challengers. Why, she defies me,
Like Turk to Christian. Women's gentle brain
Could not drop forth such giant-rude invention,
Such Ethiope words, blacker in their effect
Than in their countenance. Will you hear the letter?
SILVIUS. So please you, for I never heard it yet;
Yet heard too much of Phebe's cruelty.
ROSALIND. She Phebes me: mark how the tyrant writes.
[*Reads*]

'Art thou god to shepherd turn'd,
    That a maiden's heart hath burn'd?'

Can a woman rail thus?
SILVIUS. Call you this railing?
ROSALIND.   'Why, thy godhead laid apart,
    Warr'st thou with a woman's heart?'

Did you ever hear such railing?

'Whiles the eye of man did woo me,
    That could do no vengeance to me.'

Meaning me a beast.

'If the scorn of your bright eyne
Have power to raise such love in mine,
Alack, in me what strange effect

740

Would they work in mild aspect!
Whiles you chid me, I did love;
How then might your prayers move!
He that brings this love to thee
Little knows this love in me;
And by him seal up thy mind,
Whether that thy youth and kind
Will the faithful offer take
Of me and all that I can make;
Or else by him my love deny,
And then I'll study how to die.'

SILVIUS. Call you this chiding?
CELIA. Alas, poor shepherd!
ROSALIND. Do you pity him? No, he deserves no pity. Wilt thou love such a woman? What, to make thee an instrument, and play false strains upon thee! Not to be endur'd! Well, go your way to her, for I see love hath made thee a tame snake, and say this to her—that if she love me, I charge her to love thee; if she will not, I will never have her unless thou entreat for her. If you be a true lover, hence, and not a word; for here comes more company.

Exit SILVIUS

Enter OLIVER

OLIVER. Good morrow, fair ones; pray you, if you know,
Where in the purlieus of this forest stands
A sheep-cote fenc'd about with olive trees?
CELIA. West of this place, down in the neighbour bottom.
The rank of osiers by the murmuring stream
Left on your right hand brings you to the place.
But at this hour the house doth keep itself;
There's none within.
OLIVER. If that an eye may profit by a tongue,
Then should I know you by description—
Such garments, and such years: 'The boy is fair,
Of female favour, and bestows himself
Like a ripe sister; the woman low,
And browner than her brother.' Are not you
The owner of the house I did inquire for?
CELIA. It is no boast, being ask'd, to say we are.

741

OLIVER. Orlando doth commend him to you both;
And to that youth he calls his Rosalind
He sends this bloody napkin. Are you he?
ROSALIND. I am. What must we understand by this?
OLIVER. Some of my shame; if you will know of me
What man I am, and how, and why, and where,
This handkercher was stain'd.
CELIA. I pray you, tell it.
OLIVER. When last the young Orlando parted from you,
He left a promise to return again
Within an hour; and, pacing through the forest,
Chewing the food of sweet and bitter fancy,
Lo, what befell! He threw his eye aside,
And mark what object did present itself.
Under an oak, whose boughs were moss'd with age,
And high top bald with dry antiquity,
A wretched ragged man, o'ergrown with hair,
Lay sleeping on his back. About his neck
A green and gilded snake had wreath'd itself,
Who with her head nimble in threats approach'd
The opening of his mouth; but suddenly,
Seeing Orlando, it unlink'd itself,
And with indented glides did slip away
Into a bush; under which bush's shade
A lioness, with udders all drawn dry,
Lay couching, head on ground, with catlike watch,
When that the sleeping man should stir; for 'tis
The royal disposition of that beast
To prey on nothing that doth seem as dead.
This seen, Orlando did approach the man,
And found it was his brother, his elder brother.
CELIA. O, I have heard him speak of that same brother;
And he did render him the most unnatural
That liv'd amongst men.
OLIVER. And well he might so do,
For well I know he was unnatural.
ROSALIND. But, to Orlando: did he leave him there,
Food to the suck'd and hungry lioness?
OLIVER. Twice did he turn his back, and purpos'd so;
But kindness, nobler ever than revenge,

And nature, stronger than his just occasion,
Made him give battle to the lioness,
Who quickly fell before him; in which hurtling
From miserable slumber I awak'd.

CELIA. Are you his brother?

ROSALIND. Was't you he rescu'd?

CELIA. Was't you that did so oft contrive to kill him?

OLIVER. 'Twas I; but 'tis not I. I do not shame
    To tell you what I was, since my conversion
    So sweetly tastes, being the thing I am.

ROSALIND. But for the bloody napkin?

OLIVER. By and by.
    When from the first to last, betwixt us two,
    Tears our recountments had most kindly bath'd,
    As how I came into that desert place—
    In brief, he led me to the gentle Duke,
    Who gave me fresh array and entertainment,
    Committing me unto my brother's love;
    Who led me instantly unto his cave,
    There stripp'd himself, and here upon his arm
    The lioness had torn some flesh away,
    Which all this while had bled; and now he fainted,
    And cried, in fainting, upon Rosalind.
    Brief, I recover'd him, bound up his wound,
    And, after some small space, being strong at heart,
    He sent me hither, stranger as I am,
    To tell this story, that you might excuse
    His broken promise, and to give this napkin,
    Dy'd in his blood, unto the shepherd youth
    That he in sport doth call his Rosalind.

                                [ROSALIND *swoons*]

CELIA. Why, how now, Ganymede! sweet Ganymede!

OLIVER. Many will swoon when they do look on blood.

CELIA. There is more in it. Cousin Ganymede!

OLIVER. Look, he recovers.

ROSALIND. I would I were at home.

CELIA. We'll lead you thither.
    I pray you, will you take him by the arm?

OLIVER. Be of good cheer, youth. You a man!
    You lack a man's heart.

The Foresters' Song   (ACT IV. SCENE II)

ACT IV. SCENE 3

ROSALIND. I do so, I confess it. Ah, sirrah, a body would think this was well counterfeited. I pray you tell your brother how well I counterfeited. Heigh-ho!

OLIVER. This was not counterfeit; there is too great testimony in your complexion that it was a passion of earnest.

ROSALIND. Counterfeit, I assure you.

OLIVER. Well then, take a good heart and counterfeit to be a man.

ROSALIND. So I do; but, i' faith, I should have been a woman by right.

CELIA. Come, you look paler and paler; pray you draw homewards. Good sir, go with us.

OLIVER. That will I, for I must bear answer back
How you excuse my brother, Rosalind.

ROSALIND. I shall devise something; but, I pray you, commend my counterfeiting to him. Will you go? *Exeunt*

ACT V. SCENE 1

The forest

Enter TOUCHSTONE *and* AUDREY

TOUCHSTONE. We shall find a time, Audrey; patience, gentle Audrey.

AUDREY. Faith, the priest was good enough, for all the old gentleman's saying.

TOUCHSTONE. A most wicked Sir Oliver, Audrey, a most vile Martext. But, Audrey, there is a youth here in the forest lays claim to you.

AUDREY. Ay, I know who 'tis; he hath no interest in me in the world; here comes the man you mean.

Enter WILLIAM

TOUCHSTONE. It is meat and drink to me to see a clown. By my troth, we that have good wits have much to answer for: we shall be flouting; we cannot hold.

WILLIAM. Good ev'n, Audrey.

AUDREY. God ye good ev'n, William.

WILLIAM. And good ev'n to you, sir.

TOUCHSTONE. Good ev'n, gentle friend. Cover thy head, cover thy head; nay, prithee be cover'd. How old are you, friend?

WILLIAM. Five and twenty, sir.

TOUCHSTONE. A ripe age. Is thy name William?

WILLIAM. William, sir.

TOUCHSTONE. A fair name. Wast born i' th' forest here?

WILLIAM. Ay, sir, I thank God.

TOUCHSTONE. 'Thank God.' A good answer. Art rich?

WILLIAM. Faith, sir, so so.

TOUCHSTONE. 'So so' is good, very good, very excellent good; and yet it is not; it is but so so. Art thou wise?

WILLIAM. Ay, sir, I have a pretty wit.

TOUCHSTONE. Why, thou say'st well. I do now remember a saying: 'The fool doth think he is wise, but the wise man knows himself to be a fool.' The heathen philosopher, when he had a desire to eat a grape, would open his lips when he put it into his mouth; meaning thereby that grapes were made to eat and lips to open. You do love this maid?

WILLIAM. I do, sir.

TOUCHSTONE. Give me your hand. Art thou learned?

WILLIAM. No, sir.

TOUCHSTONE. Then learn this of me: to have is to have; for it is a figure in rhetoric that drink, being pour'd out of a cup into a glass, by filling the one doth empty the other; for all your writers do consent that ipse is he; now, you are not ipse, for I am he.

WILLIAM. Which he, sir?

TOUCHSTONE. He, sir, that must marry this woman. Therefore, you clown, abandon—which is in the vulgar leave—the society—which in the boorish is company—of this female—which in the common is woman—which together is: abandon the society of this female; or, clown, thou perishest; or, to thy better understanding, diest; or, to wit, I kill thee, make thee away, translate thy life into death, thy liberty into bondage. I will deal in poison with thee, or in bastinado, or in steel; I will bandy with thee in faction; I will o'er-run thee with policy; I will kill thee a hundred and fifty ways; therefore tremble and depart.

AUDREY. Do, good William.

WILLIAM. God rest you merry, sir.   *Exit*

Enter CORIN

CORIN. Our master and mistress seeks you; come away, away.

TOUCHSTONE. Trip, Audrey, trip, Audrey. I attend, I attend.

Exeunt

SCENE 2

The forest

Enter ORLANDO *and* OLIVER

ORLANDO. Is't possible that on so little acquaintance you should like her? that but seeing you should love her? and loving woo? and, wooing, she should grant? and will you persever to enjoy her?

OLIVER. Neither call the giddiness of it in question, the poverty of her, the small acquaintance, my sudden wooing, nor her sudden consenting; but say with me, I love Aliena; say with her that she loves me; consent with both that we may enjoy each other. It shall be to your good; for my father's house and all the revenue that was old Sir Rowland's will I estate upon you, and here live and die a shepherd.

ORLANDO. You have my consent. Let your wedding be tomorrow. Thither will I invite the Duke and all's contented followers. Go you and prepare Aliena; for, look you, here comes my Rosalind.

Enter ROSALIND

ROSALIND. God save you, brother.

OLIVER. And you, fair sister.   *Exit*

ROSALIND. O, my dear Orlando, how it grieves me to see thee wear thy heart in a scarf!

ORLANDO. It is my arm.

747

ROSALIND. I thought thy heart had been wounded with the claws of a lion.

ORLANDO. Wounded it is, but with the eyes of a lady.

ROSALIND. Did your brother tell you how I counterfeited to swoon when he show'd me your handkercher?

ORLANDO. Ay, and greater wonders than that.

ROSALIND. O, I know where you are. Nay, 'tis true. There was never any thing so sudden but the fight of two rams and Cæsar's thrasonical brag of 'I came, saw, and overcame.' For your brother and my sister no sooner met but they look'd; no sooner look'd but they lov'd; no sooner lov'd but they sigh'd; no sooner sigh'd but they ask'd one another the reason; no sooner knew the reason but they sought the remedy—and in these degrees have they made a pair of stairs to marriage, which they will climb incontinent, or else be incontinent before marriage. They are in the very wrath of love, and they will together. Clubs cannot part them.

ORLANDO. They shall be married to-morrow; and I will bid the Duke to the nuptial. But, O, how bitter a thing it is to look into happiness through another man's eyes! By so much the more shall I to-morrow be at the height of heart-heaviness, by how much I shall think my brother happy in having what he wishes for.

ROSALIND. Why, then, to-morrow I cannot serve your turn for Rosalind?

ORLANDO. I can live no longer by thinking.

ROSALIND. I will weary you, then, no longer with idle talking. Know of me then—for now I speak to some purpose—that I know you are a gentleman of good conceit. I speak not this that you should bear a good opinion of my knowledge, insomuch I say I know you are; neither do I labour for a greater esteem than may in some little measure draw a belief from you, to do yourself good, and not to grace me. Believe then, if you please, that I can do strange things. I have, since I was three year old, convers'd with a magician, most profound in his art and yet not damnable. If you do love Rosalind so near the heart as your gesture cries it out, when your brother marries Aliena shall you marry her. I know into what straits of fortune she is driven; and

it is not impossible to me, if it appear not inconvenient to
you, to set her before your eyes to-morrow, human as she
is, and without any danger.

ORLANDO. Speak'st thou in sober meanings?

ROSALIND. By my life, I do; which I tender dearly, though I
say I am a magician. Therefore put you in your best array,
bid your friends; for if you will be married to-morrow,
you shall; and to Rosalind, if you will.

Enter SILVIUS *and* PHEBE

Look, here comes a lover of mine, and a lover of hers.

PHEBE. Youth, you have done me much ungentleness
To show the letter that I writ to you.

ROSALIND. I care not if I have. It is my study
To seem despiteful and ungentle to you.
You are there follow'd by a faithful shepherd;
Look upon him, love him; he worships you.

PHEBE. Good shepherd, tell this youth what 'tis to love.

SILVIUS. It is to be all made of sighs and tears;
And so am I for Phebe.

PHEBE. And I for Ganymede.

ORLANDO. And I for Rosalind.

ROSALIND. And I for no woman.

SILVIUS. It is to be all made of faith and service;
And so am I for Phebe.

PHEBE. And I for Ganymede.

ORLANDO. And I for Rosalind.

ROSALIND. And I for no woman.

SILVIUS. It is to be all made of fantasy,
All made of passion, and all made of wishes;
All adoration, duty, and observance,
All humbleness, all patience, and impatience,
All purity, all trial, all obedience;
And so am I for Phebe.

PHEBE. And so am I for Ganymede.

ORLANDO. And so am I for Rosalind.

ROSALIND. And so am I for no woman.

PHEBE. If this be so, why blame you me to love you?

SILVIUS. If this be so, why blame you me to love you?

ORLANDO. If this be so, why blame you me to love you?

ROSALIND. Why do you speak too, 'Why blame you me to love you?'

ORLANDO. To her that is not here, nor doth not hear.

ROSALIND. Pray you, no more of this; 'tis like the howling of Irish wolves against the moon. [*To* SILVIUS] I will help you if I can. [*To* PHEBE] I would love you if I could.— To-morrow meet me all together. [*To* PHEBE] I will marry you if ever I marry woman, and I'll be married to-morrow. [*To* ORLANDO] I will satisfy you if ever I satisfied man, and you shall be married to-morrow. [*To* SILVIUS] I will content you if what pleases you contents you, and you shall be married to-morrow. [*To* ORLANDO] As you love Rosalind, meet. [*To* SILVIUS] As you love Phebe, meet;— and as I love no woman, I'll meet. So, fare you well; I have left you commands.

SILVIUS. I'll not fail, if I live.

PHEBE. Nor I.

ORLANDO. Nor I.   *Exeunt*

SCENE 3

The forest

Enter TOUCHSTONE *and* AUDREY

TOUCHSTONE. To-morrow is the joyful day, Audrey; to-morrow will we be married.

AUDREY. I do desire it with all my heart; and I hope it is no dishonest desire to desire to be a woman of the world. Here come two of the banish'd Duke's pages.

Enter two PAGES

FIRST PAGE. Well met, honest gentleman.

TOUCHSTONE. By my troth, well met. Come sit, sit, and a song.

SECOND PAGE. We are for you; sit i' th' middle.

FIRST PAGE. Shall we clap into't roundly, without hawking, or spitting, or saying we are hoarse, which are the only prologues to a bad voice?

SECOND PAGE. I'faith, i'faith; and both in a tune, like two gipsies on a horse.

SONG

It was a lover and his lass,
 With a hey, and a ho, and a hey nonino,
That o'er the green corn-field did pass
 In the spring time, the only pretty ring time,
When birds do sing, hey ding a ding, ding.
Sweet lovers love the spring.

Between the acres of the rye,
 With a hey, and a ho, and a hey nonino,
These pretty country folks would lie,
 In the spring time, &c.

This carol they began that hour,
 With a hey, and a ho, and a hey nonino,
How that a life was but a flower,
 In the spring time, &c.

And therefore take the present time,
 With a hey, and a ho, and a hey nonino,
For love is crowned with the prime,
 In the spring time, &c.

TOUCHSTONE. Truly, young gentlemen, though there was no great matter in the ditty, yet the note was very untuneable.

FIRST PAGE. You are deceiv'd, sir; we kept time, we lost not our time.

TOUCHSTONE. By my troth, yes; I count it but time lost to hear such a foolish song. God buy you; and God mend your voices. Come, Audrey. *Exeunt*

SCENE 4

The forest

Enter DUKE SENIOR, AMIENS, JAQUES, ORLANDO, OLIVER, *and* CELIA

DUKE SENIOR. Dost thou believe, Orlando, that the boy Can do all this that he hath promised?

751

ORLANDO. I sometimes do believe and sometimes do not:
As those that fear they hope, and know they fear.

Enter ROSALIND, SILVIUS, *and* PHEBE

ROSALIND. Patience once more, whiles our compact is urg'd:
You say, if I bring in your Rosalind,
You will bestow her on Orlando here?
DUKE SENIOR. That would I, had I kingdoms to give with
her.
ROSALIND. And you say you will have her when I bring her?
ORLANDO. That would I, were I of all kingdoms king.
ROSALIND. You say you'll marry me, if I be willing?
PHEBE. That will I, should I die the hour after.
ROSALIND. But if you do refuse to marry me,
You'll give yourself to this most faithful shepherd?
PHEBE. So is the bargain.
ROSALIND. You say that you'll have Phebe, if she will?
SILVIUS. Though to have her and death were both one thing.
ROSALIND. I have promis'd to make all this matter even.
Keep you your word, O Duke, to give your daughter;
You yours, Orlando, to receive his daughter;
Keep your word, Phebe, that you'll marry me,
Or else, refusing me, to wed this shepherd;
Keep your word, Silvius, that you'll marry her
If she refuse me; and from hence I go,
To make these doubts all even.
                                   Exeunt ROSALIND *and* CELIA
DUKE SENIOR. I do remember in this shepherd boy
Some lively touches of my daughter's favour.
ORLANDO. My lord, the first time that I ever saw him
Methought he was a brother to your daughter.
But, my good lord, this boy is forest-born,
And hath been tutor'd in the rudiments
Of many desperate studies by his uncle,
Whom he reports to be a great magician,
Obscured in the circle of this forest.

Enter TOUCHSTONE *and* AUDREY

JAQUES. There is, sure, another flood toward, and these

couples are coming to the ark. Here comes a pair of very
strange beasts which in all tongues are call'd fools.

TOUCHSTONE. Salutation and greeting to you all!

JAQUES. Good my lord, bid him welcome. This is the motley-
minded gentleman that I have so often met in the forest.
He hath been a courtier, he swears.

TOUCHSTONE. If any man doubt that, let him put me to my
purgation. I have trod a measure; I have flatt'red a lady;
I have been politic with my friend, smooth with mine
enemy; I have undone three tailors; I have had four quarrels, and like to have fought one.

JAQUES. And how was that ta'en up?

TOUCHSTONE. Faith, we met, and found the quarrel was upon
the seventh cause.

JAQUES. How seventh cause? Good my lord, like this fellow.

DUKE SENIOR. I like him very well.

TOUCHSTONE. God 'ild you, sir; I desire you of the like. I
press in here, sir, amongst the rest of the country copula-
tives, to swear and to forswear, according as marriage
binds and blood breaks. A poor virgin, sir, an ill-favour'd
thing, sir, but mine own; a poor humour of mine, sir, to
take that that no man else will. Rich honesty dwells like
a miser, sir, in a poor house; as your pearl in your foul
oyster.

DUKE SENIOR. By my faith, he is very swift and sententious.

TOUCHSTONE. According to the fool's bolt, sir, and such
dulcet diseases.

JAQUES. But, for the seventh cause: how did you find the
quarrel on the seventh cause?

TOUCHSTONE. Upon a lie seven times removed—bear your
body more seeming, Audrey—as thus, sir. I did dislike the
cut of a certain courtier's beard; he sent me word, if I said
his beard was not cut well, he was in the mind it was. This
is call'd the Retort Courteous. If I sent him word again
it was not well cut, he would send me word he cut it to
please himself. This is call'd the Quip Modest. If again it
was not well cut, he disabled my judgment. This is call'd
the Reply Churlish. If again it was not well cut, he would
answer I spake not true. This is call'd the Reproof Valiant.
If again it was not well cut, he would say I lie. This is

call'd the Countercheck Quarrelsome. And so to the Lie
Circumstantial and the Lie Direct.

JAQUES. And how oft did you say his beard was not well
cut?

TOUCHSTONE. I durst go no further than the Lie Circumstantial, nor he durst not give me the Lie Direct; and so we
measur'd swords and parted.

JAQUES. Can you nominate in order now the degrees of the
lie?

TOUCHSTONE. O, sir, we quarrel in print by the book, as you
have books for good manners. I will name you the degrees.
The first, the Retort Courteous; the second, the Quip
Modest; the third, the Reply Churlish; the fourth, the Reproof Valiant; the fifth, the Countercheck Quarrelsome;
the sixth, the Lie with Circumstance; the seventh, the Lie
Direct. All these you may avoid but the Lie Direct; and
you may avoid that too with an If. I knew when seven
justices could not take up a quarrel; but when the parties
were met themselves, one of them thought but of an If, as:
'If you said so, then I said so.' And they shook hands, and
swore brothers. Your If is the only peace-maker; much
virtue in If.

JAQUES. Is not this a rare fellow, my lord?
He's as good at any thing, and yet a fool.

DUKE SENIOR. He uses his folly like a stalking-horse, and
under the presentation of that he shoots his wit.

Enter HYMEN, ROSALIND, *and* CELIA. *Still music*

HYMEN.   Then is there mirth in heaven,
           When earthly things made even
               Atone together.
           Good Duke, receive thy daughter;
           Hymen from heaven brought her,
               Yea, brought her hither,
           That thou mightst join her hand with his,
           Whose heart within his bosom is.

ROSALIND. [*To* DUKE] To you I give myself, for I am yours.
    [*To* ORLANDO] To you I give myself, for I am yours.

DUKE SENIOR. If there be truth in sight, you are my daughter.

ORLANDO. If there be truth in sight, you are my Rosalind.

PHEBE. If sight and shape be true,
  Why then, my love adieu!
ROSALIND. I'll have no father, if you be not he;
  I'll have no husband, if you be not he;
  Nor ne'er wed woman, if you be not she.
HYMEN.   Peace, ho! I bar confusion;
      'Tis I must make conclusion
        Of these most strange events.
      Here's eight that must take hands
      To join in Hymen's bands,
        If truth holds true contents.
      You and you no cross shall part;
      You and you are heart in heart;
      You to his love must accord,
      Or have a woman to your lord;
      You and you are sure together,
      As the winter to foul weather.
      Whiles a wedlock-hymn we sing,
      Feed yourselves with questioning,
      That reason wonder may diminish,
      How thus we met, and these things finish.

SONG

      Wedding is great Juno's crown;
        O blessed bond of board and bed!
      'Tis Hymen peoples every town;
        High wedlock then be honoured.
      Honour, high honour, and renown,
      To Hymen, god of every town!

DUKE SENIOR. O my dear niece, welcome thou art to me!
  Even daughter, welcome in no less degree.
PHEBE. I will not eat my word, now thou art mine;
  Thy faith my fancy to thee doth combine.

Enter JAQUES DE BOYS

JAQUES DE BOYS. Let me have audience for a word or two.
  I am the second son of old Sir Rowland,
  That bring these tidings to this fair assembly.
  Duke Frederick, hearing how that every day

Men of great worth resorted to this forest,
Address'd a mighty power; which were on foot,
In his own conduct, purposely to take
His brother here, and put him to the sword;
And to the skirts of this wild wood he came,
Where, meeting with an old religious man,
After some question with him, was converted
Both from his enterprise and from the world;
His crown bequeathing to his banish'd brother,
And all their lands restor'd to them again
That were with him exil'd. This to be true
I do engage my life.
DUKE SENIOR. Welcome, young man.
Thou offer'st fairly to thy brothers' wedding:
To one, his lands withheld; and to the other,
A land itself at large, a potent dukedom.
First, in this forest let us do those ends
That here were well begun and well begot;
And after, every of this happy number,
That have endur'd shrewd days and nights with us,
Shall share the good of our returned fortune,
According to the measure of their states.
Meantime, forget this new-fall'n dignity,
And fall into our rustic revelry.
Play, music; and you brides and bridegrooms all,
With measure heap'd in joy, to th' measures fall.
JAQUES. Sir, by your patience. If I heard you rightly,
The Duke hath put on a religious life,
And thrown into neglect the pompous court.
JAQUES DE BOYS. He hath.
JAQUES. To him will I. Out of these convertites
There is much matter to be heard and learn'd.
[*To* DUKE] You to your former honour I bequeath;
Your patience and your virtue well deserves it.
[*To* ORLANDO] You to a love that your true faith doth
  merit;
[*To* OLIVER] You to your land, and love, and great allies;
[*To* SILVIUS] You to a long and well-deserved bed;
[*To* TOUCHSTONE] And you to wrangling; for thy loving
  voyage

Is but for two months victuall'd.—So to your pleasures;
I am for other than for dancing measures.
DUKE SENIOR. Stay, Jaques, stay.
JAQUES. To see no pastime I. What you would have
I'll stay to know at your abandon'd cave.　　　　　*Exit*
DUKE SENIOR. Proceed, proceed. We will begin these rites,
As we do trust they'll end, in true delights.
　　　　　　　　　　　　　[A dance]　*Exeunt*

EPILOGUE

ROSALIND. It is not the fashion to see the lady the epilogue;
but it is no more unhandsome than to see the lord the prologue. If it be true that good wine needs no bush, 'tis true
that a good play needs no epilogue. Yet to good wine they
do use good bushes; and good plays prove the better by
the help of good epilogues. What a case am I in then, that
am neither a good epilogue, nor cannot insinuate with you
in the behalf of a good play! I am not furnish'd like a beggar; therefore to beg will not become me. My way is to
conjure you; and I'll begin with the women. I charge you,
O women, for the love you bear to men, to like as much of
this play as please you; and I charge you, O men, for the
love you bear to women—as I perceive by your simp'ring
none of you hates them—that between you and the women
the play may please. If I were a woman, I would kiss as
many of you as had beards that pleas'd me, complexions
that lik'd me, and breaths that I defied not; and, I am sure,
as many as have good beards, or good faces, or sweet
breaths, will, for my kind offer, when I make curtsy, bid
me farewell.

The Taming of the Shrew

THE TAMING OF THE SHREW

IN 1594 there appeared in quarto a play called *The Taming of a Shrew*. Twenty years later Shakespeare's colleagues printed *The Shrew* in the First Folio. What is the relation of these plays to each other?

Three answers have been given: one, that *a Shrew* is a play that Shakespeare took over from some earlier dramatist and rewrote as *The Shrew;* two, that both *a Shrew* and *The Shrew* are descended from a lost Shrew play; three, that *a Shrew* is nothing more than a surreptitious version of *The Shrew* put together by someone who had seen Shakespeare's comedy.

That *a Shrew* is not an original play but the ill-digested fragments of an earlier version, its many confusions clearly demonstrate; to explain this muddled imitation by inventing a third play as the original seems superfluous as Shakespeare's *The Shrew* is by itself sufficient to explain the features of the fraudulent version. It is true there are some minor confusions in *The Shrew* but not of a kind that warrant the creation of a completely unknown play to explain them. What slight confusion there is arises from the complexities Shakespeare himself created by combining two very distinct sources to form his action.

For that part of his plot that centres in Bianca the dramatist found his idea in a comedy by Ariosto or in an English translation of the Italian original. Ariosto's comedy *I Suppositi* was a verse revision of his prose original. George Gascoigne published an English version with the title *The Supposes*. Here we have the lover who disguises himself as a servant to have access to the daughter of the house. His servant disguised as his master pretends to offer himself as a wooer of the lady, and hopes by this device to protect her from other suitors. He has however to bring forward his own father to guarantee his offers to the girl's father; naturally a pretending parent has to be found and as in Shakespeare the arrival of the young master's real father exposes the conspiracy but ratifies the lovers' bargain.

With this intrigue which in *The Shrew* has Bianca as its

PETRUCHIO. *Nay, come again,*
Good Kate; I am a gentleman
(ACT II. SCENE I)

object, Shakespeare combined the Petruchio-Katherina affair. Bianca and Katherina are now sisters and Shakespeare has cleverly dovetailed the two parts together. The taming part of the play has given offence to those who feel that it makes a hero of a rather brutal fortune-hunting character. But Petruchio belongs to a type that Shakespeare enjoyed repeating in his early years, the anti-romantic who is really more romantic than those who delight in the vocabulary rather than in the realities of romance; and the wager that he wins over the others at the end is the token of something more than the triumph of selfishness and brutality.

To prevent all misunderstanding Shakespeare represents his play as performed before a deluded tinker. The Prologue or Induction opening with the quarrel between Sly and the hostess of the tavern must have had as a pendant a final scene in which the tinker restored to his rags and wakened from his dream of greatness exchanges reproaches once more with his hostess before returning to encounter his own domestic problem. Such an epilogue is preserved however imperfectly in the Bad Quarto, and this report for all its obvious faults allows us to see how Shakespeare must have ended his entertainment. The absence of this finale from the Folio must be due to carelessness or some error in the handling of the copy; that it once formed part of Shakespeare's play there need be no doubt.

The play may be assigned to an early stage in Shakespeare's development as a dramatist. When Lord Strange's company (later the Chamberlain's and then the King's men) returned from touring the provinces in 1594 and, with the passing of the plague, re-established themselves in London, they opened with a short season of plays by Shakespeare that included *The Shrew, Hamlet* in an early version, and *Titus Andronicus.* These pieces were not new, and doubtless went back to the years before 1592-4, for from 1592 the theatres were closed during the severest plague of Elizabeth's reign. In its boisterous knockabout situations *The Shrew* resembles *The Comedy of Errors.* Yet in spite of these primitive features *The Shrew* is still a successful stage piece. Shakespeare contrived to mix with his farce something that gives it a lasting or ever-renewed youthfulness and brio.

INTRODUCTION

The stage-history of *The Taming of the Shrew* provides an admirable illustration of the adaptation to which so many of Shakespeare's plays have been subjected during the centuries since the dramatist's death. Till this century few actors thought it necessary or desirable to present the plays as the text directed; interpretations, transpositions, as well as the inevitable cuts, were the rule rather than the exception. Some plays were largely rewritten and into this group fell *The Shrew*.

When Pepys saw *The Shrew*, after the Restoration, he found the language of the principal part hardly intelligible, for what was then performed was an adaptation called *Sauny the Scott, or The Taming of the Shrew* in which the part of Grumio was enlarged and played in a dialect that baffled Pepys. Yet this version that contained much additional horseplay and fooling was in its day as successful as *Kiss Me Kate*, the most recent adaptation of Shakespeare's original.

A LORD
CHRISTOPHER SLY, *a tinker*
HOSTESS, PAGE, PLAYERS, } *Persons in the Induction*
    HUNTSMEN, SERVANTS

BAPTISTA MINOLA, *a gentleman of Padua*
VINCENTIO, *a merchant of Pisa*
LUCENTIO, *son to Vincentio, in love with Bianca*
PETRUCHIO, *a gentleman of Verona, a suitor to Katherina*
GREMIO } *suitors to Bianca*
HORTENSIO
TRANIO } *servants to Lucentio*
BIONDELLO
GRUMIO } *servants to Petruchio*
CURTIS
A PEDANT

KATHERINA, *the shrew* } *daughters to Baptista*
BIANCA
A WIDOW

Tailor, Haberdasher, *and* Servants *attending on* Baptista *and Petruchio*

SCENE:

Padua, and PETRUCHIO's *house in the country*

The Taming of the Shrew

INDUCTION. SCENE 1

Before an alehouse on a heath

Enter HOSTESS *and* SLY

SLY. I'll pheeze you, in faith.

HOSTESS. A pair of stocks, you rogue!

SLY. Y'are a baggage; the Slys are no rogues. Look in the chronicles: we came in with Richard Conqueror. Therefore, paucas pallabris; let the world slide. Sessa!

HOSTESS. You will not pay for the glasses you have burst?

SLY. No, not a denier. Go by, Saint Jeronimy, go to thy cold bed and warm thee.

HOSTESS. I know my remedy; I must go fetch the third-borough. *Exit*

SLY. Third, or fourth, or fifth borough, I'll answer him by law. I'll not budge an inch, boy; let him come, and kindly.

[*Falls asleep*]

Wind horns. Enter a LORD *from hunting, with his train*

LORD. Huntsman, I charge thee, tender well my hounds;
Brach Merriman, the poor cur, is emboss'd;
And couple Clowder with the deep-mouth'd brach.
Saw'st thou not, boy, how Silver made it good
At the hedge corner, in the coldest fault?
I would not lose the dog for twenty pound.

FIRST HUNTSMAN. Why, Belman is as good as he, my lord;
He cried upon it at the merest loss,
And twice to-day pick'd out the dullest scent;
Trust me, I take him for the better dog.

LORD. Thou art a fool; if Echo were as fleet,
I would esteem him worth a dozen such.
But sup them well, and look unto them all;
To-morrow I intend to hunt again.

765

FIRST HUNTSMAN. I will, my lord.

LORD. What's here? One dead, or drunk?
See, doth he breathe?

SECOND HUNTSMAN. He breathes, my lord. Were he not
warm'd with ale,
This were a bed but cold to sleep so soundly.

LORD. O monstrous beast, how like a swine he lies!
Grim death, how foul and loathsome is thine image!
Sirs, I will practise on this drunken man.
What think you, if he were convey'd to bed,
Wrapp'd in sweet clothes, rings put upon his fingers,
A most delicious banquet by his bed,
And brave attendants near him when he wakes,
Would not the beggar then forget himself?

FIRST HUNTSMAN. Believe me, lord, I think he cannot choose.

SECOND HUNTSMAN. It would seem strange unto him when
he wak'd.

LORD. Even as a flatt'ring dream or worthless fancy.
Then take him up, and manage well the jest:
Carry him gently to my fairest chamber,
And hang it round with all my wanton pictures;
Balm his foul head in warm distilled waters,
And burn sweet wood to make the lodging sweet;
Procure me music ready when he wakes,
To make a dulcet and a heavenly sound;
And if he chance to speak, be ready straight,
And with a low submissive reverence
Say 'What is it your honour will command?'
Let one attend him with a silver basin
Full of rose-water and bestrew'd with flowers;
Another bear the ewer, the third a diaper,
And say 'Will't please your lordship cool your hands?'
Some one be ready with a costly suit,
And ask him what apparel he will wear;
Another tell him of his hounds and horse,
And that his lady mourns at his disease;
Persuade him that he hath been lunatic,
And, when he says he is, say that he dreams,
For he is nothing but a mighty lord.
This do, and do it kindly, gentle sirs;

It will be pastime passing excellent,
  If it be husbanded with modesty.
FIRST HUNTSMAN. My lord, I warrant you we will play our
  part
  As he shall think by our true diligence
  He is no less than what we say he is.
LORD. Take him up gently, and to bed with him;
  And each one to his office when he wakes.
                    [SLY *is carried out. A trumpet sounds*]
  Sirrah, go see what trumpet 'tis that sounds—
                                        Exit SERVANT
  Belike some noble gentleman that means,
  Travelling some journey, to repose him here.

              Re-enter a SERVINGMAN

  How now! who is it?
SERVANT. An't please your honour, players
  That offer service to your lordship.
LORD. Bid them come near.

              Enter PLAYERS

  Now, fellows, you are welcome.
PLAYERS. We thank your honour.
LORD. Do you intend to stay with me to-night?
PLAYER. So please your lordship to accept our duty.
LORD. With all my heart. This fellow I remember
  Since once he play'd a farmer's eldest son;
  'Twas where you woo'd the gentlewoman so well.
  I have forgot your name; but, sure, that part
  Was aptly fitted and naturally perform'd.
PLAYER. I think 'twas Soto that your honour means.
LORD. 'Tis very true; thou didst it excellent.
  Well, you are come to me in happy time,
  The rather for I have some sport in hand
  Wherein your cunning can assist me much.
  There is a lord will hear you play to-night;
  But I am doubtful of your modesties,
  Lest, over-eying of his odd behaviour,
  For yet his honour never heard a play,
  You break into some merry passion

767

And so offend him; for I tell you, sirs,
If you should smile, he grows impatient.
PLAYER. Fear not, my lord; we can contain ourselves,
Were he the veriest antic in the world.
LORD. Go, sirrah, take them to the buttery,
And give them friendly welcome every one;
Let them want nothing that my house affords.

Exit one with the PLAYERS

Sirrah, go you to Barthol'mew my page,
And see him dress'd in all suits like a lady;
That done, conduct him to the drunkard's chamber,
And call him 'madam,' do him obeisance.
Tell him from me—as he will win my love—
He bear himself with honourable action,
Such as he hath observ'd in noble ladies
Unto their lords, by them accomplished;
Such duty to the drunkard let him do,
With soft low tongue and lowly courtesy,
And say 'What is't your honour will command,
Wherein your lady and your humble wife
May show her duty and make known her love?'
And then with kind embracements, tempting kisses,
And with declining head into his bosom,
Bid him shed tears, as being overjoyed
To see her noble lord restor'd to health,
Who for this seven years hath esteemed him
No better than a poor and loathsome beggar.
And if the boy have not a woman's gift
To rain a shower of commanded tears,
An onion will do well for such a shift,
Which, in a napkin being close convey'd,
Shall in despite enforce a watery eye.
See this dispatch'd with all the haste thou canst;
Anon I'll give thee more instructions. *Exit a* SERVINGMAN
I know the boy will well usurp the grace,
Voice, gait, and action, of a gentlewoman;
I long to hear him call the drunkard 'husband';
And how my men will stay themselves from laughter
When they do homage to this simple peasant.
I'll in to counsel them; haply my presence

May well abate the over-merry spleen,
Which otherwise would grow into extremes.   *Exeunt*

SCENE 2

A bedchamber in the LORD's *house*

Enter aloft SLY, *with* ATTENDANTS; *some with apparel, basin
and ewer, and other appurtenances; and* LORD

SLY. For God's sake, a pot of small ale.

FIRST SERVANT. Will't please your lordship drink a cup of
sack?

SECOND SERVANT. Will't please your honour taste of these
conserves?

THIRD SERVANT. What raiment will your honour wear to-
day?

SLY. I am Christophero Sly; call not me 'honour' nor 'lordship.' I ne'er drank sack in my life; and if you give me any
conserves, give me conserves of beef. Ne'er ask me what
raiment I'll wear, for I have no more doublets than backs,
no more stockings than legs, nor no more shoes than feet
—nay, sometime more feet than shoes, or such shoes as my
toes look through the overleather.

LORD. Heaven cease this idle humour in your honour!
O, that a mighty man of such descent,
Of such possessions, and so high esteem,
Should be infused with so foul a spirit!

SLY. What, would you make me mad? Am not I Christopher
Sly, old Sly's son of Burton Heath; by birth a pedlar, by
education a cardmaker, by transmutation a bear-herd, and
now by present profession a tinker? Ask Marian Hacket,
the fat ale-wife of Wincot, if she know me not; if she say
I am not fourteen pence on the score for sheer ale, score
me up for the lying'st knave in Christendom. What! I am
not bestraught. [*Taking a pot of ale*] Here's—

THIRD SERVANT. O, this it is that makes your lady mourn!

SECOND SERVANT. O, this is it that makes your servants
droop!

LORD. Hence comes it that your kindred shuns your house,

769

As beaten hence by your strange lunacy.
O noble lord, bethink thee of thy birth!
Call home thy ancient thoughts from banishment,
And banish hence these abject lowly dreams.
Look how thy servants do attend on thee,
Each in his office ready at thy beck.
Wilt thou have music? Hark! Apollo plays,   [*Music*]
And twenty caged nightingales do sing.
Or wilt thou sleep? We'll have thee to a couch
Softer and sweeter than the lustful bed
On purpose trimm'd up for Semiramis.
Say thou wilt walk: we will bestrew the ground.
Or wilt thou ride? Thy horses shall be trapp'd,
Their harness studded all with gold and pearl.
Dost thou love hawking? Thou hast hawks will soar
Above the morning lark. Or wilt thou hunt?
Thy hounds shall make the welkin answer them
And fetch shrill echoes from the hollow earth.
FIRST SERVANT. Say thou wilt course; thy greyhounds are as swift
   As breathed stags; ay, fleeter than the roe.
SECOND SERVANT. Dost thou love pictures? We will fetch thee straight
   Adonis painted by a running brook,
   And Cytherea all in sedges hid,
   Which seem to move and wanton with her breath
   Even as the waving sedges play wi' th' wind.
LORD. We'll show thee Io as she was a maid
   And how she was beguiled and surpris'd,
   As lively painted as the deed was done.
THIRD SERVANT. Or Daphne roaming through a thorny wood,
   Scratching her legs, that one shall swear she bleeds
   And at that sight shall sad Apollo weep,
   So workmanly the blood and tears are drawn.
LORD. Thou art a lord, and nothing but a lord.
   Thou hast a lady far more beautiful
   Than any woman in this waning age.
FIRST SERVANT. And, till the tears that she hath shed for thee
   Like envious floods o'er-run her lovely face,

770

She was the fairest creature in the world;
And yet she is inferior to none.
SLY. Am I a lord and have I such a lady?
Or do I dream? Or have I dream'd till now?
I do not sleep: I see, I hear, I speak;
I smell sweet savours, and I feel soft things.
Upon my life, I am a lord indeed,
And not a tinker, nor Christopher Sly.
Well, bring our lady hither to our sight;
And once again, a pot o' th' smallest ale.
SECOND SERVANT. Will't please your Mightiness to wash your
    hands?
O, how we joy to see your wit restor'd!
O, that once more you knew but what you are!
These fifteen years you have been in a dream;
Or, when you wak'd, so wak'd as if you slept.
SLY. These fifteen years! by my fay, a goodly nap.
But did I never speak of all that time?
FIRST SERVANT. O, yes, my lord, but very idle words;
For though you lay here in this goodly chamber,
Yet would you say ye were beaten out of door;
And rail upon the hostess of the house,
And say you would present her at the leet,
Because she brought stone jugs and no seal'd quarts.
Sometimes you would call out for Cicely Hacket.
SLY. Ay, the woman's maid of the house.
THIRD SERVANT. Why, sir, you know no house nor no such
    maid,
Nor no such men as you have reckon'd up,
As Stephen Sly, and old John Naps of Greece,
And Peter Turph, and Henry Pimpernell;
And twenty more such names and men as these,
Which never were, nor no man ever saw.
SLY. Now, Lord be thanked for my good amends!
ALL. Amen.

Enter the PAGE *as a lady, with* ATTENDANTS

SLY. I thank thee; thou shalt not lose by it.
PAGE. How fares my noble lord?
SLY. Marry, I fare well; for here is cheer enough.

771

Where is my wife?

PAGE. Here, noble lord; what is thy will with her?

SLY. Are you my wife, and will not call me husband?
My men should call me 'lord'; I am your goodman.

PAGE. My husband and my lord, my lord and husband;
I am your wife in all obedience.

SLY. I know it well. What must I call her?

LORD. Madam.

SLY. Al'ce madam, or Joan madam?

LORD. Madam, and nothing else; so lords call ladies.

SLY. Madam wife, they say that I have dream'd
And slept above some fifteen year or more.

PAGE. Ay, and the time seems thirty unto me,
Being all this time abandon'd from your bed.

SLY. 'Tis much. Servants, leave me and her alone.

Exeunt SERVANTS

Madam, undress you, and come now to bed.

PAGE. Thrice noble lord, let me entreat of you
To pardon me yet for a night or two;
Or, if not so, until the sun be set.
For your physicians have expressly charg'd,
In peril to incur your former malady,
That I should yet absent me from your bed.
I hope this reason stands for my excuse.

SLY. Ay, it stands so that I may hardly tarry so long. But I
would be loath to fall into my dreams again. I will therefore tarry in despite of the flesh and the blood.

Enter a MESSENGER

MESSENGER. Your honour's players, hearing your amend-
ment,
Are come to play a pleasant comedy;
For so your doctors hold it very meet,
Seeing too much sadness hath congeal'd your blood,
And melancholy is the nurse of frenzy.
Therefore they thought it good you hear a play
And frame your mind to mirth and merriment,
Which bars a thousand harms and lengthens life.

SLY. Marry, I will; let them play it. Is not a comonty a
Christmas gambold or a tumbling-trick?

PAGE. No, my good lord, it is more pleasing stuff.
SLY. What, household stuff?
PAGE. It is a kind of history.
SLY. Well, we'll see't. Come, madam wife, sit by my side
and let the world slip; we shall ne'er be younger.
[*They sit down*]
A flourish of trumpets announces the play

ACT I. SCENE 1

Padua. A public place

Enter LUCENTIO *and his man* TRANIO

LUCENTIO. Tranio, since for the great desire I had
To see fair Padua, nursery of arts,
I am arriv'd for fruitful Lombardy,
The pleasant garden of great Italy,
And by my father's love and leave am arm'd
With his good will and thy good company,
My trusty servant well approv'd in all,
Here let us breathe, and haply institute
A course of learning and ingenious studies.
Pisa, renowned for grave citizens,
Gave me my being and my father first,
A merchant of great traffic through the world,
Vincentio, come of the Bentivolii;
Vincentio's son, brought up in Florence,
It shall become to serve all hopes conceiv'd,
To deck his fortune with his virtuous deeds.
And therefore, Tranio, for the time I study,
Virtue and that part of philosophy
Will I apply that treats of happiness
By virtue specially to be achiev'd.
Tell me thy mind; for I have Pisa left
And am to Padua come as he that leaves
A shallow plash to plunge him in the deep,
And with satiety seeks to quench his thirst.

773

TRANIO. Mi perdonato, gentle master mine;
I am in all affected as yourself;
Glad that you thus continue your resolve
To suck the sweets of sweet philosophy.
Only, good master, while we do admire
This virtue and this moral discipline,
Let's be no Stoics nor no stocks, I pray,
Or so devote to Aristotle's checks
As Ovid be an outcast quite abjur'd.
Balk logic with acquaintance that you have,
And practise rhetoric in your common talk;
Music and poesy use to quicken you;
The mathematics and the metaphysics,
Fall to them as you find your stomach serves you.
No profit grows where is no pleasure ta'en;
In brief, sir, study what you most affect.
LUCENTIO. Gramercies, Tranio, well dost thou advise.
If, Biondello, thou wert come ashore,
We could at once put us in readiness,
And take a lodging fit to entertain
Such friends as time in Padua shall beget.

Enter BAPTISTA *with his two daughters,* KATHERINA
and BIANCA; GREMIO, *a pantaloon;* HORTENSIO,
suitor to BIANCA. LUCENTIO *and* TRANIO *stand by*

But stay awhile; what company is this?
TRANIO. Master, some show to welcome us to town.
BAPTISTA. Gentlemen, importune me no farther,
For how I firmly am resolv'd you know;
That is, not to bestow my youngest daughter
Before I have a husband for the elder.
If either of you both love Katherina,
Because I know you well and love you well,
Leave shall you have to court her at your pleasure.
GREMIO. To cart her rather. She's too rough for me.
There, there, Hortensio, will you any wife?
KATHERINA. [*To* BAPTISTA] I pray you, sir, is it your will
To make a stale of me amongst these mates?
HORTENSIO. Mates, maid! How mean you that? No mates
for you,

774

Unless you were of gentler, milder mould.
KATHERINA. I' faith, sir, you shall never need to fear;
Iwis it is not halfway to her heart;
But if it were, doubt not her care should be
To comb your noddle with a three-legg'd stool,
And paint your face, and use you like a fool.
HORTENSIO. From all such devils, good Lord deliver us!
GREMIO. And me, too, good Lord!
TRANIO. Husht, master! Here's some good pastime toward;
That wench is stark mad or wonderful froward.
LUCENTIO. But in the other's silence do I see
Maid's mild behaviour and sobriety.
Peace, Tranio!
TRANIO. Well said, master; mum! and gaze your fill.
BAPTISTA. Gentlemen, that I may soon make good
What I have said—Bianca, get you in;
And let it not displease thee, good Bianca,
For I will love thee ne'er the less, my girl.
KATHERINA. A pretty peat! it is best
Put finger in the eye, an she knew why.
BIANCA. Sister, content you in my discontent.
Sir, to your pleasure humbly I subscribe;
My books and instruments shall be my company,
On them to look, and practise by myself.
LUCENTIO. Hark, Tranio, thou mayst hear Minerva speak!
HORTENSIO. Signior Baptista, will you be so strange?
Sorry am I that our good will effects
Bianca's grief.
GREMIO. Why will you mew her up,
Signior Baptista, for this fiend of hell,
And make her bear the penance of her tongue?
BAPTISTA. Gentlemen, content ye; I am resolv'd.
Go in, Bianca. _Exit_ BIANCA
And for I know she taketh most delight
In music, instruments, and poetry,
Schoolmasters will I keep within my house
Fit to instruct her youth. If you, Hortensio,
Or, Signior Gremio, you, know any such,
Prefer them hither; for to cunning men
I will be very kind, and liberal

To mine own children in good bringing-up;
And so, farewell. Katherina, you may stay;
For I have more to commune with Bianca. *Exit*

KATHERINA. Why, and I trust I may go too, may I not?
What! shall I be appointed hours, as though, belike,
I knew not what to take and what to leave? Ha! *Exit*

GREMIO. You may go to the devil's dam; your gifts are so good here's none will hold you. There! Love is not so great, Hortensio, but we may blow our nails together, and fast it fairly out; our cake's dough on both sides. Farewell; yet, for the love I bear my sweet Bianca, if I can by any means light on a fit man to teach her that wherein she delights, I will wish him to her father.

HORTENSIO. So will I, Signior Gremio; but a word, I pray. Though the nature of our quarrel yet never brook'd parle, know now, upon advice, it toucheth us both—that we may yet again have access to our fair mistress, and be happy rivals in Bianca's love—to labour and effect one thing specially.

GREMIO. What's that, I pray?

HORTENSIO. Marry, sir, to get a husband for her sister.

GREMIO. A husband? a devil.

HORTENSIO. I say a husband.

GREMIO. I say a devil. Think'st thou, Hortensio, though her father be very rich, any man is so very a fool to be married to hell?

HORTENSIO. Tush, Gremio! Though it pass your patience and mine to endure her loud alarums, why, man, there be good fellows in the world, an a man could light on them, would take her with all faults, and money enough.

GREMIO. I cannot tell; but I had as lief take her dowry with this condition: to be whipp'd at the high cross every morning.

HORTENSIO. Faith, as you say, there's small choice in rotten apples. But, come; since this bar in law makes us friends, it shall be so far forth friendly maintain'd till by helping Baptista's eldest daughter to a husband we set his youngest free for a husband, and then have to't afresh. Sweet Bianca! Happy man be his dole! He that runs fastest gets the ring. How say you, Signior Gremio?

GREMIO. I am agreed; and would I had given him the best

horse in Padua to begin his wooing that would thoroughly
woo her, wed her, and bed her, and rid the house of her!
Come on.   *Exeunt* Gremio *and* Hortensio
Tranio. I pray, sir, tell me, is it possible
  That love should of a sudden take such hold?
Lucentio. O Tranio, till I found it to be true,
  I never thought it possible or likely.
  But see! while idly I stood looking on,
  I found the effect of love in idleness;
  And now in plainness do confess to thee,
  That art to me as secret and as dear
  As Anna to the Queen of Carthage was—
  Tranio, I burn, I pine, I perish, Tranio,
  If I achieve not this young modest girl.
  Counsel me, Tranio, for I know thou canst;
  Assist me, Tranio, for I know thou wilt.
Tranio. Master, it is no time to chide you now;
  Affection is not rated from the heart;
  If love have touch'd you, nought remains but so:
  'Redime te captum quam queas minimo.'
Lucentio. Gramercies, lad. Go forward; this contents;
  The rest will comfort, for thy counsel's sound.
Tranio. Master, you look'd so longly on the maid.
  Perhaps you mark'd not what's the pith of all.
Lucentio. O, yes, I saw sweet beauty in her face,
  Such as the daughter of Agenor had,
  That made great Jove to humble him to her hand,
  When with his knees he kiss'd the Cretan strand.
Tranio. Saw you no more? Mark'd you not how her sister
  Began to scold and raise up such a storm
  That mortal ears might hardly endure the din?
Lucentio. Tranio, I saw her coral lips to move,
  And with her breath she did perfume the air;
  Sacred and sweet was all I saw in her.
Tranio. Nay, then 'tis time to stir him from his trance.
  I pray, awake, sir. If you love the maid,
  Bend thoughts and wits to achieve her. Thus it stands:
  Her elder sister is so curst and shrewd
  That, till the father rid his hands of her,
  Master, your love must live a maid at home;

And therefore has he closely mew'd her up,
Because she will not be annoy'd with suitors.
LUCENTIO. Ah, Tranio, what a cruel father's he!
But art thou not advis'd he took some care
To get her cunning schoolmasters to instruct her?
TRANIO. Ay, marry, am I, sir, and now 'tis plotted.
LUCENTIO. I have it, Tranio.
TRANIO. Master, for my hand,
Both our inventions meet and jump in one.
LUCENTIO. Tell me thine first.
TRANIO. You will be schoolmaster,
And undertake the teaching of the maid—
That's your device.
LUCENTIO. It is. May it be done?
TRANIO. Not possible; for who shall bear your part
And be in Padua here Vincentio's son;
Keep house and ply his book, welcome his friends,
Visit his countrymen, and banquet them?
LUCENTIO. Basta, content thee, for I have it full.
We have not yet been seen in any house,
Nor can we be distinguish'd by our faces
For man or master. Then it follows thus:
Thou shalt be master, Tranio, in my stead,
Keep house and port and servants, as I should;
I will some other be—some Florentine,
Some Neapolitan, or meaner man of Pisa.
'Tis hatch'd, and shall be so. Tranio, at once
Uncase thee; take my colour'd hat and cloak.
When Biondello comes, he waits on thee;
But I will charm him first to keep his tongue.
TRANIO. So had you need.   [*They exchange habits*]
In brief, sir, sith it your pleasure is,
And I am tied to be obedient—
For so your father charg'd me at our parting:
'Be serviceable to my son' quoth he,
Although I think 'twas in another sense—
I am content to be Lucentio,
Because so well I love Lucentio.
LUCENTIO. Tranio, be so because Lucentio loves;
And let me be a slave t' achieve that maid

Whose sudden sight hath thrall'd my wounded eye.

Enter BIONDELLO

Here comes the rogue. Sirrah, where have you been?
BIONDELLO. Where have I been! Nay, how now! where are
  you?
  Master, has my fellow Tranio stol'n your clothes?
  Or you stol'n his? or both? Pray, what's the news?
LUCENTIO. Sirrah, come hither; 'tis no time to jest,
  And therefore frame your manners to the time.
  Your fellow Tranio here, to save my life,
  Puts my apparel and my count'nance on,
  And I for my escape have put on his;
  For in a quarrel since I came ashore
  I kill'd a man, and fear I was descried.
  Wait you on him, I charge you, as becomes,
  While I make way from hence to save my life.
  You understand me?
BIONDELLO. I, sir? Ne'er a whit.
LUCENTIO. And not a jot of Tranio in your mouth:
  Tranio is chang'd into Lucentio.
BIONDELLO. The better for him; would I were so too!
TRANIO. So could I, faith, boy, to have the next wish after,
  That Lucentio indeed had Baptista's youngest daughter.
  But, sirrah, not for my sake but your master's, I advise
  You use your manners discreetly in all kind of companies.
  When I am alone, why, then I am Tranio;
  But in all places else your master Lucentio.
LUCENTIO. Tranio, let's go.
  One thing more rests, that thyself execute—
  To make one among these wooers. If thou ask me why—
  Sufficeth, my reasons are both good and weighty. *Exeunt*

The Presenters above speak

FIRST SERVANT. My lord, you nod; you do not mind the play.
SLY. Yes, by Saint Anne do I. A good matter, surely; comes
  there any more of it?
PAGE. My lord, 'tis but begun.

SLY. 'Tis a very excellent piece of work, madam lady.
Would 'twere done!   [*They sit and mark*]

SCENE 2

Padua. Before HORTENSIO's *house*

Enter PETRUCHIO *and his man* GRUMIO

PETRUCHIO. Verona, for a while I take my leave,
To see my friends in Padua; but of all
My best beloved and approved friend,
Hortensio; and I trow this is his house.
Here, sirrah Grumio, knock, I say.
GRUMIO. Knock, sir! Whom should I knock?
Is there any man has rebus'd your worship?
PETRUCHIO. Villain, I say, knock me here soundly.
GRUMIO. Knock you here, sir? Why, sir, what am I, sir, that
I should knock you here, sir?
PETRUCHIO. Villain, I say, knock me at this gate,
And rap me well, or I'll knock your knave's pate.
GRUMIO. My master is grown quarrelsome. I should knock
you first,
And then I know after who comes by the worst.
PETRUCHIO. Will it not be?
Faith, sirrah, an you'll not knock I'll ring it;
I'll try how you can sol-fa, and sing it.
                        [*He wrings him by the ears*]
GRUMIO. Help, masters, help! My master is mad.
PETRUCHIO. Now knock when I bid you, sirrah villain!

Enter HORTENSIO

HORTENSIO. How now! what's the matter? My old friend
Grumio and my good friend Petruchio! How do you all at
Verona?
PETRUCHIO. Signior Hortensio, come you to part the fray?
'Con tutto il cuore ben trovato' may I say.
HORTENSIO. Alla nostra casa ben venuto,
Molto honorato signor mio Petrucio.
Rise, Grumio, rise; we will compound this quarrel.

GRUMIO. Nay, 'tis no matter, sir, what he 'leges in Latin.
If this be not a lawful cause for me to leave his service—
look you, sir: he bid me knock him and rap him soundly,
sir. Well, was it fit for a servant to use his master so; being,
perhaps, for aught I see, two and thirty, a pip out?
Whom would to God I had well knock'd at first,
Then had not Grumio come by the worst.

PETRUCHIO. A senseless villain! Good Hortensio,
I bade the rascal knock upon your gate,
And could not get him for my heart to do it.

GRUMIO. Knock at the gate? O heavens! Spake you not
these words plain: 'Sirrah knock me here, rap me here,
knock me well, and knock me soundly'? And come you
now with 'knocking at the gate'?

PETRUCHIO. Sirrah, be gone, or talk not, I advise you.

HORTENSIO. Petruchio, patience; I am Grumio's pledge;
Why, this's a heavy chance 'twixt him and you,
Your ancient, trusty, pleasant servant Grumio.
And tell me now, sweet friend, what happy gale
Blows you to Padua here from old Verona?

PETRUCHIO. Such wind as scatters young men through the
world
To seek their fortunes farther than at home,
Where small experience grows. But in a few,
Signior Hortensio, thus it stands with me:
Antonio, my father, is deceas'd,
And I have thrust myself into this maze,
Haply to wive and thrive as best I may;
Crowns in my purse I have, and goods at home,
And so am come abroad to see the world.

HORTENSIO. Petruchio, shall I then come roundly to thee
And wish thee to a shrewd ill-favour'd wife?
Thou'dst thank me but a little for my counsel,
And yet I'll promise thee she shall be rich,
And very rich; but th'art too much my friend,
And I'll not wish thee to her.

PETRUCHIO. Signior Hortensio, 'twixt such friends as we
Few words suffice; and therefore, if thou know
One rich enough to be Petruchio's wife,
As wealth is burden of my wooing dance,

Be she as foul as was Florentius' love,
As old as Sibyl, and as curst and shrewd
As Socrates' Xanthippe or a worse—
She moves me not, or not removes, at least,
Affection's edge in me, were she as rough
As are the swelling Adriatic seas.
I come to wive it wealthily in Padua;
If wealthily, then happily in Padua.
GRUMIO. Nay, look you, sir, he tells you flatly what his
mind is. Why, give him gold enough and marry him to a
puppet or an aglet-baby, or an old trot with ne'er a tooth
in her head, though she has as many diseases as two and
fifty horses. Why, nothing comes amiss, so money comes
withal.
HORTENSIO. Petruchio, since we are stepp'd thus far in,
I will continue that I broach'd in jest.
I can, Petruchio, help thee to a wife
With wealth enough, and young and beauteous;
Brought up as best becomes a gentlewoman;
Her only fault, and that is faults enough,
Is—that she is intolerable curst,
And shrewd and froward so beyond all measure
That, were my state far worser than it is,
I would not wed her for a mine of gold.
PETRUCHIO. Hortensio, peace! thou know'st not gold's effect.
Tell me her father's name, and 'tis enough;
For I will board her though she chide as loud
As thunder when the clouds in autumn crack.
HORTENSIO. Her father is Baptista Minola,
An affable and courteous gentleman;
Her name is Katherina Minola,
Renown'd in Padua for her scolding tongue.
PETRUCHIO. I know her father, though I know not her;
And he knew my deceased father well.
I will not sleep, Hortensio, till I see her;
And therefore let me be thus bold with you
To give you over at this first encounter,
Unless you will accompany me thither.
GRUMIO. I pray you, sir, let him go while the humour lasts.
O' my word, and she knew him as well as I do, she would

think scolding would do little good upon him. She may perhaps call him half a score knaves or so. Why, that's nothing; and he begin once, he'll rail in his rope-tricks. I'll tell you what, sir: an she stand him but a little, he will throw a figure in her face, and so disfigure her with it that she shall have no more eyes to see withal than a cat. You know him not, sir.

HORTENSIO. Tarry, Petruchio, I must go with thee,
For in Baptista's keep my treasure is.
He hath the jewel of my life in hold,
His youngest daughter, beautiful Bianca;
And her withholds from me, and other more,
Suitors to her and rivals in my love;
Supposing it a thing impossible—
For those defects I have before rehears'd—
That ever Katherina will be woo'd.
Therefore this order hath Baptista ta'en,
That none shall have access unto Bianca
Till Katherine the curst have got a husband.

GRUMIO. Katherine the curst!
A title for a maid of all titles the worst.

HORTENSIO. Now shall my friend Petruchio do me grace,
And offer me disguis'd in sober robes
To old Baptista as a schoolmaster
Well seen in music, to instruct Bianca;
That so I may by this device at least
Have leave and leisure to make love to her,
And unsuspected court her by herself.

Enter GREMIO *with* LUCENTIO *disguised as* CAMBIO

GRUMIO. Here's no knavery! See, to beguile the old folks, how the young folks lay their heads together! Master, master, look about you. Who goes there, ha?

HORTENSIO. Peace, Grumio! It is the rival of my love. Petruchio, stand by awhile.

GRUMIO. A proper stripling, and an amorous!

[They stand aside]

GREMIO. O, very well; I have perus'd the note.
Hark you, sir; I'll have them very fairly bound—
All books of love, see that at any hand;

And see you read no other lectures to her.
You understand me—over and beside
Signior Baptista's liberality,
I'll mend it with a largess. Take your paper too,
And let me have them very well perfum'd;
For she is sweeter than perfume itself
To whom they go to. What will you read to her?
LUCENTIO. Whate'er I read to her, I'll plead for you
  As for my patron, stand you so assur'd,
  As firmly as yourself were still in place;
  Yea, and perhaps with more successful words
  Than you, unless you were a scholar, sir.
GREMIO. O this learning, what a thing it is!
GRUMIO. O this woodcock, what an ass it is!
PETRUCHIO. Peace, sirrah!
HORTENSIO. Grumio, mum!   [Coming forward]
  God save you, Signior Gremio!
GREMIO. And you are well met, Signior Hortensio.
  Trow you whither I am going? To Baptista Minola.
  I promis'd to enquire carefully
  About a schoolmaster for the fair Bianca;
  And by good fortune I have lighted well
  On this young man; for learning and behaviour
  Fit for her turn, well read in poetry
  And other books—good ones, I warrant ye.
HORTENSIO. 'Tis well; and I have met a gentleman
  Hath promis'd me to help me to another,
  A fine musician to instruct our mistress;
  So shall I no whit be behind in duty
  To fair Bianca, so beloved of me.
GREMIO. Beloved of me—and that my deeds shall prove.
GRUMIO. And that his bags shall prove.
HORTENSIO. Gremio, 'tis now no time to vent our love.
  Listen to me, and if you speak me fair
  I'll tell you news indifferent good for either.
  Here is a gentleman whom by chance I met,
  Upon agreement from us to his liking,
  Will undertake to woo curst Katherine;
  Yea, and to marry her, if her dowry please.
GREMIO. So said, so done, is well.

784

Hortensio, have you told him all her faults?

PETRUCHIO. I know she is an irksome brawling scold;
If that be all, masters, I hear no harm.

GREMIO. No, say'st me so, friend? What countryman?

PETRUCHIO. Born in Verona, old Antonio's son.
My father dead, my fortune lives for me;
And I do hope good days and long to see.

GREMIO. O sir, such a life with such a wife were strange!
But if you have a stomach, to't a God's name;
You shall have me assisting you in all.
But will you woo this wild-cat?

PETRUCHIO. Will I live?

GRUMIO. Will he woo her? Ay, or I'll hang her.

PETRUCHIO. Why came I hither but to that intent?
Think you a little din can daunt mine ears?
Have I not in my time heard lions roar?
Have I not heard the sea, puff'd up with winds,
Rage like an angry boar chafed with sweat?
Have I not heard great ordnance in the field,
And heaven's artillery thunder in the skies?
Have I not in a pitched battle heard
Loud 'larums, neighing steeds, and trumpets' clang?
And do you tell me of a woman's tongue,
That gives not half so great a blow to hear
As will a chestnut in a farmer's fire?
Tush! tush! fear boys with bugs.

GRUMIO. For he fears none.

GREMIO. Hortensio, hark:
This gentleman is happily arriv'd,
My mind presumes, for his own good and ours.

HORTENSIO. I promis'd we would be contributors
And bear his charge of wooing, whatsoe'er.

GREMIO. And so we will—provided that he win her.

GRUMIO. I would I were as sure of a good dinner.

Enter TRANIO, *bravely apparelled as* LUCENTIO,
and BIONDELLO

TRANIO. Gentlemen, God save you! If I may be bold,
Tell me, I beseech you, which is the readiest way
To the house of Signior Baptista Minola?

BIONDELLO. He that has the two fair daughters; is't he you
  mean?
TRANIO. Even he, Biondello.
GREMIO. Hark you, sir, you mean not her to—
TRANIO. Perhaps him and her, sir; what have you to do?
PETRUCHIO. Not her that chides, sir, at any hand, I pray.
TRANIO. I love no chiders, sir. Biondello, let's away.
LUCENTIO. [*Aside*] Well begun, Tranio.
HORTENSIO. Sir, a word ere you go.
  Are you a suitor to the maid you talk of, yea or no?
TRANIO. And if I be, sir, is it any offence?
GREMIO. No; if without more words you will get you hence.
TRANIO. Why, sir, I pray, are not the streets as free
  For me as for you?
GREMIO. But so is not she.
TRANIO. For what reason, I beseech you?
GREMIO. For this reason, if you'll know,
  That she's the choice love of Signior Gremio.
HORTENSIO. That she's the chosen of Signior Hortensio.
TRANIO. Softly, my masters! If you be gentlemen,
  Do me this right—hear me with patience.
  Baptista is a noble gentleman,
  To whom my father is not all unknown,
  And, were his daughter fairer than she is,
  She may more suitors have, and me for one.
  Fair Leda's daughter had a thousand wooers;
  Then well one more may fair Bianca have;
  And so she shall: Lucentio shall make one,
  Though Paris came in hope to speed alone.
GREMIO. What, this gentleman will out-talk us all!
LUCENTIO. Sir, give him head; I know he'll prove a jade.
PETRUCHIO. Hortensio, to what end are all these words?
HORTENSIO. Sir, let me be so bold as ask you,
  Did you yet ever see Baptista's daughter?
TRANIO. No, sir, but hear I do that he hath two:
  The one as famous for a scolding tongue
  As is the other for beauteous modesty.
PETRUCHIO. Sir, sir, the first's for me; let her go by.
GREMIO. Yea, leave that labour to great Hercules,
  And let it be more than Alcides' twelve.

786

PETRUCHIO. Sir, understand you this of me, in sooth:
The youngest daughter, whom you hearken for,
Her father keeps from all access of suitors,
And will not promise her to any man
Until the elder sister first be wed.
The younger then is free, and not before.
TRANIO. If it be so, sir, that you are the man
Must stead us all, and me amongst the rest;
And if you break the ice, and do this feat,
Achieve the elder, set the younger free
For our access—whose hap shall be to have her
Will not so graceless be to be ingrate.
HORTENSIO. Sir, you say well, and well you do conceive;
And since you do profess to be a suitor,
You must, as we do, gratify this gentleman,
To whom we all rest generally beholding.
TRANIO. Sir, I shall not be slack; in sign whereof,
Please ye we may contrive this afternoon,
And quaff carouses to our mistress' health;
And do as adversaries do in law—
Strive mightily, but eat and drink as friends.
GRUMIO, BIONDELLO. O excellent motion! Fellows, let's be
gone.
HORTENSIO. The motion's good indeed, and be it so.
Petruchio, I shall be your ben venuto.   *Exeunt*

ACT II. SCENE 1

Padua. BAPTISTA's *house*

Enter KATHERINA *and* BIANCA

BIANCA. Good sister, wrong me not, nor wrong yourself,
To make a bondmaid and a slave of me—
That I disdain; but for these other gawds,
Unbind my hands, I'll pull them off myself,
Yea, all my raiment, to my petticoat;

Or what you will command me will I do,
So well I know my duty to my elders.
KATHERINA. Of all thy suitors here I charge thee tell
Whom thou lov'st best. See thou dissemble not.
BIANCA. Believe me, sister, of all the men alive
I never yet beheld that special face
Which I could fancy more than any other.
KATHERINA. Minion, thou liest. Is't not Hortensio?
BIANCA. If you affect him, sister, here I swear
I'll plead for you myself but you shall have him.
KATHERINA. O then, belike, you fancy riches more:
You will have Gremio to keep you fair.
BIANCA. Is it for him you do envy me so?
Nay, then you jest; and now I well perceive
You have but jested with me all this while.
I prithee, sister Kate, untie my hands.
KATHERINA. [Strikes her] If that be jest, then all the rest was
so.

Enter BAPTISTA

BAPTISTA. Why, how now, dame! Whence grows this inso-
lence?
Bianca, stand aside—poor girl! she weeps.
[*He unbinds her*]
Go ply thy needle; meddle not with her.
For shame, thou hilding of a devilish spirit,
Why dost thou wrong her that did ne'er wrong thee?
When did she cross thee with a bitter word?
KATHERINA. Her silence flouts me, and I'll be reveng'd.
[*Flies after* BIANCA]
BAPTISTA. What, in my sight? Bianca, get thee in.
Exit BIANCA
KATHERINA. What, will you not suffer me? Nay, now I see
She is your treasure, she must have a husband;
I must dance bare-foot on her wedding-day,
And for your love to her lead apes in hell.
Talk not to me; I will go sit and weep,
Till I can find occasion of revenge.   *Exit* KATHERINA
BAPTISTA. Was ever gentleman thus griev'd as I?
But who comes here?

ACT II. SCENE 1

Enter GREMIO, *with* LUCENTIO *in the habit of a mean man;* PETRUCHIO, *with* HORTENSIO *as a musician; and* TRANIO, *as* LUCENTIO, *with his boy,* BIONDELLO, *bearing a lute and books*

GREMIO. Good morrow, neighbour Baptista.
BAPTISTA. Good morrow, neighbour Gremio.
  God save you, gentlemen!
PETRUCHIO. And you, good sir! Pray, have you not a daughter
  ter
  Call'd Katherina, fair and virtuous?
BAPTISTA. I have a daughter, sir, call'd Katherina.
GREMIO. You are too blunt; go to it orderly.
PETRUCHIO. You wrong me, Signior Gremio; give me leave.
  I am a gentleman of Verona, sir,
  That, hearing of her beauty and her wit,
  Her affability and bashful modesty,
  Her wondrous qualities and mild behaviour,
  Am bold to show myself a forward guest
  Within your house, to make mine eye the witness
  Of that report which I so oft have heard.
  And, for an entrance to my entertainment,
  I do present you with a man of mine,
                      [*Presenting* HORTENSIO]
  Cunning in music and the mathematics,
  To instruct her fully in those sciences,
  Whereof I know she is not ignorant.
  Accept of him, or else you do me wrong—
  His name is Licio, born in Mantua.
BAPTISTA. Y'are welcome, sir, and he for your good sake;
  But for my daughter Katherine, this I know,
  She is not for your turn, the more my grief.
PETRUCHIO. I see you do not mean to part with her;
  Or else you like not of my company.
BAPTISTA. Mistake me not; I speak but as I find.
  Whence are you, sir? What may I call your name?
PETRUCHIO. Petruchio is my name, Antonio's son,
  A man well known throughout all Italy.
BAPTISTA. I know him well; you are welcome for his sake.
GREMIO. Saving your tale, Petruchio, I pray,

789

Let us that are poor petitioners speak too.
Bacare! you are marvellous forward.

PETRUCHIO. O, pardon me, Signior Gremio! I would fain be doing.

GREMIO. I doubt it not, sir; but you will curse your wooing. Neighbour, this is a gift very grateful, I am sure of it. To express the like kindness, myself, that have been more kindly beholding to you than any, freely give unto you this young scholar [*Presenting* LUCENTIO] that hath been long studying at Rheims; as cunning in Greek, Latin, and other languages, as the other in music and mathematics. His name is Cambio. Pray accept his service.

BAPTISTA. A thousand thanks, Signior Gremio. Welcome, good Cambio. [*To* TRANIO] But, gentle sir, methinks you walk like a stranger. May I be so bold to know the cause of your coming?

TRANIO. Pardon me, sir, the boldness is mine own
That, being a stranger in this city here,
Do make myself a suitor to your daughter,
Unto Bianca, fair and virtuous.
Nor is your firm resolve unknown to me
In the preferment of the eldest sister.
This liberty is all that I request—
That, upon knowledge of my parentage,
I may have welcome 'mongst the rest that woo,
And free access and favour as the rest.
And toward the education of your daughters
I here bestow a simple instrument,
And this small packet of Greek and Latin books.
If you accept them, then their worth is great.

BAPTISTA. Lucentio is your name? Of whence, I pray?

TRANIO. Of Pisa, sir; son to Vincentio.

BAPTISTA. A mighty man of Pisa. By report
I know him well. You are very welcome, sir.
Take you the lute, and you the set of books;
You shall go see your pupils presently.
Holla, within!

Enter a SERVANT

Sirrah, lead these gentlemen

To my daughters; and tell them both
These are their tutors. Bid them use them well.

Exit SERVANT *leading* HORTENSIO *carrying the lute
and* LUCENTIO *with the books*

We will go walk a little in the orchard,
And then to dinner. You are passing welcome,
And so I pray you all to think yourselves.
PETRUCHIO. Signior Baptista, my business asketh haste,
And every day I cannot come to woo.
You knew my father well, and in him me,
Left solely heir to all his lands and goods,
Which I have bettered rather than decreas'd.
Then tell me, if I get your daughter's love,
What dowry shall I have with her to wife?
BAPTISTA. After my death, the one half of my lands
And, in possession, twenty thousand crowns.
PETRUCHIO. And for that dowry, I'll assure her of
Her widowhood, be it that she survive me,
In all my lands and leases whatsoever.
Let specialities be therefore drawn between us,
That covenants may be kept on either hand.
BAPTISTA. Ay, when the special thing is well obtain'd,
That is, her love; for that is all in all.
PETRUCHIO. Why, that is nothing; for I tell you, father,
I am as peremptory as she proud-minded;
And where two raging fires meet together,
They do consume the thing that feeds their fury.
Though little fire grows great with little wind,
Yet extreme gusts will blow out fire and all.
So I to her, and so she yields to me;
For I am rough, and woo not like a babe.
BAPTISTA. Well mayst thou woo, and happy be thy speed
But be thou arm'd for some unhappy words.
PETRUCHIO. Ay, to the proof, as mountains are for winds,
That shake not though they blow perpetually.

Re-enter HORTENSIO, *with his head broke*

BAPTISTA. How now, my friend! Why dost thou look so
  pale?
HORTENSIO. For fear, I promise you, if I look pale.
BAPTISTA. What, will my daughter prove a good musician?
HORTENSIO. I think she'll sooner prove a soldier:
  Iron may hold with her, but never lutes.
BAPTISTA. Why, then thou canst not break her to the lute?
HORTENSIO. Why, no; for she hath broke the lute to me.
  I did but tell her she mistook her frets,
  And bow'd her hand to teach her fingering,
  When, with a most impatient devilish spirit,
  'Frets, call you these?' quoth she 'I'll fume with them.'
  And with that word she struck me on the head,
  And through the instrument my pate made way;
  And there I stood amazed for a while,
  As on a pillory, looking through the lute,
  While she did call me rascal fiddler
  And twangling Jack, with twenty such vile terms,
  As she had studied to misuse me so.
PETRUCHIO. Now, by the world, it is a lusty wench;
  I love her ten times more than e'er I did.
  O, how I long to have some chat with her!
BAPTISTA. Well, go with me, and be not so discomfited;
  Proceed in practice with my younger daughter;
  She's apt to learn, and thankful for good turns.
  Signior Petruchio, will you go with us,
  Or shall I send my daughter Kate to you?
PETRUCHIO. I pray you do.   *Exeunt all but* PETRUCHIO
  I'll attend her here,
  And woo her with some spirit when she comes.
  Say that she rail; why, then I'll tell her plain
  She sings as sweetly as a nightingale.
  Say that she frown; I'll say she looks as clear
  As morning roses newly wash'd with dew.
  Say she be mute, and will not speak a word;
  Then I'll commend her volubility,
  And say she uttereth piercing eloquence.
  If she do bid me pack, I'll give her thanks,
  As though she bid me stay by her a week;
  If she deny to wed, I'll crave the day

When I shall ask the banns, and when be married.
But here she comes; and now, Petruchio, speak.

Enter KATHERINA

Good morrow, Kate—for that's your name, I hear.
KATHERINA. Well have you heard, but something hard of
  hearing:
They call me Katherine that do talk of me.
PETRUCHIO. You lie, in faith, for you are call'd plain Kate,
  And bonny Kate, and sometimes Kate the curst;
  But, Kate, the prettiest Kate in Christendom,
  Kate of Kate Hall, my super-dainty Kate,
  For dainties are all Kates, and therefore, Kate,
  Take this of me, Kate of my consolation—
  Hearing thy mildness prais'd in every town,
  Thy virtues spoke of, and thy beauty sounded,
  Yet not so deeply as to thee belongs,
  Myself am mov'd to woo thee for my wife.
KATHERINA. Mov'd! in good time! Let him that mov'd you
  hither
Remove you hence. I knew you at the first
You were a moveable.
PETRUCHIO. Why, what's a moveable?
KATHERINA. A join'd-stool.
PETRUCHIO. Thou hast hit it. Come, sit on me.
KATHERINA. Asses are made to bear, and so are you.
PETRUCHIO. Women are made to bear, and so are you.
KATHERINA. No such jade as you, if me you mean.
PETRUCHIO. Alas, good Kate, I will not burden thee!
  For, knowing thee to be but young and light—
KATHERINA. Too light for such a swain as you to catch;
  And yet as heavy as my weight should be.
PETRUCHIO. Should be! should—buzz!
KATHERINA. Well ta'en, and like a buzzard.
PETRUCHIO. O, slow-wing'd turtle, shall a buzzard take thee?
KATHERINA. Ay, for a turtle, as he takes a buzzard.
PETRUCHIO. Come, come, you wasp; i' faith, you are too
  angry.
KATHERINA. If I be waspish, best beware my sting.
PETRUCHIO. My remedy is then to pluck it out.

KATHERINA. Ay, if the fool could find it where it lies.

PETRUCHIO. Who knows not where a wasp does wear his sting?
In his tail.

KATHERINA. In his tongue.

PETRUCHIO. Whose tongue?

KATHERINA. Yours, if you talk of tales; and so farewell.

PETRUCHIO. What, with my tongue in your tail? Nay, come again,
Good Kate; I am a gentleman.

KATHERINA. That I'll try.   [*She strikes him*]

PETRUCHIO. I swear I'll cuff you, if you strike again.

KATHERINA. So may you lose your arms.
If you strike me, you are no gentleman;
And if no gentleman, why then no arms.

PETRUCHIO. A herald, Kate? O, put me in thy books!

KATHERINA. What is your crest—a coxcomb?

PETRUCHIO. A combless cock, so Kate will be my hen.

KATHERINA. No cock of mine: you crow too like a craven.

PETRUCHIO. Nay, come, Kate, come; you must not look so sour.

KATHERINA. It is my fashion, when I see a crab.

PETRUCHIO. Why, here's no crab; and therefore look not sour.

KATHERINA. There is, there is.

PETRUCHIO. Then show it me.

KATHERINA. Had I a glass I would.

PETRUCHIO. What, you mean my face?

KATHERINA. Well aim'd of such a young one.

PETRUCHIO. Now, by Saint George, I am too young for you.

KATHERINA. Yet you are wither'd.

PETRUCHIO. 'Tis with cares.

KATHERINA. I care not.

PETRUCHIO. Nay, hear you, Kate—in sooth, you scape not so.

KATHERINA. I chafe you, if I tarry; let me go.

PETRUCHIO. No, not a whit; I find you passing gentle.
'Twas told me you were rough, and coy, and sullen,
And now I find report a very liar;
For thou art pleasant, gamesome, passing courteous,
But slow in speech, yet sweet as springtime flowers.

Thou canst not frown, thou canst not look askance,
Nor bite the lip, as angry wenches will,
Nor hast thou pleasure to be cross in talk;
But thou with mildness entertain'st thy wooers;
With gentle conference, soft and affable.
Why does the world report that Kate doth limp?
O sland'rous world! Kate like the hazel-twig
Is straight and slender, and as brown in hue
As hazel-nuts, and sweeter than the kernels.
O, let me see thee walk. Thou dost not halt.
KATHERINA. Go, fool, and whom thou keep'st command.
PETRUCHIO. Did ever Dian so become a grove
As Kate this chamber with her princely gait?
O, be thou Dian, and let her be Kate;
And then let Kate be chaste, and Dian sportful!
KATHERINA. Where did you study all this goodly speech?
PETRUCHIO. It is extempore, from my mother wit.
KATHERINA. A witty mother! witless else her son.
PETRUCHIO. Am I not wise?
KATHERINA. Yes, keep you warm.
PETRUCHIO. Marry, so I mean, sweet Katherine, in thy bed.
And therefore, setting all this chat aside,
Thus in plain terms: your father hath consented
That you shall be my wife; your dowry 'greed on;
And will you, nill you, I will marry you.
Now, Kate, I am a husband for your turn;
For, by this light, whereby I see thy beauty,
Thy beauty that doth make me like thee well,
Thou must be married to no man but me;
For I am he am born to tame you, Kate,
And bring you from a wild Kate to a Kate
Conformable as other household Kates.

Re-enter BAPTISTA, GREMIO, *and* TRANIO

Here comes your father. Never make denial;
I must and will have Katherine to my wife.
BAPTISTA. Now, Signior Petruchio, how speed you with my
daughter?
PETRUCHIO. How but well, sir? how but well?
It were impossible I should speed amiss.

BAPTISTA. Why, how now, daughter Katherine, in your dumps?

KATHERINA. Call you me daughter? Now I promise you
You have show'd a tender fatherly regard
To wish me wed to one half lunatic,
A mad-cap ruffian and a swearing Jack,
That thinks with oaths to face the matter out.

PETRUCHIO. Father, 'tis thus: yourself and all the world
That talk'd of her have talk'd amiss of her.
If she be curst, it is for policy,
For she's not froward, but modest as the dove;
She is not hot, but temperate as the morn;
For patience she will prove a second Grissel,
And Roman Lucrece for her chastity.
And, to conclude, we have 'greed so well together
That upon Sunday is the wedding-day.

KATHERINA. I'll see thee hang'd on Sunday first.

GREMIO. Hark, Petruchio; she says she'll see thee hang'd first.

TRANIO. Is this your speeding? Nay, then good-night our part!

PETRUCHIO. Be patient, gentlemen. I choose her for myself;
If she and I be pleas'd, what's that to you?
'Tis bargain'd 'twixt us twain, being alone,
That she shall still be curst in company.
I tell you 'tis incredible to believe.
How much she loves me—O, the kindest Kate!
She hung about my neck, and kiss on kiss
She vied so fast, protesting oath on oath,
That in a twink she won me to her love.
O, you are novices! 'Tis a world to see
How tame, when men and women are alone,
A meacock wretch can make the curstest shrew.
Give me thy hand, Kate; I will unto Venice,
To buy apparel 'gainst the wedding-day.
Provide the feast, father, and bid the guests;
I will be sure my Katherine shall be fine.

BAPTISTA. I know not what to say; but give me your hands.
God send you joy, Petruchio! 'Tis a match.

GREMIO, TRANIO. Amen, say we; we will be witnesses.

PETRUCHIO. Father, and wife, and gentlemen, adieu.
I will to Venice; Sunday comes apace;
We will have rings and things, and fine array;
And kiss me, Kate; we will be married a Sunday.
Exeunt PETRUCHIO *and* KATHERINA *severally*
GREMIO. Was ever match clapp'd up so suddenly?
BAPTISTA. Faith, gentlemen, now I play a merchant's part,
And venture madly on a desperate mart.
TRANIO. 'Twas a commodity lay fretting by you;
'Twill bring you gain, or perish on the seas.
BAPTISTA. The gain I seek is quiet in the match.
GREMIO. No doubt but he hath got a quiet catch.
But now, Baptista, to your younger daughter:
Now is the day we long have looked for;
I am your neighbour, and was suitor first.
TRANIO. And I am one that love Bianca more
Than words can witness or your thoughts can guess.
GREMIO. Youngling, thou canst not love so dear as I.
TRANIO. Greybeard, thy love doth freeze.
GREMIO. But thine doth fry.
Skipper, stand back; 'tis age that nourisheth.
TRANIO. But youth in ladies' eyes that flourisheth.
BAPTISTA. Content you, gentlemen; I will compound this
strife.
'Tis deeds must win the prize, and he of both
That can assure my daughter greatest dower
Shall have my Bianca's love.
Say, Signior Gremio, what can you assure her?
GREMIO. First, as you know, my house within the city
Is richly furnished with plate and gold,
Basins and ewers to lave her dainty hands;
My hangings all of Tyrian tapestry;
In ivory coffers I have stuff'd my crowns;
In cypress chests my arras counterpoints,
Costly apparel, tents, and canopies,
Fine linen, Turkey cushions boss'd with pearl,
Valance of Venice gold in needle-work;
Pewter and brass, and all things that belongs
To house or housekeeping. Then at my farm
I have a hundred milch-kine to the pail,

Six score fat oxen standing in my stalls,
And all things answerable to this portion.
Myself am struck in years, I must confess;
And if I die to-morrow this is hers,
If whilst I live she will be only mine.

TRANIO. That 'only' came well in. Sir, list to me:
I am my father's heir and only son;
If I may have your daughter to my wife,
I'll leave her houses three or four as good
Within rich Pisa's walls as any one
Old Signior Gremio has in Padua;
Besides two thousand ducats by the year
Of fruitful land, all which shall be her jointure.
What, have I pinch'd you, Signior Gremio?

GREMIO. Two thousand ducats by the year of land!
[*Aside*] My land amounts not to so much in all.—
That she shall have, besides an argosy
That now is lying in Marseilles road.
What, have I chok'd you with an argosy?

TRANIO. Gremio, 'tis known my father hath no less
Than three great argosies, besides two galliasses,
And twelve tight galleys. These I will assure her,
And twice as much whate'er thou off'rest next.

GREMIO. Nay, I have off'red all; I have no more;
And she can have no more than all I have;
If you like me, she shall have me and mine.

TRANIO. Why, then the maid is mine from all the world
By your firm promise; Gremio is out-vied.

BAPTISTA. I must confess your offer is the best;
And let your father make her the assurance,
She is your own. Else, you must pardon me;
If you should die before him, where's her dower?

TRANIO. That's but a cavil; he is old, I young.

GREMIO. And may not young men die as well as old?

BAPTISTA. Well, gentlemen,
I am thus resolv'd: on Sunday next you know
My daughter Katherine is to be married;
Now, on the Sunday following shall Bianca
Be bride to you, if you make this assurance;
If not, to Signior Gremio.

And so I take my leave, and thank you both.
GREMIO. Adieu, good neighbour.   *Exit* BAPTISTA
  Now, I fear thee not.
  Sirrah young gamester, your father were a fool
  To give thee all, and in his waning age
  Set foot under thy table. Tut, a toy!
  An old Italian fox is not so kind, my boy.   *Exit*
TRANIO. A vengeance on your crafty withered hide!
  Yet I have fac'd it with a card of ten.
  'Tis in my head to do my master good:
  I see no reason but suppos'd Lucentio
  Must get a father, call'd suppos'd Vincentio;
  And that's a wonder—fathers commonly
  Do get their children; but in this case of wooing
  A child shall get a sire, if I fail not of my cunning.   *Exit*

ACT III. SCENE 1

Padua. BAPTISTA's *house*

Enter LUCENTIO *as* CAMBIO, HORTENSIO *as* LICIO, *and* BIANCA

LUCENTIO. Fiddler, forbear; you grow too forward, sir.
  Have you so soon forgot the entertainment
  Her sister Katherine welcome'd you withal?
HORTENSIO. But, wrangling pedant, this is
  The patroness of heavenly harmony.
  Then give me leave to have prerogative;
  And when in music we have spent an hour,
  Your lecture shall have leisure for as much.
LUCENTIO. Preposterous ass, that never read so far
  To know the cause why music was ordain'd!
  Was it not to refresh the mind of man
  After his studies or his usual pain?
  Then give me leave to read philosophy,
  And while I pause serve in your harmony.
HORTENSIO. Sirrah, I will not bear these braves of thine.
BIANCA. Why, gentlemen, you do me double wrong

799

To strive for that which resteth in my choice.
I am no breeching scholar in the schools,
I'll not be tied to hours nor 'pointed times,
But learn my lessons as I please myself.
And to cut off all strife: here sit we down;
Take you your instrument, play you the whiles!
His lecture will be done ere you have tun'd.

HORTENSIO. You'll leave his lecture when I am in tune?

LUCENTIO. That will be never—tune your instrument.

BIANCA. Where left we last?

LUCENTIO. Here, madam:
'Hic ibat Simois, hic est Sigeia tellus,
Hic steterat Priami regia celsa senis.'

BIANCA. Construe them.

LUCENTIO. 'Hic ibat' as I told you before—'Simois' I am Lucentio—'hic est' son unto Vincentio of Pisa—'Sigeia tellus' disguised thus to get your love—'Hic steterat' and that Lucentio that comes a-wooing—'Priami' is my man Tranio—'regia' bearing my port—'celsa senis' that we might beguile the old pantaloon.

HORTENSIO. Madam, my instrument's in tune.

BIANCA. Let's hear. O fie! the treble jars.

LUCENTIO. Spit in the hole, man, and tune again.

BIANCA. Now let me see if I can construe it: 'Hic ibat Simois' I know you not—'hic est Sigeia tellus' I trust you not—'Hic steterat Priami' take heed he hear us not—'regia' presume not—'celsa senis' despair not.

HORTENSIO. Madam, 'tis now in tune.

LUCENTIO. All but the bass.

HORTENSIO. The bass is right; 'tis the base knave that jars.
[Aside] How fiery and forward our pedant is!
Now, for my life, the knave doth court my love.
Pedascule, I'll watch you better yet.

BIANCA. In time I may believe, yet I mistrust.

LUCENTIO. Mistrust it not—for sure, Æacides
Was Ajax, call'd so from his grandfather.

BIANCA. I must believe my master; else, I promise you,
I should be arguing still upon that doubt;
But let it rest. Now, Licio, to you.
Good master, take it not unkindly, pray,

That I have been thus pleasant with you both.
HORTENSIO. [*To* LUCENTIO] You may go walk and give me
    leave awhile;
My lessons make no music in three parts.
LUCENTIO. Are you so formal, sir? Well, I must wait,
    [*Aside*] And watch withal; for, but I be deceiv'd,
Our fine musician groweth amorous.
HORTENSIO. Madam, before you touch the instrument
To learn the order of my fingering,
I must begin with rudiments of art,
To teach you gamut in a briefer sort,
More pleasant, pithy, and effectual,
Than hath been taught by any of my trade;
And there it is in writing fairly drawn.
BIANCA. Why, I am past my gamut long ago.
HORTENSIO. Yet read the gamut of Hortensio.
BIANCA. [*Reads*]
    ' "Gamut" I am, the ground of all accord—
    "A re" to plead Hortensio's passion—
    "B mi" Bianca, take him for thy lord—
    "C fa ut" that loves with all affection—
    "D sol re" one clef, two notes have I—
    "E la mi" show pity or I die.'
Call you this gamut? Tut, I like it not!
Old fashions please me best; I am not so nice
To change true rules for odd inventions.

Enter a SERVANT

SERVANT. Mistress, your father prays you leave your books
And help to dress your sister's chamber up.
You know to-morrow is the wedding-day.
BIANCA. Farewell, sweet masters, both; I must be gone.
                        Exeunt BIANCA *and* SERVANT
LUCENTIO. Faith, mistress, then I have no cause to stay.   *Exit*
HORTENSIO. But I have cause to pry into this pedant;
Methinks he looks as though he were in love.
Yet if thy thoughts, Bianca, be so humble
To cast thy wand'ring eyes on every stale—
Seize thee that list. If once I find thee ranging,
Hortensio will be quit with thee by changing.   *Exit*

SCENE 2

Padua. Before BAPTISTA'S *house*

Enter BAPTISTA, GREMIO, TRANIO *as* LUCENTIO, KATHERINA, BIANCA, LUCENTIO *as* CAMBIO, *and* ATTENDANTS

BAPTISTA. [*To* TRANIO] Signior Lucentio, this is the 'pointed day
That Katherine and Petruchio should be married,
And yet we hear not of our son-in-law.
What will be said? What mockery will it be
To want the bridegroom when the priest attends
To speak the ceremonial rites of marriage!
What says Lucentio to this shame of ours?
KATHERINA. No shame but mine; I must, forsooth, be forc'd
To give my hand, oppos'd against my heart,
Unto a mad-brain rudesby, full of spleen,
Who woo'd in haste and means to wed at leisure.
I told you, I, he was a frantic fool,
Hiding his bitter jests in blunt behaviour;
And, to be noted for a merry man,
He'll woo a thousand, 'point the day of marriage,
Make friends invited, and proclaim the banns;
Yet never means to wed where he hath woo'd.
Now must the world point at poor Katherine,
And say 'Lo, there is mad Petruchio's wife,
If it would please him come and marry her!'
TRANIO. Patience, good Katherine, and Baptista too.
Upon my life, Petruchio means but well,
Whatever fortune stays him from his word.
Though he be blunt, I know him passing wise;
Though he be merry, yet withal he's honest.
KATHERINA. Would Katherine had never seen him though!
Exit, weeping, followed by BIANCA *and others*
BAPTISTA. Go, girl, I cannot blame thee now to weep,
For such an injury would vex a very saint;
Much more a shrew of thy impatient humour.

Enter BIONDELLO

BIONDELLO. Master, master! News, and such old news as you never heard of!

BAPTISTA. Is it new and old too? How may that be?

BIONDELLO. Why, is it not news to hear of Petruchio's coming?

BAPTISTA. Is he come?

BIONDELLO. Why, no, sir.

BAPTISTA. What then?

BIONDELLO. He is coming.

BAPTISTA. When will he be here?

BIONDELLO. When he stands where I am and sees you there.

TRANIO. But, say, what to thine old news?

BIONDELLO. Why, Petruchio is coming—in a new hat and an old jerkin; a pair of old breeches thrice turn'd; a pair of boots that have been candle-cases, one buckled, another lac'd; an old rusty sword ta'en out of the town armoury, with a broken hilt, and chapeless; with two broken points; his horse hipp'd, with an old motley saddle and stirrups of no kindred; besides, possess'd with the glanders and like to mose in the chine, troubled with the lampass, infected with the fashions, full of windgalls, sped with spavins, rayed with the yellows, past cure of the fives, stark spoil'd with the staggers, begnawn with the bots, sway'd in the back and shoulder-shotten, near-legg'd before, and with a half-cheek'd bit, and a head-stall of sheep's leather which, being restrained to keep him from stumbling, hath been often burst, and now repaired with knots; one girth six times piec'd, and a woman's crupper of velure, which hath two letters for her name fairly set down in studs, and here and there piec'd with pack-thread.

BAPTISTA. Who comes with him?

BIONDELLO. O, sir, his lackey, for all the world caparison'd like the horse—with a linen stock on one leg and a kersey boot-hose on the other, gart'red with a red and blue list; an old hat, and the humour of forty fancies prick'd in't for a feather; a monster, a very monster in apparel, and not like a Christian footboy or a gentleman's lackey.

TRANIO. 'Tis some odd humour pricks him to this fashion;
Yet oftentimes he goes but mean-apparell'd.

BAPTISTA. I am glad he's come, howsoe'er he comes.

BIONDELLO. Why, sir, he comes not.

BAPTISTA. Didst thou not say he comes?

BIONDELLO. Who? that Petruchio came?

BAPTISTA. Ay, that Petruchio came.

BIONDELLO. No, sir; I say his horse comes with him on his back.

BAPTISTA. Why, that's all one.

BIONDELLO. Nay, by Saint Jamy,
I hold you a penny,
A horse and a man
Is more than one,
And yet not many.

Enter PETRUCHIO *and* GRUMIO

PETRUCHIO. Come, where be these gallants? Who's at home?

BAPTISTA. You are welcome, sir.

PETRUCHIO. And yet I come not well.

BAPTISTA. And yet you halt not.

TRANIO. Not so well apparell'd
As I wish you were.

PETRUCHIO. Were it better, I should rush in thus.
But where is Kate? Where is my lovely bride?
How does my father? Gentles, methinks you frown;
And wherefore gaze this goodly company
As if they saw some wondrous monument,
Some comet or unusual prodigy?

BAPTISTA. Why, sir, you know this is your wedding-day.
First were we sad, fearing you would not come;
Now sadder, that you come so unprovided.
Fie, doff this habit, shame to your estate,
An eye-sore to our solemn festival!

TRANIO. And tell us what occasion of import
Hath all so long detain'd you from your wife,
And sent you hither so unlike yourself?

PETRUCHIO. Tedious it were to tell, and harsh to hear;
Sufficeth I am come to keep my word,
Though in some part enforced to digress,
Which at more leisure I will so excuse
As you shall well be satisfied withal.
But where is Kate? I stay too long from her;

The morning wears, 'tis time we were at church.

TRANIO. See not your bride in these unreverent robes;
  Go to my chamber, put on clothes of mine.

PETRUCHIO. Not I, believe me; thus I'll visit her.

BAPTISTA. But thus, I trust, you will not marry her.

PETRUCHIO. Good sooth, even thus; therefore ha' done with
    words;
  To me she's married, not unto my clothes.
  Could I repair what she will wear in me
  As I can change these poor accoutrements,
  'Twere well for Kate and better for myself.
  But what a fool am I to chat with you,
  When I should bid good-morrow to my bride
  And seal the title with a lovely kiss!

                    Exeunt PETRUCHIO *and* GRUMIO

TRANIO. He hath some meaning in his mad attire.
  We will persuade him, be it possible,
  To put on better ere he go to church.

BAPTISTA. I'll after him and see the event of this.

        Exeunt BAPTISTA, GREMIO, BIONDELLO, *and* ATTENDANTS

TRANIO. But to her love concerneth us to add
  Her father's liking; which to bring to pass,
  As I before imparted to your worship,
  I am to get a man—whate'er he be
  It skills not much; we'll fit him to our turn—
  And he shall be Vincentio of Pisa,
  And make assurance here in Padua
  Of greater sums than I have promised.
  So shall you quietly enjoy your hope
  And marry sweet Bianca with consent.

LUCENTIO. Were it not that my fellow schoolmaster
  Doth watch Bianca's steps so narrowly,
  'Twere good, methinks, to steal our marriage;
  Which once perform'd, let all the world say no,
  I'll keep mine own despite of all the world.

TRANIO. That by degrees we mean to look into
  And watch our vantage in this business;
  We'll over-reach the greybeard, Gremio,
  The narrow-prying father, Minola,
  The quaint musician, amorous Licio—

All for my master's sake, Lucentio.

Re-enter GREMIO

Signior Gremio, came you from the church?
GREMIO. As willingly as e'er I came from school.
TRANIO. And is the bride and bridegroom coming home?
GREMIO. A bridegroom, say you? 'Tis a groom indeed,
A grumbling groom, and that the girl shall find.
TRANIO. Curster than she? Why, 'tis impossible.
GREMIO. Why, he's a devil, a devil, a very fiend.
TRANIO. Why, she's a devil, a devil, the devil's dam.
GREMIO. Tut, she's a lamb, a dove, a fool, to him!
I'll tell you, Sir Lucentio: when the priest
Should ask if Katherine should be his wife,
'Ay, by gogs-wouns' quoth he, and swore so loud
That, all amaz'd, the priest let fall the book;
And as he stoop'd again to take it up,
This mad-brain'd bridegroom took him such a cuff
That down fell priest and book, and book and priest.
'Now take them up,' quoth he 'if any list.'
TRANIO. What said the wench, when he rose again?
GREMIO. Trembled and shook, for why he stamp'd and
swore
As if the vicar meant to cozen him.
But after many ceremonies done
He calls for wine: 'A health!' quoth he, as if
He had been abroad, carousing to his mates
After a storm; quaff'd off the muscadel,
And threw the sops all in the sexton's face,
Having no other reason
But that his beard grew thin and hungerly
And seem'd to ask him sops as he was drinking.
This done, he took the bride about the neck,
And kiss'd her lips with such a clamorous smack
That at the parting all the church did echo.
And I, seeing this, came thence for very shame;
And after me, I know, the rout is coming.
Such a mad marriage never was before.
Hark, hark! I hear the minstrels play.   [*Music plays*]

Enter PETRUCHIO, KATHERINA, BIANCA, BAPTISTA, HORTENSIO,
GRUMIO, *and train*

PETRUCHIO. Gentlemen and friends, I thank you for your
  pains.
  I know you think to dine with me to-day,
  And have prepar'd great store of wedding cheer
  But so it is—my haste doth call me hence,
  And therefore here I mean to take my leave.
BAPTISTA. Is't possible you will away to-night?
PETRUCHIO. I must away to-day before night come.
  Make it no wonder; if you knew my business,
  You would entreat me rather go than stay.
  And, honest company, I thank you all
  That have beheld me give away myself
  To this most patient, sweet, and virtuous wife.
  Dine with my father, drink a health to me.
  For I must hence; and farewell to you all.
TRANIO. Let us entreat you stay till after dinner.
PETRUCHIO. It may not be.
GREMIO. Let me entreat you.
PETRUCHIO. It cannot be.
KATHERINA. Let me entreat you.
PETRUCHIO. I am content.
KATHERINA. Are you content to stay?
PETRUCHIO. I am content you shall entreat me stay;
  But yet not stay, entreat me how you can.
KATHERINA. Now, if you love me, stay.
PETRUCHIO. Grumio, my horse.
GRUMIO. Ay, sir, they be ready; the oats have eaten the
  horses.
KATHERINA. Nay, then,
  Do what thou canst, I will not go to-day;
  No, nor to-morrow, not till I please myself.
  The door is open, sir; there lies your way;
  You may be jogging whiles your boots are green;
  For me, I'll not be gone till I please myself.
  'Tis like you'll prove a jolly surly groom
  That take it on you at the first so roundly.
PETRUCHIO. O Kate, content thee; prithee be not angry.
KATHERINA. I will be angry; what hast thou to do?

807

Father, be quiet; he shall stay my leisure.

GREMIO. Ay, marry, sir, now it begins to work.

KATHERINA. Gentlemen, forward to the bridal dinner.
I see a woman may be made a fool
If she had not a spirit to resist.

PETRUCHIO. They shall go forward, Kate, at thy command.
Obey the bride, you that attend on her;
Go to the feast, revel and domineer,
Carouse full measure to her maidenhead;
Be mad and merry, or go hang yourselves.
But for my bonny Kate, she must with me.
Nay, look not big, nor stamp, nor stare, nor fret;
I will be master of what is mine own—
She is my goods, my chattels, she is my house,
My household stuff, my field, my barn,
My horse, my ox, my ass, my any thing,
And here she stands; touch her whoever dare;
I'll bring mine action on the proudest he
That stops my way in Padua. Grumio,
Draw forth thy weapon; we are beset with thieves;
Rescue thy mistress, if thou be a man.
Fear not, sweet wench; they shall not touch thee, Kate;
I'll buckler thee against a million.

Exeunt PETRUCHIO, KATHERINA, *and* GRUMIO

BAPTISTA. Nay, let them go, a couple of quiet ones.

GREMIO. Went they not quickly, I should die with laughing.

TRANIO. Of all mad matches, never was the like.

LUCENTIO. Mistress, what's your opinion of your sister?

BIANCA. That, being mad herself, she's madly mated.

GREMIO. I warrant him, Petruchio is Kated.

BAPTISTA. Neighbours and friends, though bride and bride-
groom wants
For to supply the places at the table,
You know there wants no junkets at the feast.
Lucentio, you shall supply the bridegroom's place;
And let Bianca take her sister's room.

TRANIO. Shall sweet Bianca practise how to bride it?

BAPTISTA. She shall, Lucentio. Come, gentlemen, let's go.

Exeunt

ACT IV. SCENE 1

Petruchio's *country house*

Enter Grumio

Grumio. Fie, fie on all tired jades, on all mad masters, and all foul ways! Was ever man so beaten? Was ever man so ray'd? Was ever man so weary? I am sent before to make a fire, and they are coming after to warm them. Now were not I a little pot and soon hot, my very lips might freeze to my teeth, my tongue to the roof of my mouth, my heart in my belly, ere I should come by a fire to thaw me. But I with blowing the fire shall warm myself; for, considering the weather, a taller man than I will take cold. Holla, ho! Curtis!

Enter Curtis

Curtis. Who is that calls so coldly?

Grumio. A piece of ice. If thou doubt it, thou mayst slide from my shoulder to my heel with no greater a run but my head and my neck. A fire, good Curtis.

Curtis. Is my master and his wife coming, Grumio?

Grumio. O, ay, Curtis, ay; and therefore fire, fire; cast on no water.

Curtis. Is she so hot a shrew as she's reported?

Grumio. She was, good Curtis, before this frost; but thou know'st winter tames man, woman, and beast; for it hath tam'd my old master, and my new mistress, and myself, fellow Curtis.

Curtis. Away, you three-inch fool! I am no beast.

Grumio. Am I but three inches? Why, thy horn is a foot, and so long am I at the least. But wilt thou make a fire, or shall I complain on thee to our mistress, whose hand—she being now at hand—thou shalt soon feel, to thy cold comfort, for being slow in thy hot office?

Curtis. I prithee, good Grumio, tell me how goes the world?

Grumio. A cold world, Curtis, in every office but thine; and therefore fire. Do thy duty, and have thy duty, for my master and mistress are almost frozen to death.

Curtis. There's fire ready; and therefore, good Grumio, the news?

GRUMIO. Why, 'Jack boy! ho, boy!' and as much news as thou wilt.

CURTIS. Come, you are so full of cony-catching!

GRUMIO. Why, therefore, fire; for I have caught extreme cold. Where's the cook? Is supper ready, the house trimm'd, rushes strew'd, cobwebs swept, the serving-men in their new fustian, their white stockings, and every officer his wedding-garment on? Be the jacks fair within, the jills fair without, the carpets laid, and everything in order?

CURTIS. All ready; and therefore, I pray thee, news.

GRUMIO. First know my horse is tired; my master and mistress fall'n out.

CURTIS. How?

GRUMIO. Out of their saddles into the dirt; and thereby hangs a tale.

CURTIS. Let's ha't, good Grumio.

GRUMIO. Lend thine ear.

CURTIS. Here.

GRUMIO. There. [Striking him]

CURTIS. This 'tis to feel a tale, not to hear a tale.

GRUMIO. And therefore 'tis call'd a sensible tale; and this cuff was but to knock at your ear and beseech list'ning. Now I begin: Imprimis, we came down a foul hill, my master riding behind my mistress—

CURTIS. Both of one horse?

GRUMIO. What's that to thee?

CURTIS. Why, a horse.

GRUMIO. Tell thou the tale. But hadst thou not cross'd me, thou shouldst have heard how her horse fell and she under her horse; thou shouldst have heard in how miry a place, how she was bemoil'd, how he left her with the horse upon her, how he beat me because her horse stumbled, how she waded through the dirt to pluck him off me, how he swore, how she pray'd that never pray'd before, how I cried, how the horses ran away, how her bridle was burst, how I lost my crupper—with many things of worthy memory, which now shall die in oblivion, and thou return unexperienc'd to thy grave.

CURTIS. By this reck'ning he is more shrew than she.

GRUMIO. Ay, and that thou and the proudest of you all

shall find when he comes home. But what talk I of this? Call forth Nathaniel, Joseph, Nicholas, Philip, Walter, Sugarsop, and the rest; let their heads be sleekly comb'd, their blue coats brush'd and their garters of an indifferent knit; let them curtsy with their left legs, and not presume to touch a hair of my master's horse-tail till they kiss their hands. Are they all ready?

CURTIS. They are.

GRUMIO. Call them forth.

CURTIS. Do you hear, ho? You must meet my master, to countenance my mistress.

GRUMIO. Why, she hath a face of her own.

CURTIS. Who knows not that?

GRUMIO. Thou, it seems, that calls for company to countenance her.

CURTIS. I call them forth to credit her.

GRUMIO. Why, she comes to borrow nothing of them.

Enter four or five SERVINGMEN

NATHANIEL. Welcome home, Grumio!

PHILIP. How now, Grumio!

JOSEPH. What, Grumio!

NICHOLAS. Fellow Grumio!

NATHANIEL. How now, old lad!

GRUMIO. Welcome, you!—how now, you!—what, you!—fellow, you!—and thus much for greeting. Now, my spruce companions, is all ready, and all things neat?

NATHANIEL. All things is ready. How near is our master?

GRUMIO. E'en at hand, alighted by this; and therefore be not—Cock's passion, silence! I hear my master.

Enter PETRUCHIO *and* KATHERINA

PETRUCHIO. Where be these knaves? What, no man at door
To hold my stirrup nor to take my horse!
Where is Nathaniel, Gregory, Philip?

ALL SERVANTS. Here, here, sir; here, sir.

PETRUCHIO. Here, sir! here, sir! here, sir! here, sir!
You logger-headed and unpolish'd grooms!
What, no attendance? no regard? no duty?
Where is the foolish knave I sent before?

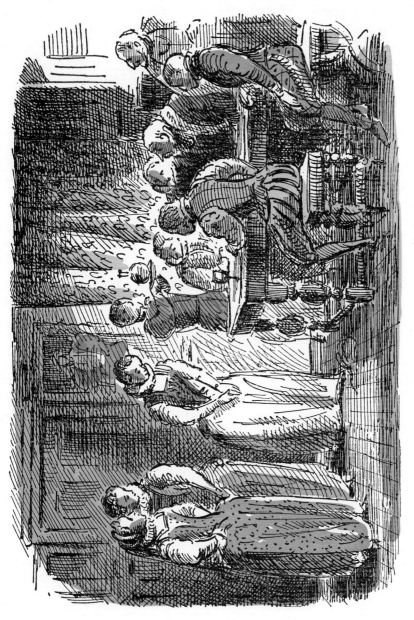

PETRUCHIO. *Katherine, I charge thee, tell these headstrong women*
What duty they do owe their lords and husbands   (ACT V. SCENE II)

GRUMIO. Here, sir; as foolish as I was before.

PETRUCHIO. You peasant swain! you whoreson malt-horse drudge!
Did I not bid thee meet me in the park
And bring along these rascal knaves with thee?

GRUMIO. Nathaniel's coat, sir, was not fully made,
And Gabriel's pumps were all unpink'd i' th' heel;
There was no link to colour Peter's hat,
And Walter's dagger was not come from sheathing;
There were none fine but Adam, Ralph, and Gregory;
The rest were ragged, old, and beggarly;
Yet, as they are, here are they come to meet you.

PETRUCHIO. Go, rascals, go and fetch my supper in.

Exeunt some of the SERVINGMEN

[*Sings*] Where is the life that late I led?
Where are those—

Sit down, Kate, and welcome. Soud, soud, soud, soud!

Re-enter SERVANTS *with supper*

Why, when, I say? Nay, good sweet Kate, be merry.
Off with my boots, you rogues! you villains, when?

[*Sings*] It was the friar of orders grey,
As he forth walked on his way—

Out, you rogue! you pluck my foot awry;
Take that, and mend the plucking off the other.
[*Strikes him*]
Be merry, Kate. Some water, here, what, ho!

Enter one with water

Where's my spaniel Troilus? Sirrah, get you hence,
And bid my cousin Ferdinand come hither:
Exit SERVINGMAN
One, Kate, that you must kiss and be acquainted with.
Where are my slippers? Shall I have some water?
Come, Kate, and wash, and welcome heartily.
You whoreson villain! will you let it fall? [*Strikes him*]

KATHERINA. Patience, I pray you; 'twas a fault unwilling.

PETRUCHIO. A whoreson, beetle-headed, flap-ear'd knave!

Come, Kate, sit down; I know you have a stomach.
Will you give thanks, sweet Kate, or else shall I?
What's this? Mutton?

FIRST SERVANT. Ay.

PETRUCHIO. Who brought it?

PETER. I.

PETRUCHIO. 'Tis burnt; and so is all the meat.
What dogs are these? Where is the rascal cook?
How durst you villains bring it from the dresser
And serve it thus to me that love it not?
There, take it to you, trenchers, cups, and all;
                                    [*Throws the meat, etc., at them*]
You heedless joltheads and unmanner'd slaves!
What, do you grumble? I'll be with you straight.
                                                Exeunt SERVANTS

KATHERINA. I pray you, husband, be not so disquiet;
The meat was well, if you were so contented.

PETRUCHIO. I tell thee, Kate, 'twas burnt and dried away,
And I expressly am forbid to touch it;
For it engenders choler, planteth anger;
And better 'twere that both of us did fast,
Since, of ourselves, ourselves are choleric,
Than feed it with such over-roasted flesh.
Be patient; to-morrow 't shall be mended.
And for this night we'll fast for company.
Come, I will bring thee to thy bridal chamber.   *Exeunt*

Re-enter SERVANTS *severally*

NATHANIEL. Peter, didst ever see the like?

PETER. He kills her in her own humour.

Re-enter CURTIS

GRUMIO. Where is he?

CURTIS. In her chamber. Making a sermon of continency to
    her,
And rails, and swears, and rates, that she, poor soul,
Knows not which way to stand, to look, to speak.
And sits as one new risen from a dream.
Away, away! for he is coming hither.   *Exeunt*

ACT IV. SCENE 1

Re-enter PETRUCHIO

PETRUCHIO. Thus have I politicly begun my reign,
And 'tis my hope to end successfully.
My falcon now is sharp and passing empty.
And till she stoop she must not be full-gorg'd,
For then she never looks upon her lure.
Another way I have to man my haggard,
To make her come, and know her keeper's call,
That is, to watch her, as we watch these kites
That bate and beat, and will not be obedient.
She eat no meat to-day, nor none shall eat;
Last night she slept not, nor to-night she shall not;
As with the meat, some undeserved fault
I'll find about the making of the bed;
And here I'll fling the pillow, there the bolster,
This way the coverlet, another way the sheets;
Ay, and amid this hurly I intend
That all is done in reverend care of her—
And, in conclusion, she shall watch all night;
And if she chance to nod I'll rail and brawl
And with the clamour keep her still awake.
This is a way to kill a wife with kindness,
And thus I'll curb her mad and headstrong humour.
He that knows better how to tame a shrew,
Now let him speak; 'tis charity to show.   *Exit*

SCENE 2

Padua. Before BAPTISTA'S *house*

Enter TRANIO *as* LUCENTIO, *and* HORTENSIO *as* LICIO

TRANIO. Is't possible, friend Licio, that Mistress Bianca
Doth fancy any other but Lucentio?
I tell you, sir, she bears me fair in hand.
HORTENSIO. Sir, to satisfy you in what I have said,
Stand by and mark the manner of his teaching.
                              [*They stand aside*]

Enter BIANCA, *and* LUCENTIO *as* CAMBIO

815

LUCENTIO. Now, mistress, profit you in what you read?

BIANCA. What, master, read you? First resolve me that.

LUCENTIO. I read that I profess, 'The Art to Love.'

BIANCA. And may you prove, sir, master of your art!

LUCENTIO. While you, sweet dear, prove mistress of my
    heart.   *[They retire]*

HORTENSIO. Quick proceeders, marry! Now tell me, I pray,
    You that durst swear that your Mistress Bianca
    Lov'd none in the world so well as Lucentio.

TRANIO. O despiteful love! unconstant womankind!
    I tell thee, Licio, this is wonderful.

HORTENSIO. Mistake no more; I am not Licio.
    Nor a musician as I seem to be;
    But one that scorn to live in this disguise
    For such a one as leaves a gentleman
    And makes a god of such a cullion.
    Know, sir, that I am call'd Hortensio.

TRANIO. Signior Hortensio, I have often heard
    Of your entire affection to Bianca;
    And since mine eyes are witness of her lightness,
    I will with you, if you be so contented,
    Forswear Bianca and her love for ever.

HORTENSIO. See, how they kiss and court! Signior Lucentio,
    Here is my hand, and here I firmly vow
    Never to woo her more, but do forswear her,
    As one unworthy all the former favours
    That I have fondly flatter'd her withal.

TRANIO. And here I take the like unfeigned oath,
    Never to marry with her though she would entreat;
    Fie on her! See how beastly she doth court him!

HORTENSIO. Would all the world but he had quite for-
    sworn!
    For me, that I may surely keep mine oath,
    I will be married to a wealthy widow
    Ere three days pass, which hath as long lov'd me
    As I have lov'd this proud disdainful haggard.
    And so farewell, Signior Lucentio.
    Kindness in women, not their beauteous looks,
    Shall win my love; and so I take my leave,
    In resolution as I swore before.   *Exit*

TRANIO. Mistress Bianca, bless you with such grace
As 'longeth to a lover's blessed case!
Nay, I have ta'en you napping, gentle love,
And have forsworn you with Hortensio.
BIANCA. Tranio, you jest; but have you both forsworn me?
TRANIO. Mistress, we have.
LUCENTIO. Then we are rid of Licio.
TRANIO. I' faith, he'll have a lusty widow now,
That shall be woo'd and wedded in a day.
BIANCA. God give him joy!
TRANIO. Ay, and he'll tame her.
BIANCA. He says so, Tranio.
TRANIO. Faith, he is gone unto the taming-school.
BIANCA. The taming-school! What, is there such a place?
TRANIO. Ay, mistress; and Petruchio is the master,
That teacheth tricks eleven and twenty long,
To tame a shrew and charm her chattering tongue.

Enter BIONDELLO

BIONDELLO. O master, master, I have watch'd so long
That I am dog-weary; but at last I spied
An ancient angel coming down the hill
Will serve the turn.
TRANIO. What is he, Biondello?
BIONDELLO. Master, a mercatante or a pedant,
I know not what; but formal in apparel,
In gait and countenance surely like a father.
LUCENTIO. And what of him, Tranio?
TRANIO. If he be credulous and trust my tale,
I'll make him glad to seem Vincentio,
And give assurance to Baptista Minola
As if he were the right Vincentio.
Take in your love, and then let me alone.

Exeunt LUCENTIO *and* BIANCA

Enter a PEDANT

PEDANT. God save you, sir!
TRANIO. And you, sir; you are welcome.
Travel you far on, or are you at the farthest?
PEDANT. Sir, at the farthest for a week or two;

But then up farther, and as far as Rome;
And so to Tripoli, if God lend me life.
TRANIO. What countryman, I pray?
PEDANT. Of Mantua.
TRANIO. Of Mantua, sir? Marry, God forbid,
And come to Padua, careless of your life!
PEDANT. My life, sir! How, I pray? For that goes hard.
TRANIO. 'Tis death for any one in Mantua
To come to Padua. Know you not the cause?
Your ships are stay'd at Venice; and the Duke,
For private quarrel 'twixt your Duke and him,
Hath publish'd and proclaim'd it openly.
'Tis marvel—but that you are but newly come,
You might have heard it else proclaim'd about.
PEDANT. Alas, sir, it is worse for me than so!
For I have bills for money by exchange
From Florence, and must here deliver them.
TRANIO. Well, sir, to do you courtesy,
This will I do, and this I will advise you—
First, tell me, have you ever been at Pisa?
PEDANT. Ay, sir, in Pisa have I often been,
Pisa renowned for grave citizens.
TRANIO. Among them know you one Vincentio?
PEDANT. I know him not, but I have heard of him,
A merchant of incomparable wealth.
TRANIO. He is my father, sir; and, sooth to say,
In count'nance somewhat doth resemble you.
BIONDELLO. [Aside] As much as an apple doth an oyster,
and all one.
TRANIO. To save your life in this extremity,
This favour will I do you for his sake;
And think it not the worst of all your fortunes
That you are like to Sir Vincentio.
His name and credit shall you undertake,
And in my house you shall be friendly lodg'd;
Look that you take upon you as you should.
You understand me, sir. So shall you stay
Till you have done your business in the city.
If this be court'sy, sir, accept of it.
PEDANT. O, sir, I do; and will repute you ever

The patron of my life and liberty.
TRANIO. Then go with me to make the matter good.
This, by the way, I let you understand:
My father is here look'd for every day
To pass assurance of a dow'r in marriage
'Twixt me and one Baptista's daughter here.
In all these circumstances I'll instruct you.
Go with me to clothe you as becomes you.   *Exeunt*

SCENE 3

PETRUCHIO's *house*

Enter KATHERINA *and* GRUMIO

GRUMIO. No, no, forsooth; I dare not for my life.
KATHERINA. The more my wrong, the more his spite appears.
What, did he marry me to famish me?
Beggars that come unto my father's door
Upon entreaty have a present alms;
If not, elsewhere they meet with charity;
But I, who never knew how to entreat,
Nor never needed that I should entreat,
Am starv'd for meat, giddy for lack of sleep;
With oaths kept waking, and with brawling fed;
And that which spites me more than all these wants—
He does it under name of perfect love;
As who should say, if I should sleep or eat,
'Twere deadly sickness or else present death.
I prithee go and get me some repast;
I care not what, so it be wholesome food.
GRUMIO. What say you to a neat's foot?
KATHERINA. 'Tis passing good; I prithee let me have it.
GRUMIO. I fear it is too choleric a meat.
How say you to a fat tripe finely broil'd?
KATHERINA. I like it well; good Grumio, fetch it me.
GRUMIO. I cannot tell; I fear 'tis choleric.
What say you to a piece of beef and mustard?
KATHERINA. A dish that I do love to feed upon.

GRUMIO. Ay, but the mustard is too hot a little.

KATHERINA. Why then the beef, and let the mustard rest.

GRUMIO. Nay, then I will not; you shall have the mustard,
  Or else you get no beef of Grumio.

KATHERINA. Then both, or one, or anything thou wilt.

GRUMIO. Why then the mustard without the beef.

KATHERINA. Go, get thee gone, thou false deluding slave,
                                                    [Beats him]
  That feed'st me with the very name of meat.
  Sorrow on thee and all the pack of you
  That triumph thus upon my misery!
  Go, get thee gone, I say.

  Enter PETRUCHIO, *and* HORTENSIO *with meat*

PETRUCHIO. How fares my Kate? What, sweeting, all amort?

HORTENSIO. Mistress, what cheer?

KATHERINA. Faith, as cold as can be.

PETRUCHIO. Pluck up thy spirits, look cheerfully upon me.
  Here, love, thou seest how diligent I am,
  To dress thy meat myself, and bring it thee.
  I am sure, sweet Kate, this kindness merits thanks.
  What, not a word? Nay, then thou lov'st it not,
  And all my pains is sorted to no proof.
  Here, take away this dish.

KATHERINA. I pray you, let it stand.

PETRUCHIO. The poorest service is repaid with thanks;
  And so shall mine, before you touch the meat.

KATHERINA. I thank you, sir.

HORTENSIO. Signior Petruchio, fie! you are to blame.
  Come, Mistress Kate, I'll bear you company.

PETRUCHIO. [*Aside*] Eat it up all, Hortensio, if thou lovest
    me.—
  Much good do it unto thy gentle heart!
  Kate, eat apace. And now, my honey love,
  Will we return unto thy father's house
  And revel it as bravely as the best,
  With silken coats and caps, and golden rings,
  With ruffs and cuffs and farthingales and things,
  With scarfs and fans and double change of brav'ry.
  With amber bracelets, beads, and all this knav'ry.

What, hast thou din'd? The tailor stays thy leisure,
To deck thy body with his ruffling treasure.

Enter TAILOR

Come, tailor, let us see these ornaments;
Lay forth the gown.

Enter HABERDASHER

What news with you, sir?
HABERDASHER. Here is the cap your worship did bespeak.
PETRUCHIO. Why, this was moulded on a porringer;
  A velvet dish. Fie, fie! 'tis lewd and filthy;
  Why, 'tis a cockle or a walnut-shell,
  A knack, a toy, a trick, a baby's cap.
  Away with it. Come, let me have a bigger.
KATHERINA. I'll have no bigger; this doth fit the time,
  And gentlewomen wear such caps as these.
PETRUCHIO. When you are gentle, you shall have one too,
  And not till then.
HORTENSIO. [*Aside*] That will not be in haste.
KATHERINA. Why, sir, I trust I may have leave to speak;
  And speak I will. I am no child, no babe.
  Your betters have endur'd me say my mind,
  And if you cannot, best you stop your ears.
  My tongue will tell the anger of my heart,
  Or else my heart, concealing it, will break;
  And rather than it shall, I will be free
  Even to the uttermost, as I please, in words.
PETRUCHIO. Why, thou say'st true; it is a paltry cap,
  A custard-coffin, a bauble, a silken pie;
  I love thee well in that thou lik'st it not.
KATHERINA. Love me or love me not, I like the cap;
  And it I will have, or I will have none. *Exit* HABERDASHER
PETRUCHIO. Thy gown? Why, ay. Come, tailor, let us see't.
  O mercy, God! what masquing stuff is here?
  What's this? A sleeve? 'Tis like a demi-cannon.
  What, up and down, carv'd like an appletart?
  Here's snip and nip and cut and slish and slash,
  Like to a censer in a barber's shop.
  Why, what a devil's name, tailor, call'st thou this?

HORTENSIO. [*Aside*] I see she's like to have neither cap nor
gown.

TAILOR. You bid me make it orderly and well,
According to the fashion and the time.

PETRUCHIO. Marry, and did; but if you be rememb'red,
I did not bid you mar it to the time.
Go, hop me over every kennel home,
For you shall hop without my custom, sir.
I'll none of it; hence! make your best of it.

KATHERINA. I never saw a better fashion'd gown,
More quaint, more pleasing, nor more commendable;
Belike you mean to make a puppet of me.

PETRUCHIO. Why, true; he means to make a puppet of thee.

TAILOR. She says your worship means to make a puppet of
her.

PETRUCHIO. O monstrous arrogance! Thou liest, thou thread,
thou thimble,
Thou yard, three-quarters, half-yard, quarter, nail,
Thou flea, thou nit, thou winter-cricket thou—
Brav'd in mine own house with a skein of thread!
Away, thou rag, thou quantity, thou remnant;
Or I shall so bemete thee with thy yard
As thou shalt think on prating whilst thou liv'st!
I tell thee, I, that thou hast marr'd her gown.

TAILOR. Your worship is deceiv'd; the gown is made
Just as my master had direction.
Grumio gave order how it should be done.

GRUMIO. I gave him no order; I gave him the stuff.

TAILOR. But how did you desire it should be made?

GRUMIO. Marry, sir, with needle and thread.

TAILOR. But did you not request to have it cut?

GRUMIO. Thou hast fac'd many things.

TAILOR. I have.

GRUMIO. Face not me. Thou hast brav'd many men; brave
not me. I will neither be fac'd nor brav'd. I say unto thee,
I bid thy master cut out the gown; but I did not bid him
cut it to pieces. Ergo, thou liest.

TAILOR. Why, here is the note of the fashion to testify.

PETRUCHIO. Read it.

GRUMIO. The note lies in's throat, if he say I said so.

TAILOR. [*Reads*] 'Imprimis, a loose-bodied gown'—

GRUMIO. Master, if ever I said loose-bodied gown, sew me in the skirts of it and beat me to death with a bottom of brown bread; I said a gown.

PETRUCHIO. Proceed.

TAILOR. [*Reads*] 'With a small compass'd cape'—

GRUMIO. I confess the cape.

TAILOR. [*Reads*] 'With a trunk sleeve'—

GRUMIO. I confess two sleeves.

TAILOR. [*Reads*] 'The sleeves curiously cut.'

PETRUCHIO. Ay, there's the villainy.

GRUMIO. Error i' th' bill, sir; error i' th' bill! I commanded the sleeves should be cut out, and sew'd up again; and that I'll prove upon thee, though thy little finger be armed in a thimble.

TAILOR. This is true that I say; an I had thee in place where, thou shouldst know it.

GRUMIO. I am for thee straight; take thou the bill, give me thy meteyard, and spare not me.

HORTENSIO. God-a-mercy, Grumio! Then he shall have no odds.

PETRUCHIO. Well, sir, in brief, the gown is not for me.

GRUMIO. You are i' th' right, sir; 'tis for my mistress.

PETRUCHIO. Go, take it up unto thy master's use.

GRUMIO. Villain, not for thy life! Take up my mistress' gown for thy master's use!

PETRUCHIO. Why, sir, what's your conceit in that?

GRUMIO. O, sir, the conceit is deeper than you think for.
Take up my mistress' gown to his master's use!
O fie, fie, fie!

PETRUCHIO. [*Aside*] Hortensio, say thou wilt see the tailor paid.—
Go take it hence; be gone, and say no more.

HORTENSIO. Tailor, I'll pay thee for thy gown to-morrow;
Take no unkindness of his hasty words.
Away, I say; commend me to thy master.   *Exit* TAILOR

PETRUCHIO. Well, come, my Kate; we will unto your father's
Even in these honest mean habiliments;
Our purses shall be proud, our garments poor;
For 'tis the mind that makes the body rich;

And as the sun breaks through the darkest clouds,
So honour peereth in the meanest habit.
What, is the jay more precious than the lark
Because his feathers are more beautiful?
Or is the adder better than the eel
Because his painted skin contents the eye?
O no, good Kate; neither art thou the worse
For this poor furniture and mean array.
If thou account'st it shame, lay it on me;
And therefore frolic; we will hence forthwith
To feast and sport us at thy father's house.
Go call my men, and let us straight to him;
And bring our horses unto Long-lane end;
There will we mount, and thither walk on foot.
Let's see; I think 'tis now some seven o'clock,
And well we may come there by dinner-time.
KATHERINA. I dare assure you, sir, 'tis almost two,
And 'twill be supper-time ere you come there.
PETRUCHIO. It shall be seven ere I go to horse.
Look what I speak, or do, or think to do,
You are still crossing it. Sirs, let't alone;
I will not go to-day; and ere I do,
It shall be what o'clock I say it is.
HORTENSIO. Why, so this gallant will command the sun.
Exeunt

SCENE 4

Padua. Before BAPTISTA's *house*

Enter TRANIO *as* LUCENTIO, *and the* PEDANT *dressed
like* VINCENTIO

TRANIO. Sir, this is the house; please it you that I call?
PEDANT. Ay, what else? And, but I be deceived,
Signior Baptista may remember me
Near twenty years ago in Genoa,
Where we were lodgers at the Pegasus.
TRANIO. 'Tis well; and hold your own, in any case,
With such austerity as longeth to a father.

ACT IV. SCENE 4

Enter BIONDELLO

PEDANT. I warrant you. But, sir, here comes your boy;
'Twere good he were school'd.
TRANIO. Fear you not him. Sirrah Biondello,
Now do your duty throughly, I advise you.
Imagine 'twere the right Vincentio.
BIONDELLO. Tut, fear not me.
TRANIO. But hast thou done thy errand to Baptista?
BIONDELLO. I told him that your father was at Venice,
And that you look'd for him this day in Padua.
TRANIO. Th'art a tall fellow; hold thee that to drink.
Here comes Baptista. Set your countenance, sir.

Enter BAPTISTA, *and* LUCENTIO *as* CAMBIO

Signior Baptista, you are happily met.
[*To the* PEDANT] Sir, this is the gentleman I told you of;
I pray you stand good father to me now;
Give me Bianca for my patrimony.
PEDANT. Soft, son!
Sir, by your leave: having come to Padua
To gather in some debts, my son Lucentio
Made me acquainted with a weighty cause
Of love between your daughter and himself;
And—for the good report I hear of you,
And for the love he beareth to your daughter,
And she to him—to stay him not too long,
I am content, in a good father's care,
To have him match'd; and, if you please to like
No worse than I, upon some agreement
Me shall you find ready and willing
With one consent to have her so bestow'd;
For curious I cannot be with you,
Signior Baptista, of whom I hear so well.
BAPTISTA. Sir, pardon me in what I have to say.
Your plainness and your shortness please me well.
Right true it is your son Lucentio here
Doth love my daughter, and she loveth him,
Or both dissemble deeply their affections;
And therefore, if you say no more than this,

825

That like a father you will deal with him,
And pass my daughter a sufficient dower,
The match is made, and all is done—
Your son shall have my daughter with consent.
TRANIO. I thank you, sir. Where then do you know best
We be affied, and such assurance ta'en
As shall with either part's agreement stand?
BAPTISTA. Not in my house, Lucentio, for you know
Pitchers have ears, and I have many servants;
Besides, old Gremio is heark'ning still,
And happily we might be interrupted.
TRANIO. Then at my lodging, an it like you.
There doth my father lie; and there this night
We'll pass the business privately and well.
Send for your daughter by your servant here;
My boy shall fetch the scrivener presently.
The worst is this, that at so slender warning
You are like to have a thin and slender pittance.
BAPTISTA. It likes me well. Cambio, hie you home,
And bid Bianca make her ready straight;
And, if you will, tell what hath happened—
Lucentio's father is arriv'd in Padua,
And how she's like to be Lucentio's wife. *Exit* LUCENTIO
BIONDELLO. I pray the gods she may, with all my heart.
TRANIO. Dally not with the gods, but get thee gone.
Exit BIONDELLO

Signior Baptista, shall I lead the way?
Welcome! One mess is like to be your cheer;
Come, sir; we will better it in Pisa.
BAPTISTA. I follow you. *Exeunt*

Re-enter LUCENTIO *as* CAMBIO, *and* BIONDELLO

BIONDELLO. Cambio.
LUCENTIO. What say'st thou, Biondello?
BIONDELLO. You saw my master wink and laugh upon you?
LUCENTIO. Biondello, what of that?
BIONDELLO. Faith, nothing; but has left me here behind to ex-
pound the meaning or moral of his signs and tokens.
LUCENTIO. I pray thee moralize them.

BIONDELLO. Then thus: Baptista is safe, talking with the deceiving father of a deceitful son.
LUCENTIO. And what of him?
BIONDELLO. His daughter is to be brought by you to the supper.
LUCENTIO. And then?
BIONDELLO. The old priest at Saint Luke's church is at your command at all hours.
LUCENTIO. And what of all this?
BIONDELLO. I cannot tell, except they are busied about a counterfeit assurance. Take your assurance of her, cum privilegio ad imprimendum solum; to th' church take the priest, clerk, and some sufficient honest witnesses.
If this be not that you look for, I have more to say,
But bid Bianca farewell for ever and a day.
LUCENTIO. Hear'st thou, Biondello?
BIONDELLO. I cannot tarry. I knew a wench married in an afternoon as she went to the garden for parsley to stuff a rabbit; and so may you, sir; and so adieu, sir. My master hath appointed me to go to Saint Luke's to bid the priest be ready to come against you come with your appendix.
Exit
LUCENTIO. I may and will, if she be so contented.
She will be pleas'd; then wherefore should I doubt?
Hap what hap may, I'll roundly go about her;
It shall go hard if Cambio go without her.   *Exit*

SCENE 5

A public road

Enter PETRUCHIO, KATHERINA, HORTENSIO, *and* SERVANTS

PETRUCHIO. Come on, a God's name; once more toward our father's.
Good Lord, how bright and goodly shines the moon!
KATHERINA. The moon? The sun! It is not moonlight now.
PETRUCHIO. I say it is the moon that shines so bright.
KATHERINA. I know it is the sun that shines so bright.
PETRUCHIO. Now by my mother's son, and that's myself,

It shall be moon, or star, or what I list,
Or ere I journey to your father's house.
Go on and fetch our horses back again.
Evermore cross'd and cross'd; nothing but cross'd!
HORTENSIO. Say as he says, or we shall never go.
KATHERINA. Forward, I pray, since we have come so far,
And be it moon, or sun, or what you please;
And if you please to call it a rush-candle,
Henceforth I vow it shall be so for me.
PETRUCHIO. I say it is the moon.
KATHERINA. I know it is the moon.
PETRUCHIO. Nay, then you lie; it is the blessed sun.
KATHERINA. Then, God be bless'd, it is the blessed sun;
But sun it is not, when you say it is not;
And the moon changes even as your mind.
What you will have it nam'd, even that it is,
And so it shall be so for Katherine.
HORTENSIO. Petruchio, go thy ways, the field is won.
PETRUCHIO. Well, forward, forward! thus the bowl should
run,
And not unluckily against the bias.
But, soft! Company is coming here.

Enter VINCENTIO

[*To* VINCENTIO] Good-morrow, gentle mistress; where
away?—
Tell me, sweet Kate, and tell me truly too,
Hast thou beheld a fresher gentlewoman?
Such war of white and red within her cheeks!
What stars do spangle heaven with such beauty
As those two eyes become that heavenly face?
Fair lovely maid, once more good day to thee.
Sweet Kate, embrace her for her beauty's sake.
HORTENSIO. 'A will make the man mad, to make a woman of
him.
KATHERINA. Young budding virgin, fair and fresh and sweet,
Whither away, or where is thy abode?
Happy the parents of so fair a child;
Happier the man whom favourable stars
Allots thee for his lovely bed-fellow.

828

PETRUCHIO. Why, how now, Kate, I hope thou art not mad!
    This is a man, old, wrinkled, faded, withered,
    And not a maiden, as thou sayst he is.
KATHERINA. Pardon, old father, my mistaking eyes,
    That have been so bedazzled with the sun
    That everything I look on seemeth green;
    Now I perceive thou art a reverend father.
    Pardon, I pray thee, for my mad mistaking.
PETRUCHIO. Do, good old grandsire, and withal make known
    Which way thou travellest—if along with us,
    We shall be joyful of thy company.
VINCENTIO. Fair sir, and you my merry mistress,
    That with your strange encounter much amaz'd me,
    My name is call'd Vincentio, my dwelling Pisa,
    And bound I am to Padua, there to visit
    A son of mine, which long I have not seen.
PETRUCHIO. What is his name?
VINCENTIO. Lucentio, gentle sir.
PETRUCHIO. Happily met; the happier for thy son.
    And now by law, as well as reverend age,
    I may entitle thee my loving father:
    The sister to my wife, this gentlewoman,
    Thy son by this hath married. Wonder not,
    Nor be not grieved—she is of good esteem,
    Her dowry wealthy, and of worthy birth;
    Beside, so qualified as may beseem
    The spouse of any noble gentleman.
    Let me embrace with old Vincentio;
    And wander we to see thy honest son,
    Who will of thy arrival be full joyous.
VINCENTIO. But is this true; or is it else your pleasure,
    Like pleasant travellers, to break a jest
    Upon the company you overtake?
HORTENSIO. I do assure thee, father, so it is.
PETRUCHIO. Come, go along, and see the truth hereof;
    For our first merriment hath made thee jealous.
                                        Exeunt all but HORTENSIO
HORTENSIO. Well, Petruchio, this has put me in heart.
    Have to my widow; and if she be froward,
    Then hast thou taught Hortensio to be untoward.   *Exit*

THE TAMING OF THE SHREW

ACT V. SCENE 1

Padua. Before LUCENTIO'S *house*

Enter BIONDELLO, LUCENTIO, *and* BIANCA; GREMIO
is out before

BIONDELLO. Softly and swiftly, sir, for the priest is ready.

LUCENTIO. I fly, Biondello; but they may chance to need thee
at home, therefore leave us.

BIONDELLO. Nay, faith, I'll see the church a your back, and
then come back to my master's as soon as I can.

Exeunt LUCENTIO, BIANCA, *and* BIONDELLO

GREMIO. I marvel Cambio comes not all this while.

Enter PETRUCHIO, KATHERINA, VINCENTIO, GRUMIO,
and ATTENDANTS

PETRUCHIO. Sir, here's the door; this is Lucentio's house;
My father's bears more toward the market-place;
Thither must I, and here I leave you, sir.

VINCENTIO. You shall not choose but drink before you go;
I think I shall command your welcome here,
And by all likelihood some cheer is toward.   [*Knocks*]

GREMIO. They're busy within; you were best knock louder.

[PEDANT *looks out of the window*]

PEDANT. What's he that knocks as he would beat down the
gate?

VINCENTIO. Is Signior Lucentio within, sir?

PEDANT. He's within, sir, but not to be spoken withal.

VINCENTIO. What if a man bring him a hundred pound or
two to make merry withal?

PEDANT. Keep your hundred pounds to yourself; he shall
need none so long as I live.

PETRUCHIO. Nay, I told you your son was well beloved in
Padua. Do you hear, sir? To leave frivolous circumstances,
I pray you tell Signior Lucentio that his father is come
from Pisa, and is here at the door to speak with him.

PEDANT. Thou liest: his father is come from Padua, and here
looking out at the window.

VINCENTIO. Art thou his father?

PEDANT. Ay, sir; so his mother says, if I may believe her.

PETRUCHIO. [*To* VINCENTIO] Why, how now, gentleman! Why, this is flat knavery to take upon you another man's name.

PEDANT. Lay hands on the villain; I believe 'a means to cozen somebody in this city under my countenance.

Re-enter BIONDELLO

BIONDELLO. I have seen them in the church together. God send 'em good shipping! But who is here? Mine old master, Vincentio! Now we are undone and brought to nothing.

VINCENTIO. [*Seeing* BIONDELLO] Come hither, crack-hemp.

BIONDELLO. I hope I may choose, sir.

VINCENTIO. Come hither, you rogue. What, have you forgot me?

BIONDELLO. Forgot you! No, sir. I could not forget you, for I never saw you before in all my life.

VINCENTIO. What, you notorious villain, didst thou never see thy master's father, Vincentio?

BIONDELLO. What, my old worshipful old master? Yes, marry, sir; see where he looks out of the window.

VINCENTIO. Is't so, indeed? [*He beats* BIONDELLO]

BIONDELLO. Help, help, help! Here's a madman will murder me. *Exit*

PEDANT. Help, son! help, Signior Baptista! *Exit from above*

PETRUCHIO. Prithee, Kate, let's stand aside and see the end of this controversy. [*They stand aside*]

Re-enter PEDANT *below;* BAPTISTA, TRANIO, *and* SERVANTS

TRANIO. Sir, what are you that offer to beat my servant?

VINCENTIO. What am I, sir? Nay, what are you, sir? O immortal gods! O fine villain! A silken doublet, a velvet hose, a scarlet cloak, and a copatain hat! O, I am undone! I am undone! While I play the good husband at home, my son and my servant spend all at the university.

TRANIO. How now! what's the matter?

BAPTISTA. What, is the man lunatic?

TRANIO. Sir, you seem a sober ancient gentleman by your habit, but your words show you a madman. Why, sir, what 'cerns it you if I wear pearl and gold? I thank my good father, I am able to maintain it.

VINCENTIO. Thy father! O villain! he is a sailmaker in Bergamo.

BAPTISTA. You mistake, sir; you mistake, sir. Pray, what do you think is his name?

VINCENTIO. His name! As if I knew not his name! I have brought him up ever since he was three years old, and his name is Tranio.

PEDANT. Away, away, mad ass! His name is Lucentio; and he is mine only son, and heir to the lands of me, Signior Vincentio.

VINCENTIO. Lucentio! O, he hath murd'red his master! Lay hold on him, I charge you, in the Duke's name. O, my son, my son! Tell me, thou villain, where is my son, Lucentio?

TRANIO. Call forth an officer.

Enter one with an OFFICER

Carry this mad knave to the gaol. Father Baptista, I charge you see that he be forthcoming.

VINCENTIO. Carry me to the gaol!

GREMIO. Stay, Officer; he shall not go to prison.

BAPTISTA. Talk not, Signior Gremio; I say he shall go to prison.

GREMIO. Take heed, Signior Baptista, lest you be cony-catch'd in this business; I dare swear this is the right Vincentio.

PEDANT. Swear if thou dar'st.

GREMIO. Nay, I dare not swear it.

TRANIO. Then thou wert best say that I am not Lucentio.

GREMIO. Yes, I know thee to be Signior Lucentio.

BAPTISTA. Away with the dotard; to the gaol with him!

VINCENTIO. Thus strangers may be hal'd and abus'd. O monstrous villain!

Re-enter BIONDELLO, *with* LUCENTIO *and* BIANCA

BIONDELLO. O, we are spoil'd; and yonder he is! Deny him, forswear him, or else we are all undone.

Exeunt BIONDELLO, TRANIO, *and* PEDANT, *as fast as may be*

LUCENTIO. [*Kneeling*] Pardon, sweet father.

VINCENTIO. Lives my sweet son?
BIANCA. Pardon, dear father.
BAPTISTA. How hast thou offended?
  Where is Lucentio?
LUCENTIO. Here's Lucentio,
  Right son to the right Vincentio,
  That have by marriage made thy daughter mine,
  While counterfeit supposes blear'd thine eyne.
GREMIO. Here's packing, with a witness, to deceive us all!
VINCENTIO. Where is that damned villain, Tranio,
  That fac'd and brav'd me in this matter so?
BAPTISTA. Why, tell me, is not this my Cambio?
BIANCA. Cambio is chang'd into Lucentio.
LUCENTIO. Love wrought these miracles. Bianca's love
  Made me exchange my state with Tranio,
  While he did bear my countenance in the town;
  And happily I have arrived at the last
  Unto the wished haven of my bliss.
  What Tranio did, myself enforc'd him to;
  Then pardon him, sweet father, for my sake.
VINCENTIO. I'll slit the villain's nose that would have sent me
  to the gaol.
BAPTISTA. [*To* LUCENTIO] But do you hear, sir? Have you
  married my daughter without asking my good will?
VINCENTIO. Fear not, Baptista; we will content you, go to;
  but I will in to be revenged for this villainy.   *Exit*
BAPTISTA. And I to sound the depth of this knavery. *Exit*
LUCENTIO. Look not pale, Bianca; thy father will not frown.
                        Exeunt LUCENTIO *and* BIANCA
GREMIO. My cake is dough, but I'll in among the rest;
  Out of hope of all but my share of the feast.   *Exit*
KATHERINA. Husband, let's follow to see the end of this ado.
PETRUCHIO. First kiss me, Kate, and we will.
KATHERINA. What, in the midst of the street?
PETRUCHIO. What, art thou asham'd of me?
KATHERINA. No, sir; God forbid; but asham'd to kiss.
PETRUCHIO. Why, then, let's home again. Come, sirrah, let's
  away.
KATHERINA. Nay, I will give thee a kiss; now pray thee,
  love, stay.

PETRUCHIO. Is not this well? Come, my sweet Kate:
Better once than never, for never too late. *Exeunt*

SCENE 2

LUCENTIO's *house*

Enter BAPTISTA, VINCENTIO, GREMIO, *the* PEDANT,
LUCENTIO, BIANCA, PETRUCHIO, KATHERINA, HOR-
TENSIO, *and* WIDOW. *The* SERVINGMEN *with*
TRANIO, BIONDELLO, *and* GRUMIO, *bringing in a
banquet*

LUCENTIO. At last, though long, our jarring notes agree;
And time it is when raging war is done
To smile at scapes and perils overblown.
My fair Bianca, bid my father welcome,
While I with self-same kindness welcome thine.
Brother Petruchio, sister Katherina,
And thou, Hortensio, with thy loving widow,
Feast with the best, and welcome to my house.
My banquet is to close our stomachs up
After our great good cheer. Pray you, sit down;
For now we sit to chat as well as eat. [*They sit*]
PETRUCHIO. Nothing but sit and sit, and eat and eat!
BAPTISTA. Padua affords this kindness, son Petruchio.
PETRUCHIO. Padua affords nothing but what is kind.
HORTENSIO. For both our sakes I would that word were true.
PETRUCHIO. Now, for my life, Hortensio fears his widow.
WIDOW. Then never trust me if I be afeard.
PETRUCHIO. You are very sensible, and yet you miss my
sense:
I mean Hortensio is afeard of you.
WIDOW. He that is giddy thinks the world turns round.
PETRUCHIO. Roundly replied.
KATHERINA. Mistress, how mean you that?
WIDOW. Thus I conceive by him.
PETRUCHIO. Conceives by me! How likes Hortensio that?
HORTENSIO. My widow says thus she conceives her tale.

PETRUCHIO. Very well mended. Kiss him for that, good
widow.
KATHERINA. 'He that is giddy thinks the world turns round.'
I pray you tell me what you meant by that.
WIDOW. Your husband, being troubled with a shrew,
Measures my husband's sorrow by his woe;
And now you know my meaning.
KATHERINA. A very mean meaning.
WIDOW. Right, I mean you.
KATHERINA. And I am mean, indeed, respecting you.
PETRUCHIO. To her, Kate!
HORTENSIO. To her, widow!
PETRUCHIO. A hundred marks, my Kate does put her down.
HORTENSIO. That's my office.
PETRUCHIO. Spoke like an officer—ha' to thee, lad.
                                    [*Drinks to* HORTENSIO]
BAPTISTA. How likes Gremio these quick-witted folks?
GREMIO. Believe me, sir, they butt together well.
BIANCA. Head and butt! An hasty-witted body
Would say your head and butt were head and horn.
VINCENTIO. Ay, mistress bride, hath that awakened you?
BIANCA. Ay, but not frighted me; therefore I'll sleep again.
PETRUCHIO. Nay, that you shall not; since you have begun,
Have at you for a bitter jest or two.
BIANCA. Am I your bird? I mean to shift my bush,
And then pursue me as you draw your bow.
You are welcome all.
                      Exeunt BIANCA, KATHERINA, *and* WIDOW
PETRUCHIO. She hath prevented me. Here, Signior Tranio,
This bird you aim'd at, though you hit her not;
Therefore a health to all that shot and miss'd.
TRANIO. O, sir, Lucentio slipp'd me like his greyhound,
Which runs himself, and catches for his master.
PETRUCHIO. A good swift simile, but something currish.
TRANIO. 'Tis well, sir, that you hunted for yourself;
'Tis thought your deer does hold you at a bay.
BAPTISTA. O, O, Petruchio! Tranio hits you now.
LUCENTIO. I thank thee for that gird, good Tranio.
HORTENSIO. Confess, confess; hath he not hit you here?
PETRUCHIO. 'A has a little gall'd me, I confess;

And, as the jest did glance away from me,
'Tis ten to one it maim'd you two outright.

BAPTISTA. Now, in good sadness, son Petruchio,
I think thou hast the veriest shrew of all.

PETRUCHIO. Well, I say no; and therefore, for assurance,
Let's each one send unto his wife,
And he whose wife is most obedient,
To come at first when he doth send for her,
Shall win the wager which we will propose.

HORTENSIO. Content. What's the wager?

LUCENTIO. Twenty crowns.

PETRUCHIO. Twenty crowns?
I'll venture so much of my hawk or hound,
But twenty times so much upon my wife.

LUCENTIO. A hundred then.

HORTENSIO. Content.

PETRUCHIO. A match! 'tis done.

HORTENSIO. Who shall begin?

LUCENTIO. That will I.
Go, Biondello, bid your mistress come to me.

BIONDELLO. I go.   *Exit*

BAPTISTA. Son, I'll be your half Bianca comes.

LUCENTIO. I'll have no halves; I'll bear it all myself.

Re-enter BIONDELLO

How now! what news?

BIONDELLO. Sir, my mistress sends you word
That she is busy and she cannot come.

PETRUCHIO. How! She's busy, and she cannot come!
Is that an answer?

GREMIO. Ay, and a kind one too.
Pray God, sir, your wife send you not a worse.

PETRUCHIO. I hope better.

HORTENSIO. Sirrah Biondello, go and entreat my wife
To come to me forthwith.   *Exit* BIONDELLO

PETRUCHIO. O, ho! entreat her!
Nay, then she must needs come.

HORTENSIO. I am afraid, sir,
Do what you can, yours will not be entreated.

Re-enter BIONDELLO

Now, where's my wife?

BIONDELLO. She says you have some goodly jest in hand:
She will not come; she bids you come to her.
PETRUCHIO. Worse and worse; she will not come! O vile,
Intolerable, not to be endur'd!
Sirrah Grumio, go to your mistress;
Say I command her come to me.   *Exit* GRUMIO
HORTENSIO. I know her answer.
PETRUCHIO. What?
HORTENSIO. She will not.
PETRUCHIO. The fouler fortune mine, and there an end.

Re-enter KATHERINA

BAPTISTA. Now, by my holidame, here comes Katherina!
KATHERINA. What is your will, sir, that you send for me?
PETRUCHIO. Where is your sister, and Hortensio's wife?
KATHERINA. They sit conferring by the parlour fire.
PETRUCHIO. Go, fetch them hither; if they deny to come,
Swinge me them soundly forth unto their husbands.
Away, I say, and bring them hither straight.
                                    Exit KATHERINA
LUCENTIO. Here is a wonder, if you talk of a wonder.
HORTENSIO. And so it is. I wonder what it bodes.
PETRUCHIO. Marry, peace it bodes, and love, and quiet life,
An awful rule, and right supremacy;
And, to be short, what not that's sweet and happy.
BAPTISTA. Now fair befall thee, good Petruchio!
The wager thou hast won; and I will add
Unto their losses twenty thousand crowns;
Another dowry to another daughter,
For she is chang'd, as she had never been.
PETRUCHIO. Nay, I will win my wager better yet,
And show more sign of her obedience,
Her new-built virtue and obedience.

Re-enter KATHERINA *with* BIANCA *and* WIDOW

See where she comes, and brings your froward wives
As prisoners to her womanly persuasion.

Katherine, that cap of yours becomes you not:
Off with that bauble, throw it underfoot.

[KATHERINA *complies*]

WIDOW. Lord, let me never have a cause to sigh
  Till I be brought to such a silly pass!
BIANCA. Fie! what a foolish duty call you this?
LUCENTIO. I would your duty were as foolish too;
  The wisdom of your duty, fair Bianca,
  Hath cost me a hundred crowns since supper-time!
BIANCA. The more fool you for laying on my duty.
PETRUCHIO. Katherine, I charge thee, tell these headstrong
    women
  What duty they do owe their lords and husbands.
WIDOW. Come, come, you're mocking; we will have no telling.
PETRUCHIO. Come on, I say; and first begin with her.
WIDOW. She shall not.
PETRUCHIO. I say she shall. And first begin with her.
KATHERINA. Fie, fie! unknit that threatening unkind brow,
  And dart not scornful glances from those eyes
  To wound thy lord, thy king, thy governor.
  It blots thy beauty as frosts do bite the meads,
  Confounds thy fame as whirlwinds shake fair buds,
  And in no sense is meet or amiable.
  A woman mov'd is like a fountain troubled—
  Muddy, ill-seeming, thick, bereft of beauty;
  And while it is so, none so dry or thirsty
  Will deign to sip or touch one drop of it.
  Thy husband is thy lord, thy life, thy keeper,
  Thy head, thy sovereign; one that cares for thee,
  And for thy maintenance commits his body
  To painful labour both by sea and land,
  To watch the night in storms, the day in cold,
  Whilst thou liest warm at home, secure and safe;
  And craves no other tribute at thy hands
  But love, fair looks, and true obedience—
  Too little payment for so great a debt.
  Such duty as the subject owes the prince,
  Even such a woman oweth to her husband;
  And when she is froward, peevish, sullen, sour,
  And not obedient to his honest will,

What is she but a foul contending rebel
And graceless traitor to her loving lord?
I am asham'd that women are so simple
To offer war where they should kneel for peace;
Or seek for rule, supremacy, and sway,
When they are bound to serve, love, and obey.
Why are our bodies soft and weak and smooth,
Unapt to toil and trouble in the world,
But that our soft conditions and our hearts
Should well agree with our external parts?
Come, come, you froward and unable worms!
My mind hath been as big as one of yours,
My heart as great, my reason haply more,
To bandy word for word and frown for frown;
But now I see our lances are but straws,
Our strength as weak, our weakness past compare,
That seeming to be most which we indeed least are.
Then vail your stomachs, for it is no boot,
And place your hands below your husband's foot;
In token of which duty, if he please,
My hand is ready, may it do him ease.
PETRUCHIO. Why, there's a wench! Come on, and kiss me,
    Kate.
LUCENTIO. Well, go thy ways, old lad, for thou shalt ha't.
VINCENTIO. 'Tis a good hearing when children are toward.
LUCENTIO. But a harsh hearing when women are froward.
PETRUCHIO. Come, Kate, we'll to bed.
    We three are married, but you two are sped.
    [To LUCENTIO] 'Twas I won the wager, though you hit
    the white;
    And being a winner, God give you good night!
                    Exeunt PETRUCHIO and KATHERINA
HORTENSIO. Now go thy ways; thou hast tam'd a curst
    shrow.
LUCENTIO. 'Tis a wonder, by your leave, she will be tam'd so.
                                            Exeunt

All's Well that Ends Well

ALL'S WELL THAT ENDS WELL

THE story Shakespeare used as the basis for the plot of *All's Well that Ends Well* he could find in William Paynter's *Palace of Pleasure*, a collection of tales issued in 1566. Paynter, who was a scholar, though Clerk of the Ordnance at the Tower of London, had read widely in the works of the foreign story-tellers and translated in his *Palace of Pleasure* a selection he made from their work. Paynter took the story Shakespeare remodelled in *All's Well* from Boccaccio's *Decameron*, where it stands as the ninth story of the third day. On that day Boccaccio's company were to discourse of those who by their exertions and tenacity acquired what they greatly admired or regained what they had lost. The story Shakespeare adapted provides an outstanding example of such successful exertion.

Boccaccio's story tells how there lived in the household of Isnard Count Roussilon a famous physician Gerard de Narbonne. The Count had a son Beltram, the physician a daughter Giletta. The children grew up together and Giletta fell in love with Beltram, and although she was rich and much sought in marriage she refused all her suitors because of the secret love she cherished for Beltram. Their fathers having died, Beltram goes to Paris and Giletta mourns at home. When the King of France fell ill however of a complaint that Gerard had known how to cure, Giletta went to Paris and persuaded the King to allow her to cure him as her father would have done. In return for her service she was to have the husband she desired. She chooses Beltram who cannot defy the King's order; but as soon as the marriage ceremony is over he sets out for Tuscany to help the Florentines against the Senesi. To his wife's messengers he replies that he will return to her only when she shall have the ring from his finger and their son in her arms. Giletta goes secretly and in disguise to Florence, substitutes herself for a lady with whom Beltram has made an assignation, and secures the ring and the child, or rather children, for she stays in Florence till she gives birth to twin sons. Meantime Beltram hearing of his wife's absence returns to his estate, and is in the midst of the feast of All Saints' Day at Roussilon when Giletta returns and presents him with his ring and his twin sons. The Count admiring her constancy and determination welcomes her as his wife and they live happily ever after.

As a story to illustrate a set theme Giletta's adventures are doubtless easily accepted; here is both the pursuit of the desired object and of its recovery when lost. Regarded however as the basis of a drama the story's limitations are at once obvious. In the original it is Giletta's story; Beltram is merely a functionary in the action; we are not to inquire into the nature or motives of his conduct. Translated into drama however a principal character who is merely a functionary raises questions that cannot be answered satisfactorily by referring us to a scheme for which he is designed. There is no context such as that into which the mere story fits to which we may appeal. The appeal is now to human nature as we know it, and Shakespeare's Bertram is judged on that standard as a young man whom no sensible girl could pursue while retaining her self-respect. Yet it is clear that in its original setting the lady's determination and the very extravagance of her devotion are her glory; and it is equally clear that Shakespeare does not intend his audience to regard her with anything but favour. What we must not do is to ignore the convention on which Shakespeare relied and offer an explanation of the action and an analysis of Shakespeare's attitude based on modern social conventions.

In the original story Beltram's conduct is taken for granted: it is felt to be natural for a man of his rank to regard a match with a social inferior as degrading. It is true there is something in human nature that will always plead against such a partial view of our human condition; and the protest against its inhumanity is common in Shakespeare and obviously found a ready response in his audience. Of the ideal queen he says

those about her
From her shall read the perfect ways of honour
And by these claims their greatness, not by blood.

His Beltram therefore has no longer the excuse of the original

Beltram for his treatment of his wife, and he therefore becomes in Shakespeare a much more odious and indeed treacherous character. In order to save our respect and liking for Helena, Shakespeare has to blacken Bertram; and yet the more he blackens Bertram the less willing are we to accept Helena's pursuit as worthy of her sense and goodness. From this dilemma there is no escape on critical lines, and Shakespeare naturally recognises this; he simply takes it for granted we will ignore the difficulty and accept his intention without question. That his audience did so we need hardly doubt; to compensate for this concession on their part he gave them good measure elsewhere.

In his *Shakespeare*, a second Folio now preserved at Windsor, Charles I added *Parolles* as an alternative title for *All's Well*. Modern criticism is divided in its verdict on this character; some readers find him not merely an unpleasant but a singularly uninteresting character, others have pronounced him one of Shakespeare's masterpieces. Charles I's entry makes it clear that even the judicious could at one time find in this character the chief interest of the play.

In spite of paradoxical attempts to regard *All's Well* as a more serious or more satisfying play than the popular comedies, it will never find a place beside *Twelfth Night* or *Midsummer Night's Dream* as one of Shakespeare's most artistic achievements. It may well be that it is an early piece, possibly that mentioned by Meres as *Love's Labours Won*, which Shakespeare revised in later years for the boards, when he was engaged in writing his succession of tragic masterpieces.

THE KING. *Upon thy certainty and confidence*
What dar'st thou venture? (ACT II. SCENE I)

THE KING OF FRANCE
THE DUKE OF FLORENCE
BERTRAM, *Count of Rousillon*
LAFEU, *an old lord*
PAROLLES, *a follower of Bertram*
TWO FRENCH LORDS, *serving with Bertram*
STEWARD
LAVACHE, *a clown* } *servants to the Countess of Rousillon*
A PAGE

COUNTESS OF ROUSILLON, *mother to Bertram*
HELENA, *a gentlewoman protected by the Countess*
A WIDOW OF FLORENCE
DIANA, *daughter to the Widow*
VIOLENTA } *neighbours and friends to the Widow*
MARIANA

Lords, Officers, Soldiers, *etc.*, French *and* Florentine

SCENE:

Rousillon; Paris; Florence; Marseilles

All's Well that Ends Well

ACT I. SCENE 1

Rousillon. The Count's *palace*

Enter Bertram, *the* Countess of Rousillon, Helena,
and Lafeu, *all in black*

Countess. In delivering my son from me, I bury a second
husband.

Bertram. And I in going, madam, weep o'er my father's
death anew; but I must attend his Majesty's command, to
whom I am now in ward, evermore in subjection.

Lafeu. You shall find of the King a husband, madam; you,
sir, a father. He that so generally is at all times good must
of necessity hold his virtue to you, whose worthiness
would stir it up where it wanted, rather than lack it where
there is such abundance.

Countess. What hope is there of his Majesty's amendment?

Lafeu. He hath abandon'd his physicians, madam; under
whose practices he hath persecuted time with hope, and
finds no other advantage in the process but only the losing
of hope by time.

Countess. This young gentlewoman had a father—O, that
'had,' how sad a passage 'tis!—whose skill was almost as
great as his honesty; had it stretch'd so far, would have
made nature immortal, and death should have play for lack
of work. Would, for the King's sake, he were living! I
think it would be the death of the King's disease.

Lafeu. How call'd you the man you speak of, madam?

Countess. He was famous, sir, in his profession, and it was
his great right to be so—Gerard de Narbon.

Lafeu. He was excellent indeed, madam; the King very
lately spoke of him admiringly and mourningly; he was
skilful enough to have liv'd still, if knowledge could be set
up against mortality.

Bertram. What is it, my good lord, the King languishes of?

Lafeu. A fistula, my lord.

BERTRAM. I heard not of it before.

LAFEU. I would it were not notorious. Was this gentlewoman the daughter of Gerard de Narbon?

COUNTESS. His sole child, my lord, and bequeathed to my overlooking. I have those hopes of her good that her education promises; her dispositions she inherits, which makes fair gifts fairer; for where an unclean mind carries virtuous qualities, there commendations go with pity—they are virtues and traitors too. In her they are the better for their simpleness; she derives her honesty, and achieves her goodness.

LAFEU. Your commendations, madam, get from her tears.

COUNTESS. 'Tis the best brine a maiden can season her praise in. The remembrance of her father never approaches her heart but the tyranny of her sorrows takes all livelihood from her cheek. No more of this, Helena; go to, no more, lest it be rather thought you affect a sorrow than to have—

HELENA. I do affect a sorrow indeed, but I have it too.

LAFEU. Moderate lamentation is the right of the dead: excessive grief the enemy to the living.

COUNTESS. If the living be enemy to the grief, the excess makes it soon mortal.

BERTRAM. Madam, I desire your holy wishes.

LAFEU. How understand we that?

COUNTESS. Be thou blest, Bertram, and succeed thy father
In manners, as in shape! Thy blood and virtue
Contend for empire in thee, and thy goodness
Share with thy birthright! Love all, trust a few,
Do wrong to none; be able for thine enemy
Rather in power than use, and keep thy friend
Under thy own life's key; be check'd for silence,
But never tax'd for speech. What heaven more will,
That thee may furnish, and my prayers pluck down,
Fall on thy head! Farewell. My lord,
'Tis an unseason'd courtier; good my lord,
Advise him.

LAFEU. He cannot want the best
That shall attend his love.

COUNTESS. Heaven bless him! Farewell, Bertram.   *Exit*

BERTRAM. The best wishes that can be forg'd in your

thoughts be servants to you! [*To* HELENA] Be comfortable
to my mother, your mistress, and make much of her.

LAFEU. Farewell, pretty lady; you must hold the credit of
your father.   *Exeunt* BERTRAM *and* LAFEU

HELENA. O, were that all! I think not on my father;
And these great tears grace his remembrance more
Than those I shed for him. What was he like?
I have forgot him; my imagination
Carries no favour in't but Bertram's.
I am undone; there is no living, none,
If Bertram be away. 'Twere all one
That I should love a bright particular star
And think to wed it, he is so above me.
In his bright radiance and collateral light
Must I be comforted, not in his sphere.
Th' ambition in my love thus plagues itself:
The hind that would be mated by the lion
Must die for love. 'Twas pretty, though a plague,
To see him every hour; to sit and draw
His arched brows, his hawking eye, his curls,
In our heart's table—heart too capable
Of every line and trick of his sweet favour.
But now he's gone, and my idolatrous fancy
Must sanctify his relics. Who comes here?

Enter PAROLLES

[*Aside*] One that goes with him. I love him for his sake;
And yet I know him a notorious liar,
Think him a great way fool, solely a coward;
Yet these fix'd evils sit so fit in him
That they take place when virtue's steely bones
Looks bleak i' th' cold wind; withal, full oft we see
Cold wisdom waiting on superfluous folly.

PAROLLES. Save you, fair queen!

HELENA. And you, monarch!

PAROLLES. No.

HELENA. And no.

PAROLLES. Are you meditating on virginity?

HELENA. Ay. You have some stain of soldier in you; let me

ask you a question. Man is enemy to virginity; how may we barricado it against him?

PAROLLES. Keep him out.

HELENA. But he assails; and our virginity, though valiant in the defence, yet is weak. Unfold to us some warlike resistance.

PAROLLES. There is none. Man, setting down before you, will undermine you and blow you up.

HELENA. Bless our poor virginity from underminers and blowers-up! Is there no military policy how virgins might blow up men?

PAROLLES. Virginity being blown down, man will quicklier be blown up; marry, in blowing him down again, with the breach yourselves made, you lose your city. It is not politic in the commonwealth of nature to preserve virginity. Loss of virginity is rational increase; and there was never virgin got till virginity was first lost. That you were made of is metal to make virgins. Virginity by being once lost may be ten times found; by being ever kept, it is ever lost. 'Tis too cold a companion; away with't.

HELENA. I will stand for 't a little, though therefore I die a virgin.

PAROLLES. There's little can be said in't; 'tis against the rule of nature. To speak on the part of virginity is to accuse your mothers; which is most infallible disobedience. He that hangs himself is a virgin; virginity murders itself, and should be buried in highways, out of all sanctified limit, as a desperate offendress against nature. Virginity breeds mites, much like a cheese; consumes itself to the very paring, and so dies with feeding his own stomach. Besides, virginity is peevish, proud, idle, made of self-love, which is the most inhibited sin in the canon. Keep it not; you cannot choose but lose by't. Out with't. Within ten year it will make itself ten, which is a goodly increase; and the principal itself not much the worse. Away with't.

HELENA. How might one do, sir, to lose it to her own liking?

PAROLLES. Let me see. Marry, ill to like him that ne'er it likes. 'Tis a commodity will lose the gloss with lying; the longer kept, the less worth. Off with't while 'tis vendible; answer the time of request. Virginity, like an old courtier,

wears her cap out of fashion, richly suited but unsuitable;
just like the brooch and the toothpick, which wear not
now. Your date is better in your pie and your porridge
than in your cheek. And your virginity, your old virginity,
is like one of our French wither'd pears: it looks ill, it eats
drily; marry, 'tis a wither'd pear; it was formerly better;
marry, yet 'tis a wither'd pear. Will you anything with it?
HELENA. Not my virginity yet.
There shall your master have a thousand loves,
A mother, and a mistress, and a friend,
A phœnix, captain, and an enemy,
A guide, a goddess, and a sovereign,
A counsellor, a traitress, and a dear;
His humble ambition, proud humility,
His jarring concord, and his discord dulcet,
His faith, his sweet disaster; with a world
Of pretty, fond, adoptious christendoms
That blinking Cupid gossips. Now shall he—
I know not what he shall. God send him well!
The court's a learning-place, and he is one—
PAROLLES. What one, i' faith?
HELENA. That I wish well. 'Tis pity—
PAROLLES. What's pity?
HELENA. That wishing well had not a body in't
Which might be felt; that we, the poorer born,
Whose baser stars do shut us up in wishes,
Might with effects of them follow our friends
And show what we alone must think, which never
Returns us thanks.

Enter PAGE

PAGE. Monsieur Parolles, my lord calls for you. *Exit* PAGE
PAROLLES. Little Helen, farewell; if I can remember thee, I
will think of thee at court.
HELENA. Monsieur Parolles, you were born under a chari-
table star.
PAROLLES. Under Mars, I.
HELENA. I especially think, under Mars.
PAROLLES. Why under Mars?

HELENA. The wars hath so kept you under that you must needs be born under Mars.

PAROLLES. When he was predominant.

HELENA. When he was retrograde, I think, rather.

PAROLLES. Why think you so?

HELENA. You go so much backward when you fight.

PAROLLES. That's for advantage.

HELENA. So is running away, when fear proposes the safety; but the composition that your valour and fear makes in you is a virtue of a good wing, and I like the wear well.

PAROLLES. I am so full of business I cannot answer thee acutely. I will return perfect courtier; in the which my instruction shall serve to naturalize thee, so thou wilt be capable of a courtier's counsel, and understand what advice shall thrust upon thee; else thou diest in thine unthankfulness, and thine ignorance makes thee away. Farewell. When thou hast leisure, say thy prayers; when thou hast none, remember thy friends. Get thee a good husband, and use him as he uses thee. So, farewell.   *Exit*

HELENA. Our remedies oft in ourselves do lie,
Which we ascribe to heaven. The fated sky
Gives us free scope; only doth backward pull
Our slow designs when we ourselves are dull.
What power is it which mounts my love so high,
That makes me see, and cannot feed mine eye?
The mightiest space in fortune nature brings
To join like likes, and kiss like native things.
Impossible be strange attempts to those
That weigh their pains in sense, and do suppose
What hath been cannot be. Who ever strove
To show her merit that did miss her love?
The King's disease—my project may deceive me,
But my intents are fix'd, and will not leave me.   *Exit*

SCENE 2

Paris. The KING'S *palace*

Flourish of cornets. Enter the KING OF FRANCE, *with letters, and divers* ATTENDANTS

KING. The Florentines and Senoys are by th' ears;
Have fought with equal fortune, and continue
A braving war.
FIRST LORD. So 'tis reported, sir.
KING. Nay, 'tis most credible. We here receive it,
A certainty, vouch'd from our cousin Austria,
With caution, that the Florentine will move us
For speedy aid; wherein our dearest friend
Prejudicates the business, and would seem
To have us make denial.
FIRST LORD. His love and wisdom,
Approv'd so to your Majesty, may plead
For amplest credence.
KING. He hath arm'd our answer,
And Florence is denied before he comes;
Yet, for our gentlemen that mean to see
The Tuscan service, freely have they leave
To stand on either part.
SECOND LORD. It well may serve
A nursery to our gentry, who are sick
For breathing and exploit.
KING. What's he comes here?

Enter BERTRAM, LAFEU, *and* PAROLLES

FIRST LORD. It is the Count Rousillon, my good lord,
Young Bertram.
KING. Youth, thou bear'st thy father's face;
Frank nature, rather curious than in haste,
Hath well compos'd thee. Thy father's moral parts
Mayst thou inherit too! Welcome to Paris.
BERTRAM. My thanks and duty are your Majesty's.
KING. I would I had that corporal soundness now,
As when thy father and myself in friendship
First tried our soldiership. He did look far

Into the service of the time, and was
Discipled of the bravest. He lasted long;
But on us both did haggish age steal on,
And wore us out of act. It much repairs me
To talk of your good father. In his youth
He had the wit which I can well observe
To-day in our young lords; but they may jest
Till their own scorn return to them unnoted
Ere they can hide their levity in honour.
So like a courtier, contempt nor bitterness
Were in his pride or sharpness; if they were,
His equal had awak'd them; and his honour,
Clock to itself, knew the true minute when
Exception bid him speak, and at this time
His tongue obey'd his hand. Who were below him
He us'd as creatures of another place;
And bow'd his eminent top to their low ranks,
Making them proud of his humility
In their poor praise he humbled. Such a man
Might be a copy to these younger times;
Which, followed well, would demonstrate them now
But goers backward.
BERTRAM. His good remembrance, sir,
Lies richer in your thoughts than on his tomb;
So in approof lives not his epitaph
As in your royal speech.
KING. Would I were with him! He would always say—
Methinks I hear him now; his plausive words
He scatter'd not in ears, but grafted them
To grow there, and to bear—'Let me not live'—
This his good melancholy oft began,
On the catastrophe and heel of pastime,
When it was out—'Let me not live' quoth he
'After my flame lacks oil, to be the snuff
Of younger spirits, whose apprehensive senses
All but new things disdain; whose judgments are
Mere fathers of their garments; whose constancies
Expire before their fashions.' This he wish'd.
I, after him, do after him wish too,
Since I nor wax nor honey can bring home,

I quickly were dissolved from my hive,
To give some labourers room.
SECOND LORD. You're loved, sir;
They that least lend it you shall lack you first.
KING. I fill a place, I know't. How long is't, Count,
Since the physician at your father's died?
He was much fam'd.
BERTRAM. Some six months since, my lord.
KING. If he were living, I would try him yet—
Lend me an arm—the rest have worn me out
With several applications. Nature and sickness
Debate it at their leisure. Welcome, Count;
My son's no dearer.
BERTRAM. Thank your Majesty.   *Exeunt* [*Flourish*]

SCENE 3

Rousillon. The COUNT's *palace*

Enter COUNTESS, STEWARD, *and* CLOWN

COUNTESS. I will now hear; what say you of this gentlewoman?
STEWARD. Madam, the care I have had to even your content
I wish might be found in the calendar of my past endeavours; for then we wound our modesty, and make foul
the clearness of our deservings, when of ourselves we publish them.
COUNTESS. What does this knave here? Get you gone, sirrah.
The complaints I have heard of you I do not all believe; 'tis
my slowness that I do not, for I know you lack not folly
to commit them and have ability enough to make such
knaveries yours.
CLOWN. 'Tis not unknown to you, madam, I am a poor
fellow.
COUNTESS. Well, sir.
CLOWN. No, madam, 'tis not so well that I am poor, though
many of the rich are damn'd; but if I may have your ladyship's good will to go to the world, Isbel the woman and I
will do as we may.
COUNTESS. Wilt thou needs be a beggar?

855

CLOWN. I do beg your good will in this case.

COUNTESS. In what case?

CLOWN. In Isbel's case and mine own. Service is no heritage; and I think I shall never have the blessing of God till I have issue o' my body; for they say barnes are blessings.

COUNTESS. Tell me thy reason why thou wilt marry.

CLOWN. My poor body, madam, requires it. I am driven on by the flesh; and he must needs go that the devil drives.

COUNTESS. Is this all your worship's reason?

CLOWN. Faith, madam, I have other holy reasons, such as they are.

COUNTESS. May the world know them?

CLOWN. I have been, madam, a wicked creature, as you and all flesh and blood are; and, indeed, I do marry that I may repent.

COUNTESS. Thy marriage, sooner than thy wickedness.

CLOWN. I am out o' friends, madam, and I hope to have friends for my wife's sake.

COUNTESS. Such friends are thine enemies, knave.

CLOWN. Y'are shallow, madam—in great friends; for the knaves come to do that for me which I am aweary of. He that ears my land spares my team, and gives me leave to in the crop. If I be his cuckold, he's my drudge. He that comforts my wife is the cherisher of my flesh and blood; he that cherishes my flesh and blood loves my flesh and blood; he that loves my flesh and blood is my friend; ergo, he that kisses my wife is my friend. If men could be contented to be what they are, there were no fear in marriage; for young Charbon the puritan and old Poysam the papist, howsome'er their hearts are sever'd in religion, their heads are both one; they may jowl horns together like any deer i' th' herd.

COUNTESS. Wilt thou ever be a foul-mouth'd and calumnious knave?

CLOWN. A prophet I, madam; and I speak the truth the next way:

> For I the ballad will repeat,
>   Which men full true shall find:
> Your marriage comes by destiny,
>   Your cuckoo sings by kind.

COUNTESS. Get you gone, sir; I'll talk with you more anon.

STEWARD. May it please you, madam, that he bid Helen come to you. Of her I am to speak.

COUNTESS. Sirrah, tell my gentlewoman I would speak with her; Helen I mean.

CLOWN. [*Sings*]

> 'Was this fair face the cause' quoth she
>   'Why the Grecians sacked Troy?
> Fond done, done fond,
>   Was this King Priam's joy?'
> With that she sighed as she stood,
> With that she sighed as she stood,
>   And gave this sentence then:
> 'Among nine bad if one be good,
> Among nine bad if one be good,
>   There's yet one good in ten.'

COUNTESS. What, one good in ten? You corrupt the song, sirrah.

CLOWN. One good woman in ten, madam, which is a purify-ing o' th' song. Would God would serve the world so all the year! We'd find no fault with the tithe-woman, if I were the parson. One in ten, quoth 'a! An we might have a good woman born before every blazing star, or at an earthquake, 'twould mend the lottery well: a man may draw his heart out ere 'a pluck one.

COUNTESS. You'll be gone, sir knave, and do as I command you.

CLOWN. That man should be at woman's command, and yet no hurt done! Though honesty be no puritan, yet it will do no hurt; it will wear the surplice of humility over the black gown of a big heart. I am going, forsooth. The busi-ness is for Helen to come hither.   *Exit*

COUNTESS. Well, now.

STEWARD. I know, madam, you love your gentlewoman en-tirely.

COUNTESS. Faith I do. Her father bequeath'd her to me; and she herself, without other advantage, may lawfully make title to as much love as she finds. There is more owing her than is paid; and more shall be paid her than she'll demand.

857

STEWARD. Madam, I was very late more near her than I think she wish'd me. Alone she was, and did communicate to herself her own words to her own ears; she thought, I dare vow for her, they touch'd not any stranger sense. Her matter was, she loved your son. Fortune, she said, was no goddess, that had put such difference betwixt their two estates; Love no god, that would not extend his might only where qualities were level; Diana no queen of virgins, that would suffer her poor knight surpris'd without rescue in the first assault, or ransom afterward. This she deliver'd in the most bitter touch of sorrow that e'er I heard virgin exclaim in; which I held my duty speedily to acquaint you withal; sithence, in the loss that may happen, it concerns you something to know it.

COUNTESS. You have discharg'd this honestly; keep it to yourself. Many likelihoods inform'd me of this before, which hung so tott'ring in the balance that I could neither believe nor misdoubt. Pray you leave me. Stall this in your bosom; and I thank you for your honest care. I will speak with you further anon.   *Exit* STEWARD

Enter HELENA

Even so it was with me when I was young.
If ever we are nature's, these are ours; this thorn
Doth to our rose of youth rightly belong;
Our blood to us, this to our blood is born.
It is the show and seal of nature's truth,
Where love's strong passion is impress'd in youth.
By our remembrances of days foregone,
Such were our faults, or then we thought them none.
Her eye is sick on't; I observe her now.
HELENA. What is your pleasure, madam?
COUNTESS. You know, Helen,
I am a mother to you.
HELENA. Mine honourable mistress.
COUNTESS. Nay, a mother.
Why not a mother? When I said 'a mother,'
Methought you saw a serpent. What's in 'mother'
That you start at it? I say I am your mother,
And put you in the catalogue of those

That were enwombed mine. 'Tis often seen
Adoption strives with nature, and choice breeds
A native slip to us from foreign seeds.
You ne'er oppress'd me with a mother's groan,
Yet I express to you a mother's care.
God's mercy, maiden! does it curd thy blood
To say I am thy mother? What's the matter,
That this distempered messenger of wet,
The many-colour'd Iris, rounds thine eye?
Why, that you are my daughter?
HELENA. That I am not.
COUNTESS. I say I am your mother.
HELENA. Pardon, madam.
    The Count Rousillon cannot be my brother:
I am from humble, he from honoured name;
No note upon my parents, his all noble.
My master, my dear lord he is; and I
His servant live, and will his vassal die.
He must not be my brother.
COUNTESS. Nor I your mother?
HELENA. You are my mother, madam; would you were—
So that my lord your son were not my brother—
Indeed my mother! Or were you both our mothers,
I care no more for than I do for heaven,
So I were not his sister. Can't no other,
But, I your daughter, he must be my brother?
COUNTESS. Yes, Helen, you might be my daughter-in-law.
God shield you mean it not! 'daughter' and 'mother'
So strive upon your pulse. What! pale again?
My fear hath catch'd your fondness. Now I see
The myst'ry of your loneliness, and find
Your salt tears' head. Now to all sense 'tis gross
You love my son; invention is asham'd,
Against the proclamation of thy passion,
To say thou dost not. Therefore tell me true;
But tell me then, 'tis so; for, look, thy cheeks
Confess it, th' one to th' other; and thine eyes
See it so grossly shown in thy behaviours
That in their kind they speak it; only sin
And hellish obstinacy tie thy tongue,

That truth should be suspected. Speak, is't so?
If it be so, you have wound a goodly clew;
If it be not, forswear't; howe'er, I charge thee,
As heaven shall work in me for thine avail,
To tell me truly.

HELENA. Good madam, pardon me.

COUNTESS. Do you love my son?

HELENA. Your pardon, noble mistress.

COUNTESS. Love you my son?

HELENA. Do not you love him, madam?

COUNTESS. Go not about; my love hath in't a bond
Whereof the world takes note. Come, come, disclose
The state of your affection; for your passions
Have to the full appeach'd.

HELENA. Then I confess,
Here on my knee, before high heaven and you,
That before you, and next unto high heaven,
I love your son.
My friends were poor, but honest; so's my love.
Be not offended, for it hurts not him
That he is lov'd of me; I follow him not
By any token of presumptuous suit,
Nor would I have him till I do deserve him;
Yet never know how that desert should be.
I know I love in vain, strive against hope;
Yet in this captious and intenible sieve
I still pour in the waters of my love,
And lack not to lose still. Thus, Indian-like,
Religious in mine error, I adore
The sun that looks upon his worshipper
But knows of him no more. My dearest madam,
Let not your hate encounter with my love,
For loving where you do; but if yourself,
Whose aged honour cites a virtuous youth,
Did ever in so true a flame of liking
Wish chastely and love dearly that your Dian
Was both herself and Love; O, then, give pity
To her whose state is such that cannot choose
But lend and give where she is sure to lose;
That seeks not to find that her search implies,

But, riddle-like, lives sweetly where she dies!
COUNTESS. Had you not lately an intent—speak truly—
  To go to Paris?
HELENA. Madam, I had.
COUNTESS. Wherefore? Tell true.
HELENA. I will tell truth; by grace itself I swear.
  You know my father left me some prescriptions
  Of rare and prov'd effects, such as his reading
  And manifest experience had collected
  For general sovereignty; and that he will'd me
  In heedfull'st reservation to bestow them,
  As notes whose faculties inclusive were
  More than they were in note. Amongst the rest
  There is a remedy, approv'd, set down,
  To cure the desperate languishings whereof
  The King is render'd lost.
COUNTESS. This was your motive
  For Paris, was it? Speak.
HELENA. My lord your son made me to think of this,
  Else Paris, and the medicine, and the King,
  Had from the conversation of my thoughts
  Haply been absent then.
COUNTESS. But think you, Helen,
  If you should tender your supposed aid,
  He would receive it? He and his physicians
  Are of a mind: he, that they cannot help him;
  They, that they cannot help. How shall they credit
  A poor unlearned virgin, when the schools,
  Embowell'd of their doctrine, have let off
  The danger to itself?
HELENA. There's something in't
  More than my father's skill, which was the great'st
  Of his profession, that his good receipt
  Shall for my legacy be sanctified
  By th' luckiest stars in heaven; and, would your honour
  But give me leave to try success, I'd venture
  The well-lost life of mine on his Grace's cure.
  By such a day and hour.
COUNTESS. Dost thou believe't?
HELENA. Ay, madam, knowingly.

COUNTESS. Why, Helen, thou shalt have my leave and love,
Means and attendants, and my loving greetings
To those of mine in court. I'll stay at home,
And pray God's blessing into thy attempt.
Be gone to-morrow; and be sure of this,
What I can help thee to thou shalt not miss.　　*Exeunt*

ACT II. SCENE 1

Paris. The KING's *palace*

Flourish of cornets. Enter the KING *with divers
young* LORDS *taking leave for the Florentine war;*
BERTRAM *and* PAROLLES; ATTENDANTS

KING. Farewell, young lords; these war-like principles
Do not throw from you. And you, my lords, farewell;
Share the advice betwixt you; if both gain all,
The gift doth stretch itself as 'tis receiv'd,
And is enough for both.
FIRST LORD. 'Tis our hope, sir,
After well-ent'red soldiers, to return
And find your Grace in health.
KING. No, no, it cannot be; and yet my heart
Will not confess he owes the malady
That doth my life besiege. Farewell, young lords;
Whether I live or die, be you the sons
Of worthy Frenchmen; let higher Italy—
Those bated that inherit but the fall
Of the last monarchy—see that you come
Not to woo honour, but to wed it; when
The bravest questant shrinks, find what you seek,
That fame may cry you aloud. I say farewell.
SECOND LORD. Health, at your bidding, serve your Majesty!
KING. Those girls of Italy, take heed of them;
They say our French lack language to deny,
If they demand; beware of being captives
Before you serve.

862

BOTH. Our hearts receive your warnings.

KING. Farewell. [*To* ATTENDANTS] Come hither to me.

The KING *retires attended*

FIRST LORD. O my sweet lord, that you will stay behind us!

PAROLLES. 'Tis not his fault, the spark.

SECOND LORD. O, 'tis brave wars!

PAROLLES. Most admirable! I have seen those wars.

BERTRAM. I am commanded here and kept a coil with
'Too young' and 'The next year' and ' 'Tis too early.'

PAROLLES. An thy mind stand to 't, boy, steal away bravely.

BERTRAM. I shall stay here the forehorse to a smock,
Creaking my shoes on the plain masonry,
Till honour be bought up, and no sword worn
But one to dance with. By heaven, I'll steal away.

FIRST LORD. There's honour in the theft.

PAROLLES. Commit it, Count.

SECOND LORD. I am your accessary; and so farewell.

BERTRAM. I grow to you, and our parting is a tortur'd body.

FIRST LORD. Farewell, Captain.

SECOND LORD. Sweet Monsieur Parolles!

PAROLLES. Noble heroes, my sword and yours are kin. Good
sparks and lustrous, a word, good metals: you shall find in
the regiment of the Spinii one Captain Spurio, with his
cicatrice, an emblem of war, here on his sinister cheek; it
was this very sword entrench'd it. Say to him I live; and
observe his reports for me.

FIRST LORD. We shall, noble Captain.

PAROLLES. Mars dote on you for his novices!   *Exeunt* LORDS
What will ye do?

Re-enter the KING

BERTRAM. Stay; the King!

PAROLLES. Use a more spacious ceremony to the noble lords;
you have restrain'd yourself within the list of too cold an
adieu. Be more expressive to them; for they wear themselves in the cap of the time; there do muster true gait; eat,
speak, and move, under the influence of the most receiv'd
star; and though the devil lead the measure, such are to be
followed. After them, and take a more dilated farewell.

BERTRAM. And I will do so.

PAROLLES. Worthy fellows; and like to prove most sinewy sword-men.   *Exeunt* BERTRAM *and* PAROLLES

Enter LAFEU

LAFEU. [*Kneeling*] Pardon, my lord, for me and for my tidings.

KING. I'll fee thee to stand up.

LAFEU. Then here's a man stands that has brought his pardon.
  I would you had kneel'd, my lord, to ask me mercy;
  And that at my bidding you could so stand up.

KING. I would I had; so I had broke thy pate,
  And ask'd thee mercy for't.

LAFEU. Good faith, across!
  But, my good lord, 'tis thus: will you be cur'd
  Of your infirmity?

KING. No.

LAFEU. O, will you eat
  No grapes, my royal fox? Yes, but you will
  My noble grapes, an if my royal fox
  Could reach them: I have seen a medicine
  That's able to breathe life into a stone,
  Quicken a rock, and make you dance canary
  With spritely fire and motion; whose simple touch
  Is powerful to araise King Pepin, nay,
  To give great Charlemain a pen in's hand
  And write to her a love-line.

KING. What her is this?

LAFEU. Why, Doctor She! My lord, there's one arriv'd,
  If you will see her. Now, by my faith and honour,
  If seriously I may convey my thoughts
  In this my light deliverance, I have spoke
  With one that in her sex, her years, profession,
  Wisdom, and constancy, hath amaz'd me more
  Than I dare blame my weakness. Will you see her,
  For that is her demand, and know her business?
  That done, laugh well at me.

KING. Now, good Lafeu,
  Bring in the admiration, that we with thee
  May spend our wonder too, or take off thine

By wond'ring how thou took'st it.

LAFEU. Nay, I'll fit you,

And not be all day neither.   *Exit* LAFEU

KING. Thus he his special nothing ever prologues.

Re-enter LAFEU *with* HELENA

LAFEU. Nay, come your ways.

KING. This haste hath wings indeed.

LAFEU. Nay, come your ways;

This is his Majesty; say your mind to him.

A traitor you do look like; but such traitors

His Majesty seldom fears. I am Cressid's uncle,

That dare leave two together. Fare you well.   *Exit*

KING. Now, fair one, does your business follow us?

HELENA. Ay, my good lord.

Gerard de Narbon was my father,

In what he did profess, well found.

KING. I knew him.

HELENA. The rather will I spare my praises towards him;

Knowing him is enough. On's bed of death

Many receipts he gave me; chiefly one,

Which, as the dearest issue of his practice,

And of his old experience th' only darling,

He bade me store up as a triple eye,

Safer than mine own two, more dear. I have so:

And, hearing your high Majesty is touch'd

With that malignant cause wherein the honour

Of my dear father's gift stands chief in power,

I come to tender it, and my appliance,

With all bound humbleness.

KING. We thank you, maiden;

But may not be so credulous of cure,

When our most learned doctors leave us, and

The congregated college have concluded

That labouring art can never ransom nature

From her inaidable estate—I say we must not

So stain our judgment, or corrupt our hope,

To prostitute our past-cure malady

To empirics; or to dissever so

Our great self and our credit to esteem

A senseless help, when help past sense we deem.
HELENA. My duty then shall pay me for my pains.
I will no more enforce mine office on you;
Humbly entreating from your royal thoughts
A modest one to bear me back again.
KING. I cannot give thee less, to be call'd grateful.
Thou thought'st to help me; and such thanks I give
As one near death to those that wish him live.
But what at full I know, thou know'st no part;
I knowing all my peril, thou no art.
HELENA. What I can do can do no hurt to try,
Since you set up your rest 'gainst remedy.
He that of greatest works is finisher
Oft does them by the weakest minister.
So holy writ in babes hath judgment shown,
When judges have been babes. Great floods have flown
From simple sources, and great seas have dried
When miracles have by the greatest been denied.
Oft expectation fails, and most oft there
Where most it promises; and oft it hits
Where hope is coldest, and despair most fits.
KING. I must not hear thee. Fare thee well, kind maid;
Thy pains, not us'd, must by thyself be paid;
Proffers not took reap thanks for their reward.
HELENA. Inspired merit so by breath is barr'd.
It is not so with Him that all things knows,
As 'tis with us that square our guess by shows;
But most it is presumption in us when
The help of heaven we count the act of men.
Dear sir, to my endeavours give consent;
Of heaven, not me, make an experiment.
I am not an impostor, that proclaim
Myself against the level of mine aim;
But know I think, and think I know most sure,
My art is not past power nor you past cure.
KING. Art thou so confident? Within what space
Hop'st thou my cure?
HELENA. The greatest Grace lending grace,
Ere twice the horses of the sun shall bring
Their fiery torcher his diurnal ring,

Ere twice in murk and occidental damp
Moist Hesperus hath quench'd his sleepy lamp,
Or four and twenty times the pilot's glass
Hath told the thievish minutes how they pass,
What is infirm from your sound parts shall fly,
Health shall live free, and sickness freely die.
KING. Upon thy certainty and confidence
What dar'st thou venture?
HELENA. Tax of impudence,
A strumpet's boldness, a divulged shame,
Traduc'd by odious ballads; my maiden's name
Sear'd otherwise; ne worse of worst—extended
With vilest torture let my life be ended.
KING. Methinks in thee some blessed spirit doth speak
His powerful sound within an organ weak;
And what impossibility would slay
In common sense, sense saves another way.
Thy life is dear; for all that life can rate
Worth name of life in thee hath estimate:
Youth, beauty, wisdom, courage, all
That happiness and prime can happy call.
Thou this to hazard needs must intimate
Skill infinite or monstrous desperate.
Sweet practiser, thy physic I will try,
That ministers thine own death if I die.
HELENA. If I break time, or flinch in property
Of what I spoke, unpitied let me die;
And well deserv'd. Not helping, death's my fee;
But, if I help, what do you promise me?
KING. Make thy demand.
HELENA. But will you make it even?
KING. Ay, by my sceptre and my hopes of heaven.
HELENA. Then shalt thou give me with thy kingly hand
What husband in thy power I will command.
Exempted be from me the arrogance
To choose from forth the royal blood of France,
My low and humble name to propagate
With any branch or image of thy state;
But such a one, thy vassal, whom I know
Is free for me to ask, thee to bestow.

KING. Here is my hand; the premises observ'd,
Thy will by my performance shall be serv'd.
So make the choice of thy own time, for I,
Thy resolv'd patient, on thee still rely.
More should I question thee, and more I must,
Though more to know could not be more to trust,
From whence thou cam'st, how tended on. But rest
Unquestion'd welcome and undoubted blest.
Give me some help here, ho! If thou proceed
As high as word, my deed shall match thy deed.

[Flourish. Exeunt]

SCENE 2

Rousillon. The COUNT'S *palace*

Enter COUNTESS *and* CLOWN

COUNTESS. Come on, sir; I shall now put you to the height of your breeding.

CLOWN. I will show myself highly fed and lowly taught. I know my business is but to the court.

COUNTESS. To the court! Why, what place make you special, when you put off that with such contempt? But to the court!

CLOWN. Truly, madam, if God have lent a man any manners, he may easily put it off at court. He that cannot make a leg, put off's cap, kiss his hand, and say nothing, has neither leg, hands, lip, nor cap; and indeed such a fellow, to say precisely, were not for the court; but for me, I have an answer will serve all men.

COUNTESS. Marry, that's a bountiful answer that fits all questions.

CLOWN. It is like a barber's chair, that fits all buttocks—the pin buttock, the quatch buttock, the brawn buttock, or any buttock.

COUNTESS. Will your answer serve fit to all questions?

CLOWN. As fit as ten groats is for the hand of an attorney, as your French crown for your taffety punk, as Tib's rush for Tom's forefinger, as a pancake for Shrove Tuesday, a morris for Mayday, as the nail to his hole, the cuckold to his horn, as a scolding quean to a wrangling knave, as the nun's lip to the friar's mouth; nay, as the pudding to his skin.

COUNTESS. Have you, I say, an answer of such fitness for all questions?

CLOWN. From below your duke to beneath your constable, it will fit any question.

COUNTESS. It must be an answer of most monstrous size that must fit all demands.

CLOWN. But a trifle neither, in good faith, if the learned should speak truth of it. Here it is, and all that belongs to't. Ask me if I am a courtier: it shall do you no harm to learn.

COUNTESS. To be young again, if we could, I will be a fool in question, hoping to be the wiser by your answer. I pray you, sir, are you a courtier?

CLOWN. O Lord, sir!—There's a simple putting off. More, more, a hundred of them.

COUNTESS. Sir, I am a poor friend of yours, that loves you.

CLOWN. O Lord, sir!—Thick, thick; spare not me.

COUNTESS. I think, sir, you can eat none of this homely meat.

CLOWN. O Lord, sir!—Nay, put me to't, I warrant you.

COUNTESS. You were lately whipp'd, sir, as I think.

CLOWN. O Lord, sir!—Spare not me.

COUNTESS. Do you cry 'O Lord, sir!' at your whipping, and 'spare not me'? Indeed your 'O Lord, sir!' is very sequent to your whipping. You would answer very well to a whipping, if you were but bound to't.

CLOWN. I ne'er had worse luck in my life in my 'O Lord, sir!' I see things may serve long, but not serve ever.

COUNTESS. I play the noble housewife with the time,
To entertain it so merrily with a fool.

CLOWN. O Lord, sir!—Why, there't serves well again.

COUNTESS. An end, sir! To your business: give Helen this,
And urge her to a present answer back;
Commend me to my kinsmen and my son. This is not much.

CLOWN. Not much commendation to them?

COUNTESS. Not much employment for you. You understand me?

CLOWN. Most fruitfully; I am there before my legs.
COUNTESS. Haste you again.   *Exeunt*

SCENE 3

Paris. The KING'S *palace*

Enter BERTRAM, LAFEU, *and* PAROLLES

LAFEU. They say miracles are past; and we have our philo-
sophical persons to make modern and familiar things super-
natural and causeless. Hence is it that we make trifles of
terrors, ensconcing ourselves into seeming knowledge
when we should submit ourselves to an unknown fear.
PAROLLES. Why, 'tis the rarest argument of wonder that hath
shot out in our latter times.
BERTRAM. And so 'tis.
LAFEU. To be relinquish'd of the artists—
PAROLLES. So I say—both of Galen and Paracelsus.
LAFEU. Of all the learned and authentic fellows—
PAROLLES. Right; so I say.
LAFEU. That gave him out incurable—
PAROLLES. Why, there 'tis; so say I too.
LAFEU. Not to be help'd—
PAROLLES. Right; as 'twere a man assur'd of a—
LAFEU. Uncertain life and sure death.
PAROLLES. Just; you say well; so would I have said.
LAFEU. I may truly say it is a novelty to the world.
PAROLLES. It is indeed. If you will have it in showing, you
shall read it in what-do-ye-call't here.
LAFEU. [*Reading the ballad title*] 'A Showing of a Heavenly
Effect in an Earthly Actor.'
PAROLLES. That's it; I would have said the very same.
LAFEU. Why, your dolphin is not lustier. 'Fore me, I speak
in respect—
PAROLLES. Nay, 'tis strange, 'tis very strange; that is the brief
and the tedious of it; and he's of a most facinerious spirit
that will not acknowledge it to be the—
LAFEU. Very hand of heaven.
PAROLLES. Ay; so I say.

870

LAFEU. In a most weak—

PAROLLES. And debile minister, great power, great transcendence; which should, indeed, give us a further use to be made than alone the recov'ry of the King, as to be—

LAFEU. Generally thankful.

Enter KING, HELENA, *and* ATTENDANTS

PAROLLES. I would have said it; you say well. Here comes the King.

LAFEU. Lustig, as the Dutchman says. I'll like a maid the better, whilst I have a tooth in my head. Why, he's able to lead her a coranto.

PAROLLES. Mort du vinaigre! Is not this Helen?

LAFEU. 'Fore God, I think so.

KING. Go, call before me all the lords in court.

Exit an ATTENDANT

Sit, my preserver, by thy patient's side;
And with this healthful hand, whose banish'd sense
Thou has repeal'd, a second time receive
The confirmation of my promis'd gift,
Which but attends thy naming.

Enter three or four LORDS

Fair maid, send forth thine eye. This youthful parcel
Of noble bachelors stand at my bestowing,
O'er whom both sovereign power and father's voice
I have to use. Thy frank election make;
Thou hast power to choose, and they none to forsake.

HELENA. To each of you one fair and virtuous mistress
Fall, when love please. Marry, to each but one!

LAFEU. I'd give bay Curtal and his furniture
My mouth no more were broken than these boys',
And writ as little beard.

KING. Peruse them well.
Not one of those but had a noble father.

HELENA. Gentlemen,
Heaven hath through me restor'd the King to health.

ALL. We understand it, and thank heaven for you.

HELENA. I am a simple maid, and therein wealthiest
That I protest I simply am a maid.

Please it your Majesty, I have done already.
The blushes in my cheeks thus whisper me:
'We blush that thou shouldst choose; but, be refused,
Let the white death sit on thy cheek for ever,
We'll ne'er come there again.'
KING. Make choice and see:
Who shuns thy love shuns all his love in me.
HELENA. Now, Dian, from thy altar do I fly,
And to imperial Love, that god most high,
Do my sighs stream. Sir, will you hear my suit?
FIRST LORD. And grant it.
HELENA. Thanks, sir; all the rest is mute.
LAFEU. I had rather be in this choice than throw ames-ace
for my life.
HELENA. The honour, sir, that flames in your fair eyes,
Before I speak, too threat'ningly replies.
Love make your fortunes twenty times above
Her that so wishes, and her humble love!
SECOND LORD. No better, if you please.
HELENA. My wish receive,
Which great Love grant; and so I take my leave.
LAFEU. Do all they deny her? An they were sons of mine
I'd have them whipt; or I would send them to th' Turk
to make eunuchs of.
HELENA. Be not afraid that I your hand should take;
I'll never do you wrong for your own sake.
Blessing upon your vows; and in your bed
Find fairer fortune, if you ever wed!
LAFEU. These boys are boys of ice; they'll none have her.
Sure, they are bastards to the English; the French ne'er got
'em.
HELENA. You are too young, too happy, and too good,
To make yourself a son out of my blood.
FOURTH LORD. Fair one, I think not so.
LAFEU. There's one grape yet; I am sure thy father drunk
wine—but if thou be'st not an ass, I am a youth of four-
teen; I have known thee already.
HELENA. [To BERTRAM] I dare not say I take you; but I
give
Me and my service, ever whilst I live,

872

Into your guiding power. This is the man.
KING. Why, then, young Bertram, take her; she's thy wife.
BERTRAM. My wife, my liege! I shall beseech your Highness,
　In such a business give me leave to use
　The help of mine own eyes.
KING. Know'st thou not, Bertram,
　What she has done for me?
BERTRAM. Yes, my good lord;
　But never hope to know why I should marry her.
KING. Thou know'st she has rais'd me from my sickly bed.
BERTRAM. But follows it, my lord, to bring me down
　Must answer for your raising? I know her well:
　She had her breeding at my father's charge.
　A poor physician's daughter my wife! Disdain
　Rather corrupt me ever!
KING. 'Tis only title thou disdain'st in her, the which
　I can build up. Strange is it that our bloods,
　Of colour, weight, and heat, pour'd all together,
　Would quite confound distinction, yet stand off
　In differences so mighty. If she be
　All that is virtuous—save what thou dislik'st,
　A poor physician's daughter—thou dislik'st
　Of virtue for the name; but do not so.
　From lowest place when virtuous things proceed,
　The place is dignified by the doer's deed;
　Where great additions swell 's, and virtue none,
　It is a dropsied honour. Good alone
　Is good without a name. Vileness is so:
　The property by what it is should go,
　Not by the title. She is young, wise, fair;
　In these to nature she's immediate heir;
　And these breed honour. That is honour's scorn
　Which challenges itself as honour's born
　And is not like the sire. Honours thrive
　When rather from our acts we them derive
　Than our fore-goers. The mere word's a slave,
　Debauch'd on every tomb, on every grave
　A lying trophy; and as oft is dumb
　Where dust and damn'd oblivion is the tomb
　Of honour'd bones indeed. What should be said?

If thou canst like this creature as a maid,
I can create the rest. Virtue and she
Is her own dower; honour and wealth from me.
BERTRAM. I cannot love her, nor will strive to do't.
KING. Thou wrong'st thyself, if thou shouldst strive to
  choose.
HELENA. That you are well restor'd, my lord, I'm glad.
  Let the rest go.
KING. My honour's at the stake; which to defeat,
  I must produce my power. Here, take her hand,
  Proud scornful boy, unworthy this good gift,
  That dost in vile misprision shackle up
  My love and her desert; that canst not dream
  We, poising us in her defective scale,
  Shall weigh thee to the beam; that wilt not know
  It is in us to plant thine honour where
  We please to have it grow. Check thy contempt;
  Obey our will, which travails in thy good;
  Believe not thy disdain, but presently
  Do thine own fortunes that obedient right
  Which both thy duty owes and our power claims;
  Or I will throw thee from my care for ever
  Into the staggers and the careless lapse
  Of youth and ignorance; both my revenge and hate
  Loosing upon thee in the name of justice,
  Without all terms of pity. Speak; thine answer.
BERTRAM. Pardon, my gracious lord; for I submit
  My fancy to your eyes. When I consider
  What great creation and what dole of honour
  Flies where you bid it, I find that she which late
  Was in my nobler thoughts most base is now
  The praised of the King; who, so ennobled,
  Is as 'twere born so.
KING. Take her by the hand,
  And tell her she is thine; to whom I promise
  A counterpoise, if not to thy estate
  A balance more replete.
BERTRAM. I take her hand.
KING. Good fortune and the favour of the King
  Smile upon this contract; whose ceremony

Shall seem expedient on the now-born brief,
And be perform'd to-night. The solemn feast
Shall more attend upon the coming space,
Expecting absent friends. As thou lov'st her,
Thy love's to me religious; else, does err.

> *Exeunt all but* LAFEU *and* PAROLLES *who stay behind,*
> *commenting of this wedding*

LAFEU. Do you hear, monsieur? A word with you.

PAROLLES. Your pleasure, sir?

LAFEU. Your lord and master did well to make his recantation.

PAROLLES. Recantation! My Lord! my master!

LAFEU. Ay; is it not a language I speak?

PAROLLES. A most harsh one, and not to be understood without bloody succeeding. My master!

LAFEU. Are you companion to the Count Rousillon?

PAROLLES. To any count; to all counts; to what is man.

LAFEU. To what is count's man: count's master is of another style.

PAROLLES. You are too old, sir; let it satisfy you, you are too old.

LAFEU. I must tell thee, sirrah, I write man; to which title age cannot bring thee.

PAROLLES. What I dare too well do, I dare not do.

LAFEU. I did think thee, for two ordinaries, to be a pretty wise fellow; thou didst make tolerable vent of thy travel; it might pass. Yet the scarfs and the bannerets about thee did manifoldly dissuade me from believing thee a vessel of too great a burden. I have now found thee; when I lose thee again I care not; yet art thou good for nothing but taking up; and that thou'rt scarce worth.

PAROLLES. Hadst thou not the privilege of antiquity upon thee—

LAFEU. Do not plunge thyself too far in anger, lest thou hasten thy trial; which if—Lord have mercy on thee for a hen! So, my good window of lattice, fare thee well; thy casement I need not open, for I look through thee. Give me thy hand.

PAROLLES. My lord, you give me most egregious indignity.

LAFEU. Ay, with all my heart; and thou art worthy of it.

PAROLLES. I have not, my lord, deserv'd it.

LAFEU. Yes, good faith, ev'ry dram of it; and I will not bate thee a scruple.

PAROLLES. Well, I shall be wiser.

LAFEU. Ev'n as soon as thou canst, for thou hast to pull at a smack o' th' contrary. If ever thou be'st bound in thy scarf and beaten, thou shalt find what it is to be proud of thy bondage. I have a desire to hold my acquaintance with thee, or rather my knowledge, that I may say in the default 'He is a man I know.'

PAROLLES. My lord, you do me most insupportable vexation.

LAFEU. I would it were hell pains for thy sake, and my poor doing eternal; for doing I am past, as I will by thee, in what motion age will give me leave. *Exit*

PAROLLES. Well, thou hast a son shall take this disgrace off me: scurvy, old, filthy, scurvy lord! Well, I must be patient; there is no fettering of authority. I'll beat him, by my life, if I can meet him with any convenience, an he were double and double a lord. I'll have no more pity of his age than I would have of—I'll beat him, and if I could but meet him again.

Re-enter LAFEU

LAFEU. Sirrah, your lord and master's married; there's news for you; you have a new mistress.

PAROLLES. I most unfeignedly beseech your lordship to make some reservation of your wrongs. He is my good lord: whom I serve above is my master.

LAFEU. Who? God?

PAROLLES. Ay, sir.

LAFEU. The devil it is that's thy master. Why dost thou garter up thy arms o' this fashion? Dost make hose of thy sleeves? Do other servants so? Thou wert best set thy lower part where thy nose stands. By mine honour, if I were but two hours younger, I'd beat thee. Methink'st thou art a general offence, and every man should beat thee. I think thou wast created for men to breathe themselves upon thee.

PAROLLES. This is hard and undeserved measure, my lord.

LAFEU. Go to, sir; you were beaten in Italy for picking a

kernel out of a pomegranate; you are a vagabond, and no
true traveller; you are more saucy with lords and honourable personages than the commission of your birth and
virtue gives you heraldry. You are not worth another
word, else I'd call you knave. I leave you.   *Exit*

Enter BERTRAM

PAROLLES. Good, very good, it is so then. Good, very good;
let it be conceal'd awhile.

BERTRAM. Undone, and forfeited to cares for ever!

PAROLLES. What's the matter, sweetheart?

BERTRAM. Although before the solemn priest I have sworn,
I will not bed her.

PAROLLES. What, what, sweetheart?

BERTRAM. O my Parolles, they have married me!
I'll to the Tuscan wars, and never bed her.

PAROLLES. France is a dog-hole, and it no more merits
The tread of a man's foot. To th' wars!

BERTRAM. There's letters from my mother; what th' import
is I know not yet.

PAROLLES. Ay, that would be known. To th' wars, my boy,
to th' wars!
He wears his honour in a box unseen
That hugs his kicky-wicky here at home,
Spending his manly marrow in her arms,
Which should sustain the bound and high curvet
Of Mars's fiery steed. To other regions!
France is a stable; we that dwell in't jades;
Therefore, to th' war!

BERTRAM. It shall be so; I'll send her to my house,
Acquaint my mother with my hate to her,
And wherefore I am fled; write to the King
That which I durst not speak. His present gift
Shall furnish me to those Italian fields
Where noble fellows strike. War is no strife
To the dark house and the detested wife.

PAROLLES. Will this capriccio hold in thee, art sure?

BERTRAM. Go with me to my chamber and advise me.
I'll send her straight away. To-morrow
I'll to the wars, she to her single sorrow.

PAROLLES. Why, these balls bound; there's noise in it. 'Tis hard:
A young man married is a man that's marr'd.
Therefore away, and leave her bravely; go.
The King has done you wrong; but, hush, 'tis so.   *Exeunt*

SCENE 4

Paris. The KING'S *palace*

Enter HELENA *and* CLOWN

HELENA. My mother greets me kindly; is she well?

CLOWN. She is not well, but yet she has her health; she's very merry, but yet she is not well. But thanks be given, she's very well, and wants nothing i' th' world; but yet she is not well.

HELENA. If she be very well, what does she ail that she's not very well?

CLOWN. Truly, she's very well indeed, but for two things.

HELENA. What two things?

CLOWN. One, that she's not in heaven, whither God send her quickly! The other, that she's in earth, from whence God send her quickly!

Enter PAROLLES

PAROLLES. Bless you, my fortunate lady!

HELENA. I hope, sir, I have your good will to have mine own good fortunes.

PAROLLES. You had my prayers to lead them on; and to keep them on, have them still. O, my knave, how does my old lady?

CLOWN. So that you had her wrinkles and I her money, I would she did as you say.

PAROLLES. Why, I say nothing.

CLOWN. Marry, you are the wiser man; for many a man's tongue shakes out his master's undoing. To say nothing, to do nothing, to know nothing, and to have nothing, is to be a great part of your title, which is within a very little of nothing.

PAROLLES. Away! th'art a knave.

CLOWN. You should have said, sir, 'Before a knave th'art a knave'; that's 'Before me th'art a knave.' This had been truth, sir.

PAROLLES. Go to, thou art a witty fool; I have found thee.

CLOWN. Did you find me in yourself, sir, or were you taught to find me? The search, sir, was profitable; and much fool may you find in you, even to the world's pleasure and the increase of laughter.

PAROLLES. A good knave, i' faith, and well fed.
Madam, my lord will go away to-night:
A very serious business calls on him.
The great prerogative and rite of love,
Which, as your due, time claims, he does acknowledge;
But puts it off to a compell'd restraint;
Whose want, and whose delay, is strew'd with sweets,
Which they distil now in the curbed time,
To make the coming hour o'erflow with joy
And pleasure drown the brim.

HELENA. What's his will else?

PAROLLES. That you will take your instant leave o' th' King,
And make this haste as your own good proceeding,
Strength'ned with what apology you think
May make it probable need.

HELENA. What more commands he?

PAROLLES. That, having this obtain'd, you presently
Attend his further pleasure.

HELENA. In everything I wait upon his will.

PAROLLES. I shall report it so.

HELENA. I pray you.   *Exit* PAROLLES
Come, sirrah.   *Exeunt*

SCENE 5

Paris. The KING's *palace*

Enter LAFEU *and* BERTRAM

LAFEU. But I hope your lordship thinks not him a soldier.

BERTRAM. Yes, my lord, and of very valiant approof.

LAFEU. You have it from his own deliverance.

BERTRAM. And by other warranted testimony.

LAFEU. Then my dial goes not true; I took this lark for a bunting.

BERTRAM. I do assure you, my lord, he is very great in knowledge, and accordingly valiant.

LAFEU. I have then sinn'd against his experience and transgress'd against his valour; and my state that way is dangerous, since I cannot yet find in my heart to repent. Here he comes; I pray you make us friends; I will pursue the amity.

Enter PAROLLES

PAROLLES. [*To* BERTRAM] These things shall be done, sir.

LAFEU. Pray you, sir, who's his tailor?

PAROLLES. Sir!

LAFEU. O, I know him well. Ay, sir; he, sir, 's a good workman, a very good tailor.

BERTRAM. [*Aside to* PAROLLES] Is she gone to the King?

PAROLLES. She is.

BERTRAM. Will she away to-night?

PAROLLES. As you'll have her.

BERTRAM. I have writ my letters, casketed my treasure,
  Given order for our horses; and to-night,
  When I should take possession of the bride,
  End ere I do begin.

LAFEU. A good traveller is something at the latter end of a dinner; but one that lies three-thirds and uses a known truth to pass a thousand nothings with, should be once heard and thrice beaten. God save you, Captain.

BERTRAM. Is there any unkindness between my lord and you, monsieur?

PAROLLES. I know not how I have deserved to run into my lord's displeasure.

LAFEU. You have made shift to run into 't, boots and spurs and all, like him that leapt into the custard; and out of it you'll run again, rather than suffer question for your residence.

BERTRAM. It may be you have mistaken him, my lord.

LAFEU. And shall do so ever, though I took him at's prayers. Fare you well, my lord; and believe this of me: there can

be no kernel in this light nut; the soul of this man is his
clothes; trust him not in matter of heavy consequence; I
have kept of them tame, and know their natures. Farewell,
monsieur; I have spoken better of you than you have or
will to deserve at my hand; but we must do good against
evil. *Exit*

PAROLLES. An idle lord, I swear.

BERTRAM. I think so.

PAROLLES. Why, do you not know him?

BERTRAM. Yes, I do know him well; and common speech
Gives him a worthy pass. Here comes my clog.

Enter HELENA

HELENA. I have, sir, as I was commanded from you,
Spoke with the King, and have procur'd his leave
For present parting; only he desires
Some private speech with you.

BERTRAM. I shall obey his will.
You must not marvel, Helen, at my course,
Which holds not colour with the time, nor does
The ministration and required office
On my particular. Prepar'd I was not
For such a business; therefore am I found
So much unsettled. This drives me to entreat you
That presently you take your way for home,
And rather muse than ask why I entreat you;
For my respects are better than they seem,
And my appointments have in them a need
Greater than shows itself at the first view
To you that know them not. This to my mother.
                                    [*Giving a letter*]
'Twill be two days ere I shall see you; so
I leave you to your wisdom.

HELENA. Sir, I can nothing say
But that I am your most obedient servant.

BERTRAM. Come, come, no more of that.

HELENA. And ever shall
With true observance seek to eke out that
Wherein toward me my homely stars have fail'd
To equal my great fortune.

881

BERTRAM. Let that go.
    My haste is very great. Farewell; hie home.
HELENA. Pray, sir, your pardon.
BERTRAM. Well, what would you say?
HELENA. I am not worthy of the wealth I owe,
    Nor dare I say 'tis mine, and yet it is;
    But, like a timorous thief, most fain would steal
    What law does vouch mine own.
BERTRAM. What would you have?
HELENA. Something; and scarce so much; nothing, indeed.
    I would not tell you what I would, my lord.
    Faith, yes:
    Strangers and foes do sunder and not kiss.
BERTRAM. I pray you, stay not, but in haste to horse.
HELENA. I shall not break your bidding, good my lord.
BERTRAM. Where are my other men, monsieur?
    Farewell! *Exit* HELENA
    Go thou toward home, where I will never come
    Whilst I can shake my sword or hear the drum.
    Away, and for our flight.
PAROLLES. Bravely, coragio! *Exeunt*

ACT III. SCENE 1

Florence. The DUKE's *palace*

Flourish. Enter the DUKE OF FLORENCE, *attended; two*
FRENCH LORDS, *with a* TROOP OF SOLDIERS

DUKE. So that, from point to point, now have you heard
    The fundamental reasons of this war;
    Whose great decision hath much blood let forth
    And more thirsts after.
FIRST LORD. Holy seems the quarrel
    Upon your Grace's part; black and fearful
    On the opposer.
DUKE. Therefore we marvel much our cousin France
    Would in so just a business shut his bosom

Against our borrowing prayers.

SECOND LORD. Good my lord,
The reasons of our state I cannot yield,
But like a common and an outward man
That the great figure of a council frames
By self-unable motion; therefore dare not
Say what I think of it, since I have found
Myself in my incertain grounds to fail
As often as I guess'd.

DUKE. Be it his pleasure.

FIRST LORD. But I am sure the younger of our nature,
That surfeit on their ease, will day by day
Come here for physic.

DUKE. Welcome shall they be
And all the honours that can fly from us
Shall on them settle. You know your places well;
When better fall, for your avails they fell.
To-morrow to th' field.   *Flourish. Exeunt*

SCENE 2

Rousillon. The COUNT'S *palace*

Enter COUNTESS *and* CLOWN

COUNTESS. It hath happen'd all as I would have had it, save that he comes not along with her.

CLOWN. By my troth, I take my young lord to be a very melancholy man.

COUNTESS. By what observance, I pray you?

CLOWN. Why, he will look upon his boot and sing; mend the ruff and sing; ask questions and sing; pick his teeth and sing. I know a man that had this trick of melancholy sold a goodly manor for a song.

COUNTESS. Let me see what he writes, and when he means to come.   [*Opening a letter*]

CLOWN. I have no mind to Isbel since I was at court. Our old ling and our Isbels o' th' country are nothing like your old ling and your Isbels o' th' court. The brains of

883

my Cupid's knock'd out; and I begin to love, as an old man
loves money, with no stomach.

COUNTESS. What have we here?

CLOWN. E'en that you have there.   *Exit*

COUNTESS. [*Reads*] 'I have sent you a daughter-in-law; she
hath recovered the King and undone me. I have wedded
her, not bedded her; and sworn to make the "not" eternal.
You shall hear I am run away; know it before the report
come. If there be breadth enough in the world, I will hold
a long distance. My duty to you.

Your unfortunate son,
BERTRAM.'

This is not well, rash and unbridled boy,
To fly the favours of so good a king,
To pluck his indignation on thy head
By the misprizing of a maid too virtuous
For the contempt of empire.

Re-enter CLOWN

CLOWN. O madam, yonder is heavy news within between
two soldiers and my young lady.

COUNTESS. What is the matter?

CLOWN. Nay, there is some comfort in the news, some comfort; your son will not be kill'd so soon as I thought he
would.

COUNTESS. Why should he be kill'd?

CLOWN. So say I, madam, if he run away, as I hear he does;
the danger is in standing to 't; that's the loss of men,
though it be the getting of children. Here they come will
tell you more. For my part, I only hear your son was run
away.   *Exit*

Enter HELENA *and the two* FRENCH GENTLEMEN

SECOND GENTLEMAN. Save you, good madam.

HELENA. Madam, my lord is gone, for ever gone.

FIRST GENTLEMAN. Do not say so.

COUNTESS. Think upon patience. Pray you, gentlemen—
I have felt so many quirks of joy and grief
That the first face of neither, on the start,
Can woman me unto 't. Where is my son, I pray you?

FIRST GENTLEMAN. Madam, he's gone to serve the Duke of
Florence.
We met him thitherward; for thence we came,
And, after some dispatch in hand at court,
Thither we bend again.
HELENA. Look on this letter, madam; here's my passport.
[*Reads*] 'When thou canst get the ring upon my finger,
which never shall come off, and show me a child begotten
of thy body that I am father to, then call me husband; but
in such a "then" I write a "never."'
This is a dreadful sentence.
COUNTESS. Brought you this letter, gentlemen?
FIRST GENTLEMAN. Ay, madam;
And for the contents' sake are sorry for our pains.
COUNTESS. I prithee, lady, have a better cheer;
If thou engrossest all the griefs are thine,
Thou robb'st me of a moiety. He was my son;
But I do wash his name out of my blood,
And thou art all my child. Towards Florence is he?
FIRST GENTLEMAN. Ay, madam.
COUNTESS. And to be a soldier?
FIRST GENTLEMAN. Such is his noble purpose; and, believe 't,
The Duke will lay upon him all the honour
That good convenience claims.
COUNTESS. Return you thither?
SECOND GENTLEMAN. Ay, madam, with the swiftest wing of
speed.
HELENA. [*Reads*] 'Till I have no wife, I have nothing in
France.'
'Tis bitter.
COUNTESS. Find you that there?
HELENA. Ay, madam.
SECOND GENTLEMAN. 'Tis but the boldness of his hand haply,
which his heart was not consenting to.
COUNTESS. Nothing in France until he have no wife!
There's nothing here that is too good for him
But only she; and she deserves a lord
That twenty such rude boys might tend upon,
And call her hourly mistress. Who was with him?
SECOND GENTLEMAN. A servant only, and a gentleman

885

Which I have sometime known.

COUNTESS. Parolles, was it not?

SECOND GENTLEMAN. Ay, my good lady, he.

COUNTESS. A very tainted fellow, and full of wickedness.
My son corrupts a well-derived nature
With his inducement.

SECOND GENTLEMAN. Indeed, good lady,
The fellow has a deal of that too much
Which holds him much to have.

COUNTESS. Y'are welcome, gentlemen.
I will entreat you, when you see my son,
To tell him that his sword can never win
The honour that he loses. More I'll entreat you
Written to bear along.

FIRST GENTLEMAN. We serve you, madam,
In that and all your worthiest affairs.

COUNTESS. Not so, but as we change our courtesies.
Will you draw near? *Exeunt* COUNTESS *and* GENTLEMEN

HELENA. 'Till I have no wife, I have nothing in France.'
Nothing in France until he has no wife!
Thou shalt have none, Rousillon, none in France
Then hast thou all again. Poor lord! is't I
That chase thee from thy country, and expose
Those tender limbs of thine to the event
Of the non-sparing war? And is it I
That drive thee from the sportive court, where thou
Wast shot at with fair eyes, to be the mark
Of smoky muskets? O you leaden messengers,
That ride upon the violent speed of fire,
Fly with false aim; move the still-piecing air,
That sings with piercing; do not touch my lord.
Whoever shoots at him, I set him there;
Whoever charges on his forward breast,
I am the caitiff that do hold him to't;
And though I kill him not, I am the cause
His death was so effected. Better 'twere
I met the ravin lion when he roar'd
With sharp constraint of hunger; better 'twere
That all the miseries which nature owes
Were mine at once. No; come thou home, Rousillon,

Whence honour but of danger wins a scar,
As oft it loses all. I will be gone.
My being here it is that holds thee hence.
Shall I stay here to do't? No, no, although
The air of paradise did fan the house,
And angels offic'd all. I will be gone,
That pitiful rumour may report my flight
To consolate thine ear. Come, night; end, day.
For with the dark, poor thief, I'll steal away.　　*Exit*

SCENE 3

Florence. Before the DUKE's *palace*

Flourish. Enter the DUKE OF FLORENCE, BERTRAM,
PAROLLES, SOLDIERS, *drum and trumpets*

DUKE. The General of our Horse thou art; and we,
Great in our hope, lay our best love and credence
Upon thy promising fortune.
BERTRAM. Sir, it is
A charge too heavy for my strength; but yet
We'll strive to bear it for your worthy sake
To th' extreme edge of hazard.
DUKE. Then go thou forth;
And Fortune play upon thy prosperous helm,
As thy auspicious mistress!
BERTRAM. This very day,
Great Mars, I put myself into thy file;
Make me but like my thoughts, and I shall prove
A lover of thy drum, hater of love.　　*Exeunt*

SCENE 4

Rousillon. The COUNT's *palace*

Enter COUNTESS *and* STEWARD

COUNTESS. Alas! and would you take the letter of her?
Might you not know she would do as she has done

By sending me a letter? Read it again.
STEWARD. [*Reads*] 'I am Saint Jaques' pilgrim, thither gone.
Ambitious love hath so in me offended
That barefoot plod I the cold ground upon,
With sainted vow my faults to have amended.
Write, write, that from the bloody course of war
My dearest master, your dear son, may hie.
Bless him at home in peace, whilst I from far
His name with zealous fervour sanctify.
His taken labours bid him me forgive;
I, his despiteful Juno, sent him forth
From courtly friends, with camping foes to live,
Where death and danger dogs the heels of worth.
He is too good and fair for death and me;
Whom I myself embrace to set him free.'
COUNTESS. Ah, what sharp stings are in her mildest words!
Rinaldo, you did never lack advice so much
As letting her pass so; had I spoke with her,
I could have well diverted her intents,
Which thus she hath prevented.
STEWARD. Pardon me, madam;
If I had given you this at over-night,
She might have been o'erta'en; and yet she writes
Pursuit would be but vain.
COUNTESS. What angel shall
Bless this unworthy husband? He cannot thrive,
Unless her prayers, whom heaven delights to hear
And loves to grant, reprieve him from the wrath
Of greatest justice. Write, write, Rinaldo,
To this unworthy husband of his wife;
Let every word weigh heavy of her worth
That he does weigh too light. My greatest grief,
Though little he do feel it, set down sharply.
Dispatch the most convenient messenger.
When haply he shall hear that she is gone
He will return; and hope I may that she,
Hearing so much, will speed her foot again,
Led hither by pure love. Which of them both
Is dearest to me I have no skill in sense
To make distinction. Provide this messenger.

My heart is heavy, and mine age is weak;
Grief would have tears, and sorrow bids me speak. *Exeunt*

SCENE 5

Without the walls of Florence

A tucket afar off. Enter an old WIDOW OF FLOR-
ENCE, *her daughter* DIANA, VIOLENTA, *and* MARI-
ANA, *with other* CITIZENS

WIDOW. Nay, come; for if they do approach the city we
shall lose all the sight.
DIANA. They say the French count has done most honourable service.
WIDOW. It is reported that he has taken their great'st commander; and that with his own hand he slew the Duke's
brother. [*Tucket*] We have lost our labour; they are gone
a contrary way. Hark! you may know by their trumpets.
MARIANA. Come, let's return again, and suffice ourselves with
the report of it. Well, Diana, take heed of this French earl;
the honour of a maid is her name, and no legacy is so
rich as honesty.
WIDOW. I have told my neighbour how you have been
solicited by a gentleman his companion.
MARIANA. I know that knave, hang him! one Parolles; a
filthy officer he is in those suggestions for the young earl.
Beware of them, Diana: their promises, enticements, oaths,
tokens, and all these engines of lust, are not the things they
go under; many a maid hath been seduced by them; and
the misery is, example, that so terrible shows in the wreck
of maidenhood, cannot for all that dissuade succession, but
that they are limed with the twigs that threatens them. I
hope I need not to advise you further; but I hope your
own grace will keep you where you are, though there
were no further danger known but the modesty which is
so lost.
DIANA. You shall not need to fear me.

Enter HELENA *in the dress of a pilgrim*

WIDOW. I hope so. Look, here comes a pilgrim. I know she will lie at my house: thither they send one another. I'll question her. God save you, pilgrim! Whither are bound?

HELENA. To Saint Jaques le Grand.
Where do the palmers lodge, I do beseech you?

WIDOW. At the Saint Francis here, beside the port.

HELENA. Is this the way?   *[A march afar]*

WIDOW. Ay, marry, is't. Hark you! They come this way.
If you will tarry, holy pilgrim,
But till the troops come by,
I will conduct you where you shall be lodg'd;
The rather for I think I know your hostess
As ample as myself.

HELENA. Is it yourself?

WIDOW. If you shall please so, pilgrim.

HELENA. I thank you, and will stay upon your leisure.

WIDOW. You came, I think, from France?

HELENA. I did so.

WIDOW. Here you shall see a countryman of yours
That has done worthy service.

HELENA. His name, I pray you.

DIANA. The Count Rousillon. Know you such a one?

HELENA. But by the ear, that hears most nobly of him;
His face I know not.

DIANA. Whatsome'er he is,
He's bravely taken here. He stole from France,
As 'tis reported, for the King had married him
Against his liking. Think you it is so?

HELENA. Ay, surely, mere the truth; I know his lady.

DIANA. There is a gentleman that serves the Count
Reports but coarsely of her.

HELENA. What's his name?

DIANA. Monsieur Parolles.

HELENA. O, I believe with him,
In argument of praise, or to the worth
Of the great Count himself, she is too mean
To have her name repeated; all her deserving
Is a reserved honesty, and that
I have not heard examin'd.

DIANA. Alas, poor lady!

'Tis a hard bondage to become the wife
Of a detesting lord.
WIDOW. I weet, good creature, wheresoe'er she is
Her heart weighs sadly. This young maid might do her
A shrewd turn, if she pleas'd.
HELENA. How do you mean?
May be the amorous Count solicits her
In the unlawful purpose.
WIDOW. He does, indeed;
And brokes with all that can in such a suit
Corrupt the tender honour of a maid;
But she is arm'd for him, and keeps her guard
In honestest defence.

Enter, with drum and colours, BERTRAM, PAROLLES, *and the whole* ARMY

MARIANA. The gods forbid else!
WIDOW. So, now they come.
That is Antonio, the Duke's eldest son;
That, Escalus.
HELENA. Which is the Frenchman?
DIANA. He—
That with the plume; 'tis a most gallant fellow.
I would he lov'd his wife; if he were honester
He were much goodlier. Is't not a handsome gentleman?
HELENA. I like him well.
DIANA. 'Tis pity he is not honest. Yond's that same knave
That leads him to these places; were I his lady
I would poison that vile rascal.
HELENA. Which is he?
DIANA. That jack-an-apes with scarfs. Why is he melan-
choly?
HELENA. Perchance he's hurt i' th' battle.
PAROLLES. Lose our drum! well.
MARIANA. He's shrewdly vex'd at something.
Look, he has spied us.
WIDOW. Marry, hang you!
MARIANA. And your courtesy, for a ring-carrier!
                    Exeunt BERTRAM, PAROLLES, *and* ARMY
WIDOW. The troop is past. Come, pilgrim, I will bring you

Where you shall host. Of enjoin'd penitents
There's four or five, to great Saint Jaques bound,
Already at my house.
HELENA. I humbly thank you.
Please it this matron and this gentle maid
To eat with us to-night; the charge and thanking
Shall be for me, and, to requite you further,
I will bestow some precepts of this virgin,
Worthy the note.
BOTH. We'll take your offer kindly.   *Exeunt*

SCENE 6

Camp before Florence

Enter BERTRAM, *and the two* FRENCH LORDS

SECOND LORD. Nay, good my lord, put him to't; let him have
his way.
FIRST LORD. If your lordship find him not a hiding, hold me
no more in your respect.
SECOND LORD. On my life, my lord, a bubble.
BERTRAM. Do you think I am so far deceived in him?
SECOND LORD. Believe it, my lord, in mine own direct knowledge, without any malice, but to speak of him as my kinsman, he's a most notable coward, an infinite and endless
liar, an hourly promise-breaker, the owner of no one good
quality worthy your lordship's entertainment.
FIRST LORD. It were fit you knew him; lest, reposing too far
in his virtue, which he hath not, he might at some great
and trusty business in a main danger fail you.
BERTRAM. I would I knew in what particular action to try
him.
FIRST LORD. None better than to let him fetch off his drum,
which you hear him so confidently undertake to do.
SECOND LORD. I with a troop of Florentines will suddenly
surprise him; such I will have whom I am sure he knows
not from the enemy. We will bind and hoodwink him so
that he shall suppose no other but that he is carried into
the leaguer of the adversaries when we bring him to our

own tents. Be but your lordship present at his examination; if he do not, for the promise of his life and in the highest compulsion of base fear, offer to betray you and deliver all the intelligence in his power against you, and that with the divine forfeit of his soul upon oath, never trust my judgment in anything.

FIRST LORD. O, for the love of laughter, let him fetch his drum; he says he has a stratagem for't. When your lordship sees the bottom of his success in't, and to what metal this counterfeit lump of ore will be melted, if you give him not John Drum's entertainment, your inclining cannot be removed. Here he comes.

Enter PAROLLES

SECOND LORD. O, for the love of laughter, hinder not the honour of his design; let him fetch off his drum in any hand.

BERTRAM. How now, monsieur! This drum sticks sorely in your disposition.

FIRST LORD. A pox on't; let it go; 'tis but a drum.

PAROLLES. But a drum! Is't but a drum? A drum so lost! There was excellent command: to charge in with our horse upon our own wings, and to rend our own soldiers!

FIRST LORD. That was not to be blam'd in the command of the service; it was a disaster of war that Cæsar himself could not have prevented, if he had been there to command.

BERTRAM. Well, we cannot greatly condemn our success. Some dishonour we had in the loss of that drum; but it is not to be recovered.

PAROLLES. It might have been recovered.

BERTRAM. It might, but it is not now.

PAROLLES. It is to be recovered. But that the merit of service is seldom attributed to the true and exact performer, I would have that drum or another, or 'hic jacet.'

BERTRAM. Why, if you have a stomach, to't, monsieur. If you think your mystery in stratagem can bring this instrument of honour again into his native quarter, be magnanimous in the enterprise, and go on; I will grace the attempt for a worthy exploit. If you speed well in it, the Duke shall both speak of it and extend to you what further becomes his greatness, even to the utmost syllable of our worthiness.

PAROLLES. By the hand of a soldier, I will undertake it.

BERTRAM. But you must not now slumber in it.

PAROLLES. I'll about it this evening; and I will presently pen down my dilemmas, encourage myself in my certainty, put myself into my mortal preparation; and by midnight look to hear further from me.

BERTRAM. May I be bold to acquaint his Grace you are gone about it?

PAROLLES. I know not what the success will be, my lord, but the attempt I vow.

BERTRAM. I know th'art valiant; and, to the possibility of thy soldiership, will subscribe for thee. Farewell.

PAROLLES. I love not many words. *Exit*

SECOND LORD. No more than a fish loves water. Is not this a strange fellow, my lord, that so confidently seems to undertake this business, which he knows is not to be done; damns himself to do, and dares better be damn'd than to do't.

FIRST LORD. You do not know him, my lord, as we do. Certain it is that he will steal himself into a man's favour, and for a week escape a great deal of discoveries; but when you find him out, you have him ever after.

BERTRAM. Why, do you think he will make no deed at all of this that so seriously he does address himself unto?

SECOND LORD. None in the world; but return with an invention, and clap upon you two or three probable lies. But we have almost emboss'd him. You shall see his fall to-night; for indeed he is not for your lordship's respect.

FIRST LORD. We'll make you some sport with the fox ere we case him. He was first smok'd by the old Lord Lafeu. When his disguise and he is parted, tell me what a sprat you shall find him; which you shall see this very night.

SECOND LORD. I must go look my twigs; he shall be caught.

BERTRAM. Your brother, he shall go along with me.

SECOND LORD. As't please your lordship. I'll leave you. *Exit*

BERTRAM. Now will I lead you to the house, and show you
The lass I spoke of.

FIRST LORD. But you say she's honest.

HELENA. *I like him well*   (ACT III. SCENE V)

BERTRAM. That's all the fault. I spoke with her but once,
And found her wondrous cold; but I sent to her,
By this same coxcomb that we have i' th' wind,
Tokens and letters which she did re-send;
And this is all I have done. She's a fair creature;
Will you go see her?
FIRST LORD. With all my heart, my lord.   *Exeunt*

SCENE 7

Florence. The WIDOW's *house*

Enter HELENA *and* WIDOW

HELENA. If you misdoubt me that I am not she,
I know not how I shall assure you further
But I shall lose the grounds I work upon.
WIDOW. Though my estate be fall'n, I was well born,
Nothing acquainted with these businesses;
And would not put my reputation now
In any staining act.
HELENA. Nor would I wish you.
First give me trust the Count he is my husband,
And what to your sworn counsel I have spoken
Is so from word to word; and then you cannot,
By the good aid that I of you shall borrow,
Err in bestowing it.
WIDOW. I should believe you;
For you have show'd me that which well approves
Y'are great in fortune.
HELENA. Take this purse of gold,
And let me buy your friendly help thus far,
Which I will over-pay and pay again
When I have found it. The Count he woos your daughter,
Lays down his wanton siege before her beauty,
Resolv'd to carry her. Let her in fine consent,
As we'll direct her how 'tis best to bear it.
Now his important blood will nought deny
That she'll demand. A ring the County wears
That downward hath succeeded in his house

From son to son some four or five descents
Since the first father wore it. This ring he holds
In most rich choice; yet, in his idle fire,
To buy his will, it would not seem too dear,
Howe'er repented after.
WIDOW. Now I see
The bottom of your purpose.
HELENA. You see it lawful then. It is no more
But that your daughter, ere she seems as won,
Desires this ring; appoints him an encounter;
In fine, delivers me to fill the time,
Herself most chastely absent. After this,
To marry her, I'll add three thousand crowns
To what is pass'd already.
WIDOW. I have yielded.
Instruct my daughter how she shall persever,
That time and place with this deceit so lawful
May prove coherent. Every night he comes
With musics of all sorts, and songs compos'd
To her unworthiness. It nothing steads us
To chide him from our eaves, for he persists
As if his life lay on't.
HELENA. Why then to-night
Let us assay our plot; which, if it speed,
Is wicked meaning in a lawful deed,
And lawful meaning in a lawful act;
Where both not sin, and yet a sinful fact.
But let's about it. *Exeunt*

ACT IV. SCENE 1

Without the Florentine camp

Enter SECOND FRENCH LORD *with five or six
other* SOLDIERS *in ambush*

SECOND LORD. He can come no other way but by this hedge-
corner. When you sally upon him, speak what terrible

language you will; though you understand it not yourselves, no matter; for we must not seem to understand him,
unless some one among us, whom we must produce for an
interpreter.

FIRST SOLDIER. Good captain, let me be th' interpreter.

SECOND LORD. Art not acquainted with him? Knows he not
thy voice?

FIRST SOLDIER. No, sir, I warrant you.

SECOND LORD. But what linsey-woolsey has thou to speak to
us again?

FIRST SOLDIER. E'en such as you speak to me.

SECOND LORD. He must think us some band of strangers i' th'
adversary's entertainment. Now he hath a smack of all
neighbouring languages, therefore we must every one be a
man of his own fancy; not to know what we speak one to
another, so we seem to know, is to know straight our purpose: choughs' language, gabble enough, and good enough.
As for you, interpreter, you must seem very politic. But
couch, ho! here he comes; to beguile two hours in a sleep,
and then to return and swear the lies he forges.

Enter PAROLLES

PAROLLES. Ten o'clock. Within these three hours 'twill be
time enough to go home. What shall I say I have done?
It must be a very plausive invention that carries it. They
begin to smoke me; and disgraces have of late knock'd too
often at my door. I find my tongue is too foolhardy; but
my heart hath the fear of Mars before it, and of his creatures, not daring the reports of my tongue.

SECOND LORD. This is the first truth that e'er thine own
tongue was guilty of.

PAROLLES. What the devil should move me to undertake the
recovery of this drum, being not ignorant of the impossibility, and knowing I had no such purpose? I must give
myself some hurts, and say I got them in exploit. Yet slight
ones will not carry it. They will say 'Came you off with
so little?' And great ones I dare not give. Wherefore,
what's the instance? Tongue, I must put you into a butter-
woman's mouth, and buy myself another of Bajazet's mule,
if you prattle me into these perils.

SECOND LORD. Is it possible he should know what he is, and be that he is?

PAROLLES. I would the cutting of my garments would serve the turn, or the breaking of my Spanish sword.

SECOND LORD. We cannot afford you so.

PAROLLES. Or the baring of my beard; and to say it was in stratagem.

SECOND LORD. 'Twould not do.

PAROLLES. Or to drown my clothes, and say I was stripp'd.

SECOND LORD. Hardly serve.

PAROLLES. Though I swore I leap'd from the window of the citadel—

SECOND LORD. How deep?

PAROLLES. Thirty fathom.

SECOND LORD. Three great oaths would scarce make that be believed.

PAROLLES. I would I had any drum of the enemy's; I would swear I recover'd it.

SECOND LORD. You shall hear one anon. [*Alarum within*]

PAROLLES. A drum now of the enemy's!

SECOND LORD. Throca movousus, cargo, cargo, cargo.

ALL. Cargo, cargo, cargo, villianda par corbo, cargo.

PAROLLES. O, ransom, ransom! Do not hide mine eyes.

[*They blindfold him*]

FIRST SOLDIER. Boskos thromuldo boskos.

PAROLLES. I know you are the Muskos' regiment,
And I shall lose my life for want of language.
If there be here German, or Dane, Low Dutch,
Italian, or French, let him speak to me;
I'll discover that which shall undo the Florentine.

FIRST SOLDIER. Boskos vauvado. I understand thee, and can speak thy tongue. Kerely-bonto, sir, betake thee to thy faith, for seventeen poniards are at thy bosom.

PAROLLES. O!

FIRST SOLDIER. O, pray, pray, pray! Manka revania dulche.

SECOND LORD. Oscorbidulchos volivorco.

FIRST SOLDIER. The General is content to spare thee yet;
And, hoodwink'd as thou art, will lead thee on
To gather from thee. Haply thou mayst inform
Something to save thy life.

PAROLLES. O, let me live,
And all the secrets of our camp I'll show,
Their force, their purposes. Nay, I'll speak that
Which you will wonder at.
FIRST SOLDIER. But wilt thou faithfully?
PAROLLES. If I do not, damn me.
FIRST SOLDIER. Acordo linta.
    Come on; thou art granted space.
            Exit, with PAROLLES *guarded. A short alarum within*
SECOND LORD. Go, tell the Count Rousillon and my brother
We have caught the woodcock, and will keep him muffled
Till we do hear from them.
SECOND SOLDIER. Captain, I will.
SECOND LORD. 'A will betray us all unto ourselves—
Inform on that.
SECOND SOLDIER. So I will, sir.
SECOND LORD. Till then I'll keep him dark and safely lock'd.
                                                        Exeunt

SCENE 2

Florence. The WIDOW's *house*

Enter BERTRAM *and* DIANA

BERTRAM. They told me that your name was Fontibell.
DIANA. No, my good lord, Diana.
BERTRAM. Titled goddess;
And worth it, with addition! But, fair soul,
In your fine frame hath love no quality?
If the quick fire of youth light not your mind,
You are no maiden, but a monument;
When you are dead, you should be such a one
As you are now, for you are cold and stern;
And now you should be as your mother was
When your sweet self was got.
DIANA. She then was honest.
BERTRAM. So should you be.
DIANA. No.
My mother did but duty; such, my lord,

As you owe to your wife.
BERTRAM. No more o' that!
I prithee do not strive against my vows.
I was compell'd to her; but I love thee
By love's own sweet constraint, and will for ever
Do thee all rights of service.
DIANA. Ay, so you serve us
Till we serve you; but when you have our roses
You barely leave our thorns to prick ourselves,
And mock us with our bareness.
BERTRAM. How have I sworn!
DIANA. 'Tis not the many oaths that makes the truth,
But the plain single vow that is vow'd true.
What is not holy, that we swear not by,
But take the High'st to witness. Then, pray you, tell me:
If I should swear by Jove's great attributes
I lov'd you dearly, would you believe my oaths
When I did love you ill? This has no holding,
To swear by him whom I protest to love
That I will work against him. Therefore your oaths
Are words and poor conditions, but unseal'd—
At least in my opinion.
BERTRAM. Change it, change it;
Be not so holy-cruel. Love is holy;
And my integrity ne'er knew the crafts
That you do charge men with. Stand no more off,
But give thyself unto my sick desires,
Who then recovers. Say thou art mine, and ever
My love as it begins shall so persever.
DIANA. I see that men make ropes in such a scarre
That we'll forsake ourselves. Give me that ring.
BERTRAM. I'll lend it thee, my dear, but have no power
To give it from me.
DIANA. Will you not, my lord?
BERTRAM. It is an honour 'longing to our house,
Bequeathed down from many ancestors;
Which were the greatest obloquy i' th' world
In me to lose.
DIANA. Mine honour's such a ring:
My chastity's the jewel of our house,

Bequeathed down from many ancestors;
Which were the greatest obloquy i' th' world
In me to lose. Thus your own proper wisdom
Brings in the champion Honour on my part
Against your vain assault.
BERTRAM. Here, take my ring;
My house, mine honour, yea, my life, be thine,
And I'll be bid by thee.
DIANA. When midnight comes, knock at my chamber window;
I'll order take my mother shall not hear.
Now will I charge you in the band of truth,
When you have conquer'd my yet maiden bed,
Remain there but an hour, nor speak to me:
My reasons are most strong; and you shall know them
When back again this ring shall be deliver'd.
And on your finger in the night I'll put
Another ring, that what in time proceeds
May token to the future our past deeds.
Adieu till then; then fail not. You have won
A wife of me, though there my hope be done.
BERTRAM. A heaven on earth I have won by wooing thee.
Exit

DIANA. For which live long to thank both heaven and me!
You may so in the end.
My mother told me just how he would woo,
As if she sat in's heart; she says all men
Have the like oaths. He had sworn to marry me
When his wife's dead; therefore I'll lie with him
When I am buried. Since Frenchmen are so braid,
Marry that will, I live and die a maid.
Only, in this disguise, I think't no sin
To cozen him that would unjustly win.   *Exit*

902

SCENE 3

The Florentine camp

Enter the two FRENCH LORDS, *and two or three* SOLDIERS

SECOND LORD. You have not given him his mother's letter?

FIRST LORD. I have deliv'red it an hour since. There is something in't that stings his nature; for on the reading it he chang'd almost into another man.

SECOND LORD. He has much worthy blame laid upon him for shaking off so good a wife and so sweet a lady.

FIRST LORD. Especially he hath incurred the everlasting displeasure of the King, who had even tun'd his bounty to sing happiness to him. I will tell you a thing, but you shall let it dwell darkly with you.

SECOND LORD. When you have spoken it, 'tis dead, and I am the grave of it.

FIRST LORD. He hath perverted a young gentlewoman here in Florence, of a most chaste renown; and this night he fleshes his will in the spoil of her honour. He hath given her his monumental ring, and thinks himself made in the unchaste composition.

SECOND LORD. Now, God delay our rebellion! As we are ourselves, what things are we!

FIRST LORD. Merely our own traitors. And as in the common course of all treasons we still see them reveal themselves till they attain to their abhorr'd ends; so he that in this action contrives against his own nobility, in his proper stream, o'erflows himself.

SECOND LORD. Is it not meant damnable in us to be trumpeters of our unlawful intents? We shall not then have his company to-night?

FIRST LORD. Not till after midnight; for he is dieted to his hour.

SECOND LORD. That approaches apace. I would gladly have him see his company anatomiz'd, that he might take a measure of his own judgments, wherein so curiously he had set this counterfeit.

FIRST LORD. We will not meddle with him till he come; for his presence must be the whip of the other.

SECOND LORD. In the meantime, what hear you of these wars?

FIRST LORD. I hear there is an overture of peace.

SECOND LORD. Nay, I assure you, a peace concluded.

FIRST LORD. What will Count Rousillon do then? Will he travel higher, or return again into France?

SECOND LORD. I perceive, by this demand, you are not altogether of his counsel.

FIRST LORD. Let it be forbid, sir! So should I be a great deal of his act.

SECOND LORD. Sir, his wife, some two months since, fled from his house. Her pretence is a pilgrimage to Saint Jaques le Grand; which holy undertaking with most austere sanctimony she accomplish'd; and, there residing, the tenderness of her nature became as a prey to her grief; in fine, made a groan of her last breath, and now she sings in heaven.

FIRST LORD. How is this justified?

SECOND LORD. The stronger part of it by her own letters, which makes her story true even to the point of her death. Her death itself, which could not be her office to say is come, was faithfully confirm'd by the rector of the place.

FIRST LORD. Hath the Count all this intelligence?

SECOND LORD. Ay, and the particular confirmations, point from point, to the full arming of the verity.

FIRST LORD. I am heartily sorry that he'll be glad of this.

SECOND LORD. How mightily sometimes we make us comforts of our losses!

FIRST LORD. And how mightily some other times we drown our gain in tears! The great dignity that his valour hath here acquir'd for him shall at home be encount'red with a shame as ample.

SECOND LORD. The web of our life is of a mingled yarn, good and ill together. Our virtues would be proud if our faults whipt them not; and our crimes would despair if they were not cherish'd by our virtues.

Enter a MESSENGER

How now? Where's your master?

SERVANT. He met the Duke in the street, sir; of whom he

hath taken a solemn leave. His lordship will next morning for France. The Duke hath offered him letters of commendations to the King.

SECOND LORD. They shall be no more than needful there, if they were more than they can commend.

FIRST LORD. They cannot be too sweet for the King's tartness. Here's his lordship now.

Enter BERTRAM

How now, my lord, is't not after midnight?

BERTRAM. I have to-night dispatch'd sixteen businesses, a month's length apiece; by an abstract of success: I have congied with the Duke, done my adieu with his nearest; buried a wife, mourn'd for her; writ to my lady mother I am returning; entertain'd my convoy; and between these main parcels of dispatch effected many nicer needs. The last was the greatest, but that I have not ended yet.

SECOND LORD. If the business be of any difficulty and this morning your departure hence, it requires haste of your lordship.

BERTRAM. I mean the business is not ended, as fearing to hear of it hereafter. But shall we have this dialogue between the Fool and the Soldier? Come, bring forth this counterfeit module has deceiv'd me like a double-meaning prophesier.

SECOND LORD. Bring him forth. [*Exeunt* SOLDIERS] Has sat i' th' stocks all night, poor gallant knave.

BERTRAM. No matter; his heels have deserv'd it, in usurping his spurs so long. How does he carry himself?

SECOND LORD. I have told your lordship already the stocks carry him. But to answer you as you would be understood: he weeps like a wench that had shed her milk; he hath confess'd himself to Morgan, whom he supposes to be a friar, from the time of his remembrance to this very instant disaster of his setting i' th' stocks. And what think you he hath confess'd?

BERTRAM. Nothing of me, has 'a?

SECOND LORD. His confession is taken, and it shall be read to his face; if your lordship be in't, as I believe you are, you must have the patience to hear it.

Enter PAROLLES *guarded, and*
FIRST SOLDIER *as interpreter*

BERTRAM. A plague upon him! muffled! He can say nothing of me.

SECOND LORD. Hush, hush! Hoodman comes. Portotartarossa.

FIRST SOLDIER. He calls for the tortures. What will you say without 'em?

PAROLLES. I will confess what I know without constraint; if ye pinch me like a pasty, I can say no more.

FIRST SOLDIER. Bosko chimurcho.

SECOND LORD. Boblibindo chicurmurco.

FIRST SOLDIER. You are a merciful general. Our General bids you answer to what I shall ask you out of a note.

PAROLLES. And truly, as I hope to live.

FIRST SOLDIER. 'First demand of him how many horse the Duke is strong.' What say you to that?

PAROLLES. Five or six thousand; but very weak and unserviceable. The troops are all scattered, and the commanders very poor rogues, upon my reputation and credit, and as I hope to live.

FIRST SOLDIER. Shall I set down your answer so?

PAROLLES. Do; I'll take the sacrament on't, how and which way you will.

BERTRAM. All's one to him. What a past-saving slave is this!

SECOND LORD. Y'are deceiv'd, my lord; this is Monsieur Parolles, the gallant militarist—that was his own phrase—that had the whole theoric of war in the knot of his scarf, and the practice in the chape of his dagger.

FIRST LORD. I will never trust a man again for keeping his sword clean; nor believe he can have everything in him by wearing his apparel neatly.

FIRST SOLDIER. Well, that's set down.

PAROLLES. 'Five or six thousand horse' I said—I will say true —'or thereabouts' set down, for I'll speak truth.

SECOND LORD. He's very near the truth in this.

BERTRAM. But I con him no thanks for't in the nature he delivers it.

PAROLLES. 'Poor rogues' I pray you say.

FIRST SOLDIER. Well, that's set down.

PAROLLES. I humbly thank you, sir. A truth's a truth—the rogues are marvellous poor.

FIRST SOLDIER. 'Demand of him of what strength they are a-foot.' What say you to that?

PAROLLES. By my troth, sir, if I were to live this present hour, I will tell true. Let me see: Spurio, a hundred and fifty; Sebastian, so many; Corambus, so many; Jaques, so many; Guiltian, Cosmo, Lodowick, and Gratii, two hundred fifty each; mine own company, Chitopher, Vaumond, Bentii, two hundred fifty each; so that the muster-file, rotten and sound, upon my life, amounts not to fifteen thousand poll; half of the which dare not shake the snow from off their cassocks lest they shake themselves to pieces.

BERTRAM. What shall be done to him?

SECOND LORD. Nothing, but let him have thanks. Demand of him my condition, and what credit I have with the Duke.

FIRST SOLDIER. Well, that's set down. 'You shall demand of him whether one Captain Dumain be i' th' camp, a Frenchman; what his reputation is with the Duke, what his valour, honesty, expertness in wars; or whether he thinks it were not possible, with well-weighing sums of gold, to corrupt him to a revolt.' What say you to this? What do you know of it?

PAROLLES. I beseech you, let me answer to the particular of the inter'gatories. Demand them singly.

FIRST SOLDIER. Do you know this Captain Dumain?

PAROLLES. I know him: 'a was a botcher's prentice in Paris, from whence he was whipt for getting the shrieve's fool with child—a dumb innocent that could not say him nay.

BERTRAM. Nay, by your leave, hold your hands; though I know his brains are forfeit to the next tile that falls.

FIRST SOLDIER. Well, is this captain in the Duke of Florence's camp?

PAROLLES. Upon my knowledge, he is, and lousy.

SECOND LORD. Nay, look not so upon me; we shall hear of your lordship anon.

FIRST SOLDIER. What is his reputation with the Duke?

PAROLLES. The Duke knows him for no other but a poor officer of mine; and writ to me this other day to turn him out o' th' band. I think I have his letter in my pocket.

FIRST SOLDIER. Marry, we'll search.

PAROLLES. In good sadness, I do not know; either it is there or it is upon a file with the Duke's other letters in my tent.

FIRST SOLDIER. Here 'tis; here's a paper. Shall I read it to you?

PAROLLES. I do not know if it be it or no.

BERTRAM. Our interpreter does it well.

SECOND LORD. Excellently.

FIRST SOLDIER. [Reads] 'Dian, the Count's a fool, and full of gold.'

PAROLLES. That is not the Duke's letter, sir; that is an advertisement to a proper maid in Florence, one Diana, to take heed of the allurement of one Count Rousillon, a foolish idle boy, but for all that very ruttish. I pray you, sir, put it up again.

FIRST SOLDIER. Nay, I'll read it first by your favour.

PAROLLES. My meaning in't, I protest, was very honest in the behalf of the maid; for I knew the young Count to be a dangerous and lascivious boy, who is a whale to virginity, and devours up all the fry it finds.

BERTRAM. Damnable both-sides rogue!

FIRST SOLDIER. [Reads]
'When he swears oaths, bid him drop gold, and take it;
After he scores, he never pays the score.
Half won is match well made; match, and well make it;
He ne'er pays after-debts, take it before.
And say a soldier, Dian, told thee this:
Men are to mell with, boys are not to kiss;
For count of this, the Count's a fool, I know it,
Who pays before, but not when he does owe it.
Thine, as he vow'd to thee in thine ear,
                              PAROLLES.'

BERTRAM. He shall be whipt through the army with this rhyme in's forehead.

FIRST LORD. This is your devoted friend, sir, the manifold linguist, and the armipotent soldier.

BERTRAM. I could endure anything before but a cat, and now he's a cat to me.

FIRST SOLDIER. I perceive, sir, by our General's looks we shall be fain to hang you.

PAROLLES. My life, sir, in any case! Not that I am afraid to die, but that, my offences being many, I would repent out the remainder of nature. Let me live, sir, in a dungeon, i' th' stocks, or anywhere, so I may live.

FIRST SOLDIER. We'll see what may be done, so you confess freely; therefore, once more to this Captain Dumain: you have answer'd to his reputation with the Duke, and to his valour; what is his honesty?

PAROLLES. He will steal, sir, an egg out of a cloister; for rapes and ravishments he parallels Nessus. He professes not keeping of oaths; in breaking 'em he is stronger than Hercules. He will lie, sir, with such volubility that you would think truth were a fool. Drunkenness is his best virtue, for he will be swine-drunk; and in his sleep he does little harm, save to his bedclothes about him; but they know his conditions and lay him in straw. I have but little more to say, sir, of his honesty. He has everything that an honest man should not have; what an honest man should have he has nothing.

SECOND LORD. I begin to love him for this.

BERTRAM. For this description of thine honesty? A pox upon him! For me, he's more and more a cat.

FIRST SOLDIER. What say you to his expertness in war?

PAROLLES. Faith, sir, has led the drum before the English tragedians—to belie him I will not—and more of his soldiership I know not, except in that country he had the honour to be the officer at a place there called Mile-end to instruct for the doubling of files—I would do the man what honour I can—but of this I am not certain.

SECOND LORD. He hath out-villain'd villainy so far that the rarity redeems him.

BERTRAM. A pox on him! he's a cat still.

FIRST SOLDIER. His qualities being at this poor price, I need not to ask you if gold will corrupt him to revolt.

PAROLLES. Sir, for a cardecue he will sell the fee-simple of his salvation, the inheritance of it; and cut th' entail from all remainders and a perpetual succession for it perpetually.

FIRST SOLDIER. What's his brother, the other Captain Dumain?

FIRST LORD. Why does he ask him of me?

FIRST SOLDIER. What's he?

PAROLLES. E'en a crow o' th' same nest; not altogether so great as the first in goodness, but greater a great deal in evil. He excels his brother for a coward; yet his brother is reputed one of the best that is. In a retreat he outruns any lackey: marry, in coming on he has the cramp.

FIRST SOLDIER. If your life be saved, will you undertake to betray the Florentine?

PAROLLES. Ay, and the Captain of his Horse, Count Rousillon.

FIRST SOLDIER. I'll whisper with the General, and know his pleasure.

PAROLLES. [Aside] I'll no more drumming. A plague of all drums! Only to seem to deserve well, and to beguile the supposition of that lascivious young boy the Count, have I run into this danger. Yet who would have suspected an ambush where I was taken?

FIRST SOLDIER. There is no remedy, sir, but you must die. The General says you that have so traitorously discover'd the secrets of your army, and made such pestiferous reports of men very nobly held, can serve the world for no honest use; therefore you must die. Come, headsman, off with his head.

PAROLLES. O Lord, sir, let me live, or let me see my death!

FIRST SOLDIER. That shall you, and take your leave of all your friends. [Unmuffling him] So look about you; know you any here?

BERTRAM. Good morrow, noble Captain.

FIRST LORD. God bless you, Captain Parolles.

SECOND LORD. God save you, noble Captain.

FIRST LORD. Captain, what greeting will you to my Lord Lafeu? I am for France.

SECOND LORD. Good Captain, will you give me a copy of the sonnet you writ to Diana in behalf of the Count Rousillon? An I were not a very coward I'd compel it of you; but fare you well.   *Exeunt* BERTRAM *and* LORDS

FIRST SOLDIER. You are undone, Captain, all but your scarf; that has a knot on't yet.

PAROLLES. Who cannot be crush'd with a plot?

FIRST SOLDIER. If you could find out a country where but

women were that had received so much shame, you might
begin an impudent nation. Fare ye well, sir; I am for
France too; we shall speak of you there.

Exit with SOLDIERS

PAROLLES. Yet am I thankful. If my heart were great,
'Twould burst at this. Captain I'll be no more;
But I will eat, and drink, and sleep as soft
As captain shall. Simply the thing I am
Shall make me live. Who knows himself a braggart,
Let him fear this; for it will come to pass
That every braggart shall be found an ass.
Rust, sword; cool, blushes; and, Parolles, live
Safest in shame. Being fool'd, by fool'ry thrive.
There's place and means for every man alive.
I'll after them.   *Exit*

SCENE 4

The WIDOW's *house*

Enter HELENA, WIDOW, *and* DIANA

HELENA. That you may well perceive I have not wrong'd
    you,
One of the greatest in the Christian world
Shall be my surety; fore whose throne 'tis needful,
Ere I can perfect mine intents, to kneel.
Time was I did him a desired office,
Dear almost as his life; which gratitude
Through flinty Tartar's bosom would peep forth,
And answer 'Thanks.' I duly am inform'd
His Grace is at Marseilles, to which place
We have convenient convoy. You must know
I am supposed dead. The army breaking,
My husband hies him home; where, heaven aiding,
And by the leave of my good lord the King,
We'll be before our welcome.
WIDOW. Gentle madam,
You never had a servant to whose trust
Your business was more welcome.

HELENA. Nor you, mistress,
Ever a friend whose thoughts more truly labour
To recompense your love. Doubt not but heaven
Hath brought me up to be your daughter's dower,
As it hath fated her to be my motive
And helper to a husband. But, O strange men!
That can such sweet use make of what they hate,
When saucy trusting of the cozen'd thoughts
Defiles the pitchy night. So lust doth play
With what it loathes, for that which is away.
But more of this hereafter. You, Diana,
Under my poor instructions yet must suffer
Something in my behalf.
DIANA. Let death and honesty
Go with your impositions, I am yours
Upon your will to suffer.
HELENA. Yet, I pray you:
But with the word the time will bring on summer,
When briers shall have leaves as well as thorns
And be as sweet as sharp. We must away;
Our waggon is prepar'd, and time revives us.
All's Well that Ends Well. Still the fine's the crown.
Whate'er the course, the end is the renown.   *Exeunt*

SCENE 5

Rousillon. The COUNT'S *palace*

Enter COUNTESS, LAFEU, *and* CLOWN

LAFEU. No, no, no, your son was misled with a snipt-taffeta
fellow there, whose villainous saffron would have made all
the unbak'd and doughy youth of a nation in his colour.
Your daughter-in-law had been alive at this hour, and your
son here at home, more advanc'd by the King than by that
red-tail'd humble-bee I speak of.
COUNTESS. I would I had not known him. It was the death
of the most virtuous gentlewoman that ever nature had
praise for creating. If she had partaken of my flesh, and

cost me the dearest groans of a mother, I could not have owed her a more rooted love.

LAFEU. 'Twas a good lady, 'twas a good lady. We may pick a thousand sallets ere we light on such another herb.

CLOWN. Indeed, sir, she was the sweet-marjoram of the sallet, or, rather, the herb of grace.

LAFEU. They are not sallet-herbs, you knave; they are nose-herbs.

CLOWN. I am no great Nebuchadnezzar, sir; I have not much skill in grass.

LAFEU. Whether dost thou profess thyself—a knave or a fool?

CLOWN. A fool, sir, at a woman's service, and a knave at a man's.

LAFEU. Your distinction?

CLOWN. I would cozen the man of his wife, and do his service.

LAFEU. So you were a knave at his service, indeed.

CLOWN. And I would give his wife my bauble, sir, to do her service.

LAFEU. I will subscribe for thee; thou art both knave and fool.

CLOWN. At your service.

LAFEU. No, no, no.

CLOWN. Why, sir, if I cannot serve you, I can serve as great a prince as you are.

LAFEU. Who's that? A Frenchman?

CLOWN. Faith, sir, 'a has an English name; but his fisnomy is more hotter in France than there.

LAFEU. What prince is that?

CLOWN. The Black Prince, sir; alias, the Prince of Darkness; alias, the devil.

LAFEU. Hold thee, there's my purse. I give thee not this to suggest thee from thy master thou talk'st of; serve him still.

CLOWN. I am a woodland fellow, sir, that always loved a great fire; and the master I speak of ever keeps a good fire. But, sure, he is the prince of the world; let his nobility remain in's court. I am for the house with the narrow gate, which I take to be too little for pomp to enter. Some that humble themselves may; but the many will be too chill and tender; and they'll be for the flow'ry way that leads to the broad gate and the great fire.

LAFEU. Go thy ways, I begin to be aweary of thee; and I tell thee so before, because I would not fall out with thee. Go thy ways; let my horses be well look'd to, without any tricks.

CLOWN. If I put any tricks upon 'em, sir, they shall be jades' tricks, which are their own right by the law of nature.

Exit

LAFEU. A shrewd knave, and an unhappy.

COUNTESS. So 'a is. My lord that's gone made himself much sport out of him. By his authority he remains here, which he thinks is a patent for his sauciness; and indeed he has no pace, but runs where he will.

LAFEU. I like him well; 'tis not amiss. And I was about to tell you, since I heard of the good lady's death, and that my lord your son was upon his return home, I moved the King my master to speak in the behalf of my daughter; which, in the minority of them both, his Majesty out of a self-gracious remembrance did first propose. His Highness hath promis'd me to do it; and, to stop up the displeasure he hath conceived against your son, there is no fitter matter. How does your ladyship like it?

COUNTESS. With very much content, my lord; and I wish it happily effected.

LAFEU. His Highness comes post from Marseilles, of as able body as when he number'd thirty; 'a will be here to-morrow, or I am deceiv'd by him that in such intelligence hath seldom fail'd.

COUNTESS. It rejoices me that I hope I shall see him ere I die. I have letters that my son will be here to-night. I shall beseech your lordship to remain with me till they meet together.

LAFEU. Madam, I was thinking with what manners I might safely be admitted.

COUNTESS. You need but plead your honourable privilege.

LAFEU. Lady, of that I have made a bold charter; but, I thank my God, it holds yet.

Re-enter CLOWN

CLOWN. O madam, yonder's my lord your son with a patch of velvet on's face; whether there be a scar under 't or no, the velvet knows; but 'tis a goodly patch of velvet. His left cheek is a cheek of two pile and a half, but his right cheek is worn bare.

LAFEU. A scar nobly got, or a noble scar, is a good liv'ry of honour; so belike is that.

CLOWN. But it is your carbonado'd face.

LAFEU. Let us go see your son, I pray you;
I long to talk with the young noble soldier.

CLOWN. Faith, there's a dozen of 'em, with delicate fine hats, and most courteous feathers, which bow the head and nod at every man. *Exeunt*

ACT V. SCENE 1

Marseilles. A street

Enter HELENA, WIDOW, *and* DIANA, *with two* ATTENDANTS

HELENA. But this exceeding posting day and night
Must wear your spirits low; we cannot help it.
But since you have made the days and nights as one,
To wear your gentle limbs in my affairs,
Be bold you do so grow in my requital
As nothing can unroot you.

Enter a GENTLEMAN

In happy time!
This man may help me to his Majesty's ear,
If he would spend his power. God save you, sir.

GENTLEMAN. And you.

HELENA. Sir, I have seen you in the court of France.

GENTLEMAN. I have been sometimes there.

HELENA. I do presume, sir, that you are not fall'n
From the report that goes upon your goodness;
And therefore, goaded with most sharp occasions,
Which lay nice manners by, I put you to

The use of your own virtues, for the which
I shall continue thankful.
GENTLEMAN. What's your will?
HELENA. That it will please you
To give this poor petition to the King;
And aid me with that store of power you have
To come into his presence.
GENTLEMAN. The King's not here.
HELENA. Not here, sir?
GENTLEMAN. Not indeed.
He hence remov'd last night, and with more haste
Than is his use.
WIDOW. Lord, how we lose our pains!
HELENA. All's Well That Ends Well yet,
Though time seem so adverse and means unfit.
I do beseech you, whither is he gone?
GENTLEMAN. Marry, as I take it, to Rousillon;
Whither I am going.
HELENA. I do beseech you, sir,
Since you are like to see the King before me,
Commend the paper to his gracious hand;
Which I presume shall render you no blame,
But rather make you thank your pains for it.
I will come after you with what good speed
Our means will make us means.
GENTLEMAN. This I'll do for you.
HELENA. And you shall find yourself to be well thank'd,
Whate'er falls more. We must to horse again;
Go, go, provide.   *Exeunt*

SCENE 2

Rousillon. The inner court of the COUNT's *palace*

Enter CLOWN *and* PAROLLES

PAROLLES. Good Monsieur Lavache, give my Lord Lafeu this
letter. I have ere now, sir, been better known to you, when
I have held familiarity with fresher clothes; but I am now,

sir, muddied in Fortune's mood, and smell somewhat strong
of her strong displeasure.

CLOWN. Truly, Fortune's displeasure is but sluttish, if it smell
so strongly as thou speak'st of. I will henceforth eat no fish
of Fortune's butt'ring. Prithee, allow the wind.

PAROLLES. Nay, you need not to stop your nose, sir; I spake
but by a metaphor.

CLOWN. Indeed, sir, if your metaphor stink, I will stop my
nose; or against any man's metaphor. Prithee, get thee
further.

PAROLLES. Pray you, sir, deliver me this paper.

CLOWN. Foh! prithee stand away. A paper from Fortune's
close-stool to give to a nobleman! Look here he comes
himself.

Enter LAFEU

Here is a pur of Fortune's, sir, or of Fortune's cat, but not
a musk-cat, that has fall'n into the unclean fishpond of her
displeasure, and, as he says, is muddied withal. Pray you,
sir, use the carp as you may; for he looks like a poor, decayed, ingenious, foolish, rascally knave. I do pity his distress in my similes of comfort, and leave him to your lordship.   *Exit*

PAROLLES. My lord, I am a man whom Fortune hath cruelly
scratch'd.

LAFEU. And what would you have me to do? 'Tis too late to
pare her nails now. Wherein have you played the knave
with Fortune, that she should scratch you, who of herself
is a good lady and would not have knaves thrive long under her? There's a cardecue for you. Let the justices make
you and Fortune friends; I am for other business.

PAROLLES. I beseech your honour to hear me one single
word.

LAFEU. You beg a single penny more; come, you shall ha't;
save your word.

PAROLLES. My name, my good lord, is Parolles.

LAFEU. You beg more than word then. Cox my passion! give
me your hand. How does your drum?

PAROLLES. O my good lord, you were the first that found
me.

917

LAFEU. Was I, in sooth? And I was the first that lost thee.

PAROLLES. It lies in you, my lord, to bring me in some grace, for you did bring me out.

LAFEU. Out upon thee, knave! Dost thou put upon me at once both the office of God and the devil? One brings thee in grace, and the other brings thee out. [*Trumpets sound*] The King's coming; I know by his trumpets. Sirrah, inquire further after me; I had talk of you last night. Though you are a fool and a knave, you shall eat. Go to; follow.

PAROLLES. I praise God for you.   *Exeunt*

SCENE 3

Rousillon. The COUNT'S *palace*

Flourish. Enter KING, COUNTESS, LAFEU, *the two* FRENCH LORDS, *with* ATTENDANTS

KING. We lost a jewel of her, and our esteem
Was made much poorer by it; but your son,
As mad in folly, lack'd the sense to know
Her estimation home.

COUNTESS. 'Tis past, my liege;
And I beseech your Majesty to make it
Natural rebellion, done i' th' blaze of youth,
When oil and fire, too strong for reason's force,
O'erbears it and burns on.

KING. My honour'd lady,
I have forgiven and forgotten all;
Though my revenges were high bent upon him
And watch'd the time to shoot.

LAFEU. This I must say—
But first, I beg my pardon: the young lord
Did to his Majesty, his mother, and his lady,
Offence of mighty note; but to himself
The greatest wrong of all. He lost a wife
Whose beauty did astonish the survey
Of richest eyes; whose words all ears took captive;
Whose dear perfection hearts that scorn'd to serve

Humbly call'd mistress.

KING. Praising what is lost
  Makes the remembrance dear. Well, call him hither;
  We are reconcil'd, and the first view shall kill
  All repetition. Let him not ask our pardon;
  The nature of his great offence is dead,
  And deeper than oblivion do we bury
  Th' incensing relics of it; let him approach,
  A stranger, no offender; and inform him
  So 'tis our will he should.
GENTLEMAN. I shall, my liege.   *Exit* GENTLEMAN
KING. What says he to your daughter? Have you spoke?
LAFEU. All that he is hath reference to your Highness.
KING. Then shall we have a match. I have letters sent me
  That sets him high in fame.

Enter BERTRAM

LAFEU. He looks well on't.
KING. I am not a day of season,
  For thou mayst see a sunshine and a hail
  In me at once. But to the brightest beams
  Distracted clouds give way; so stand thou forth;
  The time is fair again.
BERTRAM. My high-repented blames,
  Dear sovereign, pardon to me.
KING. All is whole;
  Not one word more of the consumed time.
  Let's take the instant by the forward top;
  For we are old, and on our quick'st decrees
  Th' inaudible and noiseless foot of Time
  Steals ere we can effect them. You remember
  The daughter of this lord?
BERTRAM. Admiringly, my liege. At first
  I stuck my choice upon her, ere my heart
  Durst make too bold a herald of my tongue;
  Where the impression of mine eye infixing,
  Contempt his scornful perspective did lend me,
  Which warp'd the line of every other favour,
  Scorn'd a fair colour or express'd it stol'n,
  Extended or contracted all proportions

To a most hideous object. Thence it came
That she whom all men prais'd, and whom myself,
Since I have lost, have lov'd, was in mine eye
The dust that did offend it.

KING. Well excus'd.
That thou didst love her, strikes some scores away
From the great compt; but love that comes too late,
Like a remorseful pardon slowly carried,
To the great sender turns a sour offence,
Crying 'That's good that's gone.' Our rash faults
Make trivial price of serious things we have,
Not knowing them until we know their grave.
Oft our displeasures, to ourselves unjust,
Destroy our friends, and after weep their dust;
Our own love waking cries to see what's done,
While shameful hate sleeps out the afternoon.
Be this sweet Helen's knell. And now forget her.
Send forth your amorous token for fair Maudlin.
The main consents are had; and here we'll stay
To see our widower's second marriage-day.

COUNTESS. Which better than the first, O dear heaven, bless!
Or, ere they meet, in me, O nature, cesse!

LAFEU. Come on, my son, in whom my house's name
Must be digested; give a favour from you,
To sparkle in the spirits of my daughter,
That she may quickly come.   [BERTRAM *gives a ring*]
By my old beard,
And ev'ry hair that's on't, Helen, that's dead,
Was a sweet creature; such a ring as this,
The last that e'er I took her leave at court,
I saw upon her finger.

BERTRAM. Hers it was not.

KING. Now, pray you, let me see it; for mine eye,
While I was speaking, oft was fasten'd to't.
This ring was mine; and when I gave it Helen
I bade her, if her fortunes ever stood
Necessitied to help, that by this token
I would relieve her. Had you that craft to reave her
Of what should stead her most?

BERTRAM. My gracious sovereign,

Howe'er it pleases you to take it so,
The ring was never hers.
COUNTESS. Son, on my life,
I have seen her wear it; and she reckon'd it
At her life's rate.
LAFEU. I am sure I saw her wear it.
BERTRAM. You are deceiv'd, my lord; she never saw it.
In Florence was it from a casement thrown me,
Wrapp'd in a paper, which contain'd the name
Of her that threw it. Noble she was, and thought
I stood engag'd; but when I had subscrib'd
To mine own fortune, and inform'd her fully
I could not answer in that course of honour
As she had made the overture, she ceas'd,
In heavy satisfaction, and would never
Receive the ring again.
KING. Plutus himself,
That knows the tinct and multiplying med'cine,
Hath not in nature's mystery more science
Than I have in this ring. 'Twas mine, 'twas Helen's,
Whoever gave it you. Then, if you know
That you are well acquainted with yourself,
Confess 'twas hers, and by what rough enforcement
You got it from her. She call'd the saints to surety
That she would never put it from her finger
Unless she gave it to yourself in bed—
Where you have never come—or sent it us
Upon her great disaster.
BERTRAM. She never saw it.
KING. Thou speak'st it falsely, as I love mine honour;
And mak'st conjectural fears to come into me
Which I would fain shut out. If it should prove
That thou art so inhuman—'twill not prove so.
And yet I know not—thou didst hate her deadly,
And she is dead; which nothing, but to close
Her eyes myself, could win me to believe
More than to see this ring. Take him away.
                              [GUARDS *seize* BERTRAM]
My fore-past proofs, howe'er the matter fall,
Shall tax my fears of little vanity,

Having vainly fear'd too little. **Away with him.**
We'll sift this matter further.
BERTRAM. If you shall prove
This ring was ever hers, you shall as easy
Prove that I husbanded her bed in Florence,
Where she yet never was. *Exit, guarded*
KING. I am wrapp'd in dismal thinkings.

Enter a GENTLEMAN

GENTLEMAN. Gracious sovereign,
Whether I have been to blame or no, I know not:
Here's a petition from a Florentine,
Who hath, for four or five removes, come short
To tender it herself. I undertook it,
Vanquish'd thereto by the fair grace and speech
Of the poor suppliant, who by this, I know,
Is here attending; her business looks in her
With an importing visage; and she told me
In a sweet verbal brief it did concern
Your Highness with herself.
KING. [*Reads the letter*] 'Upon his many protestations to marry me when his wife was dead, I blush to say it, he won me. Now is the Count Rousillon a widower; his vows are forfeited to me, and my honour's paid to him. He stole from Florence, taking no leave, and I follow him to his country for justice. Grant it me, O King! in you it best lies; otherwise a seducer flourishes, and a poor maid is undone.
DIANA CAPILET.'
LAFEU. I will buy me a son-in-law in a fair, and toll for this. I'll none of him.
KING. The heavens have thought well on thee, Lafeu,
To bring forth this discov'ry. Seek these suitors.
Go speedily, and bring again the Count.
Exeunt ATTENDANTS
I am afeard the life of Helen, lady,
Was foully snatch'd.
COUNTESS. Now, justice on the doers!

Enter BERTRAM, *guarded*

KING. I wonder, sir, sith wives are monsters to you,
  And that you fly them as you swear them lordship,
  Yet you desire to marry.

Enter WIDOW *and* DIANA

What woman's that?
DIANA. I am, my lord, a wretched Florentine,
  Derived from the ancient Capilet.
  My suit, as I do understand, you know,
  And therefore know how far I may be pitied.
WIDOW. I am her mother, sir, whose age and honour
  Both suffer under this complaint we bring,
  And both shall cease, without your remedy.
KING. Come hither, Count; do you know these women?
BERTRAM. My lord, I neither can nor will deny
  But that I know them. Do they charge me further?
DIANA. Why do you look so strange upon your wife?
BERTRAM. She's none of mine, my lord.
DIANA. If you shall marry,
  You give away this hand, and that is mine;
  You give away heaven's vows, and those are mine;
  You give away myself, which is known mine;
  For I by vow am so embodied yours
  That she which marries you must marry me,
  Either both or none.
LAFEU. [*To* BERTRAM] Your reputation comes too short for
  my daughter; you are no husband for her.
BERTRAM. My lord, this is a fond and desp'rate creature
  Whom sometime I have laugh'd with. Let your Highness
  Lay a more noble thought upon mine honour
  Than for to think that I would sink it here.
KING. Sir, for my thoughts, you have them ill to friend
  Till your deeds gain them. Fairer prove your honour
  Than in my thought it lies!
DIANA. Good my lord,
  Ask him upon his oath if he does think
  He had not my virginity.
KING. What say'st thou to her?
BERTRAM. She's impudent, my lord,
  And was a common gamester to the camp.

DIANA. He does me wrong, my lord; if I were so
  He might have bought me at a common price.
  Do not believe him. O, behold this ring,
  Whose high respect and rich validity
  Did lack a parallel; yet, for all that,
  He gave it to a commoner o' th' camp,
  If I be one.
COUNTESS. He blushes, and 'tis it.
  Of six preceding ancestors, that gem
  Conferr'd by testament to th' sequent issue,
  Hath it been ow'd and worn. This is his wife:
  That ring's a thousand proofs.
KING. Methought you said
  You saw one here in court could witness it.
DIANA. I did, my lord, but loath am to produce
  So bad an instrument; his name's Parolles.
LAFEU. I saw the man to-day, if man he be.
KING. Find him, and bring him hither. *Exit an* ATTENDANT
BERTRAM. What of him?
  He's quoted for a most perfidious slave,
  With all the spots o' th' world tax'd and debauch'd,
  Whose nature sickens but to speak a truth.
  Am I or that or this for what he'll utter
  That will speak anything?
KING. She hath that ring of yours.
BERTRAM. I think she has. Certain it is I lik'd her,
  And boarded her i' th' wanton way of youth.
  She knew her distance, and did angle for me,
  Madding my eagerness with her restraint,
  As all impediments in fancy's course
  Are motives of more fancy; and, in fine,
  Her infinite cunning with her modern grace
  Subdu'd me to her rate. She got the ring;
  And I had that which any inferior might
  At market-price have bought.
DIANA. I must be patient.
  You that have turn'd off a first so noble wife
  May justly diet me. I pray you yet—
  Since you lack virtue, I will lose a husband—
  Send for your ring, I will return it home,

And give me mine again.

BERTRAM. I have it not.

KING. What ring was yours, I pray you?

DIANA. Sir, much like
The same upon your finger.

KING. Know you this ring? This ring was his of late.

DIANA. And this was it I gave him, being abed.

KING. The story, then, goes false you threw it him
Out of a casement.

DIANA. I have spoke the truth.

Enter PAROLLES

BERTRAM. My lord, I do confess the ring was hers.

KING. You boggle shrewdly; every feather starts you.
Is this the man you speak of?

DIANA. Ay, my lord.

KING. Tell me, sirrah—but tell me true I charge you,
Not fearing the displeasure of your master,
Which, on your just proceeding, I'll keep off—
By him and by this woman here what know you?

PAROLLES. So please your Majesty, my master hath been an
honourable gentleman; tricks he hath had in him, which
gentlemen have.

KING. Come, come, to th' purpose. Did he love this woman?

PAROLLES. Faith, sir, he did love her; but how?

KING. How, I pray you?

PAROLLES. He did love her, sir, as a gentleman loves a
woman.

KING. How is that?

PAROLLES. He lov'd her, sir, and lov'd her not.

KING. As thou art a knave and no knave.
What an equivocal companion is this!

PAROLLES. I am a poor man, and at your Majesty's command.

LAFEU. He's a good drum, my lord, but a naughty orator.

DIANA. Do you know he promis'd me marriage?

PAROLLES. Faith, I know more than I'll speak.

KING. But wilt thou not speak all thou know'st?

PAROLLES. Yes, so please your Majesty. I did go between
them, as I said; but more than that, he loved her—for indeed he was mad for her, and talk'd of Satan, and of

Limbo, and of Furies, and I know not what. Yet I was in that credit with them at that time that I knew of their going to bed; and of other motions, as promising her marriage, and things which would derive me ill will to speak of; therefore I will not speak what I know.

KING. Thou hast spoken all already, unless thou canst say they are married; but thou art too fine in thy evidence; therefore stand aside.

This ring, you say, was yours?

DIANA. Ay, my good lord.

KING. Where did you buy it? Or who gave it you?

DIANA. It was not given me, nor I did not buy it.

KING. Who lent it you?

DIANA. It was not lent me neither.

KING. Where did you find it then?

DIANA. I found it not.

KING. If it were yours by none of all these ways,
How could you give it him?

DIANA. I never gave it him.

LAFEU. This woman's an easy glove, my lord; she goes off and on at pleasure.

KING. This ring was mine, I gave it his first wife.

DIANA. It might be yours or hers, for aught I know.

KING. Take her away, I do not like her now;
To prison with her. And away with him.
Unless thou tell'st me where thou hadst this ring,
Thou diest within this hour.

DIANA. I'll never tell you.

KING. Take her away.

DIANA. I'll put in bail, my liege.

KING. I think thee now some common customer.

DIANA. By Jove, if ever I knew man, 'twas you.

KING. Wherefore hast thou accus'd him all this while?

DIANA. Because he's guilty, and he is not guilty.
He knows I am no maid, and he'll swear to't:
I'll swear I am a maid, and he knows not.
Great King, I am no strumpet, by my life;
I am either maid, or else this old man's wife.
                                        [*Pointing to* LAFEU]

KING. She does abuse our ears; to prison with her.

DIANA. Good mother, fetch my bail. Stay, royal sir;
                                          Exit WIDOW
The jeweller that owes the ring is sent for,
And he shall surety me. But for this lord
Who hath abus'd me as he knows himself,
Though yet he never harm'd me, here I quit him.
He knows himself my bed he hath defil'd;
And at that time he got his wife with child.
Dead though she be, she feels her young one kick;
So there's my riddle: one that's dead is quick—
And now behold the meaning.

              Re-enter WIDOW *with* HELENA

KING. Is there no exorcist
Beguiles the truer office of mine eyes?
Is't real that I see?
HELENA. No, my good lord;
'Tis but the shadow of a wife you see,
The name and not the thing.
BERTRAM. Both, both; O, pardon!
HELENA. O, my good lord, when I was like this maid,
I found you wondrous kind. There is your ring,
And, look you, here's your letter. This it says:
'When from my finger you can get this ring,
And are by me with child,' &c. This is done.
Will you be mine now you are doubly won?
BERTRAM. If she, my liege, can make me know this clearly,
I'll love her dearly, ever, ever dearly.
HELENA. If it appear not plain, and prove untrue,
Deadly divorce step between me and you!
O my dear mother, do I see you living?
LAFEU. Mine eyes smell onions; I shall weep anon. [*To* PA-
ROLLES] Good Tom Drum, lend me a handkercher. So, I
thank thee. Wait on me home, I'll make sport with thee;
let thy curtsies alone, they are scurvy ones.
KING. Let us from point to point this story know,
To make the even truth in pleasure flow.
[*To* DIANA] If thou beest yet a fresh uncropped flower,
Choose thou thy husband, and I'll pay thy dower;
For I can guess that by thy honest aid

Thou kept'st a wife herself, thyself a maid.—
Of that and all the progress, more and less,
Resolvedly more leisure shall express.
All yet seems well; and if it end so meet,
The bitter past, more welcome is the sweet.   [*Flourish*]

EPILOGUE

KING. The King's a beggar, now the play is done.
All is well ended if this suit be won,
That you express content; which we will pay
With strife to please you, day exceeding day.
Ours be your patience then, and yours our parts;
Your gentle hands lend us, and take our hearts.
Exeunt omnes

Twelfth Night;

or,

What You Will

MALVOLIO. *My masters, are you mad?*
(ACT II. SCENE III)

TWELFTH NIGHT

THE CENTRAL SITUATION—Olivia's falling in love with the disguised Viola; Viola's acting as the messenger for the man she loves; Viola's brother arriving to content Olivia and allow Viola herself to have Orsino—Shakespeare had already outlined in *Two Gentlemen of Verona*. In that early comedy he had combined elements from Montemayor's *Diana* with the original situation as designed by the author or authors of *Gl'Ingannati*, overlaying something of the asperity of the Italian original with the courtliness of the Spanish version. In *Twelfth Night* Shakespeare remoulds the situation entirely to his own mind; we do not feel here that he is tempering one version with the other; he knows now what the situation that he has had in mind so long can yield him and he redesigns it solely with reference to his own intention.

Not only had Shakespeare had the central situation in mind for a number of years; he had, if the traces that scholars have so carefully collected can be trusted, studied the situation in several versions; for from the original *Gl'Ingannati* depends a whole chain of imitations and adaptations with Shakespeare's own play as the wonderful conclusion of the series.

The transformation Shakespeare was to work on the original material can best be appreciated by a lightning survey of the development of European comedy. Modern comedy was born in Ferrara, its father being the poet Ariosto. He set the example of adapting classical Latin comedy that the Italian authors of the *commedia erudita* or 'learned comedy' followed. The classical convention that forbade the author to present on his stage a respectable unmarried young woman was at first evaded by disguising the heroine as a boy and so providing for more romantic situations than could otherwise have been achieved. The cynical and harsher tone of the older comedy was softened by this innovation and the way prepared for the later romantic treatment of the love intrigue. *Gl'Ingannati* is an admirable example of the Italian *commedia erudita*; it is still what may be called *bourgeois* comedy, reflecting the attitudes that are supposed to be de-

931

noted by that term. The heroine Laelia is not like Viola reluctantly true to her master's service. Laelia has no scruples in telling Isabella (Shakespeare's Olivia) that if she dismisses Flaminio (Orsino in Shakespeare) perhaps her new passion for Laelia may prosper; nor does she maintain towards Flaminio the reticence of a Viola. Flaminio himself is coarse as well as unfaithful. *Twelfth Night* marks the end of the transformation from the classical to the romantic comedy.

Shakespeare's poetry of course adds the last enchantment to the transformation. Instead of the witty prose of the Italian comedy Shakespeare finds a music for his scenes that overflows in some of his loveliest verse. Nor is there any loss of virility in Shakespeare's treatment of the theme, for there is no lack in his Illyria of keen wits and sharp tongues to mock or correct the aberrations of self-love. The additions of Sir Toby and Sir Andrew Aguecheek, Maria, Feste, and Malvolio to the scene are a further contribution by Shakespeare to the gaiety and variety of the piece.

Just as the first recorded performance of *Comedy of Errors* was at a celebration given by one of the Inns of Court, so *Twelfth Night* is first heard of as an entertainment at the Middle Temple on 2nd February 1602. John Manningham of that society made this record in his diary:

> At our feast wee had a play called Twelve Night, or What You Will, much like the Commedy of Errores, or Menechmi in Plautus, but most like and neere to that in Italian called *Inganni*.

Manningham refers to the identical twins in the *Menaechmi* of Plautus that Shakespeare took over in his *Comedy of Errors;* but, as these were male twins, *Twelfth Night* was obviously more like a play in which the twins were brother and sister. There were several plays with the title *Gl'Inganni*, of which Shakespeare could have known two. They give various versions of the Viola-Sebastian tangle, and in that by Curzio Gonzaga, published in 1592, the disguised heroine assumes the name Cesare, which seems to have suggested the Cesario of Shakespeare. There are resemblances of this sort, the apparent echo of a name or phrase, that seem to connect Shakespeare's *Twelfth Night* not only with *Gl'Ingannati* and with one of the *Gl'Inganni* but with prose versions of the original Italian plot by Bandello, Belleforest, and Barnabe Rich whose *Apolonius and Silla,* one of the discourses in *Riche his Farewell to the Military Profession* (1581) gives a variation in English of the theme. Rich, like Cinthio before him, uses a shipwreck to provide a complication and so does Shakespeare.

These links with what we may call the *Ingannati* family would, if sound, entitle us to say that Shakespeare had by his reading prepared himself pretty thoroughly for his own treatment of the situation. After all Shakespeare was a professional playwright; it would be natural for him to acquaint himself with the matters of his profession. Molière, another professional, was a great reader and had a quick eye for what he could turn to account; to those who accused him of plagiarism he replied with the old phrase *Je prends mon bien où je le trouve.* We need not believe that Shakespeare had a duller eye or a less retentive memory, or that he was slower to develop the possibilities he detected in older material. Till then there is evidence to support another view of Shakespeare's methods of work, *Twelfth Night* may serve as the perfect illustration of Shakespeare's power of assimilating and recombining the elements of a situation, which he had seen tried in various combinations, so that he could at last present us with its most human and interesting arrangement.

ORSINO, *Duke of Illyria*
SEBASTIAN, *brother of Viola*
ANTONIO, *a sea captain, friend of Sebastian*
A SEA CAPTAIN, *friend of Viola*
VALENTINE
CURIO } *gentlemen attending on the Duke*
SIR TOBY BELCH, *uncle of Olivia*
SIR ANDREW AGUECHEEK
MALVOLIO, *steward to Olivia*
FABIAN
FESTE, *a clown* } *servants to Olivia*

OLIVIA, *a rich countess*
VIOLA, *sister of Sebastian*
MARIA, *Olivia's waiting woman*

Lords, Priests, Sailors, Officers, Musicians, *and* Attendants

SCENE:

A city in Illyria; and the sea-coast near it

Twelfth Night

ACT I. SCENE 1

The DUKE's *palace*

Enter ORSINO, *Duke of Illyria,* CURIO, *and other* LORDS;
MUSICIANS *attending*

DUKE. If music be the food of love, play on,
Give me excess of it, that, surfeiting,
The appetite may sicken and so die.
That strain again! It had a dying fall;
O, it came o'er my ear like the sweet sound
That breathes upon a bank of violets,
Stealing and giving odour! Enough, no more;
'Tis not so sweet now as it was before.
O spirit of love, how quick and fresh art thou!
That, notwithstanding thy capacity
Receiveth as the sea, nought enters there,
Of what validity and pitch soe'er,
But falls into abatement and low price
Even in a minute. So full of shapes is fancy,
That it alone is high fantastical.
CURIO. Will you go hunt, my lord?
DUKE. What, Curio?
CURIO. The hart.
DUKE. Why, so I do, the noblest that I have.
O, when mine eyes did see Olivia first,
Methought she purg'd the air of pestilence!
That instant was I turn'd into a hart,
And my desires, like fell and cruel hounds,
E'er since pursue me.

Enter VALENTINE

How now! what news from her?
VALENTINE. So please my lord, I might not be admitted,
But from her handmaid do return this answer:
The element itself, till seven years' heat,

935

Shall not behold her face at ample view;
But like a cloistress she will veiled walk,
And water once a day her chamber round
With eye-offending brine; all this to season
A brother's dead love, which she would keep fresh
And lasting in her sad remembrance.
DUKE. O, she that hath a heart of that fine frame
To pay this debt of love but to a brother,
How will she love when the rich golden shaft
Hath kill'd the flock of all affections else
That live in her; when liver, brain, and heart,
These sovereign thrones, are all supplied and fill'd,
Her sweet perfections, with one self king!
Away before me to sweet beds of flow'rs:
Love-thoughts lie rich when canopied with bow'rs.

Exeunt

SCENE 2

The sea-coast

Enter VIOLA, *a* CAPTAIN, *and* SAILORS

VIOLA. What country, friends, is this?
CAPTAIN. This is Illyria, lady.
VIOLA. And what should I do in Illyria?
My brother he is in Elysium.
Perchance he is not drown'd—what think you, sailors?
CAPTAIN. It is perchance that you yourself were saved.
VIOLA. O my poor brother! and so perchance may he be.
CAPTAIN. True, madam, and, to comfort you with chance,
Assure yourself, after our ship did split,
When you, and those poor number saved with you,
Hung on our driving boat, I saw your brother,
Most provident in peril, bind himself—
Courage and hope both teaching him the practice—
To a strong mast that liv'd upon the sea;
Where, like Arion on the dolphin's back,
I saw him hold acquaintance with the waves
So long as I could see.
VIOLA. For saying so, there's gold.

Mine own escape unfoldeth to my hope,
Whereto thy speech serves for authority,
The like of him. Know'st thou this country?

CAPTAIN. Ay, madam, well; for I was bred and born
Not three hours' travel from this very place.

VIOLA. Who governs here?

CAPTAIN. A noble duke, in nature as in name.

VIOLA. What is his name?

CAPTAIN. Orsino.

VIOLA. Orsino! I have heard my father name him.
He was a bachelor then.

CAPTAIN. And so is now, or was so very late;
For but a month ago I went from hence,
And then 'twas fresh in murmur—as, you know,
What great ones do the less will prattle of—
That he did seek the love of fair Olivia.

VIOLA. What's she?

CAPTAIN. A virtuous maid, the daughter of a count
That died some twelvemonth since, then leaving her
In the protection of his son, her brother,
Who shortly also died; for whose dear love,
They say, she hath abjur'd the company
And sight of men.

VIOLA. O that I serv'd that lady,
And might not be delivered to the world,
Till I had made mine own occasion mellow,
What my estate is!

CAPTAIN. That were hard to compass,
Because she will admit no kind of suit—
No, not the Duke's.

VIOLA. There is a fair behaviour in thee, Captain;
And though that nature with a beauteous wall
Doth oft close in pollution, yet of thee
I will believe thou hast a mind that suits
With this thy fair and outward character.
I prithee, and I'll pay thee bounteously,
Conceal me what I am, and be my aid
For such disguise as haply shall become
The form of my intent. I'll serve this duke:
Thou shalt present me as an eunuch to him;

It may be worth thy pains, for I can sing
And speak to him in many sorts of music,
That will allow me very worth his service.
What else may hap to time I will commit;
Only shape thou silence to my wit.
CAPTAIN. Be you his eunuch and your mute I'll be;
When my tongue blabs, then let mine eyes not see.
VIOLA. I thank thee. Lead me on.   *Exeunt*

SCENE 3

OLIVIA's *house*

Enter SIR TOBY BELCH *and* MARIA

SIR TOBY. What a plague means my niece to take the death
of her brother thus? I am sure care's an enemy to life.
MARIA. By my troth, Sir Toby, you must come in earlier o'
nights; your cousin, my lady, takes great exceptions to
your ill hours.
SIR TOBY. Why, let her except before excepted.
MARIA. Ay, but you must confine yourself within the modest
limits of order.
SIR TOBY. Confine! I'll confine myself no finer than I am.
These clothes are good enough to drink in, and so be these
boots too; an they be not, let them hang themselves in
their own straps.
MARIA. That quaffing and drinking will undo you; I heard
my lady talk of it yesterday, and of a foolish knight that
you brought in one night here to be her wooer.
SIR TOBY. Who? Sir Andrew Aguecheek?
MARIA. Ay, he.
SIR TOBY. He's as tall a man as any's in Illyria.
MARIA. What's that to th' purpose?
SIR TOBY. Why, he has three thousand ducats a year.
MARIA. Ay, but he'll have but a year in all these ducats; he's
a very fool and a prodigal.
SIR TOBY. Fie that you'll say so! He plays o' th' viol-de-
gamboys, and speaks three or four languages word for

word without book, and hath all the good gifts of nature.

MARIA. He hath indeed, almost natural; for, besides that he's a fool, he's a great quarreller; and but that he hath the gift of a coward to allay the gust he hath in quarrelling, 'tis thought among the prudent he would quickly have the gift of a grave.

SIR TOBY. By this hand, they are scoundrels and subtractors that say so of him. Who are they?

MARIA. They that add, moreover, he's drunk nightly in your company.

SIR TOBY. With drinking healths to my niece; I'll drink to her as long as there is a passage in my throat and drink in Illyria. He's a coward and a coystrill that will not drink to my niece till his brains turn o' th' toe like a parish-top. What, wench! Castiliano vulgo! for here comes Sir Andrew Agueface.

Enter SIR ANDREW AGUECHEEK

AGUECHEEK. Sir Toby Belch! How now, Sir Toby Belch!

SIR TOBY. Sweet Sir Andrew!

AGUECHEEK. Bless you, fair shrew.

MARIA. And you too, sir.

SIR TOBY. Accost, Sir Andrew, accost.

AGUECHEEK. What's that?

SIR TOBY. My niece's chambermaid.

AGUECHEEK. Good Mistress Accost, I desire better acquaintance.

MARIA. My name is Mary, sir.

AGUECHEEK. Good Mistress Mary Accost—

SIR TOBY. You mistake, knight. 'Accost' is front her, board her, woo her, assail her.

AGUECHEEK. By my troth, I would not undertake her in this company. Is that the meaning of 'accost'?

MARIA. Fare you well, gentlemen.

SIR TOBY. An thou let part so, Sir Andrew, would thou mightst never draw sword again!

AGUECHEEK. An you part so, mistress, I would I might never draw sword again. Fair lady, do you think you have fools in hand?

MARIA. Sir, I have not you by th' hand.

AGUECHEEK. Marry, but you shall have; and here's my hand.

MARIA. Now, sir, thought is free. I pray you, bring your hand to th' butt'ry-bar and let it drink.

AGUECHEEK. Wherefore, sweetheart? What's your metaphor?

MARIA. It's dry, sir.

AGUECHEEK. Why, I think so; I am not such an ass but I can keep my hand dry. But what's your jest?

MARIA. A dry jest, sir.

AGUECHEEK. Are you full of them?

MARIA. Ay, sir, I have them at my fingers' ends; marry, now I let go your hand, I am barren. *Exit* MARIA

SIR TOBY. O knight, thou lack'st a cup of canary! When did I see thee so put down?

AGUECHEEK. Never in your life, I think; unless you see canary put me down. Methinks sometimes I have no more wit than a Christian or an ordinary man has; but I am a great eater of beef, and I believe that does harm to my wit.

SIR TOBY. No question.

AGUECHEEK. An I thought that, I'd forswear it. I'll ride home to-morrow, Sir Toby.

SIR TOBY. Pourquoi, my dear knight?

AGUECHEEK. What is 'pourquoi'—do or not do? I would I had bestowed that time in the tongues that I have in fencing, dancing, and bear-baiting. Oh, had I but followed the arts!

SIR TOBY. Then hadst thou had an excellent head of hair.

AGUECHEEK. Why, would that have mended my hair?

SIR TOBY. Past question; for thou seest it will not curl by nature.

AGUECHEEK. But it becomes me well enough, does't not?

SIR TOBY. Excellent; it hangs like flax on a distaff, and I hope to see a huswife take thee between her legs and spin it off.

AGUECHEEK. Faith, I'll home to-morrow, Sir Toby. Your niece will not be seen, or if she be, it's four to one she'll none of me; the Count himself here hard by woos her.

SIR TOBY. She'll none o' th' Count; she'll not match above her degree, neither in estate, years, nor wit; I have heard her swear't. Tut, there's life in't, man.

AGUECHEEK. I'll stay a month longer. I am a fellow o' th'

strangest mind i' th' world; I delight in masques and revels sometimes altogether.

SIR TOBY. Art thou good at these kickshawses, knight?

AGUECHEEK. As any man in Illyria, whatsoever he be, under the degree of my betters; and yet I will not compare with an old man.

SIR TOBY. What is thy excellence in a galliard, knight?

AGUECHEEK. Faith, I can cut a caper.

SIR TOBY. And I can cut the mutton to't.

AGUECHEEK. And I think I have the back-trick simply as strong as any man in Illyria.

SIR TOBY. Wherefore are these things hid? Wherefore have these gifts a curtain before 'em? Are they like to take dust, like Mistress Mall's picture? Why dost thou not go to church in a galliard and come home in a coranto? My very walk should be a jig; I would not so much as make water but in a sink-a-pace. What dost thou mean? Is it a world to hide virtues in? I did think, by the excellent constitution of thy leg, it was form'd under the star of a galliard.

AGUECHEEK. Ay, 'tis strong, and it does indifferent well in a flame-colour'd stock. Shall we set about some revels?

SIR TOBY. What shall we do else? Were we not born under Taurus?

AGUECHEEK. Taurus? That's sides and heart.

SIR TOBY. No, sir; it is legs and thighs. Let me see thee caper. Ha, higher! Ha, ha, excellent!   *Exeunt*

SCENE 4

The DUKE's *palace*

Enter VALENTINE, *and* VIOLA *in man's attire*

VALENTINE. If the Duke continue these favours towards you, Cesario, you are like to be much advanc'd; he hath known you but three days, and already you are no stranger.

VIOLA. You either fear his humour or my negligence, that you call in question the continuance of his love. Is he inconstant, sir, in his favours?

VALENTINE. No, believe me.

Enter DUKE, CURIO, *and* ATTENDANTS

VIOLA. I thank you. Here comes the Count.
DUKE. Who saw Cesario, ho?
VIOLA. On your attendance, my lord, here.
DUKE. Stand you awhile aloof. Cesario,
  Thou know'st no less but all; I have unclasp'd
  To thee the book even of my secret soul.
  Therefore, good youth, address thy gait unto her;
  Be not denied access, stand at her doors,
  And tell them there thy fixed foot shall grow
  Till thou have audience.
VIOLA. Sure, my noble lord,
  If she be so abandon'd to her sorrow
  As it is spoke, she never will admit me.
DUKE. Be clamorous and leap all civil bounds,
  Rather than make unprofited return.
VIOLA. Say I do speak with her, my lord, what then?
DUKE. O, then unfold the passion of my love,
  Surprise her with discourse of my dear faith!
  It shall become thee well to act my woes:
  She will attend it better in thy youth
  Than in a nuncio's of more grave aspect.
VIOLA. I think not so, my lord.
DUKE. Dear lad, believe it,
  For they shall yet belie thy happy years
  That say thou art a man: Diana's lip
  Is not more smooth and rubious; thy small pipe
  Is as the maiden's organ, shrill and sound,
  And all is semblative a woman's part.
  I know thy constellation is right apt
  For this affair. Some four or five attend him—
  All, if you will, for I myself am best
  When least in company. Prosper well in this,
  And thou shalt live as freely as thy lord
  To call his fortunes thine.
VIOLA. I'll do my best
  To woo your lady. [*Aside*] Yet, a barful strife!
  Whoe'er I woo, myself would be his wife.

SCENE 5

Olivia's *house*

Enter Maria *and* Clown

Maria. Nay, either tell me where thou hast been, or I will not open my lips so wide as a bristle may enter in way of thy excuse; my lady will hang thee for thy absence.

Clown. Let her hang me. He that is well hang'd in this world needs to fear no colours.

Maria. Make that good.

Clown. He shall see none to fear.

Maria. A good lenten answer. I can tell thee where that saying was born, of 'I fear no colours.'

Clown. Where, good Mistress Mary?

Maria. In the wars; and that may you be bold to say in your foolery.

Clown. Well, God give them wisdom that have it; and those that are fools, let them use their talents.

Maria. Yet you will be hang'd for being so long absent; or to be turn'd away—is not that as good as a hanging to you?

Clown. Many a good hanging prevents a bad marriage; and for turning away, let summer bear it out.

Maria. You are resolute, then?

Clown. Not so, neither; but I am resolv'd on two points.

Maria. That if one break, the other will hold; or if both break, your gaskins fall.

Clown. Apt, in good faith, very apt! Well, go thy way; if Sir Toby would leave drinking, thou wert as witty a piece of Eve's flesh as any in Illyria.

Maria. Peace, you rogue, no more o' that. Here comes my lady. Make your excuse wisely, you were best. *Exit*

Enter Olivia *and* Malvolio

Clown. Wit, an't be thy will, put me into good fooling! Those wits that think they have thee do very oft prove fools; and I that am sure I lack thee may pass for a wise man. For what says Quinapalus? 'Better a witty fool than a foolish wit.' God bless thee, lady!

943

OLIVIA. Take the fool away.

CLOWN. Do you not hear, fellows? Take away the lady.

OLIVIA. Go to, y'are a dry fool; I'll no more of you. Besides, you grow dishonest.

CLOWN. Two faults, madonna, that drink and good counsel will amend; for give the dry fool drink, then is the fool not dry. Bid the dishonest man mend himself: if he mend, he is no longer dishonest; if he cannot, let the botcher mend him. Anything that's mended is but patch'd; virtue that transgresses is but patch'd with sin, and sin that amends is but patch'd with virtue. If that this simple syllogism will serve, so; if it will not, what remedy? As there is no true cuckold but calamity, so beauty's a flower. The lady bade take away the fool; therefore, I say again, take her away.

OLIVIA. Sir, I bade them take away you.

CLOWN. Misprision in the highest degree! Lady, 'Cucullus non facit monachum'; that's as much to say as I wear not motley in my brain. Good madonna, give me leave to prove you a fool.

OLIVIA. Can you do it?

CLOWN. Dexteriously, good madonna.

OLIVIA. Make your proof.

CLOWN. I must catechize you for it, madonna.
Good my mouse of virtue, answer me.

OLIVIA. Well, sir, for want of other idleness, I'll bide your proof.

CLOWN. Good madonna, why mourn'st thou?

OLIVIA. Good fool, for my brother's death.

CLOWN. I think his soul is in hell, madonna.

OLIVIA. I know his soul is in heaven, fool.

CLOWN. The more fool, madonna, to mourn for your brother's soul being in heaven. Take away the fool, gentlemen.

OLIVIA. What think you of this fool, Malvolio? Doth he not mend?

MALVOLIO. Yes, and shall do, till the pangs of death shake him. Infirmity, that decays the wise, doth ever make the better fool.

CLOWN. God send you, sir, a speedy infirmity, for the better increasing your folly! Sir Toby will be sworn that I am no

944

fox; but he will not pass his word for twopence that you are no fool.

OLIVIA. How say you to that, Malvolio?

MALVOLIO. I marvel your ladyship takes delight in such a barren rascal; I saw him put down the other day with an ordinary fool that has no more brain than a stone. Look you now, he's out of his guard already; unless you laugh and minister occasion to him, he is gagg'd. I protest I take these wise men that crow so at these set kind of fools no better than the fools' zanies.

OLIVIA. O, you are sick of self-love, Malvolio, and taste with a distemper'd appetite. To be generous, guiltless, and of free disposition, is to take those things for bird-bolts that you deem cannon bullets. There is no slander in an allow'd fool, though he do nothing but rail; nor no railing in a known discreet man, though he do nothing but reprove.

CLOWN. Now Mercury endue thee with leasing, for thou speak'st well of fools!

Re-enter MARIA

MARIA. Madam, there is at the gate a young gentleman much desires to speak with you.

OLIVIA. From the Count Orsino, is it?

MARIA. I know not, madam; 'tis a fair young man, and well attended.

OLIVIA. Who of my people hold him in delay?

MARIA. Sir Toby, madam, your kinsman.

OLIVIA. Fetch him off, I pray you; he speaks nothing but madman. Fie on him! [*Exit* MARIA] Go you, Malvolio: if it be a suit from the Count, I am sick, or not at home—what you will to dismiss it. [*Exit* MALVOLIO] Now you see, sir, how your fooling grows old, and people dislike it.

CLOWN. Thou hast spoke for us, madonna, as if thy eldest son should be a fool; whose skull Jove cram with brains! For—here he comes—one of thy kin has a most weak pia mater.

Enter SIR TOBY

OLIVIA. By mine honour, half drunk! What is he at the gate, cousin?

SIR TOBY. A gentleman.

OLIVIA. A gentleman! What gentleman?

SIR TOBY. 'Tis a gentleman here. [*Hiccups*] A plague o' these pickle-herring! How now, sot!

CLOWN. Good Sir Toby!

OLIVIA. Cousin, cousin, how have you come so early by this lethargy?

SIR TOBY. Lechery! I defy lechery. There's one at the gate.

OLIVIA. Ay, marry; what is he?

SIR TOBY. Let him be the devil an he will, I care not; give me faith, say I. Well, it's all one. *Exit*

OLIVIA. What's a drunken man like, fool?

CLOWN. Like a drown'd man, a fool, and a madman: one draught above heat makes him a fool; the second mads him; and a third drowns him.

OLIVIA. Go thou and seek the crowner, and let him sit o' my coz; for he's in the third degree of drink, he's drown'd; go look after him.

CLOWN. He is but mad yet, madonna, and the fool shall look to the madman. *Exit*

Re-enter MALVOLIO

MALVOLIO. Madam, yond young fellow swears he will speak with you. I told him you were sick; he takes on him to understand so much, and therefore comes to speak with you. I told him you were asleep; he seems to have a foreknowledge of that too, and therefore comes to speak with you. What is to be said to him, lady? He's fortified against any denial.

OLIVIA. Tell him he shall not speak with me.

MALVOLIO. Has been told so; and he says he'll stand at your door like a sheriff's post, and be the supporter to a bench, but he'll speak with you.

OLIVIA. What kind o' man is he?

MALVOLIO. Why, of mankind.

OLIVIA. What manner of man?

MALVOLIO. Of very ill manner; he'll speak with you, will you or no.

OLIVIA. Of what personage and years is he?

MALVOLIO. Not yet old enough for a man, nor young enough for a boy; as a squash is before 'tis a peascod, or a codling when 'tis almost an apple; 'tis with him in standing water, between boy and man. He is very well-favour'd, and he speaks very shrewishly; one would think his mother's milk were scarce out of him.

OLIVIA. Let him approach. Call in my gentlewoman.

MALVOLIO. Gentlewoman, my lady calls.   *Exit*

Re-enter MARIA

OLIVIA. Give me my veil; come, throw it o'er my face; We'll once more hear Orsino's embassy.

Enter VIOLA

VIOLA. The honourable lady of the house, which is she?

OLIVIA. Speak to me; I shall answer for her. Your will?

VIOLA. Most radiant, exquisite, and unmatchable beauty—I pray you tell me if this be the lady of the house, for I never saw her. I would be loath to cast away my speech; for, besides that it is excellently well penn'd, I have taken great pains to con it. Good beauties, let me sustain no scorn; I am very comptible, even to the least sinister usage.

OLIVIA. Whence came you, sir?

VIOLA. I can say little more than I have studied, and that question's out of my part. Good gentle one, give me modest assurance if you be the lady of the house, that I may proceed in my speech.

OLIVIA. Are you a comedian?

VIOLA. No, my profound heart; and yet, by the very fangs of malice I swear, I am not that I play. Are you the lady of the house?

OLIVIA. If I do not usurp myself, I am.

VIOLA. Most certain, if you are she, you do usurp yourself; for what is yours to bestow is not yours to reserve. But this is from my commission. I will on with my speech in your praise, and then show you the heart of my message.

OLIVIA. Come to what is important in't. I forgive you the praise.

VIOLA. Alas, I took great pains to study it, and 'tis poetical.

OLIVIA. It is the more like to be feigned; I pray you keep it in. I heard you were saucy at my gates, and allow'd your approach rather to wonder at you than to hear you. If you

947

be not mad, be gone; if you have reason, be brief; 'tis not
that time of moon with me to make one in so skipping a
dialogue.

MARIA. Will you hoist sail, sir? Here lies your way.

VIOLA. No, good swabber, I am to hull here a little longer.
Some mollification for your giant, sweet lady.

OLIVIA. Tell me your mind.

VIOLA. I am a messenger.

OLIVIA. Sure, you have some hideous matter to deliver, when
the courtesy of it is so fearful. Speak your office.

VIOLA. It alone concerns your ear. I bring no overture of
war, no taxation of homage: I hold the olive in my hand;
my words are as full of peace as matter.

OLIVIA. Yet you began rudely. What are you? What would
you?

VIOLA. The rudeness that hath appear'd in me have I learn'd
from my entertainment. What I am and what I would are
as secret as maidenhead—to your ears, divinity; to any
other's, profanation.

OLIVIA. Give us the place alone; we will hear this divinity.
[*Exeunt* MARIA *and* ATTENDANTS] Now, sir, what is your
text?

VIOLA. Most sweet lady—

OLIVIA. A comfortable doctrine, and much may be said of it.
Where lies your text?

VIOLA. In Orsino's bosom.

OLIVIA. In his bosom! In what chapter of his bosom?

VIOLA. To answer by the method: in the first of his heart.

OLIVIA. O, I have read it; it is heresy. Have you no more to
say?

VIOLA. Good madam, let me see your face.

OLIVIA. Have you any commission from your lord to negotiate with my face? You are now out of your text; but we
will draw the curtain and show you the picture. [*Unveiling*] Look you, sir, such a one I was this present. Is't not
well done?

VIOLA. Excellently done, if God did all.

OLIVIA. 'Tis in grain, sir; 'twill endure wind and weather.

VIOLA. 'Tis beauty truly blent, whose red and white
Nature's own sweet and cunning hand laid on.

Lady, you are the cruell'st she alive,
If you will lead these graces to the grave,
And leave the world no copy.

OLIVIA. O, sir, I will not be so hard-hearted; I will give out
divers schedules of my beauty. It shall be inventoried, and
every particle and utensil labell'd to my will: as—item, two
lips indifferent red; item, two grey eyes with lids to them;
item, one neck, one chin, and so forth. Were you sent
hither to praise me?

VIOLA. I see you what you are: you are too proud;
But, if you were the devil, you are fair.
My lord and master loves you—O, such love
Could be but recompens'd though you were crown'd
The nonpareil of beauty!

OLIVIA. How does he love me?

VIOLA. With adorations, fertile tears,
With groans that thunder love, with sighs of fire.

OLIVIA. Your lord does know my mind; I cannot love him.
Yet I suppose him virtuous, know him noble,
Of great estate, of fresh and stainless youth;
In voices well divulg'd, free, learn'd, and valiant,
And in dimension and the shape of nature
A gracious person; but yet I cannot love him.
He might have took his answer long ago.

VIOLA. If I did love you in my master's flame,
With such a suff'ring, such a deadly life,
In your denial I would find no sense;
I would not understand it.

OLIVIA. Why, what would you?

VIOLA. Make me a willow cabin at your gate,
And call upon my soul within the house;
Write loyal cantons of contemned love
And sing them loud even in the dead of night;
Halloo your name to the reverberate hills,
And make the babbling gossip of the air
Cry out 'Olivia!' O, you should not rest
Between the elements of air and earth
But you should pity me!

OLIVIA. You might do much.
What is your parentage?

VIOLA. Above my fortunes, yet my state is well:
I am a gentleman.
OLIVIA. Get you to your lord.
I cannot love him; let him send no more—
Unless perchance you come to me again
To tell me how he takes it. Fare you well.
I thank you for your pains; spend this for me.
VIOLA. I am no fee'd post, lady; keep your purse;
My master, not myself, lacks recompense.
Love make his heart of flint that you shall love;
And let your fervour, like my master's, be
Plac'd in contempt! Farewell, fair cruelty.   *Exit*
OLIVIA. 'What is your parentage?'
'Above my fortunes, yet my state is well:
I am a gentleman.' I'll be sworn thou art;
Thy tongue, thy face, thy limbs, actions, and spirit,
Do give thee five-fold blazon. Not too fast! Soft, soft!
Unless the master were the man. How now!
Even so quickly may one catch the plague?
Methinks I feel this youth's perfections
With an invisible and subtle stealth
To creep in at mine eyes. Well, let it be.
What ho, Malvolio!

Re-enter MALVOLIO

MALVOLIO. Here, madam, at your service.
OLIVIA. Run after that same peevish messenger,
  The County's man. He left this ring behind him,
  Would I or not. Tell him I'll none of it.
  Desire him not to flatter with his lord,
  Nor hold him up with hopes; I am not for him.
  If that the youth will come this way to-morrow,
  I'll give him reasons for't. Hie thee, Malvolio.
MALVOLIO. Madam, I will.   *Exit*
OLIVIA. I do I know not what, and fear to find
  Mine eye too great a flatterer for my mind.
  Fate, show thy force: ourselves we do not owe;
  What is decreed must be; and be this so!   *Exit*

ACT II. SCENE 1

The sea-coast

Enter ANTONIO *and* SEBASTIAN

ANTONIO. Will you stay no longer; nor will you not that I
go with you?

SEBASTIAN. By your patience, no. My stars shine darkly over
me; the malignancy of my fate might perhaps distemper
yours; therefore I shall crave of you your leave that I may
bear my evils alone. It were a bad recompense for your
love to lay any of them on you.

ANTONIO. Let me know of you whither you are bound.

SEBASTIAN. No, sooth, sir; my determinate voyage is mere extravagancy. But I perceive in you so excellent a touch of
modesty that you will not extort from me what I am
willing to keep in; therefore it charges me in manners the
rather to express myself. You must know of me then, Antonio, my name is Sebastian, which I call'd Roderigo; my
father was that Sebastian of Messaline whom I know
you have heard of. He left behind him myself and a sister,
both born in an hour; if the heavens had been pleas'd,
would we had so ended! But you, sir, alter'd that; for
some hour before you took me from the breach of the sea
was my sister drown'd.

ANTONIO. Alas the day!

SEBASTIAN. A lady, sir, though it was said she much re-
sembled me, was yet of many accounted beautiful; but
though I could not with such estimable wonder overfar believe that, yet thus far I will boldly publish her: she bore a
mind that envy could not but call fair. She is drown'd already, sir, with salt water, though I seem to drown her
remembrance again with more.

ANTONIO. Pardon me, sir, your bad entertainment.

SEBASTIAN. O good Antonio, forgive me your trouble.

ANTONIO. If you will not murder me for my love, let me be
your servant.

SEBASTIAN. If you will not undo what you have done—that is,
kill him whom you have recover'd—desire it not. Fare ye
well at once; my bosom is full of kindness, and I am yet so

near the manners of my mother that, upon the least occasion more, mine eyes will tell tales of me. I am bound to
the Count Orsino's court. Farewell. *Exit*

ANTONIO. The gentleness of all the gods go with thee!
I have many enemies in Orsino's court,
Else would I very shortly see thee there.
But come what may, I do adore thee so
That danger shall seem sport, and I will go. *Exit*

SCENE 2

A street

Enter VIOLA *and* MALVOLIO *at several doors*

MALVOLIO. Were you not ev'n now with the Countess
Olivia?

VIOLA. Even now, sir; on a moderate pace I have since
arriv'd but hither.

MALVOLIO. She returns this ring to you, sir; you might have
saved me my pains, to have taken it away yourself. She
adds, moreover, that you should put your lord into a desperate assurance she will none of him. And one thing
more: that you be never so hardy to come again in his
affairs, unless it be to report your lord's taking of this.
Receive it so.

VIOLA. She took the ring of me; I'll none of it.

MALVOLIO. Come, sir, you peevishly threw it to her; and her
will is it should be so return'd. If it be worth stooping for,
there it lies in your eye; if not, be it his that finds it. *Exit*

VIOLA. I left no ring with her; what means this lady?
Fortune forbid my outside have not charm'd her!
She made good view of me; indeed, so much
That methought her eyes had lost her tongue,
For she did speak in starts distractedly.
She loves me, sure: the cunning of her passion
Invites me in this churlish messenger.
None of my lord's ring! Why, he sent her none.
I am the man. If it be so—as 'tis—
Poor lady, she were better love a dream.

Disguise, I see thou art a wickedness
Wherein the pregnant enemy does much.
How easy is it for the proper-false
In women's waxen hearts to set their forms!
Alas, our frailty is the cause, not we!
For such as we are made of, such we be.
How will this fadge? My master loves her dearly,
And I, poor monster, fond as much on him;
And she, mistaken, seems to dote on me.
What will become of this? As I am man,
My state is desperate for my master's love;
As I am woman—now alas the day!—
What thriftless sighs shall poor Olivia breathe!
O Time, thou must untangle this, not I;
It is too hard a knot for me t' untie!   *Exit*

SCENE 3

OLIVIA'S *house*

Enter SIR TOBY *and* SIR ANDREW

SIR TOBY. Approach, Sir Andrew. Not to be abed after midnight is to be up betimes; and 'diluculo surgere' thou
know'st—
AGUECHEEK. Nay, by my troth, I know not; but I know to
be up late is to be up late.
SIR TOBY. A false conclusion! I hate it as an unfill'd can. To
be up after midnight and to go to bed then is early; so that
to go to bed after midnight is to go to bed betimes. Does
not our lives consist of the four elements?
AGUECHEEK. Faith, so they say; but I think it rather consists
of eating and drinking.
SIR TOBY. Th'art a scholar; let us therefore eat and drink.
Marian, I say! a stoup of wine.

Enter CLOWN

AGUECHEEK. Here comes the fool, i' faith.
CLOWN. How now, my hearts! Did you never see the picture
of 'we three'?

953

SIR TOBY. Welcome, ass. Now let's have a catch.

AGUECHEEK. By my troth, the fool has an excellent breast. I had rather than forty shillings I had such a leg, and so sweet a breath to sing, as the fool has. In sooth, thou wast in very gracious fooling last night, when thou spok'st of Pigrogromitus, of the Vapians passing the equinoctial of Queubus; 'twas very good, i' faith. I sent thee sixpence for thy leman; hadst it?

CLOWN. I did impeticos thy gratillity; for Malvolio's nose is no whipstock. My lady has a white hand, and the Myrmidons are no bottle-ale houses.

AGUECHEEK. Excellent! Why, this is the best fooling, when all is done. Now, a song.

SIR TOBY. Come on, there is sixpence for you. Let's have a song.

AGUECHEEK. There's a testril of me too; if one knight give a—

CLOWN. Would you have a love-song, or a song of good life?

SIR TOBY. A love-song, a love-song.

AGUECHEEK. Ay, ay; I care not for good life.

CLOWN sings

O mistress mine, where are you roaming?
O, stay and hear; your true love's coming,
    That can sing both high and low.
Trip no further, pretty sweeting;
Journeys end in lovers meeting,
    Every wise man's son doth know.

AGUECHEEK. Excellent good, i' faith!

SIR TOBY. Good, good!

CLOWN sings

What is love? 'Tis not hereafter;
Present mirth hath present laughter;
    What's to come is still unsure.
In delay there lies no plenty,
Then come kiss me, sweet and twenty;
    Youth's a stuff will not endure.

AGUECHEEK. A mellifluous voice, as I am true knight.
SIR TOBY. A contagious breath.
AGUECHEEK. Very sweet and contagious, i' faith.
SIR TOBY. To hear by the nose, it is dulcet in contagion. But shall we make the welkin dance indeed? Shall we rouse the night-owl in a catch that will draw three souls out of one weaver? Shall we do that?
AGUECHEEK. An you love me, let's do't. I am dog at a catch.
CLOWN. By'r lady, sir, and some dogs will catch well.
AGUECHEEK. Most certain. Let our catch be 'Thou knave.'
CLOWN. 'Hold thy peace, thou knave' knight? I shall be constrain'd in't to call thee knave, knight.
AGUECHEEK. 'Tis not the first time I have constrained one to call me knave. Begin, fool: it begins 'Hold thy peace.'
CLOWN. I shall never begin if I hold my peace.
AGUECHEEK. Good, i' faith! Come, begin.   [*Catch sung*]

Enter MARIA

MARIA. What a caterwauling do you keep here! If my lady have not call'd up her steward Malvolio, and bid him turn you out of doors, never trust me.
SIR TOBY. My lady's a Cataian, we are politicians, Malvolio's a Peg-a-Ramsey, and   [*Sings*]
                 Three merry men be we.
Am not I consanguineous? Am I not of her blood? Tilly-vally, lady.   [*Sings*]
            There dwelt a man in Babylon,
            Lady, lady.
CLOWN. Beshrew me, the knight's in admirable fooling.
AGUECHEEK. Ay, he does well enough if he be dispos'd, and so do I too; he does it with a better grace, but I do it more natural.
SIR TOBY. [*Sings*] O' the twelfth day of December—
MARIA. For the love o' God, peace!

Enter MALVOLIO

MALVOLIO. My masters, are you mad? Or what are you? Have you no wit, manners, nor honesty, but to gabble like tinkers at this time of night? Do ye make an ale-house of my lady's house, that ye squeak out your coziers' catches without any mitigation or remorse of voice? Is there no respect of place, persons, nor time, in you?

SIR TOBY. We did keep time, sir, in our catches. Sneck up!

MALVOLIO. Sir Toby, I must be round with you. My lady bade me tell you that, though she harbours you as her kinsman, she's nothing allied to your disorders. If you can separate yourself and your misdemeanours, you are welcome to the house; if not, and it would please you to take leave of her, she is very willing to bid you farewell.

SIR TOBY. [Sings] Farewell, dear heart, since I must needs be gone.

MARIA. Nay, good Sir Toby.

CLOWN. [Sings] His eyes do show his days are almost done.

MALVOLIO. Is't even so?

SIR TOBY. [Sings] But I will never die.   [Falls down]

CLOWN. [Sings] Sir Toby, there you lie.

MALVOLIO. This is much credit to you.

SIR TOBY. [Sings] Shall I bid him go?

CLOWN. [Sings] What an if you do?

SIR TOBY. [Sings] Shall I bid him go, and spare not?

CLOWN. [Sings] O, no, no, no, no, you dare not.

SIR TOBY. [Rising] Out o' tune, sir! Ye lie. Art any more than a steward? Dost thou think, because thou art virtuous, there shall be no more cakes and ale?

CLOWN. Yes, by Saint Anne; and ginger shall be hot i' th' mouth too.

SIR TOBY. Th'art i' th' right. Go, sir, rub your chain with crumbs. A stoup of wine, Maria!

MALVOLIO. Mistress Mary, if you priz'd my lady's favour at anything more than contempt, you would not give means for this uncivil rule; she shall know of it, by this hand.

Exit

MARIA. Go shake your ears.

AGUECHEEK. 'Twere as good a deed as to drink when a man's ahungry, to challenge him the field, and then to break promise with him and make a fool of him.

SIR TOBY. Do't, knight. I'll write thee a challenge; or I'll deliver thy indignation to him by word of mouth.

MARIA. Sweet Sir Toby, be patient for to-night; since the youth of the Count's was to-day with my lady, she is

much out of quiet. For Monsieur Malvolio, let me alone
with him; if I do not gull him into a nayword, and make
him a common recreation, do not think I have wit enough
to lie straight in my bed. I know I can do it.

SIR TOBY. Possess us, possess us; tell us something of him.

MARIA. Marry, sir, sometimes he is a kind of Puritan.

AGUECHEEK. O, if I thought that, I'd beat him like a dog.

SIR TOBY. What, for being a Puritan? Thy exquisite reason,
dear knight?

AGUECHEEK. I have no exquisite reason for't, but I have reason good enough.

MARIA. The devil a Puritan that he is, or anything constantly
but a time-pleaser; an affection'd ass that cons state without
book and utters it by great swarths; the best persuaded of
himself, so cramm'd, as he thinks, with excellencies that it is
his grounds of faith that all that look on him love him; and
on that vice in him will my revenge find notable cause to
work.

SIR TOBY. What wilt thou do?

MARIA. I will drop in his way some obscure epistles of love;
wherein, by the colour of his beard, the shape of his leg,
the manner of his gait, the expressure of his eye, forehead,
and complexion, he shall find himself most feelingly per-
sonated. I can write very like my lady, your niece; on a
forgotten matter we can hardly make distinction of our
hands.

SIR TOBY. Excellent! I smell a device.

AGUECHEEK. I have't in my nose too.

SIR TOBY. He shall think, by the letters that thou wilt drop,
that they come from my niece, and that she's in love with
him.

MARIA. My purpose is, indeed, a horse of that colour.

AGUECHEEK. And your horse now would make him an ass.

MARIA. Ass, I doubt not.

AGUECHEEK. O, 'twill be admirable!

MARIA. Sport royal, I warrant you. I know my physic will
work with him. I will plant you two, and let the fool make
a third, where he shall find the letter; observe his construction of it. For this night, to bed, and dream on the event.
Farewell.   *Exit*

SIR TOBY. Good night, Penthesilea.

AGUECHEEK. Before me, she's a good wench.

SIR TOBY. She's a beagle true-bred, and one that adores me. What o' that?

AGUECHEEK. I was ador'd once too.

SIR TOBY. Let's to bed, knight. Thou hadst need send for more money.

AGUECHEEK. If I cannot recover your niece, I am a foul way out.

SIR TOBY. Send for money, knight; if thou hast her not i' th' end, call me Cut.

AGUECHEEK. If I do not, never trust me; take it how you will.

SIR TOBY. Come, come, I'll go burn some sack; 'tis too late to go to bed now. Come, knight; come, knight.　*Exeunt*

SCENE 4

The DUKE's *palace*

Enter DUKE, VIOLA, CURIO, *and* OTHERS

DUKE. Give me some music. Now, good morrow, friends.
　Now, good Cesario, but that piece of song,
　That old and antique song we heard last night;
　Methought it did relieve my passion much,
　More than light airs and recollected terms
　Of these most brisk and giddy-paced times.
　Come, but one verse.

CURIO. He is not here, so please your lordship, that should sing it.

DUKE. Who was it?

CURIO. Feste, the jester, my lord; a fool that the Lady Olivia's father took much delight in. He is about the house.

DUKE. Seek him out, and play the tune the while.

　　　　　　　　　　　　Exit CURIO. [*Music plays*]
　Come hither, boy. If ever thou shalt love,
　In the sweet pangs of it remember me;
　For such as I am all true lovers are,

Unstaid and skittish in all motions else
Save in the constant image of the creature
That is belov'd. How dost thou like this tune?
VIOLA. It gives a very echo to the seat
Where Love is thron'd.
DUKE. Thou dost speak masterly.
My life upon't, young though thou art, thine eye
Hath stay'd upon some favour that it loves;
Hath it not, boy?
VIOLA. A little, by your favour.
DUKE. What kind of woman is't?
VIOLA. Of your complexion.
DUKE. She is not worth thee, then. What years, i' faith?
VIOLA. About your years, my lord.
DUKE. Too old, by heaven! Let still the woman take
An elder than herself; so wears she to him,
So sways she level in her husband's heart.
For, boy, however we do praise ourselves,
Our fancies are more giddy and unfirm,
More longing, wavering, sooner lost and won,
Than women's are.
VIOLA. I think it well, my lord.
DUKE. Then let thy love be younger than thyself,
Or thy affection cannot hold the bent;
For women are as roses, whose fair flow'r
Being once display'd doth fall that very hour.
VIOLA. And so they are; alas, that they are so!
To die, even when they to perfection grow!

Re-enter CURIO *and* CLOWN

DUKE. O, fellow, come, the song we had last night.
Mark it, Cesario; it is old and plain;
The spinsters and the knitters in the sun,
And the free maids that weave their thread with bones,
Do use to chant it; it is silly sooth,
And dallies with the innocence of love,
Like the old age.
CLOWN. Are you ready, sir?
DUKE. Ay; prithee, sing. [*Music*]

959

FESTE'S SONG

Come away, come away, death;
And in sad cypress let me be laid;
Fly away, fly away, breath,
I am slain by a fair cruel maid.
My shroud of white, stuck all with yew,
    O, prepare it!
My part of death no one so true
    Did share it.

Not a flower, not a flower sweet,
On my black coffin let there be strown;
Not a friend, not a friend greet
My poor corpse where my bones shall be thrown;
A thousand thousand sighs to save,
    Lay me, O, where
Sad true lover never find my grave,
    To weep there!

DUKE. There's for thy pains.
CLOWN. No pains, sir; I take pleasure in singing, sir.
DUKE. I'll pay thy pleasure, then.
CLOWN. Truly, sir, and pleasure will be paid one time or another.
DUKE. Give me now leave to leave thee.
CLOWN. Now the melancholy god protect thee; and the tailor make thy doublet of changeable taffeta, for thy mind is a very opal. I would have men of such constancy put to sea, that their business might be everything, and their intent everywhere: for that's it that always makes a good voyage of nothing. Farewell. *Exit* CLOWN
DUKE. Let all the rest give place.
                    Exeunt CURIO *and* ATTENDANTS
Once more, Cesario,
Get thee to yond same sovereign cruelty.
Tell her my love, more noble than the world,
Prizes not quantity of dirty lands;
The parts that fortune hath bestow'd upon her,
Tell her I hold as giddily as Fortune;
But 'tis that miracle and queen of gems

That Nature pranks her in attracts my soul.
VIOLA. But if she cannot love you, sir?
DUKE. I cannot be so answer'd.
VIOLA. Sooth, but you must.
   Say that some lady, as perhaps there is,
   Hath for your love as great a pang of heart
   As you have for Olivia. You cannot love her;
   You tell her so. Must she not then be answer'd?
DUKE. There is no woman's sides
   Can bide the beating of so strong a passion
   As love doth give my heart; no woman's heart
   So big to hold so much; they lack retention.
   Alas, their love may be call'd appetite—
   No motion of the liver, but the palate—
   That suffer surfeit, cloyment, and revolt;
   But mine is all as hungry as the sea,
   And can digest as much. Make no compare
   Between that love a woman can bear me
   And that I owe Olivia.
VIOLA. Ay, but I know—
DUKE. What dost thou know?
VIOLA. Too well what love women to men may owe.
   In faith, they are as true of heart as we.
   My father had a daughter lov'd a man,
   As it might be perhaps, were I a woman,
   I should your lordship.
DUKE. And what's her history?
VIOLA. A blank, my lord. She never told her love,
   But let concealment, like a worm i' th' bud,
   Feed on her damask cheek. She pin'd in thought;
   And with a green and yellow melancholy
   She sat like Patience on a monument,
   Smiling at grief. Was not this love indeed?
   We men may say more, swear more, but indeed
   Our shows are more than will; for still we prove
   Much in our vows, but little in our love.
DUKE. But died thy sister of her love, my boy?
VIOLA. I am all the daughters of my father's house,
   And all the brothers too—and yet I know not.
   Sir, shall I to this lady?

DUKE. Ay, that's the theme.
To her in haste. Give her this jewel; say
My love can give no place, bide no denay.   *Exeunt*

SCENE 5

OLIVIA'S *garden*

Enter SIR TOBY, SIR ANDREW, *and* FABIAN

SIR TOBY. Come thy ways, Signior Fabian.
FABIAN. Nay, I'll come; if I lose a scruple of this sport let
me be boil'd to death with melancholy.
SIR TOBY. Wouldst thou not be glad to have the niggardly
rascally sheep-biter come by some notable shame?
FABIAN. I would exult, man; you know he brought me out o'
favour with my lady about a bear-baiting here.
SIR TOBY. To anger him we'll have the bear again; and we
will fool him black and blue—shall we not, Sir Andrew?
AGUECHEEK. And we do not, it is pity of our lives.

Enter MARIA

SIR TOBY. Here comes the little villain.
How now, my metal of India!
MARIA. Get ye all three into the box-tree. Malvolio's coming
down this walk. He has been yonder i' the sun practising
behaviour to his own shadow this half hour. Observe him,
for the love of mockery, for I know this letter will make
a contemplative idiot of him. Close, in the name of jesting!
[*As the men hide she drops a letter*] Lie thou there; for
here comes the trout that must be caught with tickling.
                                                    Exit

Enter MALVOLIO

MALVOLIO. 'Tis but fortune; all is fortune. Maria once told
me she did affect me; and I have heard herself come thus
near, that, should she fancy, it should be one of my complexion. Besides, she uses me with a more exalted respect
than any one else that follows her. What should I think
on't?

SIR TOBY. Here's an overweening rogue!

FABIAN. O, peace! Contemplation makes a rare turkey-cock of him; how he jets under his advanc'd plumes!

AGUECHEEK. 'Slight, I could so beat the rogue—

SIR TOBY. Peace, I say.

MALVOLIO. To be Count Malvolio!

SIR TOBY. Ah, rogue!

AGUECHEEK. Pistol him, pistol him.

SIR TOBY. Peace, peace!

MALVOLIO. There is example for't: the Lady of the Strachy married the yeoman of the wardrobe.

AGUECHEEK. Fie on him, Jezebel!

FABIAN. O, peace! Now he's deeply in; look how imagination blows him.

MALVOLIO. Having been three months married to her, sitting in my state—

SIR TOBY. O, for a stone-bow to hit him in the eye!

MALVOLIO. Calling my officers about me, in my branch'd velvet gown, having come from a day-bed—where I have left Olivia sleeping—

SIR TOBY. Fire and brimstone!

FABIAN. O, peace, peace!

MALVOLIO. And then to have the humour of state; and after a demure travel of regard, telling them I know my place as I would they should do theirs, to ask for my kinsman Toby—

SIR TOBY. Bolts and shackles!

FABIAN. O, peace, peace, peace! Now, now.

MALVOLIO. Seven of my people, with an obedient start, make out for him. I frown the while, and perchance wind up my watch, or play with my—some rich jewel. Toby approaches; curtsies there to me—

SIR TOBY. Shall this fellow live?

FABIAN. Though our silence be drawn from us with cars, yet peace.

MALVOLIO. I extend my hand to him thus, quenching my familiar smile with an austere regard of control—

SIR TOBY. And does not Toby take you a blow o' the lips then?

MALVOLIO. Saying 'Cousin Toby, my fortunes having cast me

on your niece give me this prerogative of speech'—
SIR TOBY. What, what?
MALVOLIO. 'You must amend your drunkenness'—
SIR TOBY. Out, scab!
FABIAN. Nay, patience, or we break the sinews of our plot.
MALVOLIO. 'Besides, you waste the treasure of your time with
a foolish knight'—
AGUECHEEK. That's me, I warrant you.
MALVOLIO. 'One Sir Andrew.'
AGUECHEEK. I knew 'twas I; for many do call me fool.
MALVOLIO. What employment have we here?
[*Taking up the letter*]
FABIAN. Now is the woodcock near the gin.
SIR TOBY. O, peace! And the spirit of humours intimate
reading aloud to him!
MALVOLIO. By my life, this is my lady's hand: these be her
very C's, her U's, and her T's; and thus makes she her great
P's. It is, in contempt of question, her hand.
AGUECHEEK. Her C's, her U's, and her T's. Why that?
MALVOLIO. [*Reads*] 'To the unknown belov'd, this, and my
good wishes.' Her very phrases! By your leave, wax. Soft!
And the impressure her Lucrece with which she uses to
seal; 'tis my lady. To whom should this be?
FABIAN. This wins him, liver and all.
MALVOLIO. [*Reads*]

'Jove knows I love,
But who?
Lips, do not move;
No man must know.'

'No man must know.' What follows? The numbers alter'd!
'No man must know.' If this should be thee, Malvolio?
SIR TOBY. Marry, hang thee, brock!
MALVOLIO. [*Reads*]

'I may command where I adore;
But silence, like a Lucrece knife,
With bloodless stroke my heart doth gore;
M. O. A. I. doth sway my life.'

FABIAN. A fustian riddle!
SIR TOBY. Excellent wench, say I.

MALVOLIO. 'M. O. A. I. doth sway my life.'
Nay, but first let me see, let me see, let me see.
FABIAN. What dish o' poison has she dress'd him!
SIR TOBY. And with what wing the staniel checks at it!
MALVOLIO. 'I may command where I adore.' Why, she may
command me: I serve her; she is my lady. Why, this is evi-
dent to any formal capacity; there is no obstruction in this.
And the end—what should that alphabetical position por-
tend? If I could make that resemble something in me.
Softly! M. O. A. I.—
SIR TOBY. O, ay, make up that! He is now at a cold scent.
FABIAN. Sowter will cry upon't for all this, though it be as
rank as a fox.
MALVOLIO. M—Malvolio; M—why, that begins my name.
FABIAN. Did not I say he would work it out?
The cur is excellent at faults.
MALVOLIO. M—But then there is no consonancy in the se-
quel; that suffers under probation: A should follow, but O
does.
FABIAN. And O shall end, I hope.
SIR TOBY. Ay, or I'll cudgel him, and make him cry 'O!'
MALVOLIO. And then I comes behind.
FABIAN. Ay, an you had any eye behind you, you might see
more detraction at your heels than fortunes before you.
MALVOLIO. M. O. A. I. This simulation is not as the former;
and yet, to crush this a little, it would bow to me, for
every one of these letters are in my name. Soft! here follows prose.

[*Reads*]

'If this fall into thy hand, revolve. In my stars I
am above thee; but be not afraid of greatness. Some are
born great, some achieve greatness, and some have greatness thrust upon 'em. Thy Fates open their hands; let thy
blood and spirit embrace them; and, to inure thyself to
what thou art like to be, cast thy humble slough and appear fresh. Be opposite with a kinsman, surly with servants;
let thy tongue tang arguments of state; put thyself into the
trick of singularity. She thus advises thee that sighs for
thee. Remember who commended thy yellow stockings,
and wish'd to see thee ever cross-garter'd. I say, remember,

965

Go to, thou art made, if thou desir'st to be so; if not, let me see thee a steward still, the fellow of servants, and not worthy to touch Fortune's fingers. Farewell. She that would alter services with thee,

THE FORTUNATE-UNHAPPY.'

Daylight and champain discovers not more. This is open. I will be proud, I will read politic authors, I will baffle Sir Toby, I will wash off gross acquaintance, I will be point-devise the very man. I do not now fool myself to let imagination jade me; for every reason excites to this, that my lady loves me. She did commend my yellow stockings of late, she did praise my leg being cross-garter'd; and in this she manifests herself to my love, and with a kind of injunction drives me to these habits of her liking. I thank my stars I am happy. I will be strange, stout, in yellow stockings, and cross-garter'd, even with the swiftness of putting on. Jove and my stars be praised! Here is yet a postscript.

[Reads] 'Thou canst not choose but know who I am. If thou entertain'st my love, let it appear in thy smiling; thy smiles become thee well. Therefore in my presence still smile, dear my sweet, I prithee.'

Jove, I thank thee. I will smile; I will do everything that thou wilt have me.   *Exit*

FABIAN. I will not give my part of this sport for a pension of thousands to be paid from the Sophy.

SIR TOBY. I could marry this wench for this device.

AGUECHEEK. So could I too.

SIR TOBY. And ask no other dowry with her but such another jest.

Enter MARIA

AGUECHEEK. Nor I neither.

FABIAN. Here comes my noble gull-catcher.

SIR TOBY. Wilt thou set thy foot o' my neck?

AGUECHEEK. Or o' mine either?

SIR TOBY. Shall I play my freedom at tray-trip, and become thy bond-slave?

AGUECHEEK. I' faith, or I either?

ACT II. SCENE 5

SIR TOBY. Why, thou hast put him in such a dream that when the image of it leaves him he must run mad.
MARIA. Nay, but say true; does it work upon him?
SIR TOBY. Like aqua-vitæ with a midwife.
MARIA. If you will then see the fruits of the sport, mark his first approach before my lady. He will come to her in yellow stockings, and 'tis a colour she abhors, and cross-garter'd, a fashion she detests; and he will smile upon her, which will now be so unsuitable to her disposition, being addicted to a melancholy as she is, that it cannot but turn him into a notable contempt. If you will see it, follow me.
SIR TOBY. To the gates of Tartar, thou most excellent devil of wit!
AGUECHEEK. I'll make one too.   *Exeunt*

ACT III. SCENE 1

OLIVIA's *garden*

Enter VIOLA, *and* CLOWN *with a tabor*

VIOLA. Save thee, friend, and thy music!
    Dost thou live by thy tabor?
CLOWN. No, sir, I live by the church.
VIOLA. Art thou a churchman?
CLOWN. No such matter, sir: I do live by the church; for I do live at my house, and my house doth stand by the church.
VIOLA. So thou mayst say the king lies by a beggar, if a beggar dwell near him; or the church stands by thy tabor, if thy tabor stand by the church.
CLOWN. You have said, sir. To see this age! A sentence is but a chev'ril glove to a good wit. How quickly the wrong side may be turn'd outward!
VIOLA. Nay, that's certain; they that dally nicely with words may quickly make them wanton.
CLOWN. I would, therefore, my sister had had no name, sir.
VIOLA. Why, man?

967

CLOWN. Why, sir, her name's a word; and to dally with that word might make my sister wanton. But indeed words are very rascals since bonds disgrac'd them.

VIOLA. Thy reason, man?

CLOWN. Troth, sir, I can yield you none without words, and words are grown so false I am loath to prove reason with them.

VIOLA. I warrant thou art a merry fellow and car'st for nothing.

CLOWN. Not so, sir; I do care for something; but in my conscience, sir, I do not care for you. If that be to care for nothing, sir, I would it would make you invisible.

VIOLA. Art not thou the Lady Olivia's fool?

CLOWN. No, indeed, sir; the Lady Olivia has no folly; she will keep no fool, sir, till she be married; and fools are as like husbands as pilchers are to herrings—the husband's the bigger. I am indeed not her fool, but her corrupter of words.

VIOLA. I saw thee late at the Count Orsino's.

CLOWN. Foolery, sir, does walk about the orb like the sun—it shines everywhere. I would be sorry, sir, but the fool should be as oft with your master as with my mistress: I think I saw your wisdom there.

VIOLA. Nay, an thou pass upon me, I'll no more with thee. Hold, there's expenses for thee.   [Giving a coin]

CLOWN. Now Jove, in his next commodity of hair, send thee a beard!

VIOLA. By my troth, I'll tell thee, I am almost sick for one; [Aside] though I would not have it grow on my chin.—Is thy lady within?

CLOWN. Would not a pair of these have bred, sir?

VIOLA. Yes, being kept together and put to use.

CLOWN. I would play Lord Pandarus of Phrygia, sir, to bring a Cressida to this Troilus.

VIOLA. I understand you, sir; 'tis well begg'd.

[Giving another coin]

CLOWN. The matter, I hope, is not great, sir, begging but a beggar: Cressida was a beggar. My lady is within, sir. I will construe to them whence you come; who you are and what you would are out of my welkin—I might say 'element' but the word is overworn.   *Exit*

VIOLA. This fellow is wise enough to play the fool;
And to do that well craves a kind of wit.
He must observe their mood on whom he jests,
The quality of persons, and the time;
And, like the haggard, check at every feather
That comes before his eye. This is a practice
As full of labour as a wise man's art;
For folly that he wisely shows is fit;
But wise men, folly-fall'n, quite taint their wit.

Enter SIR TOBY *and* SIR ANDREW

SIR TOBY. Save you, gentleman!
VIOLA. And you, sir.
AGUECHEEK. Dieu vous garde, monsieur.
VIOLA. Et vous aussi; votre serviteur.
AGUECHEEK. I hope, sir, you are; and I am yours.
SIR TOBY. Will you encounter the house? My niece is desirous you should enter, if your trade be to her.
VIOLA. I am bound to your niece, sir; I mean, she is the list of my voyage.
SIR TOBY. Taste your legs, sir; put them to motion.
VIOLA. My legs do better understand me, sir, than I understand what you mean by bidding me taste my legs.
SIR TOBY. I mean, to go, sir, to enter.
VIOLA. I will answer you with gait and entrance. But we are prevented.

Enter OLIVIA *and* MARIA

Most excellent accomplish'd lady, the heavens rain odours on you!
AGUECHEEK. That youth's a rare courtier—'Rain odours' well!
VIOLA. My matter hath no voice, lady, but to your own most pregnant and vouchsafed ear.
AGUECHEEK. 'Odours,' 'pregnant,' and 'vouchsafed'—I'll get 'em all three all ready.
OLIVIA. Let the garden door be shut, and leave me to my hearing. [*Exeunt all but* OLIVIA *and* VIOLA] Give me your hand, sir.

Viola. My duty, madam, and most humble service.
Olivia. What is your name?
Viola. Cesario is your servant's name, fair Princess.
Olivia. My servant, sir! 'Twas never merry world
Since lowly feigning was call'd compliment.
Y'are servant to the Count Orsino, youth.
Viola. And he is yours, and his must needs be yours:
Your servant's servant is your servant, madam.
Olivia. For him, I think not on him; for his thoughts,
Would they were blanks rather than fill'd with me!
Viola. Madam, I come to whet your gentle thoughts
On his behalf.
Olivia. O, by your leave, I pray you:
I bade you never speak again of him;
But, would you undertake another suit,
I had rather hear you to solicit that
Than music from the spheres.
Viola. Dear lady—
Olivia. Give me leave, beseech you. I did send,
After the last enchantment you did here,
A ring in chase of you; so did I abuse
Myself, my servant, and, I fear me, you.
Under your hard construction must I sit,
To force that on you in a shameful cunning
Which you knew none of yours. What might you think?
Have you not set mine honour at the stake,
And baited it with all th' unmuzzled thoughts
That tyrannous heart can think? To one of your receiving
Enough is shown: a cypress, not a bosom,
Hides my heart. So, let me hear you speak.
Viola. I pity you.
Olivia. That's a degree to love.
Viola. No, not a grize; for 'tis a vulgar proof
That very oft we pity enemies.
Olivia. Why, then, methinks 'tis time to smile again.
O world, how apt the poor are to be proud!
If one should be a prey, how much the better
To fall before the lion than the wolf!   [Clock strikes]
The clock upbraids me with the waste of time.
Be not afraid, good youth; I will not have you;

OLIVIA. *Why, this is very midsummer madness* (ACT III. SCENE IV)

And yet, when wit and youth is come to harvest,
Your wife is like to reap a proper man.
There lies your way, due west.

VIOLA. Then westward-ho!
Grace and good disposition attend your ladyship!
You'll nothing, madam, to my lord by me?

OLIVIA. Stay.
I prithee tell me what thou think'st of me.

VIOLA. That you do think you are not what you are.

OLIVIA. If I think so, I think the same of you.

VIOLA. Then think you right: I am not what I am.

OLIVIA. I would you were as I would have you be!

VIOLA. Would it be better, madam, than I am?
I wish it might, for now I am your fool.

OLIVIA. O, what a deal of scorn looks beautiful
In the contempt and anger of his lip!
A murd'rous guilt shows not itself more soon
Than love that would seem hid: love's night is noon.
Cesario, by the roses of the spring,
By maidhood, honour, truth, and every thing,
I love thee so that, maugre all thy pride,
Nor wit nor reason can my passion hide.
Do not extort thy reasons from this clause,
For that I woo, thou therefore hast no cause;
But rather reason thus with reason fetter:
Love sought is good, but given unsought is better.

VIOLA. By innocence I swear, and by my youth,
I have one heart, one bosom, and one truth,
And that no woman has; nor never none
Shall mistress be of it, save I alone.
And so adieu, good madam; never more
Will I my master's tears to you deplore.

OLIVIA. Yet come again; for thou perhaps mayst move
That heart which now abhors to like his love.   *Exeunt*

SCENE 2

OLIVIA's *house*

Enter SIR TOBY, SIR ANDREW, *and* FABIAN

AGUECHEEK. No, faith, I'll not stay a jot longer.

SIR TOBY. Thy reason, dear venom, give thy reason.

FABIAN. You must needs yield your reason, Sir Andrew.

AGUECHEEK. Marry, I saw your niece do more favours to the Count's servingman than ever she bestow'd upon me; I saw't i' th' orchard.

SIR TOBY. Did she see thee the while, old boy? Tell me that.

AGUECHEEK. As plain as I see you now.

FABIAN. This was a great argument of love in her toward you.

AGUECHEEK. 'Slight! will you make an ass o' me?

FABIAN. I will prove it legitimate, sir, upon the oaths of judgment and reason.

SIR TOBY. And they have been grand-jurymen since before Noah was a sailor.

FABIAN. She did show favour to the youth in your sight only to exasperate you, to awake your dormouse valour, to put fire in your heart and brimstone in your liver. You should then have accosted her; and with some excellent jests, fire-new from the mint, you should have bang'd the youth into dumbness. This was look'd for at your hand, and this was baulk'd. The double gilt of this opportunity you let time wash off, and you are now sail'd into the north of my lady's opinion; where you will hang like an icicle on a Dutchman's beard, unless you do redeem it by some laudable attempt either of valour or policy.

AGUECHEEK. An't be any way, it must be with valour, for policy I hate; I had as lief be a Brownist as a politician.

SIR TOBY. Why, then, build me thy fortunes upon the basis of valour. Challenge me the Count's youth to fight with him; hurt him in eleven places. My niece shall take note of it; and assure thyself there is no love-broker in the world can more prevail in man's commendation with woman than report of valour.

973

FABIAN. There is no way but this, Sir Andrew.

AGUECHEEK. Will either of you bear me a challenge to him?

SIR TOBY. Go, write it in a martial hand; be curst and brief; it is no matter how witty, so it be eloquent and full of invention. Taunt him with the license of ink; if thou thou'st him some thrice, it shall not be amiss; and as many lies as will lie in thy sheet of paper, although the sheet were big enough for the bed of Ware in England, set 'em down; go about it. Let there be gall enough in thy ink, though thou write with a goose-pen, no matter. About it.

AGUECHEEK. Where shall I find you?

SIR TOBY. We'll call thee at the cubiculo. Go.

Exit SIR ANDREW

FABIAN. This is a dear manakin to you, Sir Toby.

SIR TOBY. I have been dear to him, lad—some two thousand strong, or so.

FABIAN. We shall have a rare letter from him; but you'll not deliver't?

SIR TOBY. Never trust me then; and by all means stir on the youth to an answer. I think oxen and wainropes cannot hale them together. For Andrew, if he were open'd and you find so much blood in his liver as will clog the foot of a flea, I'll eat the rest of th' anatomy.

FABIAN. And his opposite, the youth, bears in his visage no great presage of cruelty.

Enter MARIA

SIR TOBY. Look where the youngest wren of nine comes.

MARIA. If you desire the spleen, and will laugh yourselves into stitches, follow me. Yond gull Malvolio is turned heathen, a very renegado; for there is no Christian that means to be saved by believing rightly can ever believe such impossible passages of grossness. He's in yellow stockings.

SIR TOBY. And cross-garter'd?

MARIA. Most villainously; like a pedant that keeps a school i' th' church. I have dogg'd him like his murderer. He does obey every point of the letter that I dropp'd to betray him. He does smile his face into more lines than is in the new map with the augmentation of the Indies. You have not

seen such a thing as 'tis; I can hardly forbear hurling things
at him. I know my lady will strike him; if she do, he'll
smile and take't for a great favour.

SIR TOBY. Come, bring us, bring us where he is.   *Exeunt*

SCENE 3

A street

Enter SEBASTIAN *and* ANTONIO

SEBASTIAN. I would not by my will have troubled you;
But since you make your pleasure of your pains,
I will no further chide you.
ANTONIO. I could not stay behind you: my desire,
More sharp than filed steel, did spur me forth;
And not all love to see you—though so much
As might have drawn one to a longer voyage—
But jealousy what might befall your travel,
Being skilless in these parts; which to a stranger,
Unguided and unfriended, often prove
Rough and unhospitable. My willing love,
The rather by these arguments of fear,
Set forth in your pursuit.
SEBASTIAN. My kind Antonio,
I can no other answer make but thanks,
And thanks, and ever thanks; and oft good turns
Are shuffl'd off with such uncurrent pay;
But were my worth as is my conscience firm,
You should find better dealing. What's to do?
Shall we go see the reliques of this town?
ANTONIO. To-morrow, sir; best first go see your lodging.
SEBASTIAN. I am not weary, and 'tis long to night;
I pray you, let us satisfy our eyes
With the memorials and the things of fame
That do renown this city.
ANTONIO. Would you'd pardon me.
I do not without danger walk these streets:
Once in a sea-fight 'gainst the Count his galleys
I did some service; of such note, indeed,

That, were I ta'en here, it would scarce be answer'd.
SEBASTIAN. Belike you slew great number of his people.
ANTONIO. Th' offence is not of such a bloody nature;
  Albeit the quality of the time and quarrel
  Might well have given us bloody argument.
  It might have since been answer'd in repaying
  What we took from them; which, for traffic's sake,
  Most of our city did. Only myself stood out;
  For which, if I be lapsed in this place,
  I shall pay dear.
SEBASTIAN. Do not then walk too open.
ANTONIO. It doth not fit me. Hold, sir, here's my purse;
  In the south suburbs, at the Elephant,
  Is best to lodge. I will bespeak our diet,
  Whiles you beguile the time and feed your knowledge
  With viewing of the town; there shall you have me.
SEBASTIAN. Why I your purse?
ANTONIO. Haply your eye shall light upon some toy
  You have desire to purchase; and your store,
  I think, is not for idle markets, sir.
SEBASTIAN. I'll be your purse-bearer, and leave you for
  An hour.
ANTONIO. To th' Elephant.
SEBASTIAN. I do remember.   *Exeunt*

SCENE 4

OLIVIA's *garden*

Enter OLIVIA *and* MARIA

OLIVIA. I have sent after him; he says he'll come.
  How shall I feast him? What bestow of him?
  For youth is bought more oft than begg'd or borrow'd.
  I speak too loud.
  Where's Malvolio? He is sad and civil,
  And suits well for a servant with my fortunes.
  Where is Malvolio?
MARIA. He's coming, madam; but in very strange manner.
  He is sure possess'd, madam.

976

OLIVIA. Why, what's the matter? Does he rave?

MARIA. No, madam, he does nothing but smile. Your ladyship were best to have some guard about you if he come; for sure the man is tainted in's wits.

OLIVIA. Go call him hither.   *Exit* MARIA
I am as mad as he,
If sad and merry madness equal be.

Re-enter MARIA *with* MALVOLIO

How now, Malvolio!

MALVOLIO. Sweet lady, ho, ho.

OLIVIA. Smil'st thou?
I sent for thee upon a sad occasion.

MALVOLIO. Sad, lady? I could be sad. This does make some obstruction in the blood, this cross-gartering; but what of that? If it please the eye of one, it is with me as the very true sonnet is: 'Please one and please all.'

OLIVIA. Why, how dost thou, man? What is the matter with thee?

MALVOLIO. Not black in my mind, though yellow in my legs. It did come to his hands, and commands shall be executed. I think we do know the sweet Roman hand.

OLIVIA. Wilt thou go to bed, Malvolio?

MALVOLIO. To bed? Ay, sweetheart, and I'll come to thee.

OLIVIA. God comfort thee! Why dost thou smile so, and kiss thy hand so oft?

MARIA. How do you, Malvolio?

MALVOLIO. At your request? Yes, nightingales answer daws!

MARIA. Why appear you with this ridiculous boldness before my lady?

MALVOLIO. 'Be not afraid of greatness.' 'Twas well writ.

OLIVIA. What mean'st thou by that, Malvolio?

MALVOLIO. 'Some are born great,'—

OLIVIA. Ha?

MALVOLIO. 'Some achieve greatness,'—

OLIVIA. What say'st thou?

MALVOLIO. 'And some have greatness thrust upon them.'

OLIVIA. Heaven restore thee!

MALVOLIO. 'Remember who commended thy yellow stockings,'—

OLIVIA. 'Thy yellow stockings?'
MALVOLIO. 'And wish'd to see thee cross-garter'd.'
OLIVIA. 'Cross-garter'd?'
MALVOLIO. 'Go to, thou art made, if thou desir'st to be so';—
OLIVIA. Am I made?
MALVOLIO. 'If not, let me see thee a servant still.'
OLIVIA. Why, this is very midsummer madness.

Enter SERVANT

SERVANT. Madam, the young gentleman of the Count Orsino's is return'd; I could hardly entreat him back; he attends your ladyship's pleasure.
OLIVIA. I'll come to him. [*Exit* SERVANT] Good Maria, let
this fellow be look'd to. Where's my cousin Toby? Let
some of my people have a special care of him; I would
not have him miscarry for the half of my dowry.

Exeunt OLIVIA *and* MARIA

MALVOLIO. O, ho! do you come near me now? No worse
man than Sir Toby to look to me! This concurs directly
with the letter: she sends him on purpose, that I may appear stubborn to him; for she incites me to that in the letter. 'Cast thy humble slough,' says she. 'Be opposite with a
kinsman, surly with servants; let thy tongue tang with
arguments of state; put thyself into the trick of singularity'
and consequently sets down the manner how, as: a sad
face, a reverend carriage, a slow tongue, in the habit of
some sir of note, and so forth. I have lim'd her; but it is
Jove's doing, and Jove make me thankful! And when she
went away now—'Let this fellow be look'd to.' 'Fellow,'
not 'Malvolio' nor after my degree, but 'fellow.' Why,
everything adheres together, that no dram of a scruple, no
scruple of a scruple, no obstacle, no incredulous or unsafe
circumstance—What can be said? Nothing that can be can
come between me and the full prospect of my hopes. Well,
Jove, not I, is the doer of this, and he is to be thanked.

Re-enter MARIA, *with* SIR TOBY *and* FABIAN

SIR TOBY. Which way is he, in the name of sanctity? If all
the devils of hell be drawn in little, and Legion himself
possess'd him, yet I'll speak to him.

FABIAN. Here he is, here he is. How is't with you, sir?

SIR TOBY. How is't with you, man?

MALVOLIO. Go off; I discard you. Let me enjoy my private; go off.

MARIA. Lo, how hollow the fiend speaks within him! Did not I tell you? Sir Toby, my lady prays you to have a care of him.

MALVOLIO. Ah, ha! does she so?

SIR TOBY. Go to, go to; peace, peace; we must deal gently with him. Let me alone. How do you, Malvolio? How is't with you? What, man, defy the devil; consider, he's an enemy to mankind.

MALVOLIO. Do you know what you say?

MARIA. La you, an you speak ill of the devil, how he takes it at heart! Pray God he be not bewitched.

FABIAN. Carry his water to th' wise woman.

MARIA. Marry, and it shall be done to-morrow morning, if I live. My lady would not lose him for more than I'll say.

MALVOLIO. How now, mistress!

MARIA. O Lord!

SIR TOBY. Prithee hold thy peace; this is not the way. Do you not see you move him? Let me alone with him.

FABIAN. No way but gentleness—gently, gently. The fiend is rough, and will not be roughly us'd.

SIR TOBY. Why, how now, my bawcock!
How dost thou, chuck?

MALVOLIO. Sir!

SIR TOBY. Ay, Biddy, come with me. What, man, 'tis not for gravity to play at cherrypit with Satan. Hang him, foul collier!

MARIA. Get him to say his prayers, good Sir Toby, get him to pray.

MALVOLIO. My prayers, minx!

MARIA. No, I warrant you, he will not hear of godliness.

MALVOLIO. Go, hang yourselves all! You are idle shallow things; I am not of your element; you shall know more hereafter.   *Exit*

SIR TOBY. Is't possible?

FABIAN. If this were play'd upon a stage now, I could condemn it as an improbable fiction.

SIR TOBY. His very genius hath taken the infection of the device, man.

MARIA. Nay, pursue him now, lest the device take air and taint.

FABIAN. Why, we shall make him mad indeed.

MARIA. The house will be the quieter.

SIR TOBY. Come, we'll have him in a dark room and bound. My niece is already in the belief that he's mad. We may carry it thus, for our pleasure and his penance, till our very pastime, tired out of breath, prompt us to have mercy on him; at which time we will bring the device to the bar and crown thee for a finder of madmen. But see, but see.

Enter SIR ANDREW

FABIAN. More matter for a May morning.

AGUECHEEK. Here's the challenge; read it. I warrant there's vinegar and pepper in't.

FABIAN. Is't so saucy?

AGUECHEEK. Ay, is't, I warrant him; do but read.

SIR TOBY. Give me. [*Reads*] 'Youth, whatsoever thou art, thou art but a scurvy fellow.'

FABIAN. Good and valiant.

SIR TOBY. [*Reads*] 'Wonder not, nor admire not in thy mind, why I do call thee so, for I will show thee no reason for't.'

FABIAN. A good note; that keeps you from the blow of the law.

SIR TOBY. [*Reads*] 'Thou com'st to the Lady Olivia, and in my sight she uses thee kindly; but thou liest in thy throat; that is not the matter I challenge thee for.'

FABIAN. Very brief, and to exceeding good sense—less.

SIR TOBY. [*Reads*] 'I will waylay thee going home; where if it be thy chance to kill me'—

FABIAN. Good.

SIR TOBY. 'Thou kill'st me like a rogue and a villain.'

FABIAN. Still you keep o' th' windy side of the law. Good!

SIR TOBY. [*Reads*] 'Fare thee well; and God have mercy upon one of our souls! He may have mercy upon mine; but my hope is better, and so look to thyself. Thy friend, as thou usest him, and thy sworn enemy,

ANDREW AGUECHEEK.'

If this letter move him not, his legs cannot. I'll give't him.

MARIA. You may have very fit occasion for't; he is now in some commerce with my lady, and will by and by depart.

SIR TOBY. Go, Sir Andrew; scout me for him at the corner of the orchard, like a bum-baily; so soon as ever thou seest him, draw; and as thou draw'st, swear horrible; for it comes to pass oft that a terrible oath, with a swaggering accent sharply twang'd off, gives manhood more approbation than ever proof itself would have earn'd him. Away.

AGUECHEEK. Nay, let me alone for swearing. *Exit*

SIR TOBY. Now will not I deliver his letter; for the behaviour of the young gentleman gives him out to be of good capacity and breeding; his employment between his lord and my niece confirms no less. Therefore this letter, being so excellently ignorant, will breed no terror in the youth: he will find it comes from a clodpole. But, sir, I will deliver his challenge by word of mouth, set upon Aguecheek a notable report of valour, and drive the gentleman—as I know his youth will aptly receive it—into a most hideous opinion of his rage, skill, fury, and impetuosity. This will so fright them both that they will kill one another by the look, like cockatrices.

Re-enter OLIVIA, *with* VIOLA

FABIAN. Here he comes with your niece; give them way till he take leave, and presently after him.

SIR TOBY. I will meditate the while upon some horrid message for a challenge.

Exeunt SIR TOBY, FABIAN, *and* MARIA

OLIVIA. I have said too much unto a heart of stone,
And laid mine honour too unchary out;
There's something in me that reproves my fault;
But such a headstrong potent fault it is
That it but mocks reproof.

VIOLA. With the same haviour that your passion bears
Goes on my master's griefs.

OLIVIA. Here, wear this jewel for me; 'tis my picture.
Refuse it not; it hath no tongue to vex you.

And I beseech you come again to-morrow.
What shall you ask of me that I'll deny,
That honour sav'd may upon asking give?
VIOLA. Nothing but this—your true love for my master.
OLIVIA. How with mine honour may I give him that
Which I have given to you?
VIOLA. I will acquit you.
OLIVIA. Well, come again to-morrow. Fare thee well;
A fiend like thee might bear my soul to hell.   *Exit*

Re-enter SIR TOBY *and* FABIAN

SIR TOBY. Gentleman, God save thee.
VIOLA. And you, sir.
SIR TOBY. That defence thou hast, betake thee to't. Of what
   nature the wrongs are thou hast done him, I know not; but
   thy intercepter, full of despite, bloody as the hunter, attends thee at the orchard end. Dismount thy tuck, be yare
   in thy preparation, for thy assailant is quick, skilful, and
   deadly.
VIOLA. You mistake, sir; I am sure no man hath any quarrel to me; my remembrance is very free and clear from
   any image of offence done to any man.
SIR TOBY. You'll find it otherwise, I assure you; therefore, if
   you hold your life at any price, betake you to your guard;
   for your opposite hath in him what youth, strength, skill,
   and wrath, can furnish man withal.
VIOLA. I pray you, sir, what is he?
SIR TOBY. He is knight, dubb'd with unhatch'd rapier and
   on carpet consideration; but he is a devil in private brawl.
   Souls and bodies hath he divorc'd three; and his incense-
   ment at this moment is so implacable that satisfaction can
   be none but by pangs of death and sepulchre. Hob-nob is
   his word—give't or take't.
VIOLA. I will return again into the house and desire some
   conduct of the lady. I am no fighter. I have heard of
   some kind of men that put quarrels purposely on others to
   taste their valour; belike this is a man of that quirk.
SIR TOBY. Sir, no; his indignation derives itself out of a very
   competent injury; therefore, get you on and give him his
   desire. Back you shall not to the house, unless you under-

take that with me which with as much safety you might
answer him; therefore on, or strip your sword stark naked;
for meddle you must, that's certain, or forswear to wear
iron about you.

VIOLA. This is as uncivil as strange. I beseech you do me this
courteous office as to know of the knight what my offence
to him is: it is something of my negligence, nothing of my
purpose.

SIR TOBY. I will do so. Signior Fabian, stay you by this
gentleman till my return.   *Exit* SIR TOBY

VIOLA. Pray you, sir, do you know of this matter?

FABIAN. I know the knight is incens'd against you, even to a
mortal arbitrement; but nothing of the circumstance more.

VIOLA. I beseech you, what manner of man is he?

FABIAN. Nothing of that wonderful promise, to read him by
his form, as you are like to find him in the proof of his
valour. He is indeed, sir, the most skilful, bloody, and fatal
opposite that you could possibly have found in any part of
Illyria. Will you walk towards him? I will make your
peace with him if I can.

VIOLA. I shall be much bound to you for't. I am one that
would rather go with sir priest than sir knight. I care not
who knows so much of my mettle.   *Exeunt*

Re-enter SIR TOBY *with* SIR ANDREW

SIR TOBY. Why, man, he's a very devil; I have not seen such
a firago. I had a pass with him, rapier, scabbard, and all,
and he gives me the stuck in with such a mortal motion
that it is inevitable; and on the answer, he pays you as
surely as your feet hit the ground they step on. They say
he has been fencer to the Sophy.

AGUECHEEK. Pox on't, I'll not meddle with him.

SIR TOBY. Ay, but he will not now be pacified; Fabian can
scarce hold him yonder.

AGUECHEEK. Plague on't; an I thought he had been valiant,
and so cunning in fence, I'd have seen him damn'd ere I'd
have challeng'd him. Let him let the matter slip, and I'll
give him my horse, grey Capilet.

SIR TOBY. I'll make the motion. Stand here, make a good

983

show on't; this shall end without the perdition of souls.
[*Aside*] Marry, I'll ride your horse as well as I ride you.

Re-enter FABIAN *and* VIOLA

[*To* FABIAN] I have his horse to take up the quarrel; I have
persuaded him the youth's a devil.

FABIAN. [*To* SIR TOBY] He is as horribly conceited of him;
and pants and looks pale, as if a bear were at his heels.

SIR TOBY. [*To* VIOLA] There's no remedy, sir: he will fight
with you for's oath sake. Marry, he hath better bethought
him of his quarrel, and he finds that now scarce to be
worth talking of. Therefore draw for the supportance of
his vow; he protests he will not hurt you.

VIOLA. [*Aside*] Pray God defend me! A little thing would
make me tell them how much I lack of a man.

FABIAN. Give ground if you see him furious.

SIR TOBY. Come, Sir Andrew, there's no remedy; the gentleman will, for his honour's sake, have one bout with you;
he cannot by the duello avoid it; but he has promis'd me,
as he is a gentleman and a soldier, he will not hurt you.
Come on; to't.

AGUECHEEK. Pray God he keep his oath! [*They draw*]

Enter ANTONIO

VIOLA. I do assure you 'tis against my will.

ANTONIO. Put up your sword. If this young gentleman
Have done offence, I take the fault on me:
If you offend him, I for him defy you.

SIR TOBY. You, sir! Why, what are you?

ANTONIO. One, sir, that for his love dares yet do more
Than you have heard him brag to you he will.

SIR TOBY. Nay, if you be an undertaker, I am for you.

[*They draw*]

Enter OFFICERS

FABIAN. O good Sir Toby, hold! Here come the officers.

SIR TOBY. [*To* ANTONIO] I'll be with you anon.

VIOLA. Pray, sir, put your sword up, if you please.

AGUECHEEK. Marry, will I, sir; and for that I promis'd you,

I'll be as good as my word. He will bear you easily and
reins well.

FIRST OFFICER. This is the man; do thy office.

SECOND OFFICER. Antonio, I arrest thee at the suit
Of Count Orsino.

ANTONIO. You do mistake me, sir.

FIRST OFFICER. No, sir, no jot; I know your favour well,
Though now you have no sea-cap on your head.
Take him away; he knows I know him well.

ANTONIO. I must obey. [*To* VIOLA] This comes with seek-
ing you;
But there's no remedy; I shall answer it.
What will you do, now my necessity
Makes me to ask you for my purse? It grieves me
Much more for what I cannot do for you
Than what befalls myself. You stand amaz'd;
But be of comfort.

SECOND OFFICER. Come, sir, away.

ANTONIO. I must entreat of you some of that money.

VIOLA. What money, sir?
For the fair kindness you have show'd me here,
And part being prompted by your present trouble,
Out of my lean and low ability
I'll lend you something. My having is not much;
I'll make division of my present with you;
Hold, there's half my coffer.

ANTONIO. Will you deny me now?
Is't possible that my deserts to you
Can lack persuasion? Do not tempt my misery,
Lest that it make me so unsound a man
As to upbraid you with those kindnesses
That I have done for you.

VIOLA. I know of none,
Nor know I you by voice or any feature.
I hate ingratitude more in a man
Than lying, vainness, babbling drunkenness,
Or any taint of vice whose strong corruption
Inhabits our frail blood.

ANTONIO. O heavens themselves!

SECOND OFFICER. Come, sir, I pray you go.

ANTONIO. Let me speak a little. This youth that you see here
I snatch'd one half out of the jaws of death,
Reliev'd him with such sanctity of love,
And to his image, which methought did promise
Most venerable worth, did I devotion.
FIRST OFFICER. What's that to us? The time goes by; away.
ANTONIO. But, O, how vile an idol proves this god!
Thou hast, Sebastian, done good feature shame.
In nature there's no blemish but the mind:
None can be call'd deform'd but the unkind.
Virtue is beauty; but the beauteous evil
Are empty trunks, o'erflourish'd by the devil.
FIRST OFFICER. The man grows mad. Away with him.
Come, come, sir.
ANTONIO. Lead me on.   *Exit with* OFFICERS
VIOLA. Methinks his words do from such passion fly
That he believes himself; so do not I.
Prove true, imagination, O, prove true,
That I, dear brother, be now ta'en for you!
SIR TOBY. Come hither, knight; come hither, Fabian; we'll
whisper o'er a couplet or two of most sage saws.
VIOLA. He nam'd Sebastian. I my brother know
Yet living in my glass; even such and so
In favour was my brother; and he went
Still in this fashion, colour, ornament,
For him I imitate. O, if it prove,
Tempests are kind, and salt waves fresh in love!   *Exit*
SIR TOBY. A very dishonest paltry boy, and more a coward
than a hare. His dishonesty appears in leaving his friend
here in necessity and denying him; and for his cowardship,
ask Fabian.
FABIAN. A coward, a most devout coward, religious in it.
AGUECHEEK. 'Slid, I'll after him again and beat him.
SIR TOBY. Do; cuff him soundly, but never draw thy sword.
AGUECHEEK. And I do not—   *Exit*
FABIAN. Come, let's see the event.
SIR TOBY. I dare lay any money 'twill be nothing yet.
                                              Exeunt

ACT IV. SCENE 1

Before OLIVIA'S *house*

Enter SEBASTIAN *and* CLOWN

CLOWN. Will you make me believe that I am not sent for
you?

SEBASTIAN. Go to, go to, thou art a foolish fellow; let me
be clear of thee.

CLOWN. Well held out, i' faith! No, I do not know you; nor
I am not sent to you by my lady, to bid you come speak
with her; nor your name is not Master Cesario; nor this is
not my nose neither. Nothing that is so is so.

SEBASTIAN. I prithee vent thy folly somewhere else.
Thou know'st not me.

CLOWN. Vent my folly! He has heard that word of some
great man, and now applies it to a fool. Vent my folly! I
am afraid this great lubber, the world, will prove a cockney. I prithee now, ungird thy strangeness, and tell me
what I shall vent to my lady. Shall I vent to her that thou
art coming?

SEBASTIAN. I prithee, foolish Greek, depart from me;
There's money for thee; if you tarry longer
I shall give worse payment.

CLOWN. By my troth, thou hast an open hand. These wise
men that give fools money get themselves a good report—
after fourteen years' purchase.

Enter SIR ANDREW, SIR TOBY, *and* FABIAN

AGUECHEEK. Now, sir, have I met you again?
[*Striking* SEBASTIAN] There's for you.

SEBASTIAN. Why, there's for thee, and there, and there.
Are all the people mad?

SIR TOBY. Hold, sir, or I'll throw your dagger o'er the house.
[*Holding* SEBASTIAN]

CLOWN. This will I tell my lady straight. I would not be in
some of your coats for two-pence. *Exit*

SIR TOBY. Come on, sir; hold.

AGUECHEEK. Nay, let him alone. I'll go another way to work
with him; I'll have an action of battery against him, if

987

there be any law in Illyria; though I struck him first, yet it's no matter for that.

SEBASTIAN. Let go thy hand.

SIR TOBY. Come, sir, I will not let you go. Come, my young soldier, put up your iron; you are well flesh'd. Come on.

SEBASTIAN. I will be free from thee. What wouldst thou now?

If thou dar'st tempt me further, draw thy sword. [*Draws*]

SIR TOBY. What, what? Nay, then I must have an ounce or two of this malapert blood from you. [*Draws*]

Enter OLIVIA

OLIVIA. Hold, Toby; on thy life, I charge thee hold.

SIR TOBY. Madam!

OLIVIA. Will it be ever thus? Ungracious wretch,
Fit for the mountains and the barbarous caves,
Where manners ne'er were preach'd! Out of my sight!
Be not offended, dear Cesario—
Rudesby, be gone!

> *Exeunt* SIR TOBY, SIR ANDREW, *and* FABIAN

I prithee, gentle friend,
Let thy fair wisdom, not thy passion, sway
In this uncivil and unjust extent
Against thy peace. Go with me to my house,
And hear thou there how many fruitless pranks
This ruffian hath botch'd up, that thou thereby
Mayst smile at this. Thou shalt not choose but go;
Do not deny. Beshrew his soul for me!
He started one poor heart of mine in thee.

SEBASTIAN. What relish is in this? How runs the stream?
Or I am mad, or else this is a dream.
Let fancy still my sense in Lethe steep;
If it be thus to dream, still let me sleep!

OLIVIA. Nay, come, I prithee. Would thou'dst be rul'd by me!

SEBASTIAN. Madam, I will.

OLIVIA. O, say so, and so be! *Exeunt*

SCENE 2

Olivia's house

Enter Maria *and* Clown

Maria. Nay, I prithee, put on this gown and this beard; make him believe thou art Sir Topas the curate; do it quickly. I'll call Sir Toby the whilst.   *Exit*

Clown. Well, I'll put it on, and I will dissemble myself in't; and I would I were the first that ever dissembled in such a gown. I am not tall enough to become the function well nor lean enough to be thought a good student; but to be said an honest man and a good housekeeper goes as fairly as to say a careful man and a great scholar. The competitors enter.

Enter Sir Toby *and* Maria

Sir Toby. Jove bless thee, Master Parson.

Clown. Bonos dies, Sir Toby; for as the old hermit of Prague, that never saw pen and ink, very wittily said to a niece of King Gorboduc 'That that is is'; so I, being Master Parson, am Master Parson; for what is 'that' but that, and 'is' but is?

Sir Toby. To him, Sir Topas.

Clown. What ho, I say! Peace in this prison!

Sir Toby. The knave counterfeits well; a good knave.

Malvolio. [*Within*] Who calls there?

Clown. Sir Topas the curate, who comes to visit Malvolio the lunatic.

Malvolio. Sir Topas, Sir Topas, good Sir Topas, go to my lady.

Clown. Out, hyperbolical fiend! How vexest thou this man! Talkest thou nothing but of ladies?

Sir Toby. Well said, Master Parson.

Malvolio. Sir Topas, never was man thus wronged. Good Sir Topas, do not think I am mad; they have laid me here in hideous darkness.

Clown. Fie, thou dishonest Satan! I call thee by the most modest terms, for I am one of those gentle ones that will

989

use the devil himself with courtesy. Say'st thou that house is dark?

MALVOLIO. As hell, Sir Topas.

CLOWN. Why, it hath bay windows transparent as barricadoes, and the clerestories toward the south north are as lustrous as ebony; and yet complainest thou of obstruction?

MALVOLIO. I am not mad, Sir Topas. I say to you this house is dark.

CLOWN. Madman, thou errest. I say there is no darkness but ignorance; in which thou art more puzzled than the Egyptians in their fog.

MALVOLIO. I say this house is as dark as ignorance, though ignorance were as dark as hell; and I say there was never man thus abus'd. I am no more mad than you are; make the trial of it in any constant question.

CLOWN. What is the opinion of Pythagoras concerning wild fowl?

MALVOLIO. That the soul of our grandam might haply inhabit a bird.

CLOWN. What think'st thou of his opinion?

MALVOLIO. I think nobly of the soul, and no way approve his opinion.

CLOWN. Fare thee well. Remain thou still in darkness: thou shalt hold th' opinion of Pythagoras ere I will allow of thy wits; and fear to kill a woodcock, lest thou dispossess the soul of thy grandam. Fare thee well.

MALVOLIO. Sir Topas, Sir Topas!

SIR TOBY. My most exquisite Sir Topas!

CLOWN. Nay, I am for all waters.

MARIA. Thou mightst have done this without thy beard and gown: he sees thee not.

SIR TOBY. To him in thine own voice, and bring me word how thou find'st him. I would we were well rid of this knavery. If he may be conveniently deliver'd, I would he were; for I am now so far in offence with my niece that I cannot pursue with any safety this sport to the upshot. Come by and by to my chamber.   *Exit with* MARIA

CLOWN. [*Sings*] Hey, Robin, jolly Robin,
    Tell me how thy lady does.

MALVOLIO. Fool!

CLOWN. [*Sings*] My lady is unkind, perdy.

MALVOLIO. Fool!

CLOWN. [*Sings*] Alas, why is she so?

MALVOLIO. Fool I say!

CLOWN. [*Sings*] She loves another—Who calls, ha?

MALVOLIO. Good fool, as ever thou wilt deserve well at my hand, help me to a candle, and pen, ink, and paper; as I am a gentleman, I will live to be thankful to thee for't.

CLOWN. Master Malvolio?

MALVOLIO. Ay, good fool.

CLOWN. Alas, sir, how fell you besides your five wits?

MALVOLIO. Fool, there was never man so notoriously abus'd; I am as well in my wits, fool, as thou art.

CLOWN. But as well? Then you are mad indeed, if you be no better in your wits than a fool.

MALVOLIO. They have here propertied me; keep me in darkness, send ministers to me, asses, and do all they can to face me out of my wits.

CLOWN. Advise you what you say: the minister is here. [*Speaking as* SIR TOPAS] Malvolio, Malvolio, thy wits the heavens restore! Endeavour thyself to sleep, and leave thy vain bibble-babble.

MALVOLIO. Sir Topas!

CLOWN. Maintain no words with him, good fellow.—Who, I, sir? Not I, sir. God buy you, good Sir Topas.—Marry, amen.—I will sir, I will.

MALVOLIO. Fool, fool, fool, I say!

CLOWN. Alas, sir, be patient. What say you, sir? I am shent for speaking to you.

MALVOLIO. Good fool, help me to some light and some paper. I tell thee I am as well in my wits as any man in Illyria.

CLOWN. Well-a-day that you were, sir!

MALVOLIO. By this hand, I am. Good fool, some ink, paper, and light; and convey what I will set down to my lady. It shall advantage thee more than ever the bearing of letter did.

CLOWN. I will help you to't. But tell me true, are you not mad indeed, or do you but counterfeit?

MALVOLIO. Believe me, I am not; I tell thee true.

CLOWN. Nay, I'll ne'er believe a madman till I see his brains.

I will fetch you light and paper and ink.

MALVOLIO. Fool, I'll requite it in the highest degree; I prithee
be gone.

CLOWN. [*Singing*]

> I am gone, sir,
>   And anon, sir,
>   I'll be with you again,
>   In a trice,
>   Like to the old Vice,
>   Your need to sustain;
>
> Who with dagger of lath,
> In his rage and his wrath,
>   Cries, Ah, ha! to the devil,
>   Like a mad lad,
>   Pare thy nails, dad.
>   Adieu, goodman devil.   *Exit*

SCENE 3

OLIVIA's *garden*

Enter SEBASTIAN

SEBASTIAN. This is the air; that is the glorious sun;
This pearl she gave me, I do feel't and see't;
And though 'tis wonder that enwraps me thus,
Yet 'tis not madness. Where's Antonio, then?
I could not find him at the Elephant;
Yet there he was; and there I found this credit,
That he did range the town to seek me out.
His counsel now might do me golden service;
For though my soul disputes well with my sense
That this may be some error, but no madness,
Yet doth this accident and flood of fortune
So far exceed all instance, all discourse,
That I am ready to distrust mine eyes
And wrangle with my reason, that persuades me
To any other trust but that I am mad,
Or else the lady's mad; yet if 'twere so,
She could not sway her house, command her followers,

Take and give back affairs and their dispatch
With such a smooth, discreet, and stable bearing,
As I perceive she does. There's something in't
That is deceivable. But here the lady comes.

Enter OLIVIA *and* PRIEST

OLIVIA. Blame not this haste of mine. If you mean well,
Now go with me and with this holy man
Into the chantry by; there, before him
And underneath that consecrated roof,
Plight me the full assurance of your faith,
That my most jealous and too doubtful soul
May live at peace. He shall conceal it
Whiles you are willing it shall come to note,
What time we will our celebration keep
According to my birth. What do you say?
SEBASTIAN. I'll follow this good man, and go with you;
And, having sworn truth, ever will be true.
OLIVIA. Then lead the way, good father; and heavens so
shine
That they may fairly note this act of mine!   *Exeunt*

ACT V. SCENE 1

Before OLIVIA's *house*

Enter CLOWN *and* FABIAN

FABIAN. Now, as thou lov'st me, let me see his letter.
CLOWN. Good Master Fabian, grant me another request.
FABIAN. Anything.
CLOWN. Do not desire to see this letter.
FABIAN. This is to give a dog, and in recompense desire my
dog again.

Enter DUKE, VIOLA, CURIO, *and* LORDS

DUKE. Belong you to the Lady Olivia, friends?
CLOWN. Ay, sir, we are some of her trappings.

DUKE. I know thee well. How dost thou, my good fellow?

CLOWN. Truly, sir, the better for my foes and the worse for my friends.

DUKE. Just the contrary: the better for thy friends.

CLOWN. No, sir, the worse.

DUKE. How can that be?

CLOWN. Marry, sir, they praise me and make an ass of me. Now my foes tell me plainly I am an ass; so that by my foes, sir, I profit in the knowledge of myself, and by my friends I am abused; so that, conclusions to be as kisses, if your four negatives make your two affirmatives, why then, the worse for my friends, and the better for my foes.

DUKE. Why, this is excellent.

CLOWN. By my troth, sir, no; though it please you to be one of my friends.

DUKE. Thou shalt not be the worse for me. There's gold.

CLOWN. But that it would be double-dealing, sir, I would you could make it another.

DUKE. O, you give me ill counsel.

CLOWN. Put your grace in your pocket, sir, for this once, and let your flesh and blood obey it.

DUKE. Well, I will be so much a sinner to be a double-dealer. There's another.

CLOWN. Primo, secundo, tertio, is a good play; and the old saying is 'The third pays for all.' The triplex, sir, is a good tripping measure; or the bells of Saint Bennet, sir, may put you in mind—one, two, three.

DUKE. You can fool no more money out of me at this throw; if you will let your lady know I am here to speak with her, and bring her along with you, it may awake my bounty further.

CLOWN. Marry, sir, lullaby to your bounty till I come again. I go, sir; but I would not have you to think that my desire of having is the sin of covetousness. But, as you say, sir, let your bounty take a nap; I will awake it anon. *Exit*

Enter ANTONIO *and* OFFICERS

VIOLA. Here comes the man, sir, that did rescue me.

DUKE. That face of his I do remember well;
Yet when I saw it last it was besmear'd

994

As black as Vulcan in the smoke of war.
A baubling vessel was he captain of,
For shallow draught and bulk unprizable,
With which such scathful grapple did he make
With the most noble bottom of our fleet
That very envy and the tongue of loss
Cried fame and honour on him. What's the matter?
FIRST OFFICER. Orsino, this is that Antonio
  That took the Phœnix and her fraught from Candy;
  And this is he that did the Tiger board
  When your young nephew Titus lost his leg.
  Here in the streets, desperate of shame and state,
  In private brabble did we apprehend him.
VIOLA. He did me kindness, sir; drew on my side;
  But in conclusion put strange speech upon me.
  I know not what 'twas but distraction.
DUKE. Notable pirate, thou salt-water thief!
  What foolish boldness brought thee to their mercies
  Whom thou, in terms so bloody and so dear,
  Hast made thine enemies?
ANTONIO. Orsino, noble sir,
  Be pleas'd that I shake off these names you give me:
  Antonio never yet was thief or pirate,
  Though I confess, on base and ground enough,
  Orsino's enemy. A witchcraft drew me hither:
  That most ingrateful boy there by your side
  From the rude sea's enrag'd and foamy mouth
  Did I redeem; a wreck past hope he was.
  His life I gave him, and did thereto add
  My love without retention or restraint,
  All his in dedication; for his sake,
  Did I expose myself, pure for his love,
  Into the danger of this adverse town;
  Drew to defend him when he was beset;
  Where being apprehended, his false cunning,
  Not meaning to partake with me in danger,
  Taught him to face me out of his acquaintance,
  And grew a twenty years removed thing
  While one would wink; denied me mine own purse,
  Which I had recommended to his use

Not half an hour before.

VIOLA. How can this be?

DUKE. When came he to this town?

ANTONIO. To-day, my lord; and for three months before,
No int'rim, not a minute's vacancy,
Both day and night did we keep company.

Enter OLIVIA *and* ATTENDANTS

DUKE. Here comes the Countess; now heaven walks on
earth.
But for thee, fellow—fellow, thy words are madness.
Three months this youth hath tended upon me—
But more of that anon. Take him aside.

OLIVIA. What would my lord, but that he may not have,
Wherein Olivia may seem serviceable?
Cesario, you do not keep promise with me.

VIOLA. Madam?

DUKE. Gracious Olivia—

OLIVIA. What do you say, Cesario? Good my lord—

VIOLA. My lord would speak; my duty hushes me.

OLIVIA. If it be aught to the old tune, my lord,
It is as fat and fulsome to mine ear
As howling after music.

DUKE. Still so cruel?

OLIVIA. Still so constant, lord.

DUKE. What, to perverseness? You uncivil lady,
To whose ingrate and unauspicious altars
My soul the faithfull'st off'rings hath breath'd out
That e'er devotion tender'd! What shall I do?

OLIVIA. Even what it please my lord, that shall become him.

DUKE. Why should I not, had I the heart to do it,
Like to the Egyptian thief at point of death,
Kill what I love?—a savage jealousy
That sometime savours nobly. But hear me this:
Since you to non-regardance cast my faith,
And that I partly know the instrument
That screws me from my true place in your favour,
Live you the marble-breasted tyrant still;
But this your minion, whom I know you love,
And whom, by heaven I swear, I tender dearly,

Him will I tear out of that cruel eye
Where he sits crowned in his master's spite.
Come, boy, with me; my thoughts are ripe in mischief:
I'll sacrifice the lamb that I do love
To spite a raven's heart within a dove.
VIOLA. And I, most jocund, apt, and willingly,
To do you rest, a thousand deaths would die.
OLIVIA. Where goes Cesario?
VIOLA. After him I love
More than I love these eyes, more than my life,
More, by all mores, than e'er I shall love wife.
If I do feign, you witnesses above
Punish my life for tainting of my love!
OLIVIA. Ay me, detested! How am I beguil'd!
VIOLA. Who does beguile you? Who does do you wrong?
OLIVIA. Hast thou forgot thyself? Is it so long?
    Call forth the holy father.   *Exit an* ATTENDANT
DUKE. Come, away!
OLIVIA. Whither, my lord? Cesario, husband, stay.
DUKE. Husband?
OLIVIA. Ay, husband; can he that deny?
DUKE. Her husband, sirrah?
VIOLA. No, my lord, not I.
OLIVIA. Alas, it is the baseness of thy fear
That makes thee strangle thy propriety.
Fear not, Cesario, take thy fortunes up;
Be that thou know'st thou art, and then thou art
As great as that thou fear'st.

Enter PRIEST

O, welcome, father!
Father, I charge thee, by thy reverence,
Here to unfold—though lately we intended
To keep in darkness what occasion now
Reveals before 'tis ripe—what thou dost know
Hath newly pass'd between this youth and me.
PRIEST. A contract of eternal bond of love,
Confirm'd by mutual joinder of your hands,
Attested by the holy close of lips,
Strength'ned by interchangement of your rings;

997

And all the ceremony of this compact
Seal'd in my function, by my testimony;
Since when, my watch hath told me, toward my grave,
I have travell'd but two hours.
DUKE. O thou dissembling cub! What wilt thou be,
When time hath sow'd a grizzle on thy case?
Or will not else thy craft so quickly grow
That thine own trip shall be thine overthrow?
Farewell, and take her; but direct thy feet
Where thou and I henceforth may never meet.
VIOLA. My lord, I do protest—
OLIVIA. O, do not swear!
Hold little faith, though thou has too much fear.

Enter SIR ANDREW

AGUECHEEK. For the love of God, a surgeon!
Send one presently to Sir Toby.
OLIVIA. What's the matter?
AGUECHEEK. Has broke my head across, and has given Sir
  Toby a bloody coxcomb too. For the love of God, your
  help! I had rather than forty pound I were at home.
OLIVIA. Who has done this, Sir Andrew?
AGUECHEEK. The Count's gentleman, one Cesario. We took
  him for a coward, but he's the very devil incardinate.
DUKE. My gentleman, Cesario?
AGUECHEEK. Od's lifelings, here he is! You broke my head
  for nothing; and that that I did, I was set on to do't by
  Sir Toby.
VIOLA. Why do you speak to me? I never hurt you.
  You drew your sword upon me without cause;
  But I bespake you fair and hurt you not.

Enter SIR TOBY *and* CLOWN

AGUECHEEK. If a bloody coxcomb be a hurt, you have hurt
  me; I think you set nothing by a bloody coxcomb. Here
  comes Sir Toby halting; you shall hear more; but if he had
  not been in drink, he would have tickl'd you othergates
  than he did.
DUKE. How now, gentleman? How is't with you?

SIR TOBY. That's all one; has hurt me, and there's th' end on't. Sot, didst see Dick Surgeon, sot?

CLOWN. O, he's drunk, Sir Toby, an hour agone; his eyes were set at eight i' th' morning.

SIR TOBY. Then he's a rogue and a passy measures pavin. I hate a drunken rogue.

OLIVIA. Away with him. Who hath made this havoc with them?

AGUECHEEK. I'll help you, Sir Toby, because we'll be dress'd together.

SIR TOBY. Will you help—an ass-head and a coxcomb and a knave, a thin fac'd knave, a gull?

OLIVIA. Get him to bed, and let his hurt be look'd to.

Exeunt CLOWN, FABIAN, SIR TOBY, *and* SIR ANDREW

Enter SEBASTIAN

SEBASTIAN. I am sorry, madam, I have hurt your kinsman;
But, had it been the brother of my blood,
I must have done no less with wit and safety.
You throw a strange regard upon me, and by that
I do perceive it hath offended you.
Pardon me, sweet one, even for the vows
We made each other but so late ago.

DUKE. One face, one voice, one habit, and two persons!
A natural perspective, that is and is not.

SEBASTIAN. Antonio, O my dear Antonio!
How have the hours rack'd and tortur'd me
Since I have lost thee!

ANTONIO. Sebastian are you?

SEBASTIAN. Fear'st thou that, Antonio?

ANTONIO. How have you made division of yourself?
An apple cleft in two is not more twin
Than these two creatures. Which is Sebastian?

OLIVIA. Most wonderful!

SEBASTIAN. Do I stand there? I never had a brother;
Nor can there be that deity in my nature
Of here and everywhere. I had a sister
Whom the blind waves and surges have devour'd.
Of charity, what kin are you to me?
What countryman, what name, what parentage?

999

VIOLA. Of Messaline; Sebastian was my father.
Such a Sebastian was my brother too;
So went he suited to his watery tomb;
If spirits can assume both form and suit,
You come to fright us.
SEBASTIAN. A spirit I am indeed,
But am in that dimension grossly clad
Which from the womb I did participate.
Were you a woman, as the rest goes even,
I should my tears let fall upon your cheek,
And say 'Thrice welcome, drowned Viola!'
VIOLA. My father had a mole upon his brow.
SEBASTIAN. And so had mine.
VIOLA. And died that day when Viola from her birth
Had numb'red thirteen years.
SEBASTIAN. O, that record is lively in my soul!
He finished indeed his mortal act
That day that made my sister thirteen years.
VIOLA. If nothing lets to make us happy both
But this my masculine usurp'd attire,
Do not embrace me till each circumstance
Of place, time, fortune, do cohere and jump
That I am Viola; which to confirm,
I'll bring you to a captain in this town,
Where lie my maiden weeds; by whose gentle help
I was preserv'd to serve this noble Count.
All the occurrence of my fortune since
Hath been between this lady and this lord.
SEBASTIAN. [*To* OLIVIA] So comes it, lady, you have been
    mistook;
But nature to her bias drew in that.
You would have been contracted to a maid;
Nor are you therein, by my life, deceiv'd;
You are betroth'd both to a maid and man.
DUKE. Be not amaz'd; right noble is his blood.
If this be so, as yet the glass seems true,
I shall have share in this most happy wreck.
[*To* VIOLA] Boy, thou hast said to me a thousand times
Thou never shouldst love woman like to me.
VIOLA. And all those sayings will I overswear;

And all those swearings keep as true in soul
As doth that orbed continent the fire
That severs day from night.
DUKE. Give me thy hand;
And let me see thee in thy woman's weeds.
VIOLA. The captain that did bring me first on shore
Hath my maid's garments. He, upon some action,
Is now in durance, at Malvolio's suit,
A gentleman and follower of my lady's.
OLIVIA. He shall enlarge him. Fetch Malvolio hither;
And yet, alas, now I remember me,
They say, poor gentleman, he's much distract.

Re-enter CLOWN, *with a letter, and* FABIAN

A most extracting frenzy of mine own
From my remembrance clearly banish'd his.
How does he, sirrah?
CLOWN. Truly, madam, he holds Belzebub at the stave's end
as well as a man in his case may do. Has here writ a letter
to you; I should have given 't you to-day morning, but as
a madman's epistles are no gospels, so it skills not much
when they are deliver'd.
OLIVIA. Open't, and read it.
CLOWN. Look then to be well edified when the fool delivers
the madman. [*Reads madly*] 'By the Lord, madam—'
OLIVIA. How now! Art thou mad?
CLOWN. No, madam, I do but read madness. An your ladyship will have it as it ought to be, you must allow vox.
OLIVIA. Prithee read i' thy right wits.
CLOWN. So I do, madonna; but to read his right wits is to
read thus; therefore perpend, my Princess, and give ear.
OLIVIA. [*To* FABIAN] Read it you, sirrah.
FABIAN. [*Reads*] 'By the Lord, madam, you wrong me, and
the world shall know it. Though you have put me into
darkness and given your drunken cousin rule over me, yet
have I the benefit of my senses as well as your ladyship. I
have your own letter that induced me to the semblance I
put on, with the which I doubt not but to do myself much
right or you much shame. Think of me as you please. I

leave my duty a little unthought of, and speak out of my injury.

THE MADLY-US'D MALVOLIO'

OLIVIA. Did he write this?

CLOWN. Ay, Madam.

DUKE. This savours not much of distraction.

OLIVIA. See him deliver'd, Fabian; bring him hither.

Exit FABIAN

My lord, so please you, these things further thought on,
To think me as well a sister as a wife,
One day shall crown th' alliance on't, so please you,
Here at my house, and at my proper cost.

DUKE. Madam, I am most apt t' embrace your offer.
[*To* VIOLA] Your master quits you; and, for your service done him,
So much against the mettle of your sex,
So far beneath your soft and tender breeding,
And since you call'd me master for so long,
Here is my hand; you shall from this time be
You master's mistress.

OLIVIA. A sister! You are she.

Re-enter FABIAN, *with* MALVOLIO

DUKE. Is this the madman?

OLIVIA. Ay, my lord, this same.
How now, Malvolio!

MALVOLIO. Madam, you have done me wrong,
Notorious wrong.

OLIVIA. Have I, Malvolio? No.

MALVOLIO. Lady, you have. Pray you peruse that letter.
You must not now deny it is your hand;
Write from it if you can, in hand or phrase;
Or say 'tis not your seal, not your invention;
You can say none of this. Well, grant it then,
And tell me, in the modesty of honour,
Why you have given me such clear lights of favour,
Bade me come smiling and cross-garter'd to you,
To put on yellow stockings, and to frown
Upon Sir Toby and the lighter people;
And, acting this in an obedient hope,

Why have you suffer'd me to be imprison'd,
Kept in a dark house, visited by the priest,
And made the most notorious geck and gull
That e'er invention play'd on? Tell me why.
OLIVIA. Alas, Malvolio, this is not my writing,
Though, I confess, much like the character;
But out of question 'tis Maria's hand.
And now I do bethink me, it was she
First told me thou wast mad; then cam'st in smiling,
And in such forms which here were presuppos'd
Upon thee in the letter. Prithee, be content;
This practice hath most shrewdly pass'd upon thee,
But, when we know the grounds and authors of it,
Thou shalt be both the plaintiff and the judge
Of thine own cause.
FABIAN. Good madam, hear me speak,
And let no quarrel nor no brawl to come
Taint the condition of this present hour,
Which I have wond'red at. In hope it shall not,
Most freely I confess myself and Toby
Set this device against Malvolio here,
Upon some stubborn and uncourteous parts
We had conceiv'd against him. Maria writ
The letter, at Sir Toby's great importance,
In recompense whereof he hath married her.
How with a sportful malice it was follow'd
May rather pluck on laughter than revenge,
If that the injuries be justly weigh'd
That have on both sides pass'd.
OLIVIA. Alas, poor fool, how have they baffl'd thee!
CLOWN. Why, 'Some are born great, some achieve greatness,
and some have greatness thrown upon them.' I was one,
sir, in this interlude—one Sir Topas, sir; but that's all one.
'By the Lord, fool, I am not mad!' But do you remember
—'Madam, why laugh you at such a barren rascal? An you
smile not, he's gagg'd'? And thus the whirligig of time
brings in his revenges.
MALVOLIO. I'll be reveng'd on the whole pack of you. *Exit*
OLIVIA. He hath been most notoriously abus'd.
DUKE. Pursue him, and entreat him to a peace;

1003

He hath not told us of the captain yet.
When that is known, and golden time **convents,**
A solemn combination shall be made
Of our dear souls. Meantime, sweet sister,
We will not part from hence. Cesario, come;
For so you shall be while you are a man;
But when in other habits you are seen,
Orsino's mistress, and his fancy's queen.

Exeunt all but the CLOWN

CLOWN *sings*

When that I was and a little tiny boy,
   With hey, ho, the wind and the rain,
A foolish thing was but a toy,
   For the rain it raineth every day.

But when I came to man's estate,
   With hey, ho, the wind and the rain,
'Gainst knaves and thieves men shut their gate,
   For the rain it raineth every day.

But when I came, alas! to wive,
   With hey, ho, the wind and the rain,
By swaggering could I never thrive,
   For the rain it raineth every day.

But when I came unto my beds,
   With hey, ho, the wind and the rain,
With toss-pots still had drunken heads,
   For the rain it raineth every day.

A great while ago the world begun,
   With hey, ho, the wind and the rain,
But that's all one, our play is done,
And we'll strive to please you every day.   *Exit*

The Winter's Tale

LEONTES. *Inch-thick, knee-deep, o'er head and ears a fork'd one*
(ACT I. SCENE II)

THE WINTER'S TALE

Doctor SIMON FORMAN, the astrologer, alchemist, and medico, saw *The Winter's Tale* performed at the Globe Theatre on 15th May 1611; he wrote out a summary of the plot and his account in his own hand, preserved in the Ashmole Collection in the Bodleian, tallies with the play as we have it. He seems to have been particularly impressed by Autolycus for that character draws from him his only bit of moralising; he describes the rascal's pranks in some detail:

Remember also the Rog that cam in all tottered like coll pixie (perhaps colt-pixie, a sprite like a horse) and howe he cosened the poor man of all his money. and after cam to the shep sher with a pedlers packe & ther cosened them again of all their money And howe he changed apparrell with the Kinge of Bonia his sonn and then how he turned Courtier &c.

and Forman concludes with this remark: 'beware of trustinge feined beggars or fawninge fellouss.'

It has been suggested that the dance of saltiers in IV, 4, three of whom are announced as having 'danced before the King,' may have been inspired by the Satyrs' dance in Ben Jonson's masque *Oberon*, performed at Court on 1st January 1611. That some of Shakespeare's company may have formed part of Jonson's band of Satyrs is not improbable; the company had (of course) in their number some well-trained dancers, and in a masque before the King some of the King's servants, for the King had extended his own patronage to Shakespeare's company, would not have been out of place. There were also tame bears in the Court performance; the Globe players obviously took advantage of the existence at this time of a tame bear to employ it in the scene in which Antigonus is pursued by the animal.

The Winter's Tale was performed at Court on 5th November 1611, as the much disputed, but genuine, Revels Accounts for the period show. In his *Bartholomew Fair* Jonson glances at the plays of Shakespeare's final period, especially

The Tempest and *The Winter's Tale* where probability seemed to him to be too little regarded. He assures his audience in his Introduction that at his Fair things will be different:

If there be never a servant-monster in the fair, who can help it, he says, nor a nest of antiques? He is loth to make nature afraid in his plays, like these that beget tales, tempests, and such like drolleries.

The servant-monster is doubtless Caliban and such characters seemed to Jonson to overstep the modesty of nature, 'to make nature afraid.' The public might enjoy Caliban, but many years were to pass before criticism could compass the circuit that would bring it to the point of view that 'the magic of the *Tempest* is lasting and universal.' To the critical Jonson it was inevitable that the Romances of which *The Winter's Tale* is so characteristic an example should appear extravagant and quite beyond the bounds of nature. Dr. Johnson felt about *Cymbeline*, the third of the Romances, much as Ben Jonson about the other two—there was not in them the matter of fact coherence these two powerful minds demanded.

Shakespeare took the material for his plot from the novel *Pandosto, The Triumph of Time*, which Robert Greene had published in 1588. He also drew on Greene's second pamphlet on *Conny-catching*; there Greene professes to give his readers an insight into the doings of tricksters and cheats and includes an account of how a Foiste robbed a farmer, who defied ordinary devices, by feigning to fall dead at his victim's feet and removing the purse of his deluded but anxious helper, much as Autolycus robs the Clown.

Greene's *Pandosto* had been reprinted in 1607 as *Dorastus and Fawnia*. Pandosto, King of Bohemia, becomes Shakespeare's Leontes, King of Sicilia, for Shakespeare reverses the relation in Greene between Sicilia and Bohemia. Shakespeare makes a number of other and more decisive alterations in the sequence of events. Pandosto's queen Bellaria dies on learning of the death of her son. This rules out the possibility of their reunion as in Shakespeare; and Greene allows his Pandosto to dispose of himself at the end by suicide when he discovers that the long-lost Fawnia for whom he has conceived a passion is his own daughter. Shakespeare rejects Greene's treatment of the erring King and his wronged queen; he keeps Hermione alive and introduces the device of the statue to give us a scene of reconciliation and final happiness. Husband and wife are restored to one another, and their child recovered by them along with Bohemia, and Bohemia's son is added for full measure.

This reconciliation forms the framework in which is set the story of Florizel and Perdita. Shakespeare recognises that his audience will feel so strongly the artistic necessity for the reunion of the elders that both spectators and readers will allow him to present it to them by means of almost any device. His difficulty lay in providing the reasons for the train of disasters that were to set the stage for the adventures of the younger generation. Shakespeare tries to meet the difficulty by presenting the jealousy of Leontes as if it were a stroke or some sudden visitation of madness or disease. An idyllic world has got to be shattered, but the more idyllic it appears the more difficult it is to believe in the stroke that destroys it.

Consequent on this Shakespeare has to divide his play into two contrasting sections and employ Time as Chorus to bridge the gap of years in which Perdita has grown to womanhood. Certainly it is the wonderful scenes in Bohemia that give the play its vitality, and it may be felt that Shakespeare was so intent on this feature of his scheme that he was reckless in the means he employed to make it so central and significant. But even Robert Bridges as he condemns as melodramatic and absurd the opening scenes admits that they are almost justified in the sequel. 'Our interests are magically shifted—the relief of the contrast almost justifies the uncomfortable distress of the earlier acts' and he recognises that 'we are gratified to find Hermione alive at the end.'

LEONTES, *King of Sicilia*
MAMILLIUS, *his son, the young Prince of Sicilia*
CAMILLO
ANTIGONUS
CLEOMENES *lords of Sicilia*
DION
POLIXENES, *King of Bohemia*
FLORIZEL, *his son, Prince of Bohemia*
ARCHIDAMUS, *a lord of Bohemia*
OLD SHEPHERD, *reputed father of Perdita*
CLOWN, *his son*
AUTOLYCUS, *a rogue*
A MARINER
A GAOLER
TIME, *as Chorus*

HERMIONE, *Queen to Leontes*
PERDITA, *daughter to Leontes and Hermione*
PAULINA, *wife to Antigonus*
EMILIA, *a lady attending on the Queen*
MOPSA
DORCAS *shepherdesses*

Other Lords, Gentlemen, Ladies, Officers, Servants, Shepherds, Shepherdesses

SCENE:

Sicilia and Bohemia

The Winter's Tale

ACT I. SCENE 1

Sicilia. The palace of LEONTES

Enter CAMILLO *and* ARCHIDAMUS

ARCHIDAMUS. If you shall chance, Camillo, to visit Bohemia, on the like occasion whereon my services are now on foot, you shall see, as I have said, great difference betwixt our Bohemia and your Sicilia.

CAMILLO. I think this coming summer the King of Sicilia means to pay Bohemia the visitation which he justly owes him.

ARCHIDAMUS. Wherein our entertainment shall shame us we will be justified in our loves; for indeed—

CAMILLO. Beseech you—

ARCHIDAMUS. Verily, I speak it in the freedom of my knowledge: we cannot with such magnificence, in so rare—I know not what to say. We will give you sleepy drinks, that your senses, unintelligent of our insufficience, may, though they cannot praise us, as little accuse us.

CAMILLO. You pay a great deal too dear for what's given freely.

ARCHIDAMUS. Believe me, I speak as my understanding instructs me and as mine honesty puts it to utterance.

CAMILLO. Sicilia cannot show himself overkind to Bohemia. They were train'd together in their childhoods; and there rooted betwixt them then such an affection which cannot choose but branch now. Since their more mature dignities and royal necessities made separation of their society, their encounters, though not personal, have been royally attorneyed with interchange of gifts, letters, loving embassies; that they have seem'd to be together, though absent; shook hands, as over a vast; and embrac'd as it were from the ends of opposed winds. The heavens continue their loves!

ARCHIDAMUS. I think there is not in the world either malice

or matter to alter it. You have an unspeakable comfort of your young Prince Mamillius; it is a gentleman of the greatest promise that ever came into my note.

CAMILLO. I very well agree with you in the hopes of him. It is a gallant child; one that indeed physics the subject, makes old hearts fresh; they that went on crutches ere he was born desire yet their life to see him a man.

ARCHIDAMUS. Would they else be content to die?

CAMILLO. Yes; if there were no other excuse why they should desire to live.

ARCHIDAMUS. If the King had no son, they would desire to live on crutches till he had one.   *Exeunt*

SCENE 2

Sicilia. The palace of LEONTES

Enter LEONTES, POLIXENES, HERMIONE, MAMILLIUS, CAMILLO, *and* ATTENDANTS

POLIXENES. Nine changes of the wat'ry star hath been
The shepherd's note since we have left our throne
Without a burden. Time as long again
Would be fill'd up, my brother, with our thanks;
And yet we should for perpetuity
Go hence in debt. And therefore, like a cipher,
Yet standing in rich place, I multiply
With one 'We thank you' many thousands moe
That go before it.

LEONTES. Stay your thanks a while,
And pay them when you part.

POLIXENES. Sir, that's to-morrow.
I am question'd by my fears of what may chance
Or breed upon our absence, that may blow
No sneaping winds at home, to make us say
'This is put forth too truly.' Besides, I have stay'd
To tire your royalty.

LEONTES. We are tougher, brother,
Than you can put us to't.

POLIXENES. No longer stay.

LEONTES. One sev'night longer.

POLIXENES. Very sooth, to-morrow.

LEONTES. We'll part the time between's then; and in that
I'll no gainsaying.

POLIXENES. Press me not, beseech you, so.
There is no tongue that moves, none, none i' th' world,
So soon as yours could win me. So it should now,
Were there necessity in your request, although
'Twere needful I denied it. My affairs
Do even drag me homeward; which to hinder
Were in your love a whip to me; my stay
To you a charge and trouble. To save both,
Farewell, our brother.

LEONTES. Tongue-tied, our Queen? Speak you.

HERMIONE. I had thought, sir, to have held my peace until
You had drawn oaths from him not to stay. You, sir,
Charge him too coldly. Tell him you are sure
All in Bohemia's well—this satisfaction
The by-gone day proclaim'd. Say this to him,
He's beat from his best ward.

LEONTES. Well said, Hermione.

HERMIONE. To tell he longs to see his son were strong;
But let him say so then, and let him go;
But let him swear so, and he shall not stay;
We'll thwack him hence with distaffs.
[*To* POLIXENES] Yet of your royal presence I'll adventure
The borrow of a week. When at Bohemia
You take my lord, I'll give him my commission
To let him there a month behind the gest
Prefix'd for's parting.—Yet, good deed, Leontes,
I love thee not a jar o' th' clock behind
What lady she her lord.—You'll stay?

POLIXENES. No, madam.

HERMIONE. Nay, but you will?

POLIXENES. I may not, verily.

HERMIONE. Verily!
You put me off with limber vows; but I,
Though you would seek t' unsphere the stars with oaths,
Should yet say 'Sir, no going.' Verily,
You shall not go; a lady's 'verily' is

As potent as a lord's. Will you go yet?
Force me to keep you as a prisoner,
Not like a guest; so you shall pay your fees
When you depart, and save your thanks. How say you?
My prisoner or my guest? By your dread 'verily,'
One of them you shall be.
POLIXENES. Your guest, then, madam:
To be your prisoner should import offending;
Which is for me less easy to commit
Than you to punish.
HERMIONE. Not your gaoler then,
But your kind hostess. Come, I'll question you
Of my lord's tricks and yours when you were boys.
You were pretty lordings then!
POLIXENES. We were, fair Queen,
Two lads that thought there was no more behind
But such a day to-morrow as to-day,
And to be boy eternal.
HERMIONE. Was not my lord
The verier wag o' th' two?
POLIXENES. We were as twinn'd lambs that did frisk i' th' sun
And bleat the one at th' other. What we chang'd
Was innocence for innocence; we knew not
The doctrine of ill-doing, nor dream'd
That any did. Had we pursu'd that life,
And our weak spirits ne'er been higher rear'd
With stronger blood, we should have answer'd heaven
Boldly 'Not guilty,' the imposition clear'd
Hereditary ours.
HERMIONE. By this we gather
You have tripp'd since.
POLIXENES. O my most sacred lady,
Temptations have since then been born to 's, for
In those unfledg'd days was my wife a girl;
Your precious self had then not cross'd the eyes
Of my young playfellow.
HERMIONE. Grace to boot!
Of this make no conclusion, lest you say
Your queen and I are devils. Yet, go on;
Th' offences we have made you do we'll answer,

If you first sinn'd with us, and that with us
You did continue fault, and that you slipp'd not
With any but with us.
LEONTES. Is he won yet?
HERMIONE. He'll stay, my lord.
LEONTES. At my request he would not.
Hermione, my dearest, thou never spok'st
To better purpose.
HERMIONE. Never?
LEONTES. Never but once.
HERMIONE. What! Have I twice said well? When was't be-
fore?
I prithee tell me; cram's with praise, and make's
As fat as tame things. One good deed dying tongueless
Slaughters a thousand waiting upon that.
Our praises are our wages; you may ride's
With one soft kiss a thousand furlongs ere
With spur we heat an acre. But to th' goal:
My last good deed was to entreat his stay;
What was my first? It has an elder sister,
Or I mistake you. O, would her name were Grace!
But once before I spoke to th' purpose—When?
Nay, let me have't; I long.
LEONTES. Why, that was when
Three crabbed months had sour'd themselves to death,
Ere I could make thee open thy white hand
And clap thyself my love; then didst thou utter
'I am yours for ever.'
HERMIONE. 'Tis Grace indeed.
Why, lo you now, I have spoke to th' purpose twice:
The one for ever earn'd a royal husband;
Th' other for some while a friend.
                    [*Giving her hand to* POLIXENES]
LEONTES. [*Aside*] Too hot, too hot!
To mingle friendship far is mingling bloods.
I have tremor cordis on me; my heart dances,
But not for joy, not joy. This entertainment
May a free face put on; derive a liberty
From heartiness, from bounty, fertile bosom,
And well become the agent. 'T may, I grant;

But to be paddling palms and pinching fingers,
As now they are, and making practis'd smiles
As in a looking-glass; and then to sigh, as 'twere
The mort o' th' deer. O, that is entertainment
My bosom likes not, nor my brows! Mamillius,
Art thou my boy?
MAMILLIUS. Ay, my good lord.
LEONTES. I' fecks!
Why, that's my bawcock. What! hast smutch'd thy nose?
They say it is a copy out of mine. Come, Captain,
We must be neat—not neat, but cleanly, Captain.
And yet the steer, the heifer, and the calf,
Are all call'd neat.—Still virginalling
Upon his palm?—How now, you wanton calf,
Art thou my calf?
MAMILLIUS. Yes, if you will, my lord.
LEONTES. Thou want'st a rough pash and the shoots that I
    have,
To be full like me; yet they say we are
Almost as like as eggs. Women say so,
That will say anything. But were they false
As o'er-dy'd blacks, as wind, as waters—false
As dice are to be wish'd by one that fixes
No bourn 'twixt his and mine; yet were it true
To say this boy were like me. Come, sir page,
Look on me with your welkin eye. Sweet villain!
Most dear'st! my collop! Can thy dam?—may't be?
Affection! thy intention stabs the centre.
Thou dost make possible things not so held,
Communicat'st with dreams—how can this be?—
With what's unreal thou coactive art,
And fellow'st nothing. Then 'tis very credent
Thou mayst co-join with something; and thou dost—
And that beyond commission; and I find it,
And that to the infection of my brains
And hard'ning of my brows.
POLIXENES. What means Sicilia?
HERMIONE. He something seems unsettled.
POLIXENES. How, my lord!
What cheer? How is't with you, best brother?

HERMIONE. You look
As if you held a brow of much distraction.
Are you mov'd, my lord?
LEONTES. No, in good earnest.
How sometimes nature will betray its folly,
Its tenderness, and make itself a pastime
To harder bosoms! Looking on the lines
Of my boy's face, methoughts I did recoil
Twenty-three years; and saw myself unbreech'd,
In my green velvet coat; my dagger muzzl'd,
Lest it should bite its master and so prove,
As ornaments oft do, too dangerous.
How like, methought, I then was to this kernel,
This squash, this gentleman. Mine honest friend,
Will you take eggs for money?
MAMILLIUS. No, my lord, I'll fight.
LEONTES. You will? Why, happy man be's dole! My brother,
Are you so fond of your young prince as we
Do seem to be of ours?
POLIXENES. If at home, sir,
He's all my exercise, my mirth, my matter;
Now my sworn friend, and then mine enemy;
My parasite, my soldier, statesman, all.
He makes a July's day short as December,
And with his varying childness cures in me
Thoughts that would thick my blood.
LEONTES. So stands this squire
Offic'd with me. We two will walk, my lord,
And leave you to your graver steps. Hermione,
How thou lov'st us show in our brother's welcome;
Let what is dear in Sicily be cheap;
Next to thyself and my young rover, he's
Apparent to my heart.
HERMIONE. If you would seek us,
We are yours i' th' garden. Shall's attend you there?
LEONTES. To your own bents dispose you; you'll be found,
Be you beneath the sky. [*Aside*] I am angling now,
Though you perceive me not how I give line.
Go to, go to!
How she holds up the neb, the bill to him!

And arms her with the boldness of a wife
To her allowing husband!

Exeunt POLIXENES, HERMIONE, *and* ATTENDANTS

Gone already!
Inch-thick, knee-deep, o'er head and ears a fork'd one!
Go, play, boy, play; thy mother plays, and I
Play too; but so disgrac'd a part, whose issue
Will hiss me to my grave. Contempt and clamour
Will be my knell. Go, play, boy, play. There have been,
Or I am much deceiv'd, cuckolds ere now;
And many a man there is, even at this present,
Now while I speak this, holds his wife by th' arm
That little thinks she has been sluic'd in's absence,
And his pond fish'd by his next neighbour, by
Sir Smile, his neighbour. Nay, there's comfort in't,
Whiles other men have gates and those gates open'd,
As mine, against their will. Should all despair
That hath revolted wives, the tenth of mankind
Would hang themselves. Physic for't there's none;
It is a bawdy planet, that will strike
Where 'tis predominant; and 'tis pow'rful, think it,
From east, west, north, and south. Be it concluded,
No barricado for a belly. Know't,
It will let in and out the enemy
With bag and baggage. Many thousand on's
Have the disease, and feel't not. How now, boy!
MAMILLIUS. I am like you, they say.
LEONTES. Why, that's some comfort.
    What! Camillo there?
CAMILLO. Ay, my good lord.
LEONTES. Go play, Mamillius; thou'rt an honest man.

Exit MAMILLIUS

Camillo, this great sir will yet stay longer.
CAMILLO. You had much ado to make his anchor hold;
    When you cast out, it still came home.
LEONTES. Didst note it?
CAMILLO. He would not stay at your petitions; made
    His business more material.
LEONTES. Didst perceive it?

[*Aside*] They're here with me already; whisp'ring, round-
ing,
'Sicilia is a so-forth.' 'Tis far gone
When I shall gust it last.—How came't, Camillo,
That he did stay?
CAMILLO. At the good Queen's entreaty.
LEONTES. 'At the Queen's' be't. 'Good' should be pertinent;
But so it is, it is not. Was this taken
By any understanding pate but thine?
For thy conceit is soaking, will draw in
More than the common blocks. Not noted, is't,
But of the finer natures, by some severals
Of head-piece extraordinary? Lower messes
Perchance are to this business purblind? Say.
CAMILLO. Business, my lord? I think most understand
Bohemia stays here longer.
LEONTES. Ha?
CAMILLO. Stays here longer.
LEONTES. Ay, but why?
CAMILLO. To satisfy your Highness, and the entreaties
Of our most gracious mistress.
LEONTES. Satisfy
Th' entreaties of your mistress! Satisfy!
Let that suffice. I have trusted thee, Camillo,
With all the nearest things to my heart, as well
My chamber-councils, wherein, priest-like, thou
Hast cleans'd my bosom—I from thee departed
Thy penitent reform'd; but we have been
Deceiv'd in thy integrity, deceiv'd
In that which seems so.
CAMILLO. Be it forbid, my lord!
LEONTES. To bide upon't: thou art not honest; or,
If thou inclin'st that way, thou art a coward,
Which hoxes honesty behind, restraining
From course requir'd; or else thou must be counted
A servant grafted in my serious trust,
And therein negligent; or else a fool
That seest a game play'd home, the rich stake drawn,
And tak'st it all for jest.
CAMILLO. My gracious lord,

I may be negligent, foolish, and fearful:
In every one of these no man is free
But that his negligence, his folly, fear,
Among the infinite doings of the world,
Sometime puts forth. In your affairs, my lord,
If ever I were wilful-negligent,
It was my folly; if industriously
I play'd the fool, it was my negligence,
Not weighing well the end; if ever fearful
To do a thing where I the issue doubted,
Whereof the execution did cry out
Against the non-performance, 'twas a fear
Which oft infects the wisest. These, my lord,
Are such allow'd infirmities that honesty
Is never free of. But, beseech your Grace,
Be plainer with me; let me know my trespass
By its own visage; if I then deny it,
'Tis none of mine.

LEONTES. Ha' not you seen, Camillo—
But that's past doubt; you have, or your eye-glass
Is thicker than a cuckold's horn—or heard—
For to a vision so apparent rumour
Cannot be mute—or thought—for cogitation
Resides not in that man that does not think—
My wife is slippery? If thou wilt confess—
Or else be impudently negative,
To have nor eyes nor ears nor thought—then say
My wife's a hobby-horse, deserves a name
As rank as any flax-wench that puts to
Before her troth-plight. Say't and justify't.

CAMILLO. I would not be a stander-by to hear
My sovereign mistress clouded so, without
My present vengeance taken. Shrew my heart!
You never spoke what did become you less
Than this; which to reiterate were sin
As deep as that, though true.

LEONTES. Is whispering nothing?
Is leaning cheek to cheek? Is meeting noses?
Kissing with inside lip? Stopping the career
Of laughter with a sigh?—a note infallible

Of breaking honesty. Horsing foot on foot?
Skulking in corners? Wishing clocks more swift;
Hours, minutes; noon, midnight? And all eyes
Blind with the pin and web but theirs, theirs only,
That would unseen be wicked—is this nothing?
Why, then the world and all that's in't is nothing;
The covering sky is nothing; Bohemia nothing;
My wife is nothing; nor nothing have these nothings,
If this be nothing.
CAMILLO. Good my lord, be cur'd
Of this diseas'd opinion, and betimes;
For 'tis most dangerous.
LEONTES. Say it be, 'tis true.
CAMILLO. No, no, my lord.
LEONTES. It is; you lie, you lie.
I say thou liest, Camillo, and I hate thee;
Pronounce thee a gross lout, a mindless slave,
Or else a hovering temporizer that
Canst with thine eyes at once see good and evil,
Inclining to them both. Were my wife's liver
Infected as her life, she would not live
The running of one glass.
CAMILLO. Who does infect her?
LEONTES. Why, he that wears her like her medal, hanging
About his neck, Bohemia; who—if I
Had servants true about me that bare eyes
To see alike mine honour as their profits,
Their own particular thrifts, they would do that
Which should undo more doing. Ay, and thou,
His cupbearer—whom I from meaner form
Have bench'd and rear'd to worship; who mayst see,
Plainly as heaven sees earth and earth sees heaven,
How I am gall'd—mightst bespice a cup
To give mine enemy a lasting wink;
Which draught to me were cordial.
CAMILLO. Sir, my lord,
I could do this; and that with no rash potion,
But with a ling'ring dram that should not work
Maliciously like poison. But I cannot
Believe this crack to be in my dread mistress,

So sovereignly being honourable.
I have lov'd thee—
LEONTES. Make that thy question, and go rot!
Dost think I am so muddy, so unsettled,
To appoint myself in this vexation; sully
The purity and whiteness of my sheets—
Which to preserve is sleep, which being spotted
Is goads, thorns, nettles, tails of wasps;
Give scandal to the blood o' th' Prince, my son—
Who I do think is mine, and love as mine—
Without ripe moving to 't? Would I do this?
Could man so blench?
CAMILLO. I must believe you, sir.
I do; and will fetch off Bohemia for't;
Provided that, when he's remov'd, your Highness
Will take again your queen as yours at first,
Even for your son's sake; and thereby for sealing
The injury of tongues in courts and kingdoms
Known and allied to yours.
LEONTES. Thou dost advise me
Even so as I mine own course have set down.
I'll give no blemish to her honour, none.
CAMILLO. My lord,
Go then; and with a countenance as clear
As friendship wears at feasts, keep with Bohemia
And with your queen. I am his cupbearer;
If from me he have wholesome beverage,
Account me not your servant.
LEONTES. This is all:
Do't, and thou hast the one half of my heart;
Do't not, thou split'st thine own.
CAMILLO. I'll do't, my lord.
LEONTES. I will seem friendly, as thou hast advis'd me.   *Exit*
CAMILLO. O miserable lady! But, for me,
What case stand I in? I must be the poisoner
Of good Polixenes; and my ground to do't
Is the obedience to a master; one
Who, in rebellion with himself, will have
All that are his so too. To do this deed,
Promotion follows. If I could find example

Of thousands that had struck anointed kings
And flourish'd after, I'd not do't; but since
Nor brass, nor stone, nor parchment, bears not one,
Let villainy itself forswear't. I must
Forsake the court. To do't, or no, is certain
To me a break-neck. Happy star reign now!
Here comes Bohemia.

Enter POLIXENES

POLIXENES. This is strange. Methinks
My favour here begins to warp. Not speak?
Good day, Camillo.
CAMILLO. Hail, most royal sir!
POLIXENES. What is the news i' th' court?
CAMILLO. None rare, my lord.
POLIXENES. The King hath on him such a countenance
As he had lost some province, and a region
Lov'd as he loves himself; even now I met him
With customary compliment, when he,
Wafting his eyes to th' contrary and falling
A lip of much contempt, speeds from me;
So leaves me to consider what is breeding
That changes thus his manners.
CAMILLO. I dare not know, my lord.
POLIXENES. How, dare not! Do not. Do you know, and dare
    not
Be intelligent to me? 'Tis thereabouts;
For, to yourself, what you do know, you must,
And cannot say you dare not. Good Camillo,
Your chang'd complexions are to me a mirror
Which shows me mine chang'd too; for I must be
A party in this alteration, finding
Myself thus alter'd with't.
CAMILLO. There is a sickness
Which puts some of us in distemper; but
I cannot name the disease; and it is caught
Of you that yet are well.
POLIXENES. How! caught of me?
Make me not sighted like the basilisk;
I have look'd on thousands who have sped the better

By my regard, but kill'd none so. Camillo—
As you are certainly a gentleman; thereto
Clerk-like experienc'd, which no less adorns
Our gentry than our parents' noble names,
In whose success we are gentle—I beseech you,
If you know aught which does behove my knowledge
Thereof to be inform'd, imprison't not
In ignorant concealment.
CAMILLO. I may not answer.
POLIXENES. A sickness caught of me, and yet I well?
  I must be answer'd. Dost thou hear, Camillo?
  I conjure thee, by all the parts of man
  Which honour does acknowledge, whereof the least
  Is not this suit of mine, that thou declare
  What incidency thou dost guess of harm
  Is creeping toward me; how far off, how near;
  Which way to be prevented, if to be;
  If not, how best to bear it.
CAMILLO. Sir, I will tell you;
  Since I am charg'd in honour, and by him
  That I think honourable. Therefore mark my counsel,
  Which must be ev'n as swiftly followed as
  I mean to utter it, or both yourself and me
  Cry lost, and so goodnight.
POLIXENES. On, good Camillo.
CAMILLO. I am appointed him to murder you.
POLIXENES. By whom, Camillo?
CAMILLO. By the King.
POLIXENES. For what?
CAMILLO. He thinks, nay, with all confidence he swears,
  As he had seen 't or been an instrument
  To vice you to't, that you have touch'd his queen
  Forbiddenly.
POLIXENES. O, then my best blood turn
  To an infected jelly, and my name
  Be yok'd with his that did betray the Best!
  Turn then my freshest reputation to
  A savour that may strike the dullest nostril
  Where I arrive, and my approach be shunn'd,
  Nay, hated too, worse than the great'st infection

That e'er was heard or read!
CAMILLO. Swear his thought over
  By each particular star in heaven and
  By all their influences, you may as well
  Forbid the sea for to obey the moon
  As or by oath remove or counsel shake
  The fabric of his folly, whose foundation
  Is pil'd upon his faith and will continue
  The standing of his body.
POLIXENES. How should this grow?
CAMILLO. I know not; but I am sure 'tis safer to
  Avoid what's grown than question how 'tis born.
  If therefore you dare trust my honesty,
  That lies enclosed in this trunk which you
  Shall bear along impawn'd, away to-night.
  Your followers I will whisper to the business;
  And will, by twos and threes, at several posterns,
  Clear them o' th' city. For myself, I'll put
  My fortunes to your service, which are here
  By this discovery lost. Be not uncertain,
  For, by the honour of my parents, I
  Have utt'red truth; which if you seek to prove,
  I dare not stand by; nor shall you be safer
  Than one condemn'd by the King's own mouth, thereon
  His execution sworn.
POLIXENES. I do believe thee:
  I saw his heart in's face. Give me thy hand;
  Be pilot to me, and thy places shall
  Still neighbour mine. My ships are ready, and
  My people did expect my hence departure
  Two days ago. This jealousy
  Is for a precious creature; as she's rare,
  Must it be great; and, as his person's mighty,
  Must it be violent; and as he does conceive
  He is dishonour'd by a man which ever
  Profess'd to him, why, his revenges must
  In that be made more bitter. Fear o'ershades me.
  Good expedition be my friend, and comfort
  The gracious Queen, part of this theme, but nothing
  Of his ill-ta'en suspicion! Come, Camillo;

I will respect thee as a father, if
Thou bear'st my life off hence. Let us avoid.
CAMILLO. It is in mine authority to command
The keys of all the posterns. Please your Highness
To take the urgent hour. Come, sir, away.　　*Exeunt*

ACT II. SCENE 1

Sicilia. The palace of LEONTES

Enter HERMIONE, MAMILLIUS, *and* LADIES

HERMIONE. Take the boy to you; he so troubles me,
'Tis past enduring.
FIRST LADY. Come, my gracious lord,
Shall I be your playfellow?
MAMILLIUS. No, I'll none of you.
FIRST LADY. Why, my sweet lord?
MAMILLIUS. You'll kiss me hard, and speak to me as if
I were a baby still. I love you better.
SECOND LADY. And why so, my lord?
MAMILLIUS. Not for because
Your brows are blacker; yet black brows, they say,
Become some women best; so that there be not
Too much hair there, but in a semicircle
Or a half-moon made with a pen.
SECOND LADY. Who taught't this?
MAMILLIUS. I learn'd it out of women's faces. Pray now,
What colour are your eyebrows?
FIRST LADY. Blue, my lord.
MAMILLIUS. Nay, that's a mock. I have seen a lady's nose
That has been blue, but not her eyebrows.
FIRST LADY. Hark ye:
The Queen your mother rounds apace. We shall
Present our services to a fine new prince
One of these days; and then you'd wanton with us,
If we would have you.
SECOND LADY. She is spread of late

Into a goodly bulk. Good time encounter her!
HERMIONE. What wisdom stirs amongst you? Come, sir, now
　I am for you again. Pray you sit by us,
　And tell's a tale.
MAMILLIUS. Merry or sad shall't be?
HERMIONE. As merry as you will.
MAMILLIUS. A sad tale's best for winter. I have one
　Of sprites and goblins.
HERMIONE. Let's have that, good sir.
　Come on, sit down; come on, and do your best
　To fright me with your sprites; you're pow'rful at it.
MAMILLIUS. There was a man—
HERMIONE. Nay, come, sit down; then on.
MAMILLIUS. Dwelt by a churchyard—I will tell it softly;
　Yond crickets shall not hear it.
HERMIONE. Come on then,
　And give't me in mine ear.

Enter LEONTES, ANTIGONUS, LORDS, *and* OTHERS

LEONTES. Was he met there? his train? Camillo with him?
FIRST LORD. Behind the tuft of pines I met them; never
　Saw I men scour so on their way. I ey'd them
　Even to their ships.
LEONTES. How blest am I
　In my just censure, in my true opinion!
　Alack, for lesser knowledge! How accurs'd
　In being so blest! There may be in the cup
　A spider steep'd, and one may drink, depart,
　And yet partake no venom, for his knowledge
　Is not infected; but if one present
　Th' abhorr'd ingredient to his eye, make known
　How he hath drunk, he cracks his gorge, his sides,
　With violent hefts. I have drunk, and seen the spider.
　Camillo was his help in this, his pander.
　There is a plot against my life, my crown;
　All's true that is mistrusted. That false villain
　Whom I employ'd was pre-employ'd by him;
　He has discover'd my design, and I
　Remain a pinch'd thing; yea, a very trick
　For them to play at will. How came the posterns

So easily open?

FIRST LORD. By his great authority;
Which often hath no less prevail'd than so
On your command.

LEONTES. I know't too well.
Give me the boy. I am glad you did not nurse him;
Though he does bear some signs of me, yet you
Have too much blood in him.

HERMIONE. What is this? Sport?

LEONTES. Bear the boy hence; he shall not come about her;
Away with him; and let her sport herself
[MAMILLIUS *is led out*]
With that she's big with—for 'tis Polixenes
Has made thee swell thus.

HERMIONE. But I'd say he had not,
And I'll be sworn you would believe my saying,
Howe'er you lean to th' nayward.

LEONTES. You, my lords,
Look on her, mark her well; be but about
To say 'She is a goodly lady' and
The justice of your hearts will thereto add
' 'Tis pity she's not honest—honourable.'
Praise her but for this her without-door form,
Which on my faith deserves high speech, and straight
The shrug, the hum or ha, these petty brands
That calumny doth use—O, I am out!—
That mercy does, for calumny will sear
Virtue itself—these shrugs, these hum's and ha's,
When you have said she's goodly, come between,
Ere you can say she's honest. But be't known,
From him that has most cause to grieve it should be,
She's an adultress.

HERMIONE. Should a villain say so,
The most replenish'd villain in the world,
He were as much more villain: you, my lord,
Do but mistake.

LEONTES. You have mistook, my lady,
Polixenes for Leontes. O thou thing!
Which I'll not call a creature of thy place,
Lest barbarism, making me the precedent,

Should a like language use to all degrees
And mannerly distinguishment leave out
Betwixt the prince and beggar. I have said
She's an adultress; I have said with whom.
More, she's a traitor; and Camillo is
A federary with her, and one that knows
What she should shame to know herself
But with her most vile principal—that she's
A bed-swerver, even as bad as those
That vulgars give bold'st titles; ay, and privy
To this their late escape.
HERMIONE. No, by my life,
Privy to none of this. How will this grieve you,
When you shall come to clearer knowledge, that
You thus have publish'd me! Gentle my lord,
You scarce can right me throughly then to say
You did mistake.
LEONTES. No; if I mistake
In those foundations which I build upon,
The centre is not big enough to bear
A school-boy's top. Away with her to prison.
He who shall speak for her is afar off guilty
But that he speaks.
HERMIONE. There's some ill planet reigns.
I must be patient till the heavens look
With an aspect more favourable. Good my lords,
I am not prone to weeping, as our sex
Commonly are—the want of which vain dew
Perchance shall dry your pities—but I have
That honourable grief lodg'd here which burns
Worse than tears drown. Beseech you all, my lords,
With thoughts so qualified as your charities
Shall best instruct you, measure me; and so
The King's will be perform'd!
LEONTES. [*To the* GUARD] Shall I be heard?
HERMIONE. Who is't that goes with me? Beseech your high-
ness
My women may be with me, for you see
My plight requires it. Do not weep, good fools;
There is no cause; when you shall know your mistress

Has deserv'd prison, then abound in tears
As I come out: this action I now go on
Is for my better grace. Adieu, my lord.
I never wish'd to see you sorry; now
I trust I shall. My women, come; you have leave.
LEONTES. Go, do our bidding; hence!

Exeunt HERMIONE, *guarded, and* LADIES

FIRST LORD. Beseech your Highness, call the Queen again.
ANTIGONUS. Be certain what you do, sir, lest your justice
  Prove violence, in the which three great ones suffer,
  Yourself, your queen, your son.
FIRST LORD. For her, my lord,
  I dare my life lay down—and will do't, sir,
  Please you t' accept it—that the Queen is spotless
  I' th' eyes of heaven and to you—I mean
  In this which you accuse her.
ANTIGONUS. If it prove
  She's otherwise, I'll keep my stables where
  I lodge my wife; I'll go in couples with her;
  Than when I feel and see her no farther trust her;
  For every inch of woman in the world,
  Ay, every dram of woman's flesh is false,
  If she be.
LEONTES. Hold your peaces.
FIRST LORD. Good my lord—
ANTIGONUS. It is for you we speak, not for ourselves.
  You are abus'd, and by some putter-on
  That will be damn'd for't. Would I knew the villain!
  I would land-damn him. Be she honour-flaw'd—
  I have three daughters: the eldest is eleven;
  The second and the third, nine and some five;
  If this prove true, they'll pay for't. By mine honour,
  I'll geld 'em all; fourteen they shall not see
  To bring false generations. They are co-heirs;
  And I had rather glib myself than they
  Should not produce fair issue.
LEONTES. Cease; no more.
  You smell this business with a sense as cold
  As is a dead man's nose; but I do see't and feel't
  As you feel doing thus; and see withal

The instruments that feel.

ANTIGONUS. If it be so,
We need no grave to bury honesty;
There's not a grain of it the face to sweeten
Of the whole dungy earth.

LEONTES. What! Lack I credit?

FIRST LORD. I had rather you did lack than I, my lord,
Upon this ground; and more it would content me
To have her honour true than your suspicion,
Be blam'd for't how you might.

LEONTES. Why, what need we
Commune with you of this, but rather follow
Our forceful instigation? Our prerogative
Calls not your counsels; but our natural goodness
Imparts this; which, if you—or stupified
Or seeming so in skill—cannot or will not
Relish a truth like us, inform yourselves
We need no more of your advice. The matter,
The loss, the gain, the ord'ring on't, is all
Properly ours.

ANTIGONUS. And I wish, my liege,
You had only in your silent judgment tried it,
Without more overture.

LEONTES. How could that be?
Either thou art most ignorant by age,
Or thou wert born a fool. Camillo's flight,
Added to their familiarity—
Which was as gross as ever touch'd conjecture,
That lack'd sight only, nought for approbation
But only seeing, all other circumstances
Made up to th' deed—doth push on this proceeding.
Yet, for a greater confirmation—
For, in an act of this importance, 'twere
Most piteous to be wild—I have dispatch'd in post
To sacred Delphos, to Apollo's temple,
Cleomenes and Dion, whom you know
Of stuff'd sufficiency. Now, from the oracle
They will bring all, whose spiritual counsel had,
Shall stop or spur me. Have I done well?

FIRST LORD. Well done, my lord.

LEONTES. Though I am satisfied, and need no more
    Than what I know, yet shall the oracle
    Give rest to th' minds of others such as he
    Whose ignorant credulity will not
    Come up to th' truth. So have we thought it good
    From our free person she should be confin'd,
    Lest that the treachery of the two fled hence
    Be left her to perform. Come, follow us;
    We are to speak in public; for this business
    Will raise us all.
ANTIGONUS. [*Aside*] To laughter, as I take it,
    If the good truth were known.   *Exeunt*

SCENE 2

Sicilia. A prison

Enter PAULINA, *a* GENTLEMAN, *and* ATTENDANTS

PAULINA. The keeper of the prison—call to him;
    Let him have knowledge who I am.   *Exit* GENTLEMAN
    Good lady!
    No court in Europe is too good for thee;
    What dost thou then in prison?

Re-enter GENTLEMAN *with the* GAOLER

    Now, good sir,
    You know me, do you not?
GAOLER. For a worthy lady,
    And one who much I honour.
PAULINA. Pray you, then,
    Conduct me to the Queen.
GAOLER. I may not, madam;
    To the contrary I have express commandment.
PAULINA. Here's ado, to lock up honesty and honour from
    Th' access of gentle visitors! Is't lawful, pray you,
    To see her women—any of them? Emilia?
GAOLER. So please you, madam,
    To put apart these your attendants, I
    Shall bring Emilia forth.

PAULINA. I pray now, call her.
Withdraw yourselves. *Exeunt* ATTENDANTS
GAOLER. And, madam,
I must be present at your conference.
PAULINA. Well, be't so, prithee. *Exit* GAOLER
Here's such ado to make no stain a stain
As passes colouring.

Re-enter GAOLER, *with* EMILIA

Dear gentlewoman,
How fares our gracious lady?
EMILIA. As well as one so great and so forlorn
May hold together. On her frights and griefs,
Which never tender lady hath borne greater,
She is, something before her time, deliver'd.
PAULINA. A boy?
EMILIA. A daughter, and a goodly babe,
Lusty, and like to live. The Queen receives
Much comfort in't; says 'My poor prisoner,
I am as innocent as you.'
PAULINA. I dare be sworn.
These dangerous unsafe lunes i' th' King, beshrew them!
He must be told on't, and he shall. The office
Becomes a woman best; I'll take't upon me;
If I prove honey-mouth'd, let my tongue blister,
And never to my red-look'd anger be
The trumpet any more. Pray you, Emilia,
Commend my best obedience to the Queen;
If she dares trust me with her little babe,
I'll show't the King, and undertake to be
Her advocate to th' loud'st. We do not know
How he may soften at the sight o' th' child:
The silence often of pure innocence
Persuades when speaking fails.
EMILIA. Most worthy madam,
Your honour and your goodness is so evident
That your free undertaking cannot miss
A thriving issue; there is no lady living
So meet for this great errand. Please your ladyship
To visit the next room, I'll presently

Acquaint the Queen of your most noble offer
Who but to-day hammer'd of this design,
But durst not tempt a minister of honour,
Lest she should be denied.

PAULINA. Tell her, Emilia,
I'll use that tongue I have; if wit flow from't
As boldness from my bosom, let't not be doubted
I shall do good.

EMILIA. Now be you blest for it!
I'll to the Queen. Please you come something nearer.

GAOLER. Madam, if't please the Queen to send the babe,
I know not what I shall incur to pass it,
Having no warrant.

PAULINA. You need not fear it, sir.
This child was prisoner to the womb, and is
By law and process of great Nature thence
Freed and enfranchis'd—not a party to
The anger of the King, nor guilty of,
If any be, the trespass of the Queen.

GAOLER. I do believe it.

PAULINA. Do not you fear. Upon mine honour, I
Will stand betwixt you and danger.   *Exeunt*

SCENE 3

Sicilia. The palace of LEONTES

Enter LEONTES, ANTIGONUS, LORDS, *and* SERVANTS

LEONTES. Nor night nor day no rest! It is but weakness
To bear the matter thus—mere weakness. If
The cause were not in being—part o' th' cause,
She, th' adultress; for the harlot king
Is quite beyond mine arm, out of the blank
And level of my brain, plot-proof; but she
I can hook to me—say that she were gone,
Given to the fire, a moiety of my rest
Might come to me again. Who's there?

FIRST SERVANT. My lord?

LEONTES. How does the boy?

FIRST SERVANT. He took good rest to-night;
'Tis hop'd his sickness is discharg'd.
LEONTES. To see his nobleness!
Conceiving the dishonour of his mother,
He straight declin'd, droop'd, took it deeply,
Fasten'd and fix'd the shame on't in himself,
Threw off his spirit, his appetite, his sleep,
And downright languish'd. Leave me solely. Go,
See how he fares. [*Exit* SERVANT] Fie, fie! no thought of
him!
The very thought of my revenges that way
Recoil upon me—in himself too mighty,
And in his parties, his alliance. Let him be,
Until a time may serve; for present vengeance,
Take it on her. Camillo and Polixenes
Laugh at me, make their pastime at my sorrow.
They should not laugh if I could reach them; nor
Shall she, within my pow'r.

Enter PAULINA, *with a* CHILD

FIRST LORD. You must not enter.
PAULINA. Nay, rather, good my lords, be second to me.
Fear you his tyrannous passion more, alas,
Than the Queen's life? A gracious innocent soul,
More free than he is jealous.
ANTIGONUS. That's enough.
SECOND SERVANT. Madam, he hath not slept to-night; com-
manded
None should come at him.
PAULINA. Not so hot, good sir;
I come to bring him sleep. 'Tis such as you,
That creep like shadows by him, and do sigh
At each his needless heavings—such as you
Nourish the cause of his awaking: I
Do come with words as medicinal as true,
Honest as either, to purge him of that humour
That presses him from sleep.
LEONTES. What noise there, ho?
PAULINA. No noise, my lord; but needful conference
About some gossips for your Highness.

LEONTES. How!
  Away with that audacious lady! Antigonus,
  I charg'd thee that she should not come about me;
  I knew she would.
ANTIGONUS. I told her so, my lord,
  On your displeasure's peril, and on mine,
  She should not visit you.
LEONTES. What, canst not rule her?
PAULINA. From all dishonesty he can: in this,
  Unless he take the course that you have done—
  Commit me for committing honour—trust it,
  He shall not rule me.
ANTIGONUS. La you now, you hear!
  When she will take the rein, I let her run;
  But she'll not stumble.
PAULINA. Good my liege, I come—
  And I beseech you hear me, who professes
  Myself your loyal servant, your physician,
  Your most obedient counsellor; yet that dares
  Less appear so, in comforting your evils,
  Than such as most seem yours—I say I come
  From your good Queen.
LEONTES. Good Queen!
PAULINA. Good Queen, my lord, good Queen—I say good
    Queen;
  And would by combat make her good, so were I
  A man, the worst about you.
LEONTES. Force her hence.
PAULINA. Let him that makes but trifles of his eyes
  First hand me. On mine own accord I'll off;
  But first I'll do my errand. The good Queen,
  For she is good, hath brought you forth a daughter;
  Here 'tis; commends it to your blessing.
                              [Laying down the child]
LEONTES. Out!
  A mankind witch! Hence with her, out o' door!
  A most intelligencing bawd!
PAULINA. Not so.
  I am as ignorant in that as you
  In so entitling me; and no less honest

Than you are mad; which is enough, I'll warrant,
As this world goes, to pass for honest.

LEONTES. Traitors!
Will you not push her out? Give her the bastard.
[*To* ANTIGONUS] Thou dotard, thou art woman-tir'd, un-
roosted
By thy Dame Partlet here. Take up the bastard;
Take't up, I say; give't to thy crone.

PAULINA. For ever
Unvenerable be thy hands, if thou
Tak'st up the Princess by that forced baseness
Which he has put upon't!

LEONTES. He dreads his wife.

PAULINA. So I would you did; then 'twere past all doubt
You'd call your children yours.

LEONTES. A nest of traitors!

ANTIGONUS. I am none, by this good light.

PAULINA. Nor I; nor any
But one that's here; and that's himself; for he
The sacred honour of himself, his Queen's,
His hopeful son's, his babe's, betrays to slander,
Whose sting is sharper than the sword's; and will not—
For, as the case now stands, it is a curse
He cannot be compell'd to 't—once remove
The root of his opinion, which is rotten
As ever oak or stone was sound.

LEONTES. A callat
Of boundless tongue, who late hath beat her husband,
And now baits me! This brat is none of mine;
It is the issue of Polixenes.
Hence with it, and together with the dam   ¶
Commit them to the fire.

PAULINA. It is yours.
And, might we lay th' old proverb to your charge,
So like you 'tis the worse. Behold, my lords,
Although the print be little, the whole matter
And copy of the father—eye, nose, lip,
The trick of's frown, his forehead; nay, the valley,
The pretty dimples of his chin and cheek; his smiles;
The very mould and frame of hand, nail, finger.

And thou, good goddess Nature, which hast made it
So like to him that got it, if thou hast
The ordering of the mind too, 'mongst all colours
No yellow in't, lest she suspect, as he does,
Her children not her husband's!

LEONTES. A gross hag!
And, lozel, thou art worthy to be hang'd
That wilt not stay her tongue.

ANTIGONUS. Hang all the husbands
That cannot do that feat, you'll leave yourself
Hardly one subject.

LEONTES. Once more, take her hence.

PAULINA. A most unworthy and unnatural lord
Can do no more.

LEONTES. I'll ha' thee burnt.

PAULINA. I care not.
It is an heretic that makes the fire,
Not she which burns in't. I'll not call you tyrant
But this most cruel usage of your Queen—
Not able to produce more accusation
Than your own weak-hing'd fancy—something savours
Of tyranny, and will ignoble make you,
Yea, scandalous to the world.

LEONTES. On your allegiance,
Out of the chamber with her! Were I a tyrant,
Where were her life? She durst not call me so,
If she did know me one. Away with her!

PAULINA. I pray you, do not push me; I'll be gone.
Look to your babe, my lord; 'tis yours. Jove send her
A better guiding spirit! What needs these hands?
You that are thus so tender o'er his follies
Will never do him good, not one of you.
So, so. Farewell; we are gone.   *Exit*

LEONTES. Thou, traitor, hast set on thy wife to this.
My child! Away with't. Even thou, that hast
A heart so tender o'er it, take it hence,
And see it instantly consum'd with fire;
Even thou, and none but thou. Take it up straight.
Within this hour bring me word 'tis done,
And by good testimony, or I'll seize thy life,

With that thou else call'st thine. If thou refuse,
And wilt encounter with my wrath, say so;
The bastard brains with these my proper hands
Shall I dash out. Go, take it to the fire;
For thou set'st on thy wife.
ANTIGONUS. I did not, sir.
These lords, my noble fellows, if they please,
Can clear me in't.
LORDS. We can. My royal liege,
He is not guilty of her coming hither.
LEONTES. You're liars all.
FIRST LORD. Beseech your Highness, give us better credit.
We have always truly serv'd you; and beseech
So to esteem of us; and on our knees we beg,
As recompense of our dear services
Past and to come, that you do change this purpose,
Which being so horrible, so bloody, must
Lead on to some foul issue. We all kneel.
LEONTES. I am a feather for each wind that blows.
Shall I live on to see this bastard kneel
And call me father? Better burn it now
Than curse it then. But be it; let it live.
It shall not neither. [*To* ANTIGONUS] You, sir, come you
    hither.
You that have been so tenderly officious
With Lady Margery, your midwife there,
To save this bastard's life—for 'tis a bastard,
So sure as this beard's grey—what will you adventure
To save this brat's life?
ANTIGONUS. Anything, my lord,
That my ability may undergo,
And nobleness impose. At least, thus much:
I'll pawn the little blood which I have left
To save the innocent—anything possible.
LEONTES. It shall be possible. Swear by this sword
Thou wilt perform my bidding.
ANTIGONUS. I will, my lord.
LEONTES. Mark, and perform it—seest thou? For the fail
Of any point in't shall not only be
Death to thyself, but to thy lewd-tongu'd wife,

Whom for this time we pardon. We enjoin thee,
As thou art liegeman to us, that thou carry
This female bastard hence; and that thou bear it
To some remote and desert place, quite out
Of our dominions; and that there thou leave it,
Without more mercy, to it own protection
And favour of the climate. As by strange fortune
It came to us, I do in justice charge thee,
On thy soul's peril and thy body's torture,
That thou commend it strangely to some place
Where chance may nurse or end it. Take it up.
ANTIGONUS. I swear to do this, though a present death
Had been more merciful. Come on, poor babe.
Some powerful spirit instruct the kites and ravens
To be thy nurses! Wolves and bears, they say,
Casting their savageness aside, have done
Like offices of pity. Sir, be prosperous
In more than this deed does require! And blessing
Against this cruelty fight on thy side,
Poor thing, condemn'd to loss!   *Exit with the child*
LEONTES. No, I'll not rear
Another's issue.

Enter a SERVANT

SERVANT. Please your Highness, posts
From those you sent to th' oracle are come
An hour since. Cleomenes and Dion,
Being well arriv'd from Delphos, are both landed,
Hasting to th' court.
FIRST LORD. So please you, sir, their speed
Hath been beyond account.
LEONTES. Twenty-three days
They have been absent; 'tis good speed; foretells
The great Apollo suddenly will have
The truth of this appear. Prepare you, lords;
Summon a session, that we may arraign
Our most disloyal lady; for, as she hath
Been publicly accus'd, so shall she have
A just and open trial. While she lives,

My heart will be a burden to me. Leave me;
And think upon my bidding.   *Exeunt*

ACT III. SCENE 1

Sicilia. On the road to the Capital

Enter CLEOMENES *and* DION

CLEOMENES. The climate's delicate, the air most sweet,
Fertile the isle, the temple much surpassing
The common praise it bears.
DION. I shall report,
For most it caught me, the celestial habits—
Methinks I so should term them—and the reverence
Of the grave wearers. O, the sacrifice!
How ceremonious, solemn, and unearthly,
It was i' th' off'ring!
CLEOMENES. But of all, the burst
And the ear-deaf'ning voice o' th' oracle,
Kin to Jove's thunder, so surpris'd my sense
That I was nothing.
DION. If th' event o' th' journey
Prove as successful to the Queen—O, be't so!—
As it hath been to us rare, pleasant, speedy,
The time is worth the use on't.
CLEOMENES. Great Apollo
Turn all to th' best! These proclamations,
So forcing faults upon Hermione,
I little like.
DION. The violent carriage of it
Will clear or end the business. When the oracle—
Thus by Apollo's great divine seal'd up—
Shall the contents discover, something rare
Even then will rush to knowledge. Go; fresh horses.
And gracious be the issue!   *Exeunt*

THE WINTER'S TALE

SCENE 2

Sicilia. A court of justice

Enter LEONTES, LORDS, *and* OFFICERS

LEONTES. This sessions, to our great grief we pronounce,
Even pushes 'gainst our heart—the party tried,
The daughter of a king, our wife, and one
Of us too much belov'd. Let us be clear'd
Of being tyrannous, since we so openly
Proceed in justice, which shall have due course,
Even to the guilt or the purgation.
Produce the prisoner.
OFFICER. It is his Highness' pleasure that the Queen
Appear in person here in court.

Enter HERMIONE, *as to her trial*, PAULINA, *and* LADIES

Silence!
LEONTES. Read the indictment.
OFFICER. [*Reads*] 'Hermione, Queen to the worthy Leontes,
King of Sicilia, thou art here accused and arraigned of high
treason, in committing adultery with Polixenes, King of
Bohemia; and conspiring with Camillo to take away the
life of our sovereign lord the King, thy royal husband: the
pretence whereof being by circumstances partly laid open,
thou, Hermione, contrary to the faith and allegiance of a
true subject, didst counsel and aid them, for their better
safety, to fly away by night.'
HERMIONE. Since what I am to say must be but that
Which contradicts my accusation, and
The testimony on my part no other
But what comes from myself, it shall scarce boot me
To say 'Not guilty.' Mine integrity
Being counted falsehood shall, as I express it,
Be so receiv'd. But thus—if pow'rs divine
Behold our human actions, as they do,
I doubt not then but innocence shall make
False accusation blush, and tyranny
Tremble at patience. You, my lord, best know—

Who least will seem to do so—my past life
Hath been as continent, as chaste, as true,
As I am now unhappy; which is more
Than history can pattern, though devis'd
And play'd to take spectators; for behold me—
A fellow of the royal bed, which owe
A moiety of the throne, a great king's daughter,
The mother to a hopeful prince—here standing
To prate and talk for life and honour fore
Who please to come and hear. For life, I prize it
As I weigh grief, which I would spare; for honour,
'Tis a derivative from me to mine,
And only that I stand for. I appeal
To your own conscience, sir, before Polixenes
Came to your court, how I was in your grace,
How merited to be so; since he came,
With what encounter so uncurrent I
Have strain'd t' appear thus; if one jot beyond
The bound of honour, or in act or will
That way inclining, hard'ned be the hearts
Of all that hear me, and my near'st of kin
Cry fie upon my grave!

LEONTES. I ne'er heard yet
That any of these bolder vices wanted
Less impudence to gainsay what they did
Than to perform it first.

HERMIONE. That's true enough;
Though 'tis a saying, sir, not due to me.

LEONTES. You will not own it.

HERMIONE. More than mistress of
Which comes to me in name of fault, I must not
At all acknowledge. For Polixenes,
With whom I am accus'd, I do confess
I lov'd him as in honour he requir'd;
With such a kind of love as might become
A lady like me; with a love even such,
So and no other, as yourself commanded;
Which not to have done, I think had been in me
Both disobedience and ingratitude
To you and toward your friend; whose love had spoke,

Ever since it could speak, from an infant, freely,
That it was yours. Now for conspiracy:
I know not how it tastes, though it be dish'd
For me to try how; all I know of it
Is that Camillo was an honest man;
And why he left your court, the gods themselves,
Wotting no more than I, are ignorant.

LEONTES. You knew of his departure, as you know
What you have underta'en to do in's absence.

HERMIONE. Sir,
You speak a language that I understand not.
My life stands in the level of your dreams,
Which I'll lay down.

LEONTES. Your actions are my dreams.
You had a bastard by Polixenes,
And I but dream'd it. As you were past all shame—
Those of your fact are so—so past all truth;
Which to deny concerns more than avails; for as
Thy brat hath been cast out, like to itself,
No father owning it—which is indeed
More criminal in thee than it—so thou
Shalt feel our justice; in whose easiest passage
Look for no less than death.

HERMIONE. Sir, spare your threats.
The bug which you would fright me with I seek.
To me can life be no commodity.
The crown and comfort of my life, your favour,
I do give lost, for I do feel it gone,
But know not how it went; my second joy
And first fruits of my body, from his presence
I am barr'd, like one infectious; my third comfort,
Starr'd most unluckily, is from my breast—
The innocent milk in it most innocent mouth—
Hal'd out to murder; myself on every post
Proclaim'd a strumpet; with immodest hatred
The child-bed privilege denied, which 'longs
To women of all fashion; lastly, hurried
Here to this place, i' th' open air, before
I have got strength of limit. Now, my liege,
Tell me what blessings I have here alive

That I should fear to die. Therefore proceed.
But yet hear this—mistake me not: no life,
I prize it not a straw, but for mine honour
Which I would free—if I shall be condemn'd
Upon surmises, all proofs sleeping else
But what your jealousies awake, I tell you
'Tis rigour, and not law. Your honours all,
I do refer me to the oracle:
Apollo be my judge!

FIRST LORD. This your request
Is altogether just. Therefore, bring forth,
And in Apollo's name, his oracle.

Exeunt certain OFFICERS

HERMIONE. The Emperor of Russia was my father;
O that he were alive, and here beholding
His daughter's trial! that he did but see
The flatness of my misery; yet with eyes
Of pity, not revenge!

Re-enter OFFICERS, *with* CLEOMENES *and* DION

OFFICER. You here shall swear upon this sword of justice
That you, Cleomenes and Dion, have
Been both at Delphos, and from thence have brought
This seal'd-up oracle, by the hand deliver'd
Of great Apollo's priest; and that since then
You have not dar'd to break the holy seal
Nor read the secrets in't.

CLEOMENES, DION. All this we swear.

LEONTES. Break up the seals and read.

OFFICER. [*Reads*] 'Hermione is chaste; Polixenes blameless;
Camillo a true subject; Leontes a jealous tyrant; his innocent babe truly begotten; and the King shall live without
an heir, if that which is lost be not found.'

LORDS. Now blessed be the great Apollo!

HERMIONE. Praised!

LEONTES. Hast thou read truth?

OFFICER. Ay, my lord; even so
As it is here set down.

LEONTES. There is no truth at all i' th' oracle.
The sessions shall proceed. This is mere falsehood.

Enter a SERVANT

SERVANT. My lord the King, the King!

LEONTES. What is the business?

SERVANT. O sir, I shall be hated to report it:
   The Prince your son, with mere conceit and fear
   Of the Queen's speed, is gone.

LEONTES. How! Gone?

SERVANT. Is dead.

LEONTES. Apollo's angry; and the heavens themselves
   Do strike at my injustice.   [HERMIONE *swoons*]
   How now, there!

PAULINA. This news is mortal to the Queen. Look down
   And see what death is doing.

LEONTES. Take her hence.
   Her heart is but o'ercharg'd; she will recover.
   I have too much believ'd mine own suspicion.
   Beseech you tenderly apply to her
   Some remedies for life.

          Exeunt PAULINA *and* LADIES *with* HERMIONE

   Apollo, pardon
   My great profaneness 'gainst thine oracle.
   I'll reconcile me to Polixenes,
   New woo my queen, recall the good Camillo—
   Whom I proclaim a man of truth, of mercy.
   For, being transported by my jealousies
   To bloody thoughts and to revenge, I chose
   Camillo for the minister to poison
   My friend Polixenes; which had been done
   But that the good mind of Camillo tardied
   My swift command, though I with death and with
   Reward did threaten and encourage him,
   Not doing it and being done. He, most humane
   And fill'd with honour, to my kingly guest
   Unclasp'd my practice, quit his fortunes here,
   Which you knew great, and to the certain hazard
   Of all incertainties himself commended,
   No richer than his honour. How he glisters
   Thorough my rust! And how his piety
   Does my deeds make the blacker!

ACT III. SCENE 2

Re-enter PAULINA

PAULINA. Woe the while!
　O, cut my lace, lest my heart, cracking it,
　Break too!
FIRST LORD. What fit is this, good lady?
PAULINA. What studied torments, tyrant, hast for me?
　What wheels, racks, fires? what flaying, boiling
　In leads or oils? What old or newer torture
　Must I receive, whose every word deserves
　To taste of thy most worst? Thy tyranny
　Together working with thy jealousies,
　Fancies too weak for boys, too green and idle
　For girls of nine—O, think what they have done,
　And then run mad indeed, stark mad; for all
　Thy by-gone fooleries were but spices of it.
　That thou betray'dst Polixenes, 'twas nothing;
　That did but show thee, of a fool, inconstant,
　And damnable ingrateful. Nor was't much
　Thou wouldst have poison'd good Camillo's honour,
　To have him kill a king—poor trespasses,
　More monstrous standing by; whereof I reckon
　The casting forth to crows thy baby daughter
　To be or none or little, though a devil
　Would have shed water out of fire ere done't;
　Nor is't directly laid to thee, the death
　Of the young Prince, whose honourable thoughts—
　Thoughts high for one so tender—cleft the heart
　That could conceive a gross and foolish sire
　Blemish'd his gracious dam. This is not, no,
　Laid to thy answer; but the last—O lords,
　When I have said, cry 'Woe!'—the Queen, the Queen,
　The sweet'st, dear'st creature's dead; and vengeance for't
　Not dropp'd down yet.
FIRST LORD. The higher pow'rs forbid!
PAULINA. I say she's dead; I'll swear't. If word nor oath
　Prevail not, go and see. If you can bring
　Tincture or lustre in her lip, her eye,
　Heat outwardly or breath within, I'll serve you
　As I would do the gods. But, O thou tyrant!

Do not repent these things, for they are heavier
Than all thy woes can stir; therefore betake thee
To nothing but despair. A thousand knees
Ten thousand years together, naked, fasting,
Upon a barren mountain, and still winter
In storm perpetual, could not move the gods
To look that way thou wert.

LEONTES. Go on, go on.
Thou canst not speak too much; I have deserv'd
All tongues to talk their bitt'rest.

FIRST LORD. Say no more;
Howe'er the business goes, you have made fault
I' th' boldness of your speech.

PAULINA. I am sorry for't.
All faults I make, when I shall come to know them.
I do repent. Alas, I have show'd too much
The rashness of a woman! He is touch'd
To th' noble heart. What's gone and what's past help
Should be past grief. Do not receive affliction
At my petition; I beseech you, rather
Let me be punish'd that have minded you
Of what you should forget. Now, good my liege,
Sir, royal sir, forgive a foolish woman.
The love I bore your queen—lo, fool again!
I'll speak of her no more, nor of your children;
I'll not remember you of my own lord,
Who is lost too. Take your patience to you,
And I'll say nothing.

LEONTES. Thou didst speak but well
When most the truth; which I receive much better
Than to be pitied of thee. Prithee, bring me
To the dead bodies of my queen and son.
One grave shall be for both. Upon them shall
The causes of their death appear, unto
Our shame perpetual. Once a day I'll visit
The chapel where they lie; and tears shed there
Shall be my recreation. So long as nature
Will bear up with this exercise, so long
I daily vow to use it. Come, and lead me
To these sorrows.   *Exeunt*

SCENE 3

Bohemia. The sea-coast

Enter ANTIGONUS *with the* CHILD, *and a* MARINER

ANTIGONUS. Thou art perfect then our ship hath touch'd
      upon
  The deserts of Bohemia?
MARINER. Ay, my lord, and fear
  We have landed in ill time; the skies look grimly
  And threaten present blusters. In my conscience,
  The heavens with that we have in hand are angry
  And frown upon 's.
ANTIGONUS. Their sacred wills be done! Go, get aboard;
  Look to thy bark. I'll not be long before
  I call upon thee.
MARINER. Make your best haste; and go not
  Too far i' th' land; 'tis like to be loud weather;
  Besides, this place is famous for the creatures
  Of prey that keep upon't.
ANTIGONUS. Go thou away;
  I'll follow instantly.
MARINER. I am glad at heart
  To be so rid o' th' business.   *Exit*
ANTIGONUS. Come, poor babe.
  I have heard, but not believ'd, the spirits o' th' dead
  May walk again. If such thing be, thy mother
  Appear'd to me last night; for ne'er was dream
  So like a waking. To me comes a creature,
  Sometimes her head on one side some another—
  I never saw a vessel of like sorrow,
  So fill'd and so becoming; in pure white robes,
  Like very sanctity, she did approach
  My cabin where I lay; thrice bow'd before me;
  And, gasping to begin some speech, her eyes
  Became two spouts; the fury spent, anon
  Did this break from her: 'Good Antigonus,
  Since fate, against thy better disposition,
  Hath made thy person for the thrower-out

Of my poor babe, according to thine oath,
Places remote enough are in Bohemia,
There weep, and leave it crying; and, for the babe
Is counted lost for ever, Perdita
I prithee call't. For this ungentle business,
Put on thee by my lord, thou ne'er shalt see
Thy wife Paulina more.' And so, with shrieks,
She melted into air. Affrighted much,
I did in time collect myself, and thought
This was so and no slumber. Dreams are toys;
Yet, for this once, yea, superstitiously,
I will be squar'd by this. I do believe
Hermione hath suffer'd death, and that
Apollo would, this being indeed the issue
Of King Polixenes, it should here be laid,
Either for life or death, upon the earth
Of its right father. Blossom, speed thee well!
                                    [*Laying down the child*]
There lie, and there thy character; there these
                                    [*Laying down a bundle*]
Which may, if fortune please, both breed thee, pretty,
And still rest thine. The storm begins. Poor wretch,
That for thy mother's fault art thus expos'd
To loss and what may follow! Weep I cannot,
But my heart bleeds; and most accurs'd am I
To be by oath enjoin'd to this. Farewell!
The day frowns more and more. Thou'rt like to have
A lullaby too rough; I never saw
The heavens so dim by day. [*Noise of hunt within*] A
     savage clamour!
Well may I get aboard! This is the chase;
I am gone for ever.   *Exit, pursued by a bear*

                Enter an old SHEPHERD

SHEPHERD. I would there were no age between ten and three
     and twenty, or that youth would sleep out the rest; for there
     is nothing in the between but getting wenches with child,
     wronging the ancientry, stealing, fighting—[*Horns*] Hark
     you now! Would any but these boil'd brains of nineteen
     and two and twenty hunt this weather? They have scar'd

away two of my best sheep, which I fear the wolf will
sooner find than the master. If any where I have them, 'tis
by the sea-side, browsing of ivy. Good luck, an't be thy
will! What have we here? [*Taking up the child*] Mercy
on's, a barne! A very pretty barne. A boy or a child, I
wonder? A pretty one; a very pretty one—sure, some
scape. Though I am not bookish, yet I can read waiting-
gentlewoman in the scape. This has been some stair-work,
some trunk-work, some behind-door-work; they were
warmer that got this than the poor thing is here. I'll take it
up for pity; yet I'll tarry till my son come; he halloo'd but
even now. Whoa-ho-hoa!

Enter CLOWN

CLOWN. Hilloa, loa!
SHEPHERD. What, art so near? If thou'lt see a thing to talk on
when thou art dead and rotten, come hither. What ail'st
thou, man?
CLOWN. I have seen two such sights, by sea and by land! But
I am not to say it is a sea, for it is now the sky; betwixt the
firmament and it you cannot thrust a bodkin's point.
SHEPHERD. Why, boy, how is it?
CLOWN. I would you did but see how it chafes, how it rages,
how it takes up the shore! But that's not to the point. O,
the most piteous cry of the poor souls! Sometimes to see
'em, and not to see 'em; now the ship boring the moon
with her mainmast, and anon swallowed with yeast and
froth, as you'd thrust a cork into a hogshead. And then
for the land service—to see how the bear tore out his
shoulder-bone; how he cried to me for help, and said his
name was Antigonus, a nobleman! But to make an end of
the ship—to see how the sea flap-dragon'd it; but first, how
the poor souls roared, and the sea mock'd them; and how
the poor gentleman roared, and the bear mock'd him, both
roaring louder than the sea or weather.
SHEPHERD. Name of mercy, when was this, boy?
CLOWN. Now, now; I have not wink'd since I saw these
sights; the men are not yet cold under water, nor the bear
half din'd on the gentleman; he's at it now.
SHEPHERD. Would I had been by to have help'd the old man!

CLOWN. I would you had been by the ship-side, to have
help'd her; there your charity would have lack'd footing.
SHEPHERD. Heavy matters, heavy matters! But look thee
here, boy. Now bless thyself; thou met'st with things dying, I with things new-born. Here's a sight for thee; look
thee, a bearing-cloth for a squire's child! Look thee here;
take up, take up, boy; open't. So, let's see—it was told me
I should be rich by the fairies. This is some changeling.
Open't. What's within, boy?
CLOWN. You're a made old man; if the sins of your youth
are forgiven you, you're well to live. Gold! all gold!
SHEPHERD. This is fairy gold, boy, and 'twill prove so. Up
with't, keep it close. Home, home, the next way! We are
lucky, boy; and to be so still requires nothing but secrecy.
Let my sheep go. Come, good boy, the next way home.
CLOWN. Go you the next way with your findings. I'll go see
if the bear be gone from the gentleman, and how much he
hath eaten. They are never curst but when they are hungry. If there be any of him left, I'll bury it.
SHEPHERD. That's a good deed. If thou mayest discern by
that which is left of him what he is, fetch me to th' sight
of him.
CLOWN. Marry, will I; and you shall help to put him i' th'
ground.
SHEPHERD. 'Tis a lucky day, boy; and we'll do good deeds
on't. *Exeunt*

ACT IV. SCENE 1

Enter TIME, *the* CHORUS

TIME. I, that please some, try all, both joy and terror
Of good and bad, that makes and unfolds error,
Now take upon me, in the name of Time,
To use my wings. Impute it not a crime
To me or my swift passage that I slide
O'er sixteen years, and leave the growth untried
Of that wide gap, since it is in my pow'r
To o'erthrow law, and in one self-born hour

ACT IV. SCENE 1

To plant and o'erwhelm custom. Let me pass
The same I am, ere ancient'st order was
Or what is now receiv'd. I witness to
The times that brought them in; so shall I do
To th' freshest things now reigning, and make stale
The glistering of this present, as my tale
Now seems to it. Your patience this allowing,
I turn my glass, and give my scene such growing
As you had slept between. Leontes leaving—
Th' effects of his fond jealousies so grieving
That he shuts up himself—imagine me,
Gentle spectators, that I now may be
In fair Bohemia; and remember well
I mention'd a son o' th' King's, which Florizel
I now name to you; and with speed so pace
To speak of Perdita, now grown in grace
Equal with wond'ring. What of her ensues
I list not prophesy; but let Time's news
Be known when 'tis brought forth. A shepherd's daughter,
And what to her adheres, which follows after,
Is th' argument of Time. Of this allow,
If ever you have spent time worse ere now;
If never, yet that Time himself doth say
He wishes earnestly you never may.   *Exit*

SCENE 2

Bohemia. The palace of POLIXENES

Enter POLIXENES *and* CAMILLO

POLIXENES. I pray thee, good Camillo, be no more importunate: 'tis a sickness denying thee anything; a death to
grant this.
CAMILLO. It is fifteen years since I saw my country; though
I have for the most part been aired abroad, I desire to lay
my bones there. Besides, the penitent King, my master,
hath sent for me; to whose feeling sorrows I might be some
allay, or I o'erween to think so, which is another spur to
my departure.

1053

POLIXENES. As thou lov'st me, Camillo, wipe not out the rest of thy services by leaving me now. The need I have of thee thine own goodness hath made. Better not to have had thee than thus to want thee; thou, having made me businesses which none without thee can sufficiently manage, must either stay to execute them thyself, or take away with thee the very services thou hast done; which if I have not enough considered—as too much I cannot—to be more thankful to thee shall be my study; and my profit therein the heaping friendships. Of that fatal country Sicilia, prithee, speak no more; whose very naming punishes me with the remembrance of that penitent, as thou call'st him, and reconciled king, my brother; whose loss of his most precious queen and children are even now to be afresh lamented. Say to me, when saw'st thou the Prince Florizel, my son? Kings are no less unhappy, their issue not being gracious, than they are in losing them when they have approved their virtues.

CAMILLO. Sir, it is three days since I saw the Prince. What his happier affairs may be are to me unknown; but I have missingly noted he is of late much retired from court, and is less frequent to his princely exercises than formerly he hath appeared.

POLIXENES. I have considered so much, Camillo, and with some care, so far that I have eyes under my service which look upon his removedness; from whom I have this intelligence, that he is seldom from the house of a most homely shepherd—a man, they say, that from very nothing, and beyond the imagination of his neighbours, is grown into an unspeakable estate.

CAMILLO. I have heard, sir, of such a man, who hath a daughter of most rare note. The report of her is extended more than can be thought to begin from such a cottage.

POLIXENES. That's likewise part of my intelligence; but, I fear, the angle that plucks our son thither. Thou shalt accompany us to the place; where we will, not appearing what we are, have some question with the shepherd; from whose simplicity I think it not uneasy to get the cause of my son's resort thither. Prithee be my present partner in this business, and lay aside the thoughts of Sicilia.

ACT IV. SCENE 2

CAMILLO. I willingly obey your command.
POLIXENES. My best Camillo! We must disguise ourselves.

Exeunt

SCENE 3

Bohemia. A road near the SHEPHERD'S *cottage*

Enter AUTOLYCUS, *singing*

When daffodils begin to peer,
　With heigh! the doxy over the dale,
Why, then comes in the sweet o' the year,
　For the red blood reigns in the winter's pale.

The white sheet bleaching on the hedge,
　With heigh! the sweet birds, O, how they sing!
Doth set my pugging tooth on edge,
　For a quart of ale is a dish for a king.

The lark, that tirra-lirra chants,
　With heigh! with heigh! the thrush and the jay,
Are summer songs for me and my aunts,
　While we lie tumbling in the hay.

I have serv'd Prince Florizel, and in my time wore three-pile; but now I am out of service.

　　　But shall I go mourn for that, my dear?
　　　　The pale moon shines by night;
　　　And when I wander here and there,
　　　　I then do most go right.

　　　If tinkers may have leave to live,
　　　　And bear the sow-skin budget,
　　　Then my account I well may give
　　　　And in the stocks avouch it.

My traffic is sheets; when the kite builds, look to lesser linen. My father nam'd me Autolycus; who, being, as I am, litter'd under Mercury, was likewise a snapper-up of unconsidered trifles. With die and drab I purchas'd this caparison; and my revenue is the silly-cheat. Gallows and knock are too powerful on the highway; beating and hanging are terrors to me; for the life to come, I sleep out the thought of it. A prize! a prize!

Enter Clown

Clown. Let me see: every 'leven wether tods; every tod yields pound and odd shilling; fifteen hundred shorn, what comes the wool to?
Autolycus. [*Aside*] If the springe hold, the cock's mine.
Clown. I cannot do 't without counters. Let me see: what am I to buy for our sheep-shearing feast? Three pound of sugar, five pound of currants, rice—what will this sister of mine do with rice? But my father hath made her mistress of the feast, and she lays it on. She hath made me four and twenty nosegays for the shearers—three-man song-men all, and very good ones; but they are most of them means and bases; but one Puritan amongst them, and he sings psalms to hornpipes. I must have saffron to colour the warden pies; mace; dates—none, that's out of my note; nutmegs, seven; a race or two of ginger, but that I may beg; four pound of prunes, and as many of raisins o' th' sun.
Autolycus. [*Grovelling on the ground*] O that ever I was born!
Clown. I' th' name of me!
Autolycus. O, help me, help me! Pluck but off these rags; and then, death, death!
Clown. Alack, poor soul! thou hast need of more rags to lay on thee, rather than have these off.
Autolycus. O sir, the loathsomeness of them offend me more than the stripes I have received, which are mighty ones and millions.
Clown. Alas, poor man! a million of beating may come to a great matter.
Autolycus. I am robb'd, sir, and beaten; my money and apparel ta'en from me, and these detestable things put upon me.
Clown. What, by a horseman or a footman?
Autolycus. A footman, sweet sir, a footman.
Clown. Indeed, he should be a footman, by the garments he has left with thee; if this be a horseman's coat, it hath seen very hot service. Lend me thy hand, I'll help thee.

Come, lend me thy hand.   [*Helping him up*]

AUTOLYCUS. O, good sir, tenderly, O!

CLOWN. Alas, poor soul!

AUTOLYCUS. O, good sir, softly, good sir; I fear, sir, my shoulder blade is out.

CLOWN. How now! Canst stand?

AUTOLYCUS. Softly, dear sir [*Picks his pocket*]; good sir, softly. You ha' done me a charitable office.

CLOWN. Dost lack any money? I have a little money for thee.

AUTOLYCUS. No, good sweet sir; no, I beseech you, sir. I have a kinsman not past three quarters of a mile hence, unto whom I was going; I shall there have money or anything I want. Offer me no money, I pray you; that kills my heart.

CLOWN. What manner of fellow was he that robb'd you?

AUTOLYCUS. A fellow, sir, that I have known to go about with troll-my-dames; I knew him once a servant of the Prince. I cannot tell, good sir, for which of his virtues it was, but he was certainly whipt out of the court.

CLOWN. His vices, you would say; there's no virtue whipt out of the court. They cherish it to make it stay there; and yet it will no more but abide.

AUTOLYCUS. Vices, I would say, sir. I know this man well; he hath been since an ape-bearer; then a process-server, a bailiff; then he compass'd a motion of the Prodigal Son, and married a tinker's wife within a mile where my land and living lies; and, having flown over many knavish professions, he settled only in rogue. Some call him Autolycus.

CLOWN. Out upon him! prig, for my life, prig! He haunts wakes, fairs, and bear-baitings.

AUTOLYCUS. Very true, sir; he, sir, he; that's the rogue that put me into this apparel.

CLOWN. Not a more cowardly rogue in all Bohemia; if you had but look'd big and spit at him, he'd have run.

AUTOLYCUS. I must confess to you, sir, I am no fighter; I am false of heart that way, and that he knew, I warrant him.

CLOWN. How do you now?

AUTOLYCUS. Sweet sir, much better than I was; I can stand

and walk. I will even take my leave of you and pace softly towards my kinsman's.

CLOWN. Shall I bring thee on the way?

AUTOLYCUS. No, good-fac'd sir; no, sweet sir.

CLOWN. Then fare thee well. I must go buy spices for our sheep-shearing.

AUTOLYCUS. Prosper you, sweet sir! *Exit* CLOWN
Your purse is not hot enough to purchase your spice. I'll be with you at your sheep-shearing too. If I make not this cheat bring out another, and the shearers prove sheep, let me be unroll'd, and my name put in the book of virtue!

[*Sings*]

Jog on, jog on, the footpath way,
    And merrily hent the stile-a;
A merry heart goes all the day,
    Your sad tires in a mile-a.   *Exit*

SCENE 4

Bohemia. The SHEPHERD'S *cottage*

Enter FLORIZEL *and* PERDITA

FLORIZEL. These your unusual weeds to each part of you
Do give a life—no shepherdess, but Flora
Peering in April's front. This your sheep-shearing
Is as a meeting of the petty gods,
And you the Queen on't.

PERDITA. Sir, my gracious lord,
To chide at your extremes it not becomes me—
O, pardon that I name them! Your high self,
The gracious mark o' th' land, you have obscur'd
With a swain's wearing; and me, poor lowly maid,
Most goddess-like prank'd up. But that our feasts
In every mess have folly, and the feeders
Digest it with a custom, I should blush
To see you so attir'd; swoon, I think,
To show myself a glass.

FLORIZEL. I bless the time
When my good falcon made her flight across

1058

Thy father's ground.

PERDITA. Now Jove afford you cause!
To me the difference forges dread; your greatness
Hath not been us'd to fear. Even now I tremble
To think your father, by some accident,
Should pass this way, as you did. O, the Fates!
How would he look to see his work, so noble,
Vilely bound up? What would he say? Or how
Should I, in these my borrowed flaunts, behold
The sternness of his presence?

FLORIZEL. Apprehend
Nothing but jollity. The gods themselves,
Humbling their deities to love, have taken
The shapes of beasts upon them: Jupiter
Became a bull and bellow'd; the green Neptune
A ram and bleated; and the fire-rob'd god,
Golden Apollo, a poor humble swain,
As I seem now. Their transformations
Were never for a piece of beauty rarer,
Nor in a way so chaste, since my desires
Run not before mine honour, nor my lusts
Burn hotter than my faith.

PERDITA. O, but, sir,
Your resolution cannot hold when 'tis
Oppos'd, as it must be, by th' pow'r of the King.
One of these two must be necessities,
Which then will speak, that you must change this purpose,
Or I my life.

FLORIZEL. Thou dearest Perdita,
With these forc'd thoughts, I prithee, darken not
The mirth o' th' feast. Or I'll be thine, my fair,
Or not my father's; for I cannot be
Mine own, nor anything to any, if
I be not thine. To this I am most constant,
Though destiny say no. Be merry, gentle;
Strangle such thoughts as these with any thing
That you behold the while. Your guests are coming.
Lift up your countenance, as it were the day
Of celebration of that nuptial which
We two have sworn shall come.

PERDITA. O Lady Fortune,
Stand you auspicious!
FLORIZEL. See, your guests approach.
Address yourself to entertain them sprightly,
And let's be red with mirth.

Enter SHEPHERD, *with* POLIXENES *and* CAMILLO, *disguised;*
CLOWN, MOPSA, DORCAS, *with* OTHERS

SHEPHERD. Fie, daughter! When my old wife liv'd, upon
This day she was both pantler, butler, cook;
Both dame and servant; welcom'd all; serv'd all;
Would sing her song and dance her turn; now here
At upper end o' th' table, now i' th' middle;
On his shoulder, and his; her face o' fire
With labour, and the thing she took to quench it
She would to each one sip. You are retired,
As if you were a feasted one, and not
The hostess of the meeting. Pray you bid
These unknown friends to's welcome, for it is
A way to make us better friends, more known.
Come, quench your blushes, and present yourself
That which you are, Mistress o' th' Feast. Come on,
And bid us welcome to your sheep-shearing,
As your good flock shall prosper.
PERDITA. [*To* POLIXENES] Sir, welcome.
It is my father's will I should take on me
The hostess-ship o' th' day. [*To* CAMILLO]
You're welcome, sir.
Give me those flow'rs there, Dorcas. Reverend sirs,
For you there's rosemary and rue; these keep
Seeming and savour all the winter long.
Grace and remembrance be to you both!
And welcome to our shearing.
POLIXENES. Shepherdess—
A fair one are you—well you fit our ages
With flow'rs of winter.
PERDITA. Sir, the year growing ancient,
Not yet on summer's death nor on the birth
Of trembling winter, the fairest flow'rs o' th' season
Are our carnations and streak'd gillyvors,

Which some call nature's bastards. Of that kind
Our rustic garden's barren; and I care not
To get slips of them.
POLIXENES. Wherefore, gentle maiden,
Do you neglect them?
PERDITA. For I have heard it said
There is an art which in their piedness shares
With great creating nature.
POLIXENES. Say there be;
Yet nature is made better by no mean
But nature makes that mean; so over that art
Which you say adds to nature, is an art
That nature makes. You see, sweet maid, we marry
A gentler scion to the wildest stock,
And make conceive a bark of baser kind
By bud of nobler race. This is an art
Which does mend nature—change it rather; but
The art itself is nature.
PERDITA. So it is.
POLIXENES. Then make your garden rich in gillyvors,
And do not call them bastards.
PERDITA. I'll not put
The dibble in earth to set one slip of them;
No more than were I painted I would wish
This youth should say 'twere well, and only therefore
Desire to breed by me. Here's flow'rs for you:
Hot lavender, mints, savory, marjoram;
The marigold, that goes to bed wi' th' sun,
And with him rises weeping; these are flow'rs
Of middle summer, and I think they are given
To men of middle age. Y'are very welcome.
CAMILLO. I should leave grazing, were I of your flock,
And only live by gazing.
PERDITA. Out, alas!
You'd be so lean that blasts of January
Would blow you through and through. Now, my fair'st
    friend,
I would I had some flow'rs o' th' spring that might
Become your time of day—and yours, and yours,
That wear upon your virgin branches yet

Your maidenheads growing. O Proserpina,
From the flowers now that, frighted, thou let'st fall
From Dis's waggon!—daffodils,
That come before the swallow dares, and take
The winds of March with beauty; violets, dim
But sweeter than the lids of Juno's eyes
Or Cytherea's breath; pale primroses,
That die unmarried ere they can behold
Bright Phœbus in his strength—a malady
Most incident to maids; bold oxlips, and
The crown-imperial; lilies of all kinds,
The flow'r-de-luce being one. O, these I lack
To make you garlands of, and my sweet friend
To strew him o'er and o'er!

FLORIZEL. What, like a corse?

PERDITA. No; like a bank for love to lie and play on;
Not like a corse; or if—not to be buried,
But quick, and in mine arms. Come, take your flow'rs.
Methinks I play as I have seen them do
In Whitsun pastorals. Sure, this robe of mine
Does change my disposition.

FLORIZEL. What you do
Still betters what is done. When you speak, sweet,
I'd have you do it ever. When you sing,
I'd have you buy and sell so; so give alms;
Pray so; and, for the ord'ring your affairs,
To sing them too. When you do dance, I wish you
A wave o' th' sea, that you might ever do
Nothing but that; move still, still so,
And own no other function. Each your doing,
So singular in each particular,
Crowns what you are doing in the present deeds,
That all your acts are queens.

PERDITA. O Doricles,
Your praises are too large. But that your youth,
And the true blood which peeps fairly through't,
Do plainly give you out an unstain'd shepherd,
With wisdom I might fear, my Doricles,
You woo'd me the false way.

FLORIZEL. I think you have

1062

As little skill to fear as I have purpose
To put you to't. But, come; our dance, I pray.
Your hand, my Perdita; so turtles pair
That never mean to part.
PERDITA. I'll swear for 'em.
POLIXENES. This is the prettiest low-born lass that ever
Ran on the green-sward; nothing she does or seems
But smacks of something greater than herself,
Too noble for this place.
CAMILLO. He tells her something
That makes her blood look out. Good sooth, she is
The queen of curds and cream.
CLOWN. Come on, strike up.
DORCAS. Mopsa must be your mistress; marry, garlic,
To mend her kissing with!
MOPSA. Now, in good time!
CLOWN. Not a word, a word; we stand upon our manners.
Come, strike up.   [*Music*]

Here a dance of SHEPHERDS *and* SHEPHERDESSES

POLIXENES. Pray, good shepherd, what fair swain is this
Which dances with your daughter?
SHEPHERD. They call him Doricles, and boasts himself
To have a worthy feeding; but I have it
Upon his own report, and I believe it:
He looks like sooth. He says he loves my daughter;
I think so too; for never gaz'd the moon
Upon the water as he'll stand and read,
As 'twere my daughter's eyes; and, to be plain,
I think there is not half a kiss to choose
Who loves another best.
POLIXENES. She dances featly.
SHEPHERD. So she does any thing; though I report it
That should be silent. If young Doricles
Do light upon her, she shall bring him that
Which he not dreams of.

Enter a SERVANT

SERVANT. O master, if you did but hear the pedlar at the
door, you would never dance again after a tabor and pipe;

no, the bagpipe could not move you. He sings several tunes faster than you'll tell money; he utters them as he had eaten ballads, and all men's ears grew to his tunes.

CLOWN. He could never come better; he shall come in. I love a ballad but even too well, if it be doleful matter merrily set down, or a very pleasant thing indeed and sung lamentably.

SERVANT. He hath songs for man or woman of all sizes; no milliner can so fit his customers with gloves. He has the prettiest love-songs for maids; so without bawdry, which is strange; with such delicate burdens of dildos and fadings, 'jump her and thump her'; and where some stretch-mouth'd rascal would, as it were, mean mischief, and break a foul gap into the matter, he makes the maid to answer 'Whoop, do me no harm, good man'—puts him off, slights him, with 'Whoop, do me no harm, good man.'

POLIXENES. This is a brave fellow.

CLOWN. Believe me, thou talkest of an admirable conceited fellow. Has he any unbraided wares?

SERVANT. He hath ribbons of all the colours i' th' rainbow; points, more than all the lawyers in Bohemia can learnedly handle, though they come to him by th' gross; inkles, caddisses, cambrics, lawns. Why he sings 'em over as they were gods or goddesses; you would think a smock were a she-angel, he so chants to the sleeve-hand and the work about the square on't.

CLOWN. Prithee bring him in; and let him approach singing.

PERDITA. Forewarn him that he use no scurrilous words in's tunes.   *Exit* SERVANT

CLOWN. You have of these pedlars that have more in them than you'd think, sister.

PERDITA. Ay, good brother, or go about to think.

Enter AUTOLYCUS, *singing*

Lawn as white as driven snow;
Cypress black as e'er was crow;
Gloves as sweet as damask roses;
Masks for faces and for noses;
Bugle bracelet, necklace amber,
Perfume for a lady's chamber;

Golden quoifs and stomachers,
For my lads to give their dears;
Pins and poking-sticks of steel—
What maids lack from head to heel.
Come, buy of me, come; come buy, come buy;
Buy, lads, or else your lasses cry.
Come, buy.

CLOWN. If I were not in love with Mopsa, thou shouldst take no money of me; but being enthrall'd as I am, it will also be the bondage of certain ribbons and gloves.

MOPSA. I was promis'd them against the feast; but they come not too late now.

DORCAS. He hath promis'd you more than that, or there be liars.

MOPSA. He hath paid you all he promis'd you. May be he has paid you more, which will shame you to give him again.

CLOWN. Is there no manners left among maids? Will they wear their plackets where they should bear their faces? Is there not milking-time, when you are going to bed, or kiln-hole, to whistle off these secrets, but you must be tittle-tattling before all our guests? 'Tis well they are whisp'ring. Clammer your tongues, and not a word more.

MOPSA. I have done. Come, you promis'd me a tawdry-lace, and a pair of sweet gloves.

CLOWN. Have I not told thee how I was cozen'd by the way, and lost all my money?

AUTOLYCUS. And indeed, sir, there are cozeners abroad; therefore it behoves men to be wary.

CLOWN. Fear not thou, man; thou shalt lose nothing here.

AUTOLYCUS. I hope so, sir; for I have about me many parcels of charge.

CLOWN. What hast here? Ballads?

MOPSA. Pray now, buy some. I love a ballad in print a-life, for then we are sure they are true.

AUTOLYCUS. Here's one to a very doleful tune: how a usurer's wife was brought to bed of twenty money-bags at a burden, and how she long'd to eat adders' heads and toads carbonado'd.

Mopsa. Is it true, think you?

Autolycus. Very true, and but a month old.

Dorcas. Bless me from marrying a usurer!

Autolycus. Here's the midwife's name to't, one Mistress Taleporter, and five or six honest wives that were present. Why should I carry lies abroad?

Mopsa. Pray you now, buy it.

Clown. Come on, lay it by; and let's first see moe ballads; we'll buy the other things anon.

Autolycus. Here's another ballad, of a fish that appeared upon the coast on Wednesday the fourscore of April, forty thousand fathom above water, and sung this ballad against the hard hearts of maids. It was thought she was a woman, and was turn'd into a cold fish for she would not exchange flesh with one that lov'd her. The ballad is very pitiful, and as true.

Dorcas. Is it true too, think you?

Autolycus. Five justices' hands at it; and witnesses more than my pack will hold.

Clown. Lay it by too. Another.

Autolycus. This is a merry ballad, but a very pretty one.

Mopsa. Let's have some merry ones.

Autolycus. Why, this is a passing merry one, and goes to the tune of 'Two maids wooing a man.' There's scarce a maid westward but she sings it; 'tis in request, I can tell you.

Mopsa. We can both sing it. If thou'lt bear a part, thou shalt hear; 'tis in three parts.

Dorcas. We had the tune on't a month ago.

Autolycus. I can bear my part; you must know 'tis my occupation. Have at it with you.

SONG

Autolycus. Get you hence, for I must go
Where it fits not you to know.

Dorcas. Whither?

Mopsa. O, whither?

Dorcas. Whither?

Mopsa. It becomes thy oath full well
Thou to me thy secrets tell.

DORCAS.   Me too! Let me go thither
MOPSA.   Or thou goest to th' grange or mill.
DORCAS.   If to either, thou dost ill.
AUTOLYCUS. Neither.
DORCAS.   What, neither?
AUTOLYCUS.   Neither.
DORCAS.   Thou hast sworn my love to be.
MOPSA.   Thou hast sworn it more to me.
            Then whither goest? Say, whither?

CLOWN. We'll have this song out anon by ourselves; my
father and the gentlemen are in sad talk, and we'll not
trouble them. Come, bring away thy pack after me.
Wenches, I'll buy for you both. Pedlar, let's have the first
choice. Follow me, girls.   *Exit with* DORCAS *and* MOPSA
AUTOLYCUS. And you shall pay well for 'em.

                              Exit AUTOLYCUS, *singing*

            Will you buy any tape,
            Or lace for your cape,
            My dainty duck, my dear-a?
            Any silk, any thread,
            Any toys for your head,
            Of the new'st and fin'st, fin'st wear-a?
            Come to the pedlar;
            Money's a meddler
            That doth utter all men's ware-a.

                    Re-enter SERVANT

SERVANT. Master, there is three carters, three shepherds, three
neat-herds, three swineherds, that have made themselves all
men of hair; they call themselves Saltiers, and they have a
dance which the wenches say is a gallimaufry of gambols,
because they are not in't; but they themselves are o' th'
mind, if it be not too rough for some that know little but
bowling, it will please plentifully.
SHEPHERD. Away! We'll none on't; here has been too much
homely foolery already. I know, sir, we weary you.
POLIXENES. You weary those that refresh us. Pray, let's see
these four threes of herdsmen.
SERVANT. One three of them, by their own report, sir, hath

danc'd before the King; and not the worst of the three but
jumps twelve foot and a half by th' squier.

SHEPHERD. Leave your prating; since these good men are
pleas'd, let them come in; but quickly now.

SERVANT. Why, they stay at door, sir. *Exit*

Here a dance of twelve SATYRS

POLIXENES. [*To* SHEPHERD] O, father, you'll know more of
that hereafter.

[*To* CAMILLO] Is it not too far gone? 'Tis time to part
them.

He's simple and tells much. [*To* FLORIZEL] How now, fair
shepherd!
Your heart is full of something that does take
Your mind from feasting. Sooth, when I was young
And handed love as you do, I was wont
To load my she with knacks; I would have ransack'd
The pedlar's silken treasury and have pour'd it
To her acceptance: you have let him go
And nothing marted with him. If your lass
Interpretation should abuse and call this
Your lack of love or bounty, you were straited
For a reply, at least if you make a care
Of happy holding her.

FLORIZEL. Old sir, I know
She prizes not such trifles as these are.
The gifts she looks from me are pack'd and lock'd
Up in my heart, which I have given already,
But not deliver'd. O, hear me breathe my life
Before this ancient sir, whom, it should seem,
Hath sometime lov'd. I take thy hand—this hand,
As soft as dove's down and as white as it,
Or Ethiopian's tooth, or the fann'd snow that's bolted
By th' northern blasts twice o'er.

POLIXENES. What follows this?
How prettily the young swain seems to wash
The hand was fair before! I have put you out.
But to your protestation; let me hear
What you profess.

FLORIZEL. Do, and be witness to't.

POLIXENES. And this my neighbour too?
FLORIZEL. And he, and more
　Than he, and men—the earth, the heavens, and all:
　That, were I crown'd the most imperial monarch,
　Thereof most worthy, were I the fairest youth
　That ever made eye swerve, had force and knowledge
　More than was ever man's, I would not prize them
　Without her love; for her employ them all;
　Commend them and condemn them to her service
　Or to their own perdition.
POLIXENES. Fairly offer'd.
CAMILLO. This shows a sound affection.
SHEPHERD. But, my daughter,
　Say you the like to him?
PERDITA. I cannot speak
　So well, nothing so well; no, nor mean better.
　By th' pattern of mine own thoughts I cut out
　The purity of his.
SHEPHERD. Take hands, a bargain!
　And, friends unknown, you shall bear witness to't:
　I give my daughter to him, and will make
　Her portion equal his.
FLORIZEL. O, that must be
　I' th' virtue of your daughter. One being dead,
　I shall have more than you can dream of yet;
　Enough then for your wonder. But come on,
　Contract us fore these witnesses.
SHEPHERD. Come, your hand;
　And, daughter, yours.
POLIXENES. Soft, swain, awhile, beseech you;
　Have you a father?
FLORIZEL. I have, but what of him?
POLIXENES. Knows he of this?
FLORIZEL. He neither does nor shall.
POLIXENES. Methinks a father
　Is at the nuptial of his son a guest
　That best becomes the table. Pray you, once more,
　Is not your father grown incapable
　Of reasonable affairs? Is he not stupid
　With age and alt'ring rheums? Can he speak, hear,

Know man from man, dispute his own estate?
Lies he not bed-rid, and again does nothing
But what he did being childish?

FLORIZEL. No, good sir;
He has his health, and ampler strength indeed
Than most have of his age.

POLIXENES. By my white beard,
You offer him, if this be so, a wrong
Something unfilial. Reason my son
Should choose himself a wife; but as good reason
The father—all whose joy is nothing else
But fair posterity—should hold some counsel
In such a business.

FLORIZEL. I yield all this;
But, for some other reasons, my grave sir,
Which 'tis not fit you know, I not acquaint
My father of this business.

POLIXENES. Let him know't.

FLORIZEL. He shall not.

POLIXENES. Prithee let him.

FLORIZEL. No, he must not.

SHEPHERD. Let him, my son; he shall not need to grieve
At knowing of thy choice.

FLORIZEL. Come, come, he must not.
Mark our contract.

POLIXENES. [Discovering himself] Mark your divorce, young
sir,
Whom son I dare not call; thou art too base
To be acknowledg'd—thou a sceptre's heir,
That thus affects a sheep-hook! Thou, old traitor,
I am sorry that by hanging thee I can but
Shorten thy life one week. And thou, fresh piece
Of excellent witchcraft, who of force must know
The royal fool thou cop'st with—

SHEPHERD. O, my heart!

POLIXENES. I'll have thy beauty scratch'd with briers and
made
More homely than thy state. For thee, fond boy,
If I may ever know thou dost but sigh
That thou no more shalt see this knack—as never

I mean thou shalt—we'll bar thee from succession;
Not hold thee of our blood, no, not our kin,
Farre than Deucalion off. Mark thou my words.
Follow us to the court. Thou churl, for this time,
Though full of our displeasure, yet we free thee
From the dead blow of it. And you, enchantment,
Worthy enough a herdsman—yea, him too
That makes himself, but for our honour therein,
Unworthy thee—if ever henceforth thou
These rural latches to his entrance open,
Or hoop his body more with thy embraces,
I will devise a death as cruel for thee
As thou art tender to't.   *Exit*

PERDITA. Even here undone!
I was not much afeard; for once or twice
I was about to speak and tell him plainly
The self-same sun that shines upon his court
Hides not his visage from our cottage, but
Looks on alike. [*To* FLORIZEL] Will't please you, sir, be
  gone?
I told you what would come of this. Beseech you,
Of your own state take care. This dream of mine—
Being now awake, I'll queen it no inch farther,
But milk my ewes and weep.

CAMILLO. Why, how now, father!
Speak ere thou diest.

SHEPHERD. I cannot speak nor think,
Nor dare to know that which I know. [*To* FLORIZEL] O
  sir,
You have undone a man of fourscore-three
That thought to fill his grave in quiet, yea,
To die upon the bed my father died,
To lie close by his honest bones; but now
Some hangman must put on my shroud and lay me
Where no priest shovels in dust. [*To* PERDITA] O cursed
  wretch,
That knew'st this was the Prince, and wouldst adventure
To mingle faith with him!—Undone, undone!
If I might die within this hour, I have liv'd
To die when I desire.   *Exit*

POLIXENES. *Pray, good shepherd, what fair swain is this*
Which dances with your daughter? (ACT IV. SCENE III)

FLORIZEL. Why look you so upon me?
I am but sorry, not afeard; delay'd,
But nothing alt'red. What I was, I am:
More straining on for plucking back; not following
My leash unwillingly.
CAMILLO. Gracious, my lord,
You know your father's temper. At this time
He will allow no speech—which I do guess
You do not purpose to him—and as hardly
Will he endure your sight as yet, I fear;
Then, till the fury of his Highness settle,
Come not before him.
FLORIZEL. I not purpose it.
I think Camillo?
CAMILLO. Even he, my lord.
PERDITA. How often have I told you 'twould be thus!
How often said my dignity would last
But till 'twere known!
FLORIZEL. It cannot fail but by
The violation of my faith; and then
Let nature crush the sides o' th' earth together
And mar the seeds within! Lift up thy looks.
From my succession wipe me, father; I
Am heir to my affection.
CAMILLO. Be advis'd.
FLORIZEL. I am—and by my fancy; if my reason
Will thereto be obedient, I have reason;
If not, my senses, better pleas'd with madness,
Do bid it welcome.
CAMILLO. This is desperate, sir.
FLORIZEL. So call it; but it does fulfil my vow:
I needs must think it honesty. Camillo,
Not for Bohemia, nor the pomp that may
Be thereat glean'd, for all the sun sees or
The close earth wombs, or the profound seas hides
In unknown fathoms, will I break my oath
To this my fair belov'd. Therefore, I pray you,
As you have ever been my father's honour'd friend,
When he shall miss me—as, in faith, I mean not
To see him any more—cast your good counsels

Upon his passion. Let myself and Fortune
Tug for the time to come. This you may know,
And so deliver: I am put to sea
With her who here I cannot hold on shore.
And most opportune to her need I have
A vessel rides fast by, but not prepar'd
For this design. What course I mean to hold
Shall nothing benefit your knowledge, nor
Concern me the reporting.

CAMILLO. O my lord,
I would your spirit were easier for advice,
Or stronger for your need.

FLORIZEL. Hark, Perdita.   *[Takes her aside]*
[*To* CAMILLO] I'll hear you by and by.

CAMILLO. He's irremovable,
Resolv'd for flight. Now were I happy if
His going I could frame to serve my turn,
Save him from danger, do him love and honour,
Purchase the sight again of dear Sicilia
And that unhappy king, my master, whom
I so much thirst to see.

FLORIZEL. Now, good Camillo,
I am so fraught with curious business that
I leave out ceremony.

CAMILLO. Sir, I think
You have heard of my poor services i' th' love
That I have borne your father?

FLORIZEL. Very nobly
Have you deserv'd. It is my father's music
To speak your deeds; not little of his care
To have them recompens'd as thought on.

CAMILLO. Well, my lord,
If you may please to think I love the King,
And through him what's nearest to him, which is
Your gracious self, embrace but my direction.
If your more ponderous and settled project
May suffer alteration, on mine honour,
I'll point you where you shall have such receiving
As shall become your Highness; where you may
Enjoy your mistress, from the whom, I see,

There's no disjunction to be made but by,
As heavens forfend! your ruin—marry her;
And with my best endeavours in your absence
Your discontenting father strive to qualify,
And bring him up to liking.

FLORIZEL. How, Camillo,
May this, almost a miracle, be done?
That I may call thee something more than man,
And after that trust to thee.

CAMILLO. Have you thought on
A place whereto you'll go?

FLORIZEL. Not any yet;
But as th' unthought-on accident is guilty
To what we wildly do, so we profess
Ourselves to be the slaves of chance and flies
Of every wind that blows.

CAMILLO. Then list to me.
This follows, if you will not change your purpose
But undergo this flight: make for Sicilia,
And there present yourself and your fair princess—
For so, I see, she must be—fore Leontes.
She shall be habited as it becomes
The partner of your bed. Methinks I see
Leontes opening his free arms and weeping
His welcomes forth; asks thee there 'Son, forgiveness!'
As 'twere i' th' father's person; kisses the hands
Of your fresh princess; o'er and o'er divides him
'Twixt his unkindness and his kindness—th'one
He chides to hell, and bids the other grow
Faster than thought or time.

FLORIZEL. Worthy Camillo,
What colour for my visitation shall I
Hold up before him?

CAMILLO. Sent by the King your father
To greet him and to give him comforts. Sir,
The manner of your bearing towards him, with
What you as from your father shall deliver,
Things known betwixt us three, I'll write you down;
The which shall point you forth at every sitting
What you must say, that he shall not perceive

But that you have your father's bosom there
And speak his very heart.
FLORIZEL. I am bound to you.
There is some sap in this.
CAMILLO. A course more promising
Than a wild dedication of yourselves
To unpath'd waters, undream'd shores, most certain
To miseries enough; no hope to help you,
But as you shake off one to take another;
Nothing so certain as your anchors, who
Do their best office if they can but stay you
Where you'll be loath to be. Besides, you know
Prosperity's the very bond of love,
Whose fresh complexion and whose heart together
Affliction alters.
PERDITA. One of these is true:
I think affliction may subdue the cheek,
But not take in the mind.
CAMILLO. Yea, say you so?
There shall not at your father's house these seven years
Be born another such.
FLORIZEL. My good Camillo,
She is as forward of her breeding as
She is i' th' rear o' our birth.
CAMILLO. I cannot say 'tis pity
She lacks instructions, for she seems a mistress
To most that teach.
PERDITA. Your pardon, sir; for this
I'll blush you thanks.
FLORIZEL. My prettiest Perdita!
But, O, the thorns we stand upon! Camillo—
Preserver of my father, now of me;
The medicine of our house—how shall we do?
We are not furnish'd like Bohemia's son;
Nor shall appear in Sicilia.
CAMILLO. My lord,
Fear none of this. I think you know my fortunes
Do all lie there. It shall be so my care
To have you royally appointed as if
The scene you play were mine. For instance, sir,

That you may know you shall not want—one word.

[They talk aside]

Re-enter AUTOLYCUS

AUTOLYCUS. Ha, ha! what a fool Honesty is! and Trust, his sworn brother, a very simple gentleman! I have sold all my trumpery; not a counterfeit stone, not a ribbon, glass, pomander, brooch, table-book, ballad, knife, tape, glove, shoe-tie, bracelet, horn-ring, to keep my pack from fasting. They throng who should buy first, as if my trinkets had been hallowed and brought a benediction to the buyer; by which means I saw whose purse was best in picture; and what I saw, to my good use I rememb'red. My clown, who wants but something to be a reasonable man, grew so in love with the wenches' song that he would not stir his pettitoes till he had both tune and words, which so drew the rest of the herd to me that all their other senses stuck in ears. You might have pinch'd a placket, it was senseless; 'twas nothing to geld a codpiece of a purse; I would have fil'd keys off that hung in chains. No hearing, no feeling, but my sir's song, and admiring the nothing of it. So that in this time of lethargy I pick'd and cut most of their festival purses; and had not the old man come in with a whoobub against his daughter and the King's son and scar'd my choughs from the chaff, I had not left a purse alive in the whole army.

CAMILLO, FLORIZEL, *and* PERDITA *come forward*

CAMILLO. Nay, but my letters, by this means being there
So soon as you arrive, shall clear that doubt.
FLORIZEL. And those that you'll procure from King Leontes?
CAMILLO. Shall satisfy your father.
PERDITA. Happy be you!
All that you speak shows fair.
CAMILLO. [*seeing* AUTOLYCUS] Who have we here?
We'll make an instrument of this; omit
Nothing may give us aid.
AUTOLYCUS. [*Aside*] If they have overheard me now—why,
hanging.
CAMILLO. How now, good fellow! Why shak'st thou so?

Fear not, man; here's no harm intended to thee.

AUTOLYCUS. I am a poor fellow, sir.

CAMILLO. Why, be so still; here's nobody will steal that from thee. Yet for the outside of thy poverty we must make an exchange; therefore discase thee instantly—thou must think there's a necessity in't—and change garments with this gentleman. Though the pennyworth on his side be the worst, yet hold thee, there's some boot.   [*Giving money*]

AUTOLYCUS. I am a poor fellow, sir. [*Aside*] I know ye well enough.

CAMILLO. Nay, prithee dispatch. The gentleman is half flay'd already.

AUTOLYCUS. Are you in earnest, sir? [*Aside*] I smell the trick on't.

FLORIZEL. Dispatch, I prithee.

AUTOLYCUS. Indeed, I have had earnest; but I cannot with conscience take it.

CAMILLO. Unbuckle, unbuckle.

FLORIZEL *and* AUTOLYCUS *exchange garments*

Fortunate mistress—let my prophecy
Come home to ye!—you must retire yourself
Into some covert; take your sweetheart's hat
And pluck it o'er your brows, muffle your face,
Dismantle you, and, as you can, disliken
The truth of your own seeming, that you may—
For I do fear eyes over—to shipboard
Get undescried.

PERDITA. I see the play so lies
That I must bear a part.

CAMILLO. No remedy.
Have you done there?

FLORIZEL. Should I now meet my father,
He would not call me son.

CAMILLO. Nay, you shall have no hat.
                                            [*Giving it to* PERDITA]
Come, lady, come. Farewell, my friend.

AUTOLYCUS. Adieu, sir.

FLORIZEL. O Perdita, what have we twain forgot!
Pray you a word.   [*They converse apart*]

ACT IV. SCENE 4

CAMILLO. *[Aside]* What I do next shall be to tell the King
Of this escape, and whither they are bound;
Wherein my hope is I shall so prevail
To force him after; in whose company
I shall re-view Sicilia, for whose sight
I have a woman's longing.
FLORIZEL. Fortune speed us!
Thus we set on, Camillo, to th' sea-side.
CAMILLO. The swifter speed the better.
            Exeunt FLORIZEL, PERDITA, *and* CAMILLO
AUTOLYCUS. I understand the business, I hear it. To have an
open ear, a quick eye, and a nimble hand, is necessary for
a cut-purse; a good nose is requisite also, to smell out work
for th' other senses. I see this is the time that the unjust
man doth thrive. What an exchange had this been without
boot! What a boot is here with this exchange! Sure, the
gods do this year connive at us, and we may do anything
extempore. The Prince himself is about a piece of iniquity
—stealing away from his father with his clog at his heels. If
I thought it were a piece of honesty to acquaint the King
withal, I would not do't. I hold it the more knavery to
conceal it; and therein am I constant to my profession.

      Re-enter CLOWN *and* SHEPHERD

Aside, aside—here is more matter for a hot brain. Every
lane's end, every shop, church, session, hanging, yields a
careful man work.
CLOWN. See, see; what a man you are now! There is no
other way but to tell the King she's a changeling and none
of your flesh and blood.
SHEPHERD. Nay, but hear me.
CLOWN. Nay—but hear me.
SHEPHERD. Go to, then.
CLOWN. She being none of your flesh and blood, your flesh
and blood has not offended the King; and so your flesh
and blood is not to be punish'd by him. Show those things
you found about her, those secret things—all but what she
has with her. This being done, let the law go whistle; I
warrant you.
SHEPHERD. I will tell the King all, every word—yea, and his

1079

son's pranks too; who, I may say, is no honest man, neither
to his father nor to me, to go about to make me the King's
brother-in-law.

CLOWN. Indeed, brother-in-law was the farthest off you
could have been to him; and then your blood had been the
dearer by I know how much an ounce.

AUTOLYCUS. [Aside] Very wisely, puppies!

SHEPHERD. Well, let us to the King. There is that in this
fardel will make him scratch his beard.

AUTOLYCUS. [Aside] I know not what impediment this complaint may be to the flight of my master.

CLOWN. Pray heartily he be at palace.

AUTOLYCUS. [Aside] Though I am not naturally honest, I am
so sometimes by chance. Let me pocket up my pedlar's
excrement. [Takes off his false beard] How now, rustics!
Whither are you bound?

SHEPHERD. To th' palace, an it like your worship.

AUTOLYCUS. Your affairs there, what, with whom, the condition of that fardel, the place of your dwelling, your names,
your ages, of what having, breeding, and anything that is
fitting to be known—discover.

CLOWN. We are but plain fellows, sir.

AUTOLYCUS. A lie: you are rough and hairy. Let me have no
lying; it becomes none but tradesmen, and they often give
us soldiers the lie; but we pay them for it with stamped
coin, not stabbing steel; therefore they do not give us the
lie.

CLOWN. Your worship had like to have given us one, if you
had not taken yourself with the manner.

SHEPHERD. Are you a courtier, an't like you, sir?

AUTOLYCUS. Whether it like me or no, I am a courtier. Seest
thou not the air of the court in these enfoldings? Hath not
my gait in it the measure of the court? Receives not thy
nose court-odour from me? Reflect I not on thy baseness
court-contempt? Think'st thou, for that I insinuate, that
toaze from thee thy business, I am therefore no courtier?
I am courtier cap-a-pe, and one that will either push on or
pluck back thy business there; whereupon I command thee
to open thy affair.

SHEPHERD. My business, sir, is to the King.

AUTOLYCUS. What advocate hast thou to him?

SHEPHERD. I know not, an't like you.

CLOWN. Advocate's the court-word for a pheasant; say you have none.

SHEPHERD. None, sir; I have no pheasant, cock nor hen.

AUTOLYCUS. How blessed are we that are not simple men!
Yet nature might have made me as these are,
Therefore I will not disdain.

CLOWN. This cannot be but a great courtier.

SHEPHERD. His garments are rich, but he wears them not handsomely.

CLOWN. He seems to be the more noble in being fantastical.
A great man, I'll warrant; I know by the picking on's teeth.

AUTOLYCUS. The fardel there? What's i' th' fardel? Wherefore that box?

SHEPHERD. Sir, there lies such secrets in this fardel and box which none must know but the King; and which he shall know within this hour, if I may come to th' speech of him.

AUTOLYCUS. Age, thou hast lost thy labour.

SHEPHERD. Why, sir?

AUTOLYCUS. The King is not at the palace; he is gone aboard a new ship to purge melancholy and air himself; for, if thou be'st capable of things serious, thou must know the King is full of grief.

SHEPHERD. So 'tis said, sir—about his son, that should have married a shepherd's daughter.

AUTOLYCUS. If that shepherd be not in hand-fast, let him fly; the curses he shall have, the tortures he shall feel, will break the back of man, the heart of monster.

CLOWN. Think you so, sir?

AUTOLYCUS. Not he alone shall suffer what wit can make heavy and vengeance bitter; but those that are germane to him, though remov'd fifty times, shall all come under the hangman—which, though it be great pity, yet it is necessary. An old sheep-whistling rogue, a ram-tender, to offer to have his daughter come into grace! Some say he shall be ston'd; but that death is too soft for him, say I. Draw our throne into a sheep-cote!—all deaths are too few, the sharpest too easy.

CLOWN. Has the old man e'er a son, sir, do you hear, an't like you, sir?

AUTOLYCUS. He has a son—who shall be flay'd alive; then 'nointed over with honey, set on the head of a wasp's nest; then stand till he be three quarters and a dram dead; then recover'd again with aqua-vitæ or some other hot infusion; then, raw as he is, and in the hottest day prognostication proclaims, shall he be set against a brick wall, the sun looking with a southward eye upon him, where he is to behold him with flies blown to death. But what talk we of these traitorly rascals, whose miseries are to be smil'd at, their offences being so capital? Tell me, for you seem to be honest plain men, what you have to the King. Being something gently consider'd, I'll bring you where he is aboard, tender your persons to his presence, whisper him in your behalfs; and if it be in man besides the King to effect your suits, here is man shall do it.

CLOWN. He seems to be of great authority. Close with him, give him gold; and though authority be a stubborn bear, yet he is oft led by the nose with gold. Show the inside of your purse to the outside of his hand, and no more ado. Remember—ston'd and flay'd alive.

SHEPHERD. An't please you, sir, to undertake the business for us, here is that gold I have. I'll make it as much more, and leave this young man in pawn till I bring it you.

AUTOLYCUS. After I have done what I promised?

SHEPHERD. Ay, sir.

AUTOLYCUS. Well, give me the moiety. Are you a party in this business?

CLOWN. In some sort, sir; but though my case be a pitiful one, I hope I shall not be flay'd out of it.

AUTOLYCUS. O, that's the case of the shepherd's son! Hang him, he'll be made an example.

CLOWN. Comfort, good comfort! We must to the King and show our strange sights. He must know 'tis none of your daughter nor my sister; we are gone else. Sir, I will give you as much as this old man does, when the business is performed; and remain, as he says, your pawn till it be brought you.

AUTOLYCUS. I will trust you. Walk before toward the sea-side; go on the right-hand; I will but look upon the hedge, and follow you.

CLOWN. We are blest in this man, as I may say, even blest.

SHEPHERD. Let's before, as he bids us. He was provided to do us good. *Exeunt* SHEPHERD *and* CLOWN

AUTOLYCUS. If I had a mind to be honest, I see Fortune would not suffer me: she drops booties in my mouth. I am courted now with a double occasion—gold, and a means to do the Prince my master good; which who knows how that may turn back to my advancement? I will bring these two moles, these blind ones, aboard him. If he think it fit to shore them again, and that the complaint they have to the King concerns him nothing, let him call me rogue for being so far officious; for I am proof against that title, and what shame else belongs to't. To him will I present them. There may be matter in it. *Exit*

ACT V. SCENE 1

Sicilia. The palace of LEONTES

Enter LEONTES, CLEOMENES, DION, PAULINA, *and* OTHERS

CLEOMENES. Sir, you have done enough, and have perform'd
A saint-like sorrow. No fault could you make
Which you have not redeem'd; indeed, paid down
More penitence than done trespass. At the last,
Do as the heavens have done: forget your evil;
With them forgive yourself.

LEONTES. Whilst I remember
Her and her virtues, I cannot forget
My blemishes in them, and so still think of
The wrong I did myself; which was so much
That heirless it hath made my kingdom, and
Destroy'd the sweet'st companion that e'er man
Bred his hopes out of.

PAULINA. True, too true, my lord.
If, one by one, you wedded all the world,

Or from the all that are took something good
To make a perfect woman, she you kill'd
Would be unparallel'd.
LEONTES. I think so. Kill'd!
She I kill'd! I did so; but thou strik'st me
Sorely, to say I did. It is as bitter
Upon thy tongue as in my thought. Now, good now,
Say so but seldom.
CLEOMENES. Not at all, good lady.
You might have spoken a thousand things that would
Have done the time more benefit, and grac'd
Your kindness better.
PAULINA. You are one of those
Would have him wed again.
DION. If you would not so,
You pity not the state, nor the remembrance
Of his most sovereign name; consider little
What dangers, by his Highness' fail of issue,
May drop upon his kingdom and devour
Incertain lookers-on. What were more holy
Than to rejoice the former queen is well?
What holier than, for royalty's repair,
For present comfort, and for future good,
To bless the bed of majesty again
With a sweet fellow to't?
PAULINA. There is none worthy,
Respecting her that's gone. Besides, the gods
Will have fulfill'd their secret purposes;
For has not the divine Apollo said,
Is't not the tenour of his oracle,
That King Leontes shall not have an heir
Till his lost child be found? Which that it shall,
Is all as monstrous to our human reason
As my Antigonus to break his grave
And come again to me; who, on my life,
Did perish with the infant. 'Tis your counsel
My lord should to the heavens be contrary,
Oppose against their wills. [*To* LEONTES] Care not for
issue;
The crown will find an heir. Great Alexander

Left his to th' worthiest; so his successor
Was like to be the best.
LEONTES. Good Paulina,
Who hast the memory of Hermione,
I know, in honour, O that ever I
Had squar'd me to thy counsel! Then, even now,
I might have look'd upon my queen's full eyes,
Have taken treasure from her lips—
PAULINA. And left them
More rich for what they yielded.
LEONTES. Thou speak'st truth.
No more such wives; therefore, no wife. One worse,
And better us'd, would make her sainted spirit
Again possess her corpse, and on this stage,
Where we offend her now, appear soul-vex'd,
And begin 'Why to me'—
PAULINA. Had she such power,
She had just cause.
LEONTES. She had; and would incense me
To murder her I married.
PAULINA. I should so.
Were I the ghost that walk'd, I'd bid you mark
Her eye, and tell me for what dull part in't
You chose her; then I'd shriek, that even your ears
Should rift to hear me; and the words that follow'd
Should be 'Remember mine.'
LEONTES. Stars, stars,
And all eyes else dead coals! Fear thou no wife;
I'll have no wife, Paulina.
PAULINA. Will you swear
Never to marry but by my free leave?
LEONTES. Never, Paulina; so be blest my spirit!
PAULINA. Then, good my lords, bear witness to his oath.
CLEOMENES. You tempt him over-much.
PAULINA. Unless another,
As like Hermione as is her picture,
Affront his eye.
CLEOMENES. Good madam—
PAULINA. I have done.
Yet, if my lord will marry—if you will, sir,

No remedy but you will—give me the office
To choose you a queen. She shall not be so young
As was your former; but she shall be such
As, walk'd your first queen's ghost, it should take joy
To see her in your arms.
LEONTES. My true Paulina,
We shall not marry till thou bid'st us.
PAULINA. That
Shall be when your first queen's again in breath;
Never till then.

Enter a GENTLEMAN

GENTLEMAN. One that gives out himself Prince Florizel,
Son of Polixenes, with his princess—she
The fairest I have yet beheld—desires access
To your high presence.
LEONTES. What with him? He comes not
Like to his father's greatness. His approach,
So out of circumstance and sudden, tells us
'Tis not a visitation fram'd, but forc'd
By need and accident. What train?
GENTLEMAN. But few,
And those but mean.
LEONTES. His princess, say you, with him?
GENTLEMAN. Ay; the most peerless piece of earth, I think,
That e'er the sun shone bright on.
PAULINA. O Hermione,
As every present time doth boast itself
Above a better gone, so must thy grave
Give way to what's seen now! Sir, you yourself
Have said and writ so, but your writing now
Is colder than that theme: 'She had not been,
Nor was not to be equall'd.' Thus your verse
Flow'd with her beauty once; 'tis shrewdly ebb'd,
To say you have seen a better.
GENTLEMAN. Pardon, madam.
The one I have almost forgot—your pardon;
The other, when she has obtain'd your eye,
Will have your tongue too. This is a creature,
Would she begin a sect, might quench the zeal

Of all professors else, make proselytes
Of who she but bid follow.

PAULINA. How! not women?

GENTLEMAN. Women will love her that she is a woman
More worth than any man; men, that she is
The rarest of all women.

LEONTES. Go, Cleomenes;
Yourself, assisted with your honour'd friends,
Bring them to our embracement.   *Exeunt*
Still, 'tis strange
He thus should steal upon us.

PAULINA. Had our prince,
Jewel of children, seen this hour, he had pair'd
Well with this lord; there was not full a month
Between their births.

LEONTES. Prithee no more; cease. Thou know'st
He dies to me again when talk'd of. Sure,
When I shall see this gentleman, thy speeches
Will bring me to consider that which may
Unfurnish me of reason.

Re-enter CLEOMENES, *with* FLORIZEL, PERDITA, *and*
ATTENDANTS

They are come.
Your mother was most true to wedlock, Prince;
For she did print your royal father off,
Conceiving you. Were I but twenty-one,
Your father's image is so hit in you,
His very air, that I should call you brother,
As I did him, and speak of something wildly
By us perform'd before. Most dearly welcome!
And your fair princess—goddess! O, alas!
I lost a couple that 'twixt heaven and earth
Might thus have stood begetting wonder as
You, gracious couple, do. And then I lost—
All mine own folly—the society,
Amity too, of your brave father, whom,
Though bearing misery, I desire my life
Once more to look on him.

FLORIZEL. By his command

Have I here touch'd Sicilia, and from him
Give you all greetings that a king, at friend,
Can send his brother; and, but infirmity,
Which waits upon worn times, hath something seiz'd
His wish'd ability, he had himself
The lands and waters 'twixt your throne and his
Measur'd, to look upon you; whom he loves,
He bade me say so, more than all the sceptres
And those that bear them living.

LEONTES. O my brother—
Good gentleman!—the wrongs I have done thee stir
Afresh within me; and these thy offices,
So rarely kind, are as interpreters
Of my behind-hand slackness! Welcome hither,
As is the spring to th' earth. And hath he too
Expos'd this paragon to th' fearful usage,
At least ungentle, of the dreadful Neptune,
To greet a man not worth her pains, much less
Th' adventure of her person?

FLORIZEL. Good, my lord,
She came from Libya.

LEONTES. Where the warlike Smalus,
That noble honour'd lord, is fear'd and lov'd?

FLORIZEL. Most royal sir, from thence; from him whose
daughter
His tears proclaim'd his, parting with her; thence,
A prosperous south-wind friendly, we have cross'd,
To execute the charge my father gave me
For visiting your Highness. My best train
I have from your Sicilian shores dismiss'd;
Who for Bohemia bend, to signify
Not only my success in Libya, sir,
But my arrival and my wife's in safety
Here where we are.

LEONTES. The blessed gods
Purge all infection from our air whilst you
Do climate here! You have a holy father,
A graceful gentleman, against whose person,
So sacred as it is, I have done sin,
For which the heavens, taking angry note,

Have left me issueless; and your father's blest,
As he from heaven merits it, with you,
Worthy his goodness. What might I have been,
Might I a son and daughter now have look'd on,
Such goodly things as you!

Enter a LORD

LORD. Most noble sir,
That which I shall report will bear no credit,
Were not the proof so nigh. Please you, great sir,
Bohemia greets you from himself by me;
Desires you to attach his son, who has—
His dignity and duty both cast off—
Fled from his father, from his hopes, and with
A shepherd's daughter.
LEONTES. Where's Bohemia? Speak.
LORD. Here in your city; I now came from him.
I speak amazedly; and it becomes
My marvel and my message. To your court
Whiles he was hast'ning—in the chase, it seems,
Of this fair couple—meets he on the way
The father of this seeming lady and
Her brother, having both their country quitted
With this young prince.
FLORIZEL. Camillo has betray'd me;
Whose honour and whose honesty till now
Endur'd all weathers.
LORD. Lay't so to his charge;
He's with the King your father.
LEONTES. Who? Camillo?
LORD. Camillo, sir; I spake with him; who now
Has these poor men in question. Never saw I
Wretches so quake. They kneel, they kiss the earth;
Forswear themselves as often as they speak.
Bohemia stops his ears, and threatens them
With divers deaths in death.
PERDITA. O my poor father!
The heaven sets spies upon us, will not have
Our contract celebrated.
LEONTES. You are married?

FLORIZEL. We are not, sir, nor are we like to be;
  The stars, I see, will kiss the valleys first.
  The odds for high and low's alike.
LEONTES. My lord,
  Is this the daughter of a king?
FLORIZEL. She is,
  When once she is my wife.
LEONTES. That 'once,' I see by your good father's speed,
  Will come on very slowly. I am sorry,
  Most sorry, you have broken from his liking
  Where you were tied in duty; and as sorry
  Your choice is not so rich in worth as beauty,
  That you might well enjoy her.
FLORIZEL. Dear, look up.
  Though Fortune, visible an enemy,
  Should chase us with my father, pow'r no jot
  Hath she to change our loves. Beseech you, sir,
  Remember since you ow'd no more to time
  Than I do now. With thought of such affections,
  Step forth mine advocate; at your request
  My father will grant precious things as trifles.
LEONTES. Would he do so, I'd beg your precious mistress,
  Which he counts but a trifle.
PAULINA. Sir, my liege,
  Your eye hath too much youth in't. Not a month
  Fore your queen died, she was more worth such gazes
  Than what you look on now.
LEONTES. I thought of her
  Even in these looks I made. [*To* FLORIZEL] But your petition
  Is yet unanswer'd. I will to your father.
  Your honour not o'erthrown by your desires,
  I am friend to them and you. Upon which errand
  I now go toward him; therefore, follow me,
  And mark what way I make. Come, good my lord.
                                    Exeunt

SCENE 2

Sicilia. Before the palace of LEONTES

Enter AUTOLYCUS *and a* GENTLEMAN

AUTOLYCUS. Beseech you, sir, were you present at this relation?

FIRST GENTLEMAN. I was by at the opening of the fardel, heard the old shepherd deliver the manner how he found it; whereupon, after a little amazedness, we were all commanded out of the chamber; only this, methought I heard the shepherd say he found the child.

AUTOLYCUS. I would most gladly know the issue of it.

FIRST GENTLEMAN. I make a broken delivery of the business; but the changes I perceived in the King and Camillo were very notes of admiration. They seem'd almost, with staring on one another, to tear the cases of their eyes; there was speech in their dumbness, language in their very gesture; they look'd as they had heard of a world ransom'd, or one destroyed. A notable passion of wonder appeared in them; but the wisest beholder that knew no more but seeing could not say if th' importance were joy or sorrow—but in the extremity of the one it must needs be.

Enter another GENTLEMAN

Here comes a gentleman that happily knows more. The news, Rogero?

SECOND GENTLEMAN. Nothing but bonfires. The oracle is fulfill'd: the King's daughter is found. Such a deal of wonder is broken out within this hour that ballad-makers cannot be able to express it.

Enter another GENTLEMAN

Here comes the Lady Paulina's steward; he can deliver you more. How goes it now, sir? This news, which is call'd true, is so like an old tale that the verity of it is in strong suspicion. Has the King found his heir?

THIRD GENTLEMAN. Most true, if ever truth were pregnant by circumstance. That which you hear you'll swear you see, there is such unity in the proofs. The mantle of Queen

Hermione's; her jewel about the neck of it; the letters of
Antigonus found with it, which they know to be his character; the majesty of the creature in resemblance of the
mother; the affection of nobleness which nature shows
above her breeding; and many other evidences—proclaim
her with all certainty to be the King's daughter. Did you
see the meeting of the two kings?

SECOND GENTLEMAN. No.

THIRD GENTLEMAN. Then you have lost a sight which was
to be seen, cannot be spoken of. There might you have beheld one joy crown another, so and in such manner that it
seem'd sorrow wept to take leave of them; for their joy
waded in tears. There was casting up of eyes, holding up
of hands, with countenance of such distraction that they
were to be known by garment, not by favour. Our
king, being ready to leap out of himself for joy of his
found daughter, as if that joy were now become a loss,
cries 'O, thy mother, thy mother!' then asks Bohemia forgiveness; then embraces his son-in-law; then again worries
he his daughter with clipping her. Now he thanks the old
shepherd, which stands by like a weather-bitten conduit of
many kings' reigns. I never heard of such another encounter, which lames report to follow it and undoes description to do it.

SECOND GENTLEMAN. What, pray you, became of Antigonus,
that carried hence the child?

THIRD GENTLEMAN. Like an old tale still, which will have
matter to rehearse, though credit be asleep and not an ear
open: he was torn to pieces with a bear. This avouches the
shepherd's son, who has not only his innocence, which
seems much, to justify him, but a handkerchief and rings
of his that Paulina knows.

FIRST GENTLEMAN. What became of his bark and his followers?

THIRD GENTLEMAN. Wreck'd the same instant of their master's death, and in the view of the shepherd; so that all the
instruments which aided to expose the child were even then
lost when it was found. But, O, the noble combat that
'twixt joy and sorrow was fought in Paulina! She had one
eye declin'd for the loss of her husband, another elevated

that the oracle was fulfill'd. She lifted the Princess from the earth, and so locks her in embracing as if she would pin her to her heart, that she might no more be in danger of losing.

FIRST GENTLEMAN. The dignity of this act was worth the audience of kings and princes; for by such was it acted.

THIRD GENTLEMAN. One of the prettiest touches of all, and that which angl'd for mine eyes—caught the water, though not the fish—was, when at the relation of the Queen's death, with the manner how she came to't bravely confess'd and lamented by the King, how attentiveness wounded his daughter; till, from one sign of dolour to another, she did with an 'Alas!'—I would fain say—bleed tears; for I am sure my heart wept blood. Who was most marble there changed colour; some swooned, all sorrowed. If all the world could have seen't, the woe had been universal.

FIRST GENTLEMAN. Are they returned to the court?

THIRD GENTLEMAN. No. The Princess hearing of her mother's statue, which is in the keeping of Paulina—a piece many years in doing and now newly perform'd by that rare Italian master, Julio Romano, who, had he himself eternity and could put breath into his work, would beguile nature of her custom, so perfectly he is her ape. He so near to Hermione hath done Hermione that they say one would speak to her and stand in hope of answer—thither with all greediness of affection are they gone, and there they intend to sup.

SECOND GENTLEMAN. I thought she had some great matter there in hand; for she hath privately twice or thrice a day, ever since the death of Hermione, visited that removed house. Shall we thither, and with our company piece the rejoicing?

FIRST GENTLEMAN. Who would be thence that has the benefit of access? Every wink of an eye some new grace will be born. Our absence makes us unthrifty to our knowledge. Let's along. *Exeunt* GENTLEMEN

AUTOLYCUS. Now, had I not the dash of my former life in me, would preferment drop on my head. I brought the old man and his son aboard the Prince; told him I heard them talk of a fardel and I know not what; but he at that time over-fond of the shepherd's daughter—so he then took her to be—who began to be much sea-sick, and himself little better, extremity of weather continuing, this mystery remained undiscover'd. But 'tis all one to me; for had I been the finder-out of this secret, it would not have relish'd among my other discredits.

Enter SHEPHERD *and* CLOWN

Here come those I have done good to against my will, and already appearing in the blossoms of their fortune.

SHEPHERD. Come, boy; I am past moe children, but thy sons and daughters will be all gentlemen born.

CLOWN. You are well met, sir. You denied to fight with me this other day, because I was no gentleman born. See you these clothes? Say you see them not and think me still no gentleman born. You were best say these robes are not gentlemen born. Give me the lie, do; and try whether I am not now a gentleman born.

AUTOLYCUS. I know you are now, sir, a gentleman born.

CLOWN. Ay, and have been so any time these four hours.

SHEPHERD. And so have I, boy.

CLOWN. So you have; but I was a gentleman born before my father; for the King's son took me by the hand and call'd me brother; and then the two kings call'd my father brother; and then the Prince, my brother, and the Princess, my sister, call'd my father father. And so we wept; and there was the first gentleman-like tears that ever we shed.

SHEPHERD. We may live, son, to shed many more.

CLOWN. Ay; or else 'twere hard luck, being in so preposterous estate as we are.

AUTOLYCUS. I humbly beseech you, sir, to pardon me all the faults I have committed to your worship, and to give me your good report to the Prince my master.

SHEPHERD. Prithee, son, do; for we must be gentle, now we are gentlemen.

CLOWN. Thou wilt amend thy life?

AUTOLYCUS. Ay, an it like your good worship.

CLOWN. Give me thy hand. I will swear to the Prince thou art as honest a true fellow as any is in Bohemia.

SHEPHERD. You may say it, but not swear it.

CLOWN. Not swear it, now I am a gentleman? Let boors and franklins say it: I'll swear it.

SHEPHERD. How if it be false, son?

CLOWN. If it be ne'er so false, a true gentleman may swear it in the behalf of his friend. And I'll swear to the Prince thou art a tall fellow of thy hands and that thou wilt not be drunk; but I know thou art no tall fellow of thy hands and that thou wilt be drunk. But I'll swear it; and I would thou wouldst be a tall fellow of thy hands.

AUTOLYCUS. I will prove so, sir, to my power.

CLOWN. Ay, by any means, prove a tall fellow. If I do not wonder how thou dar'st venture to be drunk not being a tall fellow, trust me not. Hark! the kings and the princes, our kindred, are going to see the Queen's picture. Come, follow us; we'll be thy good masters.   *Exeunt*

SCENE 3

Sicilia. A chapel in PAULINA's *house*

Enter LEONTES, POLIXENES, FLORIZEL, PERDITA, CAMILLO,
PAULINA, LORDS *and* ATTENDANTS

LEONTES. O grave and good Paulina, the great comfort
That I have had of thee!

PAULINA. What, sovereign sir,
I did not well, I meant well. All my services
You have paid home; but that you have vouchsaf'd,
With your crown'd brother and these your contracted
Heirs of your kingdoms, my poor house to visit,
It is a surplus of your grace, which never
My life may last to answer.

LEONTES. O Paulina,
We honour you with trouble; but we came
To see the statue of our queen. Your gallery
Have we pass'd through, not without much content
In many singularities; but we saw not
That which my daughter came to look upon,
The statue of her mother.

PAULINA. As she liv'd peerless,
So her dead likeness, I do well believe,
Excels whatever yet you look'd upon
Or hand of man hath done; therefore I keep it
Lonely, apart. But here it is. Prepare
To see the life as lively mock'd as ever
Still sleep mock'd death. Behold; and say 'tis well.
[PAULINA *draws a curtain, and discovers* HERMIONE
standing like a statue]
I like your silence; it the more shows off
Your wonder; but yet speak. First, you, my liege.
Comes it not something near?
LEONTES. Her natural posture!
Chide me, dear stone, that I may say indeed
Thou art Hermione; or rather, thou art she
In thy not chiding; for she was as tender
As infancy and grace. But yet, Paulina,
Hermione was not so much wrinkled, nothing
So aged as this seems.
POLIXENES. O, not by much!
PAULINA. So much the more our carver's excellence,
Which lets go by some sixteen years and makes her
As she liv'd now.
LEONTES. As now she might have done,
So much to my good comfort as it is
Now piercing to my soul. O, thus she stood,
Even with such life of majesty—warm life,
As now it coldly stands—when first I woo'd her!
I am asham'd. Does not the stone rebuke me
For being more stone than it? O royal piece,
There's magic in thy majesty, which has
My evils conjur'd to remembrance, and
From thy admiring daughter took the spirits,
Standing like stone with thee!
PERDITA. And give me leave,
And do not say 'tis superstition that
I kneel, and then implore her blessing. Lady,
Dear queen, that ended when I but began,
Give me that hand of yours to kiss.
PAULINA. O, patience!

The statue is but newly fix'd, the colour's
Not dry.

CAMILLO. My lord, your sorrow was too sore laid on,
Which sixteen winters cannot blow away,
So many summers dry. Scarce any joy
Did ever so long live; no sorrow
But kill'd itself much sooner.

POLIXENES. Dear my brother,
Let him that was the cause of this have pow'r
To take off so much grief from you as he
Will piece up in himself.

PAULINA. Indeed, my lord,
If I had thought the sight of my poor image
Would thus have wrought you—for the stone is mine—
I'd not have show'd it.

LEONTES. Do not draw the curtain.

PAULINA. No longer shall you gaze on't, lest your fancy
May think anon it moves.

LEONTES. Let be, let be.
Would I were dead, but that methinks already—
What was he that did make it? See, my lord,
Would you not deem it breath'd, and that those veins
Did verily bear blood?

POLIXENES. Masterly done!
The very life seems warm upon her lip.

LEONTES. The fixture of her eye has motion in't,
As we are mock'd with art.

PAULINA. I'll draw the curtain.
My lord's almost so far transported that
He'll think anon it lives.

LEONTES. O sweet Paulina,
Make me to think so twenty years together!
No settled senses of the world can match
The pleasure of that madness. Let't alone.

PAULINA. I am sorry, sir, I have thus far stirr'd you; but
I could afflict you farther.

LEONTES. Do, Paulina;
For this affliction has a taste as sweet
As any cordial comfort. Still, methinks,
There is an air comes from her. What fine chisel

Could ever yet cut breath? Let no man mock me,
For I will kiss her.

PAULINA. Good my lord, forbear.
The ruddiness upon her lip is wet;
You'll mar it if you kiss it; stain your own
With oily painting. Shall I draw the curtain?

LEONTES. No, not these twenty years.

PERDITA. So long could I
Stand by, a looker-on.

PAULINA. Either forbear,
Quit presently the chapel, or resolve you
For more amazement. If you can behold it,
I'll make the statue move indeed, descend,
And take you by the hand, but then you'll think—
Which I protest against—I am assisted
By wicked powers.

LEONTES. What you can make her do
I am content to look on; what to speak
I am content to hear; for 'tis as easy
To make her speak as move.

PAULINA. It is requir'd
You do awake your faith. Then all stand still;
Or those that think it is unlawful business
I am about, let them depart.

LEONTES. Proceed.
No foot shall stir.

PAULINA. Music, awake her: strike.   *[Music]*
'Tis time; descend; be stone no more; approach;
Strike all that look upon with marvel. Come;
I'll fill your grave up. Stir; nay, come away.
Bequeath to death your numbness, for from him
Dear life redeems you. You perceive she stirs.
           [HERMIONE comes down from the pedestal]
Start not; her actions shall be holy as
You hear my spell is lawful. Do not shun her
Until you see her die again; for then
You kill her double. Nay, present your hand.
When she was young you woo'd her; now in age
Is she become the suitor?

LEONTES. O, she's warm!

If this be magic, let it be an art
Lawful as eating.
POLIXENES. She embraces him.
CAMILLO. She hangs about his neck.
If she pertain to life, let her speak too.
POLIXENES. Ay, and make it manifest where she has liv'd,
Or how stol'n from the dead.
PAULINA. That she is living,
Were it but told you, should be hooted at
Like an old tale; but it appears she lives
Though yet she speak not. Mark a little while.
Please you to interpose, fair madam. Kneel,
And pray your mother's blessing. Turn, good lady;
Our Perdita is found.
HERMIONE. You gods, look down,
And from your sacred vials pour your graces
Upon my daughter's head! Tell me, mine own,
Where hast thou been preserv'd? Where liv'd? How found
Thy father's court? For thou shalt hear that I,
Knowing by Paulina that the oracle
Gave hope thou wast in being, have preserv'd
Myself to see the issue.
PAULINA. There's time enough for that,
Lest they desire upon this push to trouble
Your joys with like relation. Go together,
You precious winners all; your exultation
Partake to every one. I, an old turtle,
Will wing me to some wither'd bough, and there
My mate, that's never to be found again,
Lament till I am lost.
LEONTES. O peace, Paulina!
Thou shouldst a husband take by my consent,
As I by thine a wife. This is a match,
And made between's by vows. Thou hast found mine;
But how, is to be question'd; for I saw her,
As I thought, dead; and have, in vain, said many
A prayer upon her grave. I'll not seek far—
For him, I partly know his mind—to find thee
An honourable husband. Come, Camillo,
And take her by the hand whose worth and honesty

Is richly noted, and here justified
By us, a pair of kings. Let's from this place.
What! look upon my brother. Both your pardons,
That e'er I put between your holy looks
My ill suspicion. This your son-in-law,
And son unto the King, whom heavens directing,
Is troth-plight to your daughter. Good Paulina,
Lead us from hence where we may leisurely
Each one demand and answer to his part
Perform'd in this wide gap of time since first
We were dissever'd. Hastily lead away.   *Exeunt*

Glossary

GLOSSARY

ABATE, to shorten, *Mid. N. Dr.*, 3.ii; to except, *L. Lab. Lost*, 5.ii; to lessen, *Tam. Shrew*, Ind. i.

ABHOR, to loathe, *Two Gent. Ver.*, 4.iii; shudder from, *Mer. Wives Win.*, 3.v.

ABJECT, despicable, *Com. Err.*, 4.iv; servile, *Mer. Ven.*, 4.i.

ABORTIVE, premature, *L. Lab. Lost*, 1.i.   [*Tem.* 1.ii.

ABSOLUTE, without qualification, ABY, to pay penalty for, *Mid. N. Dr.*, 3.ii.

ACCOMMODATIONS, resources, *M. Meas.*, 3.i.   [3.iv.

ACCOMPLISH, to furnish, *Mer. Ven.*,

ACHE, pronounced 'aitch' at *Much Ado*, 3.iv, where it is represented by H.

ACHERON, one of the five rivers of the lower world, *Mid. N. Dr.*, 3.ii.

ADAM, (i) *the picture of old Adam*, because the officer had a coat of strong leather, and Adam, after the Fall, wore skins, *Com. Err.*, 4.iii; (ii) Adam Bell, famous as an archer, *Much Ado*, 1.i.

ADAMANT, lode-stone, *Mid. N. Dr.*, 2.i.

ADDITION, title, *All's Well*, 2.iii.

ADDRESS, to prepare, *As You Like*, 5.iv.

ADMIRATION, wonder, *Win. Tale*, 5.ii.

ADMISSION, tire of Venetian admittance, in Venetian fashion, *Mer. Wives Win.*, 3.iii.

ADOPTIOUS, *adoptious christendoms*, names given (by love), *All's Well*, 1.i.

ADVERTISEMENT, information, warning, *All's Well*, 4.iii.   [2.iv.

ADVICE, thought, *Two Gent. Ver.*,

AFFECT, to love, *Tw. Night*, 2.v.

AFFECTION, affectation, *L. Lab. Lost*, 5.i.   [5.i.

AFFRONT, to confront, *Win. Tale*,

AFFY, to betroth, *Tam. Shrew*, 4.iv.

AGATE, a stone used in seal-rings suitable for carving, *L. Lab. Lost*, 2.i.

AGLET-BABY, small figure on lace-tag, *Tam. Shrew*, 1.ii.

A-HOLD, directly into the wind, *Tem.*, 1.i.

AIM, *cry aim*, exclaim 'good shot,' *Mer. Wives Win.*, 3.ii.

AJAX, Greek hero (with pun on 'jakes'), *L. Lab. Lost*, 5.ii.

A-LIFE, dearly, *Win. Tale*, 4.iv.

ALL-HALLOND EVE, Hallowe'en, eve of All Saints' day, *M. Meas.*, 2.i.

ALL-HALLOWMAS, All Saints' day, 1st Nov., *Mer. Wives Win.*, 1.i.

ALL HID, hide and seek, *L. Lab. Lost*, 4.iii.

ALLICHOLY, melancholy, *Mer. Wives Win.*, 1.iv.

AMES-ACE, both aces, lowest throw with two dice, *All's Well*, 2.iii.

AMORT, *all amort*, almost dead, *Tam. Shrew*, 4.iii.

ANATOMY, skeleton, *Com. Err.*, 5.i.

ANGEL, gold coin with image of angel, worth about ten shillings, *Mer. Ven.*, 2.vii.

ANTHROPOPHAGINIAN, man-eater, *Mer. Wives Win.*, 4.v.

AQUA-VITÆ, whisky, *Mer. Wives Win.*, 2.ii.   [*Win.*, 1.i.

ARMIGERO, esquire, *Mer. Wives*

ARMIPOTENT, strong in arms, *L. Lab. Lost*, 5.ii.

ATE, goddess of mischief, *more Ates*, more provocation, *L. Lab. Lost*, 5.ii.

ATONE, agree, *As You Like*, 5.iv.

AWFUL, law-abiding, *Two Gent. Ver.*, 4.i.

BACARE, go back, *Tam. Shrew*, 2.i.

BACK-FRIEND, the officer who arrests you from behind, *Com. Err.*, 4.ii.

BACK-TRICK, a movement in some dance, *Tw. Night*, 1.iii.

BAFFLE, shame, *Tw. Night*, 2.v.

BAIT, to set on dogs at a tethered bear, to assail, *Tw. Night*, 3.i; to catch as with a bait, *Com. Err.*, 2.i.

BALDRICK, cross belt from shoulder to carry bugle, *Much Ado*, 1.i.

BALK, to miss a chance, *Tw. Night*, 3.ii; chop logic, *Tam. Shrew*, 1.i.

BANBURY CHEESE, a thin milk cheese, *Mer. Wives Win.*, 1.i.

BANDY, to exchange words, or strokes (as at tennis), *L. Lab. Lost*, 5.ii.   [2.ii.

BARBASON, a devil, *Mer. Wives Win.*,

BARFUL, difficult, *Tw. Night*, 1.iv.

BARM, yeast, *Mid. N. Dr.*, 2.i.

BARNE, child, *Much Ado*, 3.iv.

BARNACLE, a goose, *Tem.*, 4.i.

GLOSSARY

BASE, *bid the base*, run, as in the game of Prisoners' Base, *Two Gent. Ver.*, 1.ii.

BASILISK, the fabled cockatrice that kills with its look, *Win. Tale*, 1.ii.

BASTA, enough, *Tam. Shrew*, 1.i.

BASTARD, sweet wine from Spain, *M. Meas.*, 3.ii.

BATE, to flutter, *Tam. Shrew*, 4.i; blunt, *L. Lab. Lost*, 1.i.

BAT-FOWLING, catching birds at night by dazzling them with a light, *Tem.*, 2.i.

BATLER, wooden instrument for beating clothes, *As You Like*, 2.iv.

BAWBLING, of small account, *Tw. Night*, 5.i.   [3.iv.

BAWCOCK, fine fellow, *Tw. Night*,

BAY, to hunt and bring to a stand, *Mid. N. Dr.*, 4.i.

BEAM, in contrast to the 'mote,' as in Matthew's gospel, *L. Lab. Lost*, 4.iii.

BEAR-HERD *or* BEAR-WARD (berrord), one who keeps a bear for exhibition, *Much Ado*, 2.i.

BEARING-CLOTH, christening robe, *Win. Tale*, 3.iii.

BELL-WETHER, leader of the flock with a bell at its neck, *As You Like*, 3.ii.   [4.iii.

BE-METE, to thrash, *Tam. Shrew*,

BENCHED, raised to authority, *Win. Tale*, 1.ii.   [1.ii.

BEN VENUTO, welcome, *Tam. Shrew*,

BERGOMASK, rustic dance, *Mid. N. Dr.*, 5.i.

BERRORD, *see* BEAR-HERD.

BESHREW (a good-natured imprecation), a plague on, *L. Lab. Lost*, 5.ii.

BETEEM, provide, *Mid. N. Dr.*, 1.i.

BIAS, (metaphor from bowls), natural tendency, *L. Lab. Lost*, 4.ii.

BILBO, sword, *Mer. Wives Win.*, 3.v.

BILL, a weapon like a pole-axe, *Much Ado*, 3.iii.

BLANK, white spot in centre of target, *Win. Tale*, 2.iii.

BLAZON, (i) coat of arms, *Mer. Wives Win.*, 5.v; (ii) description, *Much Ado*, 2.i.   [5.i.

BLEAR, to hoodwink, *Tam. Shrew*,

BLOCK, wooden mould for hats, *Much Ado*, 1.i.

BLOW, to puff up, *Tw. Night*, 2.v; defile, *Tem.*, 3.i.

BOB, quip, *As You Like*, 2.vii.

BODKIN, sharp-pointed instrument, *Win. Tale*, 3.iii.

BOLT, arrow, *Mid. N. Dr.*, 2.i.

BOLT, to sift, *Win. Tale*, 4.iv.

BOMBARD, leather bottle, *Tem.*, 2.ii.

BOMBAST, cotton-wool stuffing, *L. Lab. Lost*, 5.ii.

BONES, rural musical instrument, *Mid. N. Dr.*, 4.i; bobbins, *Tw. Night*, 2.iv.

BOOT, profit, *Tam. Shrew*, 5.ii.

BOOT-HOSE, long stocking, *Tam. Shrew*, 3.ii.   [*Tem.*, 4.i.

BOSKY, with trees and undergrowth, *All's Well*, 4.iii.

BOTCHER, a patcher of old clothes, *All's Well*, 4.iii.

BOTTOM, (i) valley, *As You Like*, 4.iii; (ii) ship, *Mer. Ven.*, 1.i; (iii) ball of thread, with *verb* meaning to wind on a core, *Two Gent. Ver.*, 3.ii.

BOURN, boundary, *Win. Tale*, 1.ii.

BRACH, hound, *Tam. Shrew*, Ind.i.

BRAVERY, display as of clothes or feelings, *Tam. Shrew*, 4.iii.

BRAWL, a dance, *L. Lab. Lost*, 3.i.

BRIB'D, stolen, *Mer. Wives Win.*, 5.v.

BROCK, badger, *Tw. Night*, 2.v.

BROWNIST, Puritan sect, *Tw. Night*, 3.ii.

BUCK, a stag, named by sportsmen according to its age: 1st fawn, 2nd pricket, 3rd sorell, 4th sore, 5th buck of the first head, 6th buck, *L. Lab. Lost*, 4.ii.

BUCKING, putting dirty clothes through the 'buck' or wash, *Mer. Wives Win.*, 3.iii.

BUCKLERSBURY, street where apothecaries sold herbs, *Mer. Wives Win.*, 3.iii.

BUFF, stout leather, *Com. Err.*, 4.ii.

BULLY, term of affection, *Mid. N. Dr.*, 4.ii.

BUM-BAILY, bailiff, *Tw. Night*, 3.iv.

BURDEN, bass accompaniment, *As You Like*, 3.ii; refrain, *Tem.*, 1.ii.

BUSKIN'D, wearing high boots, *Mid. N. Dr.*, 2.i.   [*Shrew*, 2.i.

BUZZARD, poor type of hawk, *Tam.*

CADDIS, garter-tape, *Win. Tale*, 4.iv.

CADMUS, founder and king of Thebes, *Mid. N. Dr.*, 4.i.

CAIN-COLOURED, reddish, *Mer. Wives Win.*, 1.iv.

CALLAT, slut, *Win. Tale*, 2.iii.

CANARY, (i) sweet wine from the Canaries, *Tw. Night*, 1.iii; (ii) Spanish dance, *All's Well*, 2.i.

CANKER, worm in flower, *Mid. N. Dr.*, 2.ii; wild rose, *Much Ado*, 1.iii.

CANON, church law, then any rule, *All's Well*, 1.i.

CANTON, song, *Tw. Night*, 1.v.

CANZONET, short song, *L. Lab. Lost*, 4.ii.

CARBONADO, to score meat for broiling, *All's Well*, 4.v.

CARCANET, necklace, *Com. Err.*, 3.i.

1103

GLOSSARY

CARDECUE, 'quart d'écu,' French silver coin, *All's Well*, 4.iii.

CARDUUS BENEDICTUS, the blessed thistle, a cure-all, *Much Ado*, 3.iv.

CARPET CONSIDERATION, for reasons other than valour, *Tw. Night*, 3.iv. [2.iii.

CATAIAN, Chinaman, *Tw. Night*, CATER-COUSINS, (quarter cousins), intimates, *Mer. Ven.*, 2.ii.

CAT-O'-MOUNTAIN, a spotted creature, *Tem.*, 4.i.

CERECLOTH, shroud of waxed linen, *Mer. Ven.*, 2.vii.

CHAMPAIGN, flat, open country, *Tw. Night*, 2.v.

CHANGELING, child adopted by fairies, *Mid. N. Dr.*, 2.i.

CHAPE, scabbard, or its metal point, *All's Well*, 4.iii. [2.i.

CHAPMAN, merchant, *L. Lab. Lost*, CHARACTER, to write, *As You Like*, 3.ii. [5.i.

CHARGE-HOUSE, school, *L. Lab. Lost*, CHEATER, officer of the Exchequer, *Mer. Wives Win.*, 1.iii.

CHEVERIL, pliable leather, *Tw. Night*, 3.i. [2.i.

CHOUGH, crow or jackdaw, *Tem.*, CICATRICE, scar, *All's Well*, 2.i.

CINQUEPACE, brisk dance, *Tw. Night*, 1.iii.

CITTERN, guitar-shaped instrument, often with carved head, *L. Lab. Lost*, 5.ii. [3.ii.

CLACK-DISH, beggar's dish, *M. Meas.*, CLEARSTORIES, upper range of windows, *Tw. Night*, 4.ii.

CLEPE, to call, *L. Lab. Lost*, 5.i.

CLERK, scholar, *Mid. N. Dr.*, 5.i.

CLEW, ball of thread, *All's Well*, 1.iii.

CLIP, embrace, *Win. Tale*, 5.ii.

CLOUT, mark at archery, *L. Lab. Lost*, 4.i.

COCK, perversion of 'God,' in oaths, *Mer. Wives Win.*, 1.i.

COCKATRICE, see BASILISK.

COCKLE, the tares that grow with the corn, so of evil disposition, *L. Lab. Lost*, 4.iii. [4.i.

COCKNEY, useless fellow, *Tw. Night*, COG, cheat, wheedle, *Mer. Wives Win.*, 3.i.

COIL, confusion, *Temp.*, 1.ii.

COISTREL, knave, *Tw. Night*, 1.iii.

COLLIED, overcast and troubled, *Mid. N. Dr.*, 1.i.

COLOUR, (often) deceitful appearance, *Two Gent. Ver.*, 4.ii.

COMBINATION, alliance, *Tw. Night*, 5.i.

COMMODITY, merchandise, *Much Ado*, 3.iii. [4.ii.

COMPETITOR, partner, *Tw. Night*,

COMPLEXION, appearance as governed by the predominant 'humour,' *L. Lab. Lost*, 1.ii.

COMPT, reckoning and so Day of Judgment, *All's Well*, 5.iii.

CON, learn, *Mid. N. Dr.*, 1.ii.

CONCEIT, thought, *Mer. Ven.*, 1.i.

CONGIED, taken ceremonious farewell, *All's Well*, 4.iii.

CONY-CATCH, to cheat, *Mer. Wives Win.*, 1.iii.

COPATAIN, high-crowned hat, *Tam. Shrew*, 5.i.

COPY, example to follow, as at head of a copy-book, *All's Well*, 1.ii.

CORANTO, a dance, *Tw. Night*, 1.iii.

CORNUTO, cuckold, *Mer. Wives Win.*, 3.v.

COROLLARY, some extra, *Tem.*, 4.i.

CORPORAL, a senior rank in Shakespeare's day, *L. Lab. Lost*, 3.i.

COSTARD, head, from name for large apple, *Mer. Wives Win.*, 3.i.

COUNTER, used with *hunting* when dogs follow the scent in the wrong direction; play on this meaning and counter = debtors' prison in *Com. Err.*, 4.ii.

COUNTERFEIT, portrait, *Mer. Ven.*, 3.ii.

COUNTER-GATE, debtors' prison, *Mer. Wives Win.*, 3.iii.

COUSIN, Coz, a relative of some kind, or courtesy title, *Much Ado*, 1.ii.

COZEN, to cheat, *Mer. Wives Win.*, 4.v.

COZIER, cobbler, *Tw. Night*, 2.iii.

CROWN-IMPERIAL, a kind of lily, *Win. Tale*, 4.iv.

CRY, pack of hounds, *Mid. N. Dr.*, 4.i. [4.ii.

CULLION, low fellow, *Tam. Shrew*, CUNNING, (i) *noun*, knowledge, skill; (ii) *adj.*, learned, clever (not always in bad sense as to-day), *Tam. Shrew*, 1.i.

CUPID'S FLOWER, love-in-idleness, the pansy, *Mid. N. Dr.*, 2.i and 4.i.

CURIOUS, careful, *All's Well*, 1.ii.

CURST, sharp in tone or temper, *Tw. Night*, 3.ii.

CUSTALORUM, nonsense for 'Custos Rotulorum,' Keeper of the Rolls, *Mer. Wives Win.*, 1.i.

CUT, working-horse or gelding, so as term of contempt, and the point of *Tw. Night*, 2.v; of dog with docked tail, *Mer. Wives Win.*, 3.iv. [*Night*, 3.i.

CYPRESS, garment of crape, *Tw.*

DAFF, put off, thrust aside, *Much Ado*, 2.iii.

DANCING HORSE, a performing horse called Morocco exhibited by its

1104

GLOSSARY

owner Banks about 1590, *L. Lab. Lost*, 1.ii.

DAPHNE, a nymph loved by Apollo and turned to a laurel tree to escape his pursuit, *Mid. N. Dr.*, 2.i.

DAUBERY, pretence, *Mer. Wives Win.*, 4.ii.

DAY-BED, couch, *Tw. Night*, 2.v.

DEBILE, feeble, *All's Well*, 2.iii.

DEBOSHED, debauched, *Tem.*, 3.ii.

DEGREE, step, stage, *As You Like*, 5.iv.

DEMI-CANNON, gun of large calibre, *Tam. Shrew*, 4.iii.

DENIER, French copper coin of small value, *Tam. Shrew*, Ind.i.

DEPOSE, assert on oath, *M. Meas.*, 5.i. [*Meas.*, 1.i.

DEPUTATION, office of deputy, *M.*

DESCANT, comment (from the term that refers to the upper and more elaborate part of a musical composition), *Two Gent. Ver.*, 1.ii.

DETERMINATE, purposed, conclusive, *Tw. Night*, 2.i.

DETERMINATION, decision, *M. Measure*, 3.ii.

DEUCE-ACE, throw of two and one at dice, *L. Lab. Lost*, 1.ii.

DIAL, watch, *As You Like*, 2.vii.

DIFFERENCE, distinction of rank or descent or character, *All's Well*, 2.iii. [*Lost*, 1.ii.

DIGRESSION, transgression, *L. Lab.*

DILEMMAS, alternatives, *All's Well*, 3.vi. [4.iv.

DISCONTENTING, vexed, *Win. Tale*,

DISCOURSE, power or process of thought, *M. Meas.*, 1.ii.

DISCOVER, to reveal what is known to the speaker, *Two Gent. Ver.*, 3.i.

DISMOUNT, draw sword from its scabbard, *Tw. Night*, 3.iv.

DISPOSE, *noun*, disposal, *Two Gent. Ver.*, 2.vii.

DISPOSITION, behaviour, mood, *As You Like*, 4.i.

DISTANCE, space between fencers, *Mer. Wives Win.*, 2.i.

DISTEMPERATURE, lack of order and so inclemency in weather or illness in man, *Mid. N. Dr.*, 2.i.

DISTINCTION, discrimination, *All's Well*, 2.iii.

DISTINCTLY, in several separate parts, *Tem.*, 1.ii. [*Tale*, 2.i.

DISTINGUISHMENT, distinction, *Win.*

DISTRACT, *adj.*, divided, and so divided in mind, crazed, *Com. Err.*, 4.iii.

DIVERS, different, *As You Like*, 3.ii.

DIVISION, arrangement, *Much Ado*, 5.i.

DOCTRINE, precept, principle, learning, *L. Lab. Lost*, 4.iii.

DOIT, a Dutch coin of small value, *Mer. Ven.*, 1.iii.

DOLLAR, English name for German thaler, a large silver coin, *Tem.*, 2.i; Shakespeare puns on dollar and dolour elsewhere.

DOMINICAL, dominical letter which was printed in red in the almanacs, so a reference to the lady's hair and complexion, *L. Lab. Lost*, 5.ii. [3.i.

DOOM, judgment, *Two Gent. Ver.*,

DOUBLET AND HOSE, the dress of a man, hence his characteristics, *As You Like*, 3.ii.

DOWLE, feather, *Tem.*, 3.iii.

DOXY, beggar's trull, *Win. Tale*, 4.iii.

DRAW DRY-FOOT, to track by the scent of the footmarks, *Com. Err.*, 4.ii. [2.ii.

DRAWER, tapster, *Mer. Wives Win.*,

DRIBBLING, falling wide of the mark, *M. Meas.*, 1.iii.

DRIFT, design, intention, *Tem.*, 5.i.

DROLLERY, puppet-show, *Tem.*, 3.iii.

DRUMBLE, to move slowly, *Mer. Wives Win.*, 3.iii.

DUCAT, gold coin of about ten shillings value, Italian silver coin, *Mer. Ven.*, 1.iii.

DUELLO, the rules and etiquette of duelling, *L. Lab. Lost*, 1.ii.

DUMP, melancholy tune, *Two Gent. Ver.*, 3.ii.

DURANCE, lasting nature, *Com. Err.*, 4.iii, with the idea of imprisonment implied.

EAN, to give birth, *Mer. Ven.*, 1.iii.

EAR, plough, cultivate, *All's Well*, 1.iii.

EARNEST, token payment as pledge of some service or obligation, *Win. Tale*, 4.iv.

ECSTASY, out of one's normal state, madness, stupor, *Tem.*, 3.iii.

EFFIGIES, image, *As You Like*, 2.vii.

EGREGIOUS, notable, *All's Well*, 2.iii.

ELD, old age, *M. Meas.*, 3.i.

ELM, the elm tree used as a prop for vines, *Com. Err.*, 2.ii.

EMBOSSED, (i) swollen, *As You Like*, 2.vii; (ii) with mouth covered with foam from exertion, *Tam. Shrew*, Ind.i.

EMPIRIC, unprofessional or quack practitioner and his type of prescription, *All's Well*, 2.i.

ENEW, to drive, as the falcon, the prey into the water, *M. Meas.*, 3.i.

ENGINE, contrivance, weapon of war, *Tem.*, 2.i.

1105

GLOSSARY

ENSCONCE, take shelter, *Mer. Wives Win.*, 3.iii.

ENTERTAIN, receive, as a follower, *Mer. Wives Win.*, 1.iii.

EPHESIAN, companion, *Mer. Wives Win.*, 4.v.

EPITHET, EPITHETON, expression, *L. Lab. Lost*, 4.ii.

ERGO, therefore, *Com. Err.*, 4.iii.

ERINGO, candied sweetmeat, *Mer. Wives Win.*, 5.v. [5.v.

EVITATE, avoid, *Mer. Wives Win.*,

EXACTLY, completely, *Tem.*, 1.ii.

EXCEPT, object, play on legal phrase 'except as before excepted' at *Tw. Night*, 1.iii.

EXCEPTION, objection, disapproval, *All's Well*, 1.ii.

EXCREMENT, what grows from the body as nails or hair, *Com. Err.*, 2.ii.

EXEMPT, separated from, free from, *As You Like*, 2.i.

EXHIBITION, a maintenance allowance, *Two Gent. Ver.*, 1.iii.

EXORCIST, one who calls up spirits, *All's Well*, 5.iii.

EXPRESSURE, expression, *Tw. Night*, 2.iii.

EXTEMPORAL, extempore, *L. Lab. Lost*, 4.ii.

EXTIRP, to weed out, *M. Meas.*, 3.ii.

EXTRAVAGANCY, wandering, *Tw. Night*, 2.i.

EYAS, young hawk in training, so *eyas-musket* of a boy at *Mer. Wives Win.*, 3.iii. [1.ii.

EYE-GLASS, lens of eye, *Win. Tale*,

FACE, to trim a garment, *Tam. Shrew*, 4.iii, punning on meaning 'to face up to.' [2.iii.

FACERINOUS, wicked, *All's Well*,

FACT, way of acting, *Win. Tale*, 3.ii. [4.i.

FACTION, a party, *Two Gent. Ver.*,

FADGE, come off, *Tw. Night*, 2.ii.

FADING, refrain of popular song, *Win. Tale*, 4.iv.

FAIRING, present, *L. Lab. Lost*, 5.ii.

FAME, rumour, *Much Ado*, 2.i; reputation, *Tw. Night*, 3.iii.

FANATICAL PHANTASIME, individual with crazy but fixed notions, *L. Lab. Lost*, 5.i.

FANTASTIC, capricious, *Two Gent. Ver.*, 2.vii. [5.i.

FANTASY, imagination, *Mid. N. Dr.*,

FAP, drunk, *Mer. Wives Win.*, 1.i.

FARBOROUGH, third borough, constable, *L. Lab. Lost*, 1.i.

FARDEL, pack or burden, *Win. Tale*, 4.iv.

FARTHINGALE, hooped petticoat, *Mer. Wives Win.*, 3.iii.

FASHIONS, a disease in horses, *Tam. Shrew*, 3.ii.

FAULT, break in the scent in hunting, *Tw. Night*, 2.v.

FAVOUR, token of someone's favour, *L. Lab. Lost*, 5.ii; features, *M. Meas.*, 4.ii.

FEAT, neat, becoming, *Tem.*, 2.i.

FEATLY, with neatness and agility, *Tem.*, 1.ii.

FEATURE, figure (not face), *Much Ado*, 3.i. [*Tale*, 2.i.

FEDARY, FEDERARY, accomplice, *Win.*

FEE, *fee-simple*, the most complete and absolute form of tenure or possession, *All's Well*, 4.iii.

FEEDER, servant, *As You Like*, 2.iv.

FESTINATELY, speedily, *L. Lab. Lost*, 3.i.

FICO, FIG, FIGO, contemptuous expression, often accompanied by insulting gesture, *Mer. Wives Win.*, 1.iii.

FIGHTS, protective screens used in fighting at sea, *Mer. Wives Win.*, 2.ii.

FIGURE, appearance, real, imaginary, or assumed, *Much Ado*, 1.i; *Mer. Wives Win.*, 4.ii; figure of speech, *Two Gent. Ver.*, 2.i. [2.ii.

FILLS, shafts, *fill-horse*, *Mer. Ven.*,

FINE, end, *All's Well*, 4.iv; conclusion of legal agreement as in *fine and recovery*, a process to break an entail and convert the tenure to fee-simple (*see* FEE-SIMPLE), *Mer. Wives Win.*, 4.ii.

FIT, spasm or attack of some disease or illness, *Com. Err.*, 4.iii.

FIVES, a disease of horses, *Tam. Shrew*, 3.ii.

FLAP-DRAGON, something served in flaming spirits at Christmas parties, *L. Lab. Lost*, 5.i; verb, to gulp down, as one would such a mouthful, *Win. Tale*, 3.iii.

FLAW, gust of wind, or passion, *M. Meas.*, 2.iii.

FLEER, to sneer, *Much Ado*, 5.i.

FLESH (to give a hound the flesh of the victim to rouse its keenness) so to introduce an untried soldier to bloodshed; *well fleshed*, having tasted success, *Tw. Night*, 4.i. [*Dr.*, 4.i.

FLEW'D, with large chaps, *Mid. N.*

FLOTE, sea, *Tem.*, 1.ii. [4.iv.

FLOWER-DE-LUCE, iris, *Win. Tale*,

FLUX, secretion, *As You Like*, 3.ii.

FOIL, *put to the foil*, overthrow, deprive of commendation, *Tem.*, 3.i.

FOIN, thrust with rapier, *Mer. Wives Win.*, 2.iii.

FOISON, harvest, *Tem.*, 4.i.

FONDLY, foolishly, *Com. Err.*, 4.ii.

GLOSSARY

FOREHORSE, leading horse as in a tandem, *All's Well*, 2.i.

FRAMPOLD, unpleasant, *Mer. Wives Win.*, 2.ii.

FRANKLIN, freeholder but not numbered among the county families, *Win. Tale*, 5.ii.

FRESHES, springs of fresh water, *Tem.*, 3.ii.

FRETS, the points marked on the neck of a stringed instrument where the fingers may stop the string, *Tam. Shrew*, 2.i.

FRIEZE, coarse cloth, *Mer. Wives Win.*, 5.v.

FRIPPERY, second-hand clothes shop, *Tem.*, 4.i.

FULLAM, kind of loaded dice, *Mer. Wives Win.*, 1.iii. [4.i.

FUSTIAN, coarse cloth, *Tam. Shrew*,

GABERDINE, kind of cloak, *Mer. Ven.*, 1.iii.

GAGE, pledge, *Mer. Ven.*, 1.i.

GAINSAY, to deny, *Win. Tale*, 3.ii.

GALEN, Greek who became physician to the Emperor Marcus Aurelius; his voluminous writings on medical topics were authoritative in Shakespeare's day, *All's Well*, 2.iii.

GALLIARD, a lively dance usually in triple time, *Tw. Night*, 1.iii.

GALLIASS, large type of galley, *Tam. Shrew*, 2.i.

GALLIMAUFRY, hotch potch, *Win. Tale*, 4.iv.

GAMUT, musical scale, *Tam. Shrew*, 3.i. [1.v.

GASKINS, wide breeches, *Tw. Night*,

GAWDS, gay trifles, *Mid. N. Dr.*, 1.i.

GECK, butt, *Tw. Night*, 5.1.

GENEROUS, well born, and so acting like a gentleman, *Tw. Night*, 1.v.

GENIUS, the spirit that is assigned to each individual as a guardian, so peculiar bent or nature, *Tw. Night*, 3.iv.

GENTILITY, gentlemanly conduct, *L. Lab. Lost*, 1.i.

GENTLE, of good birth, *Win. Tale*, 4.iv. [4.iv.

GERMAN, GERMANE, akin, *Win. Tale*,

GEST, time limit, *Win. Tale*, 1.ii.

GHOSTLY, concerned with spiritual welfare, *M. Meas.*, 4.iii.

GIG, whipping-top, *L. Lab. Lost*, 4.iii.

GIGLET, -OT, a wanton, *M. Meas.*, 5.i.

GILLYVOR, gillyflower, *Win. Tale*, 4.iv. [*Like*, 2.vii.

GLANCE, satirical comment, *As You*

GLASS, hour glass, *Tem.*, 1.ii.

GLEEK, to joke, gibe, *Mid. N. Dr.*, 3.i.

GOD-DEN, GOD-I-GODEN (and similar forms) God give you good even! *L. Lab. Lost*, 4.i.

GOD DILD YOU, God yield, or repay, you! *As You Like*, 3.iii.

GOOD YEAR, a common exclamation, without any particular meaning, *Mer. Wives Win.*, 1.iv.

GOSS, gorse, *Tem.*, 4.i.

GOSSIP, one associated with parents at baptism of their child, a god-parent, *Win. Tale*, 2.iii.

GOSSIPING, enjoying the 'gossips' feast' at the 'rebirth' of the lost sons, *Com. Err.*, 5.i.

GOURD, loaded dice, *Mer. Wives Win.*, 1.iii. [5.i.

GOVERNMENT, control, *Mid. N. Dr.*,

GRACEFUL, blest with the grace of God, *Win. Tale*, 5.i.

GRAFT, to insert shoots and so to incorporate, *All's Well*, 1.ii.

GRAIN, *in grain*, dyed in a colour that will not wash out, *Tw. Night*, 1.v. [*Mer. Ven.*, 2.ii.

GRAMERCY, expression of thanks,

GRANGE, a lonely house in the country, *M. Meas.*, 3.i.

GRATE, to fret, annoy, *Mer. Wives Win.*, 2.ii.

GRATULATE, gratifying, *M. Meas.*, 5.i.

GREASILY, indecently, *L. Lab. Lost*, 4.i. [*Night*, 4.i.

GREEK, light fellow or wench, *Tw.*

GREENSLEEVES, a ballad tune not tending to godliness, *Mer. Wives Win.*, 2.i.

GRIEVANCE, inconvenience, affliction, *Two Gent. Ver.*, 1.i.

GRIEVE, regret, *Win. Tale*, 4.i.

GRIZE, step, *Tw. Night*, 3.i.

GROAT, fourpenny piece, *Mer. Wives Win.*, 1.i.

GUARD, trimming to a garment, *M. Meas.*, 3.i.

GUILDER, Dutch coin, but for money generally, *Com. Err.*, 1.i.

GUST, taste, *Tw. Night*, 1.iii.

GYVES, fetters, *M. Meas.*, 4.ii.

H, *see* ACHE, *Much Ado*, 3.iv.

HABILIMENTS, costume, *Tam. Shrew*, 4.iii.

HABIT, costume, (sometimes combined with idea of corresponding) demeanour, *As You Like*, 3.ii.

HABITED, dressed, *Win. Tale*, 4.iv.

HACK, of doubtful meaning, *Mer. Wives Win.*, 2.i.

HACKNEY, promiscuous wench, *L. Lab. Lost*, 3.i.

HAGGARD, wild female hawk in training, *Tam. Shrew*, 4.i.

HAIR, *against the hair*, contrary to nature, *Mer. Wives Win.*, 2.iii.

GLOSSARY

HALBERD, axe-like weapon with long handle, *Com. Err.*, 5.i.

HALF-CHEEK'D, applied to inefficient or deficient bit, *Tam. Shrew*, 3.ii.

HALIDOM, HOLIDAME, an oath (on holy relics) reduced by Shakespeare's time to a mere asseveration, *Two Gent. Ver.*, 4.ii.

HARBINGER, forerunner, *Mid. N. Dr.*, 3.ii. [5.i.

HAY, country dance, *L. Lab. Lost*,

HAZARD, game with dice, so to venture, *Mer. Ven.*, 2.ix.

HECATE, divinity of classical antiquity, associated with ghost world and worshipped in triform shape at cross-roads; *triple Hecate*, as Cynthia in heaven, Diana on earth, and Proserpine in hell, *Mid. N. Dr.*, 5.i.

HEFT, heaving, *Win. Tale*, 2.i.

HEROD, the ranting character of Herod in the Miracle plays, *Mer. Wives Win.*, 2.i.

HEST, command, *L. Lab. Lost*, 5.ii.

HIGH AND LOW, dice loaded to throw high or low numbers, *Mer. Wives Win.*, 1.iii.

HIGHT, named, *L. Lab. Lost*, 1.i.

HIND, female deer, *As You Like*, 3.ii.

HINT, occasion, *Tem.*, 1.ii.

HIPPED, lame, owing to injury to hipbone, *Tam. Shrew*, 3.ii.

HOBBY-HORSE, 'the figure of a horse' fastened round the waist of a morris dancer; the antics of this particular character in the dance were offensive to the Puritans, and so of a loose character, *L. Lab. Lost*, 3.i. [4.ii.

HOLDING, consistency, *All's Well*,

HOLIDAME, see HALIDOM.

HOLY THISTLE, see CARDUUS BENEDICTUS.

HONORIFICABILITUDINITATIBUS, ablative plural of medieval Latin word; stock example of long word, *L. Lab. Lost*, 5.i.

HORN-BOOK, sheet containing alphabet, etc., for children, protected with transparent covering of horn, *L. Lab. Lost*, 5.i.

HOSE, includes various types of breeches and clothing (not stockings) for the lower limbs, *Two Gent. Ver.*, 2.vii.

HOX, hamstring, *Win. Tale*, 1.ii.

HOY, ferry, small vessel, *Com. Err.*, 4.iii.

HULL, to furl sails and drift with the tide, *Tw. Night*, 1.v.

HUMOUR, corresponding to the four elements (earth, air, fire, water) were the four humours—black bile, blood, bile, phlegm. According as one or other predominated in a man's system so his temperament was choleric or phlegmatic or melancholy, and his complexion in keeping. The term was overworked, and parodied in Nym's use of it, e.g. *Mer. Wives Win.*, 1.i.

HYMEN, whose presence was invoked at Greek marriages, and so became regarded as god of marriage; the torch was one of his symbols, *Tem.*, 4.i.

HYPERBOLE, figure of speech characterised by exaggeration, *L. Lab. Lost*, 5.ii.

IDEA, image, *Much Ado*, 4.i.

IGNOMINY, IGNOMY, disgrace, *M. Meas.*, 2.iv.

IGNORANT, causing ignorance, *Win. Tale*, 1.ii. [4.iii.

IMAGINARY, deceptive, *Com. Err.*,

IMBRUE, cover with blood, *Mid. N. Dr.*, 5.i.

IMMEDIATELY, for that particular case, *Mid. N. Dr.*, 1.i.

IMP, child, *L. Lab. Lost*, 5.ii.

IMPART, express, *Mer. Ven.*, 3.ii.

IMPEACH, to expose to judgment, *Mid. N. Dr.*, 2.i.

IMPEACHMENT, reproach, *Two Gent. Ver.*, 1.iii.

IMPERTINENCY, IMPERTINENT, what is beside the point, *Tem.*, 1.ii.

IMPETICOS, put into the packet of his long motley coat, *Tw. Night*, 2.iii.

IMPORT, content, *All's Well*, 2.iii.

IMPORTANCE, importunity, *Tw. Night*, 5.i. [2.i.

IMPORTANT, importunate, *Much Ado*,

IMPORTUNE, require, *M. Meas.*, 1.i.

IMPOSITION, charge, *M. Meas.*, 1.ii; *Mer. Ven.*, 1.ii.

IMPUDENT, shameless, *All's Well*, 4.iii.

IMPUGN, question the process, *Mer. Ven.*, 4.i.

IMPUTATION, report, *Mer. Ven.*, 1.iii.

INCAPABLE, beyond the capacity, *Tem.*, 1.ii.

INCARNATION and similar formations used of the devil are comic versions of 'incarnate,' *Mer. Ven.*, 2.ii.

INCONTINENT, at once (with pun on normal sense), *As You Like*, 5.ii.

INCONY, fine, *L. Lab. Lost*, 3.i.

INCORPORATE, bound up together, *Mid. N. Dr.*, 3.ii. [1.i.

INDIRECT, treacherous, *As You Like*,

INDIRECTLY, not straightforwardly, *M. Meas.*, 4.vi.

INDUSTRIOUS, zealous, *Tem.*, 4.i.

INDUSTRY, diligence, *Two Gen. Ver.*, 1.iii.

GLOSSARY

INEQUALITY (meaning doubtful), difference in rank, or unequal to the case, *M. Meas.*, 5.i.

INFLUENCE, what flows in from the stars and affects the character or destiny of man, *M. Meas.*, 3.i.

INFORMAL, without reason, *M. Meas.*, 5.i.

INKLE, tape, *Win. Tale*, 4.iv.

INLAND, familiar with good society, *As You Like*, 3.ii. (inland, near centres of culture).

INSINUATE, to assume a cordial form of address, *Win. Tale*, 4.iv.

INSTALMENT, stall seat in chapel, *Mer. Wives Win.*, 5.v.

INTELLIGENT, informative, communicative, *Win. Tale*, 1.ii.

INTENIBLE, unable to retain, *All's Well*, 1.iii.

INTERLUDE, an early type of dramatic entertainment, *Mid. N. Dr.*, 1.ii.

IWIS, assuredly, *Tam. Shrew*, 1.i.

JACK, often used to indicate contempt, *Mer. Wives Win.*, 1.iv; with reference to knave at cards, *Tem.*, 4.i; associated with 'Jill' as common name and as measure of drink, *Tam. Shrew*, 4.i.

JACK-A-LENT, dummy set up at Lent as a cock-sky, *Mer. Wives Win.*, 5.v. [*Well*, 3.v.

JACK-AN-APES, vain fellow, *All's*

JADE, poor class of horse, *Tam. Shrew*, 1.ii.

JAY, bedizened wench, *Mer. Wives Win.*, 3.iii. [3.i.

JEALOUS, suspicious, *Two Gen. Ver.*,

JEALOUSY, fear, *Tw. Night*, 3.iii.

JERK, sharp stroke of wit or whip, *L. Lab. Lost*, 4.ii.

JERKIN, sleeveless jacket worn over doublet, for hard wear, often made of leather, *Tam. Shrew*, 3.ii.

JET, strut, *Tw. Night*, 2.v.

JIG, brisk dance, *Much Ado*, 2.i.

JILL, see JACK.

JOINT-STOOL (*join-, join'd-*), stool carefully carpentered, *Tam. Shrew*, 2.i.

JOURNAL, daily, *M. Meas.*, 4.iii.

JOWL, to dash, *All's Well*, 1.iii.

JUDAS, tradition gave him red hair, *As You Like*, 3.iv.

JUMP, to agree, *Mer. Ven.*, 2.ix.

JUVENAL, youth, *L. Lab. Lost*, 1.ii.

KEEL, cool, keep pot from boiling over, *L. Lab. Lost*, 5.ii.

KEN, to know, *Mer. Wives Win.*, 1.iii.

KENNEL, channel, gutter, *Tam. Shrew*, 4.iii.

KERNEL, seed, pip, *All's Well*, 2.iii.

KERSEY, coarse woollen cloth, *L. Lab. Lost*, 5.ii.

KIBE, chilblain, *Tem.*, 2.i.

KICKSHAWS, fancy trifle of food or deportment, *Tw. Night*, 1.iii.

KICKY-WICKY, wife, *All's Well*, 2.iii.

KILN-HOLE (doubtful), *Mer. Wives Win.*, 4.ii.

KINDLE, (term used of the littering of rabbits) born, *As You Like*, 3.ii.

KINDLY, according to nature, *Much Ado*, 4.i.

KISSING-COMFIT, comfit for sweetening breath, *Mer. Wives Win.*, 5.v.

KNAP, to bite, *Mer. Ven.*, 3.i.

KNAVE, a servant, *Mer. Wives Win.*, 3.v.

KNOT-GRASS, a weed thought to check the growth of animals, so derisively at *Mid. N. Dr.*, 3.ii.

KNOTTED, *curious-knotted*, elaborately laid out, *L. Lab. Lost*, 1.i.

LABEL, attached on a slip or 'label' to her will, *Tw. Night*, 1.v.

LABRAS, lips (labra), *Mer. Wives Win.*, 1.i.

LACE, to trim a garment with, *Much Ado*, 3.iv; laced *mutton*, courtesan, *Two Gent. Ver.*, 1.i.

LADY-SMOCK, flower, *L. Lab. Lost*, 5.ii. [*Tem.*, 4.i.

LAMP, *Hymen's lamps*, torches,

LAMPASS, disease of horses, *Tam. Shrew*, 3.ii.

LAND-DAMN, the context makes the general meaning of 'punish' clear, but the precise meaning is doubtful, *Win. Tale*, 2.i.

LAPLAND, regarded as the haunt of witches and sorcerers, *Com. Err.*, 4.iii.

LAPSE, *lapsed*, arrested (tho' how it comes to mean this is not clear), *Tw. Night*, 3.iii. [4.vi.

LARD, to enrich, *Mer. Wives Win.*,

LATCH, to touch, *Mid. N. Dr.*, 3.ii.

LATH, *dagger of lath*, of wood, *Tw. Night*, 4.ii.

LATTEN, an alloy like brass, *Mer. Wives Win.*, 1.i. [2.i.

LAUGHTER, a sitting of eggs, *Tem.*,

LEAGUER, camp, *All's Well*, 3.vi.

LEARN, to teach, *Tem.*, 1.ii.

LEASING, lying, *Tw. Night*, 1.v.

LEER, complexion, *As You Like*, 4.i; glance, *Mer. Wives Win.*, 1.iii.

LEET, court under jurisdiction of lord of the manor, *Tam. Shrew*, Ind.ii.

LEGION, name taken by unclean spirit in Mark, v.9, 'for we are many'; so host of fiends, *Tw. Night*, 3.iv.

LEIGER, ambassador, representative, *M. Meas.*, 3.i.

GLOSSARY

LEMAN, sweetheart, *Tw. Night*, 2.iii.

LENTEN, *lenten entertainment*, poor reception, meagre like the restricted diet of Lent, *Tw. Night*, 1.v.

L'ENVOY, conclusion of poem, marked off as such by form, *L. Lab. Lost*, 3.i.

LESS (sometimes used in negative or virtual negative expressions where meaning is 'more'), *Win. Tale*, 3.ii.

LET, to prevent, *Two Gent. Ver.*, 3.i.

LETHE, 'the river of oblivion' in the underworld whose waters caused forgetfulness of one's past existence, *Tw. Night*, 4.i.

LETTER, *affect the letter*, employ alliteration, *L. Lab. Lost*, 4.ii.

LETTERED, learned, *L. Lab. Lost*, 5.i.

LEVEL, aim (from gunnery), *All's Well*, 2.i.   [5.i.

LEWD, of the baser sort, *Much Ado*,

LEWDSTER, lecherous person, *Mer. Wives Win.*, 5.iii.

LIABLE, fit, *L. Lab. Lost*, 5.i.

LIBBARD, leopard, *L. Lab. Lost*, 5.ii.

LIBERAL, *liberal arts*, those suitable for a gentleman, *Tem.*, 1.ii; going beyond manners, gross, *Mer. Ven.*, 2.ii.

LIBERTY, licence, *M. Meas.*, 1.iii.

LIEF, *had as leif*, would as willingly, *As You Like*, 3.ii.

LIGHT O' LOVE, dance tune, light wench, *Much Ado*, 3.iv.

LIMBER, not rigid, *Win. Tale*, 1.ii.

LIMBO, slang for prison, *Com. Err.*, 4.ii.

LIME, *limed*, held, as a bird with bird-lime, *Tw. Night*, 3.iv; to doctor wine or sack with lime, *Mer. Wives Win.*, 1.iii.

LINE-GROVE, grove of lime-trees, *Tem.*, 5.i.   [*Shrew*, 4.i.

LINK, torch, used as blacking, *Tam.*

LINSEY-WOOLSEY, mixture of flax and wool; so unintelligible medley at *All's Well*, 4.i.

LIST, strip of cloth, *Tam. Shrew*, 3.ii.

LIVELIHOOD, life, animal vigour, *All's Well*, 1.i.   [5.iii.

LIVELY, like life itself, *Win. Tale*,

LIVER, regarded as seat of more violent passions: love, courage, anger, *Tw. Night*, 1.i; *As You Like*, 3.ii; *livers white as milk*, of cowards, *Mer. Ven.*, 3.ii.

LIVER-VEIN, style of a lover, *L. Lab. Lost*, 4.iii.

LOOSE, *at his very loose*, at the moment of discharge, *L. Lab. Lost*, 5.ii.

LORD'S SAKE, *for the Lord's sake*, the formula in which those imprisoned for debt begged alms of the passersby, *M. Meas.*, 4.iii.

LOVE-IN-IDLENESS, pansy, *Mid. N. Dr.*, 2.i.

LOZEL, rascal, *Win. Tale*, 2.iii.

LUBBER, lout, *Tw. Night*, 4.i.

LUCE, pike, *Mer. Wives Win.*, 1.i.

LUNE, mad fit, *Win. Tale*, 2.ii; spelt 'lines' at *Mer. Wives Win.*, 4.ii.

LURCH, steal, *Mer. Wives Win.*, 2.ii.

LURE, dummy bird to entice hawk to return, *Tam. Shrew*, 4.i.

LUXURIOUS, lascivious, *Much Ado*, 4.i.

MACHIAVEL, regarded as the type of ruthless schemer, *Mer. Wives Win.*, 3.i.

MACULATE, spotted, impure, *L. Lab. Lost*, 1.ii.

MADRIGAL, song (though the 'madrigal' was a part-song of a very special type), *Mer. Wives Win.*, 3.i.

MAGNIFICO, Venetian magnate, *Mer. Ven.*, 3.ii.

MAIN-COURSE, mainsail, *Tem.*, 1.i.

MALAPERT, presumptuous, *Tw. Night*, 4.i.

MALIGNANT, exerting evil influence, *Two Gent. Ver.*, 3.i.

MALMSEY, sweet wine, *L. Lab. Lost*, 5.ii.

MALT-HORSE, brewer's dray-horse, *Tam. Shrew*, 4.i.

MAN, to tame a hawk, *Tam. Shrew*, 4.i.

MANAGE, training or handling of a horse, *L. Lab. Lost*, 5.ii.

MANNER, the stolen article when found on the thief, so caught in the act, *Win. Tale*, 4.iv. *L. Lab. Lost*, 1.i (where the company of a woman was the unlawful possession).   [*Tem.*, 4.i.

MANTLE, scum on stagnant water,

MARGENT, margin of book, *L. Lab. Lost*, 5.ii; commentary or explanation written in margin, *L. Lab. Lost*, 2.i.

MARK, a sum of money (not a coin) value 13s. 4d., *Com. Err.*, 1.ii.

MARMOSET, small monkey, *Tem.*, 2.ii.

MARTLET, house-martin, swallow, *Mer. Ven.*, 2.ix.

MATE, bewilder, *Com. Err.*, 3.ii.

MAUGRE, in spite of, *Tw. Night*, 3.i.

MEACOCK, feeble, cowardly, *Tam. Shrew*, 2.i.

MEAL, stain, *M. Meas.*, 4.ii.

MEAN, middle part, tenor or alto, *L. Lab. Lost*, 5.ii; singer of such a part, *Win. Tale*, 4.iii.

MECHANICAL, manual worker, *Mid. N. Dr.*, 3.ii.

GLOSSARY

MEDICINE, the elixir of life or alchemist's stone that turned all to gold, *All's Well*, 5.iii.

MEDLAR, a tree whose fruit is eaten when almost rotten (with pun on 'meddler'), *As You Like*, 3.ii.

MELANCHOLY, of various kinds, see *As You Like*, 4.i.

MERCATANTE, merchant, *Tam. Shrew*, 4.ii.

MERCURY, messenger of the gods, so messenger, *Mer. Wives Win.*, 2.ii; patron of rogues and cheats, *Win. Tale*, 4.iii.

MERE, complete, absolute, *Mer. Wives Win.*, 4.v.

MESS, four, usual number in subdivisions of company at banquet, *L. Lab. Lost*, 4.iii.

METAMORPHOSE, transform, *Two Gent. Ver.*, 1.i.

METE, *mete-yard*, measuring stick, *Tam. Shrew*, 4.iii; aim at, *L. Lab. Lost*, 4.i.

METHEGLIN, spiced drink, *L. Lab. Lost*, 5.ii.

MEW, shut up, *Mid. N. Dr.*, 1.i.

MICKLE, *cp*. Scots 'muckle,' great, *Com. Err.*, 3.i.

MIDDLE-EARTH, between heaven and hell, *Mer. Wives Win.*, 5.v.

MIGHT, *might not merit*, the intention not the performance, *Mid. N. Dr.*, 5.i.

MILE-END, where train-bands drilled, *All's Well*, 4.iii.

MILLINER, vendor of gloves, hats, etc., *Win. Tale*, 4.iv.

MILL-SIXPENCE, milled coin, not hammered as older pieces, *Mer. Wives Win.*, 1.i.   [*Dr.*, 3.ii.

MINIMUS, of smallest size, *Mid. N.*

MISGRAFFED, unsuitably mated, *Mid. N. Dr.*, 1.i.

MISPRISION, (i) undervaluing, scorning, *All's Well*, 2.iii; (ii) mistaking, *Mid. N. Dr.*, 3.ii.

MODERN, ordinary, commonplace, *As You Like*, 2.vii; *modern grace*, common attractions, *All's Well*, 5.iii.

MODEST, reasonable, *Tw. Night*, 1.v.

MODESTLY, without exaggeration, *Much Ado*, 2.iii.

MODESTY, reasonable limits, *Tam. Shrew*, Ind.i.

MODULE, copy, *All's Well*, 4.iii.

MOME, dolt, *Com. Err.*, 3.i.

MONARCHO, title assumed by mad Italian as emperor of the world, so of those with such notions, *L. Lab. Lost*, 4.i.

MONTANT, fencing term for particular thrust, *Mer. Wives Win.*, 2.iii.

MONUMENTAL, *ring*, a memento from the possessor's ancestors, *All's Well*, 4.iii.

MOONISH, fickle, changing like the moon, *As You Like*, 3.ii.

MOP, grimace, *Tem.*, 4.i.

MOPE, wander in body or mind, *Tem.*, 5.i.

MORRIS, MORRIS-DANCE, costume dance of fantastic kind; characters included Robin Hood, Maid Marian, *All's Well*, 2.ii; *nine men's morris*, a game played on squares cut in the turf, *Mid. N. Dr.*, 2.i.

MORT, the note on the horn that announces the death of the deer, *Win. Tale*, 1.ii.

MOSE, *in the chine*, of horses, glanders, *Tam. Shrew*, 3.ii.

MOTION, puppet-show, *Win. Tale*, 4.iii; *Two Gent. Ver.*, 2.i.

MOTLEY, cloth woven of green and yellow threads, *As You Like*, 2.vii; *Tam. Shrew*, 3.ii; *coat*, long coat to ankles, worn by idiots or professional fools.

MOUNTEBANK, quack, *Com. Err.*, 1.ii.

MOW, grimace, *Tem.*, 4.i.

MURRAIN, plague, *Tem.*, 3.ii.

MUSCADEL, strong sweet wine, *Tam. Shrew*, 3.ii.

MUSIC, musicians, *Mer. Ven.*, 5.i.

MUSK, secretion from musk-deer, *Mer. Wives Win.*, 2.ii.

MUTINY, dispute, *L. Lab. Lost*, 1.i.

MUTUAL, common (as in 'Our Mutual Friend'), *Mer. Ven.*, 5.i.

MYNHEERS (suggested for 'Anheires'), sirs, *Mer. Wives Win.*, 2.i.

MYRMIDONS, followers of Achilles, *Tw. Night*, 2.iii.   [4.ii.

MYSTERY, craft, calling, *M. Meas.*,

NAIL, measure of length for cloth, one-sixteenth of a yard, *Tam. Shrew*, 4.iii.

NAPKIN, handkerchief, *As You Like*, 4.iii.   [2.i.

NAYWARD, opposite belief, *Win. Tale*,

NAYWORD, byword, *Tw. Night*, 2.iii; password, *Mer. Wives Win.*, 5.ii.

NAZARITE, of Nazareth, *Mer. Ven.*, 1.iii (the term 'Nazarene' was introduced by the Authorized Version of 1611).

NEAF, fist, *Mid. N. Dr.*, 4.i.

NEAR-LEGGED, *before*, fore-legs close, *Tam. Shrew*, 3.ii.

NEAT, animal, ox, cow, calf, *Win. Tale*, 1.ii.

NEB, mouth, *Win. Tale*, 1.ii.

NEEZE, sneeze, *Mid. N. Dr.*, 2.i.

NICE, coy, shy, mannerly, fastidious, *All's Well*, 5.i; *nice wenches*, those affecting shyness, wantons, *L. Lab. Lost*, 3.i.

I I I I

GLOSSARY

NICELY, subtly, ingeniously, *Tw. Night*, 3.i.

NICHOLAS, *Saint*, patron saint, of boys and scholars, *Two Gent. Ver.*, 3.i.

NICK, *out of all nick*, beyond reckoning (nicks used on sticks to keep reckoning), *Two Gent. Ver.*, 4.ii. [*Ado*, 3.iv.

NIGHTGOWN, dressing-gown, *Much*

NOBLE, a gold coin worth 6s. 8d. (with pun on angel), *Much Ado*, 2.iii.

NOISE, often applied to musical sounds, *Tem.*, 3.ii.

NOLE, head, *Mid. N. Dr.*, 3.ii.

NON-COME, Dogberry's term is of doubtful meaning, *Much Ado*, 3.v.

NONPAREIL, without an equal, *Tw. Night*, 1.v. [4.v.

NOSE-HERB, scented plant, *All's Well*,

NOVUM, a game with dice, in which throws of nine and five were important, *L. Lab. Lost*, 5.ii (the five characters were to enact the Nine Worthies).

NUMBERS, verses, *L. Lab. Lost*, 4.iii.

NUNCIO, messenger, *Tw. Night*, 1.iv.

NUT-HOOK, beadle, *Mer. Wives Win.*, 1.i.

O, *yon fiery oes and eyes of light*, the stars, *Mid. N. Dr.*, 3.ii.

OBLIGATION, bond, *Mer. Wives Win.*, 1.i.

OBLIGED, *obliged faith*, pledged, *Mer. Ven.*, 2.vi.

OBLOQUY, shame, *All's Well*, 4.ii.

OBSCENE, abominable, *L. Lab. Lost*, 1.i.

OBSEQUIOUS, showing proper duty, *M. Meas.*, 2.iv.

OBSERVANCE, attention required by respect or love, *All's Well*, 2.v.

OBSERVATION, of a rite, *Mid. N. Dr.*, 4.i; of life itself, *As You Like*, 2.vii.

OBSTRUCTION, *obstruction in the blood*, hindrance, *Tw. Night*, 3.iv; *cold obstruction*, death, where all that makes for life is shut off, *M. Meas.*, 3.i.

OCCASION, *quarrelling with occasion*, deliberately misunderstanding the situation, *Mer. Ven.*, 3.v.

OD's, UD's, form of 'God' in oaths and exclamations, *As You Like*, 3.v.

OEILLADES, inviting glances, *Mer. Wives Win.*, 1.iii.

O'ERFLOURISH'D, decorated outwardly, *Tw. Night*, 3.iv.

O'ERPARTED, given too difficult a part, *L. Lab. Lost*, 5.ii.

OFFICE, to act as servant, *All's Well*, 3.ii.

OLD, extreme (in some form), *Tam. Shrew*, 3.ii.

OPPOSITE, adversary, *Tw. Night*, 3.iv; *adj.*, hostile, unfriendly, *Tw. Night*, 2.v.

ORB, circle, *Mid. N. Dr.*, 2.i (fairy rings); the circle or sphere in which the planets were supposed to move, so of Diana or the moon, *Much Ado*, 4.i.

ORDINARY, meal (from name given to meal in a tavern), *All's Well*, 2.iii.

ORTHOGRAPHY, orthographer, pedantic in his use of words, *Much Ado*, 2.iii.

OSTENT, show, appearance, *Mer. Ven.*, 2.ii. [4.i.

OSTENTATION, display, *Much Ado*,

OTHERGATES, in another and very different way, *Tw. Night*, 5.i.

OUNCE, lynx, *Mid. N. Dr.*, 2.ii.

OUPHE, elf, goblin, *Mer. Wives Win.*, 5.v.

OUT-VIE, to outbid (as at cards), *Tam. Shrew*, 2.i.

OVERTURE, disclosure, declaration, *Tw. Night*, 1.v.

OWE, to possess, *Tem.*, 1.ii.

OYES, (*Fr.* oyez) the call of the public crier to secure attention, *Mer. Wives Win.*, 5.v.

PACE, training (as of horses), discipline, *All's Well*, 4.v.

PACK, to plot, *pack'd*, confederate, *Much Ado*, 5.i; *Com. Err.*, 5.i.

PACKING, plotting, *Tam. Shrew*, 5.i.

PAGEANT (the wagon on which a scene in the Miracle plays was staged at the various stations appointed for performance) so of a ship, *Mer. Ven.*, 1.i; a show, sometimes with the notion of unreality or deception, *Tem.*, 4.i.

PAIN, toil, *L. Lab. Lost.*, 1.i.

PAINFUL, toilsome, *Tam. Shrew*, 5.ii.

PAINTED, specious, false, *As You Like*, 2.i.

PAINTED CLOTH, canvas hangings painted with figures and moral sentences were a cheap substitute for figured tapestries; *right painted cloth*, the answer taken from the mottoes, etc., on the hangings, *As You Like*, 3.ii.

PALABRAS, *paucas pallabris*, few words, *Tam. Shrew*, Ind.i; *Much Ado*, 3.v.

PALE, enclosure, *Com. Err.*, 2.i.

PALMER, pilgrim, *All's Well*, 3.v.

PANTALOON, originally a stock character in Italian comedy; withered dotard—so figure of old age, *As You Like*, 2.vii.

1112

GLOSSARY

PANTLER, pantry-man, *Win. Tale*, 4.iv.

PARACELSUS, Swiss alchemist of early 16th century; criticised academic medical opinion as represented in Galen; *Both of Galen and Paracelsus*, all schools of medical thought, *All's Well*, 2.iii.

PARAGON, perfect example, *Tem.*, 2.i.

PARCEL, group, *Mer. Ven.*, 1.ii.

PARD, panther or leopard, *As You Like*, 2.vii.

PARISH-TOP, kept to provide recreation in cold weather, *Tw. Night*, 1.iii.

PARITOR, summoner to the Bishop's court (the pranks inspired by Cupid giving him most work), *L. Lab. Lost*, 3.i.

PARLE, conversation, *Two Gent. Ver.*, 1.ii.

PARLOUS, perilous, *As You Like*, 3.ii.

PARTS, abilities, talents, *As You Like*, 1.i.

PARTIAL, favour, *M. Meas.*, 2.i.

PARTI-COATED, motley, the garb of the fool, *L. Lab. Lost*, 5.ii.

PARTLET, *Dame Partlet*, traditional name for the hen, *Win. Tale*, 2.iii.

PASH, head, *Win. Tale*, 1.ii.

PASSADO, a lunge in rapier fighting, *L. Lab. Lost*, 1.ii.

PASSANT (of heraldic figures), walking, *Mer. Wives Win.*, 1.i.

PASSING, surpassing, *Two Gent. Ver.*, 2.i.

PASSION, Christ's sufferings (in oaths, etc.), *Mer. Wives Win.*, 3.i; a passionate speech, *Mid. N. Dr.*, 5.i; *verb*, feel sorrow, *Tem.*, 5.i.

PASSY, *measures pavin* (from Italian passamezzo pavana), a variety of pavan, which was slow and stately, *Tw. Night*, 5.i.

PATCH, fool, *Mid. N. Dr.*, 3.ii.

PATENT, *virgin patent*, privilege of liberty as maid, *Mid. N. Dr.*, 1.i.

PATINE, circular metal plate (patine, plate used in the Eucharist), *Mer. Ven.*, 5.i.

PAUNCH, pierce his belly, *Tem.*, 3.ii.

PAVIN, see PASSY.

PEACH, proclaim, *M. Meas.*, 4.iii.

PEAK, to sneak, *Mer. Wives Win.*, 3.v.

PEARL, cataract (with play on usual sense), *Two Gent. Ver.*, 5.ii.

PECULIAR, belonging to particular individual, personal, *M. for Meas.*, 1.ii.

PEDANT, schoolmaster, *Tw. Night*, 3.ii; *pedascule* (contemptuously), pedant, *Tam. Shrew*, 3.i.

PEISE, *peize the time*, make it heavy and slow, *Mer. Ven.*, 3.ii.

PELION, the giants placed Mount Ossa on Mount Pelion in their attempt to scale the heavens, *Mer. Wives Win.*, 2.i.

PELTING, paltry, *Mid. N. Dr.*, 2.i.

PENSIONERS, royal body-guard, formed by Henry VIII, *Mer. Wives Win.*, 2.ii.

PEPIN, father of Charlemagne, and so someone who lived long ago, *L. Lab. Lost*, 4.i.

PERDURABLY, *fin'd*, eternally punished, *M. Meas.*, 3.i.

PERDY (*French*, par dieu), *Tw. Night*, 4.ii.

PEREGRINATE, with the affectations of one who has seen the world, *L. Lab. Lost*, 5.i.

PEREMPTORY, unabashed, *L. Lab. Lost*, 4.iii.

PERFECT, certain, *Cym.*, 3.i; *verb*, to instruct, *M. Meas.*, 4.iii.

PERFECTION, performance, *M. Meas.*, 3.i.

PERFORCE, forcibly, *Com. Err.*, 4.iii.

PERFUMER, one who kept the rooms fresh with perfume, *Much Ado*, 1.iii.

PERJURE, *noun*, a perjurer, *L. Lab. Lost*, 4.iii; *perjur'd note*, the paper pinned to the perjurer setting out his guilt, *L. Lab. Lost*, 4.iii.

PERPEND, ponder, *As You Like*, 3.ii.

PERSONAGE, figure, *Mid. N. Dr.*, 3.ii.

PERSPECTIVE, a picture that appeared coherent and intelligible only from one particular point of view, illusion, *Tw. Night*, v.i.

PERTAUNT-LIKE, 'pertaunt' was perhaps a winning declaration at the card game of Post and Pair—perhaps a hand of four Queens—*L. Lab. Lost*, 5.ii.

PHANTASIME, a fantastic fellow, *L. Lab. Lost*, 4.i.

PHEEZE, castigate, *Tam. Shrew*, Ind. 1; *Pheazar*, comic formation, *Mer. Wives Win.*, 1.iii.

PHILOMEL, the nightingale, *Mid. N. Dr.*, 2.ii.

PHILOSOPHER, *weeping*, Heraclitus, *Mer. Ven.*, 1.ii.

PHOEBE, PHOEBUS, the moon-goddess, the sungod, *Mid. N. Dr.*, 1.i and 1.ii (Phibbus).

PHOENIX, a unique wonder, *All's Well*, 1.i.

PHYSIC, cure, *As You Like*, 1.i.

PIA MATER, brain, *Tw. Night*, 1.v.

PICKED, finical, *L. Lab. Lost*, 5.i.

PICKT-HATCH, a quarter of ill-repute in London, *Mer. Wives Win.*, 2.ii.

PIKE, spike on buckler, *Much Ado*, 5.ii.

1113

GLOSSARY

PILCHER, pilchard, *Tw. Night*, 3.i.

PIN, peg in the centre of target, *L. Lab. Lost.*, 4.i; *pin and web*, cataract, blindness, *Win. Tale*, 1.ii; *pin buttock*, narrow buttock, *All's Well*, 2.ii.

PINFOLD, pound for stray animals, *Two Gent. Ver.*, 1.i.

PIONED, *pioned and twilled brims*, meaning doubtful, *Tem.*, 4.i.

PIP, *a pip out*, thirty-two when thirty-one (at card game) is needed, *Tam. Shrew*, 1.ii.

PIPE-WINE, wine from cask, *Mer. Wives Win.*, 3.ii.

PITCH, height, *Tw. Night*, 1.i.

PLACKET, slit in petticoat to allow it to slip on, *Win. Tale*, 4.iv.

PLAIN-SONG, *cuckoo*, which sings a simple fixed tune, *Mid. N. Dr.*, 3.i.

PLANCHED, of boards, *M. Meas.*, 4.i.

PLANTAIN, plant with broad flat leaves, thought good for wounds, *L. Lab. Lost*, 3.i.

PLANTATION, colonization, settlement, *Tem.*, 2.i.

PLASH, pool, *Tam. Shrew*, 1.i.

PLAUSIBLE, pleased, *M. Meas.*, 3.i.

PLAUSIVE, persuasive, *All's Well*, 1.ii; plausible, cunning, *All's Well*, 4.i.

PLEACHED, *thicked-pleached alley*, the boughs closely intertwined, *Much Ado*, 1.ii.

PLEASANT, jocular, *M. Meas.*, 3.ii.

PLEASE-MAN, toady, *L. Lab. Lost*, 5.ii.

PLUME, plumage, *Tem.*, 3.iii.

POINT, lace for keeping hose attached to doublet, *Tam. Shrew*, 3.ii; *point-devise*, in all particulars, precisely, *Tw. Night*, 2.v.

POISE, weight, balance, *M. Meas.*, 2.iv.

POKE, pocket, *As You Like*, 2.vii.

POKING-STICKS, for ruffs, *Win. Tale*, 4.iv.

POLE-CLIPT, *vineyard*, the poles perhaps for the vines to climb on, *Tem.*, 4.i.

POLITIC, *politic authors*, writers on state affairs, *Tw. Night*, 2.v.

POLITICIAN, intriguer, *Tw. Night*, 2.iii.

POMANDER, scent-ball, *Win. Tale*, 4.iv.

POMEWATER, kind of apple, *L. Lab. Lost*, 4.ii.

POOR-JOHN, salted fish, *Tem.*, 2.ii.

PORRIDGE, pottage or soup, *Com. Err.*, 2.ii.

PORT, (i) gate, *All's Well*, 3.v; (ii) rank, wealth, *Mer. Ven.*, 3.ii.

POSSESSION, possessed as by an evil spirit, *Com. Err.*, 5.i.

POSSET, 'night-cap' of hot milk and spiced liquor, *Mer. Wives Win.*, 5.v.

POST, *sheriff's post*, sheriff's noticeboard, *Tw. Night*, 1.v; doorpost of tavern, *Com. Err.*, 1.ii.

POST, courier, *Mer. Ven.*, 5.i; *in post*, in haste (as with posthorses), *Com. Err.*, 1.ii.

POSTERN, side-door, *Win. Tale*, 1.ii.

POSY, inscription inside a ring, *Mer. Ven.*, 5.i.

POTTLE, two-quart measure, so tankard, *Mer. Wives Win.*, 2.i.

PRACTICE, intrigue, treachery, *Tw. Night*, 5.i.

PRACTISE, use some device, plot, *Much Ado*, 2.i.

PRAISE, *praise in departing*, keep your praise till the end of the entertainment, *Tem.*, 3.iii.

PREAMBULATE, to go before, *L. Lab. Lost*, 5.i.

PRECEDENCE, what is said before, *L. Lab. Lost*, 3.i.

PRECEDENT, example, *L. Lab. Lost*, 1.ii.

PRECEPTIAL, *preceptial medicine*, suitable precepts or advice on conduct, *Much Ado*, 5.i.

PRECISE, scrupulous, puritanical, *M. Meas.*, 1.iii (also at 3.i, where the Folio reads 'prenzie').

PRECISIAN, puritan-like adviser, *Mer. Wives Win.*, 2.i.

PRE-CONTRACT, engagement of marriage, *M. Meas.*, 4.i.

PREDOMINANT, in the ascendant or influential position, *All's Well*, 1.i.

PREGNANT, full of resource, *Tw. Night*, 2.ii.

PREJUDICATE, pass judgment on a matter before it is formally raised, *All's Well*, 1.ii.

PREPARATIONS, accomplishments, *Mer. Wives Win.*, 2.ii.

PREROGATIVE, precedence, *Tam. Shrew*, 3.i; *All's Well*, 2.iv.

PRESAGE, promise, *Tw. Night*, 3.ii.

PRESENCE, company, *Mid. N. Dr.*, 1.i.

PRESENT, immediate, *M. Meas.*, 2.iv; *present money*, ready money, *Mer. Ven.*, 3.ii.

PRESENTATION, show, disguise, *As You Like*, 5.iv.

PRESS, *pressing to death*, refers to the pressing to death, with weights, of accused who would not plead, *M. Meas.*, 5.i.

PRESTER JOHN, a fabled and mysterious king of the East or Ethiopia, *Much Ado*, 2.i.

PRESUPPOS'D, *forms presuppos'd*, dressed as the false letter suggested, *Tw. Night*, 5.i.

PRETENCE, purpose, *Win. Tale*, 3.ii.

1114

GLOSSARY

PREVENT, anticipate, *Tw. Night*, 3.i.

PRICK, *noun*, to mark centre of target, *L. Lab. Lost*, 4.i.

PRICKET, *see* BUCK.

PRIG, thief, *Win. Tale*, 4.iii.

PRIMERO, card-game, *Mer. Wives Win.*, 4.v.

PRINCIPALITY, Principalities, Archangels, and Angels, formed the third order of Heavenly beings, *Two Gent. Ver.*, 2.iv.

PRISCIAN, Roman grammarian, *a little scratch'd*, his rules violated somewhat, *L. Lab. Lost*, 5.i. [2.i.

PRIVILEGE, justification, *Mid. N. Dr.*,

PRIZE, contest, *Mer. Ven.*, 3.ii.

PRIZER, prize-fighter, *As You Like*, 2.iii. [2.v.

PROBATION, examination, *Tw. Night*,

PROCEEDER, *quick proceeders*, with play on idea of proceeding to a university degree in Arts, *Tam. Shrew*, 4.ii. [*Dr.*, 5.i.

PRODIGIOUS, of evil omen, *Mid. N.*

PROGENY, offspring, a daughter of *L. Lab. Lost*, 5.ii.

PROGNOSTICATION, according to the almanac's forecast, *Win. Tale*, 4.iv.

PROLIXIOUS, time-wasting, *M. Meas.*, 2.iv.

PROLONG, postpone, *Much Ado*, 4.i.

PROMETHEAN, life-giving, like the fire Prometheus stole from heaven, *L. Lab. Lost*, 4.iii.

PROPER-FALSE, good-looking but deceitful at heart, *Tw. Night*, 2.ii.

PROPERTY, to treat as a mere inanimate thing, *Tw. Night*, 4.ii.

PROPOSE, purpose, *Much Ado*, 3.i.

PROVINCIAL, of a particular province and subject to his superior there, *M. Meas.*, 5.i.

PUGGING, thieving (doubtful), *Win. Tale*, 4.iii.

PUNK, harlot, *Mer. Wives Win.*, 2.ii.

PUNTO, thrust in fencing, *Mer. Wives Win.*, 2.iii.

PURGATION, clearance of guilt, *Win. Tale*, 3.ii.

PURLIEU, land bordering forest, *As You Like*, 4.iii.

PURPLE-IN-GRAIN, *see* GRAIN.

PUSH-PIN, children's game, *L. Lab. Lost*, 4.iii.

PUTTER-OUT *of five for one*, the voyager who put down a sum with a dealer on condition that he obtained on return five times the original, but forfeited the lot if he failed to return by a fixed date, *Tem.*, 3.iii.

PYTHAGORAS, the Greek philosopher who is supposed to have believed in the transmigration of souls, *As You Like*, 3.ii.

QUAINT, charming, delicate, *Mid. N. Dr.*, 2.ii; *quaint mazes*, intricate paths, *Mid. N. Dr.*, 2.i.

QUALIFY, to moderate, *M. Meas.*, 1.i.

QUALITY, profession, *Two Gent. Ver.*, 4.i. [1.i.

QUANTITY, proportion, *Mid. N. Dr.*,

QUEAN, wench, *All's Well*, 2.ii.

QUEASY, squeamish, *Much Ado*, 2.i.

QUESTANT, seeker for fame, *All's Well*, 2.i.

QUESTION, *in contempt of*, without doubt, *Tw. Night*, 2.v.

QUICK, living, *Win. Tale*, 4.iv; pregnant, *L. Lab. Lost*, 5.ii.

QUICKEN, to make alive, *Tem.*, 3.i.

QUILLET, quibble, *L. Lab. Lost*, 4.iii.

QUINTAIN, a post to tilt at, *As You Like*, 1.ii.

QUINTESSENCE, the fifth essence in the four elements (earth, air, fire, water), so the most subtle manifestation, *As You Like*, 3.ii.

QUIP, retort, *As You Like*, 5.iv.

QUIRK, shock, *All's Well*, 3.ii; turn of mind, *Tw. Night*, 3.iv.

QUIT, require, *M. Meas.*, 5.i; release, *Tw. Night*, 5.i.

QUITTANCE, acquittance, *Mer. Wives Win.*, 1.i. [4.iv.

QUOIF, close-fitting cap, *Win. Tale*,

QUONDAM, former, *L. Lab. Lost*, 5.i.

QUONIAM, since, because, *L. Lab. Lost*, 5.ii.

QUOTE, indicate (as a reference in a book does), *L. Lab. Lost*, 2.i; to interpret, *L. Lab. Lost*, 5.ii.

QUOTIDIAN, a fever that comes on every day, *As You Like*, 3.ii.

RABATO, a kind of stiff collar, *Much Ado*, 3.iv.

RACE, herd, *Mer. Ven.*, 5.i; strain, e.g., *sensual race*, lust, *M. Meas.*, 2.iv.

RACE, RAZE, *race of ginger*, root of ginger, *Win. Tale*, 4.iii.

RACK, *leave not a rack*, not even a cloud, *Tem.*, 4.i.

RACKERS, distorters, *L. Lab. Lost*, 5.i.

RAISINS O' THE SUN, sun-dried grapes, *Win. Tale*, 4.iii.

RANK, overgrown, gross, stinking, *As You Like*, 2.vii.

RAP, *rapt*, absorbed, *Tem.*, 1.ii.

RASCAL, a lean and worthless deer, *As You Like*, 3.iii.

RATE, estimation, *Tem.*, 2.i; style of living, *Mer. Ven.*, 1.i.

RATHER, *the rather*, the sooner, *All's Well*, 3.v; *ratherest*, most of all, *L. Lab. Lost*, 4.ii.

RATIFY, *only numbers ratified*, correct in form only, *L. Lab. Lost*, 4.ii.

GLOSSARY

RATOLORUM, corruption of Custos Rotulorum (Keeper of the Rolls), *Mer. Wives Win.*, 1.i.

RAVEL, become tangled, *Two Gent. Ver.*, 3.ii.

RAVIN, *adj.*, ravenous, *All's Well*, 3.ii; *verb*, devour, *M. Meas.*, 1.ii.

RAY'D, bemired, *Tam. Shrew*, 4.i.

RAZE, lay flat, *M. Meas.*, 2.ii; *razure*, *M. Meas.*, 5.i.

REACH, *raught to*, amounted to, *L. Lab. Lost*, 4.ii.

READ, to give learned instruction in, *Tam. Shrew*, 1.ii.   [5.i.

REASON, observation, *L. Lab. Lost*,

REAVE, *reft* (participle), taken from, *Com. Err.*, 1.i.

REBATE, blunt, *M. Meas.*, 1.iv.

RECHEAT, call on hunting-horn (so of cuckold's horns), *Much Ado*, 1.i.

RECK, to heed, *As You Like*, 2.iv.

RECKLESS, heedless, *Two Gent. Ver.*, 5.ii.

RECOLLECT, *recollected terms*, artificial diction, *Tw. Night*, 2.iv.

RECOMMEND, deliver, *Tw. Night*, 5.i.

RECORD, sing, *Two Gent. Ver.*, 5.iv.

RECORDER, kind of flageolet, *Mid. N. Dr.*, 5.i.   [*Ver.*, 3.i.

RECOURSE, admittance, *Two Gent.*

RECOVERY, *see* FINE.

RECREATION, refreshment, *L. Lab. Lost*, 4.ii.

RECTOR, ruler, *All's Well*, 4.iii.

RED LATTICE, *red-lattice phrases*, language of alehouse, *Mer. Wives Win.*, 2.ii.

REECHY, smoky, *Much Ado*, 3.iii.

REED VOICE, piping voice, *Mer. Ven.*, 3.iv.

REFEL, refute, *M. Meas.*, 5.i.

REINS, loins, *Mer. Wives Win.*, 3.v.

RELIGIOUS, conscientious, *Tw. Night*, 3.iv.

RELINQUISH, *relinquish'd of the artists*, given up by doctors, *All's Well*, 2.iii.

REMAINDER, *cut the entail from all remainders*, (legal terms) give away all that may remain after he has parted with his (inheritance) salvation, *All's Well*, 4.iii; *remainder biscuit*, left over after voyage, *As You Like*, 2.vii.

REMISSION, *apt remission*, ready pardon, *M. Meas.*, 5.i.

REMONSTRANCE, *rash remonstrance*, sudden demonstration, *M. Meas.*, 5.i.

REMORSEFUL, compassionate, *Two Gent. Ver.*, 4.iii.

RENDER, report, *As You Like*, 4.iii.

RENEGADO, turncoat, *Tw. Night*, 3.ii.

REPAIR, to return, *Mid. N. Dr.*, 4.i.

REPASTURE, food, *L. Lab. Lost*, 4.i.

REPETITION, reference to the past, *All's Well*, 5.iii.

REPLENISHED, full, complete, *Win. Tale*, 2.i.   [4.ii.

REPLICATION, reply, *L. Lab. Lost*, REQUIRING, request, *M. Meas.*, 3.i.

REQUIT, repaid, *Tem.*, 3.iii.

RERE-MICE, bats, *Mid. N. Dr.*, 2.ii.

RESEMBLANCE, probability, *M. Meas.*, 4.ii.

RESPECT, *noun*, regard, *Tw. Night*, 2.iii; *without respect*, apart from its proper context, *Mer. Ven.*, 5.i; *verb*, consider, *Com. Err.*, 4.iv.

RESPECTIVE, regardful, *Mer. Ven.*, 5.i.

REST, term from card game of primero signifying the stake on which the game turned, its loss ending the game—so hazarding everything or making an end of the matter, *Mer. Ven.*, 2.ii.

RETORT, give back, *Mer. Wives Win.*, 2.ii.

RETROGRADE, with apparent backward motion in the heavens, *All's Well*, 1.i.   [1.v.

REVERBERATE, re-echoing, *Tw. Night*, REVERSE, back-handed thrust in fencing, *Mer. Wives Win.*, 2.iii.

REVIEW, see again, *Win. Tale*, 4.iv.

REVOLVE, turn over in mind, *Tw. Night*, 2.v.

RHENISH, Rhine wine, *Mer. Ven.*, 1.ii.

RHEUM, a flow of tears, saliva, etc.; *rheumatic diseases*, diseases brought on by such an excessive flow, *Mid. N. Dr.*, 2.i.

RIALTO, the Exchange of Venice, *Mer. Ven.*, 1.iii.   [*Well*, 3.v.

RING-CARRIER, a go-between, *All's*

RIPE, *sinking-ripe*, ready to sink, *Com. Err.*, 1.i; *Mid. N. Dr.*, 5.i.

RIVAL, partner, *Mid. N. Dr.*, 3.ii.

ROAD, roadstead, *Mer. Ven.*, 1.i.

ROGUE, vagrant, *Win. Tale*, 4.iii.

ROMAN, *Roman hand*, the Roman or Italian hand that replaced the English style of writing, *Tw. Night*, 3.iv.   [*Wives Win.*, 4.ii.

RONYON, scabby creature, *Mer.*

ROPE-TRICKS, knavery (Grumio's word for rhetoric), *Tam. Shrew*, 1.ii.   [*N. Dr.*, 2.ii.

ROUNDEL, a dance in a circle, *Mid.*

ROYNISH, scurvy, *As You Like*, 2.ii.

RUDESBY, rude fellow, *Tam. Shrew*, 3.ii.

RUSSET, homespun cloth, so plain, genuine, *L. Lab. Lost*, 5.ii; *russetpated*, grey-headed, *Mid. N. Dr.*, 3.ii.

SACK, a white wine of Sherry class from Spain or Canaries, *Tem.*, 2.ii.

GLOSSARY

SACKERSON, a performing bear at Paris garden, *Mer. Wives Win.*, 1.i.

SAD, serious, grave; *speak sad brow and true maid*, in all truth and sincerity, *As You Like*, 3.ii.

SAFFRON, crocus-yellow (alluding to yellow starch'd ruffs, etc.), *All's Well*, 4.v.

SAIN, *tofore been sain*, said before, *L. Lab. Lost*, 3.i.

SALE-WORK, ordinary ready-made quality, *As You Like*, 3.v.

SALT, wanton, *M. Meas.*, 5.i.

SALTIERS, perhaps for 'Satyrs,' *Win. Tale*, 4.iv.

SANCTIMONIOUS, sacred, *Tem.*, 4.i; hypocritical, *M. Meas.*, 1.ii.

SANDBLIND, almost blind, *Mer. Ven.*, 2.ii. [4.i.

SANDED, sand colour'd, *Mid. N. Dr.*,

SANS, without, *As You Like*, 2.vii.

SATURN, planet under which saturnine and morose characters were born, *Much Ado*, 1.iii.

SCAMELS, (various suggestions, e.g., seamells, seamews), *Tem.*, 2.ii.

SCARRE, (meaning uncertain), *All's Well*, 4.ii. [2.ix.

SCHEDULE, document, list, *Mer. Ven.*,

SCHOOLS, the learned faculties (here medical), *All's Well*, 1.iii.

SCIENCE, knowledge, *All's Well*, 5.iii.

SCION, cutting for grafting, *Win. Tale*, 4.iv.

SCONCE, fort, so of some protection, *Com. Err.*, 2.ii; the head, *Com. Err.*, 1.ii.

SCORCH, cut, *Com. Err.*, 5.i.

SCORE, the notch on a tally (stick) to record debt, *Tam. Shrew*, Ind.ii.

SCRIP, document, *Mid. N. Dr.*, 1.ii; *scrip and scrippage*, shepherd's pouch and contents, *As You Like*, 3.ii. [5.i.

SCRUBBED, undersized, *Mer. Ven.*,

SCUT, tail of a deer, *Mer. Wives Win.*, 5.v.

SEA-COAL, coal carried by sea from Newcastle, *Mer. Wives Win.*, 1.iv.

SEAL, *seal'd quarts*, measures stamped as correct, *Tam. Shrew*, Ind.ii.

SECOND, a support, *Win. Tale*, 2.iii.

SECURE, free from suspicion, *Mer. Wives Win.*, 2.i; *securely*, carelessly, *Mer. Wives Win.*, 2.ii.

SEE, *the See*, Rome, *M. Meas.*, 3.ii.

SEEMING, outward show true or false, *Win. Tale*, 4.iv; *Much Ado*, 4.i.

SE'NNIGHT, week (from ancient custom of beginning day at sunset), *As You Like*, 3.ii.

SENSELESS, without feelings, *Com. Err.*, 4.iv.

SENSIBLE, capable of physical or spiritual feeling, *Mid. N. Dr.*, 5.i.

SENTENCE, moral saying, maxim, *Mer. Ven.*, 1.ii.

SENTENTIOUS, full of wise saws, *As You Like*, 5.iv.

SEQUENT, following, *M. Meas.*, 5.i.

SEQUESTER, *sequest'red stag*, separated from the herd, *As You Like*, 2.i.

SERE, withered, *Com. Err.*, 4.ii.

SERGEANT, bailiff, *Com. Err.*, 4.ii.

SERPIGO, skin disease, *M. Meas.*, 3.i.

SEVERAL, a private enclosure as opposed to common land, *L. Lab. Lost*, 2.i.

SHEEP-BITER, term of abuse, *Tw. Night*, 2.v.

SHEER, *for sheer ale*, for ale alone, *Tam. Shrew*, Ind.ii.

SHENT, blamed, *Tw. Night*, 4.ii.

SHIFT, contrive to help oneself or another, *Tem.*, 5.i.

SHIP-TIRE, type of head-dress, *Mer. Wives Win.*, 3.iii. [2.v.

SHOT, reckoning, *Two Gent. Ver.*,

SHOULDER-SHOTTEN, damaged in the shoulder, *Tam. Shrew*, 3.ii.

SHOVEL-BOARD, *Edward shovel-board*, shilling of Edward VI's reign used for shove-halfpenny, *Mer. Wives Win.*, 1.i.

SHREWD, shrewish, *Mid. N. Dr.*, 3.ii; malicious, *All's Well*, 3.v.

SHRIEVE, sheriff, *All's Well*, 4.iii.

SHRIFT, confession and absolution, *M. Meas.*, 4.ii.

SICLE, shekel, *M. Meas.*, 2.ii.

SIEGE, seat, *M. Meas.*, 4.ii.

SILLY, helpless, *Two Gent. Ver.*, 4.i.

SIMPLE, an ingredient in a compound, *As You Like*, 4.i.

SINGULARITY, *trick of singularity*, habit of being different from others, *Tw. Night*, 2.v.

SINGULE, to single out, *L. Lab. Lost*, 5.i.

SINISTER, left, *All's Well*, 2.i.

SIR-REVERENCE, corruption of 'save your reverence,' *Com. Err.*, 3.ii.

SISTER, *Sisters Three*, the three Fates, *Mid. N. Dr.*, 5.i.

SKILL, *it skills not*, it is no matter, *Tw. Night*, 5.i. [2.i.

SKIPPER, giddy youth, *Tam. Shrew*,

SLEEVE-HAND, wristband, *Win. Tale*, 4.iv. [3.iv.

'SLID, by God's eyelid, *Tw. Night*,

'SLIGHT, by God's light, *Tw. Night*, 2.v. [3.ii.

SLOPS, wide breeches, *Much Ado*,

SLUBBER, to scamp, *Mer. Ven.*, 2.viii.

SMOCK, woman's undergarment, so a woman at *All's Well*, 2.i.

1117

GLOSSARY

SMOKE, drive from hiding with smoke, so expose to criticism, *All's Well*, 3.vi.

SMUG, spick and span, *Mer. Ven.*, 3.i.

SNECK-UP, expression of contempt, *Tw. Night*, 2.iii.

SNIPT-TAFFETA, *snipt-taffeta fellow*, over-dressed creature, *All's Well*, 4.v.

SNUFF, *to take in snuff*, to resent, *L. Lab. Lost*, 5.ii.

SOB, a rest during which a horse recovers its wind, so punningly at *Com. Err.*, 4.iii.

SOLE, unique, *L. Lab. Lost*, 2.i.

SOLEMNITY, festivity, *Two Gent. Ver.*, 5.iv.

SONTIES, saints, *Mer. Ven.*, 2.ii.

SOP, cake, or wafer, in wine, *Tam. Shrew*, 3.ii. [2.v.

SOPHY, Shah of Persia, *Tw. Night*,

SORE, SOREL, see BUCK.

SORT, *noun*, rank, *M. Meas.*, 4.iv; *many in sort*, many together, *Mid. N. Dr.*, 3.ii; *verb*, choose, *Two Gent. Ver.*, 3.ii.

SOUTH SEA, *South Sea of Discovery*, a lengthy voyage in unknown Pacific, *As You Like*, 3.ii.

SOWTER, cobbler, as name of hound at *Tw. Night*, 2.v.

SPAVINS, joint-disease of horses, *Tam. Shrew*, 3.ii.

SPHERE, *music from the spheres*, the sun, moon, and planets were supposed to be carried round the earth on concentric spheres, whose motions produced a harmonious sound, *Tw. Night*, 3.i.

SPLEEN, regarded as seat of anger, pugnacity, violent laughter, *M. Meas.*, 2.ii.

SPRAG, quick, *Mer. Wives Win.*, 4.i.

SPRINGE, snare, *Win. Tale*, 4.iii.

SQUARE, to quarrel, *Mid. N. Dr.*, 2.i; *squarer*, quarreller, *Much Ado*, 1.i.

SQUASH, unripe peascod, *Mid. N. Dr.*, 3.i.

SQUIER, carpenter's rule, *L. Lab. Lost*, 5.ii.

STAGGERS, disease in animals accompanied by giddiness, *Tam. Shrew*, 3.ii. [*Err.*, 2.i.

STALE, bait, *Tem.*, 4.i; dupe, *Com.*

STAMP, coin, *Mer. Wives Win.*, 3.iv.

STANDING-BED, standing in sense that it could not be pushed under another like a truckle-bed, *Mer. Wives Win.*, 4.v.

STANIEL, poor type of hawk, *Tw. Night*, 2.v.

STAPLE, quality of fibre in wool, etc., *L. Lab. Lost*, 5.i.

STATE, *cons state*, gets up matters of state, *Tw. Night*, 2.iii; chair of authority or dignity, *Tw. Night*, 2.v.

STATUTE-CAP, to help the wool trade Parliament made the wearing of woollen caps compulsory on Sundays, *L. Lab. Lost*, 5.ii.

STIGMATICAL, marked as wicked by some deformity, *Com. Err.*, 4.ii.

STILL, *adverb*, always; *still-vex'd Bermoothes*, always storm bound, *Tem.*, 1.ii. [2.i.

STOCCADO, thrust, *Mer. Wives Win.*,

STOCK-FISH, dried cod, softened before cooking by beating, *Tem.*, 3.ii. [3.ii.

STOMACH, inclination, *As You Like*,

STONE-BOW, cross-bow for discharging stones, *Tw. Night*, 2.v.

STOUP, flagon, *Tw. Night*, 2.iii.

STOVER, fodder, *Tem.*, 4.i.

STRANGENESS, reserve, *Tw. Night*, 4.i.

STRIKE, shed evil influence, *Win. Tale*, 1.ii. [3.iv.

STUCK, see STOCCADO; *Tw. Night*,

STYLE, title, *Mer. Wives Win.*, 2.ii.

SUBSCRIBE, sign one's name, *L. Lab. Lost*, 1.i; proclaim, *Much Ado*, 5.ii.

SUCCEED, follow as a consequence, *All's Well*, 2.iii.

SUCCESS, *in whose success*, as their issue, *Win. Tale*, 1.ii.

SUCCESSION, those coming after in like condition, *All's Well*, 3.v.

SUGGEST, tempt, *Two Gent. Ver.*, 3.i.

SUPPOSE, *counterfeit supposes*, false presumptions, *Tam. Shrew*, 5.i.

SWABBER, sailor who cleans up, *Tw. Night*, 1.v.

SWARTH, swath, *Tw. Night*, 2.iii.

SWAY'D, *sway'd in the back* (of horse), weak-backed, *Tam. Shrew*, 3.ii.

SWINGE, whip, *Two Gent. Ver.*, 2.i.

SYMPATHIZE, *sympathized error*, error shared in by all, *Com. Err.*, 5.i.

SYMPATHY, harmony (in age, rank, etc.), *Mid. N. Dr.*, 1.i.

TABLE (*-s*), wood or canvas for painting on, *All's Well*, 1.i; palm of hand, *Mer. Ven.*, 2.ii; backgammon, *L. Lab. Lost*, 5.ii.

TABOR, drum, *Tw. Night*, 3.i.

TAFFETA, *changeable taffeta*, shot silk, *Tw. Night*, 2.iv.

TAINT, to infect, to corrupt, *Mer. Wives Win.*, 5.v.

TALL, of a fine specimen of its kind (*often ironical*), *Tw. Night*, 1.iii.

TARTAR, TARTARUS, hell, *Tw. Night*, 2.v.

TASK, impose a task, *L. Lab. Lost*, 2.i.

GLOSSARY

TAWDRY-LACE, necklace (originally from St. Audrey's fair), *Win. Tale*, 4.iv.

TAX, TAXATION, censure, *All's Well*, 2.i; *As You Like*, 1.ii.

TEEN, grief, *Tem.*, 1.ii.

TENDER, regard, *Com. Err.*, 5.i.

TERMINATION, word, *Much Ado*, 2.i.

TESTER, sixpence, *Mer. Wives Win.*, 1.iii.

TESTRIL, see TESTER.

THIN-BELLY, *thin-belly doublet*, unlined over belly, *L. Lab. Lost*, 3.i.

THIRD, thread, *Tem.*, 4.i.

THRACIAN, *Thracian singer*, Orpheus, *Mid. N. Dr.*, 5.i.

THRASONICAL, boastful (from Thraso, bragging soldier in *Eunuchus* of Terence), *As You Like*, 5.ii.

THREE-MAN SONG-MEN, singers of three-part catches, *Win. Tale*, 4.iii.

THREE-PILE, rich velvet, *Win. Tale*, 4.iii; *three-pil'd hyperboles*, extravagant exaggerations, *L. Lab. Lost*, 5.ii.

THROE, pain, *Tem.*, 2.i.

THRUM, *thread and thrum*, good and bad, *Mid. N. Dr.*, 5.i; *thrumm'd hat*, witch-cap of weaver's ends, *Mer. Wives Win.*, 4.ii.

TIGHT, sound, *Tem.*, 5.i.

TINCT, the grand elixir of the alchemists, *All's Well*, 5.iii.

TIRE, head-dress, *Mer. Wives Win.*, 3.iii (so *tire-valiant* is a particular style). [*N. Dr.*, 3.i.

TIRING-HOUSE, dressing-room, *Mid.*

TOAST, toast in wine, *Mer. Wives Win.*, 3.v. [4.iv.

TOAZE, TOUZE, to draw, *Win. Tale*,

TOD, 28 lb. of wool, *Win. Tale*, 4.iii.

TOIL, net, trap, *L. Lab. Lost*, 4.iii.

TOKEN, *Lord's tokens*, marks of plague and so of death, of infection of love, *L. Lab. Lost*, 5.ii.

TOLL, pay the seller's tax to market authorities, *All's Well*, 5.iii.

TONGS, *the tongs and the bones*, a percussion instrument, like the triangle, and clappers, *Mid. N. Dr.*, 4.i.

TOUZE, to tear, *M. Meas.*, 5.i.

TRAIN, to entice, *Com. Err.*, 3.ii.

TRANSLATE, transform, *Mid. N. Dr.*, 3.i.

TRASH, to curb a hound's impetuosity by adding weight to the collar, *Tem.*, 1.ii.

TRAVERSE, *quite traverse*, missing aim with the lance at tilting and breaking it crosswise on the opponent, *As You Like*, 3.iv.

TRAY-TRIP, game with dice in which three (trey) was the important throw, *Tw. Night*, 2.v.

TREY, throw of three with dice, *L. Lab. Lost*, 5.ii.

TRICK, fashion, *M. Meas.*, 5.i.

TRICKING, furnishings, *Mer. Wives Win.*, 4.iv.

TRIPLE, third, *All's Well*, 2.i.

TROPHY, memorial, *All's Well*, 2.iii.

TRUCKLE-BED, low bed that could be pushed under standing-bed, *Mer. Wives Win.*, 4.v.

TRUNK SLEEVE, wide sleeve, *Tam. Shrew*, 4.iii. [*Tem.*, 1.i.

TRY, *bring her to try*, into the wind,

TUITION, protection, *Much Ado*, 1.i.

TUN-DISH, funnel, *M. Meas.*, 3.ii.

UMBER, earthy brown colour, *As You Like*, 1.iii. [*Ver.*, 4.iv.

UNADVIS'D, inadvertently, *Two Gent.*

UNBATED, unabated, *Mer. Ven.*, 2.vi.

UNBRAIDED, fresh and new, *Win. Tale*, 4.iv.

UNCASE, undress, *Tam. Shrew*, 1.i.

UNCONFIRMED, uninstructed, *Much Ado*, 3.iii.

UNCOUTH, unfamiliar and fearsome, *As You Like*, 2.vi.

UNDERBORNE, lined, *Much Ado*, 3.iv.

UNDERTAKER, venturer, *Tw. Night*, 3.iv.

UNEXPRESSIVE, beyond all praise, *As You Like*, 3.ii.

UNPINK'D, still lacking their pierced pattern, *Tam. Shrew*, 4.i.

UNPREGNANT, barren of purpose, *M. Meas.*, 4.iv. [5.i.

UNPRIZABLE, worthless, *Tw. Night*,

URCHIN, hedgehog, *Temp.*, 1.ii; hobgoblin, *Mer. Wives Win.*, 4.iv.

URINAL, doctor's glass for testing urine, *Two Gent. Ver.*, 2.i.

USANCE, interest, *Mer. Ven.*, 1.iii.

USE, interest, *M. Meas.*, 1.i.

VAIL, to lower, *M. Meas.*, 5.i.

VALIDITY, worth, *All's Well*, 5.iii.

VASTIDITY, measureless space, *M. Meas.*, 3.i.

VELURE, velvet, *Tam. Shrew*, 3.ii.

VENUE, VENEY, thrust, *L. Lab. Lost*, 5.i; hit at fencing, *Mer. Wives Win.*, 1.i.

VENTRICLE, one of the three divisions into which the brain was supposed to be divided, *L. Lab. Lost*, 4.ii.

VIA, *interjection*, go on! *Mer. Ven.*, 2.ii.

VICE, the Vice was a character in the morality plays, presented often as a buffoon, *Tw. Night*, 4.ii.

GLOSSARY

VIOL-DE-GAMBOYS, *viol da gamba*, being held between the knees like the cello, *Tw. Night*, 1.iii.

VIRGINALLING, fingering, as if playing on the virginals, *Win. Tale*, 1.ii.

VIRTUOUS, potent, *Mid. N. Dr.*, 3.ii.

VISITATION, affliction (of love), and visit, *Tem.*, 3.i.

VISITOR, like clergyman coming to console the afflicted, *Tem.*, 2.i.

VISOR, VIZARD, mask, *Much Ado*, 2.i.

VOUCH, testimony, *M. Meas.*, 2.iv.

WAFT, beckon, *Mer. Ven.*, 5.i; move, *Win. Tale*, 1.ii.   [4.i.

WAFTAGE, passage by sea, *Com. Err.*,

WAG, to go along, *Much Ado.*, 5.i.

WAGGON, chariot, *Win. Tale*, 4.iv.

WAIST, mid part of ship, *Tem.*, 1.ii.

WAKE, celebration of some holy day, beginning the evening before, *Win. Tale*, 4.iii.   [2.ii.

WARD, defence, *Mer. Wives Win.*,

WARDEN, pear, *Win. Tale*, 4.iii.

WARE, *bed of Ware*, at Ware in Hertfordshire, famous for its size (now in the Victoria and Albert Museum), *Tw. Night*, 3.ii.

WARP, distort, *All's Well*, 5.iii; change, *As You Like*, 2.vii.   [1.i.

WARRANTY, permission, *Mer. Ven.*,

WARREN, game preserve, *Much Ado*, 2.i; *warrener*, game-keeper, *Mer. Wives Win.*, 1.iv.

WASSAIL, (originally the salutation on drinking) carousing, *L. Lab. Lost*, 5.ii.

WATCH, to tame hawk by denying it sleep, *Tam. Shrew*, 4.i.

WEATHER-FEND, shelter, *Tem.*, 5.i.

WEED, garment, *Mid. N. Dr.*, 2.i.

WELKIN, sky, *Tem.*, 1.ii.

WEZAND, windpipe, *Tem.*, 3.ii.

WHEEL, spinning-wheel (a turning wheel being emblem of Fortune), *As You Like*, 1.ii; *Turn i' the wheel*, going round to turn the spit for the roast, *Com. Err.*, 3.ii.

WHEY, pale, *Mer. Wives Win.*, 1.iv.

WHIRLIGIG, top (turning like Fortune's wheel), *Tw. Night*, 5.i.

WHIST, hushed, *Tem.*, 1.ii.

WHITE, play on white of target and name of Bianca, *Tam. Shrew*, 5.ii.

WHITING-TIME, bleaching-time, *Mer. Wives Win.*, 3.iii.

WHITSTER, bleacher, *Mer. Wives Win.*, 3.iii.   [1.i.

WIDE-CHAPPED, open-mouthed, *Tem.*,

WIMPLED, hooded, blind, *L. Lab. Lost*, 3.i.

WINCOT, Wilmecot (home of Shakespeare's mother), *Tam. Shrew*, Ind.ii.

WIND, *i' the wind*, detected as one spots game by scent, *All's Well*, 3.vi; *windy side of*, safe side of, *Tw. Night*, 3.iv.

WINDGALLS, disease of horse's fetlock, *Tam. Shrew*, 3.ii.

WIND'RING, (perhaps wandering or winding), *Tem.*, 4.i.   [3.iv.

WISE WOMAN, witch, *Tw. Night*,

WITTOL, complacent cuckold, *Mer. Wives Win.*, 2.ii.   [2.i.

WOOD, mad, frantic, *Mid. N. Dr.*,

WOODCOCK, a fool (like the stupid bird), *Much Ado*, 5.i.

WOODMAN, hunter (so of women), *M. Meas.*, 4.iii.

WOOLLEN, *lie in the woollen*, in blankets and no sheets, or in the grave (the shroud being by law of wool), *Much Ado*, 2.i.

WOOLWARD, with woollen inner garment, *L. Lab. Lost*, 5.ii.

WORLD, *go to the world*, marry, *Much Ado*, 2.i; *woman of the world*, married woman, *As You Like*, 5.iii.

WORT, (i) vegetable, *Mer. Wives Win.*, 1.i; (ii) unfermented beer, *L. Lab. Lost*, 5.ii.

WORTHY, deserved, of praise or blame, *All's Well*, 4.iii.

WREST, misinterpret, *Much Ado*, 3.iv.

WROTH, misfortune, *Mer. Ven.*, 2.ix.

WRY-NECK'D, *fife*, played with head turned to side, *Mer Ven.*, 2.v.

YARE, quick and efficient, *Tw. Night*, 3.iv; (of a ship), *Tem.*, 5.i.

YCLEPED, called, *L. Lab. Lost*, 1.i.

YEARN, grieve, *Mer. Wives Win.*, 3.v.   [*Win.*, 1.iii.

YELLOWNESS, jealousy, *Mer. Wives Win.*,

YELLOWS, jaundice (of horses), *Tam. Shrew*, 3.ii.

YEST, YEAST, froth, *Win. Tale*, 3.iii.

YOKE, pair, *Mer. Wives Win*, 2.i.

YOUNKER, younger son, novice, *Mer. Ven.*, 2.vi.

ZANY, a fool's 'stooge,' *Tw. Night*, 1.v.   [*Tem.*, 1.ii.

ZENITH, the culmination of his life, *Zodiac*, year (in which sun completes its course through the Zodiac), *M. Meas.*, 1.ii.